MEN AT WAR

MEN AT WAR

The Best War Stories
of All Time

EDITED

with an Introduction

BY

ERNEST HEMINGWAY

Based on a plan by William Kozlenko

BRAMHALL HOUSE
NEW YORK

d e f g h
BRAMHALL 1979 EDITION
Manufactured in the United States of America

Library of Congress Cataloging in Publication Data

Hemingway, Ernest, 1899-1961, comp.
    Men at war.

    1. War stories.   I. Title.
PZ1.H38Mef   1979   [PN6071.W35]   808.83'9'3
ISBN 0-517-02084-X   79-21785

To

JOHN, PATRICK AND GREGORY HEMINGWAY

EDITOR'S NOTE

The editor wishes to thank Colonel Charles Sweeny, Lt. Col. John W. Thomason, and Maxwell E. Perkins for the invaluable aid and advice they have given in the editing of this book.

PUBLISHER'S NOTE

Acknowledgments are due to William Kozlenko for the plan from which this book was developed, and for the suggestion of a number of the stories; also to Edmund Fuller, Fred C. Rodewald, Albert Seadler and the many others whose suggestions and contributions helped to make this book.

Table of Contents

vii

WAR IS THE PROVINCE OF UNCERTAINTY

WAR IS THE PROVINCE OF CHANCE

WAR IS THE PROVINCE OF FRICTION

WAR DEMANDS RESOLUTION, FIRMNESS, AND STAUNCHNESS

WAR DEMANDS RESOLUTION, FIRMNESS, AND STAUNCHNESS
(*Continued*)

WAR IS FOUGHT BY HUMAN BEINGS

Introduction

BY

ERNEST HEMINGWAY

Edited for the 1955 edition.

THIS book will not tell you how to die. Some cheer-leaders of war can always get out a pamphlet telling the best way to go through that small but necessary business at the end. PM may have published it already in a special Sunday issue with pictures. They might even have it bound up as a companion piece to the issue I read in November 1941 entitled "How We Can Lick Japan in Sixty Days."

No. This book will not tell you how to die. This book will tell you, though, how all men from the earliest times we know have fought and died. So when you have read it you will know that there are no worse things to be gone through than men have been through before.

When you read the account of Saint Louis the IX's Crusade you will see that no expeditionary force can ever have to go through anything as bad as those men endured. We have only to fight as well as the men who stayed and fought at Shiloh. It is not necessary that we should fight better. There can be no such thing as better. And no thing that can ever happen to you from the air can ever be worse than the shelling men lived through on the Western Front in 1916 and 1917. The worst generals it would be possible to develop by a process of reverse selection of brains carried on over a period of a thousand years could never make a worse mess than Passchendaele and Gallipoli. Yet we won that war and we must win this one.

The editor of this anthology, who took part and was wounded in the last war to end war, hates war and hates all the politicians whose mismanagement, gullibility, cupidity, selfishness and ambition brought on this present war and made it inevitable. But once we have a war there is only one thing to do. It must be won. For defeat brings worse things than any that can ever happen in a war.

Regardless of how this war was brought on, step by step, in the Democracies' betrayal of the only countries that fought or were ready to fight to prevent it, there is only one thing now to do. We must win it. We must win it at all costs and as soon as possible. We must win it never forgetting what we are fighting for, in order that while we are fighting Fascism we do not slip into the ideas and ideals of Fascism.

For many years you heard American people speak who admired Mussolini because he made the trains run on time in Italy. It never seemed to occur to them that we made the trains run on time in America without Fascism.

We can fight a total war without becoming totalitarians if we do not stand on our mistakes to try and cover them; our military; our political and our naval mistakes; and learn from the winners; rather than copy the methods of the losers because they have been at the business of losing for so long.

The Germans are not successful because they are supermen. They are simply practical professionals in war who have abandoned all the old theories and shibboleths which had accumulated to such a point that military thought had completely stagnated, and who have developed the practical use of weapons and tactics to the highest point of common sense that has ever been reached. It is at that point that we can take over if no dead hand of last-war thinking lies on the high command; and we can thank the enemy for having done all this preliminary work for us.

The part this book can play in the winning of this war is to furnish certain information from former times.

When you go to war as a boy you have a great illusion of immortality. Other people get killed; not you. It can happen to other people; but not to you. Then when you are badly wounded the first time you lose that illusion and you know it can happen to you. After being severely wounded two weeks before my nineteenth birthday I had a bad time until I figured it out that nothing could happen to me that had not happened to all men before me. Whatever I had to do men had always done. If they had done it then I could do it too and the best thing was not to worry about it.

I was very ignorant at nineteen and had read little and I remember the sudden happiness and the feeling of having a permanent protecting talisman when a young British officer I met when in the hospital first wrote out for me, so that I could remember them, these lines:

"By my troth, I care not: a man can die but once; we owe God a death . . . and let it go which way it will, he that dies this year is quit for the next."

That is probably the best thing that is written in this book and, with nothing else, a man can get along all right on that. But I would have given anything for a book like this which showed what all the other men that we are a part of had gone through and how it had been with them. As nearly as it is possible to do so with only a thousand pages this book tells you how it was for all those who came before us from the shepherd boy who used his sling that day on a certain scrubby hillside to the moment when Admiral Fitch turned to Captain Sherman on the deck of the aircraft carrier *Lexington* and said, "Well, Fred, I guess it's time to get the men off."

The material has not been grouped chronologically but is rather placed under certain arbitrary heads and divisions. These divisions were made by probably the most intelligent writer on the metaphysics of war that ever lived, General Karl von Clausewitz.

There could have been more divisions; just as the book could have been twice as long. But something over a thousand pages is as large a book as can be handled and packed easily. Sometime there might be another volume to go with this one. After this war when things can be written without causing offense between allies I hope to live to read the true accounts of Hong Kong, Bataan, Singapore, Java, Burma, and the rest. I saw the preparation for all that and I have heard accounts of some of it from bitter young officers. But there has been no understanding writing on any of it up to the date this book is published.

In the last war there was no really good true war book during the entire four years of the war. The only true writing that came through during the war was in poetry. One reason for this is that poets are not arrested as quickly as prose writers would be if they wrote critically since the latter's meaning, if they are good writers, is too uncomfortably clear. The last war, during the years 1915, 1916, 1917, was the most colossal, murderous, mismanaged butchery that has ever taken place on earth. Any writer who said otherwise lied. So the writers either wrote propaganda, shut up, or fought. Of those who fought many died and we shall never know who were the fine writers who would have come out of the war who died in it instead.

But after the war the good and true books finally started to come out. They were mostly all by writers who had never written or published anything before the war. The writers who were established before the war had nearly all sold out to write propaganda during it and most of them never recovered their honesty afterwards. All of their reputations steadily slumped because a writer should be of as great probity and honesty as a priest of God. He is either honest or not, as a woman is either chaste or not, and after one piece of dishonest writing he is never the same again.

A writer's job is to tell the truth. His standard of fidelity to the truth should be so high that his invention, out of his experience, should produce a truer account than anything factual can be. For facts can be observed badly; but when a good writer is creating something, he has time and scope to make it of an absolute truth. If, during a war, conditions are such that a writer cannot publish the truth because its publication would do harm to the State he should write and not publish. If he cannot make a living without publishing he can work at something else. But if he ever writes something which he knows in his inner self is not true, for no matter what patriotic motives, then he is finished. After the war the people will have none of him because he, whose obligation is to tell them truth, has lied to them. And he will never be at peace with himself because he has deserted his one complete obligation.

Sometimes this loss of his good name will not show during his lifetime because such critics, as have also sold out in wartime, will keep his reputation bolstered up along with their own, so long as they are functioning. But when such a writer dies, or a new generation of critics comes, the whole thing collapses.

In selecting the material for this book I found nothing that was useable in the books which were published during the last war. The nearest thing to useable material was an account of a trench raid by Arthur Guy Empey who wrote that glorified mug's-eye view of trench warfare called "Over the Top." But it was such a pitiful piece of bravado writing beside the solid magnificence of Private Frank Richard's writing that it was like comparing the Brooklyn Dodger fan who jumps on the field and slugs an umpire with the beautiful professional austerity of Arky Vaughan, the Brooklyn third baseman. Read Frank Richards, who also wrote that neglected masterpiece, "Old Soldier Sahib," for the finest account of the last war by a professional soldier serving in the ranks that has ever been written.

To clean away the scent of Private Peat that still lingers in the corners of our lecture halls and sweetens our library shelves this book publishes a part of "Her Privates We" originally published, unexpurgated, in a limited edition in England as, "The Middle Parts of Fortune." It is the finest and noblest book of men in war that I have ever read. I read it over once each year to remember how things really were so that I will never lie to myself nor to anyone else about them.

As they get further and further away from a war they have taken part in all men have a tendency to make it more as they wish it had been rather than how it really was. So each year in July, the anniversary of the month when I got the big wound, I read "The Middle Parts of Fortune" and it all comes back again as though it were not yesterday, nor long ago, but as though it were this morning before daylight and you were waiting there, dry-mouthed, for it to start.

The only good war book to come out during the last war was "Under Fire" by Henri Barbusse. He was the first one to show us, the boys who went from school or college to the last war, that you could protest, in anything besides poetry, the gigantic useless slaughter and lack of even elemental intelligence in generalship that characterized the Allied conduct of that war from 1915 through 1917. His whole book was a protest and an attitude. The attitude was that he hated it. But when you came to read it over to try to take something permanent and representative from it the book did not stand up.

Its greatest quality was his courage in writing it when he did. But the writers who came after him wrote better and truer than he did. They had learned to tell the truth without screaming. Screaming, necessary though it may be to attract attention at the time, reads badly in later years.

I would have liked to include something from "Three Soldiers" by John Dos Passos which, written under the influence of Barbusse, was the first attempt at a realistic book about the war written by an American. But in spite of its great merit, like Barbusse, as a pioneering book, on rereading it did not stand up. Try to read it yourself and you will see what I mean. The dialogue rings false and the actual combat is completely unconvincing. There are books like that which are as exciting as a fine new play when they come out and, when you return to them after years, are as dead as the scenery of that play if you should happen on it in a storage house.

It has always been a problem to know why certain writing dates and goes bad in this manner. I think it is probably due, as much as anything, to the improper use of slang due to a defective ear. There are certain words which are a permanent, but usually unpunishable part of the language. They are how men have talked actually, when under stress for hundred of years. But to substitute slang expressions for these words, slang being a language which becomes a dead language at least every three years, makes a defect in writing which causes it to die as fast as the slang expressions die. It is the "Twenty-three skiddo" and "Ish ka bibble" school of American writing. Its pall, and the lack of all clarity in the combat scenes, is what makes the Dos Passos book unreadable today. But the writing of it was as valuable a pioneering feat in American letters as some minor Lewis or Clark's expedition into the Northwest.

There was no real literature of our Civil War, excepting the forgotten "Miss Ravenall's Conversion" by J. W. De Forest, until Stephen Crane wrote "The Red Badge of Courage." This is published entire and unabridged in this book. Crane wrote it before he had ever seen any war. But he had read the contemporary accounts, had heard the old soldiers, they were not so old then, talk, and above all he had seen Matthew Brady's wonderful photographs. Creating his story out of this material he wrote that great boy's dream of war that was to be truer to how war is than any war the boy who wrote it would ever live to see. It is one of the finest books of our literature and I included it entire because it is all as much of one piece as a great poem is.

If you want to find out how perfect a piece of writing is try to cut it for the purpose of making a selection for an anthology. I do not mean how good a thing is. There is no better writing on war than there is in Tolstoy but it is so huge and overwhelming that any amount of fights and battles can be chopped out of it and maintain all their truth and vigor and you feel no crime in the cutting. Actually "War and Peace" would be greatly improved by cutting; not by cutting the action, but by removing some of the parts where Tolstoy tampered with the truth to make it fit his conclusions. The Crane book, though, could not be cut at all. I am sure he cut it all himself as he wrote it to the exact measure of the poem it is.

Tolstoy carries the contempt of the man of common sense who has been a soldier for most generalship to such a length that it reaches true absurdity. Most generalship is as bad as he believes it to be but he took one of the few really great generals of the world and, inspired by a mystic nationalism, tried to show that this general, Napoleon, did not truly intervene in the direction of his battles but was simply a puppet at the mercy of forces completely beyond his control. Yet when he was writing of the Russians Tolstoy showed in the greatest and truest detail how the operations were directed. His hatred and contempt for Napoleon makes the only weakness in that great book of men at war.

I love "War and Peace" for the wonderful, penetrating and true descriptions of war and of people but I have never believed in the great Count's thinking. I wish there could have been someone in his confidence with authority to remove his heaviest and worst thinking and keep him simply inventing truly. He could invent more with more insight and truth than anyone who ever lived. But his ponderous and

Messianic thinking was no better than many another evangelical professor of history and I learned from him to distrust my own Thinking
with a capital T and to try to write as truly, as straightly, as objectively
and as humbly as possible.

The account of Bagration's rearguard action in this book is the
finest and best understood relation of such an action that I have ever
read and it gives an understanding, by presenting things on a small
enough scale to be completely comprehended, of what a battle is that
no one has ever bettered. I prefer it to the account of Borodino, magnificent though that is. Then, too, from Tolstoy is the wonderful account of young Petya's first action and his death published here in the
selection that has been titled, badly enough, for it is about much more
than that and it has been presented from the viewpoint of an aristocrat, "The People's War." It has all the happiness, and freshness
and nobility of a boy's first encounter with the business of war and
it is as true as the "Red Badge of Courage" is true although the two
boys had little in common except their youth and that they were
first facing that thing which no one knows about who has not done it.

They represent, too, the difference between a first cavalry action
and the first action of a foot soldier. A man with a horse is never
as alone as a man on foot, for a horse will take you where you cannot
make your own legs go. Just as a mechanized force, not by virtue of
their armor, but by the fact that they move mechanically, will advance
into situations where you could put neither men nor animals; neither
get them up there nor hold them there.

After mechanized troops have had enough experience, so that they
appreciate accurately the degree of danger involved in their movements, then the same limits in what they will do are reached. It has
been one of the great advantages, in the tank warfare in Northern
Africa, which the Germans have held that their Commander in Chief
has always been up with the tanks to see that his orders have been
carried out rather than to assume they would be carried out simply
because they had been given. He could thus make decisions on the
spot and change orders which had become impossible of execution.
He was there in person to see that they were obeyed.

In the civil war in Spain the tanks of both sides in early 1937 were
completely vulnerable to the effective Russian anti-tank gun, which was
employed on the Republican side, and to the even better German anti-
tank weapon which was being first used then by the Franco troops,
and there were never enough tanks to use them in proper force so that
their possibilities had to always be deduced rather than proven. There

we learned much about the mentality of men in armored vehicles functioning under the worst possible conditions for their morale.

I have seen a French tank company commander turn up at five o'clock in the morning for an attack so drunk he could not stand, having tried, with brandy, to bolster himself up to have nerve enough to make the attack which he was convinced, from careful study of the ground the day before, was hopeless in the force with which it had to be made. He never got his tanks up to the starting point and was shot, quite properly, that afternoon with only one week more to go on the time he had enlisted for. He had been a good officer at the start, but the necessity to do things in insufficient force and the constant improvement of the German anti-tank guns had, coupled with the approach of the end of his term of enlistment, made him worthless and dangerous.

We learned later that the attack had been a complete surprise. The anti-tank guns which had been in that sector had been removed to another part of the front where the attack had been expected and the French officer could have completed his enlistment with a victorious action. But it was a relief to everyone when he was shot because the amount of fear he was carrying around with him was dangerous, disgusting, and embarrassing. In the next action, a week later, when his tanks were used, very sound elements of infantry were detailed to keep close behind the disgraced tanks with anti-tank grenades and blow them up if they did not keep moving as ordered.

The moral of this digression is, as stated above, that a horse will carry a man in his first action where his legs might not go; and a mechanized vehicle will carry him further than a horse will go; but finally no mechanized vehicle is any better than the heart of the man who handles the controls. So learn about the human heart and the human mind in war from this book. There is much about them in here.

The best account of actual human beings behaving during a world shaking event is Stendhal's picture of young Fabrizio at the battle of Waterloo. That account is more like war and less like the nonsense written about it than any other writing could possibly be. Once you have read it you will have been at the battle of Waterloo and nothing can ever take that experience from you. You will have to read Victor Hugo's account of the same battle, which is a fine, bold, majestic painting of the whole tragedy, to find out what you saw there as you rode with the boy; but you will have actually seen the field of Waterloo already whether you understood it or not. You will have seen a small piece of war as closely and as clearly with Stendhal as any man has ever written of it. It is the classic account of a routed army and beside it all of Zola's piled on detail in his "Debacle" is as dead and unconvincing as a steel engraving. Stendhal served with Napoleon and saw some of the greatest battles of the world. But all he ever wrote about war is the one long passage from "Le Chartreuse de Parme" which is included, complete, in this book.

It was at Waterloo that General Cambronne, when called on to surrender, was supposed to have said, "The Old Guard dies but never surrenders!" What Cambronne actually said was, "Merde!" which the French, when they do not wish to pronounce it, still refer to as, "the word of Cambronne." It corresponds to our four letter word for manure. All the difference between the noble and the earthy accounts of war is contained in the variance between these two quotations. The whole essence of how men speak in actual war is in Stendhal.

There are good accounts of sea fighting in this book from Trafalgar through the *Monitor* and the *Merrimac* to Dewey in Manila Bay and the wonderful account of the destruction of the Russian fleet by Admiral Togo's forces. In that account, which is one of the finest that I know of fighting in armored ships before the introduction of the airplane into naval warfare, you see what men could go through, with their spirits unconquered, in a battle which most Americans had completely forgotten.

Our last two naval fights, before this war, the destruction of the Spanish fleet off Santiago de Cuba and Dewey's action in Manila Bay, had been pushovers. There are no more pushovers to be fought now and if more people had read "Tsushima" there would not have been such a pushover psychology in our navy before Pearl Harbor. All through the Pacific and the Far East in 1941 I heard about the general incapacity and worthlessness of "those Little Monkeys." All the oil they had was what we, the Dutch and the British sold them and the quantity they split with the Russians on Sakhalin Island to their North. They had to have the oil if they were ever to be a first class power. So they edged down toward it. Finally we told them they could go no further toward the oil. At that moment it was perfectly clear that we would have to fight them.

When that moment arrives, whether it is in a barroom fight or in a war, the thing to do is to hit your opponent the first punch and hit him as hard as possible. But we were a great and noble power and they relied on our nobility and kept men talking to us while they prepared to hit. They had hit once before against Russia without warning. In Washington they seemed to have forgotten that. We kept on talking. As a matter of fact, I believe we were talking to them at the moment when it happened. So we had Pearl Harbor.

It is not in my province in this book to examine further into the causes of Pearl Harbor. A commission has reported on its immediate causes and fixed some of the blame. After the war there will be more blame to fix. In the meantime it has happened. There is nothing this book can ever do about it. But it can show you something about our enemy so that they will not be taken lightly. "Tsushima" makes interesting reading. There is nothing about monkeys in it at all.

Naval war has been changed completely and fundamentally by two events; the sinking of the wooden ships by the *Merrimac* which introduced the armored vessel, and the sinking of the *Prince of Wales* and the *Repulse* off Malaya. The British attack on the Italian warships in Taranto harbor with torpedo planes was the prelude to the *Prince of Wales* and *Repulse* loss but since the naval authorities continued to think of the *Prince of Wales* as unsinkable by air-attack the later event was the real turning point.

Since then there have been the two accounts of the battle of the Coral Seas and the battle of Midway which mark the third and fourth phases of the evolution of naval warfare. The first of these is the evolution and supreme employ of the aircraft carrier so that two fleets might never be in contact and yet fight destructive actions exclusively with the planes from their carriers; actions which if carried to their furthest conclusion could result in mutual destruction of all planes and their carrier bases involved. The second showed the ability of land based planes to beat off and destroy a fleet accompanied by aircraft carriers.

The implications of these two actions are too vast to go into in an introduction to this book.

There is no material on Commando raids in this book. But since those raiders, who due to the lack of action in the west from the fall of France until an invasion of the continent is undertaken, have been publicized very extensively, this book instead presents an account of that greatest pre-Commando raid of raids, the bottling up of Zeebrugge. If anyone ever sneers to you about the bravery of the British have him read that account.

This war is only a continuation of the last war. France was not beaten in 1940. France was beaten in 1917. Singapore was not really lost in 1942. It was lost at Gallipoli and on the Somme and in the mud of Passchendaele. Austria was not destroyed in 1938. Austria was destroyed in the battle of Vittorio-Veneto at the end of October in 1918. It was really lost and gone when it failed to beat Italy after Caporetto in the great Austrian victory offensive of the 15th of June, 1918.

All of history is of one piece and it is ourselves, who bore the least weight of casualties in 1917 and 1918, who have to bear the most to defeat Germany this time. Once a nation has entered into a policy of foreign wars, there is no withdrawing. If you do not go to them then they will come to you. It was April, 1917 that ended our isolation —it was not Pearl Harbor.

But there will be no lasting peace, nor any possibility of a just peace, until *all lands* where the people are ruled, exploited and governed by any government whatsoever against their consent are given their freedom. This premise has implications which have no place in this introduction.

There is no space to comment on each of the selections in this book. You will discover for yourself the fascination and lucidity of Sir Charles Oman, the great commentator and historian of the art of war in the Middle Ages. I wish that the two selections from his work could have been fifty. As it is, you have in "The Battle of Hastings" the account of the last great effort to use the Teutonic infantry tactics which had once ruled Europe against the rising tide of the feudal cavalry, which was to be the dominant arm for the next two hundred and fifty years until it, in turn, succumbed to the English longbow at Crecy.

In "The Battle of Arsouf" you see the classic example of the patience and endurance it takes in men to lure a harassing enemy to close combat and can admire without reserve the generalship of King Richard. In that meeting between the Saracens and the Franks, war took on the aspect of a part of the intercourse of the human race just as it had in the Battle of Hastings and as it was to have in the great fighting between Cortez and the followers of Montezuma and in all the encounters that were grouped under that first division in the book.

Since war is made up of all the elements under which certain selections are listed in this book and since all the selections deal with war, many of them would fit as well under one head as under another. Especially, since war is the province of chance, are there many other stories that could be classified under that fifth division of material.

For wonderful narratives of the part chance plays in our history, read, "The Wrong Road," by Marquis James to really understand the fate of Major André and for excitement read, "The Stolen Railroad Train," by the same author. For excitement and for a great story which should do much to make us appreciate and understand our British allies, read, "Turn About," by William Faulkner.

Charles Nordhoff and James Norman Hall's account of an all day air fight is as different from modern war in the air as the battle of Cannae is from a Commando raid; but you can appreciate the element of chance when you realize that but for the lucky appearance of a French Spad pilot, we would never have had the "Mutiny on the Bounty" trilogy. That is, if it is autobiographical. If it isn't, read it anyway.

That *War is the province of friction and that everything is very simple in war, but the simplest thing is difficult,* no better example proves than Major General J. F. C. Fuller's account of Gallipoli. We had Masefield's account of Gallipoli, which is a poet's record of heroism and suffering. But I believe the men who died there would rather that Fuller's account be published. I do not agree with General Fuller's politics and he has written many things to which I am absolutely opposed. But his account of Gallipoli remains as something that we can learn from greatly and it contains the type of necessary criticism which has been mentioned earlier in this introduction.

Criticism of the friction at Gettysburg is presented in Lt. Col. John W. Thomason's story, "The Stars in Their Courses." It presents much else too and it is a fine story as are all of his other stories in this book. It is a great loss they could not be illustrated by his drawings which are so excellent and added so much to the edition of General Marbot's Memoirs which he edited.

There is quite a bit of Marbot in this book and if you like it, you must read it all. It is worth learning French to read the three volumes of his memoirs alone. None of the four great young cavalry leaders of Napoleon left memoirs. Colbert was killed by a sniper in Spain, Sainte-Croix was hit by a shell from an English gunboat in the same Peninsular campaign; Lasalle was killed at Wagram when the battle was all but over, and Montbrun died at Borodino. You know about the life they led and their battles, though, from reading Marbot. That he should have lived to write the book is a miracle.

When reading the memoirs of fighting soldiers, I am always

reminded of the story of old Marshal Lefebvre who was entertaining a boyhood friend who could not conceal his envy of the Marshal-Duke's elaborate residence in Paris. "So you are jealous, eh?" the Marshal peered at him. "Eh bien, come out to the garden and I'll have twenty shots at you at thirty paces. If I miss you, then you can have the house and grounds and all that's in it. I was shot at a thousand times from as close range as that before I got this house."

Of the stories that you must not miss in this book, one of the finest is, "After the Final Victory," by Agnes Smedley. In it she has gotten that absolute determination to win, the unthinkability of defeat no matter what the odds or how long the time that they must go, that has characterized the Chinese people. Under conditions that are inconceivable to Western people, they have fought for five years. Their great illusion was that we would enter the war finally and then the Japanese would be quickly destroyed. Now, having lost almost all the advantages they held when we were neutral, they are our second front against Japan; a second front which must be nurtured with more than promises and a little aviation aid.

China's resistance has been taken too much for granted, just as Russia's was. It cannot be dismissed with praise, fine words or simply money, and a few planes, no matter how superb are the pilots that fly them. The greatest danger that the allied cause faces is the possible disillusion of the people of China and Russia in regard to their allies. China must have aid in greatly increasing amounts. No enchantment with the possibility of immediate and flashy successes elsewhere should divert the long term necessity for sending that aid to China no matter what sacrifices are involved.

This introduction is written by a man, who, having three sons to whom he is responsible in some ways for having brought them into this unspeakably balled-up world, does not feel in any way detached or impersonal about the entire present mess we live in. Therefore, be pleased to regard this introduction as absolutely personal rather than impersonal writing.

This book has been edited in order that those three boys, as they grow to the age where they can appreciate it and use it and will need it, can have the book that will contain truth about war as near as we can come by it, which was lacking to me when I needed it most. It will not replace experience. But it can prepare for and supplement experience. It can serve as a corrective after experience.

This year, the mother of the oldest boy, who is eighteen, had asked me to have a talk with him about the war in case he should be worried about it in any way. So when we were driving back in the car from the airfield where he had just flown in to spend the few days of vacation that were all he would get before the summer term started at college, I said, "Mother thought you might be worried a little about the war and going to it and all."

"No, Papa," he said. "Don't you worry about that. I'm not worried at all."

"The one thing I really know," I told him, "is that worrying doesn't do any good about anything."

"Don't you worry," he said. "I'm not worried."

That was the end of that conversation. No, worrying does no good. Neither for children nor for their parents. A good soldier does not worry. He knows that nothing happens until it actually happens and you live your life up until then. Danger only exists at the moment of danger. To live properly in war, the individual eliminates all such things as potential danger. Then a thing is only bad when it is bad. It is neither bad before nor after. Cowardice, as distinguished from panic, is almost always simply a lack of ability to suspend the functioning of the imagination. Learning to suspend your imagination and live completely in the very second of the present minute with no before and no after is the greatest gift a soldier can acquire. It, naturally, is the opposite of all those gifts a writer should have. That is what makes good writing by good soldiers such a rare thing and why it is so prized when we have it.

You never know how people will react to war. Take self-inflicted wounds. In one famous International Brigade which fought at the battle of Guadalajara so valiantly and well that they made history there in that eight-day battle, there were thirty-seven self-inflicted wounds in the first afternoon the Brigade was in action. That was panic. There is a sure cure for self-inflicted wounds; much more efficacious than court-martial and execution when the offense is proven as was practiced in the world war.

It was discovered in the snow and mud of the plateau above Brihuega with that March wind blowing against the constant rolling roar of automatic weapon fire and it consists of loading all the self-inflicted wounded into a truck; taking away their coats and blankets so their comrades in the lines can have that much more warmth; and driving them back to the town of Guadalajara where all the men's wounds were dressed, and then returning the bandaged men to their sections in the line.

After that treatment there were no more self-inflicted wounds in that Brigade except head wounds. Any man who would rather shoot himself in the head than run the chance that the enemy might eventually do that same thing can be, and is, written off as a hopeless coward and listed under, "Died of Wounds and Other Causes."

There was much trouble with self-inflicted wounds in Italy during the last war. The men became very skillful at it and often a pair would team up to shoot each other, usually wrapping sandbags around the arm or leg, to avoid any evidence of a close discharge of the rifle. Others would hold copper coins in their armpits to get a yellow cast of complexion and simulate jaundice. Others deliberately contracted venereal disease in order to leave the lines. There were doctors in Milan who did a thriving trade in injecting paraffin under the kneecaps of their clients to induce lameless. Mussolini himself was wounded superficially in the legs and backside by the premature explosion of an Italian trench mortar in the early years of the war and never returned to the front. I have often thought that all his martial bombast and desire for military glory was a defense mechanism, formed against his own knowledge of how frightened he had been in the world war and the ignominious exit he had made from it at the first opportunity.

Against the type of cowardice, or more often panic and stupidity, that produces self-inflicted wounds, I will always remember one marvelous story of the deprecation the truly brave man can feel for them. Evan Shipman, one of my oldest friends, a fine poet and good prose writer, had gone to France in order to drive an ambulance on the Loyalist side in the Spanish Civil War. Our State Department had refused to validate his passport for Spain, so he took the smuggler's route over the Pyrenees border between France and Spain with a group of recruits for the International Brigades. They were all caught by the French gendarmerie and sentenced to a jail term in Toulouse.

Being jailed made Evan so indignant that he determined, instead of driving an ambulance, that he would enlist in the infantry of the Brigades. After coming out of jail he successfully entered Spain by another route and in a short time was at the front, and in the battle of Brunete, one of the fiercest fought of all that war. He fought all through the battle with exemplary courage, staying with the Franco-Belge battalion to whom he had been attached as an interpreter and a runner, and fighting in the fine stand they made against orders which prevented a rout at the very most critical time, and on the last day was severely wounded.

I did not see him for some months and when I did he was pale, ragged, limping and profoundly cheerful.

"Tell me about when you were wounded," I said by the time we had settled down to a drink.

"Why, Hem, it was absolutely nothing. It was nothing at all. I never felt a thing."

"What do you mean, you didn't feel a thing?" The machine gun bullet had gone through his thigh from one side to the other.

"Why, it was really nothing. You see I was unconscious at the time."

"Yes?"

"You see the planes had just caught us in the open and bombed us and I was unconscious at the time. So I didn't feel a thing when they came down and machine gunned us. Really, Hem, it was absolutely nothing. I've hardly even thought of it as a wound. It was almost like having an anaesthetic beforehand."

He turned his drink around in his hand and then said, "Hem, I can never thank you enough for having brought me over here. I was very upset that you might be worried about me. I want you to know that being in Spain is the happiest time I have ever had in my life. Please believe me, Hem. You really must believe me absolutely."

You can set that against all the self-inflicted wound cases. It was because of Evan that I finally insisted "The Red Badge of Courage" must be published entire in this book. Evan Shipman is a private now in an Armored unit of the U. S. Army. He was turned down innumerable times by medical examiners, but finally built up enough weight to get a doctor to pass him. He wrote me from where his unit is stationed, "I picked up a copy of 'The Red Badge of Courage,' here in the library and it seems even better than when I first read it." So I thought, on rereading it that it better be in and all of it in.

There is no space now to recommend all the other things you should absolutely read in this book. If I did not think they were all good they would not be in.

This collection of stories, accounts, and narratives is an attempt to give a true picture of men at war. It is not a propaganda book. It seeks to instruct and inform rather than to influence anyone's opinion. Its only and absolute standard for inclusion has been the soundness and truth of the material.

I have seen much war in my lifetime and I hate it profoundly. But there are worse things than war; and all of them come with defeat. The more you hate war, the more you know that once you are forced into it, for whatever reason it may be, you have to win it. You have to win it and get rid of the people that made it and see that, this time, it never comes to us again. We who took part in the last war to end wars are not going to be fooled again. This war is going to be fought until that objective is achieved; if it takes a hundred years if necessary, and no matter whom we have to fight to gain that objective in the end.

We will also fight this war to enjoy the rights and privileges conveyed to us by the Declaration of Independence, the Constitution of the United States, and the Bill of Rights, and woe to anyone who has any plans for taking those rights and privileges away from us under any guise or for any reason whatsoever.

During a war censorship can conceal mistakes, blunders and acts of almost criminal misjudgment and negligence. These occur in all wars. But after the war is over, all of these acts have to be paid for. The people fight the war and in the end the people know what has really happened. In spite of all censorship that can be imposed, the people always finally know in the end because enough of them have been there.

It is very easy to fool the people at the start of a war and run it on a confidential basis. But later the wounded start coming back and the actual news spreads. Then, finally, when we have won, the men who fought the war come home. There will be millions of them who will come home knowing how things were. A government which wants to keep the confidence of its people after the war, or during the last stages of it, should take the people into its confidence and tell them everything that they can know, bad as well as good, so long as their knowing of it does not help the enemy. Covering up errors to save the men who make them can only lead to a lack of confidence which can be one of the greatest dangers a nation can face.

I am sure that as the war progresses, our government will realize the necessity of telling the people the truth, the whole truth, and nothing but the truth, in everything that does not aid the enemy, because times are coming in this war when the government will need the complete and absolute confidence of all citizens if this country is to endure.

The subtitles and quotations at the beginning of the first seven sections of this book are from ON WAR by General Karl von Clausewitz: Kegan Paul, Trench, Trubner & Co., London; E. P. Dutton & Co., New York.

WAR IS PART OF THE INTERCOURSE
OF THE HUMAN RACE

*W*E SAY, therefore, War belongs not to the province of Arts or Sciences, but to the province of social life. It is a conflict of great interests which is settled by bloodshed and only in that is it different from others. It would be better, instead of comparing it with Art, to liken it to business competition, which is also a conflict of human interests and activities; and it is still more like State politics, which again, on its part, may be looked upon as a kind of business competition on a great scale. Besides, State politics is the womb in which War is developed, in which its outlines lie hidden in a rudimentary state, like the qualities of living creatures in their embryos.

The Invasion of Britain

BY

JULIUS CAESAR

DURING the short part of summer which remained, Cæsar, although in these countries, as all Gaul lies toward the north, the winters are early, nevertheless resolved to proceed into Britain, because he discovered that in almost all the wars with the Gauls succors had been furnished to our enemy from that country; and even if the time of year should be insufficient for carrying on the war, yet he thought it would be of great service to him if he only entered the island, and saw into the character of the people, and got knowledge of their localities, harbors, and landing-places, all which were for the most part unknown to the Gauls. For neither does anyone except merchants generally go thither, nor even to them was any portion of it known, except the sea-coast and those parts which are opposite to Gaul. Therefore, after having called up to him the merchants from all parts, he could learn neither what was the size of the island, nor what or how numerous were the nations which inhabited it, nor what system of war they followed, nor what customs they used, nor what harbors were convenient for a great number of large ships.

He sends before him Caius Volusenus with a ship of war, to acquire a knowledge of these particulars before he in person should make a descent into the island, as he was convinced that this was a judicious measure. He commissioned him to thoroughly examine into all matters, and then return to him as soon as possible. He himself proceeds to the Morini with all his forces. He orders ships from all parts of the neighboring countries, and the fleet which the preceding summer he had built for the war with the Venĕti, to assemble in this place. In the meantime, his purpose having been discovered, and reported to the Britons by merchants, ambassadors come to him from several states of the island, to promise that they will give hostages, and submit to the government of the Roman people. Having given them an audience, he after promising liberally, and exhorting them to continue in that purpose, sends them back to their own country, and [dispatches] with them Commius, whom, upon subduing the Atrebătes, he had created king there, a man whose courage and conduct he esteemed, and who he thought would be faithful to him, and whose influence ranked highly in those countries. He orders him to visit as many states as he could, and persuade them to embrace the protection of the Roman people, and apprize

From: Caesar's *Commentaries*.

3

them that he would shortly come thither. Volusenus, having viewed the localities as far as means could be afforded one who dared not leave his ship and trust himself to barbarians, returns to Cæsar on the fifth day, and reports what he had there observed.

While Cæsar remains in these parts for the purpose of procuring ships, ambassadors come to him from a great portion of the Morini, to plead their excuse respecting their conduct on the late occasion; alleging that it was as men uncivilized, and as those who were unacquainted with our custom, that they had made war upon the Roman people, and promising to perform what he should command. Cæsar, thinking that this had happened fortunately enough for him, because he neither wished to leave an enemy behind him, nor had an opportunity for carrying on a war, by reason of the time of year, nor considered that employment in such trifling matters was to be preferred to his enterprise on Britain, imposes a large number of hostages; and when these were brought, he received them to his protection. Having collected together, and provided about eighty transport ships, as many as he thought necessary for conveying over two legions, he assigned such [ships] of war as he had besides to the quæstor, his lieutenants, and officers of cavalry. There were in addition to these eighteen ships of burden which were prevented, eight miles from that place, by winds, from being able to reach the same port. These he distributed among the horse; the rest of the army, he delivered to Q. Titurius Sabinus and L. Aurunculeius Cotta, his lieutenants, to lead into the territories of the Menapii and those cantons of the Morini from which ambassadors had not come to him. He ordered P. Sulpicius Rufus, his lieutenant, to hold possession of the harbor, with such a garrison as he thought sufficient.

These matters being arranged, finding the weather favorable for his voyage, he set sail about the third watch, and ordered the horse to march forward to the further port, and there embark and follow him. As this was performed rather tardily by them, he himself reached Britain with the first squadron of ships, about the fourth hour of the day, and there saw the forces of the enemy drawn up in arms on all the hills. The nature of the place was this: the sea was confined by mountains so close to it that a dart could be thrown from their summit upon the shore. Considering this by no means a fit place for disembarking, he remained at anchor till the ninth hour, for the other ships to arrive there. Having in the meantime assembled the lieutenants and military tribunes, he told them both what he had learned from Volusenus, and what he wished to be done; and enjoined them (as the principle of military matters, and especially as maritime affairs, which have a precipitate and uncertain action, required) that all things should be performed by them at a nod and at the instant. Having dismissed them, meeting both with wind and tide favorable at the same time, the signal being given and the anchor weighed, he advanced about seven miles from that place, and stationed his fleet over against an open and level shore.

But the barbarians, upon perceiving the design of the Romans, sent forward their cavalry and charioteers, a class of warriors of whom it is their practice to make great use in their battles, and following with the rest of their forces, endeavored to prevent our men landing. In this was the greatest difficulty, for the following reasons, namely, because our ships, on account of their great size, could be stationed only in deep water; and our soldiers, in places unknown to them, with their hands embarrassed, oppressed with a large and heavy weight of armor, had at the same time to leap from the ships, stand amid the waves, and encounter the enemy; whereas they, either on dry ground, or advancing a little way into the water, free in all their limbs, in places thoroughly known to them, could confidently throw their weapons and spur on their horses, which were accustomed to this kind of service. Dismayed by these circumstances and altogether untrained in this mode of battle, our men did not all exert the same vigor and eagerness which they had been wont to exert in engagements on dry ground.

When Cæsar observed this, he ordered the ships of war, the appearance of which was somewhat strange to the barbarians and the motion more ready for service, to be withdrawn a little from the transport vessels, and to be propelled by their oars, and be stationed toward the open flank of the enemy, and the enemy to be beaten off and driven away, with slings, arrows, and engines: which plan was of great service to our men; for the barbarians being startled by the form of our ships and the motions of our oars and the nature of our engines, which was strange to them, stopped, and shortly after retreated a little. And while our men were hesitating [whether they should advance to the shore], chiefly on account of the depth of the sea, he who carried the eagle of the tenth legion, after supplicating the gods that the matter might turn out favorably to the legion, exclaimed, "Leap, fellow soldiers, unless you wish to betray your eagle to the enemy. I, for my part, will perform my duty to the commonwealth and my general." When he had said this with a loud voice, he leaped from the ship and proceeded to bear the eagle toward the enemy. Then our men, exhorting one another that so great a disgrace should not be incurred, all leaped from the ship. When those in the nearest vessels saw them, they speedily followed and approached the enemy.

The battle was maintained vigorously on both sides. Our men, however, as they could neither keep their ranks, nor get firm footing, nor follow their standards, and as one from one ship and another from another assembled around whatever standards they met, were thrown into great confusion. But the enemy, who were acquainted with all the shallows, when from the shore they saw any coming from a ship one by one, spurred on their horses, and attacked them while embarrassed; many surrounded a few, others threw their weapons upon our collected forces on their exposed flank. When Cæsar observed this, he ordered the boats of the ships of war and the spy sloops to be filled with soldiers, and sent them up to the succor of those whom he had observed in distress. Our men, as soon as they made good their footing on dry ground, and all their comrades had joined them, made an attack upon the enemy, and put them to flight, but could not pursue them very far, because the horse had not been able to maintain their course at sea and reach the island. This alone was wanting to Cæsar's accustomed success.

The enemy being thus vanquished in battle, as soon as they recovered after their flight, instantly sent ambassadors to Cæsar to negotiate about peace. They promised to give hostages and perform what he should command. Together with these ambassadors came Commius the Altrebatian, who, as I have above said, had been sent by Cæsar into Britain. Him they had seized upon when leaving his ship, although in the character of ambassador he bore the general's commission to them, and thrown into chains: then after the battle was fought, they sent him back, and in suing for peace cast the blame of that act upon the common people, and entreated that it might be pardoned on account of their indiscretion. Cæsar, complaining, that after they had sued for peace, and had voluntarily sent ambassadors into the continent for that purpose, they had made war without a reason, said that he would pardon their indiscretion, and imposed hostages, a part of whom they gave immediately; the rest they said they would give in a few days, since they were sent for from remote places. In the meantime they ordered their people to return to the country parts, and the chiefs assembled from all quarters, and proceeded to surrender themselves and their states to Cæsar.

A peace being established by these proceedings four days after we had come into Britain, the eighteen ships, to which reference has been made above, and which conveyed the cavalry, set sail from the upper port with a gentle gale, when, however, they were approaching Britain and were seen from the camp, so great a storm suddenly arose that none of them could maintain their course at sea; and some were taken back to the same port from which they had started;—others, to their great danger, were driven to the lower part of the island, nearer to the west; which, however, after having cast anchor, as they were getting filled with water, put out to sea through necessity in a stormy night, and made for the continent.

It happened that night to be full moon, which usually occasions very high tides in that ocean; and that circumstance was unknown to our men. Thus, at the same time, the tide began to fill the ships of war which Cæsar had provided to convey over his army, and which he had drawn up on the strand; and the storm began to dash the ships of burden which were riding at anchor against each other; nor was any means afforded our men of either managing them or of rendering any service. A great many ships having been wrecked, inasmuch as the rest, having lost their cables, anchors, and other tackling, were unfit for sailing, a great confusion, as would necessarily happen, arose throughout the army; for there were no other ships in which they could be conveyed back, and all things which are of service in repairing vessels were wanting, and, corn for the winter had not been provided in those places, because it was understood by all that they would certainly winter in Gaul.

On discovering these things the chiefs of Britain, who had come up after the battle was fought to perform those conditions which Cæsar had imposed, held a conference, when they perceived that cavalry, and ships, and corn were wanting to the Romans, and discovered the small number of our soldiers from the small extent of the camp (which, too, was on this account more limited than ordinary, because Cæsar had conveyed over his legions without baggage), and thought that the best plan was to renew the war, and cut off our men from corn and provisions and protract the affair till winter; because they felt confident, that, if they were vanquished or cut off from a return, no one would afterward pass over into Britain for the purpose of making war. Therefore, again entering into a conspiracy, they began to depart from the camp by degrees and secretly bring up their people from the country parts.

But Cæsar, although he had not as yet discovered their measures, yet, both from what had occurred to his ships, and from the circumstance that they had neglected to give the promised hostages, suspected that the thing would come to pass which really did happen. He therefore provided remedies against all contingencies; for he daily conveyed corn from the country parts into the camp, used the timber and brass of such ships as were most seriously damaged for repairing the rest, and ordered whatever things besides were necessary for this object to be brought to him from the continent. And thus, since that business was executed by the soldiers with the greatest energy, he effected that, after the loss of twelve ships, a voyage could be made well enough in the rest.

While these things are being transacted, one legion had been sent to forage, according to custom, and no suspicion of war had arisen as yet, and some of the people remained in the country parts, others went backward and forward to the camp, they who were on duty at the gates of the camp reported to Cæsar that a greater dust than was usual was seen in that direction in which the legion had marched. Cæsar, suspecting that which was [really the case],—that some new enterprise was undertaken by the barbarians, ordered the two cohorts which were on duty, to march into that quarter with him, and two other cohorts to relieve them on duty; the rest to be armed and follow him immediately. When he had advanced some little way from the camp, he saw that his men were overpowered by the enemy and scarcely able to stand their ground, and that, the legion being crowded together, weapons were being cast on them from all sides. For as all the corn was reaped in every part with the exception of one, the enemy, suspecting that our men would repair to that, had concealed themselves in the woods during the night. Then attacking them suddenly, scattered as they were, and when they had laid aside their arms, and were engaged in reaping, they killed a small number, threw the rest into confusion, and surrounded them with their cavalry and chariots.

Their mode of fighting with their chariots is this: firstly, they drive about in all directions and throw their weapons and generally break the ranks of the enemy with the very dread of their horses and the noise of their wheels; and when they have worked themselves in between the troops of horse, leap from their chariots and engage on foot. The charioteers in the meantime withdraw some little distance from the battle, and so place themselves with the chariots that, if their masters are overpowered by the number of the enemy, they may have a ready retreat to their own troops. Thus they display in battle the speed of horse, [together with] the firmness of infantry; and by daily practice and exercise attain to such expertness that they are accustomed, even on a declining and steep place, to check their horses at full speed, and manage and turn them in an instant and run along the pole, and stand on the yoke, and thence betake themselves with the greatest celerity to their chariots again.

Under these circumstances, our men being dismayed by the novelty of this mode of battle, Cæsar most seasonably brought assistance; for upon his arrival the enemy paused, and our men recovered from their fear; upon which thinking the time unfavorable for provoking the enemy and coming to an action, he kept himself in his own quarter, and, a short time having intervened, drew back the legions into the camp. While these things are going on, and all our men engaged, the rest of the Britons, who were in the fields, departed. Storms then set in for several successive days, which both confined our men to the camp and hindered the enemy from attacking us. In the meantime the barbarians dispatched messengers to all parts, and reported to their people the small number of our soldiers, and how good an opportunity was given for obtaining spoil and for liberating themselves forever, if they should only drive the Romans from their camp. Having by these means speedily got together a large force of infantry and of cavalry, they came up to the camp.

Although Cæsar anticipated that the same thing which had happened on former occasions would then occur—that, if the enemy were routed, they would escape from danger by their speed; still, having got about thirty horse, which Commius the Atrebatian, of whom mention has been made, had brought over with him [from Gaul], he drew up the legions in order of battle before the camp. When the action commenced, the enemy were unable to sustain the attack of our men long, and turned their backs; our men pursued them as far as their speed and strength permitted, and slew a great number of them; then, having destroyed and burned everything far and wide, they retreated to their camp.

The same day, ambassadors sent by the enemy came to Cæsar to negotiate a peace. Cæsar doubled the number of hostages which he had before demanded; and ordered that they should be brought over to the continent, because, since the time of the equinox was near, he did not consider that, with his ships out of repair, the voyage ought to be deferred till winter. Having met with favorable weather, he set sail a little after midnight, and all his fleet arrived safe at the continent, except two of the ships of burden which could not make the same port which the other ships did, and were carried a little lower down.

When our soldiers, about 300 in number, had been drawn out of these two ships, and were marching to the camp, the Morini, whom Cæsar, when setting forth for Britain, had left in a state of peace, excited by the hope of spoil, at first surrounded them with a small number of men, and ordered them to lay down their arms, if they did not wish to be slain; afterward however, when they, forming a circle, stood on their defense, a shout was raised and about 6000 of the enemy soon assembled; which being reported, Cæsar sent all the cavalry in the camp as a relief to his men. In the meantime our soldiers sustained the attack of the enemy, and fought most valiantly for more than four hours, and, receiving but few wounds themselves, slew several of them. But after our cavalry came in sight, the enemy, throwing away their arms, turned their backs, and a great number of them were killed.

The day following Cæsar sent Labienus, his lieutenant, with those legions which he had brought back from Britain, against the Morini, who had revolted; who, as they had no place to which they might retreat, on account of the drying up of their marshes (which they had availed themselves of as a place of refuge the preceding year), almost all fell into the power of Labienus. In the meantime Cæsar's lieutenants, Q. Titurius and L. Cotta, who had led the legions into the territories of the Menapii, having laid waste all their lands, cut down their corn and burned their houses, returned to Cæsar because the Menapii had all concealed themselves in their thickest woods. Cæsar fixed the winter quarters of all the legions among the Belgæ. Thither only two British states sent hostages; the rest omitted to do so. For these successes, a thanksgiving of twenty days was decreed by the senate upon receiving Cæsar's letter.

The Battle of Hastings, 1066 A.D.

BY

CHARLES OMAN

As THE last great example of an endeavour to use the old infantry tactics of the Teutonic races against the now fully-developed cavalry of feudalism, we have to describe the battle of Hastings, a field which has been fought over by modern critics almost as fiercely as by the armies of Harold Godwineson and William the Bastard.

About the political and military antecedents of the engagement we have no need to speak at length. Suffice it to say that the final defeat of the old English thegnhood was immediately preceded by its most striking victory. In the summer of 1066 the newly-chosen King Harold was forced to watch two enemies at once. The Norman Duke William had openly protested against the election that had taken place in January, and was known to be gathering a great army and fleet at St. Valery. Harold knew him well, and judged him a most formidable enemy; he had called out the available naval strength of his realm, and a strong squadron was waiting all through June, July, and August, ranging between the Isle of Wight and Dover, ready to dispute the passage of the Channel. At the same time the earls and sheriffs had been warned to have the land forces of the realm ready for mobilisation, and the king with his housecarles lay by the coast in Sussex waiting for news. Duke William came not, for many a week; his host took long to gather, and when his ships were ready, August turned out a month of persistent storm and northerly winds, unsuited for the sailing of a great armament.

Meanwhile there was danger from the North also. King Harold's rebel brother, Earl Tostig, had been hovering off the coast with a small squadron, and had made a descent on the Humber in May, only to be driven away by the Northumbrian Earl Edwin. But Tostig had leagued himself with Harald Hardrada, the warlike and greedy King of Norway, and a Norse invasion was a possibility, though it seemed a less immediate danger than the Norman threat to the South Coast. September had arrived before either of the perils materialised.

By a most unlucky chance the crisis came just when the English fleet had run out of provisions, after keeping the sea for three months. On September 8, Harold ordered it round to London to revictual, and to refit, for it had suffered in the hard weather. It was to resume its cruising as soon as

From: *History of the Art of War in the Middle Ages,* by Charles Oman.

possible. Seven days later came the news that a Norwegian fleet of three hundred sail had appeared off the Yorkshire coast, and had ravaged Cleveland and taken Scarborough. Harold was compelled to commit the guard of the Channel to the winds, which had hitherto served him well, and to fly north with his housecarlès to face Hardrada's invasion. On his way he got the disastrous message that the two Earls Edwin of Northumbria and Morkar of Mercia had been beaten in a pitched battle at Fulford, in front of York (September 20), and that the city was treating for surrender. Pressing on with all possible speed, the English king arrived at York in time to prevent this disaster, and the same afternoon he brought the Norsemen to action at Stamford Bridge on the Derwent, seven miles from the city. Here he inflicted on them an absolutely crushing defeat—Hardrada was slain, so was the rebel Earl Tostig, and the invading host was so nearly exterminated that the survivors fled on only twenty-four ships, though they had brought three hundred into the Humber.

The details of the fight are absolutely lost—we cannot unfortunately accept one word of the spirited narrative of the *Heimskringla,* for all the statements in it that can be tested are obviously incorrect. Harold *may* have offered his rebel brother pardon and an earldom, and have promised his Norse ally no more than the famous "seven feet of English earth, since his stature is greater than that of other men." The Vikings *may* have fought for long hours in their shieldring, and have failed at evening only, when their king had been slain by a chance arrow. But we cannot trust a saga which says that Morkar was King Harold Godwineson's brother, and fell at Fulford; that Earl Waltheof (then a child) took part in the fight, and that the English army was mostly composed of cavalry and archers. The whole tale of the *Heimskringla* reads like a version of the battle of Hastings transported to Stamford Bridge by some incredible error. The one detail about it recorded in the Anglo-Saxon Chronicle, namely, that the fighting included a desperate defence of a bridge against the pursuing English, does *not* appear in the Norse narrative at all. We can only be sure that both sides must have fought on foot in the old fashion of Viking and Englishman, "hewing at each other across the war-linden" till the beaten army was well-nigh annihilated.

Meanwhile, on September 28—two days after Stamford Bridge—William of Normandy had landed at Pevensey, unhindered either by the English fleet, which was refitting at London, or by the king's army, which had gone north to repel the Norwegians. The invaders began to waste the land, and met with little resistance, since the king and his chosen warriors were absent. Only at Romney, as we are told, did the landsfolk stand to their arms and beat off the raiders.

Meanwhile, the news of William's landing was rapidly brought to Harold at York, and reached him—as we are told—at the very moment when he was celebrating by a banquet his victory over the Northmen. The king received the message on October 1 or October 2: he immediately hurried southward to London with all the speed that he could make. The victorious army of Stamford Bridge was with him, and the North Country levies of Edwin and Morkar were directed to follow as fast as they were able. Harold reached London on the 7th or 8th of October, and stayed there a few days to gather in the fyrd of the neighbouring shires of the South Midlands. On the 11th he marched forth from the city to face Duke William, though his army was still incomplete. The slack or treacherous earls of the North had not yet brought up their contingents, and the men of the western shires had not been granted time enough to reach the mustering place. But Harold's heart had been stirred by the reports of the cruel ravaging of Kent and Sussex by the Normans, and he was resolved to put his cause to the arbitrament of battle as quickly as possible, though the delay of a few days would per-haps have doubled his army. A rapid march of two days brought him to the outskirts of the Andredsweald, within touch of the district on which William had for the last fortnight been exercising his cruelty.

Harold took up his position at the point where the road from London to Hastings first leaves the woods, and comes forth into the open land of the coast. The chosen ground was the lonely hill above the marshy bottom of Senlac, on which the ruins of Battle Abbey stand, but then marked to the chronicler only by "the hoar apple tree" on its ridge, just as Ashdown had been marked two centuries before by its aged thorn.

The Senlac position consists of a hill some 1100 yards long and 150 yards broad, joined to the main bulk of the Wealden Hills by a sort of narrow isthmus with steep descents on either side. The road from London to Hast-ings crosses the isthmus, bisects the hill at its highest point, and then sinks down into the valley, to climb again the opposite ridge of Telham Hill. The latter is considerably the higher of the two, reaching 441 feet above the sea-level, while Harold's hill is but 275 at its summit. The English hill has a fairly gentle slope towards the south, the side which looked towards the enemy, but on the north the fall on either side of the isthmus is so steep as to be almost precipitous. The summit of the position, where it is crossed by the road, is the highest point. Here it was that King Harold fixed his two banners, the Dragon of Wessex, and his own standard of the Fighting Man.

The position was very probably one that had served before for some army of an older century, for we learn from the best authorities that there lay about it, especially on its rear, ancient banks and ditches, in some places scarped to a precipitous slope. Perhaps it may have been the camp of some part of Alfred's army in 893–894, when, posted in the east end of the Andredsweald, between the Danish fleet which had come ashore at Lymne and the other host which had camped at Middleton, he endeavoured from his central position to restrain their ravages in Kent and Sussex. No place indeed could have been more suited for a force observing newly-landed foes. It covers the only road from London which then pierced the Andredsweald, and was so close to its edge that the defenders could seek shelter in the impenetrable woods if they wished to avoid a battle.

The hill above the Senlac bottom, therefore, being the obvious position to take, for an army whose tactics compelled it to stand upon the defensive,

Harold determined to offer battle there. We need not believe the authorities who tell us that the King had been thinking of delivering a night attack upon the Normans, if he should chance to find them scattered abroad on their plundering, or keeping an inefficient lookout. It was most unlikely that he should dream of groping in the dark through eight miles of rolling ground, to assault a camp whose position and arrangements must have been unknown. His army had marched hard from London, had apparently only reached Senlac at nightfall, and must have been tired out. Moreover, Harold knew William's capacities as a general, and could not have thought it likely that he would be caught unprepared. It must have seemed to him a much more possible event that the Norman might refuse to attack the strong Senlac position, and offer battle in the open and nearer the sea. It was probably in anticipation of some such chance that Harold ordered his fleet, which had run back into the mouth of the Thames in very poor order some four weeks back, to refit itself and sail round the North Foreland, to threaten the Norman vessels now drawn ashore under the cover of a wooden castle at Hastings. He can scarcely have thought it likely that William would retire over seas on the news of his approach, so the bringing up of the fleet must have been intended either to cut off the Norman retreat in the event of a great English victory on land, or to so molest the invader's stranded vessels that he would be forced to return to the shore in order to defend them.

The English position is said by one narrator of the battle to have been entrenched. According to Wace, the latest and the most diffuse of our authorities, Harold ordered his men to rear a fence of plaited woodwork from the timber of the forest which lay close at their backs. But the earlier chroniclers, without exception, speak only of the shield-wall of the English, of their dense mass covering the crest of the hill, and of relics of ancient fortifications, the *antiquus agger* and *frequentia fossarum*, and *fovea magna* mentioned above. There is nothing inconceivable in the idea of Harold's having used the old Danish device of palisading a camp, save that he had arrived only on the preceding night, and that his army was weary. In the morning hours of October 14 little could have been done, though between daybreak and the arrival of the Norman host there were certainly three long hours. But it is difficult to suppose that if any serious entrenching had been carried out, the earlier Norman narrators of the fight would have refrained from mentioning it, since the more formidable the obstacles opposed to him, the more notable and creditable would have been the triumph of their duke. And the Bayeux Tapestry, which (despite all destructive criticism) remains a primary authority for the battle, appears to show no traces of any breastwork covering the English front. Probably Wace, writing from oral tradition ninety years after the battle, had heard something of the *frequentia fossarum* mentioned by William of Poictiers, and the *agger* described by Orderic, and translated them into new entrenchments, which he described as works of the best military type of his day.

From end to end of the crest of the hill the English host was ranged in one great solid mass. Probably its line extended from the high road, which crosses the summit nearer to its eastern than to its western side, for some 200 yards to the left, as far as the head of the small steep combe (with a rivulet at its bottom) which lies 200 yards to the due east of the modern parish church; while on the other, or western, side of the high road, the battle-front was much longer, running from the road as far as the upper banks of the other ravine (with a forked brook flowing out of it from two sources) which forms the western flank of the hill. From the road to this ravine there must have been a front of 800 or 850 yards. Harold's two standards were, as we know, set up on the spot which was afterwards marked by the high altar of Battle Abbey. His standing-place must therefore have been in the left-centre rather than in the absolute middle-front of the line. But the spot was dictated by the lie of the ground—here is the actual highest point of the hill, 275 feet above sea-level, while the greater part of the position is along the 250 feet contour. It was the obvious place for the planting of standards to be visible all around, and a commander standing by them could look down from a slight vantage-ground on the whole front of his host.

In this array, the English centre being slightly curved forward, its flank slightly curved back, the army looked to the Normans more like a circular mass than a deployed line. Although the Northumbrian and West-country levies were still missing, the army must have numbered many thousands, for the fyrd of south and central England was present in full force, and stirred to great wrath by the ravages of the Normans. It is impossible to guess at the strength of the host: the figures of the chroniclers, which sometimes swell up to hundreds of thousands, are wholly useless. As the position was about 1100 yards long, and the space required by a single warrior swinging his axe or hurling his javelin was some three feet, the front rank must have been at least some eleven hundred or twelve hundred strong. The hilltop was completely covered by the English, whose spear-shafts appeared to the Normans like a wood, so that they cannot have been a mere thin line: if they were some eight or ten deep, the total must have reached ten or eleven thousand men. Of these the smaller part must have been composed of the fully-armed warriors, the king's housecarles, the thegnhood, and the wealthier and better-equipped freemen, the class owning some five hides of land. The rudely-armed levies of the fyrd must have constituted the great bulk of the army: they bore, as the Bayeux Tapestry shows, the most miscellaneous arms—swords, javelins, clubs, axes, a few bows, and probably even rude instruments of husbandry turned to warlike uses. Their only defensive armour was the round or kite-shaped shield: body and head were clothed only in the tunic and cap of everyday wear.

In their battle array we know that the well-armed housecarles—perhaps two thousand chosen and veteran troops—were grouped in the centre around the king and the royal standards. The fyrd, divided no doubt according to its shires, was ranged on either flank. Presumably the thegns and other fully-armed men formed its front ranks, while the peasantry stood

behind and backed them up, though at first only able to hurl their weapons
at the advancing foe over the heads of their more fully-equipped fellows.

We must now turn to the Normans. Duke William had undertaken his
expedition not as the mere feudal head of the barons of Normandy, but
rather as the managing director of a great joint-stock company for the
conquest of England, in which not only his own subjects, but hundreds of
adventurers, poor and rich, from all parts of western Europe had taken
shares. At the assembly of Lillebonne the Norman baronage had refused
in their corporate capacity to undertake the vindication of their duke's
claims on England. But all, or nearly all, of them had consented to serve
under him as volunteers, bringing not merely their usual feudal contingent,
but as many men as they could get together. In return they were to receive
the spoils of the island kingdom if the enterprise went well. On similar
terms William had accepted offers of help from all quarters: knights and
sergeants flocked in, ready, "some for land and some for pence," to back
his claim. It seems that, though the native Normans were the core of the
invading army, yet the strangers considerably outnumbered them on the
muster-rolls. Great nobles like Eustace Count of Boulogne, the Breton
Count Alan Fergant, and Haimar of Thouars were ready to risk their lives
and resources on the chance of an ample profit. French, Bretons, Flemings,
Angevins, knights from the more distant regions of Aquitaine and Loth-
aringia, even—if Guy of Amiens speaks truly—stray fighting men from
among the Norman conquerors of Naples and Sicily, joined the host.

Many months had been spent in the building of a fleet at the mouth
of the Dive. Its numbers, exaggerated to absurd figures by many chroniclers,
may possibly have reached the six hundred and ninety-six vessels given to
the duke by the most moderate estimate. What was the total of the warriors
which it carried is as uncertain as its own numbers. If any analogies may
be drawn from contemporary hosts, the cavalry must have formed a very
heavy proportion of the whole. In continental armies the foot-soldiery were
so despised that an experienced general devoted all his attention to increasing the numbers of his horse. If we guess that there may have been three
thousand or even four thousand mounted men, and eight thousand or nine
thousand foot-soldiers, we are going as far as probability carries us, and
must confess that our estimate is wholly arbitrary. The most modest figure
given by the chroniclers is sixty thousand fighting men; but, considering
their utter inability to realise the meaning of high numbers, we are dealing
liberally with them if we allow a fifth of that estimate.

After landing at Pevensey on September 28, William had moved to
Hastings and built a wooden castle there for the protection of his fleet. It
was then in his power to have moved on London unopposed, for Harold was
only starting on his march from York. But the duke had resolved to fight
near his base, and spent the fortnight which was at his disposal in the systematic harrying of Kent and Sussex. When his scouts told him that Harold
was at hand, and had pitched his camp by Senlac hill, he saw that his
purpose was attained; he would be able to fight at his own chosen moment,

and at only a few miles' distance from his ships. At daybreak on the morn ing of October 14, William bade his host get in array, and marched over the eight miles of rolling ground which separate Hastings and Senlac. When they reached the summit of the hill at Telham, the English position came in sight, on the opposite hill, not much more than a mile away.

On seeing the hour of conflict at hand, the duke and his knights drew on their mail-shirts, which, to avoid fatigue, they had not yet assumed, and the host was arrayed in battle order. The form which William had chosen was that of three parallel corps, each containing infantry and cavalry. The centre was composed of the native contingents of Normandy; the left mainly of Bretons and men from Maine and Anjou; the right, of French and Flemings. But there seem to have been some Normans in the flanking divisions also. The duke himself, as was natural, took command in the centre, the wings fell respectively to the Breton Count Alan Fergant and to Eustace of Boulogne: with the latter was associated Roger of Mont-gomery, a great Norman baron.

In each division there were three lines: the first was composed of bow-men mixed with arbalesters: the second was composed of foot-soldiery armed not with missile weapons but with pike and sword. Most of them seem to have worn mail-shirts, unlike the infantry of the English fyrd. In the rear was the really important section of the army, the mailed knights. We may presume that William intended to harass and thin the English masses with his archery, to attack them seriously with his heavy infantry, who might perhaps succeed in getting to close quarters and engaging the enemy hand to hand; but evidently the crushing blow was to be given by the great force of horsemen who formed the third line of each division.

The Normans deployed on the slopes of Telham, and then began their advance over the rough valley which separated them from the English position.

When they came within range, the archery opened upon the English, and not without effect; at first there must have been little reply to the showers of arrows, since Harold had but very few bowmen in his ranks. The shield-wall, moreover, can have given but a partial protection, though it no doubt served its purpose to some extent. When, however, the Normans advanced farther up the slope, they were received with a furious discharge of missiles of every kind, javelins, lances, taper-axes, and even—if William of Poictiers is to be trusted—rude weapons more appropriate to the neo-lithic age than to the eleventh century, great stones bound to wooden handles and launched in the same manner that was used for the casting-axe. The archers were apparently swept back by the storm of missiles, but the heavy armed foot pushed up to the front of the English line and got to hand-to-hand fighting with Harold's men. They could, however, make not the least impression on the defenders, and were perhaps already recoiling when William ordered up his cavalry. The horsemen rode up the slope al-ready strewn with corpses, and dashed into the fight. Foremost among them was a minstrel named Taillefer, who galloped forward cheering on his comrades, and playing like a *jougleur* with his sword, which he kept casting into the air and then catching again. He burst right through the shield-wall and into the English line, where he was slain after cutting down several opponents. Behind him came the whole Norman knighthood, chanting their battle-song, and pressing their horses up the slope as hard as they could ride. The foot-soldiery dropped back—through the intervals between the three divisions, as we may suppose—and the duke's cavalry dashed against the long front of the shield-wall, whose front rank men they may have swept down by their mere impetus. Into the English mass, however, they could not break: there was a fearful crash, and a wild interchange of blows, but the line did not yield at any point. Nay, more, the assailants were ere long abashed by the fierce resistance that they met; the English axes cut through shield and mail, lopping off limbs and felling even horses to the ground. Never had the continental horsemen met such infantry before. After a space the Bretons and Angevins of the left wing felt their hearts fail, and recoiled down the hill in wild disorder, many men unhorsed and overthrown in the marshy bottom at the foot of the slope. All along the line the onset wavered, and the greater part of the host gave back, though the centre and right did not fly in wild disorder like the Bretons. A rumour ran along the front that the duke had fallen, and William had to bare his head and to ride down the ranks, crying that he lived, and would yet win the day, before he could check the retreat of his warriors. His brother Odo aided him to rally the waverers, and the greater part of the host was soon restored to order.

As it chanced, the rout of the Norman left wing was destined to bring nothing but profit to William. A great mass of the shire-levies on the English right, when they saw the Bretons flying, came pouring after them down the hill. They had forgotten that their sole chance of victory lay in keeping their front firm till the whole strength of the assailant should be exhausted. It was mad to pursue when two-thirds of the hostile army was intact, and its spirit still unbroken. Seeing the tumultuous crowd rushing after the flying Bretons, William wheeled his centre and threw it upon the flank of the pursuers. Caught in disorder, with their ranks broken and scattered, the rash peasantry were ridden down in a few moments. Their light shields, swords, and javelins availed them nothing against the rush of the Norman horse, and the whole horde, to the number of several thousands, were cut to pieces. The great bulk of the English host, how-ever, had not followed the routed Bretons, and the duke saw that his day's work was but begun. Forming up his disordered squadrons, he ordered a second general attack on the line. Then followed an encounter even more fierce than the first. It would appear that the fortune of the Normans was somewhat better in this than in the earlier struggle: one or two temporary breaches were made in the English mass, probably in the places where it had been weakened by the rash onset of the shire-levies an hour before. Gyrth and Leofwine, Harold's two brothers, fell in the forefront of the fight, the former by William's own hand, if we may trust one good contemporary authority. Yet, on the whole, the duke had got little profit by his assault: the English had suffered severe loss, but their long line of shields and axes still crowned the slope, and their cries of "Out! out!" and "Holy Cross!" still rang forth in undaunted tones.

A sudden inspiration then came to William, suggested by the disaster which had befallen the English right in the first conflict. He determined to try the expedient of a feigned flight, a stratagem not unknown to Bretons and Normans of earlier ages. By his orders a considerable portion of the assailants suddenly wheeled about and retired in seeming disorder. The English thought, with more excuse on this occasion than on the last, that the enemy was indeed routed, and for the second time a great body of them broke the line and rushed after the retreating squadrons. When they were well on their way down the slope, William repeated his former procedure. The intact portion of his host fell upon the flanks of the pursuers, while those who had simulated flight faced about and attacked them in front. The result was again a foregone conclusion: the disordered men of the fyrd were hewn to pieces, and few or none of them escaped back to their comrades on the height. But the slaughter in this period of the fight did not fall wholly on the English; a part of the Norman troops who had carried out the false flight suffered some loss by falling into a deep ditch,—perhaps the remains of old entrenchments, perhaps the "rhine" which drained the Senlac bottom,—and were there smothered or trodden down by the comrades who rode over them. But the loss at this point must have been insignificant compared with that of the English.

Harold's host was now much thinned and somewhat shaken, but, in spite of the disasters which had befallen them, they drew together their thinned ranks, and continued the fight. The struggle was still destined to endure for many hours, for the most daring onsets of the Norman chivalry could not yet burst into the serried mass around the standards. The bands which had been cut to pieces were mere shire-levies, and the well-armed housecarles had refused to break their ranks, and still formed a solid core for the remainder of the host.

The fourth act of the battle consisted of a series of vigorous assaults by the duke's horsemen, alternating with volleys of arrows poured in during the intervals between the charges. The Saxon mass was subjected to exactly the same trial which befell the British squares in the battle of Waterloo— incessant charges by a gallant cavalry mixed with a destructive hail of missiles. Nothing could be more maddening than such an ordeal to the infantry-soldier, rooted to the spot by the necessities of his formation. The situation was frightful: the ranks were filled with wounded men unable to retire to the rear through the dense mass of their comrades, unable even to sink to the ground for the hideous press. The enemy was now attacking on both flanks: shields and mail had been riven: the supply of missile spears had given out: the English could but stand passive, waiting for the night or for the utter exhaustion of the enemy. The cavalry onsets must have been almost a relief compared with the desperate waiting between the acts, while the arrow-shower kept beating in on the thinning host. We have indications that, in spite of the disasters of the noon, some of the English made yet a third sally to beat off the archery. Individuals worked to frenzy by the weary standing still, seem to have occasionally burst out of the line to swing axe or sword freely in the open and meet a certain death. But the mass held firm—"a strange manner of battle," says William of Poictiers, "where the one side works by constant motion and ceaseless charges, while the other can but endure passively as it stands fixed to the sod. The Norman arrow and sword worked on: in the English ranks the only movement was the dropping of the dead: the living stood motionless." Desperate as was their plight, the English still held out till evening; though William himself led charge after charge against them, and had three horses killed beneath him, they could not be scattered while their king still survived and their standards still stood upright. It was finally the arrow rather than the sword that settled the day: the duke is said to have bade his archers shoot not point-blank, but with a high trajectory, so that the shafts fell all over the English host, and not merely on its front ranks. One of these chance shafts struck Harold in the eye and gave him a mortal wound. The arrow-shower, combined with the news of the king's fall, at last broke up the English host: after a hundred ineffective charges, a band of Norman knights burst into the midst of the mass, hewed Harold to pieces as he lay wounded at the foot of his banners, and cut down both the Dragon of Wessex and the Fighting Man.

The remnant of the English were now at last constrained to give ground: the few thousands—it may rather have been the few hundreds—who still clung to the crest of the bloodstained hill turned their backs to the foe and sought shelter in the friendly forest in their rear. Some fled on foot through the trees, some seized the horses of the thegns and housecarles from the camp and rode off upon them. But even in retreat they took some vengeance on the conquerors. The Normans, following in disorder, swept down the steep slope at the back of the hill, scarped like a glacis and impassable for horsemen,—the back defence, as we have conjectured, of some ancient camp of other days. Many of the knights, in the confused evening light, plunged down this trap, lost their footing, and lay floundering, man and horse, in the ravine at the bottom. Turning back, the last of the English swept down on them and cut them to pieces before resuming their flight. The Normans thought for a moment that succours had arrived to join the English—and, indeed, Edwin and Morkar's Northern levies were long overdue. The duke himself had to rally them, and to silence the fainthearted counsels of Eustace of Boulogne, who bade him draw back when the victory was won. When the Normans came on more cautiously, following, no doubt, the line of the isthmus and not plunging down the slopes, the last of the English melted away into the forest and disappeared. The hard day's work was done.

The stationary tactics of the phalanx of axemen had failed decisively before William's combination of archers and cavalry, in spite of the fact that the ground had been favourable to the defensive. The exhibition of desperate courage on the part of the English had only served to increase the number of the slain. Of all the chiefs of the army, only Esegar the Staller and Leofric, Abbot of Bourne, are recorded to have escaped, and both of them were dangerously wounded. The king and his brothers, the stubborn housecarles, and the whole thegnhood of Southern England had perished on the field. The English loss was never calculated; practically it amounted to the entire army. Nor is it possible to guess that of the Normans: one chronicle gives twelve thousand,—the figure is absurd, and the authority is not a good or a trustworthy one for English history. But whatever was the relative slaughter on the two sides, the lesson of the battle was unmistakable. The best of infantry, armed only with weapons for close fight and destitute of cavalry support, were absolutely helpless before a capable general who knew how to combine the horseman and the archer. The knights, if unsupported by the bowmen, might have surged for ever against the impregnable shield-wall. The archers, unsupported by the knights, could easily have been driven off the field by a general charge. United by the skilful hand of William, they were invincible.

The French Crusade, 1249-1250 A.D.

BY

JEAN DE JOINVILLE

As soon as the month of March was come, it was proclaimed, by orders of the king, that all vessels should be laden and ready to sail whenever the king should command. All things being ready, the king, the queen, and their households embarked on board their different ships. On the Friday preceding Whitsunday, the king ordered every one to follow him on the morrow, and proceed to Egypt; and on the morrow, being Saturday, every vessel made sail, which was a pleasant sight to see, for it seemed as if the whole sea, as far as the sight could reach, was covered with cloth, from the great quantity of sails that were spread to the wind, there being 1,800 vessels great and small.

There was much joy in the whole army on the arrival of the count de Poitiers, the king's brother; and shortly after the king assembled his barons and council, and asked them what route he should pursue, whether to Alexandria or to Babylon? The count Peter of Brittany, with several other barons, were of opinion that the king should march to Alexandria, because there was a good harbour for boats and vessels, to bring provision to the army. But this plan was not approved of by the count d'Artois, who said he would never march to Alexandria until he should have been at Babylon, which was the seat of empire in Egypt. He added, among other reasons, that whoever wished to kill a snake, should begin with the head. To this opinion the king assented, and gave up the former plan.

At the beginning of Advent, the king and his whole army began their march toward Babylon, according to the advice given by the count d'Artois. On the road near to Damietta, we met a branch of the great river; and the king was advised to halt a day, until a dam should be thrown across, that the army might pass. This was easily done; and the river was stopped so level that it did not overflow, and might be crossed with facility.

What did the sultan do? He sent craftily to the king five hundred of his best-mounted troops, saying they were come to assist him, but in reality to delay him as much as possible. On St. Nicholas's day, the king commanded his army to mount their horses, and forbade any of his people to dare to hurt, in any way, one of the Turks or Saracens whom the sultan had sent to him. Now it happened, that when the Saracens perceived the king's army was in motion, and heard that the king had forbidden any one

From: *Memoirs of St. Louis IX.*

to touch them, they advanced with great courage in a body toward the Templars, who had the van of the army. One of these Turks gave a knight in the first rank so heavy a blow with his battle-axe as felled him under the feet of Sir Reginald de Bicher's horse, who was marshal of the Templars.

The marshal, seeing this, cried out to his men-at-arms,—"Now, companions, attack them, in the name of God! for I cannot longer suffer thus." He instantly stuck spurs into his horse, and charged the Saracens, followed by the whole army. The horses of the Turks were worn down and tired, while ours were fresh and hearty, which caused their misfortune; for I have since heard that not one escaped being slain or drowned in the sea.

It is proper that I say something here of the river which runs through Egypt, and which comes from the terrestrial paradise; for such things should be known to those who are desirous of understanding the subject I am writing on. This river differs from all others, for the more brooks fall into a large river, the more it is divided into small streamlets, and spread over a country; but this river has not such aids, and seems always the same. When arrived in Egypt, it spreads its waters over the country. About the period of St. Remy's day, it expands itself into seven branches, and thence flows over the plains. When the waters are retired, the labourers appear, and till the ground with ploughs without wheels, and then sow wheat, barley, rice, and cummin, which succeed so well that it is not possible to have finer crops.

No one can say whence this annual increase of water comes, except from God's mercy. Were it not to happen, Egypt would produce nothing, from the very great heat of that country; for it is near to the rising sun, and it scarcely ever rains but at very long intervals.

This river is quite muddy, from the crowds of people of that and other countries who, towards evening, come thither to seek water to drink. They put into their vessels which hold it four almonds or four beans, which they shake well, and on the morrow it is wondrous clear and fit to drink. When this river enters Egypt, there are expert persons, accustomed to the business, who may be called the fishermen of this stream, and who in the evenings cast their nets into the water, and in the mornings frequently find many spices in them, which they sell into these countries dearly, and by weight; such as cinnamon, ginger, rhubarb, cloves, lignum-aloes, and other good things. It is the report of the country, that they come from the terrestrial paradise, and that the wind blows them down from these fine trees, as it does in our forests the old dry wood. What falls into the river is brought down with it, and collected by merchants, who sell it to us by weight.

I heard in the country of Babylon, that the sultan had frequently attempted to learn whence this river came, by sending experienced persons to follow the course of it. They carried with them a bread called biscuit, for they would not have found any on their route, and on their return reported, that they had followed the course of the river until they came to a large mountain of perpendicular rocks, which it was impossible to climb, and over these rocks fell the river. It seemed to them, that on the top of this mountain were many trees; and they said they had seen there many strange wild beasts, such as lions, serpents, elephants, and other sorts, which came to gaze at them as they ascended the river. These travellers, not daring to advance further, returned to the sultan.

Now, to pursue my subject, this river, on entering Egypt, spreads its branches over the plain: one of them flows to Damietta, another to Alexandria, another to Tunis, and another to Rexi. To this branch which runs by Rexi, the king of France marched with his whole army, and encamped between the Damietta branch and that of Rexi. We found the sultan encamped with his entire force on the opposite bank of the Rexi branch, to prevent and oppose our passage. It was easy for him to do this, for none of us could have crossed unless we had stripped ourselves naked, as there were no other means to pass.

The king determined to have a causeway made, to enable him to pass over to the Saracens; and to guard those employed on it, he had built two beffrois,[1] called *chas-chateils*.[2] There were two towers in front of these beffrois, and two houses in their rear, to receive the things the Saracens threw upon their machines, of which they had sixteen that did wonders. The king ordered eighteen machines to be constructed, under the direction of a man namd Jousselin de Courvant, who was the inventor and undertaker; and with these engines did each army play on the other. The king's brother was on guard over the cats in the daytime, and we other knights guarded them at night.

These chas-chateils were finished the week before Christmas, and then the causeway was set about in earnest; but as fast as we advanced, the Saracens destroyed it. They dug, on their side of the river, wide and deep holes in the earth, and as the water recoiled from our causeway it filled these holes with water, and tore away the banks; so that what we had been employed on for three weeks or a month, they ruined in one or two days; they also very much annoyed, by their arrows, our people who were carrying materials for the dam.

The Turks, after the death of their sultan, who died of the disorder

---

[1] The beffroy was a warlike machine in the form of a tower, made of wood, having different stories, which was drawn near to the walls of a town, and the stories filled with a proper number of soldiers, who shot from their bows and cross-bows over the walls, against the defenders of the place. These machines were usually moved on four wheels, and to prevent the Greek fire from hurting them, they were covered with boiled horse or bullock skins. Froissart, in his first volume, chap. 108, thus describes the beffrois: "The English had constructed two large towers, of great beams of wood, three stories high; each tower was placed on wheels, and covered over with prepared leather, to shelter those within from fire, and from the arrows: in each story were 100 archers." William of Malmesbury, in the fourth book of his History of England, calls this machine *berfroy*. This word *beffroy* (belfry) has since been applied to the highest towers of frontier towns, wherein a sentinel is placed to watch for their security, and with a bell for him to strike on to alarm the inhabitants and guards at the gates. This bell has afterwards been employed to mark the hour for the retreat of the inhabitants to their houses, and the garrisons to their quarters, and other public uses.

[2] The cat was properly a machine made in the form of a covered gallery which was fastened to the walls to afford shelter to the sappers. Ravedicus, in the second book of the History of Frederic I. c. 63, describing the siege of Crema, says that the inhabitants, to defend themselves against those who scaled the walls, or who descended on their walls from beffrois and towers of wood, made use of cats to enable them to attack the enemy within their machines.

he was seized with when before Hamault, chose for their chief a Saracen named Sacedun, son of the sheik, whom the emperor Ferrait had made a knight.

Shortly after this, Sacedun sent part of his army to cross near Damietta, and to a small town called Sourmesac, which is on the Rexi branch, that from that quarter they might fall on us. On Christmas day, whilst I and all my people were at dinner with my companion Pierre d'Avalon, the Saracens entered our camp, and slew many of our poor soldiers who had strayed into the fields.

We instantly mounted our horses to attack them; and well timed was it for my lord Perron, our host, who had quitted the camp on the first alarm; for before we could overtake him, the Saracens had made him prisoner, and were carrying him off with his brother, the lord Du Val. We pushed our horses forward, attacked the Saracens, and rescued these two good knights, whom they had already, by their blows, struck to the ground, and brought them back to the camp. The Templars, who were within hearing, formed a bold and determined rear-guard.

The Turks continued to make repeated attacks on us in that quarter with much courage, until our army had closed up the canal toward Damietta, from that branch to the one of Rexi.

This Sacedun, chief of the Turks, was held to be the most able and courageous of all the infidels. He bore on his banners the arms of the emperor who had made him a knight; his banner had several bends, on one of which he bore the same arms with the sultan of Aleppo, and on another bend on the side were the arms of the sultan of Babylon. His name was, as I said before, Sacedun, son of the sheik, which signifies the same in their language as to say the son of the old man. His name had great weight with them; for they are a people, it is said, who pay much honour to such old men as have in their youth been especially careful to preserve their characters from reproach. This chief, as it was told the king by his spies, boasted, that on St. Sebastian's day next coming, he would dine in the king's tent.

When the king heard this, he replied, that he would take good care to prevent it. He then drew his army in closer array, orders for which were given to the men-at-arms; and to the count d'Artois, brother to the king, was given the command of the beffrois and machines. The king, and the count d'Anjou, who was afterwards king of Sicily, took on them the guard of the army, on the side of Babylon; and the count de Poitiers, with me, seneschal of Champagne, had the guard on the side toward Damietta.

Not long after this, the chief of the Turks, before named, crossed with his army into the island that lies between the Rexi and Damietta branches, where our army was encamped, and formed a line of battle, extending from one bank of the river to the other. The count d'Anjou, who was on the spot, attacked the Turks, and defeated them so completely that they took to flight, and numbers were drowned in each of the branches of the Nile.

A large body, however, kept their ground, whom we dared not attack, on account of their numerous machines, by which they did us great injury with the divers things cast from them. During the attack on the Turks by the count d'Anjou, the count Guy de Ferrois, who was in his company, galloped through the Turkish force, attended by his knights, until they came to another battalion of Saracens, where they performed wonders. But at last he was thrown to the ground with a broken leg, and was led back by two of his knights, supporting him by the arms.

You must know there was difficulty in withdrawing the count d'Anjou from this attack, wherein he was frequently in the utmost danger, and was ever after greatly honoured for it.

Another large body of Turks made an attack on the count de Poitiers and me; but be assured they were very well received, and served in like manner. It was well for them that they found their way back by which they had come; but they left behind great numbers of slain. We returned safely to our camp without having scarcely lost any of our men.

One night the Turks brought forward an engine, called by them *la perriere,* a terrible engine to do mischief, and placed it opposite to the chas-chateils, which Sir Walter de Curel and I were guarding by night. From this engine they flung such quantities of Greek fire,[1] that it was the most horrible sight ever witnessed. When my companion, the good Sir

[1] This fire was so called, because it was first invented among the Greeks by Callinicus the architect, a native of Heliopolis, a town in Syria, under Constantinus Barbatus; and likewise because the Greeks were for a long time the only people who preserved the use of it, which they very rarely communicated to any of their allies. Anna Comnena says, that this fire was made with pitch and other gums from trees, mixed with sulphur, and the whole ground together. Abbon, in the first book of the Wars of Paris, has given the composition of it in these verses:

"Addit eis oleum, ceramque, picemque ministrans,
Mixta simul liquefacta foco ferventia valde,
Quæ Danis cervice comas uruntque trahuntque."

The author of the History of Jerusalem, p. 1167, makes oil a part of the composition: at least, he names it, "oleum incendarium, quod ignem Græcum vocant." It may perhaps be naphtha, which Procopius, in the fourth book of the War of the Goths, ch. 11, says, the Greeks call Μηδείας ελαιον, and the Medes *naphtha*, which Lambecius, in his observations on Codinus, thinks should be corrected to Μηδίας ελαιον, oil of Media, and that for this reason the same Greeks have given to this artificial fire the name of Μηδιχου πορ, which is met with in Cinnamus, p. 308, and in Codinus, p. 7 of the royal edition. There are others, however, who imagine naphtha was called Μηδειας ελαιον, or πορ, because Medea, according to Pliny (l. 2, ch. 105), burnt her husband Jason with this fire. Whatever may be thought of this, Procopius, in the part quoted, informs us, that in the composition of this artificial fire, there was a mixture of naphtha with sulphur and bitumen. Vanoccio Biringuccio, in the tenth book of his Pyrotechny, chap. 9, has described all the materials that form part of the artificial fireworks which the Greeks made use of to burn the vessels of their enemies. The Greeks made use of this fire when at sea, in two ways; first by fire-ships filled with this fire, that were floated among the enemies' fleet, and thus set them on fire. Fire-ships were used before the time of the emperor Constantinus Barbatus, for Theophanes informs us, p. 100, that under the empire of Leon le Grand, Genseric, king of Africa, burnt with vessels that were filled with dry wood and other combustibles, and which he floated down the stream, the whole of the Grecian fleet. Secondly, by artificial fires on the prows of these vessels, placed in large tubes of copper, through which they blew them into the enemy's ships. With regard to the use of the Greek fire in battles on land, it was different, for soldiers were then supplied with copper tubes, and blew it through them on their enemies.—See Anna Comnena, in the 13th book of her Alexiade. Sometimes they threw sharp bolts of iron, covered with tow, well oiled and pitched, with which they set fire to the engines. Joinville speaks of this fire, "and they opened a very quick fire upon us with balls made of the Greek fire." Sometimes this fire was put into phials and pots, and it was also discharged from perrieres and cross-bows. Albert d'Aix, l. 7, ch. 5, remarks, that "hujus ignis genus aqua erat inextinguibile;" but there were other materials by which it could be extinguished, namely, vinegar and sand. Jacques de Vitry, l. 3, ch. 84, adds urine as an extinguisher; and Cinnamus, in the place before quoted, says that ships were frequently covered with cloths dipped in vinegar, to prevent the bad effects of this fire.

Walter, saw this shower of fire, he cried out, "Gentlemen, we are all lost without remedy; for should they set fire to our chas-chateils we must be burnt; and if we quit our post we are for ever dishonoured; from which I conclude, that no one can possibly save us from this peril but God, our benignant Creator; I therefore advise all of you, whenever they throw any of this Greek fire, to cast yourselves on your hands and knees, and cry for mercy to our Lord, in whom alone resides all power."

As soon, therefore, as the Turks threw their fires, we flung ourselves on our hands and knees, as the wise man had advised; and this time they fell between our two cats into a hole in front, which our people had made to extinguish them; and they were instantly put out by a man appointed for that purpose. This Greek fire, in appearance, was like a large tun, and its tail was of the length of a long spear; the noise which it made was like to thunder; and it seemed a great dragon of fire flying through the air, giving so great a light with its flame, that we saw in our camp as clearly as in broad day. Thrice this night did they throw the fire from la perriere, and four times from cross-bows.

Each time that our good king St. Louis heard them make these discharges of fire, he cast himself on the ground, and with extended arms and eyes turned to the heavens, cried with a loud voice to our Lord, and shedding heavy tears, said, "Good Lord God Jesus Christ, preserve thou me, and all my people;" and believe me, his sincere prayers were of great service to us. At every time the fire fell near us, he sent one of his knights to know how we were, and if the fire had hurt us. One of the discharges from the Turks fell beside a chas-chateil, guarded by the men of the Lord Courtenay, struck the bank of the river in front, and ran on the ground toward them burning with flame. One of the knights of this guard instantly came to me, crying out,—"Help us, my lord, or we are burnt; for there is a long train of Greek fire, which the Saracens have discharged, that is running straight for our castle."

We immediately hastened thither, and good need was there; for as the knight had said, so it was. We extinguished the fire with much labour and difficulty; for the Saracens, in the meantime, kept up so brisk a shooting from the opposite bank, that we were covered with arrows and bolts.

The count of Anjou, brother to the king, guarded these castles during the day, and annoyed the Saracen army with his cross-bows. It was ordered by the king, that after the count of Anjou should have finished his daily guard, we, and others of my company, should continue it during the night. We suffered much pain and uneasiness; for the Turks had already broken and damaged our tandies and defences. Once these Turkish traitors advanced their perriere in the daytime, when the count d'Anjou had the guard, and had brought together all their machines, from which they threw Greek fires on our dams, over the river, opposite to our tandies and defences, which completely prevented any of the workmen from shewing themselves; and our two chas-chateils were in a moment destroyed and burnt. The count d'Anjou was almost mad at seeing this; for they were under his guard, and like one out of his senses, wanted to throw himself into the fire to extinguish it, whilst I and my knights returned thanks to God; for if they had delayed this attack to the night, we must have all been burnt.

The king, on hearing what had happened, made a request to each of his barons, that they would give him as much of the largest timbers from their ships that were on the coast as they could spare, and have them transported to where the army lay; for there was not any timber near fit to make use of. After the king had made this request, they all aided him to the utmost; and before the new chas-chateils were finished, the timber employed was estimated to be worth upwards of 10,000 livres. You may guess from this that many boats were destroyed, and that we were then in the utmost distress.

When the chas-chateils were completed, the king would not have them fixed, or pointed, until the count of Anjou resumed the guard: he then ordered that they should be placed on the exact spot where the others had been burnt. This he did to recover the honour of his said brother, under whose guard the two others had been destroyed. As the king had ordered, so it was done; which the Saracens observing, they brought thither all their machines, and, coupling them together, shot at our new chas-chateils vigorously. When they perceived that our men were afraid of going from one castle to the other, for fear of the showers of stones which they were casting, they advanced the perriere directly opposite to them, and again burnt them with their Greek fires. I and my knights returned thanks to God for this second escape. Had they waited until night to make the attack, when the guard would have devolved to us, we must all have been burnt with them.

The king, seeing this, was, as well as his army, much troubled, and he called his barons to council, to consider what should be done; for they now perceived themselves that it would be impossible to throw a causeway over the river to cross to the Turks and Saracens, as our people could not make such advance on their side, but they were more speedily ruined by the Turks on the other.

Sir Humbert de Beaujeu, constable of France, then addressed the king, and said, that a Bedouin had lately come to him to say, that if we would give him 500 golden besants, he would shew a safe ford, which might easily be crossed on horseback. The king replied, that he most cheerfully granted this, provided he spoke the truth; but the man would on no account shew the ford before the money demanded was paid.

It was determined by the king, that the duke of Burgundy, and the nobles beyond sea his allies, should guard the army from the alarms of the Saracens; whilst he, with his three brothers, the counts of Poitiers, Artois, and Anjou, who was afterward king of Sicily, as I have said before, should with their attendants on horseback make trial of the ford the Bedouin was to shew them. The day appointed for this purpose was Shrove-Tuesday, which, when arrived, we all mounted our horses, and, armed at all points, followed the Bedouin to the ford.

On our way thither, some advanced too near the banks of the river, which being soft and slippery, they and their horses fell in and were drowned. The king seeing it, pointed it out to the rest, that they might be more careful and avoid similar danger. Among those that were drowned was that valiant knight Sir John d'Orleans, who bore the banner of the army. When we came to the ford, we saw, on the opposite bank, full 300 Saracen cavalry ready to defend this passage. We entered the river, and our horses found a tolerable ford with firm footing, so that by ascending the stream we found an easy shore, and, through God's mercy, we all crossed over with safety. The Saracens, observing us thus cross, fled away with the utmost despatch.

Before we set out, the king had ordered that the Templars should form the van, and the count d'Artois, his brother, should command the second division of the army; but the moment the count d'Artois had passed the ford with all his people, and saw the Saracens flying, they stuck spurs into their horses and galloped after them; for which those who formed the van were much angered at the count d'Artois, who could not make any answer, on account of Sir Foucquault du Melle, who held the bridle of his horse; and Sir Foucquault, being deaf, heard nothing the Templars were saying to the count d'Artois, but kept bawling out "Forward, forward!"

When the Templars perceived this, they thought they should be dishonoured if they allowed the count d'Artois thus to take the lead, and with one accord they spurred their horses to their fastest speed, pursuing the Saracens through the town of Massoura, as far the plains before Babylon; but on their return the Turks shot at them plenty of arrows, and other artillery, as they repassed through the narrow streets of the town. The count d'Artois and the lord de Coucy, of the name of Raoul, were there slain, and as many as 300 other knights. The Templars lost, as their chief informed me, full fourteen score men-at-arms and horses. My knights, as well as myself, noticing on our left a large body of Turks who were arming, instantly charged them; and when we were advanced into the midst of them, I perceived a sturdy Saracen mounting his horse, which was held by one of his esquires by the bridle, and while he was putting his hand on the saddle to mount, I gave him such a thrust with my spear, which I pushed as far as I was able, that he fell down dead. The esquire, seeing his lord dead, abandoned master and horse; but, watching my motions, on my return struck me with his lance such a blow between the shoulders as drove me on my horse's neck, and held me there so tightly that I could not draw my sword, which was girthed round me. I was forced to draw another sword which was at the pommel of my saddle, and it was high time; but, when he saw I had my sword in my hand, he withdrew his lance, which I had seized, and ran from me.

It chanced that I and my knights had traversed the army of the Saracens, and saw here and there different parties of them, to the amount of about 6,000, who, abandoning their quarters, had advanced into the plain. On perceiving that we were separated from the main body, they boldly attacked us, and slew Sir Hugues de Trichatel, lord d'Escoflans, who bore the banner of our company. They also made prisoner Sir Raoul de Wanon, of our company, whom they had struck to the ground. As they were carrying him off, my knights and myself knew him, and instantly hastened, with great courage, to assist him, and deliver him from their hands. In returning from this engagement the Turks gave me such heavy blows, that my horse, not being able to withstand them, fell on his knees, and threw me to the ground over his head. I very shortly replaced my shield on my breast, and grasped my spear, during which time the Lord Errat d'Esmeray, whose soul may God pardon! advanced towards me, for he had also been struck down by the enemy; and we retreated together towards an old ruined house to wait for the king, who was coming, and I found means to recover my horse.

As we were going to this house, a large body of Turks came galloping towards us, but passed on to a party of ours whom they saw hard by: as they passed, they struck me to the ground, with my shield over my neck, and galloped over me, thinking I was dead; and indeed I was nearly so. When they were gone, my companion, Sir Errart, came and raised me up, and we went to the walls of the ruined house. Thither also had retired Sir Hugues d'Escosse, Sir Ferreys de Loppei, Sir Regnault de Menoncourt, and several others; and there also the Turks came to attack us, more bravely than ever, on all sides. Some of them entered within the walls, and were a long time fighting with us at spear's length, during which my knights gave me my horse, which they held, lest he should run away, and at the same time so vigorously defended us against the Turks, that they were greatly praised by several able persons who witnessed their prowess.

Sir Hugues d'Escosse was desperately hurt by three great wounds in the face and elsewhere. Sir Raoul and Sir Ferreys were also badly wounded in their shoulders, so that the blood spouted out just like to a tun of wine when tapped. Sir Errart d'Esmeray was so severely wounded in the face by a sword, the stroke of which cut off his nose, that it hung down over his mouth. In this severe distress, I called to my mind St. James, and said, "Good Lord St. James, succour me, I beseech thee; and come to my aid in this time of need." I had scarcely ended my prayer, when Sir Errart said to me, "Sir, if I did not think you might suppose it was done to abandon you, and save myself, I would go to my lord of Anjou, whom I see on the plain, and beg he would hasten to your help." "Sir Errart," I replied, "you will do me great honour and pleasure, if you will go and seek succour to save our lives; for your own also is in great peril;" and I said truly, for he died of the wound he had received. All were of my opinion that he should seek for assistance; and I then quitting hold of the rein of his bridle, he galloped towards the count d'Anjou, to request he would support us in the danger we were in.

There was a great lord with him who wished to detain him, but the good prince would not attend to what he urged, but, spurring his horse, galloped towards us followed by his men. The Saracens, observing them coming, left us; but when on their arrival they saw the Saracens carrying away their prisoner, Sir Raould de Wanon, badly wounded, they hastened to recover him, and brought him back in a most pitiful state.

Shortly after, I saw the king arrive with all his attendants, and with a terrible noise of trumpets, clarions, and horns. He halted on an eminence, with his men-at-arms, for something he had to say; and I assure you I never saw so handsome a man under arms. He was taller than any of his troop by the shoulders; and his helmet, which was gilded, was handsomely placed on his head; and he bore a German sword in his hand.

Soon after he had halted, many of his knights were observed intermixed with the Turks: their companions instantiy rushed into the battle among them; and you must know, that in this engagement were performed, on both sides, the most gallant deeds that were ever done in this expedition to the Holy Land; for none made use of the bow,[1] cross-bow, or other artillery. But the conflict consisted of blows given to each other by battle-axes, swords, butts of spears, all mixed together. From all I saw, my knights and myself, all wounded as we were, were very impatient to join the battle with the others.

Shortly after one of my esquires, who had once fled from my banner, came to me, and brought me one of my Flemish war-horses: I was soon mounted, and rode by the side of the king, whom I found attended by that discreet man, Sir John de Valeri. Sir John seeing the king desirous to enter into the midst of the battle, advised him to make for the riverside, on the right, in order that in case there should be any danger, he might have support from the duke of Burgundy and his army, which had been left behind to guard the camp; and likewise that his men might be refreshed, and have wherewith to quench their thirst; for the weather was at this moment exceedingly hot.

The king sent orders for his barons, knights, and others of his council, to quit the Turkish army, and on their arrival, demanded their counsel, what was best to be done. Several answered, that the good knight, Sir John de Valeri, now by his side, would give him the best advice. Then, according to the former opinion of Sir John de Valeri, which many agreed was good, the king turned to the right hand, and advanced toward the river.

[1] To kill an enemy by the bow, cross-bow, or other artillery, has never been esteemed by the French an action of valour. They only valued blows from the hand, sword, or lance, which required address and skill; and it was for this reason, that, in process of time, they forbade the use of cross-bows, arrows, and poisoned darts: it was not sufficient to destroy the enemy by any means whatever, it was necessary that he should be conquered by fair force, and with such arms as displayed the dexterity of the person using them. It is certain that the above-mentioned arms have been forbidden at various times by the popes, and particularly at the council held at Rome under Pope Innocent II. in the year 1139, ch. 29. The emperor Conrad was one of the Christian princes who forbade their use for similar reasons. From whence it is easy to judge, that we must interpret favourably the terms of the Breton poet, when, in the second book of his Philippiade, he says that Richard I., king of England, invented cross-bows; it must be explained by his meaning that King Richard revived the use of them during his reign. This is so strictly true, that in every action we read of in the histories of the first crusades, they made use of bows and cross-bows.

As this was doing, Sir Humbert de Beaujeu, constable of France, came up, and told the king that his brother, the count d'Artois, was much pressed in a house at Massoura, where, however, he defended himself gallantly, but that he would need speedy assistance; and entreated the king to go to his aid. The king replied, "Constable, spur forward, and I will follow you close." I also, the lord de Joinville, said to the constable, that I would be one of his knights, and follow him in such a case as this.

All of us now galloped straight to Massoura, and were in the midst of the Turkish army, when we were instantly separated from each other by the greater power of the Saracens and Turks. Shortly after, a serjeant at mace of the constable, with whom I was, came to him, and said the king was surrounded by the Turks, and his person in imminent danger. You may suppose our astonishment and fears, for there were between us and where the king was full one thousand or twelve hundred Turks, and we were only six persons in all. I said to the constable, that since it was impossible for us to make our way through such a crowd of Turks, it would be much better to wheel round and get on the other side of them. This we instantly did. There was a deep ditch on the road we took between the Saracens and us; and, had they noticed us, they must have slain us all: but they were solely occupied with the king, and the larger bodies: perhaps also they might have taken us for some of their friends. As we thus gained the river, following its course downward between it and the road, we observed that the king had ascended it, and that the Turks were sending fresh troops after him. Both armies now met on the banks, and the event was miserably unfortunate; for the weaker part of our army thought to cross over to the division of the duke of Burgundy, but that was impossible from their horses being worn down, and the extreme heat of the weather. As we descended the river, we saw it covered with lances, pikes, shields, men and horses, unable to save themselves from death.

When we perceived the miserable state of our army, I advised the constable to remain on this side of the river, to guard a small bridge that was hard by; "for if we leave it," added I, "the enemy may come and attack the king on this side; and if our men be assaulted in two places, they must be discomfited."

There then we halted; and you may believe me when I say, that the good king performed that day the most gallant deeds that ever I saw in any battle. It was said, that had it not been for his personal exertions, the whole army would have been destroyed; but I believe that the great courage he naturally possessed was that day doubled by the power of God, for he forced himself wherever he saw his men in any distress, and gave such blows with battle-axe and sword, it was wonderful to behold.

The lord de Courtenay and Sir John de Salenay one day told me, that at this engagement six Turks caught hold of the bridle of the king's horse, and were leading him away; but this virtuous prince exerted himself with such bravery in fighting the six Turks, that he alone freed himself from them; and that many, seeing how valiantly he defended himself, and the great courage he displayed, took greater courage themselves, and abandoning the passage they were guarding, hastened to support the king.

After some little time, the count Peter of Brittany came to us who were guarding the small bridge from Massoura, having had a most furious skirmish. He was so badly wounded in the face that the blood came out of his mouth, as if it had been full of water, and he vomited it forth. The count was mounted on a short, thick, but strong horse, and his reins and the pommel of his saddle were cut and destroyed, so that he was forced to hold himself by his two hands round the horse's neck for fear the Turks, who were close behind him, should make him fall off. He did not, however, seem much afraid of them, for he frequently turned round, and gave them many abusive words, by way of mockery.

Towards the end of this battle, Sir John de Soissons and Sir Peter de Nouille, surnamed Cayer, came to us: they had suffered much from the blows they had received by remaining behind in the last battle. The Turks, seeing them, began to move to meet them, but observing us who were guarding the bridge, with our faces towards them, suffered them to pass, suspecting that we should have gone to their succour, as we certainly should have done. I addressed the count de Soissons, who was my cousin-german: "Sir, I beg that you will remain here to guard this bridge. You will act right in so doing; for, if you leave it, the Turks whom you see before you will advance to attack us, and the king may thus have his enemies in front and rear at the same moment." He asked, if he should stay, would I remain with him? to which I most cheerfully assented.

The constable, hearing our conversation and agreement, told me to defend this bridge, and not on any account to quit it, and that he would go and seek for succour. I was sitting quietly there on my horse, having my cousin Sir John de Soissons on my right and Sir Peter de Nouille on my left hand, when a Turk, galloping from where the king was, struck Sir Peter de Nouille so heavy a blow with his battle-axe on the back as felled him on the neck of his horse, and then crossed the bridge full speed to his own people, imagining that we would abandon our post and follow him, and thus they might gain the bridge. When they perceived that we would on no account quit our post, they crossed the rivulet, and placed themselves between it and the river; on which we marched towards them in suchwise that we were ready to charge them, if they had further advanced.

In our front were two of the king's heralds: the name of one was Guillaume de Bron, and that of the other John de Gaymaches; against whom the Turks, who, as I have said, had posted themselves between the rivulet and river, led a rabble of peasants of the country, who pelted them with clods of earth and large stones. At last, they brought a villanous Turk, who thrice flung Greek fires at them; and by one of them was the tabard of Guillaume de Bron set on fire; but he soon threw it off, and good need had he, for if it had set fire to his clothes, he must have been burnt. We were also covered with these showers of stones and arrows which the Turks discharged at the two heralds.

I luckily found near me a gaubison [1] of coarse cloth which had belonged to a Saracen, and turning the slit part inward, I made a sort of shield, which was of much service to me; for I was only wounded by their shots in five places, whereas my horse was hurt in fifteen. Soon after, as God willed it, one of my vassals of Joinville brought me a banner with my arms, and a long knife for war, which I was in want of; and then, when these Turkish villains, who were on foot, pressed on the heralds, we made a charge on them, and put them instantly to flight.

Thus when the good count de Soissons and myself were returned to our post on the bridge, after chasing away these peasants, he rallied me, saying, "Seneschal, let us allow this rabble to bawl and bray; and, by the 'Cresse Dieu,'" his usual oath, "you and I will talk over this day's adventures in the chambers of our ladies."

It happened that towards evening, about sunset, the constable, Sir Humbert de Beaujeu, brought us the king's cross-bows that were on foot; and they drew up in one front, while we, horsemen, dismounted under shelter of the cross-bows. The Saracens, observing this, immediately took to flight, and left us in peace. The constable told me that we had behaved well in thus guarding the bridge; and bade me go boldly to the king, and not quit him until he should be dismounted in his pavilion. I went to the king, and at the same moment Sir John de Valeri joined, and requested of him, in the name of the lord de Chastillon, that the said lord might command the rear guard, which the king very willingly granted. The king then took the road to return to his pavilion, and raised the helmet from his head, on which I gave him my iron skull-cap, which was much lighter, that he might have more air.

Thus as we were riding together, Father Henry, prior of the hospital of Ronnay, who had crossed the river, came to him and kissed his hand, fully armed, and asked if he had heard any news of his brother, the count d'Artois. "Yes," replied the king, "I have heard all;" that is to say, that he knew well he was now in paradise. The prior, thinking to comfort him for the death of his brother, continued, "Sire, no king of France has ever reaped such honour as you have done; for with great intrepidity have you and your army crossed a dangerous river to combat your enemies; and have been so very successful, that you have put them to flight and gained the field, together with their warlike engines, with which they had wonderfully annoyed you, and concluded the affair by taking possession this day of their camp and quarters."

The good king replied, that God should be adored for all the good he had granted him; and then heavy tears began to fall down his cheeks, which many great persons noticing, were oppressed with anguish and compassion, on seeing him thus weep, praising the name of God, who had enabled him to gain the victory.

[1] It should be *gambison*, which is the name of this sort of dress. Roger Hoveden, in the year 1181, uses the word *wanbasia*, and in page 614 that of *wanbais*. The gambison was a quilted dress, well stuffed with wool, that had been soaked in, and beat up with vinegar, which Pliny, in the 48th chapter of his 8th book, says resists iron.

When we arrived at our quarters, we found great numbers of Saracens on foot holding the cords of a tent which some of our servants were erecting, and pulling against them with all their might. The master of the Temple, who had the command of the vanguard, and myself, charged this rabble, and made them run away. The tent remained, therefore, with us; not, however, that there was any great fight, for which reason many boasters were put to shame. I could readily mention their names, but I abstain from doing so because they are deceased; and we ought not to speak ill of the dead. Of Sir Guyon de Malvoisin I am willing to speak, for the constable and I met him on the road, returning from Massoura, bearing himself gallantly, although hard pressed by the Turks, who closely pursued him; for after they had dispersed the count of Brittany and his battalion, as I have before said, they followed the lord Guyon and his company. He had not suffered much in this engagement, for he and his people had most courageously behaved; which is not to be wondered at, when, as I have heard from those who knew him and his family, almost all his knights were of his kindred and lineage, and his men-at-arms his liege vassals. This gave them the greater confidence in their chief.

After we had discomfited the Turks, and driven them out of their quarters, the Bedouins, who are a powerful people, entered the camp of the Saracens and Turks, and seized and carried off whatever they could find, and all that the Saracens and Turks had left behind them. I was much surprised at this; for the Bedouins are subjects and tributary to the Saracens; but I never heard that they were treated the worse by the Saracens for what they had thus pillaged. They said it was their usual custom to fall on the weakest, which is the nature of dogs; for when there is one dog pursued by another, and a shouting made after him, all the other dogs fall on him.

As my subject requires it, I shall say something concerning these Bedouins, and what sort of people they be. The Bedouins reside in deserts and mountains, and have no great faith in Mahomet, like the Turks, but believe in the religion of Aly, who, they say, was uncle to Mahomet. They are persuaded that when any one of them dies for the service of his lord, or when attempting any good design, his soul enters a superior body, and is much more comfortable than it was before; this makes them ready to die at the command of their superiors or elders. These Bedouins do not reside in town or city, but always lie in the fields and deserted places, where, whenever the weather is bad, they, their wives and children, make themselves an habitation, by sticking into the ground poles connected by hoops, like to what women use in drying their washed clothes; and over these hoops they throw skins of their large sheep, which they call skins of Somas, tanned with alum. The Bedouins have large pelisses of coarse hair, which cover their whole bodies, and when evening comes, or when it is cold or wet, they wrap themselves up in them, and retire to rest. Those who follow war have their horses feeding near them during the night, and have only to take off their bridles, and let them eat. In the morning they spread their pelisses to the sun, and, when dry, rub them, so that they do not appear as if they had been wetted. They never are armed for combat, for they say, and believe, that no one can die but at his appointed hour: they have likewise a mode of cursing, alluding to their faith, when they swear at their children, saying, "Be thou accursed, like him who arms himself for fear of death." In battle they use only a sword, made after the Turkish manner, and are clothed in linen robes like to surplices. They are an ugly race, and hideous to look at; for their hair and beards are long and black. They live on the superabundance of the milk from their herds; and their numbers are not to be counted; for they dwell in the kingdoms of Jerusalem, Egypt, and throughout all the lands of the Saracens and infidels, to whom they are tributary.

Now I am on the subject of the Bedouins, I must say that I have seen, since my return from the Holy Land, some calling themselves Christians, who hold similar faith with the Bedouins; for they maintain that no man can die before his determined time, happen what may, which is a falsehood. I consider such a belief the same as if they should say that God had not the power to assist or hurt us, nor to lengthen or abridge our lives, which is heresy. On the contrary, I declare that we ought to put our whole faith in him who is all-powerful, and may, according to his good pleasure, send us death sooner or later. This is the opposite to the faith of the Bedouins, who firmly believe the day of death to each person is determined infallibly, without any possibility of prolonging or shortening the time.

To return to the original matter, and continue my history. In the evening of this severe engagement that I spoke of, and when we had taken up our quarters in those from whence we had driven the Saracens, my people brought me, from the main army, a tent, which the master of the Templars, who had the command of the van, had given me. I had it pitched on the right of those machines we had won from the enemy, as each of us was eager for repose: indeed we had need of it, from the wounds and fatigues we had suffered in the late battle.

Before daybreak, however, we were alarmed by the cries of "To arms, to arms!" and I made my chamberlain rise, who lay by my side, to go and see what was the matter. He was not long in returning, much frightened, and crying out, "My lord, up instantly; for the Saracens have entered the camp, both horse and foot, and have already defeated the guard which the king had appointed for our security, and to defend the engines we had won from them."

These engines were in front of the king's pavilions, and of us who were near to him. I immediately rose, threw a cuirass on my back, and put my iron skull-cap on my head; and having roused our people, wounded as we were, we drove the Saracens from the engines which they were so anxious to recover.

The king, seeing that scarcely any of us had armour on, sent Sir Walter de Chastillon, who posted himself between us and the Turks, for the better

guard of the engines. After Sir Walter had several times repulsed the
enemy, who made frequent attempts during the night to carry off these
engines, the Saracens, finding they could not succeed, retreated to a
large body of their horse, that were drawn up opposite to our lines, to
prevent us from surprising their camp, which was in their rear.

Six of the principal Turks dismounted, armed from head to foot, and
made themselves a rampart of large stones, as a shelter from our cross-
bows, and from thence shot volleys of arrows, which often wounded many
of our men. When I and my men-at-arms who had the guard of that
quarter saw their stone rampart, we took counsel together, and resolved
that, during the ensuing night, we would destroy this rampart, and bring
away the stones.

Now I had a priest called John de Waysy,[1] who, having overheard our
counsel and resolution, did not wait so long, but set out alone towards
the Saracens, with his cuirass on, his cap of iron, and his sword under his
arm. When he was near the enemy, who neither thought of nor suspected
any one coming against them thus alone, he rushed furiously on, sword
in hand, and gave such blows to these six captains, that they could
not defend themselves, and took to flight, to the great astonishment of the
other Turks and Saracens.

When the Turks saw their leaders fly, they stuck spurs into their
horses, and charged the priest, who was returning to our army, whence
had sallied fifty of our men to oppose them, as they were pursuing him
on horseback: the Turks would not meet them, but wheeled off two or
three times. It happened, however, that during these wheelings, one of our
men threw his dagger [2] at a Turk, and hit him between the ribs: he carried off the dagger, but it caused his death. The other Turks, seeing this,
were more shy than before, and never dared to approach while our men
were carrying away the stones of the rampart. My priest was well known
ever after by the whole army, who said when they saw him, "That is the
priest who, single-handed, defeated the Saracens."

These things happened during the first day of Lent; and this same day
the Saracens elected another chief, in the place of their late chief, Sacedun,
of whom mention has been made, and who died in the battle of Shrove-
Tuesday; at the same time, probably, that the good count d'Artois, brother
to the king St. Louis, was slain. This new chief found among the other

[1] Anna Comnena, in the 292nd page of the tenth book of her Alexiade, reproaches the
Latins for their clergy putting on armour, and with sword and lance hastening to the field
of battle when they have but just received the order of priesthood, which is directly forbidden by the Greeks. Petrus Diaconus, in the fourth book of the Chronicle of Monte
Cassino, makes the same charge. Doubtless it is not without reason that the Greeks have
so often made this reproach to the Latins; seeing that although it has been forbidden by
all the councils for priests to handle arms, or interfere in battles as combatants, yet notwithstanding they are there to be found fighting like seculars. Thus we read that Ebles, abbot of
St. Germain des Près, and Gosselin, bishop of Paris, fought valiantly against the Normans,
who had besieged the capital of France. The clergy not only fought against the infidels,
but against the Christians; witness the bishop of Beauvais, who, at the battle of Bovines,
struck the earl of Salisbury to the ground with his battle-axe.
[2] The word dague is still in use for a small knife or dagger. The Spaniards call it dagas,
the English dagger. The statutes of William, king of Scotland, cap. 23:—"habeat equum,
habergeon, capitium e ferro et cultellum, qui dicitur dagger."

dead the body of the count d'Artois, who had shewn great intrepidity in this battle, magnificently dressed, becoming a prince; and this chief took the count's coat of armour, and, to give courage to the Turks and Saracens, had it hoisted before them, telling them it was the coat-armour of the king their enemy, who had been slain in battle; adding, "My lords, this should make you exert yourselves the more, for body without head is nothing, nor is an army without prince or chief to be feared. I advise, and you ought to have confidence in me, that we increase the force of our attacks on them; and on Friday next we must conquer and gain the battle, since they have now lost their commander." All who heard him cheerfully agreed to follow his advice.

You must know that the king had many spies in the Saracen army, who, having overheard their plans, knew their intentions, and how they meant to act. Some of them informed the king of the intended attack of the enemy, and that they believed him dead and the army without a leader.

Upon this, the king summoned all his captains, and commanded them to have their men-at-arms completely armed, and ready drawn up before their tents at midnight, and then to advance as far as the lines which had been made to prevent the Saracens entering the camp on horseback, although they were so constructed that they might pass them on foot. This was punctually executed according to the king's orders.

You may suppose that the plan the Saracen chief had proposed and adopted he lost no time in putting into execution.

On the Friday morning, by sunrise, 4,000 knights, well armed and mounted, were drawn up in battalions, alongside our army, which lay on the banks of the river toward Babylon, and extending as far as a town called Ressil. When the Pagan chief had thus drawn up his 4,000 knights in front of our army, he then brought another large body of Saracens on foot, and in such numbers that they surrounded all the other side of it. After doing this, he drew up at a short distance other bodies in conjunction with the power of the sultan of Babylon, to succour and aid each of the two former, as occasion might occur.

The chief of the Saracens, having now completed the arrangement of his army, advanced on horseback alone, to view and make his observations on the manner in which the king's army was formed; and where he saw ours was the strongest or weakest, he strengthened or diminished his own. After this he ordered 3,000 Bedouins, whose nature and character I have described, to march in front of the troops under the command of the duke of Burgundy, which were posted between the two branches of the Nile, thinking that part of the king's army might be under the duke, and his own so much the weaker, and that these Bedouins would effectually prevent the duke from affording any support to the king.

All these operations of the infidel chief took him up until about mid-day. This done, he ordered the nacaires and drums to be loudly sounded, according to the mode of the Turks, which is certainly very surprising to those who have not been accustomed to hear them; and then both horse and foot began to be in motion on all sides. I will speak first of the battalion under the count d'Anjou, which received the first attack, being posted the nearest to Babylon. The enemy advanced in a chequered manner, like to a game of chess: for their infantry ran towards our men, and burnt them with Greek fires, which they cast from instruments made for that purpose. On the other hand, the Turkish cavalry charged them with such rapidity and success, that the battalion of the count d'Anjou was defeated. He himself was on foot among his knights, very uncomfortably situated.

When news was brought to the king of the danger his brother was in, nothing could check his ardour; nor would he wait for any one, but, sticking spurs to his horse, galloped into the midst of the battle, lance in hand, to where his brother was, and gave most deadly blows to the Turks, hastening always to where he saw the greatest crowd. He suffered many hard blows; and the Saracens covered all his horse's tail and rump with Greek fires. You may be assured that at such a time he had God in his heart and mind; and in good truth our Lord in this distress befriended him, and so far assisted him, that the king rescued his brother, the count d'Anjou, and drove the Turks before him without the lines.

Next to the battalion of the count d'Anjou was that commanded by Sir Guy de Guivelins, and his brother Baldwin, which joined the battalion of that bold and gallant man Sir Walter de Chastillon. He had with him numbers of chivalrous knights; and these two battalions behaved so vigorously against the Turks, that they were neither any way broken nor conquered.

The next battalion, however, fared but badly, under the command of Friar William de Sonnac, master of the Temple, who had with him the remnant of the men-at-arms that had survived the battle of Shrove-Tuesday, which had been so severely murderous. The master of the Temple, having but few men, made of the engines that had been taken from the enemy, a sort of rampart in his front; this, nevertheless, availed him nothing, for the Templars having added to them many planks of fir-wood, the Saracens burnt them with their Greek fires; and seeing there were but few to oppose them, they waited not until they were destroyed, but vigorously attacking the Templars, defeated them in a very short time. It is certain, that in the rear of the Templars there was about an acre of ground so covered with bolts, darts, arrows, and other weapons, that you could not see the earth beneath them, such showers of these had been discharged against the Templars by the Saracens. The commander of this battalion had lost an eye in the preceding battle of Shrove-Tuesday; and in this he lost the other, and was slain: God have mercy on his soul!

Sir Guy de Malvoisin, a bold and valiant captain of another battalion, was severely wounded in the body; and the Saracens perceiving his gallant conduct and address, shot Greek fire at him incessantly, so that at one time when he was hit by it, his people had much difficulty to extinguish it. But notwithstanding this, he stood bold and firm, unconquered by the Pagans.

From the battalion of Sir Guy de Malvoisin, the lines which enclosed our army descended to where I was, within a stone's cast of the river, and passed by the division of the lord William earl of Flanders, which extended to that branch of the river which entered the sea. Our battalion was posted opposite, and on that bank of the river where Sir Guy de Malvoisin was. The Saracens, observing the appearance of the division of the earl of Flanders fronting them, dared not make any attack on us, for which I thanked God, as neither my knights nor myself could put on any armour, on account of the wounds we had received in the engagement of the Tuesday, which rendered it impossible to wear any defensive clothing.

The Lord William of Flanders and his battalion did wonders; they gallantly and fiercely attacked the Turks on horseback and on foot, and performed great deeds of arms. Seeing their prowess, I ordered my crossbows to shoot strongly at the Turks, who were on horseback at this engagement; and the moment they felt themselves or horses wounded by the arrows, they instantly took flight, and abandoned their infantry. The earl of Flanders and his division, observing the Turks fly by, passed the lines, and charged the Pagans, who were on foot, killing great numbers, and bringing off many targets. Among others, Sir Gaultier de la Horgne, who bore the banner of the count d'Aspremont, displayed much courage.

Adjoining this battalion was that of my lord the count de Poitiers, brother to the king; it was composed solely of infantry, and the only person on horseback was the count, which was unfortunate for him; for the Turks defeated this battalion, and made the count prisoner. They would surely have carried him away, had not the butchers, and all the other traffickers, men and women, who supplied the army with provision, hearing that the Turks were carrying off the count de Poitiers, set up a great shout, and rushed on the Saracens with such fury that they rescued the count de Poitiers, and drove the Turks beyond the lines.

The next battalion to that of the count de Poitiers was the weakest of the whole army, and commanded by Sir Josserant de Brançon, whom my lord de Poitiers had brought with him to Egypt. This division was also formed of dismounted knights, Sir Josserant and his son Sir Henry being the only persons on horseback. The Turks broke this battalion on all sides, on which Sir Josserant and his son fell on the rear of the Turks, and cut them down with their swords. They pressed the enemy so much that they frequently turned on them again, leaving the main body of his men. In the end this would have been fatal; for the Turks must have slain the whole, if Sir Henry de Cone, a wise and valiant knight of the division under the duke of Burgundy, well knowing the weakness of the lord de Brançon's battalion, had not, every time he saw the Turks make their charge on it, ordered the king's cross-bows to shoot at them. He exerted himself so effectually that the lord de Brançon escaped from this danger, but lost twelve of the twenty knights whom it was said he had, without counting other men-at-arms. He himself, however, was the victim of the wounds he received in the service of God, who, we are bound to believe, has well rewarded him for it.

This lord was my uncle, and I heard him on his death-bed say, that he had in his time been in thirty-six battles or warlike skirmishes, and had borne off the prize of arms in most. Of some of them I have a remembrance; for once being in the army of the count de Mascon, who was his cousin, he came to me and a brother of mine on a Good Friday, and said to us, "Come my nephews with all your men, and join us in charging these Germans, who are destroying the monastery of Mascon."

We were instantly on horseback, and hastened to attack the Germans, whom, with hard blows of sword and lance, we drove from the monastery, where many were killed and wounded. When this was done, the good man fell on his knees before the altar, and cried with a loud voice to our Lord, praying that he would be pleased to have mercy on his soul, that he might die for his service, to the end that he might be entitled to the reward of paradise. I have related this, that you may know, as I firmly believe, that God has granted to him the request he then made.

After this battle was ended, the king summoned all his barons, knights, and other great lords, to whom, when assembled, he thus kindly addressed himself: "My lords and friends, you have all now witnessed the great grace which God our Creator has of late shewn us, and continues to do so daily, for which we are bounden to return him our thanksgiving. Last Tuesday, which was Shrovetide, we, aided by him, dislodged our enemies from their quarters, of which we have gained the possession. This Friday, which is now passed, we have defended ourselves against them, very many of us being without arms, while they were completely armed on horseback, and on their own ground." Many more fair speeches did he make; and the good king dwelt much upon what had passed, to comfort and give them courage and faith in God.

In pursuing the subject-matter of my book it is necessary now and then to make digressions, and to inform you of the manner in which the sultan supported his men-at-arms, and how his armies were supplied. It is true that the greater part of his chivalry was composed of foreigners, whom the merchants trading by sea had bought when young, and whom the Egyptians purchased by order of their sultan. They came mostly from the east; for when an eastern king[1] had defeated in battle another neighbouring monarch, the victor, and his people, seized the subjects of the vanquished, whom they sold to merchants, who bought them, as I have said, to sell again in Egypt. The children born from these captives the sultan supported and educated, and when their beards appeared, they were taught to draw the bow, by way of amusement; and when he was in a jocund mood they displayed their skill before him.

As they increased in strength, their small bows were exchanged for

[1] It is still the custom of the Turks to compose their principal military force, the Janissaries, from tributary children, sent for this purpose every fifth year by commissaries established in the provinces. These children are carried off from Christians, and are instructed in the Turkish religion, and trained up to military exercises. Soldiers, thus educated, and unacquainted with their parents and birth, only acknowledge the Grand Signor for their father and protector, which is one of the best political maxims of the infidels, although contrary to the law of nature.

others of greater weight, and proportioned to their powers. These youths bore the arms of the sultan, and were called his *Bahairiz*. When their beards were grown, the sultan made them knights; and their emblazonments were like his, of pure gold, save that to distinguish them, they added bars of vermilion, with roses, birds, griffins, or any other difference as they please. They were called the band of *La Hauleca,* which signifies the archers of the king's guard; and were always about the person of the sultan to defend him. When the sultan went to war they were quartered near him as his body-guard.

He had, besides these, other guards still nearer to his person, such as porters and minstrels, who played upon their instruments from the break of day until the sultan rose; and in the evenings sounded the retreat. Their instruments made so loud a noise, that those who were near them could not hear each other speak; and their notes were distinctly heard throughout the army. During the daytime, they dared on no account play on them, without express orders from the commander of the Hauleca.

When the sultan wanted any thing, or wished to give orders to his men-at-arms, he mentioned it to the above commander, who ordered the minstrels to sound their Saracen horns, drums, and nacaires; and to this sound the whole of the chiefs drew up before their sultan's tent, to whom the commander of the Hauleca told the good pleasure of the sultan, which they instantly obeyed to the utmost of their power. Whenever the sultan went personally to war, he nominated from such of the knights of the Hauleca as shewed the most courage and abilities an admiral, or captain over the men-at-arms, and according as they rose in merit, the more the sultan gave them; by which means every one of them tried who should surpass the other to the utmost.

The manner of the sultan's acting towards them was, that whenever any one of the knights of the Hauleca had, by his prowess and chivalry, gained a sufficiency, so that he was no longer in want, and could live independent, the sultan, for fear he should dethrone or kill him, had him arrested and thrown into prison, where he was secretly put to death, and then he took possession of all the fortune his wife and children might have had left to them. An example of this happened while I was in that country; for the sultan had imprisoned those who, by their valor and address, had made prisoners of the counts of Montfort and Bar; and from envy and jealousy, and from his dread of them, had them put to death. He acted in like manner to the Boudendars, who are his subjects; for when they had defeated the king of Armenia, and came to inform him of the event, they found him hunting wild beasts. Having dismounted to make their obeisance, and thinking, as they had behaved so well, they should be recompensed, he eyed them maliciously, and said he should not return their salute, for they had made him lose his chase; and ordered their heads to be struck off.

To return to our subject. The sultan, lately deceased, had left a son, who was twenty-five years old, well informed, prudent, and already full of malice. The last sultan, fearing he might dethrone him, kept him at a distance from his person, and had given him a kingdom in the East; but the moment his father was dead, the admirals of Babylon sent for him, and made him their sultan. On taking possession of his dignity, he deprived the constable, marshals, and seneschals of his father of their golden wands, and the offices which they held, and gave them to those whom he had brought with him from the East.

This caused great discontent in those who had been removed, as also in those of the council of his late father, who suspected strongly that he would act by them, after seizing their wealth, in the same manner as the sultan had done by those who had taken the counts of Montfort and of Bar, as already related. They therefore unanimously agreed to put him to death, and found means of obtaining from those called La Hauleca, who were the sultan's guard, a promise to murder him.

After the two battles I have mentioned, which were marvelously sharp and severe, the one on Shrove-Tuesday, and the other the first Friday in Lent, another great misfortune befel our army. At the end of eight or ten days, the bodies of those who had been slain in these two engagements, and thrown into the Nile, rose to the top of the water. It was said, this always happens when the gall is burst and rotten. These bodies floated down the river until they came to the small bridge that communicated with each part of our army; and the arch was so low it almost touched the water, and prevented the bodies passing underneath. The river was covered with them from bank to bank, so that the water could not be seen a good stone's throw from the bridge upward.

The king hired one hundred labourers, who were full eight days in separating the bodies of the Christians from the Saracens, which were easily distinguishable: the Saracen bodies they thrust under the bridge by main force, and floated them down to the sea; but the Christians were buried in deep graves, one over the other. God knows how great was the stench, and what misery it was to see the bodies of such noble and worthy persons lying so exposed. I witnessed the chamberlain of the late count d'Artois seeking the body of his master, and many more hunting after the bodies of their friends; but I never heard that any who were thus seeking their friends amidst such an infectious smell ever recovered their healths. You must know, that we ate no fish the whole Lent but eelpouts, which is a gluttonous fish, and feeds on dead bodies. From this cause, and from the bad air of the country, where it scarcely ever rains a drop, the whole army was infected by a shocking disorder, which dried up the flesh on our legs to the bone, and our skins became tanned as black as the ground, or like an old boot that has long lain behind a coffer. In addition to this miserable disorder, those affected by it had another sore complaint in the mouth, from eating such fish, that rotted the gums, and caused a most stinking breath. Very few escaped death that were thus attacked; and the surest symptom of its being fatal was a bleeding at the nose, for when that took place none ever recovered.

The better to cure us, the Turks, who knew our situation, fifteen days afterward attempted to starve us, by means I shall now tell you. These villainous Turks had drawn their galleys overland, and launched them again below our army, so that those who had gone to Damietta for provision never returned, to the great astonishment of us all. We could not imagine the reason of this, until one of the galleys of the earl of Flanders, having forced a passage, informed us how the sultan had launched his vessels, by drawing them overland, below us, so that the Turks watched all galleys going toward Damietta, and had already captured fourscore of ours, and killed their crews.

By this means all provision was exceedingly dear in the army; and when Easter arrived, a beef was sold for eighty livres, a sheep for thirty livres, a hog for thirty livres, a muid of wine for ten livres, an egg for sixpence, and everything else in proportion.

When the king and his barons saw this, and that there was not any remedy for it, they advised the king to march the army from near Babylon, and join that of the duke of Burgundy, which was on the other bank of the river that flowed to Damietta. For the security of his retreat, the king had erected a barbican in front of the small bridge I have so often mentioned; and it was constructed in suchwise that it might be entered on each side on horseback. As soon as this barbican was finished, the whole host armed; for the Turks made a vigorous attack, observing our intentions to join the duke of Burgundy's army on the opposite side of the river.

During the time we were entering the barbican, the enemy fell on the rear of our army, and took prisoner Sir Errart de Valeri; but he was soon rescued by his brother, Sir John de Valeri. The king, however, and his division never moved until the baggage and arms had crossed the river; and then we all passed after the king, except Sir Gaultier de Chastillon, who commanded the rear-guard in the barbican.

When the whole army had passed, the rear-guard was much distressed by the Turkish cavalry; for from their horses they could shoot point blank, as the barbican was low. The Turks on foot threw large stones and clods of earth in their faces, without the guard being able to defend themselves. They would infallibly have been destroyed, if the count d'Anjou, brother to the king, and afterwards king of Sicily, had not boldly gone to their rescue, and brought them off in safety.

The day preceding Shrovetide I saw a thing which I must relate. On the vigil of that day died a very valiant and prudent knight, Sir Hugh de Landricourt, one under my banner; and during his burial, six of my knights talked so loud they disturbed the priest as he was saying mass: on this I arose, and bade them be silent; for it was unbecoming gentlemen thus to talk whilst the mass was celebrating. But they burst into laughter, and told me they were talking of marrying the widow of Sir Hugh, now in his bier. I rebuked them sharply, and said such conversation was indecent and improper, for that they had too soon forgotten their companion.

Now it happened on the morrow, when the first grand battle took place, although we may laugh at their follies, God took such vengeance on them, that of all the six not one escaped death, and remained unburied. The wives of the whole six re-married. This makes it credible, that God leaves no such conduct unpunished. With regard to myself, I fared little better, for I was grievously wounded in the battle of Shrove-Tuesday. I had, besides, the disorder in my legs and mouth before spoken of, and such a rheum in my head it ran through my mouth and nostrils. In addition, I had a double fever, called a quartan, from which God defend us! and with these illnesses was I confined to my bed the half of Lent.

My poor priest was likewise as ill as myself; and one day when he was singing mass before me as I lay in my bed, at the moment of the elevation of the host, I saw him so exceedingly weak that he was near fainting; but when I perceived he was on the point of falling to the ground, I flung myself out of bed, sick as I was, and taking my coat, embraced him, and bade him be at his ease, and take courage from him whom he held in his hands. He recovered some little; but I never quitted him until he had finished the mass, which he completed, and this was the last, for he never after celebrated another, but died. God receive his soul!

To return to our history. It is true there were some parleys between the councils of the king and of the sultan, respecting a peace; and a day was appointed for the further discussion of it. The basis of the treaty was agreed on,—namely, that the king should restore to the sultan Damietta, and the sultan should surrender to the king the realm of Jerusalem. He was also to take proper care of the sick in Damietta, and to give up the salted provision that was there, for neither Turk nor Saracen eat of it, and likewise the engines of war; but the king was to send for all these things from Damietta.

The end of this was, that the sultan demanded what security the king would give him for the surrender of Damietta; and it was proposed that he should detain as prisoner one of the king's brothers, either the count de Poitiers, or the count d'Anjou, until it were effected. But the Turks refused to accept of any other hostage than the person of the king.

To this the gallant knight, Sir Geoffry de Sergines, replied, that the Turks should never have the king's person; and that he would rather they should all be slain than it should be said they had given their king in pawn; and thus matters remained.

The disorder I spoke of very soon increased so much in the army that the barbers were forced to cut away very large pieces of flesh from the gums, to enable their patients to eat. It was pitiful to hear the cries and groans of those on whom this operation was performing; they seemed like to the cries of women in labour, and I cannot express the great concern all felt who heard them.

The good king, St. Louis, witnessing the miserable condition of a great part of his army, raised his hands and eyes to heaven, blessing our Lord for all he had given him, and seeing that he could not longer remain where he was, without perishing himself as well as his army, gave orders to march on the Tuesday evening after the octave of Easter, and return to Damietta.

He issued his commands to the masters of the galleys to have them ready to receive on board the sick, and convey them to Damietta. He likewise gave his orders to Josselin de Corvant, and to other engineers, to cut the cords which held the bridges between us and the Saracens; but they neglected them, which was the cause of much evil befalling us.

Perceiving that everyone was preparing to go to Damietta, I withdrew to my vessel, with two of my knights, all that I had remaining of those that had accompanied me, and the rest of my household. Towards evening, when it began to grow dark, I ordered my captain to raise the anchor, that we might float down the stream; but he replied, that he dared not obey me, for that between us and Damietta were the large galleys of the sultan, which would infallibly capture us.

The king's seamen had made great fires on board their galleys, to cherish the unfortunate sick; and many others in the same state were waiting on the banks of the river for vessels to take them on board. As I was advising my sailors to make some little way, I saw, by the light of the fires, the Saracens enter our camp, and murder these sick that were waiting on the banks of the Nile; and as my men were raising the anchor, and we began to move downward, the sailors who were to take the sick on board advanced with their boats; but seeing the Saracens in the act of killing them, they retreated to their large galleys, cut their cables, and fell down on my small bark.

I expected every moment they would have sunk me; but we escaped this imminent danger, and made some way down the river. The king had the same illness as the rest of his army, with a dysentery, which, had he pleased, he might have prevented, by living on board his larger vessels; but he said, he had rather die than leave his people. The king, observing us make off, began to shout and cry to us to remain, and likewise ordered some heavy bolts to be shot at us, to stop our course until we should have his orders to sail.

I will now break the course of my narration, and say in what manner the king was made prisoner, as he told me himself. I heard him say, that he had quitted his own battalion and men-at-arms, and, with Sir Geoffry de Sergines, had joined the battalion of Sir Gaultier de Chastillon, who commanded the rear division. The king was mounted on a small courser, with only a housing of silk; and of all his men-at-arms, there was only with him the good knight Sir Geoffry de Sergines, who attended him as far as the town of Casel, where the king was made prisoner. But before the Turks could take him, I heard say, that Sir Geoffry de Sergines defended him in like manner as a faithful servant does the cup of his master from flies; for every time the Saracens approached him, Sir Geoffry guarded him with vigorous strokes of the blade and point of his sword, and it seemed as if his courage and strength were doubled.

By dint of gallantry he drove them away from the king, and thus conducted him to Casel, where, having dismounted at a house, he laid the king in the lap of a woman who had come from Paris, thinking that every moment must be his last, for he had no hopes that he could ever pass that day without dying.

Shortly after arrived Sir Philip de Montfort, who told the king that he had just seen the admiral of the sultan, with whom he had formerly treated for a truce, and that if it were his good pleasure, he would return to him again, and renew it. The king entreated him so to do, and declared he would abide by whatever terms they should agree on.

Sir Philip de Montfort returned to the Saracens, who had taken their turbans from their heads, and gave a ring, which he took off his finger, to the admiral, as a pledge of keeping the truce, and that they would accept the terms as offered, and of which I have spoken.

Just at this moment a villainous traitor of an apostate sergeant, named Marcel, set up a loud shout to our people, and said, "Sir knights, surrender yourselves; the king orders you by me so to do, and not to cause yourselves to be slain." At these words, all were thunderstruck; and thinking the king had indeed sent such orders, they each gave up their arms and staves to the Saracens.

The admiral, seeing the Saracens leading the king's knights as their prisoners, said to Sir Philip de Montfort, that he would not agree to any truce, for that the army had been made prisoners. Sir Phillip was greatly astonished at what he saw, for he was aware that, although he was sent as ambassador to settle a truce, he should likewise be made prisoner, and knew not to whom to have recourse. In Pagan countries, they have a very bad custom, that when any ambassadors are despatched from one king or sultan to another, to demand or conclude a peace, and one of these princes dies, and the treaty is not concluded before that event takes place, the ambassador is made prisoner, wherever he may be, and whether sent by sultan or king.

You must know, that we who had embarked on board our vessels, thinking to escape to Damietta, were not more fortunate than those who had remained on land; for we were also taken, as you shall hear. It is true, that during the time we were on the river, a dreadful tempest of wind arose, blowing towards Damietta, and with such force that, unable to ascend the stream, we were driven towards the Saracens. The king, indeed, had left a body of knights, with orders to guard the invalids on the banks of the river; but it would not have been of any use to have made for that part, as they had all fled. Towards the break of day, we arrived at the pass where the sultan's galleys lay, to prevent any provisions being sent from Damietta to the army, who, when they perceived us, set up a great noise, and shot at us and such of our horsemen as were on the banks, with large bolts armed with Greek fire, so that it seemed as if the stars were falling from the heavens.

When our mariners had gained the current, and we attempted to push forward, we saw the horsemen whom the king had left to guard the sick flying towards Damietta. The wind became more violent than ever, and drove us against the bank of the river. On the opposite shore were immense numbers of our vessels that the Saracens had taken, which we feared to approach; for we plainly saw them murdering their crews, and throwing the dead bodies into the water, and carrying away the trunks and arms they had thus gained.

Because we would not go near the Saracens, who menaced us, they shot plenty of bolts; upon which, I put on my armour, to prevent such as were well aimed from hurting me. At the stern of my vessel were some of my people, who cried out to me, "My lord, my lord; our steersman, because the Saracens threaten us, is determined to run us on shore, where we shall be all murdered." I instantly rose up, for I was then very ill, and, advancing with my drawn sword, declared I would kill the first person who should attempt to run us on the Saracen shore. The sailors replied, that it was impossible to proceed, and that I must determine which I would prefer, to be landed on the shore, or to be stranded on the mud of the banks in the river. I preferred, very fortunately, as you shall hear, being run on a mud bank in the river to being carried on shore, where I saw our men murdered, and they followed my orders.

It was not long ere we saw four of the sultan's large galleys making toward us, having full a thousand men on board. I called upon my knights to advise me how to act, whether to surrender to the galleys of the sultan or to those who were on the shore. We were unanimous, that it would be more advisable to surrender to the galleys that were coming, for then we might have a chance of being kept together; whereas, if we gave ourselves up to those on the shore, we should certainly be separated, and perhaps sold to the Bedouins, of whom I have before spoken. To this opinion, however, one of my clerks would not agree, but said it would be much better for us to be slain, as then we should go to paradise; but we would not listen to him, for the fear of death had greater influence over us.

Seeing that we must surrender, I took a small case that contained my jewels and relics, and cast it into the river. One of my sailors told me, that if I would not let him tell the Saracens I was cousin to the king, we should all be put to death. In reply, I bade him say what he pleased. The first of these galleys now came athwart us, and cast anchor close to our bow. Then, as I firmly believe, God sent to my aid a Saracen, who was a subject of the emperor. Having on a pair of trousers of coarse cloth, and swimming straight to my vessel, he embraced my knees, and said, "My lord, if you do not believe what I shall say, you are a lost man. To save yourself you must leap into the river, which will be unobserved by the crew, who are solely occupied with the capture of your bark." He had a cord thrown to me from their galley on the escot of my vessel, and I leaped into the water followed by the Saracen, who indeed saved me, and conducted me to the galley; for I was so weak I staggered, and should have otherwise sunk to the bottom of the river.

I was drawn into the galley, wherein were fourteen score men, besides those who had boarded my vessel, and this poor Saracen held me fast in his arms. Shortly after, I was landed, and they rushed upon me to cut my throat: indeed, I expected nothing else, for he that should do it would imagine he had acquired honour.

This Saracen who had saved me from drowning would not quit hold of me, but cried out to them, "The king's cousin! the king's cousin!"

I felt the knife at my throat, and had already cast myself on my knees on the ground; but God delivered me from this peril by the aid of the poor Saracen, who led me to the castle where the Saracen chiefs were assembled.

When I was in their presence, they took off my coat of mail; and from pity, seeing me so very ill, they flung over me one of my own scarlet coverlids, lined with minever, which my lady-mother had given me. Another brought me a white leathern girdle, with which I girthed my coverlid around me. One of the Saracen knights gave me a small cap, which I put on my head; but I soon began to tremble, so that my teeth chattered, as well from the fright I had had as from my disorder.

On my complaining of thirst, they brought me some water in a pot; but I had no sooner put it to my mouth, and began drinking, than it ran back through my nostrils. God knows what a pitiful state I was in; for I looked for death rather than life, having an imposthume in my throat. When my attendants saw the water run thus through my nostrils, they began to weep and to be very sorrowful.

The Saracen who had saved me asked my people why they wept; they gave him to understand, that I was nearly dead, from an imposthume in the throat which was choking me. The good Saracen, having always great compassion for me, went to tell this to one of the Saracen knights, who bade him to be comforted, for that he would give me something to drink that should cure me in two days. This he did; and I was soon well, through God's grace, and the beverage which the Saracen knight gave me.

Soon after my recovery, the admiral of the sultan's galleys sent for me, and demanded if I were cousin to the king, as it was said. I told him I was not, and related why it had been reported, and that one of my mariners had advised it through fear of the Saracens in the galleys, for that otherwise they would put us to death. The admiral replied, that I had been very well advised, or we should have been all murdered without fail, and thrown into the river. The admiral again asked me, if I had any acquaintance with the emperor Ferry of Germany, then living, and if I were of his lineage; I answered truly, that I had heard my mother say I was his second cousin. The admiral replied, that he would love me the better for it.

Thus, as we were eating and drinking, he sent for an inhabitant of Paris to come to me, who, on his entrance, seeing what we were doing, exclaimed, "Ah, sir, what are you about?" "What am I about!" replied I. When he informed me, on the part of God, that I was eating meat on a Friday. On which, I suddenly threw my trencher behind me; and the admiral, noticing it, asked of my friendly Saracen, who was always with me, why I had left off eating. He told him, because it was a Friday, which I had forgotten. The admiral said, that God could never be displeased, because I had done it unknowingly. You must know, that the legate who had accompanied the king frequently reproached me for fasting when thus ill, and when there was not any statesman but myself left with the king, and that I should hurt myself by fasting. But notwithstanding this, and that I was a prisoner, I never failed to fast every Friday on bread and water.

On the Sunday after we had been made prisoners, the admiral ordered all that had been taken on the Nile to be brought from the castle, on the banks of the river. In my presence, my chaplain was dragged from the hold of the galley; but, on coming to the open air, he fainted, and the Saracens killed him instantly before my eyes, and flung him into the stream. His clerk, from the disorder he had caught when with the army, being unable to stand, they cast a mortar on his head, killed him, and flung him after his master.

In the like manner did they deal with the other prisoners; for as they were drawn out of the hold of the galleys wherein they had been confined, there were Saracens purposely posted, who, on seeing any one weak or ill, killed him and threw him into the water. Such was the treatment of the unfortunate sick. Seeing this tyranny, I told them, through the interpretation of my Saracen, that they were doing very wrong, and contrary to the commands of Saladin the pagan, who had declared it unlawful to put to death anyone to whom they had given salt and bread. They made answer, that they were destroying men of no use, for that they were too ill with their disorders to do any service.

After this they brought before me my mariners, and said they had all denied their faith. I replied I did not believe it, but that their fears of death might have caused them to say so, and that the moment they found themselves in another country they would return to their own religion.

The admiral added to this, that he believed firmly what I said, for that Saladin had declared, that a Christian was never known to make a good pagan, nor a good Saracen a Christian. The admiral, soon after, made me mount a palfrey, and we rode side by side over a bridge to the place where St. Louis and his men were prisoners.

At the entrance of a large pavilion we found a secretary writing down the names of the prisoners by orders of the sultan. I was there forced to declare my name, which I no way wished to conceal, and it was written down with the others. As we entered this pavilion the Saracen, who had preserved my life, and had always followed me, said, "Sir, you must excuse me, but I cannot follow you further. I advise and entreat that you will never quit the hand of this young boy whom you have with you, otherwise the Saracens will murder him." The boy's name was Bartholomew de Montfaucon, son to the lord Montfaucon de Bar.

When my name was written down, the admiral led me and the little boy to the tent where were the barons of France, and more than ten thousand other persons with them. On my entrance, every one seemed to testify great pleasure at seeing me again; and for some time nothing could be heard for their noisy joy, as they concluded I had been murdered.

Thus as we were together, hoping, through the grace of God, we should not long remain in this state, a rich Saracen led us into another tent, where we had miserable cheer. Numbers of knights and other men were confined in a large court, surrounded with walls of mud. The guards of this prison led them out one at a time, and asked each if he would become a renegado: those that answered in the affirmative were put aside, but those who refused, instantly had their heads cut off.

Shortly after, the council of the sultan sent for us, and demanded to whom it was most agreeable they should deliver the sultan's message. We unanimously answered, by means of an interpreter, who spoke both French and Saracen, to the count Peter of Brittany. This was the message: "My lords, the sultan asks by us if you wish to be free, and what you are willing to give for your liberty?"

To this the earl of Brittany replied, that we all heartily wished to be delivered from the hands of the sultan, who had made us suffer most unreasonably. But when the council of the sultan asked if we would not be willing to give for our ransom some of the castles of the barons of the Holy Land, the earl of Brittany answered, that we could not possibly comply; for these castles and strong places belonged to the emperor of Germany, now on the throne, and who would never consent to the sultan holding any fiefs under him.

The council then asked if we would not surrender some of the castles belonging to the Knights Templars, or to the hospital of Rhodes, for our deliverance. The earl replied, that that was equally impossible; for it would be contrary to the accustomed oath which the governors or lords of such castles take on their investiture, when they solemnly swear to God that they will never surrender these castles for the deliverance of any man whatever.

The Saracens then spoke together, saying, that it did not appear we had any desire to regain our liberty; and that they would send us those who well knew how to use their swords, to treat us as the others had been dealt with, and on that they left us.

Not long after the sultan's council had departed, a tall old Saracen, of goodly appearance, came to us, accompanied by a great multitude of young Saracens, each of whom had a large sword by his side, which alarmed us much. The old Saracen asked us, by means of an interpreter, who spoke and understood our language well, if it were true that we believed in one only God, who had been born for our salvation, was crucified to death, and after three days rose again to save us. We answered, that what he had heard was perfectly true. On this he replied, that since it was so, we ought not to be cast down for any persecutions we might suffer for his sake; and that we had not as yet endured death for him, as he had done for us; and since he had the power to raise himself from the dead, it would not be long before he would deliver us.

The old Saracen then went away with all the young men, without doing anything more, which rejoiced me exceedingly; for I really thought the intent of his visit was to cut our heads off. It was not long after this before we heard news of our deliverance.

The sultan's council soon returned to us again, and said the king had exerted himself so effectually, that he had succeeded in obtaining our liberty. They ordered us to send four of our company to hear and know the terms on which we were to have our freedom. To this end we deputed the lords John de Valeri, Philip de Montfort, Baldwin de Ebelin, seneschal of Cyprus, and his brother, the constable of Cyprus, who was one of the handsomest and best-informed knights I ever knew, and who loved greatly the people of that country.

These four knights were not long in bringing us the terms of our liberty. In order to try the king, the sultan's council had made the same demands from him as from us; but it pleased God that the good king, St. Louis, made similar answers to what we had done through the mouth of count Peter of Brittany. The council, seeing the king would not comply with their demands, threatened to put him in the bernicles,[1] which is the greatest torture they can inflict on anyone. The bernicles are formed of two thick blocks of wood, fastened together at the top; and when they use this mode of torture, they lay the person on his side, between these two blocks, passing his legs through broad pins; they then fix the upper block on the sufferer, and make a man sit on him, by which means all the small bones of his legs are broken or dislocated. To increase the torture, at the end of three days they replace his legs, which are now greatly swollen, in the bernicles, and break them again, which is the most cruel thing ever heard; and they tie his head down with bullock's sinews, for fear he should move himself while in them.

The good king held all their menaces cheap, and said, that since he was their prisoner they might do to him whatever they pleased. The Saracens finding they could not conquer the king by threats, came to him, and asked how much money he would give the sultan for his ransom, in addition to Damietta, which was to be surrendered. The king replied, that if the sultan would be contented with a reasonable ransom, he would write to the queen to pay it for himself and his army. The Saracens asked why he wanted to write to the queen. He answered, that it was but reasonable he should do so, for that she was his wife and companion. The council then went to the sultan to know what sum he required from the king; and on their return told the king, that if the queen would pay a million of golden besants, equal at that time to 500,000 livres, she would, by so doing, obtain the king's liberty. The king then asked them, on their oath, should the queen pay

---

[1] This engine of torture appears to have been made of pieces of wood pierced with holes, into which the legs of criminals were put: they were placed at such distances from each other, and forced to so great an extension of the legs as caused very great pain, for the criminals could not draw them back again. The holes in these pieces of wood were at various distances, and the legs of the criminal were inserted into those that extended them to a greater or lesser distance, according to the heinousness of the crime or the pains to be inflicted.

these 500,000 livres, would the sultan consent to his deliverance. On this, they again returned to the sultan to know if he would bind himself by such a promise, and brought back his answer, that he was very willing so to do.

The council then took their oaths to the punctual fulfilment of this agreement, which, when done, the king engaged to pay cheerfully, for the ransom of his army, 500,000 livres; and that for his own ransom he would surrender the town of Damietta to the sultan; for he was of a rank whose bodily ransom could not be estimated by the value of money.

When the sultan heard the good disposition of the king, he said, "By my faith, the Frenchman is generous and liberal, when he does not condescend to bargain about so large a sum of money, but has instantly complied with the first demand. Go, and tell him from me," added the sultan, "that I make him a present of 100,000 livres, so that he will have only to pay 400,000."

The sultan then commanded that all of the principal nobles, and great officers of the king, should be embarked in four of the largest galleys, and conducted to Damietta. In the galley on board of which I was shipped, were the good count Peter of Brittany, William count of Flanders, John, the good count de Soissons, Sir Humbert de Beaujeu, constable of France, and those two excellent knights and brothers, Sir Baldwin and Sir Guy d'Ebelin.

The captain of the galley made us land before a large house which the sultan had erected on the banks of the river, where there was a handsome tower made of poles of fir-wood, and covered with painted cloth. At the entrance a great pavilion had been pitched, where the admirals of the sultan left their swords and staves whenever they wanted to speak with him. Passing this pavilion, there was another very handsome gateway, that led to the great hall of the sultan, and adjoining was a tower like unto the first, by which they mounted to the chamber of the sultan. In the midst of this lodgment was a handsome lawn, on which another tower larger than the others, whence the sultan made his observations on the surrounding country, and on each army. There was in this lawn an alley that led to the river, at the end of which the sultan had made a summer-house on the strand to bathe himself. This summer-house was formed of trelliswork, covered with Indian linen, to prevent anyone seeing what passed within-side. All the towers were likewise covered with cloth.

We arrived before this lodging on the Thursday preceding the feast of the Ascension of our Lord. Near to it the king had landed, to hold a parley with the sultan in a pavilion, and it was then agreed that the ensuing Saturday the king should go to Damietta.

Just as we were on our departure for Damietta, to surrender to the sultan, the admiral of the present sultan's father shewed great dissatisfaction with the reigning monarch. Although he had been the principal author of his having been sent for on his father's death at Damietta, to succeed to the throne, he had much disappointed the admiral by dismissing him from his office of constable, and others from their marshalships and seneschalships, to provide for those who had accompanied him to Egypt.

They therefore held a council, when he said,—"My lords, you see how much the sultan has dishonoured us, by depriving us of those governments and honours with which his father had entrusted us. Such conduct, you may be assured, will induce him, when once master of the castle and fortresses of Damietta, to have us arrested and put to death in his prisons, through fear that in process of time we may take our revenge on him; as his grandfather did to the admiral and the others who had made the counts de Bar and de Montfort prisoners. It will be therefore more to our advantage that we destroy him before he escape out of our hands."

This was unanimously assented to; and they instantly went to practise with the band of the Hauleca, who, as I have said before, are those who have the guard of the sultan's person. They made to them remonstrances on the subject similar to those which they had made among themselves, and required of them to slay the sultan, which they promised to do.

One day the sultan invited the knights of the Hauleca to dine with him. After the dinner, when he had taken leave of his admirals, and was about to retire to his chamber, one of these knights, who bore the sultan's sword, struck him a blow on the hand, which cut up his arm between the four fingers. The sultan, turning to his admirals, who had been the instigators of it, said, "My lords, I make my complaint to you against the knights of the Hauleca, who have endeavoured to kill me, as you may see by my hand." They all replied, that it was much better he should be slain than that he murder them, as he would assuredly do if once in possession of the fortresses of Damietta.

The conspirators acted with great caution, for they ordered the sultan's trumpets and nacaires to sound for the assembling of the army to know the sultan's will. The admirals and their accomplices told them, Damietta was taken, that the sultan was marching thither, and ordered them to arm and follow him. Instantly all armed, and set off, full gallop, towards Damietta. We were much frightened, on noticing what was going forward, for we really believed Damietta had been stormed.

The sultan, though wounded, being aware of the malice of his enemies, who had conspired against his person, fled to the high tower near his chamber which I mentioned; for those of the Hauleca had already destroyed his other pavilions, and were surrounding that in which he had hidden himself. Within this tower were three of his ecclesiastics, who had dined with him, who bade him descend. He replied, he would willingly descend, if they would answer for his safety; but they replied that they would make him come down by force, for that he was not yet arrived at Damietta. They then discharged some Greek fire into the tower, which being made only of fir and linen cloth, as I have before said, the whole was in a blaze; and I promise you, I never beheld so fine nor so sudden a bonfire.

When the sultan saw the fire gaining ground on all sides, he descended into the lawn, of which I have spoken, and ran for the river; but in his flight one of the Hauleca struck him a severe blow on the ribs with a sword, and then he flung himself, with the sword in him, into the Nile. Nine other knights pursued and killed him while in the water, near the side of the galley.

One of the foresaid knights, whose name was Faracataic, seeing the sultan dead, cut him in twain, and tore the heart from his body. On coming to the king with his hands all bloody, he said, "What wilt thou give me who have slain thine enemy, who, had he lived, would have put thee to death?" But the good king St. Louis made no answer whatever to this demand.

The deed being done, about thirty of them entered our galley with their swords drawn, and their battle-axes on their necks. I asked Sir Baldwin d'Ebelin, who understood Saracenic, what they were saying. And he replied, that they said they were come to cut off our heads; and shortly after I saw a large body of our men on board confessing themselves to a monk of La Trinité, who had accompanied the count of Flanders. With regard to myself, I no longer thought of any sin or evil I had done, but that I was about to receive my death: in consequence, I fell on my knees at the feet of one of them, and, making the sign of the cross, said, "Thus died St. Agnes." Sir Guy d'Ebelin, constable of Cyprus, knelt beside me, and confessed himself to me; and I gave him such absolution as God was pleased to grant me the power of bestowing; but of all the things he had said to me, when I arose up I could not remember one of them.

We were confined in the hold of the galley, and laid heads and heels together. We thought it had been so ordered because they were afraid of attacking us when we were in a body, and that they would destroy us one at a time. This danger lasted the whole night. I had my feet right on the face of the count Peter of Brittany, whose feet, in return, were beside my face. On the morrow we were taken out of the hold, and the admirals sent to inform us that we might renew the treaties we had made with the sultan. Those who were able went thither; but the earl of Brittany, the constable of Cyprus, and myself, who were grievously ill, remained on board.

The earl of Flanders, the count de Soissons, and the others who had gone to parley with the admirals, related to us the convention for our delivery; and the admirals promised, that as soon as Damietta should be surrendered to them, they would give liberty to the king and the other great personages now prisoners.

They told them, that had the sultan lived, he would have had the king beheaded, with the others; and that, contrary to the treaties entered into, and the promises made to the king, he had already transported to Babylon several of their most considerable men; that they had slain the sultan, because they knew well that the moment he should have been master of Damietta he would have had them instantly murdered, or would have put them to death when in confinement.

By this new agreement, the king was to swear to leave at their disposal 200,000 livres before he quitted the river, and the other 200,000 he should pay in Acre. They declared they would detain, for their security, all the sick in Damietta, the cross-bows, armours, machines, and salted meats, until the king should send for them, and should have paid the balance of his ransom.

The oath, which was on this occasion to be taken by the king and the admirals, was drawn up; and on the part of the admirals it ran thus; that in case they failed in their conventions with the king, they would own themselves dishonoured like those who for their sins went on a pilgrimage to Mecca, bareheaded, or like to those who divorced their wives, and took them again. By their law, no one can divorce his wife and cohabit with her again, before he has witnessed some other person lying in bed with her. The third oath was, that they would own themselves blasted and dishonoured, like a Saracen who should eat pork.

The king accepted the above oaths, because Master Nicolle, of Acre, who knew their manners well, assured him they could not swear more strongly. After the admirals had taken the oath above mentioned, they had one such as they wished him to take written down, and gave it to the king. This oath had been drawn up according to the advice of some renegado Christians, whom they had with them. It ran thus, that in case the king did not fulfil the conventions he had entered into with them, he might be deprived forever of the presence of God, of his worthy mother, of the twelve apostles, and of all the saints of both sexes in Paradise. This oath the king took. The other was, that if the king broke his word he should be reputed perjured, as a Christian who had denied God, his baptism, and his faith; and in despite of God would spit on his cross, and trample it under foot. But when the king heard this oath read, he declared he would never take it.

The admirals, hearing the king had refused to take the oath which they had required of him, sent in haste for Master Nicolle, of Acre, to tell him they were greatly dissatisfied with him, and discontented with the king; for that they had sworn every oath he had desired, and now, in his turn, he had refused to comply with the oaths offered to him on their part. Master Nicolle told the king that he was certain, that unless he took the oaths as prescribed, the Saracens would behead him and all his people.

The king replied, that they might act according to their pleasure, but that for his part he would rather die a good Christian than live under the anger of God, his blessed mother, and his saints. At that time, the patriarch of Jerusalem was with the king; he was eighty years old, or thereabout, and had once before gained the good-will of the Saracens for the king, and was then come to him to assist in his delivery from them. It was the custom among the Pagans and Christians, that in case any two princes were at war with each other, and one of them should die during the time ambassadors were sent to either, the ambassadors were, in such case, to remain prisoners, whether in pagan land or in Christendom; and because the sultan, lately murdered, had granted a safe-conduct to this patriarch, he was become a prisoner to the Saracens as well as ourselves.

The admirals perceiving the king was not to be frightened by their menaces, one of them said to the others, that it was the patriarch who had thus advised him; and if they would allow him to act, he would force the king to take the oath, for he would cut off the head of the patriarch, and make it fly into the king's lap. The rest would not agree to this; but they seized the good patriarch, and tied him to a post in the presence of the king and bound his hands behind his back so tightly, that they soon swelled as big as his head; and the blood spouted out from several parts of his hands. From the sufferings he endured, he cried out, "Ah! sire, sire, swear boldly; for I take the whole sin of it on my own soul, since it is by this means alone you may have the power to fulfil your promises." I know not whether the oath was taken at last; but however that may be, the admirals at length held themselves satisfied with the oaths of the king and his lords then present.

When the knights of the Hauleca had slain the sultan, the admirals ordered their trumpets and nacaires to sound merrily before the king's tent; and it was told the king, that the admirals had holden a council and were very desirous to elect him sultan of Babylon. The king one day asked me, if I were of opinion, that if the kingdom of Babylon had been offered him, he ought to have taken it? I answered, that if he had, he would have done a foolish thing, seeing they had murdered their lord. Notwithstanding this, the king told me he should have scarcely refused it.

This project only failed from the admirals saying among themselves, that the king was the proudest Christian they ever knew; and that, if they elected him sultan, he would force them to turn Christians, or have them put to death. This they said from observing, that whenever he quitted his lodgings, he made the sign of the cross on the ground, and crossed his body all over. The Saracens added, that if their Mahomet had allowed them to suffer the manifold evils that God had caused the king to undergo, they would never have had any confidence in him, nor paid him their adorations.

Not long after the conventions had been completed between the king and the admirals, it was determined that on the morrow of the feast of the Ascension of our Lord, Damietta should be surrendered to the Turks, and the king and all the other prisoners set at liberty. Our four galleys were anchored before the bridge of Damietta, where a pavilion had been pitched for the king's landing.

About sunrise of the appointed day, Sir Geoffry de Sergines went to the town of Damietta to deliver it to the admirals, and instantly the flags of the sultan were displayed from the walls. The Saracen knights entered the town, and drank of the wines they found there, insomuch that the greater part were drunk. One of them came on board our galley with his naked sword reeking with blood, telling us that he had killed six of our countrymen, which was a brutal thing for any knight or other to boast of.

Before the surrender of Damietta, the queen had embarked with all our people on board the ships, except the poor sick, whom the Saracens were bound by their oath to take care of, and give up on the payment of 200,000 livres, as has been mentioned. They were also to restore the war machines, salted meats, which they never eat, and our armour; but these infidel dogs, on the contrary, killed all the sick, and cut to pieces the machines and other things which they had promised to take care of and restore at the proper time and place. They made a great heap of the whole, and set it on fire; and it was so immense, the fire blazed from the Friday to the Sunday following.

After they had thus killed, destroyed, and set fire to all they could lay hands on, we that ought to have had our liberties at sunrise remained until sunset without eating or drinking, and the king suffered equally with us. The admirals were disputing together, and seemed inclined to put us to death. One of them, addressing the others, said, "My lords, if you will believe me and these beside me, we will kill the king and all the great persons with him, and then for forty years to come we need not fear them; for their children are young, and we have possession of Damietta, which will likewise be our security."

Another Saracen, named Scebrecy, a native of Morentaigne, opposed this, and remonstrated with the others, that if they should slay the king, just after they had killed their sultan, it would be said that the Egyptians were the most disloyal and iniquitous race of men in the world. The admiral, who was desirous of our deaths, replied by palliating arguments. He said, that indeed they had been to blame in slaying their sultan, because it was contrary to the law of Mahomet, who had commanded them to guard their sovereign as the apple of their eye, and he shewed them this commandment written down in a book which he held in his hand. "But," added he, "listen, my lords, to another commandment," and, turning over the leaves of his book, read to them the commandment of Mahomet, that for the security of the faith, the law permitted the death of an enemy. Then, turning his speech to his former purpose, he continued, "Now consider the sin we have committed in killing the sultan, against the positive command of our prophet, and the great evil we shall again do if we suffer the king to depart, and if we do not put him to death, in spite of the assurances of safety he may have had from us, for he is the greatest enemy to our law and religion."

One of the admirals that were against us, thinking we should be slain, came to the bank of the river, and shouted out in Saracen to those who were on board our galleys, and taking off his turban made signs, and told them, they were to carry us back to Babylon. The anchors were instantly raised, and we were carried a good league up the river. This caused great grief to all of us, and many tears fell from our eyes, for we now expected nothing but death.

However, as God willed it, who never is forgetful of his servants, it was agreed among the admirals, about sunset, that we should have our liberty, and we were in consequence brought back to Damietta. Our galleys were moored close to the shore, and we requested permission to land; but they would not allow it until we had refreshed ourselves, for the Saracens said it would be a shame for the admirals to discharge us fasting from their prison.

Shortly after they sent us provision from the army; that is to say, loaves of cheese that had been baked in the sun to prevent the worms from collecting in them, with hard eggs, which had been boiled four or five days, and the shells of which, in honour to us, they had painted with various colours. When we had eaten some little, they put us on shore, and we went towards the king, whom the Saracens were conducting from the pavilion where they had detained him, toward the water-side. There were full 20,000 Saracens on foot surrounding the king, girded with swords.

It chanced that a Genoese galley was on the river opposite to the king, on board of which there appeared but one man, who, the moment he saw the king, whistled, and instantly fourscore cross-bows, well equipped, with their bows bent and arrows placed, leaped on the deck from below. The Saracens no sooner saw them, than, panic struck, they ran away like sheep, and not more than two or three stayed with the king.

The Genoese cast a plank on shore, and took on board the king, his brother the count d'Anjou, who was afterward king of Sicily, Sir Geoffry de Sergines, Sir Philip de Nemours, the marshal of France, the master of the Trinity, and myself. The count de Poitiers remained prisoner with the Saracens until the king should send the 200,000 livres which he was bound to pay before he quitted the river.

The Saturday after the Ascension, which was the morrow of our deliverance, the earl of Flanders, the count de Soissons, and many other great lords, came to take leave of the king. He entreated them to delay going until his brother, the count de Poitiers, should have his liberty; but they replied it was not possible, for their galleys were on the point of sailing.

They embarked on board their galleys on their return to France, and with them was the earl of Brittany, who was grievously sick. He did not live three weeks, but died at sea.

The king, uneasy at the situation of his brother, was very anxious to pay the 200,000 livres; and the whole of Saturday and Sunday were employed in it. They paid the money according to weight, and each weighing was to the amount of 10,000 livres. Towards evening of the Sunday, the king's servant, occupied in this payment, sent him word they still wanted 30,000 livres. There were then with the king only the count d'Anjou, the marshal of France, the master of the Trinity and myself, all the rest being engaged in paying the ransom. I said to the king it would be much better to ask the commander and marshal of the Knights Templars to lend him the 30,000 livres to make up the sum, than to risk his brother longer with such people.

Father Stephen d'Outricourt, master of the Temple, hearing the advice I gave the king, said to me, "Lord de Joinville, the counsel you give the king is wrong and unreasonable; for you know we receive every farthing on our oath; and that we cannot make any payments but to those who give us their oaths in return."

The marshal of the Temple, thinking to satisfy the king, said, "Sire, don't attend to the dispute and contention of the lord de Joinville and our commander. For it is as he has said; we cannot dispose of any of the money entrusted to us, but for the means intended, without acting contrary to our oaths, and being perjured. Know, that the seneschal has ill-advised you to take by force, should we refuse you a loan; but in this you will act according to your will. Should you, however, do so, we will make ourselves amends from the wealth you have in Acre." When I heard this menace from them to the king, I said to him, that if he pleased I would go and seek the sum, which he commanded me to do.

I instantly went on board one of the galleys of the Templars, and, seeing a coffer, of which they refused to give me the keys, I was about to break it open with a wedge in the king's name; but the marshal, observing I was in earnest, ordered the keys to be given me. I opened the coffer, took out the sum wanting, and carried it to the king, who was much rejoiced at my return. Thus was the whole payment of the two hundred thousand livres completed for the ransom of the count de Poitiers. Before it was all paid, there were some who advised the king to withhold it until the Saracens had delivered up his brother; but he replied, that since he had promised it, he would pay the whole before he quitted the river.

As he said this, Sir Philip de Montfort told the king, that the Saracens had miscounted one scale weight, which was worth ten thousand livres. The king was greatly enraged at this, and commanded Sir Philip, on the faith he owed him as his liege man, to pay the Saracens these ten thousand livres, should they in fact not have been paid. He added, that he would never depart until the uttermost penny of the two hundred thousand livres were paid.

Several persons, perceiving the king was not as yet out of danger from the Saracens, often entreated him to retire to a galley that was waiting for him at sea, to be out of their hands, and at length prevailed on him so to do, for he said that he believed he had now fulfilled his oath.

We now began to make some way at sea, and had advanced a full league without saying a word to each other on the concern we felt to have left the count de Poitiers in prison. In a very short time, Sir Philip de Montfort, who had remained to make good the payment of the ten thousand livres, approached us, calling out to the king, "Sire, sire, wait for your brother the count de Poitiers, who is following you in this other galley." The king then said to those near him, "Light up, light up!" and there was great joy among us all on the arrival of the king's brother. A poor fisherman having hastened to the countess of Poitiers, and told her he had seen the count at liberty from the Saracens, she ordered twenty livres parisis to be given him, and each then went to his galley.

The Battle of Arsouf, 1191 A.D.

BY

CHARLES OMAN

AFTER a siege of nearly two years, Acre had been recovered by the Franks on July 12, 1191. The garrison had laid down its arms and surrendered to the kings of France and England, after having protracted its defence to the last possible moment. Saladin had done his best to succour the place, and delivered perpetual assaults on the camp of the besiegers, but all to no purpose. Seeing that there was no hope of relief, and that Acre must fall by assault in a few days, the Emirs Karakush and Mashtoub opened the gates, after promising that they would induce the Sultan to pay two hundred thousand bezants as ransom for the garrison, and also to restore the True Cross and fifteen hundred Christian prisoners, the survivors of the disaster of Tiberias, who were in chains at Damascus and elsewhere.

For some weeks after the fall of the great fortress, the Christians remained encamped in and around Acre, while Saladin still observed them from his camp on the mountain to the east. The delay was caused partly by the exhaustion of the victors, partly by the necessity for repairing the shattered walls of the city, partly by the protracted negotiations concerning the ransom of the garrison. Meanwhile, Philip of France took his way homeward amidst the curses of the whole army, swearing that on his return he would be a quiet and peaceful neighbour to the dominions of the King of England. "How faithfully he kept his oath is sufficiently notorious to all men, for the moment that he got back he stirred up the land, and set Normandy in an uproar." He left the bulk of his army in the camp under the Duke of Burgundy and Henry Count of Champagne.

The attempts to come to an agreement with Saladin failed hopelessly. Into the ugly story of the massacre of the Turkish garrison, when their ransom was not forthcoming, we need not enter. On Tuesday, August 20, Richard and the Duke of Burgundy beheaded the two thousand six hundred unfortunate captives, and all chance of peace was gone. Two days after, the crusading army set out upon its march.

Richard had as his objective Jerusalem, whose recovery was the main end of the Crusade. But to move directly from Acre on the Holy City is impossible. The mountains of Ephraim interpose a barrier too difficult to be attempted when an alternative route is possible. For a march on Jerusalem the best base is Jaffa, and to that place Richard resolved to transfer

From: *History of the Art of War in the Middle Ages,* by Charles Oman.

himself and his army. He accordingly arranged that the host should march along the great Roman road beside the sea by Haifa, Athlit, Caesarea, and Arsouf, while the fleet should advance parallel with it, and communicate with it at every point where it is possible to get vessels close to the shore. This co-operation was all-important, for the army was lamentably deficient in means of transport, and depended on the ships for its food. So few were the beasts of burden, that a great part of the impedimenta had to be borne on the backs of the infantry, who loaded themselves with tents, flour-bags, and miscellaneous necessaries of all kinds. Nearly half of them were employed in porter's work, and thereby taken out of the ranks when the host began to move forward. No food was to be found on the way, for Saladin had already ravaged the shore, and dismantled Haifa, Caesarea, and Arsouf.

It was obvious that the Crusaders would be harassed by Saladin the moment that they started on their march. The temptation to assail a host strung out in one thin column along many miles of road would certainly draw the Turks down from their strongholds in the hills. Richard had therefore to provide an order of march which should be convertible at a moment's notice into an order of battle. His front, rear, and left flank were all equally liable to assault. Only the right would always be covered by the proximity of the sea.

In view of this danger the king made the best disposition possible. Next the sea moved the beasts of burden and the infantry employed to carry loads. Inland from them were the cavalry, distributed into compact bands and spaced out at equal intervals all along the line of march. Inland again from the cavalry were the main body of infantry, marching in a continuous column, and so covering the whole eastern flank of the army. Though the contingents were placed so close that no gaps were left between them, they were for purposes of organization divided into twelve bodies, to each of which there was attached one of the cavalry corps, which marched level with it. Thus there were twelve divisions of foot and twelve of horse; these smaller units were united into five main corps, of which the exact composition is not easy to ascertain. The Templars and Hospitallers, who knew the country well, and had in their ranks many "Turcopoles," i.e., horse-bowmen armed like the Turks and specially fit to cope with them, took the van and the rear, the two points of greatest danger, on alternate days. With the centre division of the army moved the royal standard of England fixed on a covered waggon drawn by four horses, like the *carroccio* which the Milanese had used at Legnano a few years before. The order of the various corps was, as we gather, somewhat varied on different days. On one occasion Richard and his own military household took the van, but usually he reserved for himself no fixed station, but rode backward and forward along the line of march with his household knights, carefully supervising the movement of the whole and lending aid wherever it was required. The heat was great, September being not yet come, and the king was determined not to harass the army by long stages. Accordingly, he moved very slowly, using only the early morning for the march, and seldom covering more than eight or ten miles in the day. Moreover, he habitually halted on each alternate day, and gave his men a full twenty-four hours (or even more) of rest. Thus the host took as much as nineteen days to cover the distance of eighty miles between Acre and Jaffa.

Throughout the march the army was incessantly worried by the attacks of the Turks, especially on the 25th and 30th of August and the 1st and 3rd of September. The respite on the 26–7–8–9th was due to the fact, that while Richard had hugged the coast from Haifa and gone round the shoulder of Mount Carmel, Saladin had struck across country, passed the hills farther east, and come down on to the neighbourhood of Caesarea, before the Crusaders, moving slowly and on a longer road, had drawn near the place. From August 30 to September 7, on the other hand, he was always within a few miles of them, waiting for his opportunity to dash down from the hills if they exposed themselves. The author of the *Itinerarium* gives an interesting description of the Turkish tactics during these days:

"The Infidels, not weighed down with heavy armour like our knights, but always able to outstrip them in pace, were a constant trouble. When charged they are wont to fly, and their horses are more nimble than any others in the world; one may liken them to swallows for swiftness. When they see that you have ceased to pursue them, they no longer fly but return upon you; they are like tiresome flies which you can flap away for a moment, but which come back the instant you have stopped hitting at them: as long as you beat about they keep off: the moment you cease, they are on you again. So the Turk, when you wheel about after driving him off, follows you home without a second's delay, but will fly again if you turn on him. When the king rode at them, they always retreated, but they hung about our rear, and sometimes did us mischief, not unfrequently disabling some of our men."

Saladin, in keeping up this incessant skirmish along the flank of the crusading host, was not merely endeavouring to weary it out. Though he only showed small bands hovering about in all directions, often but thirty or fifty strong, he was always waiting close at hand with his main army. He kept it hidden in the hills, hoping that the Franks would some day be goaded into making a reckless charge upon his skirmishers. If they would only break their line by a disorderly advance, he would pounce down, penetrate into the gap, and sweep all before him. King Richard, however, kept his men in such good order that in the whole three weeks of the march they never gave the Sultan the opportunity that he longed for. The king himself and his meinie would occasionally swoop out upon bands that came too close, but the main order of march was never broken. Only on one occasion, on the first day of the march from the Belus (August 25), did the Turks get a chance of slipping in while the rearguard was passing a defile, and then the Crusaders closed up so quickly that the assailants had to fly, after accomplishing nothing more than the plunder of a little baggage. Boha-ed-din's account of the Crusaders' march is as well worth quoting as the note on the Turkish attack which we have cited from the *Itinerarium*. He is describing the events of Saturday, August 31.

"The enemy moved in order of battle: their infantry marched between us and their cavalry, keeping as level and firm as a wall. Each foot-soldier had a thick cassock of felt, and under it a mail-shirt so strong that our arrows made no impression on them. They, meanwhile, shot at us with crossbows, which struck down horse and man among the Moslems. I noted among them men who had from one to ten shafts sticking in their backs, yet trudged on at their ordinary pace and did not fall out of their ranks. The infantry were divided into two halves: one marched so as to cover the cavalry, the other moved along the beach and took no part in the fighting, but rested itself. When the first half was wearied, it changed places with the second and got its turn of repose. The cavalry marched between the two halves of the infantry, and only came out when it wished to charge. It was formed in three main corps: in the van was Guy, formerly King of Jerusalem, with all the Syrian Franks who adhered to him; in the second were the English and French; in the rear the sons of the Lady of Tiberias and other troops. In the centre of their army there was visible a waggon carrying a tower as high as one of our minarets, on which was planted the king's banner. The Franks continued to advance in this order, fighting vigorously all the time: the Moslems sent in volleys of arrows from all sides, endeavouring to irritate the knights and to worry them into leaving their rampart of infantry. But it was all in vain: they kept their temper admirably and went on their way without hurrying themselves in the least, while their fleet sailed along the coast parallel with them till they arrived at their camping-place for the night. They never marched a long stage, because they had to spare the foot-soldiery, of whom the half not actively engaged was carrying the baggage and tents, so great was their want of beasts of burden. It was impossible not to admire the patience which these people showed: they bore crushing fatigue, though they had no proper military administration, and were getting no personal advantage. And so they finally pitched their camp on the farther side of the river of Caesarea."

From the 29th August to the 6th September, Saladin had been perpetually seeking an opportunity for delivering a serious attack. But the caution and discipline which Richard had imposed upon his army foiled all the hopes of the Infidel. It became evident that, if the Christians were to be stopped before they reached Jaffa, a desperate attempt must be made to break in upon them, in spite of their orderly march and firm array. Saladin resolved, therefore, to try the ordeal of battle in the ground between the Nahr-el-Falaik (the river of Rochetaille) and Arsouf. There was every opportunity for hiding his host till the moment of conflict, for in this district one of the few forests of Palestine, the "Wood of Arsouf," runs parallel to the sea for more than twelve miles. It was a thick oak wood covering all the lower spurs of the mountains, and reaching in some places to within three thousand yards of the beach. Two days of Richard's itinerary (the 5th and 7th of September) ran between this forest and the sea. He was not less conscious than Saladin of the advantage which the cover would give to an enemy plotting a sudden attack. Accordingly he warned the army on the 5th that they might have to fight a general engagement on that day, and took every precaution to prevent disorder. But the Turks held back, and the first half of the forest was passed in safety. On the 6th September the Crusaders rested, protecting their camp by the large marsh which lies inland from the mouth of the Nahr-el-Falaik; this impassable ground, the modern Birket-el-Ramadan, extending for two miles north and south, and three miles east and west, covers completely a camp placed by the river mouth.

On the 7th the English king gave orders to move on: the day's march was to cover the six miles from the Nahr-el-Falaik to the dismantled town of Arsouf. The road lies about three-quarters of a mile inland from the beach, generally passing along the slope of a slight hill: between it and the foot of the wooded mountains there was an open valley varying from a mile to two miles in breadth. The forest on the rising ground was known to conceal the whole of Saladin's host, whose scouts were visible in all directions.

On this day Richard divided his army into twelve divisions, each consisting of a large body of infantry and a small squadron of knights. The foot-soldiery formed a continuous line, with the crossbowmen in the outermost rank. The impedimenta and the infantry told off to guard them moved as usual close to the sea. The order of the march of the twelve divisions is not clearly given to us; we know that the first consisted on this day of the Templars, with their knights, Turcopoles, and foot-sergeants. The next three consisted mainly of Richard's own subjects—Bretons and the Angevins forming the second, Poitevins (under Guy, the titular King of Jerusalem) the third, and Normans and English the fourth: the last-named corps had charge of the waggon bearing the great standard. Seven corps were made up from the French, the barons of Syria, and the miscellaneous small contingents from other lands. Lastly, the Hospitallers brought up the rear. Probably the French contingents were divided into four "battles," under (1) James d'Avesnes, (2) the Count of Dreux and his brother the Bishop of Beauvais, (3) William des Barres and William de Garlande, (4) Drogo, Count of Merle. Henry, Count of Champagne was charged with the duty of keeping out on the left flank to watch for the breaking forth of the Turks from the woods. The Duke of Burgundy, the commander of the French host, rode by Richard's side up and down the line, keeping order and ready to give aid wherever it was wanted. The whole twelve corps were divided into five divisions, but it is not stated how they were thus distributed. Some of the five must have included three, some only two, of the brigaded bodies of horse and foot.

Saladin allowed the whole Christian host to emerge from the camp and proceed some little way along the road before he launched his army upon them. While threatening the whole of the long line of march, he had resolved to throw the main weight of his attack upon the rearguard. Evidently he hoped to produce a gap, by allowing the van and centre to proceed, while delaying the rear by incessant assaults. If the Hospitallers and the divisions next to them could be so harassed that they were forced to halt or even to charge, while the the van still went on its way, it was obvious that a break in the continuous wall of infantry would occur. Into this opening Saladin would have thrown his reserves, and then have trusted to fighting the battle out with an enemy split into at least two fractions and probably more. He had, as we shall see, wholly underrated the prudence and generalship of King Richard, and was preparing for himself a bloody repulse.

The Crusaders were well upon their way when the Moslems suddenly burst out from the woods. In front were swarms of skirmishers both horse and foot—black Soudanese archers, wild Bedouins, and the terrible Turkish horse-bowmen. Behind were visible deep squadrons of supports—the Sultan's mailed Mamelukes and the contingents of all the princes and emirs of Egypt, Syria, and Mesopotamia. The whole space, two miles broad, between the road and the forest, was suddenly filled with these imposing masses. "All over the face of the land you could see the well-ordered bands of the Turks, myriads of parti-coloured banners, marshalled in troops and squadrons; of mailed men alone there appeared to be more than twenty thousand. With unswerving course, swifter than eagles, they swept down upon our line of march. The air was turned black by the dust that their hoofs cast up. Before the face of each emir went his musicians, making a horrid din with horns, trumpets, drums, cymbals, and all manner of brazen instruments, while the troops behind pressed on with howls and cries of war. For the Infidels think that the louder the noise, the bolder grows the spirit of the warrior. So did the cursed Turks beset us before, behind, and on the flank, and they pressed in so close that for two miles around there was not a spot of the bare earth visible; all was covered by the thick array of the enemy."

While some of the Turks rode in between the head of the army and its goal at Arsouf, and others followed the rearguard along the road, the majority closed in upon the left flank and plied their bows against the wall of infantry and the clumps of horsemen slowly pacing behind it. The pressure seems to have been hardest upon the rear, where the right wing of the Turks delivered a most desperate attack upon the squadron of the Hospitallers and the infantry corps which covered them. The French divisions opposite the Turkish centre were less hardly pressed; the English, Poitevins, and Templars in the van, though constantly engaged, were never seriously incommoded.

In spite of the fury of the attack, the Crusaders for some time pursued their way without the least wavering or hesitation. The crossbowmen gave the Turks back bolt for bolt, and wrought more harm than they suffered, since their missiles were heavier and possessed more penetrating power than those of the enemy. The cavalry in the centre of the column rode slowly on, though their horses soon began to suffer from the incessant rain of arrows. Many knights had to dismount from mortally wounded chargers, and to march lance in hand among the foot. Others picked up crossbows, stepped into the front rank of the infantry and revenged themselves by shooting down the Turkish horses.

The slow march southward went on for some time; the infantry held firm as a wall, and no opportunity was given for the enemy to break in. Saladin, seeing that he was making no progress, flung himself among the skirmishers, followed only by two pages leading spare horses, and continued to urge his men on and to press them closer in on the Frankish foot. The stress soon became very severe in the rear division of King Richard's host, which was exposed to a double fire from flank and rear. Some of the crossbowmen began to waver, but the majority held firm, forced though they were to walk backwards with their faces to the pursuing enemy, for, when they turned for a moment to move on, the Turks rushed in so fiercely that there was grave danger that the corps of the Hospitallers might be broken up. "They had laid their bows aside, and were now thundering upon the rearguard with their scimitars and maces like smiths upon anvils!"

The Grand Master of the Hospitallers repeatedly sent forward to the king, asking leave to charge. The horses were being shot down one by one, he complained, and the knights could no longer endure this passive kind of battle, in which they were struck themselves, but not allowed to strike back. Richard returned the reply that the rear was on no account to break their order: he had settled that there should be a general charge of the whole line when he bade six trumpets blow; before the signal no one must move. His design was evidently to get the whole Turkish army committed to close combat before he rode out upon it. At present the rear alone was seriously engaged: the van and centre were only being harassed from a distance. Moreover, there would be great advantage in waiting till the van had reached Arsouf, whose gardens and houses would give good cover for its flank when the moment for the decisive charge came.

In obedience to these orders, the Hospitallers endured for some time longer, but they were growing restive and angry as horse after horse fell, and man after man was disabled by arrows in the parts of his body which the armour did not fully protect. Presently the whole rear division lurched forward in disorder and joined the French corps which was marching immediately in front of it. At last, just when the head of the army had nearly reached the walls of Arsouf, the patience of the rear was wholly exhausted. Ere the king had bade the six trumpets sound, but (as it would seem) only just before the moment that he would have chosen, the Hospitallers burst forth. The ringleaders in this piece of indiscipline were two of their leaders, their marshal and a notable knight named Baldwin de Carron, who suddenly wheeled their horses, raised the war-cry of St. George, and dashed out through the infantry upon the Infidels. Those immediately about them followed; then the French divisions ranged next them took up the movement. It spread all down the line, and Richard himself, seeing the die cast, was constrained to allow the cavalry of the van and centre to follow up the attack. To the Saracens it bore the appearance of a preconcerted movement. "On a sudden," says Boha-ed-din, "we saw the cavalry of the enemy, who were now drawn together in three main masses, brandish their lances, raise their war-cry, and dash out at us. The infantry suddenly opened up gaps in their line to let them pass through." Thus the attack of the Crusaders was delivered in échelon, the left (*i.e.* the rear) leading, the centre starting a moment after, and the right (*i.e.* the van) a little later than the centre.

The Turks did not endure for a moment the onset of the dreaded knights of the west. The sudden change of the crusading army from a passive defence to a vigorous offensive came so unexpectedly upon them, that they broke and fled with disgraceful promptness. Nothing can be more frank than Boha-ed-din's account of the behavior of his master's host. "On our side," he says, "the rout was complete. I was myself in the centre: that corps having fled in confusion, I thought to take refuge with the left wing, which was the nearest to me; but when I reached it, I found it also in full retreat, and making off no less quickly than the centre. Then I rode to the right wing, but this had been routed even more thoroughly than the left. I turned accordingly to the spot where the Sultan's bodyguard should have served as a rallying-point for the rest. The banners were still upright and the drum beating, but only seventeen horsemen were round them."

In the northern end of the battle, where the Hospitallers and the French corps immediately in front of them were already in close contact with the foe at the moment of the charge, a dreadful slaughter of the Infidels took place. The rush of the Crusaders dashed horse and foot together into a solid mass, which could not easily escape, and the knights were able to take a bloody revenge for the long trial of endurance to which they had been exposed since daybreak. Before the Moslems could scatter and disperse to the rear, they had been mown down by thousands. In the centre and the southern end of the battle the Turks had an easier flight, since their pursuers were not so close. Here the contact and the slaughter must have been much less. We know from the author of the *Itinerarium* that the English and Norman knights who formed the fourth division, counting from the van, never reached the flying enemy, though they followed in échelon the movement of the rear and centre corps. The same was probably the case with the other three corps of the van, for King Richard, in his letter to the Abbot of Clairvaux, states that only four of his twelve divisions were seriously engaged, and that these four alone really defeated the whole host of Saladin.

Having pursued the Turks more than a mile, the Crusaders halted and began to re-form—there was no rash pursuit like that which had so often ruined the Franks in earlier fields. Those of the Infidels who still kept their heads, ceased to fly when they were no longer pursued, and turned to cut off the scattered knights, who had pushed far to the front, and were now riding back to fall into line with their comrades. Of these some few were cut off and slain—among them James d'Avesnes, a notable knight, who had commanded one of the rear divisions of the line of march. Among those of the Turks who rallied most quickly and came back first to the fight was Taki-ed-din, Saladin's nephew, with seven hundred horsemen who followed his yellow banner.

When the Christian line was once more in order, Richard led it on to a second charge; the Turks broke again and made no stand. Yet when the king cautiously halted his men, after sweeping the enemy backward for another mile, there was still a considerable body which turned back and once more showed fight. A third and final charge sent them flying into the forest, which was now close at their backs. Here they dispersed in all directions, and made no further attempt to resist. Richard, however, would not pursue them among the thickets, and led back his horsemen at leisure to Arsouf, where the infantry had now pitched their camp.

That evening many of the foot-soldiery and camp-followers went out to the field of battle, where they stripped the dead and found much valuable plunder, since the Turks, like the Mamelukes in later days, were wont to carry their money sewed up in their waist-belts or under their clothing. They reported that they had counted thirty-two emirs among the slain, and more than seven thousand of the rank and file, Boha-ed-din names as the most prominent of the Moslems who had fallen Mousec, the prince of the Kurds, and two emirs named Kaimaz-el-Adeli and Ligoush. Among the Christians, James of Avesnes was the only man of distinction who was slain: their total loss was under seven hundred men.

So ended this important and interesting fight, the most complete and typical of all the victories of the Franks over their enemies. The old morals of the earlier engagements are once more repeated in it. With a judicious combination of horse and foot, and a proper exercise of caution, the Crusader might be certain of victory. But we note that Richard, though new to the wars of the East, shows far more self-restraint, wisdom, and generalship than any of his predecessors. He could have driven off Saladin at any time during the day, but his object was not merely to chase away the Turks for a moment, but to inflict on them a blow which should disable them for a long period. This could only be done by luring them to close combat; hence came the passive tactics of the first half of the day. The victory would have been still more effective, as the author of the *Itinerarium* remarks, if the charge had been delivered a little later. But the precipitate action of the marshal of the Hospitallers caused it to be made a moment earlier than the king had intended. Nevertheless, the results of the fight were very well marked. Saladin reassembled his army, but he never dared close in upon his enemy again: he resumed his old policy of demonstrations and skirmishes. As Boha-ed-din remarks, the spirit of the Moslem army was completely broken. Recognising that he could not hold the open country against the Franks, the Sultan at once dismantled all the fortresses of Southern Palestine—Ascalon, Gaza, Blanche-Garde, Lydda, Ramleh, and the rest. He dared not leave garrisons in them, for he was fully aware that his men would not hold firm: the fate of the defenders of Acre and the result of the fight of Arsouf were always before their eyes, and they would not have maintained themselves for long. How well founded was this fear became sufficiently evident from the one exception which Saladin made to his rule. He left a force in Darum, the last fortress of Palestine on the way to Egypt. Richard made a dash against it with the knights of his own household alone, a force inferior to the garrison in number. Yet so half-hearted had the Moslems grown, that the king stormed the place in four days. The Turks surrendered the citadel on the bare promise of life, though, if they had shown a tithe of the courage of the garrison of Acre, they would certainly have been able to hold out for weeks, if not for months.

Arsouf therefore gave the Franks the whole coast-land of Southern Palestine. After repairing the walls of Jaffa, to serve them as a basis for the attack on Jerusalem, they were free to resume the offensive. But the jealousies and divisions in the host ruined the campaign which had begun so brilliantly, and, though there were several gallant feats of arms performed during the stay of Richard in Palestine, the Holy City was never recovered, and the war ended in a treaty which did no more than confirm the Syrian Franks in the possession of the coast-region which the English king had reconquered for them.

The Death of Montezuma

BY

WILLIAM HICKLING PRESCOTT

THE palace of Axayacatl, in which the Spaniards were quartered, was, as the reader may remember, a vast, irregular pile of stone buildings, having but one floor, except in the centre, where another story was added, consisting of a suite of apartments which rose like turrets on the main building of the edifice. A vast area stretched around, encompassed by a stone wall of no great height. This was supported by towers or bulwarks at certain intervals, which gave it some degree of strength, not, indeed, as compared with European fortifications, but sufficient to resist the rude battering enginery of the Indians. The parapet had been pierced here and there with embrasures for the artillery, which consisted of thirteen guns; and smaller apertures were made in other parts for the convenience of the arquebusiers. The Spanish forces found accommodations within the great building; but the numerous body of Tlascalan auxiliaries could have had no other shelter than what was afforded by barracks or sheds hastily constructed for the purpose in the spacious court-yard. Most of them, probably, bivouacked under the open sky, in a climate milder than that to which they were accustomed among the rude hills of their native land. Thus crowded into a small and compact compass, the whole army could be assembled at a moment's notice; and, as the Spanish commander was careful to enforce the strictest discipline and vigilance, it was scarcely possible that he could be taken by surprise. No sooner, therefore, did the trumpet call to arms, as the approach of the enemy was announced, than every soldier was at his post, the cavalry mounted, the artillery-men at their guns, and the archers and arquebusiers stationed so as to give the assailants a warm reception.

On they came, with the companies, or irregular masses, into which the multitude was divided, rushing forward each in its own dense column, with many a gay banner displayed, and many a bright gleam of light reflected from helmet, arrow, and spear-head, as they were tossed about in their disorderly array. As they drew near the inclosure, the Aztecs set up a hideous yell, or rather that shrill whistle used in fight by the nations of Anahuac, which rose far above the sound of shell and atabal, and their other rude instruments of warlike melody. They followed this by a tempest of missiles,— stones, darts, and arrows,—which fell thick as rain on the besieged, while

From: *The Conquest of Mexico.*

70

volleys of the same kind descended from the crowded terraces in the neighborhood.

The Spaniards waited until the foremost column had arrived within the best distance for giving effect to their fire, when a general discharge of artillery and arquebuses swept the ranks of the assailants, and mowed them down by hundreds. The Mexicans were familiar with the report of these formidable engines, as they had been harmlessly discharged on some holiday festival; but never till now had they witnessed their murderous power. They stood aghast for a moment, as with bewildered looks they staggered under the fury of the fire; but, soon rallying, the bold barbarians uttered a piercing cry, and rushed forward over the prostrate bodies of their comrades. A second and third volley checked their career, and threw them into disorder, but still they pressed on, letting off clouds of arrows; while their comrades on the roofs of the houses took more deliberate aim at the combatants in the court-yard. The Mexicans were particularly expert in the use of the sling; and the stones which they hurled from their elevated positions on the heads of their enemies did even greater execution than the arrows. They glanced, indeed, from the mail-covered bodies of the cavaliers, and from those who were sheltered under the cotton panoply, or *escaupil*. But some of the soldiers, especially the veterans of Cortés, and many of their Indian allies, had but slight defences, and suffered greatly under this stony tempest.

The Aztecs, meanwhile, had advanced close under the walls of the intrenchment; their ranks broken and disordered, and their limbs mangled by the unintermitting fire of the Christians. But they still pressed on, under the very muzzle of the guns. They endeavored to scale the parapet, which, from its moderate height, was in itself a work of no great difficulty. But the moment they showed their heads above the rampart, they were shot down by the unerring marksmen within, or stretched on the ground by a blow of a Tlascalan *maquahuitl*. Nothing daunted, others soon appeared to take the place of the fallen, and strove, by raising themselves on the writhing bodies of their dying comrades, or by fixing their spears in the crevices of the wall, to surmount the barrier. But the attempt proved equally vain.

Defeated here, they tried to effect a breach in the parapet by battering it with heavy pieces of timber. The works were not constructed on those scientific principles by which one part is made to overlook and protect another. The besiegers, therefore, might operate at their pleasure, with but little molestation from the garrison within, whose guns could not be brought into a position to bear on them, and who could mount no part of their own works for their defence, without exposing their persons to the missiles of the whole besieging army. The parapet, however, proved too strong for the efforts of the assailants. In their despair they endeavored to set the Christian quarters on fire, shooting burning arrows into them, and climbing up so as to dart their firebrands through the embrasures. The principal edifice was of stone. But the temporary defences of the Indian allies, and other parts of the exterior works, were of wood. Several of these took fire, and the flames spread rapidly among the light, combustible materials. This was a disaster for which the besieged were wholly unprepared. They had little water, scarcely enough for their own consumption. They endeavored to extinguish the flames by heaping on earth. But in vain. Fortunately the great building was of materials which defied the destroying element. But the fire raged in some of the outworks, connected with the parapet, with a fury which could only be checked by throwing down a part of the wall itself, thus laying open a formidable breach. This, by the general's order, was speedily protected by a battery of heavy guns, and a file of arquebusiers, who kept up an incessant volley through the opening on the assailants.

The fight now raged with fury on both sides. The walls around the palace belched forth an unintermitting sheet of flames and smoke. The groans of the wounded and dying were lost in the fiercer battle-cries of the combatants, the roar of the artillery, the sharper rattle of the musketry, and the hissing sound of Indian missiles. It was the conflict of the European with the American; of civilized man with the barbarian; of the science of the one with the rude weapons and warfare of the other. And as the ancient walls of Tenochtitlan shook under the thunders of the artillery,—it announced that the white man, the destroyer, had set his foot within her precincts.

Night at length came, and drew her friendly mantle over the contest. The Aztec seldom fought by night. It brought little repose, however, to the Spaniards, in hourly expectation of an assault; and they found abundant occupation in restoring the breaches in their defences, and in repairing their battered armor. The beleaguering host lay on their arms through the night, giving token of their presence, now and then, by sending a stone or shaft over the battlements, or by a solitary cry of defiance from some warrior more determined than the rest, till all other sounds were lost in the vague, indistinct murmurs which float upon the air in the neighborhood of a vast assembly.

The ferocity shown by the Mexicans seems to have been a thing for which Cortés was wholly unprepared. His past experience, his uninterrupted career of victory with a much feebler force at his command, had led him to underrate the military efficiency, if not the valor, of the Indians. The apparent facility, with which the Mexicans had acquiesced in the outrages on their sovereign and themselves, had led him to hold their courage, in particular, too lightly. He could not believe the present assault to be any thing more than a temporary ebullition of the populace, which would soon waste itself by its own fury. And he proposed, on the following day, to sally out and inflict such chastisement on his foes as should bring them to their senses, and show who was master in the capital.

With early dawn, the Spaniards were up and under arms; but not before their enemies had given evidence of their hostility by the random missiles, which, from time to time, were sent into the inclosure. As the grey light of morning advanced, it showed the besieging army far from being diminished in numbers, filling up the great square and neighboring avenues in more dense array than on the preceding evening. Instead of a confused, disorderly rabble, it had the appearance of something like a regular force, with its battalions distributed under their respective banners, the devices of which showed a contribution from the principal cities and districts in the Valley. High above the rest was conspicuous the ancient standard of Mexico, with its well known cognizance, an eagle pouncing on an ocelot, emblazoned on a rich mantle of feather-work. Here and there priests might be seen mingling in the ranks of the besiegers, and, with frantic gestures, animating them to avenge their insulted deities.

The greater part of the enemy had little clothing save the *maxtlatl*, or sash round the loins. They were variously armed, with long spears tipped with copper, or flint, or sometimes merely pointed and hardened in the fire. Some were provided with slings, and others with darts having two or three points, with long strings attached to them, by which, when discharged, they could be torn away again from the body of the wounded. This was a formidable weapon, much dreaded by the Spaniards. Those of a higher order wielded the terrible *maquahuitl*, with its sharp and brittle blades of obsidian. Amidst the motley bands of warriors, were seen many whose showy dress and air of authority intimated persons of high military consequence. Their breasts were protected by plates of metal, over which was thrown the gay surcoat of feather-work. They wore casques resembling, in their form, the head of some wild and ferocious animal, crested with bristly hair, or overshadowed by tall and graceful plumes of many a brilliant color. Some few were decorated with the red fillet bound round the hair, having tufts of cotton attached to it, which denoted by their number that of the victories they had won, and their own preëminent rank among the warriors of the nation. The motley assembly plainly showed that priest, warrior, and citizen had all united to swell the tumult.

Before the sun had shot his beams into the Castilian quarters, the enemy were in motion, evidently preparing to renew the assault of the preceding day. The Spanish commander determined to anticipate them by a vigorous sortie, for which he had already made the necessary dispositions. A general discharge of ordnance and musketry sent death far and wide into the enemy's ranks, and, before they had time to recover from their confusion, the gates were thrown open, and Cortés, sallying out at the head of his cavalry, supported by a large body of infantry and several thousand Tlascalans, rode at full gallop against them. Taken thus by surprise, it was scarcely possible to offer much resistance. Those who did were trampled down under the horses' feet, cut to pieces with the broadswords, or pierced with the lances of the riders. The infantry followed up the blow, and the rout for the moment was general.

But the Aztecs fled only to take refuge behind a barricade, or strong work of timber and earth, which had been thrown across the great street through which they were pursued. Rallying on the other side, they made a gallant stand, and poured in turn a volley of their light weapons on the Spaniards, who, saluted with a storm of missiles at the same time, from the terraces of the houses, were checked in their career, and thrown into some disorder.

Cortés, thus impeded, ordered up a few pieces of heavy ordnance, which soon swept away the barricades, and cleared a passage for the army. But it had lost the momentum acquired in its rapid advance. The enemy had time to rally and to meet the Spaniards on more equal terms. They were attacked in flank, too, as they advanced, by fresh battalions, who swarmed in from the adjoining streets and lanes. The canals were alive with boats filled with warriors, who, with their formidable darts searched every crevice or weak place in the armor of proof, and made havoc on the unprotected bodies of the Tlascalans. By repeated and vigorous charges, the Spaniards succeeded in driving the Indians before them; though many, with a desperation which showed they loved vengeance better than life, sought to embarrass the movements of their horses by clinging to their legs, or, more successfully strove to pull the riders from their saddles. And woe to the unfortunate cavalier who was thus dismounted,—to be despatched by the brutal *maquahuitl*, or to be dragged on board a canoe to the bloody altar of sacrifice!

But the greatest annoyance which the Spaniards endured was from the missiles from the *azoteas*, consisting often of large stones, hurled with a force that would tumble the stoutest rider from his saddle. Galled in the extreme by these discharges, against which even their shields afforded no adequate protection, Cortés ordered fire to be set to the buildings. This was no very difficult matter, since, although chiefly of stone, they were filled with mats, cane-work, and other combustible materials, which were soon in a blaze. But the buildings stood separated from one another by canals and drawbridges, so that the flames did not easily communicate to the neighboring edifices. Hence, the labor of the Spaniards was incalculably increased, and their progress in the work of destruction—fortunately for the city—was comparatively slow. They did not relax their efforts, however, till several hundred houses had been consumed, and the miseries of a conflagration, in which the wretched inmates perished equally with the defenders, were added to the other horrors of the scene.

The day was now far spent. The Spaniards had been everywhere victorious. But the enemy, though driven back on every point, still kept the field. When broken by the furious charges of the cavalry, he soon rallied behind the temporary defences, which, at different intervals, had been thrown across the streets, and, facing about, renewed the fight with undiminished courage, till the sweeping away of the barriers by the cannon of the assailants left a free passage for the movements of their horse. Thus the action was a succession of rallying and retreating, in which both parties suffered much, although the loss inflicted on the Indians was probably tenfold greater than that of the Spaniards. But the Aztecs could better afford the loss of a hundred lives than their antagonists that of one. And, while the Spaniards showed an array broken, and obviously thinned in numbers, the Mexican army, swelled by the tributary levies which flowed in upon it from the neighboring streets, exhibited, with all its losses, no sign of diminution. At length, sated with carnage, and exhausted by toil and hunger, the Spanish commander drew off his men, and sounded a retreat.

On his way back to his quarters, he beheld his friend, the secretary Duero, in a street adjoining, unhorsed, and hotly engaged with a body of Mexicans, against whom he was desperately defending himself with his poniard. Cortés, roused at the sight, shouted his war-cry, and, dashing into the midst of the enemy, scattered them like chaff by the fury of his onset; then, recovering his friend's horse, he enabled him to remount, and the two cavaliers, striking their spurs into their steeds, burst through their opponents and joined the main body of the army. Such displays of generous gallantry were not uncommon in these engagements, which called forth more feats of personal adventure than battles with antagonists better skilled in the science of war. The chivalrous bearing of the general was emulated in full measure by Sandoval, De Leon, Olid, Alvarado, Ordaz, and his other brave companions, who won such glory under the eye of their leader, as prepared the way for the independent commands which afterwards placed provinces and kingdoms at their disposal.

The undaunted Aztecs hung on the rear of their retreating foes, annoying them at every step by fresh flights of stones and arrows; and, when the Spaniards had reëntered their fortress, the Indian host encamped around it, showing the same dogged resolution as on the preceding evening. Though true to their ancient habits of inaction during the night, they broke the stillness of the hour by insulting cries and menaces, which reached the ears of the besieged. "The gods have delivered you, at last, into our hands," they said; "Huitzilopotchli has long cried for his victims. The stone sacrifice is ready. The knives are sharpened. The wild beasts in the palace are roaring for their offal. And the cages," they added, taunting the Tlascalans with their leanness, "are waiting for the false sons of Anahuac, who are to be fattened for the festival!" These dismal menaces, which sounded fearfully in the ears of the besieged, who understood too well their import, were mingled with piteous lamentations for their sovereign, whom they called on the Spaniards to deliver up to them.

Cortés suffered much from a severe wound which he had received in the hand in the late action. But the anguish of his mind must have been still greater, as he brooded over the dark prospect before him. He had mistaken the character of the Mexicans. Their long and patient endurance had been a violence to their natural temper, which, as their whole history proves, was arrogant and ferocious beyond that of most of the races of Anahuac. The restraint, which, in deference to their monarch, more than to their own fears, they had so long put on their natures, being once removed, their passions burst forth with accumulated violence. The Spaniards had encountered in the Tlascalan an open enemy, who had no grievance to complain of, no wrong to redress. He fought under the vague apprehension only of some coming evil to his country. But the Aztec, hitherto the proud lord of the land, was goaded by insult and injury, till he reached that pitch of self-devotion, which made life cheap, in comparison with revenge. Armed thus with the energy of despair, the savage is almost a match for the civilized man; and a whole nation, moved to its depths by a common feeling, which swallows up all selfish considerations of personal interest and safety, becomes, whatever be its resources, like the earthquake and the tornado, the most formidable among the agencies of nature.

Considerations of this kind may have passed through the mind of Cortés, as he reflected on his own impotence to restrain the fury of the Mexicans, and resolved, in despite of his late supercilious treatment of Montezuma, to employ his authority to allay the tumult,—an authority so successfully exerted in behalf of Alvarado, at an earlier stage of the insurrection. He was the more confirmed in his purpose, on the following morning, when the assailants, redoubling their efforts, succeeded in scaling the works in one quarter, and effecting an entrance into the inclosure. It is true, they were met with so resolute a spirit, that not a man, of those who entered, was left alive. But, in the impetuosity of the assault, it seemed, for a few moments, as if the place was to be carried by storm.

Cortés now sent to the Aztec emperor to request his interposition with his subjects in behalf of the Spaniards. But Montezuma was not in the humor to comply. He had remained moodily in his quarters ever since the general's return. Disgusted with the treatment he had received, he had still further cause for mortification in finding himself the ally of those who were the open enemies of his nation. From his apartment he had beheld the tragical scenes in his capital, and seen another, the presumptive heir to his throne, taking the place which he should have occupied at the head of his warriors, and fighting the battles of his country. Distressed by his position, indignant at those who had placed him in it, he coldly answered, "What have I to do with Malinche? I do not wish to hear from him. I desire only to die. To what a state has my willingness to serve him reduced me!" When urged still further to comply by Olid and father Olmedo, he added, "It is of no use. They will neither believe me, nor the false words and promises of Malinche. You will never leave these walls alive." On being assured, however, that the Spaniards would willingly depart, if a way were opened to them by their enemies, he at length—moved, probably, more by a desire to spare the blood of his subjects, than of the Christians—consented to expostulate with his people.

In order to give the greater effect to his presence, he put on his imperial robes. The *tilmatli*, his mantle of white and blue, flowed over his shoulders, held together by its rich clasp of the green *chalchivitl*. The same precious gem, with emeralds of uncommon size, set in gold, profusely ornamented other parts of his dress. His feet were shod with the golden sandals, and his brows covered by the *copilli*, or Mexican diadem, resembling in form the pontifical tiara. Thus attired, and surrounded by a guard of Spaniards and several Aztec nobles, and preceded by the golden wand, the symbol of sovereignty, the Indian monarch ascended the central turret of the palace. His presence was instantly recognised by the people, and, as the royal retinue advanced along the battlements, a change, as if by magic, came over the scene. The clang of instruments, the fierce cries of the assailants, were hushed, and a deathlike stillness pervaded the whole assembly, so fiercely agitated, but a few moments before, by the wild tumult of war! Many prostrated themselves on the ground; others bent the knee; and all turned with eager expectation towards the monarch, whom they had been taught to reverence with slavish awe, and from whose countenance they had been wont to turn away as from the intolerable splendors of divinity! Montezuma saw his advantage; and, while he stood thus confronted with his awe-struck people, he seemed to recover all his former authority and confidence, as he felt himself to be still a king. With a calm voice, easily heard over the silent assembly, he is said by the Castilian writers to have thus addressed them.

"Why do I see my people here in arms against the palace of my fathers? Is it that you think your sovereign a prisoner, and wish to release him? If so, you have acted rightly. But you are mistaken. I am no prisoner. The strangers are my guests. I remain with them only from choice, and can leave them when I list. Have you come to drive them from the city? That is unnecessary. They will depart of their own accord, if you will open a way for them. Return to your homes, then. Lay down your arms. Show your obedience to me who have a right to it. The white men shall go back to their own land; and all shall be well again within the walls of Tenochtitlan."

As Montezuma announced himself the friend of the detested strangers, a murmur ran through the multitude; a murmur of contempt for the pusillanimous prince who could show himself so insensible to the insults and injuries for which the nation was in arms! The swollen tide of their passions swept away all the barriers of ancient reverence, and, taking a new direction, descended on the head of the unfortunate monarch, so far degenerated from his warlike ancestors. "Base Aztec," they exclaimed, "woman, coward, the white men have made you a woman,—fit only to weave and spin!" These bitter taunts were soon followed by still more hostile demonstrations. A chief, it is said, of high rank, bent a bow or brandished a javelin with an air of defiance against the emperor, when, in an instant, a cloud of stones and arrows descended on the spot where the royal train was gathered. The Spaniards appointed to protect his person had been thrown off their guard by the respectful deportment of the people during their lord's address. They now hastily interposed their bucklers. But it was too late. Montezuma was wounded by three of the missiles, one of which, a stone, fell with such violence on his head, near the temple, as brought him senseless to the ground. The Mexicans, shocked at their own sacrilegious act, experienced a sudden revulsion of feeling, and, setting up a dismal cry, dispersed panic-struck, in different directions. Not one of the multitudinous array remained in the great square before the palace!

The unhappy prince, meanwhile was borne by his attendants to his apartments below. On recovering from the insensibility caused by the blow, the wretchedness of his condition broke upon him. He had tasted the last bitterness of degradation. He had been reviled, rejected, by his people. The meanest of the rabble had raised their hands against him. He had nothing more to live for. It was in vain that Cortés and his officers endeavored to soothe the anguish of his spirit and fill him with better thoughts. He spoke not a word in answer. His wound, though dangerous, might still, with skilful treatment, not prove mortal. But Montezuma refused all the remedies prescribed for it. He tore off the bandages as often as they were applied, maintaining, all the while, the most determined silence. He sat with eyes dejected, brooding over his fallen fortunes, over the image of ancient majesty, and present humiliation. He had survived his honor. But a spark of his ancient spirit seemed to kindle in his bosom, as it was clear he did not mean to survive his disgrace.—From this painful scene the Spanish general and his followers were soon called away by the new dangers which menaced the garrison.

Opposite to the Spanish quarters, at only a few rods' distance, stood the great *teocalli* of Huitzilopotchli. This pyramidal mound, with the sanctuaries that crowned it, rising altogether to the height of near a hundred and fifty feet, afforded an elevated position that completely commanded the palace of Axayacatl, occupied by the Christians. A body of five or six hundred Mexicans, many of them nobles and warriors of the highest rank, had got possession of the *teocalli*, whence they discharged such a tempest of arrows on the garrison, that no one could leave his defences for a moment without imminent danger; while the Mexicans, under shelter of the sanctuaries, were entirely covered from the fire of the besieged. It was obviously necessary to dislodge the enemy, if the Spaniards would remain longer in their quarters.

Cortés assigned this service to his chamberlain, Escobar, giving him a hundred men for the purpose, with orders to storm the *teocalli*, and set fire to the sanctuaries. But that officer was thrice repulsed in the attempt, and, after the most desperate efforts, was obliged to return with considerable loss, and without accomplishing his object.

Cortés, who saw the immediate necessity of carrying the place, determined to lead the storming party himself. He was then suffering much from the wound in his left hand, which had disabled it for the present. He made the arm serviceable, however, by fastening his buckler to it, and, thus crippled, sallied out at the head of three hundred chosen cavaliers, and several thousand of his auxiliaries.

In the court-yard of the temple he found a numerous body of Indians prepared to dispute his passage. He briskly charged them, but the flat, smooth stones of the pavement were so slippery, that the horses lost their footing, and many of them fell. Hastily dismounting, they sent back the animals to their quarters, and, renewing the assault, the Spaniards succeeded without much difficulty in dispersing the Indian warriors, and opening a free passage for themselves to the *teocalli*. This building, as the reader may remember, was a huge pyramidal structure, about three hundred feet square at the base. A flight of stone steps on the outside, at one of the angles of the mound, led to a platform, or terraced walk, which passed round the building until it reached a similar flight of stairs directly over the preceding, that conducted to another landing as before. As there were five bodies or divisions of the *teocalli*, it became necessary to pass round its whole extent four times, or nearly a mile, in order to reach the summit, which, it may be recollected, was an open area, crowned only by the two sanctuaries dedicated to the Aztec deities.

Cortés, having cleared a way for the assault, sprang up the lower stairway, followed by Alvarado, Sandoval, Ordaz, and the other gallant cavaliers of his little band, leaving a file of arquebusiers and a strong corps of Indian allies to hold the enemy in check at the foot of the monument. On the first landing, as well as on the several galleries above, and on the summit, the Aztec warriors were drawn up to dispute his passage. From their elevated position they showered down volleys of lighter missiles, together with heavy stones, beams, and burning rafters, which, thundering along the stairway, overturned the ascending Spaniards, and carried desolation through their ranks. The more fortunate, eluding or springing over these obstacles, succeeded in gaining the first terrace; where, throwing themselves on their enemies, they compelled them, after a short resistance, to fall back. The assailants pressed on, effectually supported by a brisk fire of the musketeers from below, which so much galled the Mexicans in their exposed situation, that they were glad to take shelter on the broad summit of the *teocalli*.

Cortés and his comrades were close upon their rear, and the two parties soon found themselves face to face on this aërial battle-field, engaged in mortal combat in presence of the whole city, as well as of the troops in the court-yard, who paused, as if by mutual consent, from their own hostilities, gazing in silent expectation on the issue of those above. The area, though somewhat smaller than the base of the *teocalli*, was large enough to afford a fair field of fight for a thousand combatants. It was paved with broad, flat stones. No impediment occurred over its surface, except the huge sacrificial block, and the temples of stone which rose to the height of forty feet, at the further extremity of the arena. One of these had been consecrated to the Cross. The other was still occupied by the Mexican war-god. The Christian and the Aztec contended for their religions under the very shadow of their respective shrines; while the Indian priests, running to and fro, with their hair wildly streaming over their sable mantles, seemed hovering in mid air, like so many demons of darkness urging on the work of slaughter!

The parties closed with the desperate fury of men who had no hope but in victory. Quarter was neither asked nor given; and to fly was impossible. The edge of the area was unprotected by parapet or battlement. The least slip would be fatal; and the combatants, as they struggled in mortal agony, were sometimes seen to roll over the sheer sides of the precipice together. Cortés himself is said to have had a narrow escape from this dreadful fate. Two warriors, of strong, muscular frames, seized on him, and were dragging him violently towards the brink of the pyramid. Aware of their intention, he struggled with all his force, and, before they could accomplish their purpose, succeeded in tearing himself from their grasp, and hurling one of them over the walls with his own arm! The story is not improbable in itself, for Cortés was a man of uncommon agility and strength. It has been often repeated; but not by contemporary history.

The battle lasted with unintermitting fury for three hours. The number of the enemy was double that of the Christians; and it seemed as if it were a contest which must be determined by numbers and brute force, rather than by superior science. But it was not so. The invulnerable armor of the Spaniard, his sword of matchless temper, and his skill in the use of it, gave him advantages which far outweighed the odds of physical strength and numbers. After doing all that the courage of despair could enable men to do, resistance grew fainter and fainter on the side of the Aztecs. One after another they had fallen. Two or three priests only survived to be led away in triumph by the victors. Every other combatant was stretched a corpse on the bloody arena, or had been hurled from the giddy heights. Yet the loss of the Spaniards was not inconsiderable. It amounted to forty-five of their best men, and nearly all the remainder were more or less injured in the desperate conflict.

The victorious cavaliers now rushed towards the sanctuaries. The lower story was of stone; the two upper were of wood. Penetrating into their recesses, they had the mortification to find the image of the Virgin and the Cross removed. But in the other edifice they still beheld the grim figure of Huitzilopotchli, with his censer of smoking hearts, and the walls of his oratory reeking with gore,—not improbably of their own countrymen! With shouts of triumph the Christians tore the uncouth monster from his niche, and tumbled him, in the presence of the horror-struck Aztecs, down the steps of the *teocalli*. They then set fire to the accursed building. The flames speedily ran up the slender towers, sending forth an ominous light over city, lake, and valley, to the remotest hut among the mountains. It was the funeral pyre of Paganism, and proclaimed the fall of that sanguinary religion which had so long hung like a dark cloud over the fair regions of Anahuac!

Having accomplished this good work, the Spaniards descended the winding slopes of the *teocalli* with more free and buoyant step, as if conscious that the blessing of Heaven now rested on their arms. They passed through the dusky files of Indian warriors in the court-yard, too much dismayed by the appalling scenes they had witnessed to offer resistance; and reached their own quarters in safety. That very night they followed up the blow by a sortie on the sleeping town, and burned three hundred houses, the horrors of conflagration being made still more impressive by occurring at the hour when the Aztecs, from their own system of warfare, were least prepared for them.

Hoping to find the temper of the natives somewhat subdued by these reverses, Cortés now determined, with his usual policy, to make them a vantage-ground for proposing terms of accommodation. He accordingly invited the enemy to a parley, and, as the principal chiefs, attended by their followers, assembled in the great square, he mounted the turret before occupied by Montezuma, and made signs that he would address them. Marina, as usual, took her place by his side, as his interpreter. The multitude gazed with earnest curiosity on the Indian girl, whose influence with the Spaniards was well known, and whose connection with the general, in particular, had led the Aztecs to designate him by her Mexican name of Malinche. Cortés, speaking through the soft, musical tones of his mistress, told his audience they must now be convinced, that they had nothing further to hope from opposition to the Spaniards. They had seen their gods trampled in the dust, their altars broken, their dwellings burned, their warriors falling on all sides. "All this," continued he, "you have brought on yourselves by your rebellion. Yet for the affection the sovereign, whom you have so unworthily treated, still bears you, I would willingly stay my hand, if you will lay down your arms, and return once more to your obedience. But, if you do not," he concluded, "I will make your city a heap of ruins, and leave not a soul alive to mourn over it!"

But the Spanish commander did not yet comprehend the character of the Aztecs, if he thought to intimidate them by menaces. Calm in their exterior and slow to move, they were the more difficult to pacify when roused; and now that they had been stirred to their inmost depths, it was no human voice that could still the tempest. It may be, however, that Cortés did not so much misconceive the character of the people. He may have felt that an authoritative tone was the only one he could assume with any chance of effect, in his present position, in which milder and more conciliatory language would, by intimating a consciousness of inferiority, have too certainly defeated its own object.

It was true, they answered, he had destroyed their temples, broken in pieces their gods, massacred their countrymen. Many more, doubtless, were yet to fall under their terrible swords. But they were content so long as for every thousand Mexicans they could shed the blood of a single white man! "Look out," they continued, "on our terraces and streets, see them still thronged with warriors as far as your eyes can reach. Our numbers are scarcely diminished by our losses. Yours, on the contrary, are lessening every hour. You are perishing from hunger and sickness. Your provisions and water are falling. You must soon fall into our hands. *The bridges are broken down, and you cannot escape!* There will be too few of you left to glut the vengeance of our Gods!" As they concluded, they sent a volley of arrows over the battlements, which compelled the Spaniards to descend and take refuge in their defences.

The fierce and indomitable spirit of the Aztecs filled the besieged with dismay. All, then, that they had done and suffered, their battles by day, their vigils by night, the perils they had braved, even the victories they had won, were of no avail. It was too evident that they had no longer the spring of ancient superstition to work upon, in the breasts of the natives, who, like some wild beast that has burst the bonds of his keeper, seemed now to swell and exult in the full consciousness of their strength. The annunciation respecting the bridges fell like a knell on the ears of the Christians. All that they had heard was too true,—and they gazed on one another with looks of anxiety and dismay.

The same consequences followed, which sometimes take place among the crew of a shipwrecked vessel. Subordination was lost in the dreadful sense of danger. A spirit of mutiny broke out, especially among the recent levies drawn from the army of Narvaez. They had come into the country from no motive of ambition, but attracted simply by the glowing reports of its opulence, and they had fondly hoped to return in a few months with their pockets well lined with the gold of the Aztec monarch. But how different had been their lot! From the first hour of their landing, they had experienced only trouble and disaster, privations of every description, sufferings unexampled, and they now beheld in perspective a fate yet more appalling. Bitterly did they lament the hour when they left the sunny fields of Cuba for these cannibal regions! And heartily did they curse their own folly in listening to the call of Velasquez, and still more, in embarking under the banner of Cortés!

They now demanded with noisy vehemence to be led instantly from the city, and refused to serve longer in defence of a place where they were cooped up like sheep in the shambles, waiting only to be dragged to slaughter. In all this they were rebuked by the more orderly, soldier-like conduct of the veterans of Cortés. These latter had shared with their general the day of his prosperity, and they were not disposed to desert him in the tempest. It was, indeed, obvious, on a little reflection, that the only chance of safety, in the existing crisis, rested on subordination and union; and that even this chance must be greatly diminished under any other leader than their present one.

Thus pressed by enemies without and by factions within, that leader was found, as usual, true to himself. Circumstances so appalling, as would have paralyzed a common mind, only stimulated his to higher action, and drew forth all its resources. He combined what is most rare, singular coolness and constancy of purpose, with a spirit of enterprise that might well be called romantic. His presence of mind did not now desert him. He calmly surveyed his condition, and weighed the difficulties which surrounded him, before coming to a decision. Independently of the hazard of a retreat in the face of a watchful and desperate foe, it was a deep mortification to surrender up the city, where he had so long lorded it as a master; to abandon the rich treasures which he had secured to himself and his followers; to forego the very means by which he hoped to propitiate the favor of his sovereign, and secure an amnesty for his irregular proceedings. This, he well knew, must, after all, be dependent on success. To fly now was to acknowledge himself further removed from the conquest than ever. What a close was this to a career so auspiciously begun! What a contrast to his magnificent vaunts! What a triumph would it afford to his enemies! The governor of Cuba would be amply revenged.

But, if such humiliating reflections crowded on his mind, the alternative of remaining, in his present crippled condition, seemed yet more desperate. With his men daily diminishing in strength and numbers, their provisions reduced so low that a small daily ration of bread was all the sustenance afforded to the soldier under his extraordinary fatigues, with the breaches every day widening in his feeble fortifications, with his ammunition, in fine, nearly expended, it would be impossible to maintain the place much longer—and none but men of iron constitutions and tempers, like the Spaniards, could have held it out so long—against the enemy. The chief embarrassment was as to the time and manner in which it would be expedient to evacuate the city. The best route seemed to be that of Tlacopan (Tacuba). For the causeway, the most dangerous part of the road, was but two miles long in that direction, and would, therefore, place the fugitives, much sooner than either of the other great avenues, on terra firma. Before his final departure, however, he proposed to make another sally in that direction, in order to reconnoitre the gound, and, at the same time, divert the enemy's attention from his real purpose by a show of active operations.

For some days, his workmen had been employed in constructing a military machine of his own invention. It was called a *manta*, and was contrived somewhat on the principle of the mantelets used in the wars of the Middle Ages. It was, however, more complicated, consisting of a tower made of light beams and planks, having two chambers, one over the other. These were to be filled with musketeers, and the sides were provided with loop-holes, through which a fire could be kept up on the enemy. The great advantage proposed by this contrivance was, to afford a defence to the troops against the missiles hurled from the terraces. These machines, three of which were made, rested on rollers, and were provided with strong ropes, by which they were to be dragged along the streets by the Tlascalan auxiliaries.

The Mexicans gazed with astonishment on this warlike machinery, and, as the rolling fortresses advanced, belching forth fire and smoke from their entrails, the enemy, incapable of making an impression on those within, fell back in dismay. By bringing the *mantas* under the walls of the houses, the Spaniards were enabled to fire with effect on the mischievous tenants of the *azoteas*, and when this did not silence them, by letting a ladder, or light drawbridge, fall on the roof from the top of the *manta*, they opened a passage to the terrace, and closed with the combatants hand to hand. They could not, however, thus approach the higher buildings, from which the Indian warriors threw down such heavy masses of stone and timber as dislodged the planks that covered the machines, or, thundering against their sides, shook the frail edifices to their foundation, threatening all within with indiscriminate ruin. Indeed, the success of the experiment was doubtful, when the intervention of a canal put a stop to their further progress.

The Spaniards now found the assertion of their enemies too well confirmed. The bridge which traversed the opening had been demolished; and, although the canals which intersected the city were, in general, of no great width or depth, the removal of the bridges not only impeded the movements of the general's clumsy machines, but effectually disconcerted those of his cavalry. Resolving to abandon the *mantas*, he gave orders to fill up the chasm with stone, timber, and other rubbish drawn from the ruined buildings, and to make a new passage-way for the army. While this labor was going on, the Aztec slingers and archers on the other side of the opening kept up a galling discharge on the Christians, the more defenceless from the nature of their occupation. When the work was completed, and a safe passage secured, the Spanish cavaliers rode briskly against the enemy, who, unable to resist the shock of the steel-clad column, fell back with precipitation to where another canal afforded a similar strong position for defence.

There were no less than seven of these canals, intersecting the great street of Tlacopan, and at every one the same scene was renewed, the Mexicans making a gallant stand, and inflicting some loss, at each, on their persevering antagonists. These operations consumed two days, when, after incredible toil, the Spanish general had the satisfaction to find the line of communication completely reëstablished through the whole length of the avenue, and the principal bridges placed under strong detachments of infantry. At this juncture, when he had driven the foe before him to the furthest extremity of the street, where it touches on the causeway, he was informed, that the Mexicans, disheartened by their reverses, desired to open a parley with him respecting the terms of an accommodation, and that their chiefs awaited his return for that purpose at the fortress. Overjoyed at the intelligence, he instantly rode back, attended by Alvarado, Sandoval, and about sixty of the cavaliers, to his quarters.

The Mexicans proposed that he should release the two priests captured in the temple, who might be the bearers of his terms, and serve as agents for conducting the negotiation. They were accordingly sent with the requisite instructions to their countrymen. But they did not return. The whole was an artifice of the enemy, anxious to procure the liberation of their religious leaders, one of whom was their *teoteuctli*, or high-priest, whose presence was indispensable in the probable event of a new coronation.

Cortés, meanwhile, relying on the prospects of a speedy arrangement, was hastily taking some refreshment with his officers, after the fatigues of the

day; when he received the alarming tidings, that the enemy were in arms
again, with more fury than ever; that they had overpowered the detachments posted under Alvarado at three of the bridges, and were busily occupied in demolishing them. Stung with shame at the facility with which he
had been duped by his wily foe, or rather by his own sanguine hopes, Cortés
threw himself into the saddle, and, followed by his brave companions,
galloped back at full speed to the scene of action. The Mexicans recoiled
before the impetuous charge of the Spaniards. The bridges were again restored; and Cortés and his cavalry rode down the whole extent of the
great street, driving the enemy, like frightened deer, at the points of their
lances. But, before he could return on his steps, he had the mortification
to find that the indefatigable foe, gathering from the adjoining lanes and
streets, had again closed on his infantry, who, worn down by fatigue, were
unable to maintain their position at one of the principal bridges. New
swarms of warriors now poured in on all sides, overwhelming the little band
of Christian cavaliers with a storm of stones, darts, and arrows, which
rattled like hail on their armor and on that of their well-barbed horses.
Most of the missiles, indeed, glanced harmless from the good panoplies of
steel, or thick quilted cotton, but, now and then, one better aimed penetrated the joints of the harness, and stretched the rider on the ground.

The confusion became greater around the broken bridge. Some of the
horsemen were thrown into the canal, and their steeds floundered wildly
about without a rider. Cortés himself, at this crisis, did more than any other
to cover the retreat of his followers. While the bridge was repairing, he
plunged boldly into the midst of the barbarians, striking down an enemy
at every vault of his charger, cheering on his own men, and spreading
terror through the ranks of his opponents by the well-known sound of his
battle-cry. Never did he display greater hardihood, or more freely expose
his person, emulating, says an old chronicler, the feats of the Roman
Cocles. In this way he stayed the tide of assailants, till the last man had
crossed the bridge, when, some of the planks having given way, he was
compelled to leap a chasm of full six feet in width, amidst a cloud of missiles, before he could place himself in safety. A report ran through the
army that the general was slain. It soon spread through the city, to the
great joy of the Mexicans, and reached the fortress, where the besieged
were thrown into no less consternation. But, happily for them, it was false.
He, indeed, received two severe contusions on the knee, but in other
respects remained uninjured. At no time, however, had he been in such
extreme danger; and his escape, and that of his companions, was esteemed
little less than a miracle. More than one grave historian refers the preservation of the Spaniards to the watchful care of their patron Apostle, St.
James, who, in these desperate conflicts, was beheld careering on his milk-
white steed at the head of the Christian squadrons, with his sword flashing lightning, while a lady robed in white—supposed to be the Virgin—
was distinctly seen by his side, throwing dust in the eyes of the infidel!
The fact is attested both by Spaniards and Mexicans,—by the latter after

their conversion to Christianity. Surely, never was there a time when the interposition of their tutelar saint was more strongly demanded.

The coming of night dispersed the Indian battalions, which, vanishing like birds of ill omen from the field, left the well-contested pass in possession of the Spaniards. They returned, however, with none of the joyous feelings of conquerors to their citadel, but with slow step and dispirited, with weapons hacked, armor battered, and fainting under the loss of blood, fasting, and fatigue. In this condition they had yet to learn the tidings of a fresh misfortune in the death of Montezuma.

The Indian monarch had rapidly declined, since he had received his injury, sinking, however, quite as much under the anguish of a wounded spirit, as under disease. He continued in the same moody state of insensibility as that already described; holding little communication with those around him, deaf to consolation, obstinately rejecting all medical remedies as well as nourishment. Perceiving his end approach, some of the cavaliers present in the fortress, whom the kindness of his manners had personally attached to him, were anxious to save the soul of the dying prince from the sad doom of those who perish in the darkness of unbelief. They accordingly waited on him, with father Olmedo at their head, and in the most earnest manner implored him to open his eyes to the error of his creed, and consent to be baptized. But Montezuma—whatever may have been suggested to the contrary—seems never to have faltered in his hereditary faith, or to have contemplated becoming an apostate; for surely he merits that name in its most odious application, who, whether Christian or pagan, renounces his religion without conviction of its falsehood. Indeed, it was a too implicit reliance on its oracles, which had led him to give such easy confidence to the Spaniards. His intercourse with them had, doubtless, not sharpened his desire to embrace their communion; and the calamities of his country he might consider as sent by his gods to punish him for his hospitality to those who had desecrated and destroyed their shrine.

When father Olmedo, therefore, kneeling at his side, with the uplifted crucifix, affectionately besought him to embrace the sign of man's redemption, he coldly repulsed the priest, exclaiming, "I have but a few moments to live, and will not at this hour desert the faith of my fathers." One thing, however, seemed to press heavily on Montezuma's mind. This was the fate of his children, especially of three daughters, whom he had by his two wives; for there were certain rites of marriage, which distinguished the lawful wife from the concubine. Calling Cortés to his bedside, he earnestly commended these children to his care, as "the most precious jewels that he could leave him." He besought the general to interest his master, the emperor, in their behalf, and to see that they should not be left destitute, but be allowed some portion of their rightful inheritance. "Your lord will do this," he concluded, "if it were only for the friendly offices I have rendered the Spaniards, and for the love I have shown them,—though it has brought me to this condition! But for this I bear them no ill-will." Such, according to Cortés himself, were the words of the dying monarch. Not long after, on the 30th of June, 1520, he expired in the arms of some of his own nobles, who still remained faithful in their attendance on his person. "Thus," exclaims a native historian, one of his enemies, a Tlascalan, "thus died the unfortunate Montezuma, who had swayed the sceptre with such consummate policy and wisdom; and who was held in greater reverence and awe than any other prince of his lineage, or any, indeed, that ever sat on a throne in this Western World. With him may be said to have terminated the royal line of the Aztecs, and the glory to have passed away from the empire, which under him had reached the zenith of its prosperity." "The tidings of his death," says the old Castilian chronicler, Diaz, "were received with real grief by every cavalier and soldier in the army who had had access to his person; for we all loved him as a father,—and no wonder, seeing how good he was." This simple, but emphatic, testimony to his desert, at such a time, is in itself the best refutation of the suspicions occasionally entertained of his fidelity to the Christians.

It is not easy to depict the portrait of Montezuma in its true colors, since it has been exhibited to us under two aspects, of the most opposite and contradictory character. In the accounts gathered of him by the Spaniards, on coming into the country, he was uniformly represented as bold and warlike, unscrupulous as to the means of gratifying his ambition, hollow and perfidious, the terror of his foes, with a haughty bearing which made him feared even by his own people. They found him, on the contrary, not merely affable and gracious, but disposed to waive all the advantages of his own position, and to place them on a footing with himself; making their wishes his law; gentle even to effeminacy in his deportment, and constant in his friendship, while his whole nation was in arms against them.—Yet these traits, so contradictory, were truly enough drawn. They are to be explained by the extraordinary circumstances of his position.

When Montezuma ascended the throne, he was scarcely twenty-three years of age. Young, and ambitious of extending his empire, he was continually engaged in war, and is said to have been present himself in nine pitched battles. He was greatly renowned for his martial prowess, for he belonged to the *Quachictin,* the highest military order of his nation, and one into which but few even of its sovereigns had been admitted. In later life, he preferred intrigue to violence, as more consonant to his character and priestly education. In this he was as great an adept as any prince of his time, and, by arts not very honorable to himself, succeeded in filching away much of the territory of his royal kinsman of Tezcuco. Severe in the administration of justice, he made important reforms in the arrangement of the tribunals. He introduced other innovations in the royal household, creating new offices, introducing a lavish magnificence and forms of courtly etiquette unknown to his ruder predecessors. He was, in short, most attentive to all that concerned the exterior and pomp of royalty. Stately and decorous, he was careful of his own dignity, and might be said to be as great an "actor of majesty" among the barbarian potentates of the New World, as Louis the Fourteenth was among the polished princes of Europe.

He was deeply tinctured, moreover, with that spirit of bigotry, which threw such a shade over the latter days of the French monarch. He received the Spaniards as the beings predicted by his oracles. The anxious dread, with which he had evaded their proffered visit, was founded on the same feelings which led him so blindly to resign himself to them on their approach. He felt himself rebuked by their superior genius. He at once conceded all that they demanded,—his treasures, his power, even his person. For their sake, he forsook his wonted occupations, his pleasures, his most familiar habits. He might be said to forego his nature; and, as his subjects asserted, to change his sex and become a woman. If we cannot refuse our contempt for the pusillanimity of the Aztec monarch, it should be mitigated by the consideration, that his pusillanimity sprung from his superstition, and that superstition in the savage is the substitute for religious principle in the civilized man.

It is not easy to contemplate the fate of Montezuma without feelings of the strongest compassion;—to see him thus borne along the tide of events beyond his power to avert or control; to see him, like some stately tree, the pride of his own Indian forests, towering aloft in the pomp and majesty of its branches, by its very eminence a mark for the thunderbolt, the first victim of the tempest which was to sweep over its native hills! When the wise king of Tezcuco addressed his royal relative at his coronation, he exclaimed, "Happy the empire, which is now in the meridian of its prosperity, for the sceptre is given to one whom the Almighty has in his keeping; and the nations shall hold him in reverence!" Alas! the subject of this auspicious invocation lived to see his empire melt away like the winter's wreath; to see a strange race drop as it were, from the clouds on his land; to find himself a prisoner in the palace of his fathers, the companion of those who were the enemies of his gods and his people; to be insulted, reviled, trodden in the dust, by the meanest of his subjects, by those who, a few months previous, had trembled at his glance; drawing his last breath in the halls of the stranger,—a lonely outcast in the heart of his own capital! He was the sad victim of destiny,—a destiny as dark and irresistible in its march, as that which broods over the mythic legends of Antiquity!

Montezuma at the time of his death, was about forty-one years old, of which he reigned eighteen. His person and manners have been already described. He left a numerous progeny by his various wives, most of whom, having lost their consideration after the Conquest, fell into obscurity, as they mingled with the mass of the Indian population. Two of them, however, a son and a daughter, who embraced Christianity, became founders of noble houses in Spain. The government, willing to show its gratitude for the large extent of empire derived from their ancestor, conferred on them ample estates and important hereditary honors; and the Counts of Montezuma and Tula, intermarrying with the best blood of Castile, intimated by their names and titles their illustrious descent from the royal dynasty of Mexico.

Montezuma's death was a misfortune to the Spaniards. While he lived, they had a precious pledge in their hands, which, in extremity, they might possibly have turned to account. Now the last link was snapped which connected them with the natives of the country. But independently of interested feelings, Cortés and his officers were much affected by his death from personal considerations, and, when they gazed on the cold remains of the ill-starred monarch, they may have felt a natural compunction, as they contrasted his late flourishing condition with that to which his friendship for them had now reduced him.

The Spanish commander showed all respect for his memory. His body, arrayed in its royal robes, was laid decently on a bier, and borne on the shoulders of his nobles to his subjects in the city. What honors, if any, indeed, were paid to his remains, is uncertain. A sound of wailing, distinctly heard in the western quarters of the capital, was interpreted by the Spaniards into the moans of a funeral procession, as it bore the body to be laid among those of his ancestors, under the princely shades of Chapoltepec. Others state, that it was removed to a burial-place in the city named Copalco and there burnt with the usual solemnities and signs of lamentation by his chiefs, but not without some unworthy insults from the Mexican populace. Whatever be the fact, the people, occupied with the stirring scenes in which they were engaged, were probably not long mindful of the monarch, who had taken no share in their late patriotic movements. Nor is it strange that the very memory of his sepulchre should be effaced in the terrible catastrophe which afterwards overwhelmed the capital, and swept away every landmark from its surface.

Who Called You Here?

BY

ERIC JENS PETERSEN

THE Halder farm lay in the northern part of the Tyrol, more than three thousand feet above the German frontier. It was not a big farm; only one hired man was needed to help run it. As long as he was able to do it, old Vincent Halder had done most of the work alone, from cow-milking to hay-making. But at seventy-five years of age he had become irritable and cranky.

"I won't eat the stuff!" he had growled when, in October 1939, his son had sent him the first packages of sausages and eggs from Poland. The family were on the verge of starvation in the Tyrol and his daughter-in-law was delighted with the parcels. "Take them away!" the old farmer added angrily.

Halder was a good Austrian and had been glad to go to war in 1915, against Italy. As a Tyrolean crack marksman he had defended his mountains. "What are you doing here? Who called you here?" he had bellowed at the enemy before he fired. Later, when the peace treaty divided the Tyrol and the southern part fell to the Italians he had protested to the government in Vienna which allowed such things. Why did no one in Austria stand up to the robbers of the South Tyrol? When the German agents came through the land telling about the Fuehrer Adolf Hitler, they said that South Tyrol would be freed if Austria joined Germany. Old man Halder believed them. And actually Hitler did march in and take North Tyrol. After waiting for six months old Vincent asked the village innkeeper when the Italians were going to get out of South Tyrol, whereupon the new constable, who wore a swastika on his arm, told him that if he did not shut his mouth and do it quickly, he would bash in his skull, for Hitler was on the friendliest terms with Italy.

Halder's son, whose face was tanned and whose beard was black—like Andreas Hofer's a hundred years before him—protected his father from more serious trouble. This son was clever. Already in the autumn of 1938 he saw war and famine looming. "I shan't join up," he had said to his wife. "I think they need people in the civil service too." So he found a job in Kufstein to do secret errands and make reports to the Gestapo. Then in September 1939, when the war broke, he disappeared for four weeks. Suddenly he sent his address—from Poland—"Balthasar Halder, Gestapo,

Lodz." And at the same time came a shipment of parcels with lard and sausages, flour, bacon and eggs.

"I won't eat it," said old Vincent sullenly. "It was stolen from Poles and Jews!"

"Poles and Jews are all criminals!" said Agatha, his daughter-in-law. "Didn't you read in the newspaper? They murdered German children!"

German children? A wide-eyed German boy stood beside them. The boy was Hans Halder, the old man's grandson. He was sixteen years old.

"Now I shall soon be a soldier, just like grandfather," thought Hans and he took the Austrian military medals out of the cupboard. But his grandfather snatched them out of his hands. "You are a German!" he said angrily. Then he wept a little.

When Hans turned seventeen—in November 1939—he entered the barracks at Kufstein. There he found Alois Ortner, the Ebeseder boy, and others. It was only a little while before that they were playing childish games or skiing together.

Their senior, a boy of twenty, was a student from Wörgl, the son of the village pharmacist.

They all cursed England and Poland. (Hardly any mention was made of the French, they had just been misled by England and would lose their land anyhow.) At the mountain barracks, they learned to shoot—but above all they learned how to ski expertly. None of them had ever dreamed that being in the army would be such good sport. Only the food was bad; but that was the same everywhere. "You mark my words," the student from Wörgl whispered. "One fine day we'll head for Switzerland! Adolf Hitler will take Switzerland! Why else should we be learning to ski?"

Nevertheless some of them still clung to the thought that they would march against Italy. "Quit talking!" was the instant response to that idea, or "Quit thinking!" At Christmas, when they had leave, they were told by Captain Rengger, "Say good-bye to your folks! We'll be off soon now!" Yet Easter came and still they had not gone.

But in April came a sudden mustering. The young soldiers were called to report with their overcoats, packs, rifles, skis and minimum rations. Where were they going skiing? The train was already whistling. Good-bye Tyrol! An hour later they were in Munich. The countryside grew warmer.

No snow anywhere. How *flat* was Germany! They traveled all one night over a lowland plain dotted with desolate dwarf trees, with not a hill in sight. Were they being taken to the Western Front? The air was misty but mild. Another night passed. At a great distance huge lights rose from the earth. They still had no idea where they were going; but in war, of course, it was necessary to be secretive. The train stopped; Prussian voices were heard.

"This must be Hamburg or Bremen!" said the son of the pharmacist. He was educated and was familiar with maps. "Perhaps we shall go to sea!"

"Why must we travel by sea?" was the astonished reaction of the Austrians.

"Everybody out! Change trains!" called the captain.

They were moved into another train. The bright lights disappeared again. This train moved cautiously, haltingly, through the dark. Now and then a searchlight flared across the night sky. A tepid breeze wafted the smell of coal and fog toward them. A black surface glinted. Was this the sea? They climbed out of the train.

The captain went through the battalion whispering, "Quiet! Spies around! We are going aboard. . . ."

"Aboard a ship?" Their hearts dropped a beat.

The captain shrugged his shoulders. "Destination unknown!" He looked serious. The youngsters liked him.

By companies they crossed quickly over wet planks and sand. It was pitch dark. Far off in the distance two lighthouses swung their rays in a circle. "Bremerhaven!" whispered the pharmacist's son who was next to Hans.

Suddenly it was as light as day. A searchlight was fixed on the marching men. To right and left of them stood long rows of marines with drawn bayonets. Through them marched the Austrians. "Are they to keep us from running away?" thought Hans Halder.

Soon they reached a huge companionway, which was dazzling bright in the beams of the searchlight; beyond it and thrown into sharp relief against the dark towered two smoke stacks. The ship emitted a howl, like that of an animal, and outlying vessels responded.

Bewildered, laden with skis, helmets, and rifles, the companies climbed up the gangway. The last of one company was crowded by the first of the next. Cabins? There were no cabins. They tramped into the cargo hold.

It was a Polish freighter and reeked of mice, sacking and rotting vegetables. Someone came across the name of the shipowners. "The filthy Poles! The swine!" They cursed. "Can't someone open a window? Where are we going anyhow?"

"To Africa!" sighed the pharmacist. "We are going out to conquer some colonies!"

"But why the skis?"

That was a logical question. But logic did not make them any happier. The sides of the boat began to sway. They were under way. The floor rose and fell.

All night they traveled. Through the cracks the youths could see it was morning outside. The student from Wörgl saw by his pocket compass that they were moving steadily northward. "Later on," he sighed, because he was still fearful of the possibility of going to Africa. "We shall probably turn west or south."

No life belts were seen. The ship's cooks brought them their usual rations: lentil mash and stale zwieback. They played cards by candlelight. Many of them smoked. The air became unbearable; but there was no porthole down in the hold of the ship. They had to climb up ladders and push through a trap door to get out on deck, and that was forbidden. This was because, as the ship's cooks explained to them, no light nor sound must be allowed to be observed from the ship.

But why they were not allowed on deck even during the daytime was not said.

Once in the night following the second day a quarrel broke out below deck.

"They should at least have showed us," grumbled Ebeseder, "how to get into a lifeboat."

"We don't need any lifeboats," another growled sarcastically, "we'll ski across the water!"

"It's because there aren't enough lifeboats. The ones they have are for the crew!"

"Are these dumb sailors better than we are?"

"I'd say so. And why not? There are fewer of them. They are a technical troop. Dolts like us just fill up the ranks."

With that Alois Ortner slapped the speaker. He didn't understand that the lad was only trying to be funny. A brawl resulted in which old scores between Kufstein and Wörgl had to be settled all over again. The pounding and wrangling grew to such proportions that some officers came down. They were officers from a Prussian detachment. They wore small gold daggers at their sides, were slim in body, smooth-shaven. They looked like beings from another world.

The officers expressed delighted surprise that the five hundred Tyrolean youngsters were punching each other's heads, were "threshing each other" as one of the officers, a tall first lieutenant, put it. It was quite natural that they should be doing this down here in the dark, foul air. "When German men are bored they fall naturally to fighting," a lieutenant of artillery concluded. "However, tomorrow everything will be different—tomorrow we'll be there!"

"There? Where?" Before the astonished eyes of the men the strangers disappeared and the trap door slammed before any answer was given them.

The youngsters lay down, all packed together like fish, squirming and steaming. There were five or six men to every straw mattress. If any one wanted more room he was free to lie on the bare floor.

Four hours later the hold was wakened. Several of the youths thought the ship had been struck. The trap door was yanked open and a yelled order came, "Every man on deck."

Eyes blurred with sweat, bewildered, dizzy after the foul atmosphere of their caged existence, the battalion came up. Nipping cold greeted them as they emerged through the trap door.

It was daylight but none could see more than ten paces ahead. The ship's huge smokestacks (they couldn't really be that big), were distorted and ghostly in the fog. The sea was calm, the waves hardly rippled. The men lined up, their hearts thumping. Their breath steamed as they coughed the bad air out of their lungs. A biting cold went through their sweat-soaked underwear.

"Are we at the North Pole?" thought Hans.

Suddenly he drew in his breath. He smelled something. It was not the sea, nor the smell of oysters and fish that came to him through the cold air. It was mountains! High mountains! As a Tyrolean he could sense the granite even though he might not see the mountains. Mountains give off a smell for the people who live on them, as the sea does for sailors.

And joy welled high in Hans Halder's heart. So he was back in the Tyrol! And they hadn't gone to Africa, as they had half-jokingly, half-seriously feared! Here was the old land smell of the Tyrol. The country's steep black cliffs towered like the pipes of a church organ—and perhaps there were green upland meadows among them where cows grazed and tinkled. There was no sweeter music on earth.

"Bazi, where do you think we are?"

"I should think we're in Scotland!" said his neighbor. "That's where the men run around in short skirts and bare knees . . . like women, the Scots are!"

"It can't be as cold as this in Scotland," said the pharmacist's son.

"Stand still there! Ten men go down to get the skis and packs! Nothing else! You have your rifles with you!" At last a familiar voice. It was that of their Tyrolean captain, Rengger.

But the unfamiliar Prussian, with his elongated face, soon came along. "Men!" he said, and his voice was so high that it cracked, "We have landed in Norway! We have outwitted the English fleet. Since early yesterday all points along the coast are firmly in German control. The Norwegian government has called our army over to help defend this friendly neutral country from an English invasion. Heil Hitler!"

"Halitlaa!" reverberated along the deck. And as though summoned by the power of that name the fog rose and was dissipated. To every eye was revealed the magnificent majesty of Norway. Black, chiseled iron mountains stretched out to the north and to the south, scrawling their jagged peaks against the sky as far as the eye could reach. And on their tops lay great heavy masses of snow.

The coast—the Tyrolean peasant boys after all had a keen eye for distances—lay some five miles away. Clouds of smoke and puffing noises began to come from the port side: these were the longboats. The transfer into them was quickly made.

Hans Halder's company was the first.

"Overcoats on!"

With their rifles between their knees, their helmets on, their skis and packs behind, they sat down. But they did not strap their packs on. That was surprising. But it was even more surprising when life belts were suddenly handed out. Now? After they were already in Norway? After a three-day sea journey during which time the British fleet had not fired a single torpedo at them?

The longboat captain was at the helm. His face was sharp and uneasily tense. They moved slowly, in a zigzag course. Once they moved in a curve, describing a wide arc away from the harbor town which lay inland up a river. It lay like a mountain village beside a river . . . In Hans Halder's company no one knew a *fjord* when he saw it.

The atmosphere turned misty again. The longboats passed jagged islands around which a light surf foamed; they went through veils of wet mist. No one understood the Prussian speech which the captain of the longboat used in talking to his boatswain. But they somehow got the idea that he was calling the Norwegians swine. "The whole harbor is dead! They didn't send us any pilot. If the fog had been thicker we should have been obliged to be out here until noon!"

The boat slowed down. A few rowboats came out from the shore and signaled. The mist blew away. Three and then four other longboats, which had left the steamer a quarter of an hour later than the first, now caught up with Hans Halder's boat. They steamed into the narrows.

Suddenly there was a thundering explosion. The rocky sides of the near-lying islands quadrupled the reverberations.

"They must be blasting rock," thought Hans.

That was the sound one heard when they used dynamite to make a hole in a mountainside. But not a stone budged on the stone cliff along which they were passing. Then the man next to him, his face chalk-white, pointed out that the fourth longboat had stopped. A black column of water and smoke had risen to the starboard and now crashed across it. For a moment the black mass obscured the sight of the whole boat. Then the sea opened, the boat staggered like a drunken animal, and plunged with a twisting motion into the depths.

Hans followed this drama of water and wood with horrified eyes. As yet he had not seen a single man but when he heard the boatswain yell, "Mines to the starboard! Four points to the right," he suddenly caught sight of clusters of drowning Tyroleans, like bees in a swarm. Several dozen of them were swimming and calling with sharp, far-away voices. Why did no one pick them up?

Hans hardly dared to turn his head. The danger must be terrible. But there was no more thunder. The seven boats, the eighth being lost, hastened up the river, which—now that they were in it they could see—was really an inlet from the sea.

"Narvik!" said the captain and that was a name none of them had ever heard before.

Land again at last! It looked like a village with its cobblestones among which the melting snow trickled. At least they had reached here alive! They even cracked a few feeble jokes with the comrades who had landed the day before and who now appeared on the shore with cups of steaming hot coffee.

"Boys, this is *real* coffee!" was the astonished ejaculation which broke from the battalion from the Tyrol. For since the Tyrol had become part of Germany none of the Tyroleans had tasted anything but *Ersatz* or coffee substitute.

In the bay lay several half-sunken hulls with long protruding cannon muzzles. "Norwegian battleships!" said the earlier arrivals proudly as though they had sent the Norwegians to the bottom with their own bare hands.

The pharmacist's son from Wörgl would have liked to ask why it was necessary to sink the Norwegian cruisers since the Norwegian government had called the Germans in. But he thought it safer not to ask any questions and, besides, dinner was more important.

There was, to be sure, no hurry about that. First they had to stand around for three or four hours before they were marched to their quarters. "I bet we get meat today!" said Karl Leittner to the Ebeseder boy. "The neutrals do have meat." But the few steaming pots that seemed to be coming their way went off in another direction. As none of them had had any breakfast, their necks grew longer and their bellies flatter.

Finally the Tyrolean boys were told off and a few Prussian officers began to take the individual battalions into the town. The streets were narrow, as narrow as the streets of Innsbruck. The town was small, and built out on spurs from the hills crowned with hospitable-looking white villas. And how high the clouds were! They were cold as winter, like tufts of cotton being spun in the bright light and blue wind. That's just the way they looked at home. And how the snow smelled! No, the sea was not for Tyroleans and they were happy as they marched along. They had forgotten the wrecked boat, the mine, the drowned men. They swung along in good order, with their fifes and drums ahead making the street resound. And yet it was not quite like that in the Tyrol: not a soul came out of the houses when the drums rolled. Not even a woman appeared at the windows.

Hans Halder's battalion, the first, marched up a hill. So the schoolhouse was to be their billet! What could be finer than a school? The soldiers laughingly tried to squeeze into the little seats. Everything was so doll-like. The little boys' and girls' copybooks and schoolbags lay scattered around. Too bad there was no one there. The Tyroleans would have loved to have some fun with the children and learn some Norwegian. But they must have left in a great hurry, almost a panic. Under the benches there were apples and sandwiches, and in the round hand of a child there was written in chalk on the blackboard: *Gud Bevare Faedrelandet.*

Hans Halder spelled it out. The pharmacist's son from Wörgl said it sounded like something about fatherland: "God protect our Fatherland!" Hans Halder was uncomfortable. It made him thoughtful to realize that the Germans were not the only ones with a fatherland.

But were they hungry! At four o'clock in the afternoon their food finally arrived; it was bread soup. They were also given canned fish in oil, little fish as big as your thumb. A hubbub arose: weren't they after all abroad, in a neutral country, with butcher shops? Or was it the same here as in Germany where all the meat was commandeered for "higher purposes?" They were furious. It was only when their own Captain Rengger talked to them in their familiar dialect and told them that things would soon be better, that their good humor was restored and they began to settle down.

Mattresses and pillows were brought up from the houses at the foot of the hill. There was plenty of opportunity to wash (the Norwegians, it seemed, were a clean people). A few sentries were detailed, then they stripped to the waist, hummed and laughed a little—and soon all the seventeen-year-old youngsters were snoring. Exhausted from the excitement of the last three days, they fell asleep.

About midnight they jumped out of their beds, with terror in their hearts, their hands clenched. At exactly midnight the world seemed to be crashing and thundering to an end. It sounded as though great chunks of stones were being dropped on the city. The boys ran out in their barefeet into the snow. There they stood in their shirttails, like a herd of sheep, and put their heads together. What was up?

The cursed sea had opened, a wall of fiery lightning storms had risen from the water, a colossal vessel which they couldn't see, and which out of the all-powerful darkness was raining flames and iron on them.

"The English!" said Ortner, and turned pale and the shock was so great to him, in his half-somnolent state, that he laid his hands together on his bare stomach under his shirt. He gagged as though he were going to be ill.

Hell had yawned. Under the grisly rain of flaming stars the harbor and the town began to fill with fires. Sirens shrieked. The harbor guns of the Germans barked helplessly in the direction of the invisible sea, whence the enemy hurled their shells in devastating parabolas. When several houses at the foot of the hill began to burn, the Tyroleans remembered their prayers. Some of them ran back into the classroom and mumbled on their knees to the Virgin Mary. What sort of heathen place was this? On the walls of a schoolroom there should be pictures, pictures of the Sacred Heart, of Jesus, and of the saints. But Protestants lived here. How horrible, and they had never thought of this when they left Kufstein! What had they thought about? How would all this end?

Meantime the yelling outside continued. An automobile, filled with Prussian officers, had roared up the hill. Several long-faced men in green had jumped out and bellowed, "You blasted idiots! Get to cover! Wait for orders inside!" The men crowded back into the building. "Lights out!" They stumbled over each other and cursed the children's benches.

In front of the school the automobile was preparing to turn around. The snow crunched under the tires. Then—sixty feet off to the left came a shell! It struck into the school garden. Snow, earth, branches of trees were hurled in the air. The officer at the wheel of the car threw up his hands: a mysterious force tore him from his seat. The others jumped out quickly and laid him in the snow. Immediately afterward, in through the windows of the schoolhouse, came a cry like nothing human. The Tyroleans held their ears so as not to listen to this uninterrupted screaming sound, which rose and rose—then stopped abruptly as though it had never begun. With pocket flashlights they went out and found the door of a shed, they carried the now silent body in, then the motor drove off again.

"A splinter from a grenade," whispered Ebeseder, "can be as sharp as a razor blade."

"Shut up," was the hushed command.

They sat in a huddle, with their packs strapped on their backs, and trembled. "If only it were daylight!" they prayed. By dawn the bombardment would stop, wouldn't it? Because the English would themselves become targets as soon as day broke. No one believed that with so much anguish and distress they could go to sleep again. And yet nearly all of them dropped off, with their coats and helmets on, their rifles in their hands, overcome by the healthy compulsion of their seventeen years.

Hans Halder slept, too, and he dreamed of his Grandfather Vincent. He had been a soldier; in his youth he had gone out to meet the Italians. "What are you doing here? Who called you here?" he had bellowed, and shaken his rifle at them. His voice rang out so loud that, in the middle of the dream the boy woke up.

The bombardment had not let up although it was getting light outside. Again a car drove up. "Companies, fall in! Double-quick march to the station!" Where was the station? They hurried down the hill so fast they made the snow fly. They ran through a few streets littered with broken glass, charred beams, an occasional corpse, looking like a doll and very unreal. No one knew how far they ran. Some of them declared they went around twice in a circle. In a neighboring street two houses were still burning. The crackling and crashing seemed so pointless, it made one think of circuses at country fairs. As usual there was no one around to put it out. "Haven't they any fire engines here?" thought Hans Halder. It was the most foolish thought which had yet come into his mind—and yet the very foolishness of not understanding what was going on was the one thing to which he could cling for support.

There, at last, was the railroad station! Now they could get out of this mantrap, out of Narvik, this cursed city on a cursed sea! It was to be hoped there were enough cars. . . . It was pleasant for Hans Halder to realize that he was marching with the first detachment. They would be sure to get away. But quickly, quickly!

As they hurried across the square in front of the station they saw flames licking the vaulted roof, way up on the left side. So they had struck this building too! And probably only a few seconds before—but the air was so full of noise that they had not heard it. By all the saints in the calendar, what did one burning station more or less matter in this world!

Into the train! Things were done in double-quick time and before another shell struck the remaining wall of the station, the train pulled out and puffed off into the mountains. Mountain air! This was different from travelling in the belly of a ship! The Tyroleans opened every window. Since no one had forbidden them to do this it was probably allowed. With a magnificent wind streaming around them they rode into a snowy valley, between gleaming mountain slopes.

"This looks like Kufstein and Wörgl!" someone exclaimed jubilantly. From a neighboring train came yodeling, and the long signal calls which the shepherds send across the great distances from valley to valley back home. Hans Halder, in relief, pulled his mouth organ out of his pocket. They had brought along the apples and cakes of chocolate they had found in the schoolhouse—these were great delicacies for German soldiers since the war had begun. "If we only had some post cards we could write home to Tyrol!"

A sudden jolt; they were thrown on top of each other, their skis and poles fell down on them. The train had stopped. What was the matter now?

They heard doors slam, then Captain Rengger came running along outside. "Everyone get out."

They jumped out into the soft snow. "What does this mean? Are we going to camp here?"

Near the railroad tracks were two farmhouses with great hoods of snow on their heads, standing like two outposts of the mountain village which lay beyond under the pale blue blazing sky.

"The tunnel has been blown up! Companies form and go through the village. Forward march! We're going over the mountain on foot. . . ."

Who had blown up the tunnel? Had the English been here? They tramped through the village. Captain Rengger forbade them to sing.

All the houses were closed but from the fresh footprints they could tell that people had just been there. Only two women with long skirts and black hoods came their way. They tripped along the high road. Their gait was artificial, they picked their way stiffly like birds. They looked like strange nuns.

"Our girls are better looking!" said Hans Halder.

They were leaving the village and the road began to rise when they came to a post office. "I'll take a chance," said Ortner to Ebeseder.

He and four others dashed into the building. It was a post office, a Norwegian post office. It looked like any other post office, except that there was no picture of Adolf Hitler. On the wall hung a large timetable; to the left there was a desk and over it hung a calendar. But the official at the window! They had never seen such a frightened face or two such pale blue eyes. Hans Halder was the bold one. He stepped up and asked for five stamped postal cards to go to the Tyrol. They all had money—no Norwegian money but some German—and the man at the window could reckon the rate of exchange.

Then something astonishing happened. The post-office official pulled his window shut with a bang! The five mountaineer boys from the Tyrol saw quite clearly that this foreign postal official would not sell them anything.

"And yet it is in office hours," thought Hans Halder, and shook his head.

"Norway has shut up shop!" said the man standing beside him and glowered at the closed window.

"The post office is mad at us, comrades!" An obstacle had arisen to prevent them from writing to their faraway homes. "All right. We won't send any of their post cards then!" The five boys straggled out with their helmets on their heads, their rifles and their skis on their backs.

The rest of the battalion was five hundred paces ahead of them up the mountainside by now. In the brilliant winter sunshine the five could see the others distinctly raise their feet as they marched. Should they get in a sweat by going after them in double-quick time? "We have run enough for one day! We'll catch up with them on top of the mountain!"

All were eagerly waiting for the moment when they could buckle on their skis. On the crest they would be sure to get that order and then they would go down the other side in great style. That much the regiment had learned.

"Halloo-daridariiii!" yodeled Ortner.

Above them on the winding road the tail end of the battalion disappeared. Now the boys would have to hurry if they were to catch up with them.

Then down a white slope to the right of them they noticed some low-flying birds, sweeping down over the dazzling snow. No, they were not birds: they were skiers, perhaps a dozen of them. They were looming bigger and bigger. "Gee, but they know their stuff!" said the pharmacist's son and stood still, clicking his tongue. Hans, too, looked up with admiration. From a distance they heard a whistle which sounded like some sporting signal.

Were they holding some championship event here?

Down from the snow field, facing them, some thirty blue-black figures were now racing. With a graceful movement they encircled the five Tyroleans. When Hans Halder recognized the small, black caps with dark ear muffs as belonging to Norwegians he was relieved. His neighbors and he had all used caps like that at home, before they had ever gone into the army. This was sport and it occurred to him that of course it was the Norwegians who had invented his beloved skis. Didn't he know a few words of Norwegian too—for instance the expression *telemark*?

His lips began to form it but he did not have time to say it.

One of the Norwegians came forward. His face was tanned by the sun, his eyes were sad but unflinching. He opened his mouth several times, then he said in a strange rhythmic German, "What are you doing here? Who called you here?"—and emptied a four-barreled revolver in Hans Halder's breast. Hans fell, amazed beyond all measure. And when the other Tyroleans saw the snow turn red they slowly raised their arms above their heads.

The Invaders

BY

RICHARD HILLARY

WE RETIRED early to bed and slept until, at two o'clock in the morning, a gillie banged on the door. Colin got up, took from the gillie's hand a telegram, opened it, and read it. It said: SQUADRON MOVING SOUTH STOP CAR WILL FETCH YOU AT EIGHT OCLOCK DENHOLM. For us, the war began that night.

At ten o'clock we were back at Turnhouse. The rest of the Squadron were all set to leave; we were to move down to Hornchurch, an airdrome twelve miles east of London on the Thames Estuary. Four machines would not be serviceable until the evening and Broody Benson, Pip Cardell, Colin, and I were to fly them down. We took off at four o'clock, some five hours after the others, Broody leading, Pip and I to each side, and Colin in the box, map reading. Twenty-four of us flew south that 10th day of August 1941: of those twenty-four eight were to fly back.

We landed at Hornchurch at about seven o'clock to receive our first shock. Instead of one section there were four Squadrons at readiness; 603 Squadron were already in action. They started coming in about half an hour after we landed, smoke stains along the leading edges of the wings showing that all the guns had been fired. They had acquitted themselves well although caught at a disadvantage of height.

"You don't have to look for them," said Brian. "You have to look for a way out."

From this flight Don MacDonald did not return.

At this time the Germans were sending over comparatively few bombers. They were making a determined attempt to wipe out our entire Fighter Force and from dawn till dusk the sky was filled with Messerschmitt 109's and 110's.

Half a dozen of us always slept at the Dispersal Hut to be ready for a surprise enemy attack at dawn. This entailed being up by 4:30, and by 5:00 o'clock having our machines warmed up and the oxygen, sights, and ammunition tested. The first Hun attack usually came over about breakfast time and from then until 8:00 o'clock at night we were almost continuously in the air. We ate when we could, baked beans and bacon and eggs being sent over from the Mess.

On the morning after our arrival I walked over with Peter Howes and

From: *Falling Through Space*, by Richard Hillary. Reynal & Hitchcock, New York.

Broody. Howes was at Hornchurch with another Squadron and worried because he had as yet shot nothing down. Every evening when we came into the Mess he would ask us how many we had got and then go over miserably to his room. His Squadron had had a number of losses and was due for relief. If ever a man needed it, it was Howes. Broody, on the other hand, was in a high state of excitement, his sharp eager face grinning from ear to ear. We left Howes at his Dispersal Hut and walked over to where our machines were being warmed up. The voice of the controller came unhurried over the loud speaker, telling us to take off, and in a few seconds we were running for our machines. I climbed into the cockpit of my plane and felt an empty sensation of suspense in the pit of my stomach. For one second time seemed to stand still and I stared blankly in front of me. I knew that morning I was to kill for the first time. That I might be killed or in any way injured did not occur to me. Later, when we were losing pilots regularly, I did consider it in an abstract way when on the ground; but once in the air, never. I knew it could not happen to me. I suppose every pilot knows that, knows it cannot happen to him; even when he is taking off for the last time, when he will not return, he knows that he cannot be killed. I wondered idly what he was like, this man I would kill. Was he young, was he fat, would he die with the Fuehrer's name on his lips, or would he die alone, in that last moment conscious of himself as a man? I would never know. Then I was being strapped in, my mind automatically checking the controls, and we were off.

We ran into them at 18,000 feet, twenty yellow-nosed Messerschmitt 109's, about five hundred feet above us. Our Squadron strength was eight, and as they came down on us we went into line astern and turned head on to them. Brian Carberry, who was leading the Section dropped the nose of his machine, and I could almost feel the leading Nazi pilot push forward on his stick to bring his guns to bear. At the same moment Brian hauled hard back on his own control stick and led us over them in a steep climbing turn to the left. In two vital seconds they lost their advantage. I saw Brian let go a burst of fire at the leading plane, saw the pilot put his machine into a half roll, and knew that he was mine. Automatically, I kicked the rudder to the left to get him at right angles, turned the gun button to "Fire," and let go in a four-second burst with full deflection. He came right through my sights and I saw the tracer from all eight guns thud home. For a second he seemed to hang motionless; then a jet of red flame shot upwards and he spun to the ground.

For the next few minutes I was too busy looking after myself to think of anything, but when, after a short while, they turned and made off over the Channel, and we were ordered to our base, my mind began to work again.

It had happened.

My first emotion was one of satisfaction, satisfaction at a job adequately done, at the final logical conclusion of months of specialized training. And then I had a feeling of the essential rightness of it all. He was dead and I was alive; it could so easily have been the other way round; and that would somehow have been right too. I realized in that moment just how lucky a fighter pilot is. He has none of the personalized emotions of the soldier, handed a rifle and bayonet and told to charge. He does not even have to share the dangerous emotions of the bomber pilot who night after night must experience that childhood longing for smashing things. The fighter pilot's emotions are those of the duelist—cool, precise, impersonal. He is privileged to kill well. For if one must either kill or be killed, as now one must, it should, I feel, be done with dignity. Death should be given the setting it deserves; it should never be a pettiness; and for the fighter pilot it never can be.

From this flight Broody Benson did not return.

During that August-September period we were always so outnumbered that it was practically impossible, unless we were lucky enough to have the advantage of height, to deliver more than one Squadron attack. After a few seconds we always broke up, and the sky was a smoke trail of individual dog-fights. The result was that the Squadron would come home individually, machines landing one after the other at intervals of about two minutes. After an hour, Uncle George would make a check-up on who was missing. Often there would be a telephone call from some pilot to say that he had made a forced landing at some other airdrome, or in a field. But the telephone wasn't always so welcome. It would be a rescue squad announcing the number of a crashed machine; then Uncle George would check it, and cross another name off the list. At that time, the losing of pilots was somehow extremely impersonal; nobody, I think, felt any great emotion—there simply wasn't time for it.

After the hard lesson of the first two days, we became more canny and determined not to let ourselves be caught from above. We would fly on the reciprocal of the course given us by the controller until we got to 15,000 feet, and then fly back again, climbing all the time. By this means we usually saw the Huns coming in below us, and were in a perfect position to deliver a Squadron attack. If caught at a disadvantage, they would never stay to fight, but always turned straight back for the Channel. We arranged a system whereby two planes always flew together—thus if one should follow a plane down the other stayed 500 feet or so above, to protect him from attack in the rear.

Often, machines would come back to their base just long enough for the ground staff, who worked with beautiful speed, to refuel them and put in a new oxygen bottle and more ammunition before taking off again. Uncle George was shot down several times but always turned up unhurt; once we thought Rusty was gone for good, but he was back leading his flight the next day; one sergeant pilot in "A" Flight was shot down four times, but he seemed to bear a charmed life.

The sun and the great height at which we flew often made it extremely difficult to pick out the enemy machines, but it was here that Shep's experience on the moors of Scotland proved invaluable. He led the guard section and always saw the Huns long before anyone else. For me the sun presented a major problem. We had dark lenses on our glasses, but I, as I have mentioned before, never wore mine. They gave me a feeling of claustrophobia. With spots on the windscreen, spots before the eyes, and a couple of spots which might be Messerschmitts, blind spots on my goggles seemed too much of a good thing; I always slipped them up on to my forehead before going into action. For this and for not wearing gloves, I paid a stiff price.

I remember once going practically to France before shooting down a 109. There were two of them, flying at sea-level and headed for the French Coast. Raspberry was flying beside me and caught one halfway across. I got right up close behind the second one and gave it a series of short bursts. It darted about in front, like a startled rabbit, and finally plunged into the sea about three miles off the French Coast.

On another occasion, I was stupid enough actually to fly over France: the sky appeared to be perfectly clear but for one returning Messerschmitt, flying very high. I had been trying to catch him for about ten minutes and was determined that he should not get away.

Eventually I caught him inland from Calais and was just about to open fire when I saw a squadron of twelve Messerschmitts coming in on my right. I was extremely frightened, but turned in towards them and opened fire at the leader. I could see his tracer going past underneath me, and then I saw his hood fly off, and the next moment they were past. I didn't wait to see anymore, but made off for home, pursued for half the distance by eleven very determined Germans. I landed a good hour after everyone else to find Uncle George just finishing his check up.

From this flight Larry Cunningham did not return.

After about a week of Hornchurch, I woke late one morning to the noise of machines running up on the airdrome. It irritated me: I had a headache.

Having been on every flight the previous day, the morning was mine to do with as I pleased. I got up slowly, gazed dispassionately at my tongue in the mirror, and wandered over to the Mess for breakfast. It must have been getting on for twelve o'clock when I came out on to the airdrome to find the usual August heat haze forming a dull pall over everything. I started to walk across the airdrome to the Dispersal Point on the far side. There were only two machines on the ground so I concluded that the squadron was already up. Then I heard a shout, and our ground crew drew up in a lorry beside me. Sergeant Ross leaned out:

"Want a lift, sir? We're going round."

"No thanks, Sergeant. I'm going to cut across."

This was forbidden for obvious reasons, but I felt like that.

"O.K., sir. See you round there."

The lorry trundled off down the road in a cloud of dust. I walked on across the landing ground. At that moment I heard the voice of the controller.

"Large enemy bombing formation approaching Hornchurch. All personnel not engaged in active duty take cover immediately."

I looked up. They were still not visible. At the Dispersal Point I saw Bubble and Pip Cardell make a dash for the shelter. Three Spitfires just landed, turned about and came past me with a roar to take off down wind. Our lorry was still trundling along the road, maybe half way round, and seemed suddenly an awfully long way from the Dispersal Point.

I looked up again, and this time I saw them—about a dozen slugs, shining in the bright sun and coming straight on. At the rising scream of the first bomb I instinctively shrugged up my shoulders and ducked my head. Out of the corner of my eye I saw the three Spitfires. One moment they were about twenty feet up in close formation; the next, catapulted apart as though on elastic. The leader went over on his back and plowed along the runway with a rending crash of tearing fabric; number 2 put a wing in and spun round on his airscrew, while the plane on the left was blasted wingless into the next field. I remember thinking stupidly, "That's the shortest flight he's ever taken," and then my feet were nearly knocked from under me, my mouth was full of dirt, and Bubble, gesticulating like a madman from the shelter entrance was yelling: "Run, you bloody fool, run!" I ran. Suddenly awakened to the lunacy of my behavior, I covered the distance to that shelter as if impelled by a rocket and shot through the entrance while once again the ground rose up and hit me, and my head smashed hard against one of the pillars. I subsided on a heap of rubble and massaged it.

"Who's here?" I asked, peering through the gloom.

"Cardell and I and three of our ground crew," said Bubble, "and, by the Grace of God, you!"

I could see by his mouth that he was still talking but a sudden concentration of the scream and crump of falling bombs made it impossible to hear him.

The air was thick with dust and the shelter shook and heaved at each explosion, yet somehow held firm. For about three minutes the bedlam continued, and then suddenly ceased. In the utter silence which followed nobody moved. None of us wished to be the first to look on the devastation which we felt must be outside. Then Bubble spoke. "Praise God!" he said. "I'm not a civilian. Of all the bloody frightening things I've ever done, sitting in that shelter was the worst. Me for the air from now on!"

It broke the tension and we scrambled out of the entrance. The runways were certainly in something of a mess. Gaping holes and great gobbets of earth were everywhere. Right in front of us a bomb had landed by my Spitfire, covering it with a shower of grit and rubble.

I turned to the aircraftsman standing beside me. "Will you get hold of Sergeant Ross and tell him to have a crew give her an inspection."

He jerked his head toward one corner of the airdrome: "I think I'd better collect the crew myself, sir. Sergeant Ross won't be doing any more inspections."

I followed his glance and saw the lorry, the roof about twenty yards away, lying grotesquely on its side. I climbed into the cockpit, and, feeling faintly sick, tested out the switches. Bubble poked his head over the side.

"Let's go over to the Mess and see what's up: all our machines will be landing down at the reserve landing field anyway."

I climbed out and walked over to find the three Spitfire pilots celebrating in the bar, quite unharmed but for a few superficial scratches, in spite of being machine-gunned by the bombers. "Operations" was undamaged: no hangar had been touched and the Officers' Mess had two windows broken.

The station commander ordered every available man and woman on to the job of repairing the airdrome surface and by four o'clock there was not a hole to be seen. Several unexploded bombs were marked off, and two lines of yellow flags were laid down to mark the runways. At five o'clock our squadron, taking off for a "flap" from the reserve field, landed safely on its home base. Thus, apart from four men killed in the lorry and a network of holes on the landing surface, there was nothing to show for ten minutes' really accurate bombing from 12,000 feet, in which several dozen sticks of bombs had been dropped. It was striking proof of the inefficacy of their attempts to wipe out our advance fighter airdromes.

Brian had a bullet through his foot, and as my machine was still out of commission, I took his place in readiness for the next show. I had had enough of the ground for one day.

Six o'clock came and went, and no call. We started to play poker and I was winning. It was agreed that we should stop at seven: should there be a "flap" before then, the game was off. I gazed anxiously at the clock. I am always unlucky at cards, but when the hands pointed to 6:55 I really began to feel my luck was on the change. But sure enough at that moment came the voice of the controller: "603 Squadron take off and patrol base: further instruction in the air."

We made a dash for our machines and within two minutes were off the ground. Twice we circled the airdrome to allow all twelve planes to get in formation. We were flying in four sections of three: red section leading, blue and green to right and left, and the three remaining planes forming a guard section above and behind us.

I was flying No. 2 in the blue section.

Over the radio came the voice of the controller: "Hullo Red Leader." And then the instructions and their acknowledgment by the leader.

As always, for the first few minutes we flew on the reciprocal of the course given until we reached 15,000 feet. We then turned about and flew on 110° in an all-out climb, thus coming out of the sun and gaining height all the way.

During the climb Uncle George was in constant touch with the ground. We were to intercept about 20 enemy fighters at 25,000 feet. I glanced across at Stapme and saw his mouth moving. That meant he was singing again. He would sometimes do this with his radio set on "send," with the result that mingled with our instructions from the ground we would hear a raucous rendering of "Night and Day." And then quite clearly over the radio I heard the German excitedly calling to each other. This was a not infrequent occurrence and it made one feel that they were right behind, although often they were some distance away. I switched my set to "send" and called out *"Halts Maul!"* and as many other choice pieces of German invective as I could remember. To my delight I heard one of them answer: "You feelthy Englishmen, we will teach you how to speak to a German." I am aware that this sounds a tall story, but several others in the Squadron were listening out and heard the whole thing.

I looked down. It was a completely cloudless sky and way below lay the English countryside, stretching lazily into the distance, a quite extraordinary picture of green and purple in the setting sun.

I took a glance at my altimeter. We were at 28,000 feet. At that moment Shep yelled "Tallyho" and dropped down in front of Uncle George in a slow dive in the direction of the approaching planes. Uncle George saw them at once.

"O.K. Lie astern."

I drew in behind Stapme and took a look at them. They were about 2,000 feet below us, which was a pleasant change, but they must have spotted us at the same moment, for they were forming a protective circle, one behind the other, which is a defense formation hard to break.

"Echelon starboard," came Uncle George's voice.

We spread out fanwise to the right.

"Going down!"

One after the other we peeled off in a power dive. I picked out one machine and switched my gun button to "Fire." At 300 yards I had him in my sights. At 200 I opened up in a long four-second burst and saw the tracer going into his nose. Then I was pulling out, so hard that I could feel my eyes dropping through my neck. Coming round in a slow climbing turn I saw that we had broken them up. The sky was now a mass of individual dog fights. Several of them had already been knocked down. One, I hoped was mine, but on pulling up I had not been able to see the result. To my left I saw Peter Pease make a head-on attack on a Messerschmitt. They were headed straight for each other and it looked as though the fire of both was striking home. Then at the last moment the Messerschmitt pulled up taking Peter's fire full in the belly. It rolled onto its back, yellow flames pouring from the cockpit, and vanished.

The next few minutes were typical. First the sky a bedlam of machines; then suddenly silence and not a plane to be seen. I noticed then that I was very tired and very hot. The sweat was running down my face in rivulets. But this was no time for vague reflections. Flying around the sky on one's own at that time was not a healthy course of action.

I still had some ammunition left. Having no desire to return to the airdrome until it had all been used to some good purpose, I took a look around the sky for some friendly fighters. About a mile away over Dungeness I saw a formation of about forty Hurricanes on patrol at 20,000 feet. Feeling that there was safety in numbers, I set off in their direction.

When about 200 yards from the rear machine, I looked down and saw 5,000 feet below another formation of fifty machines flying in the same direction. Flying stepped up like this was an old trick of the Huns, and I was glad to see we were adopting the same tactics. But as though hit by a douche of cold water, I suddenly woke up. There were far more machines flying together than we could ever muster over one spot. I took another look at the rear machine in my formation, and sure enough, there was the Swastika on its tail. Yet they all seemed quite oblivious of my presence. I had the sun behind me and a glorious opportunity. Closing in to 150 yards I let go a three-second burst into the rear machine. It flicked onto its back and spun out of sight. Feeling like an irresponsible schoolboy who has perpetrated some crime which must inevitably be found out, I glanced round me. Still nobody seemed disturbed. I suppose I could have repeated the performance on the next machine, but I felt that it was inadvisable to tempt Providence too far. I did a quick half roll and made off home, where I found to my irritation that Raspberry, as usual had three planes down to my one.

There was to be a concert on the Station that night, but as I had to be up at five the next morning for Dawn Patrol, I had a quick dinner and two beers, and went to bed, feeling not unsatisfied with the day.

Perhaps the most amusing though painful experience which I had was when I was shot down acting as arse-end Charlie to a Squadron of Hurricanes. Arse-end Charlie is the man who weaves backwards and forwards above and behind the Squadron to protect them from attack from the rear. There had been the usual dog fights over the South Coast, and the Squadron had broken up. Having only fired one snap burst, I climbed up in search of friendly Spitfires, but found instead a squadron of Hurricanes flying round the sky at 18,000 feet in sections of stepped-up threes, but with no rear guard. So I joined on. I learned within a few seconds the truth of the old warning, "Beware of the Hun in the Sun." I was making pleasant little sweeps from side to side, and peering earnestly into my mirror when, from out of the sun and dead astern, bullets started appearing along my port wing. There is an appalling tendency to sit and watch this happen without taking any action, as though mesmerized by a snake; but I managed to pull myself together and go into a spin, at the same time attempting to call up the Hurricanes and warn them, but I found that my radio had been shot away. At first there appeared to be little damage done and I started to climb up again, but black smoke began pouring out of the engine and there was an unpleasant smell of escaping glycol. I thought I had better get home while I could; but as the wind-screen was soon covered with oil I realized that I couldn't make it and decided instead to put down at Lympne, where there was an airdrome. Then I realized that I wasn't going to make Lympne either—I was going at full boost and only clocking 90 miles per hour, so I decided that I had better put down in the nearest field before I stalled and spun in. I chose a cornfield and put the machine down on its belly. Fortunately nothing caught fire, and I had just climbed out and switched off the petrol, when to my amazement I saw an ambulance coming through the gate. This I thought was real service, until the corporal and two orderlies who climbed out started cantering away in the opposite direction, their necks craned up to the heavens. I looked up and saw about 50 yards away a parachute, and suspended on the air, his legs dangling vaguely, Colin. He was a little burned about his face and hands but quite cheerful.

We were at once surrounded by a bevy of officers and discovered that we had landed practically in the back garden of a Brigade cocktail party. A salvage crew from Lympne took charge of my machine, a doctor took charge of Colin, and the rest took charge of me, handing me double whiskies for the nerves at a laudable rate. I was put up that night by the Brigadier, who thought I was suffering from a rather severe shock, largely because by dinner time I was so pie-eyed that I didn't dare open my mouth but answered all his questions with a glassy stare. The next day I went up to London by train, a somewhat incongruous figure, carrying a helmet and parachute. The prospect of a long and tedious journey by tube to Hornchurch did not appeal to me, so I called up the Air Ministry and demanded a car and a WAAF. I was put on to the good lady in charge of transport, a sergeant, who protested apologetically that she must have the authorization of a Wing Commander. I told her forcibly that at this moment I was considerably more important than any Wing Commander, painted a vivid picture of the complete disorganization of Fighter Command in the event of my not being back at Hornchurch within an hour, and clinched the argument by telling her that my parachute was a military secret which must on no account be seen in a train. By the afternoon I was flying again.

That evening there was a terrific attack on Hornchurch and for the first time since coming south, I saw some bombers. There were twelve Dornier 215's flying in close formation at about 12,000 feet, and headed back for France. I was on my way back to the airdrome when I first sighted them about 5,000 feet below me. I dived straight down in a quarter head-on attack. It seemed quite impossible to miss, and I pressed the button. Nothing happened, I had already fired all my ammunition. I could not turn back, so I put both my arms over my head and went straight through the formation, never thinking I'd get out of it unscratched. I landed on the airdrome with the machine riddled with bullets, but quite serviceable.

From this flight Bubble Waterson did not return.

And so August drew to a close with no slackening of pressure in the enemy offensive. Yet the Squadron showed no signs of strain, and I personally was content. This was what I had waited for, waited for nearly a year; and I was not disappointed. If I felt anything, it was a sensation of relief. We had little time to think, and each day brought new action. No one thought of the future: sufficient unto the day was the emotion thereof. At night one switched off one's mind like an electric light.

It was one week after Bubble went that I fell through space into the North Sea.

The Massacre at Matanzas Inlet, 1565

BY

PEDRO MENÉNDEZ DE AVILÉS

THE sufferings and dangers which the Adelantado and those who returned with him from the San Mateo, encountered on that day he left, and on the second and third day, until they arrived at St. Augustine, were so great as to be beyond belief, except to those who saw them; because on that day he set out from San Mateo, when they had gone about 2 leagues [and] it was about 2 o'clock in the afternoon, they entered a wood through which they had previously passed, and having gone therein half a league, they found much water; and thinking they would get out of it quickly, they proceeded over half a league farther, finding more and more water, in such manner that they could not go forward; and when they went back the streams were more swollen, and there was more water in the woods. They lost their way in such wise that they knew not whether they were going forward or back: [the Adelantado] wished to search for a place where they could halt and build a fire by which to rest during that night: none could he find: he wanted to climb the trees: they were so high and straight that it was not possible: there he felt himself entirely lost, and his companions were discouraged, not knowing what remedy could meet the situation. He made a soldier, the most agile he could find, climb a very high tree to discover any dry or level spot; this soldier said, when he had reached the top, that all he could see was water, and that there was no dry or level land: the Adelantado ordered him to look and see if there were any indication as to which way the sun was moving: he said there was none: he ordered him to remain there until later: God willed that the weather cleared a little, and the soldier saw where the sun was setting, and pointed out the place.

The Adelantado recognized the direction in which he had to emerge from the woods, as there was no undergrowth and the trees were far apart. By cutting down some pines for the places where there was a great depth of water, he came out by a deep and narrow river, which he had crossed with the men when he went from St. Augustine to San Mateo, although not at that point. He had the trees which were at the river's edge cut down at the foot with 5 hatchets the soldiers carried, in such a way that they fell across to the other side of the river; and they passed over with much peril, and in so doing, two soldiers miraculously escaped

From: *Pedro Menéndez de Avilés.*

110

drowning. He ordered the man who had climbed the tree, to go up another one, and he discovered dry land in a place by which they had passed before; and they reached the path and went to take up their quarters in a spot where they made great fires and dried their clothing, for it was all soaked with water; and toward daybreak it began to rain very hard, and as it was already light, they set out. It took them 3 days to arrive in St. Augustine, for owing to the victory Our Lord had given them, they did not feel the journey, nor the hardships thereof, in the desire they had to give this good news to their comrades: one league before reaching St. Augustine, that soldier [who had climbed the tree] begged the Adelantado as a favor to allow him to go ahead to announce the welcome tidings; the Adelantado granted this to him. The people who had remained there held them for lost, because of the bad weather they had had and the news given them by those who had returned, as they knew that they had no kind of food, powder nor wicks; but when the good news came, 4 priests who were there immediately set out, holding the cross aloft, and followed by all the sea and land forces, the women and children, in a procession, singing the *Te Deum Laudamus;* they received the Adelantado with great pleasure and rejoicing, everyone laughing and weeping for joy, praising God for so great a victory; and so they escorted the Adelantado in triumph to the intrenchment and settlement of St. Augustine, where he related to them in detail the very great mercy which Our Lord had shown them through his victory. He presently ordered the two armed ships to be made ready; and within 2 days, being about to depart with them for San Mateo, there came tidings that the 2 French ships had already left the bar; so he sent one of his vessels with artillery, powder and ammunition in order that they should be in the fort, and everything be in a good state of defence; and he occupied himself in fortifying [St. Augustine] as well as he could, to await the French armada if it should come there. The following day some Indians arrived, who told them by signs that 4 leagues away there were many Christians who could not pass an arm of the sea, even though it was narrow, which is a river inside a bar, that they were compelled of necessity to cross in order to reach St. Augustine.

Then the Adelantado took with him 40 soldiers that afternoon, and after midnight he came near that arm of the sea, where he halted. In the morning, leaving his soldiers in ambush, from the top of a tree he discovered what was going on: he saw many people and two flags on the other side of the river, and the said Adelantado, to prevent them from crossing, approached close enough for them to count his men, so that they might think that there were many [behind]. When they [saw they] were discovered, one man presently swam across: he was a Frenchman, and said that the people there were all French; that they had been shipwrecked in a storm and had all escaped.

The Adelantado asked him what Frenchmen they were.

He said there were 200 persons, captains and soldiers of Juan Ribao, Viceroy and Captain-General of that land for the King of France.

The Adelantado asked if they were Catholics or Lutherans. He said that they were all Lutherans of the new religion; although the Adelantado already knew this, for they had said this when he met their armada, and the women and children whose lives he had spared when he captured the fort, had told him so; and he had found within the fort 6 coffers full of books bound and gilt-edged, all concerning the new religion; [he knew] also that they did not say mass, and that their Lutheran faith was preached to them every afternoon; he had ordered those books to be burned, not leaving one.

The Adelantado asked him why he had come. He said that their captain had sent him to see what people they were.

The Adelantado asked if he wished to return.

He replied that he did, but that he wanted to know who they were.

This man spoke very clearly, for he was a Gascon, from San Juan de Luz.

Then the Adelantado told him that he should tell his captain that he [the Adelantado] was the Viceroy and Captain-General of that land for the King, Don Felipe; that he was called Pedro Menéndez; that he was there with some soldiers to find out who they were, as they [the Spaniards] had had news the day before that they were there and were arriving at that hour.

The Frenchman went with that message, and returned presently, begging that safe-conduct be given to his captain and to 4 other gentlemen who wished to come to see [the Adelantado], and that a boat be loaned him which the Adelantado kept there, which had then come down the river with supplies. He told the Frenchman to say to his captain that he could come over in safety, under the pledge of his word; and he sent for them at once with the boat, and they came immediately.

The Adelantado, with about 10 persons, received him very well, and he commanded the others to keep back a little among some bushes, in order that they might all be seen, in such wise that the French might think that there were more men.

One of these Frenchmen said that he was the captain of those people, and that they had been wrecked in a storm, with 4 galleons and several shallops belonging to the King of France, which had foundered within 20 leagues of one another; that they were the men belonging to one of those ships, and they desired that the Adelantado should favor them by lending them the boat with which to cross that arm of the sea, and another 4 leagues from there, which was that of St. Augustine, as they wished to go to a fort they had 20 leagues from there: this was the fort that the Adelantado had taken from them.

The Adelantado asked them if they were Catholics or Lutherans.

The captain said that they were all of the new religion.

Then the Adelantado said to them:

"Gentlemen, your fort has been captured, and the people therein killed, except the women and the boys under 15 years; and in order that you may know for certain that this is so, there are many things [from there] among some of the soldiers who are here; there are also 2 Frenchmen whom I brought with me because they said they were Catholics: be seated here and dine and I will send you the 2 Frenchmen and the things that those soldiers have taken from the fort, that you may satisfy yourselves."

The Adelantado did this, ordering food to be given them, and he sent them the 2 Frenchmen and many things that the soldiers had taken in the fort, so that they might see them; and he withdrew to eat with his men; and an hour from then, seeing that the Frenchmen had dined, he went over to them and asked them if they believed what he had told them.

They said they did, and begged him as a mercy to give them ships and supplies wherewith they could go to France.

The Adelantado replied that he would willingly do so, if they were Catholics and if he had the ships therefor, but that he did not have them as he had sent two to San Mateo with the artillery; and that they were to take the Frenchwomen and children to Santo Domingo, and seek supplies; the other was to go to Spain with dispatches to his Majesty concerning what had happened to them in those parts.

The French captain answered that he might grant them all their lives, and they would remain with him until there should be ships for France, since they were not at war, and the Kings of Spain and France were brothers and friends.

The Adelantado replied that that was the truth, and that he would aid Catholics and friends, understanding that he served both Kings thereby; but that as they belonged to the new religion he held them to be enemies, and would wage against them a war of fire and blood, and carry it on with all possible cruelty against those he should find in that land and on that sea, where he was Viceroy and Captain-General for his King; and that he came to implant the Holy Gospel in that land, in order that the Indians might be enlightened and come to the knowledge of the holy Catholic faith of Jesus Christ, Our Lord, as it is preached in the Roman church; that if they wanted to give up their flags and arms to him and place themselves at his mercy, they could do so, in order that he might do with them what God should direct him; or that they could do what they wished, for any other truce or friendship they must not form with him; and although the French captain replied, nothing else could be obtained from the Adelantado. And so the French captain went to his men in the boat wherein he had come, saying that he was going to tell them what was occurring, and to decide what they must do, and that within 2 hours he would return with the answer.

The Adelantado told him that they should do what appeared best to them, and that he would wait.

When 2 hours had gone by, that same French captain returned with the same gentlemen, and told the Adelantado that there were many noble-men over yonder, who would give him 50 thousand ducats as ransom in exchange for his granting them all their lives.

The Adelantado replied to him that although he was a poor soldier, he did not wish to give such a sign of weakness as to appear covetous to them; that when it was his duty to be liberal and merciful, it must be without any interested motive.

The French captain persisted in this: the Adelantado undeceived him, [saying] that if the earth were to join with the sky, he should do no more than what he had told him; and so the French captain returned to where his men were, telling the Adelantado that he would return at once with what had been agreed upon; and he came back within half an hour, bring-ing the flags in the boat, and about 60 arquebuses, 20 pistols, a quantity of swords and bucklers, and some helmets and breastplates; and he came to where the Adelantado was and said that all those Frenchmen gave themselves up to his mercy, and he surrendered the flags and arms. Then the Adelantado ordered 20 soldiers to enter the boat to bring the French-men over, ten at a time: the river was narrow and easy to cross; and he instructed Diego Florez de Valdés, the Admiral of the fleet, to receive the flags and arms, and go in the boat to bring the Frenchmen across; [he ordered] that the soldiers should not give them ill treatment; and the Adelantado withdrew from the shore a distance of about two arquebuse shots, behind a sand dune, among some bushes, where the men in the approaching boat, who were bringing the French, could not see him: then he said to the French captain and the other 8 Frenchmen who were with him:

"Gentlemen, I have but few soldiers, and they are not very experienced; and you are many, and if you are not bound, it would be an easy thing for you to avenge yourselves on us for the death of your people whom we killed when we took the fort; and so it is necessary that you march with your hands tied behind you, to a place 4 leagues from here where I have my camp."

The Frenchmen replied that so it should be done; and with the ropes from the soldiers' fuses they fastened their hands behind them very securely; and the ten who came over [each time] in the boat could not see those whose hands were being tied behind them, until they met them, because it was expedient so to do in order that the Frenchmen who had not crossed the river, might not understand what was happening and be warned; and thus 208 Frenchmen were bound, of whom the Adelantado asked if there were any Catholics among them who might wish to confess: eight of them said that they were Catholics: these he took away from there and placed them in the boat to be sent up the river to St. Augustine: the others replied that they were of the new religion, and held themselves to be very good Christians; that that was their faith, and no other.

The Adelantado commanded that they should march, after having first given them food and drink when they arrived in tens, before they were bound; this was done before the next ten came; and he told one of his captains, who is called . . . that he was to march with them in the vanguard, and that at a cross-bow shot's distance from there he would find a line which he [the Adelantado] would draw with a *jineta* [1] he carried in his hand; [that place] was a sandy stretch over which they had to march to the Fort of St. Augustine; that there he was to kill them all, and he ordered the captain who came with the rear-guard to do likewise; and so was it done, and they were all left there dead; and that night he returned to St. Augustine toward dawn, because the sun had already set when those men died.

On the day following that on which the Adelantado had arrived in St. Augustine, the same Indians came as before, and said that many more Christians were on the other side of the river than there were previously. The Adelantado realized that this must be the party of Juan Ribao, General of the Lutherans on land and sea, whom they called the Viceroy of that country for the King of France, and he set forth at once with 150 soldiers, [marching] well in order, and at midnight he arrived and quartered himself where he had been the first time. At dawn he came near the river, and scattered his men, and as the daylight grew stronger he saw many people on the other side of the river, two arquebuse shots away, and a raft made to take them across to the point where the Adelantado was. Presently the Frenchmen, when they saw the Adelantado and his men, sounded an alarm and unfurled a royal standard and two field banners, playing their fifes and beating their drums in very good order; and they offered battle to the Adelantado, who had commanded his men to sit down to breakfast, and make no demonstration of anger whatever. He himself walked along the shore with his Admiral and two other captains, paying no attention to the anger and battle stir of the Frenchmen, in such manner that they stopped running, and in battle array as they were, they halted, stopped playing the fifes and drums, and, sounding a bugle, they raised a white cloth in token of peace.

The Adelantado called at once to another bugler he had with him, a very good one, and drew from his pocket a small cloth, and began to wave it as a signal of peace.

A Frenchman got on the raft, and asked in a loud voice that we should go across to them.

A reply was sent to them by order of the Adelantado, that if they wished anything they should come to where he was, since they had the raft and they called to him: he who was on the raft answered that it was a poor one whereon to cross, because of the strong current; [he asked] that they send him a canoe which was there, belonging to some Indians.

The Adelantado told him that he should swim across for it, under the pledge of his word: then a French sailor came over, but the Adelantado

---

[1] A short lance with a gilded point, and a tassel as an ornament, which in ancient times was the insignia of Spanish captains of industry.

would not consent that he should speak: he ordered him to take the canoe and go to tell his captain that if he wanted anything of the Adelantado, he should send to tell him, since it was the French captain who had called to the Adelantado. That sailor returned presently with a gentleman who said he was the sergeant major of Juan Ribao, Viceroy and Captain-General of that country for the King of France, and that Juan Ribao sent him to say that he had been shipwrecked with a fleet in a storm at sea, and that he had with him there about 350 Frenchmen; that it was his purpose to go to a fort he had 20 leagues from there; that he wished the Adelantado to do him the favor of lending him boats wherein to cross that river, and another there was 4 leagues from there, and that he desired to know if they were Spaniards and who their captain was.

The Adelantado replied that they were Spaniards, and that their captain was he with whom the sergeant was speaking, who was called Pedro Menéndez; that he should tell his General that the Adelantado had taken the fort which Juan Ribao said he had 20 leagues from there, and had slain the Frenchmen therein, and others who had come from the ship-wrecked fleet, because they had ill conducted themselves; and they walked to the place where the French lay dead, and he showed them to him, [telling him to inform his General] that he had no reason left for wishing to cross the river to his fort.

The sergeant, with great composure, without showing any sign of grief at what the Adelantado said to him, asked him if he would do him the kindness to send one of his gentlemen to tell that to his General, so that they might negotiate regarding their safe-conduct because his General was very tired, and he wished that the Adelantado would go to see him in a boat he had there; and the Adelantado answered him thus:

"Brother, go with God's blessing and give the reply which has been given you; and if your General should wish to come to speak with me, I give him my word that he can come and return safely, with about 5 or 6 companions whom he may bring with him from those of his council, so that he may follow the advice which suits him best." And so that gentleman left with that message.

Within half an hour he returned to accept the safe-conduct that the Adelantado had given, and to ask for the boat, which the Adelantado would not give him, sending him to say that they might take it from him; that Juan Ribao could come across in the canoe, which was safe, since the river was narrow; and thus that gentleman again went back, and presently came Juan Ribao, whom the Adelantado received very well, with 8 other gentlemen who came with him, all of very fine address and appearance, holding positions of authority, and he had a collation served to them from a certain barrel of preserves, and gave them some drink; and he said that he would give them food if they wished it.

Juan Ribao answered with much humility, rendering thanks for the kind reception given him; and said that in order to cheer their spirits, which were sad because of the news of their comrades' death, they wished to breakfast with the preserves and wine, and that for the time being they wanted no other food; and thus they did.

Juan Ribao said that those comrades of his who lay dead there, and he saw them near by, might have been deceived [concerning the capture of the fort], and that he did not wish to be: then [the Adelantado] commanded that each one of the soldiers who were there should come with whatever he had from the fort, and the things Juan Ribao saw were so many that he held it for certain that was the truth; although he had already heard that news, and could not believe it, because among the French was a barber whom the Adelantado had ordered killed with the rest, who had remained for dead among the others, for at the first knife-thrust given him he let himself fall, pretending he was dead; and when Juan Ribao had arrived there the barber had swum over to him, and he [the barber] held it for certain that the Adelantado had deceived them in saying that the fort was captured when it was not, and so had Juan Ribao up to that time.

The Adelantado said that in order that they should believe it fully and satisfy themselves thereof, Juan Ribao should speak apart with two Frenchmen who were there, and he did so; and then he came toward the Adelantado, and told him that he was certain that all he had told him was the truth, and that what was happening to him might happen to the Adelantado; that since their Kings were brothers and such great friends, the Adelantado should treat him like a friend, giving him ships and supplies wherewith he could go to France.

The Adelantado replied to him as he had to the first Frenchmen upon whom he had worked justice, and Juan Ribao in discussion with him was unable to obtain anything else: then Juan Ribao said to him that he wished to report to his men, for there were many noblemen among them, and he would return or send an answer as to what he should decide to do: within 3 hours Juan Ribao came back in the canoe and said that there were different opinions among his men, as some wished to place themselves at the Adelantado's mercy, and others did not.

The Adelantado replied that he cared nothing whether they all came, or came in part, or did not come, any of them; they should do what seemed best to them, since they were free to do so.

Juan Ribao told the Adelantado that half of them were willing to place themselves at his mercy, and would pay as ransom more than one hundred thousand ducats; and the other half could pay more, as there were among them wealthy persons of large income who intended to settle in that land.

The Adelantado answered: "It would grieve me deeply to lose such a good ransom and booty, for I have dire need of that help to aid me in the conquest and colonizing of this country; it is my duty, in the name of my King, to spread therein the Holy Gospel."

Juan Ribao used much cunning here, to see if it might be of use to him, because it seemed to him that the Adelantado, on account of greed for the money that they could give him, would not kill Juan Ribao or those who entrusted themselves to his clemency; it appeared to him that the Adelantado's not killing them, through an agreement that Juan Ribao would make with him, would be worth more to him than 200 thousand ducats; and he told the Adelantado that he would return to his people with the answer; that because it was late he begged him to have the kindness to remain there until the day following, when he would come with the decision that might be agreed upon.

The Adelantado replied that he would wait, and told him to rejoin his men as the sun was already setting; and in the morning Juan Ribao returned in the canoe and delivered to the Adelantado two royal standards, one of the King of France, the other of the Admiral; two field banners, a gilt sword and dagger, a very fine gilt helmet, a buckler, a pistol, a seal he had with him, which the Admiral of France had given him to stamp all the edicts he should issue and titles he might give. He said to the Adelantado that about 150 persons of the 350 with him, were willing to come and place themselves at the Adelantado's mercy; that the others had departed that night, and that the boat should go over for those who wished to come, and for their arms.

The Adelantado immediately directed that Captain Diego Florez de Valdés, the Admiral of his armada, should have them brought over as he had the others, ten at a time; and taking Juan Ribao behind the sand dune, between the bushes, where he had taken the others, he had his hands and those of all the rest, tied behind their backs, as was done to the previous ones, telling them that they had to march 4 leagues on land, and by night, so that he could not allow them to go unbound; and when they were all tied, he asked them if they were Catholics or Lutherans, and if there were any who wished to confess.

Juan Ribao answered that he and all those who were there were of the new religion, and he began to sing the psalm, *Domine memento mei;* and when it was finished he said that from earth they came, and unto earth must they return; that twenty years more or less were of little account; that the Adelantado was to do with them as he wished. And the Adelantado, giving the order that they should march, as he had to the others, in the same order and to the same line in the sand, commanded that the same be done to all of them as to the others: he only spared the fifers, drummers, trumpeters, and 4 more who said that they were Catholics, in all 16 persons: all the others were put to the knife.

*WAR IS THE PROVINCE OF DANGER, AND
THEREFORE COURAGE ABOVE ALL
THINGS IS THE FIRST QUALITY
OF A WARRIOR*

*C*OURAGE *is of two kinds: First, physical courage, or courage in presence of danger to the person; and next, moral courage, or courage before responsibility, whether it be before the judgment seat of external authority or of the inner power, the conscience. We only speak here of the first.*

Courage before danger to the person, again, is of two kinds. First it may be indifference to danger, whether it proceeds from the organism of the individual, contempt of death or habit. In any of these kinds it is to be regarded as a permanent condition.

Secondly, courage may proceed from positive motives, such as personal pride, patriotism, enthusiasm of any kind. In this case courage is not so much a normal condition as an impulse. We may conceive that the two kinds act differently. The first kind is more certain, because it has become a second nature, never forsakes the man; the second often leads him farther. In the first there is more of firmness, in the second of boldness. The first leaves the judgment clearer, the second raises its power at times, but often bewilders it. The two combined make up the most perfect kind of courage.

The Red Badge of Courage

BY

STEPHEN CRANE

CHAPTER I

THE cold passed reluctantly from the earth, and the retiring fogs revealed an army stretched out on the hills, resting. As the landscape changed from brown to green, the army awakened, and began to tremble with eagerness at the noise of rumors. It cast its eyes upon the roads, which were growing from long troughs of liquid mud to proper thoroughfares. A river, amber-tinted in the shadow of its banks, purled at the army's feet; and at night, when the stream had become of a sorrowful blackness, one could see across it the red, eyelike gleam of hostile camp fires set in the low brows of distant hills.

Once a certain tall soldier developed virtues and went resolutely to wash a shirt. He came flying back from a brook waving his garment bannerlike. He was swelled with a tale he had heard from a reliable friend, who had heard it from a truthful cavalryman, who had heard it from his trustworthy brother, one of the orderlies at division headquarters. He adopted the important air of a herald in red and gold.

"We're goin' t' move t' morrah—sure," he said pompously to a group in the company street. "We're goin' 'way up the river, cut across, an' come around in behint 'em."

To his attentive audience he drew a loud and elaborate plan of a very brilliant campaign. When he had finished, the blue-clothed men scattered into small arguing groups between the rows of squat brown huts. A Negro teamster who had been dancing upon a cracker box with the hilarious encouragement of two-score soldiers was deserted. He sat mournfully down. Smoke drifted lazily from a multitude of quaint chimneys.

"It's a lie! that's all it is—a thunderin' lie!" said another private loudly. His smooth face was flushed, and his hands were thrust sulkily into his trousers' pockets. He took the matter as an affront to him. "I don't believe the derned old army's ever going to move. We're set. I've got ready to move eight times in the last two weeks, and we ain't moved yet."

The tall soldier felt called upon to defend the truth of a rumor he himself had introduced. He and the loud one came near to fighting over it.

A corporal began to swear before the assemblage. He had just put a costly board floor in his house, he said. During the early spring he had refrained from adding extensively to the comfort of his environment because he had felt that the army might start on the march at any moment. Of late, however, he had been impressed that they were in a sort of eternal camp.

Many of the men engaged in a spirited debate. One outlined in a peculiarly lucid manner all the plans of the commanding general. He was opposed by men who advocated that there were other plans of campaign. They clamored at each other, numbers making futile bids for the popular attention. Meanwhile, the soldier who had fetched the rumor bustled about with much importance. He was continually assailed by questions.

"What's up, Jim?"

"Th' army's goin' t' move."

"Ah, what yeh talkin' about? How yeh know it is?"

"Well, yeh kin b'lieve me er not, jest as yeh like. I don't care a hang."

There was much food for thought in the manner in which he replied. He came near to convincing them by disdaining to produce proofs. They grew much excited over it.

There was a youthful private who listened with eager ears to the words of the tall soldier and to the varied comments of his comrades. After receiving a fill of discussions concerning marches and attacks, he went to his hut and crawled through an intricate hole that served it as a door. He wished to be alone with some new thoughts that had lately come to him.

He lay down on a wide bunk that stretched across the end of the room. In the other end, cracker boxes were made to serve as furniture. They were grouped about the fireplace. A picture from an illustrated weekly was upon the log walls, and three rifles were paralleled on pegs. Equipments hung on handy projections, and some tin dishes lay upon a small pile of firewood. A folded tent was serving as a roof. The sunlight, without, beating upon it, made it glow a light yellow shade. A small window shot an oblique square of whiter light upon the cluttered floor. The smoke from the fire at times neglected the clay chimney and wreathed into the room, and this flimsy chimney of clay and sticks made endless threats to set ablaze the whole establishment.

The youth was in a little trance of astonishment. So they were at last going to fight. On the morrow, perhaps, there would be a battle, and he would be in it. For a time he was obliged to labor to make himself believe. He could not accept with assurance an omen that he was about to mingle in one of those great affairs of the earth.

He had, of course, dreamed of battles all his life—of vague and bloody conflicts that had thrilled him with their sweep and fire. In visions he had seen himself in many struggles. He had imagined peoples secure in the shadow of his eagle-eyed prowess. But awake he had regarded battles as crimson blotches on the pages of the past. He had put them as things of the bygone with his thought-images of heavy crowns and high castles. There was a portion of the world's history which he had regarded as the time of wars, but it, he thought, had been long gone over the horizon and had disappeared forever.

From his home his youthful eyes had looked upon the war in his own country with distrust. It must be some sort of a play affair. He had long despaired of witnessing a Greeklike struggle. Such would be no more, he had said. Men were better, or more timid. Secular and religious education had effaced the throat-grappling instinct, or else firm finance held in check the passions.

He had burned several times to enlist. Tales of great movements shook the land. They might not be distinctly Homeric, but there seemed to be much glory in them. He had read of marches, sieges, conflicts, and he had longed to see it all. His busy mind had drawn for him large pictures extravagant in color, lurid with breathless deeds.

But his mother had discouraged him. She had affected to look with some contempt upon the quality of his war ardor and patriotism. She could calmly seat herself and with no apparent difficulty give him many hundreds of reasons why he was of vastly more importance on the farm than on the field of battle. She had had certain ways of expression that told him that her statements on the subject came from a deep conviction. Moreover, on her side, was his belief that her ethical motive in the argument was impregnable.

At last, however, he had made firm rebellion against this yellow light thrown upon the color of his ambitions. The newspapers, the gossip of the village, his own picturings, had aroused him to an uncheckable degree. They were in truth fighting finely down there. Almost every day the newspapers printed accounts of a decisive victory.

One night, as he lay in bed, the winds had carried to him the clangoring of the church bell as some enthusiast jerked the rope frantically to tell the twisted news of a great battle. This voice of the people rejoicing in the night had made him shiver in a prolonged ecstasy of excitement. Later, he had gone down to his mother's room and had spoken thus: "Ma, I'm going to enlist."

"Henry, don't you be a fool," his mother had replied. She had then covered her face with the quilt. There was an end to the matter for that night.

Nevertheless, the next morning he had gone to a town that was near his mother's farm and had enlisted in a company that was forming there. When he had returned home his mother was milking the brindle cow. Four others stood waiting. "Ma, I've enlisted," he had said to her diffidently. There was a short silence. "The Lord's will be done, Henry," she had finally replied, and had then continued to milk the brindle cow.

When he had stood in the doorway with his soldier's clothes on his back, and with the light of excitement and expectancy in his eyes almost defeating the glow of regret for the home bonds, he had seen two tears leaving their trails on his mother's scarred cheeks.

Still, she had disappointed him by saying nothing whatever about returning with his shield or on it. He had privately primed himself for a beautiful scene. He had prepared certain sentences which he thought could be used with touching effect. But her words destroyed his plans. She had doggedly peeled potatoes and addressed him as follows: "You watch out, Henry, an' take good care of yerself in this here fighting business—you watch out, an' take good care of yerself. Don't go a-thinkin' you can lick the hull rebel army at the start, because yeh can't. Yer jest one little feller amongst a hull lot of others, and yeh've got to keep quiet an' do what they tell yeh. I know how you are, Henry.

"I've knet yeh eight pair of socks, Henry, and I've put in all yer best shirts, because I want my boy to be jest as warm and comf'able as anybody in the army. Whenever they get holes in 'em, I want yeh to send 'em rightaway back to me, so's I kin dern 'em.

"An' allus be careful an' choose yer comp'ny. There's lots of bad men in the army, Henry. The army makes 'em wild, and they like nothing better than the job of leading off a young feller like you, as ain't never been away from home much and has allus had a mother, an' a-learning 'em to drink and swear. Keep clear of them folks, Henry. I don't want yeh to ever do anything, Henry, that yeh would be 'shamed to let me know about. Jest think as if I was a-watchin' yeh. If yeh keep that in yer mind allus, I guess yeh'll come out about right.

"Yeh must allus remember yer father, too, child, an' remember he never drunk a drop of licker in his life, and seldom swore a cross oath.

"I don't know what else to tell yeh, Henry, excepting that yeh must never do no shirking, child, on my account. If so be a time comes when yeh have to be kilt or do a mean thing, why; Henry, don't think of anything 'cept what's right, because there's many a woman has to bear up 'ginst sech things these times, and the Lord'll take keer of us all.

"Don't forgit about the socks and the shirts, child; and I've put a cup of blackberry jam with yer bundle, because I know yeh like it above all things. Good-by, Henry. Watch out, and be a good boy."

He had, of course, been impatient under the ordeal of this speech. It had not been quite what he expected, and he had borne it with an air of irritation. He departed feeling vague relief.

Still, when he had looked back from the gate, he had seen his mother kneeling among the potato parings. Her brown face, upraised, was stained with tears, and her spare form was quivering. He bowed his head and went on, feeling suddenly ashamed of his purposes.

From his home he had gone to the seminary to bid adieu to many schoolmates. They had thronged about him with wonder and admiration. He had felt the gulf now between them and had swelled with calm pride. He and some of his fellows who had donned blue were quite overwhelmed with privileges for all of one afternoon, and it had been a very delicious thing. They had strutted.

A certain light-haired girl had made vivacious fun at his martial spirit, but there was another and darker girl whom he had gazed at steadfastly, and he thought she grew demure and sad at sight of his blue and brass. As he had walked down the path between the rows of oaks, he had turned his head and detected her at a window watching his departure. As he perceived her, she had immediately begun to stare up through the high tree branches at the sky. He had seen a good deal of flurry and haste in her movement as she changed her attitude. He often thought of it.

On the way to Washington his spirit had soared. The regiment was fed and caressed at station after station until the youth had believed that he must be a hero. There was a lavish expenditure of bread and cold meats, coffee, and pickles and cheese. As he basked in the smiles of the girls and was patted and complimented by the old men, he had felt growing within him the strength to do mighty deeds of arms.

After complicated journeyings with many pauses, there had come months of monotonous life in a camp. He had had the belief that real war was a series of death struggles with small time in between for sleep and meals; but since his regiment had come to the field the army had done little but sit still and try to keep warm.

He was brought then gradually back to his old ideas. Greeklike struggles would be no more. Men were better, or more timid. Secular and religious education had effaced the throat-grappling instinct, or else firm finance held in check the passions.

He had grown to regard himself merely as a part of a vast blue demonstration. His province was to look out, as far as he could, for his personal comfort. For recreation he could twiddle his thumbs and speculate on the thoughts which must agitate the minds of the generals. Also, he was drilled and drilled and reviewed, and drilled and drilled and reviewed.

The only foes he had seen were some pickets along the river bank. They were a sun-tanned, philosophical lot, who sometimes shot reflectively at the blue pickets. When reproached for this afterward, they usually expressed sorrow, and swore by their gods that the guns had exploded without their permission. The youth, on guard duty one night, conversed across the stream with one of them. He was a slightly ragged man, who spat skillfully between his shoes and possessed a great fund of bland and infantile assurance. The youth liked him personally.

"Yank," the other had informed him, "yer a right dum good feller." This sentiment, floating to him upon the still air, had made him temporarily regret war.

Various veterans had told him tales. Some talked of gray, bewhiskered hordes who were advancing with relentless curses and chewing tobacco with unspeakable valor; tremendous bodies of fierce soldiery who were sweeping along like the Huns. Others spoke of tattered and eternally hungry men who fired despondent powders. "They'll charge through hell's fire an' brimstone t' git a holt on a haversack, an' sech stomachs ain't a-lastin' long," he was told. From the stories, the youth imagined the red, live bones sticking out through slits in the faded uniforms.

Still, he could not put a whole faith in veterans' tales, for recruits were their prey. They talked much of smoke, fire, and blood, but he could not tell how much might be lies. They persistently yelled, "Fresh fish!" at him, and were in no wise to be trusted.

However, he perceived now that it did not greatly matter what kind of soldiers he was going to fight, so long as they fought, which fact no one disputed. There was a more serious problem. He lay in his bunk pondering upon it. He tried to mathematically prove to himself that he would not run from a battle.

Previously he had never felt obliged to wrestle too seriously with this question. In his life he had taken certain things for granted, never challenging his belief in ultimate success, and bothering little about means and roads. But here he was confronted with a thing of moment. It had suddenly appeared to him that perhaps in a battle he might run. He was forced to admit that as far as war was concerned he knew nothing of himself.

A sufficient time before he would have allowed the problem to kick its heels at the outer portals of his mind, but now he felt compelled to give serious attention to it.

A little panic-fear grew in his mind. As his imagination went forward to a fight, he saw hideous possibilities. He contemplated the lurking menaces of the future, and failed in an effort to see himself standing stoutly in the midst of them. He recalled his visions of broken-bladed glory, but in the shadow of the impending tumult he suspected them to be impossible pictures.

He sprang from the bunk and began to pace nervously to and fro. "Good Lord, what's th' matter with me?" he said aloud.

He felt that in this crisis his laws of life were useless. Whatever he had learned of himself was here of no avail. He was an unknown quantity. He saw that he would again be obliged to experiment as he had in early youth. He must accumulate information of himself, and meanwhile he resolved to remain close upon his guard lest those qualities of which he knew nothing should everlastingly disgrace him. "Good Lord!" he repeated in dismay.

After a time the tall soldier slid dexterously through the hole. The loud private followed. They were wrangling.

"That's all right," said the tall soldier as he entered. He waved his hand expressively. "You can believe me or not, jest as you like. All you got to do is to sit down and wait as quiet as you can. Then pretty soon you'll find out I was right."

His comrade grunted stubbornly. For a moment he seemed to be searching for a formidable reply. Finally he said: "Well, you don't know everything in the world, do you?"

"Didn't say I knew everything in the world," retorted the other sharply. He began to stow various articles snugly into his knapsack.

The youth, pausing in his nervous walk, looked down at the busy figure. "Going to be a battle, sure, is there, Jim?" he asked.

"Of course there is," replied the tall soldier. "Of course there is. You jest wait 'til tomorrow, and you'll see one of the biggest battles ever was. You jest wait."

"Thunder!" said the youth.

"Oh, you'll see fighting this time, my boy, what'll be regular out-and-out fighting," added the tall soldier, with the air of a man who is about to exhibit a battle for the benefit of his friends.

"Huh!" said the loud one from a corner.

"Well," remarked the youth, "like as not this story'll turn out jest like them others did."

"Not much it won't," replied the tall soldier, exasperated. "Not much it won't. Didn't the cavalry all start this morning?" He glared about him. No one denied his statement. "The cavalry started this morning," he continued. "They say there ain't hardly any cavalry left in camp. They're going to Richmond, or some place, while we fight all the Johnnies. It's some dodge like that. The regiment's got orders, too. A feller what seen 'em go to headquarters told me a little while ago. And they're raising blazes all over camp—anybody can see that."

"Shucks!" said the loud one.

The youth remained silent for a time. At last he spoke to the tall soldier. "Jim!"

"What?"

"How do you think the reg'ment'll do?"

"Oh, they'll fight all right, I guess, after they once get into it," said the other with cold judgment. He made a fine use of the third person. "There's been heaps of fun poked at 'em because they're new, of course, and all that; but they'll fight all right, I guess."

"Think any of the boys 'll run?" persisted the youth.

"Oh, there may be a few of 'em run, but there's them kind in every regiment, 'specially when they first goes under fire," said the other in a tolerant way. "Of course it might happen that the hull kit-and-boodle might start and run, if some big fighting came first-off, and then again they might stay and fight like fun. But you can't bet on nothing. Of course they ain't never been under fire yet, and it ain't likely they'll lick the hull rebel army all-to-oncet the firs' time; but I think they'll fight better than some, if worse than others. That's the way I figger. They call the reg'ment 'Fresh fish' and everything; but the boys come of good stock, and most of 'em 'll fight like sin after they oncet git shootin'," he added, with a mighty emphasis on the last four words.

"Oh, you think you know——" began the loud soldier with scorn.

The other turned savagely upon him. They had a rapid altercation, in which they fastened upon each other various strange epithets.

The youth at last interrupted them. "Did you ever think you might run yourself, Jim?" he asked. On concluding the sentence he laughed as if he had meant to aim a joke. The loud soldier also giggled.

The tall private waved his hand. "Well," said he profoundly, "I've thought it might get too hot for Jim Conklin in some of them scrimmages, and if a whole lot of boys started and run, why, I s'pose I'd start and run. And if I once started to run, I'd run like the devil, and no mistake. But if everybody was a-standing and a-fighting, why, I'd stand and fight. Be jiminey, I would. I'll bet on it."

"Huh!" said the loud one.

The youth of this tale felt gratitude for these words of his comrade. He had feared that all of the untried men possessed a great and correct confidence. He now was in a measure reassured.

CHAPTER II

THE next morning the youth discovered that his tall comrade had been the fast-flying messenger of a mistake. There was much scoffing at the latter by those who had yesterday been firm adherents of his views, and there was even a little sneering by men who had never believed the rumor. The tall one fought with a man from Chatfield Corners and beat him severely.

The youth felt, however, that his problem was in no wise lifted from him. There was, on the contrary, an irritating prolongation. The tale had created in him a great concern for himself. Now, with the newborn question in his mind, he was compelled to sink back into his old place as part of a blue demonstration.

For days he made ceaseless calculations, but they were all wondrously unsatisfactory. He found that he could establish nothing. He finally concluded that the only way to prove himself was to go into the blaze, and then figuratively to watch his legs to discover their merits and faults. He reluctantly admitted that he could not sit still and with a mental slate and pencil derive an answer. To gain it, he must have blaze, blood, and danger, even as a chemist requires this, that, and the other. So he fretted for an opportunity.

Meanwhile he continually tried to measure himself by his comrades. The tall soldier, for one, gave him some assurance. This man's serene unconcern dealt him a measure of confidence, for he had known him since childhood, and from his intimate knowledge he did not see how he could be capable of anything that was beyond him, the youth. Still, he thought that his comrade might be mistaken about himself. Or, on the other hand, he might be a man heretofore doomed to peace and obscurity, but, in reality, made to shine in war.

The youth would have liked to have discovered another who suspected himself. A sympathetic comparison of mental notes would have been a joy to him.

He occasionally tried to fathom a comrade with seductive sentences. He looked about to find men in the proper mood. All attempts failed to bring forth any statement which looked in any way like a confession to those doubts which he privately acknowledged in himself. He was afraid to make an open declaration of his concern, because he dreaded to place some unscrupulous confidant upon the high plane of the unconfessed from which elevation he could be derided.

In regard to his companions his mind wavered between two opinions, according to his mood. Sometimes he inclined to believing them all heroes. In fact, he usually admitted in secret the superior development of the higher qualities in others. He could conceive of men going very insignificantly about the world bearing a load of courage unseen, and, although he had known many of his comrades through boyhood, he began to fear that his judgment of them had been blind. Then, in other moments, he flouted these theories, and assured himself that his fellows were all privately wondering and quaking.

His emotions made him feel strange in the presence of men who talked excitedly of a prospective battle as of a drama they were about to witness, with nothing but eagerness and curiosity apparent in their faces. It was often that he suspected them to be liars.

He did not pass such thoughts without severe condemnation of himself. He dinned reproaches at times. He was convicted by himself of many shameful crimes against the gods of traditions.

In his great anxiety his heart was continually clamoring at what he considered the intolerable slowness of the generals. They seemed content to perch tranquilly on the river bank, and leave him bowed down by the weight of a great problem. He wanted it settled forthwith. He could not long bear such a load, he said. Sometimes his anger at the commanders reached an acute stage, and he grumbled about the camp like a veteran.

One morning, however, he found himself in the ranks of his prepared regiment. The men were whispering speculations and recounting the old rumors. In the gloom before the break of the day their uniforms glowed a deep purple hue. From across the river the red eyes were still peering. In the eastern sky there was a yellow patch like a rug laid for the feet of the coming sun; and against it, black and pattern-like, loomed the gigantic figure of the colonel on a gigantic horse.

From off in the darkness came the trampling of feet. The youth could occasionally see dark shadows that moved like monsters. The regiment stood at rest for what seemed a long time. The youth grew impatient. It was unendurable the way these affairs were managed. He wondered how long they were to be kept waiting.

As he looked all about him and pondered upon the mystic gloom, he began to believe that at any moment the ominous distance might be aflare, and the rolling crashes of an engagement come to his ears. Staring once at the red eyes across the river, he conceived them to be growing larger, as the orbs of a row of dragons advancing. He turned toward the colonel and saw him lift his gigantic arm and calmly stroke his mustache.

At last he heard from along the road at the foot of the hill the clatter of a horse's galloping hoofs. It must be the coming of orders. He bent forward, scarce breathing. The exciting clickety-click, as it grew louder and louder, seemed to be beating upon his soul. Presently a horseman with jangling equipment drew rein before the colonel of the regiment. The two held a short, sharp-worded conversation. The men in the foremost ranks craned their necks.

As the horseman wheeled his animal and galloped away he turned to shout over his shoulder, "Don't forget that box of cigars!" The colonel mumbled in reply. The youth wondered what a box of cigars had to do with war.

A moment later the regiment went swinging off into the darkness. It was now like one of those moving monsters wending with many feet. The air was heavy, and cold with dew. A mass of wet grass, marched upon, rusted like silk.

There was an occasional flash and glimmer of steel from the backs of all these huge crawling reptiles. From the road came creakings and grumblings as some surly guns were dragged away.

The men stumbled along still muttering speculations. There was a subdued debate. Once a man fell down, and as he reached for his rifle a comrade, unseen, trod upon his hand. He of the injured fingers swore bitterly and aloud. A low tittering laugh went among his fellows.

Presently they passed into a roadway and marched forward with easy strides. A dark regiment moved before them, and from behind also came the tinkle of equipments on the bodies of marching men.

The rushing yellow of the developing day went on behind their backs. When the sunrays at last struck full and mellowingly upon the earth, the youth saw that the landscape was streaked with two long, thin, black columns which disappeared on the brow of a hill in front and rearward vanished in a wood. They were like two serpents crawling from the cavern of the night.

The river was not in view. The tall soldier burst into praises of what he thought to be his powers of perception.

Some of the tall one's companions cried with emphasis that they, too, had evolved the same thing, and they congratulated themselves upon it. But there were others who said that the tall one's plan was not the true one at all. They persisted with other theories. There was a vigorous discussion.

The youth took no part in them. As he walked along in careless line he was engaged with his own eternal debate. He could not hinder himself from dwelling upon it. He was despondent and sullen, and threw shifting glances about him. He looked ahead, often expecting to hear from the advance the rattle of firing.

But the long serpents crawled slowly from hill to hill without bluster of smoke. A dun-colored cloud of dust floated away to the right. The sky overhead was of a fairy blue.

The youth studied the faces of his companions, ever on the watch to detect kindred emotions. He suffered disappointment. Some ardor of the air which was causing the veteran commands to move with glee—almost with song—had infected the new regiment. The men began to speak of victory as of a thing they knew. Also, the tall soldier received his vindication. They were certainly going to come around in behind the enemy. They expressed commiseration for that part of the army which had been left upon the river bank, felicitating themselves upon being a part of a blasting host.

The youth, considering himself as separated from the others, was saddened by the blithe and merry speeches that went from rank to rank. The company wags all made their best endeavors. The regiment tramped to the tune of laughter.

The blatant soldier often convulsed whole files by his biting sarcasms aimed at the tall one.

And it was not long before all the men seemed to forget their mission. Whole brigades grinned in unison, and regiments laughed.

A rather fat soldier attempted to pilfer a horse from a dooryard. He planned to load his knapsack upon it. He was escaping with his prize when a young girl rushed from the house and grabbed the animal's mane. There followed a wrangle. The young girl, with pink cheeks and shining eyes, stood like a dauntless statue.

The observant regiment, standing at rest in the roadway, whooped at once, and entered whole-souled upon the side of the maiden. The men became so engrossed in this affair that they entirely ceased to remember their own large war. They jeered the piratical private, and called attention to various defects in his personal appearance; and they were wildly enthusiastic in support of the young girl.

To her, from some distance, came bold advice. "Hit him with a stick."

There were crows and catcalls showered upon him when he retreated without the horse. The regiment rejoiced at his downfall. Loud and vociferous congratulations were showered upon the maiden, who stood panting and regarding the troops with defiance.

At nightfall the column broke into regimental pieces, and the fragments went into the fields to camp. Tents sprang up like strange plants. Camp fires, like red, peculiar blossoms, dotted the night.

The youth kept from intercourse with his companions as much as circumstances would allow him. In the evening he wandered a few paces into the gloom. From this little distance the many fires, with the black forms of men passing to and fro before the crimson rays, made weird and satanic effects.

He lay down in the grass. The blades pressed tenderly against his cheek. The moon had been lighted and was hung in a treetop. The liquid stillness of the night enveloping him made him feel vast pity for himself. There was a caress in the soft winds; and the whole mood of the darkness, he thought, was one of sympathy for himself in his distress.

He wished, without reserve, that he was at home again making the endless rounds from the house to the barn, from the barn to the fields, from the fields to the barn, from the barn to the house. He remembered he had often cursed the brindle cow and her mates, and had sometimes flung milking stools. But, from his present point of view, there was a halo of happiness about each of their heads, and he would have sacrificed all the brass buttons on the continent to have been enabled to return to them. He told himself that he was not formed for a soldier. And he mused seriously upon the radical differences between himself and those men who were dodging implike around the fires.

As he mused thus he heard the rustle of grass, and, upon turning his head, discovered the loud soldier. He called out, "Oh, Wilson!"

The latter approached and looked down. "Why, hello, Henry; is it you? What you doing here?"

"Oh, thinking," said the youth.

The other sat down and carefully lighted his pipe. "You're getting blue, my boy. You're looking thundering peeked. What the dickens is wrong with you?"

"Oh, nothing," said the youth.

The loud soldier launched then into the subject of the anticipated fight. "Oh, we've got 'em now!" As he spoke his boyish face was wreathed in a gleeful smile, and his voice had an exultant ring. "We've got 'em now. At last, by the eternal thunders, we'll lick 'em good!"

"If the truth was known," he added, more soberly, "*they've* licked *us* about every clip up to now; but this time—this time—we'll lick 'em good!"

"I thought you was objecting to this march a little while ago," said the youth coldly.

"Oh, it wasn't that," explained the other. "I don't mind marching, if there's going to be fighting at the end of it. What I hate is this getting moved here and moved there, with no good coming of it, as far as I can see, excepting sore feet and damned short rations."

"Well, Jim Conklin says we'll get a plenty of fighting this time."

"He's right for once, I guess, though I can't see how it come. This time we're in for a big battle, and we've got the best end of it, certain sure. Gee rod! how we will thump 'em!"

He arose and began to pace to and fro excitedly. The thrill of his enthusiasm made him walk with an elastic step. He was sprightly, vigorous, fiery in his belief in success. He looked into the future with clear, proud eye, and he swore with the air of an old soldier.

The youth watched him for a moment in silence. When he finally spoke his voice was as bitter as dregs. "Oh, you're going to do great things, I s'pose!"

The loud soldier blew a thoughtful cloud of smoke from his pipe. "Oh, I don't know," he remarked with dignity; "I don't know. I s'pose I'll do as well as the rest. I'm going to try like thunder." He evidently complimented himself upon the modesty of this statement.

"How do you know you won't run when the time comes?" asked the youth.

"Run?" said the loud one; "run?—of course not!" He laughed.

"Well," continued the youth, "lots of good-a-'nough men have thought they was going to do great things before the fight, but when the time come they skedaddled."

"Oh, that's all true, I s'pose," replied the other; "but I'm not going to skedaddle. The man that bets on my running will lose his money, that's all." He nodded confidently.

"Oh, shucks!" said the youth. "You ain't the bravest man in the world, are you?"

"No, I ain't," exclaimed the loud soldier indignantly; "and I didn't say I was the bravest man in the world, neither. I said I was going to do my share of fighting—that's what I said. And I am, too. Who are you, anyhow? You talk as if you thought you was Napoleon Bonaparte." He glared at the youth for a moment, and then strode away.

The youth called in a savage voice after his comrade: "Well, you needn't git mad about it!" But the other continued on his way and made no reply.

He felt alone in space when his injured comrade had disappeared. His failure to discover any mite of resemblance in their viewpoints made him more miserable than before. No one seemed to be wrestling with such a terrific personal problem. He was a mental outcast.

He went slowly to his tent and stretched himself on a blanket by the side of the snoring tall soldier. In the darkness he saw visions of a thousand-tongued fear that would babble at his back and cause him to flee, while others were going coolly about their country's business. He admitted that he would not be able to cope with this monster. He felt that every nerve in his body would be an ear to hear the voices, while other men would remain stolid and deaf.

And as he sweated with the pain of these thoughts, he could hear low, serene sentences. "I'll bid five." "Make it six." "Seven." "Seven goes."

He stared at the red, shivering reflection of a fire on the white wall of his tent until, exhausted and ill from the monotony of his suffering, he fell asleep.

CHAPTER III

WHEN another night came the columns, changed to purple streaks, filed across two pontoon bridges. A glaring fire wine-tinted the waters of the river. Its rays, shining upon the moving masses of troops, brought forth here and there sudden gleams of silver or gold. Upon the other shore a dark and mysterious range of hills was curved against the sky. The insect voices of the night sang solemnly.

After this crossing the youth assured himself that at any moment they might be suddenly and fearfully assaulted from the caves of the lowering woods. He kept his eyes watchfully upon the darkness.

But his regiment went unmolested to a camping place, and its soldiers slept the brave sleep of wearied men. In the morning they were routed out with early energy, and hustled along a narrow road that led deep into the forest.

It was during this rapid march that the regiment lost many of the marks of a new command.

The men had begun to count the miles upon their fingers, and they grew tired. "Sore feet an' damned short rations, that's all," said the loud soldier. There were perspiration and grumblings. After a time they began to shed their knapsacks. Some tossed them unconcernedly down; others hid them carefully, asserting their plans to return for them at some convenient time. Men extricated themselves from thick shirts. Presently few carried anything but their necessary clothing, blankets, haversacks, canteens, and arms and ammunition. "You can now eat and shoot," said the tall soldier to the youth. "That's all you want to do."

There was sudden change from the ponderous infantry of theory to the light and speedy infantry of practice. The regiment, relieved of a burden, received a new impetus. But there was much loss of valuable knapsacks, and, on the whole, very good shirts.

But the regiment was not yet veteranlike in appearance. Veteran regiments in the army were likely to be very small aggregations of men. Once, when the command had first come to the field, some perambulating veterans, noting the length of their column, had accosted them thus: "Hey, fellers, what brigade is that?" And when the men had replied that they formed a regiment and not a brigade, the older soldiers had laughed, and said, "O Gawd!"

Also, there was too great a similarity in the hats. The hats of a regiment should properly represent the history of headgear for a period of years. And, moreover, there were no letters of faded gold speaking from the colors. They were new and beautiful, and the color bearer habitually oiled the pole.

Presently the army again sat down to think. The odor of the peaceful pines was in the men's nostrils. The sound of monotonous axe blows rang through the forest, and the insects, nodding upon their perches, crooned like old women. The youth returned to his theory of a blue demonstration.

One gray dawn, however, he was kicked in the leg by the tall soldier, and then, before he was entirely awake, he found himself running down a wood road in the midst of men who were panting from the first effects of speed. His canteen banged rhythmically upon his thigh, and his haversack bobbed softly. His musket bounced a trifle from his shoulder at each stride and made his cap feel uncertain upon his head.

He could hear the men whisper jerky sentences: "Say—what's all this—about?" "What th' thunder—we—skedaddlin' this way fer?" "Billie—keep off m' feet. Yeh run—like a cow." And the loud soldier's shrill voice could be heard: "What th' devil they in sich a hurry for?"

The youth thought the damp fog of early morning moved from the rush of a great body of troops. From the distance came a sudden spatter of firing.

He was bewildered. As he ran with his comrades he strenuously tried to think, but all he knew was that if he fell down those coming behind would tread upon him. All his faculties seemed to be needed to guide him over and past obstructions. He felt carried along by a mob.

The sun spread disclosing rays, and, one by one, regiments burst into view like armed men just born of the earth. The youth perceived that the time had come. He was about to be measured. For a moment he felt in the face of his great trial like a babe, and the flesh over his heart seemed very thin. He seized time to look about him calculatingly.

But he instantly saw that it would be impossible for him to escape from the regiment. It inclosed him. And there were iron laws of tradition and law on four sides. He was in a moving box.

As he perceived this fact it occurred to him that he had never wished to come to the war. He had not enlisted of his free will. He had been dragged by the merciless government. And now they were taking him out to be slaughtered.

The regiment slid down a bank and wallowed across a little stream. The mournful current moved slowly on, and from the water, shaded black, some white bubble eyes looked at the men.

As they climbed the hill on the farther side artillery began to boom. Here the youth forgot many things as he felt a sudden impulse of curiosity. He scrambled up the bank with a speed that could not be exceeded by a blood-thirsty man.

He expected a battle scene.

There were some little fields girted and squeezed by a forest. Spread over the grass and in among the tree trunks, he could see knots and waving lines of skirmishers who were running hither and thither and firing at the landscape. A dark battle line lay upon a sun-struck clearing that gleamed orange color. A flag fluttered.

Other regiments floundered up the bank. The brigade was formed in line of battle, and after a pause started slowly through the woods in the rear of the receding skirmishers, who were continually melting into the scene to appear again farther on. They were always busy as bees, deeply absorbed in their little combats.

The youth tried to observe everything. He did not use care to avoid trees and branches, and his forgotten feet were constantly knocking against stones or getting entangled in briers. He was aware that these battalions with their commotions were woven red and startling into the gentle fabric of softened greens and browns. It looked to be a wrong place for a battle field.

The skirmishers in advance fascinated him. Their shots into thickets and at distant and prominent trees spoke to him of tragedies—hidden, mysterious, solemn.

Once the line encountered the body of a dead soldier. He lay upon his back staring at the sky. He was dressed in an awkward suit of yellowish brown. The youth could see that the soles of his shoes had been worn to the thinness of writing paper, and from a great rent in one the dead foot projected piteously. And it was as if fate had betrayed the soldier. In death it exposed to his enemies that poverty which in life he had perhaps concealed from his friends.

The ranks opened covertly to avoid the corpse. The invulnerable dead man forced a way for himself. The youth looked keenly at the ashen face. The wind raised the tawny beard. It moved as if a hand were stroking it. He vaguely desired to walk around and around the body and stare; the impulse of the living to try to read in dead eyes the answer to the Question.

During the march the ardor which the youth had acquired when out of view of the field rapidly faded to nothing. His curiosity was quite easily satisfied. If an intense scene had caught him with its wild swing as he came to the top of the bank, he might have gone roaring on. This advance upon Nature was too calm. He had opportunity to reflect. He had time in which to wonder about himself and to attempt to probe his sensations.

Absurd ideas took hold upon him. He thought that he did not relish the landscape. It threatened him. A coldness swept over his back, and it is true that his trousers felt to him that they were no fit for his legs at all.

A house standing placidly in distant fields had to him an ominous look. The shadows of the woods were formidable. He was certain that in this vista there lurked fierce-eyed hosts. The swift thought came to him that the generals did not know what they were about. It was all a trap. Suddenly those close forests would bristle with rifle barrels. Ironlike brigades would appear in the rear. They were all going to be sacrificed. The generals were stupids. The enemy would presently swallow the whole command. He glared about him, expecting to see the stealthy approach of his death.

He thought that he must break from the ranks and harangue his comrades. They must not all be killed like pigs; and he was sure it would come to pass unless they were informed of these dangers. The generals were idiots to send them marching into a regular pen. There was but one pair of eyes in the corps. He would step forth and make a speech. Shrill and passionate words came to his lips.

The line, broken into moving fragments by the ground, went calmly on through fields and woods. The youth looked at the men nearest him, and saw, for the most part, expressions of deep interest, as if they were investigating something that had fascinated them. One or two stepped with overvaliant airs as if they were already plunged into war. Others walked as upon thin ice. The greater part of the untested men appeared quiet and absorbed. They were going to look at war, the red animal— war, the blood-swollen god. And they were deeply engrossed in this march.

As he looked the youth gripped his outcry at his throat. He saw that even if the men were tottering with fear they would laugh at his warning. They would jeer him, and, if practicable, pelt him with missiles. Admitting that he might be wrong, a frenzied declamation of the kind would turn him into a worm.

He assumed, then, the demeanor of one who knows that he is doomed alone to unwritten responsibilities. He lagged, with tragic glances at the sky.

He was surprised presently by the young lieutenant of his company, who began heartily to beat him with a sword, calling out in a loud and insolent voice: "Come, young man, get up into ranks there. No skulking 'll do here." He mended his pace with suitable haste. And he hated the lieutenant, who had no appreciation of fine minds. He was a mere brute.

After a time the brigade was halted in the cathedral light of a forest. The busy skirmishers were still popping. Through the aisles of the wood could be seen the floating smoke from their rifles. Sometimes it went up in little balls, white and compact.

During this halt many men in the regiment began erecting tiny hills in front of them. They used stones, sticks, earth, and anything they thought might turn a bullet. Some built comparatively large ones, while others seemed content with little ones.

This procedure caused a discussion among the men. Some wished to fight like duelists, believing it to be correct to stand erect and be, from their feet to their foreheads, a mark. They said they scorned the devices of the cautious. But the others scoffed in reply, and pointed to the veterans on the flanks who were digging at the ground like terriers. In a short time there was quite a barricade along the regimental fronts. Directly, however, they were ordered to withdraw from that place.

This astounded the youth. He forgot his stewing over the advance movement. "Well, then, what did they march us out here for?" he demanded of the tall soldier. The latter with calm faith began a heavy explanation, although he had been compelled to leave a little protection of stones and dirt to which he had devoted much care and skill.

When the regiment was aligned in another position each man's regard for his safety caused another line of small intrenchments. They ate their noon meal behind a third one. They were moved from this one also. They were marched from place to place with apparent aimlessness.

The youth had been taught that a man became another thing in a battle. He saw his salvation in such a change. Hence this waiting was an ordeal to him. He was in a fever of impatience. He considered that there was denoted a lack of purpose on the part of the generals. He began to complain to the tall soldier. "I can't stand this much longer," he cried. "I don't see what good it does to make us wear out our legs for nothin'." He wished to return to camp, knowing that this affair was a blue demonstration; or else to go into a battle and discover that he had been a fool in his doubts, and was, in truth, a man of traditional courage. The strain of present circumstances he felt to be intolerable.

The philosophical tall soldier measured a sandwich of cracker and pork and swallowed it in a nonchalant manner. "Oh, I suppose we must go reconnoitering around the country jest to keep 'em from getting too close, or to develop 'em, or something."

"Huh!" cried the loud soldier.

"Well," cried the youth, still fidgeting, "I'd rather do anything 'most than go tramping 'round the country all day doing no good to nobody and jest tiring ourselves out."

"So would I," said the loud soldier. "It ain't right. I tell you if anybody with any sense was a-runnin' this army it——"

"Oh, shut up!" roared the tall private. "You little fool. You little damn' cuss. You ain't had that there coat and them pants on for six months, and yet you talk as if——"

"Well, I wanta do some fighting anyway," interrupted the other. "I didn't come here to walk. I could 'ave walked to home—'round an 'round the barn, if I jest wanted to walk."

The tall one, red-faced, swallowed another sandwich as if taking poison in despair.

But gradually, as he chewed, his face became again quiet and contented. He could not rage in fierce argument in the presence of such sandwiches. During his meals he always wore an air of blissful contemplation of the food he had swallowed. His spirit seemed then to be communing with the viands.

He accepted new environment and circumstance with great coolness, eating from his haversack at every opportunity. On the march he went along with the stride of a hunter, objecting to neither gait nor distance. And he had not raised his voice when he had been ordered away from three little protective piles of earth and stone, each of which had been an engineering feat worthy of being made sacred to the name of his grandmother.

In the afternoon the regiment went out over the same ground it had taken in the morning. The landscape then ceased to threaten the youth. He had been close to it and become familiar with it.

When, however, they began to pass into a new region, his old fears of stupidity and incompetence reassailed him, but this time he doggedly let them babble. He was occupied with his problem, and in his desperation he concluded that the stupidity did not greatly matter.

Once he thought he had concluded that it would be better to get killed directly and end his troubles. Regarding death thus out of the corner of his eye, he conceived it to be nothing but rest, and he was filled with a momentary astonishment that he should have made an extraordinary commotion over the mere matter of getting killed. He would die; he would go to some place where he would be understood. It was useless to expect appreciation of his profound and fine senses from such men as the lieutenant. He must look to the grave for comprehension.

The skirmish fire increased to a long clattering sound. With it was mingled far-away cheering. A battery spoke.

Directly the youth would see the skirmishers running. They were pursued by the sound of musketry fire. After a time the hot, dangerous flashes of the rifles were visible. Smoke clouds went slowly and insolently across the fields like observant phantoms. The din became crescendo, like the roar of an oncoming train.

A brigade ahead of them and on the right went into action with a rending roar. It was as if it had exploded. And thereafter it lay stretched in the distance behind a long gray wall, that one was obliged to look twice at to make sure that it was smoke.

The youth, forgetting his neat plan of getting killed, gazed spellbound. His eyes grew wide and busy with the action of the scene. His mouth was a little ways open.

Of a sudden he felt a heavy and sad hand laid upon his shoulder. Awakening from his trance of observation he turned and beheld the loud soldier.

"It's my first and last battle, old boy," said the latter, with intense gloom. He was quite pale and his girlish lip was trembling.

"Eh?" murmured the youth in great astonishment.

"It's my first and last battle, old boy," continued the loud soldier. "Something tells me——"

"What?"

"I'm a gone coon this first time and—and I w-want you to take these here things—to—my—folks." He ended in a quavering sob of pity for himself. He handed the youth a little packet done up in a yellow envelope.

"Why, what the devil——" began the youth again.

But the other gave him a glance as from the depths of a tomb, and raised his limp hand in a prophetic manner and turned away.

CHAPTER IV

The brigade was halted in the fringe of a grove. The men crouched among the trees and pointed their restless guns out at the fields. They tried to look beyond the smoke.

Out of this haze they could see running men. Some shouted information and gestured as they hurried.

The men of the new regiment watched and listened eagerly, while their tongues ran on in gossip of the battle. They mouthed rumors that had flown like birds out of the unknown.

"They say Perry has been driven in with big loss."

"Yes, Carrott went t' th' hospital. He said he was sick. That smart lieutenant is commanding 'G' Company. Th' boys say they won't be under Carrott no more if they all have t' desert. They allus knew he was a ——"

"Hannises' batt'ry is took."

"It ain't either. I saw Hannises' batt'ry off on th' left not more'n fifteen minutes ago."

"Well——"

"Th' general, he ses he is goin' t' take th' hull command of th' 304th when we go inteh action, an' then he ses we'll do sech fightin' as never another one reg'ment done."

"They say we're catchin' it over on th' left. They say th' enemy driv' our line inteh a devil of a swamp an' took Hannises' batt'ry."

"No sech thing. Hannises' batt'ry was 'long here 'bout a minute ago."

"That young Hasbrouck, he makes a good off'cer. He ain't afraid 'a nothin'."

"I met one of th' 148th Maine boys an' he ses his brigade fit th' hull rebel army fer four hours over on th' turnpike road an' killed about five thousand of 'em. He ses one more sech fight as that an' th' war 'll be over."

"Bill wasn't scared either. No, sir! It wasn't that. Bill ain't a-gittin' scared easy. He was jest mad, that's what he was. When that feller trod on his hand, he up an' sed that he was willin' t' give his hand t' his country, but he be dumbed if he was goin' t' have every dumb bushwacker in th' kentry walkin' 'round on it. So he went t' th' hospital disregardless of th' fight. Three fingers was crunched. Th' dern doctor wanted t' amputate 'm, an' Bill, he raised a heluva row, I hear. He's a funny feller."

The din in front swelled to a tremendous chorus. The youth and his fellows were frozen to silence. They could see a flag that tossed in the smoke angrily. Near it were the blurred and agitated forms of troops. There came a turbulent stream of men across the fields. A battery changing position at a frantic gallop scattered the stragglers right and left.

A shell screaming like a storm banshee went over the huddled heads of the reserves. It landed in the grove, and exploding redly flung the brown earth. There was a little shower of pine needles.

Bullets began to whistle among the branches and nip at the trees. Twigs and leaves came sailing down. It was as if a thousand axes, wee and invisible, were being wielded. Many of the men were constantly dodging and ducking their heads.

The lieutenant of the youth's company was shot in the hand. He began to swear so wondrously that a nervous laugh went along the regimental line. The officer's profanity sounded conventional. It relieved the tightened senses of the new men. It was as if he had hit his fingers with a tack hammer at home.

He held the wounded member carefully away from his side so that the blood would not drip upon his trousers.

The captain of the company, tucking his sword under his arm, produced a handkerchief and began to bind with it the lieutenant's wound. And they disputed as to how the binding should be done.

The battle flag in the distance jerked about madly. It seemed to be struggling to free itself from an agony. The billowing smoke was filled with horizontal flashes.

Men running swiftly emerged from it. They grew in numbers until it was seen that the whole command was fleeing. The flag suddenly sank down as if dying. Its motion as it fell was a gesture of despair.

Wild yells came from behind the walls of smoke. A sketch in gray and red dissolved into a moblike body of men who galloped like wild horses.

The veteran regiments on the right and left of the 304th immediately began to jeer. With the passionate song of the bullets and the banshee shrieks of shells were mingled loud cat-calls and bits of facetious advice concerning places of safety.

But the new regiment was breathless with horror. "Gawd! Saunders's got crushed!" whispered the man at the youth's elbow. They shrank back and crouched as if compelled to await a flood.

The youth shot a swift glance along the blue ranks of the regiment. The profiles were motionless, carven; and afterward he remembered that the color sergeant was standing with his legs apart, as if he expected to be pushed to the ground.

The following throng went whirling around the flank. Here and there were officers carried along on the stream like exasperated chips. They were striking about them with their swords and with their left fists, punching every head they could reach. They cursed like highwaymen.

A mounted officer displayed the furious anger of a spoiled child. He raged with his head, his arms, and his legs.

Another, the commander of the brigade, was galloping about bawling. His hat was gone and his clothes were awry. He resembled a man who had come from bed to go to a fire. The hoofs of his horse often threatened the heads of the running men, but they scampered with singular fortune. In this rush they were apparently all deaf and blind. They heeded not the largest and longest of the oaths that were thrown at them from all directions.

Frequently over this tumult could be heard the grim jokes of the critical veterans; but the retreating men apparently were not even conscious of the presence of an audience.

The battle reflection that shone for an instant in the faces on the mad current made the youth feel that forceful hands from heaven would not have been able to have held him in place if he could have got intelligent control of his legs.

There was an appalling imprint upon these faces. The struggle in the smoke had pictured an exaggeration of itself on the bleached cheeks and in the eyes wild with one desire.

The sight of this stampede exerted a flood-like force that seemed able to drag sticks and stones and men from the ground. They of the reserves had to hold on. They grew pale and firm, and red and quaking.

The youth achieved one little thought in the midst of this chaos. The composite monster which had caused the other troops to flee had not then appeared. He resolved to get a view of it, and then, he thought he might very likely run better than the best of them.

CHAPTER V

THERE were moments of waiting. The youth thought of the village street at home before the arrival of the circus parade on a day in the spring. He remembered how he had stood, a small, thrillful boy, prepared to follow the dingy lady upon the white horse, or the band in its faded chariot. He saw the yellow road, the lines of expectant people, and the sober houses. He particularly remembered an old fellow who used to sit upon a cracker box in front of the store and feign to despise such exhibitions. A thousand details of color and form surged in his mind. The old fellow upon the cracker box appeared in middle prominence.

Some one cried, "Here they come!"

There was rustling and muttering among the men. They displayed a feverish desire to have every possible cartridge ready to their hands. The boxes were pulled around into various positions, and adjusted with great care. It was as if seven hundred new bonnets were being tried on.

The tall soldier, having prepared his rifle, produced a red handkerchief of some kind. He was engaged in knitting it about his throat with exquisite attention to its position, when the cry was repeated up and down the line in a muffled roar of sound.

"Here they come! Here they come!" Gun locks clicked.

Across the smoke-infested fields came a brown swarm of running men who were giving shrill yells. They came on, stooping and swinging their rifles at all angles. A flag, tilted forward, sped near the front.

As he caught sight of them the youth was momentarily startled by a thought that perhaps his gun was not loaded. He stood trying to rally his faltering intellect so that he might recollect the moment when he had loaded, but he could not.

A hatless general pulled his dripping horse to a stand near the colonel of the 304th. He shook his fist in the other's face. "You've got to hold 'em back!" he shouted, savagely; "you've got to hold 'em back!"

In his agitation the colonel began to stammer. "A-all r-right, General, all right, by Gawd! We-we'll do our—we-we'll d-d-do—do our best, General." The general made a passionate gesture and galloped away. The colonel, perchance to relieve his feelings, began to scold like a wet parrot. The youth, turning swiftly to make sure that the rear was unmolested, saw the commander regarding his men in a highly resentful manner, as if he regretted above everything his association with them.

The man at the youth's elbow was mumbling, as if to himself: "Oh, we're in for it now! oh, we're in for it now!"

The captain of the company had been pacing excitedly to and fro in the rear. He coaxed in schoolmistress fashion, as to a congregation of boys with primers. His talk was an endless repetition. "Reserve your fire, boys —don't shoot till I tell you—save your fire—wait till they get close up— don't be damned fools——"

Perspiration streamed down the youth's face, which was soiled like that of a weeping urchin. He frequently, with a nervous movement, wiped his eyes with his coat sleeve. His mouth was still a little way open.

He got the one glance at the foe-swarming field in front of him, and instantly ceased to debate the question of his piece being loaded. Before he was ready to begin—before he had announced to himself that he was about to fight—he threw the obedient, well-balanced rifle into position and fired a first wild shot. Directly he was working at his weapon like an automatic affair.

He suddenly lost concern for himself, and forgot to look at a menacing fate. He became not a man but a member. He felt that something of which he was a part—a regiment, an army, a cause, or a country—was in a crisis. He was welded into a common personality which was dominated by a single desire. For some moments he could not flee, no more than a little finger can commit a revolution from a hand.

If he had thought the regiment was about to be annihilated perhaps he could have amputated himself from it. But its noise gave him assurance. The regiment was like a firework that, once ignited, proceeds superior to circumstances until its blazing vitality fades. It wheezed and banged with a mighty power. He pictured the ground before it as strewn with the discomfited.

There was a consciousness always of the presence of his comrades about him. He felt the subtle battle brotherhood more potent even than the cause for which they were fighting. It was a mysterious fraternity born of the smoke and danger of death.

He was at a task. He was like a carpenter who has made many boxes, making still another box, only there was furious haste in his movements. He, in his thought, was careering off in other places, even as the carpenter who as he works whistles and thinks of his friend or his enemy, his home or a saloon. And these jolted dreams were never perfect to him afterward, but remained a mass of blurred shapes.

Presently he began to feel the effects of the war atmosphere—a blistering sweat, a sensation that his eyeballs were about to crack like hot stones. A burning roar filled his ears.

Following this came a red rage. He developed the acute exasperation of a pestered animal, a well-meaning cow worried by dogs. He had a mad feeling against his rifle, which could only be used against one life at a time. He wished to rush forward and strangle with his fingers. He craved a power that would enable him to make a world-sweeping gesture and brush all back. His impotency appeared to him, and made his rage into that of a driven beast.

Buried in the smoke of many rifles his anger was directed not so much against the men whom he knew were rushing toward him as against the swirling battle phantoms which were choking him, stuffing their smoke robes down his parched throat. He fought frantically for respite for his senses, for air, as a babe being smothered attacks the deadly blankets.

There was a blare of heated rage mingled with a certain expression of intentness on all faces. Many of the men were making low-toned noises with their mouths, and these subdued cheers, snarls, imprecations, prayers, made a wild, barbaric song that went as an undercurrent of sound, strange and chantlike with the resounding chords of the war march.

The man at the youth's elbow was babbling. In it there was something soft and tender like the monologue of a babe. The tall soldier was swearing in a loud voice. From his lips came a black procession of curious oaths. Of a sudden another broke out in a querulous way like a man who has mislaid his hat. "Well, why don't they support us? Why don't they send supports? Do they think——"

The youth in his battle sleep heard this as one who dozes hears.

There was a singular absence of heroic poses. The men bending and surging in their haste and rage were in every impossible attitude. The steel ramrods clanked and clanged with incessant din as the men pounded them furiously into the hot rifle barrels. The flaps of the cartridge boxes were all unfastened, and bobbed idiotically with each movement. The rifles, once loaded, were jerked to the shoulder and fired without apparent aim into the smoke or at one of the blurred and shifting forms which, upon the field before the regiment, had been growing larger and larger like puppets under a magician's hand.

The officers, at their intervals, rearward, neglected to stand in picturesque attitudes. They were bobbing to and fro roaring directions and encouragements. The dimensions of their howls were extraordinary. They expended their lungs with prodigal wills. And often they nearly stood upon their heads in their anxiety to observe the enemy on the other side of the tumbling smoke.

The lieutenant of the youth's company had encountered a soldier who had fled screaming at the first volley of his comrades. Behind the lines these two were acting a little isolated scene. The man was blubbering and staring with sheeplike eyes at the lieutenant, who had seized him by the collar and was pommeling him. He drove him back into the ranks with many blows. The soldier went mechanically, dully, with his animal-like eyes upon the officer. Perhaps there was to him a divinity expressed in the voice of the other—stern, hard, with no reflection of fear in it. He tried to reload his gun, but his shaking hands prevented. The lieutenant was obliged to assist him.

The men dropped here and there like bundles. The captain of the youth's company had been killed in an early part of the action. His body lay stretched out in the position of a tired man resting, but upon his face there was an astonished and sorrowful look, as if he thought some friend had done him an ill turn. The babbling man was grazed by a shot that made the blood stream widely down his face. He clapped both hands to his head. "Oh!" he said, and ran. Another grunted suddenly as if he had been struck by a club in the stomach. He sat down and gazed ruefully. In his eyes there was mute, indefinite reproach. Farther up the line a man, standing behind a tree, had had his knee joint splintered by a ball. Immediately he had dropped his rifle and gripped the tree with both arms. And there he remained, clinging desperately and crying for assistance that he might withdraw his hold upon the tree.

At last an exultant yell went along the quivering line. The firing dwindled from an uproar to a last vindictive popping. As the smoke slowly eddied away, the youth saw that the charge had been repulsed. The enemy were scattered into reluctant groups. He saw a man climb to the top of the fence, straddle the rail, and fire a parting shot. The waves had receded, leaving bits of dark *débris* upon the ground.

Some in the regiment began to whoop frenziedly. Many were silent. Apparently they were trying to contemplate themselves.

After the fever had left his veins, the youth thought that at last he was going to suffocate. He became aware of the foul atmosphere in which he had been struggling. He was grimy and dripping like a laborer in a foundry. He grasped his canteen and took a long swallow of the warmed water.

A sentence with variations went up and down the line. "Well, we've helt 'em back. We've helt 'em back; derned if we haven't." The men said it blissfully, leering at each other with dirty smiles.

The youth turned to look behind him and off to the right and off to the left. He experienced the joy of a man who at last finds leisure in which to look about him.

Under foot there were a few ghastly forms motionless. They lay twisted in fantastic contortions. Arms were bent and heads were turned in incredible ways. It seemed that the dead men must have fallen from some great height to get into such positions. They looked to be dumped out upon the ground from the sky.

From a position in the rear of the grove a battery was throwing shells over it. The flash of the guns startled the youth at first. He thought they were aimed directly at him. Through the trees he watched the black figures of the gunners as they worked swiftly and intently. Their labor seemed a complicated thing. He wondered how they could remember its formula in the midst of confusion.

The guns squatted in a row like savage chiefs. They argued with abrupt violence. It was a grim pow-wow. Their busy servants ran hither and thither.

A small procession of wounded men were going drearily toward the rear. It was a flow of blood from the torn body of the brigade.

To the right and to the left were the dark lines of other troops. Far in front he thought he could see lighter masses protruding in points from the forest. They were suggestive of unnumbered thousands.

Once he saw a tiny battery go dashing along the line of the horizon. The tiny riders were beating the tiny horses.

From a sloping hill came the sound of cheerings and clashes. Smoke welled slowly through the leaves.

Batteries were speaking with thunderous oratorical effort. Here and there were flags, the red in the stripes dominating. They splashed bits of warm color upon the dark lines of troops.

The youth felt the old thrill at the sight of the emblem. They were like beautiful birds strangely undaunted in a storm.

As he listened to the din from the hillside, to a deep pulsating thunder that came from afar to the left, and to the lesser clamors which came from many directions, it occurred to him that they were fighting, too, over there, and over there, and over there. Heretofore he had supposed that all the battle was directly under his nose.

As he gazed around him the youth felt a flash of astonishment at the blue, pure sky and the sun gleaming on the trees and fields. It was surprising that Nature had gone tranquilly on with her golden process in the midst of so much devilment.

CHAPTER VI

THE youth awakened slowly. He came gradually back to a position from which he could regard himself. For moments he had been scrutinizing his person in a dazed way as if he had never before seen himself. Then he picked up his cap from the ground. He wriggled in his jacket to make a more comfortable fit, and kneeling relaced his shoe. He thoughtfully mopped his reeking features.

So it was all over at last! The supreme trial had been passed. The red, formidable difficulties of war had been vanquished.

He went into an ecstasy of self-satisfaction. He had the most delightful sensations of his life. Standing as if apart from himself, he viewed that last scene. He perceived that the man who had fought thus was magnificent.

He felt that he was a fine fellow. He saw himself even with those ideals which he had considered as far beyond him. He smiled in deep gratification.

Upon his fellows he beamed tenderness and good will. "Gee! ain't it hot, hey?" he said affably to a man who was polishing his streaming face with his coat sleeves.

"You bet!" said the other, grinning sociably. "I never seen sech dumb hotness." He sprawled out luxuriously on the ground. "Gee, yes! An' I hope we don't have no more fightin' till a week from Monday."

There were some handshakings and deep speeches with men whose features were familiar, but with whom the youth now felt the bonds of tied hearts. He helped a cursing comrade to bind up a wound of the shin.

But, of a sudden, cries of amazement broke out along the ranks of the new regiment. "Here they come ag'in! Here they come ag'in!" The man who had sprawled upon the ground started up and said, "Gosh!"

The youth turned quick eyes upon the field. He discerned forms begin to swell in masses out of a distant wood. He again saw the tilted flag speeding forward.

The shells, which had ceased to trouble the regiment for a time, came swirling again, and exploded in the grass or among the leaves of the trees. They looked to be strange war flowers bursting into fierce bloom.

The men groaned. The luster faded from their eyes. Their smudged countenances now expressed a profound dejection. They moved their stiffened bodies slowly, and watched in sullen mood the frantic approach of the enemy. The slaves toiling in the temple of this god began to feel rebellion at his harsh tasks.

They fretted and complained each to each. "Oh, say, this is too much of a good thing! Why can't somebody send us supports?"

"We ain't never goin' to stand this second banging. I didn't come here to fight the hull damn' rebel army."

There was one who raised a doleful cry. "I wish Bill Smithers had trod on my hand, insteader me treddin' on his'n." The sore joints of the regiment creaked as it painfully floundered into position to repulse.

The youth stared. Surely, he thought, this impossible thing was not about to happen. He waited as if he expected the enemy to suddenly stop, apologize, and retire bowing. It was all a mistake.

But the firing began somewhere on the regimental line and ripped along in both directions. The level sheets of flame developed great clouds of smoke that tumbled and tossed in the mild wind near the ground for a moment, and then rolled through the ranks as through a gate. The clouds were tinged an earthlike yellow in the sunrays and in the shadow were a sorry blue. The flag was sometimes eaten and lost in this mass of vapor, but more often it projected, sun-touched, resplendent.

Into the youth's eyes there came a look that one can see in the orbs of a jaded horse. His neck was quivering with nervous weakness and the muscles of his arms felt numb and bloodless. His hands, too, seemed large and awkward as if he was wearing invisible mittens. And there was a great uncertainty about his knee joints.

The words that comrades had uttered previous to the firing began to recur to him. "Oh, say, this is too much of a good thing! What do they take us for—why don't they send supports? I didn't come here to fight the hull damned rebel army."

He began to exaggerate the endurance, the skill, and the valor of those who were coming. Himself reeling from exhaustion, he was astonished beyond measure at such persistency. They must be machines of steel. It was very gloomy struggling against such affairs, wound up perhaps to fight until sundown.

He slowly lifted his rifle and catching a glimpse of the thickspread field he blazed at a cantering cluster. He stopped then and began to peer as best he could through the smoke. He caught changing views of the ground covered with men who were all running like pursued imps, and yelling.

To the youth it was an onslaught of redoubtable dragons. He became like the man who lost his legs at the approach of the red and green monster. He waited in a sort of a horrified, listening attitude. He seemed to shut his eyes and wait to be gobbled.

A man near him who up to this time had been working feverishly at his rifle suddenly stopped and ran with howls. A lad whose face had borne an expression of exalted courage, the majesty of he who dares give his life, was, at an instant, smitten abject. He blanched like one who has come to the edge of a cliff at midnight and is suddenly made aware. There was a revelation. He, too, threw down his gun and fled. There was no shame in his face. He ran like a rabbit.

Others began to scamper away through the smoke. The youth turned his head, shaken from his trance by this movement as if the regiment was leaving him behind. He saw the few fleeting forms.

He yelled then with fright and swung about. For a moment, in the great clamor, he was like a proverbial chicken. He lost the direction of safety. Destruction threatened him from all points.

Directly he began to speed toward the rear in great leaps. His rifle and cap were gone. His unbuttoned coat bulged in the wind. The flap of his cartridge box bobbed wildly, and his canteen, by its slender cord, swung out behind. On his face was the horror of those things which he imagined.

The lieutenant sprang forward bawling. The youth saw his features wrathfully red, and saw him make a dab with his sword. His one thought of the incident was that the lieutenant was a peculiar creature to feel interested in such matters upon this occasion.

He ran like a blind man. Two or three times he fell down. Once he knocked his shoulder so heavily against a tree that he went headlong.

Since he had turned his back upon the fight his fears had been wondrously magnified. Death about to thrust him between the shoulder blades was far more dreadful than death about to smite him between the eyes. When he thought of it later, he conceived the impression that it is better to view the appalling than to be merely within hearing. The noises of the battle were like stones; he believed himself liable to be crushed.

As he ran on he mingled with others. He dimly saw men on his right and on his left, and he heard footsteps behind him. He thought that all the regiment was fleeing, pursued by these ominous crashes.

In his flight the sound of these following footsteps gave him his one meager relief. He felt vaguely that death must make a first choice of the men who were nearest; the initial morsels for the dragons would be then those who were following him. So he displayed the zeal of an insane sprinter in his purpose to keep them in the rear. There was a race.

As he, leading, went across a little field, he found himself in a region of shells. They hurtled over his head with long wild screams. As he listened he imagined them to have rows of cruel teeth that grinned at him. Once one lit before him and the livid lightning of the explosion effectually barred the way in his chosen direction. He groveled on the ground and then springing up went careering off through some bushes.

He experienced a thrill of amazement when he came within view of a battery in action. The men there seemed to be in conventional moods, altogether unaware of the impending annihilation. The battery was disputing with a distant antagonist and the gunners were wrapped in admiration of their shooting. They were continually bending in coaxing postures over the guns. They seemed to be patting them on the back and encouraging them with words. The guns, stolid and undaunted, spoke with dogged valor.

The precise gunners were coolly enthusiastic. They lifted their eyes every chance to the smoke-wreathed hillock from whence the hostile battery addressed them. The youth pitied them as he ran. Methodical idiots! Machine-like fools! The refined joy of planting shells in the midst of the other battery's formation would appear a little thing when the infantry came swooping out of the woods.

The face of a youthful rider, who was jerking his frantic horse with an abandon of temper he might display in a placid barnyard, was impressed deeply upon his mind. He knew that he looked upon a man who would presently be dead.

Too, he felt a pity for the guns, standing, six good comrades, in a bold row.

He saw a brigade going to the relief of its pestered fellows. He scrambled upon a wee hill and watched it sweeping finely, keeping formation in difficult places. The blue of the line was crusted with steel color, and the brilliant flags projected. Officers were shouting.

This sight also filled him with wonder. The brigade was hurrying briskly to be gulped into the infernal mouths of the war god. What manner of men were they, anyhow? Ah, it was some wondrous breed! Or else they didn't comprehend—the fools.

A furious order caused commotion in the artillery. An officer on a bounding horse made maniacal motions with his arms. The teams went swinging up from the rear, the guns were whirled about, and the battery scampered away. The cannon with their noses poked slantingly at the ground grunted and grumbled like stout men, brave but with objections to hurry.

The youth went on, moderating his pace since he had left the place of noises.

Later he came upon a general of division seated upon a horse that pricked its ears in an interesting way at the battle. There was a great gleaming of yellow and patent leather about the saddle and bridle. The quiet man astride looked mouse-colored upon such a splendid charger.

A jingling staff was galloping hither and thither. Sometimes the general was surrounded by horsemen and at other times he was quite alone. He looked to be much harassed. He had the appearance of a business man whose market is swinging up and down.

The youth went slinking around this spot. He went as near as he dared trying to overhear words. Perhaps the general, unable to comprehend chaos, might call upon him for information. And he could tell him. He knew all concerning it. Of a surety the force was in a fix, and any fool could see that if they did not retreat while they had opportunity—why——

He felt that he would like to thrash the general, or at least approach and tell him in plain words exactly what he thought him to be. It was criminal to stay calmly in one spot and make no effort to stay destruction. He loitered in a fever of eagerness for the division commander to apply to him.

As he warily moved about, he heard the general call out irritably: "Tompkins, go over an' see Taylor, an' tell him not t' be in such an all-fired hurry; tell him t' halt his brigade in th' edge of th' woods; tell him t' detach a reg'ment—say I think th' center 'll break if we don't help it out some; tell him t' hurry up."

A slim youth on a fine chestnut horse caught these swift words from the mouth of his superior. He made his horse bound into a gallop almost from a walk in his haste to go upon his mission. There was a cloud of dust.

A moment later the youth saw the general bounce excitedly in his saddle. "Yes, by heavens, they have!" The officer leaned forward. His face was aflame with excitement. "Yes, by heavens, they've held 'im! They've held 'im!"

He began to blithely roar at his staff: "We'll wallop 'im now. We'll wallop 'im now. We've got 'em sure." He turned suddenly upon an aid: "Here —you—Jones—quick—ride after Tompkins—see Taylor—tell him t' go in—everlastingly—like blazes—anything."

As another officer sped his horse after the first messenger, the general beamed upon the earth like a sun. In his eyes was a desire to chant a pæan. He kept repeating, "They've held 'em, by heavens!"

His excitement made his horse plunge, and he merrily kicked and swore at it. He held a little carnival of joy on horseback.

CHAPTER VII

THE youth cringed as if discovered in a crime. By heavens, they had won after all! The imbecile line had remained and become victors. He could hear cheering.

He lifted himself upon his toes and looked in the direction of the fight. A yellow fog lay wallowing on the treetops. From beneath it came the clatter of musketry. Hoarse cries told of an advance.

He turned away amazed and angry. He felt that he had been wronged.

He had fled, he told himself, because annihilation approached. He had done a good part in saving himself, who was a little piece of the army. He had considered the time, he said, to be one in which it was the duty of every little piece to rescue itself if possible. Later the officers could fit the little pieces together again, and make a battle front. If none of the little pieces were wise enough to save themselves from the flurry of death at such a time, why, then, where would be the army? It was all plain that he had proceeded according to very correct and commendable rules. His actions had been sagacious things. They had been full of strategy. They were the work of a master's legs.

Thoughts of his comrades came to him. The brittle blue line had withstood the blows and won. He grew bitter over it. It seemed that the blind ignorance and stupidity of those little pieces had betrayed him. He had been overturned and crushed by their lack of sense in holding the position, when intelligent deliberation would have convinced them that it was impossible. He, the enlightened man who looks afar in the dark, had fled because of his superior perceptions and knowledge. He felt a great anger against his comrades. He knew it could be proved that they had been fools.

He wondered what they would remark when later he appeared in camp. His mind heard howls of derision. Their destiny would not enable them to understand his sharper point of view.

He began to pity himself acutely. He was ill used. He was trodden beneath the feet of an iron injustice. He had proceeded with wisdom and from the most righteous motives under heaven's blue only to be frustrated by hateful circumstances.

A dull, animal-like rebellion against his fellows, war in the abstract, and fate grew within him. He shambled along with bowed head, his brain in a tumult of agony and despair. When he looked loweringly up, quivering at each sound, his eyes had the expression of those of a criminal who thinks his guilt and his punishment great, and knows that he can find no words.

He went from the fields into a thick wood, as if resolved to bury himself. He wished to get out of hearing of the cracking shots which were to him like voices.

The ground was cluttered with vines and bushes, and the trees grew close and spread out like bouquets. He was obliged to force his way with much noise. The creepers, catching against his legs, cried out harshly as their sprays were torn from the barks of trees. The swishing saplings tried to make known his presence to the world. He could not conciliate the forest. As he made his way, it was always calling out protestations. When he separated embraces of trees and vines the disturbed foliages waved their arms and turned their face leaves toward him. He dreaded lest these noisy motions and cries should bring men to look at him. So he went far, seeking dark and intricate places.

After a time the sound of musketry grew faint and the cannon boomed in the distance. The sun, suddenly apparent, blazed among the trees. The insects were making rhythmical noises. They seemed to be grinding their teeth in unison. A woodpecker stuck his impudent head around the side of a tree. A bird flew on lighthearted wing.

Off was the rumble of death. It seemed now that Nature had no ears.

This landscape gave him assurance. A fair field holding life. It was the religion of peace. It would die if its timid eyes were compelled to see blood. He conceived Nature to be a woman with a deep aversion to tragedy.

He threw a pine cone at a jovial squirrel, and he ran with chattering fear. High in a treetop he stopped, and, poking his head cautiously from behind a branch, looked down with an air of trepidation.

The youth felt triumphant at this exhibition. There was the law, he said. Nature had given him a sign. The squirrel, immediately upon recognizing danger, had taken to his legs without ado. He did not stand stolidly baring his furry belly to the missile, and die with an upward glance at the sympathetic heavens. On the contrary, he had fled as fast as his legs could carry him; and he was but an ordinary squirrel, too—doubtless no philosopher of his race. The youth wended, feeling that Nature was of his mind. She re-enforced his argument with proofs that lived where the sun shone.

Once he found himself almost into a swamp. He was obliged to walk upon bog tufts and watch his feet to keep from the oil mire. Pausing at one time to look about him he saw, out at some black water, a small animal pounce in and emerge directly with a gleaming fish.

The youth went again into the deep thickets. The brushed branches made a noise that drowned the sounds of cannon. He walked on, going from obscurity into promises of a greater obscurity.

At length he reached a place where the high, arching boughs made a chapel. He softly pushed the green doors aside and entered. Pine needles were a gentle brown carpet. There was a religious half light.

Near the threshold he stopped, horror-stricken at the sight of a thing. He was being looked at by a dead man who was seated with his back against a columnlike tree. The corpse was dressed in a uniform that once had been blue, but was now faded to a melancholy shade of green. The eyes, staring at the youth, had changed to the dull hue to be seen on the side of a dead fish. The mouth was open. Its red had changed to an appalling yellow. Over the gray skin of the face ran little ants. One was trundling some sort of a bundle along the upper lip.

The youth gave a shriek as he confronted the thing. He was for moments turned to stone before it. He remained staring into the liquid-looking eyes. The dead man and the living man exchanged a long look. Then the youth cautiously put one hand behind him and brought it against a tree. Leaning upon this he retreated, step by step, with his face still toward the thing. He feared that if he turned his back the body might spring up and stealthily pursue him.

The branches, pushing against him, threatened to throw him over upon it. His unguided feet, too, caught aggravatingly in brambles; and with it all he received a subtle suggestion to touch the corpse. As he thought of his hand upon it he shuddered profoundly.

At last he burst the bonds which had fastened him to the spot and fled, unheeding the underbrush. He was pursued by a sight of the black ants swarming greedily upon the gray face and venturing horribly near to the eyes.

After a time he paused, and, breathless and panting, listened. He imagined some strange voice would come from the dead throat and squawk after him in horrible menaces.

The trees about the portals of the chapel moved soughingly in a soft wind. A sad silence was upon the little guarding edifice.

CHAPTER VIII

THE trees began softly to sing a hymn of twilight. The sun sank until slanted bronze rays struck the forest. There was a lull in the noises of insects as if they had bowed their beaks and were making a devotional pause. There was silence save for the chanted chorus of the trees.

Then, upon this stillness, there suddenly broke a tremendous clangor of sounds. A crimson roar came from the distance.

The youth stopped. He was transfixed by this terrific medley of all noises. It was as if worlds were being rended. There was the ripping sound of musketry and the breaking crash of artillery.

His mind flew in all directions. He conceived the two armies to be at each other panther fashion. He listened for a time. Then he began to run in the direction of the battle. He saw that it was an ironical thing for him to be running thus toward that which he had been at such pains to avoid. But he said, in substance, to himself that if the earth and the moon were about to clash, many persons would doubtless plan to get upon the roofs to witness the collision.

As he ran, he became aware that the forest had stopped its music, as if at last becoming capable of hearing the foreign sounds. The trees hushed and stood motionless. Everything seemed to be listening to the crackle and clatter and ear-shaking thunder. The chorus pealed over the still earth.

It suddenly occurred to the youth that the fight in which he had been was, after all, but perfunctory popping. In the hearing of this present din he was doubtful if he had seen real battle scenes. This uproar explained a celestial battle; it was tumbling hordes a-struggle in the air.

Reflecting, he saw a sort of humor in the point of view of himself and his fellows during the late encounter. They had taken themselves and the enemy very seriously and had imagined that they were deciding the war. Individuals must have supposed that they were cutting the letters of their names deep into everlasting tablets of brass, or enshrining their reputations forever in the hearts of their countrymen, while, as to fact, the affair would appear in printed reports under a meek and immaterial title. But he saw that it was good, else, he said, in battle every one would surely run save forlorn hopes and their ilk.

He went rapidly on. He wished to come to the edge of the forest that he might peer out.

As he hastened, there passed through his mind pictures of stupendous conflicts. His accumulated thought upon such subjects was used to form scenes. The noise was as the voice of an eloquent being, describing.

Sometimes the brambles formed chains and tried to hold him back. Trees, confronting him, stretched out their arms and forbade him to pass. After its previous hostility this new resistance of the forest filled him with a fine bitterness. It seemed that Nature could not be quite ready to kill him.

But he obstinately took roundabout ways, and presently he was where he could see long gray walls of vapor where lay battle lines. The voices of cannon shook him. The musketry sounded in long irregular surges that played havoc with his ears. He stood regardant for a moment. His eyes had an awestruck expression. He gawked in the direction of the fight.

Presently he proceeded again on his forward way. The battle was like the grinding of an immense and terrible machine to him. Its complexities and powers, its grim processes, fascinated him. He must go close and see it produce corpses.

He came to a fence and clambered over it. On the far side, the ground was littered with clothes and guns. A newspaper, folded up, lay in the dirt. A dead soldier was stretched with his face hidden in his arm. Farther off there was a group of four or five corpses keeping mournful company. A hot sun had blazed upon the spot.

In this place the youth felt that he was an invader. This forgotten part of the battle ground was owned by the dead men, and he hurried, in the vague apprehension that one of the swollen forms would rise and tell him to begone.

He came finally to a road from which he could see in the distance dark and agitated bodies of troops, smoke-fringed. In the lane was a blood-stained crowd streaming to the rear. The wounded men were cursing, groaning, and wailing. In the air, always, was a mighty swell of sound that it seemed could sway the earth. With the courageous words of the artillery and the spiteful sentences of the musketry mingled red cheers. And from this region of noises came the steady current of the maimed.

One of the wounded men had a shoeful of blood. He hopped like a schoolboy in a game. He was laughing hysterically.

One was swearing that he had been shot in the arm through the commanding general's mismanagement of the army. One was marching with an air imitative of some sublime drum major. Upon his features was an unholy mixture of merriment and agony. As he marched he sang a bit of doggerel in a high and quavering voice:

> "Sing a song 'a vic'try,
> A pocketful 'a bullets,
> Five an' twenty dead men
> Baked in a—pie."

Parts of the procession limped and staggered to this tune.

Another had the gray seal of death already upon his face. His lips were curled in hard lines and his teeth were clinched. His hands were bloody from where he had pressed them upon his wound. He seemed to be awaiting the moment when he should pitch headlong. He stalked like the specter of a soldier, his eyes burning with the power of a stare into the unknown.

There were some who proceeded sullenly, full of anger at their wounds, and ready to turn upon anything as an obscure cause.

An officer was carried along by two privates. He was peevish. "Don't joggle so, Johnson, yeh fool," he cried. "Think m' leg is made of iron? If yeh can't carry me decent, put me down an' let some one else do it."

He bellowed at the tottering crowd who blocked the quick march of his bearers. "Say, make way there, can't yeh? Make way, dickens take it all."

They sulkily parted and went to the roadsides. As he was carried past they made pert remarks to him. When he raged in reply and threatened them, they told him to be damned.

The shoulder of one of the tramping bearers knocked heavily against the spectral soldier who was staring into the unknown.

The youth joined this crowd and marched along with it. The torn bodies expressed the awful machinery in which the men had been entangled.

Orderlies and couriers occasionally broke through the throng in the roadway, scattering wounded men right and left, galloping on, followed by howls. The melancholy march was continually disturbed by the messengers, and sometimes by bustling batteries that came swinging and thumping down upon them, the officers shouting orders to clear the way.

There was a tattered man, fouled with dust, blood and powder stain from hair to shoes, who trudged quietly at the youth's side. He was listening with eagerness and much humility to the lurid descriptions of a bearded sergeant. His lean features wore an expression of awe and admiration. He was like a listener in a country store to wondrous tales told among the sugar barrels. He eyed the story-teller with unspeakable wonder. His mouth was agape in yokel fashion.

The sergeant, taking note of this, gave pause to his elaborate history while he administered a sardonic comment. "Be keerful, honey, you'll be a-ketchin' flies," he said.

The tattered man shrank back abashed.

After a time he began to sidle near to the youth, and in a different way try to make him a friend. His voice was gentle as a girl's voice and his eyes were pleading. The youth saw with surprise that the soldier had two wounds, one in the head, bound with a blood-soaked rag, and the other in the arm, making that member dangle like a broken bough.

After they had walked together for some time the tattered man mustered sufficient courage to speak. "Was pretty good fight, wasn't it?" he timidly said. The youth, deep in thought, glanced up at the bloody and grim figure with its lamblike eyes, "What?"

"Was pretty good fight, wa'n't it?"

"Yes," said the youth shortly. He quickened his pace.

But the other hobbled industriously after him. There was an air of apology in his manner, but he evidently thought that he needed only to talk for a time, and the youth would perceive that he was a good fellow.

"Was pretty good fight, wa'n't it?" he began in a small voice, and then he achieved the fortitude to continue. "Dern me if I ever see fellers fight so. Laws, how they did fight! I knowed th' boys 'd like it when they onct got square at it. Th' boys ain't had no fair chanct up t' now, but this time they showed what they was. I knowed it 'd turn out this way. Yeh can't lick them boys. No, sir! They're fighters, they be."

He breathed a deep breath of humble admiration. He had looked at the youth for encouragement several times. He received none, but gradually he seemed to be absorbed in his subject.

"I was talkin' 'cross pickets with a boy from Georgie, onct, an' that boy, he ses, 'Your fellers 'll all run like hell when they onct hearn a gun,' he ses. 'Mebbe they will,' I ses, 'but I don't b'lieve none of it,' I ses; 'an' b'jiminey,' I ses back t' 'um, 'mebbe your fellers 'll all run like hell when they onct hearn a gun,' I ses. He larfed. Well, they didn't run t'-day, did they, hey? No, sir! They fit, an' fit, an' fit."

His homely face was suffused with a light of love for the army which was to him all things beautiful and powerful.

After a time he turned to the youth. "Where yeh hit, ol' boy?" he asked in a brotherly tone.

The youth felt instant panic at this question, although at first its full import was not borne in upon him.

"What?" he asked.

"Where yeh hit?" repeated the tattered man.

"Why," began the youth, "I—I—that is—why—I——"

He turned away suddenly and slid through the crowd. His brow was heavily flushed, and his fingers were picking nervously at one of his buttons. He bent his head and fastened his eyes studiously upon the button as if it were a little problem.

The tattered man looked after him in astonishment.

CHAPTER IX

THE youth fell back in the procession until the tattered soldier was not in sight. Then he started to walk on with the others.

But he was amid wounds. The mob of men was bleeding. Because of the tattered soldier's question he now felt that his shame could be viewed. He was continually casting sidelong glances to see if the men were contemplating the letters of guilt he felt burned into his brow.

At times he regarded the wounded soldiers in an envious way. He conceived persons with torn bodies to be peculiarly happy. He wished that he, too, had a wound, a red badge of courage.

The spectral soldier was at his side like a stalking reproach. The man's eyes were still fixed in a stare into the unknown. His gray, appalling face had attracted attention in the crowd, and men, slowing to his dreary pace, were walking with him. They were discussing his plight, questioning him and giving him advice. In a dogged way he repelled them, signing to them to go on and leave him alone. The shadows of his face were deepening and his tight lips seemed holding in check the moan of great despair. There could be seen a certain stiffness in the movements of his body, as if he were taking infinite care not to arouse the passion of his wounds. As he went on, he seemed always looking for a place, like one who goes to choose a grave.

Something in the gesture of the man as he waved the bloody and pity-ing soldiers away made the youth start as if bitten. He yelled in horror. Tottering forward he laid a quivering hand upon the man's arm. As the latter slowly turned his waxlike features toward him, the youth screamed: "Gawd! Jim Conklin!"

The tall soldier made a little commonplace smile. "Hello, Henry," he said.

The youth swayed on his legs and glared strangely. He stuttered and stammered. "Oh, Jim—oh, Jim—oh, Jim———"

The tall soldier held out his gory hand. There was a curious red and black combination of new blood and old blood upon it. "Where yeh been, Henry?" he asked. He continued in a monotonous voice, "I thought mebbe yeh got keeled over. There's been thunder t' pay t'-day. I was worryin' about it a good deal."

The youth still lamented. "Oh, Jim—oh, Jim—oh, Jim———"

"Yeh know," said the tall soldier, "I was out there." He made a careful gesture. "An', Lord, what a circus! An', b'jiminey, I got shot—I got shot. Yes, b'jiminey, I got shot." He reiterated this fact in a bewildered way, as if he did not know how it came about.

The youth put forth anxious arms to assist him, but the tall soldier went firmly on as if propelled. Since the youth's arrival as a guardian for his friend, the other wounded men had ceased to display much inter-est. They occupied themselves again in dragging their own tragedies toward the rear.

Suddenly, as the two friends marched on, the tall soldier seemed to be overcome by a terror. His face turned to a semblance of gray paste. He clutched the youth's arm and looked all about him, as if dreading to be overheard. Then he began to speak in a shaking whisper:

"I tell yeh what I'm 'fraid of, Henry—I'll tell yeh what I'm 'fraid of. I'm 'fraid I'll fall down—an' then yeh know—them damned artillery wagons—they like as not 'll run over me. That's what I'm 'fraid of———"

The youth cried out to him hysterically: "I'll take care of yeh, Jim! I'll take care of yeh! I swear t' Gawd I will!"

"Sure—will yeh, Henry?" the tall soldier beseeched.

"Yes—yes—I tell yeh—I'll take care of yeh, Jim!" protested the youth. He could not speak accurately because of the gulpings in his throat.

But the tall soldier continued to beg in a lowly way. He now hung babe-like to the youth's arm. His eyes rolled in the wildness of his terror. "I was allus a good friend t' yeh, wa'n't I, Henry? I've allus been a pretty good feller, ain't I? An' it ain't much t' ask, is it? Jest t' pull me along outer th' road? I'd do it fer you, wouldn't I, Henry?"

He paused in piteous anxiety to await his friend's reply.

The youth had reached an anguish where the sobs scorched him. He strove to express his loyalty, but he could only make fantastic gestures.

However, the tall soldier seemed suddenly to forget all those fears. He became again the grim, stalking specter of a soldier. He went stonily forward. The youth wished his friend to lean upon him, but the other always shook his head and strangely protested. "No—no—no—leave me be—leave me be——"

His look was fixed again upon the unknown. He moved with mysterious purpose, and all of the youth's offers he brushed aside. "No—no—leave me be—leave me be——"

The youth had to follow.

Presently the latter heard a voice talking softly near his shoulders. Turning he saw that it belonged to the tattered soldier. "Ye'd better take 'im outa th' road, pardner. There's a batt'ry comin' helitywhoop down th' road an' he'll git runned over. He's a goner anyhow in about five minutes—yeh kin see that. Ye'd better take 'im outa th' road. Where th' blazes does he git his stren'th from?"

"Lord knows!" cried the youth. He was shaking his hands helplessly.

He ran forward presently and grasped the tall soldier by the arm. "Jim! Jim!" he coaxed, "come with me."

The tall soldier weakly tried to wrench himself free. "Huh," he said vacantly. He stared at the youth for a moment. At last he spoke as if dimly comprehending. "Oh! Inteh th' fields? Oh!"

He started blindly through the grass.

The youth turned once to look at the lashing riders and jouncing guns of the battery. He was startled from this view by a shrill outcry from the tattered man.

"Gawd! He's runnin'!"

Turning his head swiftly, the youth saw his friend running in a staggering and stumbling way toward a little clump of bushes. His heart seemed to wrench itself almost free from his body at this sight. He made a noise of pain. He and the tattered man began a pursuit. There was a singular race.

When he overtook the tall soldier he began to plead with all the words he could find. "Jim—Jim—what are you doing—what makes you do this way—you'll hurt yerself."

The same purpose was in the tall soldier's face. He protested in a dulled way, keeping his eyes fastened on the mystic place of his intentions. "No—no—don't tech me—leave me be—leave me be——"

The youth, aghast and filled with wonder at the tall soldier, began quaveringly to question him. "Where yeh goin', Jim? What you thinking about? Where you going? Tell me, won't you, Jim?"

The tall soldier faced about as upon relentless pursuers. In his eyes there was a great appeal. "Leave me be, can't yeh? Leave me be fer a minnit."

The youth recoiled. "Why, Jim," he said, in a dazed way, "what's the matter with you?"

The tall soldier turned and, lurching dangerously, went on. The youth and the tattered soldier followed, sneaking as if whipped, feeling unable to face the stricken man if he should again confront them. They began to have thoughts of a solemn ceremony. There was something ritelike in these movements of the doomed soldier. And there was a resemblance in him to a devotee of a mad religion, blood-sucking, muscle-wrenching, bone-crushing. They were awed and afraid. They hung back lest he have at command a dreadful weapon.

At last, they saw him stop and stand motionless. Hastening up, they perceived that his face wore an expression telling that he had at last found the place for which he had struggled. His spare figure was erect; his bloody hands were quietly at his side. He was waiting with patience for something that he had come to meet. He was at the rendezvous. They paused and stood, expectant.

There was a silence.

Finally, the chest of the doomed soldier began to heave with a strained motion. It increased in violence until it was as if an animal was within and was kicking and tumbling furiously to be free.

This spectacle of gradual strangulation made the youth writhe, and once as his friend rolled his eyes, he saw something in them that made him sink wailing to the ground. He raised his voice in a last supreme call.

"Jim—Jim—Jim——"

The tall soldier opened his lips and spoke. He made a gesture. "Leave me be—don't tech me—leave me be——"

There was another silence while he waited.

Suddenly, his form stiffened and straightened. Then it was shaken by a prolonged ague. He stared into space. To the two watchers there was a curious and profound dignity in the firm lines of his awful face.

He was invaded by a creeping strangeness that slowly enveloped him. For a moment the tremor of his legs caused him to dance a sort of hideous hornpipe. His arms beat wildly about his head in expression of implike enthusiasm.

His tall figure stretched itself to its full height. There was a slight rending sound. Then it began to swing forward, slow and straight, in the manner of a falling tree. A swift muscular contortion made the left shoulder strike the ground first.

The body seemed to bounce a little way from the earth. "God!" said the tattered soldier.

The youth had watched, spellbound, this ceremony at the place of meeting. His face had been twisted into an expression of every agony he had imagined for his friend.

He now sprang to his feet and, going closer, gazed upon the pastelike face. The mouth was open and the teeth showed in a laugh.

As the flap of the blue jacket fell away from the body, he could see that the side looked as if it had been chewed by wolves.

The youth turned, with sudden, livid rage, toward the battlefield. He shook his fist. He seemed about to deliver a philippic.

"Hell——"

The red sun was pasted in the sky like a wafer.

CHAPTER X

The tattered man stood musing.

"Well, he was reg'lar jim-dandy fer nerve, wa'n't he," said he finally in a little awe-struck voice. "A reg'lar jim-dandy." He thoughtfully poked one of the docile hands with his foot. "I wonner where he got 'is stren'th from? I never seen a man do like that before. It was a funny thing. Well, he was a reg'lar jim-dandy."

The youth desired to screech out his grief. He was stabbed, but his tongue lay dead in the tomb of his mouth. He threw himself again upon the ground and began to brood.

The tattered man stood musing.

"Look-a-here, pardner," he said, after a time. He regarded the corpse as he spoke. "He's up an' gone, ain't 'e, an' we might as well begin t' look out fer ol' number one. This here thing is all over. He's up an' gone, ain't 'e? An' he's all right here. Nobody won't bother 'im. An' I must say I ain't enjoying any great health m'self these days."

The youth, awakened by the tattered soldier's tone, looked quickly up. He saw that he was swinging uncertainly on his legs and that his face had turned to a shade of blue.

"Good Lord!" he cried, "you ain't goin' t'—not you, too."

The tattered man waved his hand. "Nary die," he said. "All I want is some pea soup an' a good bed. Some pea soup," he repeated dreamfully.

The youth arose from the ground. "I wonder where he came from. I left him over there." He pointed. "And now I find 'im here. And he was coming from over there, too." He indicated a new direction. They both turned toward the body as if to ask it a question.

"Well," at length spoke the tattered man, "there ain't no use in our stayin' here an' tryin' t' ask him anything."

The youth nodded an assent wearily. They both turned to gaze for a moment at the corpse.

The youth murmured something.

"Well, he was a jim-dandy, wa'n't 'e?" said the tattered man as if in response.

They turned their backs upon it and started away. For a time they stole softly, treading with their toes. It remained laughing there in the grass.

"I'm commencin' t' feel pretty bad," said the tattered man, suddenly breaking one of his little silences. "I'm commencin' t' feel pretty damn' bad."

The youth groaned. "O Lord!" He wondered if he was to be the tortured witness of another grim encounter.

But his companion waved his hand reassuringly. "Oh, I'm not goin' t' die yit! There's too much dependin' on me fer me t' die yit. No, sir! Nary die; I *can't*! Ye'd oughta see th' swad a' chil'ren I've got, an' all like that."

The youth glancing at his companion could see by the shadow of a smile that he was making some kind of fun.

As they plodded on the tattered soldier continued to talk. "Besides, if I died, I wouldn't die th' way that feller did. That was th' funniest thing. I'd jest flop down, I would. I never seen a feller die th' way that feller did.

"Yeh know Tom Jamison, he lives next door t' me up home. He's a nice feller, he is, an' we was allus good friends. Smart, too. Smart as a steel trap. Well, when we was a-fightin' this afternoon, all-of-a-sudden he begin t' rip up an' cuss an' beller at me. 'Yer shot, yeh blamed infernal!'—he swear horrible—he ses t' me. I put up m' hand t' m' head an' when I looked at m' fingers, I seen, sure 'nough, I was shot. I give a holler an' begin t' run, but b'fore I could git away another one hit me in th' arm an' whirl' me clean 'round. I got skeared when they was all a-shootin' b'hind me an' I run t' beat all, but I cotch it pretty bad. I've an idee I'd a' been fightin' yit, if t'wasn't fer Tom Jamison."

Then he made a calm announcement: "There's two of 'em—little ones—but they're beginnin' t' have fun with me now. I don't b'lieve I kin walk much furder."

They went slowly on in silence. "Yeh look pretty peeked yerself," said the tattered man at last. "I bet yeh 've got a worser one than yeh think. Ye'd better take keer of yer hurt. It don't do t' let sech things go. It might be inside mostly, an' them plays thunder. Where is it located?" But he continued his harangue without waiting for a reply. "I see' a feller git hit plum in th' head when my reg'ment was a-standin' at ease onct. An' everybody yelled out to 'im; Hurt, John? Are yeh hurt much? 'No,' ses he. He looked kinder surprised, an' he went on tellin' 'em how he felt. He sed he didn't feel nothin'. But, by dad, th' first thing that feller knowed he was dead. Yes, he was dead—stone dead. So, yeh wanta watch out. Yeh might have some queer kind 'a hurt yerself. Yeh can't never tell. Where is your'n located?"

The youth had been wriggling since the introduction of this topic. He now gave a cry of exasperation and made a furious motion with his hand. "Oh, don't bother me!" he said. He was enraged against the tattered man, and could have strangled him. His companions seemed ever to play intolerable parts. They were ever upraising the ghost of shame on the stick of their curiosity. He turned toward the tattered man as one at bay. "Now, don't bother me," he repeated with desperate menace.

"Well, Lord knows I don't wanta bother anybody," said the other. There was a little accent of despair in his voice as he replied, "Lord knows I've gota 'nough m' own t' tend to."

The youth, who had been holding a bitter debate with himself and casting glances of hatred and contempt at the tattered man, here spoke in a hard voice. "Good-by," he said.

The tattered man looked at him in gaping amazement. "Why—why, pardner, where yeh goin'?" he asked unsteadily. The youth looking at him, could see that he, too, like the other one, was beginning to act dumb and animal-like. His thoughts seemed to be floundering about in his head. "Now—now—look—a—here, you Tom Jamison—now—I won't have this —this here won't do. Where—where yeh goin'?"

The youth pointed vaguely. "Over there," he replied.

"Well, now look—a—here—now," said the tattered man, rambling on in idiot fashion. His head was hanging forward and his words were slurred. "This thing won't do, now, Tom Jamison. It won't do. I know yeh, yeh pig-headed devil. Yeh wanta go trompin' off with a bad hurt. It ain't right —now—Tom Jamison—it ain't. Yeh wanta leave me take keer of yeh, Tom Jamison. It ain't—right—it ain't—fer yeh t' go—trompin off—with a bad hurt—it ain't—ain't—ain't right—it ain't."

In reply the youth climbed a fence and started away. He could hear the tattered man bleating plaintively.

Once he faced about angrily. "What?"

"Look—a—here, now, Tom Jamison—now—it ain't——"

The youth went on. Turning at a distance he saw the tattered man wandering about helplessly in the field.

He now thought that he wished he was dead. He believe that he envied those men whose bodies lay strewn over the grass of the fields and on the fallen leaves of the forest.

The simple questions of the tattered man had been knife thrusts to him. They asserted a society that probes pitilessly at secrets until all is apparent. His late companion's chance persistency made him feel that he could not keep his crime concealed in his bosom. It was sure to be brought plain by one of those arrows which cloud the air and are constantly pricking, discovering, proclaiming those things which are willed to be forever hidden. He admitted that he could not defend himself against this agency. It was not within the power of vigilance.

CHAPTER XI

HE BECAME aware that the furnace roar of the battle was growing louder. Great brown clouds had floated to the still heights of air before him. The noise, too, was approaching. The woods filtered men and the fields became dotted.

As he rounded a hillock, he perceived that the roadway was now a crying mass of wagons, teams, and men. From the heaving tangle issued exhortations, commands, imprecations. Fear was sweeping it all along. The cracking whips bit and horses plunged and tugged. The white-topped wagons strained and stumbled in their exertions like fat sheep.

The youth felt comforted in a measure by this sight. They were all retreating. Perhaps, then, he was not so bad after all. He seated himself and watched the terror-stricken wagons. They fled like soft, ungainly animals. All the roarers and lashers served to help him to magnify the dangers and horrors of the engagement that he might try to prove to himself that the thing with which men could charge him was in truth a symmetrical act. There was an amount of pleasure to him in watching the wild march of this vindication.

Presently the calm head of a forward-going column of infantry appeared in the road. It came swiftly on. Avoiding the obstructions gave it the sinuous movement of a serpent. The men at the head butted mules with their musket stocks. They prodded teamsters indifferent to all howls. The men forced their way through parts of the dense mass by strength. The blunt head of the column pushed. The raving teamsters swore many strange oaths.

The commands to make way had the ring of a great importance in them. The men were going forward to the heart of the din. They were to confront the eager rush of the enemy. They felt the pride of their onward movement when the remainder of the army seemed trying to dribble down this road. They tumbled teams about with a fine feeling that it was no matter so long as their column got to the front in time. This importance made their faces grave and stern. And the backs of the officers were very rigid.

As the youth looked at them the black weight of his woe returned to him. He felt that he was regarding a procession of chosen beings. The separation was as great to him as if they had marched with weapons of flame and banners of sunlight. He could never be like them. He could have wept in his longings.

He searched about in his mind for an adequate malediction for the indefinite cause, the thing upon which men turn the words of final blame. It—whatever it was—was responsible for him, he said. There lay the fault.

The haste of the column to reach the battle seemed to the forlorn young man to be something much finer than stout fighting. Heroes, he thought, could find excuses in that long seething lane. They could retire with perfect self-respect and make excuses to the stars.

He wondered what those men had eaten that they could be in such haste to force their way to grim chances of death. As he watched, his envy grew until he thought that he wished to change lives with one of them. He would have liked to have used a tremendous force, he said, throw off himself and become a better. Swift pictures of himself, apart, yet in himself, came to him—a blue desperate figure leading lurid charges with one knee forward and a broken blade high—a blue, determined figure standing before a crimson and steel assault, getting calmly killed on a high place before the eyes of all. He thought of the magnificent pathos of his dead body.

These thoughts uplifted him. He felt the quiver of war desire. In his ears, he heard the ring of victory. He knew the frenzy of a rapid successful charge. The music of the trampling feet, the sharp voices, the clanking arms of the column near him made him soar on the red wings of war. For a few moments he was sublime.

He thought that he was about to start for the front. Indeed, he saw a picture of himself, dust-stained, haggard, panting, flying to the front at the proper moment to seize and throttle the dark, leering witch of calamity.

Then the difficulties of the thing began to drag at him. He hesitated, balancing awkwardly on one foot.

He had no rifle; he could not fight with his hands, said he resentfully to his plan. Well, rifles could be had for the picking. They were extraordinarily profuse.

Also, he continued, it would be a miracle if he found his regiment. Well, he could fight with any regiment.

He started forward slowly. He stepped as if he expected to tread upon some explosive thing. Doubts and he were struggling.

He would truly be a worm if any of his comrades should see him returning thus, the marks of his flight upon him. There was a reply that the intent fighters did not care for what happened rearward saving that no hostile bayonets appeared there. In the battle-blur his face would, in a way, be hidden, like the face of a cowled man.

But then he said that his tireless fate would bring forth, when the strife lulled for a moment, a man to ask of him an explanation. In imagination he felt the scrutiny of his companions as he painfully labored through some lies.

Eventually, his courage expended itself upon these objections. The debates drained him of his fire.

He was not cast down by this defeat of his plan, for, upon studying the affair carefully, he could not but admit that the objections were very formidable.

Furthermore, various ailments had begun to cry out. In their presence he could not persist in flying high with the wings of war; they rendered it almost impossible for him to see himself in a heroic light. He tumbled headlong.

He discovered that he had a scorching thirst. His face was so dry and grimy that he thought he could feel his skin crackle. Each bone of his body had an ache in it, and seemingly threatened to break with each movement. His feet were like two sores. Also, his body was calling for food. It was more powerful than a direct hunger. There was a dull, weight-like feeling in his stomach, and, when he tried to walk, his head swayed and he tottered. He could not see with distinctness. Small patches of green mist floated before his vision.

While he had been tossed by many emotions, he had not been aware of ailments. Now they beset him and made clamor. As he was at last compelled to pay attention to them, his capacity for self-hate was multiplied. In despair, he declared that he was not like those others. He now conceded it to be impossible that he should ever become a hero. He was a craven loon. Those pictures of glory were piteous things. He groaned from his heart and went staggering off.

A certain mothlike quality within him kept him in the vicinity of the battle. He had a great desire to see and to get news. He wished to know who was winning.

He told himself that, despite his unprecedented suffering, he had never lost his greed for a victory, yet, he said, in a half-apologetic manner to his conscience, he could not but know that a defeat for the army this time might mean many favorable things for him. The blows of the enemy would splinter regiments into fragments. Thus, many men of courage, he considered, would be obliged to desert the colors and scurry like chickens. He would appear as one of them. They would be sullen brothers in distress, and he could then easily believe he had not run any farther or faster than they. And if he himself could believe in his virtuous perfection, he conceived that there would be small trouble in convincing all others.

He said, as if in excuse for this hope, that previously the army had encountered great defeats and in a few months had shaken off all blood and tradition of them, emerging as bright and valiant as a new one; thrusting out of sight the memory of disaster, and appearing with the valor and confidence of unconquered legions. The shrilling voices of the people at home would pipe dismally for a time, but various generals were usually compelled to listen to these ditties. He of course felt no compunctions for proposing a general as a sacrifice. He could not tell who the chosen for the barbs might be, so he could center no direct sympathy upon him. The people were afar and he did not conceive public opinion to be accurate at long range. It was quite probable they would hit the wrong man who, after he had recovered from his amazement would perhaps spend the rest of his days in writing replies to the songs of his alleged failure. It would be very unfortunate, no doubt, but in this case a general was of no consequence to the youth.

In a defeat there would be a roundabout vindication of himself. He thought it would prove, in a manner, that he had fled early because of his superior powers of perception. A serious prophet upon predicting a flood should be the first man to climb a tree. This would demonstrate that he was indeed a seer.

A moral vindication was regarded by the youth as a very important thing. Without salve, he could not, he thought, wear the sore badge of his dishonor through life. With his heart continually assuring him that he was despicable, he could not exist without making it, through his actions, apparent to all men.

If the army had gone gloriously on he would be lost. If the din meant that now his army's flags were tilted forward he was a condemned wretch. He would be compelled to doom himself to isolation. If the men were advancing, their indifferent feet were trampling upon his chances for a successful life.

As these thoughts went rapidly through his mind, he turned upon them and tried to thrust them away. He denounced himself as a villain. He said that he was the most unutterably selfish man in existence. His mind pictured the soldiers who would place their defiant bodies before the spear of the yelling battle fiend, and as he saw their dripping corpses on an imagined field, he said that he was their murderer.

Again he thought that he wished he was dead. He believed that he envied a corpse. Thinking of the slain, he achieved a great contempt for some of them, as if they were guilty for thus becoming lifeless. They might have been killed by lucky chances, he said, before they had had opportunities to flee or before they had been really tested. Yet they would receive laurels from tradition. He cried out bitterly that their crowns were stolen and their robes of glorious memories were shams. However, he still said that it was a great pity he was not as they.

A defeat of the army had suggested itself to him as a means of escape from the consequences of his fall. He considered, now, however, that it was useless to think of such a possibility. His education had been that success for that mighty blue machine was certain; that it would make victories as a contrivance turns out buttons. He presently discarded all his speculations in the other direction. He returned to the creed of soldiers.

When he perceived again that it was not possible for the army to be defeated, he tried to bethink him of a fine tale which he could take back to his regiment, and with it turn the expected shafts of derision.

But, as he mortally feared these shafts, it became impossible for him to invent a tale he felt he could trust. He experimented with many schemes, but threw them aside one by one as flimsy. He was quick to see vulnerable places in them all.

Furthermore, he was much afraid that some arrow of scorn might lay him mentally low before he could raise his protecting tale.

He imagined the whole regiment saying: "Where's Henry Fleming? He run, didn't 'e? Oh, my!" He recalled various persons who would be quite sure to leave him no peace about it. They would doubtless question him with sneers, and laugh at his stammering hesitation. In the next engagement they would try to keep watch of him to discover when he would run.

Wherever he went in camp, he would encounter insolent and lingeringly cruel stares. As he imagined himself passing near a crowd of comrades, he could hear some one say, "There he goes!"

Then, as if the heads were moved by one muscle, all the faces were turned toward him with wide, derisive grins. He seemed to hear some one make a humorous remark in a low tone. At it the others all crowed and cackled. He was a slang phrase.

CHAPTER XII

THE column that had butted stoutly at the obstacles in the roadway was barely out of the youth's sight before he saw dark waves of men come sweeping out of the woods and down through the fields. He knew at once that the steel fibers had been washed from their hearts. They were bursting from their coats and their equipments as from entanglements. They charged down upon him like terrified buffaloes.

Behind them blue smoke curled and clouded above the treetops, and through the thickets he could sometimes see a distant pink glare. The voices of the cannon were clamoring in interminable chorus.

The youth was horror-stricken. He stared in agony and amazement. He forgot that he was engaged in combating the universe. He threw aside his mental pamphlets on the philosophy of the retreated and rules for the guidance of the damned.

The fight was lost. The dragons were coming with invincible strides. The army, helpless in the matted thickets and blinded by the overhanging night, was going to be swallowed. War, the red animal, war, the blood-swollen god, would have bloated fill.

Within him something bade to cry out. He had the impulse to make a rallying speech, to sing a battle hymn, but he could only get his tongue to call into the air: "Why—why—what—what's th' matter?"

Soon he was in the midst of them. They were leaping and scampering all about him. Their blanched faces shone in the dusk. They seemed, for the most part, to be very burly men. The youth turned from one to another of them as they galloped along. His incoherent questions were lost. They were heedless of his appeals. They did not seem to see him.

They sometimes gabbled insanely. One huge man was asking of the sky: "Say, where de plank road? Where de plank road!" It was as if he had lost a child. He wept in his pain and dismay.

Presently, men were running hither and thither in all ways. The artillery booming, forward, rearward, and on the flanks made jumble of ideas of direction. Landmarks had vanished into the gathered gloom. The youth began to imagine that he had got into the center of the tremendous quarrel, and he could perceive no way out of it. From the mouths of the fleeing men came a thousand wild questions, but no one made answers.

The youth, after rushing about and throwing interrogations at the heedless bands of retreating infantry, finally clutched a man by the arm. They swung around face to face.

"Why—why——" stammered the youth struggling with his balking tongue.

The man screamed: "Let go me! Let go me!" His face was livid and his eyes were rolling uncontrolled. He was heaving and panting. He still grasped his rifle, perhaps having forgotten to release his hold upon it. He tugged frantically, and the youth being compelled to lean forward was dragged several paces.

"Let go me! Let go me!"

"Why—why——" stuttered the youth.

"Well, then!" bawled the man in a lurid rage. He adroitly and fiercely swung his rifle. It crushed upon the youth's head. The man ran on.

The youth's fingers had turned to paste upon the other's arm. The energy was smitten from his muscles. He saw the flaming wings of lightning flash before his vision. There was a deafening rumble of thunder within his head.

Suddenly his legs seemed to die. He sank writhing to the ground. He tried to arise. In his efforts against the numbing pain he was like a man wrestling with a creature of the air.

There was a sinister struggle.

Sometimes he would achieve a position half erect, battle with the air for a moment, and then fall again, grabbing at the grass. His face was of a clammy pallor. Deep groans were wrenched from him.

At last, with a twisting movement, he got upon his hands and knees, and from thence, like a babe trying to walk, to his feet. Pressing his hands to his temples he went lurching over the grass.

He fought an intense battle with his body. His dulled senses wished him to swoon and he opposed them stubbornly, his mind portraying unknown dangers and mutilations if he should fall upon the field. He went tall soldier fashion. He imagined secluded spots where he could fall and be unmolested. To search for one he strove against the tide of his pain.

Once he put his hand to the top of his head and timidly touched the wound. The scratching pain of the contact made him draw a long breath through his clinched teeth. His fingers were dabbed with blood. He regarded them with a fixed stare.

Around him he could hear the grumble of jolted cannon as the scurrying horses were lashed toward the front. Once, a young officer on a besplashed charger nearly ran him down. He turned and watched the mass of guns, men, and horses sweeping in a wide curve toward a gap in a fence. The officer was making excited motions with a gauntleted hand. The guns followed the teams with an air of unwillingness, of being dragged by the heels.

Some officers of the scattered infantry were cursing and railing like fishwives. Their scolding voices could be heard above the din. Into the unspeakable jumble in the roadway rode a squadron of cavalry. The faded yellow of their facings shone bravely. There was a mighty altercation.

The artillery were assembling as if for a conference.

The blue haze of evening was upon the field. The lines of forest were long purple shadows. One cloud lay along the western sky partly smothering the red.

As the youth left the scene behind him, he heard the guns suddenly roar out. He imagined them shaking in black rage. They belched and howled like brass devils guarding a gate. The soft air was filled with the tremendous remonstrance. With it came the shattering peal of opposing infantry. Turning to look behind him, he could see sheets of orange light illumine the shadowy distance. There were subtle and sudden lightnings in the far air. At times he thought he could see heaving masses of men.

He hurried on in the dusk. The day had faded until he could barely distinguish place for his feet. The purple darkness was filled with men who lectured and jabbered. Sometimes he could see them gesticulating against the blue and somber sky. There seemed to be a great ruck of men and munitions spread about in the forest and in the fields.

The little narrow roadway now lay lifeless. There were overturned wagons like sun-dried boulders. The bed of the former torrent was choked with the bodies of horses and splintered parts of war machines.

It had come to pass that his wound pained him but little. He was afraid to move rapidly, however, for a dread of disturbing it. He held his head very still and took many precautions against stumbling. He was filled with anxiety, and his face was pinched and drawn in anticipation of the pain of any sudden mistake of his feet in the gloom.

His thoughts, as he walked, fixed intently upon his hurt. There was a cool, liquid feeling about it and he imagined blood moving slowly down under his hair. His head seemed swollen to a size that made him think his neck to be inadequate.

The new silence of his wound made much worriment. The little blistering voices of pain that had called out from his scalp were, he thought, definite in their expression of danger. By them he believed that he could measure his plight. But when they remained ominously silent he became frightened and imagined terrible fingers that clutched into his brain.

Amid it he began to reflect upon various incidents and conditions of the past. He bethought him of certain meals his mother had cooked at home, in which those dishes of which he was particularly fond had occupied prominent positions. He saw the spread table. The pine walls of the kitchen were glowing in the warm light from the stove. Too, he remembered how he and his companions used to go from the schoolhouse to the bank of a shaded pool. He saw his clothes in disorderly array upon the grass of the bank. He felt the swash of the fragrant water upon his body. The leaves of the overhanging maple rustled with melody in the wind of youthful summer.

He was overcome presently by a dragging weariness. His head hung forward and his shoulders were stooped as if he were bearing a great bundle. His feet shuffled along the ground.

He held continuous arguments as to whether he should lie down and sleep at some near spot, or force himself on until he reached a certain haven. He often tried to dismiss the question, but his body persisted in rebellion and his senses nagged at him like pampered babies.

At last he heard a cheery voice near his shoulder: "Yeh seem t' be in a pretty bad way, boy?"

The youth did not look up, but he assented with thick tongue. "Uh!"

The owner of the cheery voice took him firmly by the arm. "Well," he said, with a round laugh, "I'm goin' your way. Th' hull gang is goin' your way. An' I guess I kin give yeh a lift." They began to walk like a drunken man and his friend.

As they went along, the man questioned the youth and assisted him with the replies like one manipulating the mind of a child. Sometimes he interjected anecdotes. "What reg'ment do yeh be'long teh? Eh? What's that? Th' 304th N' York? Why, what corps is that in? Oh, it is? Why, I thought they wasn't engaged t'-day—they're 'way over in th' center. Oh, they was, eh? Well, pretty nearly everybody got their share 'a fightin' t'-day. By dad, I give myself up fer dead any number 'a times. There was shootin' here an' shootin' there, an' hollerin' here an' hollerin' there, in th' damn' darkness, until I couldn't tell t' save m' soul which side I was on. Sometimes I thought I was sure 'nough from Ohier, an' other-times I could a' swore I was from th' bitter end of Florida. It was th' most mixed up dern thing I ever see. An' these here hull woods is a reg'lar mess. It'll be a miracle if we find our reg'ments t'-night. Pretty soon, though, we'll meet a-plenty of guards an' provost-guards, an' one thing an' another. Ho! there they go with an off'cer, I guess. Look at his hands a-draggin'. He's got all th' war he wants, I bet. He won't be talkin' so big about his reputation an' all when they go t' sawin' off his leg. Poor feller! My brother's got whiskers jest like that. How did yeh git 'way over here, anyhow? Your reg'ment is a long way from here, ain't it? Well, I guess we can find it. Yeh know there was a boy killed in my comp'ny t'-day that I thought th' world an' all of. Jack was a nice feller. By ginger, it hurt like thunder t' see ol' Jack jest git knocked flat. We was a-standin' purty peaceable for a spell, 'though there was men runnin' ev'ry way all 'round us, an' while we was a-standin' like that, 'long come a big fat feller. He began t' peck at Jack's elbow, an' he ses: 'Say, where's th' road t' th' river?' An' Jack, he never paid no attention, an' th' feller kept on a-peckin' at his elbow an' sayin': 'Say, where's th' road t' th' river?' Jack was a-lookin' ahead all th' time tryin' t' see th' Johnnies comin' through th' woods, an' he never paid no attention t' this big fat feller fer a long time, but at last he turned 'round an' he ses: 'Ah, go t' hell an' find th' road t' th' river!' An' jest then a shot slapped him bang on th' side th' head. He was a sergeant, too. Them was his last words. Thunder, I wish we was sure 'a findin' our reg'ments t'-night. It's goin' t' be long huntin'. But I guess we kin do it."

In the search that followed, the man of the cheery voice seemed to the youth to possess a wand of a magic kind. He threaded the mazes of the tangled forest with a strange fortune. In encounter with guards and patrols he displayed the keenness of a detective and the valor of a gamin. Obstacles fell before him and became of assistance. The youth, with his chin still on his breast, stood woodenly by while his companion beat ways and means out of sullen things.

The forest seemed a vast hive of men buzzing about in frantic circles, but the cheery man conducted the youth without mistakes, until at last he began to chuckle with glee and self-satisfaction. "Ah, there yeh are! See that fire?"

The youth nodded stupidly.

"Well, there's where your reg'ment is. An' now, good-by, ol' boy, good luck t' yeh."

A warm and strong hand clasped the youth's languid fingers for an instant, and then he heard a cheerful and audacious whistling as the man strode away. As he who had so befriended him was thus passing out of his life, it suddenly occurred to the youth that he had not once seen his face.

CHAPTER XIII

The youth went slowly toward the fire indicated by his departed friend. As he reeled, he bethought him of the welcome his comrades would give him. He had a conviction that he would soon feel in his sore heart the barbed missiles of ridicule. He had no strength to invent a tale; he would be a soft target.

He made vague plans to go off into the deeper darkness and hide, but they were all destroyed by the voices of exhaustion and pain from his body. His ailments, clamoring, forced him to seek the place of food and rest, at whatever cost.

He swung unsteadily toward the fire. He could see the forms of men throwing black shadows in the red light, and as he went nearer it became known to him in some way that the ground was strewn with sleeping men.

Of a sudden he confronted a black and monstrous figure. A rifle barrel caught some glinting beams. "Halt! halt!" He was dismayed for a moment, but he presently thought that he recognized the nervous voice. As he stood tottering before the rifle barrel, he called out: "Why, hello, Wilson, you— you here?"

The rifle was lowered to a position of caution and the loud soldier came slowly forward. He peered into the youth's face. "That you, Henry?"

"Yes it's—it's me."

"Well, well, ol' boy," said the other, "by ginger, I'm glad t' see yeh! I give yeh up fer a goner. I thought yeh was dead sure enough." There was husky emotion in his voice.

The youth found that now he could barely stand upon his feet. There was a sudden sinking of his forces. He thought he must hasten to produce his tale to protect him from the missiles already at the lips of his redoubtable comrades. So, staggering before the loud soldier, he began: "Yes, yes. I've—I've had an awful time. I've been all over. Way over on th' right. Ter'ble fightin' over there. I had an awful time. I got separated from th' reg'ment. Over on th' right, I got shot. In th' head. I never see sech fightin'. Awful time. I don't see how I could a' got separated from th' reg'ment. I got shot, too."

His friend had stepped forward quickly. "What? Got shot? Why didn't yeh say so first? Poor ol' boy, we must—hol' on a minnit; what am I doin'? I'll call Simpson."

Another figure at that moment loomed in the gloom. They could see that it was the corporal. "Who yeh talkin' to, Wilson?" he demanded. His voice was anger-toned. "Who yeh talkin' to? Yeh th' derndest sentinel—why— hello, Henry, you here? Why, I thought you was dead four hours ago! Great Jerusalem, they keep turnin' up every ten minutes or so! We thought we'd lost forty-two men by straight count, but if they keep on a-comin' this way, we'll get th' comp'ny all back by mornin' yit. Where was yeh?"

"Over on th' right. I got separated"—began the youth with considerable glibness.

But his friend had interrupted hastily. "Yes, an' he got shot in th' head an' he's in a fix, an' we must see t' him right away." He rested his rifle in the hollow of his left arm and his right around the youth's shoulder.

"Gee, it must hurt like thunder!" he said.

The youth leaned heavily upon his friend. "Yes, it hurts—hurts a good deal," he replied. There was a faltering in his voice.

"Oh," said the corporal. He linked his arm in the youth's and drew him forward. "Come on, Henry. I'll take keer 'a yeh."

As they went on together the loud private called out after them: "Put 'im t' sleep in my blanket, Simpson. An'—hol' on a minnit—here's my canteen. It's full 'a coffee. Look at his head by th' fire an' see how it looks. Maybe it's a pretty bad un. When I git relieved in a couple 'a minnits, I'll be over an' see t' him."

The youth's senses were so deadened that his friend's voice sounded from afar and he could scarcely feel the pressure of the corporal's arm. He submitted passively to the latter's directing strength. His head was in the old manner hanging forward upon his breast. His knees wobbled.

The corporal led him into the glare of the fire. "Now, Henry," he said, "let's have look at yer ol' head."

The youth sat down obediently and the corporal, laying aside his rifle, began to fumble in the bushy hair of his comrade. He was obliged to turn the other's head so that the full flush of the fire light would beam upon it. He puckered his mouth with a critical air. He drew back his lips and whistled through his teeth when his fingers came in contact with the splashed blood and the rare wound.

"Ah, here we are!" he said. He awkwardly made further investigations. "Jest as I thought," he added, presently. "Yeh've been grazed by a ball. It's raised a queer lump jest as if some feller had lammed yeh on th' head with a club. It stopped a-bleedin' long time ago. Th' most about it is that in th' mornin' yeh'll feel that a number ten hat wouldn't fit yeh. An' your head'll be all het up an' feel as dry as burnt pork. An' yeh may git a lot 'a other sicknesses, too, by mornin'. Yeh can't never tell. Still, I don't much think so. It's jest a damn' good belt on th' head, an' nothin' more. Now, you jest sit here an' don't move, while I go rout out th' relief. Then I'll send Wilson t' take keer 'a yeh."

The corporal went away. The youth remained on the ground like a parcel. He stared with a vacant look into the fire.

After a time he aroused, for some part, and the things about him began to take form. He saw that the ground in the deep shadows was cluttered with men, sprawling in every conceivable posture. Glancing narrowly into the more distant darkness, he caught occasional glimpses of visages that loomed pallid and ghostly, lit with a phosphorescent glow. These faces expressed in their lines the deep stupor of the tired soldiers. They made them appear like men drunk with wine. This bit of forest might have appeared to an ethereal wanderer as a scene of the result of some frightful debauch.

On the other side of the fire the youth observed an officer asleep, seated bolt upright, with his back against a tree. There was something perilous in his position. Badgered by dreams, perhaps, he swayed with little bounces and starts, like an old, toddy-stricken grandfather in a chimney corner. Dust and stains were upon his face. His lower jaw hung down as if lacking strength to assume its normal position. He was the picture of an exhausted soldier after a feast of war.

He had evidently gone to sleep with his sword in his arms. These two had slumbered in an embrace, but the weapon had been allowed in time to fall unheeded to the ground. The brass-mounted hilt lay in contact with some parts of the fire.

Within the gleam of rose and orange light from the burning sticks were other soldiers, snoring and heaving, or lying deathlike in slumber. A few pairs of legs were struck forth, rigid and straight. The shoes displayed the mud or dust of marches and bits of rounded trousers, protruding from the blankets, showed rents and tears from hurried pitchings through the dense brambles.

The fire crackled musically. From it swelled light smoke. Overhead the foliage moved softly. The leaves, with their faces turned toward the blaze, were colored shifting hues of silver, often edged with red. Far off to the right, through a window in the forest, could be seen a handful of stars lying, like glittering pebbles, on the black level of the night.

Occasionally, in this low-arched hall, a soldier would arouse and turn his body to a new position, the experience of his sleep having taught him of uneven and objectionable places upon the ground under him. Or, perhaps, he would lift himself to a sitting posture, blink at the fire for an unintelligent moment, throw a swift glance at his prostrate companion, and then cuddle down again with a grunt of sleepy content.

The youth sat in a forlorn heap until his friend, the loud young soldier, came, swinging two canteens by their light strings. "Well, now, Henry, ol' boy," said the latter, "we'll have yeh fixed up in jest about a minnit."

He had the bustling ways of an amateur nurse. He fussed around the fire and stirred the sticks to brilliant exertions. He made his patient drink largely from the canteen that contained the coffee. It was to the youth a delicious draught. He tilted his head afar back and held the canteen long to his lips. The cool mixture went caressingly down his blistered throat. Having finished, he sighed with comfortable delight.

The loud young soldier watched his comrade with an air of satisfaction. He later produced an extensive handkerchief from his pocket. He folded it into a manner of bandage and soused water from the other canteen upon the middle of it. This crude arrangement he bound over the youth's head, tying the ends in a queer knot at the back of the neck.

"There," he said, moving off and surveying his deed, "yeh look like th' devil, but I bet yeh feel better."

The youth contemplated his friend with grateful eyes. Upon his aching and swelling head the cold cloth was like a tender woman's hand.

"Yeh don't holler ner say nothin'," remarked his friend approvingly. "I know I'm a blacksmith at takin' keer 'a sick folks, an' yeh never squeaked. Yer a good un, Henry. Most 'a men would a' been in th' hospital long ago. A shot in th' head ain't foolin' business."

The youth made no reply, but began to fumble with the buttons of his jacket.

"Well, come, now," continued his friend, "come on. I must put yeh t' bed an' see that yeh git a good night's rest."

The other got carefully erect, and the loud young soldier led him among the sleeping forms lying in groups and rows. Presently he stooped and picked up his blankets. He spread the rubber one upon the ground and placed the woolen one about the youth's shoulders.

"There now," he said, "lie down an' git some sleep."

The youth, with his manner of doglike obedience, got carefully down like a crone stooping. He stretched out with a murmur of relief and comfort. The ground felt like the softest couch.

But of a sudden he ejaculated: "Hol' on a minnit! Where you goin' t' sleep?"

His friend waved his hand impatiently. "Right down there by yeh."

"Well, but hol' on a minnit," continued the youth. "What yeh goin' t' sleep in? I've got your——"

The loud young soldier snarled: "Shet up an' go on t' sleep. Don't be makin' a damn' fool 'a yerself," he said severely.

After the reproof the youth said no more. An exquisite drowsiness had spread through him. The warm comfort of the blanket enveloped him and made a gentle languor. His head fell forward on his crooked arm and his weighted lids went slowly down over his eyes. Hearing a splatter of musketry from the distance, he wondered indifferently if those men sometimes slept. He gave a long sigh, snuggled down into his blankets, and in a moment was like his comrades.

CHAPTER XIV

WHEN the youth awoke it seemed to him that he had been asleep for a thousand years, and he felt sure that he opened his eyes upon an unexpected world. Gray mists were slowly shifting before the first efforts of the sunrays. An impending splendor could be seen in the eastern sky. An icy dew had chilled his face, and immediately upon arousing he curled farther down into his blankets. He stared for a while at the leaves overhead, moving in a heraldic wind of the day.

The distance was splintering and blaring with the noise of fighting. There was in the sound an expression of a deadly persistency, as if it had not begun and was not to cease.

About him were the rows and groups of men that he had dimly seen the previous night. They were getting a last draught of sleep before the awakening. The gaunt, careworn features and dusty figures were made plain by this quaint light at the dawning, but it dressed the skin of the men in corpselike hues and made the tangled limbs appear pulseless and dead. The youth started up with a little cry when his eyes first swept over this motionless mass of men, thick-spread upon the ground, pallid, and in strange postures. His disordered mind interpreted the hall of the forest as a charnel place. He believed for an instant that he was in the house of the dead, and he did not dare to move lest these corpses start up, squalling and squawking. In a second, however, he achieved his proper mind. He swore a complicated oath at himself. He saw that this somber picture was not a fact of the present, but a mere prophecy.

He heard then the noise of a fire crackling briskly in the cold air, and turning his head, he saw his friend pottering busily about a small blaze. A few other figures moved in the fog, and he heard the hard cracking of axe blows.

Suddenly there was a hollow rumbling of drums. A distant bugle sang faintly. Similar sounds, varying in strength, came from near and far over the forest. The bugles called to each other like brazen gamecocks. The near thunder of the regimental drums rolled.

The body of men in the woods rustled. There was a general uplifting of heads. A murmuring of voices broke upon the air. In it there was much bass of grumbling oaths. Strange gods were addressed in condemnation of the early hours necessary to correct war. An officer's peremptory tenor rang out and quickened the stiffened movement of the men. The tangled limbs unraveled. The corpse-hued faces were hidden behind fists that twisted slowly in the eye sockets.

The youth sat up and gave vent to an enormous yawn. "Thunder!" he remarked petulantly. He rubbed his eyes, and then putting up his hand felt carefully of the bandage over his wound. His friend, perceiving him to be awake, came from the fire. "Well, Henry, ol' man, how do yeh feel this mornin'?" he demanded.

The youth yawned again. Then he puckered his mouth to a little pucker. His head, in truth, felt precisely like a melon, and there was an unpleasant sensation at his stomach.

"Oh, Lord, I feel pretty bad," he said.

"Thunder!" exclaimed the other. "I hoped ye'd feel all right this mornin'. Let's see th' bandage—I guess it's slipped." He began to tinker at the wound in rather a clumsy way until the youth exploded.

"Gosh-dern it!" he said in sharp irritation; "you're the hangdest man I ever saw! You wear muffs on your hands. Why in good thunderation can't you be more easy? I'd rather you'd stand off an' throw guns at it. Now, go slow, an' don't act as if you was nailing down carpet."

He glared with insolent command at his friend, but the latter answered soothingly. "Well, well, come now, an' git some grub," he said. "Then, maybe, yeh'll feel better."

At the fireside the loud young soldier watched over his comrade's wants with tenderness and care. He was very busy marshaling the little black vagabonds of tin cups and pouring into them the streaming, iron colored mixture from a small and sooty tin pail. He had some fresh meat, which he roasted hurriedly upon a stick. He sat down then and contemplated the youth's appetite with glee.

The youth took note of a remarkable change in his comrade since those days of camp life upon the river bank. He seemed no more to be continually regarding the proportions of his personal prowess. He was not furious at small words that pricked his conceits. He was no more a loud young soldier. There was about him now a fine reliance. He showed a quiet belief in his purposes and his abilities. And this inward confidence evidently enabled him to be indifferent to little words of other men aimed at him.

The youth reflected. He had been used to regarding his comrade as a blatant child with an audacity grown from his inexperience, thoughtless, headstrong, jealous, and filled with a tinsel courage. A swaggering babe accustomed to strut in his own dooryard. The youth wondered where had been born these new eyes; when his comrade had made the great discovery that there were many men who would refuse to be subjected by him. Apparently, the other had now climbed a peak of wisdom from which he could perceive himself as a very wee thing. And the youth saw that ever after it would be easier to live in his friend's neighborhood.

His comrade balanced his ebony coffee cup on his knee. "Well, Henry," he said, "what d'yeh think th' chances are? D'yeh think we'll wallop 'em?"

The youth considered for a moment. "Day-be'fore-yesterday," he finally replied, with boldness, "you would 'a' bet you'd lick the hull kit-an'-boodle all by yourself."

His friend looked a trifle amazed. "Would I?" he asked. He pondered. "Well, perhaps I would," he decided at last. He stared humbly at the fire.

The youth was quite disconcerted at this surprising reception of his remarks. "Oh, no, you wouldn't either," he said, hastily trying to retrace.

But the other made a deprecating gesture. "Oh, yeh needn't mind, Henry," he said. "I believe I was a pretty big fool in those days." He spoke as after a lapse of years.

There was a little pause.

"All th' officers say we've got th' rebs in a pretty tight box," said the friend, clearing his throat in a commonplace way. "They all seem t' think we've got 'em jest where we want 'em."

"I don't know about that," the youth replied. "What I seen over on th' right makes me think it was th' other way about. From where I was. it looked as if we was gettin' a good poundin' yestirday."

"D'yeh think so?" inquired the friend. "I thought we handled 'em pretty rough yestirday."

"Not a bit," said the youth. "Why, lord, man, you didn't see nothing of the fight. Why!" Then a sudden thought came to him. "Oh! Jim Conklin's dead."

His friend started. "What? Is he? Jim Conklin?"

The youth spoke slowly. "Yes. He's dead. Shot in th' side."

"Yeh don't say so. Jim Conklin . . . poor cuss!"

All about them were other small fires surrounded by men with their little black utensils. From one of these near came sudden sharp voices in a row. It appeared that two light-footed soldiers had been teasing a huge, bearded man, causing him to spill coffee upon his blue knees. The man had gone into a rage and had sworn comprehensively. Stung by his language, his tormentors had immediately bristled at him with a great show of resenting unjust oaths. Possibly there was going to be a fight.

The friend arose and went over to them, making pacific motions with his arms. "Oh, here, now, boys, what's th' use?" he said. "We'll be at th' rebs in less'n an hour. What's th' good fightin' 'mong ourselves?"

One of the light-footed soldiers turned upon him red-faced and violent. "Yeh needn't come around here with yer preachin'. I s'pose yeh don't approve 'a fightin' since Charley Morgan licked yeh; but I don't see what business this here is 'a yours or anybody else."

"Well, it ain't," said the friend mildly. "Still I hate t' see——"

That was a tangled argument.

"Well, he——," said the two, indicating their opponent with accusative forefingers.

The huge soldier was quite purple with rage. He pointed at the two soldiers with his great hand, extended clawlike. "Well, they——"

But during this argumentative time the desire to deal blows seemed to pass, although they said much to each other. Finally the friend returned to his old seat. In a short while the three antagonists could be seen together in an amiable bunch.

"Jimmie Rogers ses I'll have t' fight him after th' battle t'-day," announced the friend as he again seated himself. "He ses he don't allow no interferin' in his business. I hate t' see th' boys fightin' 'mong themselves."

The youth laughed. "Yer changed a good bit. Yeh ain't at all like yeh was. I remember when you an' that Irish feller——" He stopped and laughed again.

"No, I didn't use t' be that way," said his friend thoughtfully. "That's true 'nough."

"Well, I didn't mean——" began the youth.

The friend made another deprecatory gesture. "Oh, yeh needn't mind, Henry."

There was another little pause.

"Th' reg'ment lost over half th' men yestirday," remarked the friend eventually. "I thought a course they was all dead, but, laws, they kep' a-comin' back last night until it seems, after all, we didn't lose but a few.

They'd been scattered all over, wanderin' around in th' woods, fightin' with other reg'ments, an' everything. Jest like you done."

"So?" said the youth.

CHAPTER XV

THE regiment was standing at order arms at the side of a lane, waiting for the command to march, when suddenly the youth remembered the little packet enwrapped in a faded yellow envelope which the loud young soldier with lugubrious words had intrusted to him. It made him start. He uttered an exclamation and turned toward his comrade.

"Wilson!"

His friend, at his side in the ranks, was thoughtfully staring down the road. From some cause his expression was at that moment very meek. The youth, regarding him with sidelong glances, felt impelled to change his purpose. "Oh, nothing," he said.

His friend turned his head in some surprise, "Why, what was yeh goin' t' say?"

"Oh, nothin'," repeated the youth.

He resolved not to deal the little blow. It was sufficient that the fact made him glad. It was not necessary to knock his friend on the head with the misguided packet.

He had been possessed of much fear of his friend, for he saw how easily questionings could make holes in his feelings. Lately, he had assured himself that the altered comrade would not tantalize him with a persistent curiosity, but he felt certain that during the first period of leisure his friend would ask him to relate his adventures of the previous day.

He now rejoiced in the possession of a small weapon with which he could prostrate his comrade at the first signs of a cross-examination. He was master. It would now be he who could laugh and shoot the shafts of derision.

His friend had, in a weak hour, spoken with sobs of his own death. He had delivered a melancholy oration previous to his funeral, and had doubtless, in the packet of letters, presented various keepsakes to relatives. But he had not died, and thus he had delivered himself into the hands of the youth.

The latter felt immensely superior to his friend, but he inclined to condescension. He adopted toward him an air of patronizing good humor.

His self-pride was now entirely restored. In the shade of its flourishing growth he stood with braced and self-confident legs, and since nothing could now be discovered he did not shrink from an encounter with the eyes of judges, and allowed no thoughts of his own to keep him from an attitude of manfulness. He had performed his mistakes in the dark, so he was still a man.

Indeed, when he remembered his fortunes of yesterday, and looked at them from a distance he began to see something fine there. He had license to be pompous and veteranlike.

His panting agonies of the past he put out of his sight.

In the present, he declared to himself that it was only the doomed and the damned who roared with sincerity at circumstance. Few but they ever did it. A man with a full stomach and the respect of his fellows had no business to scold about anything that he might think to be wrong in the ways of the universe, or even with the ways of society. Let the unfortunates rail; the others may play marbles.

He did not give a great deal of thought to these battles that lay directly before him. It was not essential that he should plan his ways in regard to them. He had been taught that many obligations of a life were easily avoided. The lessons of yesterday had been that retribution was a laggard and blind. With these facts before him he did not deem it necessary that he should become feverish over the possibilities of the ensuing twenty-four hours. He could leave much to chance. Besides, a faith in himself had secretly blossomed. There was a little flower of confidence growing within him. He was now a man of experience. He had been out among the dragons, he said, and he assured himself that they were not so hideous as he had imagined them. Also, they were inaccurate; they did not sting with precision. A stout heart often defied, and, defying, escaped.

And, furthermore, how could they kill him who was the chosen of gods and doomed to greatness?

He remembered how some of the men had run from the battle. As he recalled their terror-struck faces he felt a scorn for them. They had surely been more fleet and more wild than was absolutely necessary. They were weak mortals. As for himself, he had fled with discretion and dignity.

He was aroused from this reverie by his friend, who, having hitched about nervously and blinked at the trees for a time, suddenly coughed in an introductory way, and spoke.

"Fleming!"

"What?"

The friend put his hand up to his mouth and coughed again. He fidgeted in his jacket.

"Well," he gulped, at last, "I guess yeh might as well give me back them letters." Dark, prickly blood had flushed into his cheeks and brow.

"All right, Wilson," said the youth. He loosened two buttons of his coat, thrust in his hand, and brought forth the packet. As he extended it to his friend the latter's face was turned from him.

He had been slow in the act of producing the packet because during it he had been trying to invent a remarkable comment upon the affair. He could conjure nothing of sufficient point. He was compelled to allow his friend to escape unmolested with his packet. And for this he took unto himself considerable credit. It was a generous thing.

His friend at his side seemed suffering great shame. As he contemplated him, the youth felt his heart grow more strong and stout. He had never been compelled to blush in such manner for his acts; he was an individual of extraordinary virtues.

He reflected, with condescending pity: "Too bad! Too bad! The poor devil, it makes him feel tough!"

After this incident, and as he reviewed the battle pictures he had seen, he felt quite competent to return home and make the hearts of the people glow with stories of war. He could see himself in a room of warm tints telling tales to listeners. He could exhibit laurels. They were insignificant; still, in a district where laurels were infrequent, they might shine.

He saw his gaping audience picturing him as the central figure in blazing scenes. And he imagined the consternation and ejaculations of his mother and the young lady at the seminary as they drank his recitals. Their vague feminine formula for beloved ones doing brave deeds on the field of battle without risk of life would be destroyed.

CHAPTER XVI

A SPUTTERING of musketry was always to be heard. Later, the cannon had entered the dispute. In the fog-filled air their voices made a thudding sound. The reverberations were continued. This part of the world led a strange, battleful existence.

The youth's regiment was marched to relieve a command that had lain long in some damp trenches. The men took positions behind a curving line of rifle pits that had been turned up, like a large furrow, along the line of woods. Before them was a level stretch, peopled with short, deformed stumps. From the woods beyond came the dull popping of the skirmishers and pickets, firing in the fog. From the right came the noise of a terrific fracas.

The men cuddled behind the small embankment and sat in easy attitudes awaiting their turn. Many had their backs to the firing. The youth's friend lay down, buried his face in his arms, and almost instantly, it seemed, he was in a deep sleep.

The youth leaned his breast against the brown dirt and peered over at the woods and up and down the line. Curtains of trees interfered with his ways of vision. He could see the low line of trenches but for a short distance. A few idle flags were perched on the dirt hills. Behind them were rows of dark bodies with a few heads sticking curiously over the top.

Always the noise of skirmishers came from the woods on the front and left, and the din on the right had grown to frightful proportions. The guns were roaring without an instant's pause for breath. It seemed that the cannon had come from all parts and were engaged in a stupendous wrangle. It became impossible to make a sentence heard.

The youth wished to launch a joke—a quotation from newspapers. He desired to say, "All quiet on the Rappahannock," but the guns refused to permit even a comment upon their uproar. He never successfully concluded the sentence. But at last the guns stopped, and among the men in the rifle pits rumors again flew, like birds, but they were now for the most part black creatures who flapped their wings drearily near to the ground and refused to rise on any wings of hope. The men's faces grew doleful from the interpreting of omens. Tales of hesitation and uncertainty on the part of those high in place and responsibility came to their ears. Stories of disaster were borne into their minds with many proofs. This din of musketry on the right, growing like a released genie of sound, expressed and emphasized the army's plight.

The men were disheartened and began to mutter. They made gestures expressive of the sentence: "Ah, what more can we do?" And it could always be seen that they were bewildered by the alleged news and could not fully comprehend a defeat.

Before the gray mists had been totally obliterated by the sunrays, the regiment was marching in a spread column that was retiring carefully through the woods. The disordered, hurrying lines of the enemy could sometimes be seen down through the groves and little fields. They were yelling, shrill and exultant.

At this sight the youth forgot many personal matters and became greatly enraged. He exploded in loud sentences. "B'jiminey, we're generaled by a lot 'a lunkheads."

"More than one feller has said that t'-day," observed a man.

His friend, recently aroused, was still very drowsy. He looked behind him until his mind took in the meaning of the movement. Then he sighed. "Oh, well, I s'pose we got licked," he remarked sadly.

The youth had a thought that it would not be handsome for him to freely condemn other men. He made an attempt to restrain himself, but the words upon his tongue were too bitter. He presently began a long and intricate denunciation of the commander of the forces.

"Mebbe, it wa'n't all his fault—not all together. He did th' best he knowed. It's our luck t' git licked often," said his friend in a weary tone. He was trudging along with stooped shoulders and shifting eyes like a man who has been caned and kicked.

"Well, don't we fight like the devil? Don't we do all that men can?" demanded the youth loudly.

He was secretly dumbfounded at this sentiment when it came from his lips. For a moment his face lost its valor and he looked guiltily about him. But no one questioned his right to deal in such words, and presently he recovered his air of courage. He went on to repeat a statement he had heard going from group to group at the camp that morning. "The brigadier said he never saw a new reg'ment fight the way we fought yestirday, didn' he? And we didn't do better than any other reg'ment, did we? Well, then, you can't say it's th' army's fault, can you?"

In his reply, the friend's voice was stern. " 'A course not," he said. "No man dare say we don't fight like th' devil. No man will ever dare say it. Th' boys fight like hell-roosters. But still—still, we don't have no luck."

"Well, then, if we fight like the devil an' don't ever whip, it must be the general's fault," said the youth grandly and decisively. "And I don't see any sense in fighting and fighting and fighting, yet always losing through some derned old lunkhead of a general."

A sarcastic man who was tramping at the youth's side, then spoke lazily. "Mebbe yeh think yeh fit th' hull battle yestirday, Fleming," he remarked.

The speech pierced the youth. Inwardly he was reduced to an abject pulp by these chance words. His legs quaked privately. He cast a frightened glance at the sarcastic man.

"Why, no," he hastened to say in a conciliating voice. "I don't think I fought the whole battle yesterday."

But the other seemed innocent of any deeper meaning. Apparently, he had no information. It was merely his habit. "Oh!" he replied in the same tone of calm derision.

The youth, nevertheless, felt a threat. His mind shrank from going nearer to the danger, and thereafter he was silent. The significance of the sarcastic man's words took from him all loud moods that would make him appear prominent. He became suddenly a modest person.

There was low-toned talk among the troops. The officers were impatient and snappy, their countenances clouded with the tales of misfortune. The troops, sifting through the forest, were sullen. In the youth's company once a man's laugh rang out. A dozen soldiers turned their faces quickly toward him and frowned with vague displeasure.

The noise of firing dogged their footsteps. Sometimes, it seemed to be driven a little way, but it always returned again with increased insolence. The men muttered and cursed, throwing black looks in its direction.

In a clear space the troops were at last halted. Regiments and brigades, broken and detached through their encounters with thickets, grew together again and lines were faced toward the pursuing bark of the enemy's infantry.

This noise, following like the yellings of eager, metallic hounds, increased to a loud and joyous burst, and then, as the sun went serenely up the sky, throwing illuminating rays into the gloomy thickets, it broke forth into prolonged pealings. The woods began to crackle as if afire.

"Whoop-a-dadee," said a man, "here we are! Everybody fightin'. Blood an' destruction."

"I was willin' t' bet they'd attack as soon as th' sun got fairly up," savagely asserted the lieutenant who commanded the youth's company. He jerked without mercy at his little mustache. He strode to and fro with dark dignity in the rear of his men, who were lying down behind whatever protection they had collected.

A battery had trundled into position in the rear and was thoughtfully shelling the distance. The regiment, unmolested as yet, awaited the moment when the gray shadows of the woods before them should be slashed by the lines of flame. There was much growling and swearing.

"Good Gawd," the youth grumbled, "we're always being chased around like rats! It makes me sick. Nobody seems to know where we go or why we go. We just get fired around from pillar to post and get licked here and get licked there, and nobody knows what it's done for. It makes a man feel like a damn' kitten in a bag. Now, I'd like to know what the eternal thunders we was marched into these woods for anyhow, unless it was to give the rebs a regular pot shot at us. We came in here and got our legs all tangled up in these cussed briers, and then we begin to fight and the rebs had an easy time of it. Don't tell me it's just luck! I know better. It's this derned old——"

The friend seemed jaded, but he interrupted his comrade with a voice of calm confidence. "It'll turn out all right in th' end," he said.

"Oh, the devil it will! You always talk like a dog-hanged parson. Don't tell me! I know——"

At this time there was an interposition by the savage-minded lieutenant, who was obliged to vent some of his inward dissatisfaction upon his men. "You boys shut right up! There's no need 'a your wastin' your breath in long-winded arguments about this an' that an' th' other. You've been jawin' like a lot 'a old hens. All you've got t' do is to fight, an' you'll get plenty 'a that t' do in about ten minutes. Less talkin' an' more fightin' is what's best for you boys. I never saw sech gabbling jackasses."

He paused, ready to pounce upon any man who might have the temerity to reply. No words being said, he resumed his dignified pacing.

"There's too much chin music an' too little fightin' in this war, anyhow," he said to them, turning his head for a final remark.

The day had grown more white, until the sun shed its full radiance upon the thronged forest. A sort of a gust of battle came sweeping toward that part of the line where lay the youth's regiment. The front shifted a trifle to meet it squarely. There was a wait. In this part of the field there passed slowly the intense moments that precede the tempest.

A single rifle flashed in a thicket before the regiment. In an instant it was joined by many others. There was a mighty song of clashes and crashes that went sweeping through the woods. The guns in the rear, aroused and enraged by shells that had been thrown burr-like at them, suddenly involved themselves in a hideous altercation with another band of guns. The battle roar settled to a rolling thunder, which was a single long explosion.

In the regiment there was a peculiar kind of hesitation denoted in the attitudes of the men. They were worn, exhausted, having slept but little and labored much. They rolled their eyes toward the advancing battle as they stood awaiting the shock. Some shrank and flinched. They stood as men tied to stakes.

CHAPTER XVII

THIS advance of the enemy had seemed to the youth like a ruthless hunting. He began to fume with rage and exasperation. He beat his foot upon the ground, and scowled with hate at the swirling smoke that was approaching like a phantom flood. There was a maddening quality in this seeming resolution of the foe to give him no rest, to give him no time to sit down and think. Yesterday he had fought and had fled rapidly. There had been many adventures. For to-day he felt that he had earned opportunities for contemplative repose. He could have enjoyed portraying to uninitiated listeners various scenes at which he had been a witness or ably discussing the processes of war with other proved men. Too it was important that he should have time for physical recuperation. He was sore and stiff from his experiences. He had received his fill of all exertions, and he wished to rest.

But those other men seemed never to grow weary; they were fighting with their old speed. He had a wild hate for the relentless foe. Yesterday, when he had imagined the universe to be against him, he had hated it, little gods and big gods; to-day he hated the army of the foe with the same great hatred. He was not going to be badgered of his life, like a kitten chased by boys, he said. It was not well to drive men into final corners; at those moments they could all develop teeth and claws.

He leaned and spoke into his friend's ear. He menaced the words with a gesture. "If they keep on chasing us, by Gawd, they'd better watch out, Can't stand *too* much."

The friend twisted his head and made a calm reply. "If they keep on a-chasin' us they'll drive us all inteh th' river."

The youth cried out savagely at this statement. He crouched behind a little tree, with his eyes burning hatefully and his teeth set in a curlike snarl. The awkward bandage was still about his head, and upon it, over his wound, there was a spot of dry blood. His hair was wondrously tousled, and some straggling, moving locks hung over the cloth of the bandage down toward his forehead. His jacket and shirt were open at the throat, and exposed his young bronzed neck. There could be seen spasmodic gulpings at his throat.

His fingers twined nervously about his rifle. He wished that it was an engine of annihilating power. He felt that he and his companions were being taunted and derided from sincere convictions that they were poor and puny. His knowledge of his inability to take vengeance for it made his rage into a dark and stormy specter, that possessed him and made him dream of abominable cruelties. The tormentors were flies sucking insolently at his blood, and he thought that he would have given his life for a revenge of seeing their faces in pitiful plights.

The winds of battle had swept all about the regiment, until the one rifle, instantly followed by others, flashed in its front. A moment later the regiment roared forth its sudden and valiant retort. A dense wall of smoke settled slowly down. It was furiously slit and slashed by the knifelike fire from the rifles.

To the youth the fighters resembled animals tossed for a death struggle into a dark pit. There was a sensation that he and his followers, at bay, were pushing back, always pushing fierce onslaughts of creatures who were slippery. Their beams of crimson seemed to get no purchase upon the bodies of their foes; the latter seemed to evade them with ease, and come through, between, around, and about with unopposed skill.

When, in a dream, it occurred to the youth that his rifle was an impotent stick, he lost sense of everything but his hate, his desire to smash into pulp the glittering smile of victory which he could feel upon the faces of his enemies.

The blue smoke-swallowed line curled and writhed like a snake stepped upon. It swung its ends to and fro in an agony of fear and rage.

The youth was not conscious that he was erect upon his feet. He did not know the direction of the ground. Indeed, once he even lost the habit of balance and fell heavily. He was up again immediately. One thought went through the chaos of his brain at the time. He wondered if he had fallen because he had been shot. But the suspicion flew away at once. He did not think more of it.

He had taken up a first position behind the little tree, with a direct determination to hold it against the world. He had not deemed it possible that his army could that day succeed, and from this he felt the ability to fight harder. But the throng had surged in all ways, until he lost directions and locations, save that he knew where lay the enemy.

The flames bit him, and the hot smoke broiled his skin. His rifle barrel grew so hot that ordinarily he could not have borne it upon his palms; but he kept on stuffing cartridges into it, and pounding them with his clanking, bending ramrod. If he aimed at some changing form through the smoke, he pulled his trigger with a fierce grunt, as if he were dealing a blow of the fist with all his strength.

When the enemy seemed falling back before him and his fellows, he went instantly forward, like a dog who, seeing his foes lagging, turns and insists upon being pursued. And when he was compelled to retire again, he did it slowly, sullenly, taking steps of wrathful despair.

Once he, in his intent hate, was almost alone, and was firing, when all those near him had ceased. He was so engrossed in his occupation that he was not aware of a lull.

He was recalled by a hoarse laugh and a sentence that came to his ears in a voice of contempt and amazement. "Yeh infernal fool, don't yeh know enough t' quit when there ain't anything t' shoot at? Good Gawd!"

He turned then and, pausing with his rifle thrown half into position, looked at the blue line of his comrades. During this moment of leisure they seemed all to be engaged in staring with astonishment at him. They had become spectators. Turning to the front again he saw, under the lifted smoke, a deserted ground.

He looked bewildered for a moment. Then there appeared upon the glazed vacancy of his eyes a diamond point of intelligence. "Oh," he said, comprehending.

He returned to his comrades and threw himself upon the ground. He sprawled like a man who had been thrashed. His flesh seemed strangely on fire, and the sounds of the battle continued in his ears. He groped blindly for his canteen.

The lieutenant was crowing. He seemed drunk with fighting. He called out to the youth: "By heavens, if I had ten thousand wild cats like you I could tear th' stomach outa this war in less'n a week!" He puffed out his chest with large dignity as he said it.

Some of the men muttered and looked at the youth in awe-struck ways. It was plain that as he had gone on loading and firing and cursing without the proper intermission, they had found time to regard him. And they now looked upon him as a war devil.

The friend came staggering to him. There was some fright and dismay in his voice. "Are yeh all right, Fleming? Do yeh feel all right? There ain't nothin' th' matter with yeh, Henry, is there?"

"No," said the youth with difficulty. His throat seemed full of knobs and burs.

These incidents made the youth ponder. It was revealed to him that he had been a barbarian, a beast. He had fought like a pagan who defends his religion. Regarding it, he saw that it was fine, wild, and, in some ways, easy. He had been a tremendous figure, no doubt. By this struggle he had overcome obstacles which he had admitted to be mountains. They had fallen like paper peaks, and he was now what he called a hero. And he had not been aware of the process. He had slept and, awakening, found himself a knight.

He lay and basked in the occasional stares of his comrades. Their faces were varied in degrees of blackness from the burned powder. Some were utterly smudged. They were reeking with perspiration, and their breaths came hard and wheezing. And from these soiled expanses they peered at him.

"Hot work! Hot work!" cried the lieutenant deliriously. He walked up and down, restless and eager. Sometimes his voice could be heard in a wild, incomprehensible laugh.

When he had a particularly profound thought upon the science of war he always unconsciously addressed himself to the youth.

There was some grim rejoicing by the men.

"By thunder, I bet this army'll never see another new reg'ment like us!"

"You bet!"

"A dog, a woman, an' a walnut tree,
    Th' more yeh beat 'em, th' better they be!

That's like us."

"Lost a piler men, they did. If an' ol' woman swep' up th' woods she'd git a dustpanful."

"Yes, an' if she'll come around ag'in in 'bout an' hour she'll git a pile more."

The forest still bore its burden of clamor. From off under the trees came the rolling clatter of the musketry. Each distant thicket seemed a strange porcupine with quills of flame. A cloud of dark smoke, as from smoldering ruins, went up toward the sun now bright and gay in the blue, enameled sky.

CHAPTER XVIII

THE ragged line had respite for some minutes, but during its pause the struggle in the forest became magnified until the trees seemed to quiver from the firing and the ground to shake from the rushing of the men. The voices of the cannon were mingled in a long and interminable row. It seemed difficult to live in such an atmosphere. The chests of the men strained for a bit of freshness, and their throats craved water.

There was one shot through the body, who raised a cry of bitter lamentation when came this lull. Perhaps he had been calling out during the fighting also, but at that time no one had heard him. But now the men turned at the woeful complaints of him upon the ground.

"Who is it? Who is it?"

"It's Jimmie Rogers. Jimmie Rogers."

When their eyes first encountered him there was a sudden halt, as if they feared to go near. He was thrashing about in the grass, twisting his shuddering body into many strange postures. He was screaming loudly. This instant's hesitation seemed to fill him with a tremendous, fantastic contempt, and he damned them in shrieked sentences.

The youth's friend had a geographical illusion concerning a stream, and he obtained permission to go for some water. Immediately canteens were showered upon him. "Fill mine, will yeh?" "Bring me some, too." "And me, too." He departed, laden. The youth went with his friend, feeling a desire to throw his heated body onto the stream and, soaking there, drink quarts.

They made a hurried search for the supposed stream, but did not find it. "No water here," said the youth. They turned without delay and began to retrace their steps.

From their position as they again faced toward the place of the fighting, they could of course comprehend a greater amount of the battle than when their visions had been blurred by the hurling smoke of the line. They could see dark stretches winding along the land, and on one cleared space there was a row of guns making gray clouds, which were filled with large flashes of orange-colored flame. Over some foliage they could see the roof of a house. One window, glowing a deep murder red, shone squarely through the leaves. From the edifice a tall leaning tower of smoke went far into the sky.

Looking over their own troops, they saw mixed masses slowly getting into regular form. The sunlight made twinkling points of the bright steel.

To the rear there was a glimpse of a distant roadway as it curved over a slope. It was crowded with retreating infantry. From all the interwoven forest arose the smoke and bluster of the battle. The air was always occupied by a blaring.

Near where they stood shells were flip-flapping and hooting. Occasional bullets buzzed in the air and spanged into tree trunks. Wounded men and other stragglers were slinking through the woods.

Looking down an aisle of the grove, the youth and his companion saw a jangling general and his staff almost ride upon a wounded man who was crawling on his hands and knees. The general reined strongly at his charger's opened and foamy mouth and guided it with dextrous horsemanship past the man. The latter scrambled in wild and torturing haste. His strength evidently failed him as he reached a place of safety. One of his arms suddenly weakened, and he fell, sliding over upon his back. He lay stretched out, breathing gently.

A moment later the small, creaking cavalcade was directly in front of the two soldiers. Another officer, riding with the skillful abandon of a cowboy, galloped his horse to a position directly before the general. The two unnoticed foot soldiers made a little show of going on, but they lingered near in the desire to overhear the conversation. Perhaps, they thought, some great inner historical things would be said.

The general, whom the boys knew as the commander of their division, looked at the other officer and spoke coolly, as if he were criticising his clothes. "Th' enemy's formin' over there for another charge," he said. "It'll be directed against Whiterside, an' I fear they'll break through there unless we work like thunder t' stop them."

The other swore at his restive horse, and then cleared his throat. He made a gesture toward his cap. "It'll be hell t' pay stoppin' them," he said shortly.

"I presume so," remarked the general. Then he began to talk rapidly and in a lower tone. He frequently illustrated his words with a pointing finger. The two infantrymen could hear nothing until finally he asked: "What troops can you spare?"

The officer who rode like a cowboy reflected for an instant. "Well," he said, "I had to order in th' 12th to help th' 76th, an' I haven't really got any. But there's th' 304th. They fight like a lot 'a mule drivers. I can spare them best of any."

The youth and his friend exchanged glances of astonishment.

The general spoke sharply. "Get 'em ready, then. I'll watch developments from here, an' send you word when t' start them. It'll happen in five minutes."

As the other officer tossed his fingers toward his cap and, wheeling his horse, started away, the general called out to him in a sober voice: "I don't believe many of your mule drivers will get back."

The other shouted something in reply. He smiled.

With scared faces, the youth and his companion hurried back to the line.

These happenings had occupied an incredibly short time, yet the youth felt that in them he had been made aged. New eyes were given to him. And the most startling thing was to learn suddenly that he was very insignificant. The officer spoke of the regiment as if he referred to a broom. Some part of the woods needed sweeping, perhaps, and he merely indicated a broom in a tone properly indifferent to its fate. It was war, no doubt, but it appeared strange.

As the two boys approached the line, the lieutenant perceived them and swelled with wrath. "Fleming—Wilson—how long does it take yeh to git water, anyhow—where yeh been to."

But his oration ceased as he saw their eyes, which were large with great tales. "We're goin' t' charge—we're goin' t' charge!" cried the youth's friend, hastening with his news.

"Charge?" said the lieutenant. "Charge? Well, b'Gawd! Now; this is real fightin'." Over his soiled countenance there went a boastful smile. "Charge? Well, b'Gawd!"

A little group of soldiers surrounded the two youths. "Are we, sure 'nough? Well, I'll be derned! Charge? What fer? What at? Wilson, you're lyin'."

"I hope to die," said the youth's friend, pitching his tones to the key of angry remonstrance. "Sure as shooting, I tell you."

And the youth spoke in re-enforcement. "Not by a blame sight, he ain't lyin'. We heard 'em talkin'."

They caught sight of two mounted figures a short distance from them. One was the colonel of the regiment and the other was the officer who had received orders from the commander of the division. They were gesticulating at each other. The soldier, pointing at them, interpreted the scene.

One man had a final objection: "How could yeh hear 'em talkin'?" But the men, for a large part, nodded, admitting that previously the two friends had spoken truth.

They settled back into reposeful attitudes with airs of having accepted the matter. And they mused upon it, with a hundred varieties of expression. It was an engrossing thing to think about. Many tightened their belts carefully and hitched at their trousers.

A moment later the officers began to bustle among the men, pushing them into a more compact mass and into a better alignment. They chased those that straggled and fumed at a few men who seemed to show by their attitudes that they had decided to remain at that spot. They were like critical shepherds struggling with sheep.

Presently, the regiment seemed to draw itself up and heave a deep breath. None of the men's faces were mirrors of large thoughts. The soldiers were bended and stooped like sprinters before a signal. Many pairs of glinting eyes peered from the grimy faces toward the curtains of the deeper woods. They seemed to be engaged in deep calculations of time and distance.

They were surrounded by the noises of the monstrous altercation between the two armies. The world was fully interested in other matters. Apparently, the regiment had its small affair to itself.

The youth, turning, shot a quick, inquiring glance at his friend. The latter returned to him the same manner of look. They were the only ones who possessed an inner knowledge. "Mule drivers—hell t' pay—don't believe many will get back." It was an ironical secret. Still, they saw no hesitation in each other's faces, and they nodded a mute and unprotesting assent when a shaggy man near them said in a meek voice: "We'll git swallowed."

CHAPTER XIX

THE youth stared at the land in front of him. Its foliage now seemed to veil powers and horrors. He was unaware of the machinery of orders that started the charge, although from the corners of his eyes he saw an officer, who looked like a boy a-horseback, come galloping, waving his hat. Suddenly he felt a straining and heaving among the men. The line fell slowly forward like a toppling wall, and, with a convulsive gasp that was intended for a cheer, the regiment began its journey. The youth was pushed and jostled for a moment before he understood the movement at all, but directly he lunged ahead and began to run.

He fixed his eye upon a distant and prominent clump of trees where he had concluded the enemy were to be met, and he ran toward it as toward a goal. He had believed throughout that it was a mere question of getting over an unpleasant matter as quickly as possible, and he ran desperately, as if pursued for a murder. His face was drawn hard and tight with the stress of his endeavor. His eyes were fixed in a lurid glare. And with his soiled and disordered dress, his red and inflamed features surmounted by the dingy rag with its spot of blood, his wildly swinging rifle and banging accoutrements, he looked to be an insane soldier.

As the regiment swung from its position out into a cleared space the woods and thickets before it awakened. Yellow flames leaped toward it from many directions. The forest made a tremendous objection.

The line lurched straight for a moment. Then the right wing swung forward; it in turn was surpassed by the left. Afterward the center careered to the front until the regiment was a wedge-shaped mass, but an instant later the opposition of the bushes, trees, and uneven places on the ground split the command and scattered it into detached clusters.

The youth, light-footed, was unconsciously in advance. His eyes still kept note of the clump of trees. From all places near it the clannish yell of the enemy could be heard. The little flames of rifles leaped from it. The song of the bullets was in the air and shells snarled among the tree-tops. One tumbled directly into the middle of a hurrying group and exploded in crimson fury. There was an instant's spectacle of a man, almost over it, throwing up his hands to shield his eyes.

Other men, punched by bullets, fell in grotesque agonies. The regiment left a coherent trail of bodies.

They had passed into a clearer atmosphere. There was an effect like a revelation in the new appearance of the landscape. Some men working madly at a battery were plain to them, and the opposing infantry's lines were defined by the gray walls and fringes of smoke.

It seemed to the youth that he saw everything. Each blade of the green grass was bold and clear. He thought that he was aware of every change in the thin, transparent vapor that floated idly in sheets. The brown or gray trunks of the trees showed each roughness of their surfaces. And the men of the regiment, with their starting eyes and sweating faces, running madly, or falling, as if thrown headlong, to queer, heaped-up corpses—all were comprehended. His mind took a mechanical but firm impression, so that afterward everything was pictured and explained to him, save why he himself was there.

But there was a frenzy made from this furious rush. The men, pitching forward insanely, had burst into cheerings, moblike and barbaric, but tuned in strange keys that can arouse the dullard and the stoic. It made a mad enthusiasm that, it seemed, would be incapable of checking itself before granite and brass. There was the delirium that encounters despair and death, and is heedless and blind to the odds. It is a temporary but sublime absence of selfishness. And because it was of this order was the reason, perhaps, why the youth wondered, afterward, what reasons he could have had for being there.

Presently the straining pace ate up the energies of the men. As if by agreement, the leaders began to slacken their speed. The volleys directed against them had had a seeming windlike effect. The regiment snorted and blew. Among some stolid trees it began to falter and hesitate. The men, staring intently, began to wait for some of the distant walls of smoke to move and disclose to them the scene. Since much of their strength and their breath had vanished, they returned to caution. They were become men again.

The youth had a vague belief that he had run miles, and he thought, in a way, that he was now in some new and unknown land.

The moment the regiment ceased its advance the protesting splutter of musketry became a steadier roar. Long and accurate fringes of smoke spread out. From the top of a small hill came level belchings of yellow flame that caused an inhuman whistling in the air.

The men, halted, had opportunity to see some of their comrades dropping with moans and shrieks. A few lay under foot, still or wailing. And now for an instant the men stood, their rifles slack in their hands, and watched the regiment dwindle. They appeared dazed and stupid. This spectacle seemed to paralyze them, overcome them with a fatal fascination. They stared woodenly at the sights, and, lowering their eyes, looked from face to face. It was a strange pause, and a strange silence.

Then, above the sounds of the outside commotion, arose the roar of the lieutenant. He strode suddenly forth, his infantile features black with rage.

"Come on, yeh fools!" he bellowed. "Come on! Yeh can't stay here. Yeh must come on." He said more, but much of it could not be understood.

He started rapidly forward, with his head turned toward the men. "Come on," he was shouting. The men stared with blank and yokel-like eyes at him. He was obliged to halt and retrace his steps. He stood then with his back to the enemy and delivered gigantic curses into the faces of the men. His body vibrated from the weight and force of his imprecations. And he could string oaths with the facility of a maiden who strings beads.

The friend of the youth aroused. Lurching suddenly forward and dropping to his knees, he fired an angry shot at the persistent woods. This action awakened the men. They huddled no more like sheep. They seemed suddenly to bethink them of their weapons, and at once commenced firing. Belabored by their officers, they began to move forward. The regiment, involved like a cart involved in mud and muddle, started unevenly with many jolts and jerks. The men stopped now every few paces to fire and load, and in this manner moved slowly on from trees to trees.

The flaming opposition in their front grew with their advance until it seemed that all forward ways were barred by the thin leaping tongues, and off to the right an ominous demonstration could sometimes be dimly discerned. The smoke lately generated was in confusing clouds that made it difficult for the regiment to proceed with intelligence. As he passed through each curling mass the youth wondered what would confront him on the farther side.

The command went painfully forward until an open space interposed between them and the lurid lines. Here, crouching and cowering behind some trees, the men clung with desperation, as if threatened by a wave. They looked wild-eyed, and as if amazed at this furious disturbance they had stirred. In the storm there was an ironical expression of their importance. The faces of the men, too, showed a lack of a certain feeling of responsibility for being there. It was as if they had been driven. It was the dominant animal failing to remember in the supreme moments the forceful causes of various superficial qualities. The whole affair seemed incomprehensible to many of them.

As they halted thus the lieutenant again began to bellow profanely. Regardless of the vindictive threats of the bullets, he went about coaxing, berating, and bedamning. His lips, that were habitually in a soft and childlike curve, were now writhed into unholy contortions. He swore by all possible deities.

Once he grabbed the youth by the arm. "Come on, yeh lunkhead!" he roared. "Come on! We'll all git killed if we stay here. We've on'y got t' go across that lot. An' then"—the remainder of his idea disappeared in a blue haze of curses.

The youth stretched forth his arm. "Cross there?" His mouth was puckered in doubt and awe.

"Certainly. Jest 'cross th' lot! We can't stay here," screamed the lieutenant. He poked his face close to the youth and waved his bandaged hand. "Come on!" Presently he grappled with him as if for a wrestling bout. It was as if he planned to drag the youth by the ear on to the assault.

The private felt a sudden unspeakable indignation against his officer. He wrenched fiercely and shook him off.

"Come on yerself, then," he yelled. There was a bitter challenge in his voice.

They galloped together down the regimental front. The friend scrambled after them. In front of the colors the three men began to bawl: "Come on! come on!" They danced and gyrated like tortured savages.

The flag, obedient to these appeals, bended its glittering form and swept toward them. The men wavered in indecision for a moment, and then with a long, wailful cry the dilapidated regiment surged forward and began its new journey.

Over the field went the scurrying mass. It was a handful of men splattered into the faces of the enemy. Toward it instantly sprang the yellow tongues. A vast quantity of blue smoke hung before them. A mighty banging made ears valueless.

The youth ran like a madman to reach the woods before a bullet could discover him. He ducked his head low, like a football player. In his haste his eyes almost closed, and the scene was a wild blur. Pulsating saliva stood at the corners of his mouth.

Within him, as he hurled himself forward, was born a love, a despairing fondness for this flag which was near him. It was a creation of beauty and invulnerability. It was a goddess, radiant, that bended its form with an imperious gesture to him. It was a woman, red and white, hating and loving, that called him with the voice of his hopes. Because no harm could come to it he endowed it with power. He kept near, as if it could be a saver of lives, and an imploring cry went from his mind.

In the mad scramble he was aware that the color sergeant flinched suddenly, as if struck by a bludgeon. He faltered, and then became motionless, save for his quivering knees.

He made a spring and a clutch at the pole. At the same instant his friend grabbed it from the other side. They jerked at it, stout and furious, but the color sergeant was dead, and the corpse would not relinquish its trust. For a moment there was a grim encounter. The dead man, swinging with bended back, seemed to be obstinately tugging, in ludicrous and awful ways, for the possession of the flag.

It was past in an instant of time. They wrenched the flag furiously from the dead man, and, as they turned again, the corpse swayed forward with bowed head. One arm swung high, and the curved hand fell with heavy protest on the friend's unheeding shoulder.

CHAPTER XX

WHEN the two youths turned with the flag they saw that much of the regiment had crumbled away, and the dejected remnant was coming back. The men, having hurled themselves in projectile fashion, had presently expended their forces. They slowly retreated, with their faces still toward the spluttering woods, and their hot rifles still replying to the din. Several officers were giving orders, their voices keyed to screams.

"Where in hell yeh goin'?" the lieutenant was asking in a sarcastic howl. And a red-bearded officer, whose voice of triple brass could plainly be heard, was commanding: "Shoot into 'em! Shoot into 'em, Gawd damn their souls!" There was a *mêlée* of screeches, in which the men were ordered to do conflicting and impossible things.

The youth and his friend had a small scuffle over the flag. "Give it t' me!" "No, let me keep it!" Each felt satisfied with the other's possession of it, but each felt bound to declare, by an offer to carry the emblem, his willingness to further risk himself. The youth roughly pushed his friend away.

The regiment fell back to the stolid trees. There it halted for a moment to blaze at some dark forms that had begun to steal upon its track. Presently it resumed its march again, curving among the tree trunks. By the time the depleted regiment had again reached the first open space they were receiving a fast and merciless fire. There seemed to be mobs all about them.

The greater part of the men, discouraged, their spirits worn by the turmoil, acted as if stunned. They accepted the pelting of the bullets with bowed and weary heads. It was of no purpose to strive against walls. It was of no use to batter themselves against granite. And from this consciousness that they had attempted to conquer an unconquerable thing there seemed to arise a feeling that they had been betrayed. They glowered with bent brows, but dangerously, upon some of the officers, more particularly upon the red-bearded one with the voice of triple brass.

However, the rear of the regiment was fringed with men, who continued to shoot irritably at the advancing foes. They seemed resolved to make every trouble. The youthful lieutenant was perhaps the last man in the disordered mass. His forgotten back was toward the enemy. He had been shot in the arm. It hung straight and rigid. Occasionally he would cease to remember it, and be about to emphasize an oath with a sweeping gesture. The multiplied pain caused him to swear with incredible power.

The youth went along with slipping, uncertain feet. He kept watchful eyes rearward. A scowl of mortification and rage was upon his face. He had thought of a fine revenge upon the officer who had referred to him and his fellows as mule drivers. But he saw that it could not come to pass. His dreams had collapsed when the mule drivers, dwindling rapidly, had wavered and hesitated on the little clearing, and then had recoiled. And now the retreat of the mule drivers was a march of shame to him.

A dagger-pointed gaze from without his blackened face was held toward the enemy, but his greater hatred was riveted upon the man, who, not knowing him, had called him a mule driver.

When he knew that he and his comrades had failed to do anything in successful ways that might bring the little pangs of a kind of remorse upon the officer, the youth allowed the rage of the baffled to possess him. This cold officer upon a monument, who dropped epithets unconcernedly down, would be finer as a dead man, he thought. So grievous did he think it that he could never possess the secret right to taunt truly in answer.

He had pictured red letters of curious revenge. "We *are* mule drivers, are we?" And now he was compelled to throw them away.

He presently wrapped his heart in the cloak of his pride and kept the flag erect. He harangued his fellows, pushing against their chests with his free hand. To those he knew well he made frantic appeals, beseeching them by name. Between him and the lieutenant, scolding and near to losing his mind with rage, there was felt a subtle fellowship and equality. They supported each other in all manner of hoarse, howling protests.

But the regiment was a machine run down. The two men babbled at a forceless thing. The soldiers who had heart to go slowly were continually shaken in their resolves by a knowledge that comrades were slipping with speed back to the lines. It was difficult to think of reputation when others were thinking of skins. Wounded men were left crying on this black journey.

The smoke fringes and flames blustered always. The youth, peering once through a sudden rift in a cloud, saw a brown mass of troops, interwoven and magnified until they appeared to be thousands. A fierce-hued flag flashed before his vision.

Immediately, as if the uplifting of the smoke had been prearranged, the discovered troops burst into a rasping yell, and a hundred flames jetted toward the retreating band. A rolling gray cloud again interposed as the regiment doggedly replied. The youth had to depend again upon his misused ears, which were trembling and buzzing from the *mêlée* of musketry and yells.

The way seemed eternal. In the clouded haze men became panic-stricken with the thought that the regiment had lost its path, and was proceeding in a perilous direction. Once the men who headed the wild procession turned and came pushing back against their comrades, screaming that they were being fired upon from points which they had considered to be toward their own lines. At this cry a hysterical fear and dismay beset the troops. A soldier, who heretofore had been ambitious to make the regiment into a wise little band that would proceed calmly amid the huge-appearing difficulties, suddenly sank down and buried his face in his arms with an air of bowing to a doom. From another a shrill lamentation rang out filled with profane illusions to a general. Men ran hither and thither, seeking with their eyes roads of escape. With serene regularity, as if controlled by a schedule, bullets buffed into men.

The youth walked stolidly into the midst of the mob, and with his flag in his hands took a stand as if he expected an attempt to push him to the ground. He unconsciously assumed the attitude of the color bearer in the fight of the preceding day. He passed over his brow a hand that trembled. His breath did not come freely. He was choking during this small wait for the crisis.

His friend came to him. "Well, Henry, I guess this is good-by—John."

"Oh, shut up, you damned fool!" replied the youth, and he would not look at the other.

The officers labored like politicians to beat the mass into a proper circle to face the menaces. The ground was uneven and torn. The men curled into depressions and fitted themselves snugly behind whatever would frustrate a bullet.

The youth noted with vague surprise that the lieutenant was standing mutely with his legs far apart and his sword held in the manner of a cane. The youth wondered what had happened to his vocal organs that he no more cursed.

There was something curious in this little intent pause of the lieutenant. He was like a babe which, having wept its fill, raises its eyes and fixes them upon a distant toy. He was engrossed in this contemplation, and the soft under lip quivered from self-whispered words.

Some lazy and ignorant smoke curled slowly. The men, hiding from the bullets, waited anxiously for it to lift and disclose the plight of the regiment.

The silent ranks were suddenly thrilled by the eager voice of the youthful lieutenant bawling out: "Here they come! Right on to us, b'Gawd!" His further words were lost in a roar of wicked thunder from the men's rifles.

The youth's eyes had instantly turned in the direction indicated by the awakened and agitated lieutenant, and he had seen the haze of treachery disclosing a body of soldiers of the enemy. They were so near that he could see their features. There was a recognition as he looked at the types of faces. Also he perceived with dim amazement that their uniforms were rather gay in effect, being light gray, accented with a brilliant-hued facing. Moreover, the clothes seemed new.

These troops had apparently been going forward with caution, their rifles held in readiness, when the youthful lieutenant had discovered them and their movement had been interrupted by the volley from the blue regiment. From the moment's glimpse, it was derived that they had been unaware of the proximity of their dark-suited foes or had mistaken the direction. Almost instantly they were shut utterly from the youth's sight by the smoke from the energetic rifles of his companions. He strained his vision to learn the accomplishment of the volley, but the smoke hung before him.

The two bodies of troops exchanged blows in the manner of a pair of boxers. The fast angry firings went back and forth. The men in blue were intent with the despair of their circumstances and they seized upon the revenge to be had at close range. Their thunder swelled loud and valiant. Their curving front bristled with flashes and the place resounded with the clangor of their ramrods. The youth ducked and dodged for a time and achieved a few unsatisfactory views of the enemy. There appeared to be many of them and they were replying swiftly. They seemed moving toward the blue regiment, step by step. He seated himself gloomily on the ground with his flag between his knees.

As he noted the vicious, wolflike temper of his comrades he had a sweet thought that if the enemy was about to swallow the regimental broom as a large prisoner, it could at least have the consolation of going down with bristles forward.

But the blows of the antagonist began to grow more weak. Fewer bullets ripped the air, and finally, when the men slackened to learn of the fight, they could see only dark, floating smoke. The regiment lay still and gazed. Presently some chance whim came to the pestering blur, and it began to coil heavily away. The men saw a ground vacant of fighters. It would have been an empty stage if it were not for a few corpses that lay thrown and twisted into fantastic shapes upon the sward.

At sight of this tableau, many of the men in blue sprang from behind their covers and made an ungainly dance of joy. Their eyes burned and a hoarse cheer of elation broke from their dry lips.

It had begun to seem to them that events were trying to prove that they were impotent. These little battles had evidently endeavored to demonstrate that the men could not fight well. When on the verge of submission to these opinions, the small duel had showed them that the proportions were not impossible, and by it they had revenged themselves upon their misgivings and upon the foe.

The impetus of enthusiasm was theirs again. They gazed about them with looks of uplifted pride, feeling new trust in the grim, always confident weapons in their hands. And they were men.

CHAPTER XXI

PRESENTLY they knew that no fighting threatened them. All ways seemed once more opened to them. The dusty blue lines of their friends were disclosed a short distance away. In the distance there were many colossal noises, but in all this part of the field there was a sudden stillness.

They perceived that they were free. The depleted band drew a long breath of relief and gathered itself into a bunch to complete its trip.

In this last length of journey the men began to show strange emotions. They hurried with nervous fear. Some who had been dark and unfaltering in the grimmest moments now could not conceal an anxiety that made them frantic. It was perhaps that they dreaded to be killed in insignificant ways after the times for proper military deaths had passed. Or, perhaps, they thought it would be too ironical to get killed at the portals of safety. With backward looks of perturbation, they hastened.

As they approached their own lines there was some sarcasm exhibited on the part of a gaunt and bronzed regiment that lay resting in the shade of trees. Questions were wafted to them.

"Where th' hell yeh been?"

"What yeh comin' back fer?"

"Why didn't yeh stay there?"

"Was it warm out there, sonny?"

"Goin' home now, boys?"

One shouted in taunting mimicry: "Oh, mother, come quick an' look at th' sojers!"

There was no reply from the bruised and battered regiment, save that one man made broadcast challenges to fist fights and the red-bearded officer walked rather near and glared in great swashbuckler style at a tall captain in the other regiment. But the lieutenant suppressed the man who wished to fist fight, and the tall captain, flushing at the little fanfare of the red-bearded one, was obliged to look intently at some trees.

The youth's tender flesh was deeply stung by these remarks. From under his creased brows he glowered with hate at the mockers. He meditated upon a few revenges. Still, many in the regiment hung their heads in criminal fashion, so that it came to pass that the men trudged with sudden heaviness, as if they bore upon their bended shoulders the coffin of their honor. And the youthful lieutenant, recollecting himself, began to mutter softly in black curses.

They turned when they arrived at their old position to regard the ground over which they had charged.

The youth in this contemplation was smitten with a large astonishment. He discovered that the distances, as compared with the brilliant measurings of his mind, were trivial and ridiculous. The stolid trees, where much had taken place, seemed incredibly near. The time, too, now that he reflected, he saw to have been short. He wondered at the number of emotions and events that had been crowded into such little spaces. Elfin thoughts must have exaggerated and enlarged everything, he said.

It seemed, then, that there was bitter justice in the speeches of the gaunt and bronzed veterans. He veiled a glance of disdain at his fellows who strewed the ground, choking with dust, red from perspiration, misty-eyed, disheveled.

They were gulping at their canteens, fierce to wring every mite of water from them, and they polished at their swollen and watery features with coat sleeves and bunches of grass.

However, to the youth there was a considerable joy in musing upon his performances during the charge. He had had very little time previously in which to appreciate himself, so that there was now much satisfaction in quietly thinking of his actions. He recalled bits of color that in the flurry had stamped themselves unawares upon his engaged senses.

As the regiment lay heaving from its hot exertions the officer who had named them as mule drivers came galloping along the line. He had lost his cap. His tousled hair streamed wildly, and his face was dark with vexation and wrath. His temper was displayed with more clearness by the way in which he managed his horse. He jerked and wrenched savagely at his bridle, stopping the hard-breathing animal with a furious pull near the colonel of the regiment. He immediately exploded in reproaches which came unbidden to the ears of the men. They were suddenly alert, being always curious about black words between officers.

"Oh, thunder, MacChesnay, what an awful bull you made of this thing!" began the officer. He attempted low tones, but his indignation caused certain of the men to learn the sense of his words. "What an awful mess you made! Good Lord, man, you stopped about a hundred feet this side of a very pretty success! If your men had gone a hundred feet farther you would have made a great charge, but as it is—what a lot of mud diggers you've got anyway!"

The men, listening with bated breath, now turned their curious eyes upon the colonel. They had a ragamuffin interest in this affair.

The colonel was seen to straighten his form and put one hand forth in oratorical fashion. He wore an injured air; it was as if a deacon had been accused of stealing. The men were wiggling in an ecstasy of excitement.

But of a sudden the colonel's manner changed from that of a deacon to that of a Frenchman. He shrugged his shoulders. "Oh, well, general, we went as far as we could," he said calmly.

"As far as you could? Did you, b'Gawd?" snorted the other. "Well, that wasn't very far, was it?" he added, with a glance of cold contempt into the other's eyes. "Not very far, I think. You were intended to make a diversion in favor of Whiterside. How well you succeeded your own ears can now tell you." He wheeled his horse and rode stiffly away.

The colonel, bidden to hear the jarring noises of an engagement in the woods to the left, broke out in vague damnations.

The lieutenant, who had listened with an air of impotent rage to the interview, spoke suddenly in firm and undaunted tones. "I don't care what a man is—whether he is a general or what—if he says th' boys didn't put up a good fight out there he's a damned fool."

"Lieutenant," began the colonel, severely, "this is my own affair, and I'll trouble you——"

The lieutenant made an obedient gesture. "All right, colonel, all right," he said. He sat down with an air of being content with himself.

The news that the regiment had been reproached went along the line.

For a time the men were bewildered by it. "Good thunder!" they ejaculated, staring at the vanishing form of the general. They conceived it to be a huge mistake.

Presently, however, they began to believe that in truth their efforts had been called light. The youth could see this convention weigh upon the entire regiment until the men were like cuffed and cursed animals, but withal rebellious.

The friend, with a grievance in his eye, went to the youth. "I wonder what he does want," he said. "He must think we went out there an' played marbles! I never see sech a man!"

The youth developed a tranquil philosophy for these moments of irritation. "Oh, well," he rejoined, "he probably didn't see nothing of it at all and got mad as blazes, and concluded we were a lot of sheep, just because we didn't do what he wanted done. It's a pity old Grandpa Henderson got killed yesterday—he'd have known that we did our best and fought good. It's just our awful luck, that's what."

"I should say so," replied the friend. He seemed to be deeply wounded at an injustice. "I should say we did have awful luck! There's no fun in fightin' fer people when everything yeh do—no matter what—ain't done right. I have a notion t' stay behind next time an' let 'em take their ol' charge an' go t' th' devil with it."

The youth spoke soothingly to his comrade. "Well, we both did good. I'd like to see the fool what'd say we both didn't do as good as we could!"

"Of course we did," declared the friend stoutly. "An' I'd break th' feller's neck if he was as big as a church. But we're all right, anyhow, for I heard one feller say that we two fit th' best in th' reg'ment, an' they had a great argument 'bout it. Another feller, 'a course, he had t' up an' say it was a lie—he seen all what was goin' on an' he never seen us from th' beginnin' t' th' end. An' a lot more struck in an' ses it wasn't a lie —we did fight like thunder, an' they give us quite a send-off. But this is what I can't stand—these everlastin' ol' soldiers, titterin' an' laughin', an' then that general, he's crazy."

The youth exclaimed with sudden exasperation: "He's a lunkhead! He makes me mad. I wish he'd come along next time. We'd show 'im what——"

He ceased because several men had come hurrying up. Their faces expressed a bringing of great news.

"O Flem, yeh jest oughta heard!" cried one, eagerly.

"Heard what?" said the youth.

"Yeh jest oughta heard!" repeated the other, and he arranged himself to tell his tidings. The others made an excited circle. "Well, sir, th' colonel met your lieutenant right by us—it was damnedest thing I ever heard—an' he ses: 'Ahem! ahem!' he ses. 'Mr. Hasbrouck!' he ses, 'by th' way, who was that lad what carried th' flag?' he ses. There, Flemin', what d' yeh think 'a that? 'Who was th' lad what carried th' flag?' he ses, an' th' lieutenant, he speaks up right away: 'That's Flemin', an' he's a jimhickey,' he ses, right away. What? I say he did. 'A jimhickey,' he ses—those 'r his words. He did, too. I say he did. If you kin tell this story better than I kin, go ahead an' tell it. Well, then, keep yer mouth shet. Th' lieutenant, he ses: 'He's a jimhickey,' an' th' colonel, he ses: 'Ahem! ahem! he is, indeed, a very good man t' have, ahem! He kep' th' flag 'way t' th' front. I saw 'im. He's a good un,' ses th' colonel. 'You bet,' ses th' lieutenant, 'he an' a feller named Wilson was at th' head 'a th' charge, an' howlin' like Indians all th' time,' he ses. 'Head a' th' charge all th' time,' he ses. 'A feller named Wilson,' he ses. There, Wilson, m'boy, put that in a letter an' send it hum t' yer mother, hay? 'A feller named Wilson,' he ses. An' th' colonel, he ses: 'Were they, indeed? Ahem! ahem! My sakes!' he ses. 'At th' head a' th' reg'ment?' he ses. 'They were,' ses th' lieutenant. 'My sakes!' ses th' colonel. He ses: 'Well, well, well,' he ses, 'those two babies?' 'They were,' ses th' lieutenant. 'Well, well,' ses th' colonel, 'they deserve t' be major generals,' he ses. 'They deserve t' be major generals.' "

The youth and his friend had said: "Huh!" "Yer lyin', Thompson." "Oh, go t' blazes!" "He never sed it." "Oh, what a lie!" "Huh!" But despite these youthful scoffings and embarrassments, they knew that their faces were deeply flushing from thrills of pleasure. They exchanged a secret glance of joy and congratulation.

They speedily forgot many things. The past held no pictures of error and disappointment. They were very happy, and their hearts swelled with grateful affection for the colonel and the youthful lieutenant.

CHAPTER XXII

When the woods again began to pour forth the dark-hued masses of the enemy the youth felt serene self-confidence. He smiled briefly when he saw men dodge and duck at the long screechings of shells that were thrown in giant handfuls over them. He stood, erect and tranquil, watching the attack begin against a part of the line that made a blue curve along the side of an adjacent hill. His vision being unmolested by smoke from the rifles of his companions, he had opportunities to see parts of the hard fight. It was a relief to perceive at last from whence came some of these noises which had been roared into his ears.

Off a short way he saw two regiments fighting a little separate battle with two other regiments. It was in a cleared space, wearing a set-apart look. They were blazing as if upon a wager, giving and taking tremendous blows. The firings were incredibly fierce and rapid. These intent regiments apparently were oblivious of all larger purposes of war, and were slugging each other as if at a matched game.

In another direction he saw a magnificent brigade going with the evident intention of driving the enemy from a wood. They passed in out of sight and presently there was a most awe-inspiring racket in the wood. The noise was unspeakable. Having stirred this prodigious uproar, and, apparently, finding it too prodigious, the brigade, after a little time, came marching airily out again with its fine formation in nowise disturbed. There were no traces of speed in its movements. The brigade was jaunty and seemed to point a proud thumb at the yelling wood.

On a slope to the left there was a long row of guns, gruff and maddened, denouncing the enemy, who, down through the woods, were forming for another attack in the pitiless monotony of conflicts. The round red discharges from the guns made a crimson flare and a high, thick smoke. Occasional glimpses could be caught of groups of the toiling artillerymen. In the rear of this row of guns stood a house, calm and white, amid bursting shells. A congregation of horses, tied to a long railing, were tugging frenziedly at their bridles. Men were running hither and thither.

The detached battle between the four regiments lasted for some time. There chanced to be no interference, and they settled their dispute by themselves. They struck savagely and powerfully at each other for a period of minutes, and then the lighter-hued regiments faltered and drew back, leaving the dark-blue lines shouting. The youth could see the two flags shaking with laughter amid the smoke remnants.

Presently there was a stillness, pregnant with meaning. The blue lines shifted and changed a trifle and stared expectantly at the silent woods and fields before them. The hush was solemn and churchlike, save for a distant battery that, evidently unable to remain quiet, sent a faint rolling thunder over the ground. It irritated, like the noises of unimpressed boys. The men imagined that it would prevent their perched ears from hearing the first words of the new battle.

Of a sudden the guns on the slope roared out a message of warning. A spluttering sound had begun in the woods. It swelled with amazing speed to a profound clamor that involved the earth in noises. The splitting crashes swept along the lines until an interminable roar was developed. To those in the midst of it it became a din fitted to the universe. It was the whirring and thumping of gigantic machinery, complications among the smaller stars. The youth's ears were filled up. They were incapable of hearing more.

On an incline over which a road wound he saw wild and desperate rushes of men perpetually backward and forward in riotous surges. These parts of the opposing armies were two long waves that pitched upon each other madly at dictated points. To and fro they swelled. Sometimes, one side by its yells and cheers would proclaim decisive blows, but a moment later the other side would be all yells and cheers. Once the youth saw a spray of light forms go in houndlike leaps toward the waving blue lines. There was much howling, and presently it went away with a vast mouthful of prisoners. Again, he saw a blue wave dash with such thunderous force against a gray obstruction that it seemed to clear the earth of it and leave nothing but trampled sod. And always in their swift and deadly rushes to and fro the men screamed and yelled like maniacs.

Particular pieces of fence or secure positions behind collections of trees were wrangled over, as gold thrones or pearl bedsteads. There were desperate lunges at these chosen spots seemingly every instant, and most of them were bandied like light toys between the contending forces. The youth could not tell from the battle flags flying like crimson foam in many directions which color of cloth was winning.

His emaciated regiment bustled forth with undiminished fierceness when its time came. When assaulted again by bullets, the men burst out in a barbaric cry of rage and pain. They bent their heads in aims of intent hatred behind the projected hammers of their guns. Their ramrods clanged loud with fury as their eager arms pounded the cartridges into the rifle barrels. The front of the regiment was a smoke-wall penetrated by the flashing points of yellow and red.

Wallowing in the fight, they were in an astonishingly short time re-smudged. They surpassed in stain and dirt all their previous appearances. Moving to and fro with strained exertion, jabbering the while, they were, with their swaying bodies, black faces, and glowing eyes, like strange and ugly fiends jigging heavily in the smoke.

The lieutenant, returning from a tour after a bandage, produced from a hidden receptacle of his mind new and portentous oaths suited to the emergency. Strings of expletives he swung lashlike over the backs of his men, and it was evident that his previous efforts had in nowise impaired his resources.

The youth, still the bearer of the colors, did not feel his idleness. He was deeply absorbed as a spectator. The crash and swing of the great drama made him lean forward, intent-eyed, his face working in small contortions. Sometimes he prattled, words coming unconsciously from him in grotesque exclamations. He did not know that he breathed; that the flag hung silently over him, so absorbed was he.

A formidable line of the enemy came within dangerous range. They could be seen plainly—tall, gaunt men with excited faces running with long strides toward a wandering fence.

At sight of this danger the men suddenly ceased their cursing monotone. There was an instant of strained silence before they threw up their rifles and fired a plumping volley at the foes. There had been no order given; the men, upon recognizing the menace, had immediately let drive their flock of bullets without waiting for word of command.

But the enemy were quick to gain the protection of the wandering line of fence. They slid down behind it with remarkable celerity, and from this position they began briskly to slice up the blue men.

These latter braced their energies for a great struggle. Often, white clinched teeth shone from the dusky faces. Many heads surged to and fro, floating upon a pale sea of smoke. Those behind the fence frequently shouted and yelped in taunts and gibelike cries, but the regiment maintained a stressed silence. Perhaps, at this new assault the men recalled the fact that they had been named mud diggers, and it made their situation thrice bitter. They were breathlessly intent upon keeping the ground and thrusting away the rejoicing body of the enemy. They fought swiftly and with a despairing savageness denoted in their expressions.

The youth had resolved not to budge whatever should happen. Some arrows of scorn that had buried themselves in his heart had generated strange and unspeakable hatred. It was clear to him that his final and absolute revenge was to be achieved by his dead body lying, torn and gluttering, upon the field. This was to be a poignant retaliation upon the officer who had said "mule drivers," and later "mud diggers," for in all the wild graspings of his mind for a unit responsible for his sufferings and commotions he always seized upon the man who had dubbed him wrongly. And it was his idea, vaguely formulated, that his corpse would be for those eyes a great and salt reproach.

The regiment bled extravagantly. Grunting bundles of blue began to drop. The orderly sergeant of the youth's company was shot through the cheeks. Its supports being injured, his jaw hung afar down, disclosing in the wide cavern of his mouth a pulsing mass of blood and teeth. And with it all he made attempts to cry out. In his endeavor there was a dreadful earnestness, as if he conceived that one great shriek would make him well.

The youth saw him presently go rearward. His strength seemed in nowise impaired. He ran swiftly, casting wild glances for succor.

Others fell down about the feet of their companions. Some of the wounded crawled out and away, but many lay still, their bodies twisted into impossible shapes.

The youth looked once for his friend. He saw a vehement young man, powder-smeared and frowzled, whom he knew to be him. The lieutenant, also, was unscathed in his position at the rear. He had continued to curse, but it was now with the air of a man who was using his last box of oaths.

For the fire of the regiment had begun to wane and drip. The robust voice, that had come strangely from the thin ranks, was growing rapidly weak.

CHAPTER XXIII

THE colonel came running along back of the line. There were other officers following him. "We must charge'm!" they shouted. "We must charge'm!" they cried with resentful voices, as if anticipating a rebellion against this plan by the men.

The youth, upon hearing the shout, began to study the distance between him and the enemy. He made vague calculations. He saw that to be firm soldiers they must go forward. It would be death to stay in the present place, and with all the circumstances to go backward would exalt too many others. Their hope was to push the galling foes away from the fence.

He expected that his companions, weary and stiffened, would have to be driven to this assault, but as he turned toward them he perceived with a certain surprise that they were giving quick and unqualified expressions of assent. There was an ominous, clanging overture to the charge when the shafts of the bayonets rattled upon the rifle barrels. At the yelled words of command the soldiers sprang forward in eager leaps. There was new and unexpected force in the movement of the regiment. A knowledge of its faded and jaded condition made the charge appear like a paroxysm, a display of the strength that comes before a final feebleness. The men scampered in insane fever of haste, racing as if to achieve a sudden success before an exhilarating fluid should leave them. It was a blind and despairing rush by the collection of men in dusty and tattered blue, over a green sward and under a sapphire sky, toward a fence, dimly outlined in smoke, from behind which spluttered the fierce rifles of enemies.

The youth kept the bright colors to the front. He was waving his free arm in furious circles, the while shrieking mad calls and appeals, urging on those that did not need to be urged, for it seemed that the mob of blue men hurling themselves on the dangerous group of rifles were again grown suddenly wild with an enthusiasm of unselfishness. From the many firings starting toward them, it looked as if they would merely succeed in making a great sprinkling of corpses on the grass between their former position and the fence. But they were in a state of frenzy, perhaps because of forgotten vanities, and it made an exhibition of sublime recklessness. There was no obvious questioning, nor figurings, nor diagrams. There was, apparently, no considered loopholes. It appeared that the swift wings of their desires would have shattered against the iron gates of the impossible.

He himself felt the daring spirit of a savage religion-mad. He was capable of profound sacrifices, a tremendous death. He had no time for dissections, but he knew that he thought of the bullets only as things that could prevent him from reaching the place of his endeavor. There were subtle flashings of joy within him that thus should be his mind.

He strained all his strength. His eyesight was shaken and dazzled by the tension of thought and muscle. He did not see anything excepting the mist of smoke gashed by the little knives of fire, but he knew that in it lay the aged fence of a vanished farmer protecting the snuggled bodies of the gray men.

As he ran a thought of the shock of contact gleamed in his mind. He expected a great concussion when the two bodies of troops crashed together. This became a part of his wild battle madness. He could feel the onward swing of the regiment about him and he conceived of a thunderous, crushing blow that would prostrate the resistance and spread consternation and amazement for miles. The flying regiment was going to have a catapultian effect. This dream made him run faster among his comrades, who were giving vent to hoarse and frantic cheers.

But presently he could see that many of the men in gray did intend to abide the blow. The smoke, rolling, disclosed men who ran, faces still turned. These grew to a crowd, who retired stubbornly. Individuals wheeled frequently to send a bullet at the blue wave.

But at one part of the line there was a grim and obdurate group that made no movement. They were settled firmly down behind posts and rails. A flag, ruffled and fierce, waved over them and their rifles dinned fiercely.

The blue whirl of men got very near, until it seemed that in truth there would be a close and frightful scuffle. There was an expressed disdain in the opposition of the little group, that changed the meaning of the cheers of the men in blue. They became yells of wrath, directed, personal. The cries of the two parties were now in sound an interchange of scathing insults.

They in blue showed their teeth; their eyes shone all white. They launched themselves as at the throats of those who stood resisting. The space between dwindled to an insignificant distance.

The youth had centered the gaze of his soul upon that other flag. Its possession would be high pride. It would express bloody minglings, near blows. He had a gigantic hatred for those who made great difficulties and complications. They caused it to be as a craved treasure of mythology, hung amid tasks and contrivances of danger.

He plunged like a mad horse at it. He was resolved it should not escape if wild blows and darings of blows could seize it. His own emblem, quivering and aflare, was winging toward the other. It seemed there would shortly be an encounter of strange beaks and claws, as of eagles.

The swirling body of blue men came to a sudden halt at close and disastrous range and roared a swift volley. The group in gray was split and broken by this fire, but its riddled body still fought. The men in blue yelled again and rushed in upon it.

The youth, in his leapings, saw, as through a mist, a picture of four or five men stretched upon the ground or writhing upon their knees with bowed heads as if they had been stricken by bolts from the sky. Tottering among them was the rival color bearer, whom the youth saw had been bitten vitally by the bullets of the last formidable volley. He perceived this man fighting a last struggle, the struggle of one whose legs are grasped by demons. It was a ghastly battle. Over his face was the bleach of death, but set upon it were the dark and hard lines of desperate purpose. With this terrible grin of resolution he hugged his precious flag to him and was stumbling and staggering in his design to go the way that led to safety for it.

But his wounds always made it seem that his feet were retarded, held, and he fought a grim fight, as with invisible ghouls fastened greedily upon his limbs. Those in advance of the scampering blue men, howling cheers, leaped at the fence. The despair of the lost was in his eyes as he glanced back at them.

The youth's friend went over the obstruction in a tumbling heap and sprang at the flag as a panther at prey. He pulled at it and, wrenching it free, swung up its red brilliancy with a mad cry of exultation even as the

color bearer, gasping, lurched over in a final throe and, stiffening convulsively, turned his dead face to the ground. There was much blood upon
the grass blades.

At the place of success there began more wild clamorings of cheers.
The men gesticulated and bellowed in an ecstasy. When they spoke it was
as if they considered their listener to be a mile away. What hats and caps
were left to them they often slung high in the air.

At one part of the line four men had been swooped upon, and they
now sat as prisoners. Some blue men were about them in an eager and
curious circle. The soldiers had trapped strange birds, and there was an
examination. A flurry of fast questions was in the air.

One of the prisoners was nursing a superficial wound in the foot. He
cuddled it, baby-wise, but he looked up from it often to curse with an
astonishing utter abandon straight at the noses of his captors. He con-
signed them to red regions; he called upon the pestilential wrath of
strange gods. And with it all he was singularly free from recognition of
the finer points of the conduct of prisoners of war. It was as if a clumsy
clod had trod upon his toe and he conceived it to be his privilege, his
duty, to use deep, resentful oaths.

Another, who was a boy in years, took his plight with great calmness and
apparent good nature. He conversed with the men in blue, studying their
faces with his bright and keen eyes. They spoke of battles and conditions.
There was an acute interest in all their faces during this exchange of viewpoints. It seemed a great satisfaction to hear voices from where all had
been darkness and speculation.

The third captive sat with a morose countenance. He preserved a
stoical and cold attitude. To all advances he made one reply without variation, "Ah, go t' hell!"

The last of the four was always silent and, for the most part, kept his
face turned in unmolested directions. From the views the youth received
he seemed to be in a state of absolute dejection. Shame was upon him, and
with it profound regret that he was, perhaps, no more to be counted in
the ranks of his fellows. The youth could detect no expression that would
allow him to believe that the other was giving a thought to his narrowed
future, the pictured dungeons, perhaps, and starvations and brutalities, liable to the imagination. All to be seen was shame for captivity and regret
for the right to antagonize.

After the men had celebrated sufficiently they settled down behind the
old rail fence, on the opposite side to the one from which their foes had been
driven. A few shot perfunctorily at distant marks.

There was some long grass. The youth nestled in it and rested, making
a convenient rail support the flag. His friend, jubilant and glorified, holding his treasure with vanity, came to him there. They sat side by side
and congratulated each other.

CHAPTER XXIV

THE roarings that had stretched in a long line of sound across the face of the forest began to grow intermittent and weaker. The stentorian speeches of the artillery continued in some distant encounter, but the crashes of the musketry had almost ceased. The youth and his friend of a sudden looked up, feeling a deadened form of distress at the waning of these noises, which had become a part of life. They could see changes going on among the troops. There were marchings this way and that way. A battery wheeled leisurely. On the crest of a small hill was the thick gleam of many departing muskets.

The youth arose. "Well, what now, I wonder?" he said. By his tone he seemed to be preparing to resent some new monstrosity in the way of dins and smashes. He shaded his eyes with his grimy hand and gazed over the field.

His friend also arose and stared. "I bet we're goin' t' git along out of this an' back over th' river," said he.

"Well, I swan!" said the youth.

They waited, watching. Within a little while the regiment received orders to retrace its way. The men got up grunting from the grass, regretting the soft repose. They jerked their stiffened legs, and stretched their arms over their heads. One man swore as he rubbed his eyes. They all groaned "O Lord!" They had as many objections to this change as they would have had to a proposal for a new battle.

They trampled slowly back over the field across which they had run in a mad scamper.

The regiment marched until it had joined its fellows. The reformed brigade, in column, aimed through a wood at the road. Directly they were in a mass of dust-covered troops, and were trudging along in a way parallel to the enemy's lines as these had been defined by the previous turmoil.

They passed within view of a stolid white house, and saw in front of it groups of their comrades lying in wait behind a neat breastwork. A row of guns were booming at a distant enemy. Shells thrown in reply were raising clouds of dust and splinters. Horsemen dashed along the line of intrenchments.

At this point of its march the division curved from the field and went winding off in the direction of the river. When the significance of this movement had impressed itself upon the youth he turned his head and looked over his shoulder toward the trampled and *débris*-strewed ground. He breathed a breath of new satisfaction. He finally nudged his friend. "Well, it's all over," he said to him.

His friend gazed backward. "B'Gawd, it is," he assented. They mused.

For a time the youth was obliged to reflect in a puzzled and uncertain way. His mind was undergoing a subtle change. It took moments for it to cast off its battleful ways and resume its accustomed course of thought. Gradually his brain emerged from the clogged clouds, and at last he was enabled to more closely comprehend himself and circumstance.

He understood then that the existence of shot and counter-shot was in the past. He had dwelt in a land of strange, squalling upheavals and had come forth. He had been where there was red of blood and black of passion, and he was escaped. His first thoughts were given to rejoicings at this fact.

Later he began to study his deeds, his failures, and his achievements. Thus, fresh from scenes where many of his usual machines of reflection had been idle, from where he had proceeded sheeplike, he struggled to marshal all his acts.

At last they marched before him clearly. From this present viewpoint he was enabled to look upon them in spectator fashion and to criticize them with some correctness, for his new condition had already defeated certain sympathies.

Regarding his procession of memory he felt gleeful and unregretting, for in it his public deeds were paraded in great and shining prominence. Those performances which had been witnessed by his fellows marched now in wide purple and gold, having various deflections. They went gayly with music. It was pleasure to watch these things. He spent delightful minutes viewing the gilded images of memory.

He saw that he was good. He recalled with a thrill of joy the respectful comments of his fellows upon his conduct.

Nevertheless, the ghost of his flight from the first engagement appeared to him and danced. There were small shoutings in his brain about these matters. For a moment he blushed, and the light of his soul flickered with shame.

A specter of reproach came to him. There loomed the dogging memory of the tattered soldier—he who, gored by bullets and faint for blood, had fretted concerning an imagined wound in another; he who had loaned his last of strength and intellect for the tall soldier; he who, blind with weariness and pain, had been deserted in the field.

For an instant a wretched chill of sweat was upon him at the thought that he might be detected in the thing. As he stood persistently before his vision, he gave vent to a cry of sharp irritation and agony.

His friend turned. "What's the matter, Henry?" he demanded. The youth's reply was an outburst of crimson oaths.

As he marched along the little branch-hung roadway among his prattling companions this vision of cruelty brooded over him. It clung near him always and darkened his view of these deeds in purple and gold. Whichever way his thoughts turned they were followed by the somber phantom of the desertion in the fields. He looked stealthily at his companions, feeling sure that they must discern in his face evidences of this pursuit. But they were plodding in ragged array, discussing with quick tongues the accomplishments of the late battle.

"Oh, if a man should come up an' ask me, I'd say we got a dum good lickin'."

"Lickin'—in yer eye! We ain't licked, sonny. We're going down here aways, swing aroun', an' come in behint 'em."

"Oh, hush, with your comin' in behint 'em. I've seen all 'a that I wanta. Don't tell me about comin' in behint——"

"Bill Smithers, he ses he'd rather been in ten hundred battles than been in that heluva hospital. He ses they got shootin' in th' nighttime, an' shells dropped plum among 'em in th' hospital. He ses sech hollerin' he never see."

"Hasbrouck? He's th' best off'cer in this here reg'ment. He's a whale."

"Didn't I tell yeh we'd come aroun' in behint 'em? Didn't I tell yeh so? We——"

"Oh, shet yer mouth!"

For a time this pursuing recollection of the tattered man took all elation from the youth's veins. He saw his vivid error, and he was afraid that it would stand before him all his life. He took no share in the chatter of his comrades, nor did he look at them or know them, save when he felt sudden suspicion that they were seeing his thoughts and scrutinizing each detail of the scene with the tattered soldier.

Yet gradually he mustered force to put the sin at a distance. And at last his eyes seemed to open to some new ways. He found that he could look back upon the brass and bombast of his earlier gospels and see them truly. He was gleeful when he discovered that he now despised them.

With the conviction came a store of assurance. He felt a quiet manhood, non-assertive but of sturdy and strong blood. He knew that he would no more quail before his guides wherever they should point. He had been to touch the great death, and found that, after all, it was but the great death. He was a man.

So it came to pass that as he trudged from the place of blood and wrath his soul changed. He came from hot plowshares to prospects of clover tranquilly, and it was as if hot plowshares were not. Scars faded as flowers.

It rained. The procession of weary soldiers became a bedraggled train, despondent and muttering, marching with churning effort in a trough of liquid brown mud under a low, wretched sky. Yet the youth smiled, for he saw that the world was a world for him, though many discovered it to be made of oaths and walking sticks. He had rid himself of the red sickness of battle. The sultry nightmare was in the past. He had been an animal blistered and sweating in the heat and pain of war. He turned now with a lover's thirst to images of tranquil skies, fresh meadows, cool brooks— an existence of soft and eternal peace.

Over the river a golden ray of sun came through the hosts of leaden rain clouds.

The Blocking of Zeebrugge

BY

SIR ARCHIBALD HURD

SITUATED on the Belgian coast, some twelve miles apart, and facing a little to the west of north, Zeebrugge was in reality but a sea-gate of the inland port of Bruges—the latter being the station to which the enemy destroyers and submarines were sent in parts from the German workshops; where they were assembled; and whence, by canal, they proceeded to sea by way of Zeebrugge and Ostend. Of these two exits, Zeebrugge, the northernmost, was considerably the nearer to Bruges and the more important—Zeebrugge being eight, while Ostend was eleven miles distant from their common base —and to receive an adequate impression of what was subsequently achieved there it is necessary to bear in mind its salient features.

Unlike Ostend, apart from its harbour, it possessed no civic importance, merely consisting of a few streets of houses clustering about its railway station, locks, wharves, and store-houses, its sandy roadstead being guarded from the sea by an immensely powerful crescentic Mole. It was into this roadstead, that the Bruges canal opened between heavy timbered break-waters, having first passed through a sea-lock, some half a mile higher up. Between the two lighthouses, each about twenty feet above high-water level, that stood upon the ends of these breakwaters, the canal was 200 yards wide, narrowing to a width, in the lock itself, of less than seventy feet.

Leading from the canal entrance to the tip of the Mole, on which stood a third lighthouse, and so out to sea, was a curved channel, about three-quarters of a mile long, kept clear by continual dredging; and this was pro-tected both by a string of armed barges and by a system of nets on its shoreward side. It was in its great sea-wall, however, some eighty yards broad and more than a mile long, that Zeebrugge's chief strength resided; and this had been utilized, since the German occupation, to the utmost ex-tent. Upon the seaward end of it, near the lighthouse, a battery of 6-inch guns had been mounted, other batteries and machine-guns being stationed at various points throughout its length. With a parapet along its outer side, some sixteen feet higher than the level of the rest of the Mole, it not only carried a railway-line but contained a sea-plane shed, and shelters for stores and *personnel*. It was connected with the shore by a light wood and steel viaduct—a pilework structure, allowing for the passage of the through-current necessary to prevent silting.

From: *Sons of the Admiralty.*

Emplaced upon the shore, on either side of this, were further batteries of heavy guns; while, to the north of the canal entrance, and at a point almost opposite to the tip of the Mole, was the Goeben Fort, containing yet other guns covering both the Mole and the harbour. Under the lee of the parapet were dug-outs for the defenders, while, under the lee of the Mole itself, was a similar shelter for the enemy's submarines and destroyers. Nor did this exhaust the harbour's defences, since it was further protected not only by minefields, but by natural shoals, always difficult to navigate, and infinitely more so in the absence of beacons.

Even to a greater extent was this last a feature of Ostend, though here the whole problem was somewhat simpler, there being no Mole, and there-fore no necessity—though equally no opportunity—for a subsidiary attack. Covered, of course, from the shore by guns of all calibres—and here it should be remembered that there were 225 of these between Nieuport and the Dutch frontier—the single object in this case was to gain the entrance, before the block ships should be discovered by the enemy, and sunk by his gunners where their presence would do no harm. Since for complete success, however, it was necessary to seal both places, and, if possible, to do so simul-taneously, it will readily be seen that, in the words of Sir Eric Geddes—the successor, as First Lord of the Admiralty, to Mr. Balfour and Sir Edward Carson—it was, "a particularly intricate operation which had to be worked strictly to timetable." It was also one that, for several months before, required the most arduous and secret toil.

Begun in 1917 while Sir John Jellicoe was still First Sea Lord, the plan ultimately adopted—there had been several previous ones, dropped for mili-tary reasons—was devised by Vice-Admiral Roger Keyes, then head of the Plans Division at the Admiralty. From the first it was realized, of course, by all concerned that the element of surprise would be the determining fac-tor; and it was therefore decided that the attempt to block the harbours should take place at night. It was also clear that, under modern conditions of star-shells and searchlights, an extensive use would have to be made of the recent art of throwing out smokescreens; and fortunately, in Com-mander Brock, Admiral Keyes had at his disposal just the man to supply this need. A Wing-Commander in the Royal Naval Air Service, in private life Commander Brock was a partner in a well-known firm of firework makers; and his inventive ability had already been fruitful in more than one direction. A first-rate pilot and excellent shot, Commander Brock was a typical English sportsman; and his subsequent death during the opera-tions, for whose success he had been so largely responsible, was a loss of the gravest description both to the Navy and the empire.

The next consideration was the choosing of the block-ships and for these the following vessels were at last selected—the *Sirius* and *Brilliant* to be sunk at Ostend, and the *Thetis, Iphigenia,* and *Intrepid* to seal the canal entrance at Zeebrugge. These were all old cruisers, and they were to be filled with cement, which when submerged would turn into concrete, fuses being so placed that they could be sunk by explosion as soon as they had reached the desired position; and it was arranged that motor-launches should accompany them in order to rescue their crews.

So far these general arrangements were applicable to both places; but, as regarded Zeebrugge, it was decided to make a diversion in the shape of a subsidiary attack on the Mole, in which men were to be landed and to do as much damage as possible. Such an attack, it was thought, would help to draw the enemy's attention from the main effort, which was to be the sinking of the block-ships, and, apart from this, would have valuable results both material and moral. For this secondary operation, three other vessels were especially selected and fitted out—two Liverpool ferry boats, the *Iris* and *Daffodil,* obtained by Captain Grant, not without some difficulty, owing to the natural reluctance of the Liverpool authorities and the impossibility of divulging the object for which they were wanted—and the old cruiser *Vindictive*. This latter vessel had been designed as a "ram" ship more than twenty years before, displacing about 5,000 tons and capable of a speed of some twenty knots. She had no armour-belt, but her bow was covered with plates, two inches thick and extending fourteen feet aft, while her deck was also protected by hardened plates, covered with nickel steel, from a half to two inches thick. Originally undergunned, she had subsequently been provided with ten 6-inch guns and eight 12-pounders.

This was the vessel chosen to convey the bulk of the landing party, and, for many weeks, under the supervision of Commander E. O. B. S. Osborne, the carpenters and engineers were hard at work upon her. An additional high deck, carrying thirteen brows or gangways, was fitted upon her port side; pom-poms and machine-guns were placed in her fighting-top; and she was provided with three howitzers and some Stokes mortars. A special flame-throwing cabin, fitted with speaking tubes, was built beside the bridge, and another on the port quarter.

It was thus to be the task of the *Vindictive* and her consorts to lay themselves alongside the Mole, land storming and demolition parties, and protect these by a barrage as they advanced down the Mole; and, in order to make this attack more effective, yet a third operation was designed. This was to cut off the Mole from the mainland, thus isolating its defenders and preventing the arrival of reinforcements; and, in order to do so, it was decided to blow up the viaduct by means of an old submarine charged with high explosives. Meanwhile the whole attempt was to be supported from out at sea by a continuous bombardment from a squadron of monitors; sea-planes and aeroplanes, weather permitting, were to render further assistance; and flotillas of destroyers were to shepherd the whole force and to hold the flanks against possible attack.

This then was the plan of campaign, one of the most daring ever conceived, and all the more so in face of the difficulty of keeping it concealed from the enemy during the long period of preparation—a difficulty enhanced in that it was not only necessary to inform each man of his particular *rôle*, but of the particular objectives of each attack and the general outline of the whole scheme. That was unavoidable since it was more than likely that, during any one of the component actions, every officer might be killed or wounded and the men themselves become responsible. Nor was it possible, even approximately, to fix a date for the enterprise, since this could only be carried out under particular conditions of wind and weather. Thus the night must be dark and the sea calm; the arrival on the other side must be at high water; and there must above all things be a following wind, since, without this, the smoke screens would be useless. Twice, when all was ready, these conditions seemed to have come, and twice, after a start had been made, the expedition had to return; and it was not until April 22nd, 1918, that the final embarkation took place.

By this time Vice-Admiral Keyes had succeeded Vice-Admiral Bacon in command of the Dover Patrol; and he was therefore in personal charge of the great adventure that he had initiated and planned with such care. Every man under him was not only a volunteer fully aware of what he was about to face, but a picked man, selected and judged by as high a standard, per-haps, as the world could have provided. Flying his own flag on the destroyer *Warwick*, Admiral Keyes had entrusted the *Vindictive* to acting Captain A. F. B. Carpenter, the *Iris* and the *Daffodil* being in the hands respectively of Commander Valentine Gibbs and Lieutenant Harold Campbell. The marines, consisting of three companies of the Royal Marine Light Infantry and a hundred men of the Royal Marine Artillery, had been drawn from the Grand Fleet, the Chatham, Portsmouth, and Devonport Depots, and were commanded by Lieutenant-Colonel Bertram Elliot. The three block-ships that were to be sunk at Zeebrugge, the *Thetis, Intrepid,* and *Iphigenia,* were in charge of Commander Ralph S. Sneyd, Lieutenant Stuart Bonham-Carter, and Lieutenant E. W. Billyard-Leake; while the old submarine *C3* that was to blow up the viaduct was commanded by Lieutenant R. D. Sandford. In control of the motor-launches, allotted to the attack on Zee-brugge, was Admiral Keyes' flag-captain, Captain R. Collins, those at Ostend being directed by Commander Hamilton Benn, M. P.—the opera-tions at the latter place being in charge of Commodore Hubert Lynes. Also acting in support, was a large body of coastal motor-boats under Lieutenant A. E. P. Wellman, and a flotilla of destroyers under Captain Wilfred Tomkinson, the general surveying of the whole field of attack—including the fixing of targets and firing-points—being in the skilful hands of Com-mander H. P. Douglas and Lieutenant-Commander F. E. B. Haselfoot.

Included among the monitors were the *Erebus* and *Terror,* each mounting 15-inch guns, to operate at Zeebrugge; and the *Prince Eugene, General Crauford,* and *Lord Clive,* carrying 12-inch guns, and the *Marshal Soult,* carrying 15-inch guns, to assist at Ostend. To the old *Vindictive* Admiral Keyes had presented a horseshoe that had been nailed for luck to her centre funnel; and, to the whole fleet, on its way across, he signalled the message, "St. George for England." Few who received that message ex-pected to return unscathed, and in the block-ships none; but it is safe to say that, in the words of Nelson, they would not have been elsewhere that night for thousands.

Such then were the forces that, on this still dark night, safely arrived at their first rendezvous and then parted on their perilous ways, some to Zeebrugge and some to Ostend. It was at a point about fifteen miles from the Belgian coast that the two parties separated; and, since it is impossible to follow them both at once, let us confine ourselves at first to the former. Theirs was the more complicated, though, as it afterwards proved, the more swiftly achieved task, the first to arrive on the scene of action, almost at the stroke of midnight, being the old cruiser *Vindictive* with her two stout little attendants. These she had been towing as far as the rendezvous; but, at this point, she had cast them off, and they were now following her, under their own steam, to assist in berthing her and to land their own parties. Ahead of them the small craft had been laying their smoke-screens, the north-east wind rolling these shorewards, while already the monitors could be heard at work bombarding the coast defences with their big guns. Accustomed as he was to such visitations, this had not aroused in the enemy any particular alarm; and it was not until the *Vindictive* and the two ferry-boats were within 400 yards of the Mole that the off-shore wind caused the smoke-screen to lift somewhat and left them exposed to the enemy. By this time the marines and bluejackets, ready to spring ashore, were mustered on the lower and main decks; while Colonel Elliot, Major Cordner, and Captain Chater, who were to lead the marines, and Captain Halahan, who was in charge of the bluejackets, were waiting on the high false deck.

It was a crucial moment, for there could be no mistaking now what was the *Vindictive's* intention. The enemy's star-shells, soaring into the sky, broke into a baleful and crimson light; while his searchlights, that had been wavering through the darkness, instantly sprang together and fastened upon the three vessels. This, as Captain Carpenter afterwards confessed, induced "an extraordinarily naked feeling," and then, from every gun that could be brought to bear, both from the Mole and the coast, there burst upon her such a fire as, given another few minutes, must inevitably have sunk her. Beneath it Colonel Elliot, Major Cordner, and Captain Halahan, all fell slain; while Captain Carpenter himself had the narrowest escape from destruction. His cap—he had left his best one at home—was two or three times over pierced by bullets, as was the case of his binoculars, slung by straps over his back; while, during the further course of the action, both his searchlight and smoke-goggles were smashed.

The surprise had so far succeeded, however, that, within less than five minutes, the *Vindictive's* bow was against the side of the Mole, and all but her upper works consequently protected from the severest of the enemy's fire. Safe—or comparatively so—as regarded her water-line, she was nevertheless still a point-blank target; her funnels were riddled over and over again, the one carrying the horse-shoe suffering least; the signal-room was smashed and the bridge blown to pieces, just as Commander Carpenter entered the flame-throwing cabin; and this in its turn, drawing the enemy's fire, was soon twisted and splintered in all directions. It was now raining; explosion followed explosion till the whole air quaked as if in torment; and meanwhile a new and unforeseen danger had just made itself apparent. Till the harbour was approached, the sea had been calm, but now a ground-swell was causing a "scend" against the Mole, adding tenfold not only to the difficulties of landing, but of maintaining the *Vindictive* at her berth. In this emergency, it was the little *Daffodil* that rose to and saved the situation. Her primary duty, although she carried a landing party, had been to push the *Vindictive* in until the latter had been secured; but, as matters were, she had to hold her against the Mole throughout the whole hour and a quarter of her stay there. Even so, the improvised gangways that had been thrust out from the false deck were now some four feet up in the air and now crashing down from the top of the parapet; and it was across these brows, splintering under their feet, and in the face of a fire that baffled description, that the marines and bluejackets had to scramble ashore with their Lewis guns, hand-grenades, and bayonets.

Under such conditions, once a man fell, there was but little hope of his regaining his feet; and it was only a lucky chance that saved one of the officers from being thus trodden to death. This was Lieutenant H. T. C. Walker, who, with an arm blown away, had stumbled and fallen on the upper deck, the eager storming parties, sweeping over him until he was happily discovered and dragged free. Let it be said at once that Lieutenant Walker bore no malice, and waved them good luck with his remaining arm. The command of the marines had now devolved upon Major Weller; and, of the 300 or so who followed him ashore, more than half were soon to be casualties. But the landing was made good; the awkward drop from the parapet was successfully negotiated thanks to the special scaling-ladders; the barrage was put down; and they were soon at hand-to-hand grips with such of the German defenders as stayed to face them. Many of these were in the dug-out under the parapets, but, seeing that to remain there was only to be bayoneted, they made a rush for some of their own destroyers that were hugging the lee of the Mole. But few reached these, however, thanks to the vigour of the marines and the fire of the machine-guns from the *Vindictive's* top, while one of the destroyers was damaged by hand-grenades and by shells lobbed over the Mole from the *Vindictive's* mortars.

Meanwhile the *Vindictive* was still the object of a fire that was rapidly dismantling all of her that was visible. A shell in her fighting-top killed every man at the guns there except Sergeant Finch of the Royal Marine Artillery, who was badly wounded, but who extricated himself from a pile of corpses, and worked his gun for a while single-handed. Another shell, bursting forward, put the whole of a howitzer crew out of action, and yet a third, finding the same place, destroyed the crew that followed.

Fierce as was the ordeal through which the *Vindictive* was passing, however, that of the *Iris* was even more so. Unprotected, as was her fellow the *Daffodil*, boring against the side of the larger *Vindictive*, the *Iris*, with her landing-party, was trying to make good her berth lower down the Mole, ahead of Captain Carpenter. Unfortunately the grapnels with which she had been provided proved to be ineffective owing to the "scend," and, with the little boat tossing up and down, and under the fiercest fire, two of the officers, Lieutenant-Commander Bradford and Lieutenant Hawkins, climbed ashore to try and make them fast. Both were killed before they succeeded, toppling into the water between the Mole and the ship, while, a little later, a couple of shells burst aboard with disastrous results. One of these, piercing the deck, exploded among a party of marines, waiting for the gangways to be thrust out, killing forty-nine and wounding seven; while another, wrecking the ward-room, killed four officers and twenty-six men. Her Captain, Commander Gibbs, had both his legs blown away, and died in a few hours, the *Iris* having been forced meanwhile to change her position, and take up another astern of the *Vindictive*.

Before this happened, however, every man aboard her, as aboard the *Vindictive, Daffodil,* and upon the Mole, had been thrilled to the bone by the gigantic explosion that had blown up the viaduct lower down. With a deafening roar and a gush of flame leaping up hundreds of yards into the night, Lieutenant Sandford had told them the good tidings of his success with the old submarine. Creeping towards the viaduct, with his little crew on deck, he had made straight for an aperture between the steel-covered piles, and to the blank amazement and apparent paralysis of the Germans crowded upon the viaduct, had rammed in the submarine up to her conning-tower before lighting the fuse that was to start the explosion.

Before himself doing this, he had put off a boat, his men needing no orders to tumble into her, followed by their commander, as soon as the fuse was fired, with the one idea of getting away as far as possible. As luck would have it, the boat's propeller fouled, and they had to rely for safety upon two oars only, pulling, as Lieutenant Sandford afterwards described it, as hard as men ever pulled before. Raked by machine-gun fire and with shells plunging all round them, most of them, including Lieutenant Sandford, were wounded; but they were finally borne to safety by an attendant picket-boat under his brother, Lieutenant-Commander F. Sandford.

That had taken place about fifteen minutes after the *Vindictive* and her consorts had reached their berths, and a few minutes before the block-ships, with *Thetis* leading, had rounded the light-house at the tip of the Mole. In order to assist these to find their bearings, an employee of Commander Brock, who had never before been to sea, had for some time been firing rockets from the after cabin of the *Vindictive;* and presently they came in sight, exposed as the *Vindictive* had been, by the partial blowing back of their smoke screen. Steaming straight ahead for their objectives, they were therefore opposed by the intensest fire; and the spirit in which they proceeded is well illustrated by what had just taken place on board the *Intrepid*. It had been previously arranged that, for the final stage of their journey, the crews of the block-ships should be reduced to a minimum; but, when the moment came to disembark the extra men, those on the *Intrepid*, so anxious were they to remain, actually hid themselves away. Many of them did in fact succeed in remaining, and sailed with their comrades into the canal.

The first to draw the enemy's fire, the *Thetis,* had the misfortune, having cleared the armed barges, to foul the nets—bursting through the gate and carrying this with her, but with her propellers gathering in the meshes and rendering her helpless. Heavily shelled, she was soon in a sinking condition, and Commander Sneyd was obliged to blow her charges, but not before he had given the line, with the most deliberate coolness, to the two following block-ships—Lieutenant Littleton, in a motor-launch, then rescuing the crew.

Following the *Thetis* came the *Intrepid*, with all her guns in full action, and Lieutenant Bonham-Carter pushed her right into the canal up to a point actually behind some of the German batteries. Here he ran her nose into the western bank, ordered his crew away, and blew her up, the engineer remaining down below in order to be able to report results. These being satisfactory, and every one having left, Lieutenant Bonham-Carter committed himself to a Carley float—a kind of lifebuoy that, on contact with the water, automatically ignited a calcium flare. Illuminated by this, the *Intrepid's* commander found himself the target of a machine-gun on the bank, and, but for the smoke still pouring from the *Intrepid*, he would probably have been killed before the launch could rescue him.

Meanwhile the *Iphigenia*, close behind, had been equally successful under more difficult conditions. With the *Intrepid's* smoke blowing back upon her, she had found it exceedingly hard to keep her course, and had rammed a dredger with a barge moored to it, pushing the latter before her when she broke free. Lieutenant Billyard-Leake, however, was able to reach his objective—the eastern bank of the canal entrance—and here he sank her in good position, with her engines still working to keep her in place. Both vessels were thus left lying well across the canal, as aeroplane photographs afterwards confirmed; and thanks to the persistent courage of Lieutenant Percy Dean, the crews of both block-ships were safely removed.

With the accompanying motor-launch unhappily sunk as she was going in, Lieutenant Dean, under fire from all sides, often at a range of but a few feet, embarked in *Motor-Launch 282* no less than 101 officers and men. He then started for home, but, learning that there was an officer still in the water, at once returned and rescued him, three men being shot at his side as he handled his little vessel. Making a second start, just as he cleared the canal entrance, his steering-gear broke down; and he had to manœuvre by means of his engines, hugging the side of the Mole to keep out of range of the guns. Reaching the harbour mouth he then, by a stroke of luck, found himself alongside the destroyer *Warwick*, who was thus able to take on board and complete the rescue of the block-ships' crews.

It was now nearly one o'clock on the morning of the 23rd; the main objects of the attack had been secured; and Captain Carpenter, watching the course of events, decided that it was time to recall his landing-parties. It had been arranged to do so with the *Vindictive's* siren, but this, like so much of her gear, was no longer serviceable; and it was necessary to have recourse to the *Daffodil's* little hooter, so feebly opposed to the roar of the guns. Throughout the whole operation, humble as her part had been, the

Daffodil had been performing yeoman's service, and, but for the fine sea-manship of Lieutenant Harold Campbell, and the efforts of her engine-room staff, it would have been quite impossible to re-embark the marines and bluejackets from the Mole. In the normal way her boilers developed some 80-lbs steam-pressure per inch; but, for the work of holding the *Vindictive* against the side of the Mole, it was necessary throughout to maintain double this pressure. All picked men, under Artificer-Engineer Sutton, the stokers held to their task in the ablest fashion; and, in ignorance of what was happening all about them, and to the muffled accompaniment of bursting shells, they worked themselves out, stripped to their vests and trousers, to the last point of exhaustion.

Nor did their colleagues on board the *Vindictive* fall in any degree short of the same high standard, as becomes clear from the account afterwards given by one of her stokers, Alfred Dingle. "My pigeon," he said, "was in the boiler-room of the *Vindictive,* which left with the other craft at two o'clock on Tuesday afternoon. We were in charge of Chief Artificer-Engineer Campbell, who was formerly a merchant-service engineer and must have been specially selected for the job. He is a splendid fellow. At the start he told us what we were in for, and that before we had finished we should have to feed the fires like mad. 'This ship was built at Chatham twenty years ago,' he said, 'and her speed is 19 knots, but if you don't get 21 knots out of her when it is wanted, well—it's up to you to do it anyway.' We cheered, and he told us, when we got the order, to get at it for all we were worth, and take no notice of anybody. We were all strong fellows, the whole thirteen of us. . . . The *Vindictive* was got to Zeebrugge; it was just before midnight when we got alongside the Mole. We had gas-masks on then, and were stoking furiously all the time, with the artificer-engineer backing us up, and joking and keeping us in the best of spirits. Nobody could have been down-hearted while he was there. There is no need to say it was awful; you know something from the accounts in the papers, al-though no written accounts could make you understand what it was really like. . . . Well, there we were, bump, bump, bump against the Mole for I don't know how long, and all the time the shells shrieking and crashing, rockets going up, and a din that was too awful for words, added to which were the cries and shrieks of wounded officers and men. . . . Several times Captain Carpenter came below and told us how things were going on. That was splendid of him, I think. He was full of enthusiasm, and cheered us up wonderfully. He was the same with the seamen and men on deck. . . . I can't help admiring the marines. They were a splendid lot of chaps, most of them seasoned men, whilst the bluejackets (who were just as good) were generally quite young men. The marines were bursting to get at the fight and were chafing under the delay all the time. . . . While we were along-side I was stoking and took off my gas-mask, as it was so much in the way. It was a silly thing to do, but I couldn't get on with the work with it on. Suddenly I smelt gas. I don't know whether it came from an ordinary shell, but I know it was not from the smoke screen, and you ought to have seen me nip round for the helmet. I forgot where I put it for the moment, and there was I running round with my hand clapped on my mouth till I found it. In the boiler-room our exciting time was after the worst was over on shore. All of a sudden the telegraph rang down, 'Full speed ahead,' and then there was a commotion. The artificer-engineer shouted 'Now for it; don't forget what you have to do—21 knots, if she never does it again.' In a minute or two the engines were going full pelt. Somebody came down and said we were still hitched on to the Mole, but Campbell said he didn't care if we towed the Mole back with us; nothing was going to stop him. As a matter of fact, we pulled away great chunks of the masonry with the grappling irons, and brought some of it back with us. Eventually we got clear of the Mole, and there was terrific firing up above. Mr. Campbell was urging us on all the time, and we were shoving in the coal like madmen. We were all singing. One of the chaps started with 'I want to go home,' and this eventually developed into a verse, and I don't think we stopped singing it for three and a half hours—pretty nearly all the time we were coming back. In the other parts of the ship there wasn't much singing, for all the killed and wounded men we could get hold of had been brought on board, and were being attended to by the doctors and sick bay men. I don't know if we did the 21 knots, but we got jolly near it, and everybody worked like a Trojan, and was quite exhausted when it was all over. When we were off Dover the Engineer-Commander came down into the boiler-room and asked Artificer-Engineer Campbell, 'What have you got to say about your men?' He replied, 'I'm not going to say anything for them or anything against them; but if I was going to hell to-morrow night I would have the same men with me.' "

Not until the Mole had been cleared of every man that could possibly be removed did the *Vindictive* break away, turning in a half-circle and belching flames from every pore of her broken funnels. That was perhaps her worst moment, for now she was exposed to every angry and awakened battery; her lower decks were already a shambles; and many of her navigating staff were killed or helpless. But her luck held; the enemy's shells fell short; and soon she was comparatively safe in the undispersed smoke-trails, with the glorious consciousness that she had indeed earned the Admiral's "Well done, *Vindictive*."

Horatius at the Bridge

BY

LIVY

BY THIS time the Tarquins had fled to Lars Porsena, king of Clusium.
There, with advice and entreaties, they besought him not to suffer them,
who were descended from the Etrurians and of the same blood and name,
to live in exile and poverty; and advised him not to let this practice of
expelling kings to pass unpunished. Liberty, they declared, had charms
enough in itself; and unless kings defended their crowns with as much
vigor as the people pursued their liberty, the highest must be reduced to
a level with the lowest; there would be nothing exalted, nothing distinguished above the rest; hence there must be an end of regal government, the
most beautiful institution both among gods and men. Porsena, thinking it
would be an honor to the Tuscans that there should be a king at Rome,
especially one of the Etrurian nation, marched towards Rome with an
army. Never before had such terror seized the Senate, so powerful was the
state of Clusium at the time, and so great the renown of Porsena. Nor did
they only dread their enemies, but even their own citizens, lest the common
people, through excess of fear should, by receiving the Tarquins into the
city, accept peace even though purchased with slavery. Many concessions
were therefore granted to the people by the Senate during that period. Their
attention, in the first place, was directed to the markets, and persons were
sent, some to the Volscians, others to Cumæ, to buy up corn. The privilege
of selling salt, because it was farmed at a high rate, was also taken into the
hands of the government, and withdrawn from private individuals; and
the people were freed from port-duties and taxes, in order that the rich,
who could bear the burden, should contribute; the poor paid tax enough
if they educated their children. This indulgent care of the fathers accordingly kept the whole state in such concord amid the subsequent severities
of the siege and famine, that the highest as well as the lowest abhorred the
name of king; nor was any individual afterwards so popular by intriguing
practices as the whole Senate was by their excellent government.

Some parts of the city seemed secured by the walls, others by the River
Tiber. The Sublician Bridge well-nigh afforded a passage to the enemy,
had there not been one man, Horatius Cocles (fortunately Rome had on
that day such a defender) who, happening to be posted on guard at the
bridge, when he saw the Janiculum taken by a sudden assault and the

From: *The History of Rome, Book II.*

221

enemy pouring down thence at full speed, and that his own party, in terror and confusion, were abandoning their arms and ranks, laying hold of them one by one, standing in their way and appealing to the faith of gods and men, he declared that their flight would avail them nothing if they deserted their post; if they passed the bridge, there would soon be more of the enemy in the Palatium and Capitol than in the Janiculum. For that reason he charged them to demolish the bridge, by sword, by fire, or by any means whatever; declaring that he would stand the shock of the enemy as far as could be done by one man. He then advanced to the first entrance of the bridge, and being easily distinguished among those who showed their backs in retreating, faced about to engage the foe hand to hand, and by his surprising bravery he terrified the enemy. Two indeed remained with him from a sense of shame: Sp. Lartius and T. Herminius, men eminent for their birth, and renowned for their gallant exploits. With them he for a short time stood the first storm of the danger, and the severest brunt of the battle. But as they who demolished the bridge called upon them to retire, he obliged them also to withdraw to a place of safety on a small portion of the bridge that was still left. Then casting his stern eyes toward the officers of the Etrurians in a threatening manner, he now challenged them singly, and then reproached them, slaves of haughty tyrants who, regardless of their own freedom, came to oppress the liberty of others. They hesitated for a time, looking round one at the other, to begin the fight; shame then put the army in motion, and a shout being raised, they hurled weapons from all sides at their single adversary; and when they all stuck in his upraised shield, and he with no less obstinacy kept possession of the bridge, they endeavored to thrust him down from it by one push, when the crash of the falling bridge was heard, and at the same time a shout of the Romans raised for joy at having completed their purpose, checked their ardor with sudden panic. Then said Cocles: "Holy Father Tiber, I pray thee, receive these arms, and this thy soldier, in thy propitious stream." Armed as he was, he leaped into the Tiber, and amid showers of darts, swam across safe to his party, having dared an act which is likely to obtain with posterity more fame than credit. The state was grateful for such valor; a statue was erected to him in the comitium, and as much land given to him as he could plow in one day. The zeal of private individuals was also conspicuous among his public honors. For amid the great scarcity, each contributed something, according to his supply, depriving himself of his own support.

Shiloh, Bloody Shiloh!

BY

LLOYD LEWIS

THE dawn came up on Sunday, April 6, to shine red on the peach blossoms that were flowering in Tennessee. Among the fluttering petals, buglers in blue uniforms stood up and their horns wailed "The-devil-is-loose, the-devil-is-loose." The routine reveille snarled through the tents and the Army of the Tennessee awakened to remember that they were soldiers face to face with another day of camp life. There had been a little scare on Friday evening when some gray cavalry had galloped up with a few cannon to annoy the outposts, but that meant nothing more than bluff. Sherman had pursued the enemy for five miles with his brigade, only to find no respectable force menacing him. On Saturday afternoon Colonel Jesse J. Appler of the Fifty-third Ohio, holding the most advanced position, had sent Sherman word that a large force of the foe was approaching, and the red-haired commander, bulging with confidence, had answered, "Take your damned regiment back to Ohio. There is no enemy nearer than Corinth." That afternoon he had wired Grant, "I do not apprehend anything like an attack upon our position."

Ever since his arrival at Pittsburgh Landing, Sherman had been listening to wild-eyed pickets rushing in with tales of massed armies "out there," and always he had found on investigation merely a few squads of Southern cavalrymen scampering away. He had had enough of these camp rumors in Kentucky and would not make the same mistake again. In Sherman's tent, his new aide-de-camp, Lieutenant John T. Taylor, asked why he didn't march out to fight the "Rebs" over in Corinth. Sherman replied, "Never mind, young man, you'll have all the fighting you want before this war is over."

Now the Confederates, looking at the red dawn, exclaimed, "The sun of Austerlitz!"—so filled were they with Napoleonic mottoes. No bugles blew; the whole Southern army stepped quietly into battle array. "Tonight we will water our horses in the Tennessee," said Johnston, his large mustachios flaring. At half-past five the brigades, spread wide, came marching through the dew, straight down the ribs of the giant fan, aiming at the Landing in the handle. Men in the ranks carried their muskets at right-shoulder shift; the skirmishers ahead bore their guns like quail-hunters.

From: *Sherman: Fighting Prophet*: Copyright 1932, by Harcourt, Brace & Co.

Johnston's battle scheme was to strike the Union right, then let the whole Southern line, as it came up, roll down the length of the Union front—a method that would begin with Sherman, proceed to Prentiss, then engage Hurlbut and W. H. L. Wallace on the left.

"What a beautiful morning this is!" said boys of the Eighty-first Ohio as they washed their faces in front of their tents, stuffed their shirt tails inside their trousers, and stretched themselves. The birds and insects sang with that especial loudness which they seemed to possess on Sundays. Breakfast was cooking. Shots popped among the trees, far away. "Those pickets again," everybody said. The Eighty-first, well to the rear—they were in W. H. L. Wallace's division—did not know that the shooting came from skirmishers whom Prentiss had sent out to reconnoiter. Prentiss, the volunteer officer, was warier than his neighbor Sherman, the trained soldier.

In Sherman's lines, so much nearer the sound of this first clash between the opposing skirmishers, there was deadly calm. One man, that timorous leader, Colonel Appler of the Fifty-third Ohio, took alarm and had his drums sound the long roll. He had cried "Wolf" so often that his men, grumbling, took their own time about falling into formation. Suddenly a private of the Twenty-fifth Missouri, one of Prentiss's outposts, stumbled out of the thicket, holding a wound and calling, "Get into line, the Rebels are coming!" Appler sent a courier to Sherman, who sent back word, "You must be badly scared over there." Neighboring regiments, accustomed to Appler's chronic uneasiness, went on with their breakfasts.

An officer of the Fifty-third who had gone into the bushes half dressed came scrambling back howling, "Colonel, the Rebels are crossing the field!" Appler hurried two companies out to see and one of their captains rushed back with the news, "The Rebels are out there thicker than fleas on a dog's back!" At that moment the quail-hunting skirmishers of the Confederate advance stalked into view within musket shot of Appler's right flank. "Look, Colonel!" an officer shouted. A Union skirmisher dashed in yelling, "Get ready, the Johnnies are here thicker than Spanish needles in a fence corner!"

"This is no place for us," wailed Appler, and ordering battalions right to meet the Southern threat, shook in his shoes. His men, who had never held a battalion drill, were confused and milled about pathetically. Cooks left their camp kettles and ran. The sick, one third of the regiment, were carried to the rear. Sherman, one orderly behind him, rode up and trained his glasses on a part of the field that was as yet clear. The quail-hunters raised their rifles. "Sherman will be shot!" cried the Fifty-third. "General, look to your right!"

The general looked, threw up his hand, snapping, "My God, we're attacked!" As he said it the Confederates fired and his orderly fell dead, the first mortality at Shiloh. "Colonel Appler, hold your position! I'll support you!" shouted Sherman, and he spurred away for reënforcements. Appler received the encouraging news, walked over to a tree, and lay down behind it, his face like ashes. His men, forming in a wavering line, began to shoot at the Confederates, whose main line, guns flashing in the sun, came out of the woods. "Retreat! Save yourselves!" bawled Appler, and jumping up from the shelter of the tree, he bounded away to the rear and so out of the Civil War. The Fifty-third wavered. Some boys followed their colonel; the rest began to shoot at the enemy.

An incessant humming was going on among the tree tops. The boys said it sounded like a swarm of bees. Then the leaden swarm drew lower and lower until men began to fall down under its stings. It was all new and puzzling. When a man fell wounded his friends dropped their guns and helped him to the rear, staring at the blood with horror and curiosity. There were no stretchers, no hospital attendants at hand, no first-aid kits. Men bled to death because no comrade knew how to stanch the flow with a twisted handkerchief. One boy of the Fifty-third was hit a glancing blow in the shin and sat down, rubbing the place and squalling loudly. It hurt, bad!

Private A. C. Voris of the Seventeenth Illinois, which stood close by, left his regiment and came over to help the leaderless Fifty-third. He had served at Fort Donelson and was therefore a veteran among these apprentice killers. Walking calmly among them, Voris taught the trembling youngsters how to use their guns. He would aim, fire, reload, and talk. "I've met the elephant before and the way to do is to keep cool and aim low." His rifle would go "Crack!" then his voice would resume: "It's just like shooting squirrels, only these squirrels have guns, that's all." The Fifty-third began to do better. Soon Voris, seeing his own regiment moving off, called "Goodby!" and left, but the Ohio boys never forgot him, even if a little later they all ran away. After their flight they re-formed, promoted Captain Jones to the colonelcy, and marched back into the fight in scattered units.

Recruits like those of the Fifty-third were scampering away from all parts of the field before nine o'clock, and soon a number, estimated by Grant to be 8,000 were hiding under the bluffs by the river screeching in terror. Grant, who had hurried down from Savannah at the first sound of guns, wasted no time trying to re-form the fugitives. "Excluding these troops who fled, panic-stricken before they had fired a shot, there was not a time," he said, "when during the day we had more than 25,000 men in line." This 25,000, however, learned the business of battle quickly. Considering their lack of training it would not have been surprising if they had all run; so said British military critics when they studied the battle years later. The average Federal stood his ground, shooting at enemies sometimes not more than thirty feet away. When the Confederates derisively shouted "Bull Run!" the Union boys gave them back "Donelson!" in a jeering bellow.

To join them came a thin trickle of soldiers who, after fleeing, regained self-command on the river bank. Surgeon Horace Wardner, Twelfth Illinois, was working among the wounded on the wharf when he heard a large splash and looked up to see a demoralized horseman trying to swim the river on horseback. Some fifty yards from shore the animal wheeled, unseating its rider, and headed back. Frantically the cavalryman caught the passing tail and was towed to land. The ducking had cooled his blood and, gathering up weapons, he mounted and rode toward the battle.

So stoutly did Sherman hold the Union right that Johnston failed in his scheme for rolling up the Federal line like a sheet of paper. With his face and red beard black with powder, Sherman dashed up and down the field, re-forming regiments as fast as they crumbled, plugging leaks in the human dike, drawing back his force, step by step, and succeeding, somehow, in keeping the stormy tide of Southerners from breaking through. Confederate batteries were shelling his force heavily and volleys of musket balls and buckshot swept the ground. One buckshot penetrated his palm, but without taking his eyes off the enemy he wrapped a handkerchief about it and thrust his hand into his breast. Another ball tore his shoulder strap, scratching the skin. Captain William Reuben Rowley, aide-de-camp to Grant, arriving to ask how the battle was going, found Sherman standing with his uninjured hand resting on a tree, his eyes watching his skirmishers.

"Tell Grant," he said, "if he has any men to spare I can use them; if not, I will do the best I can. We are holding them pretty well just now—pretty well—but it's hot as hell."

Four horses had died between Sherman's knees. At the death of the first, Lieutenant Taylor dismounted and handed his reins to the general. Swinging into the saddle, Sherman said, "Well, my boy, didn't I promise you all the fighting you could do?" Albert D. Richardson, collecting descriptions of Sherman from his men after the battle, said that at this point in the encounter:

All around him were excited orderlies and officers, but though his face was besmeared with powder and blood, battle seemed to have cooled his usually hot nerves.

Other soldiers said that during the battle Sherman hadn't waved his arms when he talked, nor talked so much, as in the past. His lips were shut tight, his eyelids narrowed to a slit. He let his cigars go out more often than in peace times. He didn't puff smoke as furiously as in camp. John Day of Battery A in the Chicago Light Artillery saw Sherman halt his spurring progress over the field by the guns, again and again. Brass missionaries, the cannoneers called their pieces, having vowed to "convert the Rebels or send 'em to Kingdom Come." Day remembered that during the fight "Sherman had trouble keeping his cigar lit and he used up all his matches and most of the men's."

Thomas Kilby Smith, officer of the Fifty-fourth Ohio, and a family friend of the Ewings, watched Sherman with worshipful eyes and wrote home, "Sherman's cheek never blanched." For the second time in his life, Sherman had found something to make him forget himself, completely, utterly. He had caught that sharp rapture of absorption as a youth painting pictures on canvas in South Carolina. Now he had found it again—the strange joy of profound selflessness. Here in the storm and thunder of Shiloh, the artist found his art. His nerves, so close to the thin skin, congealed into ice. Sometimes when he held his horse motionless for a period, studying the enemy, the dead and wounded piled high before him. He did not notice them, yet they were the same boys for whose safety he had worried himself in Louisville to the brink of lunacy.

Soldiers around him thought he saw and foresaw everything. When his right wing fell back, he grinned, saying, "I was looking for that," and loosed a battery that halted the charging Confederates in stricken postures. When his chief of staff, Major Dan Sanger, pointed out Southern cavalry charging the battery, Sherman produced two companies of infantry that had been held for this emergency. They shot riders from saddles while Sherman went on with his cannonade.

For all its absorption, his mind—perhaps his subconscious mind—was photographing hideous pictures, sharp negatives, and storing them away. Later on they would become vivid positives:

. . . our wounded mingled with rebels, charred and blackened by the burning tents and grass, crawling about begging for some one to end their misery . . . the bones of living men crushed beneath the cannon wheels coming left about . . . 10,000 men lying in a field not more than a mile by half a mile.

The field of which he spoke was a cocklebur meadow in the front. Across it Beauregard had sent his Irish-born dare-devil General Patrick R. Cleburne, to lose one third of the brigade in the fury of Sherman's fire. Probably all that saved the life of Cleburne was an accident; his horse stumbled at the start of the charge, sinking the general in the mud and separating him from his command. When the day was done, many observers said that a man could have walked all over the cocklebur meadow using bodies for stepping-stones.

Novitiates though the Northern boys might be at the profession of war, most of them were trained squirrel-shooters who, once they had mastered the complexities of the newfangled muskets, did lavish execution at point-blank range. After the first flurry, nothing could terrify them, not even the Rebel yell that had first been heard at Fort Donelson. This incoherent battle cry was distinguished by a peculiar shrillness from the deeper shouts of the Federals.

By ten o'clock the Northerners had steadied enough to begin counter-charges, the Twentieth Illinois, for instance, fighting back and forth through its camps a half-dozen times. At this hour Grant, making the rounds, had ridden quietly up to Sherman, upon whom the full fury of Southern determination continued to fall. Grant said that he had anticipated Sherman's need of cartridges, and that he was satisfied the enemy could be held. He said that he was needed more elsewhere and galloped away. It was their first meeting under fire, and in the smoke they gauged each other. Later Grant said, "In thus moving along the line, I never deemed it important to stay long with Sherman."

It was at this hour of 10 A.M. that the battle settled into what most of those participants who survived the war would describe as the fiercest they ever saw. Regiments mixed, blue and gray, in the hit-trip-smother. Men carried away confused memories—awful sheets of flame . . . the endless zip-zip of musket balls, canister . . . the shudder of grapeshot . . . dirt, gravel, twigs, pieces of bark, flying in their faces . . . splinters like knives ripping open bodies . . . men tearing paper cartridges, ramming them down musket barrels, capping the guns, firing, and as likely as not forgetting to remove the ramrods, not missing them, in fact, until they saw them quivering like arrows in the throats of enemies fifty feet away. Sense and hearing were stunned by the crash of exploding powder and the death shrieks of boys. Fountains of warm wet blood sprayed on the faces and hands of the living, brains spattered on coat sleeves. Men moved convulsively, wondering whether this moment—now—would be their last. When the Fifty-fifth Illinois retreated into a blind ravine, Confederates slaughtered them from the gully edge. "It was like shooting into a flock of sheep," said Major Whitfield of the Ninth Mississippi, and years later he was still saying, "I never saw such cruel work during the war."

Prentiss, who had been forced slowly backward, finally anchored his regiments in a sunken road and by a concentrated fire was achieving a carnage hitherto unimagined by any one of the youths involved. The Hornet's Nest, the Southerners called this sector as they worked in it for six hours, trampling their own dead and wounded. Federals noted how the charging lines would wave like standing grain when a volley cut through them. Others said the lines when hit wobbled like a loose rope shaken at one end. At times the graycoats simply bent their heads as to a sleet storm. For beginners the Southerners were as brave as the Federals, and vice versa—farm boys all, learning a new trade.

A young private of the Fourteenth Illinois came up to Lieutenant Colonel Cam, fumbling at his entrails, which were trying to escape through a great slit in his abdomen, made by a passing shell. The slippery intestines kept working through his fingers. "Oh, Colonel, what shall I do?" he pleaded. Cam laid him gently behind a tree, whipped tears off his own cheeks, then walked back into the killing. Johnson, an officer of the same regiment, spurred his horse after an elderly Confederate officer, shot him through the body, reached out and seized his victim by the hair. To his horror the whole scalp came off as the Southerner slipped dead from the saddle. A roar of laughter arose above the battle clash, and Johnson saw that he held a wig.

Private Robert Oliver of the Fifty-fifth Illinois saw Private James Goodwin walk off the field resembling Mephistopheles in a play: "He looked like he had been dipped in a barrel of blood." Goodwin carried seven bullet holes in his skin. The Union Sergeant Lacey saw George F. Farwell, a company bugler, sitting against a tree reading a letter. Lacey shook him and found that he was dead, his sightless eyes still fast upon his wife's handwriting. Colonel (afterwards General) Joseph Wheeler of the Southern force said, "The Yankee bullets were so thick I imagined if I held up a bushel basket it would fill in a minute." A boy of the Fifty-third Ohio, joining another outfit, was wounded and sent to the rear, but was soon back saying, "Captain, give me a gun, this damned fight ain't got any rear." Units were surrounded at times without knowing it and were rescued only by the equality of their enemy's ignorance.

Lieutenant James H. Wilson of Grant's staff caught a youth starting for the rear, shook him, and called him a coward. The soldier protested indignantly. "I've only lost confidence in my colonel," he said. Private Sam Durkee of Waterhouse's Battery, close to Sherman often during the day, felt a blow on the seat of his trousers as he bent over his cannon, and looking around, he saw the heels of his lieutenant's horse flirting past. Durkee yelled above the cannonade, "Why did you let your horse kick me?" "I didn't," screamed the officer. Sam felt his posterior with his hand and found blood. "Oh, I'm wounded!" he screeched. Ed Russell, thumbing the vent of a cannon near by, went down with a solid shot through his abdomen, lived twenty minutes, and shook hands with every man in the battery before he died. Men with lung wounds lay heaving, every breath hissing through holes in their chests.

The most ghastly killing of all took place when Albert Sidney Johnston assailed the Peach Orchard, a knob left of the Union center. Hurlbut, defending it, placed his men on their stomachs in a double row to shoot Johnston's men like rabbits "a-settin'." Before such a blast the Confederate boys at length withered and refused to try again. Johnston rode along the front. In one hand he carried a small tin cup that he had picked up in the sack of a Union camp and forgotten to drop. He touched bayonets with it, crying, "Men, they are stubborn; we must use the bayonet!" The Southern boys admitted that Johnston was magnificent and that his horse Fire-eater was beautiful, but they did not want to go into that sheet-flame death again. Suddenly Johnston swung his horse toward the foe and shouted, "Come, I will lead you!" Boys felt hot blood in their veins once more and, rushing past him, took the Peach Orchard, although they left comrades in rows behind them.

Fire-eater was hit four times. Johnston's clothes were pierced, one ball ripping the sole of his boot. He flapped the sole, laughing— "They didn't trip me that time!" Then he reeled. Searching hands could at first find no wound, but at length came upon a boot full of blood. Johnston was dead at two-thirty in the afternoon. A tourniquet might have saved him from the thigh wound that drained his life.

The capture of the Peach Orchard was not decisive. Hurlbut fell back to another strong position, and his men fired so rapidly as to shave down saplings and thickets as if with gardeners' shears. Between the lines thirsty men from both forces drank side by side. Wounded soldiers died while drinking, staining the water red. The Bloody Pool, it was called long afterwards.

In the retirement from the orchard, two wounded gunners tried to move their cannon with one horse. Mud stalled them. They decided to give up.

Just then a stray bullet obligingly struck the horse at the base of the tail and with an astonished snort and lurch the animal took the gun off to safety.

Battered slowly, steadily backward, Grant did not lose confidence. At 3 P.M. he calmly began to assemble cannon on high ground near the Landing, parking the guns wheel to wheel and collecting enough ammunition for a final burst of flame, which at close quarters was expected to destroy any possible number of assailants.

At 4 P.M. the crisis of the battle came. In nine hours of fighting the Confederates had captured 23 cannon, and pushed the Union line back a mile or more. At the beginning Sherman had prevented them from turning the Union flank, yet they had seized three out of five Northern division camps, shooting some Federals in night clothes among the tent ropes. Some of the attackers who reached the camps so suddenly owed their success to their blue uniforms, Union batteries having let them advance unmolested. These rows of tents had helped save the Northern battle line from complete breakage, for the Confederates halted to loot the camps. It had been almost twelve hours since many of them had eaten, and they forgot the battle in their hunger for the half-cooked breakfasts standing on Union fires. They rifled haversacks, drank whisky, and read the letters of Federal privates that fluttered on tent floors.

The Confederates had been at fault, too, in attacking in long lines on so rough and broken a front. The battle had promptly split up into many individual struggles, with coöperation between generals impossible. Bragg, smashing fiercely at Prentiss, finally surrounded him, but could find no brother Confederate to push in through the open spaces on right and left to divide the Union line into three sections. By the time Prentiss had surrendered to save the lives of his remaining 2,000 men, Grant had patched up a solid front line again, Sherman and McClernand had fallen back into a more solid array, and the Federals waited for the next assault.

It never came. Beauregard, succeeding to the Confederate command on Johnston's death, saw that his men had had enough. Many had left their posts to go over and stare at the Union prisoners. Organization was broken, officers were separated from men, losses had been frightful. Furthermore, a dull, heavy, and monotonous pum-pum had begun to sound from the river. Two Union gunboats, escorting Buell's army in its advance up the stream, had begun to throw shells into the Confederate lines.

Shortly after six o'clock that morning, Grant had sent word for Buell's advance guard, under General "Bull" Nelson of Kentucky, to make haste. A steamer with rush orders had gone on to tell Buell at Savannah to bring up his whole force. To his men Buell seemed negligent as he listened to the distant guns. Boys of the Fifty-first Indiana Volunteers said he was "seemingly unconcerned—a condition of mind and heart almost universally attributed to him by the men of his command." Their regimental historian described the scene:

Colonel Streight stormed around at a great rate and Captain Will Searce became so impatient that he cried like a child and railed out against Buell, characterizing him as a rebel. Looking up he saw Buell not forty feet away. He had certainly heard the remark but took no notice. We paced up and down the bank like caged animals.

Although there was no convincing proof of the not uncommon charge that Buell's loyalty was doubtful, the man had too much of his friend McClellan's jealousies and prima donna's outlook ever to fit into the Western way of war. Twenty-two years after Shiloh, Sherman wrote James B. Fry, one of Buell's officers:

General Grant believes, and we all do, that you [Buell's army] were derelict in coming by the short line . . . so deliberately and slowly as to show a purpose, while Sidney Johnston moved around by the longer line and made his concentration and attack on us before you arrived, and long after you should have been there to help us on the *first day*.

Buell arrived at the Landing in mid-afternoon, in advance of his men, and concluded from the sight of 8,000 fugitives at the wharf that the Army of the Tennessee had been defeated. He later insisted that Grant, whom he soon met, gave him a similar impression. But Sherman, who conversed with Grant at almost the same time, declared that the latter had talked quite differently, saying that at Donelson he had noticed that there came a time "when either side was ready to give way if the other showed a bold front." He had decided to be the bold one, and had won. Now, he said, the enemy had shot its bolt and with Buell's force available by morning, victory was sure.

Near dusk, Sherman, meeting Buell and Fry, told them that the Army of the Tennessee had 18,000 men in line, that Lew Wallace's 6,000 "had just come in and that I had orders from General Grant in person to attack at daylight the next morning." He was glad Buell had come, but thought victory certain even without him. Buell regarded this as a poor way to welcome him, "the savior of the day."

The battle dwindled as twilight spread. Grant and Sherman had narrow escapes at almost the same moment. A shell, missing Grant, tore the whole head, except for a strip of chin, from a captain beside him, ripped a cantle from a saddle behind him, and bowled on to clip both legs from one of Nelson's men as he came up from the river bank.

Sherman was swinging into his saddle when his horse pranced sufficiently to tangle around his neck the reins held by Major Hammond. As he bowed while Hammond raised the reins, a cannon ball cut the straps two inches below the major's hand and tore the crown and back rim of Sherman's hat.

Up from the Landing poured Nelson's men, stepping over piles of wounded on the wharf. The 8,000 fugitives had already trampled these bloody victims, sailors had dragged heavy cables across them, and they were now so caked with mud and dried blood that they were as black as Negroes.

The fresh legions cursed the cowards at the Landing. They thought them as terrorized as sheep who have been visited by killer dogs. In answer to these taunts, the deserters answered, *"You'll* catch it; *you'll* see. They'll cut you to pieces!" Nelson wanted to fire upon them. Colonel Jacob Ammen, the Virginia-born leader of a Union brigade, found his way blocked by a clergyman who exhorted the refugees, "Rally for God and country! Oh, rally round the flag! Oh, rally!" Always a pious Episcopalian, Ammen forgot himself this once and burst out, "Shut-up, you God-damned old fool! Get out of the way!"

The first of Nelson's men to reach the top were Rousseau's brigade—the Kentuckians who had originally disliked Sherman at Muldraugh's Hill. Now when they saw him with his hat in tatters, black powder on his red beard, his hand bandaged, they put their hats on their bayonets and cheered for Old Sherman. He pretended not to notice, but he remembered it always. It was the first really good word he had had since the beginning of the war.

While the Union officers rearranged their battered forces, Bragg had been moaning, "My God! My God!" because Beauregard would not order the one final charge that, Bragg was sure, would bring complete victory. But several days later he admitted to his wife that "our force was disorganized, demoralized and exhausted and hungry." Some of his men he described as

too lazy to hunt the enemy's camps for provisions. They were mostly out of ammunition and though millions of cartridges were around them, not one officer in ten supplied his men. . . . Our failure is entirely due to a want of discipline and a want of officers. Universal suffrage, furloughs and whisky have ruined us.

It was just such a letter as Sherman would have written had he been in Bragg's shoes.

That night Bragg and Beauregard slept in Sherman's vacated tent. Near by, the captive Prentiss slept among Confederates he had known before the war. He twitted his hosts about the defeat awaiting them on the morrow. "Do you hear that?" he would say, awakening them in the night, when the boom of the United States Navy cannon came from the river, Colonel Nathan Bedford Forrest, lately a slave-trader, now an unmilitary but surpassingly warlike cavalry leader in the Southern army, walked through the bivouacs of his men confiding to brother officers, "If the enemy attack us in the morning they will whip us like hell."

Grant was riding through the Union camps with substantially the same message, hunting out his commanders in the chaos to tell them that he was going to attack at daylight. To general Rusling, he said quietly, "Whichever side takes the initiative in the morning will make the other retire, and Beauregard will be mighty smart if he attacks before I do."

Across the torn field, men slept with the roar of the gunboats and the screams of the wounded ripping the air. Hospitals had broken down. Surgeons, swamped with work, did what they could, slicing and sawing in desperate haste. Flies had been blackening wounds all day. A mixture of whisky and chloroform was the only antiseptic, and when it was poured on mangled flesh it brought out maggots "on a canter," as the sufferers grimly said. Rain fell, bringing misery to the tentless warriors and relief to the burning lips of the sufferers.

When the lightning flashed the wet and weary Confederates saw sickening sights all around them—naked, bloating flesh, ghastly white faces—and they heard the moaning refrains, "Water! Water!" in the storm. A. H. Mecklin, a Bible student who had joined a Mississippi regiment, thought he heard wild hogs in the bushes. "Through the dark I heard the sound of hogs quarreling over their carnival feasts." He admitted, however, that the sound was not unmistakable."

As the night grew gray with morning, Lieutenant William George Stevenson, of Beauregard's staff, rode the field searching for his chief. Stevenson had seen a cannon ball take off the head of an earlier mount and was sick of everything. His new horse balked at a little ravine. He said afterward:

He hesitated and I glanced down to detect the cause. The rain had washed leaves out of the narrow channel down the gully some six inches wide, leaving the hard clay exposed. Down this pathway ran a band of blood nearly an inch thick, filling the channel. Striking my rowels into the horse to escape the horrible sight, he plunged his foot into the stream of blood and threw the already thickening mass in ropy folds up on the dead leaves on the bank.

Through both battered and bleeding armies ran the folk saying, "Nobody ever wins who starts a battle on a Sunday."

Monday saw sharp, bitter fighting but victory for the North was certain. General Lew Wallace with 5,000 men arrived and took their places in the line. Wallace had started early on Sunday morning to march the five miles to Shiloh Meeting-house, but had wandered around the country all day within sound of the battle without being able to find it. Whether the mistake was his or that of Grant's aides was a matter of dispute for years to come. Beauregard, calling the roll at dawn, found only half of his original 40,000 men at hand—and these were disorganized. Nevertheless the Confederates fought stoutly for eight hours more.

At 3 P.M. on Monday Grant, gathering up fragments of regiments led them in one last charge that broke Confederate resistance, and Shiloh was won. That evening the cold, drizzling rain resumed, gradually turning to sleet and hail that bruised the butchered Southern boys who lay in the young spring grass or who had been piled like bags of grain into open wagons for the jolting trip to Corinth. Against orders, Confederate privates crowded into the tent of General Breckinridge and stood there packed and wretched while the water ran in under the tent flap. In defeat they had lost their awe of great men.

The hail pelted Union wounded too, as they lay shrieking on the field of victory; it knocked from the trees the last few peach blossoms that the bullets had spared.

How David Slew Goliath

FROM

THE BIBLE

Now the Philistines gathered together their armies to battle, and were gathered together at Shochoh, which belongeth to Judah, and pitched between Shochoh and Azekah, in Ephes-dammim. And Saul and the men of Israel were gathered together, and pitched by the valley of Elah, and set the battle in array against the Philistines. And the Philistines stood on a mountain on the one side, and Israel stood on a mountain on the other side: and there was a valley between them.

And there went out a champion out of the camp of the Philistines, named Goliath, of Gath, whose height was six cubits and a span. And he had an helmet of brass upon his head, and he was armed with a coat of mail; and the weight of the coat was five thousand shekels of brass. And he had greaves of brass upon his legs, and a target of brass between his shoulders. And the staff of his spear was like a weaver's beam; and his spear's head weighed six hundred shekels of iron: and one bearing a shield went before him.

And he stood and cried unto the armies of Israel, and said unto them, Why are ye come out to set your battle in array? am not I a Philistine, and ye servants to Saul? choose you a man for you, and let him come down to me. If he be able to fight with me, and to kill me, then will we be your servants: but if I prevail against him, and kill him, then shall ye be our servants, and serve us. And the Philistine said, I defy the armies of Israel this day; give me a man, that we may fight together.

When Saul and all Israel heard those words of the Philistine, they were dismayed, and greatly afraid.

Now David was the son of that Ephrathite of Beth-lehem-judah, whose name was Jesse; and he had eight sons: and the man went among men for an old man in the days of Saul. And the three eldest sons of Jesse went and followed Saul to the battle: and the names of his three sons that went to the battle were Eliab the firstborn, and next unto him Abinadab, and the third Shammah. And David was the youngest: and the three eldest followed Saul. But David went and returned from Saul to feed his father's sheep at Beth-lehem.

And the Philistine drew near morning and evening, and presented himself forty days. And Jesse said unto David his son, Take now for thy brethren

From: *The Bible.*

234

an ephah of this parched corn, and these ten loaves, and run to the camp to thy brethren; And carry these ten cheeses unto the captain of their thousand, and look how thy brethren fare, and take their pledge.

Now Saul, and they, and all the men of Israel, were in the valley of Elah, fighting with the Philistines. And David rose up early in the morning, and left the sheep with a keeper, and took, and went, as Jesse had commanded him; and he came to the trench, as the host was going forth to the fight, and shouted for the battle. For Israel and the Philistines had put the battle in array, army against army. And David left his carriage in the hand of the keeper of the carriage, and ran into the army, and came and saluted his brethren. And as he talked with them, behold, there came up the champion, the Philistine of Gath, Goliath by name, out of the armies of the Philistines, and spake according to the same words: and David heard them.

And all the men of Israel, when they saw the man, fled from him, and were sore afraid. And the men of Israel said, Have ye seen this man that is come up? surely to defy Israel is he come up: and it shall be, that the man who killeth him, the king will enrich him with great riches, and will give him his daughter, and make his father's house free in Israel.

And David spake to the men that stood by him, saying, What shall be done to the man that killeth this Philistine, and taketh away the reproach from Israel? for who is this uncircumcised Philistine, that he should defy the armies of the living God?

And the people answered him after this manner, saying, So shall it be done to the man that killeth him.

And Eliab his eldest brother heard when he spake unto the men; and Eliab's anger was kindled against David, and he said, Why camest thou down hither? and with whom hast thou left those few sheep in the wilderness? I know thy pride, and the naughtiness of thine heart; and thou art come down that thou mightest see the battle.

And David said, What have I now done? Is there not a cause? And he turned from him toward another, and spake after the same manner: and the people answered him again after the former manner. And when the words were heard which David spake, they rehearsed them before Saul: and he sent for him.

And David said to Saul, Let no man's heart fail because of him; thy servant will go and fight with this Philistine.

And Saul said to David, Thou art not able to go against him: for thou art but a youth, and he a man of war from his youth.

And David said unto Saul, Thy servant kept his father's sheep, and there came a lion, and a bear, and took a lamb out of the flock: And I went out after him, and smote him, and delivered it out of his mouth: and when he arose against me, I caught him by his beard, and smote him, and slew him. Thy servant slew both the lion and the bear: and this uncircumcised Philistine shall be as one of them, seeing he hath defied the armies of the living God. David said moreover, The Lord that delivered me out of the paw of the lion, and out of the paw of the bear, He will deliver me out of the hand of this Philistine. And Saul said unto David, Go, and the Lord be with thee.

And Saul armed David with his armour, and he put an helmet of brass upon his head; also he armed him with a coat of mail. And David girded his sword upon his armour, and he assayed to go; for he had not proved it. And David said unto Saul, I cannot go with these; for I have not proved them. And David put them off him.

And he took his staff in his hand, and chose him five smooth stones out of the brook, and put them in a shepherd's bag which he had, even in a scrip; and his sling was in his hand: and he drew near to the Philistine.

And the Philistine came on and drew near unto David; and the man that bare the shield went before him. And when the Philistine looked about, and saw David, he disdained him: for he was but a youth, and ruddy, and of a fair countenance.

And the Philistine said unto David, Am I a dog, that thou comest to me with staves? And the Philistine cursed David by his gods. And the Philistine said to David, Come to me, and I will give thy flesh unto the fowls of the air, and to the beasts of the field.

Then said David to the Philistine, Thou comest to me with a sword, with a spear, and with a shield: but I come to thee in the name of the Lord of hosts, the God of the armies of Israel, whom thou hast defied. This day will the Lord deliver thee into mine hand; and I will smite thee, and take thine head from thee and I will give the carcases of the host of the Philistines this day unto the fowls of the air, and to the wild beasts of the earth; that all the earth may know that there is a God in Israel. And all this assembly shall know that the Lord saveth not with sword and spear: for the battle is the Lord's, and He will give you into our hands.

And it came to pass, when the Philistine arose, and came and drew nigh to meet David, that David hasted, and ran toward the army to meet the Philistine. And David put his hand in his bag, and took thence a stone, and slang it, and smote the Philistine in his forehead, that the stone sunk into his forehead; and he fell upon his face to the earth.

So David prevailed over the Philistine with a sling and with a stone, and smote the Philistine, and slew him; but there was no sword in the hand of David. Therefore David ran, and stood upon the Philistine, and took his sword, and drew it out of the sheath thereof, and slew him, and cut off his head therewith. And when the Philistines saw their champion was dead, they fled.

And the men of Israel and of Judah arose, and shouted, and pursued the Philistines, until thou come to the valley, and to the gates of Ekron. And the wounded of the Philistines fell down by the way to Shaaraim, even unto Gath, and unto Ekron. And the children of Israel returned from chasing after the Philistines, and they spoiled their tents. And David took the head of the Philistine, and brought it to Jerusalem; but he put his armour in his tent.

And when Saul saw David go forth against the Philistine, he said unto

Abner, the captain of the host, Abner, whose son is this youth? And Abner said, As thy soul liveth, O king, I cannot tell. And the king said, Inquire thou whose son the stripling is.

And as David returned from the slaughter of the Philistine, Abner took him, and brought him before Saul with the head of the Philistine in his hand. And Saul said to him, Whose son art thou, thou young man? And David answered, I am the son of thy servant Jesse the Bethlehemite.

The Fight on the Hilltop

BY

ERNEST HEMINGWAY

EL SORDO was making his fight on a hilltop. He did not like this hill and when he saw it he thought it had the shape of a chancre. But he had had no choice except this hill and he had picked it as far away as he could see it and galloped for it, the automatic rifle heavy on his back, the horse laboring, barrel heaving between his thighs, the sack of grenades swinging against one side, the sack of automatic rifle pans banging against the other, and Joaquín and Ignacio halting and firing, halting and firing to give him time to get the gun in place.

There had still been snow then, the snow that had ruined them, and when his horse was hit so that he wheezed in a slow, jerking, climbing stagger up the last part of the crest, splattering the snow with a bright, pulsing jet, Sordo had hauled him along by the bridle, the reins over his shoulder as he climbed. He climbed as hard as he could with the bullets spatting on the rocks, with the two sacks heavy on his shoulders, and then, holding the horse by the mane, had shot him quickly, expertly, and tenderly just where he had needed him, so that the horse pitched, head forward down to plug a gap between two rocks. He had gotten the gun to firing over the horse's back and he fired two pans, the gun clattering, the empty shells pitching into the snow, the smell of burnt hair from the burnt hide where the hot muzzle rested, him firing at what came up to the hill, forcing them to scatter for cover, while all the time there was a chill in his back from not knowing what was behind him. Once the last of the five men had reached the hilltop the chill went out of his back and he had saved the pans he had left until he would need them.

There were two more horses dead along the slope and three more were dead here on the hilltop. He had only succeeded in stealing three horses last night and one had bolted when they tried to mount him bareback in the corral at the camp when the first shooting had started.

Of the five men who had reached the hilltop three were wounded. Sordo was wounded in the calf of his leg and in two places in his left arm. He was very thirsty, his wounds had stiffened, and one of the wounds in his left arm was very painful. He also had a bad headache and as he lay waiting for the planes to come he thought of a joke in Spanish. It was, *"Hay que tomar la muerte como si fuera aspirina,"* which means, "You will have to take death as an aspirin." But he did not make the joke aloud. He grinned

From: *For Whom the Bell Tolls*: Copyright 1940, by Ernest Hemingway. Scribners.

somewhere inside the pain in his head and inside the nausea that came whenever he moved his arm and looked around at what was left of his band.

The five men were spread out like the points of a five-pointed star. They had dug with their knees and hands and made mounds in front of their heads and shoulders with the dirt and piles of stones. Using this cover, they were linking the individual mounds up with stones and dirt. Joaquín, who was eighteen years old, had a steel helmet that he dug with and he passed dirt in it.

He had gotten this helmet at the blowing up of the train. It had a bullet hole through it and every one had always joked at him for keeping it. But he had hammered the jagged edges of the bullet hole smooth and driven a wooden plug into it and then cut the plug off and smoothed it even with the metal inside the helmet.

When the shooting started he had clapped this helmet on his head so hard it banged his head as though he had been hit with a casserole and, in the last lung-aching, leg-dead, mouth-dry, bullet-spatting, bullet-cracking, bullet-singing run up the final slope of the hill after his horse was killed, the helmet had seemed to weigh a great amount and to ring his bursting forehead with an iron band. But he had kept it. Now he dug with it in a steady, almost machine-like desperation. He had not yet been hit.

"It serves for something finally," Sordo said to him in his deep, throaty voice.

"*Resistir y fortificar es vencer,*" Joaquín said, his mouth stiff with the dryness of fear which surpassed the normal thirst of battle. It was one of the slogans of the Communist party and it meant, "Hold out and fortify, and you will win."

Sordo looked away and down the slope at where a cavalryman was sniping from behind a boulder. He was very fond of this boy and he was in no mood for slogans.

"What did you say?"

One of the men turned from the building that he was doing. This man was lying flat on his face, reaching carefully up with his hands to put a rock in place while keeping his chin flat against the ground.

Joaquín repeated the slogan in his dried-up boy's voice without checking his digging for a moment.

"What was the last word?" the man with his chin on the ground asked.

"*Vencer,*" the boy said. "Win."

"*Mierda,*" the man with his chin on the ground said.

"There is another that applies to here," Joaquín said, bringing them out as though they were talismans, "Pasionaria says it is better to die on your feet than to live on your knees."

"*Mierda* again," the man said and another man said, over his shoulder, "We're on our bellies, not our knees."

"Thou, Communist. Do you know your Pasionaria has a son thy age in Russia since the start of the movement?"

"It's a lie," Joaquín said.

"*Qué va,* it's a lie," the other said. "The dynamiter with the rare name told me. He was of thy party, too. Why should he lie?"

"It's a lie," Joaquín said. "She would not do such a thing as keep a son hidden in Russia out of the war."

"I wish I were in Russia," another of Sordo's men said. "Will not thy Pasionaria send me now from here to Russia, Communist?"

"If thou believest so much in thy Pasionaria, get her to get us off this hill," one of the men who had a bandaged thigh said.

"The fascists will do that," the man with his chin in the dirt said.

"Do not speak thus," Joaquín said to him.

"Wipe the pap of your mother's breast off thy lips and give me a hatful of that dirt," the man with his chin on the ground said. "No one ot us will see the sun go down this night."

El Sordo was thinking: It is shaped like a chancre. Or the breast of a young girl with no nipple. Or the top cone of a volcano. You have never seen a volcano, he thought. Nor will you ever see one. And this hill is like a chancre. Let the volcano alone. It's late now for the volcanos.

He looked very carefully around the withers of the dead horse and there was a quick hammering of firing from behind a boulder well down the slope and he heard the bullets from the submachine gun thud into the horse. He crawled along behind the horse and looked out of the angle between the horse's hindquarters and the rock. There were three bodies on the slope just below him where they had fallen when the fascists had rushed the crest under cover of the automatic rifle and submachine gunfire and he and the others had broken down the attack by throwing and rolling down hand grenades. There were other bodies that he could not see on the other sides of the hill crest. There was no dead ground by which attackers could approach the summit and Sordo knew that as long as his ammunition and grenades held out and he had as many as four men they could not get him out of there unless they brought up a trench mortar. He did not know whether they had sent to La Granja for a trench mortar. Perhaps they had not, because surely, soon, the planes would come. It had been four hours since the observation plane had flown over them.

This hill is truly like a chancre, Sordo thought, and we are the very pus of it. But we killed many when they made that stupidness. How could they think that they would take us thus? They have such modern armament that they lose all their sense with overconfidence. He had killed the young officer who had led the assault with a grenade that had gone bouncing and rolling down the slope as they came up it, running, bent half over. In the yellow flash and gray roar of smoke he had seen the officer dive forward to where he lay now like a heavy, broken bundle of old clothing marking the farthest point that the assault had reached. Sordo looked at this body and then, down the hill, at the others.

They are brave but stupid people, he thought. But they have sense enough now not to attack us again until the planes come. Unless, of course, they have a mortar coming. It would be easy with a mortar. The mortar was the normal thing and he knew that they would die as soon as a mortar came up, but when he thought of the planes coming up he felt as naked on that hilltop as though all of his clothing and even his skin had been removed. There is no nakeder thing than I feel, he thought. A flayed rabbit is as well covered as a bear in comparison. But why should they bring planes? They could get us out of here with a trench mortar easily. They are proud of their planes, though, and they will probably bring them. Just as they were so proud of their automatic weapons that they made that stupidness. But undoubtedly they must have sent for a mortar, too.

One of the men fired. Then jerked the bolt and fired again, quickly.

"Save thy cartridges," Sordo said.

"One of the sons of the great whore tried to reach that boulder," the man pointed.

"Did you hit him?" Sordo asked, turning his head with difficulty.

"Nay," the man said. "The fornicator ducked back."

"Who is a whore of whores is Pilar," the man with his chin in the dirt said. "That whore knows we are dying here."

"She could do no good," Sordo said. The man had spoken on the side of his good ear and he had heard him without turning his head. "What could she do?"

"Take these sluts from the rear."

"*Qué va*," Sordo said. "They are spread around a hillside. How would she come on them? There are a very hundred and fifty of them. Maybe more now."

"But if we hold out until dark," Joaquín said.

"And if Christmas comes on Easter," the man with his chin on the ground said.

"And if thy aunt had *cojones* she would be thy uncle," another said to him. "Send for thy Pasionaria. She alone can help us."

"I do not believe that about the son," Joaquín said. "Or if he is there he is training to be an aviator or something of that sort."

"He is hidden there for safety," the man told him.

"He is studying dialectics. Thy Pasionaria has been there. So have Lister and Modesto and others. The one with the rare name told me."

"That they should go to study and return to aid us," Joaquín said.

"That they should aid us now," another man said. "That all the cruts of Russian sucking swindlers should aid us now." He fired and said, "*Me cago en tal;* I missed him again."

"Save thy cartridges and do not talk so much or thou wilt be very thirsty," Sordo said. "There is no water on this hill."

"Take this," the man said and rolling on his side he pulled a wineskin that he wore slung from his shoulder over his head and handed it to Sordo. "Wash thy mouth out, old one. Thou must have much thirst with thy wounds."

"Let all take it," Sordo said.

"Then I will have some first," the owner said and squirted a long stream into his mouth before he handed the leather bottle around.

"Sordo, when thinkest thou the planes will come?" the man with his chin in the dirt asked.

"Any time," said Sordo. "They should have come before."

"Do you think these sons of the great whore will attack again?"

"Only if the planes do not come."

He did not think there was any need to speak about the mortar. They would know it soon enough when the mortar came.

"God knows they've enough planes with what we saw yesterday."

"Too many," Sordo said.

His head hurt very much and his arm was stiffening so that the pain of moving it was almost unbearable. He looked up at the bright, high blue early summer sky as he raised the leather wine bottle with his good arm. He was fifty-two years old and he was sure this was the last time he would see that sky.

He was not at all afraid of dying but he was angry at being trapped on this hill which was only utilizable as a place to die. If we could have gotten clear, he thought. If we could have made them come up the long valley or if we could have broken loose across the road it would have been all right. But this chancre of a hill. We must use it as well as we can and we have used it very well so far.

If he had known how many men in history have had to use a hill to die on it would not have cheered him any for, in the moment he was passing through, men are not impressed by what has happened to other men in similar circumstances any more than a widow of one day is helped by the knowledge that other loved husbands have died. Whether one has fear of it or not, one's death is difficult to accept. Sordo had accepted it but there was no sweetness in its acceptance even at fifty-two, with three wounds and him surrounded on a hill.

He joked about it to himself but he looked at the sky and at the far mountains and he swallowed the wine and he did not want it. If one must die, he thought, and clearly one must, I can die. But I hate it.

Dying was nothing and he had no picture of it nor fear of it in his mind. But living was a field of grain blowing in the wind on the side of a hill. Living was a hawk in the sky. Living was an earthen jar of water in the dust of the threshing with the grain flailed out and the chaff blowing. Living was a horse between your legs and a carbine under one leg and a hill and a valley and a stream with trees along it and the far side of the valley and the hills beyond.

Sordo passed the wine bottle back and nodded his head in thanks. He leaned forward and patted the dead horse on the shoulder where the muzzle of the automatic rifle had burned the hide. He could still smell the burnt hair. He thought how he had held the horse there, trembling, with the fire around them, whispering and cracking, over and around them like a curtain, and had carefully shot him just at the intersection of the cross-lines between the two eyes and the ears. Then as the horse pitched down he had dropped down behind his warm, wet back to get the gun to going as they came up the hill.

"*Eras mucho caballo,*" he said, meaning, "Thou wert plenty of horse."

El Sordo lay now on his good side and looked up at the sky. He was lying on a heap of empty cartridge hulls but his head was protected by the rock and his body lay in the lee of the horse. His wounds had stiffened badly and he had much pain and he felt too tired to move.

"What passes with thee, old one?" the man next to him asked.

"Nothing. I am taking a little rest"

"Sleep," the other said. "*They* will wake us when they come."

Just then some one shouted from down the slope.

"Listen, bandits!" the voice came from behind the rocks where the closest automatic rifle was placed. "Surrender now before the planes blow you to pieces."

"What is it he says?" Sordo asked.

Joaquín told him. Sordo rolled to one side and pulled himself up so that he was crouched behind the gun again.

"Maybe the planes aren't coming," he said. "Don't answer them and do not fire. Maybe we can get them to attack again."

"If we should insult them a little?" the man who had spoken to Joaquín about La Pasionaria's son in Russia asked.

"No," Sordo said. "Give me thy big pistol. Who has a big pistol?"

"Here."

"Give it to me." Crouched on his knees he took the big 9 mm. Star and fired one shot into the ground beside the dead horse, waited, then fired again four times at irregular intervals. Then he waited while he counted sixty and then fired a final shot directly into the body of the dead horse. He grinned and handed back the pistol.

"Reload it," he whispered, "and that every one should keep his mouth shut and no one shoot."

"*Bandidos!*" the voice shouted from behind the rocks.

No one spoke on the hill.

"*Bandidos!* Surrender now before we blow thee to little pieces."

"They're biting," Sordo whispered happily.

As he watched, a man showed his head over the top of the rocks. There was no shot from the hilltop and the head went down again. El Sordo waited, watching, but nothing more happened. He turned his head and looked at the others who were all watching down their sectors of the slope. As he looked at them the others shook their heads.

"Let no one move," he whispered.

"Sons of the great whore," the voice came now from behind the rocks again.

"Red swine. Mother rapers. Eaters of the milk of thy fathers."

Sordo grinned. He could just hear the bellowed insults by turning his good ear. This is better than the aspirin, he thought. How many will we get? Can they be that foolish?

The voice had stopped again and for three minutes they heard nothing and saw no movement. Then the sniper behind the boulder a hundred yards down the slope exposed himself and fired. The bullet hit a rock and ricocheted with a sharp whine. Then Sordo saw a man, bent double, run from the shelter of the rocks where the automatic rifle was across the open ground to the big boulder behind which the sniper was hidden. He almost dove behind the boulder.

Sordo looked around. They signalled to him that there was no movement on the other slopes. El Sordo grinned happily and shook his head. This is ten times better than the aspirin, he thought, and he waited, as happy as only a hunter can be happy.

Below on the slope the man who had run from the pile of stones to the shelter of the boulder was speaking to the sniper.

"Do you believe it?"

"I don't know," the sniper said.

"It would be logical," the man, who was the officer in command, said. "They are surrounded. They have nothing to expect but to die."

The sniper said nothing.

"What do you think?" the officer asked.

"Nothing," the sniper said.

"Have you seen any movement since the shots?"

"None at all."

The officer looked at his wrist watch. It was ten minutes to three o'clock.

"The planes should have come an hour ago," he said. Just then another officer flopped in behind the boulder. The sniper moved over to make room for him.

"Thou, Paco," the first officer said. "How does it seem to thee?"

The second officer was breathing heavily from his sprint up and across the hillside from the automatic rifle position.

"For me it is a trick," he said.

"But if it is not? What a ridicule we make waiting here and laying siege to dead men."

"We have done something worse than ridiculous already," the second officer said. "Look at that slope."

He looked up the slope to where the dead were scattered close to the top. From where he looked the line of the hilltop showed the scattered rocks, the belly, projecting legs, shod hooves jutting out, of Sordo's horse, and the fresh dirt thrown up by the digging.

"What about the mortars?" asked the second officer.

"They should be here in an hour. If not before."

"Then wait for them. There has been enough stupidity already."

"*Bandidos!*" the first officer shouted suddenly, getting to his feet and putting his head well up above the boulder so that the crest of the hill looked much closer as he stood upright. "Red swine! Cowards!"

The second officer looked at the sniper and shook his head. The sniper looked away but his lips tightened.

The first officer stood there, his head all clear of the rock and with his hand on his pistol butt. He cursed and vilified the hilltop. Nothing happened. Then he stepped clear of the boulder and stood there looking up the hill.

"Fire, cowards, if you are alive," he shouted. "Fire on me who has no fear of any Red that ever came out of the belly of the great whore."

This last was quite a long sentence to shout and the officer's face was red and congested as he finished.

The second officer, who was a thin sunburned man with quiet eyes, a thin, long-lipped mouth and a stubble of beard over his hollow cheeks, shook his head again. It was this officer who was shouting who had ordered the first assault. The young lieutenant who was dead up the slope had been the best friend of this other lieutenant who was named Paco Berrendo and who was listening to the shouting of the captain, who was obviously in a state of exaltation.

"Those are the swine who shot my sister and my mother," the captain said. He had a red face and a blond, British-looking moustache and there was something wrong about his eyes. They were a light blue and the lashes were light, too. As you looked at them they seemed to focus slowly. Then "Reds," he shouted, "Cowards!" and commenced cursing again.

He stood absolutely clear now and, sighting carefully, fired his pistol at the only target that the hilltop presented: the dead horse that had belonged to Sordo. The bullet threw up a puff of dirt fifteen yards below the horse. The captain fired again. The bullet hit a rock and sung off.

The captain stood there looking at the hilltop. The Lieutenant Berrendo was looking at the body of the other lieutenant just below the summit. The sniper was looking at the ground under his eyes. Then he looked up at the captain.

"There is no one alive up there," the captain said. "Thou," he said to the sniper, "go up there and see."

The sniper looked down. He said nothing.

"Don't you hear me?" the captain shouted at him.

"Yes, my captain," the sniper said, not looking at him.

"Then get up and go." The captain still had his pistol out. "Do you hear me?"

"Yes, my captain."

"Why don't you go, then?"

"I don't want to, my captain."

"You don't *want* to?" The captain pushed the pistol against the small of the man's back. "You don't *want* to?"

"I am afraid, my captain," the soldier said with dignity.

Lieutenant Berrendo, watching the captain's face and his odd eyes, thought he was going to shoot the man then.

"Captain Mora," he said.

"Lieutenant Berrendo?"

"It is possible the soldier is right."

"That he is right to say he is afraid? That he is right to say he does not *want* to obey an order?"

"No. That he is right that it is a trick."

"They are all dead," the captain said. "Don't you hear me say they are all dead?"

"You mean our comrades on the slope?" Berrendo asked him. "I agree with you."

"Paco," the captain said, "don't be a fool. Do you think you are the only one who cared for Julián? I tell you the Reds are dead. Look!"

He stood up, then put both hands on top of the boulder and pulled himself up, kneeing-up awkwardly, then getting on his feet.

"Shoot," he shouted, standing on the gray granite boulder and waved both his arms. "Shoot me! Kill me!"

On the hilltop El Sordo lay behind the dead horse and grinned.

What a people, he thought. He laughed, trying to hold it in because the shaking hurt his arm.

"Reds," came the shout from below. "Red canaille. Shoot me! Kill me!"

Sordo, his chest shaking, barely peered past the horse's crupper and saw the captain on top of the boulder waving his arms. Another officer stood by the boulder. The sniper was standing at the other side. Sordo kept his eye where it was and shook his head happily.

"Shoot me," he said softly to himself. "Kill me!" Then his shoulders shook again. The laughing hurt his arm and each time he laughed his head felt as though it would burst, but the laughter shook him again like a spasm.

Captain Mora got down from the boulder.

"Now do you believe me, Paco?" he questioned Lieutenant Berrendo.

"No," said Lieutenant Berrendo.

"*Cojones!*" the captain said. "Here there is nothing but idiots and cowards."

The sniper had gotten carefully behind the boulder again and Lieutenant Berrendo was squatting beside him.

The captain, standing in the open beside the boulder, commenced to shout filth at the hilltop. There is no language so filthy as Spanish. There are words for all the vile words in English and there are other words and expressions that are used only in countries where blasphemy keeps pace with the austerity of religion. Lieutenant Berrendo was a very devout Catholic. So was the sniper. They were Carlists from Navarra and while both of them cursed and blasphemed when they were angry they regarded it as a sin which they regularly confessed.

As they crouched now behind the boulder watching the captain and listening to what he was shouting, they both disassociated themselves from him and what he was saying. They did not want to have that sort of talk on their consciences on a day in which they might die. Talking thus will not bring luck, the sniper thought. Speaking thus of the *Virgen* is bad luck. This one speaks worse than the Reds.

Julián is dead, Lieutenant Berrendo was thinking. Dead there on the slope on such a day as this is. And this foul mouth stands there bringing more ill fortune with his blasphemies.

Now the captain stopped shouting and turned to Lieutenant Berrendo. His eyes looked stranger than ever.

"Paco," he said, happily, "you and I will go up there."

"Not me."

"What?" The captain had his pistol out again.

I hate these pistol brandishers, Berrendo was thinking. They cannot give an order without jerking a gun out. They probably pull out their pistols when they go to the toilet and order the move they will make.

"I will go if you order me to. But under protest," Lieutenant Berrendo told the captain.

"Then I will go alone," the captain said. "The smell of cowardice is too strong here."

Holding his pistol in his right hand, he strode steadily up the slope. Berrendo and the sniper watched him. He was making no attempt to take any cover and he was looking straight ahead of him at the rocks, the dead horse, and the fresh-dug dirt of the hilltop.

El Sordo lay behind the horse at the corner of the rock, watching the captain come striding up the hill.

Only one, he thought. We get only one. But from his manner of speaking, he is *caza mayor*. Look at him walking. Look what an animal. Look at him stride forward. This one is for me. This one I take with me on the trip. This one coming now makes the same voyage I do. Come on, Comrade Voyager. Come striding. Come right along. Come along to meet it. Come on. Keep on walking. Don't slow up. Come right along. Come as thou art coming. Don't stop and look at those. That's right. Don't even look down. Keep on coming with your eyes forward. Look, he has a moustache. What do you think of that? He runs to a moustache, the Comrade Voyager. He is a captain. Look at his sleeves. I said he was *caza mayor*. He has the face of an *Inglés*. Look. With a red face and blond hair and blue eyes. With no cap on and his moustache is yellow. With blue eyes. With pale blue eyes. With pale blue eyes with something wrong with them. With pale blue eyes that don't focus. Close enough. Too close. Yes, Comrade Voyager. Take it. Comrade Voyager.

He squeezed the trigger of the automatic rifle gently and it pounded back three times against his shoulder with the slippery jolt the recoil of a tripoded automatic weapon gives.

The captain lay on his face on the hillside. His left arm was under him. His right arm that had held the pistol was stretched forward of his head. From all down the slope they were firing on the hill crest again.

Crouched behind the boulder, thinking that now he would have to sprint across that open space under fire, Lieutenant Berrendo heard the deep hoarse voice of Sordo from the hilltop.

"*Bandidos!*" the voice came. "*Bandidos!* Shoot me! Kill me!"

On the top of the hill El Sordo lay behind the automatic rifle laughing so that his chest ached, so that he thought the top of his head would burst.

"*Bandidos,*" he shouted again happily. "Kill me, *bandidos!*" Then he shook his head happily. We have lots of company for the Voyage, he thought.

He was going to try for the other officer with the automatic rifle when he would leave the shelter of the boulder. Sooner or later he would have to leave it. Sordo knew that he could never command from there and he thought he had a very good chance to get him.

Just then the others on the hill heard the first sound of the coming of the planes.

El Sordo did not hear them. He was covering the down-slope edge of the boulder with his automatic rifle and he was thinking: when I see him he will be running already and I will miss him if I am not careful. I could shoot behind him all across that stretch. I should swing the gun with him and ahead of him. Or let him start and then get on him and ahead of him. I will try to pick him up there at the edge of the rock and swing just ahead of him. Then he felt a touch on his shoulder and he turned and saw the gray, fear-drained face of Joaquín and he looked where the boy was pointing and saw the three planes coming.

At this moment Lieutenant Berrendo broke from behind the boulder and, with his head bent and his legs plunging, ran down and across the slope to the shelter of the rocks where the automatic rifle was placed.

Watching the planes, Sordo never saw him go.

"Help me to pull this out," he said to Joaquín and the boy dragged the automatic rifle clear from between the horse and the rock.

The planes were coming on steadily. They were in echelon and each second they grew larger and their noise was greater.

"Lie on your backs to fire at them," Sordo said. "Fire ahead of them as they come."

He was watching them all the time. "*Cabrones! Hijos de puta!*" he said rapidly.

"Ignacio!" he said. "Put the gun on the shoulder of the boy. Thou!" to Joaquín, "Sit there and do not move. Crouch over. More. No. More."

He lay back and sighted with the automatic rifle as the planes came on steadily.

"Thou, Ignacio, hold me the three legs of that tripod." They were dangling down the boy's back and the muzzle of the gun was shaking from the jerking of his body that Joaquín could not control as he crouched with bent head hearing the droning roar of their coming.

Lying flat on his belly and looking up into the sky watching them come, Ignacio gathered the legs of the tripod into his two hands and steadied the gun.

"Keep thy head down," he said to Joaquín. "Keep thy head forward."

"Pasionaria says 'Better to die on thy—' " Joaquín was saying to himself as the drone came nearer them. Then he shifted suddenly into "Hail Mary, full of grace, the Lord is with thee; Blessed art thou among women and Blessed is the fruit of thy womb, Jesus. Holy Mary, Mother of God, pray for us sinners now and at the hour of our death. Amen. Holy Mary, Mother of God," he started, then he remembered quickly as the roar came now unbearably and started an act of contrition racing in it, "Oh my God, I am heartily sorry for having offended thee who art worthy of all my love——"

Then there were the hammering explosions past his ears and the gun barrel hot against his shoulder. It was hammering now again and his ears were deafened by the muzzle blast. Ignacio was pulling down hard on the tripod and the barrel was burning his back. It was hammering now in the roar and he could not remember the act of contrition.

All he could remember was at the hour of our death. Amen. At the hour of our death. Amen. At the hour. At the hour. Amen. The others all were firing. Now and at the hour of our death. Amen.

Then, through the hammering of the gun, there was the whistle of the air splitting apart and then in the red black roar the earth rolled under his knees and then waved up to hit him in the face and then dirt and bits of rock were falling all over and Ignacio was lying on him and the gun was lying on him. But he was not dead because the whistle came again and the earth rolled under him with the roar. Then it came again and the earth lurched under his belly and one side of the hilltop rose into the air and then fell slowly over them where they lay.

The planes came back three times and bombed the hilltop but no one on the hilltop knew it. Then the planes machine-gunned the hilltop and went away. As they dove on the hill for the last time with their machine guns hammering, the first plane pulled up and winged over and then each plane did the same and they moved from echelon to V-formation and went away into the sky in the direction of Segovia.

Keeping a heavy fire on the hilltop, Lieutenant Berrendo pushed a patrol up to one of the bomb craters from where they could throw grenades onto the crest. He was taking no chances of any one being alive and waiting for them in the mess that was up there and he threw four grenades into the confusion of dead horses, broken and split rocks, and torn yellow-stained explosive-stinking earth before he climbed out of the bomb crater and walked over to have a look.

No one was alive on the hilltop except the boy Joaquín, who was unconscious under the dead body of Ignacio. Joaquín was bleeding from the nose and from the ears. He had known nothing and had no feeling since he had suddenly been in the very heart of the thunder and the breath had been wrenched from his body when the one bomb struck so close and Lieutenant Berrendo made the sign of the cross and then shot him in the back of the head, as quickly and as gently, if such an abrupt movement can be gentle, as Sordo had shot the wounded horse.

Lieutenant Berrendo stood on the hilltop and looked down the slope at his own dead and then across the country seeing where they had galloped before Sordo had turned at bay here. He noticed all the dispositions that had been made of the troops and then he ordered the dead men's horses to be brought up and the bodies tied across the saddles so that they might be packed in to La Granja.

"Take that one, too," he said. "The one with his hands on the automatic rifle. That should be Sordo. He is the oldest and it was he with the gun. No. Cut the head off and wrap it in a poncho." He considered a minute. "You might as well take all the heads. And of the others below on the slope and where we first found them. Collect the rifles and pistols and pack that gun on a horse."

Then he walked down to where the lieutenant lay who had been killed in the first assault. He looked down at him but did not touch him.

"*Qué cosa más mala es la guerra,*" he said to himself, which meant, "What a bad thing war is."

Then he made the sign of the cross again and as he walked down the hill he said five Our Fathers and five Hail Marys for the repose of the soul of his dead comrade. He did not wish to stay to see his orders being carried out.

The Last Battle of King Arthur

BY

SIR THOMAS MALORY

THEN much people drew unto King Arthur. And then King Arthur drew
him with his host down by the seaside, westward toward Salisbury; and
there was a day assigned betwixt King Arthur and Sir Mordred, that they
should meet upon a down beside Salisbury, and not far from the seaside;
and this day was assigned on a Monday after Trinity Sunday, whereof
King Arthur was passing glad, that he might be avenged upon Sir Mordred.

So upon Trinity Sunday at night, King Arthur dreamed that Sir Gawaine
had warned him that if he fought on the morn he should be slain. Then
the king commanded Sir Lucan the Butler, and his brother Sir Bedivere,
with two bishops with them, and charged them in any wise, an they might,
Take a treaty for a month day with Sir Mordred, and spare not, proffer
him lands and goods as much as ye think best. So then they departed, and
came to Sir Mordred, where he had a grim host of an hundred thousand
men. And there they entreated Sir Mordred long time; and at the last
Sir Mordred was agreed for to have Cornwall and Kent, by Arthur's days:
after, all England, after the days of King Arthur.

Then were they condescended that King Arthur and Sir Mordred should
meet betwixt both their hosts, and everych of them should bring fourteen
persons; and they came with this word unto Arthur. Then said he: I am
glad that this is done: and so he went into the field. And when Arthur
should depart, he warned all his host that an they see any sword drawn:
Look ye come on fiercely, and slay that traitor, Sir Mordred, for I in no
wise trust him. In like wise Sir Mordred warned his host. And so they met
as their appointment was, and so they were agreed and accorded thoroughly; and wine was fetched, and they drank. Right soon came an adder
out of a little heath bush, and it stung a knight on the foot. And when the
knight felt him stung, he looked down and saw the adder, and then he drew
his sword to slay the adder, and thought of none other harm. And when
the host on both parties saw that sword drawn, then they blew beams,
trumpets, and horns, and shouted grimly. And so both hosts dressed them
together. And thus they fought all the long day, and never stinted till the
noble knights were laid to the cold earth; and ever they fought still till it
was near night, and by that time was there an hundred thousand laid dead

From: *Le Morte D'Arthur.*

upon the down. Then was Arthur wood wroth out of measure, when he saw his people so slain from him.

Then the king looked about him, and then was he ware, of all his host and of all his good knights, were left no more alive but two knights; that was Sir Lucan the Butler, and his brother Sir Bedivere, and they were full sore wounded. Jesu mercy, said the king, where are all my noble knights become? Then was King Arthur ware where Sir Mordred leaned upon his sword among a great heap of dead men. Now give me my spear, said Arthur unto Sir Lucan, for yonder I have espied the traitor that all this woe hath wrought. Sir, let him be, said Sir Lucan, for he is unhappy; and if ye pass this unhappy day, ye shall be right well revenged upon him. Good lord, remember ye of your night's dream, and what the spirit of Sir Gawaine told you this night; yet God of his great goodness hath preserved you hitherto. Therefore, for God's sake, my lord, leave off by this, for blessed by God ye have won the field, for here we be three alive, and with Sir Mordred is none alive; and if ye leave off now this wicked day of destiny is past. Tide me death, betide me life, saith the king, now I see him yonder alone he shall never escape mine hands, for at a better avail shall I never have him. God speed you well, said Sir Bedivere.

Then the king gat his spear in both his hands, and ran toward Sir Mordred crying: Traitor, now is thy deathday come. And when Sir Mordred heard Sir Arthur, he ran until him with his sword drawn in his hand. And there King Arthur smote Sir Mordred under the shield, with a foin of his spear, throughout the body, more than a fathom. And when Sir Mordred felt that he had his death wound he thrust himself with the might that he had up to the bur of King Arthur's spear. And right so he smote his father Arthur, with his sword holden in both his hands, on the side of the head, that the sword pierced the helmet and the brain-pan, and therewithal Sir Mordred fell stark dead to the earth; and the noble Arthur fell in a swoon to the earth, and there he swooned ofttimes. And Sir Lucan the Butler and Sir Bedivere ofttimes heaved him up. And so weakly they led him betwixt them both, to a little chapel not far from the seaside. And when the king was there he thought him well eased.

Then Sir Lucan saw by the moonlight, how that pillers and robbers were come into the field, and who that were not dead all out, there they slew them for their harness and their riches. When Sir Lucan understood this work, he came to the king as soon as he might, and told him all what he had heard and seen. Therefore by my rede, said Sir Lucan, it is best that we bring you to some town. I would it were so, said the king. But I may not stand, mine head works so. Ah Sir Launcelot, said King Arthur, this day have I sore missed thee: alas, that ever I was against thee, for now have I my death, whereof Sir Gawaine me warned in my dream.

Then Sir Lucan took up the king the one part, and Sir Bedivere the other part, and in the lifting Sir Lucan fell in a swoon, and therewith the noble knight's heart brast. Alas, said the king, this is to me a full heavy sight, to see this noble duke so die for my sake, for he would have holpen me, that had more need of help than I. Alas, he would not complain him, his heart was so set to help me: now Jesu have mercy upon his soul! Then Sir Bedivere wept for the death of his brother. Leave this mourning and weeping, said the king, for all this will not avail me; for wit thou well an I might live myself, the death of Sir Lucan would grieve me evermore; but my time hieth fast, said the king. Therefore, said Arthur unto Sir Bedivere, take thou Excalibur, my good sword, and go with it to yonder water side, and when thou comest there I charge thee throw my sword in that water, and come again and tell me what thou there seest.

So Sir Bedivere departed, and by the way he beheld that noble sword, that the pommel and the haft was all of precious stones; and then he said to himself: If I throw this rich sword in the water, thereof shall never come good, but harm and loss. And then Sir Bedivere hid Excalibur under a tree. And so, as soon as he might, he came again unto the king, and said he had been at the water, and had thrown the sword into the water. What saw thou there? said the king. Sir, he said, I saw nothing but waves and winds. That is untruly said of thee, said the king, therefore go though lightly again, and do my commandment; as thou art to me lief and dear, spare not, but throw it in. Then Sir Bedivere returned again, and took the sword in his hand; and then him thought sin and shame to throw away that noble sword, and so eft he hid the sword, and returned again, and told to the king that he had been at the water, and done his commandment. What saw thou there?" said the king. Sir, he said, I saw nothing but the waters wap and waves wan. Ah, traitor untrue, said King Arthur, now hast thou betrayed me twice. Who would have weened that thou, that hast been to me so lief and dear, and thou art named a noble knight, would betray me for the richness of the sword? But now go again lightly, for thy long tarrying putteth me in great jeopardy of my life, for I have taken cold. And but if thou do now as I bid thee, if ever I may see thee, I shall slay thee with mine own hands; for thou wouldst for my rich sword see me dead.

Then Sir Bedivere departed, and went to the sword, and lightly took it up, and went to the water side; and there he bound the girdle about the hilts, and then he threw the sword as far into the water as he might; and there came an arm and an hand above the water and met it, and caught it, and so shook it thrice and brandished, and then vanished away the hand with the sword in the water. So Sir Bedivere came again to the king, and told him what he saw. Alas, said the king, help me hence, for I dread me I have tarried over long. Then Sir Bedivere took the king upon his back, and so went with him to that water side. And when they were at the water side, even fast by the bank hoved a little barge with many fair ladies in it, and among them all was a queen, and all they had black hoods, and all they wept and shrieked when they saw King Arthur. Now put me into the barge, said the king. And so he did softly; and there received him three queens with great mourning; and so they set them down, and in one of their laps King Arthur laid his head. And then that queen said: Ah, dear brother, why have ye tarried so long from me? alas, this wound on your head hath caught over-much cold. And so then they rowed from the land, and Sir Bedivere beheld all those ladies go from him. Then Sir Bedivere cried: Ah my lord Arthur, what shall become of me, now ye go from me and leave me here alone among mine enemies? Comfort thyself, said the king, and do as well as thou mayst, for in me is no trust for to trust in; for I will into the vale of Avilion to heal me of my grievous wound: and if thou hear never more of me, pray for my soul. But ever the queens and ladies wept and shrieked, that it was pity to hear. And as soon as Sir Bedivere had lost sight of the barge, he wept and wailed, and so took the forest; and so he went all that night, and in the morning he was ware betwixt two holts hoar, of a chapel and an hermitage.

Then was Sir Bedivere glad, and thither he went; and when he came into the chapel, he saw where lay an hermit grovelling on all four, there fast by a tomb was new graven. When the hermit saw Sir Bedivere he knew him well, for he was but little to-fore Bishop of Canterbury, that Sir Mordred banished. Sir, said Bedivere, what man is there interred that ye pray so fast for? Fair son, said the hermit, I wot not verily, but by deeming. But this night, at midnight, here came a number of ladies, and brought hither a dead corpse, and prayed me to bury him; and here they offered an hundred tapers, and they gave me an hundred besants. Alas, said Sir Bedivere, that was my lord King Arthur, that here lieth buried in this chapel. Then Sir Bedivere swooned; and when he awoke he prayed the hermit he might abide with him still there, to live with fasting and prayers. For from hence will I never go, said Sir Bedivere, by my will, but all the days of my life here to pray for my lord Arthur. So there bode Sir Bedivere with the hermit that was to-fore Bishop of Canterbury, and there Sir Bedivere put upon him poor clothes, and served the hermit full lowly in fasting and in prayers.

Thus of Arthur I find never more written in books that be authorised, nor more of the very certainty of his death heard I never read, but thus was he led away in a ship wherein were three queens; that one was King Arthur's sister, Queen Morgan le Fay; the other was the Queen of Northgalis; the third was the Queen of the Waste Lands. Also there was Nimue, the chief lady of the lake, that had done much for King Arthur. More of the death of King Arthur could I never find, but that ladies brought him to his burials; and such one was buried there, that the hermit bare witness that sometime was Bishop of Canterbury, but yet the hermit knew not in certain that he was verily the body of King Arthur: for this tale Sir Bedivere, knight of the Table Round, made it to be written.

Yet some men say in many parts of England that King Arthur is not dead, but had by the will of our Lord Jesu into another place; and men say that he shall come again, and he shall win the holy cross. I will not say it shall be so, but rather I will say: here in this world he changed his life. But many men say that there is written upon his tomb this verse: hic jacet Arthurus, Rex quondam, Rexque futurus. Thus leave I here Sir

Bedivere with the hermit, that dwelled that time in a chapel besides Glastonbury, and there was his hermitage. And so they lived in their prayers, and fastings, and great abstinence. And when Queen Guenever understood that King Arthur was slain, and all the noble knights, Sir Mordred and all the remnant, then the queen stole away, and five ladies with her, and so she went to Almesbury; and there she let make herself a nun, and ware white clothes and black, and great penance she took, as ever did sinful lady in this land, and never creature could make her merry; but lived in fasting, prayers, and alms-deeds, that all manner of people marvelled how virtuously she was changed.

At All Costs

BY

RICHARD ALDINGTON

"Blast!"

Captain Hanley, commanding "B" Company, stumbled over a broken duckboard and fell forward against the side of the trench. His tilted helmet shielded his face, but the trench wall felt oozy and soggy to his naked hand as he tried to steady himself.

"Mind that hole, Parker."

"Very good, sir."

He felt wet mud soaking through his breeches above the short gum boots, and his right sleeve was wet to the elbow. He fumbled in his gas bag, also wet with slimy mud, to see that the mask goggles were unbroken. O.K., but he swore again with a sort of exasperated groan over the crashing bruise on his right knee.

"Are you 'it, sir?"

"No, I only fell in that mucking hole again. I've told the ser'ant-major umpteen times to get it mended. One of these days the brigadier'll fall into it and then there'll be hell to pay. Help me find my torch. I hope the bloody thing isn't broken."

The two men groped in the darkness, fingering the slimy mud and tilted broken duckboards. Suddenly they crashed helmets.

"Sorry, sir."

"All right, sorry."

"Doesn't seem to be 'ere, sir."

"Never mind, we'll look for it in the morning."

They stumbled on cautiously. The trench was very deep (old German communication), very dark, very shell-smashed, very muddy. A black, heavy-clouded night, about an hour before dawn. Occasionally a strange ghostly glow appeared as a distant Very light was fired, and made for them a near dark horizon of tumbled shell-tormented parapet. The trench swerved, and Hanley dimly made out the shape of three crosses—Canadians. Halfway. Fifty yards farther on was another turn, where a piece of corrugated iron revetment had been flung onto the top of the high parapet, where its jagged outline looked like a grotesque heraldic dragon.

It had been an ideal night for gas and would be an ideal dawn—heavy, windless, foggy—for a surprise attack. Hanley had been up and about the

From: *Roads to Glory*, by permission of the Author.

256

trenches most of the night. Since that rotten gas attack on the Somme, where he lost twenty-three men, he took no risks. Up and down the trenches, warning the N.C.O.'s to look out for gas. Now he was on the way to his advance posts. Be there in case of an attack. . . .

Splash, squelch, splodge. Somebody coming towards them.

"Who are you?"

"Mockery."

"Is that the word tonight, Parker?"

"Yessir."

"That you, Hanley?" Voice coming towards them.

"Hullo, Williams. I thought you were in Hurdle Alley?"

"I was, but I thought I'd have a look at these posts. They're a hell of a way from the front line."

"I know. Damn this organization in depth. Are they all right?"

"Yes. He sent over about forty minnies, Ser'ant Cramp said, but no casualties. He was flipping over some of those flying pineapples when I left."

From their own back areas came an irregular but ceaseless crashing of artillery. Heavy shells shrilled high above them as they swooped at enemy communications and night parties.

"Strafing the old Boche a good bit tonight," said Williams.

"Yes, it's been quite heavy. Might almost be a windup at H.Q."

"Boche are very quiet tonight."

"Yes; well, cheerio. Tell Thompson to keep our breakfast hot; and don't stand down until I get back."

"Right you are, cheerio."

Hanley visited his posts. They were established in a ruined and unre-paired German trench at the foot of a long forward slope. This had once been the British front line, but was now held only by scattered observation posts, with the main front line several hundred yards to the rear. The British bombardment increased, and the shrill scream of the passing shells was almost continuous. Very lights and rockets went up from the German lines. Hanley cursed the loss of his torch—damned difficult to get about without it. He came to the first post.

"You there, Ser'ant Tomlinson?"

A figure moved in the darkness.

"Yes, sir."

"Anything to report?"

"No, sir."

"Mr. Williams said there were some minnies and pineapples."

"Yes, sir, but it's very quiet, sir."

"Um. Any patrols still out?"

"No, sir, all in."

"Very well. Carry on, ser'ant."

"Very good, sir."

Much the same news at the other posts. Hanley returned to Number 1

post, nearest the communication trench, at dawn. The men were standing
to. Hanley got on the fire-step in a shell-smashed abandoned bay, and
watched with his glasses slung round his neck. The artillery had died down
to a couple of batteries, when the first perceptible lightening of the air came.
Hanley felt cold in his mud-soaked breeches and tunic. Very gradually, very
slowly, the darkness dissipated, as if thin imperceptible veils were being
rolled up in a transformation scene. The British wire became visible. In
the trembling misty light No Man's Land seemed alive with strange shapes
and movements. Hanley pressed cold hands on his hot eyes, puffy with
lack of sleep. He looked again. Yes, yes, surely, they were climbing over the
parapet and lying down in front. He seized a rifle leaning against the trench,
loaded with an S.O.S. rocket bomb. Funny Sergeant Tomlinson and the men
were so silent. Perhaps he was imagining things, the same old dawn-mirage
movement which had been responsible for so many false alarms. He waited
a couple of minutes with closed eyes, and then looked very carefully through
his glasses. Silly ass! The men coming over the parapets were the German
wire pickets. He put the rifle down, glad the men had not seen him, and
went round the traverse to Sergeant Tomlinson and Parker.

"Stand to for another twenty minutes, ser'ant, and then let two men
from Number 2 post and two from Number 4 go and get your breakfasts."

"Very good, sir."

On the way back Hanley found his torch—the glass bulb was smashed;
like most things in this bloody war, he reflected. Well, they'd passed another
dawn without an attack—that was something. He got on a fire-step in the
main line and took another look. A cloudy but rainless morning. Not a sign
of life in the enemy trenches, scarcely a sound. He gave the order to stand
down, and sent Parker to join his section for breakfast.

The company dugout was a large one, built as the headquarters of a
German battalion. It was remarkably lousy. Hanley threw his torch,
revolver-belt, and helmet on his wire and sacking bed, and sat down on a
box beside a small table laid with four knives and forks on a newspaper.
He felt tired, too tired even to enjoy the hot bacon and eggs which formed
the infantry officers' best meal of the day. The three subalterns chatted.
Hanley pushed away his plate and stood up.

"I'm going to turn in. Tell the signaller to wake me if anything important
happens."

"Right-o."

Hanley hung up his revolver and helmet, arranged his pack as a pillow,
swung himself still booted and wet onto the bed, and wrapped himself in a
blanket. For a few minutes he lay drowsily, listening to the throb of blood
in his head and the quiet mutter of the other officers. His eyes still ached
even when shut. He drowsed, then half awoke as he remembered that he
had not indented for enough ammunition, decided that could wait, and—
was dead asleep.

Hanley opened his eyes and lay quite still. Why were they talking so loudly? In a flash he was wide awake and swung up, sitting with his legs over the side of the bed. The colonel. Damn! Being found asleep like that! And, of course, the colonel would not know that he had been up and down the line all night. Damn! Well, never mind. He gave one dab with both hands at his rumpled hair, and stood up.

"Good morning, sir."

"Oh, good morning, Hanley. Williams said you'd been up all night. Sorry to disturb you."

"Quite all right, sir."

A large-scale trench map of their sector was spread on the table, half concealing another smaller-scale artillery map of the whole district.

"Just sit down for a few minutes, Hanley. I've got important news."

The other officers grouped beside them, gazing at the colonel and listening.

"Very important news," the colonel went on in a slow voice, "and not particularly pleasant, I'm afraid."

He pulled a neat bundle of documents from his pocket, opened one labelled "SECRET AND CONFIDENTIAL" and spread it on the table. They all gazed at it—the inexorable decree of Fate—and then again at the colonel, the agent of that Fate, of all their fates.

"That is a confidential document from Corps Headquarters. I'll tell you briefly what it is, and you can look it over afterwards. The night before last the division on our left made an identification raid, and captured a prisoner. From this and other information it seems certain that we shall be attacked —tomorrow morning—about an hour before dawn."

Each of the four company officers drew a short imperceptible breath, glanced at each other and then quickly away. Hanley leaned his elbow on the table.

"Yes, sir?"

"It will be a surprise attack, with a very short but violent preliminary bombardment." The colonel spoke very slowly and deliberately, looking down absently at the map, and gently twisting the lowest button of his tunic with the fingers of his right hand. "All reports confirm our information, and the Air Force report great enemy activity behind the lines. You heard the bombardment of their communications last night."

"Yes, sir."

There was complete silence in the dugout, as the colonel paused. A pile of tin plates fell with a clatter in the servants' compartment. None of the officers moved. Hanley noticed how clean the colonel's gas bag was.

"There will probably be twenty to thirty German divisions in the attack, which will be on a sixteen-mile front. We are about in the middle."

"Yes, sir."

The colonel moved on his box. He stretched out all the fingers of his left hand, and tapped rapidly on the table alternately with the stretched little finger and thumb.

"The Canadian Corps and several reserve divisions are being brought up at once to occupy a position about five miles to our rear. They cannot fully man the whole battle line before three tomorrow afternoon. Our duty is to delay the enemy advance until that time or longer. Our positions must be held at all costs, to the last man."

There was a long silence. The colonel ceased drumming with his fingers and looked at them.

"Have you any questions to ask?"

"Yes, sir. Am I to leave my posts out?"

"Two hours before dawn, you will withdraw them to strengthen your own line. One section, with a sergeant and a subaltern, will remain at the end of the communication trench. The subaltern will be a volunteer. His duty is to fire a green light when the German attacking line reaches him. The artillery barrage will then shorten to defend your line. You, Hanley, will have a Very-light pistol loaded with a red light, and you will fire it when the first German jumps into your trench. The object, of course, is to inform the artillery when they must shorten the defensive barrage."

"Yes, sir."

"Any more questions?"

"No, sir, not for the moment."

"You'll arrange with your officers, Hanley, as to which shall volunteer to fire the green light."

"Very good, sir."

"And I want you to come to a conference of company officers with the brigadier at Battalion Headquarters this afternoon."

"Very good, sir. What time?"

"Oh, make it three o'clock."

"Very well, sir."

The colonel rose.

"You know your battle positions, of course; but we'll discuss that this afternoon. Oh, by the bye, I'm sending up green envelopes for everyone in the company this morning. The letters must be sent down by runner at four. Of course, not a word about the attack must be mentioned either to N.C.O.'s or men until after the letters have gone."

"Of course, sir."

"And—er—naturally you will not mention the matter yourselves."

"No, sir, of course not."

"All right. Good-bye. Will you come along with me, Hanley? I should like to walk round your main defense line with you."

"Very good, sir."

There was silence in the dugout. They could hear the colonel and Hanley scuffling up the low dugout stairs. Williams tapped a cigarette on his case and bent down to light it at the candle burning on the table. He puffed a mouthful of smoke, with a twist to his lips.

"Well, that's that. Napoo, eh?"

"Looks like it."

"What about a drink?"

"Right-o."

Williams shouted:

"Thomp-sooon."

From the distance came a muffled: "Sir?"

A Tommy appeared in the doorway.

"Bring us a bottle of whisky and the mugs."

"Very good, sir."

All that day Hanley was in a state of dazed hebetude, from which he emerged from time to time. He felt vaguely surprised that everything was so much as usual. There were sentries at their posts, runners going along the trenches, an occasional airplane overhead, a little artillery—just the ordinary routine of trench warfare. And yet within twenty-four hours their trenches would be obliterated, he and thousands with him would be dead, obliterated, unless by some chance, some odd freak, he was made prisoner. He heard repeated over and over again in his head the words: "Position must be held at all costs, position must be held at all costs." He felt suddenly angry. Held at all costs! All jolly fine and large to write from the safety of Montreuil, but what about those who had to make good such dramatic sentiments with their lives? The front was ridiculously denuded of men—why, his own under-strength company held very nearly a battalion front, and had a flank to guard as well. If they fought like madmen and stood to the last man, they might hold up three waves—an hour at most. And they were asked to hold out for nearly twelve hours! Ridiculous, good God, ridiculous!

He found the colonel shaking him by the arm.

"What's the matter with you, Hanley? You don't seem to hear what I'm saying."

"I beg your pardon, sir. I——"

"I think you ought to bring a Lewis gun up to this point. You've got an excellent field of fire here."

"Very good, sir."

Hanley noted the change to be made in his field service message book. They walked on, and the colonel made various other suggestions—so many orders—which Hanley duly noted. The colonel paused at the corner of the communication trench leading to Battalion Headquarters. He waved to the orderlies to stand apart.

"We'll discuss the general plan of defense at the conference this afternoon. Make a note of anything that occurs to you, any information you want, and bring it up."

"Right, sir."

The colonel hesitated a moment.

"It's a very difficult position, Hanley, I know, but we must all do our duty."

"Of course, sir."

"I shall lead the counter-attack of the Reserve Company myself."

"Yes, sir."

"A great deal depends on our putting up a good show."

"Yes, sir."

"I suggest you go round to the dugout and speak to all your men this evening. Put a good face on it, you know. Tell them we are all prepared, and shall easily beat off the attack, and that reinforcements are being hurried up to relieve us. And above all impress upon them that these trenches *must* be held at all costs."

"Very good, sir."

The colonel held out his hand.

"I may not have another opportunity to speak to you in private. Good-bye, and the best of luck. I know you'll do your duty."

"Thank you, sir. Good-bye."

"Good-bye."

When Hanley stooped under the low entrance of the dugout chamber, the three subalterns were seated round the table with flushed cheeks, talking loudly. The whisky bottle was more than half-empty. A sudden spurt of anger shot through him. He strode up to the table and knocked the cork level with the top of the bottle neck with one hard smack of his hand. He spoke harshly:

"What's this nonsense?"

Williams, the eldest of the three subalterns, answered, half-defiantly, half-ashamedly:

"We're only having a drink. Where's the harm?"

"Only a drink! Before lunch! Now, look here, you fellows. The whisky that's left in that bottle is all that's going to be drunk in this mess between now and dawn tomorrow. Understand? One of the damned stupidities of this damned war is that every officer thinks it's the thing to be a boozer. It isn't. The men don't drink. They get a tablespoon of rum a day. Why should we make sots of ourselves? We're responsible for their lives. See? And we're responsible for these trenches. We've got to leave 'em on stretchers or stay here and manure 'em. See? We've got a bloody rotten job ahead of us, a stinking rotten job, and I wish those who ordered it were here to carry out their own damned orders. But they're not. Not bloody likely. But the people at home trust us. We're responsible to them, first and foremost. We took on the job, and we've got to carry it out. And carry it out dead bloody sober. Got me?"

The men were silent, looking sheepishly at the newspaper on the table with its wet rings from mug bottoms. Hanley took an empty mug and tossed some of the whisky from William's mug into it.

"Drink up. Here's hell!"

They drank.

Hanley shouted:

"Thomp-soooon!"

Thompson appeared in the door.

"Take those mugs away."

"Very good, sir."

"How many bottles of whisky have you?"

"Three, sir."

"Bring them here, and a sandbag."

"Very good, sir."

Hanley scribbled a few words in his message book, and tore out the slip. He put the bottles in the sandbag.

"Parker!"

Parker in his turn appeared.

"Sir?"

"Take that sandbag down to Battalion H.Q. Give it to one of the officers, and bring back his signed receipt."

"Very good, sir."

The other officers exchanged glances. Williams, who had his back turned to Hanley, made a grimace of derision. The others frowned at him.

Hanley was busy throughout the day, making arrangements, giving orders, attending the conference—which lasted a long time—and going round to speak to the men. He only had time to write a very brief letter to his wife, enclosing one still briefer for his father. He wrote calmly, almost coldly in his effort to avoid emotion and self-pity. He even managed to squeeze out a joke for each letter. As soon as they were finished the two letters vanished in the open sandbag containing the company mail, and the runner started at once for Headquarters. Somehow it was a relief to have those letters gone. The last links with England, with life, were broken. Finished, done with, almost forgotten. It was easier to carry on now.

But was it? There was that damned business of the volunteer subaltern. Hanley rubbed his clenched fist against his cheek, and found that he had forgotten to shave. He called his servant and told him to bring some hot water in a cigarette tin. Shaving for the last time. Hardly worth it, really. Still, must be done. Morale, and all that.

He shaved carefully. One of the subalterns went out to relieve the officer on duty. One was asleep. Williams was writing a situation report. Hanley bit the back of his hand hard, then shoved both hands in his breeches pockets, looking at William's bent head.

"Williams!"

Williams looked up.

"Yes?"

"There's this business of the volunteer to——"

"Oh, that's all settled."

"Settled!"

"Yes. I'm going."

"You're going! But you've only been married two months."

"Yes. That's why I thought I'd like to get it over as quickly as possible."

"But I was going to put your platoon at the end of Hurdle Alley. You might just be able to get back to battalion, you know."

"And feel a swine for the rest of my life—which would be about two hours? Thanks. No, I'd rather get it over, if you don't mind, Hanley."

"Oh, all right."

They were silent. Then Hanley said:

"Well, I'll just go and talk to the men . . . er . . . So long."

"So long."

All working parties were cancelled to give the men as much rest as possible, but there was inevitably a lot of extra work, bringing up ammunition, rations, and water. As soon as dusk fell the whole Reserve Company and some pioneers came up to strengthen the wire. The British artillery was ceaselessly active. Hardly a shot came from the German lines—an ominous sign.

After dinner Hanley lay down to sleep for a few hours. Must be as fresh as possible. He wrapped the blanket up to his chin and shut his eyes. The other three off duty were lying down, too. But Hanley could not sleep. It was all so strange, so strange, and yet so ordinary. Just like any other night, and yet the last night. Inevitably the last night? How could they escape, with orders to hold on at all costs? Half of them would go in the bombardment, which would be terrific. Bombs, bullets, and bayonets would finish off the rest. The dugouts would be wrecked with bombs and high explosive charges. A few of the wounded might be picked up later. A few of the men might escape down Hurdle Alley after the officers were gone. But no, the N.C.O.'s could be relied on to hold out to the last. They were done for, napoo. No après la guerre for *them*—bon soir, toodle-oo, good-byeeee. The silly words repeated and repeated in his brain until he hated them. He opened his eyes and gazed at the familiar dugout. His wire bed was at an angle to the others, and he could see the shapes of Williams and the two other officers muffled up silent in their blankets—as still and silent as they would be in twenty-four hours' time. There was the candle burning in the holder roughly bent from a tin biscuit box. The flame was absolutely steady in the airless, earthy smelling dugout. There were the boxes for seats, the table with its maps, tins of cigarettes, chits, and the five mugs beside the whisky bottle for the last parting drink. The bare, murky walls of chalk were damp and clammy-looking with condensed breath. The revolvers, helmets, and gas bags were hung at the bed-heads. He listened to the other men breathing, and felt an absurd regret at leaving the dugout to be smashed. After all, that and other dugouts like it were the only home they had known for months and months. Breaking up the happy home! He became aware that he felt a bit sickish, that he had been feeling like that for several hours, and pretending not to.

He gently drew his wrist from under the blanket and looked at his luminous watch. Eleven thirty-five. He had to be up at two—must get some sleep. With almost a start he noticed that Williams was looking at his own watch in the same stealthy way. So he couldn't sleep either. Poor devil. Profoundly, almost insanely in love with that wife of his. Poor devil. But still, for the matter of that, so was Hanley in love with his wife. His heart seemed to turn in his body, and he felt an acute pain in the muscles above it as he suddenly realized fully that it was all over, that he would never see her again, never feel her mouth pressed to his, never again touch her lovely, friendly body. He clutched his hand over his face until it hurt to prevent himself from groaning. God, what bloody agony! O God, he'd be a mass of dead rotting decay, and she'd still be young and beautiful and alert and desirable, O God, and her life would run on, run on, there'd be all the grief and the sorrowing for her and tears in a cold widowed bed, O God, but the years would run on and she'd still be young and desirable, and somebody else would want her, some youngster, some wangler, and youth and her flesh and life would be clamorous, and her bed would no longer be cold and widowed. O God, God. Something wet ran down his cheek. Not a tear, but the cold clammy sweat from his forehead. God, what agony!

Hanley suddenly sat up. If he was suffering like that, Williams must be suffering, too. Better to get up and pretend to talk than lie and agonize like that. He got out of bed. Williams raised his head:

"What's up. It isn't two, is it?"

The other men looked up, too, showing that neither of them had been asleep. Hanley shivered and rubbed his hands to warm them in the chill dugout.

"No, only five to twelve. But I couldn't sleep. Hope I don't disturb you. Benson must be relieved in a few minutes," he added inconsequently.

The other three rolled out of bed and stood stretching and rubbing their hands.

"Too cold to sleep in this damned damp place," said one of them.

"What about a drink?"

"If you have it now, you can't have it later on," said Hanley. "Better wait until two."

Williams put on his equipment and helmet and went up to relieve Benson. The others sat on the boxes trying to talk. Benson came down.

"Anything on?" asked Hanley casually.

"Lots of lights, ordinary strafing on their side. A hell of a bombardment from our side."

"Perhaps if they see we've got wind of it, they'll postpone the attack?" suggested the youngest officer.

"Rot," said Benson. "They know jolly well that all this part of the line has been denuded to feed the Fifth Army. They'll attack, all right."

They were silent. Hanley looked at his watch. Five past twelve. How damnably slowly the time went; and yet these were their last minutes on earth. He felt something had to be done.

"Let's have a hand at bridge."

"What, tonight, now?"

"Well, why not? It's no good sitting here grumping like owls, and you don't suggest a prayer meeting, do you?"

The last suggestion was met with oaths of a forcible nature. Hanley cleared the table and threw down the cards.

"Cut for deal."

Just before two, Hanley slipped into his breeches pocket the ten francs he had won, and stood up. He put on trench coat and muffler, tried his broken torch for about the twentieth time, then threw it down disgustedly and fitted on his equipment. The subaltern who was to relieve Williams on trench duty was already dressed and waiting. Hanley put on his hat and turned to the others.

"I'll come round and see you after you've taken up battle positions; but if by any chance I don't see you again—cheerio."

"Cheerio."

They found Williams, his runner, and a sergeant waiting in the trench outside the dugout entrance.

"Anything doing?"

"Nothing particular. I went on patrol. Their wire's got gaps cut, with knife-rests in the gaps, all the way along."

"Um."

"Lot of signal rockets, too."

"I see. Our artillery seems to have ceased altogether."

"Saving ammunition for the show."

"Be more sensible to strafe now while the Boche is taking up battle positions."

"Oh, well, that's the staff's job, not ours."

Hanley, Williams, the sergeant, two runners, started for the Outpost Line. The trench was drier, the night not so dark, with faint stars mistily gleaming among light clouds. Weather clearing up—just the Boche's luck again. The five men moved along without talking, absorbed partly in a strange anxious preoccupation, partly in keeping upright on the slippery trench. Hanley and Williams, of course, knew the full extent of their danger, had faced the ultimate despair, passed beyond revolt or hope. The sergeant still hoped—that he might be wounded and taken prisoner. The two men only knew they were "in for a show." All were dry-mouthed, a little sickish with apprehension, a little awkward in all their movements; the thought of deserting their posts never even occurred to them.

They passed the three Canadian crosses, distinctly outlined on the quiet sky; then the dragon piece of corrugated iron. At the end of the communication trench they found waiting the men from the four posts, under a sergeant. Hanley spoke in low tones—there might be advance patrols lying just outside their wire.

"All your men present, ser'ant?"

"Yes, sir."

"Right. You know your orders. See that each section joins its own platoon, and then report to your own platoon commander. Don't waste time."

"Very good, sir."

The line of men filed past them in the darkness. For the hundredth time Hanley noticed the curious pathos of fatigue in these silent moving figures —the young bodies somehow tired to age and apathy. When they had gone he took Williams a little aside.

"If I were you, I should see that each of you occupies a separate bay. Get in the first bay yourself, then the runner, then the sergeant. They won't dare try to bolt back past you. Besides—er—there's more chance if you're spread out."

"I was wondering what happens if all three of us are knocked out before the Boche actually gets into the trench, and so no green light is fired?"

"Oh, we must risk that. Besides, there are similar volunteer parties on every company front."

"I see."

"I took a compass bearing from the fire-step outside Company H.Q. yesterday, so I shan't miss your light. I expect they'll be on us ten minutes later. Perhaps we'll beat off the first two or three attacks."

"Yes. Perhaps."

They were silent. Then Hanley made an effort.

"Well, good-bye, old man. Best of luck."

"Best of luck, good-bye."

They were too shy and English even to shake hands.

It was past three when Hanley and Parker got back to their own line and found the whole company standing to in battle positions. Hanley kept his signallers on the first floor of the big dugout. He sent off to Battalion Headquarters the code message which meant they were in battle positions and all ready. He took a candle and went down to the lower dugout, where they had spent so many nights. It looked barer and damper than ever, empty except for the bare sacking beds, the boxes, the table.

Outside in the trench the air was moist and fresh. He took two Very pistols, one loaded with green, one with red, and laid them on either side of him on the parapet. Hanley was at the extreme left of the bay, with two riflemen to his right. Twenty yards to his left was the communication trench leading to the outpost line, now blocked with wire and knife-rests, and guarded by a bombing section.

A signaller came up from the dugout with a message. Hanley went down and read it by the light of a candle. He noticed the bowed back and absorbed look of a signaller tapping out a message on a Fullerphone. The message he had received simply reiterated the order that their positions were to be held at all costs. Hanley felt angry, screwed up the piece of paper and stuffed it in his pocket. Damn them, how many more times did they think that order had to be given? He returned to the trench, and resumed his watch.

3.50 A.M. One battery of German guns languidly firing on back areas —pretense that all was as usual.

3.52 A.M. Signal rockets all along the German line. Then silence.

3.55 A.M. Two miles to his right a fierce bombardment, stretching over several miles. The battle had begun.

3.57 A.M. Two miles to his left another bombardment. The British artillery on their own front opened up a defensive barrage.

4 A.M. With a terrific crash, which immediately blotted out the roar of the other bombardments, the German artillery on their own front came into action. Hanley half-recoiled. He had been in several big bombardments, and thought he had experienced the utmost limit of artillery. But this was more tremendous, more hellish, more appalling than anything he had experienced. The trench of the outpost line was one continuous line of red, crashing trench mortars and shells. The communication trench was plastered with five-nines. Shells were falling all along their own line—he heard the sharp cry "Stretcher-bearer" very faintly from somewhere close at hand.

The confusion and horror of a great battle descended on him. The crash of shells, the roar of the guns, the brilliant flashes, the eerie piercing scream of a wounded man, the rattle of the machine guns, the Lewis guns, the two riflemen beside him madly working the bolts of their rifles and fumbling as with trembling hands they thrust in a fresh clip of cartridges—all somehow perceived, but thrust aside in his intense watch. A green light went up about half a mile to the left, then another a little nearer. Hanley stared more intently in the direction of Williams's post—and found himself saying over and over again without knowing he was saying it: "O God, help him, O God, help him, O God, help him."

Suddenly two green lights appeared, one fired straight up as a signal —probably Williams—the other almost along the ground, as if fired at somebody—probably the runner, wounded or in a panic. Sergeant dead, no doubt—Williams and his runner dead, too, by now. Hanley fired a green light. Two minutes later the British barrage shortened.

Hanley grasped the Very pistol loaded with red. Their turn now.

"Stretcher-bearer, stretcher-bearer!"

Crash! A shell right on their bay.

Hanley staggered and felt a fearful pain in his right knee where a shell splinter had hit him. In the faint light of dawn he saw vaguely that one of the riflemen lay huddled on the fire-step, leaving his rifle still on the parapet; the other man had been blown backwards into the trench, and lay with his feet grimly and ludicrously caught in a torn piece of revetment. His helmet had been knocked from his head.

Faint pops of bombs to his immediate left—they were coming up the communication trench. He peered into the steel-smashed light of dawn, but saw only smoke and the fierce red flash of explosions.

Suddenly, to his left, he saw German helmets coming up the communication trench—they had passed the wire barrier! He looked to his right—a little knot of Germans had got through the wire—a Lewis gun swept them away like flies. He felt the blood running down his leg.

Somebody was standing beside him. A voice, far off, was speaking:

"Bombing attack beaten off, sir."

"Very good, carry on."

"There's only two of us left, sir."

"Carry on."

"Very good, sir."

More Germans on the right; another, longer row coming up the communication trench. Then, suddenly, Germans seemed to spring up in every direction. Hanley fired six shots from his Webley at those in front. He saw others falling hit, or jumping into the trench on either side.

A red light shot up straight in the air. A second later two bombs fell in the bay. A torn, crumpled figure collapsed sideways. The Germans reorganized, while the moppers-up did their job.

The Pass of Thermopylae
430 B.C.
BY
CHARLOTTE YONGE

"Stranger, bear this message to the Spartans, that we lie here obedient to their laws." [1]

THERE was trembling in Greece. "The Great King," as the Greeks called the chief potentate of the East, whose domains stretched from the Indian Caucasus to the Ægæus, from the Caspian to the Red Sea, was marshalling his forces against the little free states that nestled amid the rocks and gulfs of the Eastern Mediterranean. Already had his might devoured the cherished colonies of the Greeks on the eastern shore of the Archipelago, and every traitor to home institutions found a ready asylum at that despotic court, and tried to revenge his own wrongs by whispering incitements to invasion. "All people, nations, and languages," was the commencement of the decrees of that monarch's court; and it was scarcely a vain boast, for his satraps ruled over subject kingdoms, and among his tributary nations he counted the Chaldean, with his learning and old civilization, the wise and steadfast Jew, the skilful Phœnician, the learned Egyptian, the wild freebooting Arab of the desert, the dark-skinned Ethiopian, and over all these ruled the keen-witted, active native Persian race, the conquerors of all the rest, and led by a chosen band proudly called the Immortal. His many capitals—Babylon the great, Susa, Persepolis, and the like—were names of dreamy splendour to the Greeks, described now and then by Ionians from Asia Minor who had carried their tribute to the king's own feet, or by courtier slaves who had escaped with difficulty from being all too serviceable at the tyrannic court. And the lord of this enormous empire was about to launch his countless host against the little cluster of states the whole of which together would hardly equal one province of the huge Asiatic realm! Moreover, it was a war not only on the men, but on their gods. The Persians were zealous adorers of the sun and of fire; they abhorred the idol-worship of the Greeks, and defiled and plundered every temple that fell in their way. Death and desolation were almost the best that could be looked for at such hands; slavery and torture from cruelly

From: *The Book of Golden Deeds.*
[1] *Simonides: Epitaph on the tomb of the Spartans who fell at Thermopylae.*

barbarous masters would only too surely be the lot of numbers should their land fall a prey to the conquerors.

True it was that ten years back the former Great King had sent his best troops to be signally defeated upon the coast of Attica; but the losses at Marathon had but stimulated the Persian lust of conquest, and the new King Xerxes was gathering together such myriads of men as should crush down the Greeks and overrun their country by mere force of numbers.

The muster-place was at Sardis, and there Greek spies had seen the multitudes assembling and the state and magnificence of the king's attendants. Envoys had come from him to demand earth and water from each state in Greece, as emblems that land and sea were his; but each state was resolved to be free, and only Thessaly, that which lay first in his path, consented to yield the token of subjugation. A council was held at the Isthmus of Corinth, and attended by deputies from all the states of Greece, to consider of the best means of defence. The ships of the enemy would coast round the shores of the Ægean Sea, the land army would cross the Hellespont on a bridge of boats lashed together, and march southwards into Greece. The only hope of averting the danger lay in defending such passages as, from the nature of the ground, were so narrow that only a few persons could fight hand to hand at once, so that courage would be of more avail than numbers.

The first of these passes was called Tempe, and a body of troops was sent to guard it; but they found that this was useless and impossible, and came back again. The next was at Thermopylæ. Look in your map of the Archipelago, or Ægean Sea, as it was then called, for the great island of Negropont, or by its old name, Eubœa. It looks like a piece broken off from the coast, and to the north is shaped like the head of a bird, with the beak running into a gulf, that would fit over it, upon the mainland, and between the island and the coast is an exceedingly narrow strait. The Persian army would have to march round the edge of the gulf. They could not cut straight across the country, because the ridge of mountains called Œta rose up and barred their way. Indeed, the woods, rocks, and precipices came down so near the seashore that in two places there was only room for one single wheel track between the steeps and the impassable morass that formed the border of the gulf on its south side. These two very narrow places were called the gates of the pass, and were about a mile apart. There was a little more width left in the intervening space; but in this there were a number of springs of warm mineral water, salt and sulphurous, which were used for the sick to bathe in, and thus the place was called Thermopylæ, or the Hot Gates. A wall had once been built across the westernmost of these narrow places, when the Thessalians and Phocians, who lived on either side of it, had been at war with one another; but it had been allowed to go to decay, since the Phocians had found out that there was a very steep, narrow mountain path along the bed of a torrent by which it was possible to cross from one territory to the other without going round this marshy coast road.

This was therefore an excellent place to defend. The Greek ships were all drawn up on the farther side of Eubœa to prevent the Persian vessels from getting into the strait and landing men beyond the pass, and a division of the army was sent off to guard the Hot Gates. The council at the Isthmus did not know of the mountain pathway, and thought that all would be safe as long as the Persians were kept out of the coast path.

The troops sent for this purpose were from different cities, and amounted to about 4,000, who were to keep the pass against two millions. The leader of them was Leonidas, who had newly become one of the two kings of Sparta, the city that above all in Greece trained its sons to be hardy soldiers, dreading death infinitely less than shame. Leonidas had already made up his mind that the expedition would probably be his death, perhaps because a prophecy had been given at the Temple at Delphi that Sparta should be saved by the death of one of her kings of the race of Hercules. He was allowed by law to take with him 300 men, and these he chose most carefully, not merely for their strength and courage, but selecting those who had sons, so that no family might be altogether destroyed. These Spartans, with their helots or slaves, made up his own share of the numbers, but all the army was under his generalship. It is even said that the 300 celebrated their own funeral rites before they set out, lest they should be deprived of them by the enemy, since, as we have already seen, it was the Greek belief that the spirits of the dead found no rest till their obsequies had been performed. Such preparations did not daunt the spirits of Leonidas and his men; and his wife, Gorgo, was not a woman to be faint-hearted or hold him back. Long before, when she was a very little girl, a word of hers had saved her father from listening to a traitorous message from the King of Persia; and every Spartan lady was bred up to be able to say to those she best loved that they must come home from battle "with the shield or on it" —either carrying it victoriously or borne upon it as a corpse.

When Leonidas came to Thermopylæ, the Phocians told him of the mountain path through the chestnut woods of Mount Œta, and begged to have the privilege of guarding it on a spot high up on the mountain side, assuring him that it was very hard to find at the other end, and that there was every probability that the enemy would never discover it. He consented, and encamping around the warm springs, caused the broken wall to be repaired and made ready to meet the foe.

The Persian army were seen covering the whole country like locusts, and the hearts of some of the southern Greeks in the pass began to sink. Their homes in the Peloponnesus were comparatively secure: had they not better fall back and reserve themselves to defend the Isthmus of Corinth? But Leonidas, though Sparta was safe below the Isthmus, had no intention of abandoning his northern allies, and kept the other Peloponnesians to their posts, only sending messengers for further help.

Presently a Persian on horseback rode up to reconnoitre the pass. He could not see over the wall, but in front of it and on the ramparts he saw the Spartans, some of them engaged in active sports, and others in combing their long hair. He rode back to the king, and told him what he had seen. Now, Xerxes had in his camp an exiled Spartan prince, named Demartus, who had become a traitor to his country, and was serving as counsellor to the enemy. Xerxes sent for him, and asked whether his countrymen were mad to be thus employed instead of fleeing away; but Demartus made answer that a hard fight was no doubt in preparation, and that it was the custom of the Spartans to array their hair with especial care when they were about to enter upon any great peril. Xerxes would, however, not believe that so petty a force could intend to resist him, and waited four days, probably expecting his fleet to assist him; but as it did not appear, the attack was made.

The Greeks, stronger men and more heavily armed, were far better able to fight to advantage than the Persians with their short spears and wicker shields, and beat them off with great ease. It is said that Xerxes three times leapt off his throne in despair at the sight of his troops being driven backwards; and thus for two days it seemed as easy to force a way through the Spartans as through the rocks themselves. Nay, how could slavish troops, dragged from home to spread the victories of an ambitious king, fight like freemen who felt that their strokes were to defend their homes and children?

But on that evening a wretched man, named Ephialtes, crept into the Persian camp, and offered, for a great sum of money, to show the mountain path that would enable the enemy to take the brave defenders in the rear. A Persian general, named Hydarnes, was sent off at nightfall with a detachment to secure this passage, and was guided through the thick forests that clothed the hillside. In the stillness of the air, at daybreak, the Phocian guards of the path were startled by the crackling of the chestnut leaves under the tread of many feet. They started up, but a shower of arrows was discharged on them, and forgetting all save the present alarm, they fled to a higher part of the mountain, and the enemy, without waiting to pursue them, began to descend.

As day dawned, morning light showed the watchers of the Grecian camp below a glittering and shimmering in the torrent bed where the shaggy forests opened; but it was not the sparkle of water, but the shine of gilded helmets and the gleaming of silvered spears! Moreover, a Cimmerian crept over to the wall from the Persian camp with tidings that the path had been betrayed; that the enemy were climbing it, and would come down beyond the Eastern Gate. Still, the way was rugged and circuitous, the Persians would hardly descend before midday, and there was ample time for the Greeks to escape before they could thus be shut in by the enemy.

There was a short council held over the morning sacrifice. Megistias, the seer, on inspecting the entrails of the slain victim, declared, as well he might, that their appearance boded disaster. Him Leonidas ordered to retire, but he refused, though he sent home his only son. There was no disgrace to an ordinary tone of mind in leaving a post that could not be held, and Leonidas recommended all the allied troops under his command to march away while yet the way was open. As to himself and his Spartans, they had made up their minds to die at their post, and there could be no doubt that the example of such a resolution would do more to save Greece than their best efforts could ever do if they were careful to reserve themselves for another occasion.

All the allies consented to retreat, except the eighty men who came from Mycæne and the 700 Thespians, who declared that they would not desert Leonidas. There were also 400 Thebans who remained; and thus the whole number that stayed with Leonidas to confront two million of enemies were fourteen hundred warriors, besides the helots or attendants on the 300 Spartans, whose number is not known, but there was probably at least one to each. Leonidas had two kinsmen in the camp, like himself claiming the blood of Hercules, and he tried to save them by giving them letters and messages to Sparta; but one answered that "he had come to fight, not to carry letters," and the other that "his deeds would tell all that Sparta wished to know." Another Spartan, named Dienices, when told that the enemy's archers were so numerous that their arrows darkened the sun, replied, "So much the better: we shall fight in the shade." Two of the 300 had been sent to a neighbouring village, suffering severely from a complaint in the eyes. One of them, called Eurytus, put on his armour, and commanded his helot to lead him to his place in the ranks; the other, called Aristodemus, was so overpowered with illness that he allowed himself to be carried away with the retreating allies. It was still early in the day when all were gone, and Leonidas gave the word to his men to take their last meal. "To-night," he said, "we shall sup with Pluto."

Hitherto he had stood on the defensive, and had husbanded the lives of his men; but he now desired to make as great a slaughter as possible, so as to inspire the enemy with dread of the Grecian name. He therefore marched out beyond the wall, without waiting to be attacked, and the battle began. The Persian captains went behind their wretched troops and scourged them on to the fight with whips! Poor wretches! they were driven on to be slaughtered, pierced with the Greek spears, hurled into the sea, or trampled into the mud of the morass; but their inexhaustible numbers told at length. The spears of the Greeks broke under hard service, and their swords alone remained; they began to fall, and Leonidas himself was among the first of the slain. Hotter than ever was the fight over his corpse, and two Persian princes, brothers of Xerxes, were there killed; but at length word was brought that Hydarnes was over the pass, and that the few remaining men were thus enclosed on all sides. The Spartans and Thespians made their way to a little hillock within the wall, resolved to let this be the place of their last stand; but the hearts of the Thebans failed them, and they came towards the Persians holding out their hands in entreaty for mercy. Quarter was given to them, but they were all branded with the king's mark as untrustworthy deserters. The helots probably at this time escaped into the mountains; while the small desperate band stood side by side on the hill still fighting to the last, some with swords, others with daggers, others even with their hands and teeth, till not one living man remained amongst them when the sun went down. There was only a mound of slain, bristled over with arrows.

Twenty thousand Persians had died before that handful of men! Xerxes asked Demaratus if there were many more at Sparta like these, and was told there were 8,000. It must have been with a somewhat failing heart that he invited his courtiers from the fleet to see what he had done to the men who dared to oppose him, and showed them the head and arm of Leonidas set up upon a cross; but he took care that all his own slain, except 1,000, should first be put out of sight. The body of the brave king was buried where he fell, as were those of the other dead. Much envied were they by the unhappy Aristodemus, who found himself called by no name but the "Coward," and was shunned by all his fellow-citizens. No one would give him fire or water, and after a year of misery he redeemed his honour by perishing in the forefront of the battle of Platæa, which was the last blow that drove the Persians ingloriously from Greece.

The Sword of the Lord and of Gideon

BY

COLONEL THEODORE ROOSEVELT

A SCANT hundred and fifty years ago the United States was but a fringe of settlements that clung to the skirts of the Atlantic. A few miles inland from the seaboard the "backwoods" stretched unbroken from north to south. The restless pioneer spirit that built our country was astir, and hardy men and brave women were pushing westward, ever westward. The rush was starting over trackless mountain and tangled forest, turbulent river and wide, shimmering plain, which never faltered until the covered wagons jolted over a crest and the broad Pacific stretched horizon-far.

To the north the stream westward flowed along the lake-shore by the Wilderness Trail. By the wagons walked the men. When there was a halt for the night children tumbled out over the tail-board like mud-turtles from a log in a pond. The families carried their scant household goods. At Oyster Bay, we have in our library a Windsor rocking-chair that went with my wife's great-great-grandparents over this trail from Vermont to the settlement of Ohio.

To the south the pioneers struck the Appalachian Mountains as the first great barrier to their advance. These ranges stretch like a bulwark down the mid-eastern part of our country. Though not high, they are rugged and very beautiful. In spring they are cloaked in green, save where some gray shoulder of rock has thrust through. In autumn they are painted by the purple pomp of changing foliage gorgeous as a columbine.

Into these mountains tramped the wilderness hunters. They were lean, silent men, clad in coonskin caps and homespun. Around their necks were slung powder-horns. They carried the heavy, smooth-bore flint-lock guns. Such men were Daniel Boone and Simon Kenton.

These lone hunters carried more than their rifles over their shoulders; they carried the destiny of a nation. They were stout fighting men. Under Braddock they were all that stood between the British regulars and massacre. During the Revolutionary War they fought notably for the colonies and independence. Morgan's rifles were composed of them. Under General Clarke they beat the Indians time and again, and won Kentucky and Ohio for the colonists.

From: *Rank and File*: Copyright 1928. Scribners.

276

In the closing years of the eighteenth century one of these wilderness hunters worked his way over the Cumberland Mountains. He wandered south along the western slope until he came to the lovely little valley now known as the "Three Forks of the Wolf." The country looked so friendly and fertile that he settled there, cleared his fields, and travelled no more. His name was Conrad Pile.

The land attracted other settlers, and soon a little community was nestling between the rugged slopes of the mountains. It was christened Pall Mall, though no one knows why. After many years of uncertainty it was assigned to the State of Tennessee.

Like most of the other settlements in these hills the people were isolated, and had but little contact with the men and women of the lowlands. They were poor, for the valley yielded a scanty living. Most of them left but rarely the mountains that surrounded their log and board cabins. Schools were almost unknown. Children worked, not as training for life, but because it was necessary to work to live. The fiery spirit still flamed, and it was from the men of the Tennessee and Kentucky Mountains that "Old Hickory" drew the raw levees that beat the pick of the veteran British regulars at New Orleans.

Perhaps the strongest force in shaping these men and women was their religion. Their faith was of the deep-rooted, zealous type that carried the Roundheads to victory under Cromwell. Their ministers were circuit-riders, who travelled weary miles to carry the gospel to their widely scattered flocks. It was the religion of the Bible, hard and narrow at times but living, and was brought into the occurrences of every-day life, not kept as a thing apart. It was not merely for Sunday consumption in a padded pew. The citizens were the spiritual as well as probably the physical descendants of the Covenanters. For their general, when forming them for battle, to ride down their lines with a sword in one hand and a Bible in the other, would not have struck them as strange but as natural.

Next to their religion they were perhaps most influenced by the wilds. Hunting or trapping in the wooded hills was the recreation of the men. The youth of the mountains were learned in woodcraft. They could shoot rapidly and accurately and were toughened by life in the open.

During the Civil War these mountains formed an isolated island of loyalty to the Union in a sea of secession. Though the majority of the people were Federals some were Confederate sympathizers, and bitter bloody feuds tore the little hill settlements.

At the dawn of the twentieth century more than a hundred years had passed since old Conrad Pile halted from his wandering in the valley of the Three Forks of the Wolf, but Pall Mall was not greatly changed. The men wore homespun, the women calico. The houses were but little improved. Indeed, the log cabin Conrad built was still in use. The people spoke a language which was not, as many believe, a corruption of English, but an old form. They used "hit" for "it," which is the old neuter form of he or him. They spoke of "you'uns," which is an old colloquial plural of you.

Over their sewing the girls sang early English ballads, long forgotten by the rest of the world. Their recreations were husking-bees and log-rolling parties. This little valley in the mountains seemed a changeless back-eddy in the march of progress. The Reverend Rosier Pile, the great-great-grand-son of Conrad, was preacher. Full 80 per cent of the people were descend-ants of the first half-dozen settlers.

Among these were William York and his wife. They had eleven children, one of whom was a strapping, red-headed young mountaineer named Alvin. The family lived in a little two-room board cabin. William York was a blacksmith by profession, but loved hunting and spent much of his time wandering over the hills.

Alvin was much like the boys of his acquaintance. His education was scant. The little mountain school he attended was open only for three months during the summer. For the rest of the year it was closed, because the children had to work, or were winter-bound in their scattered homes on the hillsides. All young York got of "book-l'arnin' " was a foundation in the "three Rs." There was other training, however, that stood him in good stead. When he was not working on the farm or at the school, he was hunting. At an early age he had been given a rifle and it was his most valued possession.

The men of Pall Mall had cleared a rough rifle-range for themselves and had competitions on Saturdays. They used the old muzzle-loading, ball-powder-and-patch rifles handed down by their forefathers. Such rifles are very accurate for perhaps seventy-five yards. Turkeys and beeves were the usual prizes. In a turkey contest they did not use a target, but the turkey itself. In one competition the turkey was tethered by its foot to a stake some hundred and forty yards from the competitors. In another it was tied behind a log forty yards distant in such fashion that only its head showed. In both instances the turkey was given freedom of action, so that the target was constantly on the move. A turkey's head is not large, and a man who can hit it when it is bobbing about is a real marksman.

John Sowders, young York's principal rival at these matches, used to "limber up" by sticking carpet-tacks in a board and driving them home with his bullets at a range of twenty-five yards.

When Alvin York and two of his brothers were well grown, their father died. The mother, however, with their aid and the small farm, managed to keep the family together. There was no money for trimmings, but everyone had enough to eat. Her tall, red-headed son for a time had a mild "fling" —drank his corn whiskey and went on parties with his contemporaries among the boys. In the mid-twenties his stern religion gripped him and he stopped drinking. He took a deeper interest in church affairs and became an elder.

Early in the spring of 1917, word came to the little mountain commu-nity that the United States had declared war on Germany. They were such a back-eddy of the country that they had heard very little of the cumulative causes. Indeed, I have been told that the men who came to enlist in the army from some of the more isolated spots in these mountains believed that we were again at war with England, and were deeply suspicious when told we were her ally. At the Three Forks of the Wolf the War was not popular. Memories of the Civil War, with its bitter interfamily feuds, were still alive in the community. Few of the young fellows volunteered. At last the draft came.

Alvin York was a husky six-footer nearly thirty years old. He did not believe in war. He felt that the New Testament definitely stood against the killing of man by man. "For all they that take the sword shall perish with the sword." He was engaged to be married and was the principal support of his mother. Pastor Pile, of whose church he was a member, firmly believed that the tenets of his church forbade war. All York had to do was to state his case. He had clear grounds on which to claim exemption, but he was made of sterner stuff. Though he believed it wrong to kill, he believed it necessary to serve his country. He refused to claim exemption or let any one make such application in his behalf.

Down to Jamestown, the county-seat, he rode on one of his two mules. He registered, was examined and passed. Back at Pall Mall he told his womenfolk the news. They grieved bitterly, but they knew that a man must seek his happiness by following what he believes to be right.

His blue card reached him in November. In a few hours he said good-by and drove in a buggy to Jamestown. He was sent to Camp Gordon near Atlanta, Ga. It was the first time he had ever been out of sight of his beloved mountains. In his diary he wrote: "I was the homesickest boy you ever seen."

After nearly three months' training he was assigned in February, 1918, to Company G, 328th Infantry, 82nd Division. This division was really a cross-section of the country. Its men were drawn from every State of the Union. They were of every racial stock that goes to make up our nation, from the descendants of colonial English to the children of lately arrived Italian immigrants. Every trade and occupation was represented among its personnel.

Now began his battle with himself as to what course it was right for him to follow. His mother had weakened at the thought that he might be killed, and together with Pastor Pile had written to the officers stating that York's religion forbade war. York himself was deeply troubled, for Pastor Pile in letters pleaded with him not to jeopardize his eternal salvation by killing man.

He turned, in his distress, to his immediate superiors, Major G. E. Buxton and Captain E. C. B. Danforth, Jr. Fortunately both were men of high principle and broad vision. They realized at once that here was no yellow-streaked malingerer but a sincere man seeking guidance.

Late one evening the three men met in the little tar-paper shack that served Buxton for quarters. There, in the hard light of the single unshaded electric bulb that dangled from the ceiling, the officers reasoned with the lanky, red-headed private. The causes that led to the War were explained in detail. Then they turned to the Bible, and by text and teaching showed that while peace was desirable it must not be a peace at any price. Though we are in the world to strive for righteousness, justice, and peace, if one of these has to be sacrificed in order to obtain the other two, it must be peace.

They read him the thirty-third chapter of Ezekiel, and told him that he and all Americans were as "the watchman" in the Bible. On them was laid the charge of guarding humanity. To fail in the task would be traitorous.

York was absolutely honest. He strove for light. Gradually he became convinced, as had his spiritual ancestors the Covenanters, that right and war were bedfellows in this instance. Once his mind was clear, there was no faltering or hesitation. If it was right to fight at all, then it was right to fight with all your might. He flung himself into the drill and training with every ounce of energy he possessed. He soon showed that his days of shooting at the Three Forks of the Wolf were not ill spent. The Enfield rifle with which the division was equipped was the best firearm he had ever used. In rapid firing at moving targets he easily outdistanced the other men.

Some months passed. The American troops had reached Europe. Instead of a division or two scattered through the line that stretched like a dike across the north of France, the Americans now had over two million men. The United States had an army in the field and was prepared to carry her share of the battle. The tide had turned, and the Allies were crushing the gray lines back. The Germans had lost the initiative.

Our army was attacking as a unit. The battle of the Argonne was raging. Through the shell-torn woods and fields, over hills and valleys, the American troops were fighting their way forward. Then came a check. The 1st Division had gone through, but the divisions on its right and left had encountered severe resistance. As a result the Regulars were thrust out in the enemies' lines, and were swept with fire from three sides. It was imperative that the lines on the right and left be advanced. The 82nd Division was selected for this mission. On October 6th they were assigned a position on the left of the 1st Division, with orders to attack on Chatel Chehery Hills.

All day on October 7th the 328th Infantry lay in shell-holes and ditches on the slopes of Hill 223, and along the road that stretched to its rear. All day long the German shrapnel and high explosive burst along their lines. Behind them and in front were the wooded slopes of the rough Argonne hills. The ground was heavy with rain, the soldiers were mud-caked and sodden with wet.

Beyond Hill 223, the farthest point of their advance, was an open valley about five hundred yards wide. On the other side of this valley rose three hills, the central one steep and rugged, the other two gently sloping. The crest of the ridge formed by these was held by a division of veteran German troops, hard-schooled by years of war.

The position was of great importance, for behind these hills lay the narrow-gauge railroad, which supplied the Germans in the forest where they had checked the advance of the American battle line.

Late in the afternoon of October 8th York's battalion, the 2nd, received its orders. It was to relieve the 1st which had seized the hill, and then to thrust due west into the German flank. The attack was to start at six next morning from Hill 223, and the final objective was the railroad.

Through the black of the night the troops stumbled up the wooded slopes and took their position. Dawn came with gray reluctance; a heavy mist drifted through the tree-tops and choked the valley below. Gradually it lifted and shredded off. Zero hour had come.

The Americans started down through the tangled undergrowth. The sun rose and swallowed the last remnants of mist, giving the Germans a fair view of the attacking troops. Immediately from all sides the hostile fire burst. High explosives shrieked through the trees, filling the air with scraps of iron and flying splinters. Shrapnel exploded in puffs of smoke and rained down its bullets on the advancing men. Through it all machine-guns spattered our advance with a rattling hurricane of lead.

When they had descended the long wooded slope they started across the open country. The flanking fire was so ferocious that the American lines melted like snow in a spring thaw. To advance was impossible. The companies lay frozen to the ground while bullets whipped over them like sleet in a northeaster.

Lieutenant Stewart, a splendid young giant from Florida, commanded a platoon in York's company. He jumped to his feet and called to his men to follow. So great was their confidence in him that they struggled up and started ahead, though it looked certain death. He had not gone ten yards before a bullet struck him shattering his right thigh, and he crashed to the ground. Though his leg was shattered his manhood was not. By a supreme effort he shoved himself erect on the one leg left, and started to hop forward. A couple of yards farther he pitched on his face. A bullet had struck him in the head and his gallant spirit had joined the hero-dead of the nation.

The platoon dropped to the ground again and lay flat. It was clear that no advance could be attempted until the guns that were sweeping the plain with flanking fire were silenced. Captain Danforth decided to send a detachment from York's platoon on this mission.

Raising his head from the ground he turned to the platoon. Sergeant Harry Parsons, an ex-vaudeville actor from New York, was commanding it. Like a well-trained soldier he was watching his company commander for orders.

The roar of the artillery drowned all sound of his voice, so Danforth pointed to the hill on the left and motioned in its direction. Parsons understood at once. Quietly but quickly he chose three squads of his platoon. The German fire had taken its toll, a third of the men were wounded or dead. Of the twenty-four who had composed these squads when they left the hill-crest half an hour ago, only sixteen remained.

The make-up of this detachment was in itself a mute comment on our country and our army. Of the sixteen soldiers, eight had English names; the other eight were men whose parents had come from Ireland, Italy, Poland, Germany, and Sweden. One of the members of this patrol was Alvin York of Tennessee, lately promoted corporal.

Sergeant Early was placed in command. He was told to outflank in any fashion possible the machine-guns that were causing the damage, and beat down their fire or destroy them.

On their bellies the men wormed their way to the woods, hitching themselves along below the bullets that swept scythelike across the field.

When they reached the cover of the trees they rose and, crouching, threaded their way to the left. Stealing from stump to stump, taking cover wherever possible, they reached the far end of the valley without casualties. Here fortune favored them, for they found a thicket that concealed them until they were nearly half-way across.

Suddenly bullets began to rattle around them, passing with the crack of a whip. They were under fire from the right flank. They must either retreat and abandon their mission or quickly pass on. Sergeant Early's decision was made without hesitation. They moved forward. In a few seconds they were clambering up the steep hillside beyond the valley. The boldness of this move protected them. The Germans were watching the hills opposite and the valley, but not the slopes on which their own guns rested. For a moment the Americans were sheltered. The soul-satisfying relief that comes to a soldier when he finds himself defiladed from fire is like waking after a severe illness to find the pain gone.

Stumbling through the brush and dead leaves they came to a wood path that led in rear of the crest. Here they halted for a moment to get their bearings and decide on the next move. To their left stretched unbroken woodlands from which no sound of firing came. To their right crackled the machine-guns they were to silence. They had succeeded in reaching a position in rear of the Germans.

While they were standing breathless, listening for any sound that might give a further clew, they caught faintly the guttural sound of Germans talking in the valley on the reverse slope of the hill. Just at this moment a twig snapped, and right ahead of them they saw two German stretcher-bearers. There was no time to be lost, for these men might give the alarm to the machine-guns, and the Americans opened fire at once. Both Germans escaped into the woods, though one was wounded. The time for discussion had passed. It was now or never. Quick as a flash Early called: "As skirmishers, forward!"

Down the bank of a small stream they plunged, and up the other side. Here the woods were thinner. Suddenly they saw just above them about fifty Germans gathered near a small board hut. The surprise of the Americans was nothing to that of the Germans, who knew themselves to be well in rear of their own lines. They had been getting their orders for a counterattack when out of the bush had burst the Americans, ragged, unshaven, with fierce eyes and gleaming bayonets.

A couple of Boches tried to reach for their rifles, but the crack of the Enfields halted them. Up went their hands, and "Kamerad!" echoed through the grove.

It was the battalion headquarters of the machine-guns. Among the group were a major and two junior officers. The Americans formed a crescent and moved toward their prisoners, who were on high ground just above them. On the left flank was Alvin York. As he approached the group the bushes became sparser. Right above him, not forty yards away, he saw German machine-guns. The Boche gunners had got the alarm. They were trying frantically to turn their guns to the rear. A few of them picked up rifles and fired at York, who stood in plain sight. The bullets burnt his face.

A command in German was shouted. At once the prisoners dropped flat on their faces. York and six of his comrades, who were now close to the Germans, did the same. Sergeant Early, with the other Americans, did not understand what was happening and remained standing. A burst of fire swept the grove.

Six of our patrol fell dead and three were wounded, including the sergeant. The surviving Americans were now among their prisoners. Probably on this account the hail of bullets was held two or three feet above the ground. There were no more casualties.

York was a comparatively green soldier. He was fighting not for the love of fighting, but for a firm conviction of the righteousness and justice of our cause. The shadows of the men who fought at Naseby and Marston Moor stood at his elbow. The spirit that inspired Cromwell and Ireton, Hampden and Vane, stirred in him. He saw "enfranchised insult" in the persons of the German soldiers, and, like the Covenanters, with a cold fury he "smote them hip and thigh."

He was in the open. Calling to his comrades, who were cloaked by the bushes and could neither see nor be seen, to stay where they were and guard the prisoners, he prepared to take the offensive. Crawling to the left through some weeds, he reached a point from which he got a clear view of the German emplacements. Just as the got there the German fire ceased. Several rose and started down the slope in the direction of the Americans to investigate. Quick as a flash York's rifle spoke. One pitched forward on his face and the rest scuttled back. Again a hail of bullets swept through the grove.

In a few minutes it slackened. York sat up and took the position used by hunters since rifles were first invented. The range to the gun-pits was that at which he had so often shot in those seemingly distant days, in his far-off home in the Tennessee mountains. This time, however, he was not shooting for sport but "battling for the Lord." He saw several German heads peering cautiously over the emplacements. He swung his rifle toward one and fired; the helmet flew up and the head disappeared. Four times more he fired before the Germans realized what was happening and ducked back.

Bullets spattered around him, splintering the tree at his elbow and covering him with slivers of wood and dust. Heedless of the danger, he watched the ridge until another head appeared. Again his rifle cracked and again the head disappeared. Hitting German heads at forty yards was easy for a man who had hit turkey heads at the same range, and whose nerves were of iron because of his belief in his cause.

The battle rested entirely on his shoulders, for the rest of the Americans were so screened by the brush that they were only able to fire a few scattered shots.

The Germans could not aim at this lone rifleman, for whenever a head appeared it was met with a bullet from the mountaineer. York was not fighting from a passion for slaughter. He would kill any one without compunction who stood in the way of victory; but it was not killing but victory for which he strove. He began calling: "Come down, you-all, and give up."

The battle went on.

At times the Boche riflemen would creep out of their emplacements, take cover behind some tree, and try to get the American. The hunter from the Cumberland Mountains was trained to note the slightest movement. The man who could see a squirrel in the tree-top could not fail to observe a German when he moved. Every time he found them and fired before they found him. That ended the story.

The Germans by this time knew that the brunt of the battle was being borne by one American. They realized they were not quick enough to kill him by frontal attack, so they sent an officer and seven men around his left flank to rush him. These crawled carefully through the brush until they were within twenty yards of him. Then with a yell they sprang up and came at him on a dead run, their fixed bayonets flashing in the sun.

The clip of cartridges in York's rifle was nearly exhausted and he had no time to reload. Dropping his Enfield he seized his automatic pistol. As they came lunging forward through the undergrowth he fired. One after another the Germans pitched forward and lay where they fell, huddled gray heaps in the tangled woods. Not only had York killed them all, but each time he had shot at the man in rear in order that the others might not halt and fire a volley on seeing their comrade fall. The machine-gun fire had slackened during the charge. Again it burst forth and again York stilled it with his rifle.

The grim, red-headed mountaineer was invincible. Almost unaided he had already killed some twenty of his opponents. The German major's nerve was shaken. He could speak English. Slowly he wriggled on his stomach to where the American sat and offered to tell the machine-gunners to surrender. "Do it and I'll treat ye white," said York.

At this moment a lone German crawled close, jumped to his feet, and hurled a grenade. It went wide, but when the Enfield spoke its bullet did not. The German pitched forward on his face, groaning. The Boche major then rose to his knees and blew his whistle shrilly. All firing ceased. He called an order to his men. Instantly they began scrambling to their feet, throwing down belts and side-arms.

The American was alert for treachery. When they were half-way down the hill, with their hands held high over their heads, he halted them. With the eyes of a backwoodsman he scanned each for weapons. There were none. The surrender was genuine.

Corporal York stood up and called to his comrades. They answered him from where they had been guarding their first prisoners. The thick grove had prevented them from taking an active part in the fighting, but they had protected York from attacks by the prisoners who would otherwise have taken him from the rear.

Sergeant Early, the leader of the patrol, was lying in the brush desperately wounded in the abdomen. York called: "Early, are you alive?"

"I am all through," groaned the sergeant. "You take command. You'll need a compass. Turn me over. You'll find mine in my pocket. Get our men back as soon as you can, and leave me here."

York had well over a hundred prisoners, as sixty had come from the machine-gun emplacements. Some of the Americans doubted the possibility of getting them back to the lines. York paid no attention to this. He formed the Germans in column of twos, placing our wounded at the rear, with prisoners to carry Sergeant Early, who could not walk. Along the flanks he stationed his surviving comrades, with instructions to keep the column closed up and to watch for treachery. He himself led, with the German major in front of him and a German officer on each side.

Before they started York had had the major explain to the men that at any sign of hostility he would shoot to kill, and the major would be the first to die. They had seen enough of the deadly prowess of the mountaineer. Not one made the attempt. He marched his column around the hill to a point from which he could probably have taken them back safely, but his mission was to clear the hill of machine-guns. He knew that some still remained on the front slope.

Turning the column to the left, he advanced on the Boche garrisons. As he approached he had the German major call to each in turn to surrender. When they did he disarmed them and added them to his train of prisoners. In only one instance did a man attempt to resist. He went to join the long roll of German dead.

York's troubles were not over. Though he had cleaned up and destroyed the machine-guns, he still had to get back to our lines with the men he had captured. To do this he had to be very careful, for so large a body of Germans marching toward our lines might well be taken for a counter-attack and mowed down with rifle-fire. Bringing all his woodcraft into play he led his long column of gray-clad prisoners over the ridge and down through the brush, until he reached the foot of the slope up which his patrol had climbed earlier in the day.

Suddenly from the brush on the other side the command "Halt!" rang out. York jumped to the front to show his uniform, and called out that he was bringing in prisoners. He was just in time to prevent casualties. The lines of our infantry opened to let the party through. As the doughboys from left and right looked between the tree-trunks they saw gray form after gray form pass. A yell of approval rang out. Some one shouted: "Are you bringing in the whole German Army?" The lines closed behind the column. Corporal York had fulfilled his mission.

In a few minutes he reported at battalion headquarters. The prisoners were counted. There were one hundred and thirty-two, including three officers, one a major. With less than a year's military training a red-headed mountaineer, practically single-handed, had fought a veteran battalion of German troops, taken thirty-five guns, killed twenty men, captured one hundred and thirty-two and the battalion commander.

For three weeks more the Division hammered its way forward. The stubborn German defense was beaten back, the Allies drove on to Sedan. Even among the fighting troops rumors of peace became more persistent. One morning word came to the front lines where the tired men stood, ankle-deep in mud—an armistice had been signed.

York had become a sergeant. He was with his company. His feat, as he saw it, was merely a part of the day's work. The officers and men of the 82nd Division, however, were very proud of him. They had reported the facts to General Headquarters. The story had spread like wild-fire, and Alvin York was famous.

During his simple country life York had never met any of the great of the world. His nearest approach to a general had been when he stood stiffly at attention while the general inspected the ranks. Now he found himself honored of all, because physical courage, especially when backed by moral worth, commands universal admiration. General Headquarters ordered him from place to place in France. A brigade review was held in his honor. He was decorated not only by the United States but also by the Allies. At Paris Poincaré, the president of the French Republic, pinned the highest decorations to his coat.

In May, 1919, he came back with his regiment to our country. Here enthusiasm ran even higher. The streets of New York were jammed with people who cheered themselves hoarse. He went to see the Stock Exchange, where no visitors are allowed on the floor. Not only was he permitted to visit the floor but business was suspended and the stockbrokers carried him around on their shoulders.

In Washington, when he went to the gallery of the House of Representatives, the congressmen stopped debate and cheered him to the echo. Great banquets were given for him, which were attended by the highest ranking civil, military, and naval officials.

In his olive-drab uniform, with his medals and shock of red hair, he was a marked man. When he walked the streets enthusiastic crowds gathered. There were men and women to greet him at the railroad-stations as he travelled back to Tennessee to be mustered out.

He was offered a contract for $75,000 to appear in a moving-picture play on the War. He was approached by vaudeville firms, who suggested tours on which they agreed to give him a salary of $1,000 a week. Newspapers were willing to pay fabulous sums for articles by him.

He was taken up on a mountain and shown the kingdoms of the world. Ninety-nine men out of a hundred would have cracked under the adulation. Ninety-nine men out of a hundred who can bear the famine worthily will lose their heads at the feast. York did not. Though his twelve months in the army had greatly broadened him, his character was still as strong and unshaken as the rock of his own hills. He refused the offers of money or position, saying rightly that these were made him only because of his feat in the Argonne. To sell his war record would be putting a price on patriotism.

As soon as he could he made his way back to his home in the mountains, his family, and his friends. There he was met by his mother in her calico bonnet, his sisters and brothers, and Grace Williams, the mountain girl to whom he was betrothed.

In a few days there was an open-air wedding at Pall Mall. It was held on the hillside. A gray ledge of rock served as altar. The new leaves of spring danced in the sunlight, casting flickering shadows on the white starched "Sunday-go-to-meeting" dresses and blue serge "store clothes" of the mountain folk, who had driven in from the surrounding country. The governor of the State officiated, assisted by Pastor Pile. The bride and groom were Grace Williams and Sergeant Alvin York, late of the United States Army.

Though York refused to sell his service record, he knew his Bible far too well to have forgotten the parable of the talents. That which it would be wrong to use for his own benefit, it would be wrong not to use for the benefit of others. His experience in the world had made him bitterly conscious of his scanty education. He realized that "wisdom excelleth folly as far as light excelleth darkness." He decided to bend his efforts toward establishing proper schools for the children of the hills.

The people of Tennessee had been collecting an Alvin York Fund. He asked them to turn it into a foundation for building schools in the mountains. All he would accept for himself was a small farm.

Deguelo

BY

MARQUIS JAMES

1

Most of the boys had been to a fandango the night before last and still felt tired and sleepy. Travis was hard put to get any work out of them. What need to work? Herrera was either a liar or a fool who believed everything he heard. Santa Anna with an army already across the Rio Grande? Preposterous! Let the excitable tenderfeet lose sleep over a tall tale such as that.

William Barret Travis was no tenderfoot in Texas. His soldiers might not take much stock in the story that Herrera had brought to Béxar, but the inhabitants seemed to view matters in a different light. These easy-going Spaniards bestirred themselves to activities difficult to assign to any light motive. An atmosphere of suppressed excitement hung over the sunlit stone and adobe town. There was a great hurrying to and fro along the narrow streets and through the white dust of the plazas. Big two-wheeled carts loaded with household goods made their way in long files over the roads that led into the country.

On the morning of February 23, 1836, Travis posted a sentinel in the tower of San Fernando Church to keep a lookout to the west and, at first sight of anything resembling Mexican troops, to ring the bell. With this precaution the Texas army of occupation very leisurely went about the business of putting the Álamo in a state of defense. The soldiers preferred to lounge about the cantinas and mix with their friendly enemies among the native population. They regretted the departure of so many comely señoritas. The town was dull enough as it was.

This boredom was relaxed, however, when shortly before noon on the twenty-third the population and garrison alike were startled by the furious clanging of the bell in the tower of the Church of San Fernando. An officer scrambled up the dark little stairway. What had the sentinel seen? He had seen Mexicans—cavalry on the heights of Alazan—their lances glittering through the mist of a fine rain. But where were they now? demanded the officer. Gone, said the sentinel—vanished at the first taps of the bell. The officer scanned the horizon. He saw nothing and the sentinel was accused of giving a false alarm. But Travis thought it prudent to investigate the soldier's story. Dr. John Sutherland and Scout John W. Smith had their horses saddled, and volunteered to reconnoiter.

That was the way of the soldiery of the Texas Revolution—time to prepare for a fight when the enemy was in sight. Texans made the poorest peace-time soldiers on earth and the best in battle, where their feats over and again seemed beyond belief. A good man was required to command them in battle or out. Buck Travis was a good man, but when there was no fighting to do he had his hands full. A few days before the incident of the sentinel in the tower, he had written a letter to Henry Smith, the Governor of Texas.

"If you had taken the trouble to answer my letter I should not now have been under the necessity of troubling you. My situation is truly awkward and delicate. Col. Neill left me in command, but wishing to give satisfaction to the volunteers here and not wishing to assume any command over them, I issued an order for the election of an officer to command them with the exception of one company of volunteers that had previously engaged to serve under me. Bowie was elected by two small companies, and since his election has been roaring drunk all the time, has assumed all command . . . turning everything topsy turvy. If I didn't feel my honor and that of my country compromitted, I would leave here instantly. . . . I hope you will order immediately some regular troops here as it is more important to occupy this post than I imagined when last I saw you. It is the Key to Texas . . . Without a foothold here, the enemy can do nothing against us. . . . I do not solicit the command of this post, but as Col. Neill . . . is anxious for me to take command, I will do it. . . . The enemy is on the Rio Grande with 1000 strong, and is making every preparation to invade us. By the 15th of March I think Texas will be invaded and every preparation should be made to receive them."

2

Governor Smith's situation was quite as "awkward and delicate" as that of the quasi-commander at San Antonio de Béxar. Three months before, in November, 1835, the Mexican province of Texas, largely settled by Americans, had revolted against Santa Anna who had repudiated the liberal professions that had actuated the Mexican people a few years earlier to win their independence of Spain. Texas had not declared its independence, but merely its opposition to the dictatorship of Santa Anna. To administer its affairs in this crisis, Texas had elected Henry Smith as Governor. An advisory Council was created to consult with Governor Smith and Sam Houston was chosen as Commander-in-Chief of the Army.

Trouble had started immediately between the Governor and his Council, and between Houston and a clique of his officers. The Mexican government's first attempt to bring Texas to time by force of arms had resulted in victory for the Texans and not a Mexican soldier remained north of the Rio Grande. But the Texas troops could not stand idleness. They wanted to keep on fighting even if they had to cross the Rio Grande to do it. Houston advised that they stay where they were and get ready to fight because the Mexicans would be back soon to give them their fill of fighting. This was the situation army officers who were jealous of Houston had been waiting for. They sneered at the Commander-in-Chief and stirred up the soldiers with oratory about carrying the war to the enemy. Governor Smith backed Houston but the Council backed the jingo officers. Smith fought the Council and was deposed from office. Houston remained loyal to Smith and was deprived of command of the army.

In the beginning Houston had planned to defend the town of San Antonio de Béxar, but when the invasionists lured away most of the garrison Houston ordered Neill, the commander at Béxar, to blow up the fortifications and leave. Neill failed to do this and was relieved by Lieutenant Colonel W. B. Travis, a red-haired Georgian of twenty-eight who had come out to Texas to practise law, but had made his reputation in the earlier skirmishes of the war. Houston paid a flying visit to the main body of his army, which under the influence of the extremists was marching toward Mexico. The officers were as unreasonable as ever, but Houston convinced enough of the soldiers of the foolhardy nature of the enterprise to break it up. In accomplishing this he also practically broke up the army and the result was greater confusion than ever in the face of what Houston knew to be an invasion of Texas by a powerful Mexican force. Already shorn of his power, there was nothing Houston could do to put the quarreling soldiery in a proper mood for cooperation. He had saved them from risking their foolish heads in the enemy's country and he had told them what the enemy was going to do to their country. Houston then disappeared among the Indian tribes of the frontier where he could really accomplish something. Mexican agents were at work among the Indians. Himself the trusted friend of the red men, Houston was not long in winning their friendship for the Texas cause, thus destroying the shrewdly conceived Mexican plan of an Indian attack on one front while they were attacking on the other.

Meantime what Houston had predicted came to pass. Santa Anna invaded Texas with seven thousand men, many of them veterans of the old war for Mexican independence, officered by experienced leaders, including soldiers of fortune of several nationalities. To oppose them Texas had about twelve hundred men in the field, scattered everywhere, poorly equipped, without discipline, under leaders who refused to support one another and with no man in the Government strong enough to enforce obedience. This was the posture of affairs in February, 1836.

At Béxar was a handful of men under Travis who was doing his best to augment his force. Jim Bowie joined the garrison with a small following which, until the fighting started, rather increased Travis's difficulties than otherwise. James Bowie was not the man he had once been—the half-legendary figure whose tremendous exploits were a tradition from St. Louis to Mexico City. In the old days Bowie was a power in northern Mexico. He had married the daughter of a grandee and, turning his abilities to less spectacular pursuits, accumulated a fortune and his family lived like royalty. Just when his wild days seemed behind him, a plague swept Bowie's beautiful wife and their children into the grave and the lion-hearted Jim almost died of grief. Nothing mattered after that. Life became a quest for activity to turn his mind from his loss. Abandoning his property, he threw himself into the Texas struggle and supported Houston in the contest that had demoralized the Texas army. With little left but blind courage and a name at which enemies still trembled, Jim Bowie then decided to stand by the wreck. His enormous form was gaunt and worn, his blue eyes unnaturally bright from the fever of tuberculosis. Whipping up his flagging forces with whisky, Jim Bowie had plunged into Béxar, determined to sell his life dearly. He could not have come to a better place.

3

Some other recruits, dressed in fringed buckskins, rode into town and, in the drawl of a southern mountaineer, their spokesman said they wanted to fight. This was Davy Crockett with his twelve Tennesseans. Davy had been a Tennessee Congressman from a backwoods district. With a good head and an amusing way about him, he had become something of a national figure. Unfortunately, he committed the error of opposing Andrew Jackson and this had lost him his seat in Congress. Texas was in the public eye and Davy had come on looking for excitement.

A few other volunteers straggled in, bringing Travis's command to the neighborhood of one hundred and forty-five men who, on February twenty-third, awaited the return of Scouts Sutherland and Smith with an indifference born of a picturesque contempt for peril. They did not have long to wait. The two horsemen were seen returning at a dead run across the plain. Travis immediately gave orders to evacuate the Béxar and occupy the Álamo Mission beyond the eastern purlieus of the town. From the way his scouts were riding, Travis knew the Mexican army was coming. Travis now had one hundred and fifty men, having gathered up a few loyal native Mexicans in the town. His first—and last—impulse was to fight.

Sutherland and Smith found their comrades in a fever of preparation to defend the Álamo. The scouts said they had seen fifteen hundred troops drawn up in line of battle, with an officer riding up and down, flourishing a sword and exhorting his men with oratory. Doctor Sutherland had injured his knee during the reconnaissance and could not walk without assistance. But he could ride and, at three o'clock in the afternoon, he sped through the Álamo gate with a message to the "Citizens of Gonzales," a little town fifty miles to the eastward. "The enemy in large force is in sight. We want men and provisions. Send them to us. We . . . are determined to defend the Álamo to the last. Give us assistance."

The message had not been long on its way when the Mexican troops filed into Béxar. A picket on the Álamo wall announced the approach of a horseman under a flag of truce. Travis suspected the object of his visit.

He sent Major Morris and Captain Marten to meet the flag. These officers received Santa Anna's demand of surrender "at discretion." They gave Travis's answer. It was a refusal—which Travis rendered the more emphatic by sending a cannon ball into the town when the Mexican emissary had withdrawn. Santa Anna replied by raising the red flag of No Quarter over the tower of San Fernando and opening on the Texans with a mortar battery. The siege of the Álamo had begun.

The following day Travis spared another of his precious men to carry to the outside world a message that has been called the most heroic in American history.

"Commandancy of the Álamo, Béxar, Feby 24th, 1836.

"To the People of Texas and All Americans in the World—

"Fellow Citizens and Compatriots: I am besieged with a thousand or more of the Mexicans under Santa Anna. I have sustained a continual Bombardment and cannonade for 24 hours and have not lost a man. The enemy has demanded a surrender at discretion, otherwise, the garrison are to be put to the sword, if the fort is taken. I have answered the demand with a cannon shot, and our flag still waves proudly from the wall. *I shall never surrender or retreat.* Then, I call on you in the name of Liberty, of patriotism and everything dear to the American character, to come to our aid with all dispatch. The enemy is receiving reinforcements daily and will no doubt increase to three or four thousand in four or five days. If this call is neglected, I am determined to sustain myself as long as possible and die like a soldier who never forgets what is due his honor and that of his country. VICTORY or DEATH.

"William Barret Travis
"Lt. Col. Comdt."

"P.S. The Lord is on our side. When the enemy appeared in sight we had not three bushels of corn. We have since found in deserted houses 80 to 90 bushels and got into the walls 20 to 30 head of Beeves."

4

The Álamo, which means the cotton-wood tree, was a mission more than one hundred years old—a large and strong establishment with superior advantages of defense. Its size was an embarrassment, however. There was a stone church, partly unroofed in previous fighting, with walls four feet thick, and two stoutly walled enclosures adjoining. The smaller of these enclosures was the convent yard; the larger, more than two acres in extent, the general plaza of the mission. Built against the walls of these enclosures were several stone buildings—a convent, a hospital, barracks, a prison. The walls varied in height from five to twenty-two feet and to defend them Travis mounted eighteen guns. At intervals scaffolds were built for riflemen. The defensive arrangements were intelligently supervised by an engineer named Jameson, but neither scientific skill nor valor could make up for the lack of men. To garrison works so extensive required a thousand troops.

Travis knew that everything depended on reenforcements, and they must come soon. Battalion after battalion of Mexican troops showed themselves on the prairie, and began to encircle the Álamo beyond the range of its guns. Batteries were pushed up and the bombardment grew heavier. Parties of Texans sallied from the walls to gather firewood and to harass the Mexican artillerymen with rifle-fire.

To whom was the beleaguered commander to appeal for aid? Travis knew something of the confusion existing in the Texan civil government, but this situation was more serious than he imagined. After taking away Governor Smith's authority, the Council members had fallen to quarrelling among themselves. Unable to assemble a quorum of their own number, the Council thus deprived Texas of even the name of a government, and left the bewildered little bands, called the army, to shift for themselves.

Travis was shifting. The largest and best equipped body of troops in Texas was the four hundred and twenty men under James W. Fannin at Goliad, one hundred and fifty miles away. In the squabble that had disorganized Texas, Fannin had been a leader of the clique against Sam Houston, while Travis had supported Houston. Nevertheless, Travis appealed to Fannin. That officer received the letter on February twenty-fifth, the third day of the siege. Three days later he carefully packed his baggage wagons and began a leisurely march toward the Álamo.

Travis sent other messages elsewhere and Henry Smith, the deposed Governor, scattered a heart-rending call far and wide. But Smith was not the type of leader to rally men for a desperate throw. The response to Travis's heroic appeals likewise was a disappointment, a black disappointment, to the besieged garrison. After seven days and seven nights of fighting not a man had come to join the defenders. But on the eighth day of battle, March first, at three o'clock in the morning, faithful Scout John W. Smith piloted through the enemy lines thirty-two settlers from Gonzales—practically all in the town who were able to bear arms. Twenty of them had left wives and children behind. The weary garrison received these recruits with a cheer. The outside world heard from at last! Hope was revived for Fannin, whose force would surely turn the tide of battle. The watch on the parapet strained his eyes at the southern prairie, but he saw only ever-increasing numbers of Mexicans methodically throwing up works behind which to maneuver with greater safety and precision.

The Gonzales men raised the strength of the Álamo defenders to about one hundred and eighty-three, not counting some twenty refugees from Béxar, mostly women and children and two or three negro slaves. So far the Texans had lost the services of only one man—Jim Bowie, who had fallen from a scaffold while helping to mount a gun. With a fight at hand Bowie and Travis had composed their differences. The main difficulty between these officers was that each had red hair. Jim Bowie crippled was still worth a half-dozen ordinary men and he hobbled about ready for the finish fight until a piercing "norther" brought on pneumonia. Half-delirious, Jim was carried to a cot and nursed by a sister of his late wife who was among the refugees.

5

The Texans suffered greatly from fatigue and loss of sleep, practically the whole command being on duty constantly. The bombardment was continuous and two hundred shells had fallen within the enclosures. The Texans replied with artillery and rifle-fire from the walls, but their ammunition was low and they saved it for the general assault they knew must come. With the red flag of No Quarter snapping in the north wind, the Texans witnessed every hour new preparations for this attack. The Mexicans were advancing batteries on all sides of the Álamo. Sallying parties of Texans made these maneuvers expensive to the enemy, but Santa Anna had men to spare and he used them. The long hunting rifles of the Texans would no sooner clear out one parcel of gunners than another squad would appear to carry on the work.

During the tenth day of the siege, March third, the enemy bombardment increased in violence and a hostile battery was planted within pistol shot of the north wall. On that day Travis received his last news from the outside. It was brought by James Butler Bonham, a colonel in the Texas military establishment before dissension had demoralized it, and now serving as a volunteer scout under Lieutenant Colonel Travis. He had carried the Commandant's message to Fannin and, regardless of what Fannin intended to do, returned alone to stand with his comrades. Bonham's report of the mission to Fannin was a blow. While the whole truth of Fannin's behavior was never known to the Álamo's defenders, Bonham left Travis with little hope of aid from the source on which the garrison had built such high expectations. Fannin's half-hearted march toward the Álamo had ended within an hour after it began. One baggage wagon broke down and Fannin had returned to camp at Goliad, without so much as sending a messenger to warn Travis to try to escape.

Fannin could have got word to Travis in time to enable him to retreat. Whether Travis would have done this is a question. The chances are he would not for, even after Bonham arrived, the escape of the garrison was possible. There would have been a fight, but most of them could have got away. But Travis had said, "I shall never surrender or retreat," and he kept his word. The men who remained with him remained on those terms. A story that has been published many times relates that Travis called his men together and drew a line on the ground with his sword. Those wishing to stay were invited to step across the line. The tradition is that Jim Bowie had his cot carried over the line and every man, save one, followed him. The story, like much Álamo literature, is legend, not history.

In any event the fact stands that no man deserted the twenty-eight-year-old leader, although abundant opportunity presented. William Barret Travis lives in the history of the world for his thirteen-day defense of the

Álamo. It is his sole claim to a renowned memory, and it is enough. The feat has few parallels in any annals. Bands of men have died, before and since, to show devotion to a cause or their loyalty to a leader they have long known and served, but this was not strictly the case of the Álamo. Texans were fighting Mexican tyranny—technically, that is. Actually most of them were fighting for the thrill of it, for fancied riches in the form of land, or because they were under the spell of professional adventurers who dominated a large part of the Texan stage. Travis, however, was no professional adventurer, which gentry, as a class, do not die needlessly for a cause. Neither had he any special claim on the loyalty of the men who followed him at the Álamo. Most of these men were unknown to him and he to them. His rank did not impress them, for Texans cared nothing for rank and proved it on every occasion. With them it was the man that counted—and Travis was the man.

6

Bonham came in at eleven o'clock in the morning. There was still a chance—a bare chance—of help from without. Three days before, March first, an attempt to reorganize the Texas civil government had been scheduled to be made at the town of Washington-on-the-Brazos, two hundred and twenty-five miles away. After talking to Bonham, Travis prepared appeals to the leaders at Washington, writing all afternoon amid a cannonade and constant interruptions by his lieutenants with more bad news: the ring of investing troops was drawing closer. The appeals of Travis embodied a temperate account of the action to date.

"The spirits of my men are still high," he wrote, "although they have had much to depress them. We have contended for ten days against an enemy whose number are variously estimated at from fifteen hundred to six thousand men. . . . A reinforcement of about one thousand men is now entering Bejar, from the west. . . .

"Col. Fannin is said to be on the march to this place with reinforcements, but I fear it is not true, as I have repeatedly sent to him for aid without receiving any. . . . I look to the colonies alone for aid; unless it arrives soon, I shall have to fight the enemy on his own terms. I will, however, do the best I can . . . and although we may be sacrificed . . . the victory will cost the enemy so dear, that it will be worse for him than defeat. I hope your honorable body will hasten on reinforcements. . . . Our supply of ammunition is limited. . . . The bearer of this will give your honorable body a statement more in detail, should he escape through the enemy's lines. God and Texas—Victory or Death."

When his official communications were finished, Travis wrote to a friend to "take care of my little boy."

Night came on. The Commandant handed his letters to Captain Albert Marten and wished him well. Marten stole through the gate into the shadows. The last of Travis's soldiers had left the Álamo.

The next day the Mexicans kept up a heavy fire of artillery, the Texans replying occasionally. The day after that, Saturday, March fifth, the bombardment eased off in the afternoon and by ten o'clock at night it had stopped altogether. Travis suspected a ruse and posted all his men, who loaded their rifles and their guns and began their twelfth night of vigil. Since the siege had begun there had been no reliefs. The entire command had been continuously on duty. Beef and cornbread had been served on the walls. This was the sole ration. There was no coffee, which would have helped to keep the men awake, and sleep was an enemy more dreaded than the Mexicans. For days men had been dozing in snatches at their guns during the thunder of bombardment. Now the roar had ceased. A silence almost tangible, a starlit southern night: the defenders of the Álamo leaned against their guns—and slept.

At two o'clock on Saturday afternoon, Santa Anna called his commanding officers to headquarters in Béxar. He distributed copies of a general order. "The time has come to strike a decisive blow upon the enemy occupying the Fortress of the Álamo. . . . Tomorrow at 4 o'clock a.m., the columns of attack shall be stationed at musket shot distance from the first entrenchments, ready for the charge, which shall commence at a signal to be given with the bugle."

The attacking columns would be four in number—one to storm each side of the Álamo simultaneously. They would be composed of fourteen hundred infantry who had enjoyed three days' rest. "The first column will carry ten ladders, two crowbars and two axes; the second, ten ladders; the third, six ladders; and the fourth, two ladders. The men carrying the ladders will sling their guns on their shoulders, to be enabled to place the ladders wherever they may be required. The men will wear neither overcoats nor blankets, or anything that will impede the rapidity of their motions. The men will have the chin straps of their caps down. . . . The arms, principally the bayonets, should be in perfect order." Behind the attacking infantry and the infantry reserve, cavalry would prowl the country to see that no man in the Álamo escaped.

7

At four o'clock in the morning the moon had risen. A mild radiance softly outlined the irregular white walls of the fortress which betrayed not the slightest sign of life. Santa Anna's orders had been carried out exactly. Noiselessly, each column of assault had taken its places to encircle the Álamo. The signal bugle sounded and the Mexican band struck up the savage air of *Deguelo,* or *Cutthroat.* The troops gave a cheer for Santa Anna and advanced at a run.

Not until the charging assailants were within easy rifle range did a sound come from the walls of the Álamo. Then a flash, a roar and a pungent curtain of smoke. The Texans had let loose their guns loaded with grapeshot and scrap iron. They followed with a deadly fire of musketry. Gaps were torn in the attacker's ranks, but the impetus of the charge carried it on.

The Texans defending the north wall sent up an exultant shout. The column of attack in front of them had recoiled and was in full retreat. East, west and south Travis's men took heart and increased their fire. The east column faltered and fell back. The west fell back. The panic spread to the south column, which had reached the walls; it broke and fled. The moonlit plain was dotted with the vague shapes of the fallen. Among the slain was Colonel Francisco Duque, commander of the north column, wounded and then trampled to death trying to stem the rout of his men.

The first assault on the Álamo had failed.

The confused masses were reformed into battalions. Battalions were regrouped for attack, commanding officers riding up and down, heartening their men. The eastern sky was growing gray and the stars were fading when the four columns again sprang forward over the pallid plain and the corpses of the dead. Once more the dim advancing lines were staggered by a broadside from the walls. The north column recoiled, the west column retired, the east column was routed. Colonel José Vincente Minon's sturdy south column tottered, but came on and applied its scaling ladders to the walls. The retreating east column veered to the right and the west column to the left. These spontaneous movements had the effect of reenforcing the flanks of the north column which, though stopped, held its ground. Officers grasped the situation and drove this combined force against the north wall in the face of a furious fire. The wall was reached, but the assailants had no will left to try to scale it. They broke and fled. On the south side the fighting was hand to hand. The Mexicans climbed their ladders, but the Texans beat them back with clubbed rifles and bowie knives.

The second assault had failed.

The break of day looked upon preparations within and without the Álamo for a renewal of the struggle. Travis and his band were in hard case. Their guns were hot and ammunition nearly gone. There had been few casualties but the men were very weary. Had the Mexicans launched their first attack as quietly as they had moved into position for it, that onslaught might have told the tale, as the Texans were sound asleep. The three pickets stationed outside the walls to observe the enemy must have been bayonetted for they gave no warning. The alarm was given by a captain on the walls. Travis was on his feet instantly. Snatching up a rifle and his sword he called to Joe, his negro servant, and ran across the plaza to a cannon at the northwest corner of the wall. "Come on, boys, the Mexicans are here!" The cheer for Santa Anna and the notes of *Deguelo* helped to rouse the men. A clink of equipment, the pat-pat of running feet and the ghostly lines took shape in the moonlight.

After two repulses the Mexican officers had some difficulty getting their men in a mood for a third attack. But the ranks were reformed, the bugle sounded and the wave surged forward, officers beating the laggards with the flats of swords. Profiting by experience, the Mexicans varied their mode of assault. Having met with no success on the fronts assigned to them, the east and west columns swung over and joined the north column to storm that rampart. The consolidated force charged across the space swept by the Texans' cannon and reached the shadow of the wall where the cannon could not be trained to play upon them. "Nor could the defenders use their muskets with accuracy," wrote a Mexican general, "because the wall having no inner banquette, they had, in order to deliver their fire, to stand on top where they could not live for a second."

The wall was cleared and the scaling ladders flung up. Mexicans tumbled over "like sheep," according to Travis's Joe. The Commander of the Álamo fell with a ball through his head as he stood behind a useless cannon and made ready to fire his rifle. The Texans met the onrush with rifles, pistols, knives and their fists, but the Mexicans were too numerous. The defenders retreated across the plaza to the barracks that formed the east wall and to the church, also on the east side.

Meantime the southern column, which had always struck vigorous blows, breached the wall and came through. A desperate fight ensued. The Mexicans fell in heaps. The Texans took refuge in a barrack building forming the west wall of the plaza and fought from room to room until not a man of their number remained alive.

On the east side of the plaza the fight went on in the barracks there. The Mexicans ended it when they dragged inside a howitzer filled with grape, which they fired through the length of the building. Fifteen Texans were found dead in front of the gun and forty Mexicans behind it. This building was used as a hospital and according to one account, Jim Bowie perished there propped up on his cot and defending himself with two pistols.

The last point taken was the church. With his rifle "Betsy," Davy Crockett and the twelve from Tennessee held the inner gate to the little churchyard, firing until they no longer had time to load. Then clubbing their rifles and drawing hunting knives from their belts, they dispatched twenty-five more of the enemy before the last backwoodsman fell. Inside the church there was a brief struggle. The most plausible account says that Bowie died there, where he had been carried so that his sister-in-law might attend him. Both versions of Bowie's death declare that he fought from his bed to the last and that his body was pitched about on the bayonets of the soldiers.

It had been agreed that the last Texan soldier alive should blow up the powder magazine in the church. A Mexican shot down Major Robert Evans as he attempted to apply a match. This seemed to complete the conquest. Across the corpse-strewn floor in a far corner huddled a little knot of women and children and a few slaves. The soldiers began to fling them about roughly. Mrs. A. M. Dickinson, the wife of a lieutenant who had perished on the walls, held her fifteen-months-old baby girl at her breast. At the woman's side crouched young Asa Walker, a wounded gunner. Mrs. Dickinson pleaded for his life, but the Mexicans ran him through, tossing "his body on their bayonets as a farmer would handle a bundle of hay."

The slanting sunlight, driving through holes in the roof, made irregular islands on the bloodstained western wall. It was eight o'clock in the morning and the Álamo had fallen.

8

General Santa Anna gave Mrs. Dickinson a horse and sent her eastward to spread the story of the Álamo and to say that such would be the story of any and all who opposed the Mexican General. Sam Houston was the first person of consequence that Mrs. Dickinson encountered.

Houston had learned of the Álamo's plight at Washington-on-the-Brazos, whither he had returned from the Indian country to help form a new government for Texas. Independence had been declared and Houston restored to the command of the armies. With four followers he set out for the front an hour after Travis's message reached Washington. Mrs. Dickinson told him it was too late to save Travis. Houston then sent for Fannin, hoping to lead that force—the only one now remaining in Texas—against the Mexicans. Again Fannin moved reluctantly and the Mexicans cornered him. He surrendered and, with his entire command of four hundred and twenty men, was lined up and shot.

To the rallying cry of "Remember the Álamo!" Sam Houston raised eight hundred men out of the ground and ruled them with a discipline that Texans never before had known. With the new government and the entire rebel population of Texas in panic and in flight, Houston managed his makeshift "army." Outmarching and outmaneuvering the Mexicans, only six weeks after the Álamo, Houston defeated Santa Anna at San Jacinto in one of the extraordinary battles of modern times.

*WAR IS THE PROVINCE OF PHYSICAL
EXERTION AND SUFFERING*

IN ORDER not to be completely overcome by them, a certain strength of body and mind is required, which, either natural or acquired, produces indifference to them. With these qualifications, under the guidance of simply a sound understanding, a man is at once a proper instrument for War; and these are the qualifications so generally to be met with amongst wild and half civilized tribes. If we go further into the demands which War makes on its votaries, then we find the powers of the understanding predominating.

Torture

BY

T. E. LAWRENCE

PROPERLY to round off this spying of the hollow land of Hauran, it was necessary to visit Deraa, its chief town. We could cut it off on north and west and south, by destroying the three railways; but it would be more tidy to rush the junction first and work outwards. Talal, however, could not venture in with me since he was too well known in the place. So we parted from him with many thanks on both sides, and rode southward along the line until near Deraa. There we dismounted. The boy, Halim, took the ponies, and set off for Nisib, south of Deraa. My plan was to walk round the railway station and town with Faris, and reach Nisib after sunset. Faris was my best companion for the trip, because he was an insignificant peasant, old enough to be my father, and respectable.

The respectability seemed comparative as we tramped off in the watery sunlight, which was taking the place of the rain last night. The ground was muddy, we were barefoot, and our draggled clothes showed the stains of the foul weather to which we had been exposed. I was in Halim's wet things, with a torn Hurani jacket, and was yet limping from the broken foot acquired when we blew up Jemal's train. The slippery track made walking difficult, unless we spread out our toes widely and took hold of the ground with them; and doing this for mile after mile was exquisitely painful to me. Because pain hurt me so, I would not lay weight always on my pains in our revolt: yet hardly one day in Arabia passed without a physical ache to increase the corroding sense of my accessory deceitfulness towards the Arabs, and the legitimate fatigue of responsible command.

We mounted the curving bank of the Palestine railway, and from its vantage surveyed Deraa Station: but the ground was too open to admit of surprise attack. We decided to walk down the east front of the defences: so we plodded on, noting German stores, barbed wire here and there, rudiments of trenches. Turkish troops were passing incuriously between the tents and their latrines dug out on our side.

At the corner of the aerodrome by the south end of the station we struck over towards the town. There were old Albatross machines in the sheds, and men lounging about. One of these, a Syrian soldier, began to question us about our villages, and if there was much 'government' where we lived. He was probably an intending deserter, fishing for a refuge. We shook him off at last and turned away. Someone called out in Turkish. We walked on deafly; but a sergeant came after, and took me roughly by the arm, saying 'The Bey wants you.' There were too many witnesses for fight or flight, so I went readily. He took no notice of Faris.

I was marched through the tall fence into a compound set about with many huts and a few buildings. We passed to a mud room, outside which was an earth platform, whereon sat a fleshy Turkish officer, one leg tucked under him. He hardly glanced at me when the sergeant brought me up and made a long report in Turkish. He asked my name: I told him Ahmed ibn Bagr, a Circassian from Kuneitra. 'A deserter?' 'But we Circassians have no military service.' He turned, stared at me, and said very slowly 'You are a liar. Enroll him in your section, Hassan Chowish, and do what is necessary till the Bey sends for him.'

They led me into a guard-room, mostly taken up by large wooden cribs, on which lay or sat a dozen men in untidy uniforms. They took away my belt, and my knife, made me wash myself carefully, and fed me. I passed the long day there. They would not let me go on any terms, but tried to reassure me. A soldier's life was not all bad. To-morrow, perhaps, leave would be permitted, if I fulfilled the Bey's pleasure this evening. The Bey seemed to be Nahi, the Governor. If he was angry, they said, I would be drafted for infantry training to the depot in Baalbek. I tried to look as though, to my mind, there was nothing worse in the world than that.

Soon after dark three men came for me. It had seemed a chance to get away, but one held me all the time. I cursed my littleness. Our march crossed the railway, where were six tracks, besides the sidings of the engine-shop. We went through a side gate, down a street, past a square, to a detached, two-storied house. There was a sentry outside, and a glimpse of others lolling in the dark entry. They took me upstairs to the Bey's room; or to his bedroom, rather. He was another bulky man, a Circassian himself, perhaps, and sat on the bed in a night-gown, trembling and sweating as though with fever. When I was pushed in he kept his head down, and waved the guard out. In a breathless voice he told me to sit on the floor in front of him, and after that was dumb; while I gazed at the top of his great head, on which the bristling hair stood up, no longer than the dark stubble on his cheeks and chin. At last he looked me over, and told me to stand up: then to turn round. I obeyed; he flung himself back on the bed, and dragged me down with him in his arms. When I saw what he wanted I twisted round and up again, glad to find myself equal to him, at any rate in wrestling.

He began to fawn on me, saying how white and fresh I was, how fine my hands and feet, and how he would let me off drills and duties, make me his orderly, even pay me wages, if I would love him.

I was obdurate, so he changed his tone, and sharply ordered me to take off my drawers. When I hesitated, he snatched at me; and I pushed him back. He clapped his hands for the sentry, who hurried in and pinioned me. The Bey cursed me with horrible threats: and made the man holding me tear my clothes away, bit by bit. His eyes rounded at the half-healed places where the bullets had flicked through my skin a little while ago. Finally he lumbered to his feet, with a glitter in his look, and began to paw me over. I bore it for a little, till he got too beastly; and then jerked my knee into him.

He staggered to his bed, squeezing himself together and groaning with pain, while the soldier shouted for the corporal and the other three men to grip me hand and foot. As soon as I was helpless the Governor regained courage, and spat at me, swearing he would make me ask pardon. He took off his slipper, and hit me repeatedly with it in the face, while the corporal braced my head back by the hair to receive the blows. He leaned forward, fixed his teeth in my neck and bit till the blood came. Then he kissed me. Afterwards he drew one of the men's bayonets. I thought he was going to kill me, and was sorry: but he only pulled up a fold of the flesh over my ribs, worked the point through, after considerable trouble, and gave the blade a half-turn. This hurt, and I winced, while the blood wavered down my side, and dripped to the front of my thigh. He looked pleased and dabbled it over my stomach with his finger-tips.

In my despair I spoke. His face changed and he stood still, then controlled his voice with an effort, to say significantly, 'You must understand that I know: and it will be easier if you do as I wish.' I was dumbfounded, and we stared silently at one another, while the men who felt an inner meaning beyond their experience, shifted uncomfortably. But it was evidently a chance shot, by which he himself did not, or would not, mean what I feared. I could not again trust my twitching mouth, which faltered always in emergencies, so at last threw up my chin, which was the sign for 'No' in the East; then he sat down, and half-whispered to the corporal to take me out and teach me everything.

They kicked me to the head of the stairs, and stretched me over a guard-bench, pommelling me. Two knelt on my ankles, bearing down on the back of my knees, while two more twisted my wrists till they cracked, and then crushed them and my neck against the wood. The corporal had run downstairs; and now came back with a whip of the Circassian sort, a thong of supple black hide, rounded, and tapering from the thickness of a thumb at the grip (which was wrapped in silver) down to a hard point finer than a pencil.

He saw me shivering, partly I think, with cold, and made it whistle over my ear, taunting me that before his tenth cut I would howl for mercy, and at the twentieth beg for the caresses of the Bey; and then he began to lash me madly across and across with all his might, while I locked my teeth to endure this thing which lapped itself like flaming wire about my body.

To keep my mind in control I numbered the blows, but after twenty lost count, and could feel only the shapeless weight of pain, not tearing claws, for which I had prepared, but a gradual cracking apart of my whole being by some too-great force whose waves rolled up my spine till they were pent within my brain, to clash terribly together. Somewhere in the place a cheap clock ticked loudly, and it distressed me that their beating was not in its time. I writhed and twisted, but was held so tightly that my struggles were useless. After the corporal ceased, the men took up, very deliberately, giving me so many, and then an interval, during which they would squabble for the next turn, ease themselves, and play unspeakably with me. This was repeated often, for what may have been no more than ten minutes. Always for the first of every new series, my head would be pulled round, to see how a hard white ridge, like a railway, darkening slowly into crimson, leaped over my skin at the instant of each stroke, with a bead of blood where two ridges crossed. As the punishment proceeded the whip fell more and more upon existing weals, biting blacker or more wet, till my flesh quivered with accumulated pain, and with terror of the next blow coming. They soon conquered my determination not to cry, but while my will ruled my lips I used only Arabic, and before the end a merciful sickness choked my utterance.

At last when I was completely broken they seemed satisfied. Somehow I found myself off the bench, lying on my back on the dirty floor, where I snuggled down, dazed, panting for breath, but vaguely comfortable. I had strung myself to learn all pain until I died, and no longer actor, but spectator, thought not to care how my body jerked and squealed. Yet I knew or imagined what passed about me.

I remember the corporal kicking with his nailed boot to get me up; and this was true, for next day my right side was dark and lacerated, and a damaged rib made each breath stab me sharply. I remembered smiling idly at him, for a delicious warmth, probably sexual, was swelling through me: and then that he flung up his arm and hacked with the full length of his whip into my groin. This doubled me half-over, screaming, or, rather, trying impotently to scream, only shuddering through my open mouth. One giggled with amusement. A voice cried, 'Shame, you've killed him.' Another slash followed. A roaring, and my eyes went black: while within me the core of life seemed to heave slowly up through the rending nerves, expelled from its body by this last indescribable pang.

By the bruises perhaps they beat me further: but I next knew that I was being dragged about by two men, each disputing over a leg as though to split me apart: while a third man rode me astride. It was momently better than more flogging. Then Nahi called. They splashed water in my face, wiped off some of the filth, and lifted me between them, retching and sobbing for mercy, to where he lay: but he now rejected me in haste, as a thing too torn and bloody for his bed, blaming their excess of zeal which had spoilt me: whereas no doubt they had laid into me much as usual, and the fault rested mainly upon my indoor skin, which gave way more than an Arab's.

So the crestfallen corporal, as the youngest and best-looking of the guard, had to stay behind, while the others carried me down the narrow stair into the street. The coolness of the night on my burning flesh, and the unmoved shining of the stars after the horror of the past hour, made me cry again.

The soldiers, now free to speak, warned me that men must suffer their officers' wishes or pay for it, as I had just done, with greater suffering.

They took me over an open space, deserted and dark, and behind the Government house to a lean-to wooden room, in which were many dusty quilts. An Armenian dresser appeared, to wash and bandage me in sleepy haste. Then all went away, the last soldier delaying by my side a moment to whisper in his Druse accent that the door into the next room was not locked.

I lay there in a sick stupor, with my head aching very much, and growing slowly numb with cold, till the dawn light came shining through the cracks of the shed, and a locomotive whistled in the station. These and a draining thirst brought me to life, and I found I was in no pain. Pain of the slightest had been my obsession and secret terror, from a boy. Had I now been drugged with it, to bewilderment? Yet the first movement was anguish: in which I struggled nakedly to my feet, and rocked moaning in wonder that it was not a dream, and myself back five years ago, a timid recruit at Khalfati, where something, less straining, of the sort had happened.

The next room was a dispensary. On its door hung a suit of shoddy clothes. I put them on slowly and unhandily, because of my swollen wrists: and from the drugs chose corrosive sublimate, as safeguard against recapture. The window looked on a long blank wall. Stiffly I climbed out, and went shaking down the road towards the village, past the few people already astir. They took no notice; indeed there was nothing peculiar in my dark broadcloth, red fez and slippers: but it was only by the full urge of my tongue silently to myself that I refrained from being foolish out of sheer fright. Deraa felt inhuman with vice and cruelty, and it shocked me like cold water when a soldier laughed behind me in the street.

By the bridge were the wells, with men and women about them. A side trough was free. From its end I scooped up a little water in my hands, and rubbed it over my face; then drank, which was precious to me; and afterwards wandered along the bottom of the valley, towards the south, unobtrusively retreating out of sight. This valley provided the hidden road by which our projected raid could attain Deraa town secretly, and surprise the Turks. So, in escaping I solved, too late, the problem which had brought me to Deraa.

Further on, a Serdi, on his camel, overtook me hobbling up the road towards Nisib. I explained that I had business there, and was already footsore. He had pity and mounted me behind him on his bony animal, to which I clung the rest of the way, learning the feelings of my adopted name-saint on his gridiron. The tribe's tents were just in front of the village, where I found Faris and Halim anxious about me, and curious to learn how I had fared. Halim had been up to Deraa in the night, and knew by the lack of rumour that the truth had not been discovered. I told them a merry tale of bribery and trickery, which they promised to keep to themselves, laughing aloud at the simplicity of the Turks.

During the night I managed to see the great stone bridge by Nisib. Not that my maimed will now cared a hoot about the Arab Revolt (or about anything but mending itself): yet, since the war had been a hobby of mine, for custom's sake I would force myself to push it through. Afterwards we took horse, and rode gently and carefully towards Azrak, without incident, except that a raiding party of Wuld Ali let us and our horses go unplundered when they heard who we were. This was an unexpected generosity, the Wuld Ali being not yet of our fellowship. Their consideration (rendered at once, as if we had deserved men's homage) momently stayed me to carry the burden, whose certainty the passing days confirmed: how in Deraa that night the citadel of my integrity had been irrevocably lost.

Tsushima

BY

FRANK THIESS

I

AT 5:05 o'clock in the morning, information regarding the position of the Russian fleet was relayed to Togo at Masanpo. Vice-Admiral Kamimura with his Second Division immediately stood out to sea through Douglas Inlet. Togo meanwhile wirelessed the Navy Department: "I have just been informed that the enemy squadron has been sighted. The fleet will forthwith proceed to sea to attack the enemy and destroy him. The weather is clear and bright, with a choppy sea."

At 6:30 o'clock in the morning the Japanese Admiral on the *Mikasa* led the four battleships and two heavy cruisers of his First Division toward the northern tip of Tsushima island. He expected to meet the enemy about 2:00 o'clock in the afternoon off the small island of Okinoshima and attack him there.

Because there was fog in the eastern channel of the Strait, the meeting took place a few miles farther west than Togo had reckoned, but otherwise exactly as both he and Rozhestvensky had expected. The two great adversaries were not only equally convinced of the inevitability of a clash, but had calculated with almost mathematical accuracy the place of the meeting and the strength of the opposing forces. Neither of them was taken by surprise. However Togo found that he had been mistaken in the Russian formation, and this mistake might have turned out disastrously for the Japanese if the superior speed of their fleet, and a tactical error by a Russian battleship, had not enabled Togo to correct the mistake.

While the Japanese main body was on the way from Masanpo, the light Japanese cruiser *Izumi* searched for the Russian squadron in the vicinity of the Goto islands. Since the *Shinano Maru* had disappeared in the fog, the exact position of Rozhestvensky's fleet was no longer known. The *Izumi's* captain was therefore delighted to see the enemy suddenly emerging from the fog northwest of the small island of Ukushima. He stubbornly clung to the Russian flank, steaming on a parallel course, and wirelessing Togo a complete description of Rozhestvensky's fleet.

At 8:00 o'clock, the *Izumi* was still following the fleet, trying to summon by wireless the Japanese Fifth, Third and Sixth Divisions for an attack on Rozhestvensky, who had hoisted the signal: "Clear for action." After making his report, the captain of the *Izumi* was ordered to join the other

From: *Voyage of Forgotten Men*: Copyright, 1937. Used by special permission of The Bobbs-Merrill Co.

ships of the Sixth Division, but took it upon himself to disregard this order, since his was the only ship able to report on the further Russian movements. For a time he lost sight of the squadron in the fog, but tracked it down again shortly afterwards. His stubbornness was rewarded, for a few hours afterward he was able to save a Japanese troop transport on the way to Korea from steaming right into the range of Rozhestvensky's guns.

When Togo crossed the eastern channel of the Strait about noon, there was no sign of the Russians. Vice-Admiral Kataoka, commanding the Fifth Division, reported to him that he had sighted the enemy on a new course: N. E. by E.

Let us see now what happened in the meantime on the Russian side. The grey silhouette of the *Izumi* was following the squadron at a safe distance. The men were angry that the Admiral did not permit them to fire at the cruiser, but, while this might have relieved the nervous tension, it would have done no damage to the *Izumi* since she kept out of range. But later the Japanese captain became reckless. He was anxious to obtain further data, and since the visibility was only four to five miles he approached within seven thousand yards of the Russian ships, risking a shell from their heavy guns.

One can understand the impotent rage of the Russian gunners. They could not comprehend why their Admiral should tolerate this annoying patrol boat and allow her to send wireless messages without ordering his cruisers to drive her away. Men who have been on the way for seven months to fight a battle have a right to become impatient when they finally have the prey before them and are not allowed to shoot. It was fortunate that their Admiral had better nerves and was able to control his impatience.

But the provocation grew even worse. After the *Izumi* had found out all there was to know and had passed these facts on to Togo, she turned and disappeared. In her place five Japanese warships appeared, far ahead to port. Led by the protected cruiser *Akitsushima*, they were the *Matsushima*, *Itsukushima*, *Hashidate* and the old battleship *Chen-Yuen*, captured from the Chinese. They accompanied the Russian fleet for a while at a distance, and then disappeared again in the mist like disembodied spirits. An hour and a half later, four other cruisers hove in sight. Steaming on a parallel course at a distance of fifty cable lengths (ten thousand yards) their shadows emerged from the haze, remained visible for a little while, were swallowed up by the fog, re-emerged, and finally disappeared altogether. There could be no longer any doubt that the Japanese were assembling their entire fleet.

At 10:20 o'clock, Admiral Rozhestvensky suddenly ordered his squadron to change to a single-column "line-ahead" formation. The change of formation took about two hours. *Togo remained ignorant of this important move.*

Dewa's Third Division, hovering in the distance while this evolution took place, did not report it to the fleet commander. Either they were too far away to notice it, or they relied on the *Izumi's* report and, expecting Rozhestvensky to retain the originally reported formation, made no attempt to check up on any change. Critics later blamed Rozhestvensky for not driving Dewa's cruisers away. But what would have been the sense of it, since any moment the Japanese main body might emerge from the fog?

But the Russian gunners could not stand the tension any longer. On the *Orel* an excited gunner was unable to contain himself and fired a shot. The first shell in the battle of Tsushima! Owing to the use of smokeless powder, the rest of the squadron could not see from what ship the shot had been fired. They thought it had come from the Admiral's flagship, and that ended their self-control.

The whole fleet, with the exception of the *Suvoroff*, unleashed a "very-well-aimed fire" (Official Japanese History) against Dewa's cruisers, which made off as fast as they could. Almost at once a signal went up on the *Suvoroff*: "Don't waste your ammunition!"

The ships ceased fire. It was exactly noon. The single-column "line-ahead " formation was completed and the crews were allowed to lunch in watches. The squadron was now in latitude 34°, between the islands of Tsushima and Ikishima. The narrowest part of the Strait had been safely negotiated. There was no sign of the enemy.

The officers went below for lunch. In the mess rooms champagne glasses were emptied as the senior officer proposed a toast: "To Their Imperial Majesties!" Their coronation anniversary had been forgotten in the excitement. (On the other side, the Japanese officers toasted their Empress whose birthday it was.) Admiral Rozhestvensky never left the bridge. The crews heard the officers' "Hurrahs," looked up casually and went on with their work. The celebration was brief and perfunctory. It was over in a few minutes.

Throughout the squadron, excitement was mounting. The men were impatient, knowing that the next time Japanese warships were sighted they would be Togo's heavy battleships. In a few hours the curtain would rise on the drama which they had steamed half-way round the world to enact.

The bearded chaplains went through the ships, the Russian double cross in their hands, murmuring prayers and sprinkling holy water. It may have seemed a futile gesture against twelve-inch shells, but to the priests it was a sacred duty. Then the "action" signal was sounded. The Second Pacific Squadron was ready for Togo.

But instead of Togo, Dewa's Third Division—the one on which the Russians had fired before—appeared again. But this time the four cruisers were not alone—they had brought the Fourth Destroyer Flotilla along. Approaching full speed at a course crossing that of the Russian squadron, they stood out of the mist far ahead to port.

The situation was similar to the one on August 19, 1904, when the appearance of Japanese torpedo boats laying drift mines had prompted Vityeft to turn off. Rozhestvensky had little reason to believe that the torpedo boats would refrain this time from trying the same maneuver, and decided to drive them off by a frontal attack. He ordered his First Division (*Suvoroff, Alexander, Borodino* and *Orel*) to turn "in succession" eight

points to starboard. After this maneuver was executed, the Admiral ordered
his division to turn "together" eight points to port. This move would have
brought the division back on its original course, but in a line-abreast
formation. The *Alexander III* misunderstood the Admiral's second order
and remainded in the wake of the flagship, while the other two ships
correctly turned into the line-abreast formation. When they saw the
Alexander still steaming in line-ahead formation they thought that they
had misunderstood the signal and turned back to follow in the *Alexander's*
wake. Unsuccessful as this maneuver was, it had the effect of driving back
Dewa's cruisers and torpedo boats, although that does not excuse the
failure of the No. 2 ship to follow the Admiral's order. The whole fleet had
to pay for it. It must have brought home once more to Rozhestvensky how
hopeless any attempt would be to execute complicated battle maneuvers
with this fleet. It remains a moot question whether the maneuver, if correctly executed, would have improved the Russian position and would
have been a better opening move for the imminent battle.

The fleet formation was now entirely changed, and we must retain a
clear picture of the disposition of the Russian ships in order to understand
the subsequent events. The *Zemchug* with her escort of two torpedo boats,
the *Biedovy* and *Buistry,* told off to protect the starboard flank of the First
Division, obediently turned when Rozhestvensky gave the signal, and thus
remained on the starboard beam. Meanwhile the rest of the fleet had
continued on the old course, while the unsuccessful maneuver of the First
Division had arranged the four battleships in a separate line-ahead formation, to starboard of the column representing the Second and Third Divisions. In other words, the squadron was again steaming in two columns
which the Admiral had wanted to avoid. The disposition of the ships was
almost the same as that of the morning (and as reported by the *Izumi*),
except that Rozhestvensky's starboard column was now slightly ahead of
the port column, made up of the Fölkersam and Nebogatoff divisions. The
Admiral realized the danger of this formation, in view of the impending
approach of the enemy's main body, and immediately ordered his division
to proceed full speed ahead, on a course N. 20 deg. E., so as to get ahead of
the other divisions and restore the single-column formation. Since he did not
wish the other ships to slacken speed, and since the two columns were
approximately 2000 yards apart, this maneuver would take approximately
a half hour. The clock showed 1:40 P.M. (Japanese time). Shortly after
2:00 o'clock the squadron could be back in the single-column line-ahead
formation.

The sea was rough, with a southwesterly wind. The visibility was somewhat better, although the horizon was still shrouded in haze.

Worried over the peril of his situation, Rozhestvensky suddenly decided
to hasten the maneuver, even at the risk of slowing up the progress of the
squadron. The *Suvoroff* therefore signaled: "Second and Third Divisions
take stations astern of the First, while retaining formation." It was too
late. Shadows emerged from the mist to northeast—toy ships, their greenish-

grey paint making them hardly distinguishable from the ocean. One by one, the heavy ships of Togo's main body appeared out of the haze.

Rozhestvensky stood with his staff on the fore upper bridge. No one spoke a word. After a little while the Admiral put down his binoculars, silently turned and went to take his station in the conning tower.

As he walked past, Captain Semenoff, still staring through his binoculars, mumbled to himself: "There they are, all six of them!"

Shaking his head, Rozhestvensky called back without stopping: "No, there are more—they are *all* there."

II

Yes, they were all there: the First and Second Japanese Divisions, led by Togo on the *Mikasa*, with his battleships and Kamimura's six heavy armored cruisers.

The distance was still too great even for the biggest guns. Togo was steaming ahead on a westerly course at fifteen knots. The two fleets were slowly moving toward each other at intersecting courses. But Togo needed time to take the enemy's measure and study his formation. At first glance, it looked as if the *Izumi's* report had been correct and as if the Russian squadron was still steaming in two columns as reported in the morning. Togo was too far away to see that this was not the case. Between the two columns he could barely make out the contours of the third column. This would be the auxiliaries, and the port column must be the weak Third Division led by Nebogatoff which he had planned to attack an hour before, but had missed owing to the overestimate of the Russian speed.

Ordering his three light cruiser divisions to attack the enemy auxiliaries, he himself approached from the east on an opposite course, intending to cross the bows of the Russian ships and get a closer view of their formation.

In a few minutes he must have realized that Rozhestvensky had tricked him. The port column was not led by the *Nicolai I* but by the much stronger *Osliabia* with the Second Battleship Division. The worst news was still to come. Directly facing him, slightly to starboard but well ahead of the *Osliabia,* the four strongest battleships of the Russian squadron were steaming under forced draught to form a single-column line-ahead formation. The maneuver was almost completed. Togo also found that what he had supposed to be the third column was really a separate division, well protected by the Russian cruisers. They had turned away from the fleet and were now steaming toward the east to leave the battle to the heavy ships. These facts changed the situation entirely, making it much less favorable than Togo had expected. In a few minutes he would get within firing range of the leading Russian battleships. After crossing their bows, he immediately turned hard to north, away from the enemy, and then started into the famous $\propto$ -loop. This was a risky maneuver, fraught with terrible danger for the Japanese fleet *if* Rozhestvensky succeeded in restoring the single-column formation while Togo's ships were still bunched together in the loop turn.

Togo decided to risk it.

On the masthead of the *Mikasa* the signal went up: *"The rise or fall of the Empire depends upon this battle; let every man do his utmost."*

For at least fifteen minutes all of Togo's ships were forced to pass approximately the same point. They would be bunched together and unable to use their guns until they had pulled out of the loop turn. If the Russians came close enough to the enemy while this maneuver was still in progress, they could bring their heavy guns to bear upon the defenseless ships and probably annihilate the whole fleet.

An incredible excitement gripped the Japanese crews as they started into the turn. Togo was playing the most dangerous game of his life. He must keep his nerve until the maneuver was completed. A figure of stone, he stood on the bridge of the *Mikasa,* his eyes constantly at the binoculars. Since the Russians might open fire at any moment, his Chief-of-Staff asked Togo to move to the safety of the armored conning tower.

The Admiral shook his head. "I am almost sixty. But you are young. Go ahead to the conning tower!" He had become again the *samurai* with two swords in his belt. The old lust of battle had awakened in him, he was playing the most exciting game of all, with life or death as the stake. If he showed fear now, how could he expect courage from his men? He continued to stare at the approaching enemy. The clock showed 2:05 o'clock.

2:05 o'clock. Rozhestvensky was standing on the conning tower of the *Suvoroff,* inside the round steel turret with its shiny tubes, electric keys and control knobs, telephone and signal apparatus, bells and porcelain switchboards. The muffled beating of the engines penetrated faintly into the silence of the conning tower. No one said a word and the officers could hear each other breathe.

The single-column formation is not yet completed. The *Borodino* (No. 3 of the First Division) is abeam the Second Division flagship *Osliabia,* while the *Orel,* the last ship of the First Division, is abeam the *Sissoi Veliki* (No. 2 of the Second Division). Eighteen minutes more to finish the maneuver, then seventeen, then sixteen. . . . In the breathless silence, the clock's ticking can be heard louder than the beating of the engines.

Now the *Mikasa* turned from south to east, pulling out of the loop. The officers at the range-finders signaled the distance: seven thousand yards. Then six thousand eight hundred yards. The men in the conning tower looked at their Admiral but he made no move. The *Mikasa* had now swung on to her new course, with the *Shikishima* following. The Russian gunners were trembling with excitement.

It was 2:08 o'clock. Distance six thousand seven hundred yards. At last Rozhestvensky spoke. "Open fire."

A few seconds later the storm broke loose.

Fountains of water splashed about the *Mikasa,* the shells creeping closer and closer as the Russians found their range. When the first twelve-inch shell exploded near the flagship, Togo hardly moved his head. Faster and faster the huge missiles came hurling through the air, striking with a deafening roar. Tons of water crashed on the *Mikasa's* deck. Flashes of lightning shot out of the bellies of the Russian ships, the detonation rumbling over the sea like an endless, invisible freight train rolling over a bridge. For ten years Togo had been waiting for this. He could wait another two minutes, until it was safe to return the fire. He noticed that the *Orel* was as yet unable to join in the fire, for she was blocked by the *Osliabia*. If his gunners aimed at the *Osliabia,* the "overs" would hit the *Orel*. He ordered the guns aimed at the *Suvoroff* and *Osliabia* only.

The *Mikasa, Shikishima* and *Fuji* had pulled out of the turn and were steaming on the new battle course E. N. E. The clock showed 2:10. And now the *Asahi* straightened out.

Togo had done it. The damages suffered by his ships were slight and the guns still intact. Now he could return the fire.

At a distance of sixty-five hundred yards the *Mikasa* opened fire. The Russians had not yet straightened out their line and the *Orel* was still prevented from joining in the bombardment, while the first Japanese "overs" already splashed about the *Osliabia*. Recognizing the danger, Rozhestvensky ordered his Second Division to turn slightly to starboard. At last, at 2:12 o'clock the *Orel* had a clear track and could bring the guns of her port foreturrets into action. At the same moment Rozhestvensky left the course N. 23° E. toward Vladivostok and veered off to the east, toward Togo.

The duel of the twenty-four heavy ships now began in earnest, but the two turns had temporarily interfered with the Russian aim, while the *Osliabia* was exposed to a concentrated bombardment from six Japanese ships. Many of the huge shells found their mark, and with every explosion they tore parts of the superstructure away. A funnel came crashing down and fires sprang up in different parts of the ship.

A direct hit smashed into one of the turrets; when the smoke cleared away a bloody mass of broken limbs and twisted steel lay where an instant before the gun crew had labored.

2:24 o'clock. The battle raged on, fought with the mathematical precision and inhuman efficiency of destruction which marks the combat of such floating engines of war. The truly terrifying character of a naval engagement lies in the fact that it is a clash of machine against machine. An airman flying high above the battle area would see only a seemingly calm procession of little ships, following one behind the other in accurately spaced distance, and emitting white puffs of smoke and darker clouds from belching funnels. Surrounded by fountains of water, he would see them proceeding with foaming prows toward an imaginary goal. But he would not be able to see what is going on deep down in the bellies of the ships.

There the stokers are shoveling mountains of coal into the glowing furnaces, working as fast as they can—and yet they might be working thus on any peaceful day in May. Only the rumbling echo of the impact of shells against the steel hulls shows the sweating stokers that up on deck unimaginable things must be happening. Fortunately they do not know what is going on above them. They cannot see the number of wounded carried to crowded sick-bays and improvised dressing stations. They do not know that part of the superstructure is burning fiercely, that enemy hits have torn gaping holes in the hulls, that engineers are working frantically to flood the wing passages and right the ship, that shells filled with poison gas are claiming their toll among the crew. Their eyes blinded with coal dust, they shovel on.

Suddenly the stokers of the *Osliabia* were shaken out of their seeming calm. The whole ship appeared to be keeling over. Like children on a slide, the men were propelled toward the gaping, fiery mouths of their furnaces. Staring at each other in horror, they could hear steam escaping from the boilers, and a terrifying, gurgling noise like the death-throes of a gigantic animal went through the ship. Then the air became difficult to breathe, and from the air-ducts at the ceiling foul, poisonous vapors descended into their case. The lights went out and only the glowing coal in the furnaces cast an eerie, red light over the scene. Their screams died in their parched, choking throats.

Perhaps they were fortunate in that they could not see what was happening on deck. The *Osliabia* was no longer a ship; she was a floating pyre, with wreckage flying about, finishing the work of destruction the shells had wrought. But the bombardment kept on, and hardly had a missile exploded when a second, and a third, and a fourth found their mark. Their whine coming closer and closer, they whizzed through the flames and smashed into the mass of debris, tearing into still smaller fragments the wreckage left from previous hits. Winches were broken like matchsticks, turrets bent and twisted, guns lifted out of their emplacements, the steel plates of the deck and hull pierced and opened to the onrushing water. But in this inferno blood-spattered gunners still manned the remaining turrets and aimed over the roaring waves at the distant grey steel colossi from which this merciless hail of shell emerged.

On the other side, too, sweating gunners stood at their posts in the suffocating steel turrets, aiming and firing the enormous shells at the *Osliabia*. With the calmness of superhuman beings, the officers at the range-finders watched the impact of the shells, reported the result and gave curt orders, all without a smile, without pride in their success, expressionless and impersonal. But the figures they called out spelled the death of a battleship.

The battle had lasted half an hour, and the *Osliabia* was reduced to a wreck—but a wreck which could still fight. A mortally wounded animal, its guts hanging out of its belly, but still clawing and biting. For a brief moment the men on the Japanese ship may have wondered how there could still be any life left in this inferno of steel splinters, blood and fire—how men could be found to aim, load and shoot under such conditions.

The first shell to hit the ship had exploded at the water line and had smashed through the cheap armor plate as if it were tin. A second shell struck just below the ten-inch gun turret and tore a hole as big as a cave. Men tried to patch it, but they were washed away by the sea which rushed in through the gaping hole like a cataract, flowing into the hold, flooding the steerage deck, putting the electric power station out of commission and destroying the controls and ammunition hoists. Another hit stove in the side of the ship abaft the ammunition magazine. The ship listed heavily to port. The engineers flooded the starboard passages and the *Osliabia* righted herself, but settled a few feet deeper, striking the water with a resounding thud. The sea poured in through the shell holes, and she shipped water through the lower gun ports as if it were drawn in with a pump. The men tried to close up the ports, but the straps and chains were smashed. Under the concentrated fire from Kamimura's cruisers, the gun turrets crumbled to pieces. The armor plate of only twelve and one-half inch thickness bent like corrugated cardboard and finally crashed down on the crew inside. As more shells struck the deck, creatures that once had names were hurled through the air like flying torches.

Nevertheless, the *Osliabia's* commander, Captain Baer, steered this helpless wreck of a battleship in the wake of the *Orel*. His stoical calm remained unbroken. But finally the coal bunkers were flooded, great seas washed over the decks and the prow of the ship pitched forward until the foredeck was almost in the water—the *Osliabia* was finished and had to fall out of line.

She was not the first ship, however, forced to leave her station. The first was the Japanese armored cruiser *Asama*. At 2:27 o'clock, twenty-three minutes before the *Osliabia*, her steering gear was smashed by a Russian shell, and she had to seek protection out of firing range. By that time the *Mikasa* had sustained ten direct hits from twelve-inch shells, although, owing to the heavier armor of the Japanese ships, the damages were mostly confined to the superstructure and the losses in men remained comparatively small. Three minutes after the *Asama* had dropped out, a Russian hit exploded on the superstructure behind the *Mikasa's* bridge. Steel splinters hurtled through the air, destroying the compass next to the spot where Togo was standing. The force of the explosion knocked down some of his staff officers. They got up, wiping the blood from their faces, and stared at the Admiral. He had not suffered a single scratch. As he glanced back at them, the ghost of a smile lay briefly on his lips. Half an hour later, the upper portion of the foremast tumbled down and the flagstaff with the Admiral's flag toppled into the water. Another flag was hoisted on the yardarm and the battle went on. The Russians, too, had found their range. In a few minutes the first gun on the *Mikasa* was put out of commission, the shot tearing away parts of the emplacement and killing the whole crew. Another shell hit the after bridge, lifted it up like a piece of cork and smashed it into tiny bits, scattering them in the water. There was a great, gaping hole in the foreturret marking the spot of another explosion. As the stretcher-bearers carried away the wounded and dead, something howled over them and blew them off their feet. Sailors ran to their assistance when a shell struck in their midst, killing everyone in the vicinity and penetrating into the depths of the ship, where it exploded with terrific force. Holes were torn in funnels, great gun barrels were lifted up and toppled overboard into the seething water.

The grimy, bloody men coughed and choked in the smoky air. Their uniforms torn to shreds, their hands raw and bleeding, their bodies singed and bruised, they went on loading and discharging the guns that remained intact. With sharp, almond-shaped eyes, narrowed to tiny slits, they stared at the flaming Russian ships. The work of destruction was progressing satisfactorily.

III

The battle approached its climax. The officers on the Russian flagship watched anxiously as Togo's column slowly drew ahead of the Russian line. The port turrets of the *Suvoroff* released salvo after salvo, but no result was visible, although we now know how effective this fire had been. While the Japanese shells were timed so as to explode on immediate contact, the Russian ammunition was designed to explode within the enemy ship, after having pierced the armor plate of the deck or hull. This circumstance, combined with the fact that smokeless powder was used, made it impossible to observe the effect of the shells from a distance. Unless masts or funnels were hit, or a conspicuous part of the superstructure was demolished, the Russians were unable to tell in the haze and smoke of battle when one of their shots had found its mark.

This difference in ammunition had a considerable psychological influence, aside from its practical importance. The Russian gunners became convinced that their marksmanship was terrible, and that in spite of their best efforts the Japanese ships were carrying on without damage. They remained unaware of the devastation caused on Togo's side, and did not know that some of the enemy ships were only with difficulty following the orders from the *Mikasa*. This misunderstanding undermined the self-confidence of the Russian crews when they were in need of every ounce of courage to bear up under the terrible Japanese bombardment.

Another vitally important factor which gave the Japanese an unquestionable superiority was the much greater speed of Togo's fleet. The two squadrons had started out on approximately parallel courses, but with his swift ships Togo was able, thirty minutes after the battle had begun, to deflect the Russian line and dictate the conditions under which the remainder of the engagement was fought.

Thus the greater speed of the Japanese ships, the destructive effect of their shells in starting fires and releasing fumes, and finally the demoralizing misunderstanding of the Russians regarding their own marksmanship all combined to instill in Rozhestvensky's men the conviction that they were doomed to defeat. Yet this knowledge only strengthened their resolution to sell their lives as dearly as possible. Again we stand in awe before the almost superhuman endurance of the Russians who, out of defeat and despair, were able to gather new strength for the unparalleled heroism displayed in this fight to a finish. As at Port Arthur and Liao-Yang, the Japanese were again impressed by the fortitude of their enemy, who did not reveal his greatest strength until he was defeated.

At Tsushima the Russians were defeated in an hour; but it required thirty-one hours to destroy them.

The tragedy of this battle began with the building of the ships. And it did *not* end after the first hour, although Togo's victory was decided by then. The subsequent events are as fantastic as the whole voyage which led up to them. In this respect, Tsushima has no parallel in history.

Instead of following the example of Vityeft, whose narrow mind had conceived of no alternative other than a straight course for Vladivostok, Rozhestvensky accepted the conditions forced upon him by the exigencies of battle. In order to remain on a course parallel with the Japanese fleet and bring the whole weight of his heavy ordnance to bear upon it, he swerved first to N. E., then east again. The success of this strategy was proved by the effect of his fire upon the *Asama,* although her falling out of line was noticed on only a few Russian ships, and was soon more than compensated by the desperate situation of the *Osliabia.* Fölkersam's battleship still remained in line, but was no longer in any condition to fight.

The Japanese firing speed was three times as fast as the Russian, and, although many of the shells went wild, was extremely effective. Togo therefore decided not only to maintain this firing speed but even increase it, until the Russians were showered with a fierce hail of steel and fire. The *Suvoroff* was still leading the squadron, and she must be destroyed to deprive the fleet of the Admiral's leadership. Togo could not be sure of his victory while Rozhestvensky lived; he knew the endurance and tenacity of this man who could not be conquered through strategy. Only shells could do that. Therefore every gun within firing of the *Suvoroff* discharged its thunder against this one ship, and the shells came as fast as the guns could be loaded by frantic crews.

The Japanese shells, their great explosive power and incendiary effect, had been fully described by foreign correspondents for many months. Semenoff had had experience with them at Shantung, and had tried to prepare the Russian sailors against the shock of this fierce bombardment. Their disadvantage, as demonstrated at Shantung, was that they exploded only when they hit nose-first, and that they were timed so as to explode immediately upon contact, and therefore did not penetrate through heavy armor.

But they seemed different at Tsushima. Semenoff observed a curious factor about these fiery crates as they came howling over the *Suvoroff*: they exploded no matter on what side they struck, and their effect seemed not the same as at Shantung. One of the first shells landed near a six-inch gun turret and tore through its steel armor as if it were paper. Another smashed into the Admiral's quarters, setting fire to the cabins. A third hit the bridge; the force of the explosion was so strong that Semenoff, who was standing on deck near the bridge, was blown off his feet. He struggled to get up, looked at his watch, noticed it was still going but had no crystal.

He found the crystal a few feet away and tried to fit it into the rim—but suddenly realized how ridiculous this was, and shoved the watch into his pocket. While he was hurrying to help put out the fires started by the explosion, a fourth and fifth shell struck the ship, sending up gigantic columns of fire, smoke and water. Through the haze, groups of men could be seen tumbling on deck or blown into the air, their arms and legs dangling ridiculously in the void, until they were smashed, broken and bleeding, against the steel deck. Lieutenant Reydkin looked out of his after starboard six-inch turrent and inquired smilingly: "Well, do you recognize it? Is this like the 10th of August?"

"Exactly the same," Semenoff lied bravely, realizing to his horror that in the nine months since the battle of Shantung the Japanese must have acquired a new type of shell which, in its destructive power, left far in the shade anything known before. "The steel plates and superstructure on the upper deck were torn to pieces, and the splinters caused many casualties. Iron ladders were crumpled up into rings, and guns were literally hurled from their mountings. Such havoc would never be caused by the simple impact of a shell, still less by that of its splinters. It could only be caused by the force of the explosion." (Semenoff.)

In the battle of Tsushima, the Japanese for the first time used shimose in combination with a new explosive invented by a South American colonel whose patent they had bought. These shells could be used only in large-caliber guns, and therefore none but the heavy armored ships were equipped with them, but they were sufficient to cause terrible destruction on any ship exposed to such bombardment. The Russian gunners had been carefully warned against the effect of the Japanese shells, but the warning was forgotten in the face of these enormous projectiles which could not be stopped by the heaviest armor plate. Driven by the wind, the fumes from the bursting shells spread over the whole deck, corroding the lungs and making the men gasp for breath. In the first hour of battle the moral effect of poison gas upon the Russians was considerable, since gas was an entirely new and terrifying weapon to them. They were inclined to sit by idly and wait for death which they felt they could not escape, and it was with great effort that their officers persuaded them that they might just as well meet it in action, instead of submitting to it without a fight.

Human nature becomes accustomed to everything. After the first effect of this hail of shells had worn off, those among the Russian sailors who were men—many who had not been, became men in these hours—began to fight back, pitting their courage against the avalanche of fire and death. They stood at their guns with singed hair and bleeding hands, returning the fire of the enemy, deriving a grim confidence from the fact that this hell could not get worse.

But even their courage could not revive the dead. And it could not undo the suffering of the wounded. Many were bleeding to death on the decks; others, their mangled bodies carried below on stretchers, groaned under the surgeons' knives or patiently awaited their turn on the operating table.

The survivors helped their injured comrades as well as they could, and hurried through the ships putting out fires, patching up the gaping holes with boards and coal sacks, and taking the places of those killed at their guns.

The Japanese meanwhile continued their work of destruction with methodical thoroughness.

Rozhestvensky still stood in the conning tower, with wounded and dead beside him, staring at the volcanoes as they hurled tons of deadly missiles against his ship. The *Suvoroff* had become the target of most of Togo's first-line ships and it did not seem that the flagship would be able to bear up much longer under such concentrated bombardment. The men on the other ships of the squadron realized this, and in the midst of the raging battle they stopped to see whether the Admiral's flag was still flying on the *Suvoroff*. They knew that their Admiral must live if they were to escape from this hell. In the gun turrets, in dressing stations and engine-rooms, everywhere, men asked each other: "What about the Admiral? Have they got him yet?" And when the answer came: "He is still in command, he is all right!" they breathed a great sigh of relief, and the wounded lay back and patiently closed their eyes. There was yet hope.

Yes, he was still in command. He stood in the conning tower, peering through the chink between the armor and the roof at the enemy who was now steaming along a flat curve, bending toward the Russian course. This move had reduced the distance between the two flagships to four thousand yards, and the Japanese were able to open up with their medium-caliber guns. The commander of the *Suvoroff*, Captain Ignatius, could not conceal his nervousness. The calmness with which Rozhestvensky held to his course did not seem justified in view of the hell raging throughout the ship. "Your Excellency, we must change the distance!" he reminded the Admiral. "They have found our range too well, and they are simply roasting us in their fire!" Rozhestvensky replied quietly: "Just wait a while. We have also found our range."

He knew that the Japanese with their fifty per cent greater speed, were bound to overtake him, enabling them to subject the Russian ships to a flanking fire. Rozhestvensky would be forced then to seek safety by turning to starboard. The longer he could put off this inevitable turn, away from the Vladivostok course, the better for the Russian squadron. As the slower of the two fleets, its only salvation lay in steaming along the arc of the inner of two huge concentric circles, with Togo relegated to the outer circle and thus unable fully to utilize his superior speed.

Thus the Japanese slowly forged ahead, while Rozhestvensky continued on the old course. By 2:40 o'clock, the *Mikasa* stood off the *Suvoroff's* port bow and Togo was able to unleash all his medium- and large-caliber guns against the Russian flagship.

The next quarter-hour must be regarded as the height of the battle. The artillery duel raged along the entire column with a ferocity defying description. Both sides knew that during these fifteen minutes the outcome would be decided, and that it would not be a decision between victory or defeat, but between survival or annihilation. The Russians exerted super-human strength to brave the Japanese fire and stay on the course chosen by their commander as the only countermove against Togo's superior fleet.

Japanese eyewitnesses reported the astounding tenacity of the enemy at this critical stage. The Russian ships were enveloped in sheets of fire, rocked by explosions, torn open by shells, and yet gunners who remained alive through this nightmare calmly aimed and returned the fire with telling effect. The Japanese knew that they had the upper hand; their swift ships, better ammunition and heavier armor protection guaranteed that. Victory to them was not a possibility but a certainty, the inevitable result of an almost mathematical equation. Therefore they could remain calm observers of this bloody spectacle. The Russians, on the other hand, were truly a "lost battalion," and yet they were spurred to rare feats of heroism by the wish to die decently at their posts.

The heavy cruiser *Asama* had repaired its steering gear, but had lost contact with the First and Second Divisions in the smoke of battle. It proceeded on the presumable course of Togo's main body, but suddenly found itself within range of the Russian battleship divisions. The *Asama's* superstructure was smashed and her bridge torn away and dumped into the water. A gaping hole in her side caused her to settle down five feet below the normal water line. The stern funnel pierced by a Russian shell, belched smoke and fire. The lower deck became flooded and the men waded in water knee-deep, the conning tower was crushed, the hull riddled with holes through which the sea washed in cascading torrents. But the *Asama's* commander still clung faithfully to his course and tried to steam after the rest of his squadron.

It was still a long way off and it was not what it had been when the *Asama* fell out of line. The Japanese First Battleship Division was fighting as it had never had to fight before. On the *Mikasa,* the *Shikishima* and *Fuji,* guns had been torn off their emplacements, masts smashed, sides stove in, deck girders twisted, heavy gun barrels broken like flimsy reeds. The *Asahi* and *Kasuga* were in somewhat better shape, while the *Nisshin* (No. 6 in the First Japanese Division) was only little better off than the Russian battleships of the first two divisions, and much worse than Nebogatoff's ships which had so far suffered very little. On the *Nisshin,* the bridge was shot to pieces, three twelve-inch guns destroyed, part of the mainmast demolished, the lifeboats drilled full of holes. But torrents of water washed the blood from her decks and the men attended to their work as calmly as before. The wounded were carried off on stretchers in the thick of battle, with the ship pitching and rolling, shaken by violent explosions; surgeons operated as if they were in a peaceful hospital on land. The calm confidence of the crew was that of men determined to live and win—not the quiet resignation of men resolved to die fighting. This confidence could not be broken; it was stronger even than the steel armor of the ship.

Courageous, disciplined and efficient, the Japanese clung to their method of finishing off the enemy ship by ship. They did not know that the *Suvoroff* was only a fighting wreck, that the *Osliabia* flew an admiral's flag while his body rested in a cement coffin under the Holy Image. They saw only that under a hail of fire the Russian column held to its easterly course, and concluded that the enemy was far from vanquished. Therefore they continued to load and aim and shoot with a rapidity and precision that filled the British observers on board the Japanese ships with admiration. They had trained a pupil who, in the short space of a few years, had become a master in the art of scientific slaughter. Not only the British observers, but the whole world paid tribute to this clever prodigy—only a few thoughtful men in Western countries began to wonder when the pupil would turn his newly acquired knowledge against his teachers.

At 2:50 o'clock the *Osliabia,* reduced to a blazing funeral pyre, was at last forced out of line and sought shelter to starboard of the Russian squadron where she was protected from the Japanese shells. By that time the entire Russian squadron had become enveloped in smoke and fumes to such an extent that Togo's ships were compelled to stop firing. The Russians were forced to do likewise, as the wind coming from the southwest blew the acrid smoke into their eyes. Rozhestvensky had achieved his objective, although at a terrible cost; he had held fast to his course and for over five miles he had steamed through hell. The Japanese, in trying to force Rozhestvensky off his course, had overshot their mark and freed the path to Vladivostok. Now he could turn behind the rear ship of Togo's first-line divisions and resume the old course N. 23 deg. E. But just at that moment the breeze freshened, dispersing the haze. The smoke cleared and visibility was restored: "higher powers" had once more frustrated Rozhestvensky's plans. Togo's ships again appeared off the *Suvoroff's* port bow and the Japanese were bearing down upon the Russian line to block its course. Guns flashed and the hail of fire was resumed.

This time it was worse than before, because the distance had become shortened to between thirty-six hundred and four thousand yards, enabling Togo to use all the ordnance of his armored divisions. The Russian flagship sustained one direct hit after another.

It was three o'clock. The Russians had lost the battle, but as yet Togo had not won it—a few minutes later the Russians made a surprise move which gave the battle a new and, for Togo, unexpectedly dangerous turn.

IV

But we must first follow the fate of the flagship.

The *Suvoroff*, once the proud leader of the squadron, had become reduced to a smoking pile of debris. Nevertheless, there was still life left in this ruin, and it took the Japanese another four hours to put the battleship out of commission.

The deck was strewn with corpses and wreckage; limp human bodies had become amalgamated with bits of wood and steel that once were a serviceable part of the great ship. These bloody, charred piles of unrecognizable composition, part organic, part inorganic, lay everywhere—a silent, weird testimony to the chaos within the ship. Through this wreckage living men fought their way, hurrying from one part of the ship to another. But were they really human, the creatures that had emerged from this holocaust? Grimy with dirt and blood, in tattered uniforms, many with makeshift dressings or with blood flowing unchecked from open wounds, they seemed part of this scene of destruction that a Breughel might have painted. They climbed over the debris, over mountains of fallen girders and twisted steel, slipped in pools of blood, stumbled over the bodies of their dead comrades—and finally came to a halt before insurmountable barriers formed by the smashed superstructure. Then they had to retrace their steps, trying to find another way to the parts of the ship where they were urgently needed.

This pitifully small band of survivors tried to be everywhere at once, chiefly to put out the innumerable fires. Like animals, they dashed right through the fire, covering their faces and bodies with wet coal sacks. There was no longer any distinction between officers and men—only between those who could, and those who could not work. Anyone not too painfully injured lent a hand to help extinguish fires. Even the gun crews worked as firemen; their guns had been put out of commission by Japanese shells. Then the supply of fire hose was running low. New hose brought up from the storerooms was quickly burned or torn by new shells. But soon the ocean would quench the fires consuming the *Suvoroff,* and no pails or hose would be needed. It would not be long before the ship at last could rest her burning body in the cool arms of the sea.

Not many men were left of the *Suvoroff's* complement of nine hundred, and these few knew their hour was fast approaching. But this knowledge no longer paralyzed them as it had done in the beginning, when they were first stunned by the Japanese hail of fire. They worked as if victory were still a possibility, and they were grateful when they found an officer alive who could show them what to do. There was a frantic movement and hustle on board the ship, and only now and then a hurrying man would stop suddenly and lift up the head of one of his dead comrades as if to wake him and ask him to lend a hand. "Oh, Reydkin!" he would exclaim, or, "Oh, it's you Bersenieff!" until a sudden detonation would make him turn in the direction of the noise. He would hurry on then, but with a slight grin on his face. The detonation meant that the *Suvoroff* was still alive and fighting back. The after twelve-inch turret was turning and firing incessantly.

Yes, they are still firing, they are still fighting, and they will continue to defend themselves to the last moment. They are keeping the promise which Captain Bukhvostoff made for all of them at the banquet tendered the officers by the gold-braided St. Petersburg crowd: "I can promise you one thing, however. All of us here, the officers of the Second Pacific Squadron, shall at least know how to die. We shall not surrender!"

It takes a long time to destroy a battleship, but the Japanese had time, and they did their job efficiently. In the conning tower of the *Suvoroff* corpses began to pile up. The range-finders and signaling devices were destroyed. At long range the guns must be aimed haphazardly. Communication lines were burned, masts splintered, controls put out of commission. The ventilators drew poison fumes instead of air into the dimly lighted caves below, where engineers under Politovsky's supervision bravely tried to stem the onrush of water. The men choked under the effect of the gas, and now and then they simply stopped and sat down in the middle of their work, praying to God for death to release them.

An officer trying to find the Admiral made his way like a mountain climber over the wreckage on deck, with shells and splinters falling all about him, stumbling and getting to his feet again until he finally reached the conning tower. As he was about to enter, the force of a terrible explosion blew him back and he saw a sight such as he had never seen before: the armored roof of the after turret was being lifted off like an old hat and whirled through the air, to crack back on to the deck with such force that the stern of the *Suvoroff* shot out of the water and even the engines stopped turning for a few seconds. On the after deck a gigantic pillar of fire, smoke and debris rose high into the air. But then the engines started pulsing again, and with a deep sigh the officer entered the conning tower.

He was met by a breathless, choking atmosphere, the acrid stench of poison fumes and the sour smell of blood. Dead men lay on the floor. The Admiral stood beside the Senior Gunnery Lieutenant Vladimirsky who, himself wounded and his face streaming with blood, had taken the place of the officer killed at the wheel. Captain Ignatius had been carried away to the sick-bay. Rozhestvensky was still staring at Togo's ships with the calm of a chemist working quietly in his laboratory. The hands which held his binoculars did not tremble; his orders came quietly and in an unruffled voice as at the time when the fleet was steaming through the cyclone. He radiated an infectious air of confidence. Even the dull thuds of exploding shells could not break through his calm.

An officer reported that most of the heavy guns had been put out of commission. Rozhestvensky merely nodded, and Vladimirsky answered in his stead: "That's why we are allowing the Japanese to shorten the distance. Now we shall be able to fight with our medium-caliber guns!" Didn't he know that many of the medium-caliber guns had also been smashed? That it was time to port the helm and get out of range of Togo's guns? But the words of this brave officer bespoke a magnificent faith. Once, long, long ago, another brave man spoke such ringing words when it was reported to him that the enemy's arrows were so numerous that they obscured the sun: "Good, then we shall fight in the shade!" That was a few thousand years ago, before there were twelve-inch guns spewing fire and destruction, but the clouds of Persian arrows were no less to be feared than the clouds sent forth from Togo's battleships. Such courage is beyond time.

The *Suvoroff* continued to steam through the hail of shells, but fire proved stronger than the courage of her crew. Again the ship reared herself out of the water as if pounded by a titanic fist; the noise of tearing steel and crunching armor plate penetrated even into the poisoned calm of the conning tower. A shower of steel splinters bombarded the tower and suddenly it became pitch-dark inside. An officer hurried out and reported breathlessly that the foremost funnel had fallen and that the boats on the spardeck were burning.

It had become impossible to maintain the present course. The Admiral turned a few points to starboard; the squadron, which had been gradually edging off in tiny jerks to the east, was now steaming on a course S.E. The two fleets proceeded again in a parallel direction.

Then a shell hit the underwater torpedo magazine of the *Suvoroff* and disabled the steering gear. The ship no longer answered the wheel. Flag-Lieutenant Kruizanovsky hurried out of the conning tower and down to the engine room. It had become necessary to steer with the engines; but before the officer reached there the battleship got out of control, wheeling about in a crazy circle, as the *Czarevich* had done on August 10th. At last the *Suvoroff* had been forced out of line; the flagship was no longer leading the squadron.

With a sickening feeling, the officers watched their squadron steam past them, all ships wrapped in smoke and flame, still firing defiantly at the enemy. The column was now led by the *Alexander* followed by the *Borodino, Orel* and *Sissoi Veliki.* Then came the *Navarin,* lying low in the water, but nevertheless proceeding at full speed. The line-ahead formation of the Russian squadron had become a somewhat disorderly column since the *Osliabia* had fallen out of line. As the remnants of the fleet steamed past the *Suvoroff,* her men forgot their own misery as they noticed that the Japanese fire, while furious, was by no means one hundred per cent accurate. Many of the shells landed far beyond the target, hitting the water one thousand and even fifteen hundred yards off the starboard beam—so far, in fact, that even the poor flagship was not safe from the "overs" although it stood far to starboard. That meant that even the crews behind the Japanese guns were only human—not demons dealing out destruction. It meant that there was still hope—hope of what? At any rate, the first thing was to get the ship under control again and steer with the engines. Rozhestvensky ordered the *Suvoroff* to fall in behind the squadron, even if only as the last ship in the column.

Suddenly the officers noticed that the *Alexander* was falling out of line. What could have happened? Had the new leader been disabled so soon? Whatever the explanation may have been, for a few minutes, which seemed like hours, the *Alexander,* the *Suvoroff* and the dying *Osliabia* all lay in one line of fire. The Japanese did not even have to aim carefully; they were bound to hit one of the three ships if they fired along this line.

The expected happened; a full hit crashed into the conning tower of the *Suvoroff,* the armored wall was split open, and a shower of white-hot iron splinters rained over the men inside. Rozhestvensky felt a sharp pain in his head; his skull had been split open and, as it turned out afterward, a part of the skull had embedded itself in his brain. But it was only a pain, no one on this ship was paying much attention to pain. And the Admiral could still see and hear, and give orders. A few minutes later some object dealt him a painful blow against the leg, and ricochetting splinters buried themselves in his back. He stumbled, men rushed to support him, and he murmured: "It is nothing, don't bother. . . ." But one really could not work there any more, perhaps it would be better to leave the tower. Vladimirsky was also bleeding profusely, but he only smiled and twirled his moustache. At that moment a man came rushing straight through the flames: Lieutenant Bogdanoff, Senior Torpedo Officer, who had watched the shell hit the conning tower and had plunged right through the fire to save his Admiral. Rozhestvensky smiled at him and motioned that everything was all right. Bogdanoff was ordered to stay in the tower and follow the course of the squadron, steering with the engines. Fortunately the engine telegraph was still working. Then there was another fearful crash and the second funnel came tumbling down on the deck. The officers glanced up casually. Only a funnel! If only the Japanese stopped firing for a moment, one could almost imagine one was on a pleasure yacht, Bogdanoff joked as he took his station at the speaking tube.

But the Japanese did not stop.

The smoke enveloped the ship like a dark cloud and it became impossible to hold a course, since all instruments, including the compass, had gone. The ship could no longer be controlled from the upper deck; it became necessary to try to reach the lower fighting position. Bogdanoff bravely attempted to clear a path for Rozhestvensky, pushing aside the burning hammocks piled up on deck as a protection against splinters, and bending back the twisted steel in his way. Singed by the flames, he had to give up the attempt; there was no longer a path over the deck. With difficulty the hatch over the armored shaft leading below was opened—after dragging away dead bodies that blocked it—and the Admiral was helped down. There he stood, cut and bleeding, but just as calm as if nothing had happened. He left the Flag Navigating Officer in the lower fighting position with orders to steer after the squadron, and himself went back on deck to find a place from which he could watch the battle and direct the movements of the ships.

Leaving a trail of blood behind him, the wounded man climbed again to the upper deck, trying to make his way through the debris and over mountains of corpses. But he could not get farther than the Holy Image on the battery deck. For an instant his eyes were arrested by a strange sight: on this ship on which everything was smashed to atoms, the icons still hung undamaged on the wall and not even the glass of the large shrine was broken. The eternal light was burning as peacefully as at any church in Russia. So there was at least one place on this ship which the shells had not yet touched! Just as there is one place deep in a human heart which no horror can touch.

But this was not the time to ponder such matters. Rozhestvensky dragged himself on to the center six-inch turret on the port side. Here, too, a mass of twisted steel and piled-up wreckage made progress impossible. He turned back to try the starboard six-inch turret. On the way a shell exploded, hurling a mass of flaming splinters through the air. One struck Rozhestvensky on the left angle and cut through the main nerve. Dragging his paralyzed foot after him, he essayed a few steps and broke down. The officers lifted him up and carried him into the turret. There he sat on a shell case, his eyes closed until he could collect himself. Then he rapped out: "Why isn't this turret firing?"

Flag-Lieutenant Kruizhanovsky appeared just at that moment and the Admiral called to him: "Find the gun captains, fall in the crews and open fire!" Kruizhanovsky rushed off.

Rozhestvensky was again commanding his ship. With broken skull, bleeding from his shoulder and his back, and with his leg nerve severed, he gave order after order. But the connections to the lower fighting position had been damaged; speaking tubes, electric indicators, telephones put out of commission. Somewhere deep down in the poisoned atmosphere of the ship, a man was steering the *Suvoroff* through the ocean, although it was impossible to get up any speed in this manner. And the sea rushed in through gaping holes, washed over the decks, extinguished the electric lights and in general played havoc with the defenseless vessel.

The Admiral at last realized that the situation had become hopeless— there was no longer any means of transmitting orders. His words were spoken into a void; his strength which had led the squadron twenty thousand miles was confined to this small turret. A mantle of oblivion mercifully descended upon the Admiral; as he sat on the cartridge box, his indomitable spirit finally conquered by nature, he fell unconscious.

The few officers still alive on the *Suvoroff* peered anxiously for a sign of the two torpedo boats *Biedovy* and *Buistry*. They had been specifically instructed before the battle to keep close to the flagship and transfer the Admiral with his staff to another ship, as soon as the *Suvoroff* appeared to be disabled. The flagship was pitching in a heavy swell, great waves clashing against her side. Meanwhile the Russian fleet was steaming out of sight in the haze, led once more by the *Alexander*, which had retaken her place at the head of the column. Suddenly Vice-Admiral Kamimura's five cruisers appeared out of the mist to cut off the squadron, and on their way they sighted the *Suvoroff*. Again all their port guns opened up against the dying ship, pouring another hail of shell upon it.

Far to the southeast the *Osliabia* floated in the sea, a helpless derelict. She had no steam in her boilers, her bow lay deeply in the water, her stern sticking out above the waves, and she was listing heavily to port. Into this sinking target, the Japanese mercilessly sank their fire. At the beginning of the battle, three lucky Japanese hits—the same devilish coincidence as at Port Arthur!—had struck in the same place, tearing a hole in her side as wide as a barn door, through which the ocean rushed in. There could no longer be any thought of saving the ship. Her commander, Captain

Baer, ordered: "Abandon ship! All hands to the boats or jump overboard!" His servant, boatswain's mate Mikhailoff, wanted to drag his master along, but Baer embraced him and then pushed him away. "Jump overboard, save yourself!" Then he disappeared in the conning tower.

Like a dying horse, the great ship rolled over on its side. The officers on the *Suvoroff* stared at the terrible spectacle through their binoculars, reduced to the rôle of impotent spectators at a sight which was so ghastly as to seem unreal. They watched the frantic struggle of men clinging to broken crags and sharp edges protruding from the overturned hull, watched them kick and stamp on each other in their fight for a foothold, and finally pull themselves up on the starboard side which was still protruding from the water.

Hardly had they got there, however, when the narrow ledge became too small for the masses of men. They clawed at each other, a struggling mass of wounded, naked men fighting desperately for survival. But they slipped and fell, tumbling head over heels down the polished armor plate which glistened like the wet scales of a huge sea monster. They bounced against the stabilizers, broke their bones as they were catapulted down this deathly chute, to end at last in the turbulent sea. Then the battleship keeled over with a sickening roar, which resounded across the ocean like the death cry of a primeval beast.

The torpedo boats *Buiny, Bravy* and *Buistry* hurried up under forced draught, trying to save the poor struggling creatures flung about by the heavy waves. But the Japanese continued to shoot. Between the torpedo boats, which were saving as many of the survivors as they could, geysers shot into the air as shells hit the water. Finally the firing slackened and the Japanese warships, their mission accomplished, turned off to the southeast.

V

Since the *Suvoroff* was forced out of line, the *Alexander* steamed at the head of the squadron, but it has never been learned who was actually in command during those hours. Nebogatoff made no move to lead the fleet, although it had been specifically arranged that he was to take over if the flagship became disabled. A typical bureaucrat, he was waiting for a signal from Rozhestvensky transferring the command to him, regardless of the fact that the *Suvoroff*, with all her means of signaling destroyed, had no way of transmitting such an order to Nebogatoff.

Lacking information on precisely what happened during those hours, it is impossible to say whether it was Captain Bukhvostoff of the *Alexander* who made the decision which gave the battle an entirely new turn. Events were occurring so fast that even on the Japanese side it had become increasingly difficult to maintain control of the situation.

The Russian squadron, led by the *Alexander,* was proceeding on the S. E. course set by Rozhestvensky just before the *Suvoroff's* steering-gear was disabled. For a while the two fleets steamed again on parallel courses, and the Japanese flanking maneuver was temporarily forestalled. The superior speed of Togo's ships enabled him, however, to force the Russian line over to starboard, tightening the concentric circles of the opposed fleets. And now once more the First and Second Divisions under Togo and Kamimura rapidly gained over the Russians and threatened to "cross their T." At this crucial moment, the *Alexander*, followed by the rest of the squadron, suddenly turned sharply to port and proceeded under full steam on a northerly course. This move completely reversed the situation, utilizing the fact that, in his eagerness to deflect the Russian line, Togo had steamed too far to the southeast, thus freeing the route to Vladivostok. Now it was the Russians who were crossing the Japanese T, but at the wrong end of the line where they were facing only the weaker rear ships of Kamimura's division. If their ordnance was still up to the task, they could subject the enemy to a deadly flanking fire while Togo's own division, at the other end of the column, would be unable to reply in kind.

Togo recognized the dangers of the situation. He immediately turned "together" eight points to port (each ship executing a right-angle turn to the left) and proceeded in this line-abreast formation on a course parallel to the direction in which the Russians were now headed. Then he turned again eight points to port, ships together, restoring the line-ahead formation, but now headed northwest, having, in effect, reversed his course. In these evolutions only Togo's own First Division was following him. Kamimura under Togo's orders was to cover the maneuver of the First Division, and the Second Division continued on the old course, thereby losing contact with Togo's ships. Ten minutes later Kamimura also turned to port along a wide arc, headed first east and then north, to follow the First Division, but found that it had disappeared in the mist. He then tried on his own to block the northerly course of the Russian squadron. With his sixteen knots he easily outsped the Russian ships, which could barely do ten knots, turned almost sixteen points (reversing his course), when he was again on the outer (northern) of the two concentric circles and once more deflected the Russian line to the east. In the process his guns poured a new rain of fire into the Russian ships.

But the Baltic squadron tenaciously held to the course N. 23 deg. E., toward Vladivostok. They fought heroically to clear this path to Russia although in vain. Far to the northwest Togo's six battleships again emerged from the haze and soon they joined with Kamimura's division in the devastating bombardment. Slowly the Russians edged away from the Japanese guns, first to the east and then to the south. The enemy divisions drew a wide semicircle about them, with Togo in the north and Kamimura in the east. The squadron was forced to retreat south, resuming the course which it had held an hour and a half before. The attempt to break through to Vladivostok had failed.

When the *Alexander* embarked on her new northerly course, the *Suvoroff* laboriously turned about and followed. The incredible happened: this almost disabled wreck held fast to its course, and continued on it at a time when the Russian main body was being forced to swing east to escape from the Japanese. Thus the *Suvoroff* found herself alone, far ahead of the rest, again the target of the whole Japanese fleet. It was an awe-inspiring and terrible sight. Her superstructure demolished, most of her ordnance gone, her armor pierced, practically defenseless, she nevertheless was still the flagship and calmly resumed the battle. Togo sent the scouting cruiser *Chihaya* with the Fourth Destroyer Flotilla against her. At that time (4:37 P.M.), the *Suvoroff* had only one serviceable piece of ordnance and a few machine guns left; nevertheless she beat back the Japanese attack. One destroyer flotilla after another steamed against her, but was driven off by this floating wreck. Finally she was hit by a torpedo—a gigantic pillar of water shot into the air, the *Suvoroff* heeled over 10 degrees, but still continued to fire, her shells causing considerable destruction among the attackers. The *Chihaya*, her hull pierced by a shell, was forced to withdraw from the battle area, and the destroyers retreated with her. They had to leave the work of finishing the valiant ship to Togo's division.

In a Japanese official publication, entitled *Nippon-Kai Tai-Kai-Sen* (The Great Battle of the Japanese Sea), an eyewitness pays tribute to the gallant men of the *Suvoroff*: "On leaving the line the flagship, though burning badly, still steamed after the fleet, but, under the fire we brought to bear upon her, she rapidly lost her foremast and both funnels, besides being completely enveloped in flames and smoke. She was so battered that scarcely anyone would have taken her for a ship, and yet, even in this pitiful condition, like the flagship which she was, she never ceased to fire as much as possible with such of her guns as were serviceable."

Most of the *Suvoroff's* boilers were now useless. The stokers and the men working below, trying to patch leaks and extinguish fires, were almost choked by the fumes, their faces were blackened by smoke, their hair burned off—they were hardly recognizable as human beings. Yet they did their work and the gunners continued to fire. Togo had fortunately disappeared over the horizon, searching for the Russian main body. When four Japanese cruisers steamed up from the south against the flagship, her crew felt almost relieved because "compared with the previous shelling, the bombardment from Dewa's light cruisers was only a flea bite." Most of the officers were wounded, including the Admiral, Captain Ignatius, Ensign Kurssel, Captain Semenoff, Lieutenants Bogdanoff and Zotoff, but nevertheless they were still able to laugh amid this scene of utter devastation. The successful skirmish with the Japanese destroyers had given them new confidence.

Togo's and Kamimura's divisions were forcing the Russian squadron to the south, but with the fleets passing and re-passing the battle had become confused and lacked a concerted strategic plan. The Official History of the Japanese Admiralty Staff mentions that "since it became finally impossible to distinguish between friend and foe, the Second Division temporarily withheld fire and resumed it only when it was possible to recognize a Russian flag flying from the masthead." Togo lost contact with the Russian squadron and tried to regain it by steaming after Kamimura's division, which was still clinging to the enemy. Soon Kamimura also lost the Russians in the smoke and haze of battle. Knowing that they had escaped south, Togo proceeded full speed in that direction; but when he got as far as the island of Okinoshima without seeing a trace of them, he realized that they had temporarily escaped.

The time was approximately 5:30 P.M. The Russian squadron was now led by the *Borodino* (the *Alexander* was limping after the *Borodino* with a heavy list), and had been able to reform its ranks in the half hour of rest before it was again engaged by Togo's battleships. The light cruiser *Izumrud* still stuck to her place near the leader.

Suddenly the men on both fleets halted in their task, staring in utter amazement at a fantastic sight: between the two lines of ships, through the haze and smoke of battle, drifted a flaming wreck without funnels or masts, firing incessantly from its single 75-millimeter gun—the *Suvoroff*! The heavy sea washed over the deck on the low-lying port side, rushed in through the gun ports of the lower battery deck, which was already below the water line, and played with the defenseless ship like a toy ball. Then a Japanese destroyer flotilla steamed up for battle and the smoke pillars of exploding shells rose from the wounded body of the flagship like gushing blood. But the other Russian ships were themselves too sorely pressed to assist their stricken comrade.

Meanwhile the Russian torpedo boat *Besuprechny* plowed through the rough swell toward the *Nicolai I* with a formal order from Rozhestvensky transferring command of the fleet to Nebogatoff and ordering him to try to escape with the squadron to Vladivostok. Old Nebogatoff nodded, hoisted the signal "Follow in my wake," and shaped course for Vladivostok—the famous course N. 23 deg. E. But it was not an easy order. Togo's division was again on a parallel course at a distance of four thousand yards, spewing fire and steel from every gun, while Kamimura's division stood out of the mist behind Togo's rear ship. The battle went on—a battle of giants unleashing the elements against each other.

VI

About five o'clock in the afternoon the Russian destroyer *Buiny* sighted a pillar of flame to the northeast, found that it was the burning *Suvoroff*, and hurried toward it to take off the Admiral.

It would be exaggeration to say that the flagship looked any worse than it had when we left it to follow the main body heading north in the unsuccessful attempt to break through to Vladivostok. Even destruction has its limits, and all the Japanese shells could do now was to stir up the debris left from previous hits. Below deck, however, in the smoky, poisonous atmosphere where lay the wounded and dying, or farther below where human creatures incessantly labored in the vapor-laden air to patch leaks, unmitigated hell was raging. Whether it was a worse hell than before is difficult to say. On this ship life was over, and even the few survivors were already in a different world. They had reached the limit of human suffering beyond which there can be only release.

Admiral Rozhestvensky had been wounded a fourth time. The men who extinguished fires, manned the guns, patched leaks, or tried to signal a torpedo boat to take off Rozhestvensky were, like the Admiral himself, only the bleeding remnants of human beings. But they had become indifferent to pain, and some said later that in those hours they did not feel it.

When the "crates" again came flying into the wounded ship, and the sailors cowered terror-stricken in a corner to wait for death, Kurssel and Bogdanoff consoled the men and tried to calm them so that they could work again. There were moments, however, when even the officers found themselves unable to lift a finger. In the midst of shrieking shells, they would simply stand smoking innumerable cigarettes, and stare at the battle unrolling before their eyes. They watched the *Alexander* forced out of line with a heavy list, her whole foredeck torn open from bowsprit to the twelve-inch gun turret, but still dragging herself after the other ships, toward Vladivostok—toward Russia! She can't make it, though, she can't last much longer. Not for her the "Blessed Land" for which they are all longing . . .

Then came the exciting moment when the men on the *Suvoroff* saw a Russian torpedo boat, the *Buiny,* approaching. Her decks were crowded with men looking like corpses pulled out of the water: they were the two hundred and seventy sailors saved from the *Osliabia*. As the *Buiny* neared the flagship, her commander, Captain Kolomeytseff, shouted through a megaphone: "Have you a boat on board to transfer the Admiral? I haven't."

At last some one had come to save the Admiral! There are miracles even in hell. But a boat? A boat on the *Suvoroff,* when there were hardly a few square inches of space left intact on the whole battleship? On the other hand, how could Rozhestvensky be transferred to the little *Buiny* without a boat?

The sea was rough, with a heavy swell, making the attempt seem even more hopeless. The Japanese Admiral Dewa, although not wounded, had found it impossible to transfer from his badly damaged flagship, the *Kasagi,* to the *Chitose,* and had to seek refuge in a Japanese port, meanwhile leaving the command of his division to Vice-Admiral Uriu. On the *Suvoroff,* however, there was no choice. Rozhestvensky must be taken off at once.

Unfortunately, the *Buiny,* bobbing up and down on the waves like a piece of cork, could not come alongside the flagship to port where, in view of the heavy list on that side, the transfer would have been easier. Since it was the leeward side, the acrid fumes and intolerable heat from the blazing ship would have suffocated the men. On the starboard side, however, the *Suvoroff* stood high out of the water—too high to jump. Out of the shell-torn hull broken guns protruded with their sharp steel edges, and iron booms and scaled-off armor plate stuck out like pointed swords. The frail torpedo boat would be smashed to atoms if, in the rough water, a wave should carry it against the sharp edges. "Where is the Admiral?" the officers shouted. "Get the Admiral, quickly!" Semenoff climbed into the six-inch gun turret and found Rozhestvensky slumped down on his box in a state of semi-consciousness, his head wrapped in a blood-stained towel.

Semenoff reported to him that a torpedo boat had arrived to transfer him to another ship. Rozhestvensky did not answer. After a while, Semenoff's words seemed to penetrate into his wandering mind and he asked for the Flag Navigating Office Philippovsky. The Admiral did not care for his life, but he wished to resume command of the squadron. His despondency of a moment ago was the despair of one stripped of his weapon. If he were transferred to another ship, he could fight again. But, as he struggled to his feet, his strength failed him and he dropped in a faint.

Kurssel, Semenoff, Bogdanoff and a boatswain quickly improvised a rough kind of raft from burned hammocks and cork vests. Meanwhile the Japanese had noticed the commotion near the flagship and again opened fire in that direction. The fountains of water where the shells crashed came nearer and nearer to the torpedo boat. With every second the danger increased.

At last the Flag Navigating Officer, for whom they had been searching frantically, was found in the lower fighting position. Semenoff shook the Admiral gently. "Your Excellency, please come out. Philippovsky is here."

Rozhestvensky lifted his head for a moment, but as the men picked him up he groaned and again lost consciousness.

He had to be carried out of the turret, but how could they get his limp body through the twisted steel door, which was stuck and could not be opened properly? They pulled and pushed and finally dragged the severely wounded Admiral by force through the narrow opening. His coat caught in the door, but another pull, and at last they had him outside. They strapped Rozhestvensky to the raft and were ready to lower him overboard —but what then? Japanese shells exploded in the water all about the ship, throwing up fountains of water and sending the little torpedo boat high up into the air like a flying fish. One moment it was on a level with the upper deck of the *Suvoroff,* the next moment it sank away as a wave carried it off. Unless the *Buiny* could come closer it would be impossible to get the Admiral safely on board.

The brave commander of the torpedo boat unhesitatingly did what few men would have done. Heedless of the shells, heedless of the mountainous waves, heedless of the razor-sharp crags and edges protruding from the battered *Suvoroff,* he brought his boat alongside the starboard bow of the flagship, to windward. And he held it there for a few breathless minutes, when any instant a wave might smash his frail craft against the torn hull. But now the *Buiny* was near enough to transfer the Admiral, although the boat was still rising and falling with the turbulent sea.

On the deck of the *Suvoroff* the men made a last frantic effort. Carrying their unconscious commander, they hurried from the after deck through the wreckage and debris to the bow embrasure. They were scorched by the heat of steel melting in the fires of the upper battery, Japanese shells were zooming over their heads, but at last they arrived their with their precious load. Deep down below them rocked the tiny *Buiny,* her deck swarming with dripping, ghost-like creatures, all staring up at them. Now a wave lifted the boat until it was almost level with the deck—now! Kolomeytseff shouted: "Throw him over!"

Balancing precariously on an open gun port, the men picked up the raft with the Admiral, swung it back and threw it through the air over to the *Buiny.*

Kolomeytseff and his men caught the raft.

"Hurrah! The Admiral is on board!" Werner von Kurssel shouted.

And all the survivors of the *Suvoroff,* the crew of the *Buiny,* the dripping ghosts saved from the *Osliabia,* took up the cry. Waving their caps, laughing and crying hysterically, they all shouted: Hurrah! The Admiral has been saved!

Some of the staff officers jumped after Rozhestvensky. The first Japanese hits began to explode on the *Suvoroff's* hull, and ricochetting steel splinters took their toll among the men on the *Buiny.* The officers on the torpedo boat shouted back to Kurssel, Bogdanoff and Viruboff, who had stayed on the flagship: "Jump overboard! Quickly, come, jump at once!"

But Kurssel roared over the noise of wind and waves: "Push off at once!" Bogdanoff leaned over the side and shouted in stentorian tones: "Don't waste another moment! Push off at once! Don't endanger the Admiral!"

Heads peered out from the battery ports of the *Suvoroff,* and up on deck, between wreckage and broken-off gun barrels, men leaned over and waved, shouting: "Push off, push off!"

For an instant Kolomeytseff stared at the men waving their caps, their faces beaming with joy—he could not leave his comrades to their fate, he must try—

Then the first direct hit crashed into the *Buiny,* putting one of the boilers out of commission. The torpedo boat shot out of the water under the impact of the shell, and got clear of the *Suvoroff.* Kolomeytseff ordered "Full speed astern." With shells crashing all around her, the *Buiny* made off at top speed.

The men on board the boat could not take their eyes from the flagship. She was heeling over so much that the red underwater part of her hull was showing. Through the smashed gun ports, fires could be seen smoldering in the depth of the ship. But on her upper deck a group of men still waved to the torpedo boat as it disappeared from view. Rozhestvensky lay on a stretcher, unconscious, his face a waxen color. He had lost a great deal of blood. The sick bay attendant Peter Kudinoff briefly examined the Admiral, then turned to the Chief-of-Staff, Flag Captain Clappier de

Colomb, and shook his head silently. The Admiral was in no condition to lead the squadron.

The *Buiny* pitched and rolled, and heavy seas washed over her low-lying deck crowded with the survivors of the *Osliabia*. Far away, wrapped in sheets of flame, the Russian fleet steamed with flashing guns. The torpedo boat followed in the direction of this blazing group of ships.

The Admiral was carried to the commander's cabin where Kudinoff dressed his wounds as well as he could with the scant means on board. There was not much left of Rozhestvensky. His skull was broken, parts of it had embedded themselves in his brain. One of his shoulder bones was fractured, the right upper thigh bone broken, a vein on his left foot was severed and blood still gushed from the wound. A dozen steel splinters had buried themselves in his back. The sick-bay attendant washed and dressed the wounds. Suddenly the Admiral opened his eyes. Kudinoff asked him softly whether he was suffering greatly. Rozhestvensky only said: "Where is the *Suvoroff*?"

Kudinoff did not answer. The Admiral's mind was wandering again, and after a while he asked angrily: "Who gave orders to strike the flag?"

The officers pointed out that the flagship had been reduced to a burning wreck and that there was nothing left on which to hoist a flag.

"Then you should have flown it from a boat-hook!"

The men did not answer. Semenoff entered, saluted, and asked the Admiral whether he felt strong enough to continue in command, and to what ship he wished to be transferred.

Rozhestvensky tried to answer, but his voice failed him. With a great effort he pulled himself together. It was not a groan that emerged from his lips, although it sounded like it—it was the dying note of a breaking string: "To Vladivostok . . . course N. 23 deg. E."

At last the merciful hand of nature wrapped him in unconsciousness, lifting the burden from his weary mind.

The Admiral's last question about his flagship was put just at the time the *Suvoroff* was nearing her end. The sun was setting in the West when the Japanese Eleventh Torpedo-Boat Flotilla under Lieutenant-Commander Fujimoto made the last attack against the dying flagship. The Japanese were anxious to destroy the *Suvoroff* before nightfall, since the ship had already withstood so many attacks and might get away under cover of darkness. The four destroyers, still fearing the claws of the dying lion, carefully approached from the starboard quarter, crossed her bows and port where the ship was defenseless, and launched their torpedoes at a distance of three hundred yards. The *Suvoroff* had no means of defending herself, and was unable to move under her own power. Three torpedoes found their mark. The wrecked ship, wrapped in clouds of black and yellow smoke, quivered under the force of the explosion, and her bow shot up into the air. Slowly, stern first, she slipped into the ocean. The tumultuous waves closed over her, leaving only a thick cloud of smoke hanging over the water where the *Suvoroff* had been. Soon the smoke, too, was dispersed by the wind . . .

For a brief moment, the Japanese gazed at the spot, then they turned and steamed off.

Lieutenant-Commander Fujimoto, when making his official report, forgot that emotion is not a proper part of a naval officer's equipment. But he was moved by the end of the *Suvoroff* which was not like the sinking of a ship; it was the death of a living creature. He wrote:

"Although much burned and still on fire—although she had been subjected to so many attacks, having been fired at by all the fleet (in the full sense of the word)—although she had only one serviceable gun—she still opened fire, showing her determination to defend herself to the last moment of her existence—so long, in fact, as she remained above water. At length, about 7 P.M., after our torpedo boats had twice attacked her, she went to the bottom."

VII

The battle took its course—but what a strange expression; where could its course lead? To what degree of suffering and destruction could it progress? To any one delving, decades later, into the blood-drenched pages of history for an account of this struggle, it becomes clear that the distinction between victor and vanquished is only temporary. It is an arbitrary criterion of achievement that only rarely reflects the merits of the individual. In the ultimate stages of tragedy, the conquered may rise above the ignominy of their position to take their places beside the victors.

The battle went on, heaping defeat and destruction upon the Russian fleet, but from it emerged deeds of heroism and comradeship which redound to the eternal glory of the Russian sailor. In this last and most terrible phase of the battle, the fleeing Russians no longer seemed fugitives, the defeated no longer vanquished—of their own free will they entered the gates of death.

In those hours, the *Alexander*, the "fate"-ship of the squadron, expiated her previous mistakes. Her fighting end was no less remarkable than that of the *Suvoroff*. Not much is known of what happened on the *Alexander*, since she sank with every member of her crew, but observers saw her, her hull pierced like a sieve, enveloped in a flowing mantle of flames, firing until the end. With a heavy list she was forced out of line, made some repairs and fell in again behind the column to continue fighting.

Shortly before seven o'clock she preceded the flagship to the bottom. Her hull rent asunder by an explosion, she keeled over and the waves began to close above her. A few small shapes were seen clambering up on her overturned keel, then the ship went down, carrying with her nearly eight hundred men.

Methodically and with inflexible determination, the Japanese finished off the Russian leaders one by one. After the end of the *Suvoroff* and *Alexander*, they concentrated their fire on the *Borodino*. The ship was forced out of line but continued to fire. It seemed natural to all that the *Borodino* should fight with the utmost bravery; like the other two battleships, she was manned by the pick of the Russian Navy and commanded by the most beloved of all Russian officers, Captain Serebrenikoff. He was a born leader, obeyed by his men because they loved him, not because of his epaulettes. When he was wounded, there was the greatest consternation on board and at the first lull in the battle the men rushed below to the sick-bay for first-hand news. During five hours of steady pounding by Togo's guns, the *Borodino* had held her place behind the *Alexander* as if steaming in a parade. From 5:30 o'clock on, when Kamimura re-established contact with the Russian squadron, the *Borodino* was exposed to heavy fire from the whole Japanese division. One of the fiery "crates" tore an enormous hole in her lower battery deck, but the damage seemed less important to the crew than Serebrenikoff's injuries. He lost a hand and one of his neck muscles was severed, but by a supreme effort he retained consciousness and calmed his desperate sailors, who were like madmen when they saw their commander wounded. They wanted to get at the Japanese with their bare fists to revenge their captain. Hardly had his wounds been bandaged when he appeared on deck, waving to his men and directing the operations of the ship.

The terrible voyage through hell began after the *Alexander* had been forced out of line, when the *Borodino* led the squadron (Nebogatoff only had the flag). For an hour, she was the target of both Japanese battleship divisions. Listing heavily, a tortured burning wreck, she finally sustained a hit in the ammunition chamber. The whole ship was torn apart by a terrific explosion and sank in a few seconds. Of the nine hundred men on board, only one was able to save himself by diving through a gun port and swimming away. A Japanese torpedo boat hauled him on board after he had been in the water for three hours.

A ship lives her own life and dies her own death, like a human being. There was something about the sinking of the *Borodino* which gave the tragedy an unusual element of greatness, a weird glamor of perfection unachieved by any of the other ships. She slipped beneath the waves as if the god of Hades were reaching out a giant hand to bring her down into the depths. Where she had disappeared a fleecy white cloud hovered for a few seconds, tinged with the first faint pink of sunset. In the midst of battle, men stopped to look at the rosy veil marking the spot where the *Borodino* had lived and suffered. Then reality asserted itself as the *Nicolai I* rumbled over the grave.

The sinking of the *Borodino* ended the day's battle. The sun slowly descended in a fiery, blood-red sunset as if dipped in the streams of blood shed so wantonly on that day. The Japanese, fighting with their faces to the west, were blinded by the dazzling light and their shots began to go wild. Was it that the gods above the clouds had at last taken pity on suffering humanity? They stripped the victors of their weapons and concealed the vanquished in the purple cloak of dusk.

Togo gave the "Cease fire" signal. Turning west, he disappeared in the shadows of approaching darkness, leaving behind him a storm cloud of torpedo boats.

In the waning hours of the evening, Admiral Rozhestvensky regained consciousness for a brief moment. Lifting up his head, he asked in a clear voice whether all the survivors of the *Suvoroff* had been saved. On hearing that only twenty had escaped, his lips quivered and a low groan escaped him. Then, in a voice which brooked no contradiction, he ordered that a torpedo boat be sent back at once to the spot where the *Suvoroff* had sunk. The waters in the vicinity must be searched thoroughly to make sure that no men were left floating in the water.

The *Biedovy* turned and sped back to the scene of battle, but an intensive search disclosed no trace of the wreck or its survivors. Only the dark blue waves of the ocean rose and fell in solemn majesty. The wind had died down and the calm of evening had descended upon the water. The first stars were appearing behind the purple clouds. The day was at last drawing to a close.

The Parisian

BY

ALDEN BROOKS

It was a terribly dark night, wet and piercing cold. The pavements were slippery with a muddy slush. They tramped along in silence; not a word; each man his own thoughts, yet each man's thoughts the same. Slowly, however, their blood warmed a little, and their shoulderstraps settled into place. The trenches were five kilometres away to the north. By the time they reached the field kitchens, the night was a little less dark; dawn was coming. There was a wee light burning. They halted beside it and wondered what was going to happen next. One or two went and knocked on the rough huts where the cooks slept. Perhaps there might be some chance of getting a little coffee.

"Coffee for us? You're crazy. Do you think they'd waste coffee on us?"

But it so happened that they had halted for just that reason. From the wee light there came a man with great buckets of hot coffee. They gathered about him and held out their tin cups. The man told them not to crowd around so, he could not see what he was doing, and there was plenty for everybody. Standing up, they gulped it down. It was hot. It warmed. Shortly afterward they were filing along the channels through the earth— the third trenches, the second trenches, then slowly into the first trenches. The watchers there rose stiffly and made room for them. A blue rocket shot up from the Germans opposite. It lit up the landscape with a weird light. The earth seemed to grow colder. Then the artillery began intermittently. Then it got to work in earnest, and for half an hour or more it tore the sky above into shreds. They became impatient. They wanted to know what they were waiting for. It was the captain.

"What in the hell is he fussing about now?"

"Oh, he's fussing about the machine-guns!"

"Oh, he's always fussing about something or other!"

"Hell, that's his business!"

Presently the captain came creeping along. He spoke in a low whisper to the young lieutenant in charge of De Barsac's section.

"Are your men ready?"

"Yes, all ready."

"You've placed your machine-guns the way I told you?"

"Yes."

From: *The Fighting Men*: Copyright 1917. Scribners.

"Good. Then, you understand, you attack right after us. Give me a few minutes, then come out and dash right up."

There was silence again. The captain moved off. Presently George snickered.

"That's all. Dash right up. Well, I'll promise you one thing, old whiskers," he murmured to a watcher by his side, "if I've got to rot and stink out here for the next month, I'll try and carry my carcass as near as I can to their nostrils rather than to yours."

"Shut up," growled Jules.

George looked around.

"God! you're not funking it, are you?"

"Oh, what do you lose? Nothing. Eh! What do you leave behind?"

"Old man, I leave behind more wives than you."

"Yes, I guess you do—yes, I guess you do—yes, I guess that's about it."

"Stop that noise," whispered the lieutenant.

The artillery fire ceased. A minute later they heard the shouts of the other company over to the left, and above the shouting, the rapid, deadly, pank-pank-pank of the German machine-guns. They stood up instinctively; they swung on their knapsacks; they drew out their bayonets and fixed them on their rifles, and while they did so, their breath steamed upon the cold, damp air. Then, standing there in a profound silence, they looked across at each other through that murky morning light and gave up now definitely everything life had brought them. It was a bitter task, much harder for some than for others; but when the lieutenant suddenly said, "At 'em, boys!" all were ready. A low, angry snarl shot from their lips. Like hunted beasts, ready to tear the first thing they met to pieces in a last death-struggle, they scrambled out of the trench. Creeping through the barbed wire, they advanced stealthily until a hail of bullets was turned upon them, then they leaped up with a mighty yell, ran some twenty paces, fell flat upon the ground, and leaped up once more. Head bent down, De Barsac plunged forward. Bullets sang and hissed about him. Every instant he expected death to strike him. He stumbled on, trying to offer it the brain and nothing else. He fell headlong over shell holes, but each time picked himself up and staggered on and on. Hours seemed to pass. He remembered George's words. Not rot here—nor here nor here—but carry one's carcass higher and higher. Finally, he heard the young lieutenant yelling: "Come on, boys, come on, we're almost there." He looked up. Clouds of smoke, bullets ripping up the earth, comrades falling about him, a few hurrying on, all huddled up like men in a terrible rain-storm. Of a sudden he found himself among barbed wire and pit holes. The white bleached face of a man, dead weeks ago, leered at him. He stepped over the putrid body and flung himself through the wire. It tore his clothes, but failed to hold him. Bullets whizzed around his head, but they all seemed to be too high. Then, of a sudden, he realized that he was actually going to reach the trench. He started up. He gripped his rifle in both hands and let out a terrible yell. He became livid with rage. Up out of the ground rose a wave of Germans. He saw George drive his bayonet into the foremost; and as the bayonet snapped off, heard him shout: "Keep it and give it to your sweetheart for a hatpin!" A tall, haggard German charged full at him. He stood his ground, parried the thrust. The German's rifle swung off to one side and exposed his body. With a savage snort he drove his bayonet into the muddy uniform. He felt it go in and in, and instinctively plunged it farther and twisted it around, then heard the wretch scream, and saw him drop his rifle and grasp at life with extended arms, and watched him fall off the bayonet and sink down, bloody hands clasped over his stomach, and a golden ring upon the fourth finger. He stood there weak and flabby. His head began to whirl. Only just in time did he ward off the vicious lunge of a sweating bearded monster. Both rifles rose up locked together into the air. Between their upstretched arms the two men glared at each other.

"Schwein!" hissed the German.

With an adroit twist, De Barsac threw the other off and brought the butt of his rifle down smack upon the moist red forehead. The fellow sank to his knees with a grunt and, eyes closed, vaguely lifted his hand toward his face. De Barsac half fell over him, turned about, and clubbed the exposed neck as hard as he could with his rifle. Bang! went the rifle almost in his sleeve. He swore angrily. But the bullet had only grazed his arm. He leaped on with a loud shout. Within a crater-like opening in the earth a wild, uproarious fight was going on. He caught one glimpse of George swinging the broken leg of a machine-gun and battering in heads right and left, then was engulfed in the melee.

A furious struggle took place—a score of Frenchmen against a score of Germans—in a cockpit of poisoned, shell-tossed earth. None thought of victory, honor. It was merely a wild, frenzied survival of the fittest, wherein each man strove to tear off, rid himself of this fiendish thing against him. Insane with fury, his senses steeped in gore, De Barsac stabbed and clubbed and stabbed; while close by his side a tall Breton, mouth ripped open with a bayonet point, lip flapping down, bellowed horribly: "Kill! Kill! Kill!"

They killed and they killed; then as the contest began to turn rapidly in their favor, their yells became short, swift exclamations of barbaric triumph; then, unexpectedly, it was all over, and the handful of them that remained understood that, by God and by Heaven, they ten, relic though they were of two hundred better men, had actually come through it all alive and on top. The lieutenant, covered with blood, his sword swinging idly from his wrist, staggered over and leaned upon De Barsac's shoulder. In his other hand he held the bespattered broken leg of the machine-gun. So George must be dead. De Barsac burst out laughing nervously. The lieutenant laughed until he had to double up with a fit of coughing. What a picnic! Others sat down, breathing heavily, and told the whole damned German army to come along and see what was waiting for them. But a bullet flew out of the heap of fallen. It burned the skin on De Barsac's forehead like a hot poker. In a twinkling all ten were on their feet again glaring like savages. The lieutenant reached the offender first. The broken leg of the machine-gun came down with an angry thud; then the rest of them turned about and swarmed over the sloping sides of the pit and exterminated, exterminated.

"He's only playing dead. Give him one just the same. Hell! Don't waste a bullet. Here let me. There, take that, sausage!"

The lieutenant climbed up and took a cautious peep over the top of the crater. There was nothing to see. A dull morning sky over a flat rising field. A bit of communicating trench blown in. Way over to the left, like something far off and unreal, the pank-pank-pank of machine-guns and the uproar of desperate fighting. Behind, on the other side, a field littered with fallen figures in light blue, many crawling slowly away.

"What's happening?" asked De Barsac, still out of breath.

"Can't see. The fighting's all over to the left. Everybody seems to have forgotten us. As far as I can judge, this was an outpost, not a real trench."

"Well, whatever it was, it's ours now," said someone.

"Well, why don't they follow us up?"

"Yes, by God, right away, or else—"

"Oh, they will soon!" said the lieutenant, "so get busy—no time to waste. Block up that opening, and fill your sand-bags, all the sand-bags you can find, and dig yourselves in."

But they stood there astonished, irritated. Yes, where were the reinforcements? If reinforcements did not come up, they were as good as rats trapped in a cage. The lieutenant had to repeat his command. Angrily they shoved the dead out of their way and dug themselves in and filled up the sand-bags and built a rampart with them along the top of the hollow. They swore darkly. No reinforcements! Not a man sent to help them! So it was death, after all. By chance they uncovered a cement trough covered with boards and earth, a sort of shelter; and down there were a great number of cartridge-bands for a machine-gun. The sight of them inspired the lieutenant. He went and busied himself over the captured machine-gun, still half buried in the dirt. Only one leg was broken off; that was all. Hurriedly he cleaned the gun and propped it up between the bags. Then he stood back and rubbed his hands together and laughed boyishly and seemed very pleased. The sun came up in the distance; it glittered upon the frost in the fields. But with it came the shells. Cursing furiously, the ten ducked down into the trough, and for an hour or more hooted at the marksmanship. Only one shell exploded in the crater. Though it shrivelled them all up, it merely tossed about a few dead bodies and left a nasty trail of gas. They became desperate savages again. Then the firing ceased, and the lieutenant scrambled out and peered through the sand-bags. He turned back quickly, eyes flashing.

"Here they come, boys!"

They jumped up like madmen and pushed their rifles through the sand-bags. The lieutenant sat down at the machine-gun. De Barsac fed the bands. Over the field came a drove of gray-coated men. Their bayonets sparkled wonderfully in the new morning light; yet they ran along all doubled up like men doing some Swedish drill. They seemed to be a vast multitude until the machine-gun began to shoot. Then the ten saw that they were not so many after all.

"Take care she doesn't jam, old man," said the lieutenant to De Barsac.

"Oh, don't worry, she isn't going to jam!"

They were both very cool.

"Ah! now she's getting into them beautifully," said the lieutenant; "look at them fall. There we go. Spit, little lady, spit; that's the way—steady, old man."

As if by some miracle the gray line of a sudden began to break up. Many less came rushing on. They were singing some guttural song. The rifles between the sand-bags answered them like tongues aflame with hate; but the machine-gun answered them even faster still, a remorseless stream of fire. Finally, there were only some seven or eight left. The lieutenant did not seem to notice them.

"You see how idiotic it all is," he said nonchalantly. "These attacks with a company or two? Why, our little friend here could have taken care of a whole battalion!"

Only one man remained. He was yelling fiercely at the top of his lungs. He looked like some devil escaped from hell. He came tearing on. Bullets would not hit him. Then he was right upon them. But he saw now he was alone and his whole expression changed. Across his eyes glistened the light film of fear. The man with the torn lip jumped up.

"Here you are," he spluttered hideously, "all yours!"

A loud report in De Barsac's ears, smoke and the muddy soles of a pair of hobnailed boots trembling against the nozzle of the machine-gun.

"Do you see what I mean?" continued the lieutenant. "What is the use of it? Did I say a battalion? Why we could have managed a whole regiment—now, then, somebody shove those pig feet out of the way, so that I can finish off the whole lot properly."

The sun came up now in earnest and warmed them; but though they sat back in their little caves and ate some of the food they had brought and then rolled cigarettes and smoked them, they were very nervous and impatient. Every so often one of them would go up the other side of the pit and look back. Always the same sight through the tangle of barbed wire— a foreground heaped with dead, a field sprinkled with fallen blue figures, and three or four hundred yards away the trenches they had come from; otherwise, not a soul. Once they waved a handkerchief on a bayonet. It only brought a shower of bullets. So that was it. After they had accomplished the impossible, they were going to be left here to die like this. A little later the shells once more began to explode about them. The aim once more was very poor, but they knew it was the prelude to another attack. Death was again angling for them—and this time—

"Here they come!" shouted the lieutenant.

They stood up and, pushing their rifles well out through the sand-bags, glanced along the barrels. They swore furiously at what they saw—twice as many of the pig-eaters as before. De Barsac anxiously fed the bands to the vibrating machine before him. The lieutenant's face was very stern and set. It had lost its boyish look. Suddenly there was a terrific explosion, clouds of smoke, and a strange new pungent odor of gas. A man·left his post and, eyes closed, turned round and round and went staggering down the slope and stumbled over a dead man and lay where he fell. They stopped firing and huddled against their caves until the lieutenant shouted out something and the machine-gun trembled again. Then there were two more frightful explosions right over their heads. Great God! It was their own artillery!

Through the fog of smoke De Barsac could only see the lieutenant, cringed up over the machine. His face became purple with rage as he hissed into De Barsac's ear his whole opinion of the matter. If he had not said anything before, it was because it was not fit that he should; but before dying now he wanted to tell one man, one other Frenchman, what he thought of a general staff who could first send men out stupidly to their slaughter, then abandon them in positions won, and finally kill them off with their own artillery. But De Barsac, now that the smoke had rolled away a little, was hypnotized by the huge gray wave roaring toward them nearer and nearer. The machine-gun seemed to be helpless among them. However many fell, others came rushing on. Then, unexpectedly, a shell skimmed just over the heads of the nine and exploded full among the advancing throngs. It was the most beautiful sight any of the nine had ever seen. The gray figures were not simply knocked over, but blown into pieces. And in quick succession came explosion after explosion. Priceless vengeance! The field seemed to be a mass of volcanoes. The ranks faltered, broke, plunged about blindly in the smoke, turned, and fled. Only a few came charging wildly on. But the trembling little machine-gun lowered its head angrily. One by one the figures went sprawling, just as if each in turn had of a sudden walked on to slippery ice. So ended the second attack. The third attack, following right after, was a fiasco. The artillery now had their measure to a yard. The shells blew up among them before they were half started. The nine along the crater top did not fire a shot. Shortly afterward they heard the roar of an aeroplane overhead. It must have been there all the time, head in the wind. Under the wings were concentric circles of red and white about a blue dot. The mere sight of it intoxicated them like champagne. And when it was all over for the moment, and the distant figure, moving off, waved his hand, they gave him a cheer it was a great pity he could not hear.

"You see, boys," said the lieutenant gayly, "he's telling us that it's all right now. Reinforcements will be up after dark."

They sat back once more and scraped the blood and muck off their uniforms and smoked and found another meal, and for want of a suitable oath mumbled abstractedly to themselves. Long, tedious hours followed. Little by little it grew colder; then, at last, the sun began to go down. A dreary, desolate landscape stretched out all around. But the thought that reinforcements would soon be coming cheered them. They rose up and got ready to go, then stood about impatiently. The lieutenant had to tell them to never mind what was going on behind them, but stick to their posts. It grew darker, and darker still. Now help would be here any minute. They heard voices; but they were mistaken. It became quite dark, night, half an hour, an hour, two hours, and still no one came, only an ever-increasing cannon fire all around them, shells whistling and screaming to and fro over their heads, red and blue rockets, cataclysms of sound ceaselessly belched into the hollow. At last they threw their knapsacks off in disgust and sat down and cursed and swore as they had never cursed or sworn before.

The night air became painfully cold. They had to stand up again and stamp about to keep warm and not fall asleep. The lieutenant told them to fire off their rifles from time to time. Jules came nearer to De Barsac.

"Ah!" grumbled De Barsac, "they're making monkeys of us."

"Yes—or else they don't know we've taken this place."

"Oh, they know that well enough. Look at the artillery. No; they don't want this hole. They never wanted it. We were never meant to get here."

"Yes," said a voice in the darkness, "it's like this: They went to Joffre and said: 'General, some damned fools have gone and taken an outpost over there.' 'The hell they have!' says Joffre. 'Why, the damned fools! Well, give them all the military medal.' 'Very well, General,' says the Johnny who brought the message, 'but they are rather hard to reach,' 'Oh, in that case,' says Joffre, 'just finish the poor devils off with a couple of shells.' "

"Look here, boys," said the lieutenant, "cut that talk out. You know, as well as I do, that Joffre had nothing to do with this—"

"Well, why the devil then doesn't he send some one up to reinforce us?"

"Well," said the lieutenant after a pause, "look at all those fireworks. There's enough iron in the air to kill ten army corps. They don't dare come up."

"Don't dare? Christ! we dared, didn't we?"

"Well, they may come up by and by."

But no one came; just the furious interchange of shells all night long. So dawn appeared once more and found them stiff, weary, half frozen, and in their dull, hollow eyes no longer a ray of hope. And soon the shells began to fall again upon the hollow. Heedlessly the young lieutenant stood up and took a long look back at those trenches from which help should come. A shell broke just above him. He was still standing upright; but the top of his head was gone, only the lower jaw remained. Blood welled up for a second, then the figure slowly sank into a heap. De Barsac took the revolver out of the clinched hand and removed the cartridge-belt. He went back and sat down at the machine-gun.

"Feed the bands, will you, when the time comes?" he said to Jules.

"Look here," said a man, "it's sure death hanging on here any longer. I'm going to make a dash back for it before it is too light."

"Stay where you are," growled De Barsac.

"No, I'm going to take my chance."

"Do you hear what I say? Get back where you belong, or I'll blow your brains out."

More shells exploded over them. They were caught unawares. They had barely time to crawl into the trough. In fact, some of them had not. The man, who at last wanted to run away, doubled himself up grotesquely and coughed blood until he slowly rolled down toward the bottom of the pit. And there amidst the smoke was the man with the torn lip, lying on one elbow, and both legs smashed off above the knees. De Barsac and Jules tried to haul him under cover.

"Don't bother, boys; no, don't bother—I'm done for now—my mouth was nothing—but this finishes me—no, you can't stop it bleeding—so get back quick—and I'm not frightened of death—I like it—really, I do—I've been waiting for it for a long time."

The bombardment continued. It soon became a tremendous affair. It was the worst bombardment any of them had ever experienced. It was as if they were trying to hide in the mouth of a volcano. They never could have imagined such a thing possible. Then it grew even worse still. The very inside of hell was torn loose and hurled at them. Sheltered though they were in the cement trough, they were slowly buried under earth and stones and wood and dead flesh. And so, while they lay there thus, suffocated by gas and smoke, blind, deaf, senseless, the bombardment went on hour after hour. In fact, it was a great wonder that any of them lived on. But they were only six. And it is always difficult to kill the last six among a crowd of dead; the very dead themselves rise up and offer protection. At last the French artillery once more began to gain the master hand, and the bombardment gradually weakened, and finally it ceased altogether. Slowly, very slowly, the six unravelled themselves. They did not recognize their surroundings. Most of the dead had disappeared, just morsels of flesh and bone and uniform, here and there. They did not recognize themselves. As for rifles, knapsacks, machine-gun, ammunition, they had no idea where any of these were. Should an attack come now, they were defenseless. But that was just the point. They had not come out to live, but to die. The bottom of the pit was more or less empty now. One by one they went and sat down there and stared stupidly at the ground. If another shell came into the crater, they would all be killed outright. But no shell came—just a nice, warm midday sun ahead. So, presently, for want of something better to do, they gathered about a blood-soaked loaf of bread, a box of sardines, a canteen full of wine, and in this cockpit of poisonous, shell-tossed earth, with only a blue sky overhead and a few distant melodious shells singing past, they ate their last meal together.

As they ate they slowly decided several things. First of all, they decided they were cursed; but that, such being the case and since it was their fate to die like this, forgotten in this bloodstained hole, they would die like men, like Frenchmen. Then they decided that this hole was their property. Back of them lay France and her millions of acres and her millions of men; but right here in the very forefront of the fighting was this sanguinary pit; it belonged to them, all six of them, and they would die defending it. Then, finally, as soldiers of experience, they decided many things about modern warfare that all the thousand and one generals and ministers did not know. They decided that knapsacks were useless, and rifles also. What one wanted was a knife, a long knife—look, about as long as that, well, perhaps a little longer—a revolver, bombs, and endless machine-guns, light and easy to carry. They agreed it was a pity none of them would survive to give these valuable conclusions to the others back there.

But after the six had finished their meal and had smoked up all the tobacco of the only man who had any left, they decided that death was not so hard upon them as they first thought. They could still meet it as it should be met. They rose stiffly and found here a spade, there a rifle, and eventually the machine-gun. Under De Barsac's direction they threw up once more a semblance of a bulwark along the top of the hollow, and to show that there was still some fight left in them, fired a few volleys at the Germans, that is to say, all the cartridges they had left, save a full magazine for that last minute when one goes under, killing as many as one can. But whether because the Germans had grown to be a trifle frightened of them, or for some other reason, they received no reply to their taunts beyond an occasional bullet—just a sweet little afternoon when people in cities flock about, straighten their shoulders, sniff the soft atmosphere, and inform each other that Spring is coming. After a time they slumped down where they were, all of them, and stretching out their wet, mud-soaked legs, fell asleep like tired children, and slept on and on until they were awakened in the dark by scores of mysterious figures who patted them on the back, told them they were all heroes, and explained how each time the German artillery had driven them back, and how all they had to do now was to take hold of the rope there and go home to Bray.

So they got up slowly and, hands upon the rope, wandered off. Once they stopped. They heard men digging away busily toward them. They said nothing. They wandered on.

But before the six could reach even the men digging toward them, the darkness was suddenly rent with stupefying explosions, and shell fragments slashed among them. They fell apart, tumbled into shell holes, rose up, fell down again, lost touch with each other, and what became of them all no one will ever know. One or two must have been killed outright; the others must have crawled about in the dark until Fate decided what she wished to do with them. It was rather a sad end; for they deserved better than this, and the Germans did not prevent reinforcements from coming up. But thus ended the six; who they were and what became of them the world will never know.

De Barsac fell flat upon his stomach and put his hands over his head. The ground shook under him. The darkness was a bedlam of endless explosions and death hisses. He rose up again and made a dash for it, a wild, frenzied dash for life and safety. But though he ran on some distance, it was blind work and the ground was littered with obstacles, and suddenly he was lying half buried under a pile of earth. He was in great pain; such that he moaned and moaned; yet he could not move, and now it was less cold and it was morning. Slowly he extricated his right arm, but his left he could not move, and he had to take the dirt away handful by handful, until the sun made his head ache. When his arm was at last uncovered, he could not move it. His whole sleeve was a mass of blood, and the sun had gone of a sudden and it was raining, and the wet ground was tossing him about again like a man in a blanket, and his leg was broken and blood was trickling into his eyes. He moaned upon his arm until the sun again made his head ache, and Jules and his father had disappeared. He asked them to stay there a little longer, but the man next him was so repulsive he could not die thus beside him. Leaning on his right elbow and pushing with his left foot, he moved away inch by inch; only the dead man followed him, or it was his brother, and he was repelled as before, so he took the canteen away from the dead man across his path and drank the stuff down. Then he began to shout at the top of his lungs. A race of bullets swished by over his head. He fell back again on his side and cried weakly into his arm. But presently he crawled on, inch by inch, until even the sun got tired watching him, and he fell down into a sort of trench. There were a lot of dead men there, but all their canteens were empty except one, and he had a great loaf of bread strapped on his knapsack. It was very good inside under the crust.

He sat up and looked around slowly. Just an empty trench, not a living soul, just the dead. How he had got here he could not remember, except that it had taken days, weeks. If his leg were not broken, he might get up now and walk away somewhere. Ah, what dirty luck! As if his arm were not enough! He judged it was late afternoon. He wondered what had happened to the others—well, he would get the machine-gun into place all by himself and kill, kill, right up to the end. Then he remembered that, of course, that was over. Yes, of course.

"I'm out of my head."

He took some more cognac out of the canteen. He found his knife and his emergency roll. Slowly he cut off his sleeve, and slowly over the great bloody hole in his arm he wound the bandage; then he emptied the iodine bottle over it, and yelled and moaned with pain. But by and by he felt better. Some one spoke to him. It was a white face among the black dead men. He gave the fellow cognac. They sat up together and ate bread and drank cognac. They talked together. All the friend had was a bullet through his chest, just a little hole, but he said it hurt him every time he tried to breathe. He belonged to the 45th. The trench here had been taken by the Germans, only the Germans had to abandon it because they had lost a trench over there to the left.

"Yes," said De Barsac. "That was us."

By and by De Barsac asked the friend if he could get up and walk. The friend said he thought he could now. So he got up and fell down, and got up and fell down, until the third time he did not fall.

"Wait," said De Barsac, "my leg's broken."

They helped each other. They went along scraping the sides of the channel. De Barsac moaned in constant agony. But they saw two men with a stretcher in the fields above. De Barsac halloed feebly. The men turned around with a start; then one of them said, with a scowl: "All right, wait a minute." Then there was the ordinary explosion overhead. They saw nothing more of the two men; just a bit of broken stretcher and canvas sticking up out of the ground and a large cloud of dark smoke rolling away fainter and fainter. The trench was muddy. The trench smelled. The whole land smelled. The earth about was all burned yellow. The clay was red. There were boards in the bottom of the trench, but the boards wabbled and one could not hop along them. They slopped and twisted about.

"Here," said the friend, "lean on me some more."

But he only fainted. So they both lay huddled up in the mud of the channel, and death came down very near them both. But De Barsac's face was lying against a tin can in the mud, and he lifted himself up and saw that it was nearly dark and he shivered with cold. He remembered the cognac. He gulped it all down. It hurt his arm, made it throb, throb, throb; but it somehow also made him feel like laughing. So he laughed; then he cried; then he laughed; all because the friend at his side was dead and he loved him. He had not known him very long, but he loved him. He turned the head up and the friend's eyes opened. He was not dead, after all. Quickly De Barsac hunted for the cognac and at last he found it. He was horrified. He had drunk it all and not left the friend any. But there were just a few drops.

"Thanks, old camel," said the friend.

De Barsac slowly got up and, after he had got up, he helped the friend up.

"Come on."

"All right."

"Here, you get on my back."

"No, you get on mine."

But they both fell again. So they decided to crawl along. Only it was growing colder and colder, and the waits were awful. Finally, the white face said:

"I'm—I'm going to sleep a little—you go on—you see—then you call me—then I'll come along."

De Barsac wondered why they had not thought of doing it that way before. He crawled on and on. At last he stopped and called back. The friend did not come the way he said he would. He was asleep of course. De Barsac started back to fetch him, only some men came along and stepped on him until they suddenly stepped off.

"Yes, he's alive."

De Barsac pointed feebly up the channel.

"He's back there," he said.

"Who?"

"The friend."

"He's delirious," said a voice.

"Well, pass him back to the stretcher-bearers and look lively with those machine-guns."

The dressing-station was all under ground and lined with straw. It was very warm, only it was also very crowded. They gave him some hot soup with vegetables in it. He lay back on the stretcher and perspired; and though he was now in very great pain, he said nothing, because he had nothing to say. The surgeon, sleeves rolled up, bent over him. He set his leg and slapped plaster about. He swabbed his head and made him nearly scream. Then he unwound the bandage on his arm and swore and stood up and said: "Too late. Put on the tag, 'Operate at once.' " It was cold between the two wheels under the open stars amid the cigarette smoke, but the ambulances in Bray made a powerful noise, and through the darkness a sergeant looked at him under a lantern and said impatiently: "Well, I don't give a damn, there isn't an inch of space left. Fire him along to Villers-Bretonneux with that convoy that's starting." The ambulance rocked and bounced over the roads, and it was twice as cold as before. He had not enough blankets. The ambulance smelled so he knew the man to his left must be dead; yes, the man to his left, not the man above, for the man above from time to time dripped hot blood upon him, now upon his neck, now upon his face. In the big shed at Villers-Bretonneux it was warm again, and he lay there upon the straw with the others while crowds of peasant people stared at them. One woman came up and offered him half an orange. He did not take it. Another woman said: "He's out of his head, poor fellow." He said: "No, I'm not." After the man on the stretcher next him had told him he was wounded in the stomach, left shoulder, and both legs, the man on the stretcher next him asked him where he came from and how things were getting on there. He said: "All right." Then the man on the stretcher next him said weakly: "Well, you seem to have picked up all the mud there is up there." So he said: "Oh, there's plenty left!" and a neat little man in black, with a red ribbon in his buttonhole, shook his head and said to a large man staring with a heavy scowl: "They're all that way, you know; a joke on their lips up to the end."

They carried him out through the crowd, and when he was opposite the bloody table under the great arc-light, the men carrying him had to stop a second and the doctor said to the man holding the end of the leg: "Bend down, idiot, haven't you ever sawed wood?" And he saw that there were beads of perspiration upon the doctor's forehead, and he wondered why. In the train it was very, very warm, only it smelled dreadfully—that same smell. He knew now it was the man in the bunk next to him that was dead, and he wanted to tell the attendant so, only the shadows on the wooden ceiling danced about as the train rushed along over bridges and through tunnels. The shadows danced about, and sometimes they were horsemen on chargers and sometimes they were just great clouds flying out across the ocean, and all the time that the shadows danced about and the train rushed on and on a man in the other end of the compartment yelled and swore. But although he called the attendants all the names a man has ever called another, the attendants did not move. One said:

"Well, if they do shunt us over on to that other service, that'll mean we'll get down to Paris now and then."

And the first man answered:

"Oh, well, anything for a change—pass me the morphine again, will you, if you're through with it."

The train stopped, and every one wanted to know where they were. One of the attendants told them, "Amiens." He was taken out slowly and carried before a man with a glossy, black beard, smoking a pipe, who read the tag on his buttonhole and wrote something on a sheet of paper. They took him out into the cold, biting wind of a railway yard and carried him across railway tracks and set the stretcher down in pools of black mud, and argued whose turn it was, while a long freight-train rolled slowly by and a man blew a whistle. The ambulance bobbed lightly over cobbles amid the clang of street-cars and the thousand noises of a city. This ambulance also smelled that same smell; but it could not be the man next him, for he was all alone. Then the ambulance ran along a smooth drive and stopped, and the flaps were opened and he was lifted out and carried into a long hallway, where a small man in red slippers scampered about and told others to come, and a white-hooded woman bent over him.

"What's the matter with him?"

"Operation."

"Yes—his left arm—the smell is sufficient indication. George, tell the doctor not to go away."

The white-hooded woman again leaned over him. Her face was wrinkled and tired, but her eyes were very beautiful—they were so gentle and so sad.

"How do you feel?"

"Yes," he mumbled.

"Poor boy! What's your name?"

"Pierre De Barsac."

She took his hand gently and held it.

"Well, Pierre, don't worry. We are going to take care of you."

A little later she said:

"Poor fellow! Are you suffering?"

Tears came into his eyes and he nodded his head.

They carried him up-stairs. They went up slowly, very carefully, and as they turned the corners of the staircase the eyes of the little man with the red slippers glittered and strained over the end of the stretcher. They undressed him. They washed him. They put him to bed. They unwound his arm. Then they stood away and stopped talking. They left him alone with a great wad of damp cotton upon his arm until the doctor came and said:

"My boy, we've got to amputate your left arm at the shoulder."

"At the shoulder," he repeated mechanically.

"Yes, it's the only thing that will save you. What's your profession?"

"Lawyer."

The doctor smiled pleasantly.

"Oh, then you are all right! An arm the less will be a distinction."

They went away. He turned over a little and looked at his arm. He realized that this was the dead thing he had so often smelled. The arm was all brown. It crackled under his finger; then came the large cotton wad where there were strips of black flesh. The hand was crumpled up like a fallen leaf. He saw the scar on his forefinger where, as a little boy, he had cut through the orange too swiftly. What a scene that was, and his mother was dead now, and his father was very old, and the hand now was going to be taken away from him! He turned his head back and cried weakly, not on account of his hand, but because he was in such pain, his arm, his leg, his head, everything. They rolled him into another room. They fussed about him. They hurt him dreadfully; but he said nothing, because he had nothing to say. Then he was back there again, beside the lieutenant, only the machine-gun jammed and he had to break the leg off and use it against the hordes of pig-eaters, and smoke, more smoke, down one's nostrils, and then it was awful, awful, never like this, and he clutched the pig-eater by the throat and swore, swore, until now more smoke came rolling into his nostrils, and the white-hooded nurse was standing by his bed.

She went away; and when he woke up again, he was all alone. There was a bandage upon his left arm; no, his left shoulder. His arm hurt much less; he felt much better. By and by he moved his right hand over. The sleeve of the nightgown was empty.

He lay there quietly a long time and looked up into the sky through some pine boughs swaying in the wind. They reminded him of other trees he knew of—trees way back there in Brittany by the seaside where he was born. They swayed beautifully to and fro, and every so often they bent over and swished against the window-pane.

Presently he smiled, smiled quietly, happily. Life, when one can live it, is such a really wonderful thing.

The March to the Sea (400 B. C.)

BY

XENOPHON

The *Anabasis* is the epic story of the retreat of ten thousand stranded Greek soldiers from the heart of Persia back home to Greece. They had gone to Persia to help Cyrus, the younger, in his fight to dethrone his brother, King Artaxerxes. Cyrus was defeated and slain in battle and the Greeks then negotiated for safe conduct out of Artaxerxes' dominions. He, however, treacherously caused the Greek generals to be seized and murdered. The ten thousand, now leaderless and stranded, faced the ordeal of a long march, without supplies, harassed by hostile troops and savage native elements, across rivers and through mountain passes, to the Black Sea and onward, home. They elected Xenophon leader and this is his account of the first and most difficult stage of their journey—the march to the sea (Book IV).

THE resolution to which they came was that they must force a passage through the hills into the territory of the Kurds; since, according to what their informants told them, when they had once passed these, they would find themselves in Armenia—the rich and large territory governed by Orontas; and from Armenia, it would be easy to proceed in any direction whatever. Thereupon they offered sacrifice, so as to be ready to start on the march as soon as the right moment appeared to have arrived. Their chief fear was that the high pass over the mountains might be occupied in advance: and a general order was issued, that after supper every one should get his kit together for starting, and repose, in readiness to follow as soon as the word of command was given.

I.—It was now about the last watch, and enough of the night remained to allow them to cross the valley under cover of darkness; when, at the word of command, they rose and set off on their march, reaching the mountains at daybreak. At this stage of the march Cheirisophus, at the head of his own division, with the whole of the light troops, led the van, while Xenophon followed behind with the heavy infantry of the rearguard, but without any light troops, since there seemed to be no danger of pursuit or attack from the rear, while they were making their way up hill. Cheirisophus reached the summit without any of the enemy perceiving him. Then he led on slowly, and the rest of the army followed, wave upon wave, cresting the summit and descending into the villages which nestled in the hollows and recesses of the hills.

Thereupon the Carduchians abandoned their dwelling-places, and with

From: *Anabasis, Book IV.*

their wives and children fled to the mountains; so there was plenty of provisions to be got for the mere trouble of taking, and the homesteads too were well supplied with a copious store of bronze vessels and utensils which the Hellenes kept their hands off, abstaining at the same time from all pursuit of the folk themselves, gently handling them, in hopes that the Carduchians might be willing to give them friendly passage through their country, since they too were enemies of the king: only they helped themselves to such provisions as fell in their way, which indeed was a sheer necessity. But the Carduchians neither gave ear, when they called to them, nor showed any other friendly sign; and now, as the last of the Hellenes descended into the villages from the pass, they were already in the dark, since, owing to the narrowness of the road, the whole day had been spent in the ascent and descent. At that instant a party of the Carduchians, who had collected, made an attack on the hindmost men, killing some and wounding others with stones and arrows—though it was quite a small body who attacked. The fact was, the approach of the Hellenic army had taken them by surprise; if, however, they had mustered in larger force at this time, the chances are that a large portion of the army would have been annihilated. As it was, they got into quarters, and bivouacked in the villages that night, while the Carduchians kept many watch-fires blazing in a circle on the mountains, and kept each other in sight all round.

But with the dawn the generals and officers of the Hellenes met and resolved to proceed, taking only the necessary number of stout baggage animals, and leaving the weaklings behind. They resolved further to let go free all the lately-captured slaves in the host; for the pace of the march was necessarily rendered slow by the quantity of animals and prisoners, and the number of non-combatants in attendance on these was excessive, while, with such a crowd of human beings to satisfy, twice the amount of provisions had to be procured and carried. These resolutions passed, they caused a proclamation by herald to be made for their enforcement.

When they had breakfasted and the march recommenced, the generals planted themselves a little to one side in a narrow place, and when they found any of the aforesaid slaves or other property still retained, they confiscated them. The soldiers yielded obedience, except where some smuggler, prompted by desire of a good-looking boy or woman, managed to make off with his prize. During this day they contrived to get along after a fashion, now fighting and now resting. But on the next day they were visited by a great storm, in spite of which they were obliged to continue the march, owing to insufficiency of provisions. Cheirisophus was as usual leading in front, while Xenophon headed the rearguard, when the enemy began a violent and sustained attack. At one narrow place after another they came up quite close, pouring in volleys of arrows and sling-stones, so that the Hellenes had no choice but to make sallies in pursuit and then again recoil, making but very little progress. Over and over again Xenophon would send an order to the front to slacken pace, when the enemy were pressing their attack severely. As a rule, when the word was so passed up, Cheirisophus slackened; but sometimes instead of slackening, Cheirisophus quickened, sending down a counter-order to the rear to follow on quickly. It was clear that there was something or other happening, but there was no time to go to the front and discover the cause of the hurry. Under these circumstances the march, at any rate in the rear, became very like a rout, and here a brave man lost his life, Cleonymus the Laconian, shot with an arrow in the ribs right through shield and corselet, as also Basias, an Arcadian, shot clean through the head.

As soon as they reached a halting-place, Xenophon, without more ado, came up to Cheirisophus, and took him to task for not having waited, "whereby," said he, "we were forced to fight and flee at the same moment; and now it has cost us the lives of two fine fellows; they are dead, and we were not able to pick up their bodies or bury them." Cheirisophus answered: "Look up there," pointing as he spoke to the mountain, "do you see how inaccessible it all is? only this one road, which you see, going straight up, and on it all that crowd of men who have seized and are guarding the single exit. That is why I hastened on, and why I could not wait for you, hoping to be beforehand with them yonder in seizing the pass: the guides we have got say there is no other way." And Xenophon replied: "But I have got two prisoners also; the enemy annoyed us so much that we laid an ambuscade for them, which also gave us time to recover our breaths; we killed some of them, and did our best to catch one or two alive—for this very reason—that we might have guides who knew the country, to depend upon."

The two were brought up at once and questioned separately: "Did they know of any other road than the one visible?" The first said *no;* and in spite of all sorts of terrors applied to extract a better answer—*no,* he persisted. When nothing could be got out of him, he was killed before the eyes of his fellow. This latter then explained: "Yonder man said he did not know, because he has got a daughter married to a husband in those parts. I can take you," he added, "by a good road, practicable even for beasts." And when asked whether there was any point on it difficult to pass, he replied that there was a col which it would be impossible to pass unless it were occupied in advance.

Then it was resolved to summon the officers of the light infantry and some of those of the heavy infantry, and to acquaint them with the state of affairs, and ask them whether any of them were minded to distinguish themselves, and would step forward as volunteers on an expedition. Two or three heavy infantry soldiers stepped forward at once—two Arcadians, Aristonymus of Methydrium, and Agasias of Stymphalus—and in emulation of these, a third, also an Arcadian, Callimachus from Parrhasia, who said he was ready to go, and would get volunteers from the whole army to join him. "I know," he added, "there will be no lack of youngsters to follow where I lead." After that they asked, "Were there any captains of light infantry willing to accompany the expedition?" Aristeas, a Chian, who on several occasions proved his usefulness to the army on such service, volunteered.

II.—It was already late afternoon, when they ordered the storming party to take a snatch of food and set off; then they bound the guide and handed him over to them. The agreement was, that if they succeeded in taking the summit they were to guard the position that night, and at daybreak to give a signal by bugle. At this signal the party on the summit were to attack the enemy in occupation of the visible pass, while the generals with the main body would bring up their succours; making their way up with what speed they might. With this understanding, off they set, two thousand strong; and there was a heavy downpour of rain, but Xenophon, with his rearguard, began advancing to the visible pass, so that the enemy might fix his attention on this road, and the party creeping round might, as much as possible, elude observation. Now when the rearguard, so advancing, had reached a ravine which they must cross in order to strike up the steep, at that instant the barbarians began rolling down great boulders, each a wagon load, some larger, some smaller; against the rocks they crashed and splintered flying like slingstones in every direction—so that it was absolutely out of the question even to approach the entrance of the pass. Some of the officers finding themselves baulked at this point, kept trying other ways, nor did they desist till darkness set in; and then, when they thought they would not be seen retiring, they returned to supper. Some of them who had been on duty in the rearguard had had no breakfast (it so happened). However, the enemy never ceased rolling down their stones all through the night, as was easy to infer from the booming sound.

The party with the guide made a circuit and surprised the enemy's guards seated round their fire, and after killing some, and driving out the rest, took their places, thinking that they were in possession of the height. As a matter of fact they were not, for above them, lay a breastlike hill skirted by the narrow road on which they had found the guards seated. Still, from the spot in question there was an approach to the enemy, who were seated on the pass before mentioned.

Here then they passed the night, but at the first glimpse of dawn they marched stealthily and in battle order against the enemy. There was a mist, so that they could get quite close without being observed. But as soon as they caught sight of one another, the trumpet sounded, and with a loud cheer they rushed upon the fellows, who did not wait their coming, but left the road and made off; with the loss of only a few lives however, so nimble were they. Cheirisophus and his men, catching the sound of the bugle, charged up by the well-marked road, while others of the generals pushed their way up by pathless routes, where each division chanced to be; the men mounting as they were best able, and hoisting one another up by means of their spears; and these were the first to unite with the party who had already taken the position by storm. Xenophon, with the rearguard, followed the path which the party with the guide had taken, since it was easiest for the beasts of burthen; one half of his men he had posted in rear of the baggage animals; the other half he had with himself. In their course they encountered a crest above the road, occupied by the enemy, whom they must either dislodge or be themselves cut off from the rest of the Hellenes. The men by themselves could have taken the same route as the rest, but the baggage animals could not mount by any other way than this.

Here then, with shouts of encouragement to each other, they dashed at the hill with their storming columns, not from all sides, but leaving an avenue of escape for the enemy, if he chose to avail himself of it. For a while, as the men scrambled up where each best could, the natives kept up a fire of arrows and darts, yet did not receive them at close quarters, but presently left the position in flight. No sooner, however, were the Hellenes safely past this crest, than they came in sight of another in front of them, also occupied, and deemed it advisable to storm it also. But now it struck Xenophon that if they left the ridge just taken unprotected in their rear, the enemy might re-occupy it and attack the baggage animals as they filed past, presenting a long extended line owing to the narrowness of the road by which they made their way. To obviate this, he left some officers in charge of the ridge—Cephisodorus, son of Cephisophon, an Athenian; Amphicrates, the son of Amphidemus, an Athenian; and Archagoras, an Argive exile—while he in person with the rest of the men attacked the second ridge; this they took in the same fashion, only to find that they had still a third knoll left, far the steepest of the three. This was none other than the mamelon mentioned as above the outpost, which had been captured over their fire by the volunteer storming party in the night. But when the Hellenes were close, the natives, to the astonishment of all, without a struggle deserted the knoll. It was conjectured that they had left their position from fear of being encircled and besieged, but the fact was that they, from their higher ground, had been able to see what was going on in the rear, and had all made off in this fashion to attack the rearguard.

So then Xenophon, with the youngest men, scaled up to the top, leaving orders to the rest to march on slowly, so as to allow the hindmost companies to unite with them; they were to advance by the road, and when they reached the level to ground arms. Meanwhile the Argive Archagoras arrived, in full flight, with the announcement that they had been dislodged from the first ridge, and that Cephisodorus and Amphicrates were slain, with a number of others besides, all in fact who had not jumped down the crags and so reached the rearguard. After this achievement the barbarians came to a crest facing the mamelon, and Xenophon held a colloquy with them by means of an interpreter, to negotiate a truce, and demanded back the dead bodies. These they agreed to restore if he would not burn their houses, and to these terms Xenophon agreed. Meanwhile, as the rest of the army filed past, and the colloquy was proceeding, all the people of the place had time to gather gradually, and the enemy formed; and as soon as the Hellenes began to descend from the mamelon to join the others where the troops were halted, on rushed the foe, in full force, with hue and cry. They reached the summit of the mamelon from which Xenophon was descending, and began rolling down crags. One man's leg was crushed to pieces. Xenophon was left by his shield-bearer, who carried off his shield, but Eurylochus of Lusia, an Arcadian hoplite, ran up to him, and threw his shield in front to protect both of them; so the two together beat a retreat, and so too the rest, and joined the serried ranks of the main body.

After this the whole Hellenic force united, and took up their quarters there in numerous beautiful dwellings, with an ample store of provisions, for there was wine so plentiful that they had it in cemented cisterns. Xenophon and Cheirisophus arranged to recover the dead, and in return restored the guide; afterwards they did everything for the dead, according to the means at their disposal, with the customary honours paid to good men.

Next day they set off without a guide; and the enemy, by keeping up a continuous battle and occupying in advance every narrow place, obstructed passage after passage. Accordingly, whenever the van was obstructed, Xenophon, from behind, made a dash up the hills and broke the barricade, and freed the vanguard by endeavouring to get above the obstructing enemy. Whenever the rear was the point attacked, Cheirisophus, in the same way, made a détour, and by endeavouring to mount higher than the barricaders, freed the passage for the rear rank; and in this way, turn and turn about, they rescued each other, and paid unflinching attention to their mutual needs. At times it happened that, the relief party having mounted, encountered considerable annoyance in their descent from the barbarians, who were so agile that they allowed them to come up quite close, before they turned back, and still escaped, partly no doubt because the only weapons they had to carry were bows and slings.

They were, moreover, excellent archers, using bows nearly three cubits long and arrows more than two cubits. When discharging the arrow, they drew the string by getting a purchase with the left foot planted forward on the lower end of the bow. The arrows pierced through shield and cuirass, and the Hellenes, when they got hold of them, used them as javelins, fitting them to their thongs. In these districts the Cretans were highly serviceable. They were under the command of Stratocles, a Cretan.

III.—During this day they bivouacked in the villages which lie above the plain of the river Centrites, which is about two hundred feet broad. It is the frontier river between Armenia and the country of the Carduchians. Here the Hellenes recruited themselves, and the sight of the plain filled them with joy, for the river was but six or seven furlongs distant from the mountains of the Carduchians. For the moment then they bivouacked right happily; they had their provisions, they had also many memories of the labours that were now passed; seeing that the last seven days spent in traversing the country of the Carduchians had been one long continuous battle, which had cost them more suffering than the whole of their troubles at the hands of the king and Tissaphernes put together. As though they were truly quit of them forever, they laid their heads to rest in sweet content.

But with the morrow's dawn they espied horsemen at a certain point across the river, armed *cap-à-pie*, as if they meant to dispute the passage.

Infantry, too, drawn up in line upon the banks above the cavalry, threatened to prevent them debouching into Armenia. These troops were Armenian and Mardian and Chaldaean mercenaries belonging to Orontas and Artuchas. The last of the three, the Chaldaeans, were said to be a free and brave set of people. They were armed with long wicker shields and lances. The banks before named on which they were drawn up were a hundred yards or more distant from the river, and the single road which was visible was one leading upwards and looking like a regular artificially constructed highway. At this point the Hellenes endeavoured to cross, but on their making the attempt the water proved to be more than breast-deep, and the river bed was rough with great slippery stones, and as to holding their arms in the water, it was out of the question—the stream swept them away—or if they tried to carry them over the head, the body was left exposed to the arrows and other missiles; accordingly they turned back and encamped there by the bank of the river.

At the point where they had themselves been last night, up on the mountains, they could see the Carduchians collected in large numbers and under arms. A shadow of deep despair again descended on their souls, whichever way they turned their eyes—in front lay the river so difficult to ford; over, on the other side, a new enemy threatening to bar the passage; on the hills behind, the Carduchians ready to fall upon their rear should they once again attempt to cross. Thus for this day and night they halted, sunk in perplexity. But Xenophon had a dream. In his sleep he thought that he was bound in fetters, but these, of their own accord, fell from off him, so that he was loosed, and could stretch his legs as freely as he wished. So at the first glimpse of daylight he came to Cheirisophus and told him that he had hopes that all things would go well, and related to him his dream.

The other was well pleased, and with the first faint gleam of dawn the generals all were present and did sacrifice; and the victims were favourable at the first essay. Retiring from the sacrifice, the generals and officers issued an order to the troops to take their breakfasts; and while Xenophon was taking his, two young men came running up to him, for every one knew that, breakfasting or supping, he was always accessible, or that even if asleep any one was welcome to awaken him who had anything to say bearing on the business of war. What the two young men had at this time to say was that they had been collecting brushwood for fire, and had presently espied on the opposite side, in among some rocks which came down to the river's brink, an old man and some women and little girls depositing, as it would appear, bags of clothes in a cavernous rock. When they saw them, it struck them that it was safe to cross; in any case the enemy's cavalry could not approach at this point. So they stripped naked, expecting to have to swim for it, and with their long knives in their hands began crossing, but going forward crossed without being wet up to the fork. Once across they captured the clothes, and came back again.

Accordingly Xenophon at once poured out a libation himself, and bade the two young fellows fill the cup and pray to the gods, who showed to him this vision and to them a passage, to bring all other blessings for them to accomplishment. When he had poured out the libations, he at once led the two young men to Cheirisophus, and they repeated to him their story. Cheirisophus, on hearing it, offered libations also, and when they had performed them, they sent a general order to the troops to pack up ready for starting, while they themselves called a meeting of the generals and took counsel how they might best effect a passage, so as to overpower the enemy in front without suffering any loss from the men behind. And they resolved that Cheirisophus should lead the van and cross with half the army, the other half still remaining behind under Xenophon, while the baggage animals and the mob of sutlers were to cross between the two divisions.

When all was duly ordered the move began, the young men pioneering them, and keeping the river on their left. It was about four furlongs' march to the crossing, and as they moved along the bank, the squadrons of cavalry kept pace with them on the opposite side.

But when they had reached a point in a line with the ford, and the cliff-like banks of the river, they ordered arms, and first Cheirisophus himself placed a wreath upon his brows, and throwing off his cloak, resumed his arms, passing the order to all the rest to do the same, and bade the captains form their companies in open order in deep columns, some to left and some to right of himself. Meanwhile the soothsayers were slaying a victim over the river, and the enemy were letting fly their arrows and slingstones; but as yet they were out of range. As soon as the victims were favourable, all the soldiers began singing the battle hymn, and with the notes of the paean mingled the shouting of the men accompanied by the shriller chant of the women, for there were many women in the camp.

So Cheirisophus with his detachment stept in. But Xenophon, taking the most active-bodied of the rearguard, began running back at full speed to the passage facing the egress into the hills of Armenia, making a feint of crossing at that point to intercept their cavalry on the river bank. The enemy, seeing Cheirisophus's detachment easily crossing the stream, and Xenophon's men racing back, were seized with the fear of being intercepted, and fled at full speed in the direction of the road which emerges from the stream. But when they were come opposite to it they raced up hill towards their mountains. Then Lycius, who commanded the cavalry, and Aeschines, who was in command of the division of light infantry attached to Cheirisophus, no sooner saw them fleeing so lustily than they were after them, and the soldiers shouted not to fall behind, but to follow them right up to the mountains. Cheirisophus, on getting across, forbore to pursue the cavalry, but advanced by the bluffs which reached to the river to attack the enemy overhead. And these, seeing their own cavalry fleeing, seeing also the heavy infantry advancing upon them, abandoned the heights above the river.

Xenophon, as soon as he saw that things were going well on the other side, fell back with all speed to join the troops engaged in crossing, for by this time the Carduchians were well in sight, descending into the plain to attack their rear.

Cheirisophus was in possession of the higher ground, and Lycius, with his little squadron, in an attempt to follow up the pursuit, had captured some stragglers of their baggage-bearers, and with them some handsome apparel and drinking-cups. The baggage animals of the Hellenes and the mob of non-combatants were just about to cross, when Xenophon turned his troops right about to face the Carduchians. *Vis-à-vis* he formed his line, passing the order to the captains each to form his company into sections, and to deploy them into line to the left, the captains of companies and lieutenants in command of sections to advance to meet the Carduchians, while the rear leaders would keep their position facing the river. But when the Carduchians saw the rearguard so stript of the mass, and looking now like a mere handful of men, they advanced all the more quickly, singing certain songs the while. Then, as matters were safe with him, Cheirisophus sent back the peltasts and slingers and archers to join Xenophon, with orders to carry out his instructions. They were in the act of recrossing, when Xenophon, who saw their intention, sent a messenger across, bidding them wait there at the river's brink without crossing; but as soon as he and his detachment began to cross they were to step in facing him in two flanking divisions right and left of them, as if in the act of crossing; the javelin men with their javelins on the thong, and the bowmen with their arrows on the string; but they were not to advance far into the stream. The order passed to his own men was: "Wait till you are within sling-shot, and the shield rattles, then sound the paean and charge the enemy. As soon as he turns, and the bugle from the river sounds for 'the attack,' you will face to the right about, the rear rank leading, and the whole detachment falling back and crossing the river as quickly as possible, every one preserving his original rank, so as to avoid trammelling one another: the bravest man is he who gets to the other side first."

The Carduchians, seeing that the remnant left was the merest handful (for many even of those whose duty it was to remain had gone off in their anxiety to protect their beasts of burden, or their personal kit, or their mistresses), bore down upon them valorously, and opened fire with sling-stones and arrows. But the Hellenes, raising the battle hymn, dashed at them at a run, and they did not await them; armed well enough for mountain warfare, and with a view to sudden attack followed by speedy flight, they were not by any means sufficiently equipped for an engagement at close quarters. At this instant the signal of the bugle was heard. Its notes added wings to the flight of the barbarians, but the Hellenes turned right about in the opposite direction, and betook themselves to the river with what speed they might. Some of the enemy, here a man and there another, perceived, and running back to the river, let fly their arrows and wounded a few; but the majority, even when the Hellenes were well across, were still to be seen pursuing their flight. The detachment which came to meet

Xenophon's men, carried away by their valour, advanced further than they had need to, and had to cross back again in the rear of Xenophon's men, and of these too a few were wounded.

IV.—The passage effected, they fell into line about midday, and marched through Armenian territory, one long plain with smooth rolling hillocks, not less than five parasangs in distance; for owing to the wars of this people with the Carduchians there were no villages near the river. The village eventually reached was large, and possessed a palace belonging to the satrap, and most of the houses were crowned with turrets; provisions were plentiful.

From this village they marched two stages—ten parasangs—until they had surmounted the sources of the river Tigris; and from this point they marched three stages—fifteen parasangs—to the river Teleboas. This was a fine stream, though not large, and there were many villages about it. The district was named Western Armenia. The lieutenant-governor of it was Tiribazus, the king's friend, and whenever the latter paid a visit, he alone had the privilege of mounting the king upon his horse. This officer rode up to the Hellenes with a body of cavalry, and sending forward an interpreter, stated that he desired a colloquy with the leaders. The generals resolved to hear what he had to say; and advancing on their side to within speaking distance, they demanded what he wanted. He replied that he wished to make a treaty with them, in accordance with which he on his side would abstain from injuring the Hellenes, if they would not burn his houses, but merely take such provisions as they needed. This proposal satisfied the generals, and a treaty was made on the terms suggested.

From this place they marched three stages—fifteen parasangs—through plain country, Tiribazus the while keeping close behind with his own forces more than a mile off. Presently they reached a palace with villages clustered round about it, which were full of supplies in great variety. But while they were encamping in the night there was a heavy fall of snow, and in the morning it was resolved to billet out the different regiments, with their generals, throughout the villages. There was no enemy in sight, and the proceeding seemed prudent, owing to the quantity of snow. In these quarters they had for provisions all the good things there are—sacrificial beasts, corn, old wines with an exquisite bouquet, dried grapes, and vegetables of all sorts. But some of the stragglers from the camp reported having seen an army, and the blaze of many watchfires in the night. Accordingly the generals concluded that it was not prudent to separate their quarters in this way, and a resolution was passed to bring the troops together again. After that they reunited, the more so that the weather promised to be fine with a clear sky; but while they lay there in open quarters, during the night down came so thick a fall of snow that it completely covered up the stacks of arms and the men themselves lying down. It cramped and crippled the baggage animals; and there was great unreadiness to get up, so gently fell the snow as they lay there warm and comfortable, and formed a blanket, except where it slipped off the sleeper's shoulders; and it was not until Xenophon roused himself to get up, and, without his cloak on, began to split wood, that quickly first one and then another got up, and taking the log away from him, fell to splitting. Thereat the rest followed suit, got up, and began kindling fires and oiling their bodies, for there was a scented unguent to be found there in abundance, which they used instead of oil. It was made from pig's fat, sesame, bitter almonds, and turpentine. There was a sweet oil also to be found, made of the same ingredients.

After this it was resolved that they must again separate their quarters and get under cover in the villages. At this news the soldiers, with much joy and shouting, rushed upon the covered houses and the provisions; but all who in their blind folly had set fire to the houses when they left them before, now paid the penalty in the poor quarters they got. From this place one night they sent off a party under Democrates, a Temenite, up into the mountains, where the stragglers reported having seen watchfires. The leader selected was a man whose judgment might be depended upon to verify the truth of the matter. With a happy gift to distinguish between fact and fiction, he had often been successfully appealed to. He went and reported that he had seen no watchfires, but he had got a man, whom he brought back with him, carrying a Persian bow and quiver, and a sagaris or battle-axe like those worn by the Amazons. When asked "from what country he came," the prisoner answered that he was "a Persian, and was going from the army of Tiribazus to get provisions." They next asked him "how large the army was, and for what object it had been collected." His answer was that "it consisted of Tiribazus at the head of his own forces, and aided by some Chalybian and Taochian mercenaries. Tiribazus had got it together," he added, "meaning to attack the Hellenes on the high mountain pass, in a defile which was the sole passage."

When the generals heard this news, they resolved to collect the troops, and they set off at once, taking the prisoner to act as guide, and leaving a garrison behind with Sophaenetus the Stymphalian in command of those who remained in the camp. As soon as they had begun to cross the hills, the light infantry, advancing in front and catching sight of the camp, did not wait for the heavy infantry, but with a loud shout rushed upon the enemy's entrenchment. The natives, hearing the din and clatter, did not care to stop, but took rapidly to their heels. But, for all their expedition, some of them were killed, and as many as twenty horses were captured, with the tent of Tiribazus, and its contents, silver-footed couches and goblets, besides certain persons styling themselves the butlers and bakers. As soon as the generals of the heavy infantry division had learnt the news, they resolved to return to the camp with all speed, for fear of an attack being made on the remnant left behind. The recall was sounded and the retreat commenced; the camp was reached the same day.

v.—The next day it was resolved that they should set off with all possible speed, before the enemy had time to collect and occupy the defile. Having got their kit and baggage together, they at once began their march through deep snow with several guides, and, crossing the high pass the same day on which Tiribazus was to have attacked them, got safely into cantonments. From this point they marched three desert stages—fifteen parasangs—to the river Euphrates, and crossed it in water up to the waist. The sources of the river were reported to be at no great distance. From this place they marched through deep snow over a flat country three stages—fifteen parasangs. The last of these marches was trying, with the north wind blowing in their teeth, drying up everything and benumbing the men. Here one of the seers suggested to them to do sacrifice to Boreas, and sacrifice was done. The effect was obvious to all in the diminished fierceness of the blast. But there was six feet of snow, so that many of the baggage animals and slaves were lost, and about thirty of the men themselves.

They spent the whole night in kindling fires; for there was fortunately no dearth of wood at the halting-place; only those who came late into camp had no wood. Accordingly those who had arrived a good while and had kindled fires were not for allowing these late-comers near their fires, unless they would in return give a share of their corn or of any other victuals they might have. Here then a general exchange of goods was set up. Where the fire was kindled the snow melted, and great trenches formed themselves down to the bare earth, and here it was possible to measure the depth of the snow.

Leaving these quarters, they marched the whole of the next day over snow, and many of the men were afflicted with "boulimia" (or hunger-faintness). Xenophon, who was guarding the rear, came upon some men who had dropt down, and he did not know what ailed them; but some one who was experienced in such matters suggested to him that they had evidently got boulimia; and if they got something to eat, they would revive. Then he went the round of the baggage train, and laying an embargo on any eatables he could see, doled out with his own hands, or sent off other able-bodied agents to distribute to the sufferers, who as soon as they had taken a mouthful got on their legs again and continued the march.

On and on they marched, and about dusk Cheirisophus reached a village, and surprised some women and girls who had come from the village to fetch water at the fountain outside the stockade. These asked them who they were. The interpreters answered for them in Persian: "They were on their way from the king to the satrap;" in reply to which the women gave them to understand that the satrap was not at home, but was away a parasang farther on. As it was late they entered with the water-carriers within the stockade to visit the headman of the village. Accordingly Cheirisophus and as many of the troops as were able got into cantonments there, while the rest of the soldiers—those namely who were unable to complete the march—had to spend the night out, without food and without fire; under the circumstances some of the men perished.

On the heels of the army hung perpetually bands of the enemy, snatching away disabled baggage animals and fighting with each other over the carcases. And in its track not seldom were left to their fate disabled soldiers, struck down with snow-blindness or with toes mortified by frost-bite. As to the eyes, it was some alleviation against the snow to march with something black before them; for their feet, the only remedy was to keep in motion without stopping for an instant, and to loose the sandal at night. If they went to sleep with the sandals on, the thong worked into the feet, and the sandals were frozen fast to them. This was partly due to the fact that, since their old sandals had failed, they wore untanned brogues made of newly-flayed ox-hides. It was owing to some such dire necessity that a party of men fell out and were left behind, and seeing a black-looking patch of ground where the snow had evidently disappeared, they conjectured it must have been melted; and this was actually so, owing to a spring of some sort which was to be seen steaming up in a dell close by. To this they had turned aside and sat down, and were loth to go a step further. But Xeno-phon, with his rearguard, perceived them, and begged and implored them by all manner of means not to be left behind, telling them that the enemy were after them in large packs pursuing; and he ended by growing angry. They merely bade him put a knife to their throats; not one step farther would they stir. Then it seemed best to frighten the pursuing enemy if possible, and prevent their falling upon the invalids. It was already dusk, and the pursuers were advancing with much noise and hubbub, wrangling and disputing over their spoils. Then all of a sudden the rearguard, in the plenitude of health and strength, sprang up out of their lair and ran upon the enemy, whilst those weary wights bawled out as loud as their sick throats could sound, and clashed their spears against their shields; and the enemy in terror hurled themselves through the snow into the dell, and not one of them ever uttered a sound again.

Xenophon and his party, telling the sick folk that next day people would come for them, set off, and before they had gone half a mile they fell in with some soldiers who had laid down to rest on the snow with their cloaks wrapped round them, but never a guard was established, and they made them get up. Their explanation was that those in front would not move on. Passing by this group he sent forward the strongest of his light infantry in advance, with orders to find out what the stoppage was. They reported that the whole army lay reposing in the same fashion. That being so, Xenophon's men had nothing for it but to bivouac in the open air also, without fire and supperless, merely posting what pickets they could under the circumstances. But as soon as it drew towards day, Xenophon despatched the youngest of his men to the sick folk behind, with orders to make them get up and force them to proceed. Meanwhile Cheirisophus had sent some of his men quartered in the village to enquire how they fared in the rear; they were overjoyed to see them, and handed over the sick folk to them to carry into camp, while they themselves continued their march forwards, and ere twenty furlongs were past reached the village in which Cheirisophus was quartered. As soon as the two divisions were met, the resolution was come to that it would be safe to billet the regiments throughout the villages; Cheirisophus remained where he was, while the rest drew lots for the villages in sight, and then, with their several detachments, marched off to their respective destinations.

It was here that Polycrates, an Athenian and captain of a company, asked for leave of absence—he wished to be off on a quest of his own; and putting himself at the head of the active men of the division, he ran to the village which had been allotted to Xenophon. He surprised within it the villagers with their headman, and seventeen young horses which were being reared as a tribute for the king, and, last of all, the headman's own daughter, a young bride only eight days wed. Her husband had gone off to chase hares, and so he escaped being taken with the other villagers. The houses were underground structures with an aperture like the mouth of a well by which to enter, but they were broad and spacious below. The entrance for the beasts of burden was dug out, but the human occupants descended by a ladder. In these dwellings were to be found goats and sheep and cattle, and cocks and hens, with their various progeny. The flocks and herds were all reared under cover upon green food. There were stores within of wheat and barley and vegetables, and wine made from barley in great big bowls; the grains of barley malt lay floating in the beverage up to the lip of the vessel, and reeds lay in them, some longer, some shorter, without joints; when you were thirsty you must take one of these into your mouth, and suck. The beverage without admixture of water was very strong, and of a delicious flavour to certain palates, but the taste must be acquired.

Xenophon made the headman of the village his guest at supper, and bade him keep a good heart; so far from robbing him of his children, they would fill his house full of good things in return for what they took before they went away; only he must set them an example, and discover some blessing or other for the army, until they found themselves with another tribe. To this he readily assented, and with the utmost cordiality showed them the cellar where the wine was buried. For this night then, having taken up their several quarters as described, they slumbered in the midst of plenty, one and all, with the headman under watch and ward, and his children with him safe in sight.

But on the following day Xenophon took the headman and set off to Cheirisophus, making a round of the villages, and at each place turning in to visit the different parties. Everywhere alike he found them faring sumptuously and merry-making. There was not a single village where they did not insist on setting a breakfast before them, and on the same table were spread half a dozen dishes at least, lamb, kid, pork, veal, fowls, with various sorts of bread, some of wheat and some of barley. When, as an act of courtesy, any one wished to drink his neighbour's health, he would drag him to the big bowl, and when there, he must duck his head and take a long pull, drinking like an ox. The headman, they insisted everywhere, must accept as a present whatever he liked to have. But he would accept nothing, except where he espied any of his relations, when he made a point of taking them off, him or her, with himself.

When they reached Cheirisophus they found a similar scene. There too the men were feasting in their quarters, garlanded with whisps of hay and dry grass, and Armenian boys were playing the part of waiters in barbaric costumes, only they had to point out by gesture to the boys what they were to do, like deaf and dumb. After the first formalities, when Cheirisophus and Xenophon had greeted one another like bosom friends, they interrogated the headman in common by means of the Persian-speaking interpreter, "What was the country?" they asked; he replied, "Armenia." And again, "For whom are the horses being bred?" "They are tribute for the king," he replied. "And the neighbouring country?" "Is the land of the Chalybes," he said; and he described the road which led to it. So for the present Xenophon went off, taking the headman back with him to his household and friends. He also made him a present of an oldish horse which he had got; he had heard that the headman was a priest of the sun, and so he could fatten up the beast and sacrifice him; otherwise he was afraid it might die outright, for it had been injured by the long marching. For himself he took his pick of the colts, and gave a colt apiece to each of his fellow-generals and officers. The horses here were smaller than the Persian horses, but much more spirited. It was here too that their friend the headman explained to them, how they should wrap small bags or sacks round the feet of the horses and other cattle when marching through the snow, for without such precautions the creatures sank up to their bellies.

VI.—When a week had passed, on the eighth day Xenophon delivered over the guide (that is to say, the village headman) to Cheirisophus. He left the headman's household safe behind in the village, with the exception of his son, a lad in the bloom of youth. This boy was entrusted to Episthenes of Amphipolis to guard; if the headman proved himself a good guide, he was to take away his son also at his departure. They finally made his house the repository of all the good things they could contrive to get together; then they broke up their camp and commenced to march, the headman guiding them through the snow unfettered. When they had reached the third stage Cheirisophus flew into a rage with him, because he had not brought them to any villages. The headman pleaded that there were none in this part. Cheirisophus struck him, but forgot to bind him, and the end of it was that the headman ran away in the night and was gone, leaving his son behind him. This was the sole ground of difference between Cheirisophus and Xenophon during the march, this combination of ill-treatment and neglect in the case of the guide. As to the boy, Episthenes conceived a passion for him, and took him home with him, and found in him the most faithful of friends.

After this they marched seven stages at the rate of five parasangs a day, to the banks of the river Phasis, which is a hundred feet broad: and thence they marched another couple of stages, ten parasangs; but at the pass leading down into the plain there appeared in front of them a mixed body of Chalybes and Taochians and Phasians. When Cheirisophus caught sight of the enemy on the pass at a distance of about three or four miles, he ceased marching, not caring to approach the enemy with his troops in column, and he passed down the order to the others: to deploy their companies to the front, that the troops might form into line. As soon as the rearguard had come up, he assembled the generals and officers, and addressed them: "The enemy, as you see, are in occupation of the mountain pass, it is time we should consider how we are to make the best fight to win it. My opinion is, that we should give orders to the troops to take their morning meal, whilst we deliberate whether we should cross the mountains to-day or to-morrow." "My opinion," said Cleanor, "is, that as soon as we have breakfasted, we should arm for the fight and attack the enemy, without loss of time, for if we fritter away to-day, the enemy who are now content to look at us, will grow bolder, and with their growing courage, depend upon it, others more numerous will join them."

After him Xenophon spoke: "This," he said, "is how I see the matter; if fight we must, let us make preparation to sell our lives dearly, but if we desire to cross with the greatest ease, the point to consider is, how we may get the fewest wounds and throw away the smallest number of good men. Well then, that part of the mountain which is visible stretches nearly seven miles. Where are the men posted to intercept us? except at the road itself, they are nowhere to be seen. It is much better then to try if possible to steal a point of this desert mountain unobserved, and before they know where we are, secure the prize, than to fly at a strong position and an enemy thoroughly prepared. Since it is much easier to march up a mountain without fighting than to tramp along a level when assailants are on either hand; and provided he has not to fight, a man will see what lies at his feet much more plainly even at night than in broad daylight in the midst of battle; and a rough road to feet that roam in peace may be pleasanter than a smooth surface with the bullets whistling about your ears. Nor is it so impossible, I take it, to steal a march, since it is open to us to go by night, when we cannot be seen, and to fall back so far that they will never notice us. In my opinion, however, if we make a feint of attacking here, we shall find the mountain chain all the more deserted elsewhere, since the enemy will be waiting for us here in thicker swarm.

"But what right have I to be drawing conclusions about stealing in your presence, Cheirisophus? for you Lacedaemonians, as I have often been told, you who belong to the 'peers,' practise stealing from your boyhood up; and it is no disgrace but honourable rather to steal, except such things as the law forbids; and in order, I presume, to stimulate your sense of secretiveness, and to make you master thieves, it is lawful for you further to get a whipping, if you are caught. Now then you have a fine opportunity of displaying your training. But take care we are not caught stealing over the mountain, or we shall catch it ourselves." "For all that," retorted Cheirisophus, "I have heard that you Athenians are clever hands at stealing the public moneys; and that too though there is fearful risk for the person so employed; but, I am told, it is your best men who are most addicted to it; if it is your best men who are thought worthy to rule. So it is a fine opportunity for yourself also, Xenophon, to exhibit your education." "And I," replied Xenophon, "am ready to take the rear division, as soon as we have supped, and seize the mountain chain. I have already got guides, for the light troops laid an ambuscade, and seized some of the cut-purse vagabonds who hung on our rear. I am further informed by them that the mountain is not inaccessible, but is grazed by goats and cattle, so that if we can once get hold of any portion of it, there will be no difficulty as regards our animals—they can cross. As to the enemy, I expect they will not even wait for us any longer, when they once see us on a level with themselves on the heights, for they do not even at present care to come down and meet us on fair ground." Cheirisophus answered: "But why should you go and leave your command in the rear? Send others rather, unless a band of volunteers will present themselves." Thereupon Aristonymus the Methydrian came forward with some heavy infantry, and Aristeas the Chian with some light troops, and Nicomachus the Oetean with another body of light troops, and they made an agreement to kindle several watch-fires as soon as they held the heights. The arrangements made, they breakfasted; and after breakfast Cheirisophus advanced the whole army ten furlongs closer towards the enemy, so as to strengthen the impression that he intended to attack them at that point.

But as soon as they had supped and night had fallen, the party under orders set off and occupied the mountain, while the main body rested where they were. Now as soon as the enemy perceived that the mountain was taken, they banished all thought of sleep, and kept many watch-fires blazing through the night. But at break of day Cheirisophus offered sacrifice, and began advancing along the road, while the detachment which held the mountain advanced *pari passu* by the high ground. The larger mass of the enemy, on his side, remained still on the mountain-pass, but a section of them turned to confront the detachment on the heights. Before the main bodies had time to draw together, the detachment on the height came to close quarters, and the Hellenes were victorious and gave chase. Meanwhile the light division of the Hellenes, issuing from the plain, were rapidly advancing against the serried lines of the enemy, whilst Cheirisophus followed up with his heavy infantry at quick march. But the enemy on the road no sooner saw their higher division being worsted than they fled, and some few of them were slain, and a vast number of wicker shields were taken, which the Hellenes hacked to pieces with their short swords and rendered useless. So when they had reached the summit of the pass, they sacrificed and set up a trophy, and descending into the plain, reached villages abounding in good things of every kind.

VII.—After this they marched into the country of the Taochians five stages—thirty parasangs—and provisions failed; for the Taochians lived in strong places, into which they had carried up all their stores. Now when the army arrived before one of these strong places—a mere fortress, without city or houses, into which a motley crowd of men and women and numerous flocks and herds were gathered—Cheirisophus attacked at once.

When the first regiment fell back tired, a second advanced, and again a third, for it was impossible to surround the place in full force, as it was encircled by a river. Presently Xenophon came up with the rearguard, consisting of both light and heavy infantry, whereupon Cheirisophus hailed him with the words: "In the nick of time you have come; we must take this place, for the troops have no provisions, unless we take it." Thereupon they consulted together, and to Xenophon's inquiry, "What it was which hindered their simply walking in?" Cheirisophus replied, "There is just this one narrow approach which you see; but when we attempt to pass by it they roll down volleys of stones from yonder overhanging crag," pointing up, "and this is the state in which you find yourself, if you chance to be caught;" and he pointed to some poor fellows with their legs or ribs crushed to bits. "But when they have expended their ammunition," said Xenophon, "there is nothing else, is there, to hinder our passing? Certainly, except yonder handful of fellows, there is no one in front of us that we can see; and of them, only two or three apparently are armed, and the distance to be traversed under fire is, as your eyes will tell you, about one hundred and fifty feet as near as can be, and of this space the first hundred is thickly covered with great pines at intervals; under cover of these, what harm can come to our men from a pelt of stones, flying or rolling? So then, there is only fifty feet left to cross, during a lull of stones." "Ay," said Cheirisophus, "but with our first attempt to approach the bush a galling fire of stones commences." "The very thing we want," said the other, "for they will use up their ammunition all the quicker; but let us select a point from which we shall have only a brief space to run across, if we can, and from which it will be easier to get back, if we wish."

Thereupon Cheirisophus and Xenophon set out with Callimachus the Parrhasian, the captain in command of the officers of the rearguard that day; the rest of the captains remained out of danger. That done, the next step was for a party of about seventy men to get away under the trees, not in a body, but one by one, every one using his best precaution; and Agasias the Stymphalian, and Aristonymus the Methydrian, who were also officers of the rearguard, were posted as supports outside the trees; for it was not possible for more than a single company to stand safely within the trees. Here Callimachus hit upon a pretty contrivance—he ran forward from the tree under which he was posted two or three paces, and as soon as the stones came whizzing, he retired easily, but at each excursion more than ten wagon-loads of rocks were expended. Agasias, seeing how Callimachus was amusing himself, and the whole army looking on as spectators, was seized with the fear that he might miss his chance of being first to run the gauntlet of the enemy's fire and get into the place. So, without a word of summons to his next neighbour, Aristonymus, or to Eurylochus of Lusia, both comrades of his, or to any one else, off he set on his own account, and passed the whole detachment. But Callimachus, seeing him tearing past, caught hold of his shield by the rim, and in the meantime Aristonymus the Methydrian ran past both, and after him Eurylochus of Lusia; for they were one and all aspirants to valour, and in that high pursuit, each was the eager rival of the rest. So in this strife of honour, the four of them took the fortress, and when they had once rushed in, not a stone more was hurled from overhead.

And here a terrible spectacle displayed itself: the women first cast their infants down the cliff, and then they cast themselves after their fallen little ones, and the men likewise. In such a scene, Aeneas the Stymphalian, an officer, caught sight of a man with a fine dress about to throw himself over, and seized hold of him to stop him; but the other caught him to his arms, and both were gone in an instant headlong down the crags, and were killed. Out of this place the merest handful of human beings were taken prisoners, but cattle and asses in abundance and flocks of sheep.

From this place they marched through the Chalybes seven stages, fifty parasangs. These were the bravest men whom they encountered on the whole march, coming cheerily to close quarters with them. They wore linen corselets reaching to the groin, and instead of the ordinary "wings" or basques, a thickly-plaited fringe of cords. They were also provided with greaves and helmets, and at the girdle a short sabre, about as long as the Laconian dagger, with which they cut the throats of those they mastered, and after severing the head from the trunk they would march along carrying it, singing and dancing, when they drew within their enemy's field of view. They carried also a spear fifteen cubits long, lanced at one end. This folk stayed in regular townships, and whenever the Hellenes passed by they invariably hung close on their heels fighting. They had dwelling-places in their fortresses, and into them they had carried up their supplies, so that the Hellenes could get nothing from this district, but supported themselves on the flocks and herds they had taken from the Taochians. After this the Hellenes reached the river Harpasus, which was four hundred feet broad. Hence they marched through the Scythenians four stages—twenty parasangs—through a long level country to more villages, among which they halted three days, and got in supplies.

Passing on from thence in four stages of twenty parasangs, they reached a large and prosperous well-populated city, which went by the name of Gymnias, from which the governor of the country sent them a guide to lead them through a district hostile to his own. This guide told them that within five days he would lead them to a place from which they could see the sea, "and," he added, "if I fail of my word, you are free to take my life." Accordingly he put himself at their head; but he no sooner set foot in the country hostile to himself than he fell to encouraging them to burn and harry the land; indeed his exhortations were so earnest, it was plain that it was for this he had come, and not out of the good-will he bore the Hellenes.

On the fifth day they reached the mountain, the name of which was Theches. No sooner had the men in front ascended it and caught sight of the sea than a great cry arose, and Xenophon, with the rearguard, catching the sound of it, conjectured that another set of enemies must surely be attacking in front; for they were followed by the inhabitants of the country, which was all aflame; indeed the rearguard had killed some and captured others alive by laying an ambuscade; they had taken also about twenty wicker shields, covered with the raw hides of shaggy oxen.

But as the shout became louder and nearer, and those who from time to time came up, began racing at the top of their speed towards the shouters, and the shouting continually recommenced with yet greater volume as the numbers increased, Xenophon settled in his mind that something extraordinary must have happened, so he mounted his horse, and taking with him Lycius and the cavalry, he galloped to the rescue. Presently they could hear the soldiers shouting and passing on the joyful word, *The sea! the sea!*

Thereupon they began running, rearguard and all, and the baggage animals and horses came galloping up. But when they had reached the summit, then indeed they fell to embracing one another—generals and officers and all—and the tears trickled down their cheeks. And on a sudden, some one, whoever it was, having passed down the order, the soldiers began bringing stones and erecting a great cairn, whereon they dedicated a host of untanned skins, and staves, and captured wicker shields, and with his own hand the guide hacked the shields to pieces, inviting the rest to follow his example. After this the Hellenes dismissed the guide with a present raised from the common store, to wit, a horse, a silver bowl, a Persian dress, and ten darics; but what he most begged to have were their rings, and of these he got several from the soldiers. So, after pointing out to them a village where they would find quarters, and the road by which they would proceed towards the land of the Macrones, as evening fell, he turned his back upon them in the night and was gone.

VIII.—From this point the Hellenes marched through the country of the Macrones in three stages,—ten parasangs, and on the first day they reached the river, which formed the boundary between the land of the Macrones and the land of the Scythenians. Above them, on their right, they had a country of the sternest and ruggedest character, and on their left another river, into which the frontier river discharges itself, and which they must cross. This was thickly fringed with trees which, though not of any great bulk, were closely packed. As soon as they came up to them, the Hellenes proceeded to cut them down in their haste to get out of the place as soon as possible. But the Macrones, armed with wicker shields and lances and hair tunics, were already drawn up to receive them immediately opposite the crossing. They were cheering one another on, and kept up a steady pelt of stones into the river, though they failed to reach the other side or do any harm.

At this juncture one of the light infantry came up to Xenophon; he had been, he said, a slave at Athens, and he wished to tell him that he recognised the speech of these people. "I think," said he, "this must be my native country, and if there is no objection I will have a talk with them." "No objection at all," replied Xenophon, "pray talk to them, and ask them first, who they are." In answer to this question they said, "they were Macrones."

"Well, then," said he, "ask them why they are drawn up in battle and want to fight with us." They answered, "Because you are invading our country." The generals bade him say: "If so, it is with no intention certainly of doing it or you any harm: but we have been at war with the king, and are now returning to Hellas, and all we want is to reach the sea." The others asked, "Were they willing to give them pledges to that effect?" They replied: "Yes, they were ready to give and receive pledges to that effect." Then the Macrones gave a barbaric lance to the Hellenes, and the Hellenes a Hellenic lance to them: "for these," they said, "would serve as pledges," and both sides called upon the gods to witness.

After the pledges were exchanged, the Macrones fell to vigorously hewing down trees and constructing a road to help them across, mingling freely with the Hellenes and fraternising in their midst, and they afforded them as good a market as they could, and for three days conducted them on their march, until they had brought them safely to the confines of the Colchians. At this point they were confronted by a great mountain chain, which however was accessible, and on it the Colchians were drawn up for battle. In the first instance, the Hellenes drew up opposite in line of battle, as though they were minded to assault the hill in that order; but afterwards the generals determined to hold a council of war, and consider how to make the fairest fight.

Accordingly Xenophon said: "I am not for advancing in line, but advise to form into column of sections. To begin with, the line," he urged, "would be scattered and thrown into disorder at once; for we shall find the mountain full of inequalities, it will be pathless here and easy to traverse there. The mere fact of first having formed in line, and then seeing the line thrown into disorder, must exercise a disheartening effect. Again, if we advance several deep, the enemy will none the less overlap us, and turn their superfluous numbers to account as best they like; while, if we march in shallow order, we may fully expect our line to be cut through and through by the thick rain of missiles and rush of men, and if this happen anywhere along the line, the whole line will equally suffer. No; my notion is to form columns by companies, covering ground sufficient with spaces between the companies to allow the last companies of each flank to be outside the enemy's flanks. Thus we shall with our extreme companies be outside the enemy's line, and the best men at the head of their columns will lead the attack, and every company will pick its way where the ground is easy; also it will be difficult for the enemy to force his way into the intervening spaces, when there are companies on both sides; nor will it be easy for him to cut in twain any individual company marching in column. If, too, any particular company should be pressed, the neighbouring company will come to the rescue, or if at any point any single company succeed in reaching the height, from that moment not one man of the enemy will stand his ground."

This proposal was carried, and they formed into columns by companies. Then Xenophon, returning from the right wing to the left, addressed the soldiers. "Men," he said, "these men whom you see in front of you are the sole obstacles still interposed between us and the haven of our hopes so long deferred. We will swallow them up whole, without cooking, if we can."

The several divisions fell into position, the companies were formed into columns, and the result was a total of something like eighty companies of heavy infantry, each company consisting on an average of a hundred men. The light infantry and bowmen were arranged in three divisions—two outside to support the left and the right respectively, and the third in the centre—each division consisting of about six hundred men.

Before starting, the generals passed the order to offer prayer; and with the prayer and battle hymn rising from their lips they commenced their advance. Cheirisophus and Xenophon, and the light infantry with them, advanced outside the enemy's line to right and left, and the enemy, seeing their advance, made an effort to keep parallel and confront them, but in order to do so, as he extended partly to right and partly to left, he was pulled to pieces, and there was a large space or hollow left in the centre of his line. Seeing them separate thus, the light infantry attached to the Arcadian battalion, under command of Aeschines, an Acarnanian, mistook the movement for flight, and with a loud shout rushed on, and these were the first to scale the mountain summit; but they were closely followed up by the Arcadian heavy infantry, under command of Cleanor of Orchomenus.

When they began running in that way, the enemy stood their ground no longer, but betook themselves to flight, one in one direction, one in another, and the Hellenes scaled the hill and found quarters in numerous villages which contained supplies in abundance. Here, generally speaking, there was nothing to excite their wonderment, but the numbers of beehives were indeed astonishing, and so were certain properties of the honey. The effect upon the soldiers who tasted the combs was, that they all went for the nonce quite off their heads, and suffered from vomiting and diarrhoea, with a total inability to stand steady on their legs. A small dose produced a condition not unlike violent drunkenness, a large one an attack very like a fit of madness, and some dropped down, apparently at death's door. So they lay, hundreds of them, as if there had been a great defeat, a prey to the cruellest despondency. But the next day, none had died; and almost at the same hour of the day at which they had eaten they recovered their senses, and on the third or fourth day got on their legs again like convalescents after a severe course of medical treatment.

From this place they marched on two stages—seven parasangs—and reached the sea at Trapezus, a populous Hellenic city on the Euxine Sea, a colony of the Sinopeans, in the territory of the Colchians. Here they halted for about thirty days in the villages of the Colchians, which they used as a base of operations to ravage the whole territory of Colchis. The men of Trapezus supplied the army with a market, entertained them, and gave them, as gifts of hospitality, oxen and wheat and wine. Further, they negotiated with them in behalf of their neighbours the Colchians, who dwelt in the plain for the most part, and from this folk also came gifts of hospitality in the shape of cattle. And now the Hellenes made preparation for the sacrifice which they had vowed, and a sufficient number of cattle came in for them to offer thank-offerings for safe guidance to Zeus the Saviour, and to Heracles, and to the other gods, according to their vows. They instituted also a gymnastic contest on the mountain side, just where they were quartered, and chose Dracontius, a Spartan (who had been banished from home when a lad, having unintentionally slain another boy with a blow of his dagger), to superintend the course, and be president of the games.

As soon as the sacrifices were over, they handed over the hides of the beasts to Dracontius, and bade him lead the way to his racecourse. He merely waved his hand and pointed to where they were standing, and said, "There, this ridge is just the place for running, anywhere, everywhere." "But how," it was asked, "will they manage to wrestle on the hard scrubby ground?" "Oh! worse knocks for those who are thrown," the president replied. There was a mile race for boys, the majority being captive lads; and for the long race more than sixty Cretans competed; there was wrestling, boxing, and the pankration. Altogether it was a beautiful spectacle. There was a large number of entries, and the emulation, with their companions, male and female, standing as spectators, was immense. There was horse-racing also; the riders had to gallop down a steep incline to the sea, and then turn and come up again to the altar, and on the descent more than half rolled head over heels, and then back they came toiling up the tremendous steep, scarcely out of a walking pace. Loud were the shouts, the laughter, and the cheers.

Vale of Tears

BY

LAURENCE STALLINGS

HUGH DOZIER was in a crowd of wounded officers from many regiments that lay in a hospital at Angers. They frequently spoke of terrain familiar to them and mentioned small wooded streams by remote farmhouses with beautiful names, pronouncing them in flat American accents with glib affection; for they were indelible in parochial remembrances, taking rank for the officers with such tocsins to the blood as Marengo and Austerlitz.

Dozier had been in hospitals now for four months, never meeting anyone from his regiment. He was lonely for men who had seen the things he had seen and who could name in memory with him the French places he could name.

The hospital was a quadrangular building surrounding a formal garden said to be very beautiful. Officers were carried through it from time to time on the way to the operating room, but the injection of morphine and atropine given as hospital routine just before a patient left his bed always dilated the eyes to such an extent that a sick man entered the garden blinking from the strange light of the sun. Hugh Dozier's only impression as he was lurched along the garden paths was one of a dazzling panorama frosted and difficult of focusing, like the little German boxes at Christmas with peep-show landscapes of snow scenes.

A beautiful girl who shone with good health and the happiness of service walked along the paths with the litter. Miss Adair was a university girl whose duty was to cheer up the patients, and she was faithful to her trust. Her slim hand smelled of a French *savon* and the diamonds in her little-finger ring caught the sun's fire and sparkled it whimsically into Hugh's eyes. Miss Adair was saying, "You'll beat it out, Dozier; you'll beat it out."

Dozier was drowsy with morphia but he knew that she was doing her part in the strange ceremony. The operation was some business about opening a sequestrum in his side. Dozier knew that he was supposed to reply to her cheerfully. These replies were really among the hardest tasks of hospitalization. There seemed to be several persons around whom one had to be cheerful to. It was hard to humor them when Dozier was sick.

There was a gentleman named Gilson who sometimes stopped by the bed in the officers' ward and stood at the foot in a kindly manner; much as a young doctor is jovial to a sick child. Gilson wore an exaggerated bonhomie that actually was distasteful when he said, "Now, old boy, let's

By permission of the Author.

377

see that old smile! Call me Gilson. That's right. Smile!" Gilson himself would glow as Dozier forced a smile. "That's the old stuff. Smile! Call me Gilson. Smile!" Gilson wore some sort of rare tunic. Like Miss Adair, he belonged to some unit not easily identified.

Miss Adair was very pretty and was never distasteful. She was about twenty years old and her flat figure was fetching in a gray whipcord tunic and short skirts that reached to her boots. Her legs were so good that she wore laced boots. She always seemed springy and sweet.

Dozier was twenty himself. This was young for an officer but he was precocious as stage children usually are. Miss Adair never came by that he did not wish she would leave off writing letters from him and giving him pieces of chocolate.

He wanted her to lean over him and take his head and hold it to her breast that must have smelled of *savon* as her hands did, taking care lest she move his body and cause too much pain. After she had held him this way for three or four hours it would have been nice if she had pressed her lips warmly against his, breathing on his face, and leaving rouge stains after she whispered, "Hurry up and get well, Hugh Dozier; you're the only patient in this hospital."

Miss Adair had never volunteered to do this, and Dozier would never ask her to. As the litter moved along through the garden she held his hand. He knew she never even suspected the thing he wished and he resolved to grow better soon, put on his uniform, and ask her some evening in the garden.

Just now she was pinning three cigarets and three matches into the hem of his surgical gown so that he would have smokes despite old Miss Broadus the supervisor, who was severe about indulgences to post-operative cases the first night after a trip downstairs to the ether hut. Miss Adair was wealthy and a good sport about breaking red tape. A girl could not buy so many things to give away unless she had independent means.

This would make it harder to ask her. Dozier knew a ludicrous story about "I love her, I love her. I, an actor and the son of a hatter." He could see Miss Adair's beautiful lips framing the bird in reply.

The litter had reached the end of the garden path and was in the passage. "I'll slip you a bottle of Château Bel Rive tonight," she said, patting his face with her edible hand. Château Bel Rive was a faint sweet Anjou wine. Well, it was better than Gilson's smile.

In the operating room it was said that a new convoy of wounded was expected at sundown. The nurses usually had some piece of news to relay during the preliminaries, chattering in far-away voices as they shifted Dozier to the hard pad and screened the other tables from him. He was glad his was not a mastoid. That other doctor had a little silver hammer and a chisel. Hugh always asked the night nurse to hang his cap with the Globe-Eagle-and-Anchor on his bedpost at night.

One of the scrubbing nurses in unbleached linen said that the new convoy was principally wounded from the Second Division. His division had just reduced a white chalk hill back of Reims known as Blanc Mont. He believed marines would be among the wounded. The nurse who gave the ether was a handsome woman. She always smiled as if she knew a secret. She placed her hand beneath his ear. The ether gluttonously ravaged the smell of Miss Adair's hand.

He resolved to ask Miss Broadus to hang his cap at the foot of his bed as soon as he shook off the anæsthesia. He decided to have the ether nurse tell her, instead. He spoke to the ether nurse but the words were lost in the cotton cone she held above his mouth.

Hugh would turn his bedside lamp so that the light shone on the red-and-gold piping of his cap. The badge would show in such a manner that every new officer passing by on a stretcher would see that the bed held a marine.

That was the doctor talking now. Hugh had better hurry off to sleep. His side had stopped hurting. Miss Adair was smiling as she winged her way along the path. They hid together in a vast orange cavern. It would have been pleasant but for the noise of the trains roaring by.

Hugh was in an officers' ward of thirty beds in a long whitewashed hall on the third floor south and the new patients seemed a long time coming. There were many of them; so many that the ward nurses had vanished. Lieutenant Freiburg hung Hugh Dozier's cap on the bedpost and arranged the lamp to shine on the piping and the badge.

Freiburg was a Jersey City policeman released for the duration to seek medals in France. He had them all, but he sometimes cried softly in his bed next to Hugh's, out of homesickness. Hugh never mentioned this afterwards and they became friends. Freiburg's arms were so powerful that he could shift around in his bed and reach across to Hugh when the nurses were too busy to minister to his wants.

Freiburg was proud of having been shot by a Polack in a Jersey City robbery and made light of his present wounds in the legs. If the hospital had been in Jersey City he could have held receptions and the police commissioner would have called on Sundays; but the French medals were too foreign to comfort him. He sometimes talked of his wife and his two children, but the surgeon on a bad morning's dressing could make him sob, "Mother, Mother," but very softly.

Hugh lay awake watching the ceiling and waiting for the steps of the stretcher bearers when they came shuffling up the stairs. The windows on the court let in the sounds of a vast, solemn moaning from the new men in litters in the garden below.

Across the aisle old Captain Jackson sat chain-lighting his cigarets and sighing, occasionally scratching his tattooed chest with his tattooed hand. The captain had weaned himself of morphine and was smoking nights, sleeping snatches during the day.

Hugh knew that Jackson was trying to recall how he had been wounded. The old man had been serving some howitzers back of Saint-Mihiel in early

September. He had awakened in early October in a long dim ward, his body a series of compound fractures in a plaster shell.

"I had my hand on the lanyard," he said. He always asked newcomers if they recalled a howitzer company in the dooryard of a small white farmhouse with a straw roof, "about a mile back of the lines somewhere near Saint-Mihiel."

"Didn't you feel a big burst? A roar, and then a sting somewhere?"

Captain Jackson would always say: "I had my hand on the lanyard." There was the gap. He awoke to find himself addicted to morphine. "We were right by a small white farmhouse with a thatched roof. An old Frenchman lived in the farmhouse."

Each new convoy might bring some officer who could recall the howitzer and the farmhouse in which the old Frenchman lived beneath a thatched roof. The captain was waiting to see.

Hugh watched the ceiling a long time. Presently there were heavy steps upon the stairs and faint cursings, and the fresh meat started in. As the orderlies lurched somnambulantly down the aisles to the vacant beds the old pensioners sat up, peering over their bedsteads to see the new ones, each one seeking his own badges and brassards of some braver day.

Lieutenant Freiburg sat forward quickly as the regimental square on the shoulder of the first stretcher case came into the light. "Hey! Fresh meat! Any youse guys from Joisey?" he shouted.

The fresh meat raised his head. "Sure; I'm from Joisey."

"W'at paht?"

"Poit Amboy."

"For the Jesus," said Freiburg, settling back into his covers.

The officer from Perth Amboy was unaffectedly lying supine upon his litter smoking a cigaret. "Ask that smarty how he'd like to take a flying smack at me," he said to the orderly as he was borne past Freiburg's bed.

The second litter held a man whose blankets reeked of ether. Dozier saw the figure on the third pluck at the tunic of the forward bearer.

"Set me down," the new one said faintly, speaking from a face bandaged crudely to leave a single blue eye shining in the bedside lamplight. They set him down and he spoke still faintly from the floor. "Who's the marine?"

Dozier from the high white bed could not see the floor. He was sandbagged too heavily to press forward. Nausea lingered from the morning.

"I'm Hugh Dozier from the Third Battalion of the Fifth. Forty-seventh Company."

"I'm Terence Delaney. Same battalion. Lieutenant in the Forty-fifth Company."

"How's Major Schlosser?" Hugh asked happily.

The voice from the floor answered weakly. "Just when I had an eye knocked out he was smoking a big cigar and standing right out in the middle of things. He was repairing a stoppage in a Hotchkiss gun."

"God!" said Dozier, happiness welling up in him. "We've still got those old Hotchkiss guns."

Things at the regiment were the same. Hugh Dozier felt fine for the first time in four months. Those French Hotchkiss guns had been a nuisance because they fired a French D.M. cartridge and it was always additional trouble to carry the ammunition supply along. When a carrier was shot down in an advance someone had to pick up his musettes and keep going, for the Hotchkiss was not chambered for American ammunition. It was good to know the battalion was still in the old routines.

"Only a few Hotchkiss left," Delaney spoke up faintly from the floor. "Mostly have the new Brownings now."

"I'll bet they're not as good as the old Hotchkiss," he said. "I had Hotchkiss at Bouresches." Dozier was sorry about the Brownings. Something new and he would never fire one.

Delaney spoiled his pleasure. "The new Brownings are marvelous. The dead and wounded are lousy with ammunition for them."

The lead bearer signaled. The two orderlies lifted the man up. "We got to move on, lieutenant."

"If you need anything," Dozier called out when the litter was raised so high he could see Delaney's face and the rough bandages, "I've got it. Just you send to me for it. I remember you now."

"I need—plenty." Delaney spoke indistinctly, folding his arms tighter to keep his belongings from rolling off his chest.

The orderlies lurched along the rubber matting to the door at the far end of the ward. The leader kicked it open with his foot and groped his way into the dark room beyond.

Jackson was speaking to a stretcher case with an artillery brassard. "We were right by a small white farmhouse with an artillery position set in the dooryard. The house had a thatched roof. I had my hand on the lanyard."

Delaney said that he needed plenty. Dozier had four months' pay in a wallet on the table by him and he could not spend fifty francs a week. An occasional quart of *rhum négrito* cost fifteen francs, but a quart lasted three or four days. He would send Delaney a quart of *rhum négrito* and a box of Bock panatellas. Maybe he smoked a pipe and would like a can of British smoking tobacco.

It would be a fine thing to order a larded quail for Delaney from the Cheval Blanc down in the town. The quail were fat. The lords of the forest were shooting bigger game in the north and the Anjou birds were almost as large as pheasant. Delaney would smell the quail tomorrow morning and forget about his eye for a time.

Bill was the orderly to be depended upon for the quail. Dozier could give Bill an extra five francs for a drink or so and the orderly would wait for the quail to be broiled and wrapped in wax papers and a white napkin. In the meantime Delaney would have a drink of *rhum* and lie upon his weak back with a feeling of being unjointed.

His eye socket would burn at first but the second drink would stop that, and the flavor of a Bock panatella would make him hungry. Dozier almost forgot the new spot in his side. The wounded were all in, and there were no more marines.

Miss Adair tiptoed into the ward and came to Dozier's bed. He lay silent and hoped he appeared weaker than he was, so that she would come closer to him. She bent over him in the gloom, greatcoat about her, hands holding a package beneath it that rustled in tissue paper.

"Hello," she said. "Tough going?"

Hugh Dozier had not thought about the going. It was not tough in the light of other times but it was best to say no with an affirmation in his voice.

"Not tough at all," he said.

"Good soldier," Miss Adair whispered.

Dozier lay with hands beneath the covers. He smelled the scented hand in the dark. It would have patted his cheek lightly, but he moved his head and pinned it to the pillow, kissing it in the velvet palm.

"Sweet boy," Miss Adair said, withdrawing her hand.

Freiburg was asleep.

"I'm too full of ether," Dozier said. "I'd ask you to kiss me."

"But I've brought you the Bel Rive," Miss Adair said.

"Christen it for me, please," Dozier said.

"Where's your glass?" She groped about the table.

"Out of the bottle," Dozier said.

"Oh. All right."

"And I, the son of a hatter," Dozier said.

"What?" Miss Adair was pulling the cork gently, bottle on the floor between her boots.

"I said no one but you would bring me wine at night," Dozier said. "You're all I think about."

"That's what I'm here for. To give you poor boys things that the hospital can't afford."

"It's the only reason?"

"Of course I like you," Miss Adair said. "I'd rather see you get well than anyone else."

"And after I get well?"

Miss Adair got the cork out without a sound. "You're silly from ether," she said. She tipped the bottle. "Here's how; give 'em a little bit o' hell for me."

Hugh Dozier had given the Germans all the hell they would ever get from him.

"There," she said in the dark, offering him the bottle.

Dozier took the wine. "Let's drink to the new marine. Lieutenant Delaney. He's in the dark room."

"Poor boy," Miss Adair said. She shivered and looked away.

"Poor nothing!" Dozier cried warmly. "He's a great guy. They used to call him the brains of the battalion. He developed the combat organization for Browning ammunition carriers."

"I know," Miss Adair said. "Don't speak of it, please." She moved away. "Good night," she said. "Sweet dreams."

What did she know about Delaney? What was it he needed plenty of? Delaney could see plain enough. He saw a marine emblem in faint lamplight. Miss Adair was as cold as a stone. Hugh Dozier went over the whole conversation, from the moment she removed her hand from his cheek. The wine was no good.

Dozier got Freiburg awake after repeated whispers and he swung down to the floor for the *rhum négrito*. They drank it in little nips until Dozier's side stopped hurting.

"It may be because I'm ill, but I love her all the time," he said.

"Of course." Freiburg had a rough responsiveness somewhere in his broad chest. "You're bound to be nuts about somebody. You got a four-months' growth."

"But I love her in a pure way. I feel like crying when she comes by."

"Go ahead and make your throw. And if you lose——" Freiburg twisted a corner of his mouth down and jerked his thumb towards his shoulder. "Get change, and go to another game."

"I don't think I'll ever love anybody but her. Sooner or later she'll feel it. I mean, see how I feel."

"She's saving it for some hinky-dink with a million dollars," Freiburg said.

The larded quail was on Delaney's tray by noon. Dozier had received word from the bath orderly that the patient had attempted both the *rhum* and the cigar. The Lieutenant Delaney returned word that he was not up to a note of thanks, but he sent the Lieutenant Dozier a gift of some battle mementos by way of thanks.

There was a German meerschaum, strong with the *ersatz* tobacco of the German infantry, an iron cross of the second class, and a pair of ladies' garters with *"Gott Mit Uns"* clasps. Hugh thought that Delaney must be a pretty funny fellow. He would give the garters to the doctor. The meerschaum was worth keeping.

The ward surgeon was a young man, prematurely bald and addicted to ferocious carbuncles on the back of his neck where a little fuzz still persisted, as if nature abhorred hair anywhere near his brain. He was a delicate operator and rarely reached the officers' ward the day after a convoy. His name was Cross.

He was possessed of a dry humor and a Jewish passion for perfection of technique that made dressings a spirited ceremony punctuated by sharp, fresh observations freely given between surgeon and patient. He reached Dozier's bedside late the following night and chose the meerschaum.

Freiburg wanted the garters. "I'll send them to my mother," he said. "They have to keep the old dame shut up, she's so strong for Germany. Every time my wife lets her out of the house she gets talking and some nosey reports her. She'll strap 'em on and think God will bless her every time she raises a knee to take a step."

There was a place in Dozier's foot that Cross always saved until last. When he chose a probe for that he usually started a conversation to cover his intention. Cross finished dressing Dozier's other wounds. He murmured something about a "small-instrument-please" to the assisting nurse. She searched the white-enameled agony-wagon for a probe and he began his conversation.

"Got another marine officer last night."

"Delaney?" Dozier flinched before Cross touched his foot, knowing the next five minutes too well. The conversation had to be maintained. Smiling for Gilson was child's play beside it. "Fellow with an eye out?"

"Awfully downhearted," Cross said, inserting the probe. "I ate that quail for him. My first meal in twenty-four hours."

"Downhearted!" Dozier gasped, straining the word through clenched teeth. "Wh-wh-what's an eye—out, anyway?"

The probe was withdrawn from the foot an instant. The surgeon looked at Dozier's thin, dark, miserable face a moment. "It isn't his eye that worries him," he said shortly.

It was curious how a probe in the left foot rang a gong in the right side of the brain. "Got it somewhere else?" Dozier said, sweating now as the gong began clanging.

"Umhummmm." Cross was inspecting the probe.

"What place?" The probe actually pierced into the brain now and the gong caught fire. "What place?" Dozier bit into his pillows and made a little moaning sound through his nose until the probe came out. Nerve came back and speech returned. "What place?"

Cross circled his eyes around towards the assisting nurse. She was bending over, moving basins from the lower deck to the top of the cart.

"The worst place," Cross said.

"He's not going to lose anything?"

The probe was going in again. It was too bad about Delaney. It was shocking. Delaney was a tall, fair youth with curly hair. Dozier recalled now that he once set his wrist watch by a special timepiece in a square platinum hunting case that Delaney carried. It was a rich man's watch.

"Oh, no," Dozier said, forgetting his foot a second. "He won't—he won't lose anything?"

There was no doubt that the nurse knew all about it. She was setting rubber tubes on a glass syringe now and opening towels that contained fresh forceps. She was working with such cool unconcern that it was apparent she was listening.

"Well," sighed Cross sadly, "well——" He lowered his bald head and squinted through steel rims at the hole in Dozier's foot. He reached his rubbered hand to the forceps the nurse was holding and received a very small probe. It was the little one he always curved into a fishhook. It was made of lead and would bend any undesirable way. "He may lose his passports," Cross said gently with more effort to discover a nice euphemism than to affect a high-flown vulgarity.

It was shocking. "He may lose them and never travel to the wars again." Miss Adair had said not to speak of it.

One heard stories from third-hand informers. But Dozier had not known any first-hand case.

"You're not kidding me," Dozier said, trembling, tears upon his cheeks, "just because—you—are—putting—that—little—probe—in—my—foot—again?"

The doctor was bending the little probe now. "What's a foot, Dozier?"

Dozier crammed the pillow into his mouth and shut his eyes, letting a loud noise go through his nose.

When he got them open again the agony-wagon was at the next bed and Freiburg was speaking with bravado. "I wish you'd let me open that hickey on your neck now. I'd like to hear the tune you'd sing."

"It's ready," Cross smiled. "You let me dig that last little spicule of rib out now without going to the operating room and I'll let you dig me out."

"You're a liar!" Freiburg said.

"Oh, no," Cross said. "Get over on your side. My turn first."

"Just a minute."

"No. It's a trade."

Cross got the bone splinter out. Then he sat on a chair by Freiburg, while the nurse held a mirror from the lavatory so that all could see and offer advice. He gave the patient a scalpel and sat motionless.

Freiburg lanced the doctor's neck, his hands trembling. As Freiburg finished, the detachment buglers began taps outside and lights winked out around the quadrangle.

Before leaving the ward, Cross made the rounds and recalled every jeer that had urged Freiburg on when he opened the carbuncle. "Bright and early to-morrow," he said, "I'm going to scrub you all up. Old bone, old tissue. And I don't want to hear a sound."

Old Jackson gave his first chuckle of his residency in the ward. "You may as well throw me away," he said.

"Oh, no," Cross said quickly. "You're all right, captain. Don't get that in your head. You're coming around beautifully."

Captain Jackson was making his début into the night life of the ward. An arc light over the gateway in the north side of the quadrangle was reflected across his bed, so that his face was flooded in a soft diffusion as he talked.

The captain had spent his boyhood in the canebrakes of Mississippi before running away and joining the army. Entering the army in the golden age of tattooing, when it was no longer confined to primitive initial pieces or severe blue floral designs, and yet before the art had degenerated into the rendering of flabby ladies in barroom attitudes, he had shown a partiality for patriotic and religious subjects; upon the captain's chest there was a Rock of Ages in bright colors and on the backs of his hands were American eagles. Because he was breaking himself of morphine the eagles unconsciously clawed at the tapestry of his chest and arms, his old body impatient for the needle the captain had willed out of his skin forever.

He wished to cook the ward a camp supper. He began with clear turtle soup, recounting the capture of the turtle and following through successive stages to its consumption, digressing to inveigh against the horrors of white flour. He served juleps after that. As the ward was supposed to be drinking them, hands chilled by the frosting on the thick glass tumblers, Jackson got his things ready for stuffing a roast wild turkey.

"Whenever you see an old razorback hog stealing away into the deep woods, taking care that none of the other hogs are follering him, it's a sign that the scoundrel knows where the sweet acorns grow. Now a wild turkey loves sweet acorns above all other natural things. And there beneath the tree is the place to build your blind. A smart hunter will kill his turkey among the acorns that nature has decreed are the proper things for his natural stuffing."

Dozier could think only of Delaney; and not of sweet acorns.

Dozier knew that he should not tell a thing such as that about Delaney. If Dozier had been hovering on the borderland among army officers, Delaney might have kept his secret. Cross should never have told Dozier. He did it to divert him from pain. Zollicoffer in the far corner of the ward was groaning loud again. Captain Jackson's voice was pitched too high. Zollicoffer had been shot through the spine and no amount of morphine was effective at night.

Dozier told, but only to divert Zollicoffer. It stopped him.

Captain Jackson dropped his roasting turkey. "If the young man don't pull through," he said softly, "and if I was a marine and he wanted a gun, I'd get him one."

"It's not everything in life," Dozier said youthfully.

"I'd put it ahead of breathing," the captain said quickly. The old man stopped the laughter that followed.

"No, boys. I'm an old man, and yet I have not laughed at a thing like that. We think we are all pretty tough because we are here minus some hide and some hair; but the young man in the dark room has an unnatural hurt. You'd as lief laugh at a mother who loses her first-born. I swear that when they bring him out of the dark room into the light of day, if there's any joking of any nature regarding the only misfortune a full-born man can suffer, I'll crouch out of this bed and kill the man who starts it."

The captain lighted a cigaret and smoked the ward into silence. Presently with the utmost gentleness he spoke to Dozier.

"Was the young man married?"

"I don't know," Dozier said. "I didn't know him so very well. He came up just before I got mine." Dozier was trying to recall. "He was awfully serious, though."

"You can't tell by that," Freiburg said quietly.

"No, you can't," Jackson said. "Nearly every man's serious when he first comes up. They pass a dead artillery mule or a shell lights too near them and they commence to settle down. They turn gay and happy after they survive the first attack, not knowing it's a way of thanking God they weren't killed. We're happy that way ourselves. But that poor boy in there can't have gay or God in his heart tonight."

He passed a furrowed brow across the back of his cigaret hand.

"I hope he gets well," said Zollicoffer soberly, speaking for the first time to the ward. It was a matter of time with Zolly. He hoped it would be soon, but the clock ticked so slowly at night.

"If he does, nothing will hold him," Freiburg said.

"Nothing ought to," Zollicoffer said. The world was lost to him.

"A dispensation of Providence can never be ignored," Jackson reflected. "And with a black patch to one eye. Did you ever notice that an old buck with one eye out and a few branches gone is always crowded by the largest following of doe? Yes, sir, I believe in the power of prayer. I'm going to pray for that young man now. If Solomon is one of your saints, Solomon in all his glory, you who are Catholics might pray to him to intercede. Freiburg is of the race of David and he can pray to old Dave, Solomon's daddy before him. Let us all pray."

Miss Adair came down the aisle in broad daylight, shamelessly holding the plate before her, rough blocks of fudge piled in a small pyramid upon it. Dozier sat up, his heart pounding.

Only the old patients knew that fudge was the supreme achievement in a military hospital. For sugar was a thing to be hoarded. Speculators hoarded sugar. Grocers hoarded sugar. Bankers hoarded sugar; and thousands of barrels of sugar were being hoarded in army warehouses. In America it was said that the people set aside sugarless days and proprietors of eating houses doled it out for treble prices.

"The men at the front need sugar," Jackson said, watching Miss Adair, "and, by God, when they get home they are going to have sugar."

Miss Adair passed Dozier's bed and continued down the aisle to the dark room, where she opened the door softly and tiptoed in, shutting out the daylight afterwards.

"The best meal I recall," Jackson said, "was the night after the two-days' preparation before Soissons. Supper came up in *marmites* and the whole thing was fermented and sour. It was raining hard and I was cold and hungry. I let the rain wet a thick slab of French bread, and then I coated it with this brown French beet sugar that I guess our mess sergeant had hoarded away from the French infantry. That was sugar, all right—the only sugar I saw near the front."

Jackson peered over at Dozier. "What's become of your friend Miss Adair these days?"

Dozier was staring at the door of the dark room.

"Bill," the captain said to the orderly, "after the young lady leaves the room beyond us, I wonder if you could go in there and steal Lieutenant Dozier a piece of fudge from that poor blind man?"

Bill smiled. "He's got a gun in the musette bag he always keeps under his head. I'd have to steal that first, I guess."

"No," the captain said. "Let him keep the gun for a while. It must be a powerfully comforting thing. It gives the imagination a jumping-off place, and saves the fancy from—well, from wandering down the impossible halls of the future."

"I wouldn't take it from him," Bill said. "Not me. No matter what Miss Broadus tells me."

Two weeks later old Miss Broadus was on the floor early. The vacant bed between Zollicoffer and the wall at the far end of the ward was being made ready for Delaney's entrance into the light. Miss Broadus was monumental in starched linens. She had retouched the hair beneath her cap to a burnt-orange color and wore long pearl drops in her ears. She carried a large vase and a handful of pithy flowers from the fading garden of the fall.

She was followed by a corps of chattering French scrub women, one of whom was rosy and strong. This woman scrubbed the floor around and beneath the vacant bed, the suds making silver watermarks upon her thick cotton stockings, her legs appearing as a lovely treat to all the patients.

Delaney was brought out and placed in the bed, none but female hands touching him, the scrub women who bore the litter exclaiming with many ooh's and la-la's at one another's gaucheries, old Miss Broadus supervising in firm, strong tones.

Dozier sat up straining against the sandbags and watched the transfer twelve beds distant. "Hello, Third Battalion!" he shouted.

"Thanks for those things," Delaney called, in a high-strung voice. He had an incipient blond beard and wore a black patch over one eye that caricatured him as a child masquerading as a pirate. His features were waxen and clear-cut, his single eye bright but uncomprehending its own savagery as it swept the long rows of beds and tension machines.

The rosy scrub woman held his musettes and belts.

"*Donnez-moi,*" Delaney said, extending his hands for his gear.

The scrub woman shook her head violently and pointed to Miss Broadus.

"*Donnez. Donnez.* Damn it, *donnez!*"

Delaney was shouting feverishly, clamoring for the musettes and attempting to leave the bed. Miss Broadus took them from Rosy, who shrugged her shoulders and spoke French to Delaney in an aggrieved tone.

"We can lock them up for you," she cooed to Delaney. No one had ever heard old Miss Broadus coo. "No one can get them. I'll keep the key. All your belongings will be safe."

"Put them under my pillow," Delaney said sharply. His voice was querulous. "Come on, snap out of it!" He seemed to be striving for authority. "Don't stand there doping off. Put them under my pillow, I say."

No one spoke that way to old Miss Broadus. She was a great nurse and everyone knew it. It wanted character to handle wounded officers. They had been accustomed to obey only other officers superior to them in rank. A medical major is discreet if he reduces the fracture in a colonel's leg. Delaney caught the belt strap of one musette and tugged strongly. Miss Broadus had been known to pin an officer down and send for a doctor of a rank one grade higher than a refractory patient's.

"The only trouble with her," Jackson said to Dozier, "she's never been betrayed. She don't know that men are weak creatures."

Old Miss Broadus put the musettes on the bed. "Now, now," she said, roaching his fair hair back from his face, "you're not to excite yourself, poor darling."

"Then put them where I say!" Delaney cried weakly, falling back to his new pillows. "Put them under my head." There was a tear of rage in his eye.

"Yes, of course I'll put them where you say. Don't slip your bandage, dear."

Someone snickered a low snicker in the bed next to Jackson. Dozier looked fiercely, but Jackson inclined his adamant body half out of bed and thrust his tattooed hand into the offending throat.

Miss Broadus arranged the musettes beneath Delaney's head and dismissed the scrub woman. The poor French-women, who gave their all in the war, were loath to leave the bed. They smoothed down the counterpane several times and jettisoned his pillows around. Miss Broadus tastefully arranged the flowers in the vase and forced the other women to leave. Then she straightened the counterpane and made his pillows comfortable.

"Here is your bell cord," she said. "You've only to ring it. I'll be here instantly. Don't you want Miss Adair to bring the English and American papers and skim through them for you?"

"Thanks," Delaney said carelessly. "Ask her to bring the French papers and translate some more."

Miss Broadus arranged the flowers a little more tastefully. She seemed reluctant to leave him alone in a big ward. She went to other bedside tables and collected magazines with a by-your-leave acquiescence and arranged them on Delaney's table into a brilliant spot of color. The heavy blankets were showing against the sick man's chin and she folded the sheet over them in a straight new margin.

It was difficult to do much for a ward bed. A ward bed was so bare. The bell cord was not to the exact height, and she rewound it neatly over the iron bar above Delaney so that the push button would be exactly to his hand. She gave counterpane and pillows a final pat and left the man supine, arranged in an attitude suggesting the crowning touch of an æsthetic undertaker.

Dozier sat watching. Miss Broadus came down the aisle as impersonal as a commanding general at an inspection. She stopped short and wheeled opposite Dozier's bed, surveying the littered counterpane.

"Just as if a pig lived in it!" she shouted.

Miss Broadus shook the tobacco crumbs and magazines from that un-happy officer's bed and cleared his drinking glass of cigarette stubs. Briskly she began to tidy his covers. Gilson came into the ward covertly, his keen eyes darting from face to face. He came instantly to Dozier's bed, scenting misery.

Gilson leaned over with genuine friendliness, his warm heart dancing in his eyes.

"This is Gilson. Call me Gilson, big boy. Let's see that old smile this morning. The old smile."

Hugh smiled miserably for him. Miss Adair permeated the ward with sandalwood and leather polish as she passed gently by the bed and down the aisle to Delaney's cot, where she sat and took his hand. Gilson moved on.

Miss Broadus stacked the magazines and books that littered the floor. As she bent above Dozier's face to secure the rough warm blankets to his chin she whispered to him.

"Be kind to Lieutenant Delaney. Cheer him up."

"I'll try," Dozier said unhappily, looking painfully toward Miss Adair.

"Write about him in your paper." Miss Broadus was smiling impishly herself.

Hugh Dozier once edited a small paper for the ward, printing out bul-letins on a roll of toilet paper every morning. It was an enterprise Miss Broadus had suppressed. "It's war time," she had said. "Folks back home are making sacrifices for us. Nothing must be wasted."

Now she was asking him to resume publication and include Delaney among the bulletins.

Gilson possessed a remarkable flair for scenting out fresh misery and overpowering it. He moved to Delaney's bed after gleaning a harvest of smiles along the hedgerows of misery.

"My name is Gilson," he said, beaming past Miss Adair and into the single eye of the patched and waxen face. "Call me Gilson, big boy. Give old Gilson the first big smile."

"Who the hell are you?" cried Delaney. "Woodrow Gilson?"

Miss Adair turned sharply; her beautiful face lighted with anger. "Don't you see the man is ill?"

After the girl had driven Gilson away she released Delaney's hand and opened a French newspaper. She translated softly, lips near the sick man's ear. Small wisps of her hair sometimes touched his face. At these times she would stuff these wisps beneath her cap and smile apologetically, rearrang-ing his black patch and roaching the hair back over his forehead.

Delaney lay immobile. Once as she read, his eye closed and he turned his face very near to hers, but a moment later he sighed and moved it away. At these times she read holding the paper with one hand, and his hand in the other. Delaney appeared to sleep. She translated all morning.

Zollicoffer was very quiet in the week following Delaney's arrival in the ward. He was a very weak man and he never spoke to Miss Adair, but he enjoyed her translations from French newspapers when she read to Delaney. The latter would sometimes say, "Pretty good, eh, Zolly?" and defer to his opinion on war strategy when Miss Adair read the column signed "Pertinax."

Zolly was a war pilot and his cap with its aviator's wings hung over his head. He knew nothing of ground maneuvers. He could not answer but would always smile. At first Miss Adair brought only the local Angers papers. After a time, when it was apparent Delaney enjoyed her translations, she began to collect Parisian papers as well.

Miss Broadus usually made Zollicoffer's bed about five times a day to keep out wrinkles and to replace the Dakin's tubes infiltrating his wounds. One morning Zollicoffer lay incredibly thin upon the hard mattress, the top sheet about his loins as Miss Broadus shook out the blankets in the anteroom. His feet were large mahogany paddles affixed to the straight rods of his tibiæ.

Miss Adair was just arriving with the papers. She was shocked but she bowed to him, her features stiffened into a sweet smile. It was shocking how thin Zollicoffer was, his bearded head sunk upon his chest, ankles crossed and arms outstretched, white sheet across his loins.

"Look at me," said Zollicoffer, smiling too.

"Why, you're just fine," the girl said.

"No," said Zolly; "I think I'll crash."

Zollicoffer shut his eyes and listened smiling to an account of a fight in the Chamber of Deputies from the columns of Le Figaro.

The nurses always set a screen about Delaney when the doctor came to dress his wounds. It was as if Delaney had the privacy of the dying. Miss Adair usually left before Cross arrived to dress the patient. Cross came that morning before she had finished translating the papers.

"Good-by, Mr. Zollicoffer," she said, pressing Delaney's hand.

Cross looked at Zollicoffer, who lay smiling with eyes closed.

Miss Broadus put screens around Delaney. Cross remained in the aisle, watching Miss Adair's fine figure as she walked from the ward. Miss Broadus came from behind the screens.

"We are ready, doctor," she said.

"Move him away," Cross said softly. He nodded to the dead boy smiling beneath his cap with its aviator's wings.

Dozier, by holding his shaving mirror above his head, could watch the young nurses walking in the quadrangle for afternoon exercise. Enlisted men got the best of everything in this war. Enlisted men were not called upon to treat nurses as gentlemen might treat ladies. There was something about an officer that either repelled a nurse or caused her to treat him with a respect that amounted to isolation.

There was a marine sergeant walking in the garden with a tall blonde nurse who only once came on duty with Cross for a morning's dressing. Dozier knew the sergeant. He occasionally came by the lieutenant's bed and sat stiffly for a brief call. Dozier had the feeling during these calls that the sergeant was being polite as he fingered the bandages on his tiny left hand and rubbed it from time to time to keep the cold out.

Once the sergeant had called at a farmhouse where Dozier was quartered. It was one of those farmhouses with white walls and a thatched roof with an old Frenchman living in it, such as Captain Jackson sought to identify. There was a girl in the farmhouse who worked with her mother at the railway station. Her mother opened and closed the gates at the crossroads when the little short-dog French trains puffed by.

Dozier paid her a franc a day for a morning's fire of twigs and a jug of hot water. He would spread his poncho on the hearth and sponge his body before getting on to the town's major's house for breakfast. The girl sometimes stood in the doorway and watched. Dozier always treated her as a gentleman should when in France to save an entire country, bathing with his back to her and making her smile innocently. Then one evening he found the girl and the sergeant spooning in the field across the canal.

The sergeant and the blonde nurse were walking aimlessly. The blonde nurse laughed heartily at something the sergeant was saying, chin close against her shoulder, and danced away, out of the shaving mirror. Maybe by the time Delaney got over his interminable crisis Dozier would be well enough to walk in the garden with Miss Adair.

There was a couple sitting back of a yew tree on a white marble bench. Dozier, by shifting precariously to the right and holding the mirror at an inclined angle, managed to get them into his vision. The mirror and the window were by way of being Dozier's recreation, now that Miss Adair was pressed so hard with other duties. He was astonished to discover the couple to be old Miss Broadus and Cross. They were only talking, however. Cross was emphasizing something.

Dozier put the mirror down and lay respectfully as the wailing wood winds and brasses of the detachment band played Chopin's "Funeral March" in the street that ran along the back of the hospital. It would be Zollicoffer's march. Zollicoffer would share the march with others that would be flag-draped in a big truck creeping along in low gear, the night orderlies made into a forlorn detachment marching by it, clumsy rifles on tired shoulders.

Usually the patients on the other side of the ward twisted to the windows when the truck went by every afternoon. Now they remained fast to beds and the ward settled into a long silence that hovered over the room until the supper trays came with bread pudding.

After supper Cross and Miss Broadus made the night rounds. Miss Broadus stopped at Dozier's bed. Cross went on, saying cautiously to Miss Broadus: "Speak to him about it."

Miss Broadus asked Dozier to request that he be moved to Zollicoffer's vacant place. "Your bed and all," she said. "We want you to make Lieutenant Delaney take some interest in the life of the ward."

"He has a lot of company," Dozier said. "Maybe he wouldn't like it."

Miss Broadus scouted such a notion. "You'd be wonderful for him," she said.

"You're the life of the ward." She smiled impishly. "Your newspaper is coming along famously. The colonel had a copy the other day."

"We're getting a better quality of paper," he said.

Miss Broadus moved down to Cross, who was busy taunting an infantryman named Harker for not taking more exercise upon two broken legs. He wagged his finger.

"If you don't, you'll pay for it in adhesions all your life. Just get out and slam down on them. Run some of the nurses around the corridors. Good for you." He winked. "Good for the nurses."

"Doctor," said Miss Broadus loudly, "Lieutenant Dozier wishes to know if he may move his bed next to Lieutenant Delaney."

"I don't think it would harm anything," Cross said. "I'll speak to him." Cross walked over to Dozier. "Go down there," Cross said under his breath, "and cut him out of that girl. She's seeing too much of him for his own good. You can do it. Just barge right in and freeze him out."

"But I might drive her away."

"That's a good idea, too," Cross said, calling the orderly to him. "Help me move this bed," he said, grasping the foot. "Just lie still, lieutenant, we'll take the whole thing along."

Delaney seemed to be sleeping. He did not wake when Dozier moved in.

When morning came Miss Adair seemed surprised to find Dozier in Zolly's place. But she was distressed to learn of poor Zolly's death.

"He was so patient and silent we hardly knew he was here, did we, Terry?" Miss Adair had tears in her eyes. "And of course I always had the feeling that I could do nothing for him. That was what just killed me."

Delaney was eager for war news. "How'd that Fifth French Army come out?"

Miss Adair placed her chair equidistant between the two marines. "I can only stay a little while this morning. I've been neglecting the enlisted men."

"It's the first time anyone ever neglected them," Dozier said.

"What's the matter?" Delaney asked, fixing his large blue eye on Miss Adair's large blue eyes.

"Nothing," she said, sitting erect and reading the papers mechanically for a half hour, Dozier inhaling deeply and Delaney silent.

Dozier knew that Miss Adair was the only girl in the world for him. He wanted to know her first name so that he might think of her as Muriel Adair or Maurine Adair or Marlene Adair. It would be something like that. If the newspapers were mailed to her it was possible her name would be printed on one of them somewhere. Without Freiburg's help now, he succeeded in touching the floor with the tips of his fingers as she read on, his eyes bursting, his head under his bed.

Suddenly Dozier saw the lower half of Miss Van Clerk, the little dark nurse with skinny legs who trundled the agony-wagon, directly against the foot of the bed. He saw her white Cuban-heeled shoes, her fuzzy cotton ankles, and the wheels of the agony-wagon. He swung himself back upon the mattress.

Cross was standing by the wagon, fastening a fresh gown. Without a word Cross drew a fresh pair of rubber gloves from a toweled package and shook the boric acid from them in clouds, and began coaxing them upon his narrow hands.

"What's the matter with me?" Dozier cried.

"You've been hanging your head down too long," Cross said, indicating that Miss Van Clerk might as well remove the dressings from the foot.

Dozier sat up and stared at Cross. Presently a great light fell upon his way. "Hey, that's unfair!" he cried. "Give me a break, doc."

Cross moved in by Miss Adair. He seemed sorry to disturb her. "Excuse me," he said gallantly, careful lest his fresh gown touch her clothing. He mumbled to Miss Van Clerk something about "a-small-instrument-please" and inspected the hole in Dozier's foot with eyes magnified in the lenses of his steel spectacles.

His spectacle case dropped to the floor. Miss Adair picked it up and put it, beneath the gown, in the doctor's pants pocket.

"With her here, too!" cried Dozier. "You're just a damned butcher."

"I must go," said Miss Adair, smiling at Cross.

"Not now," Delaney said with annoyance. "They'll be through with him in a minute."

"I'll remember that," Cross said, lost in contemplation of the foot.

"I didn't mean that," Dozier apologized. "But you're really not going to put that probe into my foot. Not at this hour. I've not assimilated my breakfast. I've not got up my nerve."

"Who said I was going to probe?" Cross was twisting a fleck of merciful cotton around the end of the probe. "I'm just going to use it as an application for a bit of iodine."

"Hell," said Dozier, perceiving that it was just a ruse by Cross, "hell, why didn't you say so? Go ahead."

His confidence returned. "Hello, Miss Van Clerk." Miss Adair was leaving. "Don't go," Dozier said. "It's not—not anything at all."

Cross chose a little fishhook probe.

"You said you wouldn't!" Dozier called sharply. Miss Adair had straightened things around Delaney's bed and was leaving.

Cross came closer. "After all," he said sincerely, "it's unbandaged now and she's gone. We may as well go ahead." Dozier hesitated. "Come," Cross said sharply, "let's show this other gyrene how an old soldier takes it." He turned to the foot and began bending the little probe with the forceps as Dozier grinned and nodded consent.

When it was over Cross was smiling. "What I should be," he said, "is a fellow like Gilson. A joy-bringer." He put his hand on Dozier's upper arm and squeezed it affectionately. "It's a tough war, isn't it?" He was winking hard, as hard as the end man in a minstrel show.

Dozier winked back. The foot was dressed and he had not made a sound. Miss Adair had gone but it was better to have the friendship of Cross. The doctor babied no one and yet commiserated a fellow by making him stand the gaff. Dozier struck at Cross with his skinny arm. The doctor struck a posture with his left hand slightly in advance of his right, crouching in the manner of Benny Leonard.

"In about three months," Dozier said, "I'll take you on." Cross was sparring, thrusting his left in fast and keeping his right hand low. "Then I'll pay you back for all that probing. I'll kick hell out of you."

"You couldn't do it," Cross said.

"Won't I be well then?"

"It wouldn't make any difference," Cross winked, throwing his right. "You never saw the day you could do it." The surgeon suddenly relaxed and soberly walked around the bed to Delaney. "How are you making it?"

"I'm not making it," Delaney sighed.

"Well, I won't dress you today," Cross said. "But it's time you were sitting up and calling some of these ward liars. None of them ever saw any war to hurt. You've seen it all. Go after them."

Delaney turned his face into the pillows. Cross tucked in his underlip and looked quizzically at Dozier. He picked up Delaney's chart and with a rubber finger traced the rising curve of the new man's temperature.

Cross raised his sandy eyebrows above the rim of the steel loops he looked through, talking pleasantly as he did so. "I used to box a lot at Johns Hopkins," he said, "my first year of medicine. Then I worked nights in a drug store and had to give it up."

"I'll bet you were good." Dozier marked the rising curve, too.

"I was getting good." Cross wanted to sit and chat, for he seemed tired of standing. After he removed the gloves and the gown he helped himself to a cigaret and smoked silently, watching Delaney. "Well," he sighed, "I've got to go open up that thorax. See you tomorrow."

After Cross had gone Dozier felt miserable about Delaney. He opened his own newspaper and called timidly: "Want me to read you the London Daily Mail?"

"Northcliffe's vulgar," Delaney said testily.

"It ain't Northcliffe; it's me," Dozier said.

Delaney wouldn't answer.

Dozier instructed Delaney in hospital etiquette. When offered sympathy such as "How-do-you-feel?" and "Did-you-pass-a-good-night?" and "Poor-fellow-does-it-pain-you-much?" Delaney had only to reply "A. P. O. N." and the matter ended there.

The letters were code for a gasping man who wished to be let very much alone. The letters were to be decoded as "ain't putting out nothing." With those words even Gilson could be placated with a twisting corner of the mouth in lieu of his rights to a broad, expansive smile.

Of course, after Gilson once heard a patient actively conversing in a ward, there seemed to be no constituted military authority in the American Expeditionary Forces capable of enjoining his rights to a large sickly smile. After new convoys had dulled a ward with long rows of A. P. O. N.'s, Gilson walked the corridors with brows knit, possibly considering in the event of another world cataclysm ways and means of breaching the conventions of wounded men and of suspending the rights of A. P. O. N.

"It's a good thing," Delaney said, opening his eye to stare at Dozier. "After all, when you're ill nothing's any good at all, unless it's a voice you love. Mothers know that there are no good words to a lullaby. Words are no good for sympathy. That's the reason lullabies have a long string of sounds without words."

"Say that again!" Dozier thought Delaney was pretty deep.

"A. P. O. N.," Delaney said.

That day he spoke no more. In the late evening Dozier printed a bulletin that "T. Delaney, 2nd Lt. U. S. M. C., was A. P. O. N." and was himself marooned in silences among others of Delaney's taciturnity. His shaving mirror no longer showed him the young nurses in the quadrangle. He could perceive a large tree in the street outside the hospital shielding an upper-story window that occasionally gave glimpses of a fat woman working at the *dentilles* of a lace loom.

After the woman lighted a lamp and began to clear the table for her evening meal, an elderly man in stiff black entered. He removed his coat and his cuffs, and then the shutters were closed.

Darkness came into the new end of the ward with no lamps by the beds of the new patients. Occasionally Freiburg hissed an unintelligible whisper down the aisle, and Harker hobbled to him with a tangerine about midnight. When Hugh scratched his matches for cigarets old Jackson circled his own cigaret ends in glowing traceries, friendly waves to a man far away in the gloom.

Hugh's fever came back the seventh day in Delaney's corner. In the late afternoon the ward walls began to accumulate small bubbles which swam in transparent sheets; and sometime after taps the four diminutive marines returned to exorcise them. They glided through the window and remained a little aloof from the bed, waiting for Hugh Dozier to have a shot of morphine. They refused to flutter very near until he had taken the narcotic.

In the old days, when Hugh first came to the hospital, they arrived regularly after the night nurse had withdrawn the needle. They approached gently as Hugh's heart became warm and sickly, and when the drug set up a full glowing the little marines carried him, their wings beating gently in the dark, out of the window and to the roof, where they moored him with an enormous Manila rope and swung him, cooling and happy, in soothing winds.

The four little men hovered warily as Hugh refused to call the night nurse, who would in turn get the night supervisor to speak to the officer of the day about dispensing l.h.t. morphine sul. ¼ gr. for the night nurse's needle. At four in the morning the officer of the day entered the ward with the night supervisor and the two of them whispered over the figure of an A. P. O. N. across the aisle. The doctor walked away, passing through the little marines, who were slowly drifting up and down the corridor three feet above the floor.

When breakfast came they were gone and Hugh's shaking hands crammed bacon and scrambled eggs into his mouth, and four large prunes. Miss Broadus bewailed this when she read his chart shortly afterwards. Cross appeared hastily in a surgical gown with cap and mask and ignored Dozier, as he, too, scanned the chart. Cross shook his head about the breakfast and eyed Miss Broadus severely.

Cross had to hurry back to the surgical, and Hugh felt better. Cross would not operate that day, and probably would not dress his wounds; so the few bubbles beginning to gather in the morning sunlight were not without silver linings.

A long time after that came sounds of trumpets and whistles and someone saying close by that an armistice had been signed in a railway car far to the north, by the several generals conducting the war. In the midst of this Bill, the orderly, and one of his friends arrived, bearing the curious black canvas stretcher belonging to the X-ray room, and Hugh went for a ride, the armistice forgotten in the novelty of going into the garden with vision unobscured by morphine and atropine.

The stretcher had to be borne down the stairway again, this time easily observed as a boxed affair with six turns. It was uncanny how Bill knew just when to angle the stretcher. Hugh marveled that Bill had carried him so many times.

In the garden the shrubs were nodding on a wide grassy plane and the sun splashed the walls with a brilliant white. Beneath Bill's feet the gravel walk crackled loudly and far away on the horizon young nurses were rushing by, starched smocks and uniforms radiating many delightful compensations after so many days of chlorides.

At the first turn in the quadrangle the party met Miss Adair in her uniform, more lovely than ever beneath skies, with her eyes shading into deep patches with blue glints far back in their centers. It made Hugh feel well to meet her this way and it was good to know that her astonishment was genuine.

"Hugh Dozier, you're not down on the operating-room list this morning." She carried some dusty flowers in her hands, rather ugly flowers, but it would not be unpleasant to get them. He stared at her from his ill-placed pillow and suddenly understood that she had used his first name.

"What's your first name?"

She smiled at that, it seemed to him tenderly, and answered, "Arlene."

Nurses who gave ether always had good skins, but their eyes as they peered down upon a man showed recesses and hollows with shadows networked into small veins. The choiceness of Arlene's eyes when she stared down upon a man lay in the absence of hollows and lines. "What's the matter? An emergency?"

Hugh knew well enough but answered, "I don't know," from some irresistible impulse to take an unfair advantage of her.

She caught his hand, then, as the stretcher moved out of the quadrangle and into a narrow passage with white-washed walls that echoed to the rattle of metal ware and the hum of dynamos, Hugh made up his mind to tell the truth, rather than have her discover it when Bill carried him to the X-ray room. There was no way of asking Bill to carry him to the operations anteroom, where patients lay on stretchers close to the floor to await their turns.

"Nothing's wrong, Arlene," he said. "Just an X-ray of my foot."

The girl watching his flushed face, he knew, was unbelieving. She put her delicate hand against his face that burned against it.

"That dreadful foot," she said, eyes deep wells of practiced pity. "I had to leave the other day." Bill was kicking open the door into the radiology unit. "I can go in here," she said. "They let me in here." She was grieving, Hugh could see. "They won't let me go into the operating room," she was saying sadly. "They let Gilson go, though."

Hugh knew that this was an outrage. "Gilson crawls under doors," he said. "They caught him in the colonel's mustache yesterday. The colonel ran to the delousing room, but Gilson hopped onto an amputation and escaped up the incinerator chimney."

Bill was setting the stretcher down outside the metal screen that walled off the X-ray lamps. He unpinned the chart from Hugh's breast and nodded to his friend to follow him to the plate room. Miss Adair dropped down on the floor by him.

"You boys just break my heart. Always gay. Just simply wonderful, you men." She was very near to him. "Even if you are silly, Hugh Dozier."

There was no offering in her eyes. Hugh thought it was a set piece. It was like a Chicago lecturer back of the lines just before he was set to ask kindness and equality for the Negro troops. Miss Adair was an A. P. O. N. in another way, for she wasn't putting out anything for Hugh Dozier. Old Freiburg was a cop but he knew his onions.

"Apple sauce," Dozier said curtly.

The girl was on her knees by the litter. She stiffened at his curtness. "What do you mean? That I'm insincere? Have I ever given you any cause to take anything for granted?"

"Listen," Hugh said. There was the slithering hiss of an X-ray lamp and the groan of a high-tension transformer somewhere over the wall. "I'm just having a picture taken. Go ladle that apple sauce somewhere else."

"You are rude," she said, tears in her eyes.

"I've got to be rude. Running me nuts this way. I'm too ill—no, I'm not sick at all—but I'm just too tired to get you out of my head."

She was leaning above him; her eyes were as big as saucers. "Do you want me to?" she whispered.

"Hell, yes."

Afterwards Dozier remembered that it really was a mechanical gesture, done with deftness and dispatch. Like old Miss Broadus administering an alcohol rub. Arlene held his head to the hard little ridge bone of her chest. Her coat was rough cord. Some sort of dinky badge that held down her tie scratched his ear. Then her breath was on his face and he supposed she was kissing him, for he knew that a thin, hard line of mouth was pressed against him.

"There!" she cried, and was gone.

Cross was standing over him, smiling. "Wipe that rouge off your face," he said. "And let's put you under a fluoroscope. I'll look at you direct."

Bill had come back with his friend and they lifted the stretcher and carried it somewhere in the black-walled austerity to a metal table where Cross manipulated sliding bars and plates and switches.

Presently Cross cut the lights off and took his arm. "I've got good news for you," he said. "You're all cleared up in that foot except a little piece."

"There's a little bit of barbed wire somewhere," Hugh said apprehensively.

"It's just a little place," Cross debated. "Look here, you are down here now. I think I'll ream it out and suture it up once and for all. After that a few stitches, but no probes any more and no dressings."

"Let's do it," said Hugh.

"Let's. But promise me two things."

"Anything," Hugh said.

"Promise me, if the thing I do ever breaks down and gives you trouble, you'll let me know. You'll be shipped off home soon, but I like to keep a record of these things. Otherwise, I don't know a thing about anything radical I do. I'll just give you a post card to mail to me. If it breaks down, you'll let me know?"

"I'll come in person."

"Good! And one other thing. You've got a good belly. Promise me you'll keep those breakfast eggs. The colonel's in the operating room. I'll get hell if you go throwing 'em all around."

"I'll save 'em for old Miss Broadus," Hugh promised.

"Good boy, Hugh!" Cross was all business. Bill and his untidy friend caught up the litter. Cross opened the door to the anteroom, where the smell of ether crept under the door from beyond.

Bill and his friend could not go farther. They set down the burden on the floor again. It was probably all arranged, for a pretty nurse with soft hands was rolling back his sleeve and sponging his arm with a wisp of cotton soaked in alcohol. There was a faint sting and his heart began to feel as if muddy water were being pumped through it very, very slowly.

Hugh thought of Miss Adair with dispassion at first. As his heart choked along at low speed she gained in his estimation. Naturally, a kiss tumbled that way upon a man's face cold seemed cold. Maybe, after all, Miss Adair loved him very deeply and was so self-sacrificing that she held herself in check lest she deprive hundreds of men of her sweet ministrations.

If she would come to his bed at night and hold hands at first, things might be different. The little marines flapped their small wings gently and picked up his body, floating it through the door into the white-tiled room beyond.

"Let's go," said Cross; then, whispering: "Hold those eggs."

Cross used nitrous oxide to knock him out, shooting the stuff through a rubber bladder. If she would come to the bed as soon as it grew dark . . .

Hugh came to life being planed up the box of stairs by the faithful Bill. His foot was in a vice and was pretty hot, but not too hot. "Did I keep those eggs somebody?" He heard his own voice far away.

"You've still got 'em," Bill said proudly.

The stalky flowers Arlene had held an hour before were now divided between his table and Delaney's. The other marine tried to hold Dozier's head some minutes later and was rebuked by old Miss Broadus, who waited until her patient had reacted before asking him if he wished anything.

"Do you need anything?" It was always asked this way. Morphine was always a dead secret. "Maybe the doctor will give you some medicine," she whispered.

Hugh Dozier wanted to say that he needed Miss Adair. He knew it would fetch her, regardless of his breakdown in the X-ray room. Miss Adair answered the calls of the stricken without regard to their moral fitness.

There was no overpowering pain to warrant such a measure, but it was better to dope off than to raise his head each time there was a light step in the ward.

"Get Doctor Cross to give me some medicine, please," Dozier said feebly. His manner indicated his assumed unfamiliarity with narcotics. "Get me a shot of hop" would have brought Miss Broadus back with a glass of water and ten grains of veronal. It was better to have the morphine, anyway. Raising his head a hundred times an hour would bring Hugh's temperature up to the boiling point in a post-operative humor.

Hugh knew that Cross had taken a chance. It was best to humor the foot. If Miss Adair came, the smell of the sandalwood would wake him up. If she came to see Delaney, the morphine would isolate him from a vindictive emotion.

Presently Lieutenant Dozier slept. He awakened in the twilight to find that one of the A. P. O. N.'s across the way had disappeared and old Jackson was in his place at the gloomy end of the ward. Jackson was a man who talked well naturally about women or about God. This grounding in the fundamentals of hospital parlance gave him priority after taps, and Dozier was warmed to think that Jackson's removal to the bed of a vanished A. P. O. N. was a piece of thoughtfulness by Cross. Jackson began a semi-religious discussion soon after the lights were turned down. It was instinctive among the causerie that talk about women, with Delaney hearing every word, would not be the more tactful subject, particularly as the conversations usually centered about the peculiarities of human behavior among the more commercial of the French nationals.

By midnight the ward wore a revivalist air. Dozier, recovering from the shocks of the day, reflecting that, in his military prime, he had carelessly tossed away several khaki-bound Testaments into rubbish cans, found himself curiously relating how, as a little boy, he had welcomed the pleasure of memorizing the catechism's beauty with the eagerness a child might have been expected to show at the gift of a pearl-handled, double-action, hand-ejector, police-safety-model, .38-caliber revolver.

"The Jews," Jackson said, in one of his attempts to bring Delaney into conversation, "had passed their golden age when the New Testament was written and were ripe for national dissolution."

Dozier did not possess the strength needed to contest this, and Delaney, smoking interminably, confined his interest to that of a polite listener.

"For one thing," Jackson argued with himself, "there was not a fight in it."

"What about Armageddon?" It was the first question Delaney had ever asked the ward.

"Only a picture show," Jackson snorted, baiting. There was no answer. "Think of the battles of the Old Testament. Of how Joshua mined and sapped the walls of Jericho. England had promised the Jews enough cordite to blow Jericho out of the water, but in the end the Jews had to float an outside six-percent debenture in New York City to purchase the necessary trinitrotoluol."

"How did Joshua detonate it in those days?" Delaney had chuckled. Delaney was showing a sign of interest.

"Joshua rigged a fulminate of mercury cap in a tube over which he ingeniously set a magnifying glass to catch the sun's rays, head on, exactly at meridian," Jackson said. "Then he marched his Israelite infantry around the walls from breakfast to noon, occasionally breaking them into open order to sing 'Bang Away at LooLoo' and ease routine. When the meridian detonated the work, he threw out the skirmishers with two divisions of Shittim pioneers and himself led the main body at zero plus ten. At zero plus thirty he sent up yellow smoke to show the main objective of Rahab's Dance Hall gained. Then ten minutes after that, General Nun, the corps headquarters chaplain, came in with the reserves and made the place a shambles. There never were such moppers-up as the Israelites. The Turks are Boy Scouts beside their memory."

Delaney was enjoying this. He was sitting up, rubbing his good eye and scratching his face beneath the new yellow beard.

"They spared no one, eh?"

Dozier knew enough Scripture to realize that Joshua's celebrated clemency at Jericho was confined to a class of women politely referred to in his Sabbath school as unfortunates. "The poor unfortunates of Jericho who were spared." But old Jackson had seized the bit and was away on treacherous ground.

"He saved the Railroad Street ma'm'selles," Jackson said. "Joshua not only possessed what we call military character, but he was also equipped, that is to say, imbued, with what the Jews of that day called 'personal magnetism.' "

The old man was embarrassed after that and talked himself clear. "Some provost guards were caught squeezing francs from two corporals of the Seventh Israelite cavalry. The two lads had taken a pair of Canaanite ma'a'selles down to Rahab's place, just to have a few dances and pick up the dialect. Josh gave the M. P.'s ten days' bread and water and loss of two years' pay. Consequently, he also broke up the graft forever, by designating Rahab's place within leave area from Saturday retreat to reveille Monday morning.

"He was an efficient general, but history also records that after a fight he was just one of the boys. A sergeant major on general staff told the colonel of the Seventh that, after Joshua departed in triumph, Rahab went around the place her kimono fastened with old Josh's Euphrates campaign medal."

The captain then scratched his tattooed chest with his tattooed hand and gave Delaney a polite opportunity to enter the conversation. But the boy across the way was down again.

For three days Jackson held the ward as barren of love lore as a seminary. A few backsliders such as Freiburg, deprived of their normal need for conversation about women, secured transfers to the convalescent ward before their returning strength warranted the capacities for self-help the other ward demanded of its patients. Few patients in the ward knew enough about religion to talk of it night after night. It was Delaney who freed the ward of its eclectic conversational style.

A single bird arrived in the ward to take a bed next to Jackson left vacant by an engineer officer named Holsteen who felt the need of conversational stimulus, and who had himself carried with the convalescents into the sun. Holsteen had been an all-around wit who solemnly every night before taps had read a case history from Krafft-Ebing in sepulchral tones, afterwards discussing the strange case of a Mr. X, of Wiesbaden, or the curious manner of Mrs. Z, of Posen, in a serious and helpful manner.

"Why, man," said Jackson, apprised of his transfer, "you can't walk a step!"

"But I can crawl," the engineer officer said. "I'm going in that ward and rid myself of my suppressed conversational desires. I'm tired of Jonah and Leviticus. I need to learn more about the two traveling salesmen."

A "single bird" in ward parlance was a lone wounded man. To arrive wounded, and a solitary traveler, indicated an importance beyond rank or military privileges. The single bird proved to be a Y. M. C. A. man. He had been painfully wounded crosswise, and had been sewed up so securely across the gluteal parts that no skin was available to accommodate bending his body. He came in upon his stomach and swore manfully when inched from stretcher to bed, ward lights going up and the ward aroused.

Miss Broadus rigged a semicircular housing of wire netting to cover his middle, over which blankets were draped, the effect being that of an angry dog in a small kennel when he craned his distorted head around at his inquisitors. He looked out angrily, barking at orderlies for food. He was a short, fat man with a ruddy face of the sort that, unfortunately for its owner, never can seem to be hungry or tired.

"But a cut of cold beef?" he pleaded. "Just anything. Cold beef and horseradish on Russian rye bread."

"I'm sorry, fellow," Bill said politely. "But the kitchen's closed and the chef's already drunk on lemon extract. I wouldn't go near him."

Jackson leaned over to him in a kindly manner. "We got just those sandwiches," he said. "But they're fifty cents this time of night. And chocolate's twenty-five extra. Hot chocolate, thirty-five."

"I haven't anything smaller than a fifty-dollar bill," the poor devil answered sincerely.

"How were you wounded?" Jackson asked sympathetically. "I didn't know a man with a fifty-dollar bill ever joined the army."

The stout one groaned. "High explosive. Our own guns . . ." He seemed suspicious. "I was selling chocolate at a crossroads. Some of our boys came by. I sold them as much as I could afford to, at cost. They unlimbered nearby. There was a short fuse, I heard afterwards."

Jackson was incredulous. "Did it burst?" He held an offering of French chocolate from which he had once bitten a gritty plug in the days of long ago. "Just casting it upon the waters," he said genially, "for I know that any time I've got seventy-five cents it'll come back."

The new patient bit into the chocolate. "I'll never forget you, brother," he said. "One good turn, you know."

Delaney was sitting up staring at the man. "I heard you preach once," he called across. "You made the eagle scream."

Jackson instantly drew him out. "This would be a lot finer war if the churches, instead of being for it, were dead set against it. Give it the irresistible appeal to the youth of the country and dispense with recruiting posters."

"I've thought about that a lot," Delaney said savagely.

Jackson was politely all ears.

Dozier whispered to Delaney. "Go right after him, boy."

"Oh, yes," Delaney answered Jackson. He added: "You see, I was a divinity student."

Dozier heard sighs of relief along the sides of the room. A divinity student. Naturally, the marine's situation, if he failed to win out, would not be difficult to bear. Alcatraz, who was a violinist, a fiddler of such parts that he was grooming for the Philharmonic for his career, had lost three fingers of his left hand. He made jokes in the bed by the corner when the barber cut his hair, saying that he had grown it long twenty-one years for nothing. But a minister had no call to be grieving over such a singular accident in that ward. It would not deprive him of his career.

"I see his view," the new man said, straining painfully to glimpse Delaney. "I think the churches will lose caste by sponsoring the war. It would have been wiser if they had opposed it. I have not enjoyed a moment of it. But a man of independent means couldn't hang back. I had to do something, even a little thing, to serve those who fight."

Delaney shouted: "You are wrong about the churches! They couldn't hold back. It's their ideal. The young man who is torn apart to save the race. It's their story. They can't welsh on their own story."

"Look here," Jackson said vaguely, "we're not really tough in this crowd. Just a few local callouses for emergencies. Let's drop this."

The man in the dog-house who had strained at his religion now swallowed a bar of gritty chocolate. He meant to use a kindly voice. In the excitement of straining to face Delaney, however, he tore at his sutures, sending quivers down his spine and pitching his voice to a scream. "You are not going to be a minister, are you?"

Delaney pondered this. "I don't know what I'll turn out to be," he said sadly.

"Then in the name of heaven," came shrilly from the dog-house, *"what are you going to be? Fish or flesh or good red herring?"*

Delaney laughed deep in his throat and quoted: "There's a divinity that shapes our ends, you know . . ." He turned his face to the wall.

A swift shape darted down the corridor to his bed. "This is Gilson. You're waking up, eh? Smile, old boy. Give us the old smile."

Delaney turned upon the man, glaring, his face that of a bearded monster. He might leap from his bed upon Gilson, who stood, craned over the foot of the bed, his warm heart in his dancing eyes. Instead, Delaney's features relaxed into a beatific smile.

"Brother," he said, shaking the man's hand. "What's that name? Gilson? Howdy, Gilson. Howdy coming, old boy? Sit down and tell me all about yourself."

Gilson sat upon the bed. "Don't excite yourself," he said. "Just smile. It'll win in a walk. The man who can smile when everything goes dead wrong."

"Did you ever hear the story," Jackson began to the new man, "of the commercial traveler who went to a lonely farm to sell the lamp chimney to the farmer's wife? I'd like to tell it to you. I've kept that story to myself since an engineer officer whispered it to me twenty days ago."

Jackson was launched upon a long detail of a rainy night, an attic room, an unexpected guest. Delaney was whispering something to Gilson, who was smiling. Dozier caught words from Jackson and from Delaney. "I'm sorry, stranger, but there's only one bedroom . . . My clothes in the locker there. Miss Broadus has the key . . . Thanks, I'll just make myself comfortable in the hayloft . . . She doesn't live with the nurses but has a room down in some hotel in Angers . . . I'd like for you to try one of these lamp chimneys, ma'am . . . Be a good boy, Gilson. It's a matter of life and death."

Delaney was whispering to Gilson, pleading. Dozier sneaked a skinny arm into the fresh fudge on Delaney's table and ate sparingly, piece after piece, until he was drowsy from the sweet. Presently he had a horrible dream.

In the dream Miss Adair proved to be Mrs. Delaney. She was more beautiful than ever. She followed lieutenant Delaney to France to be near him. She and Delaney were married on the docks in 1917. She had given birth to a baby girl. It was staying at her grandmother's in the country while Mrs. Delaney visited France.

"Are you sure it's a girl?" Delaney asked her.

"Quite sure. She tried to enlist in the marines and was rejected." She wrung her hands over a bar of sandalwood soap, as if washing her hands of Delaney forever. The dream scurried on through a sequence of unpleasant situations. It was about to end with Dozier, harrowed by his infelicities, rushing single-handed to attack the entire German army. Bayonet brandished high, he charged forward fiercely . . .

Old Miss Broadus was shaking Hugh Dozier. Dozier awakened guiltily and looked about the cold ward. Miss Broadus was crying, probably because Mrs. Delaney was sending him to his death. The ward was quiet but for her sobbing and a long spluttering snore against the pillows beneath the dog-house, which had fine acoustical properties.

"Where is he?" Miss Broadus sobbed out the words.

Delaney's bed was empty but for a field locker opened upon it, shaving tackle and underwear littering the covers.

Bill emerged from beneath the bed. "Sorry," he said, "but the gun's gone."

"I told you to steal it from him."

"Then you told me not to, you recall."

"I'll have you discharged."

"A little irregular, but the war's over and it'd be a big help," Bill said.

Miss Broadus caught Dozier by his shoulder and tried to shake the truth from him. Dozier, awakened, observed that Miss Adair was on the far side of the bed. The situation was difficult of realizing. Either he was attacking a German line single-handed and had been shot down and was now in delirium imagining Miss Adair and Bill and old Miss Broadus were weeping by Delaney's empty bed, or they were by the empty bed and he had dreamed about Mrs. Delaney and Delaney's little girl and the Germans.

"Answer truthfully!" Miss Broadus shouted. "You know you helped him get his clothing."

Dozier gazed at a foot embedded in three hundred pounds of sand. "I might have knitted him a pair of socks," he said, "but I ran no errands for him." It was brutal for Miss Adair to cry that way right before his eyes.

"Miss Adair said he tried to force entrance into her room at one o'clock. After he had gone, she became alarmed and got me."

"I asked him how he got his uniform," Miss Adair sobbed in a faint kitten's wheezing; almost inaudibly. "He said marines always had friends."

Miss Broadus came in with a hoarse note of grief.

"You sent him to his death. Out in the woods in some lonely spot."

"A lonely spot's best," Dozier said, lighting a cigaret and taking a calm view for Miss Adair's benefit. "But you leave him alone and he'll come home, wagging his tail behind him."

Miss Broadus wept. "That poor boy out in the woods with his brains blown out."

"He had been drinking heavily," Miss Adair added to her grief-stricken memories of Lieutenant Delaney's strange midnight call. "He said he needed me. I drove him away."

"Don't wake everybody," Dozier bleated, now fully awake. "You two! Give the man a chance to slip back before the colonel's around here with an arc light."

There was a shout below, and a joyous bellow of "Turn out the guard!" in a stentorian voice.

"Never mind the guard!" old Jackson shouted.

The ward awoke to the racket below. Someone was cursing to wake the hospital, and there was a bellow of "Take your hands off me, soldier!" There was a falling body on the first flight of the box stairs, some tramping and evidently the smash of a surgical cart thrown out of a window.

Lights went up. The ward was brilliant in the sudden shimmer. Delaney came clattering down the aisle, a good six-foot-two. He was singing snatches from "Rolling Down to Rio" and was in full fighting kit, buttons gleaming and brassards flashing.

"I saw the armadillo dillowing in his armor . . ."

Miss Broadus was herself again, starched and adamant. "Lieutenant Delaney." She confronted him. "Do you know what you're going to do?"

Delaney flung the dog-house from the Y. M. C. A. man, who blinked and tried to cover himself with his handkerchief.

"You want to know, too, I suppose? Well, I'm going to be an anthro-pol-o-gist. Going to study the earliest habits of man."

Gilson came in, smiling. "How's the old boy?" he said.

"Socko!" Delaney shouted as he swung, and Gilson was rendered A.P.O.N. "Here's a grin for you!" Delaney roared, looking into Gilson's closed eyes.

The officer of the day brought two strange orderlies from the shell-shocked ward.

"Is he shell-shocked?" Miss Adair was afraid of shell-shocked men.

So many shell-shocked men were only pretending. So many of them dared to take liberties . . .

The two unknown bearers undressed Delaney, who began to sleep soundly just as Gilson was waking up. They carried him away on a stretcher, Miss Broadus following the pall. She proudly bore a service automatic, forty-five caliber, and two musette bags.

"Don't cry, Arlene," Dozier said manfully; "don't cry, darling."

"You're so sweet," she said, following Miss Broadus.

Hugh Dozier's casts were removed the day before Christmas and he sat in a wheel chair by the window next to old Jackson's bed wondering how a world could be so large as to contain trees and several houses, a train and even a few sheep.

He was reclining gratefully, a flash of rum concealed in blankets over his lap. From time to time he sipped the rum through a tube which Jackson had lent him, "plucked," the old man said, "from the very fiber of my being."

"Hello, Dozier!"

It was a fine resonant voice that came from a very tall young man, bearded to the ears, the ensemble of new uniform set off by a black patch. "Too bad you can't be out. You've had a tough time, they say."

Dozier ignored Delaney.

"Does it still pain you much?" Delaney seemed solicitous.

"A.P.O.N.," Dozier mumbled dreamily. Damn these fellows with piddling wounds who came in, made a four-weeks' racket, and were on the boulevards again with only an eye out, bloated from fudge.

Delaney sat in the window a moment and swung his long legs. "Lend me a thousand francs, Dozier. You can't have any use for that much in years. The government will look after your simple needs."

Dozier turned to Captain Jackson. "Were you interrupted?" he asked. "Go on with your story. The farmer put his younger daughter in the crib with the baby . . ."

"After all," Delaney argued, "because you missed out so badly on the X-ray floor is no reason you'll be a spoil-sport and deny me the thousand francs to win her."

"Oh," said Dozier. She had been cruel enough to tell that. "If that's what you want it for, there's a thousand in the purse by my bed there. But do you know fifty other marines to share the first week's expense?"

"I'll start with you, anyway," Delaney said.

"Just send the money back to Hugh Dozier, Base Twenty-seven, Angers, any time in the next five years," Captain Jackson said helpfully, scratching his chest.

"Hello!" Delaney called, seizing Dozier's purse. "Scratching them off for the long winter, eh?" He came closer and inspected the tattoo on the captain's chest more closely. "How's the art this season?"

Jackson spat upon the floor. After all, it was his ward; his and Dozier's, with all the others gone, and Christmas coming tomorrow.

"I asked," Delaney said, cupping his hands, "how's the art this season?"

"I just won the blue in the still-life exhibition," Jackson answered coolly. "How does it look through your glass eye?"

Delaney turned the patch to Jackson and counted himself out a thousand francs from Dozier's purse. He looked again at Jackson's chest. "Not so good," he said pleasantly. "Too bad it's got to stay that way, isn't it? If you were a marine now, you could grow enough hair to cover it."

Jackson knocked his pipe out against his plaster cast. "Listen, young man," he begged earnestly, "do you know what I do to little marines before I've had my breakfast?"

Delaney made a note in a little book that he owed "H. Dozier, Lt. U. S. M. C. Hdq., Washington, D. C., $200," and turned blandly to Jackson. "No," he said. "What do you do to little marines before you've gummed your porridge?"

"I throw them down." Jackson rested his mild blue eyes on the younger man. "Then I take my knife, and I cut their tonsils out."

"I guess I'd better leave," Delaney said to Dozier. "I've still got my tonsils. Thanks for the big note. A fool and his money . . ."

"Both of us," said Dozier.

"Toodle-doo." Delaney was gone, waving a handsome salute.

"I've been in the army thirty years," Jackson remarked to the wall across the aisle, "and I've still got no more sense than to take official announcements as sincerely as if they were rumors."

Cross came in on his afternoon rounds. Somehow, he had managed a pair of breeches that were cut to fashion. He usually seemed to be carrying cantaloupes in his kneecaps, with putties of raw yellow pigskin worn much as detachable cuffs were when his grandfather was a surgeon.

Cross looked surprisingly well in doeskin facings. He wore boots he might have stolen from an English colonel after two years of service. He also wore the best ribbon the French could afford a doctor of his rank.

"Just dropped by to say farewell," he said.

"Who'll dress me?" Jackson was unhappy.

"New man," Cross said. "Better man than I am."

"Going home?" Dozier hoped he had come to say he would take Dozier along.

"No," said Cross; "going to Germany. Want to see what the Heinies are doing about semilunar cartilages when the capsule's dry."

"Always working," Dozier said.

"Not always," Cross said. "Going to make this pleasure as well as business."

"Pleasure!" said Jackson. "In Germany? With France prostrate at your feet?"

"Mrs. Cross is going with me," he said.

"Where's the madam? Didn't know there was one."

"Oh," Cross said, looking through his steel loops, "I thought I'd tell you. I got married this afternoon."

"When?" said Captain Jackson.

"Right after doing the prettiest graft on a humerus you ever saw," Cross replied. "Took a piece of shin bone and made a triangulation. The neck of the humerus was gone an inch, but I jammed on a splice with the scapula just the same. Fellow will get a pretty good arm."

Cross seemed tired. He lighted one of Jackson's cigarets and took a few puffs. From long habit he flexed the tendon Achilles of Jackson's right ankle and from a habit of equal duration old Jackson shut his eyes tightly and put his scalp back, lifting his ears by internal forces. "Don't forget to tell the new surgeon to keep that foot jammed in a Cabot splint," he said.

Cross moved over to Dozier's foot. "You got a good foot," he said. He smiled. "You had me going that day on the floor of the X-ray room."

Dozier eyed Cross sullenly. "Was that why you gave me the ether?"

Cross had fine hands. He worked the toes on Dozier's foot with practiced delicacy. "You got a good foot, didn't you?"

"Was that why you gave me the ether?"

"You drop me a card if it ever breaks down on you," Cross said, replacing the sock and the blankets.

Dozier was ugly. "And you drop me one," Dozier said.

"Arlene looks after the wounded men," Cross said, nodding to Arlene, who appeared in the doorway, waiting. Cross gathered his cap and gloves. "I hate to leave my two old patients," he said, looking about the ward where empty beds aired their burlaps, Miss Broadus and her eagle eye forgotten.

"We'll never meet such wonderful men again," Mrs. Cross said impulsively. "They just kill me. So patient. Never complaining. Heroes all."

"We'll never meet anybody like you," Dozier said, looking her almost sternly in the eye. He wanted her to know that she had hurt him.

Cross patted both men on the back and Arlene kissed them. "We must go," she said to Cross. She explained to his patients that, being a doctor, he was helpless. "I know I'll just have to do everything for him all his life," she said. "I've already started leaving him places and walking ahead." She had started. "I'll go find Lieutenant Delaney now and tell him good-by."

Cross finished his cigaret. He carefully put it out, in the captain's drinking glass. He gave a little friendly wave with his gloves.

He moved to the door, and turned again to look at Dozier. He waited for Dozier to say something.

"All the luck in the world," Dozier said finally. "It's a swell foot, you know." He grinned. "You got to it just in the nick of time."

"Good boy," Cross said, and clattered down the stairs.

There were big tears in Dozier's eyes.

"I know," said Jackson softly. "I hate a change of doctors, too." He also knew his cue to talk. "I wish there was a chimney piece here."

Dozier, choking, took a little suck of rum. "Why?"

"Well," Jackson said, "it's Christmas Eve. You and me might hang up our plaster casts."

The Odyssey of Three Slavs

BY

ALDEN BROOKS

IVAN, Feodor, and Petro, all three of them, came from a Province of Bessarabia. Ivan was large and strong; on the march he moved along like an elephant. Feodor was quick and nimble, and clever with his hands. As for Petro, though he was not as strong as Ivan nor as clever as Feodor, he could dance and sing better than any in the whole regiment. The three were great friends.

For months they and their comrades were drilled morning and afternoon, day after day, in the use of the rifle and the bayonet and shown how to dig trenches. The work was often tiring and difficult, but it was all a wonderful new experience; good food at every meal; stout clothes to wear; strong boots under one's feet; companionship with the simplest and greatest of men; hours, not always of poverty and drudgery, but sometimes of recreation and laughter; and ever throbbing in one's heart devotion to the Little Father and worship of our Lady of Kazan, Blessed Mother of God; and whom God protects none can harm.

When they were at last sent up to the front, impatient lest the war be ended before they had done their share, they were forced to wait many days in the rear. There were not enough rifles and cartridges for every one, and those ahead had first to die and drop their weapons before others could come up. But early one autumn morning they were at last crouching near the firing-line, marvelling at the weird noises overhead and the thunder all around, and suddenly whole swarms of Germans rushed out of the woods close by and, shooting and stabbing many, surrounded the rest of them and quickly rushed them off through the forest. Stunned, shameful, they hung their heads and stumbled along, praying with beating hearts to the Little Father that he might pardon them for having surrendered without fighting.

Then down the broad wood road came the yells of the Cossacks on their horses; and all of them swayed and split asunder, and in among them terribly thrust, leapt the horses, foaming, bleeding at the mouth, teeth showing, and whips hissed their leaden bullets about and swords thumped and rifles went off, and each of them grappled with the enemy by his side. When most of the Germans had been killed, and the Cossacks had searched all the pockets of the living and the dead, and all had equipped themselves

From: *The Fighting Men*: Copyright 1917. Scribners.

with rifles and cartridge cases, they turned and led back between them those of the enemy who still could walk.

Unfortunately, after that they lost their way in the forest, and the Cossacks rode on ahead and never returned, and some said take this opening, and others that, and in the end they trooped out of the forest into a land where the whole sky was black with the smoke of naphtha wells burning, and came into the very midst of thousands and thousands of soldiers who suddenly were not their brethren at all, but the enemy. Then one by one they gave up hope, dropped rifles, and amid much shouting and laughing let themselves be shoved into a large barbed-wire pen where there was only one thing for them to do—throw themselves upon the grass and, saying nothing to each other, try to forget that they had ever been born.

That afternoon, when the sun was only one tree high, they were on their feet again tramping along between cavalrymen down a dusty road lined with hundreds of wagons, cannon, and ambulances. Once, as they waded through a muddy stream, each could flop, tumble down, hold head to take a drink; but afterwards, staggering out, each must walk on faster than before, faster and faster, on and on, faster now than human legs could go. Finally, towards the very end of daylight, when none felt he could walk a verst further, they stumbled down to a halt in a railway-yard and then did as they were told, climbed wearily one after the other into freight cars. Almost before the last could push his way in, doors were shoved past their crowded backs and closed. And towards morning, to jerk all awake, the train began to move slowly away.

Behind closed doors they travelled all day long. At the top of the car there were narrow openings where the air rushed in and many could look out. At first, most of the time, standing or sunk to the floor, they drooped on each other and tried to sleep the hunger away. But finally, as often as the train stopped, all would struggle up and push and try to look out to see what food was being brought to them. Once, towards nightfall, as they rolled through the back of a great city and rumbled past hundreds and hundreds of dirty houses, the train came to a stop under a great building lit with many lights. Of a sudden all the windows up there were filled with a rush of men and women. Some wore shades over their foreheads; others leaned far out and waved their hands derisively; all were laughing, and presently all began to shout, "Russe Caput! Russki Caputsski!"

None of the men in the freight-cars answered back. Those nearest the openings remained dully staring, scowling. The train rolled on again. It passed into the darkness of the open country. It continued all night. In the car where were Ivan, Feodor, and Petro two of the company died before morning.

That next morning, however, the doors were pushed back by new soldiers they had not seen before and there on the ground in front of each car were buckets of water and a large basket filled with pieces of black bread. While one of the soldiers counted aloud, each could jump down, take a drink, take a piece of bread, then climb back into the car. And

Feodor jumped out twice and Petro twice and taking besides their own pieces the pieces belonging to the dead at the end of the car climbed back to share, in friendliness and sorrow, with whoever was most hungry.

That afternoon the train stopped for good. Outside beyond the fences of the station there were so many people shouting and cursing and waving their fists at them that they expected on leaving the freight-cars to be torn to pieces. Yet when they passed out, they passed between lines of soldiers, and now in all the people behind there was never one word.

The prison camp was on the other side of the town. It was a large muddy field with here and there lines of low sheds. All around were high walls of barbed wire. Beyond the wire walked sentinels carrying rifles with bayonets. In the middle of the camp was a raised platform. Upon it sat two soldiers beside a machine-gun.

There were other prisoners in the camp, men of all nations. But it was among the men of their own race that the newcomers wandered. A great sadness was over all of them. They had little to say to one another.

"Brother, greeting! Christ is risen!"

"He is risen indeed!"

For some days Ivan, Feodor, and Petro were troubled to learn the ways of the camp. And all these others in strange uniform were their friends. Yet when the men in blue, the men from France, came to talk to them, it was impossible to speak to each other, though each talked with his hand and made pictures in the dirt.

It was the men from England, however, who gave them the most astonishment, for many of these did not wear trousers like men, but skirts like women—except that they wore their skirts higher than any good woman ever wore. Also these same men from England would take off their blouses and, wrapping them up in a ball, would kick them about in the dirt, or mud even, and bump each other down with their hips until all stood red and sweating and out of breath. Or then they would take off their stockings and, winding them around their fists, stand close to each other and, nodding this way that way, hit at each other hour after hour. Once they asked Ivan to come and try the same. But the first thing Ivan knew, the big freckled-face man hit him out of turn a terrible blow on the nose and, almost knocking him off his feet, brought the blood from his nose into his hands. Then, while Ivan was standing with the others around him, telling him how to let the blood drop freely on the ground, Ivan suddenly clinched his fists in and threw his arms back and sent two of those standing-by flat on the ground. And then it was that the Frenchmen laughed so much.

But the gnawing hunger within soon held all their thoughts. From the first train-hours it had grown and grown. Now, when the bugle blew for dinner or supper, they would rush towards the big cauldrons with the others like a stampede, then wait pushing and shoving, though it was only to receive ever the same thin watery mess not much better than the stuff thrown to the pigs at home. Yet for last-comers there was often not even enough of this.

Twice a week most of the men from France, England, Belgium, received bundles filled with every kind of food. But for Russians never were there any such bundles. The best Russians could do, when the wagons came, was to stand and watch the French and English open their packages, then, crowded together, hold out a hand and keep eyes always on the ground for crumbs.

Meanwhile Ivan, Feodor, and Petro, sleeping together on two bundles of straw, grew filthier and filthier. The fleas and the white lice multiplied upon them. Also the weather grew colder and colder. Finally, all the camp became a lake of wet snow and mud. During the dark nights the only thing to do was again to say nothing and, close together, try to keep the cold from freezing each to death.

But the hunger was always the worst. Never anything solid to eat. Sometimes it happened that in their dreams they would find themselves home again with the snow falling lightly through the pine trees, the sleigh bells jingling merrily, and there, within doors next roaring hearth, there would be tables loaded with corn, fish, beans, bread, pies, honey-mead, vodka, everything imaginable; then the torture of it was at its very worst, for though they ate and ate and ate, never was there one moment of satisfaction, always the terrible gnawing within continued, and finally they would wake suddenly wild with hunger, half out of their heads, and in the chill early morning air go prowling over the camp like half-starving wolves.

In the swill-pails back of the kitchen they could now and then find bits of rotting meat, or dirty potatoes, or wilted leaves of wormy cabbage, but how many other wolves were there always there to push and struggle against! Or then if some morning one had the luck to be first at the pail, have it all to oneself a moment to pull over, then one of the cooks would be sure to steal up and give one a terrible blow over the back with a stick or his belt buckle.

One afternoon a man in uniform, writing at a table in the low window over the kitchens, placed a piece of bread upon the window-ledge and beckoned those below to take it. There were wild rushes; but the window-ledge was too high and the bread always too far back. Also the man had a heavy brass ruler, and every time he would bang down on fingers that might stretch in. Then Feodor called Ivan and Petro to him; and a minute later, while Ivan leaned against the house and Petro fought the others off, Feodor came forward with a bouncing little run and leaped nimbly upon Ivan's back and snatched the bread so quickly off the window-ledge that the man's ruler only swung against the air, while the penholder in his mouth knocked against the side of the window.

A few days later Petro and Ivan came before the kitchens again, and while Petro danced for them and afterwards Ivan lifted Petro high in the air with one arm, Feodor crept to the back of the tent and through a slit passed his hand into the sacks of potatoes and filled his pockets full. For several days they worked the same trick, cooking the potatoes afterwards in a can. Then there were so many potatoes missing that a watch was kept and Feodor was caught hand in the sack.

They took Feodor and tied him to the punishing post in the middle of the camp, tied him so that only his toes touched the ground, and left him there for hours until from aching and groaning his eyes closed and his body hung unconscious on the ropes.

So after that Ivan, Feodor, and Petro saw that they would never be able to conquer the hunger. Soon now the day would come when like others in the camp they would drop to the ground with the fever and then one after the other, hands tied with a rope, be carried out on the stretcher never to return.

Yet one evening a German came to take from Feodor the ikon he had hammered out of a tin cover and he left in exchange a sausage. And the eating of that sausage was something to remember. Once more they set nooses for mice under the sheds and Petro cut marks upon the beams to bring evil luck to the mice. And thereafter, like a spread of wild fire, there was sudden trade throughout the camp in all the things Russians could make. Even visitors from outside came to buy. From tin cans, old boxes, cardboards, rope, grew now each day food for the stomach, more food, better food. Warmer blood returned, also harder strength. In the store, where before Russians never entered, Russians now entered to buy.

"Brother, if we are forgotten, we have many hands."

"We are the tall men, brother."

One of the Frenchmen had an accordion. Occasionally now he lent it to Petro and the others. To drive the Devil away they gathered together and danced in turn and chanted hymns and clapped their hands and clicked their heels until their eyes glittered with memories of the homelands. The music they made all together was so strange and wonderful that they drew great crowds about them, crowds of English, French, Belgians, Germans even, who stood there watching and then, when it was all over, unfolded their arms, smiled at each other, and shook their heads as much as to say, "Ah, these Russians!"

But, in a few weeks, old cans, old boxes, all material, grew very scarce. The good luck had turned.

The weather became less cold and the days lengthened until all at once it was the real spring in the tops of the trees beyond the barbed wire; yet there was no spring in the camp, not the smallest blade of green grass— only the same spaces of dirt and mud and the eternal rusty thickets of barbed wire; no wind talking in trees or blowing the manes of horses on the plains; no birds even in the sky. Though they understood now that if they searched and hunted long for material and worked hard the awful hunger might be kept away, they understood too that where once the better had been, the worse had returned. And now the terrible forgotten loneliness had become like a sharp pain in their hearts. Working day after day with worn fingers and the fleas and the lice running over them, they knew this was the end. Never would they go forth again into the market-places and the forests, but sitting thus remain all the days of their life.

Once in the winter time they had thought of trying to escape through the wires and run wildly away from the bullets of the sentinels, but they gave up thinking so when they learnt that the big black wire between the other two rows was a wire that burned if one but touched it—a trick of the Devil brought straight from Hell by the Germans. Once an Englishman in skirts, caught beneath it, lay there for days until his face began to turn black. No; as it was written, so must it be. Here for their sins must they live to the end.

There sat down beside the three one morning a small Frenchman with a pointed beard and who was cleanly dressed and had the hands of a noble. At first all scowled thinking that he had come to learn to make the things they were making. But to their almost unbelieving eyes it was to hand them from his pocket cake with raisins in it and pieces of the sweet food called chocolate, and what he most wanted to learn was to speak their own language. They dropped tools and came upright on their knees before him to take both his hands and thank him and bless him. But, smiling, he pushed them back and motioned to them to go on working.

From that time forward he came to them every day. In the beginning they had to laugh when he tried to speak as they did. But as the days passed they saw that he was learning to speak their language well, so well that the day came when they could understand all he wished to say. And as he ever continued on certain days to bring them sweet food, they saw more and more surely that he was the living answer to all their prayers. And though he would always smile and push them away, they sat ready then for his every wish. Among themselves they called him the Little Father.

The day came when the Little Father could speak their language even better than they could speak it themselves, for he could write it on paper after the manner of one of the Poles who had also taught him. Further, by another miracle, he rid them of all their fleas and lice.

When some men from distant countries came to visit the camp and see that all was well and ask questions, it was the Little Father who stood up and pointing to Ivan, Feodor, and Petro, said, "Look at the filth these Russians are kept in! Can they never be given water to wash in?" And half an hour later, Ivan, Feodor, and Petro, alone of all the Russians in the camp, were taken out and given better clothes and brought before the men from distant countries.

When the Germans scraped each man's arm and put into it the poison of the Devil, it was the Little Father who stopped the poison from working by only placing two fingers on Ivan's arm and saying, "Brother, fear no more, the poison shall not hurt."

One afternoon the Little Father sat beside them so long saying nothing and gazing at the wires that the three feared some sickness of the camp had stolen into him. But finally he said, "Brothers, the time has come."

"The time for what?" asked Petro.

"The time to escape."

"Escape!" said Feodor. "But how? Through the wires that burn and past the sentinels and the blood-hounds?"

"Even so."

With that Ivan, Feodor, and Petro turned and looked at the wires. But they could not understand how they were to escape through the three fences. And they remembered again the hideous face of the Englishman in skirts who had lain for days in black death under the middle wire. But at last Feodor said, "Little Father, we obey."

"Even though it may mean death?"

"If we are to die, we shall die; but if we are to live, we shall live."

Ivan and Petro nodded their heads for they knew Feodor had spoken the truth.

First Feodor must make from an old horseshoe a pair of pinchers by cutting it in two and grinding the two pieces to sharp edges and riveting them together with a nail. Also he must take an iron band from the beams under the shed and twist and sharpen it into a strong earth-scraper. Then each must listen well to what was told him.

At the fall of darkness three nights later, when the bugle blew to call everyone into the sheds, Ivan, Feodor, and Petro and the Little Father did not follow with the others. They continued working in the shadows until the last of those sitting near had risen and gone away, then they slid quickly under the shed and turned and lay waiting on their stomachs. And not before another twenty minutes, or half an hour, would the roll be called, and then it would be almost night.

Above their heads was the trampling of feet on the boards and the many voices of those in the shed. Outside their dark shelter, in the dusk, twice they saw the vague legs of sentinels walking slowly past the wires. Then the stir on the boards above began to die down a little. Then it began to grow darker and darker. And lying flat, faces off the earth, hearts thumping, Ivan, Feodor, and Petro waited for the Little Father to move and knew that whatever was to happen had already begun.

One of the arc-lights of the camp near by spluttered and suddenly a clear grey light brightened the earth all around outside the rim of the shed. The tangle of the wires stood out from the dark beyond. To the left at some distance was a sentinel approaching with rifle and bayonet on his shoulder. To the right, much nearer, came another sentinel slowly with two blood-hounds behind him on the leash. Between the two men, through the wires and sharp on the ground like a black patch, fell the shadow of the thick cement pole holding the arc-light.

The sentinels, meeting, stood and talked together in low voices. Then they walked on again, and now further and further away from each other. Already the Little Father was out from under the shed, and creeping hidden in the dark path towards the first wire fence.

There was a dull metallic twang. Then another. To the three under the shed the twangs were like rifle shots; yet above in the shed there was now the loud scuffling of feet for the roll-call. With wide-staring eyes they watched the Little Father pass through the first fence and come to the great middle wires that burn. And now it seemed that everyone must see him, despite the darkness of the path, for he was up on his knees scraping and scraping, scraping the earth from beneath the lowest burning wire. Would he never finish! But before any could believe it he was through. He was wriggling on. Or was he already lying in crumpled death like the Englishman? Another dull twang made their hearts leap. And another. They could hardly see him any longer. They waited breathless. But see, yes, he was lying flat in the shadow way beyond. And lifting his hand the way he said he would.

Like a snake Feodor slid from under the shed and twisted into the black path. After him followed Petro. Ivan for a moment hesitated trembling. To pass under the burning wire as the Little Father had, could he of the big chest do the same? He blew out his cheeks, lips bubbling, eyes staring. But Feodor and Petro were already gone. Out he pulled and flopped along the dark path like a huge rabbit. Through the hole in the first fence, where the wires were pulled back, he went without thinking. It was those thick middle wires that drew his eyes out and made the sweat roll from him. And the dip underneath was very small, and only to touch the wire lightly was to burn in death. Pressing cheek hard to the earth he pushed his head through, waited breathing deeply. Then he obeyed as the Little Father had told, "bring arms around flat forward and pull." Slowly he pulled his body inch by inch along. And now the hot wire was right over his spine and he could pull no more. Yet after another pull it was only the legs that were left. He was through the wire. He rose to his feet and leapt forward. He dove into the hole of the third fence and his back caught and the fence shook. The fence rattled and creaked for yards while he pulled and stumbled and pulled.

"Halt! Wer da!"

With a final lunge Ivan tore free, but the sentinel seeing him came running forward, blowing the whistle in his mouth loudly, and bayonet out to spear. Up from the dark path sprang the Little Father and swung the scraper down on the sentinel's neck. The whistling stopped abruptly. The sentinel tumbled forward, and Feodor came leaping, boots forward upon him.

They turned and all four abreast ran wildly straight ahead into the darkness. Bullets whistled everywhere, and all was noise behind, rifles banging, dogs yelping, whistles blowing, and now the pan-pan-pan of the machine-gun and a great light-path sweeping round in the sky. They came tumbling eight-footed into a road that went cross-ways. They hid a second from the bullets behind its bank, then, bent-over, galloped along the asphalt to the right. They came tearing down further into trees. Ahead down the road, distant street lights. "This way!" cried the Little Father. They swerved in sharp through the trees. They rushed across a waste space and through gardens. They cut away from lighted houses in trees. They heard shouting now all around. They were blocked by a long high wall. And behind was the baying of blood-hounds. "Up!" said the Little Father and placed head to the wall.

Like cats the three Russians scrambled in turn from his back to the top of the wall. Then, lying over, Ivan and Feodor bent down and seizing his wrists, pulled him bodily to the top. They leapt down the other side.

More trees; across a sort of park; grass lawns; and now another wall. Up and over as before. Another road, lonelier and darker. "It returns to the camp," cried Feodor, stopping and pointing at the great light-path in the sky.

"On!" called the Little Father, "they will search less this way."

Suddenly from around a corner ahead came straight towards them down the road a bouncing trolley-car full of light. They dove to one side, lay flat waiting. In another minute, it flashed past noisily. It was gone. They leapt up, ran on. They approached nearer the base of the great light-path dancing on their right. They came dangerously beside it. But now it was behind them. Now it was the low hedges and the telegraph poles and the darkness ahead.

The road was strong under their feet. They ran, then they walked, then they ran some more, then again they walked. There were no more distances, distances were all the same. At a brook that passed under the road the Little Father suddenly stopped. He said, looking back at the sky where there was no more light, "Let us not forget the blood-hounds, nor the cars that can speed."

After the Little Father, Feodor, Petro, and Ivan splashed into the brook. Now walking on sand, now in mud, though always in the water that cooled, they pushed and splashed and stumbled on. And, if there were often bushes to push aside, there were also sweet-smelling meadows, and frogs croaking ahead and again now behind, and willow trees, and freedom at last.

Then when they rested ten minutes on the bank, the moon began to rise over the dark trees in the far away. The Little Father pointing said, "There is our guide. And this way is Russia and that way, France." And a little later he said, "Brothers, the longest way to France is the better and cleverest way."

In the moonlight that had brought them once more together Ivan, Feodor, and Petro sat in silence. Then Feodor spoke. "Little Father, as you command, so we obey."

They returned to the brook. Slowly they waded on. And on and on. The air grew colder, the water grew colder. At last a new grey dawn-light began to creep into the sky. And now, not a great distance ahead, off the lowlands, was a high long road passing across the brook. Near a large alder-bush, spreading its limbs out each side of the stream, the Little Father went no further. Here the whole day they must stop and rest, hiding themselves deep from the terrible danger all around. "Yet first let us eat." From the small bag off his shoulder, he had always been carrying, he took forth bread and sausages and small pieces of sweet food. The three said nothing because they knew that there was nothing he would let them say. But there was no water soaking in any of it as he had feared.

They slept under the alder-bush until it was afternoon, now first one and then the other keeping watch. Then after the bag had been brought forth again and emptied of all its food, they lay low and watched the high road in front and the people always going by upon it. Many were on bicycles and, according to the Little Father, most were prisoner hunting, and the danger was never greater.

Then it was two women and a fat man; and when they came to the tall bridge over the brook, one of the women hopped off her bicycle and pointed to the lowlands, even to the alder-bush. But the man, not looking round, kept riding straight on, swinging his arm forward. So the woman stepped onto her bicycle, hopped up, and went off, twisting this way and that after the others.

When it was dark once more, finally they slipped into the water. The wind had come up and soon the night became black and noisy. But never would the Little Father leave the stream, even to follow on the bank, until at last there were houses. And then on long roads in the dark there was rain often and hardly ever moonlight to guide. And at last under the wet lead sky of another dawn coming there was hunger and tired legs and more houses and danger in the falling shadows bristling like dogs all around and no place to hide.

Down by the stream the dark building they crept to was a barn across a dirt way from a mill. The mill was covered with vines. There behind its windows human folk still lay sleeping. But in the barn the cow stalls were empty and there were lofts overhead. They climbed after the Little Father quickly up the cleats of a wooden support. In the far corner of the loft was a stack of flat hay. While the rain blew stronger on the barn outside, all four shoved legs and bodies into the hay as if under a blanket.

Ivan, who had the first watch, lay face in the straw and looked out through a knot hole. And then hardly had the Little Father begun to breathe deep beside him than down there, across the way, the mill door opened and out came a man and went to a shed and, taking a bicycle, pushed it and jumped on it and rode away. Behind from the doorway came a woman and looked up at the barn and then went and turned into the shed and turned again and sat down in its shadows.

At first, Ivan had been in great fear of the woman lest she might come to the barn. But now she was sitting in the shadows, as his grandmother used to sit, arms crossed into her sleeves.

He sank lower in the hay. The cold began to leave him. To keep from falling asleep he said his prayers over and over again. Then he started up. He had nearly fallen asleep. What would the others have said! Great ox! Great stomach! And yet sleep now came back over him like a caressing woman, and seemed even to rub her face against his cheek. He lifted right up. If only he could walk, sing, have someone to talk to. Of a sudden he remembered that the Little Father had said that if he heard or saw anyone, he was to wake him. His hand was lying out on the straw. Ivan touched it. At once the Little Father was awake looking out of the knot-hole.

One after another they came quickly down the cleats from the loft; for it was clear to the Little Father that the woman was watching while the man went for help. They had been seen entering.

They stood huddled in the doorway not knowing what to do; for there was no other way of leaving the barn and yet here the woman would see them if they went out. Then the Little Father said, "Since we are seen, nothing matters; let us be bold to take profit."

In file they walked out like men just walking around a barn and going up to a road. But when the woman gave a cry and drew back deeper in the shed, they turned and ran straight to the mill, entered its doorway.

A large room; a kitchen range simmering in one corner; food on the table; two half-dressed children playing on the floor; many shining articles everywhere. The four darted about the room. For Pedro it was a large thick loaf of white bread and a round of cheese; for Feodor, out of a cupboard pulled open, it was a half-cut ham and a large knife and eggs in a small tin bucket; for Ivan it was two bottles of beer and a basket of red apples; and for the Little Father it was lumps of sugar crowded into his pockets, a blanket torn from the bed, matches, a newspaper, and at the last minute a map with little flags in it, torn from the wall.

As they rushed out of the door, one after the other, the woman before them screamed and screamed and grabbed Petro, the last, arms full. He twisted, broke away, and with a whoop and a leap dashed after the others. They swerved down round the mill. In the mill-race was a boat. They scrambled into it and quickly the Little Father began to row away. Petro stood up on the stern and, hugging the loaf, blew kisses to the woman, and smacked his backside.

The stream went swift and the Little Father rowed swifter. In a few minutes was a small wooden bridge. "Out!" he said. And when they were on the bank waiting, he turned to the boat and shoved it away hard down stream.

On the narrow road between the fields, no one in sight. But full daylight was now upon them, and clear to the distances rose no shelter. Joy went from them. Slowly they stopped running. Now they would be caught like escaped cattle on a plain.

To the left was a wheat field. "Here!" said the Little Father. And, as he explained to them, each from a different place stepped backward into the wheat-field slowly and pulled up the blades behind. In the middle they joined together. And there upon the wet earth and the blanket, and while the rain again began to fall, they sat heads together and sucked eggs and drank beer and munched bread, listening all the time for any one coming.

But no one came.

No one ever came. Only the slow wagons passing on the road.

So they lay there three days and two nights. "For if we are caught," said the Little Father, "the prison we shall lie in will be the Devil and his Hell to this one; therefore let us be our own prisoners." And while he lay elbows propped on the ground and read the paper and turned it over and back how many times, or studied the map, they cut the wheat—except at night when each could stand up in turn—and wove it into mats for all to lie close upon together and hold the blanket over them.

Twice in the dark the Little Father stepped forth to fetch water from the stream in the bottles. But the third night all four stepped forth. And all stepped off quickly, almost running; for each knew that although there was now no more food, the great danger was once more behind them.

Thereafter, each night, they saw that they were walking away from it in the moonlight more and more—however near it might again be in front, or in the distances all around. And the day times they rested, in wet and shine, in the wheat fields and the rye, and ate stolen cabbages, carrots, apples, and even the grain of the wheat itself.

Often now on the map, the Little Father would show them where they were walking and heading for. Here was the land called Switzerland; and here was a great forest to cross and the river called Rhine; and here was France. And whenever the Little Father's finger would come to France, his eyes would brighten and he would tell of France—France the land all men love, even Germans; because there all men walk free and the sun shines down softly, as it does upon no other place on earth.

Also, when there were no more stories to be read from the map, he would try now to teach them how to write. First, each in the square of earth before him learnt to write his own name, then the names of each other, and then it was the names of all the countries fighting and so many other names that they almost forgot their own and had to begin all over again. But finally there was one name they never forgot, the name of the Little Father. All the time and upon everything they wrote it—Marcel. Petro even took the lucky needle from his collar and started to prick the name on his arm. But before he had finished, a great misfortune happened. Trying to push the needle better into the wood-handle he broke the needle short. Then all three, Ivan, Feodor, and Petro, sat silent in sadness and gloom, for each knew that however much the Little Father might laugh and say, no, it was written down that soon the luck was to turn against them.

But they walked quicker and peering sharper all around. And at last they entered the great forest and each night could cover greater distance than ever before. One early morning, while the stars faded away from the sky, they came out on a ledge, and down there through the fog-mist was more and more a wide river and a large plain, and in the distant hills the dull booming of cannon.

They stood close to a wooden bench while the Little Father with stretched finger showed it all and the far away mountains of France. Now let them hide well and this night they would cross the river and the plain and climbing over there, move to the left past the city called Basle and find anywhere ahead the land Switzerland where there were less guards and safety.

Darkness came again and in it they twisted down the land and crossing roads and railroads, at last with great trouble reached the wide dark river.

When all had tied bundles better about them, they sank one by one into the cold stream and struck out. The water grew less cold. They swam steadily, flowing with the current. Gradually they approached the dark opposite shore, Ivan in the lead.

Then Ivan rose and waded forth, but stepped on loose rocks and fell back in the water with a heavy splash. Almost immediately from behind on the river a light-path shot out and began to sweep over the waters. Ivan crawled out, and after him scrambled Feodor and Petro; but the Little Father with the blanket round his shoulder was still some distance behind. Swiftly along the shore came the light-path brightly lighting rocks, reeds, and bushes. It swept past them, then swept back, fixed upon the head of the Little Father in the water. At first he lay without motion like a log or any piece of wood; but the light-path upon him growing broader all the time and the lively pit-pit-pit of a boat growing always louder, of a sudden he turned and splashed for the shore. A loud yell on the river, then the flash and the bang of a rifle; more flashes and bangs; bullets hissing; the lighted river spouting. Upright in shallow water, the Little Father suddenly crumpled, fell forward on the rocks.

Like wild men Ivan, Feodor, and Petro flung themselves from the reeds. Six hands pulled him from the water. They dragged him up, dragged him further back into the bushes and rocks, and all the while the white light was like daylight on the leaves about them. And now the bullets were zipping and tearing terribly just above and all around. Laying the Little Father upon his back behind a small boulder, in its shadow they huddled close over him and watched that life might return. He did not move. His face was red with streams of blood. He was dead.

Then, the light-flare holding steady all around and the bullets continually tearing through the bushes, these three, Ivan, Feodor, and Petro, knelt in a silence all their own and peered at each other with wild flashing eyes that told their devotion to the body of this holy man and their determination to preserve it from the enemy at all costs.

Feodor settled the matter. While Ivan knelt, over his back was placed the body of the Little Father. With that Feodor rose and waving his arms dashed noisily away to the right, trampling through the bushes. Of a sudden the light-flare and the bullets jumped after him, and there was darkness about the rock like a candle put out. Then, with the Little Father on his back, Ivan lifted up and plunged away, straight through the bushes and the darkness, Petro behind holding the legs. On Ivan drove. Stumbling rocks, young trees, deeper bushes, nothing could stop him. And when at last the light-flare suddenly came sweeping back and held broader and higher and dimmer over their heads, before them was a road, and Feodor running swiftly upon it, and now telling, hand bleeding, that men were landing from the river and to keep hurrying on, over the road, straight ahead, to where, in the land beyond, the light showed, as the Little Father had said, a railroad track and a canal.

Bent low, like a large snail, Ivan crossed over the iron rails. And after they had climbed, all helping, to the canal path, they moved slowly along it, then stopped, slid into cold water again, and between them swam the Little Father to the other side. And so, Feodor and Petro struggling in vain to lift Ivan from his knee and receive the body themselves, on they went.

Hours long they continued. And, struggling no more between them, now one now another in turn carrying the body, under the stars they crossed through the land, keeping always away from the far twinkling lights on the left. Only when the land began to rise everywhere into woods, too rough and dark to go further through, did they stop. And lying exhausted in ferns about the body of the Little Father they decided that in the new dawnlight, here in these trees, would they dig a grave and bury him, and over him place a cross with his name that none should disturb.

However, that next morning when the three were digging earth with the knife and tree slabs, the body of the Little Father of a sudden moved. All three stopped digging and stared with wild eyes, for they saw that the Holy Spirit of the Little Father had returned from the dead into his body, even as it did into the body of the Lord Christ. Hearts trembling, it seemed that their own lives must pour out in return. But as they knelt around and bent over him the weak cry from his pained face was the word, "Water!"

While Petro galloped to the tumbling brook near-by with Ivan's bottle, Feodor and Ivan tried to place him more comfortably head up on the rolled blanket. They gave him of the water sip by sip and washed his face and made bandages of their sleeves for his head, his legs, his shoulder. Then, some time later, his eyes opened and fixed upon them. Then his eyes understood.

After he lay there weakly listening to Feodor explain, his voice spoke slowly and he told them that he was shot now too badly ever to escape, but they must go on.

Feodor shook his head.

"We do not leave you."

"You must."

"No. Without you we are lost."

Ivan hunched his big shoulders, said, "We will carry you."

Petro with dancing eyes seized Feodor's hand and showed, zip, across its gash of dried blood how the bad luck had at last passed.

The Little Father's head fell back and his eyes again closed, yet words now came louder and harsher from him, and ordered how they must leave him by a roadside and then, the land Switzerland being near, climb straight through the forest, with the cannon tapping always on their right cheek and the sun setting on their left . . .

But they listened no more, rose quickly from their knees. And a little later, with the Little Father lying in the blanket and the blanket suspended from a sapling, they started off through the trees, Petro and Ivan holding the sapling on their shoulders, and Feodor in the lead.

All day long they climbed slowly, heavily, up through the forest. The daylight guided them, but it did not hide them. And often the two behind had to wait long for the third in front to come back and give the word to move on. In the afternoon, as many as ten times they saw soldiers. Once they had to pass within several yards of four playing cards upon a rock. Once to draw a sentinel away from a gullet between a sharp rise of the land Petro had to creep into the underbrush to make a noise like a whining lost hound and hold the sentinel standing away whistling. And always the land never went straight, but higher and higher, and there were many flies. And finally the very Devil himself entered into the body of the Little Father and made him twist about in the blanket and knock the stick away that kept the blanket from choking him and yell until only by stuffing moss in his mouth could they move on.

Yet, more and more weary, hungry, on they went, and though at times it seemed they could never get the heavy-swinging sapling higher, and more and more the darkness began to steal through the trees, always they climbed. At last they came out so high above all the land around that even the tree-tops were below them, and the cannon now came on one cheek, now on the other. Then it was too dark among all the rocks to go any further, and between the rocks was a sort of cave. Here they would wait until daylight.

They knew it was dangerous to crawl in, for in such places, as the Little Father had often explained, escaped prisoners were always first looked for. But the Little Father was again trying to moan and scream, and they knew too they could not keep his mouth bandaged all night.

It was very dark and cold in the cave. There were so many rocks that there was hardly place to lay the Little Father down. But when they took the bandage off his mouth he did not groan or cry. At once they fell down among the rocks about him and lay knowing nothing more.

Feodor woke with a start to find daylight full in the cave and the Little Father lying eyes open. He hurried to give him the last of the water they had saved. But the Little Father only wished to be lifted outside and see where they were. Carefully over the rocks the three carried him into the open.

They heard the cannon thundering away behind them. They seemed to be on the top of the world. For miles and miles they could see down over forests and rivers and towns, and the sun was rising brightly in the sky. The Little Father sank back on the ground.

At first they thought from the look in his eyes that he was to begin the yelling again, but as they watched they saw that in his eyes there were tears rising. And now, half crying, half laughing, he told them that the land right below was the land of France, that he knew the country well, that the town in the distance was Saint Hippolyte, and that this terrible mountain was indeed Mount Terrible. Three big Russian fools that they were, they had not only crossed the frontier, but nearly passed over the corner of Switzerland into France; and now all they had to do was to drop, slide, go one foot before the other down the slope into the fields of France.

So after a minute these three, Ivan, Feodor, and Petro, looked up from the Little Father and, turning around, gazed once more over the rivers and the fields and the towns below all shining in the sunlight. A great, heavy joy was in their throats. But they were too weary, too bruised, too hungry to do more than stand there scowling, as men sometimes do when, toiling up from slavery, by this road and by that, the sunlight of freedom at last bursts upon them.

WAR IS THE PROVINCE OF UNCERTAINTY

THREE-FOURTHS of those things upon which action in War must be calculated, are hidden more or less in the clouds of great uncertainty. Here, then, above all, a fine and penetrating mind is called for, to search out the truth by the tact of its judgment.

An average intellect may, at one time, perhaps hit upon this truth by accident; an extraordinary courage, at another, may compensate for the want of this tact; but in the majority of cases the average result will always bring to light the deficient understanding.

Gold from Crete

BY

C. S. FORESTER

THE officers of H.M.S. *Apache* were sizing up the Captain D. at the same time that he was doing the same to them. A Captain D.—captain commanding destroyers—was a horrible nuisance on board if, as in this case, the ship in which he elected—or was compelled by circumstances—to hoist his distinguishing pennant was not fitted as a flotilla leader. The captain needed cabin space himself, and he brought with him a quartet of staff officers who also needed cabin space. Physically, that meant that four out of the seven officers already on board the *Apache* would be more uncomfortable than usual, and in a destroyer that meant a great deal. More than that; morally the effect was still more profound. It meant that with a captain on board, even if he tried not to interfere with the working of the ship, the commander and the other officers, and the lower deck ratings as well, for the matter of that, felt themselves under the scrutiny of higher authority. The captain's presence would introduce something of the atmosphere of a big ship, and it would undoubtedly cut short the commander's pleasure in his independent command.

So Commander Hammett and his officers eyed Captain Crowe and his staff, when they met on the scorching iron deck of the *Apache* in Alexandria harbor, without any appearance of hospitality. They saw a big man, tall and a little inclined to bulk, who moved with a freedom and ease that hinted at a concealed athleticism. His face was tanned so deeply that it was impossible to guess at his complexion, but under the thick black brows there were a pair of gray eyes that twinkled irrepressibly. They knew his record, of course—much of it was to be read in the rows of colored ribbon on his chest. There was the D.S.O. he had won as a midshipman at Zeebrugge in 1918—before Sublieutenant Chesterfield had been born—and they knew that they had only to look up the official account of that action to find exactly what Crowe had done there; but everyone knew that midshipmen do not receive D.S.O.'s for nothing. The spot of silver that twinkled on the red-and-blue ribbon told of the bar he had received for the part he had played at Narvik last year—not to many men is it given to be decorated for distinguished services twenty-two years apart and still to be hardly entering on middle age. There was the red ribbon that one or two

From: The Saturday Evening Post. By permission of the Author.

of them recognized as the Bath, and a string of other gay colors that ended in the Victory and General Service ribbons of the last war.

The introductions were brief—most of the officers had at least a nodding acquaintance with one another already. Commander Hammett presented his first lieutenant, Garland, and the other officers down to Sublieutenants Chesterfield and Lord Edward Mortimer, R.N.V.R.—this last was a fattish and untidy man in the late thirties whose yachting experience had miraculously brought him out of Mayfair drawing rooms and dropped him on the hard steel deck of the *Apache*—and Crowe indicated his flotilla gunnery officer and navigating officer and signals officer and secretary.

"We will proceed as soon as convenient, Commander," said Crowe, issuing his first order.

"Aye, aye, sir," said Hammett, as twenty generations of seamen had answered before him. But at least the age of consideration given to omens had passed; it did not occur to Hammett to ponder on the significance of the fact that Crowe's first order had been one of action.

"Get yourselves below and sort yourselves out," said Crowe to his staff, and as they disappeared he walked forward and ran lightly up to the bridge.

Hammett gave his orders—Crowe was glad to note that he did so without even a side glance out of the tail of his eye at the captain at the end of the bridge—and the ship broke into activity. In response to one order, the yeoman of signals on the bridge bellowed an incomprehensible string of words down to the signal bridge. It passed through Crowe's mind that yeomen of signals were always as incomprehensible as railway porters calling out the names of stations in England, but the signal rating below understood what was said to him, which was all that mattered. A string of colored flags ran up the halyards, and a moment later the yeoman of signals was bellowing the replies received. The flagship gave permission to proceed; the fussy tug out there by the antisubmarine net began to pull open the gate. The brow was pulled in, the warps cast off. The telegraph rang, the propeller began to turn, and the *Apache* trembled a little as she moved away. Everything was done as competently as possible; the simple operation was a faint indication that Crowe would not have to worry about the *Apache* in action, but could confine his attention to the handling of his whole flotilla of twelve destroyers, if and when he should ever succeed in gathering them all together.

A movement just below him caught his attention. The antiaircraft lookouts were being relieved. At the .50 gun here on the starboard side a burly seaman was taking over the earphones and the glasses. He was a huge man, but all Crowe could see of him, besides his huge bulk and the top of his cap, was his cropped red hair and a wide expanse of neck and ear, burned a solid brick red from the Mediterranean sun. Then there were a pair of thick wrists covered with dense red hair, and two vast hands that held the glasses as they swept back and forth, back and forth, over the sky from horizon to zenith in ceaseless search for hostile planes. At that moment there were six seamen employed on that task in different parts of the deck, and so exacting was the work that a quarter of an hour every hour was all that could be asked of any man.

Commander Hammett turned at that moment and caught the captain's eye.

"Sorry to intrude on you like this, Hammett," said Crowe.

"No intrusion at all, sir. Glad to have you, of course."

Hammett could hardly say anything else, poor devil, thought Crowe, before he went on: "Must be a devilish nuisance being turned out of your cabin, all the same."

"Not nearly as much nuisance as to the other officers, sir," said Hammett. "When we're at sea I never get aft to my sleeping cabin at all. Turn in always in my sea cabin."

Perfectly true, thought Crowe. No destroyer captain would think of ever going more than one jump from the bridge at sea.

"Nice of you to spare my feelings," said Crowe, with a grin. It had to be said in just the right way—Crowe could guess perfectly well at Hammett's resentment at his presence.

"Not at all, sir," said Hammett briefly.

Sublieutenant Chesterfield gave a fresh course to the quartermaster at this moment and changed the conversation.

They were clear of the mine fields now and almost out of sight of the low shore. The myriad Levantine spies would have a hard time to guess whither they were bound.

"We'll be in visual touch with the flotilla at dawn, sir," said Hammett.

"Thank you. I'll let you know if there's any change of plan," replied Crowe.

He ran down the naked steel ladder to the deck, and walked aft, past the quadruple torpedo tubes and the two pairs of 4.7's towering above him. On the blast screen a monkey sat and gibbered at him, gesticulating with withered little hands. Crowe hated monkeys; he liked dogs and could tolerate cats; he had been shipmates with pets of all species from goats to baby hippopotamuses, but monkeys were his abomination. He hated the filthy little things, their manners and their habits. He ignored this one stolidly as he walked past it to the accompaniment of screamed monkey obscenities. If he were in command of this destroyer he would have seen to it that the little beast did not remain long on board to plague him; as it was, he thought ruefully to himself, as he was in the immeasurably higher position of commanding a flotilla, he would have to endure its presence for fear of hurting the feelings of those under his command.

Down below, Paymaster Lieutenant Scroggs, his secretary, was waiting for him in the day cabin. Scroggs was looking through a mass of message forms—intercepted wireless messages which gave, when pieced together, a vague and shadowy picture of the progress of the fighting in Crete.

"I don't like the looks of it at all, sir," said Scroggs.

Neither did Crowe, but he could see no possible good in saying so. His hearty and sanguine temperament could act on bad news, but refused to dwell on it. He had digested the contents of those messages long ago, and he had no desire to worry himself with them again.

"We'll know more about it when we get there," he said cheerfully. "I shan't want you for a bit, Scroggs."

Scroggs acted on the hint and left the cabin, while Crowe sat himself at the table and drew the note paper to him and began his Thursday letter:

My dear Miriam: There has been little enough happening this week——

On Thursdays he wrote to Miriam; on Mondays, Tuesdays and Wednesdays he wrote respectively to Jane and Susan and Dorothy. On Fridays he wrote to old friends of his own sex, and he kept Saturdays to clear off arrears of official correspondence, and he hoped on Sundays never to take a pen in hand.

He often thought about using a typewriter and doing four copies at once, but Miriam and Dorothy and Jane and Susan were not fools—he would never have bothered about them in the first place if they were—and they could spot a carbon copy anywhere. There was nothing for it but to write toilsomely to each one by hand, although it did not matter if he repeated the phraseology; no one of those girls knew any of the others, thank God, and if they did, they wouldn't compare notes about him, seeing what a delicate affair each affair was.

Scroggs re-entered the room abruptly. "Message just arrived, sir," he said, passing over the decoded note.

It was for Captain D. from the vice admiral, Alexandria, and was marked "Priority." It ran: MUCH GREEK GOLD AWAITING SHIPMENT MERKA BAY. REMOVE IF POSSIBLE. ENDS.

"Not acknowledged, of course?" said Crowe.

"No, sir," said Scroggs.

Any acknowledgment would violate standing orders for wireless silence. "All right, Scroggs. I'll call you when I want you."

Crowe sat and thought about this new development. "Much Greek gold." A thousand pounds? A million pounds? The Greek government gold reserves must amount to a good deal more than a million pounds. If Crete was going to be lost—and it looked very much as if it was going to be—it would be highly desirable to keep that much gold from falling into the hands of the Germans. But it was the "if possible" that complicated the question. Actually it was a compliment—it gave him discretion. It was for him to decide whether to stake the *Apache* against the gold, but it was the devil of a decision to make. The ordinary naval problem was easy by comparison, for the value of the *Apache* could be easily computed against other standards. It would always be worth while, for instance, to risk the *Apache* in exchange for a chance to destroy a light cruiser. But in exchange for gold? When she was built, the *Apache* cost less than half a million sterling, but that was in peacetime. In time of war, destroyers might be considered to be worth their weight in gold—or was that strictly true?

There was the question of the odds, too. If he took the *Apache* into

Merka Bay tomorrow at dawn and risked the Stukas, what would be the chances of getting her out again? Obviously, if he were quite sure of it, he should try for the gold; and on the other hand, if he were sure that she would be destroyed, it would not be worth making the attempt, not for all the gold in the Americas. The actual odds lay somewhere between the one extreme and the other—two to one against success, say. Was it a profitable gamble to risk the *Apache* on a two-to-one chance, in the hope of gaining an indefinite number of millions?

He had only to raise his voice to summon the staff that a thoughtful government had provided. Three brilliant young officers, all graduates of the Naval Staff College, and the main reason for their presence on board was to advise. Crowe thought about his staff and grinned to himself. They would tell him, solemnly, the very things he had just been thinking out for himself, and, after all that, the ultimate decision would still lie with him alone. There could be no shifting of that responsibility—and Crowe suddenly realized that he did not want to shift it. Responsibility was the air he breathed. He sat making up his mind, while the *Apache* rose and fell gently on the Mediterranean swell and the propellers throbbed steadily; he still held the message in idle fingers, and looked at it with unseeing eyes. When at last he rose, he had reached his decision, and it remained only to communicate it to his staff to tell them that he intended to go into Merka Bay to fetch away some gold, and to look over the chart with them and settle the details.

That was what he did, and the flotilla gunnery officer and the signals officer and the navigating officer listened to him attentively. It was only a matter of a few minutes to decide on everything. Rowles, the navigating officer, measured off the distance on his dividers, while the others asked questions that Crowe could not answer. Crowe had not the least idea how much gold there was in Crete. Nor could he say offhand how much a million sterling in gold should weigh. Nickleby, the gunner, came to a conclusion about that, after a brief glance at his tables of specific gravities and a minute with his slide rule. "About ten tons, there or thereabouts," he announced.

"This is troy weight, twelve ounces to the pound, you know," cautioned Holby, the signals officer.

"Yes, I allowed for that," said Nickleby triumphantly.

"But what about inflations?" demanded Rowles, looking up from the map. "I heard you say something about an ounce being worth four pounds —you know what I mean, four sovereigns. But that's a long time ago, when people used to buy gold. Now it's all locked up and it's doubled in value, pretty nearly. So a million would weigh twenty tons."

"Five tons, you mean, stupid," said Holby. That started another argument as to whether inflation would increase or diminish the weight of a million sterling.

Crowe listened to them for a moment and then left them to it. There was still a little while left before dinner, and he had to finish that letter.

As the *Apache* turned her bows toward Merka Bay, Crowe took up his pen again:

  . . . little enough happening this week, but it is most infernally hot and I suppose it will get hotter as the year grows older. I have thought about you a great deal, of course——

That damned monkey was chattering at him through the scuttle. It was bad enough to have to grind out this weekly letter to Miriam, without having monkeys to irritate one. The monkey was far more in Crowe's thoughts than the Stukas he would be facing at any moment. The Stukas were something to which he had devoted all the consideration the situation demanded; it would do him no good to think about them further. But that monkey would not let Crowe stop thinking about him. Crowe cursed again.

  . . . especially that dinner we had at the Berkeley, when we had to keep back behind the palms so that old Lady Crewkerne shouldn't see us. I wonder what the poor old thing is doing now——

That was half a page, anyway, in Crowe's large handwriting. He had only to finish the page and make some appearance of a wholehearted attempt on the second. He scribbled on steadily, half his mind on the letter and the other half divided between the monkey, the approach of dinnertime, Hammett's attitude and the heat. He was not aware of the way in which somewhere inside him his mental digestion was still at work on the data for the approaching operation. With a sigh of relief he wrote:

                                        Always yours,
                                          GEORGE

and added at the foot, for the benefit of the censor:
From Captain George Crowe, C.B., DSO., R.N.

The worst business of the day was over and he could dine with a clear conscience, untroubled until morning.

The dark hours that followed midnight found the *Apache* in Merka Bay. She had glided silently in and had dropped anchor unobserved by anyone, apparently, while all around her in the distance were the signs and thunder of war. Overhead in the darkness had passed droning death, not once or twice but many times, passing by on mysterious and unknown errands. Crowe, on the bridge beside Hammett, had heard the queer bumbling of German bombers, the more incisive note of fighter planes. Out on the distant horizon along the coast they had seen the great flashes of the nightmare battle that was being fought out there, sometimes the pyrotechnic sparkle of antiaircraft fire, and they had heard the murmur of the firing. Now Nickleby had slipped ashore in the dinghy to make contact with the Greeks.

"He's the devil of a long time, sir," grumbled Rowles. "We'll never get away before daylight, at this rate."

"I never expected to," said Crowe soothingly. He felt immeasurably older than Rowles as he spoke, immeasurably wiser. Rowles was still young enough to have illusions, to expect everything to go off without delay or friction, something in the manner of a staff exercise on paper. If Rowles was still so incorrigibly optimistic after a year and a half of war, he could not be expected ever to improve in this respect.

"The bombers'll find us, though, sir," said Rowles. "Just listen to that one going over!"

"Quite likely," said Crowe. He had already weighed the possible loss of the *Apache* and her company against the chances of saving the gold, and he had no intention of working through the pros and cons again.

"Here he comes now," said Hammett suddenly; his quick ear had caught the spash of oars before anyone else.

Nickleby swung himself aboard and groped his way through the utter darkness to the bridge to make his report.

"It's all right," he said. "The gold's there. It's in lorries hidden in a gully half a mile away and they've sent for it. The jetty here's usable, thank God. Twelve feet of water at the end—took the soundings myself."

"Right," said Crowe. "Stand by to help Commander Hammett con the ship up to the jetty."

Merka Bay is a tiny crack in the difficult southern shore of Crete. It is an exposed anchorage giving no more than fifteen feet of water, but it serves a small fleet of fishing craft in peacetime, which explains the existence of the jetty, and from the village there runs an obscure mountain track, winding its way through the mountains of the interior, over which, apparently, the lorries with the gold had been brought when the fighting in the island began to take a serious turn. Crowe blessed the forethought of the Greeks while Hammett, with infinite care in the utter blackness, edged the *Apache* up the bay to the little pier, the propellers turning ever so gently and the lead going constantly.

They caught the loom of the pier and brought the *Apache* alongside. Two seamen jumped with warps, and as they dropped clove hitches over the bollards, Crowe suddenly realized that they had not had to fumble for the bollards. The utter pitchy blackness had changed into something distinctly less; when he looked up, the stars were not so vividly distinct. It was the first faint beginning of dawn.

There was a chattering group on the pierhead—four women and a couple of soldiers in ragged khaki uniforms. They exchanged voluble conversation with the interpreter on the main deck.

"The gold's coming, sir," reported that individual to Crowe.

"How much of it?"

"Forty-two tons, they say, sir."

"Metric tons, that'll be," said Holby to Nickleby. "How much d'you make that to be?"

"Metric tons are as near as dammit to our ton," said Nickleby irritably.

"The difference in terms of gold ought to amount to something, though," persisted Holby, drawing Nickleby deftly with the ease of long practice. "Let's have a rough estimate, anyway."

"Millions and millions," said Nickleby crossly. "Ten million pounds—twenty million pounds—thirty million—don't ask me."

"The knight of the slide rule doesn't bother himself about trifles like an odd ten million pounds," said Holby.

"Shut up!" broke in Rowles. "Here it comes."

In the gray dawn they could see a long procession of shabby old trucks bumping and lurching over the stony lane down to the jetty. All except one halted at the far end; the first one came creeping toward them along the pier.

An elderly officer scrambled down from the cab and saluted in the direction of the bridge.

"We got the bar gold in the first eight trucks, sir," he called in the accent of Chicago. "Coins in the other ones."

"He sounds just like an American," said Rowles.

"Returned immigrant, probably," said Holby. "Lots of 'em here. Made their little pile and retired to their native island to live like dukes on two-pence a week, until this schemozzle started."

"Poor devils," said Rowles.

Sublieutenant Lord Edward Mortimer was supervising a working party engaged in bringing the gold on board the *Apache*.

"Where do you propose to put the stuff?" said Crowe to Hammett.

"It's heavy enough, God knows," was the reply. "It's got to be low and in the center line. Do you mind if I put it in your day cabin?"

"Not at all. I think that's the best place at the moment."

Certainly it was heavy; gold is about ten times as heavy as the same bulk of coal.

The seamen who were receiving the naked bars from the Greeks in the lorry were deceived by their smallness, and more than once let them drop as the weight came upon them. A couple of the bars, each a mere foot long and three inches wide and high, made a load a man could only just stagger under. It gave the hurrying seamen a ludicrous appearance, as if they were soldiering on the job, to see them laboring with so much difficulty under such absurdly small loads. The men were grinning and excited at carrying these enormous fortunes.

"Hardly decent to see that gold all naked," said Rowles.

"Don't see any sign of receipts or bookkeeping," said Nickleby. "Old Scroggs'll break a blood vessel."

"No time for that," said Holby, glancing up to the sky. The action recalled to them all the danger in which they lay; each of them wondered how long it would be before the Stukas found them out.

The first lorry was unloaded by now, and driven away, its place being taken by the second. An unending stream of gold bars was being carried into the *Apache*. The second lorry was replaced by the third, and the third by the fourth. And then they heard the sound of dread—the high incisive note of a fighting plane. It came from the direction of the sea, but it was not a British plane. Swiftly it came, with the monstrous unnatural speed of its kind, not more than five hundred feet above the water. They could see plainly enough the swastika marking on the tail and the crosses on the wings.

"Open fire," said Hammett into the voice tube.

Crowe was glad to see that there was no trace of hurry or excitement in his voice.

All through the night the gun crews had been ready for instant action. The long noses of the 4.7's rose with their usual appearance of uncanny intelligence under the direction of Garland at the central control. Then they bellowed out, and along with their bellowing came the raving clamor of the pom-poms and the heavy machine guns. The plane swerved and circled. The .50-caliber gun under the end of the bridge beside Crowe followed it round, its din deafening Crowe. He looked down and noticed the grim concentration on the face of the red-haired seaman at the handles.

But that plane was moving at three hundred and more miles an hour; it had come and gone in the same breath, apparently unhit. It seemed to skim the steep hills that fringed the bay and vanished beyond them.

"It's calling the bombers this very minute," said Holby, savagely glaring after it. "How much longer have we got to stay here?"

Crowe heard the remark; naval thought had not changed in this respect at least, that the first idea of a naval officer should be now, as it had been in Nelson's day, to get his precious ship away from the dangerous and inhospitable shore and out to sea, where he could find freedom of maneuver, whether it was battle or storm that threatened him.

"That's the last of the bars, sir," called the English-speaking Greek officer. "Here's the coin coming."

Coins in sacks, coins in leather bags, coins in wooden boxes—sovereigns, louis d'or, double eagles, napoleons, Turkish pounds, twenty-mark pieces, dinars—the gold of every country in the world, drained out of every country in the Balkans, got away by a miracle before the fall of Athens and now being got out of Crete. The bags and sacks were just as deceptively heavy as the bars had been, and the naval ratings grinned and joked as they heaved them into the ship.

The first lorry full of coin had been emptied, and the second was driving onto the jetty when the first bombers arrived. They came from inland, over the hills, and were almost upon the ship, in consequence, before they were sighted. The guns blazed out furiously while each silver shape in turn swept into position, like the figures in some three-dimensional country dance, and then put down their noses and came racing down the air, engines screaming. Crowe had been through this before, and he did not like it. It called for nerve to stand and look death in the eye as it came tearing down at him. He had seen men dive for shelter, instinctively and futilely, behind the compass or even the canvas dodger, and he did not blame them in the least. He would do the same himself if he were not so determined that the mind of George Crowe should be as well exercised as his body. To watch like this called for as much effort as to put in a strong finish after a twenty-mile run, and he leaned back against the rail and kept his eyes on the swooping death.

At the last possible second the hurtling plane leveled off and let go its bomb. Crowe saw the ugly black blob detach itself from the silver fabric at the same second as the note of the plane's engine changed from a scream to a snarl. The bomb fell and burst in the shallows a few yards from the *Apache's* bows and an equal distance from the pier. A colossal geyser of black mud followed along with the terrific roar of the explosion. Mud and water rained down on the *Apache,* drenching everyone on deck, while the little ship leaped frantically in the wave. Crowe heard and felt the forward warp that held her to the jetty snap with the jerk. He could never be quite sure afterward whether he had seen, or merely imagined, the sea bottom revealed in a wide ring where the force of the explosion swept the water momentarily away. But he certainly noted, as a matter of importance, that bombs dropped in shallows of a few feet did not have nearly the damaging effect of a near miss in deeper water.

The second plane's nose was already down and pointing at them as the *Apache* swung to her single warp—Mortimer was busy replacing the broken one. Crowe forced himself again to look up, and he saw the thing that followed. A shell from one of the forward guns hit the plane straight on the nose; Crowe, almost directly behind the gun, saw—or afterward thought he had seen—the tiny black streak of not a hundredth of a second's duration, that marked the passage of the shell up to the target. One moment the plane was there, sharp and clear against the pale blue of sky; the next moment there was nothing at all. The huge bomb had exploded in its rack—at a height of two thousand feet the sound of the explosion was negligible, or else Crowe missed it in his excitement. The plane disappeared, and after that the eye became conscious of a wide circular smudge widening against the blue sky, fringed with tiny black fragments making a seemingly leisurely descent downward to the sea. And more than that; the third bomber had been affected by the explosion—the pilot must have been killed or the controls jammed. Crowe saw it wheel across his line of vision, skating through the air like a flipped playing card, the black crosses clearly visible. Nose first, it hit the sea close into the shore, vanished into a smother of foam, and then the tail reappeared, protruding above the surface while the nose remained fixed in the bottom.

It was a moment or two before Crowe was able to realize that the *Apache* was temporarily safe; one bomber had missed and the other two were destroyed. He became conscious that he was leaning back against the rail with a rigidity that was positively painful—his shoulder joints were hurting him. A little sheepishly he made himself relax; he grinned at his staff and took a turn or two along the bridge.

Down on the main deck Mortimer had made fast again. But somehow one of the containers of the gold coins had broken in the excitement. The deck was running with gold; the scuppers were awash with sovereigns.

"Leave that as it is for now!" bellowed Hammett, standing shoulder to shoulder with Crowe as he leaned over the rail of the *Apache*. "Get the rest of the stuff on board!"

Crowe turned and met Hammett's eye. "It looks to me," said Crowe, with a jerk of his thumb at the heaped gold on the *Apache's* deck, "as if this would be the best time in the world to ask the Admiralty for a rise in pay."

"Yes," said Hammett shortly, with so little appreciation of the neatness of the jest that Crowe made a mental note that money was apparently a sacred subject to Hammett and had better not in future be made a target for levity—presumably Hammett had an expensive family at home, or something. But Hammett was looking at him with a stranger expression than even that assumption warranted. Crowe raised his eyebrows questioningly.

"There's mud on your face, sir," said Hammett. "Lots of it."

Crowe suddenly remembered the black torrent that had drenched him when the bomb burst in the shallows. He looked down; his coat and his white trousers were thinly coated with gray mud, and it dawned upon him that his skin was wet inside his clothes. He put his hand to his face and felt the mud upon it; the damp handkerchief that he brought from his pocket came away smeared with the stuff; he must be a comic-looking sight. He tried to wipe his face clean, and found that his day-old beard hindered the process decidedly.

"That's the lot, sir!" called the Greek officer.

"Thank you," replied Hammett. "Cast off, Mortimer, if you please."

Hammett strode hastily back to the engine-room voice tube, and Crowe was left still wiping vainly at the mud. He guessed it had probably got streaky by now. He must be a sight for the gods.

Those idiots on his staff had let him grin at them and walk up and down the bridge without telling him how he looked.

The *Apache* vibrated sharply with one propeller going astern and another forward, and she swung away from the pier.

"Good luck, sir!" called the Greek officer.

"Same to you, and thank you, sir!" shouted Crowe in return.

"The poor devils'll need all the luck that's going if Jerry lays his hands on them," commented Nickleby. "Wish we could take 'em with us."

"No orders for evacuation yet," said Holby.

The *Apache* had got up speed by now and was heading briskly out to sea, the long v of her wash breaking white upon the beaches. Hammett was as anxious as anyone to get where he had sea room to maneuver before the next inevitable attack should come. Soon she was trembling to her full thirty-six knots, and the green steep hills of Crete were beginning to lose their clarity.

"Here they come!" exclaimed Nickleby.

Out of the mountains of Crete they came, three of them once more, tearing after the *Apache* with nearly ten times her speed.

Hammett turned and watched them as the guns began to speak, and Crowe watched Hammett, ready to take over the command the instant he should feel it necessary. But Hammett was steady enough, looking up with puckered eyes, the gray stubble on his cheeks catching the light.

The bombers wasted no time in reconnoitering. Straight through the shell bursts they came, steadied on the *Apache's* course, and then the leader put down its nose and screamed down in its dive.

"Hard-a-starboard!" said Hammett to the quartermaster.

The *Apache* heeled and groaned under extreme helm applied at full speed, and she swung sharply round. Once a dive bomber commits itself to its dive, it is hard for it to change its course along with its target's. Crowe's mathematical brain plunged into lightning calculations. The bomber started at about fifteen thousand feet or more—call it three miles; three hundred miles an hour. The hundredth of an hour; thirty-six seconds, but that's not allowing for acceleration. Twenty-five seconds would be more like it—say twenty before the ship began to answer her helm. The *Apache* was doing thirty-six knots. In twenty seconds that would be—let's see— almost exactly one fifth of a mile, but that did not mean to say that she would be one fifth of a mile off her course, because she would be following a curved path. A hundred and fifty yards, say, and the bomber would be able to compensate for some of that. A likely miss would be between fifty and a hundred yards.

Crowe's quick brain did its job just in time. The bomber leveled off as it let go its bomb, the thing clearly silhouetted against the sky.

"Midships!" ordered Hammett to the quartermaster. The bomb hit the water and exploded seventy-five yards from the *Apache's* port quarter, raising a vast fountain of gray water, far higher than the *Apache's* stumpy mainmast.

"Well done, Hammett!" called Crowe, but softly, so as not to distract the man as he stood gauging the direction of the second bomber's attack.

The *Apache* was coming out of her heel as she steadied on her new course.

"Hard-a-port!" said Hammett, and she began to snake round in the other direction.

The crescendo scream was repeated, but this time the pilot had tried to out-think the captain of the destroyer. The bomb fell directly in the *Apache's* wake and not more than forty yards astern. She leaped madly at the blow, flinging everyone on the bridge against the rail. And the pilot, as he tore over the ship, turned loose his machine guns; Crowe heard the bullets flick past him, through all the din of the gunfire.

The *Apache* was coming round so fast that soon she would be crossing her own wake. The third bomber was evidently so confused that he lost his head, and the bomb fell farther away than the first one did. Now all three were heading northward again, pursued vainly for a second or two by the *Apache's* fire.

So they were safe now. They had taken the gold and had paid nothing for it.

Crowe looked aft to where a sailor began to sweep the remaining gold coins into a little heap with a Squeegee, and he wondered whether any destroyer's scuppers had ever before run with gold.

Then he looked forward and then down at the crew of the .50-caliber gun. It was with a shock that he saw that the red-haired sailor was dead; the limp corpse, capless, lay neglected, face in arms, on the steel plating, while the other two hands were still at work inserting a new belt. He had been thinking that the *Apache* had escaped scot-free, and now he saw that she had paid in blood for that gold. A wave of reaction overtook him. Not all the gold in the world was worth a life. He felt a little sick.

The first-aid detachment had come up now, and were turning the body over. A heavy hand fell to the deck with a thump; Crowe saw the reddish hair on the wrist that he had noticed earlier. And then his sickness passed. Forty-two tons of gold; millions and millions sterling. Hitler was starving for gold. Gold would buy the allegiance of Arab tribesmen or neutral statesmen, might buy from Turkey the chrome that he needed so desperately or from Spain the alliance for which he thirsted. That gold might have cost England a million other lives. Through his decision England had given one life for the gold. It was a bargain well worth it.

Harper's Ferry

BY

LEONARD EHRLICH

JOHN BROWN slipped from the cot. It was still dark; the day would soon come. He dressed silently, with care; Owen, Oliver, and Jeremiah Anderson were asleep about him. He went into the kitchen, closing the door gently. He lit the lamp. Then he got the stove going with a wood fire; set up the huge kettle for coffee that the men would take, and a pot of water for his own tea. He shivered. The ague which had seeped into his body during the secret hunted days in the Kansas swamps, was still strong in his blood. He shivered with it, feeling a flush along his throat; and knew that the day coming boded rain.

He took his Bible from the chest, and went to the window. A dimmest gray began to show in the sky. The Sabbath is here, he thought; and it will be given to His work. It will be hallowed, but not rest from labor. And as he stood there with the book unopened in his hand, he felt a joy sweep over him:

I am not in a dream. I am John Brown here in the kitchen, with a fire going and the smell of coffee in my nostrils. I am John Brown, a man doing the common duties of life, living in this world. But I am more than John Brown. I have no desires that are my own, because I have passed beyond all desires. I am not in a dream, I smell the coffee, but I am two. I am the clay, yet the self which is He. I exist, yet I do not save in His will. I am not in a dream, the light breaks outside, I hear a crow. It is the Sabbath, the day of our labor.

And almost all things are by the law purged with blood; and without shedding of blood is no remission.

Rain clouded the window in a slow dismal fall; a wind shook it to a devil's tattoo. Owen Brown sat on the porch, with a rifle under his old coat. Inside the men thronged the room, very still. Stevens was reading solemnly in his deep vibrant voice:

"Whereas, Slavery, throughout its entire existence in the United States is none other than a most barbarous, unprovoked and unjustifiable War of one portion of its citizens upon another portion; the only conditions of which are perpetual imprisonment and hopeless servitude or absolute ex-

From: *God's Angry Man*: Copyright 1932. Simon & Schuster.

termination; in utter disregard and violation of those eternal and self-evident truths set forth . . . therefore, we citizens, and the oppressed people, do for the time being ordain and establish the following Provisional Constitution. . . ."

". . . And now, gentlemen," said the old man. "Let me press this one thing on your minds. You all know how dear life is to you, and how dear your lives are to your friends; and in remembering that, consider that the lives of others are dear to them as yours are to you. Do not, therefore, take the life of anyone if you can possibly avoid it. But if it is necessary to take life in order to save your own, then make sure work of it."

The hours moved slowly. The men oiled their rifles, tightened the iron pikes on the wood-shafts; then they waited. The old man sat in the gloom of the kitchen, writing a letter by the lamp-light.

Night came. They ate the meal which their Commander-in-Chief had prepared, the last meal they would eat in this farmhouse; they had heard the old man say the last grace.

He took down a tattered old cap from the wall, the battletorn Kansas cap.

"Men. Get your arms. We will proceed to the Ferry."

At 7:05 in the morning of Monday, October 16, 1859, the Baltimore & Ohio train bound from the West to Baltimore arrived at the small village of Monocacy, Maryland. Before it came to a full stop, Phelps the conductor leaped from the caboose and went scrambling up the runway to the telegraph office. At 7:07 the operator was furiously tapping out a message to the master of transportation at Baltimore:

"Train held up five hours at Harper's Ferry by insurrectionists. One hundred and fifty strong. Baggage-master killed. Say they have come to free slaves. Leader says this is last train to pass bridge east or west. If attempted will be at peril of lives. Telegraph wires cut east and west of Ferry. Notify authorities at once."

By 10:27 the head of the Baltimore & Ohio, John W. Garret, had telegraphed to President Buchanan of the United States; John Floyd, Secretary of War; Governor Wise of Virginia; and Major-General George Stewart, commanding the First Light Division, Maryland Volunteers. By noon three companies of artillery from Fort Monroe, a detachment of Marines from the Washington navy-yard, and the Fredericksburg militia were speeding toward the scene of the reported disturbance; Colonel Robert E. Lee of the Second United States Cavalry in command, Lieutenant J. E. B. Stuart second in command.

Floyd, Secretary of War, pale, pacing back and forth in his Washington office, remembered a letter which some weeks ago had come to him. He had swept it into the basket as the work of a crank, a madman. ("Sir: . . . information of a movement of so great importance that I feel it my duty to

impart it to you without delay . . . having for its general object the liberation of slaves by insurrection . . . he has been in Canada during the
winter, drilling the Negroes there. . . .") Floyd had been too busy with
certain furtive affairs of his own to pay attention to such a fantastic letter.
For who could know, perhaps some day soon the South would have great
need for guns and powder and cannon. Floyd, the United States' War
Secretary was in his heart more truly Floyd of Virginia. He was seeing to
it well and secretly that huge supplies of military stores were being shifted
from Northern arsenals to the South. Now, remembering the letter he
cursed himself.

And in a thousand cities through the nation men were reading their newspapers with incredulous excitement:

". . . The statements are fully confirmed. Two hundred Negroes and
one hundred whites are in revolt, all armed with Minnie rifles, spears and
pistols. They have all the arsenal buildings in their possession and access to
thousands of weapons. They expect, it is said, a reinforcement of twelve
hundred slaves by morning. . . ."

". . . Every light in the town had been previously extinguished by the
lawless mob. All the streets, every road and lane leading to the Ferry has
been barricaded and guarded. . . ."

". . . He has refused to let anything pass. All the east-bound trains are
lying west of the Ferry. Your correspondent has just seen a letter from
a merchant of the town, which was carried by two boys over the mountain,
and who had to swim the river in order to escape. The letter states that
almost all the leading citizens have been imprisoned and many have been
killed. Beckham the Mayor was shot twice by the gang, and died. They
are said to be disguised, the whites being painted as blacks. . . ."

". . . The ringleader, who is said to be named Anderson, made his appearance at Harper's Ferry five or six days ago, and since that time has
been driving around the place in an elegant barouche drawn by four
horses. . . ."

". . . The captain of the outlaw band was an old man with a white
beard. He was heard to say in addressing the conductor 'If you knew me
and understood my motives as well as I and others understand them you
would not blame me so much.' "

". . . The citizens were in a terrible state of consternation, most of them
being shut up in their houses, and not a light to be seen in the streets or
anywhere. It is difficult to describe the excitement throughout the entire
section. Rumors of every sort are flying about. As yet it is impossible to
divine the cause of this outbreak. Some are of the opinion it is a bold concerted scheme to rob the Government pay-house of funds deposited there
on Saturday. We are informed by others that the leader of the rioters is a
noted Abolitionist agent of the Underground Railroad. He is from Troy,
New York and has made frequent visits to the Ferry. His conduct toward

the black people had been noticed on other occasions and involved him in suspicion. He is represented as a most desperate and dangerous man, and one who is likely to cause a great deal of trouble before he will yield. The marauder chief was heard to exclaim, 'If you knew my heart and history you would not blame me.' The Negroes rely upon him, and will implicitly obey his directions. There are said to be more than six hundred armed slaves and whites. . . ."

They had buckled on their arms. They had thrown the long gray shawls over their shoulders and filed out to the cold wet darkness of the fall night, the Sabbath night. Owen had driven the horse and wagon to the door; it was filled with pikes, faggots, a sledge-hammer, and a crow-bar. The old man clambered up. "Come, boys," he said. The wagon began to creak down the lane, the men swinging behind, two and two, hiding their rifles under the shawls. Watson as he moved by found Owen's hand; they gave a quick deep squeeze. Edwin Coppoc, in the last of the line, halted for an instant, embraced his young brother, their lips meeting. Then, to the three remaining behind at the farmhouse, Owen, frail Merriam, and Barclay Coppoc, their comrades became shadows fading in the damp lonely night.

A bad wind was blowing up from the river-gloom. The little fat man walked slowly across the bridge, swinging the lantern, pressing his coat tighter about himself. He yawned, shivering a little, thinking vaguely: twelve noon to twelve the middle of the night is a rotten long dull time to mind a bridge, nothing ever happens, the sleepiest job in the sleepiest town. For seventeen years Will Williams had been watching the Potomac train-crossing and having the same drowsy glum feeling as the night closed on. Will Williams came to his tiny watch-coop at the Maryland entrance of the bridge. He settled inside on his bench with a sigh; he relaxed, nothing coming in till the 1:25 A.M. west-to-Baltimore. He carefully drew the stub of a cigar from his outer breast pocket. He put it into his mouth, rolled it luxuriously, bit on it. He lit a match, he——

"Come out of there!"

Will Williams' jaw hung. The match burned down to his fingers. A big man with a black beard and shining eyes stood in the coop door; Williams stared down the glistening barrel of a rifle.

"Come out, quick."

"Quit jokin'."

He came out, scared and incredulous. A lean young fellow was standing there too, with a rifle. "Quit jokin'," Williams kept saying. Then from the darkness a wagon came creaking on to the bridge and fat Williams saw a line of men. He saw their set hard faces, the shine of rifle-barrels; it was no joke. But it must be a joke. Why, there was Cook, John Cook the boy who tended the canal-lock. He knew the boy well, he'd married sweet Mary Turner, blessed luck. And there was that old gentleman sitting up on the seat, Mr. Smith, the new farmer at the Kennedy place, Isaac Smith who had a quick straight way and you respected him. Why, they were up to some joke! But Will Williams felt the rifle murderous against his paunch.

"Oliver Brown. Will Thompson. Newby. Guard the bridge. Await orders. The rest, follow me."

Now they were moving along the bridge. Now they were over, they were in Harper's Ferry. They went along the narrow street; passed the railroad station with its green flaring lights; passed the saloon, seeing no one and not being seen. The wet night was with them; folks were close by hearth-fires, not dreaming danger. The Ferry had known its last belligerent men during the Revolution, beyond the remembrance of living citizens. This October of 1859 they would as soon expect lava to rage up from the gentle Virginia hills as bloodshed in their streets, as eighteen men moving desperate in the night with guns, like ghosts risen from a grave. Suddenly ahead the whole village darkened, lights dotting the obscurity clean up the Bolivar Heights suddenly snuffed out. Tidd was at work. In another instant the armory loomed black by the Potomac bank. Old Dan Whelan would be drowsing in the arsenal yard. Thousands of arms would come into their possession. Hazlett and Jeremiah Anderson crept forward to the gate.

Five miles south of the Ferry, in an upstairs room of his plantation, Colonel Lewis Washington, great-grandnephew of the First President, slept fitfully. Downstairs, hanging above the fireplace, were an old pistol and a sword. The pistol had been presented to George Washington by Lafayette; the sword was the gift of Frederick the Great.

A little after midnight Lewis Washington stirred in his bed, vague sounds threading his sleep. Then two loud knocks came upon the heavy oak door. He sat up, startled. "Open up!" a voice boomed. He slipped from the bed, thrust his feet hastily into slippers, and went in his nightshirt to the door. He pulled it open. Four men stood there with levelled rifles. One, a Negro, held a burning flambeau.

"You're our prisoner," said the black-bearded man. "Get into your clothes."

Washington stared. "Will you have the courtesy to tell me what this means?"

"Yes. You're coming with us. And your slaves too. Get dressed, quick."

He prodded the thunderstruck Washington with his rifle. The colonel dressed, as in a fantastic dream. "Where are you taking me?" he asked, trying to speak with dignity as he slipped on a boot.

"Osawatomie Brown wants to see you."

"And who, pray, is Osawatomie Brown?"

"Have you never heard of Kansas?"

They went downstairs. The colonel's sister, gray-haired, wrapped in a dressing gown, sat proud in an arm-chair. Her look was eloquent: Lewis, cowhide these ruffians out of the house. Old Bettina, the Negress, was glaring defiantly at two armed men. One was a mulatto, the other a slim dark fellow.

"Good evening, Colonel Washington," the dark fellow said.

"Mr. Cook! What does this outrage mean?"

"I've been trying to calm Miss Washington. You will come to no harm."

"What does it mean, I say?"

"We're freeing the slaves of the South. We're prepared to do it."

The black-bearded man broke in roughly, "Enough talk. You, Mr. Washington, take down that sword, and that pistol too. Quick. . . . Now hand the sword over to Emperor Green. . . . Now the pistol, to Leary."

The Southerner was pale with the indignity.

"It's Captain Brown's orders," said Cook, half-proud, half-ashamed. "He said we'd start the work with a symbol."

Tidd came in growling through the front door: "The wagon's ready."

"Sir, your carriage awaits you." Stevens bowed low in mockery.

They went out, leaving the two women behind in the darkness. In the driveway was the colonel's small phaeton. Behind it was a large four-horse farm wagon. Six slaves stood startled and bewildered by the wagon. "Come on and fight to get free," Tidd had told them. Now they looked fearfully at their master, cringing. Colonel Washington stepped up into the carriage with hauteur. He felt more like himself now that he was out of his nightshirt. Stevens got beside him, taking the reins. The rest, whites and Negroes, climbed into the wagon. The first hostage was taken. The first bondmen were freed.

A little past twelve, Pat Higgins, night-watchman, walked out on the Maryland bridge to relieve Will Williams. A shameful night, he growled in his thought, may it go quick. He puffed on his pipe as he trudged along the trestle and cursed himself for not bringing his ancient outer coat.

"Halt!"

Three forms rose dark before him. Instantly, intuitively, Higgins turned and began to run. A rifle sounded, a bullet snipped a furrow in the Irishman's scalp. His leathery old body dodged from side to side up the trestle. He made the town entrance and leaped behind the wing of the station. He stood listening; there was only silence again.

At 1:25 the Baltimore & Ohio train drew in at the Ferry. ". . . but I didn't know what 'halt' mint any more than a hog knows about a holiday!" said Patrick Higgins in great excitement to the conductor, Phelps. "There's no sign anywhere of Will, and sure there's somethin' evil about!"

Phelps and the engineer, half-incredulous, walked up the tracks to investigate. Rifle-fire came from the bridge. Hastily the train was backed away out of danger. Phelps ran to the telegraph office. The wires had been cut.

Shephard Hayward, a free Negro and baggage master at the Ferry, rolled his hand-truck down the platform as the train came in. It was a good job. He had held it for seven years now and they had been the happiest of his life. The little fund at the bank was growing; the whites all respected

him, only yesterday old Mayor Beckham himself had inquired in a true
friendly fashion about his family in the small new house at the foot of the
Heights, was the boy better and how was the flower-bed coming along. It
was a good deal for a "nigger" to have reached such a secure place in a
Southern community, to have pulled himself up from the slime to a man's
place. Shephard Hayward, not seeing the watchman about, not seeing the
swing of Higgins' red lamp, walked around the corner of the hotel and
on toward the bridge to look for him; Shephard Hayward walked crooning
to himself. Dangerfield Newby, Negro with a wife and seven children
enslaved, waiting with rifle poised over the railing, saw a man moving up
in the dimness of the trestle. His finger trembled on the trigger. He called
"Stop!" The man kept moving up, Newby's finger pulled in sharp. Shephard Hayward gave a little choked cry, he turned and staggered back along
the bridge. Just over the end he dropped and lay moaning, with a bullet
and agonized bewilderment in his heart. The first deathblow for the cause
of blacks had been struck.

Back at the darkened farmhouse, Owen Brown, Merriam and the Coppoc
boy were waiting through the slow fearful hours. They could only wait.
Their share would come later. The others would put the spark to the
touchwood; these three would heap the fuel. When the first bullet cut to
a soft living wall of flesh, making it dead; when the first oppressor sank
lifeless before a black man's eyes, showing a way to freedom, the slaves
would come in wild crowds to the Kennedy farm. These three would give
them guns, old Brown had said; this was the point from which their
strength would swell, would swirl. Now his son and the two boys waited
throbbing, hoping.

And soon through the hills a boy of the South was streaking on a horse.
By dawn he would be in Charlestown, eight miles away. By dawn the
alarm bells would be ringing, tolling on—insurrection, civil war. The
Jefferson Guards, men and boys with old muskets and squirrel-guns,
would be falling into line before the court-house. In Martinsburg from bed
or breakfast men would hurry armed to the town square. Bells ringing
terror over the countryside, bells tolling, slaves rising bloody, the Shepherdstown troop forming, the Hamtramck Guards rushing, tighter, tighter
the net drawing about an old man and some boys.

The first gray cold light came into the arsenal yard. The men were ranged
about the gate with rifles, watching the still empty street. Across the town
the bell of the Lutheran church had begun a steady ominous ringing. Close
by the watch-house some of the prisoners paced, scared and hollow-eyed.
Forty-two had been brought in during the night; now the rest were huddled
inside. The handful of liberated slaves stood stupidly about, furtively trailing their pikes, ashamed to look full at the masters they were guarding.
They were cold, they were hungry, the cabins on the plantations would be

warm, food would be smelling good in the fires. But they were afraid of the old man with the fierce eyes. He kept moving about the yard, watching everything like a hawk. Now he strode over to Lewis Washington standing pale and outraged against the wall. The sword of Frederick was gripped in the old man's hand. He held it proudly, as if it were a true fit weapon for this leader. He began to speak to Washington, earnestly; his words were almost an appeal for justification:

"I am very attentive to you, sir. I may get the worst of it in my first encounter, and if so your life is worth as much as mine. I took you first for the moral effect it would give our cause having one of your name as prisoner." Or again turning to the prisoner of illustrious lineage: "You will find a fire in there, sir. It is quite cold this morning." But Washington would never answer, as if it were beneath him, and all the time his keen glance would take in the other—the gleaming bluish mettle of the eyes, the stiff whitening hair projecting close above on the low brow, the mouth like a sabre-thrust—and even as he hated the sight of the face he felt its awful unsmiling strength.

Just before daylight, in the flare of torches, the old man had addressed the prisoners, "I came here from Kansas, and this is a slave state. I want to free all the slaves, and I have possession now of the armory. I hope that no harm will come to you. But if the citizens interfere I must only burn the town, and there will be blood. I am here in the name of the Great Jehovah."

As the first grayness was showing, the Baltimore & Ohio train began to pull up very slowly to the bridge entrance. At three o'clock old Brown had sent word to the conductor by a Negro that the train might proceed; but Phelps would not trust the word; surely the arches or timbers were cut. The old man left the armory now and walked out on the trestle with Phelps to reassure him. The train drew across, took on speed, soon was lost wailing in the swell of the hills, in the direction of Monocacy. (Bend low over the keys, operator, tap tap frantic tap to Buchanan to Lee to Governor tapping drawing the net tighter ever tighter!) Meanwhile Boerly the grocer stepped from his doorway a little beyond the arsenal to see what the unusual early noises were about, the church bells ringing so strangely, a train whistling through the town at such an hour. Boerly was broad and red-faced, he was the town's wit, the jolly-man. He could take two ends of a cider cask in his huge hands and hoist it up on the counter to be bunged, and he and his childless "old lady" would drink more of it than they sold. Now, in his blue cotton shirt, his face shining red with a fresh cold wash, he stepped out into the street, into the autumn air, the brisk living day. Three steps from the door a bullet ploughed his brain. He fell with his head twisted in the gutter, his bare white feet sticking up grotesquely above the walk, the blood oozing down the red shining cheek. Dauphin Thompson, white as the mists rising in the wooded heights, stared aghast; the smoking carbine quivered in his nerveless hands. His young vision had not connected the vague beautiful idea of Liberty with men stiffening in the streets.

Kagi, holding the rifleworks with Copeland and Leary, saw the train pull across the bridge, and smiled calm and bitter. The old fool, he thought, why did he let it pass? The news will spread hours before we want it to. We could have held these farmers off indefinitely, but this will mean the troops. Kagi felt the imploring harassed eyes of yellow Leary upon him, the proud fine eyes of Copeland the Oberlin student, and the same question was in each pair, what now, what now? Poor devils, thought Kagi, this does mean everything for you, this does mean your hope, your life. Instantly he took out a small note-book and pencil from his pocket:

"Get back over Maryland bridge to hills. Why do you linger? Your purpose accomplished, terror struck through country and blacks roused. Trapped here if stay. Kagi."

In the armory yard too the men were wondering, apprehensive. For a short time they had been stirred to vast hope, flushed with the incredible success of the plan. Everything had gone like clock-work, all the vital points were theirs: the Potomac bridge was under guard, Kagi held the rifleworks, Hazlett and Osborn Perry the arsenal, they themselves the armory. They had hostages. But now a fear began to grip them. Where were the hordes of slaves, where was Owen leading down thousands to their aid? From time to time they turned their heads from the gate to look back at the old man. They felt the golden minutes slipping; but he gave them no sign, only stood there with that cold-frenzied face. He seemed to be waiting possessed of some deep invincible secret, and somehow, seeing him thus, blindly they had faith—save one. Look, thought Stewart Taylor, he is paralyzed, he does not know what to do now. He has thought nothing out further than this. He has the town, but what he shall do with it he does not know. Every minute of delay rouses the country more, and still we stand here guarding a yard. Kill, burn, escape, advance, die, only do something that will achieve a positive end. But no, behold God and one man overturning the universe!

Now old Brown was portioning out to the prisoners the coffee and biscuits which he had ordered brought in from the Wager House (he would himself take nothing nor would he give his men any for fear the food had been poisoned). Now he was opening the gate to allow young Reason Cross to return home for a moment under guard. "My aunt will be frantic with worry," pleaded the lame boy with the long patrician face. "I have been out all night. She will think I am killed. She is very ill. I'll come back." Or old Brown would be talking courteously to the huddled prisoners: "I think after a while, possibly, I shall be enabled to release you, but only on the condition of getting your friends to send in a stout Negro as a ransom, as a new member of the army of the Lord."

The sun rose up over the Bolivar Heights. The sun ran blazing cold golden down the stained autumn hills into the Ferry streets. The dawn swiftly sharply brightened blue, the Potomac caught rays, the Shenandoah, and there was a gleaming over the pure morning waters; but death in the town, panic in the town, and the Lutheran bell tolling, tolling. For years patrols had ridden and men had watched the night-roads; now the dreaded thing was upon them, slaves in revolt, slave-stealers murdering and pillaging. There must be thousands of the vengeful whites and blacks; only men with powerful numbers would dare to attack the slave border. And with the rise of the sun the whole populace was gathered upon the Bolivar hill, the women and young ones clustered in terror higher up, the townsmen running about, shouting, dazed. Some few had weapons, ancient flintlocks, axes, small rusty fowling-pieces. Starry, the young doctor, rode on his sorrel from group to stricken group, trying to calm them, to get them into some kind of organization. But far down the central street they could see a heap in the gutter, Boerly dead; they were doomed. In their apprehension they seemed not to observe the very slaves they dreaded shrinking in their midst, terror-struck equally with the masters.

"Tell Kagi, stand firm," the old man said, crumpling the paper in his hand. Stevens stood there, hesitating. "We could make it," he said, not meeting his leader's eyes, looking off to the gates. "We have the bridge."

"No."

"You owe the men a chance. We'll be hemmed in. There's no sight of Owen and the slaves."

"The slaves will come."

"Kagi's in danger."

"Yes. I know."

"Kagi's exposed, he's isolated."

"Tell Kagi, stand firm."

Stevens' hand came up in a half-salute. (He had once been in the Army, a soldier in the Mexican war under Taylor; had been tried for "mutiny, engaging in a drunken riot and assaulting Major Blake of First United States Dragoons"; he had escaped into Kansas.) Now his eyes gleamed with a proud fatal look as he strode quickly to the gates. Stand firm, throbbed in the old man's mind, the slaves will come, the slaves will come. Not back, we must not go back. It will mean the ruin of my plan, we will be at the beginning again. And I am old, it is the last of my strength. His eyes fastened hungrily upon the bridge entrance. They must come, the labor of his life hung on it. We will move into Africa, he thought fiercely, or we will die here. Let Kagi call, let Stevens plead, have we not sworn to a sacrifice? No, not back. Ahead, southward, down into the great Black Way, or let us die here.

Now among the townsmen the first paralyzing consternation was over; they saw that they had vastly overrated the number of the raiders, that the little band in the yard was receiving no reinforcement, that the separated detachments could be harassed and cut off. A boy came running up excited: he had discovered that one of the end workshops beyond the confines of the yard was open; it was filled with guns that had been placed there for protection against possible freshets at high water. There was a rush for the shop. Soon men were sniping from the houses nearby, and the rocks and trees of the lower hill. By ten o'clock a steady point-blank fire was being directed upon the armory and the yard. The bullets splintered and spattered about the prisoners shrinking in the flimsy watch house.

A handkerchief on a rifle showed in the yard, a flag of truce. Joseph Brua, one of the hostages, slipped through the gates. In a silence, he called up, pleading: "For God's sake, stop shooting! You endanger the lives of your friends! The captain offers you a truce! Leave the armory in his possession and let the firing stop on both sides!" Brua ran back, the gates opened, he slipped in. Immediately the shooting began anew, heavier. Old Brown was fighting for time; but his parley had only succeeded in convincing the townsmen that the raiders were on the defensive. Soon the "miners" were being attacked at each point. A dozen men crossed the Potomac a short distance above the Ferry, sneaked down the tow-path of the canal and concealed themselves in the brush above the bridge entrance. Oliver Brown, Newby and Will Thompson were exposed on the trestle to a cunning, almost unanswerable fire. Another party crossed the Shenandoah and took a sheltered position opposite Kagi at the rifleworks. Hazlett and the consumptive Osborn Perry, across the street from the yard, alone had a fighting chance; they had the arsenal building at their backs, and then the Shenandoah.

It was a question of time. On one side the Jefferson Guards, speeding by train, the Shepherdstown troop, the Winchesters, the Hamtramck battalion, Lee, Stuart, the Marines; on the other an old man staring at the bridge entrance: they will come, they will come!

It was noon. The machinists, the workers of the arsenal would have been leaving the buildings; some to sit in the yard with their lunch boxes, out in the warming sun; others to walk home through the quiet streets for a hot meal. But now above the desultory cracking of rifles a sudden murderous fusillade blazed in the direction of the bridge, then a great mingled sound rose, the running tramp of many feet, voices shouting. Old Brown leaped for the gate, his eyes taking on a wild life. At last! At last! The slaves were coming, Owen was leading down the slaves! Then even as the thought formed exultant, a man came running from the trestle entrance, two followed hard behind—Will, Newby, Oliver. They were fleeing toward the armory. The slaves had not come. The Jefferson Guards had come. A blackness crushed down upon the old man's heart. But swiftly he flung the gate open, calling with fierceness: "Cover them up!" and strode into the street. The raiders followed to a man, forming a desperate deadly line. The Jefferson Guards came in a ragged rush. The little band held. The old man cried "Let go on them!" There was a volley; the attackers halted, then scattered hastily, toward the Wager House. The guns behind had been silent, as if the townsmen were merely witness to the drama of the maneuver. But now as the detachment of three came panting up to the gates a sniper hidden in a house at the foot of the heights took quick savage aim; fired. Halfway up the street Newby staggered, Dangerfield Newby dropped with a ball through the arteries of his throat, instantly dead. Slave woman, slave mother of seven slave children, do not write again of Newby's babe "just commenced to crawl"; do not beg: "buy us soon, for if you don't get me somebody else will." Bow your head in the fields, in the darkness by the cabin croon your darkened heart out: "Oh dear Danger-field, come this fall without fail, money or no money I want to see you so much, that is one bright hope I have before me."

The other half of the Charlestown men had meanwhile come down from Bolivar Heights and occupied the saloon on the Shenandoah side. A detachment had swarmed into the houses between the hill and the arsenal, from which they were sending a direct fire into the yard. Tighter, tighter the net. Now there was no way of retreat into Maryland, no means of communication with the Kennedy farm, they were cut off from Kagi at the rifleworks, from Hazlett and Osborn Perry in the arsenal.

"Oliver. Was there no sign of your brother?"

"There was no sign."

The men heard, and the last hope died on their faces. Leeman's eyes desperately sought the rear gate. He was the youngest, only eighteen. But the Potomac lay there, a full half-mile across; a man swimming could never make it, he would be riddled by a hundred guns. Leeman's eyes hungered upon the river. He was the youngest. They were all so young, they might have been boys in a college—Dauphin twenty-one, Edwin Coppoc twenty-four, Barclay twenty, Hazlett twenty-two, Tidd twenty-five, so young Watson, Merriam, Copeland, Cook, Stewart Taylor twenty-two, Will Thompson twenty-six, Oliver twenty, oh so young and doom in their hearts, there was no sign of Owen.

And the old man with the flowing white beard and the sunken terrible eyes stood there, shooting, ordering, brooding defiantly: it was not over, he was not beaten. Time, only time, and they would yet come through; flaming in his mind was the thought of Owen. Aye, no surrender, the protection of night would surely bring them in; even now they must be lying on Maryland Heights, waiting for the darkness. Hold on, stand firm, this is the labor of my life. And the hostages, he thought, he still had them as an overpowering threat. Long ago a concerted attack could have wiped out his band, but in such a charge the prisoners would also go down, and these Southerners would never sacrifice their kindred. He, John Brown, would not hesitate thus; let there be a true just reason and he would offer up every life. But these men would not; and now John Brown went into the watch-house. He surveyed the forty-odd prisoners. "I want you, sir," he said, pointing at Lewis Washington. "Come, Mr. Brua. And you, sir. . . . And you. . . ." Eleven of them, the most prominent, were taken from the watch-room and crowded into the back part of the small engine-house. Then the old man ordered in the slaves he had armed, and posted the remnant of his men close about. The engine-house would be their last refuge. That, and the hostages.

"Gentlemen, you are the most influential." With stiff dignity he addressed the chosen prisoners, with solemnity as in a speech. "I have only to say now that you will share the same fate that your friends extend to my men."

The Shepherdstown troop was in, the Hamtramck Guards, three companies from Martinsburg; a thousand surrounded the town. But the struggle was not alone against the desperate odds of men. Time. Time. "Will Thompson!" called the old man.

Agatha Thompson's boy came up.

"Take the lame fellow with you into the street. Keep him ahead of you. Treat with them for a stop to the firing."

A moment later Will Thompson was a prisoner in the Wager House. Time, time, night will bring them in, beat in the old man's head. "Stevens! Watson Brown!" The two came up, waited. "Put a handkerchief on your gun. Take Mr. Kitzmiller with you and negotiate so that we may leave the yard."

"Captain Brown," said Stevens. "You saw what happened to Thompson."

"You have my orders."

"Damn your——! Why don't you run things so we'll have a chance? . . . You have the prisoners! Put a bullet in one, throw him out of the gate! Send a nigger to say we'll kill 'em all if we can't get clear!"

"You have my orders. We will injure no unarmed men."

Stevens glared at Watson. The boy stood blanched, his eyes pleading: I have Bell, I want to live, the babe's just born. But no, there was the face like granite, unrelenting: let the grand reason that one course is right and another wrong be kept continually before your mind. The boy turned his face, hopeless, undone, toward the street, toward his fate. And into the blackbearded man's eyes again came the fiercely proud fatal look. His hand rose sharp in the habitual half-salute, and the man who once in the far West had been imprisoned for insubordination under a commuted sentence of death, now strode to the engine-house door.

"Kitzmiller!"

The two raiders and the prisoner walked slowly across the yard. Stevens was waving his rifle high; it was topped with a white handkerchief. The firing ceased, save at a distance where Kagi was trapped. Watson Brown opened the gate entrance. Kitzmiller went first, shrinking with fear. The three began to walk slowly up the street, toward the Wager House. Ten feet. Fifteen, the surrounding stillness deep. Twenty. Twenty-five, a rolling whining volley, rifles recoiling in the upper windows of the saloon. Stevens slumped, the white handkerchief dropping, slugs in his side and breast. Watson plunged to his knees, face agonized, his hand clutching his belly. Kitzmiller was clumping frantically toward the hotel. Watson Brown got to one knee. Again the intense silence, with a devil's tattoo faint down the rifleworks. Watson Brown began to drag himself back up the street, dropping, writhing, rising, moaning, a hundred shamed staring eyes riveted.

Watson Brown reached the gate, suddenly there was another rattle of firing, poured in from the hillside. But not at Watson. Leeman the imp-eyed was taking his chance for life.

He had seen two comrades shot down. He went icy trembling cold, then like a madness the blood rushed in his head. Suddenly swift as a hound he whipped for the rear gate. He sprang clawing, slipping, then fell back. The volley rattled, he sprang again, held, pulled up, leaped the seven-foot gate. He darted along the river ledge. It ceased, it turned down sharp to the water. Leeman stood quivering still, his eyes moving like a cornered weasel's. The rifles were finding the range, bullets were crumbling the shale at his feet. Leeman slid down the bank to the water's edge. He pulled out his bowie, slashed at the accoutrements, the cartridge belt, the rifle-sling, flung his two revolvers away, tore off his boots; and ran into the river. He waded furiously a dozen steps, he cast himself upon the waters and began to swim. All about him the bullets were flicking up white jets. He made for the cover of a tiny green-rock islet fifty yards out. Now the militiamen were down to the water, now ten of them were wading out. Leeman draggled up on the islet, a bullet smashed his shoulder. He lay there, pant-ing, at bay, watching the men wade closer, closer through the shallows with guns uplifted. Leeman threw up his arms, gasped, "Don't shoot! I sur-render!" But they came on, one eagerly savagely in the lead, bearing his rifle high. An instant later Billy Leeman was dead, half his head blown away. All afternoon the boy's body lying on the edge of the rock, hands dangling in the water, blood staining the water, would be a target for hundreds of marksmen. Later it would slide down somehow and float in slow ghastly eddies toward the bridge.

Joseph Brua said, "I will go." He walked past the old man, crossed the yard. As he went without fear down the street toward Stevens sprawled in the gutter, a shot flicked the walk. But it was the only one; he was recognized. Brua lifted huge Stevens to his back. He sagged under the burden, moving in a zig-zag toward the Wager House. He went up the steps, went in. He came out alone and walked back toward the yard. He took his place again among the prisoners in the engine-house.

"A doctor is looking after him," he said.

"Thank you, sir," said old Brown.

But Brua's act was like a briefest gleam in a mad black chaos—snuffed out by the beating drowning lust. Gentle old Fontaine Beckham, Mayor of the Ferry and chief agent for the railroad, nervously ventured out on the trestlework, despite warnings. His heart was sickened, oh this violence in his streets, poor dead Shephard Hayward his helper. He must do some-thing. Maybe he could reason with these outlaws, stop the bloodshed.

Edwin Coppoc, crouching in the doorway of the engine-house, saw a man sneak behind the water tank near the bridge. The young Quaker levelled his rifle; you murderers, you filthy murderers, he cried inside him-self, thinking of Watson Brown all torn in the engine-house. The man showed his head. Coppoc fired, missed. Behind him, Alstadt the slave-owner cried, "It's Beckham, it's old Mayor Beckham! Don't fire!" Young Terence Burns laughed hysterically, "For God's sake, don't fire!" Coppoc fired, the dark wings again brushed the little town, and Fontaine Beckham crumpled upon the timbers. *Peace, Quaker, peace, thou shalt not kill.* And in Will Book No. 16 page 142 Jefferson Court Records, Charlestown, a recent entry showed that Fontaine Beckham (he was the greatest friend of the black man in all the country) had provided for the liberation upon his death of one Isaac Gilbert, Negro, his slave-wife and three children. The Quaker boy's shot had liberated them.

The two men ran toward the Wager House, Chambers the saloon-keeper, and young Harry Hunter. "The bitches, the god-damned bitches!" Hunter was crying. "They murdered my uncle!" The two men rushed up the steps of the Hotel, burst savagely into the room where Will Thompson was being guarded. In another moment they were dragging him out by the throat. They headed for the trestle where Beckham had fallen, and the crowd mad for revenge followed howling. "I don't care!" Will Thompson kept crying blindly as they dragged him, "Kill me, I don't care! Eighty million will rise up to free the slaves! I don't care!" Hunter and Chambers placed their revolvers against Thompson's head. "Die, you bastard!" They fired, he twisted crazily, before he fell a dozen balls had ploughed his young body. They threw him through the opening in the trestle, he dropped forty feet to the river rocks. All day Will Thompson's carcass would be riddled, his white face ghastly with agony of death staring up.

And you, Kagi, look out! They're creeping up, they're closing in on you! Oh Kagi, quick, breathe in the last sweet shining air, Oh drink the sun with your eyes! Bullets bullets close about thick as a tomb thick fatal shutting out light. Back, Kagi, back, Copeland and Leary, climb hard, desperate up on the Winchester tracks. Leap down, splash gasp swish into the ice of the waters Shenandoah. Storm of lead behind, Virginia guns opposite in a blazing wall of hate. Turn desperate, not back, not forward, turn with the downflow, east as the river flows to the sea, labor, wrench, the flat rock juts. Scream, Leary, flail screaming the stained waters, own no more the workin' place an' the honey-bab just born, cough gurgle blood, nevermore be back befo' the summer turns. Old Kagi, here it is, cease wondering, now you know the last darkness. Sink easily, move with the waters moving seaward, flow deep to the peace of the dark shining Sea the Father ancient before earth. Tremble, Copeland, alone alive. Be dragged back, a nigger living is sport. Knot the white handkerchiefs, townsmen tie them tight, lynch lynch nigger Copeland the student of Oberlin.

Now the rifleworks are empty. Now they are silent.

Night is down. They are hemmed in at the armory. The men from Martinsburg, trainmen chiefly, charged into the yard at dusk, many falling, and

the raiders are hemmed in the engine-house. It will be their last stand.
Night is down. There is no shooting. The militia are picketing the engine-
house; their work is done, soon the Marines will be in, the majesty the
power of Government. A thousand men surround the tiny stone-building.
Inside are eleven prisoners, four trembling slaves, one dead boy, two dying
boys, five living raiders—Edwin Coppoc, Jeremiah Anderson, Dauphin
Thompson, Emperor Green, and the Commander-in-Chief of the "Provisional Army," John Brown. Loop-holes have been knocked in the stone
wall. The five men stand there, waiting in the obscurity, their rifles to hand.

*The moon besieged between Saturn and Mars . . . the Lord of the First
in a streaming Sign or infested of the Malevolents, and the depositor of the
Light of Time being also in a violent Sign and afflicted. . . .*

Stewart Taylor lies dead in the engine-house.

On the brick floor close by the Canadian, Oliver Brown is moaning,
bleeding his life away.

Watson Brown lies breathing quietly, deeper deeper into the gathering
Darkness.

A message comes in, under cover of truce: Surrender. The painful
peasant hand writes:

"Captain John Brown answers—In consideration of all my men, whether
living, or dead, or wounded, being soon safely in and delivered up to me at
this point with all their arms and ammunition, we will then take our
prisoners and cross the Potomac bridge, a little beyond which we will set
them at liberty; after which we can negotiate about the Government
property as may be best. Also we require the delivery of our horse and
wagon at the hotel. John Brown." The torch flared in the yard, outlining
a form. "Approach!" the old man called back. The man came close slowly.
Old Brown opened the door a hand's breadth; he held the sword of
Frederick. The other raiders with cocked carbines stared out into the darkness; they were ready for trickery.

"What do you want?"

"I want to speak to you under a truce. Let me in. It is for your own
good."

The door opened a little wider. The man slipped through, bearing the
torch. The doors shut.

"I am Sinn. Captain Sinn of the Fredericksburg Company."

"Well, sir?"

The militiaman looked about the engine-house, saw the exhausted prisoners, the slaves, the prostrate boys, the four raiders by the loop-holes.
God, what madness, he thought.

"Surrender," he said. "You have no chance."

"You have my terms."

"There can be no terms."

"You shot my men down like dogs under a flag of truce. And I, I had full possession of the town, I could have massacred every soul, burned it to ashes. These prisoners, they are not scratched, I have given them every courtesy. And you say no terms."

"Men who take up arms as outlaws must expect to be shot down like dogs."

"Sir, we knew what we would have to go through before coming here. I have weighed the responsibility. I will not shrink from it now."

"Sinn!" It was Brua. "For mercy's sake, let them leave! They've been punished enough. His two sons are dying here."

The militiaman said, "It can't be, Mr. Brua." He turned to the old man again. "I wish to avoid danger to these citizens. I wish to save your men from further bloodshed. I beg you, surrender. I promise you protection from the crowds, a safe——"

"You have my terms. A free way to the mountains."

A groan came from Oliver Brown. Sinn looked down, watched the boy by the dim light of the torch; felt pity.

"You have no chance. For the last time, I beg you. Give in."

"We will die just here."

Sinn bowed, turned to the door. Old Brown opened it. Sinn looked back once again, his eyes lingered over the three forms lying on the brick floor. "I'll send in the company's doctor," he said; and went.

They stood there in the dark, in the silence, waiting, waiting.

"Father."

The old man went to the bearded boy.

"Father. I'm dying."

"The surgeon is coming. Have courage, Watson."

"Oh, I mustn't die. But I'm dying."

"I would help you, my son, if I could."

The old man walked back, took his place by the loop-hole again.

The surgeon came. "Good evening," he said. The old man held the torch as the Southerner kneeled by Oliver.

"He is my son," the old man said.

"Tell them to kill me," Mary Brown's youngest boy whispered. "I can't stand it."

The other's hands were swift and tender about his torn breast.

"Tell them to kill me. They won't kill me."

The doctor rose. His eyes met old Brown's. He moved to Watson's form; kneeled.

"He is my son too."

Quickly again the doctor rose, gathering his things together with finality. He went to the door.

"Will my sons live?" asked the old man.

"No," the lips formed. "They will not live." The old man handed the torch back to the doctor who stood there an instant, thinking: I will always remember this. Strange, tragic. Men killing, conversing with one another, aiding the wounded, then killing again. "I will try to come again in the morning," he said; "good night," and went.

The old man stood once more in his place, holding the still watch. Now he trembled and his eyes were unseeing:

"O Lord God of truth, my rock and my fortress, have mercy upon me, for I am afflicted! Mine eye is consumed with grief, yea, my soul and my flesh! I trust in Thee, I say: Thou art my Lord. For this God is our God for ever and ever, He will be our guide even unto death."

In the engine-house the raiders kept the vigil. "I will come again in the morning," the doctor had said. But he would not come, they knew it; their fate would come, storming the hold at dawn. It was bitterly cold, a chill as of death lay about the stone floors and walls. The outside night, cloudy, moonless, crept through the loop-holes, deepening the blackness within. The drunken shouts of the militiamen had ceased. They were resting from the heat of the day's valor; Dangerfield Newby's ears had been sliced from his head, the brutal indignities to his cold stiff body had been tired of; the poor white wretches from Loudon Heights had scavenged the dead; the riddled hulk of Will Thompson down in the trestle rocks was this hour being granted its first ghastly peace. A new sound was in the silence, the slow disciplined tread of the Marine guard cordon about the engine-house. "Rest," said the old man; "we have till morning"; and the prisoners and the Negroes and the raiders lay unsleeping side by side on the stone floor. He was still at his place by the door, now forty hours without food, without sleep; calling from time to time in the stillness of the night: "Men, are you awake?" And always there was the moaning of the dying boys.

"Father!"

"I am here, Oliver."

"I can't stand it! Shoot me!"

"No, Oliver. Have patience."

"Please! please! Oh, Martha would do it for me!"

"No, my son. I think you will get well."

Then later in the grievous black silence: "Father!"

"If you must die, die like a man does."

And golden Dolph Thompson, his hair matted with grime and blood, sat by the side of Watson; held the carbine in one hand, with the other stroked the head of his sister's young husband; rocked, heartbroken, Oh Wat, Wat, as the doomed boy sobbed with anguish; and the words which Brua had spoken earlier mingled with his present grief for a single throbbing horror.

"You are committing treason," Brua had said, "treason against your government."

Dolph Thompson had stared. "No, that isn't true! Captain Brown! Is it true that we are committing treason against our government?"

"Yes, I think it is, Dauphin. I think it is true."

"Then I won't fight more! I came to free slaves! I won't fight more, I won't commit treason!"

But the old man was at a distance, in this desperate lost moment he was far in the dream which his life had been. Yes, gentlemen, ran in his mind, ran so incalculably that he would never know whether it was speech or thought, if you realized my past history, if you knew my heart, you would not blame me for being here. I went to Kansas and the pro-slavery people from Kentucky and Virginia hunted me down like a wild animal. I lost one of my sons there. Yes, gentlemen, we are Abolitionists from the North, we've come to take and release your slaves. Our organization is large, and must succeed. I suffered much in Kansas. I expect to suffer here, in the cause of human freedom. I have been well known as Old Brown of Kansas. I shed blood on Potawatomie. Slaveholders I regard as robbers and murderers, and I have sworn to abolish slavery and liberate my fellow men. And now I am here. . . . I have failed. . . . Two of my sons were killed here today.

"Oliver!" the old man called in the gloom.
No answer. Silence.
"I guess he's dead," old Brown said.

Custer

FREDERIC F. VAN DE WATER

THE 7th Cavalry was coming up the valley with massed trumpeters in advance. Forked star-and-stripe guidons were uneasy specks of color above the dark river of horsemen, and low dust blew away beneath the trampling hoofs. The head of the column vanished in a hollow, emerged magnified, and behind it, marching fours flowed interminably down the farther slope.

Custer's men were on the move once more, riding from the glamour of the past into legend. Their chief smiled proudly as the splendid regiment drew near. The red-faced trumpeters swung out of line, and, still sounding their hosannahs, halted beside the reviewing party to play the regiment through.

Young Charley Varnum, chief of scouts, leads his followers past—the swarthy Bouyer in half-Indian garb; Reynolds with his felon-infected right hand in a sling; Herendeen, the courier who is there to carry back Custer's tidings to Terry; the bearded Fred Girard, the grinning black Isaiah Dorman, interpreters; Mark Kellogg, the correspondent, astride a mule; Bloody Knife and the twenty-four Arikara scouts, sullen men with loose black hair blowing beneath bandeaus of cloth or buckskin; the tall merry Crows lent by Gibbon—Goes Ahead, White Man Runs Him, Curly, Half Yellow Face, White Swan, Hairy Moccasin. These pass above the low blowing dust and behind them like the clangor of the bugles made flesh, with jangling arms and squeaking leather, moves the rippling blue and yellow mass of the regiment.

Dry brown men who remember Washita, sunburned recruits whose saddle soreness is still an acute memory, faces that grin, faces that frown in the shadows of the slouch hats' brims—these, and the chargers' tossing heads that sweep past, four by four; these and the flickering guidons and the beat of carbines against the burdened saddles; these, and the mincing mules whose packs even now are slipping askew, all are to be part of their leader's fame. Past him and Terry and Gibbon they ride to become eternal satellites to the glory, heart-stirring as the shouting trumpets, of George Armstrong Custer. Terry takes the salutes of officers riding at the head of their troops and calls to each a kindly word of farewell.

The last fours swing past. The last rebellious mule is shepherded along. The trumpeters hush their clamor and fall in behind as the column moves

From: *Glory Hunter*: Copyright 1934. Used by special permission of Bobbs-Merrill Co.

461

up the ridge whose farther slope leads into the Rosebud Valley. Custer smiles at the compliments of Terry and Gibbon, clasps hands with them and wheels to follow the regiment whose boasted power is enough to abolish all Indians on the plains. Gibbon, in jest or out of his knowledge of the man, calls after him:

"Now, Custer! Don't be greedy! Wait for us!"

The buckskin clad horseman raises a hand in acknowledgment.

"No," he calls back cryptically, "I won't," and gallops off. Under the gray sky, the cold wind sings through the sage as Terry, Gibbon and the rest ride back to the *Far West*.

He was committed to the flood. George Armstrong Custer rode over the ridge his regiment had crossed and down to the rising tide of ordained calamity, which was to be the agent, but not the author, of his death.

The twelve troops, with their lagging mules, splashed through a ford near the mouth of the Rosebud, a clear, pebbly-bottomed, slightly alkaline stream, and marched up its far bank. Above, the clouds split and showed blue sky. Sunlight, blazing through, turned the dust of the march to gold. Men, who repacked the burdens that slipped from mules or prodded the lagging creatures onward, sweated while they swore.

For eight miles, the valley was broad. Thereafter, for the additional four they marched that day, bluffs shouldered in on either hand. They bivouacked in timber at the foot of a rocky height. Grass was plentiful and there were many fish in the stream. Men found, when camp had been made, that the strange mood which had oppressed their leader the day before, the gloom which the excitement of departure had banished, now had returned and again possessed him.

The valley was roofed by sunset when a trumpet stuttered officers' call. The regiment's sole major, its captains and lieutenants, assembled about their leader's camp-bed and those who in the past had been fired by, and those who had mocked at, Custer's flaring elation when a trail led toward battle, were depressed by his dismal air even before he spoke officially.

"It was not," Godfrey recalls, "a cheerful assemblage."

Nor was it the headlong, sublimely self-confident Custer of old who talked to his subordinates in a singularly placating tone. Custer spoke of his reliance on his officers—he who heretofore had felt the need of dependence on no one. The sad voice professed trust in their judgment, discretion and loyalty.

It recited instructions for the marches ahead—no further trumpet calls, "boots and saddles" at five A. M., each troop commander to be responsible for the welfare of his command in all things except the start and the camping place on each day's journey. These were to be ordered by Custer himself. The pack-mules attached to each troop hereafter were to be herded together in the column's rear under command of Lieutenant E. C. Mathey.

Thereafter, with a puzzling air of self-justification, Custer explained to his astounded officers, who never had been informed of reasons for his acts, why he had refused the offer of Brisbin's Squadron of the 2nd Cavalry. Godfrey's report of that confidence reveals his chief's blindness to logic.

Custer told the uneasy circle about him that he expected to meet not more than fifteen hundred Indians. He believed that the 7th Cavalry alone could defeat these. If they could not, there was no regiment in the service that could. Wherefore, the addition of a squadron under Brisbin— equal in strength to at least a third of Custer's present force—could not affect the issue. Furthermore, the inclusion of four troops of the 2nd would be certain to mar the harmony of the 7th and cause jealousy. It was for the same shaky reason that he had refused the offer of Low's Gatlings.

After this strange baring of a normally reticent spirit, the plaintive voice revealed a startling purpose. Godfrey reports it thus:

"Troop officers were cautioned to husband their rations and the strength of their mules and horses, as we might be out for a great deal longer time than that for which we were rationed, as he intended to follow the trail until we could get the Indians, even if it took us to the Indian agencies on the Missouri River or in Nebraska."

The council ended on the identical note of appeal that had launched it. Custer begged his officers to bring him either then or later, whatever suggestions they might have for expediting the march. Dazedly, the men rose and walked away. Lieutenant Wallace strode beside Godfrey and at length broke the silence.

"Godfrey," said Wallace, "I believe General Custer is going to be killed. I have never heard him talk in that way before."

Stars appeared in the crooked strip of sky above the valley. The voice of the river grew as sleep settled over the bivouac and darkness intensified the mental gloom of those still awake. Red men, as well as white, were subject to the oppressive dread. About their camp-fire, Bouyer, the half-breed Sioux, Half Yellow Face, the Crow, and Bloody Knife conversed in sign talk. As Godfrey passed, Bouyer checked him with apprehensive questions. The guide heard without conviction the soldier's boast that the 7th Cavalry could whip the Sioux.

"Well," he shrugged. "I can tell you we're going to have a God-damned big fight."

Stars swung above the sleeping regiment; above the *Far West*, tied for the night a few hours' run up-stream from the Rosebud's mouth; above the bivouac of Gibbon's column, en route for the Bighorn. Reveille did not sound in the 7th Cavalry's camp on the morning of June twenty-third. At three o'clock, the horse guards shook the troopers from their slumbers.

Sunlight slanted through smoke of spent camp-fires when the column moved at five A. M. Already a screen of scouts—Arikaras, Crows and whites—had gone forward under Varnum. Custer led the regiment out.

The reorganized pack-train was massed at the column's tail and Benteen's H Troop brought up the rear. Mules strayed and straggled and lost their packs.

Encroaching bluffs blocked the regiment's advance. In the first three miles, the column forded the Rosebud five times. Then, on the right, the valley widened. Five miles farther along the timber-dotted level bank Custer found the trail he sought.

There were many circles of packed earth where lodges had stood. Bent brush showed where wickiups—temporary shelters—had been fashioned. Grazing ponies had "clipped the grass, almost like a lawn mower" and beyond the litter of the camp, a broad trail ran up-stream churned by hoofs, raked by dragging lodge-poles.

Scouts gathered about Custer. He shook his head and turning to Lieutenant Varnum, said:

"Here's where Reno made the mistake of his life. He had six troops of cavalry and rations enough for a number of days. He'd have made a name for himself if he'd pushed on after them."

The hunt was up. The buckskin-clad horseman pushed forward and behind him the mounting metallic roar told of the cavalry's quickened pace. Five miles they hurried and then were forced to halt and wait for the pack-train to catch up. When the mules at last rejoined the column, it pushed on, forded the Rosebud, rode fifteen miles up the left bank, crossed the stream again and camped in the old wreckage of Indian travel on the right shore. On either side the stream, hills rolled back, lightly timbered, scored by deep ravines. There was scant grazing that night for horses that had done thirty-three miles.

Fires were extinguished after supper. Men slept soddenly beneath the sparkling sky. This arched above the Gibbon column, in bivouac on the Yellowstone's north bank opposite the Bighorn's mouth; above the *Far West,* tied up farther down-stream. The stern-wheeler came abreast of Gibbon's command on the morning of June twenty-fourth shortly after the 7th Cavalry had resumed its march.

At daybreak, Crow scouts had reported to Custer that the trail ahead was broader and fresher. In the face of these tidings he could not bear to match his pace to the deliberation of the mule-hampered column. He took two troops and rode far in advance. Almost every loop of the river now was stamped with the circles of vanished lodges. Broken branches and pony droppings and the ashes of fires told him how swiftly he was over-hauling the quarry.

Custer and his escort passed the lashed sapling framework of a dance lodge and a brown withered object swung therefrom in the wind. Crows identified it as a white man's scalp, probably of a 2nd Cavalry trooper killed in a brush with the Sioux during Gibbon's march down the Yellowstone. Crows also reported that over the ridge to the right lay the head-waters of Tullock's Creek and that they had seen what looked like smoke signals down its valley.

At noon, Custer halted and when his regiment rejoined him, ordered coffee made. Varnum and the scouts had ridden on ahead. While the column rested on the Rosebud's right bank, Custer summoned his officers. They gathered where his headquarters flag, staff thrust in the earth, whipped in the steady blast of a south wind, and again at this conference something was wrong. It may have been the nervousness of their leader; it may have been prescience of impending disaster. Whatever its source, many of the officers were in the jumpy state of mind that is receptive to ill omen.

They heard their commander's tidings. The trail was freshening hourly. Custer believed the smoke reported from the Tullock's Valley to be only mist. When scouts in the advance sent back word, the regiment would move on, but with increased caution. Each troop would take a separate course so as to diminish the dust of the march.

The officers were dismissed. As Godfrey started to leave, the wind blew over Custer's headquarters flag. It fell toward the rear. Godfrey recovered and replanted it. It fell toward the rear. He picked it up and dug its staff into the earth, supporting it against a sage-brush. It stood now but some of those who had marked its double fall saw an augury of defeat.

At four, scouts returned and reported to Custer. He led his regiment forward and again they forded the Rosebud. The stream's left bank was ridged by the passage of unnumbered lodge poles. Hourly, the wide trail of the Sioux grew heavier and fresher. The regiment camped at seven-forty-five below a bluff. It had marched twenty-six miles. Fires were small and soon extinguished. Horses were not unsaddled. Mules retained their packs. The whisper ran through the bivouac that scouts still were following the trail, which had left the river's edge and now inclined westward. If it crossed the divide into the valley of the Little Bighorn, so rumor muttered, the regiment would march that night. Meanwhile, weary men rolled up in their blankets and caught what sleep they could. At the mouth of Tullock's Creek, forty-five miles distant in a beeline, Terry camped with the men of Gibbon's column.

Gibbon himself lay on the *Far West* while the boat worked her way up the Bighorn. He had been stricken with intestinal colic and did not rejoin his command until June twenty-sixth.

A company of infantry and a Gatling had been left on the Yellowstone's north bank to guard the command's surplus stores. The rest of the infantry, Brisbin's Squadron of the 2nd Cavalry and two Gatlings had been ferried across the stream and had marched up the Bighorn to the Tullock's mouth.

Earlier in the day, twelve of the bravest of Gibbon's Crows had been sent to scout up Tullock's Creek. They had gone ten miles, seen a wounded buffalo and had stampeded back. They were afraid of the Sioux.

In Custer's camp men slept and horses and mules had grazed. Beyond the wide scar of the Indian trail, grass was abundant, for the Sioux had not tarried here. At nine that night the scouts returned. Reno's earlier report had been correct. The trail ran over the divide into the valley of the Little Bighorn.

Circumstance deals Custer one more thrust. It had small subsequent part in the development of the tragedy. His own hands, his own headstrong, headlong spirit contrived it. Yet fate intervenes here, as accessory.

The trail he has followed has been made, so his scouts have told him, by four hundred lodges. There have been wickiups too. In all, perhaps fifteen hundred warriors have crossed the Wolf Mountains into the Little Bighorn Valley. This is the estimate Custer has given his officers. It is probably accurate. But these fifteen hundred warriors are only a fraction of the host assembled on the Little Bighorn. A portion, and only a portion, of the greatest mobilization of Indian might this continent ever saw had met Crook on the upper reaches of the Rosebud June seventeenth and had beaten him back. The Indians whom Custer followed had taken no part in that fight. They were additional reenforcements to the hostiles, but the man who followed them had no knowledge of this.

Circumstance or the luck whose darling Custer had been, turns against him now as his scouts report and he sends his orderlies to wake and summon his officers. He does not know that Crook has been defeated. He is rashly certain that the Sioux he follows are all his regiment will have to face. This is fate's part in his destruction.

Officers, roused by the questing orderlies, stumbled through windrows of slumbering men and toward the bright speck in the gloom that was a candle on Custer's table. The conference was brief.

Custer told his blinking and disheveled subordinates the course of the trail and his intention of getting as close to the top of the divide as possible before daybreak, there to hide and attack on the twenty-sixth. He ordered them to be ready to march at eleven-thirty. Varnum with Reynolds, Bouyer, the Crows and some Arikaras had been sent to a peak overlooking the farther valley. Lieutenant Hare of Troop K was detailed to command the remaining scouts.

The officers returned to their troops. Gradually, as the hour for the march approached, the valley filled with clamor. Soldiers, freshly wakened, found their mounts and sought their places in the column by a universal and noisy game of blind man's buff. Mules brayed and horses whinnied. Officers bawled for strayed members of their troops and these shouted back. The clatter of arms and equipment, the tumult of voices filled the black valley with confused and doleful sound.

They were to march at eleven-thirty. They did not get under way till after midnight. The reassembling of the regiment took time. There was renewed difficulty with the mules and it was an interminable job for Mathey and Keogh, who had the rear-guard, to collect the beasts and start them forward. At last Custer, with Fred Girard, interpreter, and Half Yellow Face, the Crow, moved out at the head of his command.

Girard was of the many who warned his chief of the Indian might. While they waited for the column to get under way, Custer asked the interpreter how many hostiles they were likely to meet. Girard told him at least twenty-five hundred but the estimate was offered to a man apparently deaf.

Once the regiment marched, the clamor and the confusion multiplied. The column's actual course is not certain, but the best evidence indicates that it strove to follow the valley of Davis Creek, a tributary of the Rosebud, up to the divide. The sky was clouded and darkness was curdled further by the mounting dust. No man could see the rider ahead of him. The blind column proceeded chiefly by scent and hearing. Men who no longer breathed dust knew that they had strayed from the line of march. Some troopers beat their tin cups against their saddles to aid those who followed. There was shouting and much heartfelt swearing and now and then an explosive rattle and thumping as a horse fell. Any Indian in a range of several miles and not stone deaf must have heard that uproarious advance.

At length, even Custer perceived the vanity of further tumultuous groping. Scouts assured him he could not possibly reach the ridge before daybreak and word was passed back, halting the disrupted column which had marched ten miles. Dawn found its scattered elements in the valley of the dwindling stream. Its water was so bitter with alkali that horses and mules would not drink it. Coffee made therefrom scored men's throats.

Dawn also found Varnum and his men asleep at the foot of a rocky pinnacle on the ridge's crest that red men called the Crow's Nest. As the dim mass took form against the paling sky, Hairy Moccasin, the smallest and most alert of the Crows, left his slumbering companions and climbed to its top. Varnum was wakened by his voice and saw the Indian stamped against gray heaven.

The Lieutenant and the others swarmed up the peak. On either hand, earth fell away in fir-dappled slopes of gray rock. Far down the eastern slant, the smoke of the 7th Cavalry's fires crept up across a watery daybreak and the Crows snarled. Did Custer think, they asked, that the Sioux were blind?

To the west, the land went down in broken steps to a wide valley where night still dwelt. They watched one another's faces grow sharper in the quickening light. They saw the timber-shielded Little Bighorn snaking its way across the plain. Then, one by one, the Indians exclaimed and stared to the north.

The morning mist seemed thicker and darker there and beneath it was the sense rather than the sight of movement, a confused wide-spread stirring. The Crows jabbered in awed voices and Reynolds said mildly: "That's the biggest pony herd any man ever saw."

"Biggest village," Bouyer amended. "A heap too big."

Light grew stronger. The sun was coming up behind gray clouds. Varnum's strained eyes were bleared by seventy hours' scouting with scant sleep.

"Look for worms," Bouyer advised him, for the movement of the vast and distant pony herd was like the pulsating and twitching of tangled angleworms. Still Varnum saw nothing, but the excitement of those about him left no room for doubt. He scribbled a hasty note to Custer and sent it down-hill by an Arikara.

The regiment, when the messenger reached it shortly before eight A. M., still rested in the valley where it had made its fires. Custer, on receiving

Varnum's note, leaped bareback on his horse and rode through his command shouting to his officers to be ready to march by eight o'clock. When he returned to the column's head, Bloody Knife approached him, face glowering with earnestness.

There were too many Sioux yonder, Custer's favorite scout told his chief. It would take days to kill them all. The Glory-Hunter laughed. The imminence of an enemy had restored his pre-battle elation.

"Oh," he retorted tolerantly, "I guess we'll get through them in one day," and swinging into the saddle, gave the order for the advance.

For two hours and a half, the regiment crawled up the hostile slope, gray rock below, gray sky above. Clouds still hid the sun's brilliance but not its heat. The air grew sultry so that the upward scrambling men and horses sweltered under an ash white sky. The regiment marched ten miles and then, a mile or so from the ridge's summit, hid in a ravine at Custer's order while he himself rode ahead to the Crow's Nest.

Varnum and his scouts still kept vigil there. Custer listened skeptically to their report of a colossal village to northward and with scarcely more credulity to the tale of Sioux who had been seen, scouting along ridges above the cavalry's advance. He stared into distance that swam in plum-colored haze and shook his head; clapped field-glasses to his eyes and looked long again. Despite the insistence of the Indians, despite the efforts of Reynolds and Bouyer to help him see, Custer rasped at last:

"I've been on the plains a good many years. My eyesight is as good as yours. I can't see anything that looks like Indian ponies."

Bouyer blurted: "If you don't find more Indians in that valley than you ever saw before, you can hang me."

"All right, all right, all right," Custer rattled with a short laugh. "It would do a damned lot of good to hang you, wouldn't it?"

In the distance hung the blue haze of lodge smoke. Dim beneath its veil crawled the enormous pony herd. Custer left the lookout, still insisting that he saw no sign of Indians; that he believed none were there. The waiting regiment had gained meanwhile more definite evidence of the presence of the Sioux.

Sergeant Curtis of Troop F had lost clothing from his saddle roll on the march up-hill. While the regiment sweated in the ravine, waiting its chief's return, Curtis obtained permission from Captain Yates to ride back in search of the missing raiment. Presently, he came galloping to report to Yates that he had found, not what he sought, but a breadbox, dropped from one of the mules. About the box had been Indians, Sioux, who had fled at his approach.

Yates told Keogh who informed Cook, the adjutant, who, when Custer returned to the hiding regiment, informed his chief.

That morning of June twenty-fifth, Terry lingered on Tullock's Creek, expecting Custer's courier. He marched three and a third miles up the valley in hope of meeting him and sent Lieutenant Bradley and fifteen mounted infantry still farther. The Crows would not go. They feared the Sioux.

From the concealing ravine on the eastern slope of the Wolf Mountains, where weary men drowsed and thirsty horses stood with drooping heads, a trumpet spoke. That brazen voice, silent for sixty hours past, tore through the sultry air, bounced echoing from the gray cliffs. It shouted officers' call, and those who had not already gathered about Custer scrambled up the ravine's side and joined him.

It was then about eleven-thirty on the morning of June twenty-fifth.

Men who had marched all the day before and most of the night were too weary for many questions; too spent perhaps to see the paradox in their leader's orders. Despite the insistence and the warnings of his scouts, Custer did not believe there were Indians in the Valley of the Little Bighorn. Since scouts and Sergeant Curtis had seen the Sioux, it would be useless to hide here any longer. The regiment would move at once toward a foe in whose existence its commander disbelieved. Each troop would march as it made ready. Benteen's men were the first to lurch up out of the ravine.

The others followed. Behind them, Mathey with seven soldiers from each troop and five or six civilian packers herded along the one hundred and sixty mules of the train. McDougall's B Troop, forty-five strong, brought up the rear.

The cloudy sky burned white before the vertical sun. Heat soaked into dusty men and sweating horses as the reformed column toiled up to the divide and went over its ridge. Five hundred and ninety-odd soldiers, plus scouts, interpreters and packers, rode down beneath a pillar of dust to the Little Bighorn.

They caught, as they crossed the summit, glimpses of an olive green valley, fifteen miles away. They marked where, to the north, heat haze was tinged with blue and wondered dully at Custer's skepticism. That surely was smoke. It was now seven minutes past twelve P. M. and the trail they followed went down-hill.

There was ground for further wonder immediately thereafter. Custer spoke to Benteen whose troop was foremost in the column. The white-haired Captain turned in his saddle, bawled an order and swung left oblique out of the line of march, moving toward a line of bluffs four miles away with Troops H, D and K—his own, Weir's and Godfrey's.

Reno, still without command, unconsulted by Custer and aggrieved, flung a question at Benteen as he passed.

"Going to those hills to drive everything before me," the Captain replied dryly and led his squadron onward. The Major had scant time to brood over this new evidence of neglect, for Cook, Custer's adjutant, rode up to him and announced:

The General directs that you take specific command of Companies M, A and G."

"Is that all?" Reno asked as the Adjutant turned and Cook flung assent over his shoulder.

The Chief Trumpeter galloped away on the course Benteen had taken and, overhauling him, delivered additional directions from Custer. If no

Indians were found on the first line of bluffs, the Captain should proceed to another farther line.

The column, meanwhile, scraped and slithered down the irregular folds of the mountainside. It followed still the Indian trail that bordered the course of a little stream, called Sundance then and later renamed Reno Creek. The Major had assumed command of Moylan's, McIntosh's and French's troops. He led them along the left bank of the watercourse. Custer, with his brother's Troop C, Smith's E, Yate's F, Keogh's I and Calhoun's L, went down along the right bank. Apprehensive Arikaras and Crows under Varnum and Hare moved before the twin columns. With Custer rode his brother Boston, his young nephew and namesake, Armstrong Reed, and Mark Kellogg, the correspondent.

Benteen was out of sight now, but Custer turned and spoke to Sergeant-Major W. W. Sharrow who trotted off, to bear to the senior Captain further elaboration of the original orders. If neither line of bluffs yielded Indians, Benteen was to move into the valley beyond and if this proved barren into the valley beyond that.

Meanwhile, in columns of twos, Custer's five troops and Reno's three rode toward the Little Bighorn. The sunless heat weighed down the men. Dust plastered the flanks and barrels of reeking horses. Ridges on either hand had closed in upon the command so that, as they descended, they caught no further sight of the valley. Stunted firs were aromatic in lifeless air that shook to the dull sound of hoofs, the quarreling voices of leather and steel, the mumbling speech of tired soldiers. Already the pack-train with all supplies and reserve ammunition had lagged behind.

So they rode for eight or ten miles, dazed by fatigue, wilted by heat—Reno's one hundred and twelve, Custer's two hundred and twenty-five men—while the stream that parted them deepened and grew vocal and the sharp pitches of the ridges flattened. Rocks and dwarfed firs crept past and vanished. Bare rolling foot-hills succeeded them, curved earthen surges, olive with the browning grass of spring. Through these the stream twisted and the trail still followed it.

When they had marched ten or twelve miles, the Indian trail ran wholly along the creek's right bank. Custer signaled with his white hat for Reno to cross. The Major obeyed. His three troops followed. The two commands moved down the stream's right side, parallel and fifty yards apart. Lieutenant Wallace, who kept the column's itinerary, looked at his watch. It was two P. M.

They had seen no Indians. The nervous scouts who preceded the column on a trail now alarmingly fresh had caught no glimpse of the Sioux. Then, in the valley before them, they saw the brown lonely cone of a single lodge. Its smoke vent was empty. No dogs, no children moved about its latched door-flaps.

Arikaras approached it with increasing boldness, at last tore open its entrance. A dead warrior lay with his gear beside him, a brother of Circling Bear, Sioux chief. He had died in the fight with Crook eight days before. As a spiteful blow against their enemies, the Arikaras set fire to the lodge.

The columns had halted. Girard, scout and interpreter, rode to a knoll. The lodge burned reluctantly with pallid flames and a towering smoke. Girard from his lookout yelled to Custer.

"Thar go yore Injuns, runnin' like devils."

Custer joined him and saw beyond the knoll some forty Sioux warriors cantering their ponies toward the river and yelping derision. He shouted for the Arikaras to follow them. They glowered and refused, nor could his scornful suggestion that they turn in their weapons and go home shake them free from terror.

There were at least some Indians in this valley despite the scoffing of Custer. He had seen them. His eager voice stiffened aching spines and tightened faces that had sagged with weariness. The twin column lunged forward at a trot, at a gallop. Side by side they roared down the valley, and Cook, veering from Custer's side, ranged his horse alongside Reno's. Orders jolted from him:

"The Indians," Cook shouted, long black whiskers streaming, "are about two and a half miles ahead and on the jump. Follow them as fast as you can and charge them and we will support you."

Reno galloped on with the Adjutant and Keogh who had followed on his charger, Comanche. Custer slackened pace so that the distance between the Major's column and his increased. It was then two-fifteen P. M.

The Indian trail the 7th had followed for days crossed to the left bank of the creek. Reno's three troops pursued it. A hill thrust in between them and Custer's command, blocking further views of the laggards. Ahead were trees and the glitter of moving water. Above foliage, a great dust-cloud rose in the northwest.

Cook and Keogh accompanied Reno's command to the river. Girard rode to another knoll that gave him clear view down-stream. There was delay at the ford. The horses waded into the Little Bighorn's flow and thrust parched muzzles deep. They would not cross until they had drunk. The Arikara scouts were unwilling to cross at all. They listened sullenly to Varnum's exhortations and some of them vanished.

Gradually Reno got his command to the farther bank. Cook and Keogh shouted, "Good luck," and turned to rejoin Custer. Girard rode down from the knoll. He had seen the source of the great dust. Beneath it were Indians, many Indians, rushing up-stream along the river's left bank. The scout hailed Cook and told of his discovery.

Cook replied: "All right. I'll go and report."

The Adjutant rode back to Custer. On the stream's far bank, Reno was forming. Varnum, half frantic, shouted to Girard that the Arikaras refused to go farther. In their own tongue, Girard lashed them and a dozen crossed the river with him, Varnum and Hare, Reynolds, Dorman, the negro, and other scouts.

Bellowing officers subdued confusion on the Little Bighorn's left bank.

Troopers guided their dripping mounts into place. The command solidified. Reno took his place at its head and gathered in his charger's rein. Nervous horses reared. The Major called:

"Take your time. There are enough ahead for all of us."

Before him rolled a plain, bordered on the left by shelving higher ground, on the right by timber-shielded loops of the river. Farther to the right, across the stream, were brown cliffs, ravine scored, and above their broken perpendiculars, treeless hills went back toward the gray, fir stippled ridges of the Wolf Mountains.

Ahead of the Major for two miles, the plain ran drab, undulant and empty. Then a peninsula of timber, thrust out to the left from the river bank, cut off more distant view and above the leafy barrier, the dust-cloud towered. Reno looked at the ranked column behind him. Beyond it, the ford was empty. No brilliant figure in buckskin led five troops into support. The Major turned to Trooper McIlargy, his striker, and bade him ride to Custer with news that the Indians were coming in force. Then, rising in his stirrups, he shouted his orders:

"Left into line. Guide center. Gallop."

The column woke. Fours shifted and wove. The line spread out across the valley and moved forward. Presently when through dust behind him, the Major still could see no sign of support, he sent Trooper Mitchell, a cook, back with further, more urgent message to Custer.

Neither McIlargy nor Mitchell ever was seen again. They were killed in passage or else they died on the heights with Custer.

The Glory-Hunter had not followed Reno to the ford. He had led his men at a trot on the Major's trail. Then, for reasons no man may ever know, Custer had swung sharply to the right and had ridden up into the brown hills to the north. The men of Keogh and Smith, Yates, Calhoun and Tom Custer had followed him down-stream above the bluffs that walled the Little Bighorn's right bank; down-stream behind the flutter of the familiar blue and red pennant; down-stream, away from Reno and into a nation's Valhalla.

Across the river in the valley below, Girard thought he glimpsed Yate's gray horse troop, riding hard along the ridges, and Lieutenant De Rudio insisted that later Custer had appeared on a height above the plain and had waved his hat.

Meanwhile, Reno went down the valley before his line and looked often over his shoulder for the promised support. Behind him galloped Moylan's Troop A and French's M, strung out across the plain with Varnum's scouts and reluctant Indians on the left against the higher ground. In the rear McIntosh's Troop G rode in reserve.

The squadron swung around the peninsula of timber that obscured the lower valley. Before them, as though earth were ablaze, the dust-cloud smoked to heaven. Above the roar of the advance, men could hear from that bilious murk high voices—Sioux voices—screeching like souls in torment, and where the dust thinned, momentarily, horsemen moved and feathers were slivers of light in the haze.

Out of that prototype of later smoke-screens, Indians darted, screaming, to fire and vanish. Up from before the charging line, sprang a Cadmean crop of warriors. Ahead of the troopers, a ravine split the plain. It was full of Sioux. And the valley behind Reno was empty of support.

Facing the half-hidden host before him, one hundred and twelve troopers seemed dauntingly few to Reno. He had not even the dubious aid of his Indian allies now. At the first whoop of the Sioux, all these save Bloody Knife and one or two more had vanished, leaving Varnum and Hare to hold the left flank with a handful of scouts. G. Troop was thrown into line to fill that gap.

Reno marked the ravine ahead. Military training, or more human caution, told him the Sioux who advanced only to retreat were not afraid. They were luring him into ambuscade. He flung up his hand and dragged on his charger's rein.

"Halt," Reno shouted before his charge had struck a single enemy, or his troopers had fired a shot. "Halt! Prepare to fight on foot."

There was a moment of plunging confusion. At least one unhappy recruit was carried on by his bolting mount into the shrill obscurity ahead, to return no more. The horse-holders, veterans all, each galloped four steeds back into the shelter of the timber. The thin line of footmen wavered and shrank from the crackle of bullets overhead, the sibilant flight of arrows. Then it steadied and began earnestly to bang away at yelping horsemen who swooped and wheeled like swallows in the yellow gloom.

The line plodded forward a hundred yards. A breath of air lifted the dust-screen an instant and men saw a host of horsemen and beyond them unnumbered lodges. The line advanced no farther. It knelt or lay and shot as rapidly as it might into the cloud ahead that hid no man knew what enormity. Sergeant Hynes of Troop A was dead. One or two more had been hit. The Sioux wheeled and came closer, blazing away at the troopers who replied quickly and blindly. The accuracy of both reds and whites was deplorable. The rapid fire heated the troopers' Springfields and cartridges jammed in the breeches. Men had to cut out the empty shells before they could shoot again.

Word came from the timber that Sioux were massing on the stream's far bank, that Sioux were crossing to get at the horses. Reno withdrew G Troop from the firing line and sent it back to protect the animals. Still, there was no sign of Custer and through the Major's mind may have crept the recollection of the scandalous regimental legend concerning another Major of the 7th Cavalry, Elliot by name.

Others were conscious of Custer's betrayal of his promise. Wallace, who had heard Cook's orders to Reno and who had remained on the firing line when McIntosh, his commander, had withdrawn his troop to the timber, bawled to Captain Moylan that some one ought to be sent to hurry up support. Both officers pled with Billy Jackson, a half-breed scout. He shook his head and waved to the rear.

"No one," he shouted, "could get through that."

There were Sioux behind as well as before the line now and more were sweeping around the weak left flank or pouring down from the heights on the left. The troopers were being surrounded on the open plain. There still was equivocal safety in the timber. The line went back to the shelter of brush and the few large trees.

Here was confusion. Officers lost their commands in the thickets. Horses plunged. Sioux bullets slashed through foliage or smacked against solid wood. Mounted Indians swarmed about the timbered peninsula, firing and screaming in high fierce voices. Others on foot worked up from the river and set the wood on fire.

Reno's ammunition was growing low, thanks to recruits who fired more for the comfort of the sound than for marksmanship. The Sioux were filtering through a line too thin to defend the entire grove. The defense bent backward from the river side of the wood. The Indians crawled forward. Dust billowed in from the plain, where screeching Sioux circled. The tangle of brush and cottonwoods filled with a brawling, fearful sound— panicky banging of guns, white shouting and savage screeching, screams of horses and the harsh rip of bullets through foliage. One hundred-odd men were surrounded by thrice their number and more Indians continually were arriving from the village. It was now about three-thirty P. M. Where was the promised support? Where was Custer?

History can not see him. Glory, for whom he rode northward through the hills, is mute. Even the route over which he led two hundred and twenty-five men to death is in dispute. All men ever will know surely of that last red hour is contained in the brief recitals of two who saw only its dawn—Daniel A. Kanipe, of Carolina, sergeant in Tom Custers Troop C, and Trumpeter John Martin, born Giovanni Martini and a Garibaldi veteran, who had been detailed from Benteen's Troop H, to serve as orderly to the Regiment's commander.

When Custer turned toward the hills, two ways were open to him. Beyond the first ridge that crowned the bluffs above the Little Bighorn, a shallow valley runs northward. Beyond a second ridge to the east of this valley, is another ravine, and many hold it was along this that the five troops rode. Since men with Reno believed they saw Custer and portions of his command on the heights and since, furthermore, he twice rode to a promontory to survey the valley below, it is probable that he led his men along the westerly ravine. They rode at a gallop. The pace was so hard that some of the weary horses gave out. The riders of two of these later joined Reno.

Somewhere, early in that rush northward, the troopers caught a glimpse of the dust-enveloped Little Bighorn. Kanipe says they cheered at the sight and Custer cried: "Hold your horses, boys. There's plenty down there for all of us."

The rounded hills cut off their view. They galloped farther. In a breathing space, Tom Custer called Kanipe, who, long after, remembered his
instructions thus:

"Go to Captain McDougall. Tell him to bring the pack train straight
across country. If any packs come loose, cut them and come on quick. A
big Indian village. If you see Captain Benteen, tell him to come quick.
A big Indian village."

Kanipe swung his horse out of line and spurred it back. The column
launched into a gallop again. At its head, the Glory-Hunter rode. Behind
his bright sorrel, Vic, pounded the horse of his orderly, Trumpeter Martin.
Here is the testimony of the last white survivor to see George Armstrong
Custer alive:

"There was a big bend on the hill; he turned these hills and went on top
of the ridge. All at once, we looked on the bottom and saw the Indian
village. At the same time we could only see children and dogs and ponies—
no Indians at all. General Custer appeared to be glad and supposed the
Indians were asleep in their tepees. We could not see the timber because
it was under the hill—nor anything of Reno's column. I rode about two
yards from General Custer.

"After he saw the village he pulled off his hat and gave a cheer and said:
'Courage, boys, we will get them and as soon as we get them, then we will
go back to our station.'

"We went more to the right from the ridge and down to a ravine that
led to the river. At the time General Custer passed the high place on the
ridge, or a little below it, he told his adjutant to send an order back to
Captain Benteen. I don't know what it was. Then the Adjutant called
me—I was right at the rear of the General—and said, 'Orderly, I want
you to take this dispatch to Captain Benteen and go as fast as you can.' "

Martin, the second messenger, rides back along the trail Kanipe already
has taken. Behind him Custer and the five troops vanish, with pounding
hoofs and the roar of equipment, in a dust-cloud that is the forerunner of
eternal glory.

From the ridge Custer has looked down upon a myriad brown cones of
lodges, stippling for more than three miles the Little Bighorn's western
bank. He has seen the earlier warnings of his scouts made manifest. He
who had scoffed at these discovers they had been underestimates. This is
the village whose existence he has doubted and it is incredibly vast.

A year later, General Hugh L. Scott, then a lieutenant in the 7th
Cavalry, came to the Little Bighorn Valley on the expedition sent to rebury
the dead. Scott counted along the stream the sites of eighteen hundred
lodges and never completed his tally. There were many wickiups as well.
Men have estimated the strength of the host that broke the 7th Cavalry
at all the way from twelve hundred and fifty to eight thousand warriors.
Scott's count proves that there must have been at least four thousand and
against them Custer rode with a total force of less than six hundred
troopers.

At first sight of that village, he should have read omen in its sinister quiet. He knew Indians too well to believe that at midday they were sleeping, as Martin reports. The trumpeter's English was faulty. Custer probably said that he had "caught the enemy napping." Elation rather than alarm seems to have possessed him, yet he sent at once to recall Benteen and the note Cook scribbled and Martin bore has the disjointed haste of panic. It read:

"Benteen, come on—big village—be quick—bring packs.

W. W. Cook.

"P. S. Bring pacs."

With that frantic message, the history of George Armstrong Custer ends. In the blank that intervenes before men found his stripped body, unnumbered theories flourish.

In the river bottom, Reno with three troops strives to hold back a rising red tide.

Miles away to the southeast, Benteen with three troops is growing weary of a "wild-goose chase" that reveals only more and more broken land and no Indians.

Miles up the trail from the divide, Mathey and eighty men struggle with the lagging pack-train.

Behind this, McDougall and his troop fume.

Martin sees the dust smoke up as Custer leads his two hundred and twenty-five down toward the Valley of the Little Bighorn. The rest of his last pursuit of Glory is hidden from men.

One more adherent rides hard to join George Armstrong Custer in death. A mile or so back along the trail, Martin, his last messenger, encounters Boston Custer. Earlier in the day the young man's horse had failed him and he had returned to the pack-train for another. He flings a question at Martin who grins and points the way. Boston spurs his mount along the endless road his brothers and nephew, Reed, and brother-in-law, Calhoun, already have taken.

Benteen had grown tired of "valley hunting." His choleric mouth grew ever tighter about the stem of his pipe. Lieutenant Gibson of his troop and six skirmishers preceded his column. Part of the time, the Captain rode ahead even of them. There had been no Indians beyond the first line of bluffs, or the second, and continually the country grew rougher, pushing him out of his original line of march toward the down-hill trail Reno and Custer had followed.

Benteen at last gave up the hunt, technically disobeying his commander's orders, and definitely turned back to rejoin Custer. The column came out of the badlands where Sundance Creek spread a marshy pool beside the trail Custer and Reno had traveled about two hours earlier. It halted there to water suffering horses. These had marched some thirty miles in fifteen hours without a drink. It was now three-thirty p. m.

As Benteen's command moved off from the pool, the first mules of the pack-train came charging down-hill, attendant troopers cursing horribly, and plunged into the water. Benteen moved on, passing the smoldering tepee that Custer's scouts had fired. Kanipe came riding. He grinned as the troopers cheered, shouted that the Indians were "on the run" and after reporting to Benteen, went on to the pack-train.

Two miles from the ford where Reno crossed, Trumpeter Martin approached, spurring a weary horse. Indians had fired on him and a bullet had wounded his mount. He had not known this till Benteen pointed it out. The Captain read Cook's message. Martin smiled confidently in response to his questions:

"Eenjuns," he reported, "eesa skedaddling."

Benteen scribbled a note to McDougall and sent Martin on up the trail, showed Cook's message to Captain Weir whose troop was in advance, and then went down toward the river at a smart trot. The valley was filled with smoke and dust and the squadron heard the far popping of gun-fire. An Indian came up from the ford, driving captured ponies ahead of him. It was Half Yellow Face, the Crow, who, when Benteen bawled a question about the soldiers, pointed toward a bluff on the column's right.

Meanwhile dust and smoke had darkened the grove where Reno's three troops were besieged. The banging of Springfields had a panicky sound. There was the lilt of imminent triumph in the Indians' yells. No responsive, reassuring cheer echoed the shouts of beleaguered officers and men. No trumpet split the tumult to signal approach of Custer's promised support. No trumpet proclaimed to the scattered troops Reno's determination to leave the timber. The Major gave the order which some heard and some did not.

Those who obeyed led their horses into a clear space in the grove's center and mounted there. As the column was forming Sioux fired pointblank from a thicket. A trooper of M screamed, "O God, I've got it!" and pitched from his horse. Bloody Knife, the valiant Arikara, was at Reno's side. The Major heard the thwack of the bullet that split his skull. Reno launched his "charge" from the timber.

He left his dead and wounded. A dozen troopers and Lieutenant De Rudio of Troop A, Herendeen, Reynolds and other scouts were deserted in the grove. At the head of Troop A in column of fours, with part of G following and M in the rear, Reno rode out and made for the ford by which he had crossed.

The plain swarmed with Indians, "thick as trees in an orchard," who gave way, wolf fashion, before the column's head, and, wolflike, ranged along its right flank to pull down the weak and laggard. Painted bodies burned dimly in the dust. The haze shook with shrill yelling and the uneven roar of gun-fire. Sioux laid their rifles across their ponies' withers and pumped lead into the fleeing column. Sioux watched until men had emptied their revolvers, then closing in, shot or stabbed them. Lieutenant Donald McIntosh of Troop G, the half-breed Indian, was killed close to the timber.

Lonesome Charley Reynolds died therein and those who later found his headless body counted sixty empty cartridges about it. Isaiah Dorman, the negro interpreter, was slain there too.

More and more Sioux ranged along the column's right flank as though the desperate troopers were buffalo. The catlike ponies leaped in toward soldiers whose guns were empty, the screaming riders slipped from sight behind their mounts when cavalrymen aimed at them.

Varnum, aghast at the mounting panic of the retreat, ran his horse to the head of Troop A, shouting:

"For God's sake, boys, don't run. Don't let them whip us."

A voice replied sharply: "I am in command here, sir!"

It was Reno's. He rode in the forefront of the retreat.

The head of the column kept fair order, but the rear frayed and was increasingly lashed by terror. The pressure of the Sioux forced the command away from the ford by which it had entered the valley. The war yell soared higher, Indian guns blazed as Troop A swung to the left and led by the Major, who had lost his hat, went over a five-foot bank into the belly-deep water of the Little Bighorn.

The stream at this point was some twenty-five feet wide, and running full. The farther bank was eight feet high with a fissure therein whereby active horsemen might scramble up. Above, the bluff rose steeply, with narrow ravines scoring its high brown wall. There were Indians on the heights firing down at the troopers. There were ever more Indians on the west bank, shooting into their backs.

No effort was made to guard the ford, or to control the order in which terrified troopers plunged their mounts into the river. The breadth of water became a stew of thrashing horses, screaming men, foam and the small brief fountains struck by bullets. The fugitives could ascend the far bank only one by one. The stream was jammed with fear-roweled cavalry fighting for that single passage, while from the rear the Sioux poured in their fire. Many died here.

Doctor De Wolf, assistant surgeon, reached the far bank and there was killed. Lieutenant Benny Hodgson, Reno's adjutant and a favorite in the regiment, was wounded as he reached the west shore. He caught the stirrup of a trooper and was towed across, only to be shot through the head as he reached the east bank.

Spurring and lashing their horses, the survivors rode them up the ravine with ungainly rabbit-like jumps. On the plateau above, the breathless, hatless Major strove to reorganize the remaining half of his command. Men saw Benteen's three troops come riding toward them through the hills. It was now about four-thirty.

Reno, a handkerchief bound about his head, was firing his revolver at Indians far out of range when Benteen's column joined the remnants of his own. Varnum, wild with grief at the death of his friend Hodgson, was blazing away, equally vainly, with a carbine.

If the Sioux had followed, they might have rolled up over the Major and Benteen as well, but the gun-fire from the valley slackened and died, save for occasional snipers' shots. The horsemen began a quick movement down the valley.

Benteen, the grimly efficient, shared his troops' cartridges with Reno's survivors and organized the defense. A semicircle of higher peaks blocked view of the village and whatever down-stream event summoned the victorious Sioux. On the hill, nerve-shattered men cursed the name of Custer. Lieutenant Hare on Godfrey's horse rode back to the pack-train to hurry it in and to bring back with him ammunition mules.

Down-stream, to the north, men heard the brawl of guns. Not all those on the hill heard volleys, though to De Rudio and others, still trapped in the timber and saved later by the withdrawal of the Indians, the concerted blasts were plain. The firing rolled away to the north, and Captain Weir of Troop D muttered to his lieutenant, Edgerly, that Reno ought to move to the support of Custer.

Edgerly assented and Weir asked whether, if Reno permitted, the Lieutenant would follow his Captain toward Custer with Troop D. Edgerly agreed and when Weir, without authorization, rode out alone over the hills toward the north, Edgerly, presuming permission had been granted, led Troop D after its commander.

They reached a height from which they could look down the valley and saw the lodges standing along the stream and the unbelievably wide and slowly shifting carpet of the pony herd. On a hill three miles away, Indians swarmed like disturbed ants. There was no sign of Custer. It was now close to five P. M.

Hare had brought in two ammunition mules, with a trooper guiding each by the bridle and another behind, lashing the stubborn brute along. McDougall's troop, Mathey and the rest of the train, arrived about five o'clock. So few Indians remained that Herendeen and eleven troopers abandoned in the timber were able to rejoin the command.

The reorganized column moved out in the direction Weir had taken, slowly and with difficulty for there were wounded and each of these had to be borne in a horse blanket by four men. At about six P. M. when the command reached the promontory where D Troop lingered, the Indians had completed the mission that had called them down-stream and were returning.

The column fell back toward its original position with French's A and Weir's D covering the retreat. The impatient Weir here learned the power of the Sioux. These came on so fast and in such numbers that the covering force turned into fugitives. Troops A and D went back like hunted rabbits. Godfrey's Troop K, dismounted, checked the pursuit and then retired. What remained of the 7th Cavalry stood at bay.

Benteen took charge of the defense, routing out skulkers, thrusting the troopers into line, barking orders with magnificent self-possession.

"Wallace," he shouted. "Form your troop here."

"Troop?" Wallace panted, grinning shakily, "I've got just three men."

"Very good. Form your three men here."

From higher ridges and peaks, that ringed the plateau where the soldiers lay, guns began to talk. The reports quickened, then blurred into a steady daunting roar. Bullets blew sand about the troopers and killed or wounded men and horses. The storm of lead continued while the sun went down, a red lacquer disk slipping through a rift in the cloud. The firing ebbed with dusk and ceased with darkness.

All night long, while the besieged fortified their position, a witches' sabbath endured in the valley. Great fires blazed and there rose wild yelling, the wailing minors of Indian song and the flat rhythm of many drums. There were trumpet calls, too, sounded in derision by some gifted Sioux, on an instrument taken from Custer's command. Troopers believed that their leader was returning or that Crook was riding to their rescue. It was a night of dread and of blasted hope, worse than terror. No one seems to have thought of going down to the river for the water they were to need so sorely on the morrow.

Some of the beleaguered were so utterly weary that they slumbered. Edgerly, waking, encountered Major Reno in the darkness and remembered how the unhappy man exclaimed: "Great God, I don't see how you can sleep!"

Up through the Bighorn Valley, Terry was marching that night of June twenty-fifth. The *Far West* was moving up-stream with Gibbon, still ill, on board. Terry had led the column across country from the valley of Tullock's Creek. His attempt at a short-cut had been disastrous. The command had become entangled in terrific badlands. Terry's Crows were frightened and more useless with every mile. There were no white guides with the column. Herendeen was with Reno's besieged command and Bouyer, who knew this country like the palm of his hand, lay dead with Custer. The infantry halted at length, completely spent. Terry pressed on with his cavalry. He had promised Custer, Terry told his staff, that he would be at the foot of the Little Bighorn Valley on June twenty-sixth.

They rode through blackness, intensified by rain. In the crooked country, Low's Gatlings got lost and were found again and the cavalry at last was stalled on a bluff above the Bighorn, from which they were guided to camp on the shore by Little Face, one of the less timorous Crows. Terry's men barely had gone to sleep when the day began for Reno's.

The seven remaining troops of the 7th Cavalry had had scant slumber. Through the hours of darkness, they had entrenched desperately, digging rifle-pits with the three spades in the command, with knives and tin cups; piling dead animals and the packs into redoubts. The horses and mules had been taken with the wounded into a hollow on the plateau. The line the troops established was horseshoe shape, with the open end toward the bluff. The ridges commanded it. When those to eastward grew sharp against a faintly paling sky, the first Indian rifle heralded dawn.

All that morning, while showers came and went, a lead storm beat upon the position. The troopers saw few Indians but a horde waited in the valley for place on the firing-line, and within carbine range hundreds invisible screeched and yelped and wreathed the peaks with the smoke of a steady fusillade that battered against barricades and frail earthworks; that killed mules and horses and hit not a few men crouched behind inadequate protections. Reno lost sixteen killed and forty-odd wounded on that hill.

Throughout the deadly blizzard, it was Benteen who best kept head and heart. It was he who by direct action and by prompting his Major, controlled the defense. The Indians crept close to his side of the horseshoe. Benteen insisted that Reno lend him French's troop from the other side of the defense and led H and M in a charge that drove back the Sioux. White-haired, erect, imperturbable, he was immune to bullets and fear.

"Captain, sorr," Sergeant Mike Madden objected, "ye tell us to keep down. It's yourself should keep down. They'll git ye."

"Oh, pshaw," Benteen grinned. "They can't hit me."

Madden later was wounded and lost a leg. It was Benteen who gave the order for a charge that Reno led to clear the other side of the horseshoe of an inward creeping enemy.

At ten that morning, the firing abated, dwindling into occasional sniping through which hardy souls stole down to the river, dived under fire across a little beach and obtained precious water for the wounded. Thereafter, the gusts of bullets came fitfully like a failing storm. There was another heavy outburst at two, with many flights of arrows, but this faded, and after three there was no firing at all. Grimed and haggard men, who long had looked at death, now stared without belief at life's incredible fairness.

Below them the valley filled with smoke. The Indians had fired the grass. At seven that evening, the handful on the hill beheld the awesome passage of the military might of the Sioux. Through the shifting smoke-screen, the Indian host moved up-stream in an enormous compact column, three miles in length, almost a mile in breadth. They marched with the deliberation of the retreating grizzly. The massed dark horsemen passed and vanished, followed by thin cheering from the survivors of the regiment that, alone, could whip all hostiles on the plains.

That noon, June twenty-sixth, Terry, the convalescent Gibbon, the cavalry and guns, reached the Valley of the Little Bighorn and waited impatiently for the infantry to catch up. Bradley and the scouts had talked that morning to three Crows, Hairy Moccasin, Goes Ahead and White Man Runs Him, who had called across the bank-full Bighorn to the disbelieving troops that Custer and all his men were dead. Thereafter all Indians still remaining with the Terry-Gibbon column had deserted.

When the infantry joined him, Terry moved ahead. It was Bradley, scouting in advance, who marked how the Sioux gathered in the distance to contest farther passage. Toward dark, the column bivouacked in hollow square. Two white scouts, Bostwick and Muggins Taylor, who had been sent to establish contact with Custer, returned angrily swearing that the country was "stiff with Sioux." In Terry's camp, the General and some others felt dread at which the rest of the officers scoffed. Nothing, the skeptical insisted, could happen to Custer, the eternally fortunate.

On the morrow, the Sioux were gone. Toward noon, Bradley and his scouts found on a hill, east of the Little Bighorn and opposite the northern end of the vanished village, the stripped bodies of many men.

Custer lay toward the northern end of a ridge whose slope went down to the river. He had fallen, not at the summit but a little way below it, and down the slope and along the ridge to the south were scattered the fragments of the command that had been burst apart and abolished by the power of the Sioux.

Some thirty men, including his brother, his nephew and most of his officers, had died close to Custer. Many of them were stripped. A few were mutilated. He himself had been shot in the left side and temple. With his dead about him he lay as, eight years earlier, the young and eager Major Elliot had lain, center of a ring of slain, on the frosty grass above the Washita.

The wounds that had killed George Armstrong Custer, Lieutenant-Colonel, 7th Cavalry, Brevet Major-General, United States of America, were not apparent. Among the blasted bodies that still bore impress of the fury which had passed over them, his was unmarred by agony or terror. He who found it wrote:

"His expression was rather that of a man who had fallen asleep and enjoyed peaceful dreams."

George Armstrong Custer well may have lain content. Glory, sought all his stormy life, was his at last and forever.

An Egg for the Major

BY

C. S. FORESTER

THE major commanding the squadron of light tanks was just as uncomfortable as he had been for a number of days. For the officer commanding a light tank there is a seat provided, a sort of steel piano stool, but, in the opinion of the major, it had been designed for men of a physique that has no counterpart on earth. If one sat on it in the normal way, with the part of one which Nature provides for sitting on on the stool, one's knees bumped most uncomfortably on the steel wall in front. And contrariwise, if one hitched oneself back and sat on one's thighs, not only was the circulation interfered with to an extent which led to cramps but also the back of one's head was sore with being bumped against the wall of the turret behind. Especially when the tank was rolling over the desert, lurching and bumping from ridge to ridge; on a road one could look after oneself, but it was weeks and weeks since the major had set eyes on a road.

He left off thinking about the sort of shape a man should be who has to pass his days in a light tank, and gave the order for the tank to stop. He climbed out through the steel door with his compass to take a fresh bearing. Out in the desert here an army had to navigate like a ship at sea, with the additional difficulty that inside the steel walls, with the spark coils to complicate matters, a compass was no use at all. The only thing to do was to get out of the tank, carry one's compass well away from its influence, and look over the featureless landscape and mark some patch of scrub, some minor rise in the ground, on which one could direct one's course. He walked stiffly away from the tank, laid the compass level and stared forward. This was perhaps the five-hundredth time he had done this, and he had learned by long experience the difficulties to be anticipated. There was never anything satisfactory directly ahead on which he could direct his course. There would be fine landmarks out to the right or left where they were no use to him, but nothing straight ahead. He would have to be content with some second best, the edge of that yellow patch on the brown, and he knew quite well that it would appear quite different when he got back into the tank again. Furthermore, it would appear more different still when they had traveled a little way toward it—there had been times long ago, when the desert was new to him, when he had found at a halt that he

From: The Saturday Evening Post. By permission of the Author.

was more than ninety degrees off his course. He was far more experienced now; five months of desultory warfare and now this last tremendous march across the desert had accustomed him to the difficulties.

Experience taught him to empty his mind of the hundreds of previous landscapes which he had memorized, to concentrate on this one, to note that yellow patch whose edge would be his guiding mark for the next ten miles, and to look back and absorb the appearance of the country in that direction as well. Then he went back to the tank, decided against the piano stool, slammed the door shut, and climbed up onto the roof before giving the word to start. On the roof he could lie on the unyielding steel to the detriment of hip and elbow, anchoring himself into position by locking his toe round the muzzle of the machine gun below him. After a time his leg would go to sleep at about the same time that his hip could bear it no longer; then he would have to change over; three changes—two turns with each foot and hip—would be as much as he could stand, and then it would be time to take a fresh bearing and go back to the piano stool and the other problem of which part to sit on.

He lounged on the steel roof while the tank pitched and rolled under him; it was as well to keep that foot firmly locked below the gun muzzle to save himself from being pitched off. It had happened to him sometimes; every-thing had happened to him at one time or another. The wind today was from ahead, which was a mercy; a gentle following wind meant that the dust of their progress kept pace with them and suffocated him. He looked away to the left and the right, and he could see a long line of great plumes of dust keeping pace with him as the other tanks of the squadron plowed their way across the desert. The major was an unimaginative man, but that spectacle never failed to move him. That long line of dust plumes sweeping across the desert had menace and sinister beauty about it. There were the high yellow clouds, and at the base of each a little dot, a nucleus, as it were, sometimes concealed from view by the inequalities of the ground, and every cloud indicated the presence of one of the tanks of his squadron. There were other clouds behind, when the major turned his gaze that way; they showed where the stragglers were trying to regain their places in the line after some necessary halt. The ones farthest back were the ones who had had track trouble or engine trouble. There could be no waiting for them, not in the face of the orders which the wireless brought in, insisting on the utmost speed in this dash across the desert.

Already in the major's mind the total of days already consumed in the march was a little vague. If he set his mind to it, he could have worked it out, but he felt as if he had done nothing all his life except lead this squadron across the desert. Something enormous and of vital importance was happening to the north, he knew—Sidi Barrani and Tobruk had fallen, but his command had been plucked out of that attack and sent off on this wide flanking sweep, and were already a little in the dark about the situation. These Italian maps were of no use at all. They showed things which simply did not exist—he could swear to that from bitter experience—and, in consequence, the major did not know within twenty miles where he was. But somewhere ahead of him there was the sea, across the great hump of Northern Africa which he was traversing, and beside the sea ran the great road which Mussolini had built, and he knew he had only to arrive on that road to start making things unpleasant for the Italians. What the situation would be when he did arrive he could not imagine in the least, but the major had absorbed the philosophy of the desert, and left that problem to be solved when it arose, wasting no mental effort on hypothetical cases which probably would have no resemblance to the reality he would encounter sooner or later.

The squadron was moving on a wide front, impressive on account of the distant plumes of dust, but even so, the width of the front was nothing compared with the immensity of the desert. They had marched five hundred miles so far, and a thousand miles to the south of them the desert extended as far as the plains of the Sudan. Sometimes the major would allow his imagination to think about these distances, but more often he thought about eggs. Tinned beef and biscuits, day after day, for more days than he could count, had had their effect. Nearly every idle thought that passed through his mind was busy with food. Sometimes he thought about kippers and haddock, sometimes about the green vegetables he had refused to eat as a little boy, but mostly he thought about eggs—boiled eggs, fried eggs, scrambled eggs—mostly boiled eggs. The lucky devils who were doing the fighting in the north were in among the villages now which Mussolini had peopled with so much effort; they would have a hen or two for certain, and a hen meant an egg. A boiled egg. For a day or two, eggs had formed a staple topic of conversation when he squatted at mealtimes with the gunner and the driver, until the major had detected a certain forbearing weariness mingled with the politeness with which his crew had received his remarks about eggs. Then he had left off talking about them; in this new kind of war, majors had to be careful not to become old bores in the eyes of the privates with whom they lived. But not being able to talk about them made him think about them all the more. The major swallowed hard in choking dust.

The sun was now right ahead of him, and low toward the horizon; the sky around it was already taking up the colors of the desert sunset, and the brassy blue overhead was miraculously blending into red and orange. To the major that only meant that the day's march was drawing to a close. Sunsets came every day, and eggs came only once a year, seemingly.

When darkness came, they halted; each tank where it happened to find itself, save for the outposts pushed forward in case the Italians should, incredibly, be somewhere near and should have the hardihood to attempt operations in the dark. The driver and the gunner came crawling out of the tank, dizzy with petrol fumes and stiff with fatigue, still a little deaf with the insensate din which had assailed their ears for the whole day. The most immediate duty was to service the tank and have it all ready for prolonged action again, but before they did that they washed their mouths round with a little of the precious water taken from the can which had ridden with them in the tank all day. It was at blood heat, and it tasted of the inside of a tank—indescribably, that is to say. But it was precious, all the same. There was always the possibility that their ration of water would not come up from the rear; and if it did, there was also the chance that there had been so much loss in the radiators during the day that no water could be spared for the men.

Once, long back, there had been a heavenly time when the day's ration had been a gallon a head a day. That had been marvelous, for a man could do simply anything with a gallon a day; he could shave, wash his face, sometimes even spare a little to wash off the irritating dust from his body. But the ration, now that they were so far from the base, was half a gallon, and a man, after a day in a tank, could drink half a gallon at a single draught if he were foolish enough to do so. Half a gallon meant only just enough water to keep thirst from coming to close quarters; only the most fussy among the men would spare a cupful for shaving, and the days when the radiators had been extra thirsty, so that the men's rations were cut in half, were days of torment.

The major and the gunner and the driver settled down in the desert for their supper. Long habit had blunted the surprise the major had once felt at finding himself, a field officer, squatting in the dust with a couple of privates, and, fortunately, long habit had done the same for the privates. Before this campaign opened they would have been tongue-tied and awkward at his presence. It had not been easy to reach adjustment, but they had succeeded—as witness the way in which, without saying a word, they had caused him to leave off talking about eggs. He was still "sir" to them, but almost the only other way in which his rank was noticeable in their personal relationships was that the two privates both suspected the major of being the guilty party in the matter of the loss of one of their three enameled mugs. They had not ventured openly to accuse him, and he remained in ignorance of their suspicions, taking it for granted that the gunner—a scatterbrained fellow—had been at fault in the matter.

It was an infernal nuisance, being short of a mug; two mugs among three of them called for a whole lot of organization, especially in the morning, when they had to clean their teeth, and sometimes to shave and sometimes to make tea—and the gunner liked his strong, and the driver liked his weak, and the major was the only one who did not want sugar in it. If ever the three of them were to quarrel, the major knew it would be over some difficulty arising out of the loss of the mug. Yet he did not see nowadays anything odd about a major worrying over the prospect of a disagreement with a couple of privates over an enameled mug.

And tonight he was additionally unlucky, because the rations for the day were a tinned meat and vegetable concoction that he particularly disliked. But the gunner and the driver were loud in their delight when they discovered what fate had brought them tonight. They ate noisily and appreciatively, while the major squatting beside them made only the merest pretense of eating and allowed his thoughts to stray back to memories of dinner at the Berkeley and the Gargantuan lunches at Simpson's in the Strand. And also of eggs.

It was dark now, and cold—before supper was over the major had to reach out for a blanket and wrap it round his shoulders as the treacherous desert wind blew chilly. The stars were out, but there was no moon yet and the darkness was impenetrable. There was nothing to do now except sleep. The major chose himself a spot where the scrub grew not too thickly, and where the rock did not jut entirely through the thin skin of earth which overlaid it. He spread his blankets over his fleabag and crawled in with the dexterity of long practice without disturbing the arrangement. The bit of tarpaulin stretched from the side of the tank to the earth kept off the dew, if there should be any, and the joints that had suffered on the steel piano stool and on the steel roof snuggled gratefully against the more kindly contact of the earth. And long habit was a help.

He awoke in the middle of the night with a shattering roar in his very ear. The driver had his own system of keeping his beloved motor warm enough to start. He slept only under two blankets, and when the cold awoke him he knew that it was necessary to warm up the motor. He would crawl out of bed, start it up, allow it to run for five minutes, and then switch it off. That meant that the light tank was always ready for instant action, but the major had never been able to acquire the habit of sleeping through the din of the motor. The only habit he had been able to form was that of cursing to himself at the driver, feebly, half awake, and then of turning over and completing his night's sleep. The gunner, on the other hand, slept stolidly through the whole racket, snoring away stubbornly—the major suspected him of dreaming about eggs.

Before dawn they were up and doing. Two inches of sand in the bottom of a petrol tin made an admirable wick; petrol soaked into it burned with an almost clear flame and heated the water for their tea in a flash. They had grown cunning lately and brushed their teeth after breakfast, using the remains of the tea for the purpose; that gave them an additional two swallows of water apiece to drink at the midmorning halt for filling up. The motor started, shatteringly noisy as usual. Then they were off, the long line of tanks heaving and rolling over the desert, the familiar plumes of dust trailing behind them, the familiar weary ache beginning to grow in the joints of the major as he settled himself on the piano stool.

The major's calculation of his position was a hazy one, and through no fault of his own. Erratic compasses, ridiculous Italian maps and strict wireless silence combined, after a march hundreds of miles long, to make it very doubtful where they were. But the major was philosophic about it. British light tanks were capable of fighting almost anything in Africa, and what they could not fight they could run away from; they had learned that lesson in innumerable untold skirmishes in the old days of the beginning of the war. The major felt ready for anything that might happen, as he stared out through the slit of the conning tower across the yellowish brown plain.

Yet all the same it is doubtful if he was really ready for the sight that met his eyes. The tank came lurching and rolling up a sharp slope. It heaved itself over the crest—the note of the motor changing ever so little as the gradient altered—and a new landscape was presented to the major's eyes.

First of all he saw the sea, the blue sea, the wonderful blue sea, flecked with white. The major wriggled on the piano stool and yelled involuntarily at the top of his voice when he saw it. That marvelous horizon, that beautiful color, that new-found sense of achievement and freedom—they were simply intoxicating. The driver and the gunner were as intoxicated as he was, screwing their necks round to grin at him, the fluffy immature beard of the gunner wagging on his chin.

And then they cleared the next curve of the crest, and the major saw the road, that long coastal road for the construction of which Mussolini had poured out so much treasure. The major had expected to see it from the moment when he had seen the sea—in fact, he was craning his neck for a sight of it. But he was not ready for the rest of what he saw. For twenty miles the road was black with the fleeing Italian army—an enormous column of men and vehicles, jamming the road from side to side, hastening westward—Bergenzoli's army escaping from Bengasi and from the wrath of the English behind them. From a point nearly ahead of them away off to the right stretched that hurrying column. From his point of vantage the major could see it looping like some monstrous water snake along the curves of the road. Now he knew why his squadron had been hurled across the desert at such a frantic speed. It had been planned to cut off Bergenzoli's retreat, and the object had been achieved, with no more than ten minutes to spare.

Those ten minutes were only to spare if the major did the right thing on the instant. But twenty years of training had prepared the major for that very purpose. He was still a hussar, even though his squadron's horses had long ago been replaced by light tanks. His mental reactions were instantaneous; there was no need to stop and ponder the situation. The trained tactical eye took in the lie of the land even while he was shouting into the wireless transmitter the vital information that he was ahead of the Italians. He saw the road and the ridge beside it, and the moment that the information had been acknowledged he was speaking again, quietly already, giving his orders to the squadron. The long line of tanks wheeled and swooped down upon the road.

So close was the race that they were barely in position before the head of the column was up to them. An hour later and the Italians would have been able to post a flank guard behind whose shelter most of them would have been able to slip away. As it was, the major just had time to give his orders to his two troops as the head of the Italian column came down upon them.

The tanks bucked themselves into position and the machine guns spoke out, pouring their fire into the trucks packed with infantry which were so recklessly coming down upon them. It was slaughter, the dire punishment of a harebrained attack. The major watched the trucks swerve off the road, saw the startled infantry come tumbling out while the machine-gun fire cut swaths through them. Truck piled upon truck. The poor devils in them were deserving of pity. At one moment they had thought themselves safe, rolling along a good road back to Tripoli, and then the next these gray monsters had come darting out of the desert across their path, spraying death.

With the checking of the head of the column, confusion spread up the road. The major could see movement dying away as each successive section bumped up against the one ahead; the sudden outburst of firing, taking everyone by surprise, was rousing panic among the weaker individuals. So much the better. From the major's point of view, there could not be too much panic. Somewhere up that column there were field guns and there were heavy tanks, and to neither of them could he offer any real resistance. The more confusion there was in the column, the longer would it take to extricate these, the only weapons that could clear its path. Time was of the utmost importance; he turned and looked back over his shoulder at where the sun was dipping toward the horizon and the blue sea. This time, by some curious chance, his mind was in a condition to take in the fact that the approaching sunset would be red and lurid. He was smiling grimly as he turned back to his work.

Someone over there was trying to urge the unarmored infantry to the attack—to certain death, in other words, in the face of the two grim little groups of tanks that opposed them. Some of them came forward to the certain death too. And the sun was nearer the horizon.

Farther back down the column frantic officers were clearing a path for the artillery. There were eddies and swirls in the mass. Trucks were being heaved off the road as the guns came through. The major took his glasses from his eyes and gave another order. The tanks curvetted and wheeled, and next moment they had a ridge of solid earth between them and the guns. There was a dreary wait—the major had time for another glance at the sun sinking in a reddened sky—before the shells began to come over. Then the major could smile; they were shrieking over the crest and a good two yards above his head before they buried themselves in the ridge behind him. But there was infantry creeping forward again; there was still the chance that he might be forced sideways out of his position and have to leave a gap through which the mob might escape. He looked at the sun again, and then out to his right, the direction from which he had come, and he felt a glow of relief. The rest of the advance guard was coming—a battalion of motorized infantry with their battery of antitank guns. Now they had a chance. But where were the cruiser tanks, the only weapons in Africa that could stop the heavy tanks when they should be able to make their way out of the column?

It had been touch and go in the first place, when the light tanks had cut off the retreat of the column. It was touch and go now, when the light tanks and five hundred British soldiers were trying to stop the advance of fifty thousand Italians. But night was close at hand. Darkness blinded the Italian gunners and paralyzed the efforts being made to clear the road for the heavy tanks. The major neatly withdrew his tanks over one more ridge, in case of a night attack—in all his extensive experience with the Italians they had never ventured a single operation in darkness—and went round his squadron to see that they were as well prepared as might be for a battle on the morrow.

The major always remembers that night as one when there was nothing he found it necessary to do. The British soldier was on the offensive. The veriest fool could see victory just ahead, victory of a crushing type, nothing less than annihilation of the enemy, if only the force of which the squadron formed a part could hold back Bergenzoli until pressure on his rear and the arrival of help to themselves should convince Bergenzoli of the hopelessness of his position. With victory depending on the proper lubrication of their tanks, on their precautions against surprise, they needed no telling, no inspection, to make them do their duty. The major was not an imaginative man, but something in his imagination was touched that night when he talked to his men. The final destruction of the Italians was what they had in mind; the fact that they would be opposed tomorrow by odds of a hundred to one, and that there was more chance of their being dead by evening than alive, did not alter their attitude in the least.

The major walked from one little group to another; the once khaki overalls worn by everyone, even himself, had been bleached almost white by exposure, and the oil stains somehow did not darken them in a bad light, so that the men he spoke to showed up as ghostly figures in the darkness. There was laughter in the voices of the ghosts he spoke to—laughter and delight in the imminent prospect of victory. And in the stillness of the desert night they could hear, across two valleys, the din of the heavy Italian tanks roaring up to take up positions for the charge that would try to clear the way for the Italians next day. That was the lullaby the major heard as he stretched out in the desert to try to snatch a couple of hours' sleep, side by side with the driver and the gunner. Only in the grave did officers and men sleep side by side until this war came.

Dawn—the first faint light that precedes dawn—showed, looming over the farther crest, the big Italian tanks which had been somehow forced forward during the night along the tangled column. They came forward ponderously, with fifty thousand men behind them, and in front of them there was only a thread of infantry, a single battery, a squadron of light tanks whose armor was only fit to keep out rifle bullets. It was as if the picadors and the matadors in the bull ring had to fight, not a single bull but a whole herd of bulls, all charging in the madness of desperation.

There is an art in the playing of a charging bull, even in the handling of a whole herd. Through a long and weary day, that was just what the major's squadron and the rest of the British force succeeded in doing. Since time immemorial—from Alexander to Hitler—it has been the fate of advance guards to be sacrificed to gain time for the maneuver of the main body, to be used to pin the enemy to the ground, so that his flank can be safely assailed. Only troops of the highest discipline and training can be trusted to fulfill such a mission, however. The Italian tanks which were recklessly handled were lured into the fire of the battery; the timid ones were prevailed upon to procrastinate. The slow retreat of the British force was over ground marked with crippled tanks and littered with Italian dead; and there were British dead there, too, and knocked-out British guns, and burned-out British tanks.

It was an exhausted British force that still confronted the Italians. The line had shrunk, so that on its left flank, toward the sea, there was an open gap through which, among the sand dunes, some of the Italians were beginning to dribble on foot, creeping along the edge of the sea in the wild hope of escaping captivity. And then, at that last moment, came the decisive blow. At least to us here it seemed the last moment. That can only be a guess—no one can dare say that the British had reached the end of their resistance. But it was at that moment, when British riflemen were fighting hard to protect their headquarters, when two thirds of the British guns were out of action, when the major's squadron was reduced to three tanks, that help arrived. From out of the desert there came a sweeping line of huge British cruiser tanks. They came charging down on the Italian flank, enormous, invulnerable and terrifying. It is impossible to guess at the miracle of organization, at the prodigy of hard work, which had brought these monstrous things across sands which had scarcely even been trodden by camels.

From out of the desert they came, wreathed in dust, spouting fire, charging down upon the tangled mass of the Italian army pent back behind the thin dam of the British line. The Italian tanks wheeled to meet them, and then and there the battle was fought out, tank to tank, under the brazen sky, over the sand where the dead already lay. The dust clouds wrapped them round, dimming the bright flames—visible even in the sunshine—which streamed from the wrecked tanks, the Viking pyres of their slain crews.

When it was over, the whole battle was finished. There was no fight left in the Italians. The desert had already vomited out three fierce attacks—first the major's light tanks, then the infantry, and last the cruiser tanks, and no one could guess what next would come forth. And from the rear came the news that the pursuing British were pressing on the rear guard; at any moment the sea might bring its quota of death, should the British ships find a channel through the sandbanks which would bring their guns within range of the huddled army. Front, rear and both flanks were open to attack, and overhead the air force was about to strike. Nor was that all. Thirst was assailing them, those unhappy fifty thousand men massed without a single well within reach. There was nothing for it but surrender.

The major watched the fifty thousand men yield up their arms; he knew that he was witness to one of the great victories of history, and he was pleased about it. Through the dreadful fatigue that was overwhelming him he also was aware that he had played a vital part in the gaining of that victory, and that somewhere in the future there would be mentions in dispatches and decorations. But his eyelids were heavy and his shoulders drooping.

Then came the gunner; his faded, oil-stained overalls made more shocking than ever by the stains of the blood of the wounded driver, and that horribly fluffy yellow beard of his, like the down on a baby chick, offending the sunlight. Now that they had reached the sea, the distillation plants would supply them with a sufficiency of water and that beard could be shaved off. But the gunner was grinning all over his face, his blue eyes nearly lost in the wrinkles round them, lines carved by the blinding light of the desert. The gunner had heard a cock crowing down beside the solitary white farmhouse toward the sea on the edge of the battlefield, and he had walked there and back on stiff legs. The gunner held out a big fist before the major, and opened the fingers like a man doing a conjuring trick. In his hand was an egg.

The Merrimac and the Monitor

BY

MARY JOHNSTON

WE WERE encamped on the Warwick River—infantry, and a cavalry company, and a battalion from New Orleans. Around us were green flats, black mud, winding creeks, waterfowl, earthworks, and what guns they could give us. At the mouth of the river across the channel we had sunk twenty canal boats, to the end that Burnside should not get by. Beside the canal boats and the guns and the waterfowl there was a deal of fever-malarial—of exposure, of wet, of mouldy bread, of homesickness and general desolation. Some courage existed, too, and singing at times. We had been down there a long time among the marshes—all winter, in fact.

"Down to our camp one morning about two weeks ago came El Capitan Colorado—General Magruder, you know—gold lace, stars, and black plume! With him came Lieutenant Wood, C.S.N. We were paraded and Lieutenant Wood made us a speech. 'The old *Merrimac*, you know, men, that was burnt last year when the Yankees left Norfolk?—well, we've raised her, and cut her down to her berth deck, and made her what we call an ironclad. An ironclad is a new man-of-war that's going to take the place of the old. The *Merrimac* is not a frigate any longer; she's the ironclad *Virginia*, and we rather think she's going to make her name remembered. She's over there at the Gosport Navy Yard, and she's almost ready. She's covered over with iron plates, and she's got an iron beak, or ram, and she carries ten guns. On the whole, she's the ugliest beauty that you ever saw! She's almost ready to send to Davy Jones' locker a Yankee ship or two. Commodore Buchanan commands her, and you know who he is! She's got her full quota of officers, and, the speaker excepted, they're as fine a set as you'll find on the high seas! But man-of-war's men are scarcer, my friends, than hen's teeth! It's what comes of having no maritime population. Every man Jack that isn't on our few little ships is in the army—and the *Virginia* wants a crew of three hundred of the bravest of the brave! Now, I am talking to Virginians and Louisianians. Many of you are from New Orleans, and that means that some of you may very well have been seamen—seamen at an emergency, anyhow! Anyhow, when it comes to an emergency Virginians and Louisianians are there to meet it—on sea or on land! Just now there is an emergency—the *Virginia's* got to have a crew. General Magruder, for all he's got only a small force with which to hold a long line—General

From: *The Long Roll.*

Magruder, like the patriot that he is, has said that I may ask this morning for volunteers. Men! any seaman among you has the chance to gather laurels from the strangest deck of the strangest ship that ever you saw! No fear for the laurels! They're fresh and green even under our belching smoke-stack. The *Merrimac* is up like the phoenix; the last state of her is greater than the first, and her name is going down in history! Louisianians and Virginians, who volunteers?'

"About two hundred volunteered. Well, Wood chose about eighty—all who had been seamen or gunners and a baker's dozen of ignoramuses besides. I came in with that portion of the elect. And off we went, in boats, across the James to the southern shore and to the Gosport Navy Yard. That was a week before the battle."

"What does it look like, Edward—the *Merrimac*?"

"It looks like Hamlet's cloud. Sometimes there is an appearance of a barn with everything but the roof submerged—or of Noah's Ark, three-fourths under water! Sometimes, when the flag is flying, she has the air of a piece of earthworks, mysteriously floated off into the river. Ordinarily, though, she is rather like a turtle, with a chimney sticking up from her shell. The shell is made of pitch-pine and oak, and it is covered with two-inch-thick plates of Tredegar iron. The beak is of cast iron, standing four feet out from the bow; that, with the rest of the old berth deck, is just awash. Both ends of the shell are rounded for pivot guns. Over the gun deck is an iron grating on which you can walk at need. There is the pilot-house covered with iron, and there is the smoke-stack. Below are the engines and boilers, condemned after the *Merrimac's* last cruise, and, since then, lying in the ooze at the bottom of the river. They are very wheezy, trembling, poor old men of the sea! It was hard work to get the coal for them to eat; it was brought at last from away out in Montgomery County, from the Price coal-fields. The guns are two 7-inch rifles, two 6-inch rifles and six 9-inch smooth-bores; ten in all.—Yes, call her a turtle, plated with iron; she looks as much like that as like anything else.

"When we eighty men from the Warwick first saw her, she was swarming with workmen. They continued to cover her over and to make impossible any drill or exercise upon her. Hammer, hammer upon belated plates from the Tredegar! Tinker, tinker with the poor old engines! Make shift here and make shift there; work through the day and work through the night, for there was a rumour abroad that the *Ericsson,* that we knew was building, was coming down the coast! There was no chance to drill, to become acquainted with the turtle and her temperament. Her species had never gone to war before, and when you looked at her there was room for doubt as to how she would behave! Officers and men were strange to one another —and the gunners could not try the guns for the swarming workmen. There wasn't so much of the Montgomery coal that it could be wasted on experiments in firing up—and indeed it seemed wise not to experiment at all with the ancient engines! So we stood about the navy yard, and looked down the Elizabeth and across the flats to Hampton Roads, where we could see the *Cumberland,* the *Congress,* and the *Minnesota,* Federal ships lying off Newport News—and the workmen riveted the last plates—and smoke began to come out of the smoke-stack—and suddenly Commodore Buchanan, with his lieutenants behind him, appeared between us and the *Merrimac*—or the *Virginia.* Most of us still call her the *Merrimac.* It was the morning of the 8th.

"We soldiers turned seamen came to attention. 'Get on board, men,'— said Commodore Buchanan. 'We are going out in the Roads and introduce a new era.' So off the workmen came and on we went—the flag officers and the lieutenants and the midshipmen and the surgeons and the volunteer aides and the men. The engineers were already below and the gunners were looking at the guns. The smoke rolled up very black, the ropes were cast off, a bugle blew, out streamed the stars and bars, all the workmen on the dock swung their hats, and down the Elizabeth moved the *Merrimac.* She moved slowly enough with her poor old engines, and she steered badly, and she drew twenty-two feet, and she was ugly, ugly, ugly—poor thing!

"Now we were opposite Craney Island, at the mouth of the Elizabeth. There's a battery there, you know, part of General Colston's line, and there are forts upon the main along the James. All these were now crowded with men, hurrahing, waving their caps. . . . As we passed Craney they were singing 'Dixie.' So we came out into the James to Hampton Roads.

"Now all the southern shore from Willoughby's Spit to Ragged Island is as grey as a dove, and all the northern shore from Old Point Comfort to Newport News is blue where the enemy has settled. In between are the shining Roads. Between the Rip Raps and Old Point swung at anchor the *Roanoke,* the *Saint Lawrence,* a number of gunboats, store ships, and transports, and also a French man-of-war. Far and near over the Roads were many small craft. The *Minnesota,* a large ship, lay half-way between Old Point and Newport News. At the latter place there is a large Federal garrison, and almost in the shadows of its batteries rode at anchor the frigate *Congress* and the sloop *Cumberland.* The first had fifty guns, the second thirty. The *Virginia* or the *Merrimac,* or the turtle, creeping out from the Elizabeth, crept slowly and puffing black smoke into the South Channel. The pilot, in his iron-clad pilot-house no bigger than a hickory nut, put her head to the northwest. The turtle began to swim toward Newport News.

"Until now not a few of us within her shell, and almost all of the soldiers on the forts along the shore, had thought her upon a trial trip only—down the Elizabeth, past Craney Island, turn at Sewell's Point, and back to the dock of the Gosport Navy Yard! When she did not turn, the cheering on the shore stopped; you felt the breathlessness. When she passed the Point and took to the South Channel, when her head turned up-stream, when she came abreast of the Middle Ground, when they saw that the turtle was going to fight, from along the shore to Craney and from Sewell's Point there arose a yell. Every man in grey yelled. They swung hat or cap; they shouted themselves hoarse. All the flags streamed suddenly out, trumpets blared, the sky lifted, and we drank the sunshine in like wine. That is, some of us did. To others it came cold like hemlock against the lip. Fear is a horrible sensation. I was dreadfully afraid——"

"Edward!"

"Dreadfully. But you see I didn't tell anyone I was afraid, and that makes all the difference! Besides, it wore off . . . It was a spring day and high tide, and the Federal works at Newport News and the *Congress* and the *Cumberland* and the more distant *Minnesota* all looked asleep in the calm, sweet weather. Washing day it was on the *Congress,* and clothes were drying in the rigging. That aspect as of painted ships, painted breast-works, a painted seapiece, lasted until the turtle reached mid-channel. Then the other side woke up. Upon the shore appeared a blue swarm—men running to and fro. Bugles signalled. A commotion, too, arose upon the *Congress* and the *Cumberland.* Her head toward the latter ship, the turtle puffed forth black smoke and wallowed across the channel. An uglier poor thing you never saw, nor a bolder! Squat to the water, belching black smoke, her engines wheezing and repining, unwieldy of management, her bottom scraping every hummock of sand in all the shoaly roads—ah, she was ugly and courageous! Our two small gunboats, the *Raleigh* and the *Beaufort,* coming from Norfolk, now overtook us,—we went on together. I was forward with the crew of the 7-inch pivot gun. I could see through the port, above the muzzle. Officers and men, we were all cooped under the turtle's shell; in order by the open ports, and the guns all ready. . . . We came to within a mile of the *Cumberland,* tall and graceful with her masts and spars and all the blue sky above. She looked a swan, and we, the ugly duckling. . . . Our ram, you know, was under water—seventy feet of the old berth deck, ending in a four-foot beak of cast iron . . . We came nearer. At three-quarters of a mile, we opened with a bow gun. The *Cumberland* answered, and the *Congress,* and their gunboats and shore batteries. Then began a frightful uproar that shook the marshes and sent the sea-birds screaming. Smoke arose, and flashing fire, and an excitement—an excitement—an excitement. Then it was that I forgot to be afraid. The turtle swam on, toward the *Cumberland,* swimming as fast as Montgomery coal and the engines that had lain at the bottom of the sea could make her go. There was a frightful noise within her shell, a humming, a shaking. The *Congress,* the gunboats, and the shore batteries kept firing broadsides. There was an enormous thundering noise, and the air was grown a sulphurous cloud. Their shot came battering like hail, and like hail it rebounded from the ironclad. We passed the *Congress,*—very close to her tall side. She gave us a withering fire. We returned it, and steered on for the *Cumberland.* A word ran from end to end of the turtle's shell, 'We are going to ram her—stand by, men!'

"Within easy range we fired the pivot gun. I was of her crew; half naked we were, powder blackened and streaming with sweat. The shell she sent burst above the *Cumberland's* stern pivot, killing or wounding most of her crew that served it . . . We went on . . . Through the port I could now see the *Cumberland* plainly, her starboard side just ahead of us, men in the shrouds and running to and fro on her deck. When we were all but on her her starboard blazed. That broadside tore up the carriage of our pivot gun, cut another off at the trunnions, and the muzzle from a third, riddled the smoke-stack and steam-pipe, carried away an anchor, and killed or wounded nineteen men . . . The *Virginia* answered with three guns; a cloud of smoke came between the ironclad and the armed sloop; it lifted— and we were on her. We struck her under the fore rigging with a dull and grinding sound. The iron beak with which we were armed was wrested off.

"The *Virginia* shivered, hung a moment, then backed clear of the *Cumberland,* in whose side there was now a ragged and a gaping hole. The pilot in the iron-clad pilot-house turned her head up-stream. The water was shoal; she had to run up the James some way before she could turn and come back to attack the *Congress.* Her keel was in the mud; she was creeping now like a land turtle, and all the iron shore was firing at her . . . She turned at last in freer water and came down the Roads. Through the port we could see the *Cumberland* that we had rammed. She had listed to port and was sinking. The water had reached her main deck; all her men were now on her spar deck, where they yet served the pivot guns. She fought to the last. A man of ours, stepping for one moment through a port to the outside of the turtle's shell, was cut in two. As the water rose and rose the sound of her guns was like a lessening thunder. One by one they stopped . . . To the last she flew her colours. The *Cumberland* went down.

"By now there had joined us the small, small James River Squadron that had been anchored far up the river. The *Patrick Henry* had twelve guns, the *Jamestown* had two, and the *Teaser* one. Down they scurried like three valiant marsh hens to aid the turtle. With the *Beaufort* and the *Raleigh* there were five valiant pigmies, and they fired at the shore batteries, and the shore batteries answered like an angry Jove with solid shot, with shell, with grape, and with canister! A shot wrecked the boiler of the *Patrick Henry,* scalding to death the men who were near . . . The turtle sunk a transport steamer lying alongside the wharf at Newport News, and then she rounded the Point and bore down upon the *Congress.*

"The frigate had showed discretion, which is the better part of valour. Noting how deeply we drew, she had slipped her cables and run aground in the shallows, where she was safe from the ram of the *Merrimac.* We could get no nearer than two hundred feet. There we took up position, and there we began to rake her, the *Beaufort,* the *Raleigh,* and the *Jamestown* giving us what aid they might. She had fifty guns, and there were the heavy shore batteries, and below her the *Minnesota.* This ship, also aground in the Middle Channel, now came into action with a roar. A hundred guns were trained upon the *Merrimac.* The iron hail beat down every point, not iron-clad that showed about our shell. The muzzles of two guns were shot away, the stanchions, the boat davits, the flagstaff. Again and again the flagstaff fell, and again and again we replaced it. At last we tied the colours to the smoke-stack. Beside the nineteen poor fellows that the *Cumberland's* guns had mowed down, we now had other killed and wounded. Commodore

Buchanan was badly hurt, and the flag lieutenant, Minor. The hundred guns thundered against the *Merrimac* and the *Merrimac* thundered against the *Congress*. The tall frigate and her fifty guns wished herself an ironclad; the swan would have blithely changed with the ugly duckling. We brought down her mainmast, we disabled her guns, we strewed her decks with blood and anguish (war is a wild beast, nothing more, and I'll hail the day when it lies slain). We smashed in her sides and we set her afire. She hauled down her colours and ran up a white flag. The *Merrimac* ceased firing and signalled to the *Beaufort*. The *Beaufort* ran alongside, and the frigate's ranking officer gave up his colours and his sword. The *Beaufort* and the *Congress's* own boats removed the crew and the wounded . . . The shore batteries, the *Minnesota*, the picket boat *Zouave*, kept up a heavy firing all the while upon the *Merrimac*, upon the *Raleigh* and the *Jamestown*, and also upon the *Beaufort*. We waited until the crew was clear of the *Congress*, and then we gave her a round of hot shot that presently set her afire from stem to stern. This done, we turned to other work.

"The *Minnesota* lay aground in the North Channel. To her aid hurrying up from Old Point came the *Roanoke* and the *Saint Lawrence*. Our own batteries at Sewell's Point opened upon these two ships as they passed, and they answered with broadsides. We fed our engines, and under a billow of black smoke ran down to the *Minnesota*. Like the *Congress*, she lay upon a sand bar, beyond fear of ramming. We could only manœuvre for deep water, near enough to her to be deadly. It was now late afternoon. I could see through the port of the bow pivot the slant sunlight upon the water, and how the blue of the sky was paling. The *Minnesota* lay just ahead; very tall she looked, another of the *Congress* breed; the old warships singing their death song. As we came on we fired the bow gun, then, lying nearer her, began with broadsides. But we could not get near enough; she was lifted high upon the sand, the tide was going out, and we drew twenty-three feet. We did her great harm, but we were not disabling her. An hour passed, and the sun drew on to setting. The *Roanoke* turned and went back under the guns of Old Point, but the *Saint Lawrence* remained to thunder at the turtle's iron shell. The *Merrimac* was most unhandy, and on the ebb tide there would be shoals enough between us and a berth for the night. . . . The *Minnesota* could not get away, at dawn she would be yet aground, and we would then take her for our prize. 'Stay till dusk, and the blessed old iron box will ground herself where Noah's flood won't float her!' The pilot ruled, and in the gold and purple sunset we drew off. As we passed, the *Minnesota* blazed with all her guns; we answered her, and answered too, the *Saint Lawrence*. The evening star was shining when we anchored off Sewell's Point. The wounded were taken ashore, for we had no place for wounded men under the turtle's shell. Commodore Buchanan leaving us, Lieutenant Catesby Ap Rice Jones took command.

"I do not remember what we had for supper. We had not eaten since early morning, so we must have had something. But we were too tired to think or to reason or to remember. We dropped beside our guns and slept, but not for long. Three hours, perhaps, we slept, and then a whisper seemed to run through the *Merrimac*. It was as though the ironclad herself had spoken, 'Come! Watch the *Congress* die!' Most of us arose from beside the guns and mounted to the iron grating above, to the top of the turtle's shell. It was a night as soft as silk; the water smooth, in long, faint, olive swells; a half-moon in the sky. There were lights across at Old Point, lights on the battery at the Rip Raps, lights in the frightened shipping, huddled under the guns of Fortress Monroe, lights along either shore. There were lanterns in the rigging of the *Minnesota* where she lay upon the sand bar, and lanterns on the *Saint Lawrence* and the *Roanoke*. As we looked a small moving light, as low as possible to the water, appeared between the *Saint Lawrence* and the *Minnesota*. A man said, 'What's that? Must be a rowboat.' Another man answered, 'It's going too fast for a rowboat—funny! right on the water like that!' 'A launch, I reckon,' said a third, 'with plenty of rowers. Now it's behind the *Minnesota*.' 'Shut up, you talkers,' said a midshipman, 'I want to look at the *Congress*!'

"Four miles away, off Newport News, lay the burning *Congress*. In the still, clear night, she seemed almost at hand. All her masts, her spars, and her rigging showed black in the heart of a great ring of firelight. Her hull, lifted high by the sandbank which held her, had round red eyes. Her ports were windows lit from within. She made a vision of beauty and one of horror. One by one, as they were reached by the flame, her guns exploded —a loud and awful sound in the night above the Roads. We stood and watched that sea picture, and we watched in silence. We are seeing giant things, and ere this war is ended we shall see more. At two o'clock in the morning the fire reached her powder magazine. She blew up. A column like the Israelite's Pillar shot to the zenith; there came an earthquake sound, sullen and deep; when all cleared there was only her hull upborne by the sand and still burning. It burned until the dawn, when it smouldered and went out."

The narrator arose, walked the length of the parlour.

"Go on, Edward. What happened at dawn?"

"We got the turtle in order, and those ancient mariners, our engines, began to work, wheezing and slow. We ran up a new flagstaff, and every man stood to the guns, and the *Merrimac* moved from Sewell's Point, her head turned to the *Minnesota,* away across, grounded on a sandbank in North Channel. The sky was as pink as the inside of a shell, and a thin white mist hung over the marshes and the shore and the great stretch of Hampton Roads. It was so thin that the masts of the ships huddled below Fortress Monroe rose clear of it into the flush of the coming sun. All their pennants were flying—the French man-of-war, and the Northern ships. At that hour the sea-gulls are abroad, searching for their food. They went past the ports, screaming and moving their silver wings.

"The *Minnesota* grew in size. Every man of us looked eagerly—from the pilot-house, from bow ports, and as we drew parallel with her from the ports of the side. We fired the bow gun as we came on, and the shot told. There was some cheering; the morning air was so fine, and the prize so sure! The turtle was in spirits—poor old turtle with her battered shell and her flag put back as fast as it was torn away! Her engines, this morning, were mortal slow and weak; they wheezed and whined, and she drew so deep that, in that shoaly water, she went aground twice between Sewell's Point and the stretch she had now reached of smooth pink water, with the sea-gulls dipping between her and the *Minnesota*. Despite the engines she was happy, and the gunners were all ready at the starboard ports——"

Leaning over, he took the poker and stirred the fire.

> " 'The best laid plans of mice and men
>   Do aften gang agley—'

"There came," said Edward, "there came from behind the *Minnesota* a cheese-box on a shingle. It had lain there hidden by her bulk since midnight. It was its single light that we had watched and thought no more of! A cheese-box on a shingle, and now it darted into the open as though a boy's arm had sent it! It was little beside the *Minnesota*. It was little even beside the turtle. There was a silence when we saw it, a silence of astonishment. It had come so quietly upon the scene—a *deus ex machina* indeed, dropped from the clouds between us and our prey. In a moment we knew it for the *Ericsson*—the looked-for ironclad we knew to be a-building. The *Monitor*, they call it. . . . The shingle was just awash; the cheese-box turned out to be a revolving turret, mail clad and carrying two large, modern guns —11-inch. The whole thing was armoured, had the best of engines, and drew only twelve feet. . . . Well the *Merrimac* had a startled breath, to be sure—there is no denying the drama of the *Monitor's* appearance—and then she righted and began firing. She gave to the cheese-box, or to the armoured turret, one after the other, three broadsides. The turret blazed and answered, and the balls rebounded from each armoured champion." He laughed. "By heaven! it was like our old favourites, Ivanhoe and De Bois-Gilbert—the ugliest squat gnomes of an Ivanhoe and of a Brian De Bois-Gilbert that ever came out of a nightmare! We thundered in the lists, and then we passed each other, turned, and again encountered. Sometimes we were a long way apart, and sometimes there was not ten feet of water be-tween those sunken decks from which arose the iron shell of the *Merrimac*, and the iron turret of the *Monitor*. She fired every seven minutes; we as rapidly as we could load. Now it was the bow gun, now the after pivot, now a full broadside. Once or twice we thought her done for, but always her turret revolved, and her 11-inch guns opened again. In her lighter draught she had a great advantage; she could turn and wind where we could not. The *Minnesota* took a hand, and an iron battery from the shore. We were striving to ram the *Ericsson*, but we could not get close to her; our iron beak, too, was sticking in the side of the sunken *Cumberland*—we could only ram with a blunt prow. The *Minnesota*, as we passed, gave us all her broadside guns—a tremendous fusillade at point-blank range, which would have sunk any ship of the swan breed. The turtle shook off shot and shell, grape and canister, and answered with her bow gun. The shell which it threw entered the side of the frigate, and, bursting amidship, exploded a store of powder and set the ship on fire. Leaving disaster aboard the *Minnesota,* we turned and sunk the tugboat *Dragon.* Then came manœuvre and manœuvre to gain position where we could ram the *Monitor.* . . .

"We got it at last. The engines made an effort like the leap of the spirit before expiring. 'Go ahead! Full speed!' We went; we bore down upon the *Monitor,* now in deeper water. But at the moment that we saw victory she turned. Our bow, lacking the iron beak, gave but a glancing stroke. It was heavy as it was; the *Monitor* shook like a man with the ague, but she did not share the fate of *Cumberland.* There was no ragged hole in her side; her armour was good, and held. She backed, gathered herself together, then rushed forward, striving to ram us in her turn. But our armour, too, was good, and held. Then she came upon the *Merrimac's* quarter, laid her bow against the shell, and fired her 11-inch guns twice in succession. We were so close, each to the other, that it was as though two duellists were standing upon the same cloak. Frightful enough was the concussion of those guns.

"That charge drove in the *Merrimac's* iron side three inches or more. The shots struck above the ports of the after guns, and every man at those guns was knocked down by the impact and bled at the nose and ears. The *Monitor* dropped astern, and again we turned and tried to ram her. But her far lighter draught put her where we could not go; our bow, too, was now twisted and splintered. Our powder was getting low. We did not spare it, we could not; we sent shot and shell continuously against the *Monitor,* and she answered in kind. *Monitor* and *Merrimac,* we went now this way, now that, the *Ericsson* much the lighter and quickest, the *Merrimac* fettered by her poor old engines, and her great length, and her twenty-three feet draught. It was two o'clock in the afternoon. . . . The duellists stepped from off the cloak, tried operations at a distance, hung for a moment in the wind of indecision, then put down the match from the gunner's hands. The *Monitor* darted from us, her head toward the shoal water known as the Middle Ground. She reached it and rested triumphant, out of all danger from our ram, and yet where she could still protect the *Minnesota.* . . . A curious silence fell upon the Roads; sullen like the hush before a thunderstorm, and yet not like that, for we had had the thunderstorm. It was the stillness, perhaps, of exhaustion. It was late afternoon, the fighting had been heavy. The air was filled with smoke; in the water were floating spars and wreckage of the ships we had destroyed. The weather was sultry and still. The dogged booming of a gun from a shore battery sounded lonely and remote as a bell buoy. The tide was falling; there were sand bars enough between us and Sewell's Point. We waited an hour. The *Monitor* was rightly content with the Middle Ground, and would not come back for all our charming. We fired at intervals, upon her, and upon the *Minnesota,* but at last our powder grew so low that we ceased. The tide continued to fall, and the pilot had much to say. . . . The red sun sank in the west; the engineers fed the ancient mariners with Montgomery coal; black smoke gushed forth, and pilots felt their way in the South Channel, and slowly, slowly back toward Sewell's Point. The day closed in a murky evening with a taste of smoke in the air. In the night-time the *Monitor* went down the Roads to Fortress Monroe, and in the morning we took the *Merrimac* into dry dock at Norfolk. Her armour was dented all over, though not pierced. Her bow was bent and twisted, the iron beak lost in the side of the *Cumberland*. Her boats were gone, and her smoke-stack as full of holes as any colander, and the engines at the last gasp. Several of the guns were injured, and coal and powder and ammunition all lacked. We put her there—the dear and ugly warship, the first of the ironclads—we put her there in dry dock, and there she's apt to stay for some weeks to come. Lieutenant Wood was sent to Richmond with the report for the president and the secretary of the navy. He carried, too, the flag of the *Congress*, and I was one of the men detailed for its charge. . . . And now I have told you of the *Merrimac* and the *Monitor*."

Manila Bay

BY

ADMIRAL GEORGE DEWEY

MANILA BAY is a spacious body of water opening out from a narrow entrance between high headlands and expanding toward a low-lying country until it has a navigable breadth of over twenty miles. On either side of the inlet are high volcanic peaks densely covered with tropical foliage, while in the passage itself lie several islands. The principal islands, Corregidor and Caballo, divide this entrance into two channels, known as Boca Grande, the great mouth, and Boca Chica, the little mouth.

Boca Chica has a width of two miles, while Boca Grande would have double this if it were not for the small island of El Fraile. This, being some distance off the main-land, practically reduces the breadth of Boca Grande to about three miles. Corregidor and Caballo are high and rocky, effectually commanding both entrances, while El Fraile, though smaller, is large enough to be well fortified and to aid in the defence of the broader channel.

No doubt the position is a strong one for defensive batteries, but the Spaniards, in keeping with their weakness for procrastination, had delayed fortifying the three islands until war appeared inevitable. Then they succeeded in mounting sufficient guns to have given our squadron a very unpleasant quarter of an hour before it met the Spanish squadron, provided the gunners had been enterprising and watchful.

Examination of these batteries after their surrender on May 2 showed that there were three 5.9-inch breech-loading rifles on Caballo Island, three 4.7-inch breech-loading rifles on El Fraile rock, and three 6.3-inch muzzle-loading rifles at Punta Restinga, commanding the Boca Grande entrance, which our squadron was to use; three 8-inch muzzle-loading rifles on Corregidor, three 7-inch muzzle-loading rifles at Punta Gorda, and two 6.3-inch breech-loading rifles at Punta Lasisi, commanding the Boca Chica entrance. The complement manning these batteries, as given by the official papers found in the commandant's office at Cavite Arsenal, was thirteen officers and two hundred and forty-six men. While the muzzle-loaders were relatively unimportant, the six modern rifles commanding the Boca Grande, at a range of a mile and a half, if accurately served, could deliver a telling fire.

A cable received from our consul-general at Singapore the day before we left Mirs Bay stated that the Boca Grande channel had been mined. His information was from the steamer *Isla de Panay*, which had just arrived at Singapore from Manila. This agreed with the accounts of Consul Williams, and with those of merchant-captains from Manila who had recently arrived in Hong Kong.

This subject of mines had been fully discussed in the conferences of myself and staff and the captains of our ships. We decided that submarine mines in Boca Grande might safely be considered a negligible quantity. First, the depth of water rendered the planting of submarine mines in Boca Grande, except by experts of much experience, a matter of great difficulty; secondly, either contact or electrical mines would deteriorate so rapidly in tropical waters as to become ineffective in a short time after being placed; and, thirdly, all agreed that the many reports of warnings to vessels, of notices that the passage was dangerous, of compulsory pilotage, and of spectacular zigzag courses appeared suspiciously like a cry of "wolf," intended to have its due effect upon a presumptuous enemy.

It was a similar course of reasoning, I recalled, that opened the Suez Canal during the Arabi Pasha rebellion. Hundreds of merchant-steamers had been blocked at the entrance to the canal in the fear of mines said to have been planted by the Egyptians, when an Italian man-of-war under the command of a torpedo expert (late Vice-Admiral Morin, minister of marine) appeared. He said that the Egyptians had hardly skill enough to lay mines properly, and if these had been laid as long as reported they were probably innocuous. So he steamed through the canal in spite of warning, and thus raised a blockade that had lasted for weeks.

The city of Manila lies upon the eastern side of Manila Bay, some twenty-five miles from the entrance, with the headland of Sangley Point and the naval station of Cavite five miles nearer. At all these places there were shore batteries, which added materially to the problem that our squadron had to solve. The batteries on the water-front of the city had thirty-nine heavy guns, four 9.4, four 5.5, two 5.9, two 4.7 breech-loading rifles; nine 8.3 muzzle-loading mortars; eighteen 6.3 muzzle-loading rifles; and eight breech-loading Krupp field pieces. At Sangley Point was a battery with two 5.9 breech-loading rifles and at Canacao one 4.7 breech-loading rifle. These three guns and three of the Manila batteries fired on our ships during the engagement. It will be noted that four guns of the Manila batteries being over 9-inch were larger calibre than any on board our ships.

Before reaching the entrance to Manila Bay there is another bay which might be made an invaluable aid to the protection of the capital and its harbor from naval attack. This is Subig Bay, situated thirty miles to the northward of Corregidor and directly upon the flank of any enemy threatening Manila. With this strategic point effectively occupied, no hostile commander-in-chief would think of passing it and leaving it as a menace to his lines of communication. But with it unoccupied the way was clear.

The Spaniards had inaugurated a small naval reservation at Olongapo, the port of Subig, and at various times appointed boards of officers to report upon the strategic advantages of the situation. So emphatic were the recommendations of these boards in favor of Subig as a naval station in place of Cavite that the change might have been made except for the strong social and official opposition, which preferred life in the capital to comparative exile in a provincial port. Therefore, the fortification of the bay had been neglected; and although at the last moment there was a nervous attempt to improvise defences, so little was done that when, on April 26, the Spanish admiral finally realized that Subig Bay was the strongest point for the defence of his fleet and of Manila, and accordingly sailed from Cavite for Subig, he found, upon arrival, that comparatively nothing had been accomplished and that the position was untenable.

Only twenty-four hours before the arrival of our scouts he got under way and steamed back to Cavite. In his official report he writes feelingly of his disgust that no guns had been mounted and that the entrance had not been mined. He was in error about the mines, however. A Spanish officer assured the executive officer of the *Concord* that eighty mines had been planted in the entrance of Subig Bay. Some fifteen others which the Spaniards had neglected to plant were found later by our officers in the Spanish storehouse at the Subig Bay naval station. In order to get their powder the insurgents had pulled up many of the eighty that had been planted.

So far as our Squadron is concerned, no doubt if we had entered Subig Bay we should have found the mines there as negligible a quantity as those which had undoubtedly been planted in Manila Bay and its entrance. I simply mention their existence to show the state of misinformation in the Spanish admiral's mind about his own resources. He naïvely adds, in continuing his report, that under the circumstances his vessels could not only have been destroyed if found in Subig Bay, but that, owing to the great depth of water, they would have been unable to save their crews in case of being sunk. What a singular lack of morale and what a strange conclusion for a naval officer!

A comparison of the relative strength of the two squadrons about to be engaged may easily be made (which, however, does not mention some twenty-five small gunboats not brought into action, but which might have been transformed into torpedo-launches for night attack or defence of the entrance to the bay).

In action we had six ships to the Spaniards' seven, but we were superior in class of vessel and in armaments. We had fifty-three guns above the 4-inch calibre and the Spaniards thirty-one; fifty-six guns under 4-inch to the Spaniards' forty-four; eight torpedo-tubes to the Spaniards' thirteen; officers and men, 1,456 to the Spaniards' 1,447. It will be seen that, in keeping with American naval precedent, we were much more heavily armed in ratio to our personnel than the enemy. Neither side had any armored ships and both fought with brown powder. The fact that we were not armored made the heavy guns of the Spanish batteries, if they were brought to bear on us, a serious consideration.

As for the batteries noted in the *Olympia's* official log as having fired on us during the battle and verified after the surrender, they were two 6.3-inch muzzle-loaders and three 9.4-inch from the Manila batteries; two 5.9-inch from the Sangley Point battery; and one 4.7-inch from the Canacao battery. All except the two muzzle-loaders mentioned were modern breech-loading rifles.

As we cruised southward after leaving Mirs Bay, the weather was such that we could continue the preparation of crews and ships for action by drilling the men again in battle drills and their stations in case of fire, and for repairing injuries to the ships by shell-fire, while we built barricades of canvas and iron to shield the gun crews, protected the sides and ammunition hoists with lengths of heavy sheet chain faked up and down over a buffer of awnings, and threw overboard much extra wood-work which, while essential to comfort in time of peace, might become ignited in an engagement. Had the Spaniards disposed of their wood-work their ships would have burned less fiercely both at Manila and at Santiago. At night all lights were extinguished except one on the taffrail to denote position, and even this was so carefully screened as to be visible only from directly astern. The presence of the squadron on the waters was denoted alone by the dark forms of the ships and the breaking of phosphorescence at their bows and in the wake of their propellers.

Now, Consul Williams, when he came on board just before our departure from Mirs Bay, had brought news which was anything but encouraging. It upset my preconceived ideas, as I had counted upon fighting in Manila Bay. Just as the consul was leaving Manila he had learned of the sailing of the Spanish squadron for Subig Bay. Thus Admiral Montojo at the last moment seemed to have realized the strategic advantage of Subig over Manila, which we had hoped he would fail to do. When we sighted land near Cape Bolinao early on the morning of May 30, the *Boston* and *Concord* were signalled to proceed at full speed to reconnoitre Subig Bay.

Later, some of our officers declared that they heard the sound of heavy guns firing in the direction which the *Boston* and *Concord* had taken. Though I could not hear any firing myself, I sent the *Baltimore* to support the two scouts if necessary, and to await the rest of the squadron at the entrance to the bay.

As the day broke the coast of Luzon, which had been indefinitely seen on the horizon, appeared clearly in outline. We kept at a distance of three or four miles as we cruised slowly, keeping our speed to that of our slowest vessel, the collier *Nanshan*. In the hope of obtaining news we overhauled some of the fishing-boats in our path, but they knew nothing of the movements of the Spanish squadron. At 3.30 in the afternoon the three ships which had been sent ahead as scouts were sighted at the entrance to the bay. I waited very anxiously for their signal. When it came, saying that no enemy had been found, I was deeply relieved. I remember that I said to Lamberton, "Now we have them."

The distance from Subig Bay to Corregidor was only thirty miles. As we had decided to run past the batteries at the entrance to Manila Bay under cover of darkness, we slowed down and finally stopped. All the commanding officers were signalled to come on board the flag-ship. When they were in my cabin, and Wildes, of the *Boston,* and Walker, of the *Concord,* had corroborated in person the import of their signals that there were no Spanish vessels in the vicinity, I said:

"We shall enter Manila Bay to-night and you will follow the motions and movements of the flag-ship, which will lead."

There was no discussion and no written order and no further particulars as to preparation. For every preparation that had occurred to us in our councils had already been made. I knew that I could depend upon my captains and that they understood my purposes. My position in relation to my captains and to all my officers and crews was happy, indeed, by contrast with that of the unfortunate Montojo, who tells in his official report of how, upon arriving at Subig Bay on the night of April 25 with six of his ships, he found that none of his orders for the defence of the bay had been executed. The four 5.9-inch guns which should have been mounted a month previously were lying on the shore; yet in landing-drill our men have often mounted guns of equal calibre on shore in twenty-four hours. Aside from the planting of the mines which have been mentioned and the sinking of three old hulks at the eastern entrance of the bay, nothing had been done.

Soon after his arrival at Subig on the 28th Admiral Montojo received the following cable from the Spanish consul at Hong Kong:

"The enemy's squadron sailed at 2 P. M. from Mirs Bay, and according to reliable accounts they sailed for Subig to destroy our squadron and then will go to Manila."

A council of war was held, and the captains of the Spanish ships unanimously voted to return to Manila rather than, as their own consul had expressed it, be destroyed where they were. So on the morning of the 29th the Spanish squadron steamed back to Cavite. The attitude of the commanding officers must have been the attitude of the personnel. Any force in such a state of mind is already half beaten. The morale of his squadron, as revealed by Montojo's report after the battle, bore out my reasoning before the war had begun, that everywhere the Spaniards would stand upon the defensive. This must mean defeat in the end, and the more aggressive and prompt our action the smaller would be our losses and the sooner peace would come.

When my captains, after receiving their final orders on board the flag-ship, had returned to their own ships, the squadron resumed its course to Corregidor. As the gloom of night gradually shut out the details of the coast, the squadron steamed quietly on toward the entrance of Manila Bay with all lights masked and the gun crews at the guns. By degrees the high land on either side loomed up out of the darkness, while the flag-ship headed for Boca Grande, which was the wider but comparatively little used channel. A light shower passed over about eleven o'clock and heavy, cumulus clouds drifting across the sky from time to time obscured the new moon. The landmarks and islands were, however, fairly visible, while compass bearings for regulating our course could readily be observed.

It was thirty-six years since, as executive officer of the *Mississippi,* I was first under fire in the passage of Forts Jackson and St. Philip under Farragut, and thirty-five years since, as executive officer, I had lost my ship in the attempted passage of the batteries of Port Hudson. Then, as now, we were dependent upon the screen of darkness to get by successfully, but then I was a subordinate and now the supreme responsibility was mine.

If the guns commanding the entrance were well served, there was danger of damage to my squadron before it engaged the enemy's squadron. If the Spaniards had shown enterprise in the use of the materials which they possessed, then we might have expected a heavy fire from the shore batteries. One who had military knowledge did not have to wait for the developments of the Russo-Japanese War to know how quickly modern guns of high velocity and low trajectory may be emplaced and how effective they may be, when fired from a stationary position, against so large a target as a ship. Had the batteries search-lights they could easily locate us, while we could locate them only by the flash of their guns.

When we were ten miles from Boca Grande we judged, as we saw signal lights flash, that we had already been sighted either by small vessels acting as scouts or by land lookouts. El Fraile was passed by the flag-ship at a distance of half a mile and was utilized as a point of departure for the course up the bay clear of the San Nicolas Shoals. When El Fraile bore due south (magnetic) the course was changed to northeast by north. We were not surprised to find the usual lights on Corregidor and Caballo Islands and the San Nicolas Shoals extinguished, as this was only a natural precaution on the part of the Spaniards.

There were no vessels, so far as we could see, cruising off the entrance, no dash of torpedo-launches which might have been expected, no sign of life beyond the signalling on shore until the rear of the column, steaming at full speed, was between Corregidor and El Fraile.

As we watched the walls of darkness for the first gun-flash, every moment of our progress brought its relief, and now we began to hope that we should get by without being fired on at all. But about ten minutes after midnight, when all except our rear ships had cleared it, the El Fraile battery opened with a shot that passed between the *Petrel* and the *Raleigh.* The *Boston, Concord, Raleigh,* and *McCulloch* returned the fire with a few shots. One 8-inch shell from the *Boston* seemed to be effective. After firing three times El Fraile was silent. There was no demonstration whatever from the Caballo battery, with its three 6-inch modern rifles, no explosion of mines, and no other resistance. We were safely within the bay. The next step was to locate the Spanish squadron and engage it.

Afterward we heard various explanations of why we were not given a warmer reception as we passed through. Some of the officers in the El Fraile battery said that their dilatoriness in opening fire was due to the fact that their men were ashore at Punta Lasisi and could not get off to their guns in time after they heard of the squadron's approach. An eye-witness on Corregidor informed me that our squadron was perfectly visible as it was passing through the entrance, but for some extraordinary reason the commanding officer gave no orders to the batteries to open fire.

Perhaps the enemy thought that he had done all that was necessary by cutting off the usual lights on Corregidor and Caballo Islands and San Nicolas Shoals for guiding mariners, and he expected that without pilots and without any knowledge of the waters we would not be guilty of such a foolhardy attempt as entering an unlighted channel at midnight.

Once through the entrance, as I deemed it wise to keep moving in order not to be taken by surprise when the ships had no headway, and as, at the same time, I did not wish to reach our destination before we had sufficient daylight to show us the position of the Spanish ships, the speed of the squadron was reduced to four knots, while we headed toward the city of Manila. In the meantime the men were allowed to snatch a little sleep at their guns; but at four o'clock coffee was served to them, and so eager were they that there was no need of any orders to insure readiness for the work to come.

Signal lights, rockets, and beacon lights along the shore, now that we were sure of grappling with the enemy, no longer concerned us. We waited for dawn and the first sight of the Spanish squadron, which I had rather expected would be at the anchorage off the city of Manila. This seemed naturally the strong position for Admiral Montojo to take up, as he would then have the powerful Manila battery, mounting the guns which have already been enumerated, to support him. But the admiral stated in his report that he had avoided this position on account of the resultant injury which the city might have received if the battle had been fought in close proximity to it.

The *Nanshan* and *Zafiro,* as there was no reserve ammunition for either to carry, had been sent, with the *McCulloch,* into an unfrequented part of the bay in order that they should sustain no injury and that they might not hamper the movements of the fighting-ships. When we saw that there were only merchantmen at the Manila anchorage, the squadron, led by the flag-ship, gradually changed its course, swinging around on the arc of a large circle leading toward the city and making a kind of countermarch, as it were, until headed in the direction of Cavite. This brought the ships within two or three miles of shore, with a distance of four hundred yards between ships, in the following order: *Olympia* (flag), *Baltimore, Raleigh, Petrel, Concord,* and *Boston.*

About 5.05 the Luneta and two other Manila batteries opened fire. Their shots passed well over the vessels. It was estimated that some had a range of seven miles. Only the *Boston* and *Concord* replied. Each sent two shells at the Luneta battery. The other vessels reserved their fire, having in mind my caution that, in the absence of a full supply of ammunition, the amount we had was too precious to be wasted when we were seven thousand miles from our base. My captains understood that the Spanish ships were our objective and not the shore fortifications of a city that would be virtually ours as soon as our squadron had control of Manila Bay.

With the coming of broad daylight we finally sighted the Spanish vessels formed in an irregular crescent in front of Cavite. The *Olympia* headed toward them, and in answer to her signal to close up, the distance between our ships was reduced to two hundred yards. The western flank of the Spanish squadron was protected by Cavite Peninsula and the Sangley Point battery, while its eastern flank rested in the shoal water off Las Pinas.

The Spanish line of battle was formed by the *Reina Cristina* (flag), *Castilla, Don Juan de Austria, Don Antonio de Ulloa, Isla de Luzón, Isla de Cuba,* and *Marqués del Deuro.*

The *Velasco* and *Lezo* were on the other (southern) side of Cavite Point, and it is claimed by the Spaniards that they took no part in the action. Some of the vessels in the Spanish battle-line were under way, and others were moored so as to bring their broadside batteries to bear to the best advantage. The *Castilla* was protected by heavy iron lighters filled with stone.

Before me now was the object for which we had made our arduous preparations, and which, indeed, must ever be the supreme test of a naval officer's career. I felt confident of the outcome, though I had no thought that victory would be won at so slight a cost to our own side. Confidence was expressed in the very precision with which the dun, war-colored hulls of the squadron followed in column behind the flag-ship, keeping their distance excellently. All the guns were pointed constantly at the enemy, while the men were at their stations waiting the word. There was no break in the monotone of the engines save the mechanical voice of the leadsman or an occasional low-toned command by the quartermaster at the conn, or the roar of a Spanish shell. The Manila batteries continued their inaccurate fire, to which we paid no attention.

The misty haze of the tropical dawn had hardly risen when at 5.15, at long range, the Cavite forts and Spanish squadron opened fire. Our course was not one leading directly toward the enemy, but a converging one, keeping him on our starboard bow. Our speed was eight knots and our converging course and ever-varying position must have confused the Spanish gunners. My assumption that the Spanish fire would be hasty and inaccurate proved correct.

So far as I could see, none of our ships was suffering any damage, while, in view of my limited ammunition supply, it was my plan not to open fire until we were within effective range, and then to fire as rapidly as possible with all of our guns.

At 5.40, when we were within a distance of 5,000 yards (two and one-half miles), I turned to Captain Gridley and said:

"You may fire when you are ready, Gridley."

While I remained on the bridge with Lamberton, Brumby, and Stickney, Gridley took his station in the conning-tower and gave the order to the battery. The very first gun to speak was an 8-inch from the forward turret of the *Olympia*, and this was the signal for all the other ships to join the action.

At about the time that the Spanish ships were first sighted, 5.06, two submarine mines were exploded between our squadron and Cavite, some two miles ahead of our column. On account of the distance, I remarked to Lamberton:

"Evidently the Spaniards are already rattled."

However, they explained afterward that the premature explosions were due to a desire to clear a space in which their ships might manœuvre.

At one time a torpedo-launch made an attempt to reach the *Olympia*, but she was sunk by the guns of the secondary battery and went down bow first, and another yellow-colored launch flying the Spanish colors ran out, heading for the *Olympia*, but after being disabled she was beached to prevent her sinking.

When the flag-ship neared the five-fathom curve off Cavite she turned to the westward, bringing her port batteries to bear on the enemy, and, followed by the squadron, passed along the Spanish line until north of and only some fifteen hundred yards distant from the Sangley Point battery, when she again turned and headed back to the eastward, thus giving the squadron an opportunity to use their port and starboard batteries alternately and to cover with their fire all the Spanish ships, as well as the Cavite and Sangley Point batteries. While I was regulating the course of the squadron, Lieutenant Calkins was verifying our position by cross-bearings and by the lead.

Three runs were thus made from the eastward and two from the westward, the length of each run averaging two miles and the ships being turned each time with port helm. Calkins found that there was in reality deeper water than shown on the chart, and when he reported the fact to me, inasmuch as my object was to get as near as possible to the enemy without grounding our own vessels, the fifth run past the Spaniards was farther inshore than any preceding run. At the nearest point to the enemy our range was only two thousand yards.

There had been no cessation in the rapidity of fire maintained by our whole squadron, and the effect of its concentration, owing to the fact that our ships were kept so close together, was smothering, particularly upon the two largest ships, the *Reina Cristina* and *Castilla*. The *Don Juan de Austria* first and then the *Reina Cristina* made brave and desperate attempts to charge the *Olympia*, but becoming the target for all our batteries they turned and ran back. In this sortie the *Reina Cristina* was raked by an 8-inch shell, which is said to have put out of action some twenty men and to have completely destroyed her steering-gear. Another shell in her forecastle killed or wounded all the members of the crews of four rapid-fire guns; another set fire to her after orlop; another killed or disabled nine men on her poop; another carried away her mizzen-mast, bringing down the ensign and the admiral's flag, both of which were replaced; another exploded in the after ammunition-room; and still another exploded in the sick-bay, which was already filled with wounded.

When she was raised from her muddy bed, five years later, eighty skeletons were found in the sick-bay and fifteen shot holes in the hull; while the many hits mentioned in Admiral Montojo's report, and his harrowing description of the shambles that his flag-ship had become when he was finally obliged to leave her, shows what execution was done to her upper works. Her loss was one hundred and fifty killed and ninety wounded, seven of these being officers. Among the killed was her valiant captain, Don Luis Cadarso, who, already wounded, finally met his death while bravely directing the rescue of his men from the burning and sinking vessel.

Though in the early part of the action our firing was not what I should have liked it to be, it soon steadied down, and by the time the *Reina Cristina* steamed toward us it was satisfactorily accurate. The *Castilla* fared little better than the *Reina Cristina*. All except one of her guns was disabled, she was set on fire by our shells, and finally abandoned by her crew after they had sustained a loss of twenty-three killed and eighty wounded. The *Don Juan de Austria* was badly damaged and on fire, the *Isla de Luzón* had three guns dismounted, and the *Marqués del Duero* was also in a bad way. Admiral Montojo, finding his flag-ship no longer manageable, half her people dead or wounded, her guns useless and the ship on fire, gave the order to abandon and sink her, and transferred his flag to the *Isla de Cuba* shortly after seven o'clock.

Victory was already ours, though we did not know it. Owing to the smoke over the Spanish squadron there were no visible signs of the execution wrought by our guns when we started upon our fifth run past the enemy. We were keeping up our rapid fire, and the flag-ship was opposite the centre of the Spanish line, when, at 7.35, the captain of the *Olympia* made a report to me which was as startling as it was unexpected. This was to the effect that on board the *Olympia* there remained only fifteen rounds per gun for the 5-inch battery.

It was a most anxious moment for me. So far as I could see, the Spanish squadron was as intact as ours. I had reason to believe that their supply of ammunition was as ample as ours was limited.

Therefore, I decided to withdraw temporarily from action for a redistribution of ammunition if necessary. For I knew that fifteen rounds of 5-inch ammunition could be shot away in five minutes. But even as we were steaming out of range the distress of the Spanish ships became evident. Some of them were perceived to be on fire and others were seeking protection behind Cavite Point. The *Don Antonio de Ulloa*, however, still retained her position at Sangley Point, where she had been moored. Moreover, the Spanish fire, with the exception of the Manila batteries, to which we had paid little attention, had ceased entirely. It was clear that we did not need a very large supply of ammunition to finish our morning's task; and happily it was found that the report about the *Olympia's* 5-inch ammunition had been incorrectly transmitted. It was that fifteen rounds had been fired per gun, not that only fifteen rounds remained.

Feeling confident of the outcome, I now signalled that the crews, who had had only a cup of coffee at 4 A. M., should have their breakfast. The public at home, on account of this signal, to which was attributed a nonchalance that had never occurred to me, reasoned that breakfast was the real reason for our withdrawing from action. Meanwhile, I improved the opportunity to have the commanding officers report on board the flag-ship.

There had been such a heavy flight of shells over us that each captain, when he arrived, was convinced that no other ship had had such good luck as his own in being missed by the enemy's fire, and expected the others to have both casualties and damages to their ships to report. But fortune was as pronouncedly in our favor at Manila as it was later at Santiago. To my gratification not a single life had been lost, and considering that we would rather measure the importance of an action by the scale of its conduct than by the number of casualties we were immensely happy. The concentration of our fire immediately we were within telling range had given us an early advantage in demoralizing the enemy, which has ever been the prime factor in naval battles. In the War of 1812 the losses of the *Constitution* were slight when she overwhelmed the *Guerrière* and in the Civil War the losses of the *Kearsarge* were slight when she made a shambles of the *Alabama*. On the *Baltimore* two officers (Lieutenant F. W. Kellogg and Ensign N. E. Irwin) and six men were slightly wounded. None of our ships had been seriously hit, and every one was still ready for immediate action.

In detail the injuries which we had received from the Spanish fire were as follows:

The *Olympia* was hulled five times and her rigging was cut in several places. One six-pound projectile struck immediately under the position where I was standing. The *Baltimore* was hit five times. The projectile which wounded two officers and six men pursued a most erratic course. It entered the ship's side forward of the starboard gangway, and just above the line of the main deck, passed through the hammock-netting, down through the deck planks and steel deck, bending the deck beam in a wardroom state-room, thence upward through the after engine-room coaming, over against the cylinder of a 6-inch gun, disabling the gun, struck and exploded a box of three-pounder ammunition, hit an iron ladder, and finally, spent, dropped on deck. The *Boston* had four unimportant hits, one causing a fire which was soon extinguished, and the *Petrel* was struck once.

At 11.16 A. M. we stood in to complete our work. There remained to oppose us, however, only the batteries and the gallant little *Ulloa*. Both opened fire as we advanced. But the contest was too unequal to last more than a few minutes. Soon the *Ulloa*, under our concentrated fire, went down valiantly with her colors flying.

The battery at Sangley Point was well served, and several times reopened fire before being finally silenced. Had this battery possessed its four other 6-inch guns which Admiral Montojo had found uselessly lying on the beach at Subig, our ships would have had many more casualties to report. Happily for us, the guns of this battery had been so mounted that they could be laid only for objects beyond the range of two thousand yards. As the course of our ships led each time within this range, the shots passed over and beyond them. Evidently the artillerists, who had so constructed their carriages that the muzzles of the guns took against the sill of the embrasure for any range under two thousand yards, thought it out of the question that an enemy would venture within this distance.

The *Concord* was sent to destroy a large transport, the *Mindanao,* which had been beached near Bacoor, and the *Petrel,* whose light draught would permit her to move in shallower water than the other vessels of the squadron, was sent into the harbor of Cavite to destroy any ships that had taken refuge there. The *Mindanao* was set on fire and her valuable cargo destroyed. Meanwhile, the *Petrel* gallantly performed her duty, and after a few shots from her 6-inch guns the Spanish flag on the government building was hauled down and a white flag hoisted. Admiral Montojo had been wounded, and had taken refuge on shore with his remaining officers and men; his loss was three hundred and eighty-one of his officers and crew, and there was no possibility of further resistance.

At 12.30 the *Petrel* signalled the fact of the surrender, and the firing ceased. But the Spanish vessels were not yet fully destroyed. Therefore, the executive officer of the *Petrel,* Lieutenant E. M. Hughes, with a whale-boat and a crew of only seven men, boarded and set fire to the *Don Juan de Austria, Isla de Cuba, Isla de Luzón, General Lezo, Coreo,* and *Marqués del Duero,* all of which had been abandoned in shallow water and left scuttled by their deserting crews. This was a courageous undertaking, as these vessels were supposed to have been left with trains to their magazines and were not far from the shore, where there were hundreds of Spanish soldiers and sailors, all armed and greatly excited. The *Manila,* an armed transport, which was found uninjured after having been beached by the Spaniards, was therefore spared. Two days later she was easily floated, and for many years did good service as a gunboat. The little *Petrel* continued her work until 5.20 P. M., when she rejoined the squadron, towing a long string of tugs and launches, to be greeted by volleys of cheers from every ship.

The order to capture or destroy the Spanish squadron had been executed to the letter. Not one of its fighting-vessels remained afloat. That night I wrote in my diary: "Reached Manila at daylight. Immediately engaged the Spanish ships and batteries at Cavite. Destroyed eight of the former, including the *Reina Cristina* and *Castilla*. Anchored at noon off Manila."

As soon as we had sunk the *Ulloa* and silenced the batteries at Sangley Point, the *Olympia,* followed by the *Baltimore* and *Raleigh,* while the *Concord* and *Petrel* were carrying out their orders, started for the anchorage off the city. The Manila batteries, which had kept up such a persistent though impotent firing all the early part of the day, were now silent and made no attempt to reopen as our ships approached the city.

Consul Williams was sent on board a British ship moored close inshore near the mouth of the Pasig River, with instructions to request her captain to be the bearer of a message to the Spanish captain-general. This message was taken ashore at 2 P. M., in the form of a note to the British consul, Mr. E. H. Rawson-Walker, who, after the departure of Mr. Williams, had assumed charge of our archives and interests, requesting him to see the captain-general, and to say to him, on my behalf, that if another shot were fired at our ships from the Manila batteries we should destroy the city. Moreover, if there were any torpedo-boats in the Pasig River they must be surrendered, and if we were allowed to transmit messages by the cable to Hong Kong the captain-general would also be permitted to use it.

Assurance came promptly that the forts would not fire at our squadron unless it was evident that a disposition of our ships to bombard the city was being made. This assurance, which was kept even during the land attack upon the city, some three months later, led me to drop anchor for the first time since we had entered the bay. From the moment that the captain-general accepted my terms the city was virtually surrendered, and I was in control of the situation, subject to my government's orders for the future. I had established a base seven thousand miles from home which I might occupy indefinitely. As I informed the secretary of the navy in my cable of May 4, our squadron controlled the bay and could take the city at any time. The only reason for awaiting the arrival of troops before demanding its surrender was the lack of sufficient force to occupy it.

In answer to the other points of my message, the captain-general, Don Basilio Augustin Davila, said that he knew of no torpedo-boats in the river, but that if there were any his honor would not allow him to surrender them. As there were none, he was quite safe in making this reservation, which did not affect the main fact, that his capital was under our guns. He refused my request about the cable. As a result he found himself cut off from all telegraphic communication with the outside world on the next morning, because I directed the *Zafiro* to cut the cable.

As the sun set on the evening of May 1, crowds of people gathered along the water-front, gazing at the American squadron. They climbed on the ramparts of the very battery that had fired on us in the morning. The *Olympia's* band, for their benefit, played "La Paloma" and other Spanish airs, and while the sea-breeze wafted the strains to their ears the poor colonel of artillery who had commanded the battery, feeling himself dishonored by his disgraceful failure, shot himself through the head.

During the mid-watch that night a steam-launch was discovered coming off from Manila. The crews went to quarters and search-lights and guns were trained upon her until she approached the *Olympia,* when she was allowed to come alongside. A Spanish official was on board. He desired permission to proceed to Corregidor to instruct the commanding officer that none of the batteries at the entrance to the bay were to fire on our ships when passing in or out. Permission was granted and he was told to return the following morning. When he came he was put on board the *Raleigh,* which was sent, with the *Baltimore* as escort, to demand the surrender of all the defences at the entrance to the bay. The surrender was made and the garrisons disarmed. The next day I had the *Boston* and *Concord* land parties, who disabled the guns and brought their breech-plugs off to the ships. All the ammunition found, as it was of a calibre unsuited to any of our guns, was destroyed.

Meanwhile, to my surprise, on the morning of May 2, the Spanish flag was seen to be again flying over the Cavite arsenal. Captain Lamberton was sent at once to inquire what it meant, and to demand a formal surrender. He went over to Cavite in the *Petrel,* and upon leaving her to go on shore gave instructions that in case he did not return within an hour she was to open fire on the arsenal. Upon landing he found the Spanish soldiers and sailors under arms, and in answer to his inquiry, what was meant by this and by the hoisting of the Spanish colors, he was informed by the Spanish commandant, Captain Sostoa, that the colors had been lowered the day before only as token of a temporary truce. Captain Lamberton's reply to this evasive excuse was an ultimatum that if the white flag were not hoisted by noon he would open fire.

Captain Sostoa then asked for time in which to refer the matter to Madrid, and this being refused, for time to refer it to the authorities at Manila. But he was informed that only an unconditional surrender of officers, men, and arms would be considered. Captain Lamberton then returned to the *Petrel,* and at 11.35 the white flag was hoisted by the order of Admiral Montojo; and it was this order, peculiarly enough, and not the loss of his squadron, that led to his court-martial upon his return to Spain. Shortly afterward all the Spanish officers and men evacuated the place. Possibly imperfect knowledge of each other's language by Captain Lamberton and Captain Sostoa led to a misunderstanding of our terms by the Spaniards. In a way this was fortunate for us, as we were in no position to take care of prisoners. We had what we needed: possession of the arsenal, with its machinery, workshops, and supplies, as a base for future operations.

To us it seems almost incomprehensible that the guns of Caballo and Corregidor and Punta Restinga failed to fire on our ships; that when our vessels were hampered by the narrow waters of the entrance there was no night attack by the many small vessels possessed by the Spaniards; and that during the action neither the *Isla de Cuba* nor the *Isla de Luzón,* each of them protected by an armored deck and fitted with two torpedo-tubes, made any attempt to torpedo our ships.

Naturally, the Spanish government attempted to make a scapegoat of poor Admiral Montojo, the victim of their own shortcomings and maladministration, and he was soon afterward ordered home and brought before a court-martial. It was some satisfaction to know that a factor in influencing the court in concluding that he had fulfilled his duty in a courageous manner was a letter from me testifying to his gallantry in the action, which I was glad to give in response to his request.

Tank Fighting in Libya

BY

ALAN MOOREHEAD

ON THE night of Nov. 17 a line of squat British Army trucks bounced over the camel's-thorn to the barbed-wire fence that divides Egypt from Libya. Engineers in greatcoats and battledress stepped down briskly in the darkness and began snipping some 20 holes in the 10-ft. thickness of the wire. There was no need for silence. A storm of extraordinary violence was sweeping across the desert and forked lightning played above the fence as the men sheared through the last strands dividing them from Libya.

Before the morning, while the same wild storm was rushing from the sea and the men read into it a portent of what was to come, the British Army passed through the broken fence into Libya. At the head rode the force of U. S.-built tanks that had never seen battle. Many of the crews were old in the desert—British youngsters of 20, maybe a little more, who had fought their way through to the coast beyond Bengasi last winter and held the southern desert flank ever since. But their vehicles were brand new—M3 light tanks with a brand new 37-mm. gun, new armor, new airplane motors that drove them forward over the rough gravel and salt-bush flats at an even noisy 10 m.p.h. Each tank commander sat up high in his open hatch holding his communication mouthpiece in his hand. The men's bedding and camping gear strapped on the open sides soaked steadily in the rain. Each vehicle bore its striped regimental colors with perhaps some painted name above like "Gladys," "Phyllis," "Betty." Each flew its pennants from its wireless antennae that waved about like an ear of corn in the wind.

Riding close upon his leading squadrons and ahead of the scattered supply columns following behind went the brigadier in command—a huge man with a strong dark face, a hawk nose, a black tank corps beret on his head and a flash of red on the lapels of his tunic. Like most of the others he had wound a khaki-woolen scarf round his neck and he gave his orders over the radio quietly, quickly, incessantly. By midday, when the clouds were breaking, the little brigade was well into Libya. Enemy outposts that had watched the advance had disappeared over the horizon to break the news to General Erwin Rommel at his headquarters near the coast. All the rest of that day U. S. tanks rode on into an empty enemy desert, meeting no opposition, sending scouts prying ahead but finding nothing.

From: *Life Magazine.* Copyright 1941 by London Daily Express.

The British plan was simple in structure but complex in detail. Four concentric rings were being laid round the enemy positions in the triangle of open desert between Tobruk, Fort Maddalena and Bardia. Wheeling northwest out of Egypt, two inner rings were closing upon Axis border pockets around Salûm, Bardia, Fort Capuzzo and Sidi Omár. The fourth and southernmost ring was describing a great arc from Maddalena northwest toward Tobruk. Stiffening and protecting these three layers like a band of metal through a slab of concrete went the British armored forces. This mass of hundreds of tanks, 25-pounder guns, armored fighting vehicles, armored cars, anti-tank guns, machine gun and ack-ack units was pledged to one essential job—to seek out Rommel's two armored divisions and destroy them. No one that first day knew where Rommel would strike or how. But lest he should choose not to strike at all and fall back westward, British tanks ran a cordon around him. It too reached from Tobruk to Maddalena. It was a host of thousands upon thousands of vehicles stretching across 100 miles of desert and with every hour expanding and changing as many thousands more came pouring through the gaps in the wire.

U. S.-built tanks took up position near Sidi Omár and in the evening, when the boys quietly boiled their tea and pried open their tins of bully, it was pretty certain that Rommel would be brought to battle on the morrow. Yet still, on the morning of the 19th, hardly a shot had been fired. I drove up to a tanks' supply column and was talking with Colonel Bonar Fellers, the American military attaché from Cairo. Then it came. For ten miles in the east between us and Egypt the horizon lit up with gun bursts. Some thought it was bombing and dispersed for shelter; the others thought it was artillery shooting on Sidi Omár. Most of them clambered into their vehicles and peered at the smoke that was gradually gathering itself into a continuous curtain on the horizon. Then clearly it sounded—that dry quick coughing that is a tank gun and nothing else. The war was starting. Rommel had come south with more than 100 of his medium tanks and the American "lights" had pitched into him.

Unless you are in a tank yourself, you don't see anything very clearly in a tank battle. The enemy appears as just a line of tiny silhouettes where the sky hits the desert, dark silhouettes shaped exactly like distant battleships, each one spitting out a yellow flash from time to time. Your own tanks, weaving in to attack disappear behind the wake of their own dust. Within a few minutes it is just so much smoke, dust, flame and noise. That is what happened now and what I have seen half a dozen times since.

"There they come," yells someone on his radio blower. Listening on a headquarters communication vehicle you hear the tanks talking to one another right in the battle. You hear:

"Get to hell out of it Bill so that I can get at this ————. Easy boy, easy boy, now at him. . . . Bill, you ————, you're blocking my way again. . . . Look out, right behind you." And through it all you hear the bursting of shells, the tearing and screaming of the tank treads, the gears grunting into reverse and forward. No one, remember, who wasn't right in this first fight had any clear idea of what was going on. We had to wait and just watch that pall of battle smoke widen, darken and move westward into the sun.

Then a staff major came out of it and told us: "They came right at us off the rising ground with the sun behind their backs. Right smack at us. They opened up with their 50-mm. gun at 1,500 yd.—much too far for our 37's. So the boys just went into the barrage hull down at 40 m.p.h. to get into range. Then they mixed it. I tell you no one on God's earth can follow what's going on. The boys are just weaving in and out between the Jerries, passing right through them, then turning and coming back into it again. They're passing 50 and 60 yd. apart and firing at point-blank range. As soon as you see a Swastika you just let fly. There's everything in the air—tracers, shells, bullets, ricochets, incendiaries and bits of red-hot metal whanging off the burning tanks. Some of the tanks are blowing right up into the air, their petrol exploding, their ammunition popping off in every direction."

R. A. F. bombers and fighters swept over but held their fire because they could not sort the battle out. Every few minutes a tank would stay out of the battle, rush to a supply vehicle, fling in petrol and shells, then zigzag into the arena again. The battle died down little by little as dusk fell, a blue-green dusk lightened in the east by the red glare of burning tanks. In the darkness tanks called to one another, found their friends, felt their way back to their own lines bringing what wounded they could. Other wounded walked back or crawled; or merely lay there in the dark with the acrid smell of cordite round them. And the piercing desert cold advanced degree by degree through the night.

The Nazis held the battlefield. Up from their lines flew star shells and Very lights in green, red, purple. Before midnight their breakdown wagons were there hooking on to partial wrecks, dragging guns and broken tracks away. The Germans were not unkind to our wounded. They took their rations but gave them hot tea, covered some with blankets, bandaged one or two sufficiently to give them a 50–50 chance of living till the next day. Many were left lying on the wet sand through the night. Marvelously, a British squadron leader, with both legs gone, survived till we picked him up in the morning. He described how the Nazis were round him all night salvaging their gear. Through the night we labored, gathered our unarmored vehicles into a close bunch, posted tanks in a ring outside.

Riding out at 5 o'clock in the morning, we watched the battle begin afresh when it was still only possible to see 100 yd. British and German tanks that had lain close to one another through the night simply aimed and blitzed off at one another again, though it was almost too cold to bear the touch of the metal. At 9 a.m. Rommel suddenly broke off and veered westward. He had lost some 30 tanks. We had learned too, at heavy cost, some of the great lessons that have governed this desert tank fighting ever since. Hear them out of the mouth of a young Scots sergeant, "We have got to get 50- and 75-mm. guns like the Germans. They start firing at 1,500 yd. and we have got to come right in to 800 yd. before our '37' can make any reply. But 'Honeys' (the group's word for American tanks) are wonderful on speed and weaving about. It would go fine if we could just get our 25-pounder artillery right up forward to cover our first advance and the R. A. F. to bomb."

The armor plating on the Honeys can take it. One German shell landing on the turret knocked the gun mounting into the British gunner's head but it didn't pierce. However, there were neat six-pounder holes through some of the turrets, close-range stuff, and the Nazi incendiaries seemed to burn the very metal off the tanks. Swiftly then on this second morning of the battle, the tank officers checked up, refilled the tanks and before nightfall they were swept into action again.

Rommel, binding most of his two armored divisions into one column, was moving westward across our line, feeling for a soft spot to burst through to the south. Finding none, he wheeled suddenly northwest and fell upon the extreme top of the British armored wing holding the Sidi Rezegh airfield near Tobruk. A U. S. force was launched in pursuit. They caught up with a Nazi supply column, demolished half of it and swept on again, fighting the German rearguard all the time.

Another night Honeys, expecting re-inforcement, sent out a staff officer to welcome a column of new tanks that hove up over the horizon. The newscomers were Germans. They charged straight through the brigade's headquarters, blowing up staff cars, petrol and food wagons while the British tanks scattered to new positions. There were moments of grim humor, too. A captured British officer tried to make a bolt for it when R. A. F. Blenheims came over bombing the German lines. A Nazi guard fired a burst from a tommy gun over his head. Out of a neighboring ditch popped a platoon of Italians with their hands up, surrendering. The Briton eventually, like hundreds of others, was recaptured. I met another officer who, with bad wounds, crawled 1,000 yd. out of the fight. Others have walked 20 or 30 miles to freedom, lying doggo by day, bluffing past challenges at night.

I stopped by a British concentration camp, just a few strands of barbed wire in the open desert, where I found 50 prisoners. The Germans kept to one group, the Italians to another. The Germans had nothing with them, the Italians all had bulging suitcases which they swiftly packed as they surrendered. A German captain from Saxony was bitter. "I've had no hot food since I was captured twelve hours ago," he told me. The men in the Honeys had not had any for three days. From that first fight nearly a fortnight ago they have never ceased fighting for more than an hour or two. Consider them now on this twelfth day of battle. There is not much left. The brigadier has lost his kit and wears a blanket wrapped round his legs. He sits on a wooden chair on top of his tank in which he has entered every engagement to direct his squadrons over the radio. He has eaten perhaps once daily, slept a few hours each night, been cut off half a dozen times and never remained more than two hours each night on one spot.

His tank is blackened with blast, chipped and holed with shell. He gives his men ten minutes to eat. At midday we attack again.

We cover the advance of infantry over last week's battlefield. It is a bare, utterly flat stretch of gravel now strewn with burnt-out tanks, a few crashed aircraft, and all the forlorn, pathetic wreckage of deadmen's clothing—bedding, mess tins, letters and papers. There is a litter of rifles which have been flung away, piles of British and German shell cases, tens of thousands of petrol tins, German water containers, broken tank tracks spilled along the sand like great lizards, up-ended trucks, biscuit and bully tins; and among all this the intermingled graveyards of British and German dead. These men were buried at the height of their battles beside their tanks. Most have a cross or some symbol like an empty cartridge belt placed by a comrade. As we pass, a half-demolished tank takes fire again. It fills the western sky with black smoke, its shells blowing off in mad, roaring volleys, its petrol sending up wave after wave of flame.

Two Messerschmitts come over machine-gunning briefly. British artillery starts up, sending its 25-pounders over our heads onto a formation of enemy tanks a mile or two ahead. R. A. F. bombers lay a 300-ft. curtain of dust and explosives across the battlefield. The Honeys deploy. The brigadier says quietly into his mouthpiece, "All right, go ahead." The British artillery covers the Honeys' first charge. It is working out the way the sergeant wanted it. The Nazis are coming on for a collision, dropping their shells among us already. One tank catches fire before it can get into action. Another hit below the turret lurches, stops, belches smoke. The wounded crew crawl out as a doctor in a little ambulance car races across. The Nazis are running right into our 25-pounder barrage and as far as the eye can see four more tanks, ours or theirs or both, are burning. In the last yellow light of the day the enemy seem to be veering east to open up a new attack. There is too much dust to see yet. I am told to go back for the night. The Honeys will stay there fighting in the dust as long as they can see.

Blowing Up a Train

BY

T. E. LAWRENCE

BLOWING up trains was an exact science when done deliberately, by a
sufficient party, with machine-guns in position. If scrambled at it might
become dangerous. The difficulty this time was that the available gunners
were Indians; who, though good men fed, were only half-men in cold and
hunger. I did not propose to drag them off without rations on an adventure
which might take a week. There was no cruelty in starving Arabs; they
would not die of a few days' fasting, and would fight as well as ever on
empty stomachs; while, if things got too difficult, there were the riding
camels to kill and eat; but the Indians, though Moslems, refused camel-
flesh on principle.

I explained these delicacies of diet. Ali at once said that it would be
enough for me to blow up the train, leaving him and the Arabs with him
to do their best to carry its wreck without machine-gun support. As, in this
unsuspecting district, we might well happen on a supply train, with civilians
or only a small guard of reservists aboard, I agreed to risk it. The decision
having been applauded, we sat down in a cloaked circle, to finish our
remaining food in a very late and cold supper (the rain had sodden the
fuel and made fire not possible) our hearts somewhat comforted by the
chance of another effort.

At dawn, with the unfit of the Arabs, the Indians moved away for Azrak,
miserably. They had started up country with me in hope of a really military
enterprise, and first had seen the muddled bridge, and now were losing this
prospective train. It was hard on them; and to soften the blow with honour
I asked Wood to accompany them. He agreed, after argument, for their
sakes; but it proved a wise move for himself, as a sickness which had been
troubling him began to show the early signs of penumonia.

The balance of us, some sixty men, turned back towards the railway.
None of them knew the country, so I led them to Minifir, where, with Zaal,
we had made havoc in the spring. The re-curved hill-top was an excellent
observation post, camp, grazing ground and way of retreat, and we sat
there in our old place till sunset, shivering and staring out over the immense plain which stretched map-like to the clouded peaks of Jebel Druse,
with Um el Jemal and her sister-villages like ink-smudges on it through the
rain.

In the first dusk we walked down to lay the mine. The rebuilt culvert of kilometre 172 seemed still the fittest place. While we stood by it there came a rumbling, and through the gathering darkness and mist a train suddenly appeared round the northern curve, only two hundred yards away. We scurried under the long arch and heard it roll overhead. This was annoying; but when the course was clear again, we fell to burying the charge. The evening was bitterly cold, with drifts of rain blowing down the valley.

The arch was solid masonry, of four metres span, and stood over a shingle water-bed which took its rise on our hill-top. The winter rains had cut this into a channel four feet deep, narrow and winding, which served us as an admirable approach till within three hundred yards of the line. There the gully widened out and ran straight towards the culvert, open to the sight of anyone upon the rails.

We hid the explosive carefully on the crown of the arch, deeper than usual, beneath a tie, so that the patrols could not feel its jelly softness under their feet. The wires were taken down the bank into the shingle bed of the watercourse, where concealment was quick; and up it as far as they could reach. Unfortunately, this was only sixty yards, for there had been difficulty in Egypt over insulated cable and no more had been available when our expedition started. Sixty yards was plenty for the bridge, but little for a train: however, the ends happened to coincide with a little bush about ten inches high, on the edge of the watercourse, and we buried them beside this very convenient mark. It was impossible to leave them joined up to the exploder in the proper way, since the spot was evident to the permanent way-patrols as they made their rounds.

Owing to the mud the job took longer than usual, and it was very nearly dawn before we finished. I waited under the draughty arch till day broke, wet and dismal, and then I went over the whole area of disturbance, spending another half-hour in effacing its every mark, scattering leaves and dead grass over it, and watering down the broken mud from a shallow rain-pool near. Then they waved to me that the first patrol was coming, and I went up to join the others.

Before I had reached them they came tearing down into their pre-arranged places, lining the watercourse and spurs each side. A train was coming from the north. Hamud, Feisal's long slave, had the exploder; but before he reached me a short train of closed box-wagons rushed by at speed. The rainstorms on the plain and the thick morning had hidden it from the eyes of our watchman until too late. This second failure saddened us further and Ali began to say that nothing would come right this trip. Such a statement held risk as prelude of the discovery of an evil eye present; so, to divert attention, I suggested new watching posts be sent far out, one to the ruins on the north, one to the great cairn of the southern crest.

The rest, having no breakfast, were to pretend not to be hungry. They all enjoyed doing this, and for a while we sat cheerfully in the rain, huddling against one another for warmth behind a breastwork of our streaming camels. The moisture made the animals' hair curl up like a fleece, so that they looked queerly dishevelled. When the rain paused, which it did frequently, a cold moaning wind searched out the unprotected parts of us very thoroughly. After a time we found our wetted shirts clammy and comfortless things. We had nothing to eat, nothing to do and nowhere to sit except on wet rock, wet grass or mud. However, this persistent weather kept reminding me that it would delay Allenby's advance on Jerusalem, and rob him of his great possibility. So large a misfortune to our lion was a half-encouragement for the mice. We would be partners into next year.

In the best circumstances, waiting for action was hard. To-day it was beastly. Even enemy patrols stumbled along without care, perfunctorily, against the rain. At last, near noon, in a snatch of fine weather, the watch-men on the south peak flagged their cloaks wildly in signal of a train. We reached our positions in an instant, for we had squatted the late hours on our heels in a streaming ditch near the line, so as not to miss another chance. The Arabs took cover properly. I looked back at their ambush from my firing point, and saw nothing but the grey hill-sides.

I could not hear the train coming, but trusted, and knelt ready for per-haps half an hour, when the suspense became intolerable, and I signalled to know what was up. They sent down to say it was coming very slowly, and was an enormously long train. Our appetites stiffened. The longer it was the more would be the loot. Then came word that it had stopped. It moved again.

Finally, near one o'clock, I heard it panting. The locomotive was evi-dently defective (all these wood-fired trains were bad), and the heavy load on the up-gradient was proving too much for its capacity. I crouched be-hind my bush, while it crawled slowly into view past the south cutting, and along the bank above my head towards the culvert. The first ten trucks were open trucks, crowded with troops. However, once again it was too late to choose, so when the engine was squarely over the mine I pushed down the handle of the exploder. Nothing happened. I sawed it up and down four times.

Still nothing happened; and I realized that it had gone out of order, and that I was kneeling on a naked bank, with a Turkish troop train crawling past fifty yards away. The bush, which had seemed a foot high, shrank smaller than a fig-leaf; and I felt myself the most distinct object in the country-side. Behind me was an open valley for two hundred yards to the cover where my Arabs were waiting, and wondering what I was at. It was impossible to make a bolt for it, or the Turks would step off the train and finish us. If I sat still, there might be just a hope of my being ignored as a casual Bedouin.

So there I sat, counting for sheer life, while eighteen open trucks, three box-waggons, and three officers' coaches dragged by. The engine panted slower and slower, and I thought every moment that it would break down. The troops took no great notice of me, but the officers were interested, and came out to the little platforms at the ends of their carriages, pointing and staring. I waved back at them, grinning nervously, and feeling an improbable shepherd in my Meccan dress, with its twisted golden circlet about my head. Perhaps the mud-stains, the wet and their ignorance made me accepted. The end of the brake van slowly disappeared into the cutting on the north.

As it went, I jumped up, buried my wires, snatched hold of the wretched exploder, and went like a rabbit uphill into safety. There I took breath and looked back to see that the train had finally stuck. It waited, about five hundred yards beyond the mine, for nearly an hour to get up a head of steam, while an officers' patrol came back and searched, very carefully, the ground where I had been seen sitting. However the wires were properly hidden: they found nothing: the engine plucked up heart again, and away they went.

Mifleh was past tears, thinking I had intentionally let the train through; and when the Serahin had been told the real cause they said 'bad luck is with us.' Historically they were right; but they meant it for a prophecy, so I made sarcastic reference to their courage at the bridge the week before, hinting that it might be a tribal preference to sit on camel-guard. At once there was uproar, the Serahin attacking me furiously, the Beni Sakhr defending. Ali heard the trouble, and came running.

When we had made it up the original despondency was half forgotten. Ali backed me nobly, though the wretched boy was blue with cold and shivering in an attack of fever. He gasped that their ancestor the Prophet had given to Sherifs the faculty of 'sight', and by it he knew that our luck was turning. This was comfort for them: my first instalment of good fortune came when in the wet, without other tool than my dagger, I got the box of the exploder open and persuaded its electrical gear to work properly once more.

We returned to our vigil by the wires, but nothing happened, and evening drew down with more squalls and beastliness, everybody full of grumbles. There was no train; it was too wet to light a cooking fire; our only potential food was camel. Raw meat did not tempt anyone that night; and so our beasts survived to the morrow.

Ali lay down on his belly, which position lessened the hunger-ache, trying to sleep off his fever. Khazen, Ali's servant, lent him his cloak for extra covering. For a spell I took Khazen under mine, but soon found it becoming crowded. So I left it to him and went downhill to connect up the exploder. Afterwards I spent the night there alone by the singing telegraph wires, hardly wishing to sleep, so painful was the cold. Nothing came all the long hours, and dawn, which broke wet, looked even uglier than usual. We were sick to death of Minifir, of railways, of train watching and wrecking, by now. I climbed up to the main body while the early patrol searched the railway. Then the day cleared a little. Ali awoke, much refreshed, and his new spirit cheered us. Hamud, the slave, produced some sticks which he had kept under his clothes by his skin all night. They were nearly dry. We shaved down some blasting gelatine, and with its hot flame got a fire going, while the Sukhur hurriedly killed a mangy camel, the best spared of our riding-beasts, and began with entrenching tools to hack it into handy joints.

Just at that moment the watchman on the north cried a train. We left the fire and made a breathless race of the six hundred yards down-hill to our old position. Round the bend, whistling its loudest, came the train, a splendid two-engined thing of twelve passenger coaches, travelling at top speed on the favouring grade. I touched off under the first driving wheel of the first locomotive, and the explosion was terrific. The ground spouted blackly into my face, and I was sent spinning, to sit up with the shirt torn to my shoulder and the blood dripping from long, ragged scratches on my left arm. Between my knees lay the exploder, crushed under a twisted sheet of sooty iron. In front of me was the scalded and smoking upper half of a man. When I peered through the dust and steam of the explosion the whole boiler of the first engine seemed to be missing.

I dully felt that it was time to get away to support; but when I moved, learnt that there was a great pain in my right foot, because of which I could only limp along, with my head swinging from the shock. Movement began to clear away this confusion, as I hobbled towards the upper valley, whence the Arabs were now shooting fast into the crowded coaches. Dizzily I cheered myself by repeating aloud in English, 'Oh, I wish this hadn't happened.'

When the enemy began to return our fire, I found myself much between the two. Ali saw me fall, and thinking that I was hard hit, ran out, with Turki and about twenty men of his servants and the Beni Sakhr, to help me. The Turks found their range and got seven of them in a few seconds. The others, in a rush, were about me—fit models, after their activity, for a sculptor. Their full white cotton drawers drawn in, bell-like, round their slender waists and ankles; their hairless brown bodies; and the love-locks plaited tightly over each temple in long horns, made them look like Russian dancers.

We scrambled back into cover together, and there, secretly, I felt myself over, to find I had not once been really hurt; though besides the bruises and cuts of the boiler-plate and a broken toe, I had five different bullet-grazes on me (some of them uncomfortably deep) and my clothes ripped to pieces.

From the watercourse we could look about. The explosion had destroyed the arched head of the culvert, and the frame of the first engine was lying beyond it, at the near foot of the embankment, down which it had rolled. The second locomotive had toppled into the gap, and was lying across the ruined tender of the first. Its bed was twisted. I judged them both beyond repair. The second tender had disappeared over the further side; and the first three waggons had telescoped and were smashed in pieces.

The rest of the train was badly derailed, with the listing coaches butted end to end at all angles, zigzagged along the track. One of them was a saloon, decorated with flags. In it had been Mehmed Jemal Pasha, commanding the Eighth Army Corps, hurrying down to defend Jerusalem against Allenby. His chargers had been in the first waggon; his motor-car was on the end of the train, and we shot it up. Of his staff we noticed a fat ecclesiastic, whom we thought to be Assad Shukair, Imam to Ahmed Jemal Pasha, and a notorious pro-Turk pimp. So we blazed at him till he dropped.

It was all long bowls. We could see that our chance of carrying the wreck was slight. There had been some four hundred men on board, and the survivors, now recovered from the shock, were under shelter and shooting hard at us. At the first moment our party on the north spur had closed, and nearly won the game. Mifleh on his mare chased the officers from the saloon into the lower ditch. He was too excited to stop and shoot, and so they got away scathless. The Arabs following him had turned to pick up some of the rifles and medals littering the ground, and then to drag bags and boxes from the train. If we had had a machine-gun posted to cover the far side, according to my mining practice, not a Turk would have escaped.

Mifleh and Adhub rejoined us on the hill, and asked after Fahad. One of the Serahin told how he had led the first rush, while I lay knocked out beside the exploder, and had been killed near it. They showed his belt and rifle as proof that he was dead and that they had tried to save him. Adhub said not a word, but leaped out of the gully, and raced downhill. We caught our breaths till our lungs hurt us, watching him; but the Turks seemed not to see. A minute later he was dragging a body behind the left-hand bank.

Mifleh went back to his mare, mounted, and took her down behind a spur. Together they lifted the inert figure on to the pommel, and returned. A bullet had passed through Fahad's face, knocking out four teeth, and gashing the tongue. He had fallen unconscious, but had revived just before Adhub reached him, and was trying on hands and knees, blinded with blood, to crawl away. He now recovered poise enough to cling to a saddle. So they changed him to the first camel they found, and led him off at once.

The Turks, seeing us so quiet, began to advance up the slope. We let them come half-way, and then poured in volleys which killed some twenty and drove the others back. The ground about the train was strewn with dead, and the broken coaches had been crowded: but they were fighting under the eye of their Corps Commander, and undaunted began to work round the spurs to outflank us.

We were now only about forty left, and obviously could do no good against them. So we ran in batches up the little stream-bed, turning at each sheltered angle to delay them by pot-shots. Little Turki much distinguished himself by quick coolness, though his straight-stocked Turkish cavalry carbine made him so expose his head that he got four bullets through his head-cloth. Ali was angry with me for retiring slowly. In reality my raw hurts crippled me, but to hide from him this real reason I pretended to be easy, interested in and studying the Turks. Such successive rests while I gained courage for a new run kept him and Turki far behind the rest.

At last we reached the hill-top. Each man there jumped on the nearest camel, and made away at full speed eastward into the desert, for an hour.

Then in safety we sorted our animals. The excellent Rahail, despite the ruling excitement, had brought off with him, tied to his saddle-girth, a huge haunch of the camel slaughtered just as the train arrived. He gave us the motive for a proper halt, five miles farther on, as a little party of four camels appeared marching in the same direction. It was our companion, Matar, coming back from his home village to Azrak with loads of raisins and peasant delicacies.

So we stopped at once, under a large rock in Wadi Dhuleil, where was a barren fig-tree, and cooked our first meal for three days. There, also, we bandaged up Fahad, who was sleepy with the lassitude of his severe hurt. Adhub, seeing this, took one of Matar's new carpets, and, doubling it across the camel-saddle, stitched the ends into great pockets. In one they laid Fahad, while Adhub crawled into the other as make-weight: and the camel was led off southward towards their tribal tents.

The other wounded men were seen to at the same time. Mifleh brought up the youngest lads of the party, and had them spray the wounds with their piss, as a rude antiseptic. Meanwhile we whole ones refreshed ourselves. I bought another mangy camel for extra meat, paid rewards, compensated the relatives of the killed, and gave prize-money, for the sixty or seventy rifles we had taken. It was small booty, but not to be despised. Some Serahin, who had gone into the action without rifles, able only to throw unavailing stones, had now two guns apiece. Next day we moved into Azrak, having a great welcome, and boasting—God forgive us—that we were victors.

WAR IS THE PROVINCE OF CHANCE

IN NO sphere of human activity is such a margin to be left for this intruder because none is so much in constant contact with him on all sides. He increases the uncertainty of every circumstance, and deranges the course of events.

From this uncertainty of all intelligence and suppositions, this continual interposition of chance, the actor in War constantly finds things different from his expectation; and this can not fail to have an influence on his plans, or at least on the presumptions connected with these plans. If this influence is so great as to render the predetermined plan completely null, then, as a rule, a new one must be substituted in its place; but at the moment the necessary data are often wanting for this, because in the course of action circumstances press for immediate decision, and allow no time to look about for fresh data, often not enough for mature consideration.

Lisette at Eylau

BY

GENERAL MARBOT

To ENABLE you to understand my story, I must go back to the autumn of 1805, when the officers of the Grand Army, among their preparations for the battle of Austerlitz, were completing their outfits. I had two good horses, the third, for whom I was looking, my charger, was to be better still. It was a difficult thing to find, for though horses were far less dear than now, their price was pretty high, and I had not much money; but chance served me admirably. I met a learned German, Herr von Aister, whom I had known when he was a professor at Sorèze. He had become tutor to the children of a rich Swiss banker, M. Scherer, established at Paris in partnership with M. Finguerlin. He informed me that M. Finguerlin, a wealthy man, living in fine style, had a large stud, in the first rank of which figured a lovely mare, called Lisette, easy in her paces, as light as a deer, and so well broken that a child could lead her. But this mare, when she was ridden, had a terrible fault, and fortunately a rare one: she bit like a bulldog, and furiously attacked people whom she disliked, which decided M. Finguerlin to sell her. She was bought for Mme. de Lauriston, whose husband, one of the Emperor's aides-de-camp, had written to her to get his campaigning outfit ready. When selling the mare, M. Finguerlin had forgotten to mention her fault, and that very evening a groom was found disembowelled at her feet. Mme. de Lauriston, reasonably alarmed, brought an action to cancel the bargain; not only did she get her verdict, but, in order to prevent further disasters, the police ordered that a written statement should be placed in Lisette's stall to inform purchasers of her ferocity, and that any bargain with regard to her should be void unless the purchaser declared in writing that his attention had been called to the notice. You may suppose that with such a character as this the mare was not easy to dispose of, and thus Herr von Aister informed me that her owner had decided to let her go for what any one would give. I offered 1,000 francs, and M. Finguerlin delivered Lisette to me, though she had cost him 5,000. This animal gave me a good deal of trouble for some months. It took four or five men to saddle her, and you could only bridle her by covering her eyes and fastening all four legs; but once you were on her back, you found her a really incomparable mount.

From: *The Adventures of General Marbot.* Scribners.

However, since while in my possession she had already bitten several people, and had not spared me, I was thinking of parting with her. But I had meanwhile engaged in my service Francis Woirland, a man who was afraid of nothing, and he, before going near Lisette, whose bad character had been mentioned to him, armed himself with a good hot roast leg of mutton. When the animal flew at him to bite him, he held out the mutton; she seized it in her teeth, and burning her gums, palate, and tongue, gave a scream, let the mutton drop, and from that moment was perfectly submissive to Woirland, and did not venture to attack him again. I employed the same method with a like result. Lisette became as docile as a dog, and allowed me and my servant to approach her freely. She even became a little more tractable towards the stablemen of the staff, whom she saw every day, but woe to the strangers who passed near her! I could quote twenty instances of her ferocity, but I will confine myself to one. While Marshal Augereau was staying at the château of Bellevue, near Berlin, the servants of the staff, having observed that when they went to dinner some one stole the sacks of corn that were left in the stable, got Woirland to unfasten Lisette and leave her near the door. The thief arrived, slipped into the stable, and was in the act of carrying off a sack, when the mare seized him by the nape of the neck, dragged him into the middle of the yard and trampled on him till she broke two of his ribs. At the shrieks of the thief, people ran up, but Lisette would not let him go till my servant and I compelled her, for in her fury she would have flown at any one else. She had become still more vicious ever since the Saxon hussar officer, of whom I have told you, had treacherously laid open her shoulder with a sabre-cut on the battlefield of Jena.

Such was the mare which I was riding at Eylau at the moment when the fragments of Augereau's army corps, shattered by a hail of musketry and cannon-balls, were trying to rally near the great cemetery. You will remember how the 14th of the line had remained alone on a hillock, which it could not quit except by the Emperor's order. The snow had ceased for the moment; we could see how the intrepid regiment, surrounded by the enemy, was waving its eagle in the air to show that it still held its ground and asked for support. The Emperor, touched by the grand devotion of these brave men, resolved to try to save them, and ordered Augereau to send an officer to them with orders to leave the hillock, form a small square, and make their way towards us, while a brigade of cavalry should march in their direction and assist their efforts. This was before Murat's great charge. It was almost impossible to carry out the Emperor's wishes, because a swarm of Cossacks was between us and the 14th, and it was clear that any officer who was sent towards the unfortunate regiment would be killed or captured before he could get to it. But the order was positive, and the marshal had to comply.

It was customary in the Imperial army for the aides-de-camp to place themselves in file a few paces from their general, and for the one who was in front to go on duty first; then, when he had performed his mission, to return and place himself last, in order that each might carry orders in his turn, and dangers might be shared equally. A brave captain of engineers, named Froissard, who, though not an aide-de-camp, was on the marshal's staff, happened to be nearest to him, and was bidden to carry the order to the 14th. M. Froissard galloped off; we lost sight of him in the midst of the Cossacks, and never saw him again nor heard what had become of him. The marshal, seeing that the 14th did not move, sent an officer named David; he had the same fate as Froissard: we never heard of him again. Probably both were killed and stripped, and could not be recognized among the many corpses which covered the ground. For the third time the marshal called, 'The officer for duty.' It was my turn.

Seeing the son of his old friend, and I venture to say his favorite aide-de-camp, come up, the kind marshal's face changed, and his eyes filled with tears, for he could not hide from himself that he was sending me to almost certain death. But the Emperor must be obeyed. I was a soldier; it was impossible to make one of my comrades go in my place, nor would I have allowed it; it would have been disgracing me. So I dashed off. But though ready to sacrifice my life I felt bound to take all necessary precautions to save it. I had observed that the two officers who went before me had gone with swords drawn, which led me to think that they had purposed to defend themselves against any Cossacks who might attack them on the way. Such defence, I thought, was ill-considered, since it must have compelled them to halt in order to fight a multitude of enemies, who would overwhelm them in the end. So I went otherwise to work, and leaving my sword in the scabbard, I regarded myself as a horseman who is trying to win a steeplechase, and goes as quickly as possible and by the shortest line towards the appointed goal, without troubling himself with what is to right or left of his path. Now, as my goal was the hillock occupied by the 14th, I resolved to get there without taking any notice of the Cossacks, whom in thought I abolished. This plan answered perfectly. Lisette, lighter than a swallow and flying rather than running, devoured the intervening space, leaping the piles of dead men and horses, the ditches, the broken gun-carriages, the half-extinguished bivouac fires. Thousands of Cossacks swarmed over the plain. The first who saw me acted like sportsmen who, when beating, start a hare, and announce its presence to each other by shouts of 'Your side! Your side!' but none of the Cossacks tried to stop me, first, on account of the extreme rapidity of my pace, and also probably because, their numbers being so great, each thought that I could not avoid his comrades farther on; so that I escaped them all, and reached the 14th regiment without either myself or my excellent mare having received the slightest scratch.

I found the 14th formed in square on the top of the hillock, but as the slope was very slight the enemy's cavalry had been able to deliver several charges. These had been vigorously repulsed, and the French regiment was surrounded by a circle of dead horses and dragoons, which formed a kind of rampart, making the position by this time almost inaccessible to cavalry;

as I found, for in spite of the aid of our men, I had much difficulty in passing over this horrible entrenchment. At last I was in the square. Since Colonel Savary's death at the passage of the Wkra, the 14th had been commanded by a major. While I imparted to this officer, under a hail of balls, the order to quit his position and try to rejoin his corps, he pointed out to me that the enemy's artillery had been firing on the 14th for an hour, and had caused it such loss that the handful of soldiers which remained would inevitably be exterminated if they went down into the plain, and that, moreover, there would not be time to prepare to execute such a movement, since a Russian column was marching on him, and was not more than a hundred paces away. 'I see no means of saving the regiment,' said the major; 'return to the Emperor, bid him farewell from the 14th of the line, which has faithfully executed his orders, and bear to him the eagle which he gave us, and which we can defend no longer: it would add too much to the pain of death to see it fall into the hands of the enemy.' Then the major handed me his eagle. Saluted for the last time by the glorious fragment of the intrepid regiment with cries of 'Vive l'Empereur!' they were going to die for him. It was the *Cæsar morituri te salutant* of Tacitus, but in this case the cry was uttered by heroes. The infantry eagles were very heavy, and their weight was increased by a stout oak pole on the top of which they were fixed. The length of the pole embarrassed me much, and as the stick without the eagle could not constitute a trophy for the enemy, I resolved with the major's consent to break it and only carry off the eagle. But at the moment when I was leaning forward from my saddle in order to get a better purchase to separate the eagle from the pole, one of the numerous cannon-balls which the Russians were sending at us went through the hinder peak of my hat, less than an inch from my head. The shock was all the more terrible since my hat, being fastened on by a strong leather strap under the chin, offered more resistance to the blow. I seemed to be blotted out of existence, but I did not fall from my horse; blood flowed from my nose, my ears, and even my eyes; nevertheless I still could hear and see, and I preserved all my intellectual faculties, although my limbs were paralyzed to such an extent that I could not move a single finger.

Meanwhile the column of Russian infantry which we had just perceived was mounting the hill; they were grenadiers wearing mitre-shaped caps with metal ornaments. Soaked with spirits, and in vastly superior numbers, these men hurled themselves furiously on the feeble remains of the unfortunate 14th, whose soldiers had for several days been living only on potatoes and melted snow; that day they had not had time to prepare even this wretched meal. Still our brave Frenchmen made a valiant defence with their bayonets, and when the square had been broken, they held together in groups and sustained the unequal fight for a long time.

During this terrible struggle several of our men, in order not to be struck from behind, set their backs against my mare's flanks, she, contrary to her practice, remaining perfectly quiet. If I had been able to move I should have urged her forward to get away from this field of slaughter. But it was absolutely impossible for me to press my legs so as to make the animal I rode understand my wish. My position was the more frightful since, as I have said, I retained the power of sight and thought. Not only were they fighting all round me, which exposed me to bayonet-thrusts, but a Russian officer with a hideous countenance kept making efforts to run me through. As the crowd of combatants prevented him from reaching me, he pointed me out to the soldiers around him, and they, taking me for the commander of the French, as I was the only mounted man, kept firing at me over their comrades' heads, so that bullets were constantly whistling past my ear. One of them would certainly have taken away the small amount of life that was still in me had not a terrible incident led to my escape from the mêlée.

Among the Frenchmen who had got their backs against my mare's near flank was a quartermaster-sergeant, whom I knew from having frequently seen him at the marshal's, making copies for him of the 'morning states.' This man, having been attacked and wounded by several of the enemy, fell under Lisette's belly, and was seizing my leg to pull himself up, when a Russian grenadier, too drunk to stand steady, wishing to finish him by a thrust in the breast, lost his balance, and the point of his bayonet went astray into my cloak, which at that moment was puffed out by the wind. Seeing that I did not fall, the Russian left the sergeant and aimed a great number of blows at me. These were at first fruitless, but one at last reached me, piercing my left arm, and I felt with a kind of horrible pleasure my blood flowing hot. The Russian grenadier with redoubled fury made another thrust at me, but, stumbling with the force which he put into it, drove his bayonet into my mare's thigh. Her ferocious instincts being restored by the pain, she sprang at the Russian, and at one mouthful tore off his nose, lips, eyebrows, and all the skin of his face, making of him a living death's-head, dripping with blood. Then hurling herself with fury among the combatants, kicking and biting, Lisette upset everything that she met on her road. The officer who had made so many attempts to strike me tried to hold her by the bridle; she seized him by his belly, and carrying him off with ease, she bore him out of the crush to the foot of the hillock, where, having torn out his entrails and mashed his body under her feet, she left him dying on the snow. Then, taking the road by which she had come, she made her way at full gallop towards the cemetery of Eylau. Thanks to the hussar's saddle on which I was sitting I kept my seat. But a new danger awaited me. The snow had begun to fall again, and great flakes obscured the daylight when, having arrived close to Eylau, I found myself in front of a battalion of the Old Guard, who, unable to see clearly at a distance, took me for an enemy's officer leading a charge of cavalry. The whole battalion at once opened fire on me; my cloak and my saddle were riddled, but I was not wounded nor was my mare. She continued her rapid course, and went through the three ranks of the battalion as easily as a snake through a hedge. But this last spurt had exhausted Lisette's strength; she had lost much blood, for one of the large veins in her thigh had been divided, and the poor animal collapsed suddenly and fell on one side, rolling me over on the other.

Stretched on the snow among the piles of dead and dying, unable to move in any way, I gradually and without pain lost consciousness. I felt as if I was being gently rocked to sleep. At last I fainted quite away without being revived by the mighty clatter which Murat's ninety squadrons advancing to the charge must have made in passing close to me and perhaps over me. I judge that my swoon lasted four hours, and when I came to my senses I found myself in this horrible position. I was completely naked, having nothing on but my hat and my right boot. A man of the transport corps, thinking me dead, had stripped me in the usual fashion, and wishing to pull off the only boot that remained, was dragging me by one leg with his foot against my body. The jerks which the man gave me no doubt had restored me to my senses. I succeeded in sitting up and spitting out the clots of blood from my throat. The shock caused by the wind of the ball had produced such an extravazation of blood, that my face, shoulders, and chest were black, while the rest of my body was stained red by the blood from my wound. My hat and my hair were full of bloodstained snow, and as I rolled my haggard eyes I must have been horrible to see. Anyhow, the transport man looked the other way, and went off with my property without my being able to say a single word to him, so utterly prostrate was I. But I had recovered my mental faculties, and my thoughts turned towards God and my mother.

The setting sun cast some feeble rays through the clouds. I took what I believed to be a last farewell of it. 'If,' thought I, 'I had only not been stripped, some one of the numerous people who pass near me would notice the gold lace on my pelisse, and, recognizing that I am a marshal's aide-de-camp, would perhaps have carried me to the ambulance. But seeing me naked, they do not distinguish me from the corpses with which I am surrounded, and, indeed, there soon will be no difference between them and me. I cannot call help, and the approaching night will take away all hope of succor. The cold is increasing: shall I be able to bear it till tomorrow, seeing that I feel my naked limbs stiffening already?' So I made up my mind to die, for if I had been saved by a miracle in the midst of the terrible mêlée between the Russians and the 14th, could I expect that there would be a second miracle to extract me from my present horrible position? The second miracle did take place in the following manner. Marshal Augereau had a valet named Pierre Dannel, a very intelligent and very faithful fellow, but somewhat given to arguing. Now it happened during our stay at La Houssaye that Dannel, having answered his master, got dismissed. In despair, he begged me to plead for him. This I did so zealously that I succeeded in getting him taken back into favor. From that time the valet had been devotedly attached to me. The outfit having been all left behind at Landsberg, he had started all out of his own head on the day of battle to bring provisions to his master. He had placed these in a very light wagon which could go everywhere, and contained the articles which the marshal most frequently required. This little wagon was driven by a soldier belonging to the same company of the transport corps as the man who had just stripped me. This latter, with my property in his hands, passed near the wagon, which was standing at the side of the cemetery, and, recognizing the driver, his old comrade, he hailed him, and showed him the splendid booty which he had just taken from a dead man.

Now you must know that when we were in cantonments on the Vistula the marshal happened to send Dannel to Warsaw for provisions, and I commissioned him to get the trimming of black astrachan taken from my pelisse, and have it replaced by gray, this having recently been adopted by Prince Berthier's aides-de-camp, who set the fashion in the army. Up to now, I was the only one of Augereau's officers who had gray astrachan. Dannel, who was present when the transport man made his display, quickly recognized my pelisse, which made him look more closely at the other effects of the alleged dead man. Among these he found my watch, which had belonged to my father and was marked with his cypher. The valet had no longer any doubt that I had been killed, and while deploring my loss, he wished to see me for the last time. Guided by the transport man he reached me and found me living. Great was the joy of this worthy man, to whom I certainly owed my life. He made haste to fetch my servant and some order-lies, and had me carried to a barn, where he rubbed my body with rum. Meanwhile some one went to fetch Dr. Raymond, who came at length, dressed the wound in my arm, and declared that the release of blood due to it would be the saving of me

My brother and my comrades were quickly round me; something was given to the transport soldier who had taken my clothes, which he returned very willingly, but as they were saturated with water and with blood, Marshal Augereau had me wrapped in things belonging to himself. The Emperor had given the marshal leave to go to Landsberg, but as his wound forbade him to ride, his aides-de-camp had procured a sledge, on which the body of a carriage had been placed. The marshal, who could not make up his mind to leave me, had me fastened up beside him, for I was too weak to sit upright.

Before I was removed from the field of battle I had seen my poor Lisette near me. The cold had caused the blood from her wound to clot, and prevented the loss from being too great. The creature had got on to her legs and was eating the straw which the soldiers had used the night before for their bivouacs. My servant, who was very fond of Lisette, had noticed her when he was helping to remove me, and cutting up into bandages the shirt and hood of a dead soldier, he wrapped her leg with them, and thus made her able to walk to Landsberg. The officer in command of the small garrison there had had the forethought to get quarters ready for the wounded, so the staff found places in a large and good inn.

In this way, instead of passing the night without help, stretched naked on the snow, I lay on a good bed surrounded by the attention of my brother, my comrades, and the kind Dr. Raymond. The doctor had been obliged to cut off the boot which the transport man had not been able to pull off, and which had become all the more difficult to remove owing to the swelling of my foot. You will see presently that this very nearly cost me my leg, and perhaps my life.

We stayed thirty-six hours at Landsberg. This rest, and the good care taken of me, restored me to the use of speech and senses, and when on the second day after the battle Marshal Augereau started for Warsaw I was able to be carried in the sledge. The journey lasted eight days. Gradually I recovered strength, but as strength returned I began to feel a sensation of icy cold in my right foot. At Warsaw I was lodged in the house that had been taken for the marshal, which suited me the better that I was not able to leave my bed. Yet the wound in my arm was doing well, the extravasated blood was becoming absorbed, my skin was recovering its natural color. The doctor knew not to what he could ascribe my inability to rise, till, hearing me complaining of my leg, he examined it, and found that my foot was gangrened. An accident of my early days was the cause of this new trouble. At Sorèze I had my right foot wounded by the unbuttoned foil of a schoolfellow with whom I was fencing. It seemed that the muscles of the part had become sensitive, and had suffered much from cold while I was lying unconscious on the field of Eylau; thence had resulted a swelling which explained the difficulty experienced by the soldier in dragging off my right boot. The foot was frostbitten, and as it had not been treated in time, gangrene had appeared in the site of the old wound from the foil. The place was covered with an eschar as large as a five-franc piece. The doctor turned pale when he saw the foot: then, making four servants hold me, and taking his knife, he lifted the eschar, and dug the mortified flesh from my foot just as one cuts the damaged part out of an apple. The pain was great, but I did not complain. It was otherwise, however, when the knife reached the living flesh, and laid bare the muscles and bones till one could see them moving. Then the doctor, standing on a chair, soaked a sponge in hot sweetened wine, and let it fall drop by drop into the hole which he had just dug in my foot. The pain became unbearable. Still, for eight days I had to undergo this torture morning and evening, but my leg was saved.

Nowadays, when promotions and decorations are bestowed so lavishly, some reward would certainly be given to an officer who had braved danger as I had done in reaching the 14th regiment; but under the Empire a devoted act of that kind was thought so natural that I did not receive the cross, nor did it ever occur to me to ask for it. A long rest having been ordered for the cure of Marshal Augereau's wound, the Emperor wrote to bid him return for treatment to France, and sent to Italy for Masséna, to whom my brother, Bro, and several of my comrades were attached. Augereau took me with him, as well as Dr. Raymond and his secretary. I had to be lifted in and out of the carriage; otherwise I found my health coming back as I got away from those icy regions towards a milder climate. My mare passed the winter in the stables of M. de Launay, head of the forage department. Our road lay through Silesia. So long as we were in that horrible Poland, it required twelve, sometimes sixteen, horses to draw the carriage at a walk through the bogs and quagmires; but in Germany we found at length civilization and real roads.

After a halt at Dresden, and ten or twelve days' stay at Frankfort, we reached Paris about March 15. I walked very lame, wore my arm in a sling, and still felt the terrible shaking caused by the wind of the cannonball; but the joy of seeing my mother again, and her kind care of me, together with the sweet influences of the spring, completed my cure. Before leaving Warsaw I had meant to throw away the hat which the ball had pierced, but the marshal kept it as a curiosity and gave it to my mother. It still exists in my possession, and should be kept as a family relic.

The Stolen Railroad Train

BY

MARQUIS JAMES

1

ON SUNDAY evening, the sixth of April, 1862, a tall, carefully dressed civilian with a heavy black beard and the inflection of the South in his speech, presented himself to the pickets of Mitchel's Division, encamped near Shelbyville, Tennessee. His papers were in order and he was admitted.

Major General O. M. Mitchel and the spy sat down over a map and it was daylight before they reached an agreement. The scheme offered by the secret agent was such that even a soldier as bold as Mitchel drew back. But step by step the civilian justified the proposal. Audacity would promote its success, he said, and success would be worth any risk. General Mitchel's caller asked for thirty picked men from whom to make his personal selections, and at length Mitchel agreed he should have them.

That forenoon thirty volunteers were culled from the veteran Second, Twenty-First and Thirty-Third Ohio Infantry Regiments, the colonels passing upon the qualifications of each man who was told that a detail was being made up for duty involving great personal peril. Though occupied with plans for a military advance, General Mitchel himself took the time to look over a few of the applicants. In the afternoon the chosen thirty were sent to Shelbyville to purchase civilian clothing and to report to J. J. Andrews, a tall civilian with a heavy beard who would be found on the streets of the town.

Shelbyville was full of soldiers, and, as soldiers often laid off their uniforms when going home on furlough, the thirty made their purchases without exciting comment. J. J. Andrews was easily identified. He sauntered about the streets, frequently entering a store to take an apparently idle interest in a soldier who was buying clothing. In the course of the afternoon all thirty approached him, singly or in small groups, for they were generally unknown to one another. He would ask what they were to report to him for. The soldiers would say that they did not know, or something of the sort. Andrews would ask them a few questions. Then in a casual tone he would say, "You may meet me to-night shortly after dark on the Wartrace Road a mile or so from town." To five or six he said, "There must be some mistake. I am not the man you are looking for." Their demeanor had not satisfied the Union spy.

Nor was Sergeant Major Marion Ross altogether satisfied with his interview. "A mile or so from town." "Shortly after dark." The instructions were so vague that he asked his friend Corporal William Pittenger what he thought of this Andrews. "I answered with enthusiasm," the Corporal related in after years. "The strong-influence this singular man never failed to exert over those who were brought in contact with him was already at work. His pensive manner, his soft voice, not louder than a woman's, his grace and dignity made me at once declare him above the ordinary type of manhood. He was more like a poet than an adventurer, but I would have trusted him to the end of the earth."

2

Such whole-hearted endorsement put Ross in entire agreement with his friend's estimate. In fact, his curiosity was now aroused and he wished that he knew more about their new leader. And General Mitchel himself would have liked to know more about James J. Andrews, but all he knew or ever learned was that he was a good spy and described himself as a resident of Flemingsburg, Kentucky.

This town was equally unsatisfied with the scope of its knowledge. Andrews had come there two years before the war—from Virginia, as he said, but he gave no particulars. Something about the man suggested an interesting past. Flemingsburg believed he "had a story."

Perhaps one person in Flemingsburg really knew. She was Elizabeth Layton to whom Mr. Andrews, after a long courtship, had just become engaged. They were to be married in two months, and a part of the bargain was that Andrews should abandon his perilous profession as a Union secret agent. The service he had proposed to Mitchel was intended to be his last. It was calculated to reveal to the world where his true loyalties lay, for in the South Andrews was known as a confidential agent of the Confederate armies.

The night following the interviews at Shelbyville was pitch dark and the rain fell in sheets. Twenty-four men, singly or in small parties, trudged through the mud of the Wartrace Road. Several of them were hopeless of meeting Andrews or anyone on such a night. Yet twenty-three of the twenty-four found him as readily as if they had had daylight and explicit directions to guide them. Andrews led them into a patch of woods near the road and began to speak in a quiet voice, stopping when the thunder was too loud for him to be heard distinctly.

He said that the expedition for which they had volunteered would take them into the enemy's country in disguise, which meant that any one captured and detected would probably be hanged as a spy. Therefore, any one unwilling to take the risk might now withdraw. Mr. Andrews paused. No one stirred and in a few sentences the speaker outlined the undertaking. In bands of two to four, the party would proceed to Marietta, Georgia, in the heart of the Confederacy, arriving on Thursday, four days hence. The following morning they would capture the north-bound mail train from Atlanta to Chattanooga, and run it to Bridgeport, Alabama, burning bridges behind them and rendering useless a hundred and thirty miles of railroad and telegraph. At Bridgeport, the party would meet Mitchel in the course of his southward advance. The destruction of these communications would paralyze the movement of southern armies in the Central West and embarrass Lee's operations in Virginia.

"I shall be in Marietta with you or before you," said Mr. Andrews, "and there will tell each man what to do."

The route from Shelbyville to Marietta was long and difficult, and Andrews gave his men a few pointers on travel. If questioned, the best thing to say was that they were Kentuckians on their way to join the southern armies. But the men were to use their heads. They had been selected because they were thought capable of independent action.

"But what if they take us at our word and insist that we enlist?" asked one.

"Oh, be looking for a special regiment that is some place else. But if diplomacy fails do not hesitate to enlist any place."

"What if they won't take us?"

"No danger about that," replied Andrews. "The difficulty is not to get in but to stay out of the rebel army."

Andrews distributed seven hundred dollars of Confederate money and shook hands with each man. "Good-by. Good-by, Sergeant. Marietta not later than five, Thursday afternoon. Now, move out, men. Not more than four together."

3

On the appointed Thursday—April 10, 1862—two of the twenty-three reached Marietta. They strolled about town until late and went to bed uneasy. All day Friday they waited without a sign of one of their comrades, so far as they were able to recognize, the party having been together but once and then in the dark. The evening train from Chattanooga, however, brought Andrews and the remainder of his men, except two who were never heard from.

Incessant rain had made traveling difficult. When the party converged at Chattanooga to take the train for Marietta, Mr. Andrews had passed the word that the raid should be postponed one day. Thus all but the two men who had outstripped their schedule by a few hours had lain over at Chattanooga. Andrew's reason for the delay was that he felt it better to run the captured train into Bridgeport a day late rather than risk getting there ahead of Mitchel whose advance, he figured, would be retarded by the weather.

At Marietta the men slept in different hotels and at dawn met Andrews in his room for final instructions. As usual the leader did not waste a word. "Buy tickets to different points up the line. Take seats in the same car. When the train stops at Big Shanty remain seated until I tell you to go. When the signal is given, if anybody interferes, shoot him."

The ranking soldier present was Sergeant Major Ross, whose courage was well known. Respectfully asking permission to speak, he suggested that the whole project be dropped or delayed for a reconsideration of all the factors involved. The delay of one day had altered everything, said Ross. Big Shanty was surrounded by troops; the line was congested by rolling stock being hurried out of Mitchel's reach; should Mitchel get to Bridgeport on time, the raiders, a day late, might miss him. Very courteously Mr. Andrews took up Ross's objections. He said the excitement and confusion caused by Mitchel's drive into Alabama would facilitate, not hinder, the flight of the fugitive train. "Boys," he concluded after dismissing the last of the sergeant major's arguments, "I will succeed in this or leave my bones in Dixie."

That was the nearest to an heroic speech that J. J. Andrews ever made. He closed his watch and picked up his tall silk hat. The depot was just across the street and there was barely time before the train came in to buy tickets.

An hour later Conductor William A. Fuller walked through the coaches. Fuller was a wiry young fellow, with a blond goatee and steady gray eyes. "Big Shanty!" he called. "Twenty minutes for breakfast."

The sleepy passengers began to scramble toward the door. Andrews rose and beckoned to William Knight, who had been designated as engineer. The station was on the right side of the track. Four Georgia regiments were encamped on the left side and a bored sentry walked his post within a few feet of the cars. Andrews and Knight got off on the side next to the camp. They strolled forward and took a look at the engine. The cab was empty. Behind the tender were three empty freight cars. Andrews stopped beside the last one.

"Uncouple here," he told Knight.

He walked to the coach where the other men were waiting. Strolling part of the way down the aisle, Andrews paused and said in an ordinary tone, "Come on, boys, it's time to go."

4

Wilson W. Brown, the relief engineer, and George D. Wilson, the fireman, swung off and darted toward the locomotive. Knight was in the cab with his hand on the throttle. Andrews signaled the others to tumble into the box-cars—all the work of probably twelve seconds. Knight pulled the throttle half-way open. The wheels spun on the track but the train did not move. Then the wheels "bit" and the engine, the three box-cars attached, shot forward with a bound that piled the box-car passengers in a heap.

They scurried to their feet to look from the doors and cheer. The start had been propitious beyond expectation. The picket, near enough to have used his bayonet, was staring in open-mouthed amazement—which, after all, was a fortunate negligence on the part of this green recruit as each of Andrews's men carried a cocked pistol in his coat.

The feeling of triumph was short-lived, however. Less than a mile from the Confederate camp the engine began to falter, which was strange, for this locomotive, the General, was rated one of the best on the Western & Atlantic road. Shortly this excellent engine stopped dead and Andrews, who was in the cab, called to the men in the cars to cut the telegraph wires. While John Scott, the smallest man in the party, was shinning up the telegraph pole, the trouble with the engine was located. The draft was shut off and the fire nearly out. Wood doused with oil soon had the firebox roaring and they were on their way again.

Nothing now, said Andrews who was not given to strong statements, could defeat them. Cutting the wires at this point was an excess precaution. There was no need for it so soon as Big Shanty lacked a telegraph office. Pursuit would be a matter of hours, the nearest engines available for this purpose being at Atlanta on the south and Kingston on the north, each about thirty miles from Big Shanty. Three south-bound trains from Chattanooga must be dealt with, but Andrews had arranged for that. He would adhere to the regular time on the mail train until Kingston was reached, and pass there a local freight, the first of these trains. After burning some eleven bridges beyond Kingston and keeping the wires cut to prevent word from getting ahead of them, the raiders could skirt Chattanooga by means of the "Y" below the town, and dash westward into Alabama where Mitchel would be waiting.

The schedule of the fast mail from Atlanta was sixteen miles an hour and Andrews had difficulty in holding his engineers down to that speed, even though the track was crooked and soft from the rains, and the rails light and worn by the constant travel of military trains. The local freight must be passed at Kingston and it would be better to take it easy en route than to get to Kingston early and have to wait. So they jogged along, stopping once to relieve a track repair gang of its tools, and again to cut wires and lift a rail. The rail-lifting was slow work as the tools they had taken were not the proper ones.

Half-way to Kingston Andrews received a surprise. Slowing up for a private switch that led to the Etowah Iron Works, five miles off the main line, he saw a locomotive fired up not forty feet from the main track. It was the veteran Yonah, owned by the iron works, and, carefully as he had explored the road, Andrews had not learned of its existence until now. Knight put on the brakes.

"We had better get rid of that," he suggested.

Andrews hesitated. "No," he said, "go ahead. It won't make any difference."

Andrews did not wish to risk a delay in meeting the freight at Kingston. Beyond Kingston he could destroy track and thwart pursuit by the Yonah as effectively as by attacking its crew and the iron works gang at the switch. The decision reveals an important difference in temperament between Andrews and his men. The men would have preferred to disable the Yonah on the spot. They were soldiers, the pick of a first-class division, and accustomed to direct methods. Andrews's way was otherwise—to avoid clashes and to *finesse* his way through tight places where the flick of an eyelash might mean death.

5

Seven miles from Kingston was Cassville, a wood and water stop. The box-car doors were closed while the engine crew replenished the tender. The wood-yard foreman strolled up, curious to know about the small train running on the schedule of the morning mail, with the mail's locomotive but none of the regular hands. Mr. Andrews had put on his silk hat in place of the cap he wore while the train was under way. This was a powder train, he said, being taken through to General Beauregard, who was in a bad way for ammunition. The wood-yard foreman wished the powder-bearers luck.

Kingston was a good-sized town. The station platform was filled with people. The branch train for Rome was there, waiting for the Atlanta mail. Knight stopped alongside it and the Rome engineer called out:

"What's up? Fuller's engine and none of his men on board."

"I have taken this train by Government authority," said Andrews, "to run powder through to Beauregard." He waved his hand toward the box-cars in which his men were shut up.

The local freight was late. Andrews could get no information beyond that. Five minutes passed. Ten, fifteen minutes. To the men in the dark box-cars they seemed like hours.

Mr. Andrews walked up and down the station platform. One or two persons recognized him and saluted respectfully. He would stop and chat for a moment, belittling the alarming stories of Mitchel's advance into Alabama. People spoke of his poise in the face of the vexatious delay of the powder train.

Finally the freight came in. Andrews hastened to ask the conductor to pull up so that the powder train could move. The conductor was willing to oblige, but indicated a red flag on the end of his train. Another train was behind, made up, the freight conductor said, of everything on wheels that could be gleaned out of Mitchel's path. "And where," asked the conductor, "did you say you were to deliver this powder to Beauregard?" "At Corinth, Mississippi," repeated Andrews. "Why, you can't get through," explained the conductor. "Mitchel is on the line at Huntsville." Andrews said he did not believe it, but the trainman said he knew, having just come from there.

Twenty minutes, thirty minutes dragged by. Andrews patrolled the station platform within ear-shot of the telegraph key. With one hand he raised his tall hat in polite greeting. The other hand enclosed the butt of a pistol in the pocket of his long black coat. Any attempt to send a suspicious message and the telegraph operator would have been a dead man. Andrews told Knight to get word to the men in the cars as to how the land lay and have them ready to fight.

Knight and his crew oiled their engine. An old switch tender who had spent a lifetime on southern railroads, hung around asking questions. The powder-train story did not concern him. The strange crew in the General's cab interested the veteran whose mind was an encyclopedia of southern railway personnel. Where had they worked? Road? Division? Knight and his helpers answered in monosyllables. Fortunately Brown had once run a locomotive on the Mobile & Ohio, but there was no evading a certain discomfort in the old-timer's boring cross-examination.

Forty minutes is a long time to wait for a train under any circumstances. There was a whistle around the curve and Andrews met the refugee train as it pulled in, shouting directions for it to take its place on the already crowded sidings. The conductor also pointed to a red flag on his last car. The refugee train was running in two sections.

Fifty minutes. One hour—and a whistle that was music to the ears of twenty-two men. Section two rumbled in. Two regular trains from the north were now overdue. A prudent conductor would not have entertained a notion of leaving Kingston then. But Andrews said he would have to take the chance of passing the trains at Adairsville, ten miles farther on.

He waved for the switch admitting his train to the main line to be opened. But the old switch tender refused to budge. He had hung up his keys in the station and said that Andrews would have to show his authority to get them. The men inside the box-cars heard the old man's defiance and got their pistols ready. Not so the mannerly Mr. Andrews whose life was filled with escapes from apprehensive moments. He laughed at the veteran's distemper and said he would get the keys. He did so, and the General was off after a delay of one hour and five minutes at Kingston, making in all an elapse of three hours and thirteen minutes from Big Shanty, thirty-two miles away.

"Push her, boys, push her," Andrews urged, and the General simply flew.

6

Well for Mr. Andrews that he had taken a chance and left for Adairsville. Four minutes after the General cleared the Kingston yards, a screaming whistle was heard from the south. The impatient passengers thought Fuller's train was coming and picked up their valises. It was Fuller—but he had not brought his train. The old Yonah rolled in, wheezing and blowing. Fuller swung off with the stunning story of the capture of the General at Big Shanty, and while the tracks were being cleared of the four trains congesting them, he managed to give a few of the details of his almost incredible pursuit.

At Big Shanty—now the town of Kenesaw—Fuller had just sat down to breakfast when a shout went up that his train had been stolen. He was on the platform in time to see the General and three box-cars glide around a curve. The station and camp were in an uproar. The dumfounded sentry stammered his story. It flashed on Fuller that the engine had been seized by deserters who would run it up the track for a few miles and take to the woods.

"Let's get her back before we are badly out of time," he shouted and, with Engineer Cain and Superintendent Murphy of the machine shops, started up the track at a dead run. Two miles out the three were winded and about to give up when they met the track gang whose tools Andrews had appropriated.

"If we can find the old Yonah at our end of the branch, we will get the scoundrels at Kingston where those extras will hold them up," said Fuller.

Before any one could reply to this observation push-car and riders, sailing down a grade, were pitched into a ditch, having struck a lifted rail.

The Yonah was overtaken just as she started to leave the main line. This old engine was full of complaints, but she had had her day, and on this day she turned back the calendar. The sixteen miles to Kingston were covered in thirteen minutes.

The crowd at the station told Fuller that his quarry had eluded him by four minutes. The conductor dashed into the telegraph office and sent a message north. He came back to the platform to hear the powder story, but, of course, did not learn that the "powder" cars were filled with armed men. Otherwise, he and his few helpers would have proceeded much more cautiously. The trains still were in a snarl on the tracks and, rather than lose any more time in switching, Fuller decided to abandon the Yonah. He uncoupled the engine of the Rome train and was off in a little better than six minutes, or about eleven minutes behind the Yankees.

The message telegraphed from Kingston did not get through because Andrews had stopped above the town in a blinding rain and cut the wires. Here the men also started to lift a rail, but their ineffective tools made clumsy work of it. Two-thirds of the rail was loose from the ties and the fugitives were about to give it up as a bad job, when the unmistakable whistle of a locomotive was heard from the south. Pursuit! It could be nothing else. The lifting of the rail became a matter of life or death. Most of the members of the party were large muscular men. They grasped the loose end of the rail, and with the strength born of peril heaved and pulled and heaved and pulled again. The iron rail snapped and the men tumbled in a heap. In an instant they were on their feet, in the cars and away.

At Adairsville the raiders were cheered by the sight of the south-bound freight waiting on the siding. At the depot Andrews received positive information that Mitchel held several miles of the railroad in Alabama. To Andrews, the Yankee raider, this was welcome news. To Andrews, the Confederate powder-train official, it presented complications. The story of the powder train was rendered absurd on its face, but the marvelous address of the spy covered up the inconsistency long enough for him to get away. This took a little time, too. He tarried to reassure the freight crew and send them south with their train. With the pursuers coming north, the freight going south, and a broken rail between them, Andrews expected his adversaries to be delayed long enough to give him the lead he needed.

To accomplish this he took further risks. The south-bound passenger train, following the freight, was overdue. The station officials advised Andrews to wait for it. Quite truthfully Andrews said he could not afford to wait, but he promised to run slowly, sending a flagman ahead on curves. Thus Andrews hoped to reach Calhoun, nine miles farther on, and deal with the passenger train there.

So as not to arouse suspicion, the General rolled cautiously away from the Adairsville depot. A quarter of a mile of this and Andrews told Knight to let her go.

7

The Yonah, ancient as she was, had been a faster locomotive than the engine Fuller took from the Rome train, but it was this fact—and an element of luck, as the conductor himself admitted—that averted disaster to the pursuit. Having struck one broken rail he was on the lookout for others, although the rain made it almost impossible to see anything. Nevertheless Fuller did see, or thought he saw, where the track had been tampered with in time to have his engineer throw the engine into reverse and stop it on the brink of the gap.

The conductor leaped from the useless locomotive and, motioning to his men to follow again, started another foot-race up the track, sliding and slipping in the mud. He had not gone far when he saw the through freight headed toward him. He flagged it down and backed it into Adairsville. The freight engine was the Texas and there was no better locomotive on the line. It was detached and with a small party of armed men started, tender forward, toward Calhoun.

Fuller believed he had the Yankees now. Andrews was thought to be running slowly for fear of colliding with the south-bound passenger train. If so, Fuller's quarry was boxed between two trains. But if Andrews had succeeded in reaching Calhoun before the passenger left, Fuller himself would risk a collision—unless he took care. Fuller did not take care. The scent was hot and he sent the Texas racing ahead.

8

To this day Knight probably holds the speed record between Adairsville and Calhoun, Georgia. The nine miles were behind the stolen engine in seven and one-half minutes—over a track on which safe running was reckoned to be sixteen miles an hour. At that the Andrews party escaped destruction by thirty seconds. The passenger train had just pulled out from the station when the wild General was seen roaring toward it. The two locomotives, screaming under the pressure of their brakes, were stopped within a few yards of each other. The passenger engineer was trembling with fright—and he was angry. He refused to back up and let Andrews pass. A crisis seemed at hand, for Andrews literally did not have a moment to lose, as he had not yet cut the wires beyond Adairsville.

The rain still fell. The passenger conductor came up to see what was the trouble. Andrews addressed him in a tone of authority. He said he had requested the removal of his passenger train in order that powder for the front might not be delayed. Now he had no alternative but to issue orders. Without a word the conductor obeyed.

The spraddling hamlet of Calhoun diminished in the distance and the Yankees breathed more easily. Sergeant Major Ross had been right about a day's delay altering things. Yesterday it would have been smooth sailing —no extra trains, no excitement on the line, the powder-train story perfection itself. By now the raiders should have been near their triumphant journey's end. But to-day difficulties had been encountered only to be overcome. Five trains passed, a pursuit shaken off by a matter of minutes, and now they were on the main line once more with an open road ahead and a broken track behind.

9

Fuller covered the nine miles to Calhoun in ten minutes—which still leaves the Yankee Knight in possession of the record, however. The passenger train was still waiting. One scare in a day had been enough for the engineer. Andrews had tried vainly to send him on his way, which would certainly have been the end of Conductor Fuller. Instead, the raider's Nemesis, saved by another stroke of luck, rushed the Texas, running backward, out of Calhoun. Fuller himself perched on the tender where he could get a better view of the track.

The General and crew were within a few minutes of the first bridge to be burned—a covered wooden structure over the Oostanaula River. Here Andrews planned to render his success secure. He stopped a couple of miles in front of the bridge to cut wires and take up track. While some of the men tugged at a rail, others collected wood to fire the bridge. This would not be easy as the downpour continued and everything was soaking wet. The toiling rail crew was having its usual difficulties when they saw a sight that would not have startled them more had it been a ghost. A locomotive whistled and hove in view, burning up the track from the south. For the first time during the chase, Fuller sighted his quarry. Those at the rail yanked like men possessed. They could not break the rail, but they bent a yard of it some inches out of line. That seemed sufficient to wreck any train and the men jumped into the box-cars and the General started off.

It did not, however, wreck the mysterious pursuer. As far as the fugitives could see the oncoming engine shot over the bent rail as if nothing was wrong. On the tender Fuller had been so engrossed in observing the men in possession of the General, that he overlooked the rail until it was too late to stop. Actually the rail had nearly thrown the pursuing crew from the cab and they thought they were lost. The bent rail was on the inside of a curve and the weight of the swiftly moving engine was on the outside rail. The bent rail simply straightened and the train kept on the track.

As for the Yankees, all their chances of getting away now depended on firing the bridge, and Andrews attempted a dramatic expedient to gain time for that. He reversed the General and charged his pursuers. When going full tilt the rear box-car was uncoupled, and the General was started forward leaving the box-car to continue the assault.

The bridge was reached. On a fair day a little oil and a faggot or two would have finished it, but it was raining harder than ever. Every stick of wood was soaked and the men kept their pistol ammunition dry with difficulty. Nevertheless a fire was kindled and coaxed to burn in one of the remaining cars. The plan was to leave the car in flames on the covered wooden bridge, but before the fire seemed the least encouraging here came the pursuers—pushing the raider's box-car in front of them. The southerners had had some more luck. On a down-grade the flying box-car might have driven them back for miles. But the hard-pressed Andrews was compelled to let it go on a level stretch. Fuller simply had reversed the Texas for a short distance, and, when the car slowed down, coupled it on and renewed the chase. When he came in sight of the bridge, Andrews was forced to flee, and, for the first time, a feeling that the fates were not on their side overtook the Union adventurers.

Certainly all the advantages of chance had gone against Andrews. Still, Fuller's pursuit had been intelligent and daring and he had made no mistakes. None can question the daring of Andrews, but he had made a grave mistake in not destroying the Yonah.

On the bridge the Texas picked up the smoking car that Andrews had tried to convert into a firebrand. Both cars were side-tracked at Reseca, a station a few hundred yards beyond the bridge.

Passing Reseca the General did not run very fast. It was plain that there was no eluding the Texas by speed alone. The Yankees tried wrecking her. As there was no time to stop and dismantle the track, a hole was rammed in the rear end of the remaining box-car, and ties and sticks of firewood were dropped out in the hope of obstructing a rail. The wood showed a maddening disposition to roll off the track, but now and then a piece stayed on and Fuller was forced by the protests of his men to slow up.

The desperate expedient was effective as long as the wood lasted, but presently it was all gone, except a few sticks which were crammed into the fire-box for a sprint to the next wood-yard. There about half a load had been thrown aboard when the Texas hove in sight, but fuel was so precious that the men continued to pile it on and Fuller had to check speed to avert a collision. Before the hard-pressed General pulled out, Andrew's men had made a barrier of ties across the track, and, while Fuller removed it, the fugitives gained a few minutes' headway in their race to the water tank a few miles farther, for the General's boilers were almost dry. When the General left the water tank, the Texas was again in view.

Andrews was now ten or twelve miles from Dalton which was a large town with a complicated arrangement of switches. Somehow the hard-pressed Yankees must gain a few minutes to take care of possible delays there. It was also equally important to cut the wires before a message could get into Dalton to raise enemies in his path. A tremendous spurt was made. Then a sudden stop by throwing the engine into reverse. Before the wheels had ceased to revolve, the diminutive Scott was out of the car and up a pole. Another party was building a barrier across the track. Another was frantically trying to wrench up a rail. Corporal Pittenger, a young law student who had got in the army with difficulty because of his thick spectacles, approached Mr. Andrews.

"We can capture that train if you are willing," he said.

"How?" asked Andrews.

Without hesitating for a word the Corporal outlined an excellent plan of attack. "Block the track and place our party in ambush. Run our engine out of sight to disarm suspicion. When they stop to remove the obstruction we'll seize their engine and reverse it against any other trains that may be in this pursuit."

Mr. Andrews said nothing for a moment. "It is a good plan," he conceded. "It is worth trying." He glanced about as if studying the landscape. His survey was interrupted by the inevitable whistle of the pursuers. His glance shifted to the men who were vainly straining to force the rail.

"All aboard, boys," he called, and the dash to Dalton began.

10

The Texas was not in sight when the General halted a hundred yards in front of the Dalton depot which was a large structure with a shed enclosing the track. Several local railwaymen came up. The powder story was useless now—what with one battered car which had been literally peeled for fire-wood and a company of correspondingly battered men. Andrews dropped from the cab to see if the switches were set for a clear track. They appeared to be. "I am running this train through to Corinth," he called out in general acknowledgment of a flood of inquiries, and, signaling Knight to proceed, caught on the engine step as it passed.

The General tore through the station shed and through the town to the great consternation of the citizens of Dalton. This consternation had not diminished when, five minutes later, Fuller's Texas rolled in merely slowing up to drop a man who bolted like a shot from a gun and literally fell upon the telegrapher's key.

At the same instant, a mile from Dalton, in plain sight of a Confederate regiment, John Scott was climbing a telegraph pole. One minute later the wire was cut, putting a period where no period was intended in Conductor Fuller's message from Dalton. But this much got through:

"GEN LEADBETTER COMMANDER AT CHATTANOOGA. MY TRAIN CAPTURED THIS A M AT BIG SHANTY EVIDENTLY BY FEDERAL SOLDIERS IN DISGUISE. THEY ARE MAKING RAPIDLY FOR CHATTANOOGA POSSIBLY WITH THE IDEA OF BURNING. . . ."

The Chattanooga commandant understood. What chance now for Andrews and his band? Every mile of flight from Fuller brought them a mile nearer to the open arms of the waiting Leadbetter.

Some distance from Dalton the road passed through a tunnel. Here was the place to turn and fight if they were ever to do it. But Andrews signaled to keep on. He meant to stake everything on the destruction of the Chickamauga River bridge. He ordered a fire built in the remaining box-car. This was hard to do. The car had been picked clean. Inside and out, it was wet and rain was still falling in torrents.

By drawing on the last quart of oil and almost the last stick of fire-wood a blaze was started. It crackled encouragingly and the spirits of the men rose with it. The little train stopped under the shelter of the bridge. As the oil burned from the surface of the wet wood the fire dropped a little. Still, the interior of the bridge shed was fairly dry and given time the flames in the car would do their work.

A fire always holds an attraction, and, as this fire meant so much to its guardians, they half forgot their peril, and tarried to watch it. It was midday and the strain since dawn had been great. It was worth the price to relax. If the fire failed a few minutes would not matter.

The blaze picked up again. It took possession of the car and tongues of flame licked the half-dry timbers of the bridge. No one had said a word for what might have been a full moment when the lookout called that the smoke of the Texas was in sight.

The burning car was uncoupled rather deliberately and one of Andrews's men, who was brave enough to tell the truth, said that his heart sank. The General limped through the village of Ringgold. Wood was gone and oil was gone, but Andrews dared not stop.

Fuller picked up the blazing car on the bridge and dropped it at Ring-gold. A few miles from there he sighted the Yankees drilling along at fifteen miles an hour. They were burning their clothing to keep moving and the journals on their engine were melting from want of oil. Their last fragment of hope was a wood-yard several miles ahead.

Fuller guessed their straits and their plan, but he lagged back. He knew that he was dealing with men who would be desperate at bay. With the whole country behind him aroused and other engines in pursuit by now, Fuller felt no call to precipitate a battle.

The General's speed fell to eight miles an hour and Fuller slacked accordingly, keeping a good quarter to half a mile in the rear.

Knight said he could not make the wood-yard. Andrews did not delay his decision.

"Jump and scatter, men, and be quick."

The men began to jump, rolling over and over until they vanished in the dripping woods beside the right-of-way. When all were off Knight reversed the engine and jumped. The old General moved off toward the pursuers, but the steam was too low for it to obtain any speed. Fuller simply reversed, ran back away and let the General come up gradually and couple on.

A troop train which had joined the pursuit was soon on the spot and the country was smothered with searchers under orders to take the "train thieves," dead or alive.

11

All were taken, the captures requiring from a few hours to ten days.

Nothing the soldiers of the North did during the war aroused the South to a greater pitch than the exploit of these twenty-one men. The newspaper *Southern Confederacy* of Atlanta declared the preservation of the railroad bridges a victory equal to Bull Run. "The mind and heart sink back at the bare contemplation of the consequences that would have followed the success" of the raid. It resulted in reorganization of railroad administration in the South.

Mr. Andrews left his bones in Dixie. He was hanged in Atlanta, ten days before the date set for his wedding. When his Kentucky fiancée read an account of it in a newspaper, the shock killed her.

The following week seven others were executed, but the sudden thrust of a Federal column interrupted the court martial of their fourteen comrades, eight of whom eventually escaped and reached the Union pickets. By this time the cry for vengeance had modulated and a few southerners went so far as to show publicly their admiration for the Yankees' valor. A year later the six who remained in Confederate hands were exchanged for their weight in important political prisoners held by the North. President Lincoln received them at the White House and listened to an account of their adventures.

"A little luck with the battles now and the war will be over," he said.

Turn About

BY

WILLIAM FAULKNER

I

THE American—the older one—wore no pink Bedfords. His breeches were of plain whipcord, like the tunic. And the tunic had no long London-cut skirts, so that below the Sam Browne the tail of it stuck straight out like the tunic of a military policeman beneath his holster belt. And he wore simple puttees and the easy shoes of a man of middle age, instead of Savile Row boots, and the shoes and the puttees did not match in shade, and the ordnance belt did not match either of them, and the pilot's wings on his breast were just wings. But the ribbon beneath them was a good ribbon, and the insigne on his shoulders were the twin bars of a captain. He was not tall. His face was thin, a little aquiline; the eyes intelligent and a little tired. He was past twenty-five; looking at him, one thought, not Phi Beta Kappa exactly, but Skull and Bones perhaps, or possibly a Rhodes scholarship.

One of the men who faced him probably could not see him at all. He was being held on his feet by an American military policeman. He was quite drunk, and in contrast with the heavy-jawed policeman who held him erect on his long, slim, boneless legs, he looked like a masquerading girl. He was possibly eighteen, tall, with a pink-and-white face and blue eyes, and a mouth like a girl's mouth. He wore a pea-coat, buttoned awry and stained with recent mud, and upon his blond head, at that unmistakable and rakish swagger which no other people can ever approach or imitate, the cap of a Royal Naval Officer.

"What's this, corporal?" the American captain said. "What's the trouble? He's an Englishman. You'd better let their M. P.'s take care of him."

"I know he is," the policeman said. He spoke heavily, breathing heavily, in the voice of a man under physical strain; for all his girlish delicacy of limb, the English boy was heavier—or more helpless—than he looked. "Stand up!" the policeman said. "They're officers!"

The English boy made an effort then. He pulled himself together, focusing his eyes. He swayed, throwing his arms about the policeman's neck, and with the other hand he saluted, his hand flicking, fingers curled a little, to his right ear, already swaying again and catching himself again. "Cheer-o, sir," he said. "Name's not Beatty, I hope."

"No," the captain said.

"Ah," the English boy said. "Hoped not. My mistake. No offense, what?"

"No offense," the captain said quietly. But he was looking at the policeman. The second American spoke. He was a lieutenant, also a pilot. But he was not twenty-five and he wore the pink breeches, the London boots, and his tunic might have been a British tunic save for the collar.

"It's one of those navy eggs," he said. "They pick them out of the gutters here all night long. You don't come to town often enough."

"Oh," the captain said. "I've heard about them. I remember now." He also remarked now that, though the street was a busy one—it was just outside a popular café—and there were many passers, soldier, civilian, women, yet none of them so much as paused, as though it were a familiar sight. He was looking at the policeman. "Can't you take him to his ship?"

"I thought of that before the captain did," the policeman said. "He says he can't go aboard his ship after dark because he puts the ship away at sundown."

"Puts it away?"

"Stand up, sailor!" the policeman said savagely, jerking at his lax burden. "Maybe the captain can make sense out of it. Damned if I can. He says they keep the boat under the wharf. Run it under the wharf at night, and that they can't get it out again until the tide goes out tomorrow."

"Under the wharf? A boat? What is this?" He was now speaking to the lieutenant. "Do they operate some kind of aquatic motorcycles?"

"Something like that," the lieutenant said. "You've seen them—the boats. Launches, camouflaged and all. Dashing up and down the harbor. You've seen them. They do that all day and sleep in the gutters here all night."

"Oh," the captain said. "I thought those boats were ship commanders' launches. You mean to tell me they use officers just to—"

"I don't know," the lieutenant said. "Maybe they use them to fetch hot water from one ship to another. Or buns. Or maybe to go back and forth fast when they forget napkins or something."

"Nonsense," the captain said. He looked at the English boy again.

"That's what they do," the lieutenant said. "Town's lousy with them all night long. Gutters full, and their M.P.'s carting them away in batches, like nursemaids in a park. Maybe the French give them the launches to get them out of the gutters during the day."

"Oh," the captain said, "I see." But it was clear that he didn't see, wasn't listening, didn't believe what he did hear. He looked at the English boy. "Well, you can't leave him here in that shape," he said.

Again the English boy tried to pull himself together. "Quite all right, 'sure you," he said glassily, his voice pleasant, cheerful almost, quite courteous. "Used to it. Confounded rough *pavé*, though. Should force French do something about it. Visiting lads jolly well deserve decent field to play on, what?"

"And he was jolly well using all of it too," the policeman said savagely. "He must think he's a one-man team, maybe."

At that moment a fifth man came up. He was a British military police-man. "Nah then," he said. "What's this? What's this?" Then he saw the Americans' shoulder bars. He saluted. At the sound of his voice the English boy turned, swaying, peering.

"Oh, hullo, Albert," he said.

"Nah then, Mr. Hope," the British policeman said. He said to the Ameri-can policeman, over his shoulder: "What is it this time?"

"Likely nothing," the American said. "The way you guys run a war. But I'm a stranger here. Here. Take him."

"What is this, corporal?" the captain said. "What was he doing?"

"He won't call it nothing," the American policeman said, jerking his head at the British policeman. "He'll just call it a thrush or a robin or some-thing. I turn into this street about three blocks back a while ago, and I find it blocked with a line of trucks going up from the docks, and the drivers all hollering ahead what the hell the trouble is. So I come on, and I find it is about three blocks of them, blocking the cross streets too; and I come on to the head of it where the trouble is, and I find about a dozen of the drivers out in front, holding a caucus or something in the middle of the street, and I come up and I say, 'What's going on here?' and they leave me through and I find this egg here laying—"

"Yer talking about one of His Majesty's officers, my man," the British policeman said.

"Watch yourself, corporal," the captain said. "And you found this offi-cer—"

"He had done gone to bed in the middle of the street, with an empty basket for a pillow. Laying there with his hands under his head and his knees crossed, arguing with them about whether he ought to get up and move or not. He said that the trucks could turn back and go around by another street, but that he couldn't use any other street, because this street was his."

"His street?"

The English boy had listened, interested, pleasant. "Billet, you see," he said. "Must have order, even in war emergency. Billet by lot. This street mine; no poaching, eh? Next street Jamie Wutherspoon's. But trucks can go by that street because Jamie not using it yet. Not in bed yet. Insomnia. Knew so. Told them. Trucks go that way. See now?"

"Was that it, corporal?" the captain said.

"He told you. He wouldn't get up. He just laid there, arguing with them. He was telling one of them to go somewhere and bring back a copy of their articles of war—"

"King's Regulations; yes," the captain said.

"—and see if the book said whether he had the right of way, or the trucks. And then I got him up, and then the captain come along. And that's all. And with the captain's permission I'll now hand him over to His Majesty's wet nur—"

"That'll do, corporal," the captain said. "You can go. I'll see to this."
The policeman saluted and went on. The British policeman was now sup-
porting the English boy. "Can't you take him home?" the captain said.
"Where are their quarters?"

"I don't rightly know, sir, if they have quarters or not. We—I usually
see them about the pubs until daylight. They don't seem to use quarters."

"You mean, they really aren't off of ships?"

"Well, sir, they might be ships, in a manner of speaking. But a man
would have to be a bit sleepier than him to sleep in one of them."

"I see," the captain said. He looked at the policeman. "What kind of
boats are they?"

This time the policeman's voice was immediate, final and completely
inflectionless. It was like a closed door. "I don't rightly know, sir."

"Oh," the captain said. "Quite. Well, he's in no shape to stay about
pubs until daylight this time."

"Perhaps I can find him a bit of a pub with a back table, where he can
sleep," the policeman said. But the captain was not listening. He was look-
across the street, where the lights of another café fell across the pavement.
The English boy yawned terrifically, like a child does, his mouth pink and
frankly gaped as a child's.

The captain turned to the policeman:

"Would you mind stepping across there and asking for Captain Bogard's
driver? I'll take care of Mr. Hope."

The policeman departed. The captain now supported the English boy,
his hand beneath the other's arm. Again the boy yawned like a weary child.
"Steady," the captain said. "The car will be here in a minute."

"Right," the English boy said through the yawn.

II

Once in the car he went to sleep immediately with the peaceful suddenness of babies, sitting between the two Americans. But though the aerodrome was only thirty minutes away, he was awake when they arrived,
apparently quite fresh, and asking for whisky. When they entered the
mess he appeared quite sober, only blinking a little in the lighted room, in
his raked cap and his awry-buttoned pea-jacket and a soiled silk muffler,
embroidered with a club insignia which Bogard recognized to have come
from a famous preparatory school, twisted about his throat.

"Ah," he said, his voice fresh, clear now, not blurred, quite cheerful,
quite loud, so that the others in the room turned and looked at him. "Jolly.
Whisky, what?" He went straight as a bird dog to the bar in the corner,
the lieutenant following. Bogard had turned and gone on to the other end
of the room, where five men sat about a card table.

"What's he admiral of?" one said.

"Of the whole Scotch navy, when I found him," Bogard said.

Another looked up. "Oh, I thought I'd seen him in town." He looked at
the guest. "Maybe it's because he was on his feet that I didn't recognize
him when he came in. You usually see them lying down in the gutter."

"Oh," the first said. He, too, looked around. "Is he one of those guys?"

"Sure. You've seen them. Sitting on the curb, you know, with a couple of limey M.P.'s hauling at their arms."

"Yes. I've seen them," the other said. They all looked at the English boy. He stood at the bar, talking, his voice loud, cheerful. "They all look like him too," the speaker said. "About seventeen or eighteen. They run those little boats that are always dashing in and out."

"Is that what they do?" a third said. "You mean, there's a male marine auxiliary to the Waacs? Good Lord, I sure made a mistake when I enlisted. But this war never was advertised right."

"I don't know," Bogard said. "I guess they do more than just ride around."

But they were not listening to him. They were looking at the guest. "They run by clock," the first said. "You can see the condition of one of them after sunset and almost tell what time it is. But what I don't see is, how a man that's in that shape at one o'clock every morning can even see a battleship the next day."

"Maybe when they have a message to send out to a ship," another said, "they just make duplicates and line the launches up and point them toward the ship and give each one a duplicate of the message and let them go. And the ones that miss the ship just cruise around the harbor until they hit a dock somewhere."

"It must be more than that," Bogard said.

He was about to say something else, but at that moment the guest turned from the bar and approached, carrying a glass. He walked steadily enough, but his color was high and his eyes were bright, and he was talking, loud, cheerful, as he came up.

"I say. Won't you chaps join—." He ceased. He seemed to remark something; he was looking at their breasts. "Oh, I say. You fly. All of you. Oh, good gad! Find it jolly, eh?"

"Yes," somebody said. "Jolly."

"But dangerous, what?"

"A little faster than tennis," another said. The guest looked at him, bright, affable, intent.

Another said quickly, "Bogard says you command a vessel."

"Hardly a vessel. Thanks, though. And not command. Ronnie does that. Ranks me a bit. Age."

"Ronnie?"

"Yes. Nice. Good egg. Old, though. Stickler."

"Stickler?"

"Frightful. You'd not believe it. Whenever we sight smoke and I have the glass, he sheers away. Keeps the ship hull down all the while. No beaver then. Had me two down a fortnight yesterday."

The Americans glanced at one another. "No beaver?"

"We play it. With basket masts, you see. See a basket mast. Beaver! One up. The Ergenstrasse doesn't count any more, though."

The men about the table looked at one another. Bogard spoke. "I see. When you or Ronnie see a ship with basket masts, you get a beaver on the other. I see. What is the Ergenstrasse?"

"She's German. Interned. Tramp steamer. Foremast rigged so it looks something like a basket mast. Booms, cables, I dare say. I didn't think it looked very much like a basket mast, myself. But Ronnie said yes. Called it one day. Then one day they shifted her across the basin and I called her on Ronnie. So we decided to not count her any more. See now, eh?"

"Oh," the one who had made the tennis remark said, "I see. You and Ronnie run about in the launch, playing beaver. H'm'm. That's nice. Did you ever pl—"

"Jerry," Bogard said. The guest had not moved. He looked down at the speaker, still smiling, his eyes quite wide.

The speaker still looked at the guest. "Has yours and Ronnie's boat got a yellow stern?"

"A yellow stern?" the English boy said. He had quit smiling, but his face was still pleasant.

"I thought that maybe when the boats had two captains, they might paint the stern yellow or something."

"Oh," the guest said. "Burt and Reeves aren't officers."

"Burt and Reeves," the other said, in a musing tone. "So they go, too. Do they play beaver too?"

"Jerry," Bogard said. The other looked at him. Bogard jerked his head a little. "Come over here." The other rose. They went aside. "Lay off of him," Bogard said. "I mean it, now. He's just a kid. When you were that age, how much sense did you have? Just about enough to get to chapel on time."

"My country hadn't been at war going on four years, though," Jerry said. "Here we are, spending our money and getting shot at by the clock, and it's not even our fight, and these limeys that would have been goose-stepping twelve months now if it hadn't been—"

"Shut it," Bogard said. "You sound like a Liberty Loan."

"—taking it like it was a fair or something. 'Jolly.' " His voice was now falsetto, lilting. " 'But dangerous, what?' "

"Sh-h-h-h," Bogard said.

"I'd like to catch him and his Ronnie out in the harbor, just once. Any harbor. London's. I wouldn't want anything but a Jenny, either. Jenny? Hell, I'd take a bicycle and a pair of water wings! I'll show him some war."

"Well, you lay off him now. He'll be gone soon."

"What are you going to do with him?"

"I'm going to take him along this morning. Let him have Harper's place out front. He says he can handle a Lewis. Says they have one on the boat. Something he was telling me—about how he once shot out a channel-marker light at seven hundred yards."

"Well, that's your business. Maybe he can beat you."

"Beat me?"

"Playing beaver. And then you can take on Ronnie."

"I'll show him some war, anyway," Bogard said. He looked at the guest. "His people have been in it three years now, and he seems to take it like a sophomore in town for the big game." He looked at Jerry again. "But you lay off him now."

As they approached the table, the guest's voice was loud and cheerful: ". . . if he got the glasses first, he would go in close and look, but, when I got them first, he'd sheer off where I couldn't see anything but the smoke. Frightful stickler. Frightful. But Ergenstrasse not counting any more. And if you make a mistake and call her, you lose two beaver from your score. If Ronnie were only to forget and call her we'd be even."

III

At two o'clock the English boy was still talking, his voice bright, innocent and cheerful. He was telling them how Switzerland had been spoiled by 1914, and instead of the vacation which his father had promised him for his sixteenth birthday, when that birthday came he and his tutor had had to do with Wales. But that he and the tutor had got pretty high and that he dared to say—with all due respect to any present who might have had the advantage of Switzerland, of course—that one could see probably as far from Wales as from Switzerland. "Perspire as much and breathe as hard, anyway," he added. And about him the Americans sat, a little hard-bitten, a little sober, somewhat older, listening to him with a kind of cold astonishment. They had been getting up for some time now and going out and returning in flying clothes, carrying helmets and goggles. An orderly entered with a tray of coffee cups, and the guest realized that for some time now he had been hearing engines in the darkness outside.

At last Bogard rose. "Come along," he said. "We'll get your togs." When they emerged from the mess, the sound of the engines was quite loud—an idling thunder. In alignment along the invisible tarmac was a vague rank of short banks of flickering blue-green fire suspended apparently in mid-air. They crossed the aerodrome to Bogard's quarters, where the lieutenant, McGinnis, sat on a cot fastening his flying boots. Bogard reached down a Sidcott suit and threw it across the cot. "Put this on," he said.

"Will I need all this?" the guest said. "Shall we be gone that long?"

"Probably," Bogard said. "Better use it. Cold upstairs."

The guest picked up the suit. "I say," he said. "I say. Ronnie and I have a do ourselves, tomor—today. Do you think Ronnie won't mind if I am a bit late? Might not wait for me."

"We'll be back before teatime," McGinnis said. He seemed quite busy with his boot. "Promise you." The English boy looked at him.

"What time should you be back?" Bogard said.

"Oh, well," the English boy said, "I dare say it will be all right. They let Ronnie say when to go, anyway. He'll wait for me if I should be a bit late."

"He'll wait," Bogard said. "Get your suit on."

"Right," the other said. They helped him into the suit. "Never been up before," he said, chattily, pleasantly. "Dare say you can see farther than from mountains, eh?"

"See more, anyway," McGinnis said. "You'll like it."

"Oh, rather. If Ronnie only waits for me. Lark. But dangerous, isn't it?"

"Go on," McGinnis said. "You're kidding me."

"Shut your trap, Mac," Bogard said. "Come along. Want some more coffee?" He looked at the guest, but McGinnis answered:

"No. Got something better than coffee. Coffee makes such a confounded stain on the wings."

"On the wings?" the English boy said. "Why coffee on the wings?"

"Stow it, I said, Mac," Bogard said. "Come along."

They recrossed the aerodrome, approaching the muttering banks of flame. When they drew near, the guest began to discern the shape, the outlines, of the Handley-Page. It looked like a Pullman coach run upslanted aground into the skeleton of the first floor of an incomplete skyscraper. The guest looked at it quietly.

"It's larger than a cruiser," he said in his bright, interested voice. "I say, you know. This doesn't fly in one lump. You can't pull my leg. Seen them before. It comes in two parts: Captain Bogard and me in one; Mac and 'nother chap in other. What?"

"No," McGinnis said. Bogard had vanished. "It all goes up in one lump. Big lark, eh? Buzzard, what?"

"Buzzard?" the guest murmured. "Oh, I say. A cruiser. Flying. I say, now."

"And listen," McGinnis said. His hand came forth; something cold fumbled against the hand of the English boy—a bottle. "When you feel yourself getting sick, see? Take a pull at it."

"Oh, shall I get sick?"

"Sure. We all do. Part of flying. This will stop it. But if it doesn't. See?"

"What? Quite. What?"

"Not overside. Don't spew it overside."

"Not overside?"

"It'll blow back in Bogy's and my face. Can't see. Bingo. Finished. See?"

"Oh, quite. What shall I do with it?" Their voices were quiet, brief, grave as conspirators.

"Just duck your head and let her go."

"Oh, quite."

Bogard returned. "Show him how to get into the front pit, will you?" he said. McGinnis led the way through the trap. Forward, rising to the slant of the fuselage, the passage narrowed; a man would need to crawl.

"Crawl in there and keep going," McGinnis said.

"It looks like a dog kennel," the guest said.

"Doesn't it, though?" McGinnis agreed cheerfully. "Cut along with you." Stooping, he could hear the other scuttling forward. "You'll find a Lewis gun up there, like as not," he said into the tunnel.

The voice of the guest came back: "Found it."

"The gunnery sergeant will be along in a minute and show you if it is loaded."

"It's loaded," the guest said; almost on the heels of his words the gun fired, a brief staccato burst. There were shouts, the loudest from the ground beneath the nose of the aeroplane. "It's quite all right," the English boy's voice said. "I pointed it west before I let it off. Nothing back there but Marine office and your brigade headquarters. Ronnie and I always do this before we go anywhere. Sorry if I was too soon. Oh, by the way," he added, "my name's Claude. Don't think I mentioned it."

On the ground, Bogard and two other officers stood. They had come up running. "Fired it west," one said. "How in hell does he know which way is west?"

"He's a sailor," the other said. "You forgot that."

"He seems to be a machine gunner too," Bogard said.

"Let's hope he doesn't forget that," the first said.

IV

Nevertheless, Bogard kept an eye on the silhouetted head rising from the round gunpit in the nose ten feet ahead of him. "He did work that gun, though," he said to McGinnis beside him. "He even put the drum on himself, didn't he?"

"Yes," McGinnis said. "If he just doesn't forget and think that that gun is him and his tutor looking around from a Welsh alp."

"Maybe I should not have brought him," Bogard said. McGinnis didn't answer. Bogard jockeyed the wheel a little. Ahead, in the gunner's pit, the guest's head moved this way and that continuously, looking. "We'll get there and unload and haul air for home," Bogard said. "Maybe in the dark— Confound it, it would be a shame for his country to be in this mess for four years and him not even to see a gun pointed in his direction."

"He'll see one tonight if he don't keep his head in," McGinnis said.

But the boy did not do that. Not even when they had reached the objective and McGinnis had crawled down to the bomb toggles. And even when the searchlights found them and Bogard signaled to the other machines and dived, the two engines snarling full speed into and through the bursting shells, he could see the boy's face in the searchlight's glare, leaned far overside, coming sharply out as a spotlighted face on a stage, with an expression upon it of childlike interest and delight. "But he's firing that Lewis," Bogard thought. "Straight too"; nosing the machine farther down, watching the pinpoints swing into the sights, his right hand lifted, waiting to drop into McGinnis' sight. He dropped his hand; above the noise of the engines he seemed to hear the click and whistle of the released bombs as the machine freed of the weight, shot zooming in a long upward bounce that carried it for an instant out of the light. Then he was pretty busy for a time, coming into and through the shells again, shooting athwart another beam that caught and held long enough for him to see the English boy leaning far over the side, looking back and down past the right wing, the undercarriage. "Maybe he's read about it somewhere," Bogard thought, turning, looking back to pick up the rest of the flight.

Then it was all over, the darkness cool and empty and peaceful and almost quiet, with only the steady sound of the engines. McGinnis climbed back into the office, and standing up in his seat, he fired the colored pistol this time and stood for a moment longer, looking backward toward where the searchlights still probed and sabered. He sat down again.

"O.K.," he said. "I counted all four of them. Let's haul air." Then he looked forward. "What's become of the King's Own? You didn't hang him onto a bomb release, did you?" Bogard looked. The forward pit was empty. It was in dim silhouette again now, against the stars, but there was nothing there now save the gun. "No," McGinnis said; "there he is. See? Leaning overside. Dammit, I told him not to spew it! There he comes back!" The guest's head came into view again. But again it sank out of sight.

"He's coming back," Bogard said. "Stop him. Tell him we're going to have every squadron in the Hun Channel group on top of us in thirty minutes."

McGinnis swung himself down and stooped at the entrance to the passage. "Get back!" he shouted. The other was almost out; they squatted so, face to face like two dogs, shouting at another above the noise of the still-unthrottled engines on either side of the fabric walls. The English boy's voice was thin and high.

"Bomb!" he shrieked.

"Yes," McGinnis shouted. "They were bombs! We gave them hell! Get back I tell you! Have every Hun in France on us in ten minutes! Get back to your gun!"

Again the boy's voice came, high, faint above the noise: "Bomb! All right?"

"Yes! Yes! All right. Back to your gun, damn you!"

McGinnis climbed back into the office. "He went back. Want me to take her awhile?"

"All right," Bogard said. He passed McGinnis the wheel. "Ease her back some. I'd just as soon it was daylight when they come down on us."

"Right," McGinnis said. He moved the wheel suddenly. "What's the matter with that right wing?" he said. "Watch it. . . . See? I'm flying on the right aileron and a little rudder. Feel it."

Bogard took the wheel a moment. "I didn't notice that. Wire somewhere, I guess. I didn't think any of those shells were that close. Watch her, though."

"Right," McGinnis said. "And so you are going with him on his boat tomorrow—today."

"Yes, I promised him. Confound it, you can't hurt a kid, you know."

"Why don't you take Collier along, with his mandolin? Then you could sail around and sing."

"I promised him," Bogard said. "Get that wing up a little."

"Right," McGinnis said.

Thirty minutes later it was beginning to be dawn; the sky was gray. Presently McGinnis said: "Well, here they come. Look at them! They look like mosquitoes in September. I hope he don't get worked up now and think he's playing beaver. If he does he'll just be one down to Ronnie, provided the devil has a beard. . . . Want the wheel?"

V

At eight o'clock the beach, the Channel, was beneath them. Throttled back, the machine drifted down as Bogard ruddered it gently into the Channel wind. His face was strained, a little tired.

McGinnis looked tired, too, and he needed a shave.

"What do you guess he is looking at now?" he said. For again the English boy was leaning over the right side of the cockpit, looking backward and downward past the right wing.

"I don't know," Bogard said. "Maybe bullet holes." He blasted the port engine. "Must have the riggers—"

"He could see some closer than that," McGinnis said. "I'll swear I saw tracer going into his back at one time. Or maybe it's the ocean he's looking at. But he must have seen that when he came over from England." Then Bogard leveled off; the nose rose sharply, the sand, the curling tide edge fled along-side. Yet still the English boy hung far overside, looking backward and downward at something beneath the right wing, his face rapt, with utter and childlike interest. Until the machine was completely stopped he continued to do so. Then he ducked down, and in the abrupt silence of the engines they could hear him crawling in the passage. He emerged just as the two pilots climbed stiffly down from the office, his face bright, eager; his voice high, excited.

"Oh, I say! Oh, good gad! What a chap! What a judge of distance! If Ronnie could only have seen! Oh, good gad! Or maybe they aren't like ours—don't load themselves as soon as the air strikes them."

The Americans looked at him. "What don't what?" McGinnis said.

"The bomb. It was magnificent; I say, I shan't forget it. Oh, I say, you know! It was splendid!"

After a while McGinnis said, "The bomb?" in a fainting voice. Then the two pilots glared at each other; they said in unison: "That right wing!" Then as one they clawed down through the trap and, with the guest at their heels, they ran around the machine and looked beneath the right wing. The bomb, suspended by its tail, hung straight down like a plumb bob beside the right wheel, its tip just touching the sand. And parallel with the wheel track was the long delicate line in the sand where its ultimate tip had dragged. Behind them the English boy's voice was high, clear, childlike:

"Frightened, myself. Tried to tell you. But realized you knew your business better than I. Skill. Marvelous. Oh, I say, I shan't forget it."

VI

A marine with a bayoneted rifle passed Bogard onto the wharf and directed him to the boat. The wharf was empty, and he didn't even see the boat until he approached the edge of the wharf and looked directly down into it and upon the backs of two stooping men in greasy dungarees, who rose and glanced briefly at him and stooped again.

It was about thirty feet long and about three feet wide. It was painted with gray-green camouflage. It was quarter-decked forward, with two blunt, raked exhaust stacks. "Good Lord," Bogard thought, "if all that deck is engine—" Just aft the deck was the control seat; he saw a big wheel, an instrument panel. Rising to a height of about a foot above the freeboard, and running from the stern forward to where the deck began, and continuing on across the after edge of the deck and thence back down the other gunwale to the stern, was a solid screen, also camouflaged, which inclosed the boat save for the width of the stern, which was open. Facing the steerman's seat like an eye was a hole in the screen about eight inches in diameter. And looking down into the long, narrow, still, vicious shape, he saw a machine gun swiveled at the stern, and he looked at the low screen—including which the whole vessel did not sit much more than a yard above water level—with its single empty forward-staring eye, and he thought quietly: "It's steel. It's made of steel." And his face was quite sober, quite thoughtful, and he drew his trench coat about him and buttoned it, as though he were getting cold.

He heard steps behind him and turned. But it was only an orderly from the aerodrome, accompanied by the marine with the rifle. The orderly was carrying a largish bundle wrapped in paper.

"From Lieutenant McGinnis to the captain," the orderly said.

Bogard took the bundle. The orderly and the marine retreated. He opened the bundle. It contained some objects and a scrawled note. The objects were a new yellow silk sofa cushion and a Japanese parasol, obviously borrowed, and a comb and a roll of toilet paper. The note said:

Couldn't find a camera anywhere and Collier wouldn't let me have his mandolin. But maybe Ronnie can play on the comb.

Mac.

Bogard looked at the objects. But his face was still quite thoughtful, quite grave. He rewrapped the things and carried the bundle on up the wharf a way and dropped it quietly into the water.

As he returned toward the invisible boat he saw two men approaching. He recognized the boy at once—tall, slender, already talking, voluble, his head bent a little toward his shorter companion, who plodded along beside him, hands in pockets, smoking a pipe. The boy still wore the pea-coat beneath a flapping oilskin, but in place of the rakish and casual cap he now wore an infantryman's soiled Balaclava helmet, with, floating behind him as though upon the sound of his voice, a curtainlike piece of cloth almost as long as a burnous.

"Hullo, there!" he cried, still a hundred yards away.

But it was the second man that Bogard was watching, thinking to himself that he had never in his life seen a more curious figure. There was something stolid about the very shape of his hunched shoulders, his slightly down-looking face. He was a head shorter than the other. His face was ruddy, too, but its mold was a profound gravity that was almost dour. It was the face of a man of twenty who has been for a year trying, even while asleep, to look twenty-one. He wore a high-necked sweater and dungaree slacks; above this a leather jacket; and above this a soiled naval officer's warmer that reached almost to his heels and which had one shoulder strap missing and not one remaining button at all. On his head was a plaid fore-and-aft deer stalker's cap, tied on by a narrow scarf brought across and down, hiding his ears, and then wrapped once about his throat and knotted with a hangman's noose beneath his left ear. It was unbelievably soiled, and with his hands elbow-deep in his pockets and his hunched shoulders and his bent head, he looked like someone's grandmother hung, say, for a witch. Clamped upside down between his teeth was a short brier pipe.

"Here he is!" the boy cried. "This is Ronnie. Captain Bogard."

"How are you?" Bogard said. He extended his hand. The other said no word, but his hand came forth, limp. It was quite cold, but it was hard, calloused. But he said no word; he just glanced briefly at Bogard and then away. But in that instant Bogard caught something in the look, something strange—a flicker; a kind of covert and curious respect, something like a boy of fifteen looking at a circus trapezist.

But he said no word. He ducked on; Bogard watched him drop from sight over the wharf edge as though he had jumped feet first into the sea. He remarked now that the engines in the invisible boat were running.

"We might get aboard too," the boy said. He started toward the boat, then he stopped. He touched Bogard's arm. "Yonder!" he hissed. "See?" His voice was thin with excitement.

"What?" Bogard also whispered; automatically he looked backward and upward, after old habit. The other was gripping his arm and pointing across the harbor.

"There! Over there. The Ergenstrasse. They have shifted her again." Across the harbor lay an ancient, rusting, sway-backed hulk. It was small and nondescript, and, remembering, Bogard saw that the foremast was a strange mess of cables and booms, resembling—allowing for a great deal of license or looseness of imagery—a basket mast. Beside him the boy was almost chortling. "Do you think that Ronnie noticed?" he hissed. "Do you?"

"I don't know," Bogard said.

"Oh, good gad! If he should glance up and call her before he notices, we'll be even. Oh, good gad! But come along." He went on; he was still chortling. "Careful," he said. "Frightful ladder."

He descended first, the two men in the boat rising and saluting. Ronnie had disappeared, save for his backside, which now filled a small hatch leading forward beneath the deck. Bogard descended gingerly.

"Good Lord," he said. "Do you have to climb up and down this every day?"

"Frightful, isn't it?" the other said, in his happy voice. "But you know yourself. Try to run a war with makeshifts, then wonder why it takes so long." The narrow hull slid and surged, even with Bogard's added weight. "Sits right on top, you see," the boy said. "Would float on a lawn, in a heavy dew. Goes right over them like a bit of paper."

"It does?" Bogard said.

"Oh, absolutely. That's why, you see." Bogard didn't see, but he was too busy letting himself gingerly down to a sitting posture. There were no thwarts; no seats save a long, thick, cylindrical ridge which ran along the bottom of the boat from the driver's seat to the stern. Ronnie had backed into sight. He now sat behind the wheel, bent over the instrument panel. But when he glanced back over his shoulder he did not speak. His face was merely interrogatory. Across his face there was now a long smudge of grease. The boy's face was empty, too, now.

"Right," he said. He looked forward, where one of the seamen had gone. "Ready forward?" he said.

"Aye, sir," the seaman said.

The other seaman was at the stern line. "Ready aft?"

"Aye, sir."

"Cast off." The boat sheered away, purring, a boiling of water under the stern. The boy looked down at Bogard. "Silly business. Do it shipshape, though. Can't tell when silly fourstriper—" His face changed again, immediate, solicitous. "I say. Will you be warm? I never thought to fetch—"

"I'll be all right," Bogard said. But the other was already taking off his oilskin. "No, no," Bogard said. "I won't take it."

"You'll tell me if you get cold?"

"Yes. Sure." He was looking down at the cylinder on which he sat. It was a half cylinder—that is, like the hot-water tank to some Gargantuan stove, sliced down the middle and bolted, open side down, to the floor plates. It was twenty feet long and more than two feet thick. Its top rose as high as the gunwales and between it and the hull on either side was just room enough for a man to place his feet to walk.

"That's Muriel," the boy said.

"Muriel?"

"Yes. The one before that was Agatha. After my aunt. The first one Ronnie and I had was Alice in Wonderland. Ronnie and I were the White Rabbit. Jolly, eh?"

"Oh, you and Ronnie have had three, have you?"

"Oh, yes," the boy said. He leaned down. "He didn't notice," he whispered. His face was again bright, gleeful. "When we come back," he said. "You watch."

"Oh," Bogard said. "The Ergenstrasse." He looked astern, and then he thought: "Good Lord! We must be going—traveling." He looked out now, broadside, and saw the harbor line fleeing past, and he thought to himself that the boat was well-nigh moving at the speed at which the Handley-Page flew, left the ground. They were beginning to bound now, even in the sheltered water, from one wave crest to the next with a distinct shock. His hand still rested on the cylinder on which he sat. He looked down at it again, following it from where it seemed to emerge beneath Ronnie's seat, to where it beveled into the stern. "It's the air in here, I suppose," he said.

"The what?" the boy said.

"The air. Stored up in here. That makes the boat ride high."

"Oh, yes. I dare say. Very likely. I hadn't thought about it." He came forward, his burnous whipping in the wind, and sat down beside Bogard. Their heads were below the top of the screen.

Astern the harbor fled, diminishing, sinking into the sea. The boat had begun to lift now, swooping forward and down, shocking almost stationary for a moment, then lifting and swooping again; a gout of spray came aboard over the bows like a flung shovelful of shot. "I wish you'd take this coat," the boy said.

Bogard didn't answer. He looked around at the bright face. "We're outside, aren't we?" he said quietly.

"Yes. . . . Do take it, won't you?"

"Thanks, no. I'll be all right. We won't be long, anyway, I guess."

"No. We'll turn soon. It won't be so bad then."

"Yes. I'll be all right when we turn." Then they did turn. The motion became easier. That is, the boat didn't bang head-on, shuddering, into the swells. They came up beneath now, and the boat fled with increased speed, with a long, sickening, yawing motion, first to one side and then the other. But it fled on, and Bogard looked astern with that same soberness with which he had first looked down into the boat. "We're going east now," he said.

"With just a spot of north," the boy said. "Makes her ride a bit better, what?"

"Yes," Bogard said. Astern there was nothing now save empty sea and the delicate needlelike cant of the machine gun against the boiling and slewing wake, and the two seamen crouching quietly in the stern. "Yes. It's easier." Then he said: "How far do we go?"

The boy leaned closer. He moved closer. His voice was happy, confidential, proud, though lowered a little: "It's Ronnie's show. He thought of it. Not that I wouldn't have, in time. Gratitude and all that. But he's the older, you see. Thinks fast. Courtesy, *noblesse oblige*—all that. Thought of it soon as I told him this morning. I said, 'Oh, I say. I've been there. I've seen it'; and he said, 'Not flying?'; and I said, 'Strewth'; and he said 'How far? No lying now'; and I said, 'Oh, far. Tremendous. Gone all night'; and he said, 'Flying all night. That must have been to Berlin'; and I said, 'I don't know. I dare say'; and he thought. I could see him thinking. Because he is the older, you see. More experience in courtesy, right thing. And he said, 'Berlin. No fun to that chap, dashing out and back with us.' And he thought and I waited, and I said, 'But we can't take him to Berlin. Too far. Don't know the way, either'; and he said—fast, like a shot—said, 'But there's Kiel'; and I knew—''

"What?" Bogard said. Without moving, his whole body sprang. "Kiel? In this?"

"Absolutely. Ronnie thought of it. Smart, even if he is a stickler. Said at once 'Zeebrugge no show at all for that chap. Must do best we can for him. Berlin,' Ronnie said. 'My gad! Berlin.' ''

"Listen," Bogard said. He had turned now, facing the other, his face quite grave. "What is this boat for?"

"For?"

"What does it do?" Then, knowing beforehand the answer to his own question, he said, putting his hand on the cylinder: "What is this in here? A torpedo, isn't it?"

"I thought you knew," the boy said.

"No," Bogard said. "I didn't know." His voice seemed to reach him from a distance, dry, cricketlike: "How do you fire it?"

"Fire it?"

"How do you get it out of the boat? When that hatch was open a while ago I could see the engines. They were right in front of the end of this tube."

"Oh," the boy said. "You pull a gadget there and the torpedo drops out astern. As soon as the screw touches the water it begins to turn, and then the torpedo is ready, loaded. Then all you have to do is turn the boat quickly and the torpedo goes on."

"You mean—" Bogard said. After a moment his voice obeyed him again. "You mean you aim the torpedo with the boat and release it and it starts moving, and you turn the boat out of the way and the torpedo passes through the same water that the boat just vacated?"

"Knew you'd catch on," the boy said. "Told Ronnie so. Airman. Tamer than yours, though. But can't be helped. Best we can do, just on water. But knew you'd catch on."

"Listen," Bogard said. His voice sounded to him quite calm. The boat fled on, yawing over the swells. He sat quite motionless. It seemed to him that he could hear himself talking to himself: "Go on. Ask him. Ask him what? Ask him how close to the ship do you have to be before you fire. . . . Listen," he said, in that calm voice. "Now, you tell Ronnie, you see. You just tell him—just say—" He could feel his voice ratting off on him again, so he stopped it. He sat quite motionless, waiting for it to come back; the boy leaning now, looking at his face. Again the boy's voice was solicitous:

"I say. You're not feeling well. These confounded shallow boats."

"It's not that," Bogard said. "I just— Do your orders say Kiel?"

"Oh, no. They let Ronnie say. Just so we bring the boat back. This is for you. Gratitude. Ronnie's idea. Tame, after flying. But if you'd rather, eh?"

"Yes, some place closer. You see, I—"

"Quite. I see. No vacations in wartime. I'll tell Ronnie." He went forward. Bogard did not move. The boat fled in long, slewing swoops. Bogard looked quietly astern, at the scudding sea, the sky.

"My God!" he thought. "Can you beat it? Can you beat it?"

The boy came back; Bogard turned to him a face the color of dirty paper. "All right now," the boy said. "Not Kiel. Nearer place, hunting probably just as good. Ronnie says he knows you will understand." He was tugging at his pocket. He brought out a bottle. "Here. Haven't forgot last night. Do the same for you. Good for the stomach, eh?"

Bogard drank, gulping—a big one. He extended the bottle, but the boy refused. "Never touch it on duty," he said. "Not like you chaps. Tame here."

The boat fled on. The sun was already down the west. But Bogard had lost all count of time, of distance. Ahead he could see white seas through the round eye opposite Ronnie's face, and Ronnie's hand on the wheel and the granite-like jut of his profiled jaw and the dead upside-down pipe. The boat fled on.

Then the boy leaned and touched his shoulder. He half rose. The boy was pointing. The sun was reddish; against it, outside them and about two miles away, a vessel—a trawler, it looked like—at anchor swung a tall mast.

"Lightship!" the boy shouted. "Theirs." Ahead Bogard could see a low, flat mole—the entrance to a harbor. "Channel!" the boy shouted. He swept his arm in both directions. "Mines!" His voice swept back on the wind. "Place filthy with them. All sides. Beneath us too. Lark, eh?"

VII

Against the mole a fair surf was beating. Running before the seas now, the boat seemed to leap from one roller to the next; in the intervals while the screw was in the air the engine seemed to be trying to tear itself out by the roots. But it did not slow; when it passed the end of the mole the boat seemed to be standing almost erect on its rudder, like a sailfish. The mole was a mile away. From the end of it little faint lights began to flicker like fireflies. The boy leaned. "Down," he said. "Machine guns. Might stop a stray."

"What do I do?" Bogard shouted. "What can I do?"

"Stout fellow! Give them hell, what? Knew you'd like it!"

Crouching, Bogard looked up at the boy, his face wild. "I can handle the machine gun!"

"No need," the boy shouted back. "Give them first innings. Sporting. Visitors, eh?" He was looking forward. "There she is. See?" They were in the harbor now, the basin opening before them. Anchored in the channel was a big freighter. Painted midships of the hull was a huge Argentine flag. "Must get back to stations!" the boy shouted down to him. Then at that moment Ronnie spoke for the first time. The boat was hurtling along now in smoother water. Its speed did not slacken and Ronnie did not turn his head when he spoke. He just swung his jutting jaw and the clamped cold pipe a little, and said from the side of his mouth a single word:

"Beaver."

The boy, stooped over what he had called his gadget, jerked up, his expression astonished and outraged. Bogard also looked forward and saw Ronnie's arm pointing to starboard. It was a light cruiser at anchor a mile away. She had basket masts, and as he looked a gun flashed from her after turret. "Oh, damn!" the boy cried. "Oh, you putt! Oh, confound you, Ronnie! Now I'm three down!" But he had already stooped again over his gadget, his face bright and empty and alert again; not sober; just calm, waiting. Again Bogard looked forward and felt the boat pivot on its rudder and head directly for the freighter at terrific speed. Ronnie now with one hand on the wheel and the other lifted and extended at the height of his head.

But it seemed to Bogard that the hand would never drop. He crouched, not sitting, watching with a kind of quiet horror the painted flag increase like a moving picture of a locomotive taken from between the rails. Again the gun crashed from the cruiser behind them, and the freighter fired point-blank at them from its poop. Bogard heard neither shot.

"Man, man!" he shouted. "For God's sake!"

Ronnie's hand dropped. Again the boat spun on its rudder. Bogard saw the bow rise, pivoting; he expected the hull to slam broadside on into the ship. But it didn't. It shot off on a long tangent. He was waiting for it to make a wide sweep, heading seaward, putting the freighter astern, and he thought of the cruiser again. "Get a broadside, this time, once we clear the freighter," he thought. Then he remembered the freighter, the torpedo, and looked back toward the freighter to watch the torpedo strike, and saw to his horror that the boat was now bearing down on the freighter again, in a skidding turn. Like a man in a dream, he watched himself rush down upon the ship and shoot past under her counter, still skidding, close enough to see the faces on her decks. "They missed and they are going to run down the torpedo and catch it and shoot it again," he thought idiotically.

So the boy had to touch his shoulder before he knew he was behind him. The boy's voice was quite calm: "Under Ronnie's seat there. A bit of a crank handle. If you'll just hand it to me—"

He found the crank. He passed it back; he was thinking dreamily: "Mac would say they had a telephone on board." But he didn't look at once to see what the boy was doing with it, for in that still and peaceful horror he was watching Ronnie, the cold pipe rigid in his jaw, hurling the boat at top speed round and round the freighter, so near that he could see the rivets in the plates. Then he looked aft, his face wild, importunate, and he saw what the boy was doing with the crank. He had fitted it into what was obviously a small windlass low on one flank of the tube near the head. He glanced up and saw Bogard's face. "Didn't go that time!" he shouted cheerfully.

"Go?" Bogard shouted. "It didn't— The torpedo—"

The boy and one of the seamen were quite busy, stooping over the windlass and the tube. "No. Clumsy. Always happening. Should think clever chaps like engineers— Happens, though. Draw her in and try her again."

"But the nose, the cap!" Bogard shouted. "It's still in the tube, isn't it? It's all right, isn't it?"

"Absolutely. But it's working now. Loaded. Screw's started turning. Get it back and drop it clear. If we should stop or slow up it would overtake us. Drive back into the tube. Bingo! What?"

Bogard was on his feet now, turned, braced to the terrific merry-go-round of the boat. High above them the freighter seemed to be spinning on her heel like a trick picture in the movies. "Let me have that winch!" he cried.

"Steady!" the boy said. "Mustn't draw her back too fast. Jam her into the head of the tube ourselves. Same bingo! Best let us. Every cobbler to his last, what?"

"Oh, quite," Bogard said. "Oh, absolutely." It was like someone else using his mouth. He leaned, braced, his hands on the cold tube, beside the others. He was hot inside, but his outside was cold. He could feel all his flesh jerking with cold as he watched the blunt, grained hand of the seaman turning the windlass in short, easy, inch-long arcs, while at the head of the tube the boy bent, tapping the cylinder with a spanner, lightly, his head turned with listening delicate and deliberate as a watchmaker. The boat rushed on in those furious, slewing turns. Bogard saw a long, drooping thread loop down from somebody's mouth, between his hands, and he found that the thread came from his own mouth.

He didn't hear the boy speak, nor notice when he stood up. He just felt the boat straighten out, flinging him to his knees beside the tube. The seaman had gone back to the stern and the boy stooped again over his gadget. Bogard knelt now, quite sick. He did not feel the boat when it swung again, nor hear the gun from the cruiser which had not dared to fire and the freighter which had not been able to fire, firing again. He did not feel anything at all when he saw the huge, painted flag directly ahead, and increasing with locomotive speed, and Ronnie's lifted hand drop. But this time he knew that the torpedo was gone; in pivoting and spinning this time the whole boat seemed to leave the water; he saw the bow of the boat shoot skyward like the nose of a pursuit ship going into a wingover. Then his outraged stomach denied him. He saw neither the geyser nor heard the detonation as he sprawled over the tube. He felt only a hand grasp him by the slack of his coat, and the voice of one of the seamen: "Steady all, sir. I've got you."

VIII

A voice roused him, a hand. He was half sitting in the narrow starboard runway, half lying across the tube. He had been there for quite a while; quite a while ago he had felt someone spread a garment over him. But he had not raised his head. "I'm all right," he said, "You keep it."

"Don't need it," the boy said. "Going home now."

"I'm sorry I—" Bogard said.

"Quite. Confounded shallow boats. Turn any stomach until you get used to them. Ronnie and I both, at first. Each time. You wouldn't believe it. Believe human stomach hold so much. Here." It was the bottle. "Good drink. Take enormous one. Good for stomach."

Bogard drank. Soon he did feel better, warmer. When the hand touched him later, he found that he had been asleep.

It was the boy again. The pea-coat was too small for him; shrunken, perhaps. Below the cuffs his long, slender, girl's wrists were blue with cold. Then Bogard realized what the garment was that had been laid over him. But before Bogard could speak, the boy leaned down, whispering; his face was gleeful: "He didn't notice!"

"What?"

"Ergenstrasse! He didn't notice that they had shifted her. Gad, I'd be just one down, then." He watched Bogard's face with bright, eager eyes. "Beaver, you know. I say. Feeling better, eh?"

"Yes," Bogard said. "I am."

"He didn't notice at all. Oh, gad! Oh, Jove!"

Bogard rose and sat on the tube. The entrance to the harbor was just ahead; the boat had slowed a little. It was just dusk. He said quietly: "Does this often happen?" The boy looked at him. Bogard touched the tube. "This. Failing to go out."

"Oh, yes. Why they put the windlass on them. That was later. Made first boat; whole thing blew up one day. So put on windlass."

"But it happens sometimes, even now? I mean, sometimes they blow up, even with the windlass?"

"Well, can't say, of course. Boats go out. Not come back. Possible. Not ever know, of course. Not heard of one captured yet, though. Possible. Not to us, though. Not yet."

"Yes," Bogard said. "Yes." They entered the harbor, the boat moving still fast, but throttled now and smooth, across the dusk-filled basin. Again the boy leaned down, his voice gleeful.

"Not a word, now!" he hissed. "Steady all!" He stood up; he raised his voice: "I say, Ronnie." Ronnie did not turn his head, but Bogard could tell that he was listening. "That Argentine ship was amusing, eh? In there. How do you suppose it got past us here? Might have stopped here as well. French would buy the wheat." He paused, diabolical—Machiavelli with the face of a strayed angel. "I say. How long has it been since we had a strange ship in here? Been months, eh?" Again he leaned, hissing. "Watch, now!" But Bogard could not see Ronnie's head move at all. "He's looking, though!" the boy whispered, breathed. And Ronnie was looking, though his head had not moved at all. Then there came into view, in silhouette against the dusk-filled sky, the vague, basket-like shape of the interned vessel's foremast. At once Ronnie's arm rose, pointing; again he spoke without turning his head, out of the side of his mouth, past the cold, clamped pipe, a single word:

"Beaver."

The boy moved like a released spring, like a heeled dog freed. "Oh, damn you!" he cried. "Oh, you putt! It's the Ergenstrasse! Oh, confound you! I'm just one down now!" He had stepped one stride completely over Bogard, and he now leaned down over Ronnie. "What?" The boat was slowing in toward the wharf, the engine idle. "Aren't I, Ronnie? Just one down now?"

The boat drifted in; the seamen had again crawled forward onto the deck. Ronnie spoke for the third and last time. "Right," he said.

IX

"I want," Bogard said, "a case of Scotch. The best we've got. And fix it up good. It's to go to town. And I want a responsible man to deliver it." The responsible man came. "This is for a child," Bogard said, indicating the package. "You'll find him in the Street of the Twelve Hours, somewhere near the Café Twelve Hours. He'll be in the gutter. You'll know him. A child about six feet long. Any English M.P. will show him to you. If he is asleep, don't wake him. Just sit there and wait until he wakes up. Then give him this. Tell him it is from Captain Bogard."

X

About a month later a copy of the English Gazette which had strayed onto an American aerodrome carried the following item in the casualty lists:

MISSING; Torpedo Boat XOOI. Midshipmen R. Boyce Smith and L. C. W. Hope, R. N. R., Boatswain's Mate Burt and Able Seaman Reeves, Channel Fleet, Light Torpedo Division. Failed to return from coast patrol duty.

Shortly after that the American Air Service headquarters also issued a bulletin:

For extraordinary valor over and beyond the routine of duty, Captain H. S. Bogard, with his crew, composed of Second Lieutenant Darrel McGinnis and Aviation Gunners Watts and Harper, on a daylight raid and without scout protection, destroyed with bombs an ammunition depot several miles behind the enemy's lines. From here, beset by enemy aircraft in superior numbers, these men proceeded with what bombs remained to the enemy's corps headquarters at Blank and partially demolished this château, and then returned safely without loss of a man.

And regarding which exploit, it might have been added, had it failed and had Captain Bogard come out of it alive, he would have been immediately and thoroughly court-martialed.

Carrying his remaining two bombs, he had dived the Handley-Page at the château where the generals sat at lunch, until McGinnis, at the toggles below him, began to shout at him, before he ever signaled. He didn't signal until he could discern separately the slate tiles of the roof. Then his hand dropped and he zoomed, and he held the aeroplane so, in its wild snarl, his lips parted, his breath hissing, thinking: "God! God! If they were all there—all the generals, the admirals, the presidents and the kings—theirs, ours—all of them."

The Trojan Horse

BY

VIRGIL

THE Grecian leaders, now disheartened by the war, and baffled by the Fates, after a revolution of so many years, build a horse to the size of a mountain, and interweave its ribs with planks of fir. This they pretend to be an offering, in order to procure a safe return; which report spread. Hither having secretly conveyed a select band, chosen by lot, they shut them up into the dark sides, and fill its capacious caverns and womb with armed soldiers. In sight of Troy lies Tenedos, an island well known by fame, and flourishing while Priam's kingdom stood: now only a bay, and a station unfaithful for ships. Having made this island, they conceal themselves in that desolate shore. We imagined they were gone, and that they had set sail for Mycenae. In consequence of this, all Troy is released from its long distress: the gates are thrown open; with joy we issue forth, and view the Grecian camp, the deserted plains, and the abandoned shore. Some view with amazement that baleful offering of the virgin Minerva, and wonder at the stupendous bulk of the horse; and Thymoetes first advises that it be dragged within the walls and lodged in the tower, whether with treacherous design, or that the destiny of Troy now would have it so. But Capys, and all whose minds had wiser sentiments, strenuously urge either to throw into the sea the treacherous snare and suspected oblation of the Greeks; or by applying flames consume it to ashes; or to lay open and ransack the recesses of the hollow womb. The fickle populace is split into opposite inclinations. Upon this, Laocoön, accompanied with numerous troop, first before all, with ardour hastens down from the top of the citadel; and while yet a great way off cries out, "O, wretched countrymen, what desperate infatuation is this? Do you believe the enemy gone? or think you any gifts of the Greeks can be free from deceit? Is Ulysses thus known to you? Either the Greeks lie concealed within this wood, or it is an engine framed against our walls, to overlook our houses, and to come down upon our city; or some mischievous design lurks beneath it. Trojans, put no faith in this horse. Whatever it be, I dread the Greeks, even when they bring gifts." Thus said, with valiant strength he hurled his massive spear against the sides and belly of the monster, where it swelled out with its jointed timbers; the weapon stood quivering, and the womb being shaken, the hollow caverns rang, and sent forth a groan. And had not the decrees of heaven been adverse, if our minds had not been infatuated, he had

From: *the Aeneid.*

576

prevailed on us to mutilate with the sword this dark recess of the Greeks; and thou, Troy, should still have stood, and thou, lofty tower of Priam, now remained!

In the meantime, behold, Trojan shepherds, with loud acclamations, came dragging to the king a youth, whose hands were bound behind him; who, to them a mere stranger, had voluntarily thrown himself in the way, to promote this same design, and open Troy to the Greeks; a resolute soul, and prepared for either event, whether to execute his perfidious purpose, or submit to inevitable death. The Trojan youth pour tumultuously around from every quarter, from eagerness to see him, and they vie with one another in insulting the captive. Now learn the treachery of the Greeks, and from one crime take a specimen of the whole nation. For as he stood among the gazing crowds perplexed, defenceless, and threw his eyes around the Trojan bans, "Ah!" says he, "what land, what seas can now receive me? or to what further extremity can I, a forlorn wretch, be reduced, for whom there is no shelter anywhere among the Greeks? and to complete my misery the Trojans too, incensed against me, sue for satisfaction with my blood." By which mournful accents our affections at once were moved towards him, and all our resentment suppressed.

At these tears we grant him his life, and pity him from our hearts. Priam himself first gives orders that the manacles and strait bonds be loosened from the man, then thus addresses him in the language of a friend: "Whoever you are, now henceforth forget the Greeks you have lost; ours you shall be: and give me an ingenuous reply to these questions: To what purpose raised they this stupendous bulk of a horse? Who was the contriver? or what do they intend? what was the religious motive? or what warlike engine is it?" he said. The other, practised in fraud and Grecian artifice, lifted up to heaven his hands, loosed from the bonds: "Troy can never be razed by the Grecian sword, unless they repent the omens at Argos, and carry back the goddess whom they had conveyed in their curved ships. And now, that they have sailed for their native Mycenae with the wind, they are providing themselves with arms; and, they will come upon you unexpected. For he declared that "if your hands should violate this offering sacred to Minerva, then signal ruin awaited Priam's empire and the Trojans. But, if by your hands it mounted into the city, that Asia, without further provocation given, would advance with a formidable war to the very walls, and our posterity be doomed to the same fate." By such treachery and artifice of perjured Sinon, the story was believed: and we, whom neither Diomede, nor Achilles, nor a siege of ten years, nor a thousand ships, had subdued, were ensnared by guile and constrained tears.

Meanwhile they urge with general voice to convey the statue to its proper seat, and implore the favour of the goddess. We make a breach in the walls, and lay open the bulwarks of the city. All keenly ply the work; and under the feet apply smooth-rolling wheels; stretch hempen ropes from the neck. The fatal machine passes over our walls, pregnant with arms. It advances, and with menacing aspect slides into the heart of the city.

O country, O Ilium, the habitation of gods, and ye walls of Troy by war renowned! Four times it stopped in the very threshold of the gate, and four times the arms resounded in its womb: yet we, heedless, and blind with frantic zeal, urge on, and plant the baneful monster in the sacred citadel. Unhappy we, to whom that day was to be the last, adorn the temples of the gods throughout the city with festive boughs. Meanwhile, the heavens change, and night advances rapidly from the ocean, wrapping in her extended shade both earth and heaven, and the wiles of the Myrmidons. The Trojans, dispersed about the walls, were hushed: deep sleep fast binds them weary in his embraces. And now the Grecian host, in their equipped vessels, set out for Tenedos, making towards the well-known shore, by the friendly silence of the quiet moonshine, as soon as the royal galley stern had exhibited the signal fire; and Sinon, preserved by the will of the adverse gods, in a stolen hour unlocks the wooden prison to the Greeks shut up in its tomb: the horse, from his expanded caverns, pours them forth to the open air. They assault the city buried in sleep, and wine. The sentinels are beaten down; and with opened gates they receive all their friends, and join the conquering bands.

Meanwhile the city is filled with mingled scenes of woe; and though my father's house stood retired and enclosed with trees, louder and louder the sounds rise on the ear, and the horrid din of arms assails. I start from sleep and, by hasty steps, gain the highest battlement of the palace, and stand with erect ears: as when a flame is driven by the furious south winds on standing corn; or as a torrent impetuously bursting in a mountain-flood desolates the fields, desolates the rich crops of corn and the labours of the ox.

Then, indeed, the truth is confirmed and the treachery of the Greeks disclosed. Now Deiphosus' spacious house tumbles down, overpowered by the conflagration; now, next to him, Ucalegon blazes: the straits of Sigaeum shine far and wide with the flames. The shouts of men and clangour of trumpets arise. My arms I snatch in mad haste: nor is there in arms enough of reason: but all my soul burns to collect a troop for the war and rush into the citadel with my fellows: fury and rage hurry on my mind, and it occurs to me how glorious it is to die in arms.

The towering horse, planted in the midst of our streets, pours forth armed troops; and Sinon victorious, with insolent triumph scatters the flames. Others are pressing at our wide-opened gates, as many thousands as ever came from populous Mycenae: others with arms have blocked up the lanes to oppose our passage; the edged sword, with glittering point, stands unsheathed, ready for dealing death: hardly the foremost wardens of the gates make an effort to fight and resist in the blind encounter. By the impulse of the gods, I hurry away into flames and arms, whither the grim Fury, whither the din and shrieks that rend the skies, urge me on. Ripheus and Iphitus, mighty in arms, join me; Hypanis and Dymas come up with us by the light of the moon, and closely adhere to my side. Whom, close united, soon as I saw resolute to engage, to animate them the more I thus begin: "Youths, souls magnanimous in vain! If it is your determined purpose to follow me in this last attempt, you see what is the situation of our affairs. All the gods, by whom this empire stood, have deserted their shrines and altars to the enemy: you come to the relief of the city in flames: let us meet death, and rush into the thickest of our armed foes. The only safety for the vanquished is to throw away all hopes of safety." Thus the courage of each youth is kindled into fury. Then, like ravenous wolves in a gloomy fog, whom the fell rage of hunger hath driven forth, blind to danger, and whose whelps left behind long for their return with thirsting jaws; through arms, through enemies, we march up to imminent death, and advance through the middle of the city: sable Night hovers around us with her hollow shade.

Who can describe in words the havoc, who the death of that night? or who can furnish tears equal to the disasters? Our ancient city, having borne sway for many years, falls to the ground: great numbers of sluggish carcasses are strewn up and down, both in the streets, in the houses, and the sacred thresholds of the gods. Nor do the Trojans alone pay the penalty with their blood: the vanquished too at times resume courage in their hearts, and the victorious Grecians fall: everywhere is cruel sorrow, everywhere terror and death in a thousand shapes.

We march on, mingling with the Greeks, but not with heaven on our side; and in many a skirmish we engage during the dark night: many of the Greeks we send down to Hades. Some fly to the ships, and hasten to the trusty shore; some through dishonest fear, scale once more the bulky horse, and lurk within the well-known womb.

Ye ashes of Troy, ye expiring flames of my country! witness, that in your fall I shunned neither darts nor any deadly chances of the Greeks. Thence we are forced away, forthwith to Priam's palace called by the outcries. Here, indeed, we beheld a dreadful fight, as though this had been the only seat of the war, as though none had been dying in all the city besides; with such ungoverned fury we see Mars raging and the Greeks rushing forward to the palace, and the gates besieged by an advancing testudo. Scaling ladders are fixed against the walls, and by their steps they mount to the very door-posts, and protecting themselves by their left arms, oppose their bucklers to the darts, while with their right hands they grasp the battlements. On the other hand, the Trojans tear down the turrets and roofs of their houses; with these weapons, since they see the extremity, they seek to defend themselves now in their last death-struggle, and tumble down the gilded rafters; others with drawn swords beset the gates below; these they guard in a firm, compact body. I mount up to the roof of the highest battlement, whence the distressed Trojans were hurling unavailing darts. With our swords assailing all around a turret, situated on a precipice, and shooting up its towering top to the stars, (whence we were wont to survey all Troy, the fleet of Greece, and all the Grecian camp,) where the topmost story made the joints more apt to give way, we tear it from its deep foundation, and push it on our foes. Suddenly tumbling down, it brings thundering desolation with it, and falls with wide havoc on the Grecian troops. But others succeed: meanwhile, neither stones, nor any sort of missile weapons, cease to fly. Just before the vestibule, and at the outer gate, Pyrrhus exults, glittering in arms and gleamy brass. At the same time, all the youth from Scyros advance to the wall, and toss brands to the roof. Pyrrhus himself in the front, snatching up a battleaxe, beats through the stubborn gates, and labours to tear the brazen posts from the hinges; and now, having hewn away the bars, he dug through the firm boards, and made a large, wide-mouthed breach. The palace within is exposed to view, and the long galleries are discovered: the sacred recesses of Priam and the ancient kings are exposed to view; and they see armed men standing at the gate.

As for the inner palace, it is filled with mingled groans and doleful uproar, and the hollow rooms all throughout howl with female yells: their shrieks strike the golden stars. Then the trembling matrons roam through the spacious halls, and in embraces hug the door-posts, and cling to them with their lips. Pyrrhus presses on with all his father's violence: nor bolts, nor guards themselves, are able to sustain. The gate, by repeated battering blows, gives way, and the door-posts, torn from their hinges, tumble to the ground. The Greeks make their way by force, burst a passage, and, being admitted, butcher the first they meet, and fill the places all about with their troops. Those fifty bedchambers, those doors, that proudly shone with barbaric gold and spoils, were leveled to the ground: where the flames relent, the Greeks take their place.

Perhaps, too, you are curious to hear what was Priam's fate. As soon as he beheld the catastrophe of the taken city, and his palace gates broken down, and the enemy planted in the middle of his private apartments, the aged monarch, with unavailing aim, buckles on his shoulders (trembling with years) arms long disused, girds himself with his useless sword, and rushes into the thickest of the foes, resolute on death. And lo! Polites, one of Priam's sons, who had escaped from the sword of Pyrrhus, through darts, through foes, flies along the long galleries, and wounded traverses the waste halls. Pyrrhus, all afire, pursues him with the hostile weapon, is just grasping him with his hand, and presses on him with the spear. Soon as he at length got into the sight and presence of his parents, he dropped down, and poured out his life with a stream of blood. Upon this, Priam, though now held in the very midst of death, yet did not forbear, nor spared his tongue and passion; and, without any force, threw a feeble dart: which was instantly repelled by the hoarse brass, and hung on the highest boss of the buckler without any execution. Pyrrhus made answer and dragged him to the very altar, trembling and sliding in the streaming gore of his son: and with his left hand grasped his twisted hair, and with his right unsheathed his glittering sword, and plunged it into his side up to the hilt. Such was the end of Priam's fate: this was the final doom allotted to him, having before his eyes Troy consumed, and its towers laid in ruins; once the proud monarch over so many nations and countries of Asia: now his mighty trunk lies extended on the shore, the head torn from the shoulders, and a nameless corpse.

Air Battle

BY

CHARLES NORDHOFF

AND

JAMES NORMAN HALL

ONE early morning in November, Harvey McKail, Golasse, and I were loafing around the messroom stove. The other members of Spad 597, with the exception of Captain Clermont, were out on an eight to ten o'clock patrol. A new motor was being installed in the captain's Spad, so he was doubtless having as luxurious a morning in his own barrack as we were in ours. The other three squadrons of Group 31 had gone off at eight-thirty to furnish protection to a lot of Brequet bombing planes sent out to drop huge bombs on ammunition dumps near Metz. McKail, Golasse and I were to go up at ten-fifteen for a high patrol so we had slept till nine, and now, a quarter of an hour later, still dressed in pyjamas, we were crunching buttered toast and drinking chocolate. McKail was reading Henry James' *Gabrielle de Bergerac,* and Golasse and I were exchanging boyhood reminiscences. Our lives up to the war had been as different as possible. His had been spent wholly in Paris; he had never been farther from the boulevards than to St. Cloud, and it was hard for him to understand what ranch life in California could be like. Still less could he picture the South Seas.

"Do you mean to say you really enjoyed being there?" he asked incredulously.

"Enjoyed it! That's a mild way of stating it," I replied. "I'm going back after the war; Forbes and I are going together if we get through."

Golasse shook his head. "You Americans are a queer lot. Well, you can have your South Sea island. Give me Paris. Give me the *Cafe Maxeville* on a fine summer evening, with a glass of *porto* on the table beside me, plenty of money to buy more when it's gone, and nothing to do till tomorrow. Give me——"

He didn't finish the sentence. Just then Old Felix came in, and his beard fairly bristled with excitement. "Gentlemen! I don't like to disturb you, but there's a Boche coming this way! I thought you might like to see him."

We rushed outside, and heard at once the far-off brisk detonations of anti-aircraft fire. It was a windless, cloudless morning; eight or ten miles away to the southeast the sky was dotted with the tiny white smoke

From: *Falcons of France,* by permission of Little, Brown & Co. and the Atlantic Monthly Press.

blossoms of French seventy-fives. The smoke from the French anti-aircraft shells was always white and that of the Germans black, so we knew at once that the plane was a Boche. He was still too far away to be seen, but we could follow his course by the shell bursts, and he was evidently coming our way.

"Another of those photographic buses," said Golasse. "Selden, there's some cold meat for us. Let's go after it. What do you say, McKail?"

I looked at my watch—a quarter to ten. "Haven't time," I said. "We're due for high patrol in half an hour."

Just then an orderly from Group headquarters scorched across the field on a motor-cycle. It was Flingot, the chauffeur who had met me at Chalons the night I joined the squadron.

"Now then! Now then!" he said. "Don't stand there looking at him. That won't win the war. Hop along, you two! Captain's orders."

He handed Golasse a penciled note which read:

"Golasse. You and Selden take off at once after that two-seater. Never mind the ten-fifteen patrol. McKail will wait for the scheduled information. Good luck!"

There was no time to dress, of course. We sprinted down the field, bearskin coats over our pyjamas. Orders had already been sent to hangars; the mechanics had trundled out our Spads and were warming up the motors by the time we had arrived. We jumped into our flying suits and were ready for the take-off within three minutes. At least I was, but Golasse's mechanics were having trouble with his motor. It spluttered and back-fired, and refused to turn up more than a thousand revolutions. Golasse was cursing and waving his arms. "Go on!" he yelled. "I'll be along in a minute." So I waved and started off alone.

My little ship had never climbed more beautifully. I took height over the aerodrome, watching it shrink and shrink until the great field with its rows of barracks and hangars looked no larger than a playing card. The horizons rolled back; soon I could see for miles in every direction, and above me, but still off to the right, the sky sparkled every little while with points of intense light where the French anti-aircraft shells were bursting. The minute puffs of smoke were climbing the sky in my direction. It looked at though the German meant to make a long sweep across the Salient and reënter his own territory somewhere to the northwest.

I turned northeast and climbed in a wide circle so that I could have the sun at my back when high enough to attack, at the same time keeping a sharp lookout for other Germans. There were none to be seen, however, but far to the eastward the sky, at about three thousand metres, was plentifully sprinkled with shell bursts, both black and white. There was no lack of aerial activity over the lines. Apparently the two-seater, taking altitude over his own territory, had sailed serenely across the front at a great height.

Presently I could make him out, a minute speck moving jauntily among the smoke blossoms. Every anti-aircraft battery along the sector seemed to be blazing away at him, and some of them were making good practice. They were putting them very close, in groups of three and four, but he moved in a leisurely fashion, flying in wide detours and circles. As I watched him I was convinced that Golasse was right in thinking it a photographic plane, sent out to take long range pictures with one of those marvelous high-altitude cameras the Germans had. The two men went about their business as calmly and methodically as though anti-aircraft fire was nothing to them and the possibility of pursuit by hostile planes had not crossed their minds.

I wondered whether they saw my Spad on their trail, climbing steadily up the sky. I could see them plainly enough now, not more than two miles away and about a thousand metres over me. "They must see me," I thought, "but it doesn't appear to worry them." Now and then they would make a wide turn, very slowly, as though they had throttled down for picture-taking, and then move leisurely on. I felt a little uneasy at their apparent disregard for me, and scrutinized the air below me, hoping to see Golasse. The sight of his Spad would have been a welcome one, but I was not to be granted it. No Golasse—no anybody save myself and the two Germans, who looked bigger and more sinister every moment.

While making a turn I was astonished to find that we were almost over the Senard aerodrome, which now appeared to be about the size of a postage stamp. I had been looking overhead constantly and had paid little attention to direction except to follow the Germans. We had turned west without knowing it, and were flying parallel to the front and about ten miles inside our lines. "Lord!" I thought. "Now's my time! What luck if I could bring down a German right over my field!" He was almost directly above me now, but still a good five hundred metres higher. Useless to pull up and fire a burst at that distance, but I was rather surprised that the observer didn't spray a few bullets in my direction. He didn't, however; at least I saw no penciled lines of smoke from tracers. They still flew in the most leisurely manner, as though they thought me not worth bothering about; and somehow their manner of flying told me that they were old pilots who knew their business thoroughly. Their ship, with its silvered undersurface and the huge black crosses on the wings, looked like a veteran too, long accustomed to making flights deep into enemy territory. By that time I had made it out to be a Rumpler.

I didn't like the way they ignored my little Spad, and felt a welcome flush of anger surging through me. "Just wait a minute, you two!" I thought. "You may be old hands at this game, and you may know that I'm a young one. Just the same you'll have to notice me."

I crept up, crept up, turning off from their course as I gained my last three hundred metres of altitude, and taking care to keep the sun at my back. "Now, my boy," I said, "go to it!"

I made a half turn to the left, at the same time crooking my forefinger around the machine-gun trigger on the joy stick, and started toward what

I considered my prey. I had made my calculations with the utmost care, so that I could attack directly from behind and a little below the two-seater, approaching him under cover of his blind spot. The only mistake I made was in forgetting, momentarily, that the two Germans might do some calculating as well. As I have said, I started toward my prey, and to my great astonishment he wasn't there.

Then I heard a sound as peculiar as it was uncomfortable—*flac! flac-flac! flac!* I knew what that meant: bullets were going through the fabric of my bus. I made a steep turn and found that the German pilot had dived suddenly about fifty metres and leveled off again so that his observer could have me in full view. And so he did have me, and was giving me a full dose with both guns. I thought certainly I was lost; the muzzles of his two guns were pointing straight at me and my Spad seemed to be hanging motionless. But he didn't have me in his sights for long. I made a diving turn and had him broadside on and a little above me again. I pulled the trigger. My gun popped once and jammed.

Of all the exasperating things that could happen in the air, a jammed gun was assuredly the worst, and it seemed always to occur at the most critical moment possible. It was by no means easy to clear a stoppage; and in order to do so it was necessary to withdraw from a fight for several moments, and a pilot was lucky if his opponent permitted him to withdraw. I was grateful to those Germans for allowing me to do so in this case. They flew steadily on, I was following at a safe distance, all the while hammering on my crank handle with the little wooden mallet we carried for such emergencies. I knew from the position of my crank handle that I had a bulged cartridge to deal with, but I got rid of it at last and went on again, full motor.

The two-seater was about half a mile in front of me now, flying at the same altitude. I gained on him rapidly, and in my excitement opened fire when still one hundred and fifty metres distant. My tracers appeared to be going directly into the plane, and yet, to my astonishment, and disgust, it showed no signs of being damaged. I must have fired between fifty and seventy-five rounds when of a sudden the Rumpler loomed up directly in front of me. I had not realized how much faster I was going, and as a result I nearly got him by running into him. He turned just as I zoomed over him, and I had a vivid glimpse of my opponents. The observer was sighting down through his camera, but looked up just as I passed and seized the handle of his guns with an air of annoyance and surprise as much as to say, "Oh——! Here's that pest back again!" The pilot turned his head over his shoulder, and I had a fleeting view of the vacant stare of his goggles and a flowing blonde moustache. I did an Immelmann turn to come back at them, and unfortunately, in making it, passed directly above them, whereupon the observer gave me another burst. I heard a loud *whang-g-g*, and knew that something had been hit, but it was not till several minutes later that I saw that one of my bracing wires had been cut through.

One of the most surprising things to me, in an air battle, was the rapidity with which two planes could separate. At one second you were close enough to see the color of your opponent's moustache and the kind of flying clothes he wore; a few seconds later, as you turned to come back, you found that he was a half a mile or even three-quarters of a mile away. Two planes flying at a combined speed of perhaps two hundred and fifty miles per hour are soon separated when going in opposite directions.

My Rumpler was still not mine. He was a long way off, and I had to do my creeping all over again. This time I determined to keep cool and reserve my fire until within fifty yards of him. He let me approach as before, and I knew that the observer was busy with his long-range camera, for I could see the muzzles of his guns pointing idly in the air. The pilot flew straight on as though so thoroughly convinced of my poor marksmanship that he meant to let me blaze away to my heart's content; but he was not quite so indifferent as that. I was still about three hundred yards distant, and had my head steadily braced against my head-rest and my sights in beautiful alignment, when the Rumpler began to rise as though being drawn up by invisible wires. Despite my resolution to keep cool, I pulled up steeply and fired a burst of fifteen or twenty rounds which doubtless missed him by twice as many yards, slipped off on a wing, and had to dive into it to regain flying speed. In doing so I lost a good fifty metres of altitude, and when I turned once more in pursuit the Rumpler was a long way ahead and climbing as though there was no limit to his ceiling. There was nothing to do but climb after him.

All this while we had not, of course, been circling over the same area. Our general direction had been east and a little north, but I had been so busy that I failed to notice how far we had gone. Now, with nothing to do but climb for a while, I took notice of landmarks. Far below to the left I saw a great stretch of wooded country, another to the right and north of that one a city. "Now, what in the world can that town be?" I thought. Chalons was the first name that occurred to me, but I knew there were no forests near Chalons. I made a more careful scrutiny and presently recognized the Cathedral of Rheims. There was no doubt of it. I had never seen Rheims from the air,—or from the ground, for that matter,—but for more than three months I had been studying aeroplane maps and photographs of the western front from the channel coast to Switzerland, and knew it better than my native California. I easily identified the Marne-Vesle canal which makes a great loop from Epernay to Rheims. We were a good thirty-five miles from Senard, and evidently the Germans meant to go still farther. The Rumpler was headed for Rheims, and within a few moments we were directly over the city at a height of fifty-five hundred metres.

At least that was my own altitude; the Rumpler was at six thousand or more, and my Spad was doing its best to lessen the advantage. The motor sounded tacky; not the full-blooded roar to which I was accustomed. Something was wrong, but I didn't know what. By the time we had left Rheims behind I had climbed another fifty metres. but that was the best I could do. And there were my Germans, not five hundred metres higher, paying no further attention to me, knowing, apparently, that the only harm I could do now would be to get into the line of vision of their camera. Then it occurred to me that they might even want me there, provided that my Spad was far enough away and cut off the view of nothing essential on the ground. It would add a bit of local color to their photographs to have a tiny French *chasse* plane clearly outlined over the towns, railroad junctions, aerodromes, ammunition dumps, and so forth, they were snapping. I could imagine them, a day or two later, bringing their developed films to their squadron or group commander, who would glance through them with interest.

"Splendid photographs, *Oberleutnant*. Just what we want."

"*Danke schön, Hauptmann.* We had excellent weather—a perfectly clear sky all the way from St. Mihiel to Rheims. It would have been impossible not to have taken good pictures."

"And you weren't molested, all that way?"

"*Nein, Hauptmann.* We had very good luck. We were heavily shelled, of course, as usual."

"Hello! Here's a Spad showing—in the photograph taken over that aerodrome near St. Hilare."

"*Bitte schön?*"

"A Spad—a French Spad. He must have been about five hundred metres under you at the time. Yes, here it is again in the picture taken over the Montagne de Rheims. He must have been following you. Didn't you know he was there?"

"Oh, *ja!* . . . *Ja, ja,* I remember now. There was a Spad that trailed us all the way from the foot of the Argonne Forest. The pilot was quite harmless. We could have bagged him easily if we'd had time."

I could all but hear this conversation taking place, and it made me so angry to think that in all probability it *would* take place that I pulled up and fired another burst at the Rumpler, although he was a quarter of a mile in front of me and as much above. And I believe that I may have been lucky enough to hit him with a stray bullet, for the pilot made a leisurely turn, banking to look at me, then leveled out on his course again. The manœuvre said, as plainly as though he had spoken, "What! *You* still there?" It was as though he had waved his hand at a fly—troublesome, perhaps, but not troublesome enough to waste time over.

So it went for another ten or fifteen minutes. After leaving Rheims the Rumpler made another wide sweep into French territory, all the way from five to eight or nine miles behind the trenches. I had a map from the Verdun Sector in my map case, but we had long since flown out of that, over country I had never before seen from the air. The German pilot showed me everything worth seeing, from the military standpoint, behind our lines: aerodromes, hospitals, ammunition and supply dumps, and the like, all quite unknown to me. I wondered why I was not joined by some other friendly plane until it occurred to me that other Spads below, seeing me, would refrain from joining up. Pilots would think: "That Rumpler is his victim. I'll not horn in on his victory. Hope he gets the blighter. Awful crust he's got, that Boche, coming all this way back." The anti-aircraft batteries, too, had ceased firing, doubtless from the fear of hitting the wrong ship; for all this while I was trailing along very close behind, vainly trying to coax my Spad up the last short slope of sky that would give me another chance to attack. It was damnable to think that A-A battery commanders were perhaps watching me through binoculars, counting on me to do something and wondering why I didn't.

"I will!" I said. "I will! Don't worry. If he gives me half a chance." I had forgotten to be afraid, or even in the least uneasy about my own skin. I had forgotten my severed bracing wire and my coughing motor. I had forgotten what time it was, how long I had been flying, how much gas I had left—everything but my intense longing to knock down the cheeky Rumpler that had already flown with impunity across seventy-five miles of French territory.

And then my chance came, more quickly than I had bargained for. The Germans had just made a circle over a flying field I was later to know very well, deep in our territory, at the village of Fareen-Tardenois. It was not an aerodrome, but a small aviation-supply depot furnished only with two hangars. The Rumpler circled over it, so I circled too, as I had already done a score of times while they took their photographs. Then, their mission over apparently, they headed due north to cross their own lines. But they held that course for no longer than a minute. Suddenly the pilot went down in a steep turn and I saw the observer seize his guns and swing them around to fire at me.

This time I was not caught napping, and I wasted no precious seconds trying to get under his tail. I turned left as the Rumpler did, and got in a beautiful burst of about thirty rounds, again broadside on, and from a distance of not more than fifty yards. The observer repaid me with a shorter burst, but a murderously accurate one. Again I heard the ominous *flac! flac-flac-flac! flac-flac!* but it was only for a second. My Spad flopped over in a half turn and came back in the opposite direction so prettily that the thought, "Did I do that?" flashed through my mind. So it was always in the air: the manoeuvres one made instinctively were always better than those made with deliberation. It was from that moment that I began to learn how to take care of myself in the air. Every old war-time pilot must have had some such illuminating experience which taught him more in three seconds than his flying instructions could do in five months. Thereafter, when I met a German ship, I kept my eye on that and let my Spad do its own manœuvring.

Turning, I found the Rumpler coming for me from a distance of two hundred yards—straight for me this time, the pilot firing the guns mounted on his motor hood. So I made for him, my guns crackling steadily. Our motors seemed to be eating each other's bullets; in fact they were, as I discovered later, but we flashed past each other, both seemingly intact. I made a vertical turn to the right and then saw something that made me shout for joy. The Rumpler was going off, and his propeller was standing stock-still. He had a "dead-stick," as we used to say. I thought for a second or two I had imagined this, for not infrequently pilots thought they saw what they hoped to see. It was true, however. The propeller was standing vertically, motionless. What a thrill it gave me to see it! "Now I've got them!" I thought. "I'll force them down in our lines!"

But the Germans had other plans about where they meant to land. They were planing very flatly, making a straight course for their own territory. I glanced at my altimeter. Forty-eight hundred metres. They had sufficient altitude to enable them to land behind their own lines if they were careful not to lose height unnecessarily. My motor was coughing and spitting as though at its last gasp, but I quickly overtook them. The rear gunner was waiting for me; I could see him turning his guns this way and that, trying to get a line on me; but his pilot was afraid of losing altitude which he could not regain, so I had little difficulty in keeping the observer guessing. He fired two or three bursts, but they went wide of the mark. "I'll have to shoot them," I thought. "These men are old hands. They can't be frightened into landing." So I went after them again, hoping that my marksmanship would be good enough to wing them both but not good enough to kill either. I had a wonderful chance now. They were planing all the while, of course, tail up at such an angle that I could see the surface of the under-body. I pressed the trigger. My gun fired twice and stopped. This time it wasn't a missfire or a bulged shell casing. I had run out through my entire belt of cartridges.

I didn't know what to do then. I had never thought of such an emergency as this. I confess that what I felt like doing was crying with vexation and disappointment. I had tried hard for that Rumpler, and to have him escape me at the last moment, when victory was all but in my hand—it was too much for me. And all the while the wide belt of desolate country that marked the trench lines was drawing nearer. Soon they would be sailing over it safely. I made a feint at an attack from the side so that both pilot and observer could see me, but that didn't frighten them in the least. The observer swung his guns round and gave me a dose of lead in the tail just as I passed under him. Had he been half a second quicker the chances are that I shouldn't be telling this story.

Help came in histrionic eleventh-hour fashion. Greased lightning decorated with tricolor *cocardes* streaked down the sky, turned left and fired, turned right and fired, flipped upside down, fired again, and vanished. I saw the German observer drop his guns and collapse in his seat as though he had been pushed down by strong, invisible hands. The little friendly plane flashed into view again; it was precisely as though it had the power of being everywhere at once, and visible or invisible as it chose. This time it came down from the side in plain view of the German pilot, but keeping well above him. The Frenchman, or whoever it was, did a barrel turn, at the same time cutting his motor down to come down on the Rumpler, but the German didn't wait for him to fire again. He turned away from his lines—slowly, and I could feel as well as see with what reluctance—and planed down into France.

We were right at his tail, the Frenchman on one side, I on the other. He was flying a Nieuport, type 27, and on the side of his fuselage was painted a black dragon, and another insignia which I made out to be a skull-and-crossbones design against a black background. I waved and he waved back, then reached out and went through the motions of shaking hands. He pulled up till he was opposite the German pilot's cockpit and I followed to the same position on the other side. The Frenchman yelled something at the Boche and pointed down. The German looked over the side and waved his hand as much as to say, "All right." I looked, too, and saw the hangars of an aerodrome off to our left front. We were all three so close together that we could see each other's faces. It gave me a curious feeling to be flying wing to wing with a Rumpler. The pilot's yellow moustache was even longer than it had seemed when I had my first fleeting view of it. The ends fluttered back in the wind around the sides of his flying helmet. The observer was crumpled down in his cockpit, his head hanging to one side. We weren't long in coming down. Two or three minutes later the German landed with his "dead-stick." The Rumpler rolled a little way and stopped, and I saw a crowd of mechanics rushing out to it. The Frenchman and I followed him down.

The People's War

BY

COUNT LEO TOLSTOY

THE battle of Borodino with the occupation of Moscow and the flight of the French, that followed without any more battles, is one of the most instructive phenomena in history.

All historians are agreed that the external activity of states and peoples in their conflicts finds expression in wars; that the political power of states and peoples is increased or diminished as the immediate result of success or defeat in war.

Strange are the historical accounts that tell us how some king or emperor, quarrelling with another king or emperor, levies an army, fights a battle with the army of his foe, gains a victory, kills three, five, or ten thousand men, and consequently subdues a state and a whole people consisting of several millions; and incomprehensible it seems that the defeat of any army, one hundredth of the whole strength of a people, should force that people to submit. Yet all the facts of history (so far as we know it) confirm the truth of the statement, that the successes or defeats of a nation's army are the causes or, at least, the invariable symptoms of the increase or diminution of the power of a nation. An army gains a victory, and immediately the claims of the conquering people are increased to the detriment of the conquered. An army is defeated, and at once the people loses its rights in proportion to the magnitude of the defeat; and if its army is utterly defeated, the people is completely conquered. So (according to history) it has been from the most ancient times up to the present. All Napoleon's earlier wars serve as illustrations of the rule. As the Austrian armies were defeated, Austria was deprived of her rights, and the rights and power of France were increased. The victories of the French at Jena and at Auerstadt destroyed the independent existence of Prussia.

But suddenly, in 1812, the French gained a victory before Moscow. Moscow was taken, and in consequence of that, with no subsequent battles, not Russia, but the French army of six hundred thousand, and then Napoleonic France itself ceased to exist. To strain the facts to fit the rules of history, to maintain that the field of Borodino was left in the hands of the Russians, or that after the evacuation of Moscow, there were battles that destroyed Napoleon's army—is impossible.

After the victory of the French at Borodino, there was no general en-

From: *War and Peace.*

gagement, nor even a skirmish of any great importance, yet the French army ceased to exist. What is the meaning of it? If it had been an example from the history of China, we could have said it was not an historical fact (the resource of historians, when anything will not fit in with their rules). If it had occurred in a conflict on a small scale, in which only small numbers of soldiers had taken part, we might have looked upon it as an exception. But all this took place before the eyes of our fathers, for whom it was a question of life and death for their country; and the war was on a larger scale than any wars we know of.

The sequel of the campaign of 1812—from Borodino to the final expulsion of the French—has proved that victories are not always a cause nor even an invariable sign of conquest; it has proved that the force that decides the fate of peoples does not lie in military leaders, nor even in armies and battles, but in something else.

The French historians, who describe the position of the French troops before they marched out of Moscow, assert that everything was in good order in the Grande Armée, except the cavalry, the artillery and the transport, and that there was no forage for the horses and cattle. There was no remedy for this defect, because the peasants of the surrounding country burned their hay rather than let the French have it.

Victory did not bring forth its usual results, because the peasants, Karp and Vlas, by no means persons of heroic feelings (after the French evacuation, they hurried with their carts to pillage Moscow), and the immense multitude of others like them burnt their hay rather than bring it to Moscow, however high the prices offered them.

Let us imagine two men, who have come out to fight a duel with swords in accordance with all the rules of the art of swordsmanship. The fencing has lasted for some time. All at once one of the combatants, feeling that he is wounded, grasping that it is no joking matter, but a question of life and death, flings away his sword, and snatching up the first cudgel that comes handy, begins to brandish that. But let us imagine that the combatant, who has so sensibly made use of the best and simplest means for the attainment of his object, should be inspired by the traditions of chivalry to try and disguise the real cause of the conflict and should persist in declaring that he had been victor in the duel in accordance with all the rules of swordsmanship. One can imagine what confusion and obscurity would arise from his description of the duel!

The duellist, who insisted on the conflict being fought in accordance with the principles of the fencer's art, stands for the French; his opponent, who flung away his sword and snatched up a cudgel, did like the Russians; and the attempted description of the duel in accordance with the rules of swordsmanship has been given us by the historians of the war.

From the time of the burning of Smolensk a war began which did not follow any of the old traditions of warfare. The burning of towns and villages, the retreat after every battle, the blow dealt at Borodino and followed by retreat, the burning of Moscow, the capture of marauders, the seizing of transports,—the whole of the irregular warfare was a departure from the rules.

Napoleon was aware of it, and from the time when he stood waiting in Moscow in the correct pose of the victorious fencer, and instead of his opponent's sword, saw the bludgeon raised against him, he never ceased complaining to Kutuzov and to the Emperor Alexander that the war was being conducted contrary to all the rules of war. (As though any rules existed for the slaughter of men!)

In spite of the complaints of the French that they did not keep to the rules, in spite of the fact that the Russians in the highest positions felt it somehow shameful to be fighting with a cudgel, and wanted to take up the correct position *en quarte* or *en tierce,* to make a skilful thrust, *en prime* and so on, the cudgel of the people's war was raised in all its menacing and majestic power; and troubling itself about no question of any one's tastes or rules, about no fine distinctions, with stupid simplicity, with perfect consistency, it rose and fell and belaboured the French till the whole invading army had been driven out.

And happy the people that will not, as the French did in 1813, saluting according to the rules, gracefully and cautiously offer the sword hilt to the magnanimous conqueror. Happy the people who, in the moment of trial, asks no questions how others would act by the recognized rules in such cases, but with ease and directness picks up the first cudgel that comes handy and deals blows with it, till resentment and revenge give way to contempt and pity.

One of the most conspicuous and advantageous departures from the so-called rules of warfare is the independent action of men acting separately against men huddled together in a mass. Such independent activity is always seen in a war that assumes a national character. In this kind of warfare, instead of forming in a crowd to attack a crowd, men disperse in small groups, attack singly and at once fly, when attacked by superior forces, and then attack again, when an opportunity presents itself. Such were the methods of the guerillas in Spain; of the mountain tribes in the Caucasus, and of the Russians in 1812.

War of this kind has been called partisan warfare on the supposition that this name defined its special significance. But this kind of warfare does not follow any rules of war, but is in direct contradiction to a well-known rule of tactics, regarded as infallible. That rule lays it down that the attacking party must concentrate his forces in order to be stronger than his opponent at the moment of conflict.

Partisan warfare (always successful, as history testifies) acts in direct contradiction of this rule.

The so-called "partisan" warfare had begun with the enemy's entrance into Smolensk. Before the irregular warfare was officially recognised by our government many thousands of the enemy's soldiers—straggling, marauding, or foraging parties—had been slain by Cossacks and peasants, who killed these men as instinctively as dogs set upon a stray mad dog. Denis Davydov was the first to feel with his Russian instinct the value of this terrible cudgel which belaboured the French, and asked no questions about the etiquette of the military art; and to him belongs the credit of the first step towards the recognition of this method of warfare.

The first detachment of irregulars—Davydov's—was formed on the 24th of August, and others soon followed. In the latter stages of the campaign these detachments became more and more numerous.

The irregulars destroyed the Grande Armée piecemeal. They swept up the fallen leaves that were dropping of themselves from the withered tree, and sometimes they shook the tree itself. By October, when the French were fleeing to Smolensk, there were hundreds of these companies, differing widely from one another in number and in character. Some were detachments that followed all the usual routine of an army, with infantry, artillery, staff-officers, and all the conveniences of life. Some consisted only of Cossacks, mounted men. Others were small bands of men, on foot and also mounted. Some consisted of peasants, or of landowners and their serfs, and remained unknown. There was a deacon at the head of such a band, who took several hundred prisoners in a month. There was the village elder's wife, Vassilisa, who killed hundreds of the French.

The latter part of October was the time when this guerilla warfare reached its height. That period of this warfare, in which the irregulars were themselves amazed at their own audacity, were every moment in dread of being surrounded and captured by the French, and never unsaddling, hardly dismounting, hid in the woods, in momentary expectation of pursuit, was already over. The irregular warfare had by now taken definite shape; it had become clear to all the irregulars what they could, and what they could not, accomplish with the French. By now it was only the commanders of detachments marching with staff-officers according to the rules at a distance from the French who considered much impossible. The small bands of irregulars who had been at work a long while, and were at close quarters with the French, found it possible to attempt what the leaders of larger companies did not dare to think of doing. The Cossacks and the peasants, who crept in among the French, thought everything possible now.

On the 22nd of October, Denisov, who was a leader of a band of irregulars, was eagerly engaged in a typical operation of this irregular warfare. From early morning he had been with his men moving about the woods that bordered the high road, watching a big convoy of cavalry baggage and Russian prisoners that had dropped behind the other French troops, and under strong escort—as he learned from his scouts and from prisoners—was making its way to Smolensk. Not only Denisov and Dolohov (who was also a leader of a small band acting in the same district) were aware of the presence of this convoy. Some generals in command of some larger detachments, with staff-officers, also knew of this convoy, and, as Denisov said, their mouths were watering for it. Two of these generals—one a Pole, the other a German—had almost at the same time sent to Denisov an invitation to join their respective detachments in attacking the convoy.

"No, friend, I wasn't born yesterday!" said Denisov, on reading these documents; and he wrote to the German that in spite of his ardent desire to serve under so brilliant and renowned a general, he must deprive himself of that happiness because he was already under the command of the Polish general. To the Pole he wrote the same thing, informing him that he was already serving under the command of the German.

Having thus disposed of that difficulty, Denisov, without communicating on the subject to the higher authorities, intended with Dolohov to attack and carry off this transport with his own small force. The transport was, on the 22nd of October, going from the village of Mikulino to the village of Shamshevo. On the left side of the road between Mikulino and Shamshevo there were great woods, which in places bordered on the road, and in places were a verst or more from the road. Denisov, with a small party of followers, had been the whole day riding about in these woods, sometimes plunging into their centre, and sometimes coming out at the edge, but never losing sight of the moving French. In the morning, not far from Mikulino, where the wood ran close to the road, the Cossacks of Denisov's party had pounced on two French waggonloads of saddles, stuck in the mud, and had carried them off into the wood. From that time right on to evening, they had been watching the movements of the French without attacking them. They wanted to avoid frightening them, and to let them go quietly on to Shamshevo, and then, joining Dolohov (who was to come that evening to a trysting-place in the wood, a verst from Shamshevo, to concert measures with them), from two sides to fall at dawn like an avalanche of snow on their heads, and to overcome and capture all of them at a blow.

Six Cossacks had been left behind, two versts from Mikulino, where the wood bordered the road. They were to bring word at once as soon as any fresh columns of French came into sight.

In front of Shamshevo, Dolohov was in the same way to watch the road to know at what distance there were other French troops. With the transport there was supposed to be fifteen hundred men. Denisov had two hundred men, and Dolohov might have as many more. But superiority in numbers was no obstacle to Denisov. There was only one thing that he still needed to know, and that was what troops these were; and for that object Denisov needed to take a "tongue" (that is some man belonging to that column of the enemy). The attack on the waggons in the morning was all done with such haste that they killed all the French soldiers in charge of the waggons, and captured alive only a little drummer-boy, who had straggled away from his own regiment, and could tell them nothing certain about the troops forming the column.

To make another descent upon them, Denisov thought, would be to risk alarming the whole column, and so he sent on ahead to Shamshevo a peasant, Tihon Shtcherbatov, to try if he could capture at least one of the French quartermasters from the vanguard.

It was a warm, rainy, autumn day. The sky and the horizon were all of the uniform tint of muddy water. Sometimes a mist seemed to be falling, and sometimes there was a sudden downpour of heavy, slanting rain.

Denisov, in a long cape and a high fur cap, both streaming with water, was riding a thin, pinched-looking, thoroughbred horse. With his head aslant, and his ears pricked up, like his horse, he was frowning at the driving rain, and anxiously looking before him. His face, which had grown thin, and was covered with a thick, short, black beard, looked wrathful.

Beside Denisov, wearing also a long cape and a high cap, and mounted on a sleek, sturdy Don horse, rode the esaul, or hetman of the Cossacks— Denisov's partner in his enterprises.

The esaul, Lovaisky, a thin man, also in a cape, and a high cap, was a long creature, flat as a board, with a pale face, flaxen hair, narrow, light eyes, and an expression of calm self-confidence both in his face and his attitude. Though it was impossible to say what constituted the peculiarity of horse and rider, at the first glance at the esaul and at Denisov, it was evident that Denisov was both wet and uncomfortable; that Denisov was a man sitting on a horse; while the esaul seemed as comfortable and calm as always, and seemed not a man sitting on a horse, but a man forming one whole with a horse—a single being enlarged by the strength of two.

A little ahead of them walked a peasant-guide, soaked through and through in his grey full coat and white cap.

A little behind, on a thin, delicate Kirghiz pony, with a flowing tail and mane, and a mouth flecked with blood, rode a young officer in a blue French military coat. Beside him rode an hussar, with a boy in a tattered French uniform and blue cap, perched upon his horse behind him. The boy held on to the hussar with hands red with cold, and kept moving his bare feet, trying to warm them, and lifting his eyebrows, gazed about him wonderingly. This was the French drummer, who had been taken in the morning.

Along the narrow, muddy, cut-up forest-track there came hussars in knots of three and four at a time, and then Cossacks; some in capes, some in French cloaks; others with horse-cloths pulled over their heads. The horses, chestnut and bay, all looked black from the soaking rain. Their necks looked strangely thin with their drenched manes, and steam rose in clouds from them. Clothes, saddles, and bridles, all were sticky and swollen with the wet, like the earth and the fallen leaves with which the track was strewn. The men sat huddled up, trying not to move, so as to keep warm the water that had already reached their skins, and not to let any fresh stream of cold rain trickle in anywhere under their seat, or at their knees or necks. In the midst of the file of Cossacks two waggons, drawn by French horses, and Cossack saddle-horses hitched on in front, rumbled over stumps and branches, and splashed through the ruts full of water.

Denisov's horse, in avoiding a puddle in the track, knocked his rider's knee against a tree.

"Ah, devil!" Denisov cried angrily; and showing his teeth, he struck his horse three times with his whip, splashing himself and his comrades with mud. Denisov was out of humour, both from the rain and hunger (no one had eaten anything since morning); and, most of all, from having no news of Dolohov, and from no French prisoner having been caught to give him information.

"We shall never have such another chance to fall on the transport as to-day. To attack them alone would be risky, and to put it off to another day—some one of the bigger leaders will carry the booty off from under our noses," thought Denisov, continually looking ahead, and fancying he saw the messenger from Dolohov he expected.

Coming out into a clearing from which he could get a view to some distance on the right, Denisov stopped.

"There's some one coming," he said.

The esaul looked in the direction Denisov was pointing to.

"There are two men coming—an officer and a Cossack. Only I wouldn't be *prepositive* that is the colonel himself," said the esaul, who loved to use words that were unfamiliar to the Cossacks. The two figures, riding downhill, disappeared from sight, and came into view again a few minutes later. The foremost was an officer, dishevelled looking, and soaked through, with his trousers tucked up above his knees; he was lashing his horse into a weary gallop. Behind him a Cossack trotted along, standing up in his stirrups. This officer, a quite young boy, with a broad, rosy face and keen, merry eyes, galloped up to Denisov, and handed him a sopping packet.

"From the general," he said. "I must apologise for its not being quite dry. . . ."

Denisov, frowning, took the packet and broke it open.

"Why, they kept telling us it was so dangerous," said the officer, turning to the esaul while Denisov was reading the letter. "But Komarov"—and he indicated the Cossack—"and I were prepared. We have both two pistol . . . But what's this?" he asked, seeing the French drummer-boy. "A prisoner? You have had a battle already? May I talk to him?"

"Rostov! Petya!" Denisov cried at that moment, running through the packet that had been given him. "Why, how was it you didn't say who you were?" and Denisov, turning with a smile, held out his hand to the officer. This officer was Petya Rostov.

Petya had been all the way preparing himself to behave with Denisov as a grown-up person and an officer should do, making no reference to their previous acquaintance. But as soon as Denisov smiled at him, Petya beamed at once, blushed with delight, and forgetting all the formal demeanour he had been intending to preserve, he began telling him how he had ridden by the French, and how glad he was he had been given this commission, and how he had already been in a battle at Vyazma, and how a certain hussar had distinguished himself in it.

"Well, I am glad to see you," Denisov interrupted him, and his face looked anxious again.

"Mihail Feoklititch," he said to the esaul, "this is from the German again, you know. He" (Petya) "is in his suite." And Denisov told the esaul that the letter, which had just been brought, repeated the German general's request that they would join him in attacking the transport. "If we don't catch them by to-morrow, he'll snatch them from under our noses," he concluded.

While Denisov was talking to the esaul, Petya, disconcerted by Denisov's cold tone, and imagining that that tone might be due to the condition of his trousers, furtively pulled them down under his cloak, trying to do so unobserved, and to maintain as martial an air as possible.

"Will your honour have any instructions to give me?" he said to Denisov, putting his hand to the peak of his cap, and going back to the comedy of adjutant and general, which he had prepared himself to perform, "or should I remain with your honour?"

"Instructions? . . ." said Denisov absently. "Well, can you stay till to-morrow?"

"Ah, please . . . May I stay with you?" cried Petya.

"Well, what were your instructions from your general—to go back at once?" asked Denisov.

Petya blushed.

"Oh, he gave me no instructions. I think I may?" he said interrogatively.

"All right, then," said Denisov. And turning to his followers, he directed a party of them to go to the hut in the wood, which they had fixed on as a resting-place, and the officer on the Kirghiz horse (this officer performed the duties of an adjutant) to go and look for Dolohov, to find out where he was, and whether he were coming in the evening.

Denisov himself, with the esaul and Petya, intended to ride to the edge of the wood near Shamshevo to have a look at the position of the French, where their attack next day was to take place.

"Come, my man," he said to their peasant guide, "take us to Shamshevo."

Denisov, Petya, and the esaul, accompanied by a few Cossacks and the hussar with the prisoner, turned to the left and crossed a ravine towards the edge of the wood.

On leaving Moscow, Petya had parted from his parents to join his regiment, and shortly afterwards had been appointed an orderly in attendance on a general who was in command of a large detachment. From the time of securing his commission, and even more since joining a regiment in active service, and taking part in the battle of Vyazma, Petya had been in a continual state of happy excitement at being grown-up, and of intense anxiety not to miss any opportunity of real heroism. He was highly delighted with all he had seen and experienced in the army, but, at the same time, he was always fancying that wherever he was not, there the most real and heroic exploits were at that very moment being performed. And he was in constant haste to be where he was not.

On the 21st of October, when his general expressed a desire to send some one to Denisov's company, Petya had so piteously besought him to send him, that the general could not refuse. But, as he was sending him off, the general recollected Petya's foolhardy behaviour at the battle of Vyazma, when, instead of riding by way of the road to take a message, Petya had galloped across the lines under the fire of the French, and had there fired a couple of pistol-shots. Recalling that prank, the general explicitly forbade Petya's taking part in any enterprise whatever that Denisov might be planning. This was why Petya had blushed and been disconcerted when Denisov asked him if he might stay. From the moment he set off till he reached the edge of the wood, Petya had fully intended to do his duty steadily, and to return at once. But when he saw the French, and saw Tihon, and learned that the attack would certainly take place that night, with the rapid transition from one view to another, characteristic of young people, he made up his mind that his general, for whom he had till that moment had the greatest respect, was a poor stick, and only a German, that Denisov was a hero, and the esaul a hero, and Tihon a hero, and that it would be shameful to leave them at a moment of difficulty.

It was getting dark when Denisov, with Petya and the esaul, reached the forester's hut. In the half-dark they could see saddled horses, Cossacks and hussars, rigging up shanties in the clearing, and building up a glowing fire in a hollow near, where the smoke would not be seen by the French. In the porch of the little hut there was a Cossack with his sleeves tucked up, cutting up a sheep. In the hut, three officers of Denisov's band were setting up a table made up of doors. Petya took off his wet clothes, gave them to be dried, and at once set to work to help the officers in fixing up a dining-table.

In ten minutes the table was ready and covered with a napkin. On the table was set vodka, a flask of rum, white bread, and roast mutton, and salt.

Sitting at the table with the officers, tearing the fat, savoury mutton with greasy fingers, Petya was in a childishly enthusiastic condition of tender love for all men and a consequent belief in the same feeling for himself in others.

"So what do you think, Vassily Fyodorovitch," he said to Denisov, "it won't matter my staying a day with you, will it?" And without waiting for an answer, he answered himself: "Why, I was told to find out, and here I am finding out . . . Only you must let me go into the middle . . . into the real . . . I don't care about rewards . . . But I do want . . ." Petya clenched his teeth and looked about him, tossing his head and waving his arm.

"Into the real, real thing . . ." Denisov said, smiling.

"Only, please, do give me a command of something altogether, so that I really might command," Petya went on. "Why, what would it be to you? Ah, you want a knife?" he said to an officer, who was trying to tear off a piece of mutton. And he gave him his pocket-knife.

The officer praised the knife.

"Please keep it. I have several like it . . ." said Petya, blushing. "Heavens! Why, I was quite forgetting," he cried suddenly. "I have some capital raisins, you know the sort without stones. We have a new canteen-keeper, and he does get first-rate things. I bought ten pounds of them. I'm fond of sweet things. Will you have some?" . . . And Petya ran out to his Cossack in the porch, and brought in some panniers in which there were five pounds of raisins. "Please take some."

"Don't you need a coffee-pot?" he said to the esaul; "I bought a famous one from our canteen-keeper! He has first-rate things. And he's very honest. That's the great thing. I'll be sure and send it you. Or perhaps your flints are worn out; that does happen sometimes. I brought some with me, I have got them here . . ." he pointed to the panniers. "A hundred flints. I bought them very cheap. You must please take as many as you want or all, indeed . . ." And suddenly, dismayed at the thought that he had let his tongue run away with him, Petya stopped short and blushed.

He began trying to think whether he had been guilty of any other blunders. And running through his recollections of the day the image of the French drummer-boy rose before his mind.

"We are enjoying ourselves, but how is he feeling? What have they done with him? Have they given him something to eat? Have they been nasty to him?" he wondered.

But thinking he had said too much about the flints, he was afraid to speak now.

"Could I ask about him?" he wondered. "They'll say: he's a boy himself, so he feels for the boy. I'll let them see to-morrow whether I'm a boy! Shall I feel ashamed if I ask?" Petya wondered. "Oh, well! I don't care," and he said at once, blushing and watching the officers' faces in dread of detecting amusement in them:

"Might I call that boy who was taken prisoner, and give him something to eat . . . perhaps . . ."

"Yes, poor little fellow," said Denisov, who clearly saw nothing to be ashamed of in this reminder. "Fetch him in here. His name is Vincent Bosse. Fetch him in."

"I'll call him in."

"Yes, do. Poor little fellow," repeated Denisov.

Petya was standing at the door as Denisov said this. He slipped in between the officers and went up to Denisov.

"Let me kiss you, dear fellow," he said. "Ah, how jolly it is! How splendid!" And, kissing Denisov, he ran out into the yard.

"Bosse! Vincent!" Petya cried, standing by the door.

"Whom do you want, sir?" said a voice out of the darkness. Petya answered that he wanted the French boy, who had been taken prisoner that day.

"Ah, Vesenny?" said the Cossack.

His name Vincent had already been transformed by the Cossacks into Vesenny, and by the peasants and the soldiers into Visenya. In both names there was a suggestion of the spring—vesna—which seemed to them to harmonise with the figure of the young boy.

"He's warming himself there at the fire. Ay, Visenya! Visenya!" voices called from one to another with laughter in the darkness. "He is a sharp boy," said an hussar standing near Petya. "We gave him a meal not long ago. He was hungry, terribly."

There was a sound of footsteps in the darkness, and the drummer-boy came splashing through the mud with his bare feet towards the door.

"Ah, that's you!" said Petya. "Are you hungry? Don't be afraid, they won't hurt you," he added, shyly and cordially touching his hand. "Come in, come in."

"Thank you," answered the drummer, in a trembling, almost childish voice, and he began wiping the mud off his feet on the threshold. Petya had a great deal he longed to say to the drummer-boy, but he did not dare. He stood by him in the porch, moving uneasily. Then he took his hand in the darkness and squeezed it. "Come in, come in," he repeated, but in a soft whisper.

"Oh, if I could only do something for him!" Petya was saying inwardly, and opening the door he ushered the boy in before him.

When the drummer-boy had come into the hut, Petya sat down at some distance from him, feeling that it would be lowering his dignity to take much notice of him. But he was feeling the money in his pocket and wondering whether it would do to give some to the drummer-boy.

Denisov gave orders for the drummer-boy to be given some vodka and mutton, and to be put into a Russian dress, so that he should not be sent off with the other prisoners, but should stay with his band. Petya's attention was diverted from the boy by the arrival of Dolohov. He had heard a great many stories told in the army of Dolohov's extraordinary gallantry and of his cruelty to the French. And therefore from the moment Dolohov entered the hut Petya could not take his eyes off him, and flinging up his head, he assumed a more and more swaggering air, that he might not be unworthy of associating even with a hero like Dolohov.

Dolohov's appearance struck Petya as strange through its simplicity. Denisov was dressed in a Cossack coat; he had let his beard grow, and had a holy image of Nikolay, the wonder-worker, on his breast. His whole manner of speaking and all his gestures were suggestive of his peculiar position. Dolohov, on the contrary, though in old days he had worn a Persian dress in Moscow, looked now like the most correct officer of the Guards. He was clean-shaven; he wore the wadded coat of the Guards with a St. George medal on a ribbon, and a plain forage cap, put on straight on his head. He took his wet cloak off in the corner and, without greeting any one, went straight up to Denisov and began at once asking questions about the matter in hand. Denisov told him of the designs the larger detachment had upon the French convoy, of the message Petya had brought, and the answer he had given to both generals. Then he told him all he knew of the position of the French.

"That's so. But we must find out what troops they are, and what are their numbers," said Dolohov; "we must go and have a look at them. We can't rush into the thing without knowing for certain how many there are of them. I like to do things properly. Come, won't one of you gentlemen like to come with me to pay them a call in their camp? I have an extra uniform with me."

"I, I . . . I'll come with you!" cried Petya.

"There's not the slightest need for you to go," said Denisov, addressing Dolohov; "and as for him I wouldn't let him go on any account."

"That's good!" cried Petya; "why shouldn't I go? . . ."

"Why, because there's no reason to."

"Oh, well, excuse me . . . because . . . because . . . I'm going, and that's all. You will take me?" he cried, turning to Dolohov.

"Why not? . . ." Dolohov answered, absently, staring into the face of the French drummer-boy.

"Have you had that youngster long?" he asked Denisov.

"We caught him to-day, but he knows nothing; I have kept him with us."

"Oh, and what do you do with the rest?" said Dolohov.

"What do I do with them? I take a receipt for them, and send them off!" cried Denisov, suddenly flushing. "And I make bold to say that I haven't a single man's life on my conscience. Is there any difficulty in your sending thirty, or three hundred men, under escort, to the town rather than stain—I say so bluntly—one's honour as a soldier?"

"It's all very well for this little count here at sixteen to talk of such refinements," Dolohov said, with a cold sneer; "but it's high time for you to drop all that."

"Why, I am not saying anything, I only say that I am certainly going with you," said Petya shyly.

"But for me and you, mate, it's high time to drop such delicacy," Dolohov went on, apparently deriving peculiar gratification from talking on a subject irritating to Denisov. "Why have you kept this lad," he said, "except because you are sorry for him? Why, we all know how much your receipts are worth. You send off a hundred men and thirty reach the town. They die of hunger or are killed on the way. So isn't it just as well to make short work of them?"

The esaul, screwing up his light-coloured eyes, nodded his head approvingly.

"That's not my affair, no need to discuss it. I don't care to have their lives on my conscience. You say they die. Well, let them. Only not through my doing."

Dolohov laughed.

"Who prevented their taking me twenty times over? But you know if they do catch me—and you too with your chivalrous sentiments—it will just be the same—the nearest aspen-tree." He paused. "We must be getting to work, though. Send my Cossack here with the pack. I have two French uniforms. Well, are you coming with me?" he asked Petya.

"I? Yes, yes, of course," cried Petya, blushing till the tears came into his eyes, and glancing at Denisov.

While Dolohov had been arguing with Denisov what should be done with prisoners, Petya had again had that feeling of discomfort and nervous hurry; but again he had not time to get a clear idea of what they were talking about. "If that's what is thought by grown-up men, famous leaders, then it must be so, it must be all right," he thought. "And the great thing is, that Denisov shouldn't dare to imagine that I must obey him, that he can order me about. I shall certainly go with Dolohov into the French camp. He can go, and so can I!"

To all Denisov's efforts to dissuade him from going, Petya replied that he too liked doing things properly and not in haphazard fashion, and that he never thought about danger to himself.

"For, you must admit, if we don't know exactly how many men there are there, it might cost the life of hundreds, and it is only we two, and so I very much wish it, and I shall certainly, most certainly go, and don't try to prevent me," he said; "it won't be any use . . ."

Petya and Dolohov, after dressing up in French uniforms and shakoes, rode to the clearing from which Denisov had looked at the French camp, and coming out of the wood, descended into the hollow in the pitch darkness. When they had ridden downhill, Dolohov bade the Cossacks accompanying him to wait there, and set off at a smart trot along the road towards the bridge. Petya, faint with excitement, trotted along beside him.

"If we are caught, I won't be taken alive. I have a pistol," whispered Petya.

"Don't speak Russian," said Dolohov, in a rapid whisper, and at that moment they heard in the dark the challenge: "Who goes there?" and the click of a gun.

The blood rushed into Petya's face, and he clutched at his pistol.

"Uhlans of the Sixth Regiment," said Dolohov, neither hastening nor slackening his horse's pace.

The black figure of a sentinel stood on the bridge.

"The password?"

Dolohov reined in his horse, and advanced at a walking pace.

"Tell me, is Colonel Gerard here?" he said.

"Password?" repeated the sentinel, making no reply and barring their way.

"When an officer makes his round, sentinels don't ask him for the password . . ." cried Dolohov, suddenly losing his temper and riding straight at the sentinel. "I ask you, is the colonel here?"

And not waiting for an answer from the sentinel, who moved aside, Dolohov rode at a walking pace uphill.

Noticing the black outline of a man crossing the road, Dolohov stopped the man, and asked where the colonel and officers were. The man, a soldier with a sack over his shoulder, stopped, came close up to Dolohov's horse, stroking it with his hand, and told them in a simple and friendly way that the colonel and the officers were higher up the hill, on the right, in the courtyard of the farm, as he called the little manor-house.

After going further along the road, from both sides of which they heard French talk round the camp-fires, Dolohov turned into the yard of the manor-house. On reaching the gate, he dismounted and walked towards a big, blazing fire, round which several men were sitting, engaged in loud conversation. There was something boiling in a cauldron on one side, and a soldier in a peaked cap and blue coat, kneeling in the bright glow of the fire, was stirring it with his ramrod.

"He's a tough customer," said one of the officers, sitting in the shadow on the opposite side of the fire.

"He'll make them run, the rabbits" (a French proverb), said the other, with a laugh.

Both paused, and peered into the darkness at the sound of the steps of Petya and Dolohov approaching with their horses.

"*Bonjour, messieurs!*" Dolohov called loudly and distinctly.

There was a stir among the officers in the shadow, and a tall officer with a long neck came round the fire and went up to Dolohov.

"Is that you, Clément?" said he. "Where the devil . . ." but becoming aware of his mistake, he did not finish, and with a slight frown greeted Dolohov as a stranger, and asked him what he could do for him. Dolohov told him that he and his comrade were trying to catch up their regiment, and asked, addressing the company in general, whether the officers knew anything about the Sixth Regiment. No one could tell them anything about it; and Petya fancied the officers began to look at him and Dolohov with unfriendly and suspicious eyes.

For several seconds no one spoke.

"If you're reckoning on some soup, you have come too late," said a voice from behind the fire, with a smothered laugh.

Dolohov answered that they had had supper, and wanted to push on further that night.

He gave their horses to the soldier who was stirring the pot, and squatted down on his heels beside the officer with the long neck. The latter never took his eyes off Dolohov, and asked him again what regiment did he belong to.

Dolohov appeared not to hear the question. Making no answer, he lighted a short French pipe that he took from his pocket, and asked the officers whether the road ahead of them were safe from Cossacks.

"The brigands are everywhere," answered an officer from behind the fire.

Dolohov said that the Cossacks were only a danger for stragglers like himself and his comrade; "he supposed they would not dare to attack large detachments," he added inquiringly.

No one replied.

"Well, now he will come away," Petya was thinking every moment, as he stood by the fire listening to the talk.

But Dolohov took up the conversation that had dropped, and proceeded to ask them point-blank how many men there were in their battalion, how many battalions they had, and how many prisoners.

When he asked about the Russian prisoners, Dolohov added:

"Nasty business dragging those corpses about with one. It would be better to shoot the vermin," and he broke into such a strange, loud laugh, that Petya fancied the French must see through their disguise at once, and he involuntarily stepped back from the fire.

Dolohov's words and laughter elicited no response, and a French officer whom they had not seen (he lay rolled up in a coat), sat up and whispered something to his companion. Dolohov stood up and called to the men who held their horses.

"Will they give us the horses or not?" Petya wondered, unconsciously coming closer to Dolohov.

They did give them the horses. *"Bonsoir, messieurs,"* said Dolohov.

Petya tried to say *"Bonsoir,"* but he could not utter a sound. The officers were whispering together. Dolohov was a long while mounting his horse, who would not stand still; then he rode out of the gate at a walking pace. Petya rode beside him, not daring to look round, though he was longing to see whether the French were running after him or not.

When they came out on to the road, Dolohov did not turn back towards the open country, but rode further along it into the village.

At one spot he stood still, listening. "Do you hear?" he said. Petya recognised the sound of voices speaking Russian, and saw round the camp-fire the dark outlines of Russian prisoners. When they reached the bridge again, Petya and Dolohov passed the sentinel, who, without uttering a word, paced gloomily up and down. They came out to the hollow where the Cossacks were waiting for them.

"Well now, good-bye. Tell Denisov, at sunrise, at the first shot," said Dolohov, and he was going on, but Petya clutched at his arm.

"Oh!" he cried, "you are a hero! Oh! how splendid it is! how jolly! How I love you!"

"That's all right," answered Dolohov, but Petya did not let go of him, and in the dark Dolohov made out that he was bending over to him to be kissed. Dolohov kissed him, laughed, and turning his horse's head, vanished into the darkness.

On reaching the hut in the wood, Petya found Denisov in the porch. He was waiting for Petya's return in great uneasiness, anxiety, and vexation with himself for having let him go.

"Thank God!" he cried. "Well, thank God!" he repeated, hearing Petya's ecstatic account. "And, damn you, you have prevented my sleeping!" he added. "Well, thank God; now, go to bed. We can still get a nap before morning."

"Yes . . . no," said Petya. "I'm not sleepy yet. Besides, I know what I am; if once I go to sleep, it will be all up with me. And besides, it's not my habit to sleep before a battle."

Petya sat for a little while in the hut, joyfully recalling the details of his adventure, and vividly imagining what was coming next day. Then, noticing that Denisov had fallen asleep, he got up and went out of doors.

It was still quite dark outside. The rain was over, but the trees were still dripping. Close by the hut could be seen the black outlines of the Cossacks' shanties and the horses tied together. Behind the hut there was a dark blur where two waggons stood with the horses near by, and in the hollow there was a red glow from the dying fire. The Cossacks and the hussars were not all asleep; there mingled with the sound of the falling drops and the munching of the horses, the sound of low voices, that seemed to be whispering.

Petya came out of the porch, looked about him in the darkness, and went up to the waggons. Some one was snoring under the waggons, and saddled horses were standing round them munching oats. In the dark Petya recognised and approached his own mare, whom he called Karabach, though she was in fact of a Little Russian breed.

"Well, Karabach, to-morrow we shall do good service," he said, sniffing her nostrils and kissing her.

"Why, aren't you asleep, sir?" said a Cossack, sitting under the waggon.

"No; but . . . Lihatchev—I believe that's your name, eh? You know I have only just come back. We have been calling on the French." And Petya gave the Cossack a detailed account, not only of his adventure, but also of his reasons for going, and why he thought it better to risk his life than to do things in a haphazard way.

"Well, you must be sleepy; get a little sleep," said the Cossack.

"No, I am used to it," answered Petya. "And how are the flints in your pistols—not worn out? I brought some with me. Don't you want any? Do take some."

The Cossack popped out from under the waggon to take a closer look at Petya.

"For, you see, I like to do everything carefully," said Petya. "Some men, you know, leave things to chance, and don't have things ready, and then they regret it. I don't like that."

"No, to be sure," said the Cossack.

"Oh, and another thing, please, my dear fellow, sharpen my sabre for me; I have blunt . . ." (but Petya could not bring out a lie) . . . "it has never been sharpened. Can you do that?"

"To be sure I can."

Lihatchev stood up, and rummaged in the baggage, and Petya stood and heard the martial sound of steel and whetstone. He clambered on to the waggon, and sat on the edge of it. The Cossack sharpened the sabre below.

"Are the other brave fellows asleep?" said Petya.

"Some are asleep, and some are awake, like us."

"And what about the boy?"

"Vesenny? He's lying yonder in the hay. He's sleeping well after his fright. He was so pleased."

For a long while after that Petya sat quiet, listening to the sounds. There was a sound of footsteps in the darkness, and a dark figure appeared.

"What are you sharpening?" asked a man coming up to the waggon.

"A sabre for the gentleman here."

"That's a good thing," said the man, who seemed to Petya to be an hussar. "Was the cup left with you here?"

"It's yonder by the wheel." The hussar took the cup. "It will soon be daylight," he added, yawning, as he walked off.

Petya must, one would suppose, have known that he was in a wood, with Denisov's band of irregulars, a verst from the road; that he was sitting on a waggon captured from the French; that there were horses fastened to it; that under it was sitting the Cossack Lihatchev sharpening his sabre; that the big, black blur on the right was the hut, and the red, bright glow below on the left the dying camp-fire; that the man who had come for the cup was an hussar who was thirsty. But Petya knew nothing of all that, and refused to know it. He was in a fairyland, in which nothing was like the reality. The big patch of shadow might be a hut certainly, but it might be a cave leading down into the very depths of the earth. The red patch might be a fire, but it might be the eye of a huge monster. Perhaps he really was sitting now on a waggon, but very likely he was sitting not on a waggon, but on a fearfully high tower, and if he fell off, he would go on flying to the earth for a whole day, for a whole month—fly and fly for ever and never reach it. Perhaps it was simply the Cossack Lihatchev sitting under the waggon; but very likely it was the kindest, bravest, most wonderful and splendid man in the world whom no one knew of. Perhaps it really was an hussar who had come for water and gone into the hollow; but perhaps he had just vanished, vanished altogether and was no more.

Whatever Petya had seen now, it would not have surprised him. He was in a land of fairy, where everything was possible.

He gazed at the sky. The sky too was an enchanted realm like the earth. It had begun to clear, and the clouds were scudding over the tree-tops, as though unveiling the stars. At times it seemed as though they were swept away, and there were glimpses of clear, black sky between them. At times these black patches looked like storm-clouds. At times the sky seemed to rise high, high overhead, and then again to be dropping down so that one could reach it with the hand.

Petya closed his eyes and began to nod. The branches dripped. There was a low hum of talk and the sound of some one snoring. The horses neighed and scuffled.

"Ozheeg, zheeg, ozheeg, zheeg . . ." hissed the sabre on the whetstone; and all at once Petya seemed to hear harmonious music, an orchestra playing some unfamiliar, solemnly sweet hymn. Petya was as musical by nature as Natasha, and far more so than Nikolay; but he had had no musical training, and never thought about music, so that the melody that came unexpectedly into his mind had a special freshness and charm for him. The music became more and more distinct. The melody grew and passed from one instrument to another. There was being played what is called a fugue, though Petya had not the slightest idea of what was meant by a fugue. Each instrument—one like a violin, others like flutes, but fuller and more melodious than violins and flutes—played its part, and before it had finished the air, melted in with another, beginning almost the same air, and with a third and a fourth; and all mingled into one harmony, and parted again, and again mingled into solemn church music, and then into some brilliant and triumphant song of victory.

"Oh yes, of course I am dreaming," Petya said to himself, nodding forward. "It is only in my ears. Perhaps, though, it's my own music. Come, again. Strike up, my music! Come! . . ."

He closed his eyes. And from various directions the sounds began vibrating as though from a distance, began to strike up, to part, and to mingle again, all joined in the same sweet and solemn hymn. "Ah how exquisite! As much as I want, and as I like it!" Petya said to himself. He tried to conduct this immense orchestra.

"Come, softly, softly, now!" And the sounds obeyed him. "Come, now fuller, livelier! More and more joyful!" And from unknown depths rose the swelling, triumphant sounds. "Now, voices, join in!" Petya commanded. And at first in the distance he heard men's voices, then women's. The voices swelled into rhythmic, triumphant fulness. Petya felt awe and joy as he drank in their marvellous beauty.

With the triumphant march of victory mingled the song of voices, and the drip of the branches and the zheeg, zheeg, zheeg of the sabre on the whetstone; and again the horses neighed and scuffled, not disturbing the harmony, but blending into it. How long it lasted, Petya could not tell; he was enjoying it, and wondering all the while at his own enjoyment, and regretting he had no one to share it with. He was waked by the friendly voice of Lihatchev.

"It's ready, your honour, you can cut the French in two now."

Petya waked up.

"Why, it's light already; it's really getting light," he cried. The horses, unseen before, were visible to the tails now, and through the leafless boughs there could be seen a watery light. Petya shook himself, jumped up, took a rouble out of his pocket, and gave it to Lihatchev, brandished his sabre to try it, and thrust it into the scabbard. The Cossacks were untying the horses and fastening the saddlegirths.

"And here is the commander," said Lihatchev.

Denisov came out of the hut, and calling to Petya, bade him get ready.

Rapidly in the twilight the men picked out their horses, tightened saddlegirths, and formed into parties. Denisov stood by the hut, giving the last orders. The infantry of the detachment moved on along the road, hundreds of feet splashing through the mud. They quickly vanished among the trees in the mist before the dawn. The esaul gave some order to the Cossacks. Petya held his horse by the bridle, eagerly awaiting the word of command to mount. His face glowed from a dip in cold water, and his eyes gleamed. He felt a chill running down his back, and a kind of rapid, rhythmic throbbing all over.

"Well, have you everything ready?" said Denisov. "Give us our horses."

They brought the horses up. Denisov was vexed with the Cossack because the saddlegirths were slack, and swore at him as he mounted his horse. Petya put his foot in the stirrup. The horse, as its habit was, made as though to nip at his leg; but Petya leaped into the saddle, unconscious of his own weight, and looking round at the hussars moving up from behind in the darkness, he rode up to Denisov.

"Vassily Fyodorovitch, you will trust me with some commission? Please . . . for God's sake . . ." he said. Denisov seemed to have forgotten Petya's existence. He looked round at him.

"One thing I beg of you," he said sternly, "to obey me and not to put yourself forward."

All the way Denisov did not say another word to Petya; he rode on in silence. By the time that they reached the edge of the wood, it was perceptibly getting light in the open country. Denisov whispered something to the esaul, and the Cossacks began riding by Petya and Denisov. When they had all passed on Denisov put his spurs to his horse, and rode downhill. Slipping and sinking back on their haunches, the horses slid down into the hollow with their riders. Petya kept beside Denisov. The tremor all over him was growing more intense. It was getting lighter and lighter, but the mist hid objects at a distance. When he had reached the bottom, Denisov looked back and nodded to the Cossack beside him.

"The signal," he said. The Cossack raised his arm, and a shot rang out. At the same moment they heard the tramp of horses galloping in front, shouts from different directions, and more shots.

The instant that he heard the first tramp of hoofs and shouts, Petya gave the rein to his horse, and lashing him on, galloped forward, heedless of Denisov, who shouted to him. It seemed to Petya that it suddenly became broad daylight, as though it were midday, at the moment when he heard the shot. He galloped to the bridge. The Cossacks were galloping along the road in front. At the bridge he jostled against a Cossack who had lagged behind, and he galloped on. In front Petya saw men of some sort—the French he supposed—running across the road from right to left. One slipped in the mud under his horse's legs.

Cossacks were crowding about a hut, doing something. A fearful scream rose out of the middle of the crowd. Petya galloped to this crowd, and the first thing he saw was the white face and trembling lower-jaw of a Frenchman, who had clutched hold of a lance aimed at his breast.

"Hurrah! . . . Mates . . . ours . . ." shouted Petya, and giving the rein to his excited horse, he galloped down the village street.

He heard firing in front. Cossacks, hussars, and tattered Russian prisoners, running up from both sides of the road, were all shouting something loud and unintelligible. A gallant-looking Frenchman, in a blue coat, with a red, frowning face, and no cap, was keeping back the hussars with a bayonet. By the time that Petya galloped up, the Frenchman had fallen. "Too late again," flashed through Petya's brain, and he galloped to the spot where he heard the hottest fire. The shots came from the yard of the manor-house where he had been the night before with Dolohov. The French were ambushing there behind the fence in among the bushes of the overgrown garden, and firing at the Cossacks who were crowding round the gates. As he rode up to the gates, Petya caught a glimpse in the smoke of Dolohov's white, greenish face, as he shouted something to the men. "Go round. Wait for the infantry!" he was shouting, just as Petya rode up to him.

"Wait? . . . Hurrah! . . ." shouted Petya, and without pausing a moment, he galloped towards the spot where he heard the shots, and where the smoke was the thickest. There came a volley of shots with the sound of bullets whizzing by and thudding into something. The Cossacks and Dolohov galloped in at the gates after Petya. In the thick, hovering smoke the French flung down their arms and ran out of the bushes to meet the Cossacks, or fled downhill towards the pond. Petya was galloping on round the courtyard, but instead of holding the reins, he was flinging up both arms in a strange way, and slanting more and more to one side in the saddle. The horse stepped on to the ashes of the fire smouldering in the morning light, and stopped short. Petya fell heavily on the wet earth. The Cossacks saw his arms and legs twitching rapidly, though his head did not move. A bullet had passed through his brain.

After parleying with the French senior officer, who came out of the house with a handkerchief on a sword to announce that they surrendered, Dolohov got off his horse and went up to Petya, who lay motionless with outstretched arms.

"Done for," he said frowning, and walked to the gate to Denisov, who was riding towards him.

"Killed?" cried Denisov, even from a distance recognising the familiar, unmistakably lifeless posture in which Petya's body was lying.

"Done for," Dolohov repeated, as though the utterance of those words afforded him satisfaction; and he walked rapidly towards the prisoners, whom the Cossacks were hurriedly surrounding. "No quarter!" he shouted to Denisov. Denisov made no reply. He went up to Petya, got off his horse, and with trembling hands turned over the blood-stained, mud-spattered face that was already turning white.

"I'm fond of sweet things. They are capital raisins, take them all," came into his mind. And the Cossacks looked round in surprise at the sound like the howl of a dog, that Denisov uttered as he turned away, walked to the fence and clutched at it.

The Wrong Road

BY

MARQUIS JAMES

1

ON THE night of the nineteenth of September, 1780, Private John Paulding of the First Westchester County Regiment of Militia, a prisoner of war in the hands of the British Army in New York City, escaped from the North Dutch Church, which had been turned into a military prison. Eluding the English sentries north of the city, he was again in Westchester County and reentered the American lines near Tarrytown.

The flight of Private Paulding did not greatly disturb His Majesty's forces. It had occurred at a moment when General Sir Henry Clinton expected to have the war won for his sovereign. Indeed, he had already written to London about the terms of peace to be offered the Colonies. Sir Henry was not an illiberal foe, nor without foresight, and so suggested rather generous conditions.

While Private Paulding had been working his cautious way northward, another soldier of the Revolution also was saying farewell to New York. Major John André was the guest of the Colonel Williams's mess that evening. Colonel Williams commanded the Eightieth Infantry of British Regulars. He was fortunate to have André at his table. None was insensible to the honor of being host to the adjutant-general of the British Army in America and right-hand man of Sir Henry Clinton. Major André was twenty-nine years old, brave, able, gay and handsome. He brought the gathering at Colonel Williams's to a close by mounting a chair and leading the singing of a resounding barracks ballad entitled, *How Stands the Glass Around?*

That was in the small hours. After a snatch of sleep John André set out on a bold adventure.

2

Sundown next day found André, as well as Private Paulding, safe within the American lines. The British officer was safe because he was on board the man-of-war *Vulture*, which was anchored off Teller's Point—now Croton Point—thirty miles up the river. But the *Vulture* dared not venture farther than the Point, beyond which the Hudson gradually narrows from a width of three miles to half a mile. Lofty cliffs look down from both sides of the stream. Those heights were fortified for miles and were vigilantly manned by more than one-fourth of Washington's army.

The loss of the Highlands of the Hudson would have opened a road for the British from the Atlantic Ocean to Canada. This would have cut the Colonies in two. The British held New York City with twelve thousand soldiery and a fleet. The sole remaining link for the passage of American troops between New England and the South was a ferry below West Point. So Washington was obliged to hold the Highlands at all hazard. To this task was allotted three thousand men. Their commander had been selected with care, Washington's choice finally falling upon Benedict Arnold.

The fortunes of the Continentals were low. Washington's army was reduced to eleven thousand four hundred men, half of whom were militia whose terms would expire in three months. Prospects for reenlistments were dark. Washington had just attempted a campaign for recruits to bring his force up to thirty-five thousand. It had failed sadly. His troops were ill clad, badly fed and rarely paid. Some had drawn no money for three years. The Treasury was empty and credit was poor. Congress was jealous of the army when it won and nagged when it did not win.

Washington based his immediate hopes on the French. Rochambeau and De Lafayette were encamped in Rhode Island with five thousand troops. While Private John Paulding and Major André, their fates soon to be curiously joined, were making their separate ways into the American lines along the Hudson, General Washington was a short distance away at Hartford, Connecticut, conferring with the French Generals about getting their men into action.

When Major André boarded the *Vulture,* his youthful head carried the details of a scheme by which he hoped to win the war practically single-handed. For fifteen months he had been at one end of the most interesting conspiracy ever laid on American soil, and now in fifteen minutes' time he expected to learn the result of these persistent efforts. Aboard the *Vulture* he was to receive a mysterious stranger, and his hopes were based on the anticipation that this caller would prove to be Major General Benedict Arnold.

3

Benedict Arnold was a singular man, possessed of many of the qualities of a capable military leader. He had done good work earlier in the war, though there has been a tendency on the part of historians and biographers to over-emphasize the brilliancy of this chapter of his career. Arnold was seldom happy in his relations with his fellow-officers and some of the reasons for this are not difficult to understand. He was a spendthrift with a short memory for personal loans. He was extremely vain and one could not always be sure that he was telling the truth. These defects of character were advertised by those who had been inconvenienced by them, and perhaps by others who were merely jealous of Arnold's abilities as a soldier.

But as Washington needed all the good men he could find he had rather taken Arnold's part, and decided on an attempt to salvage the good in him and put it to the service of the Colonial cause. To this end, when the British evacuated Philadelphia, Arnold was given the command there with a small force. Philadelphia was a soft and desirable berth, but Arnold was lately out of bed and his wounds still troubled him.

The smart society of Philadelphia appealed to the luxury-loving General and his health and spirits were restored quickly enough. As a matter of course he met Peggy Shippen, one of the belles of the city and daughter of a rich Tory. During the previous winter when the British were in Philadelphia living on the fat of the land and Washington a few miles away at Valley Forge, the Shippen mansion had been the scene of many splendid entertainments for His Majesty's officers. Now Benedict Arnold was received with equal honors and attentions.

The American Commander professed his love for Peggy at once, but success did not immediately prosper this courtship because Peggy's heart had been at least half won already by a young gentleman who was fighting on the other side. His name was John André.

Nevertheless, in a few months, the captivating Major General and beautiful Peggy Shippen were married. The bridegroom rented a large house and shortly owed eighteen thousand dollars. With tradesmen pressing for payment, his situation was uncomfortable. Perhaps Arnold appealed to his wealthy Tory father-in-law, but if he did it seems to have been without the result the embarrassed debtor sought. At any rate, all we know is that General Arnold undertook most extraordinary means of replenishing his purse. He wrote a letter to New York and signed it "John Moore."

Some time thereafter Washington ordered his commandant at Philadelphia to field duty again, assigning him to the vital post of West Point. This unexpected change suited "John Moore's" plans so well that Arnold was disturbed a little at first. Could Washington suspect anything? In any event a greater degree of caution could do no harm.

4

Accordingly, the next time Benedict Arnold shut himself in a room to write a letter to New York he signed it "Gustavus." This letter was addressed to Sir Henry Clinton and took up matters precisely where "John Moore" had left off. Indeed it was written in the same obviously disguised hand. The first of the "John Moore" letters had purported to be from an American general who was willing to turn his coat. As Clinton's adjutant it fell to the lot of Peggy Shippen's old suitor, John André, to respond to this communication. Thus the correspondence had developed, but in such guarded form that little progress was made. André signed his letters "John Anderson." He assumed the rôle of a merchant in New York. The letters were couched in the terms of mercantile transactions, and in the course of numerous exchanges a code was developed which baffles experts to this day. André and Clinton appear not to have been sure that "John Moore" and "Gustavus" was Arnold, and, if so, that Arnold really was sincere in his treasonable proposals. But when Arnold went to West Point, he had something tangible to offer to the British and the negotiations took on new life.

André had not forgotten Peggy Shippen who was a mother now. When dispatching code messages to "Gustavus," the chivalrous Major sometimes sent along ribbons and other pretty things for Mrs. Arnold's little boy. Finally the more serious aspects of the correspondence came to a head. Clinton resolved to discover if "Gustavus ' were in truth Arnold and if he would hand over West Point, the key to the Highland forts, for a consideration. It was arranged that the author of the "Gustavus" letters should come aboard the *Vulture* and meet André there. "Gustavus" was to devise a legitimate military excuse for openly visiting the British war-ship under a flag of truce.

On the appointed date, André arrived aboard the *Vulture* about fifteen minutes early for the interview. But he waited for his visitor long beyond this quarter of an hour. No Arnold appeared that day or the next. André was disappointed, also suspicious. Either Arnold had cold feet or his proposed treason was a stratagem to entice André into the American lines. Luckily the Major was aboard a war-ship in the river, and could get back safely.

André had about made up his mind to return to New York when, on the second night, at ten o'clock, a rowboat approached the *Vulture* under a flag of truce. Arnold was not in it, however. The passenger identified himself as Joshua Hett Smith, a wealthy American whom the British regarded as a rebel, though Joshua's brother was a well-known Tory. Smith asked to speak to André, and told him that General Arnold had found it impossible to come aboard, but was anxious to meet André—or "Anderson," as Smith called him—on shore.

This was not the bargain "Gustavus" had made. He was to meet André on the ship.

5

Before sending André up the Hudson, Sir Henry Clinton had given his adjutant explicit instructions on three points. He was not to remove his uniform. He was not to enter the American lines on shore. He was to receive nothing from Arnold in writing. The caution which prompted these directions is obvious. But André was a daring young man. Dazzling rewards seemed within his grasp. He was willing to risk everything—and did so. Despite the urgent remonstrances of the captain of the *Vulture* he climbed down into the boat with Smith and they were pulled toward the western shore.

Rightly enough André found Arnold waiting on the edge of a fir thicket below the village of Haverstraw. He led the Englishman into the tangle of trees, telling Smith to wait by the river bank. The civilian resented this exclusion. He wanted to be in on what was happening, or rather, what he fancied to be happening. Smith was the dupe and tool of Arnold, and had no suspicion of the real business that was afoot. But what the story Arnold had told him of that evening's work lacked in truth was made up by ingenious plausibility.

It was midnight and there was no moon. In the darkness of the fir thicket André could not see his hand before him. But he could hear Arnold's voice, and that voice had not spoken long before the young Englishman dismissed any qualms which the eerie circumstances of his adventure may have formed in his mind concerning his disobedience of orders in going ashore. The American outlined a project which must fairly have taken away André's breath. Arnold would surrender not only the supremely important Highland forts, but he would contrive the capture of George Washington by the British Army!

The plot was to be carried out in such a way as to give the traitor a coat of whitewash for historical purposes. There was to be no open surrender. The British were to embark an expedition at New York, ostensibly for the Chesapeake. But the ships would head up the river instead, and attack. Arnold would have his troops distributed so as to render this "surprise" certain of success. The date was fixed for September twenty-seventh. This was only five days off. On September twenty-seventh Washington was due at West Point on his return from Hartford. Arnold would so arrange that, in the confusion of the action, the Commander-in-Chief and his staff should fall into British hands. Thus the last prop would be knocked from under the Colonial cause. Arnold, of course, would be "captured," too— taken fighting. As a "prisoner" he would reflect on his situation, decide that the Colonies were beaten, and sue for the King's mercy. This would be forthcoming, with additional rewards in the form of a brigadier-general's commission in the British Army and ten thousand pounds in gold.

Arnold gave André a series of documents describing the fortifications and the Americans' plans of defense. No one knows why André accepted these papers. The gist of them could easily have been committed to memory. The best guess seems to be that André wanted to make sure that Arnold was in his power. The documents were all in Arnold's handwriting and they established his treason.

The conspirators had so much to say to each other that the coming of dawn found them still talking. They adjourned to Joshua Hett Smith's house on a bluff four miles away to finish. En route they passed an American picket. Arnold gave the countersign and received a salute. André hurried by, thankful for the blue cape which reached to his boot tops and concealed his uniform. At Smith's they ate breakfast. Then, everything settled, André prepared to leave in the rowboat for the *Vulture*, and hasten to New York to apprise Sir Henry Clinton of the wonderful news.

Just then a cannon shot was heard. It was followed by another and another. The conspirators ran to a window. Smith's house commanded a view of the river for miles. The watchers saw the *Vulture* enveloped in smoke. She was under fire from the east bank of the river. André was frightened. Had Arnold deceived him? Arnold was thunderstruck. Had his treachery been discovered? The cannonade lasted for an hour, and the *Vulture* was driven down-stream, leaving André high and dry.

6

Arnold was soon able to relieve the tension in some degree. He convinced André that he had not been deceived. He boldly assumed that by no possible chance could the attack on the *Vulture* have been due to the discovery of his plot. And in this General Arnold was correct. An impetuous Canadian had caused all the trouble—little suspecting the full extent of it. History has slight acquaintance with his name, and the same thing is true of several other contributors to this drama. It was James Livingston, and he was the colonel of the Second Canadian Regiment, part of a tiny expeditionary force which friendly Canadians had sent to help the American cause.

The presence of the *Vulture* in American waters off Teller's Point, safely out of range of the Highland forts, had annoyed Colonel Livingston. He liked action. Two or three times he had asked Arnold to lend him a cannon, so he could drag it down the river and shoot up the *Vulture*. Naturally, Arnold evaded these requests. Finally, by his own devices, Livingston got an old brass four-pounder. He asked Colonel John Lamb, commanding the artillery, for some powder, but the old artillery-man demurred, saying it would be a waste of ammunition to fire at a ship with a four-pounder. But Livingston insisted and finally Lamb issued a small quantity of powder to humor his friend. Then Livingston borrowed a work-horse of William Teller, whose farm occupied Teller's Point, and dragged the gun out to the tip of this projection of land. He did this at night while Arnold and André were whispering in the fir thicket on the other side of the river. In the morning Colonel Livingston began shooting. The *Vulture* was taken by surprise and utterly unprepared for action. Livingston and his handful of men soon had the satisfaction of seeing the British war-ship retreat down the river.

Major André passed an anxious day at the Smith house despite Arnold's assurances that everything would work out all right. It was arranged for Mr. Smith to escort André overland to the British lines. Arnold provided the two with passes. Smith insisted that André exchange his uniform for civilian clothes. André protested that he had no other clothing. Smith went to a closet and brought out a suit of his own—a second-best ensemble which the fastidious André looked at with double disdain, but very reluctantly he put it on. Once out of uniform he knew he became a spy. Of course, he could have thrown away the papers Arnold had given him. Then, if he were taken, his captors might have a hard time proving very much. But André kept the papers. He believed them worth the risk.

At dusk that evening the pair set out on horseback. It was Friday, September 22, 1780. Ferrying to the east side of the river, they landed at Peekskill. The first man they met was Colonel Livingston, still in great spirits over his private fight with the *Vulture*. He knew Smith and invited him and his young friend to supper, but they hastily pleaded another engagement and headed south over a hilly back-country road. At eight-thirty they were challenged by a sentry and taken before an officer who held up a lantern and looked at their passes. The passes were recognized, and, as a special consideration to gentlemen traveling under the personal protection of General Arnold, the officer urged the pair to put up for the night. He said the road was unsafe to travel in the dark. André wanted to go on regardless of the road, but Smith refused and they remained for the night, occupying the same bed. André kept his boots on and did not sleep a wink. Moreover, he disturbed his companion's rest by pricking his bare skin with spurs.

Next morning they were on the road at dawn. Arnold's passes worked like charms, but near Yorktown Heights the horsemen rode squarely into Colonel Samuel Webb of the Third Connecticut Infantry. André said his hair stood on end. Webb knew André well. The acquaintance had been made when the American was a prisoner of war. But for some reason Webb failed to recognize the British officer and the two rode on. When within fifteen miles of the British lines, danger seemed past. There were no more American patrols out, except possibly a few militiamen, and "John Anderson" had General Arnold's personal pass. So Mr. Smith turned back and André continued on alone.

As Smith had some business of his own to attend to at Fishkill, he thought that while on the east bank he might as well go there before returning home. He reached Fishkill that evening and stayed overnight. The next day George Washington and his staff rode into the village, on their way from Hartford to West Point. Smith called to pay his respects and the Commander-in-Chief asked him to remain for dinner.

7

About nine o'clock in the morning André reached McKeel's Corners, now in the village of Pleasantville. He stopped at the gate of Staats Hammond's house, six or seven miles from the British outposts, and safety. Hammond was a sergeant in the First Westchester County Militia, and at home in bed with a wound. Looking from a window, he saw David and Sally, his children, get a drink of water for the good-looking stranger. With a small boy's impulse toward conversation, David remarked that there was an American patrol at Young's Tavern a mile down the road. André decided not to put his pass to another test unless necessary. He thanked the children, gave Sally sixpence and turned his horse, taking the roundabout road to White Plains which goes by way of Tarrytown.

As a matter of fact David's information was incorrect. The direct road to White Plains was unguarded, but the Tarrytown road was not. A patrol of seven young men of the First Westchester, under a sergeant, had been sent out to watch roads to New York. Primarily the patrol was looking for "cow boys," or marauders who drove off Westchester cattle and sold them to the British quartermasters. The patrol divided to watch two roads. John Paulding, in charge of two other privates, took up a position on the outskirts of Tarrytown. Paulding's companions were David Williams and Isaac Van Wart.

Although a home guard organization, the ranks of the First Westchester contained a number of experienced soldiers. Both Paulding and Williams had served in the Continental, or Regular, Army, Williams having been discharged with frozen feet after the Quebec campaign. Westchester militiamen made no pretense at wearing uniforms. They wore whatever they could find. This morning Paulding had on a long green coat, such as was issued to Hessian troops serving with the British—a castoff acquired while he was a prisoner of war in New York City. A neighbor woman in Tarrytown put up a lunch for the soldiers. Another neighbor loaned them a deck of cards, and the three men sat under a tree to pass their watch as comfortably as possible.

Presently John André galloped up, trying to read a map without slackening the pace of his horse. They halted him.

"Gentlemen, I hope you belong to our party," said André in answer to the challenge.

"What party is that?" asked Paulding guardedly.

"The lower party," said André, meaning the British who were down the river.

Paulding said they did. These words were a great relief to André, who thereupon committed the astonishing blunder which so mystifies historians.

"I am a British officer," he said. "I have been up the country on particular business."

Later André himself declared he could not explain his words and he did not claim—as often has been said—that Paulding's coat misled him. The explanation probably lay in André's anxiety and fatigue. Several small circumstances indicate that his nerves were on edge, for instance, his addressing three country yokels as "gentlemen."

It was unnecessary for Paulding to continue a deception which had served its end. He announced that he and his companions were American soldiers and that André was a prisoner.

André tried to correct his unfortunate slip by saying he, too, was an American, and had claimed otherwise only to establish the identity of his questioners. He displayed Arnold's pass to prove it. This document had never been questioned before. Sentry after sentry had passed it. But Paulding, an old soldier, was suspicious—without knowing exactly why, being by no means certain that he had found a questionable character. Later he said that, if André had shown the pass at first, they would have permitted him to proceed immediately.

Paulding ordered André to dismount and submit to search. The Arnold papers were found in the prisoner's shoes. They meant nothing to Williams or to Van Wart who could not read. The papers were handed to Paulding who was no scholar, and he pored over them for a long time.

"He's a spy!" he announced finally.

André became persuasive. He offered his horse, saddle, bridle, and a hundred guineas for his freedom.

"We would not let you go for a thousand guineas," said Paulding, naming what he considered an impossible sum.

"Then I will give you ten thousand," said André. That was more money than the three poor farmers knew was in the world. André said two of them could hold him as a hostage while the other rode to New York for the money.

The services of Paulding, Williams and Van Wart were not for sale, however. They marched their prisoner twelve miles to the nearest American post and turned him over to Lieutenant Colonel John Jameson, commanding the Second Light Dragoons.

8

If John André had displayed poor judgment when confronted by the three militiamen, he made up for it in the presence of the Colonel. He assured Jameson that it was a great mistake to detain him, which fact could be established if the Colonel would communicate with General Arnold. The Colonel was half convinced and sent André, accompanied by Lieutenant Solomon Allen and a squad of Connecticut militia, for an interview with Arnold at West Point. But the Colonel mitigated this error of judgment by giving the papers that had been found on André to another messenger to deliver to General Washington, who was known to be somewhere on the road between Hartford and Arnold's headquarters.

Colonel Jameson's bungling actions are inexplicable, except to say that no suspicion of Arnold's disloyalty entered his mind. He gave Lieutenant Allen a letter to Arnold, detailing the story of the capture as related by Paulding. He described the papers found on André, saying he thought them "of a very dangerous tendency" for an unexplained civilian to be carrying around. He said that he had sent the originals to Washington. One might assume that perhaps Colonel Jameson was led into this blunder because he did not recognize that the treasonable papers were in Arnold's handwriting—his natural, and not his disguised hand. But Jameson knew Arnold's handwriting perfectly. His act was one of sheer stupidity.

The question now was, which of three things would happen first: André reach Arnold, Washington reach Arnold, or Washington receive the papers betraying Arnold's treachery before Arnold could take steps to intercept them?

This was the state of affairs on the afternoon of Saturday, September twenty-third. A little later Major Benjamin Tallmadge rode up to Colonel Jameson's headquarters. He had been on outpost duty and finding out what had happened was aghast at the Colonel's action. He suggested that the prisoner—who still called himself "Anderson"—should immediately be recalled and detained until Washington had had a chance to see the captured papers. Jameson refused to do this but at length he yielded to a compromise. A courier was dispatched with an order to Allen to bring

André back, after which Allen was to proceed to Arnold's headquarters alone and deliver Jameson's letter to Arnold. Jameson insisted on the delivery of this letter.

The courier overtook Allen and André within a few miles of Arnold's headquarters, and the prisoner was turned back on the brink of safety.

9

The next day was Sunday, September twenty-fourth.

André was turned over to Tallmadge for safe-keeping. The moment Tallmadge laid eyes on the prisoner he was sure "Anderson" was no civilian —and his manners unmistakably were British. André was removed to South Salem, a remote village in the Westchester hills, where he was comfortably lodged, provided with a clean shirt and surrounded by a guard of twenty dragoons. André chatted pleasantly with a few of the American officers and then asked for a pen and paper. These were provided. The prisoner amused his guard for a while by making facetious sketches of himself and his captors. Then he wrote a letter, addressed to General Washington, and handed it to Major Tallmadge to read. It began:

"What I have said as yet concerning myself was in the justifiable attempt to be extricated, but I am too little accustomed to duplicity to have succeeded. . . . The person in your possession is Major John André, adjutant general to the British Army."

Tallmadge increased his guard and sent the letter on its way.

The next day was Monday, September twenty-fifth.

Dispatching a messenger in advance to apprise Arnold of his coming, General Washington, his staff, and the Marquis de Lafayette crossed the river en route to West Point. The receipt of this message was an unpleasant surprise for General Arnold, who had not expected his chief until September twenty-seventh when he had arranged the "surprise" attack by the British and the capture of Washington. Arnold did the correct thing, however. He sent an orderly with a note expressing the hope that the Commander-in-Chief and his party would arrive by breakfast time. Washington responded that they would be there for breakfast.

But the Commander-in-Chief had hardly landed on the western bank when he decided to inspect some of the defenses of the locality. De Lafayette asked if this could not be postponed so as not to keep Mrs. Arnold waiting breakfast.

"Ah, Marquis," replied Washington. "You young men are all in love with Mrs. Arnold. Go and breakfast with her and tell her not to wait for me."

De Lafayette remained with Washington and, instead, Colonel Alexander Hamilton, Washington's Chief of Staff, rode on to inform Mrs. Arnold of the delay and ask her not to postpone her meal.

General Arnold, his wife and the General's staff were waiting breakfast when Hamilton arrived. They asked him to join them and the meal was served. Mrs. Arnold delighted the company with her usual vivacity, but her husband was preoccupied. Washington's early arrival had upset the plan he had given André. By what devices could he detain his chief for three days? That might be done, but then how was he to explain the lax state of his defenses which were prepared to make the British success swift and simple?

Presently a messenger entered. He came from Washington to say that the Commander-in-Chief had finished his inspection and was on his way to Arnold's house.

In a few moments another courier arrived. He was Lieutenant Allen from Colonel Jameson's headquarters. He delivered to Arnold the Colonel's letter.

Never once in his life did Arnold's amazing powers of self-command desert him. No muscle of his face moved as he read the overwhelming news of André's capture.

Folding the note, he placed it in his pocket and calmly concluded an anecdote which Allen's entrance had interrupted. Then he arose and begged to be excused, saying that a trivial emergency required his presence at the defenses, but that he would return as soon as he could and welcome the Commander-in-Chief. Asking to speak to Mrs. Arnold in private, he took her up-stairs and told her he was obliged to flee for his life on the instant, and that they might never meet again. Peggy Shippen fainted.

10

An hour later Washington arrived, and, being informed that General Arnold was at the defenses, the Commander-in-Chief went to find him. He did not find him, however. Leaving his wife insensible, Arnold had kissed his sleeping baby boy, leaped on a horse and ridden down an almost precipitous cliff to the river. There he had boarded a small army sailing scow and fled to the British war-ship *Vulture,* which had come back up the river in search of news of André.

In the middle of the afternoon Washington retraced his steps toward Arnold's headquarters, perplexed at his inability to discover the slightest trace of the General. Alexander Hamilton saw the Commander approaching and hurried to meet him. Colonel Hamilton's countenance was grave. During Washington's absence the courier from Jameson had arrived with the papers that had been found on André. This messenger had been trailing the Commander for twenty-four hours. Another runner had delivered the letter of the providentially detained André. As Washington's Chief of Staff and confidential adviser, Hamilton had opened both communications. Briefly Hamilton sketched the terrible story, including the flight of Arnold and the hysterical condition of his wife, which confirmed everything.

Washington was stunned. Turning to Lafayette he exclaimed: "Whom can we trust now?"

The next few hours reveal much of the essence of the man who won America's independence simply because he had a heart for any fortune. Already the Colonies' cause was reeling. Defeats, desertions, doubts—they had been multiplying fast of late—and, on top of all, the revelation that one of the ablest generals, commanding the most vital of defenses, had gone over to the enemy. None knew how deeply the conspiracy went—who was friend, who was foe in the West Point Garrison. Washington's very life might have been in peril from desperate confederates of Arnold in the American lines. A British attack on a betrayed army was expected at any hour.

With devastating energy Washington summoned reenforcements. He transferred troops and commanders to break up any possible traitorous combinations within the ranks, and directed the hundred and one details of putting the Highlands of the Hudson in readiness to resist to the last gasp.

The attack never came, the chief reason being that Washington himself was in possession of the papers containing the British plan of assault which an American general had laid down. Washington could not guess this, however. All he knew was that the British fleet had prepared to sail on what appeared to be a business-like mission. Yet it did not leave New York Harbor. Nothing, simply nothing, happened. From their actions, the British seemed to have been too dazed by the discovery of their scheme and the capture of André to do anything. They needed a Washington.

André was tried as a spy. On the court-martial sat three noblemen who were major generals in the Continental army—De Lafayette of France, Baron von Steuben of Prussia and the American-born Lord Stirling. Washington had no wish to punish André alone; Arnold was the man he wanted. He permitted a young sergeant major from Virginia to risk his life in a rash and unsuccessful attempt to kidnap Arnold on the streets of New York and carry him into the American lines for trial.

The pleasant manners of André endeared him to his captors. At his trial the compunctions of a gentleman impelled the doomed man to try to shield Arnold at his own expense. Or was this a last, little service of chivalry to Peggy Shippen? There has always been a mystery as to the extent of Peggy Shippen's knowledge of this affair. For André himself there was no defense. The evidence against him was unanswerable. The laws of war recognized but one penalty. On the second day of October, 1780, nine days after his capture, Major John André shaved and dressed himself in his uniform with great care. He climbed upon an army baggage wagon, which answered the purpose of a scaffold, and died with perfect courage. His body rests in Westminster Abbey.

11

George Washington obtained medals, pensions and bonuses of land for Privates Paulding, Williams and Van Wart. The Commander-in-Chief himself bestowed the medals and invited the soldiers to dinner. This was an unprecedented honor. Washington was an aristocrat and an austere disciplinarian. During the terrible winter at Valley Forge, he had severely punished a captain for eating with his men.

Taking leave of his guests Washington gave each of them a brace of pistols as his personal presents. He said they would need them as they might expect "to be hunted like partridges." Something of that sort happened. A great outcry, in which many patriotic Americans mistakenly joined, went up against the three soldiers. On the floor of Congress they were called outlaws and thieves, and the implication that they surrendered André because he would not buy his liberty finds a place in several histories. But they outlived much of this malice and at a green old age each died in his bed.

The Corvette Claymore

BY

VICTOR HUGO

ONE of the carronades of the battery, a twenty-four pounder, had got loose.

This is perhaps the most formidable of ocean accidents. Nothing more terrible can happen to a vessel in open sea and under full sail.

A gun that breaks its moorings becomes suddenly some indescribable supernatural beast. It is a machine which transforms itself into a monster. This mass turns upon its wheels, has the rapid movements of a billiard-ball; rolls with the rolling, pitches with the pitching; goes, comes, pauses, seems to meditate; resumes its course, rushes along the ship from end to end like an arrow, circles about, springs aside, evades, rears, breaks, kills, exterminates. It is a battering-ram which assaults a wall at its own caprice. Moreover, the battering-ram is metal, the wall wood. It is the entrance of matter into liberty. One might say that this eternal slave avenges itself. It seems as if the power of evil hidden in what we call inanimate objects finds a vent and bursts suddenly out. It has an air of having lost patience, of seeking some fierce, obscure retribution; nothing more inexorable than this rage of the inanimate. The mad mass has the bound of a panther, the weight of the elephant, the agility of the mouse, the obstinacy of the axe, the unexpectedness of the surge, the rapidity of lightning, the deafness of the tomb. It weighs ten thousand pounds, and it rebounds like a child's ball. Its flight is a wild whirl abruptly cut at right angles. What is to be done? How to end this? A tempest ceases, a cyclone passes, a wind falls, a broken mast is replaced, a leak is stopped, a fire dies out; but how to control this enormous brute of bronze? In what way can one attack it?

You can make a mastiff hear reason, astound a bull, fascinate a boa, frighten a tiger, soften a lion; but there is no resource with that monster,— a cannon let loose. You cannot kill it,—it is dead; at the same time it lives. It lives with a sinister life bestowed on it by Infinity.

The planks beneath it give it play. It is moved by the ship, which is moved by the sea, which is moved by the wind. This destroyer is a plaything. The ship, the waves, the blasts, all aid it; hence its frightful vitality. How to assail this fury of complication? How to fetter this monstrous mechanism for wrecking a ship? How foresee its coming and goings, its returns, its stops, its shocks? Any one of these blows upon the sides may stave out the vessel. How divine its awful gyrations! One has to deal with

From: *Ninety-Three.*

623

a projectile which thinks, seems to possess ideas, and which changes its direction at each instant. How stop the course of something which must be avoided? The horrible cannon flings itself about, advances, recoils, strikes to the right, strikes to the left, flees, passes, disconcerts, ambushes, breaks down obstacles, crushes men like flies. The great danger of the situation is in the mobility of its base. How combat an inclined plane which has caprices? The ship, so to speak, has lightning imprisoned in its womb which seeks to escape; it is like thunder rolling above an earthquake.

In an instant the whole crew were on foot. The fault was the chief gunner's; he had neglected to fix home the screw-nut of the mooring-chain, and had so badly shackled the four wheels of the carronade that the play given to the sole and frame had separated the platform, and ended by breaking the breeching. The cordage had broken, so that the gun was no longer secure on the carriage. The stationary breeching which prevents recoil was not in use at that period. As a heavy wave struck the port, the carronade, weakly attached, recoiled, burst its chain, and began to rush wildly about. Conceive, in order to have an idea of this strange sliding, a drop of water running down a pane of glass.

At the moment when the lashings gave way the gunners were in the battery, some in groups, others standing alone, occupied with such duties as sailors perform in expectation of the command to clear for action. The carronade, hurled forward by the pitching, dashed into this knot of men, and crushed four at the first blow; then, flung back and shot out anew by the rolling, it cut in two a fifth poor fellow, glanced off to the larboard side, and struck a piece of the battery with such force at to unship it. Then rose the cry of distress which had been heard. The men rushed toward the ladder; the gun-deck emptied in the twinkling of an eye. The enormous cannon was left alone. She was given up to herself. She was her own mistress, and mistress of the vessel. She could do what she willed with both. This whole crew, accustomed to laugh in battle, trembled now. To describe the universal terror would be impossible.

Captain Boisberthelot and Lieutenant Vieuville, although both intrepid men, stopped at the head of the stairs, and remained mute, pale, hesitating, looking down on the deck. Some one pushed them aside with his elbow and descended.

It was their passenger, the peasant,—the man of whom they had been speaking a moment before.

When he reached the foot of the ladder, he stood still.

The cannon came and went along the deck. One might have fancied it the living chariot of the Apocalypse. The marine-lantern, oscillating from the ceiling, added a dizzying whirl of lights and shadows to this vision. The shape of the cannon was undistinguishable from the rapidity of its course; now it looked black in the light, now it cast weird reflections through the gloom.

It kept on its work of destruction. It had already shattered four other pieces, and dug two crevices in the side, fortunately above the water-line, though they would leak in case a squall should come on. It dashed itself frantically against the frame-work; the solid tie-beams resisted, their curved form giving them great strength, but they creaked ominously under the assaults of this terrible club, which seemed endowed with a sort of appalling ubiquity, striking on every side at once. The strokes of a bullet shaken in a bottle would not be madder or more rapid. The four wheels passed and repassed above the dead men, cut, carved, slashed them, till the five corpses were a score of stumps rolling about the deck; the heads seem to cry out; streams of blood twisted in and out of the planks with every pitch of the vessel. The ceiling, damaged in several places, began to gape. The whole ship was filled with the awful tumult.

The captain promptly recovered his composure, and at his order the sailors threw down into the deck everything which could deaden and check the mad rush of the gun,—mattresses, hammocks, spare sails, coils of rope, extra equipments, and the bales of false assignats of which the corvette carried a whole cargo; an infamous deception which the English considered a fair trick in war.

But what could these rags avail? No one dared descend to arrange them in any useful fashion, and in a few instants they were mere heaps of lint.

There was just sea enough to render an accident as complete as possible. A tempest would have been desirable,—it might have thrown the gun upside down; and the four wheels once in the air, the monster could have been mastered. But the devastation increased. There were gashes and even fractures in the masts, which, imbedded in the woodwork of the keel, pierce the decks of ships like great round pillars. The mizzen-mast was cracked, and the main-mast itself was injured under the convulsive blows of the gun. The battery was being destroyed. Ten pieces out of the thirty were disabled; the breaches multiplied in the side, and the corvette began to take in water.

The old passenger, who had descended to the gun-deck, looked like a form of stone stationed at the foot of the stairs. He stood motionless, gazing sternly about upon the devastation. Indeed, it seemed impossible to take a single step forward.

Each bound of the liberated carronade menaced the destruction of the vessel. A few minutes more and shipwreck would be inevitable.

They must perish or put a summary end to the disaster. A decision must be made—but how?

What a combatant—this cannon!

They must check this mad monster. They must seize this flash of lightning. They must overthrow this thunderbolt.

Boisberthelot said to La Vieuville—

"Do you believe in God, Chevalier?"

Le Vieuville replied—

"Yes. No. Sometimes."

"In a tempest?"

"Yes; and in moments like this."

"Only God can aid us here," said Boisberthelot.

All were silent: the cannon kept up its horrible fracas.

The waves beat against the ship; their blows from without responded to the strokes of the cannon.

It was like two hammers alternating.

Suddenly, into the midst of this sort of inaccessible circus, where the escaped cannon leaped and bounded, there sprang a man with an iron bar in his hand. It was the author of this catastrophe—the gunner whose culpable negligence had caused the accident; the captain of the gun. Having been the means of bringing about the misfortune, he desired to repair it. He had caught up a handspike in one fist, a tiller-rope with a slipping-noose in the other, and jumped down into the gun-deck.

Then a strange combat began, a titantic strife—the struggle of the gun against the gunner; a battle between matter and intelligence; a duel between the inanimate and the human.

The man was posted in an angle, the bar and rope in his two fists; backed against one of the riders, settled firmly on his legs as on two pillars of steel, livid, calm, tragic, rooted as it were in the planks, he waited.

He waited for the cannon to pass near him.

The gunner knew his piece, and it seemed to him that she must recognize her master. He had lived a long while with her. How many times he had thrust his hand between her jaws! It was his tame monster. He began to address it as he might have done his dog.

"Come!" said he. Perhaps he loved it.

He seemed to wish that it would turn toward him.

But to come toward him would be to spring upon him. Then he would be lost. How to avoid its crush? There was the question. All stared in terrified silence.

Not a breast respired freely, except perchance that of the old man who alone stood in the deck with the two combatants, a stern second.

He might himself be crushed by the piece. He did not stir.

Beneath them, the blind sea directed the battle.

At the instant when, accepting this awful hand-to-hand contest, the gunner approached to challenge the cannon, some chance fluctuation of the waves kept it for a moment immovable, as if suddenly stupefied.

"Come on!" the man said to it. It seemed to listen.

Suddenly it darted upon him. The gunner avoided the shock.

The struggle began—struggle unheard of. The fragile matching itself against the invulnerable. The thing of flesh attacking the brazen brute. On the one side blind force, on the other a soul.

The whole passed in a half-light. It was like the indistinct vision of a miracle.

A soul—strange thing; but you would have said that the cannon had one also—a soul filled with rage and hatred. This blindness appeared to have eyes. The monster had the air of watching the man. There was—one might have fancied so at least—cunning in this mass. It also chose its moment. It became some gigantic insect of metal, having, or seeming to have, the will of a demon. Sometimes this colossal grasshopper would strike the low ceiling of the gun-deck, then fall back on its four wheels like a tiger upon its four claws, and dart anew on the man. He, supple, agile, adroit, would glide away like a snake from the reach of these lightning-like movements. He avoided the encounters; but the blows which he escaped fell upon the vessel and continued the havoc.

An end of broken chain remained attached to the carronade. This chain had twisted itself, one could not tell how, about the screw of the breech-button. One extremity of the chain was fastened to the carriage. The other, hanging loose, whirled wildly about the gun and added to the danger of its blows.

The screw held it like a clinched hand, and the chain multiplying the strokes of the battering-ram by its strokes of a thong, made a fearful whirlwind about the cannon—a whip of iron in a fist of brass. This chain complicated the battle.

Nevertheless, the man fought. Sometimes, even, it was the man who attacked the cannon. He crept along the side, bar and rope in hand, and the cannon had the air of understanding, and fled as if it perceived a snare. The man pursued it, formidable, fearless.

Such a duel could not last long. The gun seemed suddenly to say to itself, "Come, we must make an end!" and it paused. One felt the approach of the crisis. The cannon, as if in suspense, appeared to have, or had—because it seemed to all a sentient being—a furious premeditation. It sprang unexpectedly upon the gunner. He jumped aside, let it pass, and cried out with a laugh, "Try again!" The gun, as if in a fury, broke a carronade to larboard; then, seized anew by the invisible sling which held it, was flung to starboard toward the man, who escaped.

Three carronades gave way under the blows of the gun; then, as if blind and no longer conscious of what it was doing, it turned its back on the man, rolled from the stern to the bow, bruising the stem and making a breach in the plankings of the prow. The gunner had taken refuge at the foot of the stairs, a few steps from the old man, who was watching.

The gunner held his handspike in rest. The cannon seemed to perceive him, and, without taking the trouble to turn itself, backed upon him with the quickness of an axe-stroke. The gunner, if driven back against the side, was lost. The crew uttered a simultaneous cry.

But the old passenger, until now immovable, made a spring more rapid than all those wild whirls. He seized a bale of the false assignats, and at the risk of being crushed, succeeded in flinging it between the wheels of the carronade. This manœuvre, decisive and dangerous, could not have been executed with more adroitness and precision by a man trained to all the exercises set down in Durosel's "Manual of Sea Gunnery."

The bale had the effect of a plug. A pebble may stop a log, a tree-branch turn an avalanche. The carronade stumbled. The gunner, in his turn, seizing this terrible chance, plunged his iron bar between the spokes of one of the hind wheels. The cannon was stopped.

It staggered. The man, using the bar as a lever, rocked it to and fro. The heavy mass turned over with a clang like a falling bell, and the gunner, dripping with sweat, rushed forward headlong and passed the slipping-noose of the tiller-rope about the bronze neck of the over-thrown monster.

It was ended. The man had conquered. The ant had subdued the mastodon; the pigmy had taken the thunderbolt prisoner.

The marines and the sailors clapped their hands.

The whole crew hurried down with cables and chains, and in an instant the cannon was securely lashed.

The gunner saluted the passenger.

"Sir," he said to him, "you have saved my life."

The old man had resumed his impassible attitude, and did not reply.

The man had conquered, but one might say that the cannon had con-quered also. Immediate ship-wreck had been avoided, but the corvette was by no means saved. The dilapidation of the vessel seemed irremediable. The sides had five breaches, one of which, very large, was in the bow. Out of the thirty carronades, twenty lay useless in their frames. The carronade, which had been captured and rechained, was itself disabled; the screw of the breech-button was forced, and the levelling of the piece impossible in consequence. The battery was reduced to nine pieces. The hold had sprung a leak. It was necessary at once to repair the damages and set the pumps to work.

The gun-deck, now that one had time to look about it, offered a terrible spectacle. The interior of a mad elephant's cage could not have been more completely dismantled.

However great the necessity that the corvette should escape observation, a still more imperious necessity presented itself—immediate safety. It had been necessary to light up the deck by lanterns placed here and there along the sides.

But during the whole time this tragic diversion had lasted, the crew were so absorbed by the one question of life or death that they noticed little what was passing outside the scene of the duel. The fog had thickened; the weather had changed; the wind had driven the vessel at will; it had got out of its route, in plain sight of Jersey and Guernsey, farther to the south than it ought to have gone, and it was surrounded by a troubled sea. The great waves kissed the gaping wounds of the corvette—kisses full of peril. The sea rocked her menacingly. The breeze became a gale. A squall, a tempest perhaps, threatened. It was impossible to see before one four oars' length.

While the crew were repairing summarily and in haste the ravages of the gun-deck, stopping the leaks and putting back into position the guns which had escaped the disaster, the old passenger had gone on deck.

He stood with his back against the main-mast.

He had paid no attention to a proceeding which had taken place on the vessel. The Chevalier La Vieuville had drawn up the marines in line on either side of the main-mast, and at the whistle of the boatswain the sailors busy in the rigging stood upright on the yards.

Count du Boisberthelot advanced toward the passenger.

Behind the captain marched a man, haggard, breathless, his dress in disorder, yet wearing a satisfied look under it all. It was the gunner who had just now so opportunely shown himself a tamer of monsters, and who had got the better of the cannon.

The count made a military salute to the unknown in peasant garb, and said to him—

"General, here is the man."

The gunner held himself erect, his eyes downcast, standing in a soldierly attitude.

Count du Boisberthelot continued—

"General, taking into consideration what this man has done, do you not think there is something for his commanders to do?"

"I think there is," said the old man.

"Be good enough to give the orders," returned Boisberthelot.

"It is for you to give them. You are the captain."

"But you are the general," answered Boisberthelot.

The old man looked at the gunner.

"Approach," said he.

The gunner moved forward a step. The old man turned toward Count du Boisberthelot, detached the cross of Saint Louis from the captain's uniform and fastened it on the jacket of the gunner.

"Hurrah!" cried the sailors.

The marines presented arms. The old passenger, pointing with his finger toward the bewildered gunner, added—

"Now let that man be shot."

Stupor succeeded the applause.

Then, in the midst of a silence like that of the tomb, the old man raised his voice. He said—

"A negligence has endangered this ship. At this moment she is perhaps lost. To be at sea is to face the enemy. A vessel at open sea is an army which gives battle. The tempest conceals, but does not absent itself. The whole sea is an ambuscade.

"Death is the penalty of any fault committed in the face of the enemy. No fault is reparable. Courage ought to be rewarded and negligence punished."

These words fell one after the other, slowly, solemnly, with a sort of inexorable measure, like the blows of an axe upon an oak.

And the old man, turning to the soldiers, added—

"Do your duty."

The man upon whose breast shone the cross of Saint Louis bowed his head.

At a sign from Count du Boisberthelot, two sailors descended between decks, then returned, bringing the hammock winding-sheet. The ship's chaplain, who since the time of sailing had been at prayer in the officers' quarters, accompanied the two sailors; a sergeant detached from the line twelve marines, whom he arranged in two ranks, six by six; the gunner, without uttering a word, placed himself between the two files. The chaplain, crucifix in hand, advanced and stood near him.

"March!" said the sergeant.

The platoon moved with slow steps toward the bow. The two sailors who carried the shroud followed.

A gloomy silence fell upon the corvette. A hurricane moaned in the distance.

A few instants later there was a flash; a report followed, echoing among the shadows; then all was silent; then came the thud of a body falling into the sea.

Miracle at Dunkirk

BY

ARTHUR D. DIVINE

I AM STILL amazed about the whole Dunkirk affair. There was from first to last a queer, medieval sense of miracle about it. You remember the old quotation about the miracle that crushed the Spanish Armada, "God sent a wind." This time "God withheld the wind." Had we had one onshore breeze of any strength at all, in the first days, we would have lost a hundred thousand men.

The pier at Dunkirk was the unceasing target of bombs and shell-fire throughout, yet it never was hit. Two hundred and fifty thousand men embarked from that pier. Had it been blasted . . .

The whole thing from first to last was covered with that same strange feeling of something supernatural. We muddled, we quarreled, everybody swore and was bad-tempered and made the wildest accusations of inefficiency and worse in high places. Boats were badly handled and broke down, arrangements went wrong.

And yet out of all that mess we beat the experts, we defied the law and the prophets, and where the Government and the Board of Admiralty had hoped to bring away 30,000 men, we brought away 335,000. If that was not a miracle, there are no miracles left.

When I heard that small boats of all sorts were to be used at Dunkirk, I volunteered at once, having no vast opinion of the navy as small-boat handlers. I had been playing with the navy off and on since the beginning of the year, mine sweeping and submarine hunting, convoying, and so on. So friends of mine at the Admiralty passed me through without formalities, and within two hours of my first telephone call I was on my way to Sheerness. From Sheerness I acted as navigator for a party of small boats round to Ramsgate, and at Ramsgate we started work. The evacuation went on for something over a week, but to me the most exciting time was the night before the last.

I was given a motorboat about as long as my drawing room at home, 30 feet. She had one cabin forward and the rest was open, but she had twin engines and was fairly fast. For crew we had one sub-lieutenant, one stoker and one gunner. For armament we had two Bren guns—one my own

From: The Reader's Digest. By permission of the Author.

631

particular pet which I had stolen—and rifles. In command of our boat we had a real live Admiral—Taylor, Admiral in charge of small boats.

We first went out to French fishing boats gathered off Ramsgate, boats from Caen and Le Havre, bright little vessels with lovely names—*Ciel de France, Ave Maria, Gratia Plena, Jeanne Antoine.* They had helped at Calais and Boulogne and in the preceding days at Dunkirk, and the men were very tired, but when we passed them new orders they set out again for Dunkirk.

They went as the leaders of the procession, for they were slow. With them went a handful of Dutch *schouts,* stumpy little coasting vessels commandeered at the collapse of Holland, each flying the white ensign of the Royal Navy, sparkling new, and each fitted out with a Lewis gun. Next went coasters, colliers, paddle steamers that in time of peace had taken trippers around the harbor for a shilling, tugs towing mud scows with brave names like *Galleon's Reach* and *Queen's Channel.*

There was a car ferry, surely on its first trip in the open sea. There were yachts; one the *Skylark*—what a name for such a mission! There were dockyard tugs, towing barges. There were sloops, mine sweepers, trawlers, destroyers. There were Thames fire floats, Belgian drifters, lifeboats from all around the coast, lifeboats from sunken ships. I saw the boats of the old *Dunbar Castle,* sunk eight months before. Rolling and pitching in a cloud of spray were open speedboats, wholly unsuited for the Channel chop.

There was the old *Brighton Belle* that carried holiday crowds in the days before the Boer War. She swept mines in the Great War, and she swept mines in this war through all the fury of last winter. I know; I sailed with her then. Coming back from her second trip to Dunkirk, she struck the wreck of a ship sunk by a magnetic mine and slowly sank. Her captain, a Conservative party agent in civil life, got 400 men safely off and at the last even saved his dog.

There was never such a fleet went to war before, I think. As I went round the western arm of the harbor near sunset, passing out orders, it brought my heart into my throat to watch them leave. They were so small! Little boats like those you see in the bight of Sandy Hook fishing on a fine afternoon. Some were frowsy, with old motorcar tires for fenders, and some of them were bright with paint and chromium—little white boats that were soon lost to view across the ruffled water. And as they went there came round from the foreland a line of fishing boats—shrimp catchers and what not, from the east coast—to join the parade.

When this armada of oddments was under way, we followed with the faster boats—Royal Air Force rescue launches, picket boats and the like— and with us went an X-lighter, a flatboat, kerosene-powered built for landing troops at Gallipoli and a veteran of *that* evacuation more than 20 years ago.

It was the queerest, most nondescript flotilla that ever was, and it was manned by every kind of Englishman, never more than two men, often only one, to each small boat. There were bankers and dentists, taxi drivers and yachtsmen, longshoremen, boys, engineers, fishermen and civil servants. There were bright-faced Sea Scouts and old men whose skins looked fiery red against their white hair. Many were poor; they had no coats, but made out with old jerseys and sweaters. They wore cracked rubber boots. They were wet, chilled to the bone, hungry; they were unarmed and unprotected, and they sailed toward the pillars of smoke and fire and the thunder of the guns, into waters already slick with the oil of sunken boats, knowing perfectly well the special kind of hell ahead. Still, they went, plugging gamely along.

I had a feeling, then and after, that this was something bigger than organization, something bigger than the mere requisitioning of boats. In a sense it was the naval spirit that has always been the foundation of England's greatness, flowering again and flowering superbly. I believe 887 was the official figure for the total of boats that took part over the ten days of the evacuation. But I think there were more than a thousand craft in all. I myself know of fishermen who never registered, waited for no orders, but, all unofficial, went and brought back soldiers. Quietly, like that.

It was dark before we were well clear of the English coast. It wasn't rough, but there was a little chop on, sufficient to make it very wet, and we soaked the Admiral to the skin. Soon, in the dark, the big boats began to overtake us. We were in a sort of dark traffic lane, full of strange ghosts and weird, unaccountable waves from the wash of the larger vessels. When destroyers went by, full tilt, the wash was a serious matter to us little fellows. We could only spin the wheel to try to head into the waves, hang on, and hope for the best.

Mere navigation was dangerous in the dark. Clouds hung low and blotted out the stars. We carried no lights, we had no signals, no means of recognition of friend or foe. Before we were halfway across we began to meet the first of the returning stream. We dodged white, glimmering bow waves of vessels that had passed astern, only to fall into the way of half-seen shapes ahead. There were shouts in the darkness, but only occasionally the indignant stutter of a horn. We went "by guess and by God."

From the halfway mark, too, there were destroyers on patrol crossing our line of passage, weaving a fantastic warp of foam through the web of our progress. There were collisions, of course. Dover for days was full of destroyers with bows stove in, coasting vessels with great gashes amidships, ships battered, scraped and scarred. The miracle is that there were not ten for every one that happened.

Even before it was fully dark we had picked up the glow of the Dunkirk flames, and now as we drew nearer the sailing got better, for we could steer by them and see silhouetted the shapes of other ships, of boats coming home already loaded, and of low dark shadows that might be the enemy motor torpedo boats.

Then aircraft started dropping parachute flares. We saw them hanging all about us in the night, like young moons. The sound of the firing and the bombing was with us always, growing steadily louder as we got nearer and nearer. The flames grew, too. From a glow they rose up to enormous plumes of fire that roared high into the everlasting pall of smoke. As we approached Dunkirk there was an air attack on the destroyers and for a little the night was brilliant with bursting bombs and the fountain sprays of tracer bullets.

The beach, black with men, illumined by the fires, seemed a perfect target, but no doubt the thick clouds of smoke were a useful screen.

When we got to the neighborhood of the mole there was a lull. The aircraft had dispersed and apparently had done no damage, for there was nothing sinking. They had been there before, however, and the place was a shambles of old wrecks, British and French, and all kinds of odds and ends. The breakwaters and lighthouse were magnificently silhouetted against the flames of burning oil tanks—enormous flames that licked high above the town. Further inshore and to the east of the docks the town itself was burning furiously, but down near the beach where we were going there was no fire and we could see rows of houses standing silent and apparently empty.

We had just got to the eastward of the pier when shelling started up. There was one battery of 5.9's down between La Panne and Nieuport that our people simply could not find and its shooting was uncannily accurate. Our place was in the corner of the beach at the mole and as they were shelling the mole, the firing was right over our heads. Nothing, however, came near us in the first spell.

The picture will always remain sharp-etched in my memory—the lines of men wearily and sleepily staggering across the beach from the dunes to the shallows, falling into little boats, great columns of men thrust out into the water among bomb and shell splashes. The foremost ranks were shoulder deep, moving forward under the command of young subalterns, themselves with their heads just above the little waves that rode in to the sand. As the front ranks were dragged aboard the boats, the rear ranks moved up, from ankle deep to knee deep, from knee deep to waist deep, until they, too, came to shoulder depth and their turn.

Some of the big boats pushed in until they were almost aground, taking appalling risks with the falling tide. The men scrambled up the sides on rope nets, or climbed hundreds of ladders, made God knows where out of new, raw wood and hurried aboard the ships in England.

The little boats that ferried from the beach to the big ships in deep water listed drunkenly with the weight of men. The big ships slowly took on lists of their own with the enormous numbers crowded aboard. And always down the dunes and across the beach came new hordes of men, new columns, new lines.

On the beach was a destroyer, bombed and burned. At the water's edge were ambulances, abandoned when their last load had been discharged.

There was always the red background, the red of Dunkirk burning. There was no water to check the fires and there were no men to be spared to fight them. Red, too, were the shell bursts, the flash of guns, the fountains of tracer bullets.

The din was infernal. The 5.9 batteries shelled ceaselessly and brilliantly. To the whistle of shells overhead was added the scream of falling bombs. Even the sky was full of noise—anti-aircraft shells, machine-gun fire, the snarl of falling planes, the angry hornet noise of dive bombers. One could not speak normally at any time against the roar of it and the noise of our own engines. We all developed "Dunkirk throat," a sore hoarseness that was the hallmark of those who had been there.

Yet through all the noise I will always remember the voices of the young subalterns as they sent their men aboard, and I will remember, too, the astonishing discipline of the men. They had fought through three weeks of retreat, always falling back, often without orders, often without support. Transports had failed. They had gone sleepless. They had been without food and water. Yet they kept ranks as they came down the beaches, and they obeyed commands.

Veterans of Gallipoli and of Mons agreed this was the hottest spot they had ever been in, yet morale held. I was told stories of French troops that rushed the boats at first so that stern measures had to be taken, but I saw nothing like that. The Frenchmen I brought off were of the rear guard, fine soldiers, still fighting fit.

Having the Admiral on board, we were not actually working the beaches but were in control of operations. We moved about as necessary, and after we had spent some time putting small boats in touch with their towing boats, the 5.9 battery off Nieuport way began to drop shells on us. It seemed pure spite. The nearest salvo was about 20 yards astern, which was close enough.

We stayed there until everybody else had been sent back, and then went pottering about looking for stragglers. While we were doing that, a salvo of shells got one of our troopships alongside the mole. She was hit clean in the boilers and exploded in one terrific crash. There were then, I suppose, about 1000 Frenchmen on the mole. We had seen them crowding along its narrow crest, outlined against the flames. They had gone out under shellfire to board the boat, and now they had to go back again, still being shelled. It was quite the most tragic thing I ever have seen in my life. We could do nothing with our little park dinghy.

While they were still filing back to the beach and the dawn was breaking with uncomfortable brilliance, we found one of our stragglers—a navy whaler. We told her people to come aboard, but they said that there was a motorboat aground and they would have to fetch off her crew. They went in, and we waited. It was my longest wait, ever. For various reasons they were terribly slow. When they found the captain of the motorboat, they stood and argued with him and he wouldn't come off anyway. Damned plucky chap. He and his men lay quiet until the tide floated them later in the day. Then they made a dash for it, and got away.

We waited for them until the sun was up before we got clear of the mole. By then, the fighting was heavy inshore, on the outskirts of the town, and actually in some of the streets.

Going home, the Jerry dive bombers came over us five times, but somehow left us alone though three times they took up an attacking position. A little down the coast, towards Gravelines, we picked up a boatload of Frenchmen rowing off. We took them aboard. They were very much bothered as to where our "ship" was, said quite flatly that it was impossible to go to England in a thing like ours. Too, too horribly dangerous!

One of the rare touches of comedy at Dunkirk was the fear of the sea among French poilus from inland towns. They were desperately afraid to forfeit solid land for the unknown perils of a little boat. When, on the last nights of the evacuation, the little boats got to the mole many refused to jump in, despite the hell of shells and bombs behind them. I saw young sublieutenants grab poilus by the collar and the seat of the pants and rush them overside into waiting launches.

There was comedy of a sort, too, in the misadventures of the boats. The yachting season hadn't begun and most of the pleasure boats had been at their winter moorings when the call came; their engines had not been serviced and they broke down in the awkwardest places. The water supply at Dunkirk had been bombed out of use in the first days, and the navy ferried water across to keep the troops alive. Some of the water went in proper water cans, but most of it was put into two-gallon gasoline tins. *Of course* some of these tins got into the gasoline dumps, with lamentable results. I ran out of gasoline myself in the angle between Dunkirk mole and the beach, with heavy shelling going on and an Admiral on board. He never even said "damn." But we were lucky. A *schout* with spare fuel was lying a mile or so from the beach, near a buoy. I got to her with my last drop of reserve.

Then, for grim humor, there is the tale of the young sublieutenant, no more than a boy, whom I saw from time to time on one side of the Channel or the other. He was sent in the early days of the show to the beach east of Gravelines, where he was told there was a pocket of English troops cut off. He landed at the beach with only a revolver and walked off into the sand dunes to hunt for them. In the darkness he suddenly saw two faint shapes moving, and called out, "Here we are, boys, come to take you off."

There was silence, and then a guttural, *"Lieber Gott!"*

"So," the boy told me, "I shot them and came away."

He had walked right into the German army.

One of the greatest surprises of the whole operation was the failure of the German E-boats—motor torpedo boats. We crossed by a path that was well lit by light buoys, spread clean across from Goodwins to Dunkirk Roads. Well-handled E-boats could have got among us in the dark and played havoc—either in the Channel or in Dunkirk Roads.

I had stopped once off one of the light buoys when a division of destroyers passed me. They could see me only as a small dark shape on the water, if at all, and had I had torpedoes I could have picked off the leaders. I might have been a German motorboat, and if the German navy had any real fighting spirit I ought to have been a German motorboat. They did

send a few boats in, and I believe they claimed one of our destroyers somewhere off La Panne, but they never pressed the attack home, never came
in force against our motley armada off the beaches. The German navy
lost a great chance.

Germany, in fact, failed in three ways at Dunkirk. Against a routed army
she failed on land to drive home her advantage, though she had strategic
and numerical superiority. She failed in the air, though with half a million
men narrowed into one small semi-circle, she should have been able—if air
power ever could be decisive—to secure decisive victory. And at sea, her
motorboats were so lamentably handled that we almost disregarded them.
For long hours on end we were sheep for the slaughtering, but we got back
to Ramsgate safely each time. There we watched the debarkations, two and
three hundred men from each of the larger boats marching in an endless
brown stream down the narrow curve of the east harbor wall. Among each
load would be five or six wounded. The hospital ships went in to Dover; at
Ramsgate we saw mainly the pitiful survivors of ships bombed on the way
over—men with their skin flayed by oil burns, torn by bomb splinters, or
wounded by machine-gun fire from the air. Most of them were unbandaged
and almost untended. They were put ashore just as they were pulled from
the water, the most pitiful wrecks of men. Yet they were surprisingly few.

Well, that's the story of Dunkirk, as I saw the show. Just afterward, I
volunteered for a new picnic farther down the coast. Our 51st Division had
got cut off with a portion of the French army in the new battle which
had developed from the Somme downward, and our job was to try to get
it away.

I was given a Brighton Beach boat as warship this time, one of those
things that takes trippers for a cruise around the bay. We left before dawn
on a Wednesday morning and made the first half of the crossing in fog.
We headed for Dieppe at first, but Dieppe had already fallen, and we
veered toward St. Valery-en-Caux, a little down the coast. I knew the place
well, having been there two or three days before war broke out. We sighted
the French coast in the early afternoon and closed to within about five
miles of it. Our destroyer escort never turned up, though we heard it
having a bright little scrap on its own just below the horizon to the south-
west.

About the middle of the afternoon, we sighted two boats rowing toward
us and picked them up. They were full of French seamen who said that
they were the last survivors of St. Valery. They had fought the Germans
from their ship with machine guns until she sank under them, and then had
rowed out of the harbor. They were very badly shot about, many of them
dead and a large number wounded. I was called onto the tug to give first
aid. We stowed them on two of our faster boats and sent the wounded off.

The German planes were buzzing around most of the time, but high up.
Just as I got back to my own boat we got the signal to scatter. Three
Heinkels had come over to deal with us.

My engine wouldn't start, as I had not been on board to see that it was warmed up, and the boat ahead of me was out of action with a fouled propeller. Neither of us could move, so we had to sit and watch the attack. The bombing was pretty good, but not good enough. For a long time it looked as if bombs from the first Heinkel were falling absolutely straight at us, tiny black specks that grew most horribly. They fell about 15 or 20 yards clear, and though they blew us sideways over the water they did us no harm.

Then the second bomber dived and dropped eight bombs, and again they fell just clear. While the third was maneuvering, my engineer got the engine going. I threw a towline to the other fellow, and we got under way. I had the flight of the bombs pretty well judged by then, and we worked clear of the third attack.

We started out for England. The bombers, having used up all their bombs, left us and we had a spell of quiet. However, big fighters came out to have another smack. We were far from the rest of the fleet and going along lamely. They attacked the others from a height, but when they came to us—thinking we were helpless, I suppose—they dived low and machine-gunned us heavily.

I was standing at the tiller, steering, and there was no sort of cover. One of the bullets got me through the middle. It felt like the kick of a mule, and knocked me away from the tiller to the bottom boards. However, there was not much real pain then, and I got up and examined myself. From the looks of the hole, I didn't think I had much of a chance. I told them to put me on the bottom boards, forward, and gave my gunner the course for the English coast. The tug picked us up after a time, and we were towed to New Haven, arriving about six next morning.

I was weak from loss of blood and wasn't betting too heavily on my chances of survival. However, I was operated on within an hour of landing, and it was found that I had been amazingly lucky. The bullet had done no serious damage.

I went to a hospital at Brighton. After three weeks the Admiralty moved me to a country hospital so that I could have a quiet rest. I didn't. We had 28 siren warnings in 20 days, and were bombed one night.

I am now back in town. The Admiralty offers me a commission, as a reward of virtue, I suppose, but the medical examiners say that I cannot go to sea. I don't want a shore job, so I have turned down the offer. I shall be a good boy and sit in an office awhile until the wound is better. Then I shall wangle my way to sea. I think I know how.

Meanwhile we are all right here. Germany is not starving us out; she is not going to invade us out; and she isn't going to air-raid us out. If I can't quite see yet how we are going to win—the method and so on—I certainly can't see how we are going to be defeated.

Twenty miles of sea is still twenty miles of sea, and the Straits of Dover are the best tank trap the world has ever devised.

WAR IS THE PROVINCE OF FRICTION

ЄVERYTHING is very simple in War, but the simplest thing is difficult. These difficulties accumulate and produce a friction which no man can imagine exactly who has not seen War.

Gallipoli

BY

MAJOR-GENERAL JOHN FREDERICK CHARLES FULLER

THE stalemate which followed the battle of the Marne was almost as decisive in its results as was that battle itself. First, Germany turned Eastwards, and from then onwards until February, 1916, she launched her legions against Russia, which country began to collapse before 1914 had run its course. Then, as I shall soon show, Great Britain also turned East, not because her small army possessed a superabundance of power, but because the German fleet refused to sacrifice itself on the British naval altar. In the middle of October the first Battle of Ypres opened and was continued until November 21, during the whole of which time Sir John French's Expeditionary Force had to hold on to its parapets by its fingertips.

Worse still, in London there was no thinking military head. The War Office had been denuded of trained Staff officers, and, according to Mr. Lloyd George, British statesmen were second rate. Not until November did Mr. Asquith, the Prime Minister, decide to establish a War Council, whilst the Committee of Imperial Defence remained inoperative. Mr. Churchill, then First Lord of the Admiralty, exclaimed: "Confronted with this deadlock, military art remained dumb; the Commanders and their General Staffs had no plan except the frontal attack which all their experience and training had led them to reject; they had no policy except the policy of exhaustion." And Mr. Lloyd George writes on December 31: "I can see no signs anywhere that our military leaders and guides are considering any plans for extricating us from our present unsatisfactory position."

Is this fair criticism? I do not think so, because the truth is that Great Britain was in no way prepared for a war on one front, let alone on two or three. It may well be correct, as Lloyd George says, that the soldier did not understand his art, yet should not the chief blame be loaded upon the shoulders of the Parliamentary system which could neither prepare for a war nor direct its course?

The fact is, a fact which must not be overlooked, that, as in 1775, so far as England was concerned this was a Parliamentary war—a war of amateur strategists. Mr. John North, in an illuminating book on the

From: *Decisive Battles*. Eyre and Spottiswoode, London.

Gallipoli campaign, says: "I have never been able to understand the professionals' sneer at the amateur strategist." No wonder, for he adds: "War is a matter of common sense," which is exactly what amateurs lack. They can readily conceive a campaign, but overlook that between conception and execution yawns an illimitable gulf of detail and technique. For example: in some long-forgotten year of the primeval world Dædalus conceived the idea of human flight; yet it was not until 1903 that two practical mechanics, Wilbur and Orville Wright, solved that problem by producing the first heavier-than-air machine. The truth is that there were far too many amateur strategists. Admiral Wemyss writes: "Everything is done at home in watertight compartments; no Minister has the slightest idea of what his neighbours and colleagues are doing . . . the men at the head of affairs are ignorant of all technique; they think they have only to say 'Do it' and it is done—wrong." And, a little later on, what does General Sir William Robertson say? "The Secretary of State for War was aiming at decisive results on the Western front; the First Lord of the Admiralty was advocating a military expedition to the Dardanelles; the Secretary of State for India was devoting his attention to a campaign in Mesopotamia . . . the Secretary for the Colonies was occupying himself with 'several small wars' in Africa; and the Chancellor of the Exchequer, Mr. Lloyd George, was attempting to secure the removal of a large part of the British Army from France to some eastern Mediterranean theatre." Five active tentacles and no head—such was the British strategical polyp.

Strange as it may seem, the conception of the Gallipoli or Dardanelles campaign pre-dated the Battle of the Marne. On August 20, M. Venizelos, the Greek Prime Minister, with the full approval of King Constantine, placed all the military and naval resources of Greece at the disposal of the Entente Powers; nevertheless, for fear of antagonising Turkey, Sir Edward Grey, British Foreign Secretary, rejected this offer. Notwithstanding this, on the 31st Mr. Churchill discussed the problem with Lord Kitchener, Secretary of State for War, and the following day "Mr. Churchill asked the Chief of the Imperial General Staff to appoint two officers to examine and work out, with two officers from the Admiralty, 'a plan for the seizure of the Gallipoli peninsula, by means of a Greek army of adequate strength, with a view to admitting a British fleet to the Sea of Marmora.'" Thus the tension between cross-purposes started, to be complicated by the fact that, at this time, Lord Fisher, First Sea Lord, was pushing for a landing in the Baltic. Such an operation required troops, and Kitchener had none to spare, consequently the Dardanelles project gained in favour, yet was complicated by the fact that the Greeks now refused to budge unless Bulgaria agreed to declare war on Turkey. So the idea was shelved, until towards the end of November two Australian Divisions arrived in Egypt; whereupon Mr. Churchill once again revived it, ordering the transports which had carried them to remain in Egypt "in case they are required for an expedition." Meanwhile, on his authority, a senseless operation of war was carried out: On November 3, two days after the British Ambassador left Constantinople, the Admiralty ordered the bombardment of the Dardanelles forts. This bombardment, said Jevad Pasha (Commandant of the fortresses) after the war, "warned me and I realised that I must spend the rest of my time in developing and strengthening the defences by every means."

From now onwards Mr. Churchill became fanatically obsessed with the idea of occupying Constantinople, in which city was located the sole munition factory in Turkey. There can be little doubt that so far as pure strategy is concerned he was right. Later, on June 5, 1915, he said: "Through the Narrows of the Dardanelles and across the ridges of the Gallipoli Peninsula lie some of the shortest paths to a triumphant peace." Yet this strategy was amateurish, because "he saw the huge prize, and tried to seize it with inadequate means." The execution of his idea depended upon Greek support, which was not forthcoming; further, England was not capable of fighting on two fronts, for though it was comparatively easy for the War Office to raise men, it was impossible in a few weeks or months to create an efficient corps of officers. Further still, the British Army was not equipped or trained for a campaign in a theatre such as Gallipoli.

The truth is that the brilliance of his conception blinded him to the requirements of its execution. Mr. North says: "The responsibility for the inauguration of the Dardanelles campaign rests upon Mr. Winston Churchill"—which is true. And Admiral Keyes says: "But if he had not committed the Government to the enterprise, they would never have looked at it"—which is also true. In brief, and against the opinion of Sir William Robertson, who became Chief of the Imperial General Staff in December, he forced his Dardanelles card on the Government, the Government being incapable of playing the game. The result was that the British Empire not so much drifted, but was pushed into a campaign which in the end proved as disastrous as that of Saratoga.

On January 1, 1915, two papers were submitted to the War Council; the first by Lieutenant-Colonel Maurice Hankey, Secretary of the Council, and the second by Mr. Lloyd George. In the former it was suggested that Germany could be struck more easily through Turkey, and that should the Black Sea be reopened, the price of wheat would fall and 350,000 tons of shipping would be released. The latter considered that the Eastern operation should be directed against Austria and be based on Salonika; but this suggestion was set aside, because it demanded a considerable number of troops.

Next day "a telegram of momentous consequence" was received from the British Ambassador at Petrograd, notifying the Cabinet of the critical position of the Russian forces in the Caucasus, when, in fact, the crisis there was all but over; whereupon Kitchener telegraphed in reply: "Please assure the Grand Duke that steps will be taken to make a demonstration against the Turks," whilst Fisher set before Mr. Churchill a grandiose plan. He strongly supported an attack on Turkey if it could be carried out immediately: 75,000 men from France were to land at Besika Bay; another landing was to be made at Alexandretta and a demonstration at Haifa. "Simultaneously the Greeks should be landed on the Gallipoli peninsula, the Bulgarians should be induced to march on Adrianople, and the Rumanians to join the Russians and Serbs in an attack on Austria. Finally, Admiral Sturdee should at the same time force the Dardanelles with ships of the Majestic and Canopus class."

Blowing the froth off this tankard of strategic ale, Churchill gulped down the idea of forcing the Dardanelles with old battleships, and telegraphed to Vice-Admiral Carden, commanding at the Dardanelles: "Do you consider the forcing of the Dardanelles by ships alone a practicable operation?" To which, on the 5th, Carden answered: "I do not consider Dardanelles can be rushed. They might be forced by extended operations with large number of ships."

This was good enough for Mr. Churchill, and though Lord Fisher, Admiral Sir Henry Jackson and Mr. Lloyd George were vehemently opposed to this proposal, in it Churchill saw the means of winning over Lord Kitchener, because it would not entail the use of troops. "So Lord Kitchener swung round to the Dardanelles plan," writes Mr. Lloyd George, "and that settled it."

On the 13th Churchill brought his project before the War Council, pointing out that if progress were not made, "the bombardment could be broken off and the fleet could steam away," which consideration won over the Government. Then, on the 15th, he telegraphed to Admiral Carden: "The sooner we can begin the better. . . . Continue to perfect your plan"; and four days later he cabled the Grand Duke Nicholas, informing him that the Government had determined to force the Dardanelles. At length, on the 28th, when the War Council met again, though Lord Fisher opposed the project and urged the greater value of his Baltic scheme, Lord Kitchener considered the naval attack of vital importance; Mr. Balfour could not imagine a more helpful operation, and Sir Edward Grey thought it would settle the attitude of the whole of the Balkans. Not a soldier was to be used; the navy alone was to force the Dardanelles and seize Constantinople.

Thus the proposal passed into the realm of action, and apparently became public property, for Lord Bertie, then British Ambassador in Paris, writes: "The Dardanelles Expedition was known only to the inner ring: Louis Mallet heard of it at a dinner from Leo (Leopold) de Rothschild, who had learnt it from Alfred de R. (Rothschild) who may have picked up the information in the course of his daily visit to Kitchener, at the War Office and 10 Downing Street. There is no such thing as a secret nowadays."

No sooner had the naval attack been agreed upon than the Salonika project was revived, and though it was turned down, out of it emerged the old question whether the ships should not be supported by a military force. So, on February 16, the War Council met again to review this question, and a decision was made to send out the 29th Division as well as to despatch troops from Egypt. Thus were the foundations of the military attack laid. Then, three days later, Kitchener said he could not spare the

29th Division, so in its stead were substituted the Australian and New Zealand divisions in Egypt. Mr. Churchill, now considering that at least 50,000 men would be required, insisted for the first time that it "would be impossible for the fleet to keep the Dardanelles open for merchant shipping." Next, on the 24th, Mr. Lloyd George asked him whether, should the naval attack fail, the army would carry out a land attack, and his answer was "No!"

The muddle in execution was now complete, and on it the first gigantic blunder was founded—namely, the futile naval bombardments of the outer forts on February 19 and 25. Though this operation was inconclusive, sufficient damage was done to allow of small parties "of 50 to 100 sailors and marines" landing on the 26th, and leisurely blowing to pieces "all the guns in Sedd-el-Bahr, as well as in the two forts on the Asiatic side," at the cost of one killed and six wounded. Thus it came about that no sooner had the War Council made up their mind not to use troops than they decided to use them, and then, having arrived at this decision, they decided to carry out the naval attack without them. Instead of waiting until the army was ready to follow up the naval barrage, on the day following the bombardment Lord Kitchener warned General Maxwell, G.O.C. Egypt, to hold in readiness 30,000 Australian and New Zealand troops under Lieutenant-General Sir W. R. Birdwood "to embark about the 9th March, in transports sent from England, 'to assist the navy . . . and to occupy any captured forts.'" Then, suddenly, on the 24th, the War Council realised that, on account of Mr. Churchill's impetuosity, they had precipitated the operation into a bottomless bog, or as the official historian writes: "If a success at the Dardanelles could win the Balkans to the Entente, a failure would have the opposite effect. The opening of the bombardment had attracted such world-wide attention that, for the sake of British prestige, the enterprise must be carried through, no matter what the cost. . . . Mr. Churchill argued that the country was absolutely committed to seeing the Dardanelles attack through."

On March 4 further landings were attempted which were met by strong opposition, and all efforts to sweep the minefields were met by heavy fire directed by searchlights. The Turks were now wide awake, so on the 5th the *Queen Elizabeth* and other warships opened an indirect bombardment on the forts in the Narrows, and continued to do so until the 12th, each shell fired bringing home to Turkey the impending danger.

Whilst this bombardment was in progress, the next gigantic blunder was made, this time by Russia, for whose benefit the operation had so largely been undertaken. On the 1st M. Venizelos informed the British Government that he was ready to land three divisions on the Gallipoli peninsula; in the circumstances this offer was as miraculous as Abraham's ram. Forthwith it was communicated to Russia, who, on the 3rd, replied: "The Russian Government could not consent to Greece participating in operations in the Dardanelles, as it would be sure to lead to complications. . . ." These centred on who should possess Constantinople, which city the British

Government had promised to Russia as her share of the world-booty once the war was won. On the 7th the Venizelos Government fell, and, on the 12th, the day the bombardment ceased, this piece of political backshish was made public. Thus Russia seized the shadow and Great Britain swallowed the substance.

On the day this suicidal refusal was made the War Council met again, and once more Kitchener refused to release the 29th Division. Then, on the 5th, he received a telegram from General Birdwood saying, "I am very doubtful if the Navy can force the passage unassisted," whereupon he changed his mind, and, assuming full responsibility for the military attack, he took over the Royal Naval Division, and, on the 16th, the 29th Division sailed.

This decision, three weeks too late, was followed by the third gigantic blunder. Having made up his mind to send the 29th Division out, a veritable scramble followed. Looking around for a General-in-Chief, he selected Sir Ian Hamilton, an officer of much war experience, who had taken part in seven colonial wars in Afghanistan, S. Africa, Egypt, Burma and India, and who in 1904–05 had accompanied the Japanese in the field. On discussing the situation with him, Lord Kitchener said: "If the fleet gets through, Constantinople will fall of itself and you will have won not a battle but the war"; yet he gave him no instructions, instead an out-of-date map, and hurried him off on the 13th, as if he were in command of a corporal's patrol. Arriving at Mudros on the 17th, General Hamilton found that Admiral J. M. de Robeck had that day replaced Admiral Carden, and that, when the 29th Division had left England, the embarkation authorities, imagining that it would land at a friendly harbour, had loaded the ships in such a way that the troops could not disembark in fighting order; therefore the transports would have to be completely discharged and reloaded. As this could not be carried out at Mudros, it had to be done at Alexandria, which meant another three weeks' delay.

The day Lord Kitchener selected Sir Ian Hamilton to command the expedition, Mr. Churchill, instead of waiting for a combined operation to be elaborated, telegraphed Admiral Carden: "We suggest for your consideration that a point has now been reached when it is necessary . . . to overwhelm the forts at the Narrows at decisive range by the fire of the largest number of guns. . . ." Such was the fourth gigantic blunder. The attack was made on the 18th, when three battleships were lost through running into an unswept minefield; whereupon de Robeck informed the Admiralty that he intended to postpone his next effort until about the middle of April, when the army would be ready to act. The truth would appear to be, as Admiral Keyes writes: "He never really wished to risk his ships again in another naval attack, after the losses of the 18th March, and he welcomed the opportunity of combining with the army in an operation which promised success without hazard to the fleet." Thus it came about that the army was called upon to pull Mr. Churchill's naval chestnuts out of the fire.

Whilst the Turks were digging for their lives, the 29th Division disembarked at Alexandria, when it was found that it had been equipped for mobile warfare in a well-roaded country, yet was deficient of guns, gun and rifle ammunition, hospital requirements and trench stores. As to secrecy there was none, one of Sir Ian Hamilton's Staff receiving "an official letter from London, sent through the ordinary post, and addressed to the 'Constantinople Field Force.' "

On the 22nd a conference was held on the *Queen Elizabeth;* of it General Hamilton writes: "The moment we sat down de Robeck told us he was quite clear he could not get through without the help of all my troops . . . the fat (that is us) is fairly in the fire." The idea of landing at Bulair was set aside, not only because it was known to be entrenched, but because "the main communications of the Turkish divisions in the peninsula did not run through or anywhere near Bulair, but down and across the Straits to the town of Gallipoli." It was therefore decided to land on the toe of the peninsula, and though this spot may have been the lesser of two evils, it offered an all but insuperable disadvantage—namely, now that the Turks were roused, the British forces would have to advance up a defile, a pass flanked not by mountains but by the sea.

The strength of the force to be employed in this most difficult operation was as follows:

	Ships	*Personnel*	*Animals*	*Vehicles*
29th Division (Alexandria)	15	17,649	3,962	692
Anzac (Alexandria)	30	25,784	6,920	1,271
Anzac (Mudros)	5	4,854	698	147
French Force (Alexandria)	22	16,762	3,511	647
R.N.D. (Port Said)	12	10,007	1,390	347
	84	75,056	16,481	3,104

Turning to the enemy, between March 18 and April 25, when the first British landing took place, the Turks were given ample time wherein to entrench and prepare the more likely beaches against invasion. Yet only on March 26 was Marshal Liman von Sanders, an exceptionally capable German officer and as we shall see a born leader of men, appointed Commander-in-Chief of the Turkish forces in the Peninsula; and that day he landed at Gallipoli and took over his command. Finding his troops strung out "en cordon," he formed them into three groups: "The 5th and 7th Divisions were stationed on the upper Saros (Xeros) Gulf; the 9th and newly organised 19th Divisions were ordered to the southern part of the peninsula; and the 11th Division was stationed on the Asiatic side, together with the 3rd, which soon arrived by boat." Though his men were miserably equipped, they possessed ample rifle ammunition, but not a single aeroplane. Nevertheless, he appreciated their fighting value, which the British did not, having forgotten Plevna and its lessons. Of them General Kannengiesser writes:

"The Turkish soldier, the 'Askar,' was the Anatolian and Thracian, slightly educated, brave, trustworthy. . . . Content with little, it never entered into his mind to dispute the authority of those above him. He followed his leader without question. . . . The Turks are glad to feel an energetic leader's will, they feel supported in the consciousness that they are being led by a strong hand against a definite objective."

Though the ultimate object of the campaign was the occupation of Constantinople, the immediate object was the forcing of the Narrows between Kilid Bahr on the European side of the Dardanelles and Chanak on the Asiatic. Here the strait shrinks to 1,600 yards in width, and it was a little north of this waist, at Nagara (Abydos), where the current is not so strong, that, in 480 B.C., Xerxes built his bridge, Alexander crossed in 334 B.C., Barbarossa in 1190 and Orkhan in 1354. Also it was here that Hero swam the Hellespont, as centuries later also did Lord Byron.

On the western flank of this narrow strip of water lies the Gallipoli peninsula. At Bulair in the north it is no more than 4,600 yards in breadth, then it widens out to about twelve miles between Suvla Point to a little north of Akbash, narrows again to four and a half miles between Gaba Tepe and Maidos, widens once more and finally tapers off to Cape Helles. Most of this tongue of land is hilly and broken, cut up by sharp valleys, cliffs and ravines which end in the eminence of Achi Baba 700 feet above sea-level.

When war was declared the sole fortifications were at Bulair, at the entrance to the Dardanelles and at the Narrows, the last two being defended by over 100 guns, of which only fourteen were modern, and all were short of ammunition. The forts Kilid Bahr and Chanak dated from the reign of Mohammed II, who built them in 1462, and built them so well that, during the bombardment of March 18, the 15-inch shells of the *Queen Elizabeth* did them little damage. Of roads there was but one, that running from Gallipoli to Maidos; consequently the main communications with Constantinople were by sea, a journey of about twelve hours.

Such in brief was the theatre of war, and from it I will now turn to Sir Ian Hamilton and his task, surely one of the most perplexing since Burgoyne's campaign of Saratoga.

Besides the British Mediterranean Expeditionary Force, he had under his command the French Corps Expéditionnaire d'Orient, roughly a division, commanded by General d'Amade. His plan was, whilst feinting at Bulair and Kum Kale, (1) to effect landings on Cape Helles at five points, from east to west beach "S" in Morto Bay, "V" and "W" on each flank of Cape Helles and "X" and "Y" on its western shore; (2) simultaneously to land another force just north of Gaba Tepe, the object of which was to advance on Maidos and take in rear such Turkish forces as might oppose the Helles landings.

The plan was an able one, but, as always, its success depended upon its execution, which demanded the highest leadership and audacity. Had these been forthcoming, in my opinion, the operation might have proved successful, for to-day we know that the Turkish garrisons were insignificant. On April 25, when the landings took place, south of Achi Baba there were but two infantry battalions and one company of engineers, at "Y" beach not a man, at "W" and "V" two companies, at "S" one platoon and at "X" twelve men. Further, only "W" and "V" were protected by wire and machine-guns.

Unfortunately, though courage was conspicuous, true leadership was not. At "W" and "V" beaches disastrous delays occurred, because the landing party at "X" was too weak. At "V" disembarkation from s.s. *River Clyde,* which had been grounded, was so fiercely opposed that the landing was held up until the 26th. At "Y," where 2,000 men stepped ashore without a shot being fired, and where for eleven hours they remained undisturbed, a complete muddle took place. Instead of advancing on Krithia unopposed they re-embarked and withdrew!

Meanwhile, the Australians and New Zealanders landed north of Gaba Tepe, one mile north of the selected beach, at a spot later to be named Anzac Cove. Their landing came as a complete surprise, and a penetration of three and a half miles was made to a spot from where the gleaming Narrows could be seen, actually the nearest point reached to them "by any allied soldier during the campaign." Then they were attacked by Mustafa Kemal, "that Man of Destiny," and driven back in such disorder that General Birdwood suggested a complete withdrawal; a request very rightly refused by Sir Ian, who replied: "You have got through the difficult business. Now you have only to dig, dig, dig until you are safe." Ominous words, for digging meant that surprise was over and that the whole operation had failed. Thus the foundations of one of the greatest tragedies in British history were scraped into the stony soil of the Gallipoli peninsula, close by where Alexander set out to conquer the Oriental world.

The landing having succeeded, though its object had not been attained, the second phase of the invasion was entered, a phase of wasteful frontal attacks, as hopeless and costly as any seen on the Western front. At Anzac, where the total area held measured barely 400 acres, no offensive was attempted until August 6; but at Helles three costly battles, based largely on the unwarranted optimism of General Hunter-Weston, commander of the 29th Division and G.O.C. of the troops in the Helles area, were fought—namely, the first, second and third battles of Krithia.

The first of these, waged between April 27 and 30, was badly conceived, and ended in chaos and a loss of some 3,000 officers and men. This failure was followed by a determined Turkish attack on May 1. It was beaten back, and, in turn, on May 6–7 was followed by the second battle of Krithia, of which Ashmead-Bartlett, an eye-witness, writes:

"I doubt whether, even at Leipsic, so many different nationalities have been brought together on the same battlefield. Side by side in the Anglo-French Army there fought English, Scottish and Irish regiments, Australians, New Zealanders, Sikhs, Punjabis, and Gurkhas, whilst our Navy was represented by the Naval Division and Marines. On the other side of the Krithia road, in the French ranks, were drawn up Frenchmen, Algerians, Zouaves, Goumiers, Senegalese, and the heterogenous elements which make up the Foreign Legion."

On the 8th this battle ended like the first of its name, but this time the casualties numbered 6,500, about 30 per cent. of the numbers engaged. Next, on the 19th, the Turks attacked again, this time against Anzac, and lost 10,000 men, the Australian and New Zealand casualties numbering only 600. Then, lastly, followed the third battle of Krithia. Covered by the fire of 78 guns, supplemented, as in all these attacks, by the guns of the fleet, the 8th Corps advanced and once again was decimated, losing 4,500 officers and men out of 16,000 engaged, whilst the French lost 2,000. In the 2nd Naval Brigade 60 officers out of 70 became casualties and over 1,000 men out of 1,900. The objective of all these attacks was Achi Baba, because it was supposed to dominate the Narrows, which as a matter of fact it did not, as was discovered by Captain Keyes, Commodore to de Robeck, after the war. Then, bled white, the military operations came to a standstill.

Meanwhile, the day after the first landing took place Italy renounced the Triple Alliance and, in accordance with the Treaty of London, threw in her lot with the Allied Powers. On May 21 she was at war with Austria, whilst Mackensen fell upon the Russians along the Dunajec and drove them in rout eastwards. Then, on June 2, Sir Ian Hamilton telegraphed Lord Kitchener saying that "the movement of a quarter of a million men against us seems to be well under way." This sent a shudder through the Government, when, on the 7th, the newly constituted Dardanelles Committee was assembled to consider three alternatives—to leave things as they were, to abandon the enterprise and evacuate the peninsula, or to send out large reinforcements. Under pressure of Lord Kitchener and Mr. Churchill the third course was adopted, and eventually it was decided to despatch five new divisions, Mr. Churchill suggesting that they should be used to occupy the Bulair isthmus. This suggestion, however, was turned down, because Admiral de Robeck considered the threat of German submarines in the Gulf of Saros too great a risk to run.

General Birdwood was also against a landing so far north; instead he favoured a big attack from Anzac, where conditions were such as to persuade anyone to fight. Of them the official historian, an eye-witness, writes:

"The heat of the noonday sun was intense; and there was little or no shade; and the scanty water supply in the trenches was rarely sufficient for men with a parching thirst. The sickening smell of unburied corpses in No Man's Land pervaded the front areas; dense clouds of infected dust were incessant; and despite the preventive care of the doctors there was such a loathsome plague of huge flies (known to the troops as 'corpse-flies') that it was difficult to eat a mouthful of food without swallowing the pests. A tin of beef or jam, as soon as opened, would be covered with a thick film of flies, and amongst the troops in the trenches small pieces of veiling, to throw over their faces at meal times or when trying to sleep, were almost beyond price."

The reinforcement of five divisions having been decided upon, it was agreed to organise three as a new corps, the 9th; whereupon Sir Ian Hamilton requested that either General Byng or General Rawlinson, both able officers then serving in France, should be given command. This was not agreed to, because both were junior to General Mahon, the Commander of the 10th Division of the 9th Corps; so, instead, Lieutenant-General the Hon. Sir Frederick Stopford was selected, and no worse choice could have been made. He was sixty-one years old, kindly, affable and incompetent, and during the war in South Africa had served as Military Secretary to Sir Redvers Buller. He had never commanded troops and at this time was a sick man.

Whilst these arrangements were in hand, General Hamilton, instead of conserving the energies of his army, launched three wasteful attacks—on June 21, June 28 and July 12–13—in the Helles area. In these he lost 7,700 British and 4,600 French officers and men—that is, approximately the effective strength of an entire division. Such generalship is hard to understand in spite of the official historian's apologies.

Once the above reinforcements were promised General Hamilton set about to consider his plan. First, it was obvious to him that the Anzac Cove area was too restricted in breadth and depth to allow of five new divisions being deployed there. Therefore, in order to gain more room, he determined to extend his base of operations by landing a force at Suvla Bay, which lay five miles to the north of the Australians and New Zealanders, and simultaneously launch two closely affiliated attacks, the object of which was the occupation of the high ground from Ejelmar Bay to Koja Chemen Tepe and thence to Baba Tepe.

This plan was an able one, for not only was it known that the Suvla area was lightly defended, but that should the Turks be surprised only four miles of open plain would have to be crossed in order to seize the surrounding hills: to the north-east the Tekke Tepe, 900 feet above sea level; to the east Anafarta Spur, 350 feet; and to the north the Kiretch Tepe, 650 feet. Could these heights be occupied within twenty-four hours, the right flank of the Turkish forces opposing the Anzac Corps would be turned, which threat would almost certainly enable General Birdwood to occupy Koja Chemen Tepe (Hill 971), the true key to the Narrows.

For this dual attack Sir Ian had at his disposal two corps, the Australian and New Zealand and the 9th. The first consisted of the 1st and 2nd Australian Divisions and the New Zealand and Australian Division, and the second of the 10th, 11th, 13th, 53rd and 54th Divisions, the last two attached. Further, in the Helles area he had the 8th Corps, consisting of the 29th, 42nd, 52nd and Royal Naval Divisions, as well as the Corps

Expéditionnaire d'Orient—now two divisions. In all thirteen divisions. Selecting Mudros, Imbros and Mitylene as his advanced bases, he established his G.H.Q. on the second of these islands.

Fixing on August 6, because it was a moonless night, as the day of attack, he decided on the following operations:

Whilst the 8th Corps held by attack the Turkish forces opposing it, General Birdwood was first to feint at Lone Pine in order to draw his enemy away from the Sari Bair heights, and then assault them and carry Hill 971, Hill Q and Chunuk Bair, all three of which were to be occupied by dawn on the 7th. For these attacks the 13th Division was added to the Anzac Corps.

To land the 11th and 10th Divisions during the night of 6th-7th south of Nibrunesi Point; the first to occupy Lala Baba, Suvla Point and Kiretch Tepe, as well as Chocolate and W Hills and Tekke Tepe (all to be gained by daylight on the 7th), whilst two brigades of the 10th Division were to advance at dawn on the 7th and make straight for the Anafarta gap in order to threaten the right rear of the Turks about Hill 971.

This plan was radically a faulty one. First, the Anzac Corps was physically worn out and the area its men would have to fight their way over was indescribably difficult. Secondly, the 10th and 11th Divisions were but half trained and the country was covered with scrub. Only the most highly trained light infantry led by the most audacious officers could have carried out a successful night advance over such country. Such men and such officers Sir Ian Hamilton did not possess, therefore his plan, however brilliantly conceived, was a gamble, for requirements must fit conceptions if execution is to succeed.

Not until July 22 was General Stopford informed of this plan, when it was impressed upon him that Chocolate and W Hills "should be captured by a 'coup de main' before daylight," also that bold and vigorous leadership was imperative. At first accepting it, soon he began to doubt it, possibly because General Mahon quite rightly considered it too intricate. Thereupon he pointed out his deficiency in artillery, and finding that all his troops were to be landed at "A," "B" and "C" beaches, which were situated south of Nibrunesi Point, against naval advice he persuaded General Hamilton to shift "A" to within the Bay and immediately north of the Cut. This was the first error, as we shall see.

The second must be attributed to Sir Ian himself—namely, secrecy run mad. No units had any idea of what was required of them; maps were not handed out until the evening of the 6th. . . . "No one except the General and Admirals knew our destination." Physically and mentally it was a plunge into the dark, and thus "in excelsis" a night operation.

The landing arrangements were carefully worked out, including the carriage of 400 tons of water, but these preparations seem so completely to have monopolised the attention of Stopford and his Staff and the landing itself, and not the advance from the beaches, so dominated their minds that the importance of capturing Chocolate and W Hills was lost sight of. This was also true of Sir Ian Hamilton, for in his final instructions issued to the 9th Corps on July 29 we read:

"Your *primary objective* will be to secure Suvla Bay. . . . Should, however, you find it possible to achieve this object with only a portion of your force, your next step will be to give such direct assistance as is in your power to the General Officer commanding Anzac in his attack on Hill 305 [Hill 971], by an advance on Biyuk Anafarta. . . . He, however, directs your special attention to the fact that the Hills Yilghin [Chocolate] and Ismail Oglu Tepe [Green] are known to contain guns which can bring fire to bear on the flank and rear of an attack on Hill 305. . . . If, therefore, it is possible *without prejudice to the attainment of your primary objective* to gain possession of those hills at an early period of your attack it will greatly facilitate the capture and retention of Hill 305."

This watering down of the plan by making the landing the objective was the third error and the root cause of the eventual disaster, for the landing itself was but a means and not the end.

The fourth error was that Stopford, having no conception of what generalship demanded, instead of landing with his troops and establishing his headquarters on shore, decided to maintain them on board the *Jonquil,* where, incidentally, he remained throughout the 7th!

If Sir Ian Hamilton's problem was a difficult one, and it certainly was, Liman von Sanders' was out of all proportion more so. Though always afraid of a landing at Bulair, he nevertheless suspected that the British object was to occupy Koja Chemen Tepe, and that therefore a landing at Suvla Bay was possible. Equally possible was a landing south of Gaba Tepe, where he sent the 9th Division under Colonel Kannengiesser. In August his distribution was as follows: Kum Kale, 3 divisions; Bulair, 3; Anzac front, 3, under Essad Pasha; south of Gaba Tepe, 2; and in the Helles area, 5. To Suvla he sent a small body of troops known as the Anafarta Detachment. It was commanded by a Bavarian officer, Major Willmer, and it consisted of three battalions, one pioneer company, one squadron of cavalry, nineteen guns and a labour battalion. An exceptionally able officer, Willmer at once saw that his detachment was too weak to repulse a landing; all he could hope to do was to delay an invader for thirty-six to forty-eight hours from gaining the Anafarta spur, after which interval of time he might expect to be reinforced. Throwing out a forward screen of posts he held the following localities:

Kiretch Tepe, 2 companies Gallipoli Gendarmerie.

Hill 10, 3 companies Broussa Gendarmerie.

Chocolate and Green Hills, 3 companies 1/31st Regiment.

Lala Baba, 1 company 1/31st Regiment with a sentry post on Nibrunesi Point.

His reserve he placed at Baka Baba—W Hills, astride the track leading from the Bay to Anafarta Sagir.

In all he had some 1,500 men wherewith to face his enemy's 25,000.

At 2.30 p.m. on the 6th the battle, which was to decide the campaign and much more besides, opened on the Helles front, but instead of carrying out a holding attack as ordered the 8th Corps Commander foolishly attempted to capture Krithia and Achi Baba. He failed to do so at a cost of 3,500 men out of the 4,000 who attacked.

Two hours later the Anzac battle opened by an attack on the Turkish position on Lone Pine. Though successful, it led to an unfortunate event, for frightening Essad Pasha, he called to his support two regiments of Kannengiesser's 9th Division, which on arrival were well placed to reinforce Chunuk Bair when it was attacked next morning.

Directly Turkish attention was concentrated on Lone Pine, two columns of troops under Generals Johnston and Cox moved through the night, for it was 7.30 p.m., to seize the Sari Bair ridge from Hill 971 to Battleship Hill. The plan of operations was complicated and impossible. Concerning this attack Ashmead-Bartlett writes:

"It was launched against positions the like of which had never been attacked before under modern conditions of warfare. The men were expected to climb mountains during the night over unexplored ground, so tortuous, broken and scrubby that, had the advance taken place during peace manœuvres, it would have been an extremely arduous task for troops to reach the summit of the Sari Bair Ridge in the prescribed time."

The right column (Johnston's) set out obscured by the shadows cast by the ships' searchlights and moved on Table Top to gain Chunuk Bair by dawn. Part lost its way and the remainder was thrown into confusion. Meanwhile the left column (Cox's) moved up the coast and swinging right set out to gain Hill 971 and Hill Q. It took the wrong track, was sniped and delayed, the men becoming utterly exhausted. Thus the entire initial operations ended in a complete fiasco, costing 650 officers and men out of the 1,250 engaged.

Whilst these mistakes were taking place, at 5.30 a.m. on the 7th, hearing that British troops were establishing themselves on Rhododendron Spur, immediately west of Chunuk Bair, Mustafa Kemal, once again at the critical spot, called up his reserve division—the 19th—and ordered it to occupy the main ridge. Simultaneously Kannengiesser's two regiments were sent by Essad Pasha to hold this same ridge from Chunuk Bair to Hill 971. Hurrying forward with a patrol Kannengiesser reached Chunuk Bair at about 7 a.m. Meanwhile Liman von Sanders, realising that the hour of crisis had struck, yet ever fearful that the main blow would be directed against Bulair, telegraphed Feizi Bey, in command there, to be vigilant, and then, realising that Sari Bair must be reinforced, at 1.30 a.m. he ordered him at all possible speed to despatch three battalions south.

Meanwhile the right column shook itself into some order, and at 10.30 a.m. on the 7th, about seven hours later, sent forward five companies to attack Chunuk Bair under cover of a land and sea bombardment; but almost immediately fire was opened on them by Kannengiesser's men and the attack collapsed. This and the fact that the left column was too exhausted to accomplish anything persuaded General Godley, in command of this operation, to call off the attack until the 8th, when General Johnston was to occupy Chunuk Bair and General Cox Hill Q and Hill 971.

In all Cox's force consisted of thirteen battalions, which he divided into four columns, the objectives of which were:

> 1st Column, Northern slopes of Chunuk Bair.
> 2nd   "   Southern peak of Hill Q.
> 3rd   "   Northern peak of Hill Q.
> 4th   "   Abdul Rahman spur and Hill 971.

Whilst the fourth advanced at 3 a.m. and was almost instantly checked, and the third and first were too scattered to advance, the second moved forward to link up with the 1/6th Gurkhas, who had occupied a position far out to its front; nevertheless, its men were too exhausted to reach them. Waiting in vain for their arrival, Major C. J. L. Allanson, O.C. 1/6th Gurkhas, at length determined to attack Hill Q on his own, and after a fierce fight he gained a lodgment 100 feet below its crest and there he dug in, when at 2 p.m. General Godley, knowing nothing about this fine advance, suspended operations until the following day.

Meanwhile Johnston ordered an advance at 3.30 a.m., which, though it started late, to his surprise met with no opposition and so the top of the ridge was gained; whereupon Lieutenant-Colonel W. G. Malone, with two companies of the Wellington Battalion, started to dig in. "The men were in high spirits. Away on their right the growing daylight was showing up the paths and tracks in rear of the enemy's lines at Anzac, now at last outflanked. Straight to their front were the shining waters of the Narrows—the goal of the expedition. Victory seemed very near."

Why the Turks had abandoned Chunuk Bair is not known; but as they were still holding firm on Battleship Hill and Hill Q, when dawn broke a devasting fire was opened on the flanks of Malone's small force. "Fighting grimly, the two Wellington companies on top of the ridge maintained their exposed positions till nearly every man was killed," and amongst them their gallant leader. Thus Chunuk Bair was lost because Hill Q had not been taken.

For the 9th General Godley determined to renew the attack. Abandoning all idea of occupying Hill 971, he limited his objective to the main ridge from Chunuk Bair to Hill Q; Johnston to assault the former and Cox the latter, whilst in between these two vital points General A. H. Baldwin, in command of the 38th Brigade of the 13th Division, was to attack. All three forces were to work in close co-operation.

As night fell Baldwin advanced along an unreconnoitred track. Long halts and delays occurred, confusion set in and the track ending in a precipice the advance was counter-marched. As this muddle was taking place, Johnston's forward troops became heavily engaged, and as Baldwin did not appear his attack on Chunuk Bair was abandoned. Meanwhile

Allanson's reinforcements having gone astray, once again he attacked on his own, and directly the bombardment lifted he gained the top of the crest, when a second bombardment started and this time fell upon his small force and drove it to its original position. Here I will let him speak for himself:

"The roar of the artillery preparation was enormous; the hill, which was almost perpendicular, seemed to leap underneath one. I recognised if we flew up the hill the moment it stopped we ought to get to the top. I put the three companies into the trenches alongside my men, and said that the moment they saw me go forward carrying a red flag, everyone was to start. I had my watch out, 5.15. I never saw such artillery preparation; the trenches were being torn to pieces, the accuracy was marvellous, as we were only just below. At 5.18 it had not stopped, and I wondered if my watch was wrong. 5.20 silence; I waited three minutes to be certain, great as the risk was. Then off we dashed, all hand in hand, a most perfect advance and a wonderful sight. . . . At the top we met the Turks; Le Marchand was down, a bayonet through the heart. I got one through my leg, and then for about what appeared ten minutes we fought hand to hand, we bit and fisted, and used rifles and pistols as clubs, and then the Turks turned and fled, and I felt a very proud man; the key of the whole peninsula was ours, and our losses had not been so very great for such a result. Below I saw the Straits, motors and wheeled transport on the roads leading to Achi Baba. As I looked round I saw we were not being supported, and thought I could help best by going after those (Turks) who had retreated in front of us. We dashed down towards Maidos, but had only got about 100 feet down when suddenly our own Navy put six 12-in. monitor shells into us; and all was terrible confusion. It was a deplorable disaster; we were obviously mistaken for Turks, and we had to get back. It was an appalling sight; the first hit a Gurkha in the face; the place was a mass of blood and limbs and screams, and we all flew back to the summit and to our old positions just below."

Thus ended the battle for the Sari Bair ridge, a battle of valour run waste and of muddle rivalled only by the landing at Suvla Bay, to which I will now turn.

This operation, as Liman von Sanders says, was "the political-military summit of the campaign," yet, unlike Sari Bair, it was a feasible operation faced by no insuperable obstacles; nevertheless, like it, it was ruined by indifferent leadership and rawness of followership. "Since the Argive host set sail for the Trojan shore no stranger collection of ships can ever have crossed the Ægean than that which converged on Suvla on the night of the 6th August, 1915." So writes the official historian; yet to me it seems that its nearest approach in British history is Burgoyne's voyage up Lake Champlain.

At 9.30 p.m. the 32nd and 33rd Brigades of the 11th Division (General F. Hammersley) in pitch darkness approached "B" beach to find it undefended. By 10 p.m. four battalions landed without a man being killed; yet dog-tired, for the men had been on their feet for seventeen hours. Lala

Baba was occupied and the way opened to the capture of Hill 10; but no one knowing exactly where it was, nothing was done. Meanwhile the 34th Brigade, under General W. H. Sitwell, entered Suvla Bay; but, as the lighters headed for "A" beach, when fifty feet from the shore they struck a reef, which so delayed the landing that dawn broke before the men could disembark. To make matters worse, the 10th Division (General Sir B. T. Mahon), which should have landed at "A" beach in order to occupy Kiretch Tepe, was in part disembarked on "C" beach and on a new one discovered north of "A." Thus its organisation was broken up, when complete confusion set in.

Orders and counter-orders now followed each other in rapid succession, whilst the Turkish sharpshooters, like the American riflemen of 1777, picked off the invaders by scores, and thus the situation remained from hour to hour. Not until daylight was fading did an attack on Chocolate Hill begin to develop, and as darkness set in it was carried as well as the eastern half of Green Hill. Meanwhile on the left little was done outside gaining a foothold on Kiretch Tepe. All the encircling hills remained in Turkish hands, yet more than half the 9th Corps, twenty-two battalions in all, had not been engaged; nevertheless, those which had had lost 100 officers and 1,600 men "or rather more than the total strength of the Turks arrayed against them."

By now not only had the whole military plan collapsed, but also the naval, for the unloading of guns, ammunition, water, supplies, carts and transport animals was vastly delayed by the general confusion. Water, though it existed in abundance, was not found; and the men having emptied their water-bottles, many went nearly mad with thirst. Mobs of them collected on the beaches and were "sucking water through holes they had made in the hoses with their bayonets."

Of the landing, as seen by the Turks, Kannengiesser writes:

"Suvla Bay lay full of ships. We counted ten transports, six warships, and seven hospital ships. On land we saw a confused mass of troops like a disturbed ant-heap. . . . Nowhere was there fighting in progress."

Throughout August 7 "General Headquarters exercised no influence over the course of the Suvla operations, and their inactivity on this day, which, in the light of after events, may be regarded as one of the crises of the World War, can only be explained as the result of over-confidence." Hearing that even Hill 10 had not been captured, why did Sir Ian Hamilton not at once proceed to Suvla? "Had he done so, and insisted upon immediate advance, the duration of the World War might have been very considerably shortened." As the Commander-in-Chief sat on his island fretting for news, General Stopford sat on his ship vastly pleased that his men had got on shore. A visit to him nearly drove Commodore Keyes "to open mutiny." Both waited for victory or defeat as if the whole operation were a horse race. Such generalship defies definition; yet it was all part and parcel of the Moltke Staff theory that Generals-in-Chief cease to command the moment they are most needed—that is, when battle begins.

Whilst Sir Ian Hamilton and Sir Frederick Stopford were still waiting for their telephone bells to ring, all was activity on the Turkish side. At 6 p.m. Willmer telegraphed Liman von Sanders that the enemy, covered by numerous warships, had landed at Nibrunesi Point. Thereupon the Turkish Commander-in-Chief, making up his mind that Bulair was safe and that his enemy's objectives were Hill 971 and Chunuk, forthwith instructed Feizi Bey to lead two of his three divisions—namely, the 7th and 12th—south. At the same time he ordered every available man on the Asiatic side of the Dardanelles to march on Chanak and cross into Europe. Also he ordered the 8th Division from Krithia to move north. His anxiety was great, because none of these reinforcements could reach him under thirty-six to forty-eight hours. Meanwhile, could Willmer's minute force hold back the invasion?—that was the problem. Definitely the answer appeared to be "No!" Then came a morsel of relief; at 7 p.m. Major Willmer reported: "The landing of hostile forces has continued all day. Estimate their present strength as at least 1½ divisions. No energetic attacks on the enemy's part have taken place. On the contrary, the enemy is advancing timidly." This anyhow meant a probable gain of twenty-four hours.

At 1 a.m., on the 8th, Willmer's command was disposed as follows: Three companies of Gallipoli Gendarmerie on the Kiretch Tepe ridge; 1,100 men and five mountain guns between south of Baka Baba to W. Hill, and two batteries on the eastern side of the Tekke Tepe ridge. His nearest reinforcements were the three battalions from Bulair, then dead beat and bivouacked two miles east of Turshun Kevi.

The 8th, that most critical day in the whole campaign, was a Sunday, and so far as the 9th Corps was concerned it was to be a day of rest, and so completely out of touch was the British Commander-in-Chief that, at 10.50 a.m., he sent Stopford the following message: "You and your troops have indeed done splendidly. Please tell Hammersley how much we hope from his able and rapid advance."

"Splendid" and "rapid"! Why, outside the muddled landing itself practically nothing had been accomplished, and, worse still, Stopford was incapable of accomplishing anything; for as the official historian writes: As on the 7th "the basic cause" of inaction on the 8th "was the absence of a resolute leadership, not only on shore but at corps headquarters and even at G.H.Q." Then he continues:

"Following a quiet night, the morning of the 8th was absolutely still. Out of a cloudless sky, the sun was shining fiercely. The enemy's guns were silent. Apart from an occasional rifle-shot on Kiretch Tepe there was not a sound of war. The sand-dunes near the Cut were crowded with resting troops. The shores of the bay were fringed with naked figures bathing. General Stopford and his chief staff officer were still on board the *Jonquil*, and had not yet been ashore."

As no news was received at G.H.Q., it was decided to send Colonel Aspinall (later on the official historian) ashore to ascertain what was taking place. At 9.30 a.m. he set out, and found the whole bay at peace. Arriving on board the *Jonquil* he met General Stopford, who was "in excellent spirits" . . . "Well, Aspinall," he said, "the men have done splendidly, and have been magnificent." "But they haven't reached the hills," replied Aspinall. "No," answered Stopford, "but they are ashore." Then he added that he intended to order a fresh advance *next day*! Thereupon Aspinall sent the following wireless message to G.H.Q.: "Just been ashore, where I found all quiet. No rifle fire, no artillery fire, and apparently no Turks. 9th Corps resting. Feel confident that golden opportunities are being lost and look upon the situation as serious."

Whilst Aspinall was ashore, news was received at G.H.Q. that Turkish troops were advancing east of Tekke Tepe, whereupon Stopford was urged to push on. Transmitting this information to his divisional commanders, he added to it that "in view of want of adequate artillery support I do not want you to attack an entrenched position held in strength"—so nothing was done.

At length Sir Ian himself decided to go ashore, which he was unable to do until 4.30 p.m., because his destroyer was having her fires drawn! Proceeding first to the *Jonquil,* he found Stopford "happy," for in that General's opinion "everything was quite all right and going well." Further, he informed him that "he had decided to postpone the occupation of the ridge [Kiretch Tepe] (which might lead to a regular battle) until next morning." Then writes Sir Ian: " 'A regular battle is just exactly what we are here for' was what I was inclined to say; but did not." Then he decided to visit Hammersley's headquarters; whereupon Stopford asked to be excused from accompanying him . . . "he had not been very fit; he had just returned from a visit to the shore [400 yards away] and he wanted to give his leg a chance."

At Hammersley's headquarters General Hamilton found reigning a chaotic peace. "Here," he writes, "was a victorious division, rested and watered, said to be unable to bestir itself, even feebly, with less than twelve hours' notice! This was what I felt, and although I did not say it probably I looked it." Thereupon he ordered an immediate attack on the Tekke Tepe ridge, which resulted in looking for units, finding them, marching them and counter-marching them; during which turmoil the first Turkish reinforcements from Bulair, dead beat, occupied the crest of the ridge. Thus all surprise vanished; from now on equal forces were to face each other in the field.

"During the whole of the 8th August," writes Kannengiesser, "the goddess of victory held the door to success wide open for Stopford, but he would not enter. . . . But nobody advanced. In short, a peaceful picture, almost like a boy scouts' field day."

"At the same time under the same sun on the other side the panting troops of the 7th and 12th Divisions were straining forward over the hills from Bulair; from the Asiatic side along the shadeless Sultan's Way; over Erenkoi the Turkish battalions and batteries were pressing towards the embarkation stations in Tchanak Kale [Chanak]. Will they arrive in time? This thought feverishly occupied the mind . . . of the Marshal who waited there by Anafarta."

Whilst the British Commander-in-Chief was looking ferocious and thinking what he was inclined to say and yet remaining dumb, Marshal Liman von Sanders was all fire and activity. Before daybreak he mounted his horse, searched for his reinforcements and found the Staff Officer of the 7th Division, who informed him that both it and the 12th were still far behind. Anxiously he looked over the battlefield at the invading horde. Between it and where he stood were 400 men on W Hills, 300 on Kiretch Tepe, and not a man in between. That evening he heard from Willmer that Feizi Bey had not arrived. He summoned him to him, and when that General told him that his troops were too exhausted to attack before the morning of the 9th, what did he do? Being no drawing-room General he dismissed him on the spot and placed Mustafa Kemal Bey in command of all troops in the Anafarta section, because, as he says, "he was a leader that delighted in responsibility."

As August 7 and 8 were days of crisis, so were the 9th and 10th days of decision. After a series of orders and counter-orders, Hammersley was instructed to carry the Anafarta spur at 5 a.m. on the 9th, and Mahon to occupy Tekke Tepe. The attack of the 11th Division opened in confusion and ended in chaos. As the leading battalion of the 32nd Brigade moved forward, Turkish reinforcements were pouring up the other side of the ridge, then a clash took place and the battalion was thrown back in confusion. "Despite the 48 hours' delay, the race for Tekke Tepe" was "lost by rather less than half an hour."

The attack of the 33rd Brigade was only a little less chaotic. As it advanced it was met by crowds of stragglers flatulent with stories of defeat. Then it met the Turks at Asmak Dere, was stopped, held its own and dug in. Meanwhile at Kiretch Tepe a short advance was made, when the attackers of the 10th Division also dug in as did General Stopford, who had now established his headquarters ashore. "Walking up the lower slope of Kiretch Tepe Sirt," writes Sir Ian Hamilton, "we found Stopford, about four or five hundred yards east of Ghazi Baba, busy with part of a Field Company of Engineers supervising the building of some splinter-proof Headquarters huts for himself and Staff. He was absorbed in the work, and he said that it would be well to make a thorough good job of the dug-outs as we should probably be here for a very long time."

Next day the 53rd Division (now landed) was thrown into the battle to retake Scimitar Hill, lost on the 9th, and to assault the Anafarta Spur. Two attacks were made, and both failed.

Commenting on these two days' fighting, Ashmead-Bartlett writes:

"No one seemed to know where the headquarters of the different brigades and divisions were to be found. The troops were hunting for water, the staffs were hunting for their troops, and the Turkish snipers were hunting for their prey. . . . Where I had seen one Turk yesterday there seemed to be ten to-day. . . . Leaving comparatively few in the trenches, large numbers descended into the unburnt scrub, and there, almost immune from artillery fire, awaited our attack. . . . Their snipers crept from bush to bush, from tree to tree, from knoll to knoll, picking off our men wherever they saw a favourable target, and were themselves left almost unmolested."

Indeed, it was Saratoga over again.

This day Mustafa Kemal Bey also attacked. Having on the 9th checked the 9th Corps, on the 10th he turned on Chunuk Bair, and having personally reconnoitred that position, he decided to recapture Rhododendron Spur. At 4.45 a.m. dense waves of Turks poured across the skyline, and sweeping over their enemy's advanced trenches captured the Pinnacle and the Farm. Then the attack exhausted itself. Thus, on the 10th, ended the Battles of Sari Bair and Suvla Bay. What were their cost to the invader? Out of 50,000 British troops, 18,000 were killed, wounded and missing. Well may Ashmead-Bartlett jot down on the 12th: "We have landed again and dug another graveyard."

The remainder of this campaign must be told in brief. Stopford was dismissed and replaced by General Sir Julian Byng, who originally had been asked for. "This is a young man's war," now wrote Lord Kitchener, just six months too late; yet Sir Ian, as responsible for the disaster, remained on to carry out on August 21–22 a wasteful frontal attack at Suvla. This last battle cost 5,300 in killed, wounded and missing out of 14,300.

The immediate result of the British failure was the mobilisation of the Bulgarian Army on September 25. Next, on October 14, Bulgaria declared war on Serbia, whereupon Lord Kitchener decided to withdraw two divisions from the Dardanelles for service at Salonika. Then the storm burst, Mackensen at the head of nine German and Austrian divisions crossing the Danube. Uskub fell on the 22nd, Nish on November 2 and Monastir was entered on December 2, Serbia being reduced to ruin, while German guns and ammunition poured into Constantinople.

On October 14 Sir Ian Hamilton was recalled to England to be replaced by Sir Charles Munro, who, landing on the 28th, on the 31st recommended the total evacuation of the British forces. This threw Mr. Asquith into a panic, and, on November 2, he decided to entrust the conduct of the war to a War Committee of not less than three and not more than five members, a change he should have initiated a year or more before. Then, on the 4th, Lord Kitchener was sent out to the Dardanelles to give a second opinion and to get rid of him, as Asquith informed Lloyd George. In turn, he sent back a half-hearted answer that evacuation was inevitable, whereupon Mr. Churchill, long superseded by Mr. Balfour as First Lord of the Admiralty, pressed for a renewal of the naval attack on the Narrows, though now its strategic purpose had vanished. In this vain attempt to spoon up spilt milk, he was strongly supported by Commodore Keyes, who rushed this idea here, there, and everywhere like a tactical bull in a strategical china shop. To him, the forcing of the Narrows meant that the "whole business" would be finished. He could not see that Germany and Turkey were now without a dividing frontier, and that once the fleet had bombarded Constantinople nothing further could have been done. Nor did he know at the time that on the German-Turkish side "a large-scale offensive with the assistance of gas was in course of preparation," though this might have been guessed.

Then, on November 27, a terrific blizzard swept the Peninsula for seventy-two hours, in which hundreds of men died of exposure. "At Suvla alone in the course of three days' storm there had been more than 5,000 cases of frost-bite, and over 200 men had been drowned or frozen to death." This storm hastened the crisis; for though General Munro had estimated that the probable losses involved in evacuation would total between thirty and forty per cent. of the personnel and matériel then on the peninsula, after much intrigue and wrangling the War Committee at first decided to evacuate Anzac and Suvla only, but later on Helles as well. The evacuation of the first two was carried out by December 20, and the last by January 9, 1915, without a single soldier killed. Thus were concluded the sole successful operations of the campaign. In all 410,000 British and 70,000 French soldiers had been landed, of whom 252,000 were killed, wounded, missing, prisoners, died of disease or evacuated sick. The Turkish casualties amounted to 218,000 men, of whom 66,000 were killed. The booty left behind was immense: "It took nearly two years to clean up the ground."

The Stars in Their Courses

BY

COLONEL JOHN W. THOMASON, JR.

"WE ALL went up to Gettysburg, the summer of '63: and some of us came back from there: and that's all, except the details. I wouldn't bother you with the details."

Thus I have heard Elder Praxiteles Swan, sometime Captain, Confederate States Army, in his great age, dismiss Lee's invasion of the North; when the grown folks talked over old battles, of summer nights on our deep gallery in Texas; a mockingbird singing meanwhile from the pear tree on the lawn. Then, invariably, my uncle Mark, late sergeant-major of the Fifth Texas Infantry, in Hood's Brigade, would launch into his anticipated denunciation of General Longstreet, who was, he held, in several thousand bitter words, gravely culpable at Gettysburg. But the Elder would comment, only, that, so far as tactics were concerned, when a man got too cock-sure of himself, he was in for trouble. As to strategy, he considered that the judgments of the Lord were true and righteous altogether —except, some of the trimmings of the same were a little hard to swallow. And he would close, always, with the same quotation, from Judges in the Old Testament; mumbled mostly to his beard. He never came right out with that passage, because, he said, he hated arguments. Yet it was his word that it told more of the truth about Lee's defeat in Pennsylvania than all the reminiscences ever written. It was—but that is ahead of the story, which I have pieced together from old letters and old books, and from remembered tales.

We heard much talk of Gettysburg, while the old men lived who, in their ardent youth, followed Lee to invade the North: to carry the war into Africa, and ring a spear against the gates of Rome, as they used to declaim at reunions. The staff colleges now consider that Gettysburg was a raid; one of the great raids of history, and nothing more. Yet the men who mounted it and made it, all in a month of days, from conception to its foredoomed consummation, and those at home whose hearts attended the army with hope and faith and prayer, saw it as a valiant people's supreme thrust at the fate that was closing in upon them: a high and gallant effort, having within itself the finest possibilities for victory and peace. Cut the enemy's railroads on the Susquehanna between his east and west: occupy

From: *Lone Star Preacher*: Copyright 1941. Scribners.

his key cities: complete, upon his army, the destruction begun at Chancel-lorsville: gain foreign recognition, and the independence of the Confederate States!

It is all written down in the histories how Lee led them up from the Rappahannock line, towards the Blue Ridge, an army clanking with victory, the name of Chancellorsville fresh and terrible on its battle flags. It is related how Lee turned his shoulder contemptuously to Hooker, bemusing the Army of the Potomac with a screen of horsemen, and cavalry fights like a string of firecrackers, all across the pleasant Virginia country between the Rappahannock and the Blue Ridge, until Ewell's stroke at Winchester sounded a thunderclap from the valley: and how Hill's Corps, and Longstreet's after him, followed in turn to the Potomac River: and how the shrill cries of the invaded Pennsylvania towns fell silent in the Washington bureaus as telegraph station after telegraph station went out: and how, swinging on an inside arc to cover the capital, the Army of the Potomac trended north about the end of June. All this, and more—

But Praxiteles' letters, from Raccoon Ford, from Snicker's Gap (he wrote it, Snigger's) in the Blue Ridge, from Williamsport and Greencastle and Chambersburg, tell of more homely things. The army was confident, he said, and high-stomached; the weather most brutally hot, between showers of rain and occasional old-fashioned gully-washers. A lot of men had sunstroke, and blind staggers, and some died from the heat. At Williamsport they forded a mid-stage Potomac, in the rain, and the commander of the Texas Brigade, General Robertson laying hands on a liquor store (through correct quartermaster procedure, of course), issued the Brigade a generous whiskey ration, lest they catch cold. They walked high and wide that day through the thin end of Maryland, wrote Praxiteles, not as disapproving as he should have been; except the 3rd Arkansas regiment of the Brigade, whose Colonel was a Good Templar and held not with the Friendly Creature: so that the 3rd Arkansas marched angry and sober, and by way of reward for being sober, had grand guard on the camp across the Pennsylvania line.

At Greencastle, the Elder wrote his wife, young Captain Tom Goree of Longstreet's Staff made him acquainted with an English Colonel following the army, who wore amazing clothes and was full of good manners and fine deportment, although, declared Praxiteles, the Colonel gargled his words so, a man couldn't understand him at all, except that he wished us well. And it was at Greencastle, Praxiteles recollects, that a large Dutch lady glowered at the marching Texans from her porch, a woman all of two ax-handles broad, with a bright United States flag draped, kerchief-wise, across her bosom. She glared, men remember, and she snorted, and she remarked loud and clear to the trees across the street, while the column went along: "Look at Pharaoh's soldiers going to the Red Sea!" Whereat the Colonel of the Fifth, abreast of her, swept off his hat and bowed to his horse's mane, and behind him in the ranks one Bill Calhoun, high private and accredited buffoon to the Fifth Texas, cried out: "Take keer, ma'am; take keer whar you fly them colors! We air Hood's boys, an' we always storm the breast-works, whar we see them colors flyin'!"—And the lady went into her house and stayed there. (Greencastle, you remember, was the place in which, some days later, the patriotic citizens turned out with axes, and chopped the wheels from under the wagons of Confederate wounded, when Imboden's train of misery toiled through from Gettysburg, and its armed escort was fighting Pleasanton, off to the flank and rear. Yet in Greencastle, no violence toward civilians is recorded——)

They marched at ease to Chambersburg, a neat red brick town in a fine farming section, untouched by war; and they lay there for two pleasant days. Old soldiers still speak with emotion of the rations they had at Chambersburg. Lee had cut adrift his communications, and was feeding off the country, and even under his unbending restrictions the quarter-masters found the pickings mighty good. They thanked their stars they weren't having to glean behind Ewell's hungry corps, further east and north. Casual and unofficial persons, strolling out from camp, benefited also in guileless ways at the hands of the provident Pennsylvania Dutch who dwelt in the land. Praxiteles and Major Martin, riding on their lawful occasions, stopped to water their horses at a farm and came away with a suckling pig, a brace of turkeys, some pullets, and as many jars of apple butter as they could stow about their saddles. Major Martin did the forag-ing, while the Elder sat his mare, grinning behind his whiskers. The Penn-sylvania Dutch were a peaceful folk, and apprehensive of violence. Look-ing at the Major, who hadn't found time for a trim recently, Praxiteles didn't wonder they showered down: Howdy Martin was a rough-hewed white man. A great many feathers blew along the wind from the oak grove where the Brigade camped; and the men turned out of their blankets, at a reasonable hour on the first day of July, positively bloated with food.

Any army is like a horse, in that it reflects the temper and the spirit of its rider. If there is an uneasiness and an uncertainty, it transmits itself through the reins, and the horse feels uneasy and uncertain. This day the atmosphere changed. The troops had heard no shots since they left Virginia, and had seen no blue coats. Their notion of their whereabouts was of the vaguest. They had crossed so many streams, and passed so many hills, and marched through so many towns. Now they took the road—the Chambers-burg Pike—with the low sun in their faces and a low mountain range ahead, and stepped out comfortably, ten minutes rest in every hour, which was routine, and indicated that nothing urgent awaited them. Riding the column on his mare, Praxiteles listened to the talk among the files and remembered the talk through the past week of marches, and it made him thoughtful.

It came to him that he, and these men, were friendless orphans in a foreign land. A land they didn't want or care about, for all its fatness. These folks up here had more, and they lived better, but you didn't like them that way. Why hadn't they—these Yankees—stayed under their own vine and figtree, and drunk from their own cisterns? Did they—Praxiteles tried to remember the name of the British tribal chieftain, captive in Imperial Rome, who looked at the marble and porphyry construction of the world's capital and said, "If they have all this, why do they want my mud huts?" Caractacus, now?—He'd neglected his classics. Towards noon, the marching began to go bad. Down on the eastern slope of the mountains, in the midst of a halt, there came across the sunlit fields and the neat orchards a sound, a known sound. Gunfire. It rolled through the hot still air. Steady gunfire—no chance collision of horse batteries. The men fell in with their heads higher, their eyes brighter. The enemy was over yonder. Now they could whip him and go home. Conquer a peace, and go home again. There was a new thrust in their legs. But the pace slowed, and dragged, and fell into halts, short spurts, and halts again. McLaws' Division led the First Corps, but McLaws' Georgians, Alabamians, Mississippians, marched as well as anybody: they wouldn't drag thisaway. A courier, trotting down the column, said it was a wagon train stopping them —great big wagon train—coming in from the left, across their front. Presently the head of the Brigade saw the thing, stretching north for miles under its own dust. "We got to wait for those damn teamsters? Whose is it? Can't be our wagons. Ewell's? Hill's? Boys, they're trying to carry off all of Pennsylvania!——"

The complaint of the ungreased wheels, and the mournful cries of the drivers, made a sort of drone in the heat, but over it you heard those guns. About this time the Commanding General rode by, cutting through the fields, Longstreet with him, on his strawberry roan. Their horses were in a lope, and General Lee, decided Praxiteles, looked alert and angry. The men stood, or squatted, went forward a few yards at a time, and halted again; and the afternoon waned into evening. There is nothing so hard on troops, or so exhausting, as waiting in ranks. Men coming down from ahead said there was fighting at a place called Gettysburg, a few miles up the road, and we were doing first-rate!

Walking wounded began to appear, pessimistic as wounded generally are: "Who y'all? Texicans? Wal, it's bad up thar. Bulford's Regulars— they got Spencers. And the Pennsylvania Bucktails—'tain't no milishy up thar—it's the ole Army of the Potomac!"

The Texans received the news with professional interest, and regarded the wounded with indifference. Man was bound to get hurt, one time or another. They observed, also, long files of dusty blue prisoners passing into the fields south of the road: that looked all right. A. P. Hill was biting into them. But the thoughtful old soldiers, talking low among themselves, were troubled and puzzled. There wasn't the right feel in the air. They seemed to be drifting, and this army wasn't used to drifting. "Well," stated Major Howdy Martin, climbing down from a rail fence and putting away his spyglass, "The Bull of the Woods"—he meant Longstreet— "knows we're here; and General Lee, he's seen us. Maybe they're waiting for Pickett" (Pickett's division off to the right and rear somewhere, guarding the flank of the army, a cavalry mission). "And when they want us, they'll send word."

But Praxiteles Swan was immensely bored. They stood on the road until after dark, until the wagon train, fourteen miles of it, was past. Then they marched rapidly for some six miles, and bivouacked on a marshy stream near the Cashtown road. In the morning, contrary to the expectations of reasonable men, they had time to cook breakfast and eat it, unmolested, although there was a battle somewhere near. And when the sun was high, they moved through the debris of yesterday's fight, and skirted the edge of a little town where a yellow brick cupola showed above the trees. Some school or other. They went a mile or so down a wooded ridge, the town on their left hand. Hill's Corps was in position on the ridge—doing nothing in particular —but beyond it, towards the town, there was a steady contention of musketry and artillery. "Gettysburg, the name of the place. The whole Yankee Army's thar," Major Martin told Praxiteles, returning from one of his rounds in quest of news—the Major loved news. "Looks to me like: we whup them, or they whup us. And we're a long way from the Brazos River, Elder Swan—" Then they waited off the road, under some trees, interminably.

A hairy fellow lounged up to Praxiteles, dismounted at the head of the Fifth, to rest his mare, and said, touching his wreck of a hat, "Elder—that is, Captain, seh—we hev been so choused around today that we hev had no time to read us a passage. And us boys thought, you might be so kind— while those generals yonder air settlin' what they're goin' to do with us——"

"Brother Scruggs, I'll be right glad to read you a passage. Don't it say, "Whoso despiseth the word shall be destroyed; but he that feareth the commandment shall be rewarded—' of course, it does: Proverbs, 13:13." He took his old Bible out of his saddlebags: the red dust of the Virginia counties was ground into its frayed leather covers. He balanced it, back exactly down, in his hand, and let it fall open: it was Praxiteles' word in the days of his preaching, that wherever your eye alighted in the Bible, there was health and comfort. The sunburnt infantrymen pressed around him, most of them taking off their hats. And Praxiteles, looking to see where the book had opened, saw that it was Jeremiah, and under his eye the verse ran "Behold, a people shall come from the north . . . they shall hold the bow and the lance; they are cruel, and will not shew mercy; their voice shall roar like the sea. . . ."

But Captain Swan of the Confederate States Army, here and now in a combat zone, did not read that selection: it didn't have quite the right pitch. He squinted, and moved so that the light came over his shoulder, all in the most natural way imaginable, and found, opening in the opposite column on the page, the 51st chapter, which is all war cries and bugle calls and rolling drums. . . . *"Thus saith the Lord; behold, I will rise up against Babylon . . . and will send unto Babylon fanners, that shall fan her, and shall empty her land . . . and spare ye not her young men; destroy ye utterly all her host. Thus the slain shall fall in the land of the Chaldeans, and they that are thrust through in her streets—"* ("like the fellow said, just now, they did those Dutchmen—in Gettysburg yesterday evening—" whispered one file to another; they had been talking to one of Heth's couriers—"don't it beat all? Don't it, now? I tell you—") —*"For this is the time of the Lord's vengeance; he will render unto her a recompense,"* boomed Praxiteles, his voice growing great. . . . *"Make bright the arrows, gather the shields; the Lord hath raised up the spirit of the Kings of the Medes: for his device is against Babylon, to destroy it—"* Then, like Dante's people, from this book they read no more.

I remember the Elder talking, perhaps to General John B. Gordon, when the knightly old gentleman was in our house, of Gettysburg. One time only. They talked sadly, and as if they were still a little puzzled. "We went up there," the Elder said, "with the feeling in us that nothing on earth—not all the Yankees that were ever mustered for war—could stop us. And they couldn't have, either, had we been handled right." Then he went over the first day, and the morning of the second and its afternoon —the standing around, the waiting. Now the day was getting on, the shadows lengthening. There was fighting over on the left, where the Second Corps curved through and beyond Gettysburg—but it was just fighting to fight, not fighting to go through. Hood rode up, and the Texas Brigade greeted him with yells—they were always Hood's Brigade. He was a lean, golden-bearded sword-blade of a man, and he reined in when he saw the Elder, and greeted him. "It's my fighting preacher! You still a captain? Have to do something about that!" He rode to the crest of the ridge, dismounted, some fifty yards away from the column, and Longstreet, stolid and heavy as ever, joined him, with black-bearded, bullet-headed McLaws. They studied a map and talked, and Hood got on his horse and trotted towards the head of his division. He led them, still behind the ridge, past McLaws' division, waiting there in ranks, and on towards the right. Presently they were clear, and the brigades went, fours left, and shook themselves out into line of battle: cohesive blocks of soldiery, with the shimmer of steel over them and their bright flags. Law on the right, then the Texans, then Semmes' brigade; and while they formed they saw a new thing in this war: artillery going ahead of the infantry. All the batteries of the First Corps were there—they trotted out, and went forward, the drivers sitting their horses like cavalry about to charge. Where the Texans formed, the ridge flattened and the trees thinned, and they could see the country ahead.

Praxiteles, out with his skirmishers—they suspended also, in the very act and article of striking—studied it carefully through his glasses. It was rough country. Up to the left—towards the center, facing McLaws—were farm buildings, a wheat field, a peach orchard, and some wood lots on rising ground: the approach was broken into compartments by stout fences of stone, or of strong post-and-rail construction. And a lot of Yankees behind the fences. Battle flags, artillery guidons, heavy blue lines, galloping officers and couriers. While he watched, the Confederate batteries, out in front, went into action: white puff-balls of smoke blossomed along the blue positions: and immediately shells began to fall again in Hood's waiting ranks:

McLaws was still in cover, behind the ridge. To Hood's front, the ground ran, broken and difficult, over a wooded knoll, towards two little hills. The Round Tops. The glass showed lots of big rocks among the trees. There were the inevitable stone fences and the post-and-rail fences, annoying to a battle line. There was some wheat, and pasture land: a stream, and country lanes that came into the Emmitsburg road along their front. Not as many Yankees showing as there were on the left, but plenty of them; what looked like a line of battle on the knoll, with skirmishers out. And a signal station on the lowest hill, the inside one, but no visible troops. Flags were busy over there, a lot of them. Praxiteles couldn't see any infantry.

While they looked, Hood rode up. "When you move, Robertson," they heard him say to the Brigadier, "put your left on the Emmitsburg road —that's it yonder—and keep touch with Law's left— By the way, send Law some of your Texas scouts. He wants to know how it is, around those hills. I think we're about past their flank——"

The horses had been sent back. Small, dapper Robertson conferred with Major Martin, and Major Martin passed the order to Praxiteles Swan. "Send a sergeant and six men to General Law, over there. No, you stay here—" Praxiteles sent a Sergeant Menifee, a bear hunter from the Big Thicket on the lower Trinity, and a squad he picked: they were gone an hour. The men fumed in the heat, and small insects bit their wet faces. Praxiteles, from his line of skirmishers ahead of the Brigade, saw Sergeant Menifee, returning in unaccustomed haste, come to where Law sat his horse watching his Alabamians: the sergeant stood at Law's stirrup, pointed at the rough little hills three-quarters of a mile out in front, and talked earnestly. Law bent to listen, then straightened in his saddle, clapped spurs to his horse, and galloped down to Hood, who was in conversation with General Robertson behind the Texans. They talked, and the long lines turned their heads to watch. These soldiers were war-wise: and much can be learned by an observant file from the demeanor of his officer.

Hood never pondered long on anything: his eyes followed the sweep of Law's arm: he slapped Law's knee, nodding emphatically. "Sellers!" he cried, over his shoulder, and the staff officer came, listened, saluted, and was gone through the woods like, said the Texans, the dogs was after him. Hood and Law fidgeted on their horses. The lines of battle, tense again, slacked off disgustedly. More waiting! said the men. We've waited all day. We've waited 'most all night. We waited most of yesterday. What's the matter with these heah slow-goin' generals we've got? Want to be sure they's enough Yankees over yonder to make a mess, before we pitch in?

Praxiteles, very curious, called to Sergeant Menifee, who was taking a breather under an apple tree and chewing tobacco: "What's over there? What are the generals worked up about? How come they got the slows?"

Menifee stood up and spat. "We was on those hills yonder, with some of the Alabama boys. Thar was nobody thar—except a signal station— 'bout an hour ago. Behind them air all the Yankee wagons. You can look right down their line—a slew of troops but you're on their flank—and behind those people yonder—," he indicated the formations to the left around the peach orchard. "Was we to get thar befo' they do—an' get some guns up—why, Elder—Captain, seh, in fifteen minutes hell would be so full of Yankees their legs would be stickin' out of the windows! Law, he saw it right away, an' said he'd tell old Hood we ought to file right a ways, and go up behind—only," said Menifee, knitting his brows, "we're waitin' too long. Even them Yankees will see it after a while, and get up some soldiers——"

Hood was riding near the halted skirmish line, his face gloomy, quite oblivious to the shells that now came thicker, when his aide returned. Praxiteles saw him clench his hands and strike his saddle bow: his face was thunderous. He yelled for his adjutant-general, instructed him, and sent him galloping. It seemed a long time before the adjutant returned, shaking his head. Then Hood went himself, at a lope towards the center: Praxiteles saw General Longstreet, hat in hand, ride out of the brush with one of McLaws' columns, and saw him talk to Hood: The Bull of the Woods was gloomy of aspect. And when Hood rode back, you could see he was angry. His division was all formed, on and behind the ridge. Law on the right flank with his South Alabama Brigade; then the Texans; then Semmes: all the division was there; all the flags with the singing battle-names upon them. Hood halted in the clear, took off his hat, and his great voice pealed: "Forward——"

The battle closed upon them. Immediately they began to lose men. Praxiteles noted that shells were coming straight down the line from the left. "McLaws—blast and confound him to everlasting torment—he didn't start!" But he had no more time for the flank—the front occupied him. The Yankee skirmishers were snug behind a stone fence, and hung on with unexpected resolution. Praxiteles shot a man with his pistol, at five yards distance, before they broke. Then the wooded knoll, immediately behind the fence, was full of Blue people, very stubborn indeed. The Texas yell rose, and the Texas lines rolled over them—but there was much blood on the rocks when they looked down from the crest into a glade at their end of the gorge between the Round Tops—place to be known to history as the Devil's Den.

Now the hills were just a few hundred yards away, they could see troops on them. Praxiteles mounted a boulder and looked to the right—Law was sweeping ahead, his battle flags slanted, his battle line beautiful to see. The fire had hardly touched him. He looked to the left—Semmes, over there, was drifting towards the center, his flank regiment hardly moving. McLaws' Division not yet in sight. The knoll had split the line of the Texans—the 3rd Arkansas, on one flank, inclined towards Semmes—the 1st Texas, on the other, towards Law. And this was no place to linger. Round shot and rifled shell were howling through the tree tops, and a growing volume of musketry.

No colonels in sight. No generals. And we can't stay here—if we don't make haste and get that high ground, they'll have us on the hip. He raised his sword and bellowed. The Texans plunged down into the glade, and met a fire that staggered them.

"Hour ago, thar warn't nobody thar—only those signal flag fellows," panted Sergeant Menifee, at Praxiteles' elbow. He had lost his hat. At the marshy stream they floundered through, he dipped a once white handkerchief in water, and now he bound it around his coarse black hair. "Hot day, Elder, hot day—" A minie went through his head, bound handkerchief and all—and the attack went on.

Yelling, for they knew better, now, than to stop for a shot, they crossed the glade and tackled the slope beyond it. They were tired men. The terrain broke such formation as they had retained. The trees were in full leaf, and every tree had its Yankee behind it. The boulders were as big as corn cribs, most of them, and to every one there seemed to be an enemy. The Texans recoiled from the slope, settled behind rocks and began a fire fight.

A succession of shrill yells pierced the crackle of musketry: men looked to the rear and saw a small soldier on a small sorrel horse, coming up at a dead run. The rider was spurring hard, and fanning his mount about the ears with his hat, and yipping, they said afterwards, like a coyote. "It's Sergeant Barbee," cried a Fifth Texas infantryman, and bit a cartridge: "It's old Hood's courier—Hiyo, Barbee! What's up? What's up?"—a dozen acquaintances called to him, from the Brenham company of the Fifth. Close to the first great rocks, the little sorrel met her bullet: she came down head first, in a terrible neck-breaking crash, turned end over end, and never moved after that. But her rider hit the ground running, and running forward. "Old Jawn Hood's shot," he panted: "I've come up to get me some Yankees—gimme a gun—gimme a gun—" He caught up an Enfield from one casualty, grabbed a cartridge box from another, and cast himself down beside a hairy sharpshooter who chewed tobacco with savage vigor, and shot cautiously around the edge of his boulder.

The rifles dinned together: minies snapped and whined around, lead sparked silver on the rocks, and men fought silently, or fought with yells; and screams and prayers and curses went up in a wild cacophony from that place. Through it Barbee's high voice cut again: "Cinders of hell," he said, "a man jest natcherly caint see what he's shootin' at from here—" A dozen yards to his right lay a boulder as big as a small cabin, and in its lee a group of men were sheltered: wounded who had dragged themselves to it: prudent men who took cover there, firing cautiously around its sides; and exhausted men, who cowered and panted like hounds under it. Barbee ran across to the rock and scrambled upon it, light as a cat-squirrel. Looking—they said afterwards, twice bigger than natural; he balanced himself, took deliberate aim, and got off his shot. He flung the Enfield away and reached down and backward— " 'Nother gun—'nother gun—" From below they thrust one up; he fired again: and they passed up another. "Got 'im, by God! Now, that officer, by the tree— Hah! 'Nother gun—" Minies whined around him; there were hoarse yells from the trees up the hill—the top of his boulder was scoured with bright hot lead—yet Praxiteles and many others, in sober judgment afterwards, attested that Barbee got off no less than twenty-five rounds before a ball in the shoulder and another in the thigh lifted him into the air and hurled him bodily into the arms of the men below him. Even then he fought himself free and struggled, crying and cursing, to get on the rock again; until he fainted from loss of blood, and Sergeant Ed Goree of the Fifth got the litter-bearers to take him off.

All this Praxiteles Swan, lying behind a boulder and taking pot-shots with a casualty's rifle as opportunity offered, observed with mounting indignation. It was not his idea of a fight at all. The heat, the immense boulders, the tangled underbrush and thick gnarled trees were enough, he considered, to bother an active man with nobody shooting at him. Add to that a weight and a volume of flying lead so solid you were surprised you didn't see it sheeted over the terrain—and it was mighty near too much! Too much for Texas, even. He saw a blue cap with a red Maltese cross on it come around a tree trunk, just where it rose from behind a boulder; saw a broad red face under the cap, moved his rifle slightly to cover it, and pressed the trigger as a bright rifle barrel slid across the rock, towards him. His Enfield smote his shoulder and white smoke blinded him: when it lifted, the cap and the face had disappeared, but the rifle remained, bright and balanced, on the rock. "You got him, Rev'rend," called a cheerful soldier a little way to his right. "You got him, old Hip an' Thigh!—" The man rolled sideways and drew his legs up, his head oddly canted back, his face away. But he didn't move any more, and a little sluggish flow of blood stained the rocks under his head. Now there was more movement up the slope: a new battle flag appeared, agitated among the branches and the rocks: and every man who saw it shot at it. It dipped, vanished, came up again, fluttered anxiously, and came to rest, leaning against a rock. Over among the Alabamians on the left, a young officer sprang on a rock, waved his sword, and made impassioned representations. They couldn't hear him, but they could see him mounting. Perhaps fifty riflemen, with a flag, rose from cover around him and they ran forward, their yells coming thinly down the smoke. There was a loud indignation of rifles in the rocks above them; they disappeared in smoke and scrub: and presently a few men crawled painfully back from where they went. Praxiteles couldn't stand it. More Yankees coming in, up there—been here long enough for us to catch our breath—pretty soon, be too many of them, altogether— He rose to his knees and raised his immense voice—"Fifth Texas—Hood's Texans—" Men turned around to look at him, and a minie ball whipped his hat off: another ripped at his sleeve, and a third, ricocheting from the boulder, seared his face with fragments of stone and splashes of hot lead.

An anger surged through him. He stood erect, and looked around. "We air going," he announced, "to take that there hill. Come on." He began to walk towards the hill. To left and right, and behind him, the Texans peered at him from their shelters. A sort of sighing moan ran from one man to another. A few of them got to their feet, and a few more, and then all of them. Somebody raised a croaking yell, and the field took it up. A shrill and angry defiance. Then they were running at the slope, covered for a little by a trick of air that left the thick smoke eddying in the low ground.

They reached the first rocks at the base of the slope, where lay fragments of the advanced blue regiments, which had come back from the first holding ground, and hung on here. The Yankee pieces were foul with a day's firing—a man had to hammer his ramrod home with a rock, after you'd shot so long. And they were tired, too. They gave back before these screeching, hairy animals, led by a giant with a fearful roaring face, that was half bristling red hair and half blood. Higher on the hill lay fellows from the State of Maine, very hard men, under a most valiant colonel named Chamberlain (Praxiteles, in later years, was studious to inform himself of such details) who this day saw fall, killed or wounded, eighty-odd of each hundred soldiers he set upon this hill. These stayed—and they fought body-to-body, hideously.

"Their fiah come down the hill in blizzards—you could lean against it. A fellow could'a swung a quart cup an' caught a peck of minies in it. That was bad, and the rocks an' the bushes was bad—and some mighty strong Yankees on top of all—No, seh, no seh. Godamighty didn't mean us to take that hill—" so they said in Texas long afterwards. But Praxiteles began to chant, in the flame and fury of it:

> "Come on, Fifth Texas,
> Come on, Fifth Texicans—
> You boys from the Brazos
> And the Trinity.
> From the Colorado, and from
> Buffalo Bayou.
> From Corpus Christi
> and Galveston—
> Come on, you Texicans,
> Remember Gaines's Mill where you broke them
> and drove them—
> Remember Freeman's Ford—
> Remember Groveton.
> Remember 2d Manassas, where
> you killed the Fire Zouaves—
> Remember Sharpsburg.
> —Remember Sharpsburg
> Where the Lord of Hosts was on our side and
> the legions of hell
> could not prevail against us—
> Remember Fredericksburg
> Where they stood in rows like corn under the sun—

(blast and confound you to everlastin' Hell-fire, Joe Ruggers, don't shoot blind over that rock—)

Remember all your battles and marches—
Come on, Fifth Texas——"

And Praxiteles Swan, halfway across a boulder, and halfway through an ardent strophe in the manner of Jeremiah, never saw the blue soldier who, from the side of the rock, rose up and swung his musket butt—there was a great pale flash of light inside the Elder's skull, and after that, nothing.

The Texans hung on, among the rocks, until dark. Then Robertson drew them back to the base of the hill. They brought off all their wounded, Praxiteles Swan among them. The next thing he knew a light was hurting his eyes, and the stars blinked over him in a velvety sky. The Brigade Surgeon, a free-thinking Presbyterian when at home, was saying: "Whatever they hit you with, you' head was harder than it was, Elder—how's that, sir? What you say? I don't quite understand you——?"

"The stars—the stars—the stars in their courses fought against Sisera," Praxiteles repeated, making each word distinct. "The stars in their courses. Judges——"

"Hold that lantern higher, orderly. So. The stars in their courses . . . Well, Elder. Yes. On the whole, I agree. Sisera got whipped. But was I you, Elder, I'd not give the boys that text. Some of your shouting Methodists in the Fifth might think you meant Marse Robert—and they wouldn't like it——"

Waterloo

BY

VICTOR HUGO

LET us go back,—that is one of the story-teller's privileges,—and put ourselves once more in the year 1815, and even a little prior to the period when the action narrated in the first part of this book took place.

If it had not rained in the night between the 17th and the 18th of June, 1815, the fate of Europe would have been different. A few drops of water, more or less, made Napoleon waver. All that Providence required in order to make Waterloo the end of Austerlitz was a little more rain, and a cloud crossing the sky out of season sufficed to overthrow the world.

The battle of Waterloo could not be begun until half-past eleven o'clock, and that gave Blücher time to come up. Why? Because the ground was moist. The artillery had to wait until it became a little firmer before they could manœuvre.

Napoleon was an artillery officer, and felt the effects of one. All his plans of battle were arranged for projectiles. The key to his victory was to make the artillery converge on one point. He treated the strategy of the hostile general like a citadel, and made a breach in it. He crushed the weak point with grape-shot; he joined and dissolved battles with artillery. There was something of the sharpshooter in his genius. To beat in squares, to pulverize regiments, to break lines, to destroy and disperse masses,—for him everything lay in this, to strike, strike, strike incessantly,—and he entrusted this task to the cannon-ball. It was a formidable method, and one which, united with genius, rendered this gloomy athlete of the pugilism of war invincible for the space of fifteen years.

On the 18th of June, 1815, he relied all the more on his artillery, because he had numbers on his side. Wellington had only one hundred and fifty-nine guns; Napoleon had two hundred and forty.

Suppose the soil dry, and the artillery capable of moving, the action would have begun at six o'clock in the morning. The battle would have been won and ended at two o'clock, three hours before the change of fortune in favour of the Prussians. How much blame attaches to Napoleon for the loss of this battle? Is the shipwreck due to the pilot?

Was it the evident physical decline of Napoleon that complicated this epoch by an inward diminution of force? Had the twenty years of war worn out the blade as it had worn the scabbard, the soul as well as the

From: *Les Misérables.*

body? Did the veteran make himself disastrously felt in the leader? In a word, was this genius, as many historians of note have thought, eclipsed? Did he go into a frenzy in order to disguise his weakened powers from himself? Did he begin to waver under the delusion of a breath of adventure? Had he become—a grave matter in a general—unconscious of peril? Is there an age, in this class of material great men, who may be called the giants of action, when genius becomes short-sighted? Old age has no hold on ideal genius; for the Dantes and Michael Angelos to grow old is to grow in greatness; is it declension for the Hannibals and the Bonapartes? Had Napoleon lost the direct sense of victory? Had he reached the point where he could no longer recognize the rock, could no longer divine the snare, no longer discern the crumbling edge of the abyss? Had he lost his power of scenting out catastrophes? He who had in former days known all the roads to victory, and who, from the summit of his chariot of lightning, pointed them out with a sovereign finger, had he now reached that state of sinister amazement when he could lead his tumultuous legions harnessed to it, to the precipice? Was he seized at the age of forty-six with a supreme madness? Was that titanic charioteer of destiny now only a Phaëton?

We do not believe it.

His plan of battle was, by the confession of all, a masterpiece. To go straight to the centre of the Allies' lines, to make a breach in the enemy, to cut them in two, to drive the British half back on Halle, and the Prussian half on Tingres, to make two shattered fragments of Wellington and Blücher, to carry Mont-Saint-Jean, to seize Brussels, to hurl the German into the Rhine, and the Englishman into the sea. All this was contained in that battle, for Napoleon. Afterwards people would see.

Of course, we do not here pretend to furnish a history of the battle of Waterloo; one of the scenes of the foundation of the drama which we are relating is connected with this battle, but this history is not our subject; this history, moreover, has been finished, and finished in a masterly manner, from one point of view by Napoleon, from another by Charras.

For our part, we leave the historians to contend; we are but a distant witness, a passer-by along the plain, a seeker bending over that soil all made of human flesh, perhaps taking appearances for realities; we have no right to oppose, in the name of science, a collection of facts which contain illusions, no doubt; we possess neither military practice nor strategic ability which authorize a system; in our opinion, a chain of accidents dominated the two captains at Waterloo; and when it becomes a question of destiny, that mysterious culprit, we judge like the people.

Those who wish to gain a clear idea of the battle of Waterloo have only to place, mentally, on the ground, a capital A. The left leg of the A is the road to Nivelles, the right one is the road to Genappe, the tie of the A is the hollow road to Ohain from Braine-l'Alleud. The top of the A is Mont-Saint-Jean, where Wellington is; the lower left tip is Hougomont, where Reille is stationed with Jérôme Bonaparte; the right tip is the Belle-

Alliance, where Napoleon is. At the centre of this point is the precise point where the final word of the battle was pronounced. It was there that the lion has been placed, the involuntary symbol of the supreme heroism of the Imperial Guard.

The triangle comprised in the top of the A, between the two limbs and the tie, is the plateau of Mont-Saint-Jean. The dispute over this plateau was the whole battle. The wings of the two armies extended to the right and left of the two roads to Genappe and Nivelles; d'Erlon facing Picton, Reille facing Hill.

Behind the point of the A, behind the plateau of Mont-Saint-Jean, is the forest of Soignes.

As for the plain itself, imagine a vast undulating sweep of ground; each ascent commands the next rise, and all the undulations mount towards Mont-Saint-Jean, and there end in the forest.

Two hostile troops on a field of battle are two wrestlers. It is a question of seizing the opponent round the waist. The one tries to throw the other. They cling at everything; a bush is a point of support; an angle of the wall offers them a rest to the shoulder; for the lack of a hovel under whose cover they can draw up, a regiment yields its ground; an unevenness in the ground, a chance turn in the landscape, a cross-path encountered at the right moment, a grove, a ravine, can stay the heel of that colossus which is called an army, and prevent its retreat. He who leaves the field is beaten; hence the necessity devolving on the responsible leader of examining the smallest clump of trees and of studying deeply the slightest rise in the ground.

The two generals had attentively studied the plain of Mont-Saint-Jean, which is known as the plain of Waterloo. In the preceding year, Wellington, with the sagacity of foresight, had examined it as the future seat of a great battle. Upon this spot, and for this duel, on the 18th of June, Wellington had the good post, Napoleon the bad post. The English army was above, the French army below.

It is almost superfluous here to sketch the appearance of Napoleon on horseback, telescope in hand, upon the heights of Rossomme, at daybreak, on June 18, 1815. All the world has seen him before we can show him. The calm profile under the little three-cornered hat of the school of Brienne, the green uniform, the white facings concealing the star of the Legion of Honour, his great coat hiding his epaulets, the corner of red ribbon peeping from beneath his vest, his leather breeches, the white horse with the saddle-cloth of purple velvet bearing on the corners crowned N's and eagles, Hessian boots over silk stockings, silver spurs, the sword of Marengo,— that whole appearance of the last of the Cæsars is present to all imagination, saluted with acclamations by some, severely regarded by others.

That figure stood for a long time wholly in the light; this arose from a certain legendary dimness evolved by the majority of heroes, and which always veils the truth of a longer or shorter time; but to-day history and daylight have arrived.

That illumination called history is pitiless; it possesses this peculiar and divine quality, that, pure light as it is, and precisely because it is wholly light, it often casts a shadow in places that had been luminous; from the same man it constructs two different phantoms, and the one attacks the other and executes justice on it, and the shadows of the despot contend with the brilliancy of the leader. Hence arises a truer measure in the definitive judgments of nations. Babylon violated diminishes Alexander, Rome enchained diminishes Cæsar, Jerusalem murdered diminishes Titus. Tyranny follows the tyrant. It is a misfortune for a man to leave behind him the night which bears his form.

All the world knows the first phase of this battle; an opening which was troubled, uncertain, hesitating, menacing to both armies, but still more so for the English than for the French.

It had rained all night, the ground was saturated, the water had accumulated here and there in the hollows of the plain as if in tubs; at some points the gear of the artillery carriages was buried up to the axles, the circingles of the horses were dripping with liquid mud. If the wheat and rye trampled down by this cohort of transports on the march had not filled in the ruts and strewn a litter beneath the wheels, all movement, particularly in the valleys, in the direction of Papelotte would have been impossible.

The battle began late. Napoleon, as we have already explained, was in the habit of keeping all his artillery well in hand, like a pistol, aiming it now at one point, now at another, of the battle; and it had been his wish to wait until the horse batteries could move and gallop freely. In order to do that it was necessary that the sun should come out and dry the soil. But the sun did not make its appearance. It was no longer the rendezvous of Austerlitz. When the first cannon was fired, the English general, Colville, looked at his watch, and saw that it was twenty-five minutes to twelve.

The action was begun furiously, with more fury, perhaps, than the Emperor would have wished, by the left wing of the French resting on Hougomont. At the same time Napoleon attacked the centre by hurling Quiot's brigade on La Haie-Sainte, and Ney pushed forward the right wing of the French against the left wing of the English, which leaned on Papelotte.

The attack on Hougomont was something of a feint; the plan was to attract Wellington thither, and to make him swerve to the left. This plan would have succeeded if the four companies of the English Guards and the brave Belgians of Perponcher's division had not held the position firmly, and Wellington, instead of massing his troops there, could confine himself to despatching thither, as reinforcements, only four more companies of Guards and one battalion of Brunswickers.

The attack of the right wing of the French on Papelotte was calculated, in fact, to overthrow the English left, to cut off the road to Brussels, to bar the passage against possible Prussians, to force Mont-Saint-Jean, to turn Wellington back on Hougomont; thence on Braine-l'Alleud, thence on Halle; nothing easier. With the exception of a few incidents this attack succeeded. Papelotte was taken; La Haie-Sainte was carried.

A detail is to be noted. There were in the English infantry, particularly in Kempt's brigade, a great many young soldiers. These recruits were valiant in the presence of our redoubtable infantry; their inexperience extricated them intrepidly from the dilemma; they performed particularly excellent service as skirmishers: the soldier skirmisher, left somewhat to himself, becomes, so to speak, his own general. These recruits displayed some of the French ingenuity and fury. These novices had dash. This displeased Wellington.

After the taking of La Haie-Sainte the battle wavered.

There is in this day an obscure interval, from mid-day to four o'clock; the middle portion of this battle is almost indistinct, and participates in the sombreness of the hand-to-hand conflict. Twilight reigns over it. We perceive vast fluctuations in the midst, a dizzy mirage, paraphernalia of war almost unknown to-day, flaming colbacks, floating sabretaches, cross-belts, cartridge-boxes for grenades, hussar dolmans, red boots with a thousand wrinkles, heavy shakos garlanded with gold lace, the almost black infantry of Brunswick mingled with the scarlet infantry of England, the English soldiers with great, white circular pads on the slopes of their shoulders for epaulets, the Hanoverian light-horse with their oblong casques of leather, with brass hands and red horse-tails, the Highlanders with their bare knees and plaids, the great white gaiters of our grenadiers; pictures, not strategic lines—what a canvas for a Salvator Rosa requires, but Gribeauval would not have liked it.

A certain amount of tempest is always mingled with a battle. *Quid obscurum, quid divinum.* Each historian traces, to some extent, the particular feature which pleases him amid this pell-mell. Whatever may be the combinations of the generals, the shock of armed masses has an incalculable ebb and flow. During the action the plans of the two leaders enter into each other and become mutually thrown out of shape. Such a point of the field of battle devours more combatants than such another, just as more or less spongy soils soak up more or less quickly the water which is poured on them. It becomes necessary to pour out more soldiers than one would like; a series of expenditures which are the unforeseen. The line of battle floats and undulates like a thread, the trails of blood gush illogically, the fronts of the armies waver, the regiments form capes and gulfs as they enter and withdraw; all these reefs are continually moving in front of each other. Where the infantry stood the artillery arrives, the cavalry rushes in where the artillery was, the battalions are like smoke. There was something there; search for it. It has disappeared; the open spots change place, the sombre folds advance and retreat, a sort of wind from the sepulchre pushes forward, hurls back, distends, and disperses these tragic multitudes. What is a battle? an oscillation? The immobility of a mathematical plan expresses a minute, not a day. To depict a battle, there is required one of those powerful painters who have chaos in their brushes. Rembrandt is better than Vandermeulen; Vandermeulen, exact at noon, lies at three o'clock. Geometry is deceptive; the hurricane alone is true. That is what confers on Folard the right to contradict Polybius. Let us add, that there is a certain moment when the battle degenerates into a combat, becomes specialized, and disperses into innumerable detailed feats, which, to borrow the expression of Napoleon himself, "belong rather to the biography of the regiments than to the history of the army." The historian has, in this case, the evident right to sum up the whole. He cannot do more than catch the principal outlines of the struggle, and it is not given to any one narrator, however conscientious he may be, to fix, absolutely, the form of that horrible cloud which is called a battle.

This, which is true of all great armed encounters, is particularly applicable to Waterloo.

Nevertheless, at a certain moment in the afternoon the battle came to a decided point.

About four o'clock the condition of the English army was serious. The Prince of Orange was in command of the centre, Hill of the right wing, Picton of the left wing. The Prince of Orange, wild and intrepid, shouted to the Dutch Belgians: "Nassau! Brunswick! Don't yield an inch!" Hill, having been weakened, had come up to the support of Wellington; Picton was dead. At the very moment when the English had captured from the French the flag of the 105th of the line, the French had killed the English general, Picton, with a bullet through the head. The battle had, for Wellington, two bases of action, Hougomont and La Haie-Sainte; Hougomont still held out, but was on fire; La Haie-Sainte was taken. Of the German battalion which defended it, only forty-two men survived; all the officers, except five, were either dead or taken prisoners. Three thousand combatants had been massacred in that barn. A sergeant of the English Guards, the foremost boxer in England, reputed invulnerable by his companions, had been killed there by a little French drummer-boy. Barny had been dislodged. Alten sabred. Many flags had been lost, one from Alten's division, and one from the battalion of Lunenburg, carried by a prince of the house of Deux-Ponts. The Scots Greys no longer existed; Ponsonby's great dragoons had been cut to pieces. That valiant cavalry had bent beneath the lancers of Bro and beneath the cuirassiers of Travers; out of twelve hundred horses, six hundred remained; out of three lieutenant-colonels, two lay on the earth,—Hamilton wounded, Mater slain. Ponsonby had fallen, pierced by seven lance-thrusts. Gordon was dead. Marsh was dead. Two divisions, the fifth and the sixth, had been annihilated.

Hougomont attacked, La Haie-Sainte taken, there now existed but one rallying-point, the centre. That point still held firm. Wellington reinforced it. He summoned thither Hill, who was at Merle-Braine; he summoned Chassé, who was at Braine-l'Alleud.

The centre of the English army, rather concave, very dense, and very compact, was strongly posted. It occupied the plateau of Mont-Saint-Jean, having behind it the village, and in front of it the slope, which was tolerably steep then. It rested on that stout stone dwelling which at that time belonged to the domain of Nivelles, standing at the crossroads—a pile of the sixteenth century, and so robust that the cannonballs rebounded from it without injuring it. All about the plateau the English had cut the hedges here and there, formed embrasures in the hawthorn-trees, thrust the throat of a cannon between two branches, embattled the shrubs. There artillery was ambushed in the brushwood. This Punic task, incontestably authorized by war, which permits traps, was so well done, that Haxo, who had been despatched by the Emperor at nine o'clock in the morning to reconnoitre the enemy's batteries, had discovered nothing of it, and had returned and reported to Napoleon that there were no obstacles except the two barricades which barred the road to Nivelles and to Genappe. It was at the season when the grain is tall: on the edge of the plateau a battalion of Kempt's brigade, the 95th, armed with carbines, was concealed in the tall wheat.

Thus assured and buttressed, the centre of the Anglo-Dutch army was in a good position. The peril of this position lay in the forest of Soignes, then adjoining the field of battle, and intersected by the ponds of Groenendael and Boitsfort. An army could not retreat thither without dissolving; the regiments would have broken up immediately there. The artillery would have been lost among the marshes. The retreat, according to many a man versed in the art of war,—though it is disputed by others,—would have been a disorganized flight.

To this centre, Wellington added one of Chassé's brigades taken from the right wing, and one of Wincke's brigades taken from the left wing, plus Clinton's division. To his English, to the regiments of Halkett, to the brigades of Mitchell, to the guards of Maitland, he gave as reinforcements and aids, the infantry of Brunswick, Nassau's contingent, Kielmansegg's Hanoverians, and Ompteda's Germans. He had thus twenty-six battalions under his hand. The right wing, as Charras says, was thrown back on the centre. An enormous battery was masked by sacks of earth at the spot where there now stands what is called the "Museum of Waterloo." Besides this, Wellington had, behind a rise in the ground, Somerset's Dragoon Guards, fourteen hundred horse strong. It was the remaining half of the justly celebrated English cavalry. Ponsonby destroyed, Somerset remained.

The battery, which, if completed, would have been almost a redoubt, was ranged behind a very low wall, backed up with a coating of bags of sand and a wide slope of earth. This work was not finished; there had been no time to make a palisade for it.

Wellington, restless but impassive, was on horseback, and there remained the whole day in the same attitude, a little in front of the old mill of Mont-Saint-Jean, which is still in existence, beneath an elm, which an Englishman, an enthusiastic vandal, purchased later on for two hundred francs, cut down, and carried off. Wellington was coldly heroic. The bullets rained about him. His aide-de-camp, Gordon, fell at his side. Lord Hill, pointing to a shell which had burst, said to him: "My lord, what are your orders in case you are killed?" "Do as I am doing," replied Wellington. To Clinton he said laconically, "To hold this spot to the last man." The day was evidently turning out ill. Wellington shouted to his old companions of Talavera, of Vittoria, of Salamanca: "Boys, can retreat be thought of? Think of old England!"

About four o'clock, the English line drew back. Suddenly nothing was visible on the crest of the plateau except the artillery and the sharp-shooters; the rest had disappeared; the regiments, dislodged by the shells and the French bullets, retreated into the hollow, now intersected by the back road of the farm of Mont-Saint-Jean; a retrograde movement took place, the English front hid itself, Wellington recoiled. "The beginning of the retreat!" cried Napoleon.

The Emperor, though ill and discommoded on horseback by a local trouble, had never been so good tempered as on that day. His impenetrability had been smiling ever since the morning. On the 18th of June, that profound soul masked by marble was radiant. The man who had been gloomy at Austerlitz was gay at Waterloo. The greatest favourites of destiny make mistakes. Our joys are composed of shadow. The supreme smile is God's alone.

Ridet Cæsar, Pompeius flebit, said the legionaires of the Fulminatrix Legion. Pompey was not destined to weep on that occasion, but it is certain that Cæsar laughed. While exploring on horseback at one o'clock on the preceding night, in storm and rain, in company with Bertrand, the hills in the neighbourhood of Rossomme, satisfied at the sight of the long line of the English camp-fires illuminating the whole horizon from Frischemont to Braine-l'Alleud, it had seemed to him that fate, to whom he had assigned a day on the field of Waterloo, was exact to the appointment; he stopped his horse, and remained for some time motionless, gazing at the lightning and listening to the thunder; and this fatalist was heard to cast into the darkness this mysterious saying, "We are in accord." Napoleon was mistaken. They were no longer in accord.

He had not slept a moment; every instant of that night was marked by a joy for him. He rode through the line of the principal outposts, halting here and there to talk to the sentinels. At half-past two, near the wood of Hougomont, he heard the tread of a column on the march; he thought at the moment that it was a retreat on the part of Wellington. He said: "It is the rear-guard of the English getting under way for the purpose of decamping. I will take prisoners the six thousand English who have just landed at Ostend." He talked expansively; he regained the animation which he had shown at his landing on the 1st of March, when he pointed out to the Grand-Marshal the enthusiastic peasant of the Gulf Juan, and cried, "Well, Bertrand, here is a reinforcement already!" On the night of the 17th to the 18th of June he made fun of Wellington. "That little Englishman needs a lesson," said Napoleon. The rain redoubled in violence; it thundered while the Emperor was speaking.

At half-past three o'clock in the morning, he lost one illusion; officers who had been despatched to reconnoitre announced to him that the enemy was not making any movement. Nothing was stirring; not a bivouac-fire had been extinguished; the English army was asleep. The silence on earth was profound; the only noise was in the heavens. At four o'clock, a peasant was brought in to him by the scouts; this peasant had served as guide to a brigade of English cavalry, probably Vivian's brigade, which was on its way to take up a position in the village of Ohain, at the extreme left. At five o'clock, two Belgian deserters reported to him that they had just quitted their regiment, and that the English army meant to fight. "All the better!" exclaimed Napoleon. "I prefer to overthrow them rather than to drive them back."

At daybreak he dismounted in the mud on the slope which forms an angle with the Plancenoit road, had a kitchen table and a peasant's chair brought to him from the farm of Rossomme, seated himself, with a truss of straw for a carpet, and spread out on the table the chart of the battle-field, saying to Soult as he did so, "A pretty chess-board."

In consequence of the rains during the night, the transports of provisions, embedded in the soft roads, had not been able to arrive by morning; the soldiers had had no sleep; they were wet and famished. This did not prevent Napoleon from exclaiming cheerfully to Ney, "We have ninety chances out of a hundred." At eight o'clock the Emperor's breakfast was brought to him. He invited several generals to it. During breakfast, it was said that Wellington had been to a ball two nights before, in Brussels, at the Duchess of Richmond's; and Soult, a rough man of war, with the face of an archbishop said, "The ball will be to-day." The Emperor jested with Ney, who had said, "Wellington will not be so simple as to wait for Your Majesty." That was his way, however. "He was fond of a joke," says Fleury de Chaboulon. "A merry humour was at the foundation of his character," says Gourgaud. "He abounded in pleasantries, which were more peculiar than witty," says Benjamin Constant. These gaieties of a giant are worthy of comment. It was he who called his grenadiers "his growlers"; he pinched their ears; he pulled their moustaches. "The Emperor did nothing but play pranks on us," is the remark of one of them. During the mysterious trip from the island of Elba to France, on the 27th of February, on the open sea, the French brig of war, *Le Zéphyr*, having encountered the brig *L'Inconstant*, on which Napoleon was concealed, and having asked the news of Napoleon from *L'Inconstant*, the Emperor, who still wore in his hat the white and violet cockade sown with bees, which he had adopted at the isle of Elba, laughingly seized the speaking-trumpet, and answered for himself, "The Emperor is quite well." A man who laughs like that is on familiar terms with events. Napoleon indulged in many fits of this laughter during the breakfast at Waterloo. After breakfast he meditated for a quarter of an hour; then two generals seated themselves on the truss of straw, pen in hand and their paper on their knees, and the Emperor dictated to them the order of battle.

At nine o'clock, at the instant when the French army ranged in echelons and moving in five columns, had deployed—the divisions in two lines, the artillery between the brigades, the music at their head; as they beat the march, with rolls on the drums and the blasts of trumpets, mighty, vast, joyous, a sea of casques, of sabres, and of bayonets on the horizon, the Emperor was touched, and twice exclaimed, "Magnificent! Magnificent!"

Between nine o'clock and half-past ten the whole army, incredible as it may appear, had taken up its position and was drawn up in six lines, forming, to repeat the Emperor's expression, "the figure of six V's." A few moments after the formation of the line, in the midst of that profound silence, like that which heralds the beginning of a storm, which precedes battle, the Emperor tapped Haxo on the shoulder, as he beheld the three batteries of twelve-pounders, detached by his orders from the corps of Erlon, Reille, and Lobau, and destined to begin the action by taking Mont-Saint-Jean, which was situated at the intersection of the Nivelles and the Genappe roads, and said to him, "There are four and twenty pretty girls, General."

Sure of the result, he encouraged with a smile, as they passed before him, the company of sappers of the first corps, which he had appointed to barricade Mont-Saint-Jean as soon as the village should be carried. All this serenity had been traversed by but a single word of human pity; perceiving on his left, at a spot where there now stands a large tomb, those admirable Scots Greys, with their superb horses, massing themselves, he said, "It is a pity."

Then he mounted his horse, advanced beyond Rossomme, and selected for his coign of vantage a contracted elevation of turf to the right of the road from Genappe to Brussels, which was his second station during the battle. The third station, the one adopted at seven o'clock in the evening, between La Belle-Alliance and La Haie-Sainte, is formidable; it is a rather lofty mound, which still exists, and behind which the guard was massed in a hollow. Around this knoll the balls rebounded from the pavements of the road, up to Napoleon himself. As at Brienne, he had over his head the whistle of the bullets and canister. Mouldy cannon-balls, old sword-blades, and shapeless projectiles, eaten up with rust, have been picked up at the spot where his horse's feet stood. *Scabra rubigine.* A few years ago, a shell of sixty pounds, still charged, and with its fuse broken off level with the bomb, was unearthed. It was at this station that the Emperor said to his guide, Lacoste, a hostile and timid peasant, who was attached to the saddle of a hussar, and who turned round at every discharge of canister and tried to hide behind Napoleon: "You ass, it is shameful! You'll get yourself killed with a ball in the back." He who writes these lines has himself found, in the friable soil of this knoll, on turning over the sand, the remains of the neck of a bomb, rotted by the oxide of six and forty years, and old fragments of iron which parted like sticks of barley sugar between the fingers.

Every one is aware that the variously inclined undulations of the plains, where the encounter between Napoleon and Wellington took place, are no longer what they were on June 18, 1815. On taking from this mournful field the wherewithal to make a monument to it, its real relief has been taken away, and history, disconcerted, no longer finds her bearings there. It has been disfigured for the sake of glorifying it. Wellington, when he beheld Waterloo once more, two years later, exclaimed, "They have altered my field of battle!" Where the huge pyramid of earth, surmounted by the lion, rises to-day, there was a crest which descended in an easy slope towards the Nivelles road, but which was almost an escarpment on the side of the highway to Genappe. The elevation of this escarpment can still be imagined by the height of the two knolls of the two great sepulchres which enclose the road from Genappe to Brussels: one, the English tomb, is on the left; the other, the German tomb, is on the right. There is no French tomb. The whole of that plain is a sepulchre for France. Thanks to the thousands of cartloads of earth employed in erecting the mound one hundred and fifty feet in height and half a mile in circumference, the plateau of Mont-Saint-Jean is now accessible by an easy slope. On the day of battle, particularly on the side of La Haie-Sainte, it was abrupt and difficult of approach. The incline there is so steep that the English cannon could not see the farm, situated in the bottom of the valley, which was the centre of the combat. On the 18th of June, 1815, the rains had still further increased this acclivity, the mud complicated the problem of the ascent, and the men not only slipped back, but stuck fast in the mire. Along the crest of the plateau ran a sort of trench whose presence it was impossible for the distant observer to guess.

What was this trench? Let us explain. Braine-l'Alleud is a Belgian village; Ohain is another. These villages, both of them hidden in hollows of the landscape, are connected by a road about a league and a half in length, which traverses the plain along its undulating level, and often enters and buries itself in the hills like a furrow, which makes a ravine of this road in certain parts. In 1815, as to-day, this road cut the crest of the plateau of Mont-Saint-Jean between the two highways from Genappe and Nivelles; only, it is now on a level with the plain; it was then a hollow way. Its two slopes have been appropriated for the monumental mound. This road was, and still is, a trench for the greater portion of its course; a hollow trench, sometimes a dozen feet in depth, and whose banks, being too steep, crumbled away here and there, particularly in winter, under driving rains. Accidents happened here. The road was so narrow at the Braine-l'Alleud entrance that a passer-by was crushed by a cart, as is proved by a stone cross which stands near the cemetery, and which gives the name of the dead, *Monsieur Bernard Debrye, Merchant of Brussels*, and the date of the accident, *February,* 1637. It was so deep on the plateau of Mont-Saint-Jean that a peasant, Mathieu Nicaise, was crushed there, in 1783, by a slide from the slope, as is stated on another stone cross, the top of which has disappeared in the excavations, but whose overturned pedestal is still visible on the grassy slope to the left of the highway between La Haie-Sainte and the farm of Mont-Saint-Jean.

On the day of battle, this hollow road whose existence was in no way indicated, bordering the crest of Mont-Saint-Jean, a trench at the top of the escarpment, a rut concealed in the soil, was invisible; that is to say, terrible.

On the morning of Waterloo, then, Napoleon was content.

He was right; the plan of battle drawn up by him was, as we have seen, really admirable.

The battle once begun, its various incidents,—the resistance of Hougomont; the tenacity of La Haie-Sainte; the killing of Dauduin; the disabling of Foy; the unexpected wall against which Soye's brigade was broken; Guilleminot's fatal heedlessness when he had neither petard nor powder sacks; the sticking of the batteries in the mud; the fifteen unescorted pieces overwhelmed in a hollow way by Uxbridge; the small effect of the shells falling in the English lines, and there embedding themselves in the rain soaked soil, and only succeeding in producing volcanoes of mud, so that the canister was turned into a splash; the inutility of Piré's demonstration on Braine-l'Alleud; all that cavalry, fifteen squadrons almost annihilated; the right wing of the English badly alarmed, the left wing poorly attacked; Ney's strange mistake in massing, instead of echelonning the four divisions of the first corps; men delivered over to grape-shot, arranged in ranks twenty-seven deep and with a frontage of two hundred; the terrible gaps made in these masses by the cannon-balls; attacking columns disorganized; the side-battery suddenly unmasked on their flank; Bourgeois, Donzelot, and Durutte compromised; Quiot repulsed; Lieutenant Vieux, that Hercules graduated at the Polytechnic School, wounded at the moment when he was beating in with an axe the door of La Haie-Sainte under the downright fire of the English barricade which barred the angle on the Genappe road; Marcognet's division caught between the infantry and the cavalry, shot down at the very muzzle of the guns amid the grain by Best and Pack, put to the sword by Ponsonby; his battery of seven pieces spiked; the Prince of Saxe-Weimar holding and guarding, in spite of the Comte d'Erlon, both Frischemont and Smohain; the flags of the 105th taken, the flags of the 45th captured; that black Prussian hussar stopped by the flying column of three hundred light cavalry on the scout between Wavre and Plancenoit; the alarming things that had been said by prisoners; Grouchy's delay; fifteen hundred men killed in the orchard of Hougomont in less than an hour; eighteen hundred men overthrown in a still shorter time about La Haie-Sainte,—all these stormy incidents passing like the clouds of battle before Napoleon, had hardly troubled his gaze and had not overshadowed his imperial face. Napoleon was accustomed to gaze steadily at war; he never added up the poignant details. He cared little for figures, provided that they furnished the total, victory; he was not alarmed if the beginnings did go astray, since he thought himself the master and the possessor at the end; he knew how to wait, supposing himself to be out of the question, and he treated destiny as his equal: he seemed to say to fate, You would not dare.

Composed half of light and half of shadow, Napoleon felt himself protected in good and tolerated in evil. He had, or thought that he had, a connivance, one might almost say a complicity, of events in his favour, which was equivalent to the invulnerability of antiquity.

Nevertheless, when one has Bérésina, Leipzig, and Fontainebleau behind one, it seems as though one might defy Waterloo. A mysterious frown becomes perceptible on the face of the heavens.

At the moment when Wellington retreated, Napoleon quivered. He suddenly beheld the plateau of Mont-Saint-Jean deserted, and the van of the English army disappear. It was rallying, but hiding itself. The Emperor half rose in his stirrups. Victory flashed from his eyes.

Wellington, driven into a corner at the forest of Soignes and destroyed—that was the definite conquest of England by France; it would be Crécy, Poitiers, Malplaquet, and Ramillies avenged. The man of Marengo was wiping out Agincourt.

So the Emperor, meditating on this terrible turn of fortune, swept his glass for the last time over all the points of the field of battle. His guard, standing behind him with grounded arms, watched him from below with a sort of religious awe. He pondered; he examined the slopes, noted the declivities, scrutinized the clumps of trees, the patches of rye, the path; he seemed to be counting each bush. He gazed with some intentness at the English barricades of the two highways,—two large masses of felled trees, the one on the road to Genappe above La Haie-Sainte, defended with two cannon, the only ones out of all the English artillery which commanded the extremity of the field of battle, and that on the road to Nivelles where gleamed the Dutch bayonets of Chassé's brigade. Near this barricade he observed the old chapel of Saint Nicholas, which stands at the angle of the cross-road near Braine-l'Alleud; he bent down and spoke in a low voice to the guide Lacoste. The guide made a negative sign with his head, which was probably perfidious.

The Emperor straightened himself up and reflected.

Wellington had withdrawn.

All that remained to do was to complete this retreat by crushing him.

Napoleon turning round abruptly, despatched an express at full speed to Paris to announce that the battle was won.

Napoleon was one of those geniuses from whom thunder issues.

He had just found his thunder-stroke.

He gave orders to Milhaud's cuirassiers to carry the plateau of Mont-Saint-Jean.

There were three thousand five hundred of them. They formed a front a quarter of a league in length. They were giants, on colossal horses. There were six and twenty squadrons of them; and they had behind them to support them Lefebvre-Desnouettes's division,—the one hundred and six picked gendarmes, the light cavalry of the Guard, eleven hundred and ninety-seven men, and the lancers of the guard of eight hundred and eighty lances. They wore casques without plumes, and cuirasses of beaten iron, with horse-pistols in their holsters, and long sabre-swords. That morning the whole army had admired them, when, at nine o'clock, with blare of trumpets and all the music playing "Let us watch o'er the Safety of the Empire," they had come in a solid column, with one of their batteries on their flank, another in their centre, and deployed in two ranks between the roads to Genappe and Frischemont, and taken up their position for battle in that powerful second line, so cleverly arranged by Napoleon, which, having on its extreme left Kellermann's cuirassiers and on its extreme right Milhaud's cuirassiers, had, so to speak, two wings of iron.

The aide-de-camp Bernard carried them the Emperor's orders. Ney drew his sword and placed himself at their head. The enormous squadrons were set in motion.

Then a formidable spectacle was seen.

The whole of the cavalry, with upraised swords, standards and trumpets flung to the breeze, formed in columns by divisions, descended, by a simultaneous movement and like one man, with the precision of a brazen battering-ram which is affecting a breach, the hill of La Belle-Alliance. They plunged into the terrible depths in which so many men had already fallen, disappeared there in the smoke, then emerging from that shadow, reappeared on the other side of the valley, still compact and in close ranks, mounting at a full trot, through a storm of grape-shot which burst upon them, the terrible muddy slope of the plateau of Mont-Saint-Jean. They ascended, grave, threatening, imperturbable; in the intervals between the musketry and the artillery, their colossal trampling was audible. Being two divisions, there were two columns of them; Wathier's division held the right, Delort's division was on the left. It seemed as though two immense steel lizards were to be seen crawling towards the crest of the plateau. They traversed the battle like a flash.

Nothing like it had been seen since the taking of the great redoubt of the Moskowa by the heavy cavalry; Murat was missing, but Ney was again present. It seemed as though that mass had become a monster and had but one soul. Each column undulated and swelled like the rings of a polyp. They could be seen through a vast cloud of smoke which was rent at intervals. A confusion of helmets, of cries, of sabres, a stormy heaving of horses amid the cannons and the flourish of trumpets, a terrible and disciplined tumult; over all, the cuirasses like the scales on the dragon.

These narrations seemed to belong to another age. Something parallel to this vision appeared, no doubt, in the ancient Orphic epics, which told of the centaurs, the old hippanthropes, those Titans with human heads and equestrian chests who scaled Olympus at a gallop, horrible, invulnerable, sublime—gods and brutes.

It was a curious numerical coincidence that twenty-six battalions rode to meet twenty-six battalions. Behind the crest of the plateau, in the shadow of the masked battery, the English infantry, formed into thirteen squares, two battalions to the square, in two lines, with seven in the first line, six in the second, the stocks of their guns to their shoulders, taking aim at that which was on the point of appearing, waited, calm, mute, motionless. They did not see the cuirassiers, and the cuirassiers did not see them. They listened to the rise of this tide of men. They heard the swelling sound of three thousand horse, the alternate and symmetrical tramp of their hoofs at full trot, the jingling of the cuirasses, the clang of the sabres, and a sort of grand and formidable breathing. There was a long and terrible silence; then, all at once, a long file of uplifted arms, brandishing sabres, appeared above the crest, and casques, trumpets, and standards, and three thousand heads with grey moustaches, shouting, "Vive l'Empereur!" All this cavalry debouched on the plateau, and it was like the beginning of an earth-quake.

All at once, a tragic incident happened; on the English left, on our right, the head of the column of cuirassiers reared up with a frightful clamour. On arriving at the culminating point of the crest, ungovernable, utterly given over to fury and their course of extermination of the squares and cannon, the cuirassiers had just caught sight of a trench or grave,—a trench between them and the English. It was the sunken road of Ohain.

It was a frightful moment. The ravine was there, unexpected, yawning, directly under the horses' feet, two fathoms deep between its double slopes; the second file pushed the first into it, and the third pushed on the second; the horses reared and fell backward, landed on their haunches, slid down, all four feet in the air, crushing and overwhelming the riders; and there being no means of retreat,—the whole column being no longer anything more than a projectile,—the force which had been acquiring to crush the English crushed the French; the inexorable ravine could only yield when filled; horses and riders rolled there pell-mell, grinding each other, forming but one mass of flesh in this gulf: when this trench was full of living men, the rest marched over them and passed on. Nearly a third of Dubois's brigade fell into that abyss.

This began the loss of the battle.

A local tradition, which evidently exaggerates matters, says that two thousand horses and fifteen hundred men were buried in the sunken road of Ohain. This figure probably comprises all the other corpses which were flung into this ravine the day after the combat.

Let us note in passing that it was Dubois's sorely tried brigade which, an hour previously, making a charge to one side, had captured the flag of the Lunenburg battalion.

Napoleon, before giving the order for this charge of Milhaud's cuiras-siers, had scrutinized the ground, but had not been able to see that hollow road, which did not even form a wrinkle on the crest of the plateau. Warned, nevertheless, and put on his guard by the little white chapel which marks its angle of juncture with the Nivelles highway, he had put a question as to the possibility of an obstacle, to the guide Lacoste. The guide had answered No. We might almost say that Napoleon's catastrophe originated in the shake of a peasant's head.

Other fatalities were yet to arise.

Was it possible for Napoleon to win that battle? We answer No. Why? Because of Wellington? Because of Blücher? No. Because of God.

Bonaparte victor at Waterloo does not harmonise with the law of the nineteenth century. Another series of facts was in preparation, in which there was no longer any room for Napoleon. The ill will of events had declared itself long before.

It was time that this vast man should fall.

The excessive weight of this man in human destiny disturbed the balance. This individual alone counted for more than the universal group. These plethoras of all human vitality concentrated in a single head; the world mounting to the brain of one man,—this would be mortal to civilization were it to last. The moment had arrived for the incorruptible and supreme equity to alter its plan. Probably the principles and the elements, on which the regular gravitations of the moral, as of the material, world depend, had complained. Smoking blood, overcrowded cemeteries, mothers in tears,— these are formidable pleaders. When the earth is suffering from too heavy a burden, there are mysterious groanings of the shades, to which the abyss lends an ear.

Napoleon had been denounced in the infinite, and his fall had been decided on. He embarrassed God.

Waterloo is not a battle; it is a transformation on the part of the Universe.

The battery was unmasked simultaneously with the ravine.

Sixty cannons and the thirteen squares darted lightning point-blank on the cuirassiers. The intrepid General Delort made the military salute to the English battery.

The whole of the flying artillery of the English had re-entered the squares at a gallop. The cuirassiers had not had even the time for reflection. The disaster of the hollow road had decimated, but not discouraged them. They belonged to that class of men who, when diminished in number, increase in courage.

Wathier's column alone had suffered in the disaster; Delort's column, which had been deflected to the left, as though he had a presentiment of an ambush, had arrived whole.

The cuirassiers hurled themselves on the English squares.

At full speed, with bridles loose, swords in their teeth, pistols in their hand,—such was the attack.

There are moments in battles in which the soul hardens the man until the soldier is changed into a statue, and when all flesh becomes granite. The English battalions, desperately assaulted, did not stir.

Then it was terrible.

All the faces of the English squares were attacked at once. A frenzied whirl enveloped them. That cold infantry remained impassive. The first rank knelt and received the cuirassiers on their bayonets, the second rank shot them down; behind the second rank the cannoneers charged their guns, the front of the square parted, permitted the passage of an eruption of grape-shot, and closed again. The cuirassiers replied by crushing them. Their great horses reared, strode across the ranks, leaped over the bayonets and fell, gigantic, in the midst of these four living walls. The cannon-balls ploughed furrows in these cuirassiers; the cuirassiers made breaches in the squares. Files of men disappeared, ground to dust under the horses. The bayonets plunged into the bellies of these centaurs; hence a hideousness of wounds which has probably never been seen anywhere else. The squares, wasted by this mad cavalry, closed up their ranks without flinching. Inexhaustible in the matter of grape-shot, they created explosions in their assailants' midst. The form of this combat was monstrous. These squares were no longer battalions, they were craters; those cuirassiers were no longer cavalry, they were a tempest. Each square was a volcano attacked by a cloud; lava combated with lightning.

The extreme right square, the most exposed of all, being in the air, was almost annihilated at the very first attack. It was formed of the 75th regiment of Highlanders. The piper in the centre dropped his melancholy eyes, filled with the reflections of the forests and the lakes in profound inattention, while men were being exterminated around him, and seated on a drum, with his pibroch under his arm, played the Highland airs. These Scotchmen died thinking of Ben Lothian, as did the Greeks remembering Argos. The sword of a cuirassier, which hewed down the bagpipes and the arm which bore it, put an end to the song by killing the singer.

The cuirassiers, relatively few in number, and still further diminished by the catastrophe of the ravine, had almost the whole English army against them, but they multiplied themselves so that each man of them was equal to ten. Nevertheless, some Hanoverian battalions yielded. Wellington saw it, and thought of his cavalry. Had Napoleon at that same moment thought of his infantry, he would have won the battle. This forgetfulness was his great and fatal mistake.

All at once, the cuirassiers, who had been the assailants, found themselves assailed. The English cavalry was at their back. Before them two squares, behind them Somerset; Somerset meant fourteen hundred dragoons of the guard. On the right, Somerset had Dornberg with the German light-horse, and on his left, Trip with the Belgian carbineers; the cuirassiers attacked on the flank and in front, before and in the rear, by infantry and cavalry, had to face all sides. What did they care? They were a whirlwind. Their valour was indescribable.

In addition to this, they had behind them the battery, which was still thundering. It was necessary that it should be so, or they could never have been wounded in the back. One of their cuirasses, pierced on the shoulder by a ball, is in the Waterloo Museum.

For such Frenchmen nothing less than such Englishmen was needed.

It was no longer a hand-to-hand *mêlée;* it was a shadow, a fury, a dizzy transport of souls and courage, a hurricane of lightning swords. In an instant the fourteen hundred dragoon guards numbered only eight hundred. Fuller, their lieutenant-colonel, fell dead. Ney rushed up with the lancers and Lefebvre-Desnouettes's light-horse. The plateau of Mont-Saint-Jean was captured, recaptured, captured again. The cuirassiers left the cavalry to return to the infantry; or, to put it more exactly, the whole of that formidable rout collared each other without releasing the other. The squares still held firm after a dozen assaults. Ney had four horses killed under him. Half the cuirassiers remained on the plateau. This struggle lasted two hours.

The English army was profoundly shaken. There is no doubt that, had they not been enfeebled in their first shock by the disaster of the hollow road, the cuirassiers would have overwhelmed the centre and decided the victory. This extraordinary cavalry petrified Clinton, who had seen Talavera and Badajoz. Wellington, three-quarters vanquished, admired heroically. He said in an undertone, "Splendid!"

The cuirassiers annihilated seven squares out of thirteen, took or spiked sixty guns, and captured from the English regiments six flags, which three cuirassiers and three chasseurs of the Guard bore to the Emperor in front of the farm of La Belle-Alliance.

Wellington's situation had grown worse. This strange battle was like a duel between two savage, wounded men, each of whom, still fighting and still resisting, is expending all his blood.

Which will be the first to fall?

The conflict on the plateau continued.

What had become of the cuirassiers? No one could have told. One thing is certain, that on the day after the battle, a cuirassier and his horse were found dead among the woodwork of the scales for vehicles at Mont-Saint-Jean, at the very point where the four roads from Nivelles, Genappe, La Hulpe, and Brussels meet and intersect each other. This horseman had pierced the English lines. One of the men who picked up the body still lives at Mont-Saint-Jean. His name is Dehaye. He was eighteen years old at that time.

Wellington felt that he was yielding. The crisis was at hand.

The cuirassiers had not succeeded, since the centre was not broken through. As every one was in possession of the plateau, no one held it, and in fact it remained, to a great extent, in the hands of the English. Wellington held the village and the plain; Ney had only the crest and the slope. They seemed rooted in that fatal soil on both sides.

But the weakening of the English seemed irremediable. The hæmorrhage of that army was horrible. Kempt, on the left wing, demanded reinforcements. "There are none," replied Wellington. Almost at that same moment, a singular coincidence which depicts the exhaustion of the two armies, Ney demanded infantry from Napoleon, and Napoleon exclaimed, "Infantry! Where does he expect me to get it? Does he think I can make it?"

Nevertheless, the English army was in the worse plight of the two. The furious onsets of those great squadrons with cuirasses of iron and breasts of steel had crushed the infantry. A few men clustered round a flag marked the post of a regiment; some battalions were commanded only by a captain or a lieutenant; Alten's division, already so roughly handled at La Haie-Sainte, was almost destroyed; the intrepid Belgians of Van Kluze's brigade strewed the rye-fields all along the Nivelles road; hardly anything was left of those Dutch grenadiers, who, intermingled with Spaniards in our ranks in 1811, fought against Wellington; and who, in 1815, rallied to the English standard, fought against Napoleon. The loss in officers was considerable. Lord Uxbridge, who had his leg buried on the following day, had a fractured knee. If, on the French side, in that tussle of the cuirassiers, Delort, l'Héritier, Colbert, Dnop, Travers, and Blancard were disabled, on the side of the English there was Alten wounded, Barne wounded, Delancey killed, Van Meeren killed, Ompteda killed, the whole of Wellington's staff decimated, and England had the heaviest loss of it in that balance of blood. The second regiment of foot-guards had lost five lieutenant-colonels, four captains, and three ensigns; the first battalion of the 30th infantry had lost 24 officers and 1200 soldiers; the 79th Highlanders had lost 24 officers wounded, 18 officers killed, 450 soldiers killed. Cumberland's Hanoverian hussars, a whole regiment, with Colonel Hacke at its head, who was destined to be tried later on and cashiered, had turned bridle in the presence of the fray, and had fled to the forest of Soignes, spreading the rout as far as Brussels. The transports, ammunition-wagons, the baggage-wagons, the wagons filled with wounded, on seeing that the French were gaining ground and approaching the forest, rushed into it. The Dutch, mowed down by the French cavalry, cried, "Alarm!" From Vert-Coucou to Groentendael, a distance of nearly two leagues in the direction of Brussels, according to the testimony of eye-witnesses who are still alive, the roads were dense with fugitives. This panic was such that it attacked the Prince de Condé at Mechlin, and Louis XVIII at Ghent. With the exception of the feeble reserve echelonned behind the ambulance established at the farm of Mont-Saint-Jean, and of Vivian's and Vandeleur's brigades, which flanked the left wing, Wellington had no cavalry left. A number of batteries lay dismounted. These facts are attested by Siborne; and Pringle, exaggerating the disaster, goes so far as to say that the Anglo-Dutch army was reduced to thirty-four thousand men. The Iron Duke remained calm, but his lips blanched. Vincent, the Austrian commissioner, Alava, the Spanish commissioner, who were present at the battle in the English staff, thought the Duke lost. At five o'clock Wellington drew out his watch, and he was heard to murmur these sinister words, "Blücher, or night!"

It was about that moment that a distant line of bayonets gleamed on the heights in the direction of Frischemont.

This was the culminating point in this stupendous drama.

The awful mistake of Napoleon is well known. Grouchy expected, Blücher arriving. Death instead of life.

Fate has these turns; the throne of the world was expected; it was Saint Helena that was seen.

If the little shepherd who served as guide to Bülow, Blücher's lieutenant, had advised him to debouch from the forest above Frischemont, instead of below Plancenoit, the form of the nineteenth century might, perhaps, have been different. Napoleon would have won the battle of Waterloo. By any other route than that below Plancenoit, the Prussian army would have come out upon a ravine impassable for artillery, and Bülow would not have arrived.

Now the Prussian general, Muffling, declares that one hour's delay, and Blücher would not have found Wellington on his feet. "The battle was lost."

It was time that Bülow should arrive, as we shall see. He had, moreover, been very much delayed. He had bivouacked at Dieu-le-Mont, and had set out at daybreak; but the roads were impassable, and his divisions stuck fast in the mud. The ruts were up to the axles of the cannons. Moreover, he had been obliged to pass the Dyle on the narrow bridge of Wavre; the street leading to the bridge had been fired by the French, so the caissons and ammunition-wagons could not pass between two rows of burning houses, and had been obliged to wait until the conflagration was extinguished. It was mid-day before Bülow's vanguard had been able to reach Chapelle-Saint-Lambert.

Had the action begun two hours earlier, it would have been over at four o'clock, and Blücher would have fallen on the battle won by Napoleon. Such are these immense risks proportioned to an infinite which we cannot comprehend.

The Emperor had been the first, as early as mid-day, to descry with his field-glass, on the extreme horizon, something which had attracted his attention. He had said, "I see over there a cloud, which seems to me to be troops." Then he asked the Duc de Dalmatie, "Soult, what do you see in the direction of Chapelle-Saint-Lambert?" The marshal, looking through his glass, answered, "Four or five thousand men, Sire." It was evidently Grouchy. But it remained motionless in the mist. All the glasses of the staff had studied "the cloud" pointed out by the Emperor. Some said: "They are columns halting." The truth is, that the cloud did not move. The Emperor detached Domon's division of light cavalry to reconnoitre in that direction.

Bülow had not moved in fact. His vanguard was very feeble, and could accomplish nothing. He was obliged to wait for the main body of the army corps, and he had received orders to concentrate his forces, before entering into line; but at five o'clock, perceiving Wellington's peril, Blücher ordered Bülow to attack, and uttered these remarkable words: "We must let the English army breathe."

A little later, the divisions of Losthin, Hiller, Hacke, and Ryssel deployed before Lobau's corps, the cavalry of Prince William of Russia debouched from the Bois de Paris, Plancenoit was in flames, and the Prussian cannon-balls began to rain even upon the ranks of the guard in reserve behind Napoleon.

The rest is known,—the irruption of a third army; the battle broken to pieces; eighty-six cannon thundering simultaneously; Pirch the first coming up with Bülow; Zieten's cavalry led by Blücher in person, the French driven back; Marcognet swept from the plateau of Ohain; Durutte dislodged from Papelotte; Donzelot and Quiot retreating; Lóbau attacked on the flank; a fresh battle precipitating itself on our dismantled regiments at nightfall; the whole English line resuming the offensive and thrust forward; the gigantic breach made in the French army; the English grape-shot and the Prussian grape-shot aiding each other; the extermination; disaster in front; disaster on the flank; the Guard entering the line in the midst of this terrible crumbling of all things.

Conscious that they were about to die, they shouted, "Long live the Emperor!" History records nothing more touching than that death rattle bursting forth in acclamations.

The sky had been overcast all day. All of a sudden, at that very moment, —it was eight o'clock in the evening,—the clouds on the horizon parted, and allowed the sinister red glow of the setting sun to pass through, athwart the elms on the Nivelles road. They had seen it rise at Austerlitz.

Each battalion of the Guard was commanded by a general for this final *dénouement*. Friant, Michel, Roguet, Harlet, Mallet, Poret de Morvan, were there. When the tall bearskins of the grenadiers of the Guard, with their large plaques bearing the eagle, appeared, symmetrical, in line, tranquil, in the midst of that combat, the enemy felt a respect for France; they thought they beheld twenty victories entering the field of battle, with wings outspread, and those who were the conquerors, believing themselves to be vanquished, retreated; but Wellington shouted, "Up, Guards, and at them!" The red regiment of English Guards, lying flat behind the hedges, sprang up, a cloud of grape-shot riddled the tricoloured flag and whistled round our eagles; all hurled themselves forwards, and the supreme carnage began. In the darkness, the Imperial Guard felt the army losing ground around it, and in the vast shock of the rout it heard the desperate flight which had taken the place of the "Long live the Emperor!" and, with flight behind it, it continued to advance, more crushed, losing more men at every step it took. There were none who hesitated, no timid men in its ranks. The soldier in that troop was as much of a hero as the general. Not a man was missing in that heroic suicide.

Ney, bewildered, great with all the grandeur of accepted death, offered himself to all blows in that tempest. He had his fifth horse killed under him there. Perspiring, his eyes aflame, foam on his lips, with uniform unbuttoned, one of his epaulets half cut off by a sword-stroke from the horse-guard, his plaque with the great eagle dented by a bullet; bleeding, bemired, magnificent, a broken sword in his hand, he said, "Come and see how a Marshal of France dies on the field of battle!" But in vain; he did not die. He was haggard and angry. At Drouet d'Erlon he hurled this question, "Are you not going to get yourself killed?" In the midst of all that artillery engaged in crushing a handful of men, he shouted: "So there is nothing for me! Oh! I should like to have all these English bullets enter my chest!" Unhappy man, thou wert reserved for French bullets!

The rout in the rear of the Guard was melancholy.

The army yielded suddenly on all sides simultaneously.—Hougomont, La Haie-Sainte, Papelotte, Plancenoit. The cry, "Treachery!" was followed by a cry of "Save yourselves who can!" An army which is disbanding is like a thaw. All yields, splits, cracks, floats, rolls, falls, collides, is precipitated. The disintegration is unprecedented. Ney borrows a horse, leaps upon it, and without hat, cravat, or sword, dashes across the Brussels road, stopping both English and French. He strives to detain the army, he recalls it to its duty, he insults it, he clings to the route. He is overwhelmed. The soldiers fly from him, shouting, "Long live Marshal Ney!" Two of Durutte's regiments go and come in affright as though tossed back and forth between the swords of the Uhlans and the fusillade of the brigades of Kempt, Best, Pack, and Ryland; the worst of hand-to-hand conflicts is the defeat; friends kill each other in order to escape; squadrons and battalions break and disperse against each other, like the tremendous foam of battle. Lobau at one extremity, and Reille at the other, are drawn into the tide. In vain does Napoleon erect walls from what is left to him of his Guard; in vain does he expend in a last effort his last serviceable squadrons. Quiot retreats before Vivian, Kellermann before Vandeleur, Lobau before Bülow, Morand before Pirch, Domon and Subervic before Prince William of Prussia; Guyot, who led the Emperor's squadrons to the charge, falls beneath the feet of the English dragoons. Napoleon gallops past the line of fugitives, harangues, urges, threatens, entreats them. All the mouths which in the morning had shouted, "Long live the Emperor!" remain gaping; they hardly recognize him. The Prussian cavalry, newly arrived, dashes forwards, flies, hews, slashes, kills, exterminates. Horses lash out, the cannons flee; the soldiers of the artillery-train unharness the caissons and use the horses to make their escape; wagons overturned, with all four wheels in the air, block the road and occasion massacres. Men are crushed, trampled down, others walk over the dead and the living. Arms are lost. A dizzy multitude fills the roads, the paths, the bridges, the plains, the hills, the valleys, the woods, encumbered by this invasion of forty thousand men. Shouts, despair, knapsacks and guns flung among the wheat, passages forced at the point of the sword, no more comrades, no more officers, no more generals, an indescribable terror. Zieten putting France to the sword at his leisure. Lions converted into goats. Such was the flight.

At Genappe, an effort was made to wheel about, to present a battle front, to draw up in line. Lobau rallied three hundred men. The entrance to the village was barricaded, but at the first volley of Prussian canister, all took to flight again, and Lobau was made prisoner. That volley of grape-shot can be seen to-day imprinted on the ancient gable of a brick building on the right of the road at a few minutes' distance before you reach Genappe.

The Prussians threw themselves into Genappe, furious, no doubt, that they were not more entirely the conquerors. The pursuit was stupendous. Blücher ordered extermination. Roguet had set the lugubrious example of threatening with death any French grenadier who should bring him a Prussian prisoner. Blücher surpassed Roguet. Duchesme, the general of the Young Guard, hemmed in at the doorway of an inn at Genappe, surrendered his sword to a huzzar of death, who took the sword and slew the prisoner. The victory was completed by the assassination of the vanquished. Let us inflict punishment, since we are writing history; old Blücher disgraced himself. This ferocity put the finishing touch to the disaster. The desperate rout traversed Genappe, traversed Quatre-Bras, traversed Gosselies, traversed Frasnes, traversed Charleroi, traversed Thuin, and only halted at the frontier. Alas! and who, then, was fleeing in that manner? The Grand Army.

This vertigo, this terror, this downfall into ruin of the highest bravery which ever astounded history,—is that causeless? No. The shadow of an enormous right is projected across Waterloo. It is the day of destiny. The force which is mightier than man produced that day. Hence the terrified wrinkle of those brows; hence all those great souls surrendering their swords. Those who had conquered Europe have fallen prone on the earth, with nothing left to say nor to do, feeling the present shadow of a terrible presence. *Hoc erat in fatis.* That day the perspective of the human race was changed. Waterloo is the hinge of the nineteenth century. The disappearance of the great man was necessary for the advent of the great age, and he, who cannot be answered, took the responsibility on himself. The panic of heroes can be explained. In the battle of Waterloo there is something more than a cloud, there is something of the meteor.

At nightfall, in a meadow near Genappe, Bernard and Bertrand seized by the skirt of his coat and detained a man, haggard, pensive, sinister, gloomy, who, dragged to that point by the current of the rout, had just dismounted, had passed the bridle of his horse over his arm, and with wild eye was returning alone to Waterloo. It was Napoleon, the immense somnambulist of this dream which had crumbled, trying once more to advance.

The Retreat from Caporetto

BY

ERNEST HEMINGWAY

AT NOON we were stuck in a muddy road about, as nearly as we could figure, ten kilometres from Udine. The rain had stopped during the forenoon and three times we had heard planes coming, seen them pass overhead, watched them go far to the left and heard them bombing on the main highroad. We had worked through a network of secondary roads and had taken many roads that were blind, but had always, by backing up and finding another road, gotten closer to Udine. Now, Aymo's car, in backing so that we might get out of a blind road, had gotten into the soft earth at the side and the wheels, spinning, had dug deeper and deeper until the car rested on its differential. The thing to do now was to dig out in front of the wheels, put in brush so that the chains could grip, and then push until the car was on the road. We were all down on the road around the car. The two sergeants looked at the car and examined the wheels. Then they started off down the road without a word. I went after them.

"Come on," I said. "Cut some brush."

"We have to go," one said.

"Get busy," I said, "and cut brush."

"We have to go," one said. The other said nothing. They were in a hurry to start. They would not look at me.

"I order you to come back to the car and cut brush," I said. The one sergeant turned. "We have to go on. In a little while you will be cut off. You can't order us. You're not our officer."

"I order you to cut brush," I said. They turned and started down the road.

"Halt," I said. They kept on down the muddy road, the hedge on either side. "I order you to halt," I called. They went a little faster. I opened up my holster, took the pistol, aimed at the one who had talked the most, and fired. I missed and they both started to run. I shot three times and dropped one. The other went through the hedge and was out of sight. I fired at him through the hedge as he ran across the field. The pistol clicked empty and I put in another clip. I saw it was too far to shoot at the second sergeant. He was far across the field, running, his head held low. I commenced to reload the empty clip. Bonello came up.

"Let me go finish him," he said. I handed him the pistol and he walked down to where the sergeant of engineers lay face down across the road.

From: *A Farewell To Arms*: Copyright 1929. Scribners.

Bonello leaned over, put the pistol against the man's head and pulled the trigger. The pistol did not fire.

"You have to cock it," I said. He cocked it and fired twice. He took hold of the sergeant's legs and pulled him to the side of the road so he lay beside the hedge. He came back and handed me the pistol.

"The son of a bitch," he said. He looked toward the sergeant. "You see me shoot him, Tenente?"

"We've got to get the brush quickly," I said. "Did I hit the other one at all?"

"I don't think so," Aymo said. "He was too far away to hit with a pistol."

"The dirty scum," Piani said. We were all cutting twigs and branches. Everything had been taken out of the car. Bonello was digging out in front of the wheels. When we were ready Aymo started the car and put it into gear. The wheels spun round throwing brush and mud. Bonello and I pushed until we could feel our joints crack. The car would not move.

"Rock her back and forth, Barto," I said.

He drove the engine in reverse, then forward. The wheels only dug in deeper. Then the car was resting on the differential again, and the wheels spun freely in the holes they had dug. I straightened up.

"We'll try her with a rope," I said.

"I don't think it's any use, Tenente. You can't get a straight pull."

"We have to try it," I said. "She won't come out any other way."

Piani's and Bonello's cars could only move straight ahead down the narrow road. We roped both cars together and pulled. The wheels only pulled sideways against the ruts.

"It's no good," I shouted. "Stop it."

Piani and Bonello got down from their cars and came back. Aymo got down. The girls were up the road about forty yards sitting on a stone wall.

"What do you say, Tenente?" Bonello asked.

"We'll dig out and try once more with the brush," I said. I looked down the road. It was my fault. I had led them up here. The sun was almost out from behind the clouds and the body of the sergeant lay beside the hedge.

"We'll put his coat and cape under," I said. Bonello went to get them. I cut brush and Aymo and Piani dug out in front and between the wheels. I cut the cape, then ripped it in two, and laid it under the wheel in the mud, then piled brush for the wheels to catch. We were ready to start and Aymo got up on the seat and started the car. The wheels spun and we pushed and pushed. But it wasn't any use.

"It's ——ed," I said. "Is there anything you want in the car, Barto?"

Aymo climbed up with Bonello, carrying the cheese and two bottles of wine and his cape. Bonello, sitting behind the wheel, was looking through the pockets of the sergeant's coat.

"Better throw the coat away," I said. "What about Barto's virgins?"

"They can get in the back," Piani said. "I don't think we are going far."

I opened the back door of the ambulance.

"Come on," I said. "Get in." The two girls climbed in and sat in the corner. They seemed to have taken no notice of the shooting. I looked back up the road. The sergeant lay in his dirty long-sleeved underwear. I got up with Piani and we started. We were going to try to cross the field. When the road entered the field I got down and walked ahead. If we could get across, there was a road on the other side. We could not get across. It was too soft and muddy for the cars. When they were finally and completely stalled, the wheels dug in to the hubs, we left them in the field and started on foot for Udine.

When we came to the road which led back toward the main highway I pointed down it to the two girls.

"Go down there," I said. "You'll meet people." They looked at me. I took out my pocket-book and gave them each a ten-lira note. "Go down there," I said, pointing. "Friends! Family!"

They did not understand but they held the money tightly and started down the road. They looked back as though they were afraid I might take the money back. I watched them go down the road, their shawls close around them, looking back apprehensively at us. The three drivers were laughing.

"How much will you give me to go in that direction, Tenente?" Bonello asked.

"They're better off in a bunch of people than alone if they catch them," I said.

"Give me two hundred lire and I'll walk straight back toward Austria," Bonello said.

"They'd take it away from you," Piani said.

"Maybe the war will be over," Aymo said. We were going up the road as fast as we could. The sun was trying to come through. Beside the road were mulberry trees. Through the trees I could see our two big moving-vans of cars stuck in the field. Piani looked back too.

"They'll have to build a road to get them out," he said.

"I wish to Christ we had bicycles," Bonello said.

"Do they ride bicycles in America?" Aymo asked.

"They used to."

"Here it is a great thing," Aymo said. "A bicycle is a splendid thing."

"I wish to Christ we had bicycles," Bonello said. "I'm no walker."

"Is that firing?" I asked. I thought I could hear firing a long way away.

"I don't know," Aymo said. He listened.

"I think so," I said.

"The first thing we will see will be the cavalry," Piani said.

"I don't think they've got any cavalry."

"I hope to Christ not," Bonello said. "I don't want to be stuck on a lance by any ——— cavalry."

"You certainly shot that sergeant, Tenente," Piani said. We were walking fast.

"I killed him," Bonello said. "I never killed anybody in this war, and all my life I've wanted to kill a sergeant."

"You killed him on the sit all right," Piani said. "He wasn't flying very fast when you killed him."

"Never mind. That's one thing I can always remember. I killed that ———— of a sergeant."

"What will you say in confession?" Aymo asked.

"I'll say, 'Bless me, father, I killed a sergeant.'" They all laughed.

"He's an anarchist," Piani said. "He doesn't go to church."

"Piani's an anarchist too," Bonello said.

"Are you really anarchists?" I asked.

"No, Tenente. We're socialists. We come from Imola."

"Haven't you ever been there?"

"No."

"By Christ it's a fine place, Tenente. You come there after the war and we'll show you something."

"Are you all socialists?"

"Everybody."

"Is it a fine town?"

"Wonderful. You never saw a town like that."

"How did you get to be socialists?"

"We're all socialists. Everybody is a socialist. We've always been socialists."

"You come, Tenente. We'll make you a socialist too."

Ahead the road turned off to the left and there was a little hill and, beyond a stone wall, an apple orchard. As the road went uphill they ceased talking. We walked along together all going fast against time.

We were on a road that led to a river. There was a long line of abandoned trucks and carts on the road leading up to the bridge. No one was in sight. The river was high and the bridge had been blown up in the centre; the stone arch was fallen into the river and the brown water was going over it. We went on up the bank looking for a place to cross. Up ahead I knew there was a railway bridge and I thought we might be able to get across there. The path was wet and muddy. We did not see any troops; only abandoned trucks and stores. Along the river bank there was nothing and no one but the wet brush and muddy ground. We went up to the bank and finally we saw the railway bridge.

"What a beautiful bridge," Aymo said. It was a long plain iron bridge across what was usually a dry river-bed.

"We better hurry and get across before they blow it up," I said.

"There's nobody to blow it up," Piani said. "They're all gone."

"It's probably mined," Bonello said. "You cross first, Tenente."

"Listen to the anarchist," Aymo said. "Make him go first."

"I'll go," I said. "It won't be mined to blow up with one man."

"You see," Piani said. "That is brains. Why haven't you brains, anarchist?"

"If I had brains I wouldn't be here," Bonello said.

"That's pretty good, Tenente," Aymo said.

"That's pretty good," I said. We were close to the bridge now. The sky had clouded over again and it was raining a little. The bridge looked long and solid. We climbed up the embankment.

"Come one at a time," I said and started across the bridge. I watched the ties and the rails for any trip-wires or signs of explosive but I saw nothing. Down below the gaps in the ties the river ran muddy and fast. Ahead across the wet countryside I could see Udine in the rain. Across the bridge I looked back. Just up the river was another bridge. As I watched, a yellow mud-colored motor car crossed it. The sides of the bridge were high and the body of the car, once on, was out of sight. But I saw the heads of the driver, the man on the seat with him, and the two men on the rear seat. They all wore German helmets. Then the car was over the bridge and out of sight behind the trees and the abandoned vehicles on the road. I waved to Aymo who was crossing and to the others to come on. I climbed down and crouched beside the railway embankment. Aymo came down with me.

"Did you see the car?" I asked.

"No. We were watching you."

"A German staff car crossed on the upper bridge."

"A staff car?"

"Yes."

"Holy Mary."

The others came and we all crouched in the mud behind the embankment, looking across the rails at the bridge, the line of trees, the ditch and the road.

"Do you think we're cut off then, Tenente?"

"I don't know. All I know is a German staff car went along that road."

"You don't feel funny, Tenente? You haven't got strange feelings in the head?"

"Don't be funny, Bonello."

"What about a drink?" Piani asked. "If we're cut off we might as well have a drink." He unhooked his canteen and uncorked it.

"Look! Look!" Aymo said and pointed toward the road. Along the top of the stone bridge we could see German helmets moving. They were bent forward and moved smoothly, almost supernaturally, along. As they came off the bridge we saw them. They were bicycle troops. I saw the faces of the first two. They were ruddy and healthy-looking. Their helmets came low down over their foreheads and the side of their faces. Their carbines were clipped to the frame of the bicycles. Stick bombs hung handle down from their belts. Their helmets and their gray uniforms were wet and they rode easily, looking ahead and to both sides. There were two—then four in line, then two, then almost a dozen; then another dozen—then one alone. They did not talk but we could not have heard them because of the noise from the river. They were gone out of sight up the road.

"Holy Mary," Aymo said.

"They were Germans," Piani said. "Those weren't Austrians."

"Why isn't there somebody here to stop them?" I said. "Why haven't they blown the bridge up? Why aren't there machine-guns along this embankment?"

"You tell us, Tenente," Bonello said.

I was very angry.

"The whole bloody thing is crazy. Down below they blow up a little bridge. Here they leave a bridge on the main road. Where is everybody? Don't they try and stop them at all?"

"You tell us, Tenente," Bonello said. I shut up. It was none of my business; all I had to do was to get to Pordenone with three ambulances. I had failed at that. All I had to do now was get to Pordenone. I probably could not even get to Udine. The hell I couldn't. The thing to do was to be calm and not get shot or captured.

"Didn't you have a canteen open?" I asked Piani. He handed it to me. I took a long drink. "We might as well start," I said. "There's no hurry though. Do you want to eat something?"

"This is no place to stay," Bonello said.

"All right. We'll start.

"Should we keep on this side—out of sight?"

"We'll be better off on top. They may come along this bridge too. We don't want them on top of us before we see them."

We walked along the railroad track. On both sides of us stretched the wet plain. Ahead across the plain was the hill of Udine. The roofs fell away from the castle on the hill. We could see the campanile and the clock-tower. There were many mulberry trees in the fields. Ahead I saw a place where the rails were torn up. The ties had been dug out too and thrown down the embankment.

"Down! Down!" Aymo said. We dropped down beside the embankment. There was another group of bicycles passing along the road. I looked over the edge and saw them go on.

"They saw us but they went on," Aymo said.

"We'll get killed up there, Tenente," Bonello said.

"They don't want us," I said. "They're after something else. We're in more danger if they should come on us suddenly."

"I'd rather walk here out of sight," Bonello said.

"All right. We'll walk along the tracks."

"Do you think we can get through?" Aymo asked.

"Sure. There aren't very many of them yet. We'll go through in the dark."

"What was that staff car doing?"

"Christ knows," I said. We kept on up the tracks. Bonello tired of walking in the mud of the embankment and came up with the rest of us. The railway moved south away from the highway now and we could see what passed along the road. A short bridge over a canal was blown up but we climbed across on what was left of the span. We heard firing ahead of us.

We came up on the railway beyond the canal. It went on straight toward the town across the low fields. We could see the line of the other railway ahead of us. To the north was the main road where we had seen the cyclists; to the south there was a small branch-road across the fields with thick trees on each side. I thought we had better cut to the south and work around the town that way and across country toward Campoformio and the main road to the Tagliamento. We could avoid the main line of the retreat by keeping to the secondary roads beyond Udine. I knew there were plenty of side-roads across the plain. I started down the embankment.

"Come on," I said. We would make for the side-road and work to the south of the town. We all started down the embankment. A shot was fired at us from the side-road. The bullet went into the mud of the embankment.

"Go on back," I shouted. I started up the embankment, slipping in the mud. The drivers were ahead of me. I went up the embankment as fast as I could go. Two more shots came from the thick brush and Aymo, as he was crossing the tracks, lurched, tripped and fell face down. We pulled him down on the other side and turned him over. "His head ought to be up-hill," I said. Piani moved him around. He lay in the mud on the side of the embankment, his feet pointing downhill, breathing blood irregularly. The three of us squatted over him in the rain. He was hit low in the back of the neck and the bullet had ranged upward and come out under the right eye. He died while I was stopping up the two holes. Piani laid his head down, wiped at his face, with a piece of the emergency dressing, then let it alone.

"The ——," he said.

"They weren't Germans," I said. "There can't be any Germans over there."

"Italians," Piani said, using the word as an epithet, "Italiani!" Bonello said nothing. He was sitting beside Aymo, not looking at him. Piani picked up Aymo's cap where it had rolled down the embankment and put it over his face. He took out his canteen.

"Do you want a drink?" Piani handed Bonello the canteen.

"No," Bonello said. He turned to me. "That might have happened to us any time on the railway tracks."

"No," I said. "It was because we started across the field."

Bonello shook his head. "Aymo's dead," he said. "Who's dead next, Tenente? Where do we go now?"

"Those were Italians that shot," I said. "They weren't Germans."

"I suppose if they were Germans they'd have killed all of us," Bonello said.

"We are in more danger from Italians than Germans," I said. "The rear guard are afraid of everything. The Germans know what they're after."

"You reason it out, Tenente," Bonello said.

"Where do we go now?" Piani asked.

"We better lie up some place till it's dark. If we could get south we'd be all right."

"They'd have to shoot us all to prove they were right the first time," Bonello said. "I'm not going to try them."

"We'll find a place to lie up as near to Udine as we can get and then go through when it's dark."

"Let's go then," Bonello said. We went down the north side of the embankment. I looked back. Aymo lay in the mud with the angle of the embankment. He was quite small and his arms were by his side, his puttee-wrapped legs and muddy boots together, his cap over his face. He looked very dead. It was raining. I had liked him as well as any one I ever knew. I had his papers in my pocket and would write to his family. Ahead across the fields was a farmhouse. There were trees around it and the farm buildings were built against the house. There was a balcony along the second floor held up by columns.

"We better keep a little way apart," I said. "I'll go ahead." I started toward the farmhouse. There was a path across the field.

Crossing the field, I did not know but that some one would fire on us from the trees near the farmhouse or from the farmhouse itself. I walked toward it, seeing it very clearly. The balcony of the second floor merged into the barn and there was hay coming out between the columns. The courtyard was of stone blocks and all the trees were dripping with the rain. There was a big empty two-wheeled cart, the shafts tipped high up in the rain. I came to the courtyard, crossed it, and stood under the shelter of the balcony. The door of the house was open and I went in. Bonello and Piani came in after me. It was dark inside. I went back to the kitchen. There were ashes of a fire on the big open hearth. The pots hung over the ashes, but they were empty. I looked around but I could not find anything to eat.

"We ought to lie up in the barn," I said. "Do you think you could find anything to eat, Piani, and bring it up there?"

"I'll look," Piani said.

"I'll look too," Bonello said.

"All right," I said. "I'll go up and look at the barn." I found a stone stairway that went up from the stable underneath. The stable smelt dry and pleasant in the rain. The cattle were all gone, probably driven off when they left. The barn was half full of hay. There were two windows in the roof, one was blocked with boards, the other was a narrow dormer window on the north side. There was a chute so that hay might be pitched down to the cattle. Beams crossed the opening down into the main floor where the hay-carts drove in when the hay was hauled in to be pitched up. I heard the rain on the roof and smelled the hay and, when I went down, the clean smell of dried dung in the stable. We could pry a board loose and see out of the south window down into the courtyard. The other window looked out on the field toward the north. We could get out of either window onto the roof and down, or go down the hay chute if the stairs were impractical. It was a big barn and we could hide in the hay if we heard any one. It seemed like a good place. I was sure we could have gotten through to the south if they had not fired on us. It was impossible that there were Germans there. They were coming from the north and down the road from Cividale. They could not have come through from the south. The Italians were even more dangerous. They were frightened and firing on anything they saw.

Last night on the retreat we had heard that there had been many Germans in Italian uniforms mixing with the retreat in the north. I did not believe it. That was one of the things you always heard in the war. It was one of the things the enemy always did to you. You did not know any one who went over in German uniform to confuse them. Maybe they did but it sounded difficult. I did not believe the Germans did it. I did not believe they had to. There was no need to confuse our retreat. The size of the army and the fewness of the roads did that. Nobody gave any orders, let alone Germans. Still, they would shoot us for Germans. They shot Aymo. The hay smelled good and lying in a barn in the hay took away all the years in between. We had lain in hay and talked and shot sparrows with an air-rifle when they perched in the triangle cut high up in the wall of the barn. The barn was gone now and one year they had cut the hemlock woods and there were only stumps, dried tree-tops, branches and fireweed where the woods had been. You could not go back. If you did not go forward what happened? You never got back to Milan. And if you got back to Milan what happened? I listened to the firing to the north toward Udine. I could hear machine-gun firing. There was no shelling. That was something. They must have gotten some troops along the road. I looked down in the half-light of the hay-barn and saw Piani standing on the hauling floor. He had a long sausage, a jar of something and two bottles of wine under his arm.

"Come up," I said. "There is the ladder." Then I realized that I should help him with the things and went down. I was vague in the head from lying in the hay. I had been nearly asleep.

"Where's Bonello?" I asked.

"I'll tell you," Piani said. We went up the ladder. Up on the hay we set the things down. Piani took out his knife with the corkscrew and drew the cork on a wine bottle.

"They have sealing-wax on it," he said: "It must be good." He smiled.

"Where's Bonello?" I asked.

Piani looked at me.

"He went away, Tenente," he said. "He wanted to be a prisoner."

I did not say anything.

"He was afraid we would get killed."

I held the bottle of wine and did not say anything.

"You see we don't believe in the war anyway, Tenente."

"Why didn't you go?" I asked.

"I did not want to leave you."

"Where did he go?"

"I don't know, Tenente. He went away."

"All right," I said. "Will you cut the sausage?"

Piani looked at me in the half-light.

"I cut it while we were talking," he said. We sat in the hay and ate the sausage and drank the wine. It must have been wine they had saved for a wedding. It was so old that it was losing its color.

"You look out of this window, Luigi," I said. "I'll go look out the other window."

We had each been drinking out of one of the bottles and I took my bottle with me and went over and lay flat on the hay and looked out the narrow window at the wet country. I do not know what I expected to see but I did not see anything except the fields and the bare mulberry trees and the rain falling. I drank the wine and it did not make me feel good. They had kept it too long and it had gone to pieces and lost its quality and color. I watched it get dark outside; the darkness came very quickly. It would be a black night with the rain. When it was dark there was no use watching any more, so I went over to Piani. He was lying asleep and I did not wake him but sat down beside him for a while. He was a big man and he slept heavily. After a while I woke him and we started.

That was a very strange night. I do not know what I had expected, death perhaps and shooting in the dark and running, but nothing happened. We waited, lying flat beyond the ditch along the main road while a German battalion passed, then when they were gone we crossed the road and went on to the north. We were very close to Germans twice in the rain but they did not see us. We got past the town to the north without seeing any Italians, then after a while came on the main channels of the retreat and walked all night toward the Tagliamento. I had not realized how gigantic the retreat was. The whole country was moving, as well as the army. We walked all night, making better time than the vehicles. My leg ached and I was tired but we made good time. It seemed so silly for Bonello to have decided to be taken prisoner. There was no danger. We had walked through two armies without incident. If Aymo had not been killed there would never have seemed to be any danger. No one had bothered us when we were in plain sight along the railway. The killing came suddenly and unreasonably. I wondered where Bonello was.

"How do you feel, Tenente?" Piani asked. We were going along the side of a road crowded with vehicles and troops.

"Fine."

"I'm tired of this walking."

"Well, all we have to do is walk now. We don't have to worry."

"Bonello was a fool."

"He was a fool all right."

"What will you do about him, Tenente?"

"I don't know."

"Can't you just put him down as taken prisoner?"

"I don't know."

"You see if the war went on they would make bad trouble for his family."

"The war won't go on," a soldier said. "We're going home. The war is over."

"Everybody's going home."

"We're all going home."

"Come on, Tenente," Piani said. He wanted to get past them.

"Tenente? Who's a Tenente? *A basso gli ufficiali!* Down with the officers!"

Piani took me by the arm. "I better call you by your name," he said.

"They might try and make trouble. They've shot some officers." We worked up past them.

"I won't make a report that will make trouble for his family." I went on with our conversation.

"If the war is over it makes no difference," Piani said. "But I don't believe it's over. It's too good that it should be over."

"We'll know pretty soon," I said.

"I don't believe it's over. They all think it's over but I don't believe it."

"*Viva la Pace!*" a soldier shouted out. "We're going home!"

"It would be fine if we all went home," Piani said. "Wouldn't you like to go home?"

"Yes."

"We'll never go. I don't think it's over."

"*Andiamo a casa!*" a soldier shouted.

"They throw away their rifles," Piani said. "They take them off and drop them down while they're marching. Then they shout."

"They ought to keep their rifles."

"They think if they throw away their rifles they can't make them fight."

In the dark and the rain, making our way along the side of the road I could see that many of the troops still had their rifles. They stuck up above the capes.

"What brigade are you?" an officer called out.

"*Brigata di Pace,*" some one shouted. "Peace Brigade!" The officer said nothing.

"What does he say? What does the officer say?"

"Down with the officer. *Viva la Pace!*"

"Come on," Piani said. We passed two British ambulances, abandoned in the block of vehicles.

"They're from Gorizia," Piani said. "I know the cars."

"They got further than we did."

"They started earlier."

"I wonder where the drivers are?"

"Up ahead probably."

"The Germans have stopped outside Udine," I said. "These people will all get across the river."

"Yes," Piani said. "That's why I think the war will go on."

"The Germans could come on," I said. "I wonder why they don't come on."

"I don't know. I don't know anything about this kind of war."

"They have to wait for their transport, I suppose."

"I don't know," Piani said. Alone he was much gentler. When he was with the others he was a very rough talker.

"Are you married, Luigi?"

"You know I am married."

"Is that why you did not want to be a prisoner?"

"That is one reason. Are you married, Tenente?"

"No."

"Neither is Bonello."

"You can't tell anything by a man's being married. But I should think a married man would want to get back to his wife," I said. I would be glad to talk about wives.

"Yes."

"How are your feet?"

"They're sore enough."

Before daylight we reached the bank of the Tagliamento and followed down along the flooded river to the bridge where all the traffic was crossing.

"They ought to be able to hold at this river," Piani said. In the dark the flood looked high. The water swirled and it was wide. The wooden bridge was nearly three-quarters of a mile across, and the river, that usually ran in narrow channels in the wide stony bed far below the bridge, was close under the wooden planking. We went along the bank and then worked our way into the crowd that were crossing the bridge. Crossing slowly in the rain a few feet above the flood, pressed tight in the crowd, the box of an artillery caisson just ahead, I looked over the side and watched the river. Now that we could not go our own pace I felt very tired. There was no exhilaration in crossing the bridge. I wondered what it would be like if a plane bombed it in the daytime.

"Piani," I said.

"Here I am, Tenente." He was a little ahead in the jam. No one was talking. They were all trying to get across as soon as they could: thinking only of that. We were almost across. At the far end of the bridge there were officers and carabinieri standing on both sides flashing lights. I saw them silhouetted against the sky-line. As we came close to them I saw one of the officers point to a man in the column. A carabiniere went in after him and came out holding the man by the arm. He took him away from the road. We came almost opposite them. The officers were scrutinizing every one in the column, sometimes speaking to each other, going forward to flash a light in some one's face. They took some one else out just before we came opposite. I saw the man. He was a lieutenant-colonel. I saw the stars in the box on his sleeve as they flashed a light on him. His hair was gray and he was short and fat. The carabiniere pulled him in behind the line of officers. As we came opposite I saw one or two of them look at me. Then one pointed at me and spoke to a carabiniere. I saw the carabiniere start for me, come through the edge of the column toward me, then felt him take me by the collar.

"What's the matter with you?" I said and hit him in the face. I saw his face under the hat, upturned mustaches and blood coming down his cheek. Another one dove in toward us.

"What's the matter with you?" I said. He did not answer. He was watching a chance to grab me. I put my arm behind me to loosen my pistol.

"Don't you know you can't touch an officer?"

The other one grabbed me from behind and pulled my arm up so that it twisted in the socket. I turned with him and the other one grabbed me around the neck. I kicked his shins and got my left knee into his groin.

"Shoot him if he resists," I heard someone say.

"What's the meaning of this?" I tried to shout but my voice was not very loud. They had me at the side of the road now.

"Shoot him if he resists," an officer said. "Take him over back."

"Who are you?"

"You'll find out."

"Who are you?"

"Battle police," another officer said.

"Why don't you ask me to step over instead of having one of these airplanes grab me?"

They did not answer. They did not have to answer. They were battle police.

"Take him back there with the others," the first officer said. "You see. He speaks Italian with an accent."

"So do you, you——," I said.

"Take him back with the others," the first officer said. They took me down behind the line of officers below the road toward a group of people in a field by the river bank. As we walked toward them shots were fired. I saw flashes of the rifles and heard the reports. We came up to the group. There were four officers standing together, with a man in front of them with a carabiniere on each side of him. A group of men were standing guarded by carabinieri. Four other carabinieri stood near the questioning officers, leaning on their carbines. They were wide-hatted carabinieri. The two who had me shoved me in with the group waiting to be questioned. I looked at the man the officers were questioning. He was the fat gray-haired little lieutenant-colonel they had taken out of the column. The questioners had all the efficiency, coldness and command of themselves of Italians who are firing and are not being fired on.

"Your brigade?"

He told them.

"Regiment?"

He told them.

"Why are you not with your regiment?"

He told them.

"Do you not know that an officer should be with his troops?"

He did.

That was all. Another officer spoke.

"It is you and such as you that have let the barbarians onto the sacred soil of the fatherland."

"I beg your pardon," said the lieutenant-colonel.

"It is because of treachery such as yours that we have lost the fruits of victory."

"Have you ever been in a retreat?" the lieutenant-colonel asked.

"Italy should never retreat."

We stood there in the rain and listened to this. We were facing the officers and the prisoner stood in front and a little to one side of us.

"If you are going to shoot me," the lieutenant-colonel said, "please shoot me at once without further questioning. The questioning is stupid." He made the sign of the cross. The officers spoke together. One wrote something on a pad of paper.

"Abandoned his troops, ordered to be shot," he said.

Two carabinieri took the lieutenant-colonel to the river bank. He walked in the rain, an old man with his hat off, a carabiniere on either side. I did not watch them shoot him but I heard the shots. They were questioning some one else. This officer too was separated from his troops. He was not allowed to make an explanation. He cried when they read the sentence from the pad of paper, and they were questioning another when they shot him. They made a point of being intent on questioning the next man while the man who had been questioned before was being shot. In this way there was obviously nothing they could do about it. I did not know whether I should wait to be questioned or make a break now. I was obviously a German in Italian uniform. I saw how their minds worked; if they had minds and if they worked. They were all young men and they were saving their country. The second army was being re-formed beyond the Tagliamento. They were executing officers of the rank of major and above who were separated from their troops. They were also dealing summarily with German agitators in Italian uniform. They wore steel helmets. Only two of us had steel helmets. Some of the carabinieri had them. The other carabinieri wore the wide hat. Airplanes we called them. We stood in the rain and were taken out one at a time to be questioned and shot. So far they had shot every one they had questioned. The questioners had that beautiful detachment and devotion to stern justice of men dealing in death without being in any danger of it. They were questioning a full colonel of a line regiment. Three more officers had just been put in with us.

"Where was his regiment?"

I looked at the carabinieri. They were looking at the newcomers. The others were looking at the colonel. I ducked down, pushed between two men, and ran for the river, my head down. I tripped at the edge and went in with a splash. The water was very cold and I stayed under as long as I could. I could feel the current swirl me and I stayed under until I thought I could never come up. The minute I came up I took a breath and went down again. It was easy to stay under with so much clothing and my boots. When I came up the second time I saw a piece of timber ahead of me and reached it and held on with one hand. I kept my head behind it and did not even look over it. I did not want to see the bank. There were shots when I ran and shots when I came up the first time. I heard them when I was almost above water. There were no shots now. The piece of timber swung in the current and I held it with one hand. I looked at the bank. It seemed to be going by very fast. There was much wood in the stream. The water was very cold. We passed the brush of an island above the water. I held onto the timber with both hands and let it take me along. The shore was out of sight now.

The Battle of Cannae

BY

LIVY

WHILST time was thus being wasted in disputes instead of deliberation, Hannibal withdrew the bulk of his army, who had been standing most of the day in order of battle, into camp. He sent his Numidians, however, across the river to attack the parties who were getting water for the smaller camp. They had hardly gained the opposite bank when with their shouting and uproar they sent the crowd flying in wild disorder, and galloping on as far as the outpost in front of the rampart, they nearly reached the gates of the camp. It was looked upon as such an insult for a Roman camp to be actually terrorised by irregular auxiliaries that one thing, and one thing alone, held back the Romans from instantly crossing the river and forming their battle line—the supreme command that day rested with Paulus.

The following day Varro, whose turn it now was, without any consultation with his colleague, exhibited the signal for battle and led his forces drawn up for action across the river. Paulus followed, for though he disapproved of the measure, he was bound to support it. After crossing, they strengthened their line with the force in the smaller camp and completed their formation. On the right, which was nearest to the river, the Roman cavalry were posted, then came the infantry; on the extreme left were the cavalry of the allies, their infantry were between them and the Roman legions. The javelin men with the rest of the light-armed auxiliaries formed the front line. The consuls took their stations on the wings, Terentius Varro on the left, Æmilius Paulus on the right.

As soon as it grew light Hannibal sent forward the Balearics and the other light infantry. He then crossed the river in person and as each division was brought across he assigned it its place in the line. The Gaulish and Spanish horse he posted near the bank on the left wing in front of the Roman cavalry; the right wing was assigned to the Numidian troopers. The centre consisted of a strong force of infantry, the Gauls and Spaniards in the middle, the Africans at either end of them. You might fancy that the Africans were for the most part a body of Romans from the way they were armed, they were so completely equipped with the arms, some of which they had taken at the Trebia, but the most part at Trasumennus. The Gauls and Spaniards had shields almost of the same shape; their swords were totally different, those of the Gauls being very long and without a point, the Spaniard, accustomed to thrust more than to cut, had a short handy sword, pointed like a dagger. These nations, more than any other, inspired terror by the vastness of their stature and their frightful appearance: the Gauls were naked above the waist, the Spaniards had taken up their position wearing white tunics embroidered with purple, of dazzling brilliancy. The total number of infantry in the field was 40,000, and there were 10,000 cavalry. Hasdrubal was in command of the left wing, Maharbal of the right; Hannibal himself with his brother Mago commanded the centre. It was a great convenience to both armies that the sun shone obliquely on them, whether it was that they had purposely so placed themselves, or whether it happened by accident, since the Romans faced the north, the Carthaginians the South. The wind, called by the inhabitants the Vulturnus, was against the Romans, and blew great clouds of dust into their faces, making it impossible for them to see in front of them.

When the battle shout was raised the auxiliaries ran forward, and the battle began with the light infantry. Then the Gauls and Spaniards on the left engaged the Roman cavalry on the right; the battle was not at all like a cavalry fight, for there was no room for manoeuvering, the river on the one side and the infantry on the other hemming them in, compelled them to fight face to face. Each side tried to force their way straight forward, till at last the horses were standing in a closely pressed mass, and the riders seized their opponents and tried to drag them from their horses. It had become mainly a struggle of infantry, fierce but short, and the Roman cavalry was repulsed and fled. Just as this battle of the cavalry was finished, the infantry became engaged, and as long as the Gauls and Spaniards kept their ranks unbroken, both sides were equally matched in strength and courage. At length after long and repeated efforts the Romans closed up their ranks, echeloned their front, and by the sheer weight of their deep column bore down the division of the enemy which was stationed in front of Hannibal's line, and was too thin and weak to resist the pressure. Without a moment's pause they followed up their broken and hastily retreating foe till they took to headlong flight. Cutting their way through the mass of fugitives, who offered no resistance, they penetrated as far as the Africans who were stationed on both wings, somewhat further back than the Gauls and Spaniards who had formed the advanced centre. As the latter fell back the whole front became level, and as they continued to give ground it became concave and crescent-shaped, the Africans at either end forming the horns. As the Romans rushed on incautiously between them, they were enfiladed by the two wings, which extended and closed round them in the rear. On this, the Romans, who had fought one battle to no purpose, left the Gauls and Spaniards, whose rear they had been slaughtering, and commenced a fresh struggle with the Africans. The contest was a very one-sided one, for not only were they hemmed in on all sides, but wearied with the previous fighting they were meeting fresh and vigorous opponents.

By this time the Roman left wing, where the allied cavalry were fronting the Numidians, had become engaged, but the fighting was slack at first owing to a Carthaginian stratagem. About 500 Numidians, carrying, besides their usual arms and missiles, swords concealed under their coats of mail, rode out from their own line with their shields slung behind their backs as though they were deserters, and suddenly leaped from their horses and flung their shields and javelins at the feet of their enemy. They were received into their ranks, conducted to the rear, and ordered to remain quiet. While the battle was spreading to the various parts of the field they remained quiet, but when the eyes and minds of all were wholly taken up with the fighting they seized the large Roman shields which were lying everywhere amongst the heaps of slain and commenced a furious attack upon the rear of the Roman line. Slashing away at backs and hips, they made a great slaughter and a still greater panic and confusion. Amidst the rout and panic in one part of the field and the obstinate but hopeless struggle in the other, Hasdrubal, who was in command of that arm, withdrew some Numidians from the centre of the right wing, where the fighting was feebly kept up, and sent them in pursuit of the fugitives, and at the same time sent the Spanish and Gaulish horse to the aid of the Africans, who were by this time more wearied by slaughter than by fighting.

Paulus was on the other side of the field. In spite of his having been seriously wounded at the commencement of the action by a bullet from a sling, he frequently encountered Hannibal with a compact body of troops, and in several places restored the battle. The Roman cavalry formed a bodyguard round him, but at last, as he became too weak to manage his horse, they all dismounted. It is stated that when some one reported to Hannibal that the consul had ordered his men to fight on foot, he remarked, "I would rather he handed them over to me bound hand and foot." Now that the victory of the enemy was no longer doubtful this struggle of the dismounted cavalry was such as might be expected when men preferred to die where they stood rather than flee, and the victors, furious at them for delaying the victory, butchered without mercy those whom they could not dislodge. They did, however, repulse a few survivors exhausted with their exertions and their wounds. All were at last scattered, and those who could regained their horses for flight. Cn. Lentulus, a military tribune, saw, as he rode by, the consul covered with blood sitting on a boulder. "Lucius Æmilius," he said, "the one man whom the gods must hold guiltless of this day's disaster, take this horse while you have still some strength left, and I can lift you into the saddle and keep by your side to protect you. Do not make this day of battle still more fatal by a consul's death, there are enough tears and mourning without that." The consul replied: "Long may you live to do brave deeds, Cornelius, but do not waste in useless pity the few moments left in which to escape from the hands of the enemy. Go, announce publicly to the senate that they must fortify Rome and make its defence strong before the victorious enemy approaches, and tell Q. Fabius privately that I have ever remembered his precepts in life and in death. Suffer me to breathe my last among my slaughtered soldiers, let me not have to defend myself again when I am no longer consul, or appear as the accuser of my colleague and protect my own innocence by throwing the guilt on another." During this conversation a crowd of fugitives came suddenly upon them, followed by the enemy, who, not knowing who the consul was, overwhelmed him with a shower of missiles. Lentulus escaped on horseback in the rush.

Then there was flight in all directions; 7000 men escaped to the smaller camp, 10,000 to the larger, and about 2000 to the village of Cannae. These latter were at once surrounded by Carthalo and his cavalry, as the village was quite unfortified. The other consul, who either by accident or design had not joined any of these bodies of fugitives, escaped with about fifty cavalry to Venusia; 45,500 infantry, 2700 cavalry—almost an equal proportion of Romans and allies—are said to have been killed. Amongst the number were both the quaestors attached to the consuls, L. Atilius and L. Furius Bibulcus, twenty-nine military tribunes, several ex-consuls, ex-praetors, and ex-ædiles (amongst them are included Cn. Servilius Geminus and M. Minucius, who was Master of the Horse the previous year and, some years before that, consul), and in addition to these, eighty men who had either been senators or filled offices qualifying them for election to the senate and who had volunteered for service with the legions. The prisoners taken in the battle are stated to have amounted to 3000 infantry and 1500 cavalry.

Such was the battle of Cannae, a battle as famous as the disastrous one at the Allia; not so serious in its results, owing to the inaction of the enemy, but more serious and more horrible in view of the slaughter of the army. For the flight at the Allia saved the army though it lost the City, whereas at Cannae hardly fifty men shared the consul's flight, nearly the whole army met their death in company with the other consul. As those who had taken refuge in the two camps were only a defenceless crowd without any leaders, the men in the larger camp sent a message to the others asking them to cross over to them at night when the enemy, tired after the battle and the feasting in honour of their victory, would be buried in sleep. Then they would go in one body to Canusium. Some rejected the proposal with scorn. "Why," they asked, "cannot those who sent the message come themselves, since they are quite as able to join us as we to join them? Because, of course, all the country between us is scoured by the enemy and they prefer to expose other people to that deadly peril rather than themselves." Others did not disapprove of the proposal, but they lacked courage to carry it out.

P. Sempronius Tuditanus protested against this cowardice. "Would you," he asked, "rather be taken prisoners by a most avaricious and ruthless foe and a price put upon your heads and your value assessed after you have been asked whether you are a Roman citizen or a Latin ally, in order that another may win honour from your misery and disgrace? Certainly not, if you are really the fellow-countrymen of L. Æmilius, who chose a noble death rather than a life of degradation, and of all the brave men who are lying in heaps around him. But, before daylight overtakes us and the enemy gathers in larger force to bar our path, let us cut our way through the men who in disorder and confusion are clamouring at our gates. Good swords and brave hearts make a way through enemies, however densely they are massed. If you march shoulder to shoulder you will scatter this loose and disorganised force as easily as if nothing opposed you. Come then with me, all you who want to preserve yourselves and the State." With these words he drew his sword, and with his men in close formation marched through the very midst of the enemy. When the Numidians hurled their javelins on the right, the unprotected side, they transferred their shields to their right arms, and so got clear away to the larger camp. As many as 600 escaped on this occasion, and after another large body had joined them they at once left the camp and came through safely to Canusium. This action on the part of defeated men was due to the impulse of natural courage or of accident rather than to any concerted plan of their own or any one's generalship.

Hannibal's officers all surrounded him and congratulated him on his victory, and urged that after such a magnificent success he should allow himself and his exhausted men to rest for the remainder of the day and the following night. Maharbal, however, the commandant of the cavalry, thought that they ought not to lose a moment. "That you may know," he said to Hannibal, "what has been gained by this battle I prophesy that in five days you will be feasting as victor in the Capitol. Follow me; I will go in advance with the cavalry; they will know that you are come before they know that you are coming." To Hannibal the victory seemed too great and too joyous for him to realise all at once. He told Maharbal that he commended his zeal, but he needed time to think out his plans. Maharbal replied: "The gods have not given all their gifts to one man. You know how to win victory, Hannibal, you do not know how to use it." That day's delay is believed to have saved the City and the empire.

The next day, as soon as it grew light, they set about gathering the spoils on the field and viewing the carnage, which was a ghastly sight even for an enemy. There all those thousands of Romans were lying, infantry and cavalry indiscriminately as chance had brought them together in the battle or the flight. Some covered with blood raised themselves from amongst the dead around them, tortured by their wounds which were nipped by the cold of the morning, and were promptly put an end to by the enemy. Some they found lying with their thighs and knees gashed but still alive; these bared their throats and necks and bade them drain what blood they still had left. Some were discovered with their heads buried in the earth, they had evidently suffocated themselves by making holes in the ground and heaping the soil over their faces. What attracted the attention of all was a Numidian who was dragged alive from under a dead Roman lying across him; his ears and nose were torn, for the Roman with hands too powerless to grasp his weapon had, in his mad rage, torn his enemy with his teeth, and while doing so expired.

After most of the day had been spent in collecting the spoils, Hannibal led his men to the attack on the smaller camp and commenced operations by throwing up a breastwork to cut off their water supply from the river. As, however, all the defenders were exhausted by toil and want of sleep, as well as by wounds, the surrender was effected sooner than he had anticipated. They agreed to give up their arms and horses, and to pay for each Roman three hundred "chariot pieces," for each ally two hundred, and for each officer's servant one hundred, on condition that after the money was paid they should be allowed to depart with one garment apiece. Then they admitted the enemy into the camp and were all placed under guard, the Romans and the allies separately.

Whilst time was being spent there, all those in the larger camp, who had sufficient strength and courage, to the number of 4000 infantry and 200 cavalry, made their escape to Canusium, some in a body, others straggling through the fields, which was quite as safe a thing to do. Those who were wounded and those who had been afraid to venture surrendered the camp on the same terms as had been agreed upon in the other camp. An immense amount of booty was secured, and the whole of it was made over to the troops with the exception of the horses and prisoners and whatever silver there might be. Most of this was on the trappings of the horses, for they used very little silver plate at table, at all events when on a campaign.

Hannibal then ordered the bodies of his own soldiers to be collected for burial; it is said that there were as many as 8000 of his best troops. Some authors state that he also had a search made for the body of the Roman consul, which he buried.

The Victory of the Americans over Burgoyne at Saratoga, 1777

BY

SIR EDWARD S. CREASY

THE war which rent away the North American colonies of England is, of all subjects in history, the most painful for an Englishman to dwell on. It was commenced and carried on by the British Ministry in iniquity and folly, and it was concluded in disaster and shame. But the contemplation of it cannot be evaded by the historian, however much it may be abhorred. Nor can any military event be said to have exercised more important influence on the future fortunes of mankind, than the complete defeat of Burgoyne's expedition in 1777; a defeat which rescued the revolted colonists from certain subjection; and which, by inducing the courts of France and Spain to attack England in their behalf, ensured the independence of the United States, and the formation of that transatlantic power which, not only America, but both Europe and Asia, now see and feel.

Still, in proceeding to describe this "decisive battle of the world," a very brief recapitulation of the earlier events of the war may be sufficient; nor shall I linger unnecessarily on a painful theme.

The five northern colonies of Massachusetts, Connecticut, Rhode Island, New Hampshire, and Vermont, usually classed together as the New England colonies, were the strongholds of the insurrection against the mother-country. The feeling of resistance was less vehement and general in the central settlement of New York; and still less so in Pennsylvania, Maryland, and the other colonies of the south, although everywhere it was formidably active. Virginia should, perhaps, be particularised for the zeal which its leading men displayed in the American cause; but it was among the descendants of the stern Puritans that the spirit of Cromwell and Vane breathed in all its fervour; it was from the New Englanders that the first armed opposition to the British crown had been offered; and it was by them that the most stubborn determination to fight to the last, rather than waive a single right or privilege, had been displayed. In 1775, they had succeeded in forcing the British troops to evacuate Boston; and the events of 1776 had made New York (which the royalists captured in that year) the principal basis of operations for the armies of the mother-country.

From: *Fifteen Decisive Battles of the World.*

A glance at the map will show that the Hudson River, which falls into the Atlantic at New York, runs down from the north at the back of the New England States, forming an angle of about forty-five degrees with the line of the coast of the Atlantic, along which the New England States are situated. Northward of the Hudson, we see a small chain of lakes communicating with the Canadian frontier. It is necessary to attend closely to these geographical points, in order to understand the plan of the operations which the English attempted in 1777, and which the battle of Saratoga defeated.

The English had a considerable force in Canada; and in 1776 had completely repulsed an attack which the Americans had made upon that province. The British Ministry resolved to avail themselves, in the next year, of the advantage which the occupation of Canada gave them, not merely for the purpose of defence, but for the purpose of striking a vigorous and crushing blow against the revolted colonies. With this view, the army in Canada was largely reinforced. Seven thousand veteran troops were sent out from England, with a corps of artillery abundantly supplied, and led by select and experienced officers. Large quantities of military stores were also furnished for the equipment of the Canadian volunteers, who were expected to join the expedition. It was intended that the force thus collected should march southward by the line of the lakes, and thence along the banks of the Hudson River. The British army in New York (or a large detachment of it) was to make a simultaneous movement northward, up the line of the Hudson, and the two expeditions were to unite at Albany, a town on that river. By these operations all communication between the northern colonies and those of the centre and south would be cut off. An irresistible force would be concentrated, so as to crush all further opposition in New England; and when this was done, it was believed that the other colonies would speedily submit. The Americans had no troops in the field that seemed able to baffle these movements. Their principal army, under Washington, was occupied in watching over Pennsylvania and the south. At any rate it was believed that, in order to oppose the plan intended for the new campaign, the insurgents must risk a pitched battle, in which the superiority of the royalists, in numbers, in discipline, and in equipment, seemed to promise to the latter a crowning victory. Without question the plan was ably formed; and had the success of the execution been equal to the ingenuity of the design, the re-conquest or submission of the thirteen United States must, in all human probability, have followed; and the independence which they proclaimed in 1776 would have been extinguished before it existed a second year. No European power had as yet come forward to aid America. It is true that England was generally regarded with jealousy and ill-will, and was thought to have acquired, at the treaty of Paris, a preponderance of dominion which was perilous to the balance of power; but though many were willing to wound, none had yet ventured to strike; and America, if defeated in 1777, would have been suffered to fall unaided.

Burgoyne had gained celebrity by some bold and dashing exploits in Portugal during the last war; he was personally as brave an officer as ever headed British troops; he had considerable skill as a tactician; and his general intellectual abilities and acquirements were of a high order. He had several very able and experienced officers under him, among whom were Major-General Phillips and Brigadier-General Frazer. His regular troops amounted, exclusively to the corps of artillery, to about seven thousand two hundred men, rank and file. Nearly half of these were Germans. He had also an auxiliary force of from two to three thousand Canadians. He summoned the warriors of several tribes of the Red Indians near the western lakes to join his army. Much eloquence was poured forth, both in America and in England, in denouncing the use of these savage auxiliaries. Yet Burgoyne seems to have done no more than Montcalm, Wolfe, and other French, American, and English generals had done before him. But, in truth, the lawless ferocity of the Indians, their unskilfulness in regular action, and the utter impossibility of bringing them under any discipline, made their services of little or no value in times of difficulty: while the indignation which their outrages inspired, went far to rouse the whole population of the invaded districts into active hostilities against Burgoyne's force.

Burgoyne assembled hs troops and confederates near the river Bouquet, on the west side of Lake Champlain. He then, on the 21st of June 1777, gave his Red Allies a war-feast, and harangued them on the necessity of abstaining from their usual cruel practices against unarmed people and prisoners. At the same time he published a pompous manifesto to the Americans, in which he threatened the refractory with all the horrors of war, Indian as well as European. The army proceeded by water to Crown Point, a fortification which the Americans held at the northern extremity of the inlet by which the water from Lake George is conveyed to Lake Champlain. He landed here without opposition; but the reduction of Ticonderoga, a fortification about twelve miles to the south of Crown Point, was a more serious matter, and was supposed to be the critical part of the expedition. Ticonderoga commanded the passage along the lakes, and was considered to be the key to the route which Burgoyne wished to follow. The English had been repulsed in an attack on it in the war with the French in 1758 with severe loss. But Burgoyne now invested it with great skill; and the American General, St. Clair, who had only an ill-equipped army of about three thousand men, evacuated it on the 5th of July. It seems evident that a different course would have caused the destruction or capture of his whole army; which, weak as it was, was the chief force then in the field for the protection of the New England States. When censured by some of his countrymen for abandoning Ticonderoga, St. Clair truly replied, "that he had lost a post, but saved a province." Burgoyne's troops pursued the retiring Americans, gained several advantages over them, and took a large part of their artillery and military stores.

The loss of the British in these engagements was trifling. The army moved southward along Lake George to Skenesborough; and thence, slowly, and with great difficulty, across a broken country, full of creeks and marshes, and clogged by the enemy with felled trees and other obstacles, to Fort Edward, on the Hudson River, the American troops continuing to retire before them.

Burgoyne reached the left bank of the Hudson River on the 30th of July. Hitherto he had overcome every difficulty which the enemy and the nature of the country had placed in his way. His army was in excellent order and in the highest spirits; and the peril of the expedition seemed over, when they were once on the bank of the river which was to be the channel of communication between them and the British army in the south.

The astonishment and alarm which these events produced among the Americans were naturally great; but in the midst of their disasters none of the colonists showed any disposition to submit. The local governments of the New England States, as well as the Congress, acted with vigour and firmness in their efforts to repel the enemy. General Gates was sent to take the command of the army at Saratoga; and Arnold, a favourite leader of the Americans, was despatched by Washington to act under him, with reinforcements of troops and guns from the main American army. Burgoyne's employment of the Indians now produced the worst possible effects. Though he laboured hard to check the atrocities which they were accustomed to commit, he could not prevent the occurrence of many barbarous outrages, repugnant both to the feelings of humanity and to the laws of civilised warfare. The American commanders took care that the reports of these excesses should be circulated far and wide, well knowing that they would make the stern New Englanders not droop, but rage. Such was their effect; and though, when each man looked upon his wife, his children, his sisters, or his aged parents, the thought of the merciless Indian "thirsting for the blood of man, woman, and child," of "the cannibal savage torturing, murdering, roasting, and eating the mangled victims of his barbarous battles," might raise terror in the bravest breasts; this very terror produced a directly contrary effect to causing submission to the royal army. It was seen that the few friends of the royal cause, as well as its enemies, were liable to be the victims of the indiscriminate rage of the savages; and thus "the inhabitants of the open and frontier countries had no choice of acting: they had no means of security left, but by abandoning their habitations and taking up arms. Every man saw the necessity of becoming a temporary soldier, not only for his own security, but for the protection and defence of those connections which are dearer than life itself. Thus an army was poured forth by the woods, mountains, and marshes, which in this part were thickly sown with plantations and villages. The Americans recalled their courage; and when their regular army seemed to be entirely wasted, the spirit of the country produced a much greater and more formidable force."

While resolute recruits, accustomed to the use of firearms, and all partially trained by service in the provincial militias, were thus flocking to the standard of Gates and Arnold at Saratoga; and while Burgoyne was engaged at Fort Edward in providing the means for the further advance of his army through the intricate and hostile country that still lay before him, two events occurred, in each of which the British sustained loss, and the Americans obtained advantage, the moral effects of which were even more important than the immediate result of the encounters. When Burgoyne left Canada, General St. Leger was detached from that province with a mixed force of about one thousand men, and some light field-pieces, across Lake Ontario against Fort Stanwix, which the Americans held. After capturing this, he was to march along the Mohawk River to its confluence with the Hudson, between Saratoga and Albany, where his force and that of Burgoyne were to unite. But, after some successes, St. Leger was obliged to retreat, and to abandon his tents and large quantities of stores to the garrison. At the very time that General Burgoyne heard of this disaster, he experienced one still more severe in the defeat of Colonel Baum with a large detachment of German troops at Bennington, whither Burgoyne had sent them for the purpose of capturing some magazines of provisions, of which the British army stood greatly in need. The Americans, augmented by continual accessions of strength, succeeded, after many attacks, in breaking this corps, which fled into the woods, and left its commander mortally wounded on the field: they then marched against a force of five hundred grenadiers and light infantry, which was advancing to Colonel Baum's assistance, under Lieutenant-Colonel Breyman; who, after a gallant resistance, was obliged to retreat on the main army. The British loss in these two actions exceeded six hundred men: and a party of American loyalists, on their way to join the army, having attached themselves to Colonel Baum's corps, were destroyed with it.

Notwithstanding these reverses, which added greatly to the spirit and numbers of the American forces, Burgoyne determined to advance. It was impossible any longer to keep up his communications with Canada by way of the lakes, so as to supply his army on his southward march; but having by unremitting exertions collected provisions for thirty days, he crossed the Hudson by means of a bridge of rafts, and, marching a short distance along its western bank, he encamped on the 14th of September on the heights of Saratoga, about sixteen miles from Albany. The Americans had fallen back from Saratoga, and were now strongly posted near Stillwater, about half-way between Saratoga and Albany, and showed a determination to recede no farther.

Meanwhile Lord Howe, with the bulk of the British army that had lain at New York, had sailed away to the Delaware, and there commenced a campaign against Washington, in which the English general took Philadelphia, and gained other showy, but unprofitable successes. But Sir Henry Clinton, a brave and skilful officer, was left with a considerable force at New York; and he undertook the task of moving up the Hudson to co-operate with Burgoyne. Clinton was obliged for this purpose to wait for reinforcements which had been promised from England, and these did not arrive till September. As soon as he received them, Clinton embarked about 3000 of his men on a flotilla, convoyed by some ships of war under Commander Hotham, and proceeded to force his way up the river, but it was long before he was able to open any communication with Burgoyne.

The country between Burgoyne's position at Saratoga and that of the Americans at Stillwater was rugged, and seamed with creeks and water-courses; but after great labour in making bridges and temporary causeways, the British army moved forward. About four miles from Saratoga, on the afternoon of the 19th of September, a sharp encounter took place between part of the English right wing, under Burgoyne himself, and a strong body of the enemy, under Gates and Arnold. The conflict lasted till sunset. The British remained masters of the field; but the loss on each side was nearly equal (from five hundred to six hundred men); and the spirits of the Americans were greatly raised by having withstood the best regular troops of the English army. Burgoyne now halted again, and strengthened his position by field-works and redoubts; and the Americans also improved their defences. The two armies remained nearly within cannon-shot of each other for a considerable time, during which Burgoyne was anxiously look-ing for intelligence of the promised expedition from New York, which, according to the original plan, ought by this time to have been approaching Albany from the south. At last, a messenger from Clinton made his way, with great difficulty, to Burgoyne's camp, and brought the information that Clinton was on his way up the Hudson to attack the American forts which barred the passage up that river to Albany. Burgoyne, in reply, on the 30th of September, urged Clinton to attack the forts as speedily as possible, stating that the effect of such an attack, or even the semblance of it, would be to move the American army from its position before his own troops. By another messenger, who reached Clinton on the 5th of October, Burgoyne informed his brother general that he had lost his communica-tions with Canada, but had provisions which would last him till the 20th. Burgoyne described himself as strongly posted, and stated that though the Americans in front of him were strongly posted also, he made no doubt of being able to force them, and making his way to Albany; but that he doubted whether he could subsist there, as the country was drained of provisions. He wished Clinton to meet him there, and to keep open a communication with New York.

Burgoyne had over-estimated his resources, and in the very beginning of October found difficulty and distress pressing him hard.

The Indians and Canadians began to desert him; while, on the other hand, Gates's army was continually reinforced by fresh bodies of the militia. An expeditionary force was detached by the Americans, which made a bold, though unsuccessful, attempt to retake Ticonderoga. And finding the number and spirit of the enemy to increase daily, and his own stores of provision to diminish, Burgoyne determined on attacking the

Americans in front of him, and by dislodging them from their position, to gain the means of moving upon Albany, or at least of relieving his troops from the straitened position in which they were cooped up.

Burgoyne's force was now reduced to less than 6000 men. The right of his camp was on some high ground a little to the west of the river; thence his entrenchments extended along the lower ground to the bank of the Hudson, the line of their front being nearly at a right angle with the course of the stream. The lines were fortified with redoubts and field-works, and on a height on the flank of the extreme right a strong redoubt was reared, and intrenchments, in a horse-shoe form, thrown up. The Hessians, under Colonel Breyman, were stationed here, forming a flank defence to Burgoyne's main army. The numerical force of the Americans was now greater than the British, even in regular troops, and the numbers of the militia and volunteers which had joined Gates and Arnold were greater still.

General Lincoln, with 2000 New England troops, had reached the American camp on the 29th of September. Gates gave him the command of the right wing, and took in person the command of the left wing, which was composed of two brigades under Generals Poor and Leonard, of Colonel Morgan's rifle corps, and part of the fresh New England Militia. The whole of the American lines had been ably fortified under the direction of the celebrated Polish General, Kosciusko, who was now serving as a volunteer in Gates's army. The right of the American position, that is to say, the part of it nearest to the river, was too strong to be assailed with any prospect of success: and Burgoyne therefore determined to endeavour to force their left. For this purpose he formed a column of 1500 regular troops, with two twelve-pounders, two howitzers, and six six-pounders. He headed this in person, having Generals Phillips, Reidesel, and Frazer under him. The enemy's force immediately in front of his lines was so strong that he dared not weaken the troops who guarded them, by detaching any more to strengthen his column of attack.

It was on the 7th of October that Burgoyne led his column forward; and on the preceding day, the 6th, Clinton had successfully executed a brilliant enterprise against two American forts which barred his progress up the Hudson. He had captured them both, with severe loss to the American forces opposed to him; he had destroyed the fleet which the Americans had been forming on the Hudson, under the protection of their forts; and the upward river was laid open to his squadron. He had also, with admirable skill and industry, collected in small vessels, such as could float within a few miles of Albany, provisions sufficient to supply Burgoyne's army for six months. He was now only a hundred and fifty-six miles distant from Burgoyne; and a detachment of 1700 men actually advanced within forty miles of Albany. Unfortunately Burgoyne and Clinton were each ignorant of the other's movements; but if Burgoyne had won his battle on the 7th, he must on advancing have soon learned the tidings of Clinton's success, and Clinton would have heard of his. A junction would soon have been made of the two victorious armies, and the great objects of the campaign might yet have been accomplished. All depended on the fortune of the column with which Burgoyne, on the eventful 7th of October 1777, advanced against the American position. There were brave men, both English and German, in its ranks; and in particular it comprised one of the best bodies of grenadiers in the British service.

Burgoyne pushed forward some bodies of irregular troops to distract the enemy's attention; and led his column to within three quarters of a mile from the left of Gates's camp, and then deployed his men into line. The grenadiers under Major Ackland, and the artillery under Major Williams, were drawn up on the left; a corps of Germans, under General Reidesel, and some British troops under General Phillips, were in the centre; and the English Light Infantry, and the 24th regiment, under Lord Balcarres and General Frazer, were on the right. But Gates did not wait to be attacked; and directly the British line was formed and began to advance, the American general, with admirable skill, caused General Poor's brigade of New York and New Hampshire troops, and part of General Leonard's brigade, to make a sudden and vehement rush against its left, and at the same time sent Colonel Morgan, with his rifle corps and other troops, amounting to 1500, to turn the right of the English. The grenadiers under Ackland sustained the charge of superior numbers nobly. But Gates sent more Americans forward, and in a few minutes the action became general along the centre, so as to prevent the Germans from detaching any help to the grenadiers. Morgan, with his riflemen, was now pressing Lord Balcarres and General Frazer hard, and fresh masses of the enemy were observed advancing from their extreme left, with the evident intention of forcing the British right, and cutting off its retreat. The English light infantry and the 24th now fell back, and formed an oblique second line, which enabled them to baffle this manœuvre, and also to succour their comrades in the left wing, the gallant grenadiers, who were overpowered by superior numbers, and, but for this aid, must have been cut to pieces.

The contest now was fiercely maintained on both sides. The English cannon were repeatedly taken and retaken; but when the grenadiers near them were forced back by the weight of superior numbers, one of the guns was permanently captured by the Americans, and turned upon the English. Major Williams and Major Ackland were both made prisoners, and in this part of the field the advantage of the Americans was decided. The British centre still held its ground; but now it was that the American general Arnold appeared upon the scene, and did more for his countrymen than whole battalions could have effected. Arnold, when the decisive engagement of the 7th of October commenced, had been deprived of his command by Gates, in consequence of a quarrel between them about the action of the 19th of September. He had listened for a short time in the American camp to the thunder of the battle, in which he had no military right to take part, either as commander or as combatant. But his excited spirit could not long endure such a state of inaction. He called for his horse, a powerful brown charger, and springing on it, galloped furiously to where the fight seemed to be the thickest. Gates saw him, and sent an aide-de-camp to recall him; but Arnold spurred far in advance, and placed himself at the head of three regiments which had formerly been under him, and which welcomed their old commander with joyous cheers. He led them instantly upon the British centre; and then galloping along the American line, he issued orders for a renewed and a closer attack, which were obeyed with alacrity, Arnold himself setting the example of the most daring personal bravery, and charging more than once, sword in hand, into the English ranks. On the British side the officers did their duty nobly; but General Frazer was the most eminent of them all, restoring order wherever the line began to waver, and infusing fresh courage into his men by voice and example. Mounted on an iron-grey charger, and dressed in the full uniform of a general officer, he was conspicuous to foes as well as to friends. The American Colonel Morgan thought that the fate of the battle rested on this gallant man's life, and calling several of his best marksmen round him, pointed Frazer out, and said: "That officer is General Frazer; I admire him, but he must die. Our victory depends on it. Take your stations in that clump of bushes, and do your duty." Within five minutes, Frazer fell mortally wounded, and was carried to the British camp by two grenadiers. Just previously to his being struck by the fatal bullet, one rifleball had cut the crupper of his saddle, and another had passed through his horse's mane close behind the ears. His aide-de-camp had noticed this, and said: "It is evident that you are marked out for particular aim; would it not be prudent for you to retire from this place?" Frazer replied: "My duty forbids me to fly from danger;" and the next moment he fell.

Burgoyne's whole force was now compelled to retreat towards their camp; the left and centre were in complete disorder, but the light infantry and the 24th checked the fury of the assailants, and the remains of the column with great difficulty effected their return to their camp; leaving six of their cannons in the possession of the enemy, and great numbers of killed and wounded on the field; and especially a large proportion of the artillerymen, who had stood to their guns until shot down or bayoneted beside them by the advancing Americans.

Burgoyne's column had been defeated, but the action was not yet over. The English had scarcely entered the camp, when the Americans, pursuing their success, assaulted it in several places with remarkable impetuosity, rushing in upon the intrenchments and redoubts through a severe fire of grape-shot and musketry. Arnold especially, who on this day appeared maddened with the thirst of combat and carnage, urged on the attack against a part of the intrenchments which was occupied by the light infantry under Lord Balcarres. But the English received him with vigour and spirit. The struggle here was obstinate and sanguinary. At length, as it grew towards evening, Arnold, having forced all obstacles, entered the works with some of the most fearless of his followers. But in this critical moment of glory and danger, he received a painful wound in the same leg which had already been injured at the assault on Quebec. To his bitter regret he was obliged to be carried back. His party still continued the attack, but the English also continued their obstinate resistance, and at last night fell, and the assailants withdrew from this quarter of the British intrenchments. But in another part the attack had been more successful. A body of the Americans, under Colonel Brooke, forced their way in through a part of the horseshoe intrenchments on the extreme right, which was defended by the Hessian reserve under Colonel Breyman. The Germans resisted well, and Breyman died in defence of his post; but the Americans made good the ground which they had won, and captured baggage, tents, artillery, and a store of ammunition, which they were greatly in need of. They had, by establishing themselves on this point, acquired the means of completely turning the right flank of the British, and gaining their rear. To prevent this calamity, Burgoyne effected during the night an entire change of position. With great skill he removed his whole army to some heights near the river, a little northward of the former camp, and he there drew up his men, expecting to be attacked on the following day. But Gates was resolved not to risk the certain triumph which his success had already secured for him. He harassed the English with skirmishes, but attempted no regular attack. Meanwhile he detached bodies of troops on both sides of the Hudson to prevent the British from recrossing that river, and to bar their retreat. When night fell, it became absolutely necessary for Burgoyne to retire again, and, accordingly, the troops were marched through a stormy and rainy night towards Saratoga, abandoning their sick and wounded, and the greater part of their baggage, to the enemy.

Before the rear-guard quitted the camp, the last sad honours were paid to the brave General Frazer, who expired on the day after the action.

He had, almost with his last breath, expressed a wish to be buried in the redoubt which had formed the part of the British lines where he had been stationed, but which had now been abandoned by the English, and was within full range of the cannon which the advancing Americans were rapidly placing in position to bear upon Burgoyne's force. Burgoyne resolved, nevertheless, to comply with the dying wish of his comrade; and the interment took place under circumstances the most affecting that have ever marked a soldier's funeral. Still more interesting is the narrative of Lady Ackland's passage from the British to the American camp, after the battle, to share the captivity and alleviate the sufferings of her husband, who had been severely wounded, and left in the enemy's power. The American historian, Lossing, has described both these touching episodes of the campaign, in a spirit that does honour to the writer as well as to his subject. After narrating the death of General Frazer on the 8th of October, he says that "It was just at sunset, on that calm October evening, that the corpse of General Frazer was carried up the hill to the place of burial within the 'great redoubt.' It was attended only by the military members of his family and Mr. Brudenell, the chaplain; yet the eyes of hundreds of both armies followed the solemn procession, while the Americans, ignorant of its true character, kept up a constant cannonade upon the redoubt. The chaplain, unawed by the danger to which he was exposed, as the cannon-balls that struck the hill threw the loose soil over him, pronounced the impressive funeral service of the Church of England with an unfaltering voice. The growing darkness added solemnity to the scene. Suddenly the irregular firing ceased, and the solemn voice of a single cannon, at measured intervals, boomed along the valley, and awakened the responses of the hills. It was a minute gun fired by the Americans in honour of the gallant dead. The moment the information was given that the gathering at the redoubt was a funeral company, fulfilling, at imminent peril, the last-breathed wishes of the noble Frazer, orders were issued to withhold the cannonade with balls, and to render military homage to the fallen brave.

"The case of Major Ackland and his heroic wife presents kindred features. He belonged to the grenadiers, and was an accomplished soldier. His wife accompanied him to Canada in 1776; and during the whole campaign of that year, and until his return to England after the surrender of Burgoyne, in the autumn of 1777, endured all the hardships, dangers, and privations of an active campaign in an enemy's country. At Chambly, on the Sorel, she attended him in illness, in a miserable hut; and when he was wounded in the battle of Hubbardton, Vermont, she hastened to him at Henesborough from Montreal, where she had been persuaded to remain, and resolved to follow the army hereafter. Just before crossing the Hudson, she and her husband had had a narrow escape from losing their lives in consequence of their tent accidentally taking fire.

"During the terrible engagement of the 7th October, she heard all the tumult and dreadful thunder of the battle in which her husband was engaged; and when, on the morning of the 8th, the British fell back in confusion to their new position, she, with the other women, was obliged to take refuge among the dead and dying; for the tents were all struck, and hardly a shed was left standing. Her husband was wounded, and a prisoner in the American camp. That gallant officer was shot through both legs. When Poor and Leonard's troops assaulted the grenadiers and artillery on the British left, on the afternoon of the 7th, Wilkinson, Gates's adjutant-general, while pursuing the flying enemy when they abandoned their battery, heard a feeble voice exclaim, 'Protect me, sir, against that boy.' He turned and saw a lad with a musket taking deliberate aim at a wounded British officer, lying in a corner of a low fence. Wilkinson ordered the boy to desist, and discovered the wounded man to be Major Ackland. He had him conveyed to the quarters of General Poor on the heights, where every attention was paid to his wants.

"When the intelligence that he was wounded and a prisoner reached his wife, she was greatly distressed, and, by the advice of her friend, Baroness Reidesel, resolved to visit the American camp, and implore the favour of a personal attendance upon her husband. On the 9th she sent a message to Burgoyne by Lord Petersham, his aide-de-camp, asking permission to depart. 'Though I was ready to believe,' says Burgoyne, 'that patience and fortitude, in a supreme degree, were to be found, as well as every other virtue, under the most tender forms, I was astonished at this proposal. After so long an agitation of spirits, exhausted not only for want of rest, but absolutely want of food, drenched in rains for twelve hours together, that a woman should be capable of such an undertaking as delivering herself to an enemy, probably in the night, and uncertain of what hands she might fall into, appeared an effort above human nature. The assistance I was able to give was small indeed. I had not even a cup of wine to offer. All I could furnish her with was an open boat, and a few lines, written upon dirty wet paper, to General Gates, recommending her to his protection.' The following is a copy of the note sent by Burgoyne to General Gates:—'Sir,—Lady Harriet Ackland, a lady of the first distinction of family, rank, and personal virtues, is under such concern on account of Major Ackland, her husband, wounded and a prisoner in your hands, that I cannot refuse her request to commit her to your protection. Whatever general impropriety there may be in persons of my situation and yours to solicit favours, I cannot see the uncommon perseverance in every female grace, and the exaltation of character of this lady, and her very hard fortune, without testifying that your attentions to her will lay me under obligations. I am, sir, your obedient servant, J. Burgoyne.' She set out in an open boat upon the Hudson, accompanied by Mr. Brudenell, the chaplain, Sarah Pollard, her waiting-maid, and her husband's valet, who had been severely wounded, while searching for his master upon the battle-field. It was about sunset when they started, and a violent storm of rain and wind, which had been increasing since the morning, rendered the voyage tedious and perilous in the extreme. It was long after dark when they reached the American outposts; the sentinel heard their oars, and hailed them. Lady Harriet returned the answer herself. The clear, silvery tones of a woman's voice amid the darkness, filled the soldier on duty with superstitious fear, and he called a comrade to accompany him to the river bank. The errand of the voyagers was made known, but the faithful guard, apprehensive of treachery, would not allow them to land until they sent for Major Dearborn. They were invited by that officer to his quarters, where every attention was paid to them, and Lady Harriet was comforted by the joyful tidings that her husband was safe. In the morning she experienced parental tenderness from General Gates, who sent her to her husband, at Poor's quarters, under a suitable escort. There she remained until he was removed to Albany."

Burgoyne now took up his last position on the heights near Saratoga; and hemmed in by the enemy, who refused any encounter, and baffled in all his attempts at finding a path of escape, he there lingered until famine compelled him to capitulate. The fortitude of the British army during this melancholy period has been justly eulogised by many historians.

At length the 13th of October arrived, and as no prospect of assistance appeared, and the provisions were nearly exhausted, Burgoyne, by the unanimous advice of a council of war, sent a messenger to the American camp to treat of a convention.

General Gates in the first instance demanded that the royal army should surrender prisoners of war. He also proposed that the British should ground their arms. Burgoyne replied, "This article is inadmissible in every extremity; sooner than this army will consent to ground their arms in their encampment, they will rush on the enemy, determined to take no quarter." After various messages, a convention for the surrender of the army was settled, which provided that "The troops under General Burgoyne were to march out of their camp with the honours of war, and the artillery of the intrenchments, to the verge of the river, where the arms and artillery were to be left. The arms to be piled by word of command from their own officers. A free passage was to be granted to the army under Lieutenant-General Burgoyne to Great Britain, upon condition of not serving again in North America during the present contest."

The articles of capitulation were settled on the 15th of October; and on that very evening a messenger arrived from Clinton with an account of his successes, and with the tidings that part of his force had penetrated as far as Esopus, within fifty miles of Burgoyne's camp. But it was too late. The public faith was pledged; and the army was, indeed, too debilitated by fatigue and hunger to resist an attack if made; and Gates certainly would have made it, if the convention had been broken off. Accordingly, on the 17th, the convention of Saratoga was carried into effect. By this convention 5790 men surrendered themselves as prisoners. The sick and wounded left in the camp when the British retreated to Saratoga, together with the numbers of the British, German, and Canadian troops, who were killed, wounded, or taken, and who had deserted in the preceding part of the expedition, were reckoned to be 4689.

The British sick and wounded who had fallen into the hands of the Americans after the battle of the 7th, were treated with exemplary humanity; and when the convention was executed, General Gates showed a noble delicacy of feeling, which deserves the highest degree of honour. Every circumstance was avoided which could give the appearance of triumph. The American troops remained within their lines until the British had piled their arms; and when this was done, the vanquished officers and soldiers were received with friendly kindness by their victors, and their immediate wants were promptly and liberally supplied. Discussions and disputes afterwards arose as to some of the terms of the convention; and the American Congress refused for a long time to carry into effect the article which provided for the return of Burgoyne's men to Europe; but no blame was imputable to General Gates or his army, who showed themselves to be generous as they had proved themselves to be brave.

Gates, after the victory, immediately despatched Colonel Wilkinson to carry the happy tidings to Congress. On being introduced into the hall, he said, "The whole British army has laid down its arms at Saratoga;

our own, full of vigour and courage, expect your order. It is for your wisdom to decide where the country may still have need for their service." Honours and rewards were liberally voted by the Congress to their conquering general and his men; "and it would be difficult (says the Italian historian, Botta) to describe the transports of joy which the news of this event excited among the Americans. They began to flatter themselves with a still more happy future. No one any longer felt any doubt about their achieving their independence. All hoped, and with good reason, that a success of this importance would at length determine France, and the other European powers that waited for her example, to declare themselves in favour of America. *There could no longer be any question respecting the future; since there was no longer the risk of espousing the cause of a people too feeble to defend themselves.*

The truth of this was soon displayed in the conduct of France. When the news arrived at Paris of the capture of Ticonderoga, and of the victorious march of Burgoyne towards Albany, events which seemed decisive in favour of the English, instructions had been immediately despatched to Nantz, and the other ports of the kingdom, that no American privateers should be suffered to enter them, except from indispensable necessity, as to repair their vessels, to obtain provisions, or to escape the perils of the sea. The American commissioners at Paris, in their disgust and despair, had almost broken off all negotiations with the French Government; and they even endeavoured to open communications with the British Ministry. But the British Government, elated with the first successes of Burgoyne, refused to listen to any overtures for accommodation. But when the news of Saratoga reached Paris, the whole scene was changed. Franklin and his brother commissioners found all their difficulties with the French government vanish. The time seemed to have arrived for the House of Bourbon to take a full revenge for all its humiliations and losses in previous wars. In December a treaty was arranged, and formally signed in the February following, by which France acknowledged *the Independent United States of America*. This was, of course, tantamount to a declaration of war with England. Spain soon followed France; and before long Holland took the same course. Largely aided by French fleets and troops, the Americans vigorously maintained the war against the armies which England, in spite of her European foes, continued to send across the Atlantic. But the struggle was too unequal to be maintained by this country for many years: and when the treaties of 1783 restored peace to the world, the independence of the United States was reluctantly recognised by their ancient parent and recent enemy, England.

The Lost Battalion

BY

THOMAS M. JOHNSON AND FLETCHER PRATT

IT WAS 8:30 on the morning of October 2, 1918, the seventh day of the Argonne drive by U. S. Division 77—"New York's own." Regiment 308, on the western edge of the forest, stumbled forward into the depressed-looking jungle of second growth and underbrush. Advance north straight ahead, the orders said, through the main German line to a position just beyond Charlevaux Brook.

Major Charles W. Whittlesey, the tall, spectacled, New England lawyer who commanded the First Battalion, looked grave. The terrain was difficult, the woods too thick to permit good artillery support. Liaison with the French army on the left was bad. His men had no blankets, no raincoats, no reserve rations, and no experience. They were draft boys from New York City's lower East Side; only 10 percent of them knew how to work a hand grenade, and as for the rifles: "I can't make the bullets go into this thing," said one. But the orders were: Go ahead, pay no attention to flanks or losses.

They went forward, against machine-gun fire. Men fell here and there— "First aid"—and the advance slowed. Finally the fire in their faces became a horizontal rainstorm. To continue straight ahead was suicide. Whittlesey swung his force to the right, up Hill 198. Crawling, sneaking from tree to tree, skirmishing by singles and twos as American soldiers have done since the days of Mad Anthony Wayne, they encountered only snipers and isolated machine-gun nests. And then—the leading patrols came upon a trench, part of the main German defense line, but deserted! The German command, counting on the unfavorable terrain to hold up the American advance, had switched most of the defenders further east.

Beyond the abandoned trench was Charlevaux Valley, and across the opposite slope ran a road, their objective point. The sun of the short October day was going down behind scurrying clouds. Whittlesey and his men topped the ridge, charged down into Charlevaux Valley like a herd of wild cattle, and spread out in a pocket at the foot of the hill beyond. The parapet of the road loomed out of the forest. Whittlesey decided to spend the night up there, protected from German artillery fire by the hill. He had 575 men with him.

Early the next morning Company K of the 307th Regiment straggled into the position. The rest of the regiment, sent to support Whittlesey's right flank, had gone astray in the forest during the night.

Soon a message arrived from the commander of the 308th in the rear: "Do not advance until you receive the order from me." The message was timed at 7 p.m.; it had taken all night to come through, so some of the runners Whittlesey had left posted behind him must have been shot or dislodged by German patrols. Whittlesey sent Company K to retrace the route of the advance, but the men soon returned with the information that the hill behind them was now alive with Germans and protected by new wire.

Whittlesey was hemmed in. What to do next? Perhaps the strictly sensible course was to smash back through the new German line. However, a general order had been issued when the Argonne offensive started: "Ground once captured must not be given up in absence of direct orders. . . . *We are not going back, but forward!*" Whittlesey, with a New England background and a lawyer's training, obeyed that order to the letter. The rest of the general advance might come up to him during the day; and he realized that his battalion, driven into the German front, exercised a paralyzing effect on the whole enemy line.

The German command, knowing that the battalion was surrounded, decided not to waste men by attacking the position in force. Heavy machine-gun fire and attacks by bomb-throwers ought to be enough to bring about its surrender.

At three o'clock that afternoon, a line of Germans advanced through the forest, heaving "potato-masher" bombs in unison, scuttling forward in the shelter of the bursts. But as soon as the line became visible to the Americans a rippling blaze of fire ran along the pocket, every shot aimed. There was a choir of shrieks; half a dozen bombs burst at the feet of the men who had meant to throw them. The attack was stopped.

For a few minutes the men of the 308th relaxed in the holes they had dug. Then the Germans opened up a trench mortar, together with all the machine guns they had cautiously shifted into position. When the storm died down a little, Major Whittlesey sent a message to the rear via carrier pigeon: "Situation very serious. Have not been able to re-establish runner posts. Need ammunition."

Dawn of October 4 found burial parties of the 308th hard at work. Instantly the German mortars tuned up, and although most of the shells pitched to the foot of the hillside, the noise shattered nerves and kept every man on edge.

The men had almost no food now, and what was worse, they could no longer get enough water. Two men had been killed trying to reach the water-hole in the valley. Finally Zip Cepeglia, a little Italian runner, took a string of canteens and hunched, rolled, slid toward a shell hole where muddy liquid had collected. His foot struck a gravel pile, sending a mini-ature avalanche over a soldier who lay behind it.

"You son-of-a—!" said the man softly but with feeling. It was too much for the overwrought runner's nerves; in spite of singing bullets he leaped to his feet: "You wanna make something of it? All right, I fight you right now!"

Someone grabbed him by the ankle. "Lay down, you crazy wop! If you want to fight, fight the Germans."

More potato-mashers came over in a shower. There were only three pigeons left, but Whittlesey had to send another call for help: "Germans still around us. Men suffering from hunger and exposure. Cannot support be sent at once?"

At noon on the 4th there came a lull in the German fire. Then, suddenly, there was a violent explosion, then two more, then three. Their own artillery, believing the battalion to be somewhat to the rear of its actual position, was accidentally bombarding it!

Shells burst in among the funk holes where the men lay helpless. Trees crashed, brush flew. All over the positions men shouted, screamed, tried frantically to burrow deeper into the earth. Twenty years later the survivors recalled that terrible period as the worst of the siege.

At the headquarters hole Major Whittlesey sat down to write an emer-gency message. Someone noticed blood on his face. "Are you hurt, sir?" Whittlesey dabbed at a shrapnel cut, shook his head irritably and went on writing.

There were two pigeons left. A soldier fumbled at the crate and one of the birds whirled through his hands and away. Whittlesey swore; the soldier pulled out the last pigeon, Cher Ami, and attached the last message, the last chance this side of hell. "We are along the road parallel 276.4. Our own artillery is dropping a barrage directly on us. For heaven's sake, stop it."

Cher Ami rose in a spiral, circled several times, and then settled down on a tree and began preening his feathers.

"Boo!" yelled Whittlesey. "Hey!" shouted the soldiers. Cher Ami was oblivious. They threw sticks at the obstinate fowl, ducking as each shell burst near them. Finally one of the men shinned up the tree and shook the branch. The bird took off.

Cher Ami reached the 77th Division pigeon loft at 4 o'clock. He had been caught in shellfire and came in with one eye gone, his breastbone broken and a leg cut away. But he delivered his message.

At 4:15 the shelling stopped, and immediately the Germans laid down heavy machine-gun fire. Twice that night parties of Germans got into the outpost lines, only to be shot down or driven back. Under the cliff, the fight-ing closed in a queer battle of words. "Gaz masks!" shouted a voice—words good, but accent foreign. "Gas masks hell!" replied an American voice, ac-companied by a shot that brought a howl from the forest—undeniably German, for while Americans grunted when hit, the Heinies wailed like banshees.

The exchange started a series. "First, Second and Third Companies, this way!" shouted an authoritative voice, deceptively American this time. Good trick, but there were no first, second or third companies in the U. S. Army. "Bring ten machine guns over here on the left!" Then a long cackle of hoots. "Order your coffins, Americans!"

But there were German-speakers among the Americans too. Corporal Speich of the 308 covered himself with glory by bellowing, *"Ach, du wint Betebren!"*—"Oh, you bunch of stink experts!" It brought down the house, and also a final shower of bullets.

October 5 dawned wretched and misty. The ground was covered with a chilling fog. The men were weak with hunger, old food cans were licked clean, even the birdseed for pigeons was eaten. From down where the wounded lay came constant calls for water. The place stank frightfully of dead men and gangrene.

Meanwhile, back at Brigade Headquarters, plans had been made for another attempt to come to Whittlesey's aid, while airplanes carried him food and munitions.

The attack petered out again in the bloody ravine before Hill 198. The planes were unable to spot their objective and had to drop their loads by guess. The Americans could hear the glad, guttural shouts as the Germans gathered the food for which they were starving, and their own hunger seemed a thousandfold increased.

Then came the shock of guns to the rear, the same sound they had heard the day before. Every head turned, every heart stood still. The barrage crept closer, closer—"Oh, my God, again?"—then jumped their position and pounded the hill ahead. This time the artillery had the range! The German mortar went silent, the machine guns coughed and stopped. Commands and shouts came from the woods above.

"Jeez, Jim, listen to those bastards yell!"

In spite of cold, hunger and wounds, the Lost Battalion, for the first time since it entered the pocket, began to enjoy itself. Nothing is so pleasant as seeing the man who has bullied you take the same treatment from a bigger bully.

All through October 6 the battalion held its position. Commanders and commanded were discovering the secret of siege—as it has been learned in all the great beleaguerments of history—that the human capacity for endurance exceeds all belief, as long as there is a leader to say, "Don't give up, we're not licked yet." And this battalion had such a leader, a man who held his men steady by his own unshaken presence.

On the morning of October 7, Whittlesey asked again for volunteers to take a message back. So far, no messenger had got through; some had been killed, some driven back by enemy fire. But now Abe Krotoshinsky, a little, stoop-shouldered Polish Jew, stepped forward with two other men. In a moment they had slipped away through the bushes toward Hill 198.

"I hope they make it," the Major said, without conviction.

That afternoon a captured American private turned up with a letter for

Major Whittlesey from the German commanding officer, demanding surrender. "It would be quite useless to resist any more," the message read. "The suffering of your wounded can be heard over here and we are appealing to your human sentiments."

Captain McMurtry, second in command, cried: "We've got them licked, or they wouldn't have sent this!"

Whittlesey, in full agreement, sent no reply. Word of the happening ran through the command by grapevine. Everywhere heads popped out of funk holes.

"What's that?"

"They want us to quit! The Major told 'em to go to hell!"

Every emotion of the dead-weary, starving, hysterical men was transformed into a wild rage at the enemy. Tired men, sick men, sat up and sharpened bayonets on pieces of stone. Wounded men, who had not fired a gun in two days, hunted for cartridges on the bodies of their dead buddies. The German attack that afternoon met the fiercest and bloodiest repulse of any yet delivered.

Later the two men who had started out with Abe Krotoshinsky came back, one with a smashed shoulder and face white with pain. Someone offered them a bit of candle to eat: "Good for the Eskimos, why not us?" The messengers had separated in the woods, lost track of Abe. "He's probably been killed," they said.

But Abe Krotoshinsky had not been killed. He had crawled from one bit of cover to another until he found himself among the German outposts. Then he had inched through the brush, sometimes within earshot of German patrols and machine-gun nests, until suddenly he heard American voices. Safe in the American lines, Abe asked for food, then gasped out the location of the battalion and its desperate need for help.

"Can you lead us back?"

"Sure. I feel good now."

That night the 307th Regiment fought its way past Hill 198 into Charlevaux Valley. Here the advance patrols began to smell the Lost Battalion long before they could see it—a frightful odor of corruption, wounds and death. Now they reached the pocket, where men were groaning and muttering in the fox holes all around. Every man they met broke into a grin, an almost foolishly happy smile. The Lost Battalion had been relieved.

Major General Alexander, commanding Division 77, was one of the first into the pocket next morning. "Where's Whittlesey?" he asked. The Major was down the hill, handing out food to his men.

"Shall I get him for you?"

"By no means. I'll go to him."

The Major's face was haggard, his uniform torn and dirty. Alexander greeted him warmly. "From now on you're Lieutenant Colonel Whittlesey."

The men cheered.

With incredible nerve, many of the 194 who had gone through that week of hell without becoming hospital cases volunteered to go up in the line again as soon as they had eaten.

WAR DEMANDS RESOLUTION, FIRMNESS,
AND STAUNCHNESS

*R*ESOLUTION *is an act of courage in single instances, and if it becomes a characteristic trait, it is a habit of the mind. But here we do not mean courage in face of bodily danger but in face of responsibility; therefore to a certain extent against moral danger . . . mere intelligence is still not courage, for we often see the cleverest people devoid of resolution. The man must, therefore, first awaken the feeling of courage, and then be guided and supported by it because in momentary emergencies the man is swayed more by his feelings than his thoughts.*

Firmness denotes the resistance of the will in relation to the force of a single blow. Staunchness in relation to a continuance of blows. Close as is the analogy between the two, and often as the one is used in the place of the other, still there is a notable difference between them which can not be mistaken. Inasmuch as firmness against a single powerful impression may have its root in the mere strength of a feeling, but staunchness must be supported rather by the understanding, for the greater the duration of an action the more systematic deliberation is connected with it, and from this staunchness partly derives its power.

Force of character leads us to a spurious variety of it—obstinacy.

Bagration's Rearguard Action

BY

COUNT LEO TOLSTOY

KUTUZOV had, on the 1st of November, received from one of his spies information that showed the army he commanded to be in an almost hopeless position. The spy reported that the French, after crossing the bridge at Vienna, were moving in immense force on Kutuzov's line of communications with the reinforcements marching from Russia. If Kutuzov were to determine to remain at Krems, Napoleon's army of a hundred and fifty thousand men would cut him off from all communications, and would surround his exhausted army of forty thousand, and he would find himself in the position of Mack before Ulm. If Kutuzov decided to leave the road leading to a junction with the Russian reinforcements, he would have to make his way with no road through unknown country to the mountains of Bohemia, pursued by the cream of the enemy's forces, and to give up all hope of effecting a junction with Buxhevden. If Kutuzov decided to march by the road from Krems to Olmütz to join the forces from Russia he ran the risk of finding the French, who had crossed the Vienna bridge, in advance of him on this road, and so being forced to give battle on the march, encumbered with all his stores and transport, with an enemy three times as numerous and hemming him in on both sides. Kutuzov chose the last course.

The French, after crossing the river, had, as the spy reported, set off at a quick march toward Znaim, which lay on Kutuzov's line of route, more than a hundred versts in front of him. To reach Znaim before the French offered the best hopes of saving the army. To allow the French to get to Znaim before him would mean exposing the whole army to a disgrace like that of the Austrians at Ulm, or to complete destruction. But to arrive there before the French with the whole army was impossible. The road of the French army from Vienna to Znaim was shorter and better than the Russians' road from Krems to Znaim.

On the night of receiving the news Kutuzov sent Bagration's advance guard of four thousand soldiers to the right over the mountains from the Krems-Znaim road to the Vienna and Znaim road. Bagration was to make a forced march, to halt facing towards Vienna and with his back to Znaim, and if he succeeded in getting on the road in advance of the French, he was to delay them as long as he could. Kutuzov himself with all the transport was making straight for Znaim.

From: *War and Peace.*

Bagration marched forty-five versts, by night in stormy weather, through the mountains, with no road, and with hungry, barefoot soldiers. Leaving a third of his men, straggling behind him, Bagration reached Hollabrunn, on the Vienna and Znaim road, a few hours before the French, who marched upon Hollabrunn from Vienna. Kutuzov needed fully another twenty-four hours to get to Znaim with all the transport, and so to save the army Bagration would have had, with his four thousand hungry and exhausted soldiers, to have kept at bay the whole army of the enemy confronting him at Hollabrunn for four-and-twenty hours, and this was obviously impossible. But a freak of fate made the impossible possible. The success of the trick that had given the Vienna bridge into the hands of the French encouraged Murat to try and take in Kutuzov too. Murat, on meeting Bagration's weak detachment on the Znaim road, supposed it to be the whole army of Kutuzov. To give this army a final and crushing defeat he waited for the troops still on the road from Vienna, and to that end he proposed a truce for three days, on the condition that neither armies should change their positions nor stir from where they were. Murat averred that negotiations for peace were now proceeding, and that he proposed a truce therefore to avoid useless bloodshed. The Austrian general, Nostits, who was in charge of the advance posts, believed the statements of Murat's messengers and retired, leaving Bagration's detachment unprotected. The other messengers rode off to the Russian line to make the same announcement about peace negotiations, and to propose a truce of three days to the Russian troops. Bagration replied that he was not authorised to accept or to decline a truce, and sent his adjutant to Kutuzov with a report of the proposition made to him.

A truce gave Kutuzov the only possibility of gaining time, of letting Bagration's exhausted forces rest, and of getting the transport and heavy convoys (the movement of which was concealed from the French) a further stage on their journey. The offer of a truce gave the one—and totally unexpected—chance of saving the army. On receiving information of it, Kutuzov promptly despatched the general-adjutant, Winzengerode, who was with him, to the enemy's camp. Winzengerode was instructed not only to accept the truce, but to propose terms of capitulation, while Kutuzov meanwhile sent his adjutants back to hasten to the utmost the transport of the luggage of the whole army along the Krems and Znaim road. Bagration's hungry and exhausted detachment alone was to cover the movements of the transport and of the whole army, by remaining stationary in face of an enemy eight times stronger numerically.

Kutuzov's anticipations were correct both as to the proposals of capitulation, which bound him to nothing, giving time for part of the transport to reach Znaim, and as to Murat's blunder being very quickly discovered. As soon as Bonaparte, who was at Schönbrunn, only twenty-five versts from Hollabrunn, received Murat's despatch and projects of truce and capitulation, he detected the deception and despatched the following letter to Murat:

To Prince Murat.

Schönbrunn, 25 Brumaire, year 1805,
at 8 *o'clock in the morning.*

"It is impossible to find terms in which to express to you my displeasure. You only command my advance guard and you have no right to make any truce without my order. You are causing me to lose the results of a campaign. Break the truce immediately and march upon the enemy. You must make a declaration to them that the general who signed this capitulation had no right to do so, and that only the Emperor of Russia has that right.

"Whenever the Emperor of Russia ratifies the aforesaid convention, however, I will ratify it; but it is only a stratagem. March on, destroy the Russian army . . . you are in a position to take its baggage and artillery.

"The Emperor of Russia's aide-de-camp is a . . . Officers are nothing when they have not powers; this one had none. . . . The Austrians let themselves be tricked about the crossing of the bridge of Vienna, you are letting yourself be tricked by one of the Emperor's aides-de-camp.

"NAPOLEON."

Bonaparte's adjutant dashed off at full gallop with this menacing letter to Murat. Not trusting his generals, Bonaparte himself advanced to the field of battle with his whole guard, fearful of letting the snared victim slip through his fingers. Meanwhile the four thousand men of Bagration's detachment, merrily lighting camp-fires, dried and warmed themselves, and cooked their porridge for the first time for three days, and not one among them knew or dreamed of what was in store for them.

Before four o'clock in the afternoon Prince Andrey, who had persisted in his petition to Kutuzov, reached Grunte, and joined Bagration. Bonaparte's adjutant had not yet reached Murat's division, and the battle had not yet begun. In Bagration's detachment, they knew nothing of the progress of events. They talked about peace, but did not believe in its possibility. They talked of a battle, but did not believe in a battle's being close at hand either.

Knowing Bolkonsky to be a favourite and trusted adjutant, Bagration received him with a commanding officer's special graciousness and condescension. He informed him that there would probably be an engagement that day or the next day, and gave him full liberty to remain in attendance on him during the battle, or to retire to the rear-guard to watch over the order of the retreat, also a matter of great importance.

"To-day, though, there will most likely be no action," said Bagration, as though to reassure Prince Andrey.

"If this is one of the common run of little staff dandies, sent here to win a cross, he can do that in the rear-guard, but if he wants to be with me, let him . . . he'll be of use, if he's a brave officer," thought Bagration. Prince Andrey, without replying, asked the prince's permission to ride around the position and find out the disposition of the forces, so that, in case of a message, he might know where to take it. An officer on duty, a handsome and elegantly dressed man, with a diamond ring on his forefinger, who spoke French badly, but with assurance, was summoned to conduct Prince Andrey.

On all sides they saw officers drenched through, with dejected faces, apparently looking for something, and soldiers dragging doors, benches, and fences from the village.

"Here we can't put a stop to these people," said the staff-officer, pointing to them. "Their commanders let their companies get out of hand. And look here," he pointed to a canteen-keeper's booth, "they gather here, and here they sit. I drove them all out this morning, and look, it's full again. I must go and scare them, prince. One moment."

"Let us go together, and I'll get some bread and cheese there," said Prince Andrey, who had not yet had time for a meal.

"Why didn't you mention it, prince? I would have offered you something."

They got off their horses and went into the canteen-keeper's booth. Several officers, with flushed and exhausted faces, were sitting at the tables, eating and drinking.

"Now what does this mean, gentlemen?" said the staff-officer, in the reproachful tone of a man who has repeated the same thing several times. "You mustn't absent yourselves like this. The prince gave orders that no one was to leave his post. Come, really, captain," he remonstrated with a muddy, thin little artillery officer, who in his stockings (he had given his boots to the canteen-keeper to dry) stood up at their entrance, smiling not quite naturally.

"Now aren't you ashamed, Captain Tushin?" pursued the staff-officer. "I should have thought you as an artillery officer ought to set an example, and you have no boots on. They'll sound the alarm, and you'll be in a pretty position without your boots on." (The staff-officer smiled.) "Kindly return to your posts, gentlemen, all, all," he added in a tone of authority.

Prince Andrey could not help smiling as he glanced at Captain Tushin. Smiling, without a word, Tushin shifted from one bare foot to the other, looking inquiringly, with his big, shrewd, and good-natured eyes, from Prince Andrey to the staff-officer.

"The soldiers say it's easier barefoot," said Captain Tushin, smiling shyly, evidently anxious to carry off his awkward position in a jesting tone. But before he had uttered the words, he felt that his joke would not do and had not come off. He was in confusion.

"Kindly go to your places," said the staff-officer, trying to preserve his gravity.

Prince Andrey glanced once more at the little figure of the artillery officer. There was something peculiar about it, utterly unsoldierly, rather comic, but very attractive.

The staff-officer and Prince Andrey got on their horses and rode on.

Riding out beyond the village, continually meeting or overtaking soldiers and officers of various ranks, they saw on the left earthworks being thrown up, still red with the freshly dug clay. Several battalions of soldiers, in their shirt-sleeves, in spite of the cold wind were toiling like white ants at these entrenchments; from the trench they saw spadefuls of red clay continually being thrown out by unseen hands. They rode up to the entrenchment, examined it, and were riding on further. Close behind the entrenchment they came upon dozens of soldiers continually running to and from the earthworks, and they had to hold their noses and put their horses to a gallop to get by the pestilential atmosphere of this improvised sewer.

"*Voilà l'agrément des camps, monsieur le prince,*" said the staff-officer. They rode up the opposite hill. From that hill they had a view of the French. Prince Andrey stopped and began looking closer at what lay before them.

"You see here is where our battery stands," said the staff-officer, pointing to the highest point, "commanded by that queer fellow sitting without his boots; from there you can see everything; let us go there, prince."

"I am very grateful to you, I'll go alone now," said Prince Andrey, anxious to be rid of the staff-officer; "don't trouble yourself further, please."

The staff-officer left him, and Prince Andrey rode on alone.

The further forward and the nearer to the enemy he went, the more orderly and cheerful he found the troops. The greatest disorder and depression had prevailed in the transport forces before Znaim, which Prince Andrey had passed that morning, ten versts from the French. At Grunte too a certain alarm and vague dread could be felt. But the nearer Prince Andrey got to the French line, the more self-confident was the appearance of our troops. The soldiers, in their great-coats, stood ranged in lines with their sergeant, and the captain was calling over the men, poking the last soldier in the line in the ribs, and telling him to hold up his hand. Soldiers were dotted all over the plain, dragging logs and brushwood, and constructing shanties, chatting together, and laughing good-humouredly. They were sitting around the fires, dressed and stripped, drying shirts and foot-gear. Or they thronged round the porridge-pots and cauldrons, brushing their boots and their coats. In one company dinner was ready, and the soldiers, with greedy faces, watched the steaming pots, and waited for the sample, which was being taken in a wooden bowl to the commissariat officer, sitting on a piece of wood facing his shanty.

In another company—a lucky one, for not all had vodka—the soldiers stood in a group round a broad-shouldered, pock-marked sergeant, who was tilting a keg of vodka, and pouring it into the covers of the canteens held out to him in turn. The soldiers, with reverential faces, lifted the covers to their mouths, drained them, and licking their lips and rubbing them with the sleeves of their coats, they walked away looking more good-humoured than before. Every face was as serene as though it were all happening not in sight of the enemy, just before an action in which at least half of the detachment must certainly be left on the field, but somewhere at home in Russia, with every prospect of a quiet halting-place. Prince Andrey rode by the Chasseur regiment, and as he advanced into the ranks of the Kiev Grenadiers, stalwart fellows all engaged in the same peaceful pursuits, not far from the colonel's shanty, standing higher than the rest, he came upon a platoon of grenadiers, before whom lay a man stripped naked. Two soldiers were holding him, while two others were brandishing supple twigs and bringing them down at regular intervals on the man's bare back. The man shrieked unnaturally. A stout major was walking up and down in front of the platoon, and regardless of the screams, he kept saying: "It's a disgrace for a soldier to steal; a soldier must be honest, honourable, and brave, and to steal from a comrade, he must be without honour indeed, a monster. Again, again!"

And still he heard the dull thuds and the desperate but affected scream. "Again, again," the major was saying.

A young officer, with an expression of bewilderment and distress in his face, walked away from the flogging, looking inquiringly at the adjutant.

Prince Andrey, coming out to the foremost line, rode along in front of it. Our line and the enemy's were far from one another at the left and also at the right flank; but in the centre, at the spot where in the morning the messengers had met, the lines came so close that the soldiers of the two armies could see each other's faces and talk together. Besides these soldiers, whose place was in that part of the line, many others had gathered there from both sides, and they were laughing, as they scrutinised the strange and novel dress and aspect of their foes.

Since early morning, though it was forbidden to go up to the line, the commanding officers could not keep the inquisitive soldiers back. The soldiers, whose post was in that part of the line, like showmen exhibiting some curiosity, no longer looked at the French, but made observations on the men who came up to look, and waited with a bored face to be relieved. Prince Andrey stopped to look carefully at the French.

"Look'ee, look'ee," one soldier was saying to a comrade, pointing to a Russian musketeer, who had gone up to the lines with an officer and was talking warmly and rapidly with a French grenadier. "I say, doesn't he jabber away fine! I bet the Frenchy can't keep pace with him. Now, then, Sidorov?"

"Wait a bit; listen. Aye, it's fine!" replied Sidorov, reputed a regular scholar at talking French.

The soldier, at whom they had pointed laughing, was Dolohov. Prince Andrey recognised him and listened to what he was saying. Dolohov, together with his captain, had come from the left flank, where his regiment was posted.

"Come, again, again!" the captain urged, craning forward and trying not to lose a syllable of the conversation, though it was unintelligible to him. "Please, go on. What's he saying?"

Dolohov did not answer the captain; he had been drawn into a hot dispute with the French grenadier. They were talking, as was to be expected, of the campaign. The Frenchman, mixing up the Austrians and the Russians, was maintaining that the Russians had been defeated and had been fleeing all the way from Ulm. Dolohov declared that the Russians had never been defeated, but had beaten the French.

"We have orders to drive you away from here, and we shall too," said Dolohov.

"You had better take care you are not all captured with all your Cossacks," said the French grenadier.

Spectators and listeners on the French side laughed.

"We shall make you dance, as you danced in Suvorov's day" (*on vous fera danser*), said Dolohov.

"What is he prating about?" said a Frenchman.

"Ancient history," said another, guessing that the allusion was to former wars. "The Emperor will show your Suvorov, like the others. . . ."

"Bonaparte . . ." Dolohov was beginning, but the Frenchman interrupted him.

"Not Bonaparte. He is the Emperor! *Sacré nom* . . ." he said angrily.

"Damnation to him, your Emperor!"

And Dolohov swore a coarse soldier's oath in Russian, and, shouldering his gun, walked away.

"Come along, Ivan Lukitch," he said to his captain.

"So that's how they talk French," said the soldiers in the line. "Now then, you, Sidorov." Sidorov winked, and, turning to the French, he fell to gabbling disconnected syllables very rapidly.

"*Kari-ma-la-ta-fa-sa-fi-mu-ter-kess-ka,*" he jabbered, trying to give the most expressive intonation to his voice.

"Ho, ho, ho! ha ha! ha ha! Oh! oo!" the soldiers burst into a roar of such hearty, good-humoured laughter, in which the French line too could not keep from joining, that after it it seemed as though they must unload their guns, blow up their ammunition, and all hurry away back to their homes. But the guns remained loaded, the port-holes in the houses and earthworks looked out as menacingly as ever, and the cannons, taken off their platforms, confronted one another as before.

After making a circuit round the whole line of the army, from the right flank to the left, Prince Andrey rode up to that battery from which the staff-officer told him that the whole field could be seen. Here he dismounted and stood by the end one of the four cannons, which had been taken off their platforms. An artilleryman on sentinel duty in front of the cannons was just confronting the officer, but at a sign being made to him, he renewed his regular, monotonous pacing. Behind the cannons stood their platforms, and still further behind, the picket-ropes and camp-fires of the artillerymen. To the left, not far from the end cannon, was a little newly rigged-up shanty, from which came the sounds of officers' voices in eager conversation. From the battery there was in fact a view of almost the whole disposition of the Russian forces, and the greater part of the enemy's. Directly facing the battery on the skyline of the opposite hill could be seen the village of Schöngraben; to the left and to the right could be discerned in three places through the smoke of the camp-fires masses of the French troops, of which the greater number were undoubtedly in the village itself and behind the hill. To the left of the village there was something in the smoke that looked like a battery, but it could not be made out clearly by the naked eye. Our right flank was stationed on a rather steep eminence, which dominated the French position. About it were disposed our infantry regiments, and on the very ridge could be seen dragoons. In the centre, where was placed Tushin's battery, from which Prince Andrey was surveying the position, there was the most sloping and direct descent to the stream that separated us from Schöngraben. On the left our troops were close to a copse, where there was the smoke of the camp-fires of our infantry, chopping wood in it. The French line was wider than ours, and it was obviously easy for the French to outflank us on both sides. Behind our position was a precipitous and deep ravine, down which it would be difficult to retreat with artillery and cavalry. Prince Andrey leaned his elbow on the cannon, and taking out a note-book, sketched for himself a plan of the disposition of the troops. In two places he made notes with a pencil, intending to speak on the points to Bagration. He meant to suggest first concentrating all the artillery in the centre, and secondly drawing the cavalry back to the further side of the ravine. Prince Andrey, who was constantly in attendance on the commander-in-chief, watching the movements of masses of men and manœuvring of troops, and also continually studying the historical accounts of battles, could not help viewing the course of the military operations that were to come only in their general features. His imagination dwelt on the broad possibilities, such as the following: "If the enemy makes the right flank the point of attack," he said to himself, "the Kiev grenadiers and Podolosky Chasseurs will have to defend their position, till the reserves from the centre come to their support. In that case the dragoons can get them in the flank and drive them back. In case of an attack on the centre, we station on this height the central battery, and under its cover we draw off the left flank and retreat to the ravine by platoons," he reasoned. . . . All the while he was on the cannon, he heard, as one often does, the sounds of the voices of the officers talking in the shanty, but he did not take in a single word of what they were saying. Suddenly a voice from the shanty impressed him by a tone of such earnestness that he could not help listening.

"No, my dear fellow," said a pleasant voice that seemed somehow familiar to Prince Andrey. "I say that if one could know what will happen after death, then not one of us would be afraid of death. That's so, my dear fellow."

Another younger voice interrupted him: "But afraid or not afraid, there's no escaping it."

"Why, you're always in fear! Fie on you learned fellows," said a third, a manly voice, interrupting both. "To be sure, you artillerymen are clever fellows, because you can carry everything with you to eat and to drink."

And the owner of the manly voice, apparently an infantry officer, laughed.

"Still one is in fear," pursued the first one, the one Prince Andrey knew. "One's afraid of the unknown, that's what it is. It's all very well to say the soul goes to heaven . . . but this we do know, that there is no heaven, but only atmosphere."

Again the manly voice interrupted.

"Come, give us a drop of your herb-brandy, Tushin," it said.

"Oh, it's the captain, who had his boots off in the booth," thought Prince Andrey, recognising with pleasure the agreeable philosophising voice.

"Herb-brandy by all means," said Tushin; "but still to conceive of a future life . . ." He did not finish his sentence.

At that moment there was a whiz heard in the air: nearer, nearer, faster and more distinctly, and faster it came; and the cannon-ball, as though not uttering all it had to say, thudded into the earth not far from the shanty, tearing up the soil with superhuman force. The earth seemed to moan at the terrible blow. At the same instant there dashed out of the shanty, before any of the rest, little Tushin with his short pipe in his mouth; his shrewd, good-humoured face was rather pale. After him emerged the owner of the manly voice, a stalwart infantry officer, who ran off to his company, buttoning his coat as he ran.

Prince Andrey mounted his horse but lingered at the battery, looking at the smoke of the cannon from which the ball had flown. His eyes moved rapidly over the wide plain. He only saw that the previously immobile masses of the French were heaving to and fro, and that it really was a battery on the left. The smoke still clung about it. Two Frenchmen on horseback, doubtless adjutants, were galloping on the hill. A small column of the enemy, distinctly visible, were moving downhill, probably to strengthen the line. The smoke of the first shot had not cleared away, when there was a fresh puff of smoke and another shot. The battle was beginning. Prince Andrey turned his horse and galloped back to Grunte to look for Prince Bagration. Behind him he heard the cannonade becoming louder and more frequent. Our men were evidently beginning to reply. Musket shots could be heard below at the spot where the lines were closest. Lemarrois had only just galloped to Murat with Napoleon's menacing letter, and Murat, abashed and anxious to efface his error, at once moved his forces to the centre and towards both flanks, hoping before evening and the arrival of the Emperor to destroy the insignificant detachment before him.

"It has begun! Here it comes!" thought Prince Andrey, feeling the blood rush to his heart. "But where? What form is my Toulon to take?" he wondered.

Passing between the companies that had been eating porridge and drinking vodka a quarter of an hour before, he saw everywhere nothing but the same rapid movements of soldiers forming in ranks and getting their guns, and on every face he saw the same eagerness that he felt in his heart. "It has begun! Here it comes! Terrible and delightful!" said the face of every private and officer. Before he reached the earthworks that were being thrown up, he saw in the evening light of the dull autumn day men on horseback crossing towards him. The foremost, wearing a cloak and an Astrachan cap, was riding on a white horse. It was Prince Bagration. Prince Andrey stopped and waited for him to come up. Prince Bagration stopped his horse, and recognising Prince Andrey nodded to him. He still gazed on ahead while Prince Andrey told him what he had been seeing.

The expression: "It has begun! it is coming!" was discernible even on Prince Bagration's strong, brown face, with his half-closed, lustreless, sleepy-looking eyes. Prince Andrey glanced with uneasy curiosity at that impassive face, and he longed to know: Was that man thinking and feeling, and what was he thinking and feeling at that moment? "Is there anything at all there behind that impassive face?" Prince Andrey wondered, looking at him. Prince Bagration nodded in token of his assent to Prince Andrey's words, and said: "Very good," with an expression that seemed to signify that all that happened, and all that was told him, was exactly what he had foreseen. Prince Andrey, panting from his rapid ride, spoke quickly. Prince Bagration uttered his words in his Oriental accent with peculiar deliberation, as though impressing upon him that there was no need of hurry. He did, however, spur his horse into a gallop in the direction of Tushin's battery. Prince Andrey rode after him with his suite. The party consisted of an officer of the suite, Bagration's private adjutant, Zherkov, an orderly officer, the staff-officer on duty, riding a beautiful horse of English breed, and a civilian official, the auditor, who had asked to be present from curiosity to see the battle. The auditor, a plump man with a plump face, looked about him with a naïve smile of amusement, swaying about on his horse, and cutting a queer figure in his cloak on his saddle among the hussars, Cossacks, and adjutants.

"This gentleman wants to see a battle," said Zherkov to Bolkonsky, indicating the auditor, "but has begun to feel queer already."

"Come, leave off," said the auditor, with a beaming smile at once naïve and cunning, as though he were flattered at being the object of Zherkov's jests, and was purposely trying to seem stupider than he was in reality.

"It's very curious, *mon Monsieur Prince*," said the staff-officer on duty (He vaguely remembered that the title *prince* was translated in some peculiar way in French, but could not get it quite right.) By this time they were all riding up to Tushin's battery, and a ball struck the ground before them.

"What was that falling?" asked the auditor, smiling naïvely.

"A French pancake," said Zherkov.

"That's what they hit you with, then?" asked the auditor. "How awful!" And he seemed to expand all over with enjoyment. He had hardly uttered the words when again there was a sudden terrible whiz, which ended abruptly in a thud into something soft, and flop—a Cossack, riding a little behind and to the right of the auditor, dropped from his horse to the ground. Zherkov and the staff-officer bent forward over their saddles and turned their horses away. The auditor stopped facing the Cossack, and looking with curiosity at him. The Cossack was dead, the horse was still struggling.

Prince Bagration dropped his eyelids, looked round, and seeing the cause of the delay, turned away indifferently, seeming to ask, 'Why notice these trivial details?" With the ease of a first-rate horseman he stopped his horse, bent over a little and disengaged his sabre, which had caught under his cloak. The sabre was an old-fashioned one, unlike what are worn now. Prince Andrey remembered the story that Suvorov had given his saber to Bagration in Italy, and the recollection was particularly pleasant to him at that moment. They had ridden up to the very battery from which Prince Andrey had surveyed the field of battle.

"Whose company?" Prince Bagration asked of the artilleryman standing at the ammunition boxes.

He asked in words: "Whose company?" but what he was really asking was, "You're not in a panic here?" And the artilleryman understood that.

"Captain Tushin's, your excellency," the red-haired, freckled artilleryman sang out in a cheerful voice, as he ducked forward.

"To be sure, to be sure," said Bagration, pondering something, and he rode by the platforms up to the end cannon. Just as he reached it, a shot boomed from the cannon, deafening him and his suite, and in the smoke that suddenly enveloped the cannon the artillerymen could be seen hauling at the cannon, dragging and rolling it back to its former position. A broad-shouldered, gigantic soldier, gunner number one, with a mop, darted up to the wheel and planted himself, his legs wide apart; while number two, with a shaking hand, put the charge into the cannon's mouth; a small man with stooping shoulders, the officer Tushin, stumbling against the cannon, dashed forward, not noticing the general, and looked out, shading his eyes with his little hand.

"Another two points higher, and it will be just right," he shouted in a shrill voice, to which he tried to give a swaggering note utterly out of keeping with his figure. "Two!" he piped. "Smash away, Medvyedev!"

Bagration called to the officer, and Tushin went up to the general, putting three fingers to the peak of his cap with a timid and awkward gesture, more like a priest blessing some one than a soldier saluting. Though Tushin's guns had been intended to cannonade the valley, he was throwing shells over the village of Schöngraben, in part of which immense masses of French soldiers were moving out.

No one had given Tushin instructions at what or with what to fire, and after consulting his sergeant, Zaharchenko, for whom he had a great respect, he had decided that it would be a good thing to set fire to the village. "Very good!" Bagration said, on the officer's submitting that he had done so, and he began scrutinizing the whole field of battle that lay unfolded before him. He seemed to be considering something. The French had advanced nearest on the right side. In the hollow where the stream flowed, below the eminence on which the Kiev regiment was stationed, could be heard a continual roll and crash of guns, the din of which was overwhelming. And much further to the right, behind the dragoons, the officer of the suite pointed out to Bagration a column of French outflanking our flank. On the left the horizon was bounded by the copse close by. Prince Bagration gave orders for two battalions from the center to go to the right to reinforce the flank. The officer of the suite ventured to observe to the prince that the removal of these battalions would leave the cannon unprotected. Prince Bagration turned to the officer of the suite and stared at him with his lustreless eyes in silence. Prince Andrey thought that the officer's observation was a very just one, and that really there was nothing to be said in reply. But at that instant an adjutant galloped up with a message from the colonel of the regiment in the hollow that immense masses of the French were coming down upon them, that his men were in disorder and retreating upon the Kiev grenadiers, Prince Bagration nodded to signify his assent and approval. He rode at a walking pace to the right, and sent an adjutant to the dragoons with orders to attack the French. But the adjutant returned half an hour later with the news that the colonel of the dragoons had already retired beyond the ravine, as a destructive fire had been opened upon him, and he was losing his men for nothing, and so he had concentrated his men in the wood.

"Very good!" said Bagration.

Just as he was leaving the battery, shots had been heard in the wood on the left too; and as it was too far to the left flank for him to go himself, Prince Bagration despatched Zherkov to tell the senior general—the general whose regiment had been inspected by Kutuzov at Braunau—to retreat as rapidly as possible beyond the ravine, as the right flank would probably not long be able to detain the enemy. Tushin, and the battalion that was to have defended his battery, was forgotten. Prince Andrey listened carefully to Prince Bagration's colloquies with the commanding officers, and to the orders he gave them, and noticed, to his astonishment, that no orders were really given by him at all, but that Prince Bagration confined himself to trying to appear as though everything that was being done of necessity, by chance, or at the will of individual officers, was all done, if not by his orders, at least in accordance with his intentions. Prince Andrey observed, however, that, thanks to the tact shown by Prince Bagration, notwithstanding that what was done was due to chance, and not dependent on the commander's will, his presence was of the greatest value. Commanding officers, who rode up to Bagration looking distraught, regained their composure; soldiers and officers greeted him cheerfully, recovered their spirits in his presence, and were unmistakably anxious to display their pluck before him.

After riding up to the highest point of our right flank, Prince Bagration began to go downhill, where a continuous roll of musketry was heard and nothing could be seen for the smoke. The nearer they got to the hollow the less they could see, and the more distinctly could be felt the nearness of the actual battlefield. They began to meet wounded men. Two soldiers were dragging one along, supporting him on each side. His head was covered with blood; he had no cap, and was coughing and spitting. The bullet had apparently entered his mouth or throat. Another one came towards them, walking pluckily alone without his gun, groaning aloud and wringing his hands from the pain of a wound from which the blood was flowing, as though from a bottle, over his greatcoat. His face looked more frightened than in pain. He had been wounded only a moment before. Crossing the road, they began going down a deep descent, and on the slope they saw several men lying on the ground. They were met by a crowd of soldiers, among them some who were not wounded. The soldiers were hurrying up the hill, gasping for breath, and in spite of the general's presence, they were talking loudly together and gesticulating with their arms. In the smoke ahead of them they could see now rows of grey coats, and the commanding officer, seeing Bagration, ran after the group of retreating soldiers, calling upon them to come back. Bagration rode up to the ranks, along which there was here and there a rapid snapping of shots drowning the talk of the soldiers and the shouts of the officers. The whole air was reeking with smoke. The soldiers' faces were all full of excitement and smudged with powder. Some were plugging with their ramrods, others were putting powder on the touch-pans, and getting charges out of their pouches, others were firing their guns. But it was impossible to see at whom they were firing from the smoke, which the wind did not lift. The pleasant hum and whiz of the bullets was repeated pretty rapidly. "What is it?" wondered Prince Andrey, as he rode up to the crowd of soldiers. "It can't be the line, for they are all crowded together; it can't be an attacking party, for they are not moving; it can't be a square, they are not standing like one."

A thin, weak-looking colonel, apparently an old man, with an amiable smile, and eyelids that half-covered his old-looking eyes and gave him a mild air, rode up to Prince Bagration and received him as though he were welcoming an honoured guest into his house. He announced to Prince Bagration that his regiment had had to face a cavalry attack of the French, that though the attack had been repulsed, the regiment had lost more than half of its men. The colonel said that the attack had been repulsed, supposing that to be the proper military term for what had happened; but he did not really know himself what had been taking place during that half hour in the troops under his command, and could not have said with any certainty whether the attack had been repelled or his regiment had been beaten by the attack. All he knew was that at the beginning of the action balls and grenades had begun flying all about his regiment, and killing men, that then some one had shouted "cavalry," and our men had begun firing. And they were firing still, though not now at the cavalry, who had disappeared, but at the French infantry, who had made their appearance in the hollow and were firing at our men. Prince Bagration nodded his head to betoken that all this was exactly what he had desired and expected. Turning to an adjutant, he commanded him to bring down from the hill the two battalions of the Sixth Chasseurs, by whom they had just come. Prince Andrey was struck at that instant by the change that had come over Prince Bagration's face. His face wore the look of concentrated and happy determination, which may be seen in a man who in a hot day takes the final run before a header into the water. The lustreless, sleepy look in the eyes, the affectation of profound thought had gone. The round, hard, eagle eyes looked ecstatically and rather disdainfully before him, obviously not resting on anything, though there was still the same deliberation in his measured movements.

The colonel addressed a protest to Prince Bagration, urging him to go back, as there it was too dangerous for him. "I beg of you, your excellency, for God's sake!" he kept on saying, looking for support to the officer of the suite, who only turned away from him.

"Only look, your excellency!" He called his attention to the bullets which were continually whizzing, singing, and hissing about them. He spoke in the tone of protest and entreaty with which a carpenter speaks to a gentleman who has picked up a hatchet. "We are used to it, but you may blister your fingers." He talked as though these bullets could not kill him, and his half-closed eyes gave a still more persuasive effect to his words. The staff-officer added his protests to the colonel, but Bagration made them no answer. He merely gave the order to cease firing, and to form so as to make room for the two battalions of reinforcements. Just as he was speaking the cloud of smoke covering the hollow was lifted as by an unseen hand and blown by the rising wind from right to left, and the opposite hill came into sight with the French moving across it. All eyes instinctively fastened on that French column moving down upon them and winding in and out over the ups and downs of the ground. Already they could see the fur caps of the soldiers, could distinguish officers from privates, could see their flag flapping against its staff.

"How well they're marching," said some one in Bagration's suite.

The front part of the column was already dipping down into the hollow. The engagement would take place then on the nearer side of the slope . . .

The remnants of the regiment that had already been in action, forming hurriedly, drew off to the right; the two battalions of the Sixth Chasseurs marched up in good order, driving the last stragglers before them. They had not yet reached Bagration, but the heavy, weighty tread could be heard of the whole mass keeping step. On the left flank, nearest of all to Bagration, marched the captain, a round-faced imposing-looking man, with a foolish and happy expression of face. It was the same infantry officer who had run out of the shanty after Tushin. He was obviously thinking of nothing at the moment, but that he was marching before his commander in fine style. With the complacency of a man on parade, he stepped springing on his muscular legs, drawing himself up without the slightest effort, as though he were swinging, and this easy elasticity was a striking contrast to the heavy tread of the soldiers keeping step with him. He wore hanging by his leg an unsheathed, slender, narrow sword (a small bent sabre, more like a toy than a weapon), and looking about him, now at the commander, now behind, he turned his whole powerful frame round without getting out of step. It looked as though all the force of his soul was directed to marching by his commander in the best style possible. And conscious that he was accomplishing this, he was happy. "Left . . . left . . . left . . ." he seemed to be inwardly repeating at each alternate step. And the wall of soldierly figures, weighed down by their knapsacks and guns, with their faces all grave in different ways, moved by in the same rhythm, as though each of the hundreds of soldiers were repeating mentally at each alternate step, "Left . . . left . . . left . . ." A stout major skirted a bush on the road, puffing and shifting his step. A soldier, who had dropped behind, trotted after the company, looking panic-stricken at his own defection. A cannon ball, whizzing through the air, flew over the heads of Prince Bagration and his suite, and in time to the same rhythm, "Left . . . left . . ." it fell into the column.

"Close the ranks!" rang out the jaunty voice of the captain. The soldiers marched in a half circle round something in the place where the ball had fallen, and an old cavalryman, an under officer, lingered behind near the dead, and overtaking his line, changed feet with a hop, got into step, and looked angrily about him. "Left . . . left . . . left . . ." seemed to echo out of the menacing silence and the monotonous sound of the simultaneous tread of the feet on the ground.

"Well done, lads!" said Prince Bagration.

"For your ex . . . slen, slen, slency!" rang out along the ranks. A surly-looking soldier, marching on the left, turned his eyes on Bagration as he shouted, with an expression that seemed to say, "We know that without telling." Another, opening his mouth wide, shouted without glancing round, and marched on, as though afraid of letting his attention stray. The order was given to halt and take off their knapsacks.

Bagration rode round the ranks of men who had marched by him, and then dismounted from his horse. He gave the reins to a Cossack, took off his cloak and handed it to him, stretched his legs and set his cap straight on his head. The French column with the officers in front came into sight under the hill.

"With God's help!" cried Bagration in a resolute, sonorous voice. He turned for one instant to the front line, and swinging his arms a little with the awkward, lumbering gait of a man always on horseback, he walked forward over the uneven ground. Prince Andrey felt that some unseen force was drawing him forward, and he had a sensation of great happiness.[1]

The French were near. Already Prince Andrey, walking beside Bagration, could distinguish clearly the sashes, the red epaulettes, even the faces of the French. (He saw distinctly one bandy-legged old French officer, wearing

[1] This was the attack of which Thiers says: "The Russians behaved valiantly and, which is rare in warfare, two bodies of infantry marched resolutely upon each other, neither giving way before the other came up." And Napoleon on St. Helena said: "Some Russian battalions showed intrepidity."

Hessian boots, who was getting up the hill with difficulty, taking hold of the bushes.) Prince Bagration gave no new command, and still marched in front of the ranks in the same silence. Suddenly there was the snap of a shot among the French, another and a third . . . and smoke rose and firing rang out in all the broken-up ranks of the enemy. Several of our men fell, among them the round-faced officer, who had been marching so carefully and complacently. But at the very instant of the first shot, Bagration looked round and shouted, "Hurrah!" "Hura . . . a . . . a . . . ah!" rang out along our lines in a prolonged roar, and out-stripping Prince Bagration and one another, in no order, but in an eager and joyous crowd, our men ran downhill after the routed French.

The attack of the Sixth Chasseurs covered the retreat of the right flank. In the centre Tushin's forgotten battery had succeeded in setting fire to Schöngraben and delaying the advance of the French. The French stayed to put out the fire, which was fanned by the wind, and this gave time for the Russians to retreat. The retreat of the centre beyond the ravine was hurried and noisy; but the different companies kept apart. But the left flank, which consisted of the Azovsky and Podolsky infantry and the Pavlograd hussars, was simultaneously attacked in front and surrounded by the cream of the French army under Lannes, and was thrown into disorder. Bagration had sent Zherkov to the general in command of the left flank with orders to retreat immediately.

Zherkov, keeping his hand still at his cap, had briskly started his horse and galloped off. But no sooner had he ridden out of Bagration's sight than his courage failed him. He was overtaken by a panic he could not contend against, and he could not bring himself to go where there was danger.

After galloping some distance towards the troops of the left flank, he rode not forward where he heard firing, but off to look for the general and the officers in a direction where they could not by any possibility be; and so it was that he did not deliver the message.

The command of the left flank belonged by right of seniority to the general of the regiment in which Dolohov was serving—the regiment which Kutuzov had inspected before Braunau. But the command of the extreme left flank had been entrusted to the colonel of the Pavlograd hussars, in which Rostov was serving. Hence arose a misunderstanding. Both commanding officers were intensely exasperated with one another, and at a time when fighting had been going on a long while on the right flank, and the French had already begun their advance on the left, these two officers were engaged in negotiations, the sole aim of which was the mortification of one another. The regiments—cavalry and infantry alike —were by no means in readiness for the engagement. No one from the common soldier to the general expected a battle; and they were all calmly engaged in peaceful occupations—feeding their horses in the cavalry, gathering wood in the infantry.

"He is my senior in rank, however," said the German colonel of the hussars, growing very red and addressing an adjutant, who had ridden up. "So let him do as he likes. I can't sacrifice my hussars. Bugler! Sound the retreat!"

But things were becoming urgent. The fire of cannon and musketry thundered in unison on the right and in the centre, and the French tunics of Lannes's sharpshooters had already passed over the milldam, and were forming on this side of it hardly out of musket-shot range.

The infantry general walked up to his horse with his quivering strut, and mounting it and drawing himself up very erect and tall, he rode up to the Pavlograd colonel. The two officers met with affable bows and concealed fury in their hearts.

"Again, colonel," the general said, "I cannot leave half my men in the wood. I *beg* you, I *beg* you," he repeated, "to occupy the *position,* and prepare for an attack."

"And I beg you not to meddle in what's not your business," answered the colonel, getting hot. "If you were a cavalry officer . . ."

"I am not a cavalry officer, colonel, but I am a Russian general, and if you are unaware of the fact . . ."

"I am fully aware of it, your excellency," the colonel screamed suddenly, setting his horse in motion and becoming purple in the face. "If you care to come to the front, you will see that this position cannot be held. I don't want to massacre my regiment for your satisfaction."

"You forget yourself, colonel. I am not considering my own satisfaction, and I do not allow such a thing to be said."

Taking the colonel's proposition as a challenge to his courage, the general squared his chest and rode scowling beside him to the front line, as though their whole difference would inevitably be settled there under the enemy's fire. They reached the line, several bullets flew by them, and they stood still without a word. To look at the front line was a useless proceeding, since from the spot where they had been standing before, it was clear that the cavalry could not act, owing to the bushes and the steep and broken character of the ground, and that the French were outflanking the left wing. The general and the colonel glared sternly and significantly at one another, like two cocks preparing for a fight, seeking in vain for a symptom of cowardice. Both stood the test without flinching. Since there was nothing to be said, and neither was willing to give the other grounds for asserting that he was the first to withdraw from under fire, they might have remained a long while standing there, mutually testing each other's pluck, if there had not at that moment been heard in the copse, almost behind them, the snap of musketry and a confused shout of voices. The French were attacking the soldiers gathering wood in the copse. The hussars could not now retreat, nor could the infantry. They were cut off from falling back on the left by the French line. Now, unfavourable as the ground was, they must attack to fight a way through for themselves.

The hussars of the squadron in which Rostov was an ensign had hardly time to mount their horses when they were confronted by the enemy.

Again, as on the Enns bridge, there was no one between the squadron and the enemy, and between them lay that terrible border-line of uncertainty and dread, like the line dividing the living from the dead. All the soldiers were conscious of that line, and the question whether they would cross it or not, and how they would cross it, filled them with excitement.

The colonel rode up to the front, made some angry reply to the questions of the officers, and, like a man desperately insisting on his rights, gave some command. No one said anything distinctly, but through the whole squadron there ran a vague rumour of attack. The command to form in order rang out, then there was the clank of sabres being drawn out of their sheaths. But still no one moved. The troops of the left flank, both the infantry and the hussars, felt that their commanders themselves did not know what to do, and the uncertainty of the commanders infected the soldiers.

"Make haste, if only they'd make haste," thought Rostov, feeling that at last the moment had come to taste the joys of the attack, of which he had heard so much from his comrades.

"With God's help, lads," rang out Denisov's voice, "forward, quick, gallop!"

The horses' haunches began moving in the front line. Rook pulled at the reins and set off of himself.

On the right Rostov saw the foremost lines of his own hussars, and still further ahead he could see a dark streak, which he could not distinguish clearly, but assumed to be the enemy. Shots could be heard, but at a distance.

"Quicker!" rang out the word of command, and Rostov felt the drooping of Rook's hindquarters as he broke into a gallop. He felt the joy of the gallop coming, and was more and more lighthearted. He noticed a solitary tree ahead of him. The tree was at first in front of him, in the middle of that border-land that had seemed so terrible. But now they had crossed it and nothing terrible had happened, but he felt more lively and excited every moment. "Ah, won't I slash at him!" thought Rostov, grasping the hilt of his sabre tightly. "Hur . . . r . . . a . . . a!" roared voices.

"Now, let him come on, whoever it may be," thought Rostov, driving the spurs into Rook, and outstripping the rest, he let him go at full gallop. Already the enemy could be seen in front. Suddenly something swept over the squadron like a broad broom. Rostov lifted his sabre, making ready to deal a blow, but at that instant the soldier Nikitenko galloped ahead and left his side, and Rostov felt as though he were in a dream being carried forward with supernatural swiftness and yet remaining at the same spot. An hussar, Bandartchuk, galloped up from behind close upon him and looked angrily at him. Bandartchuk's horse started aside, and he galloped by.

"What's the matter? I'm not moving? I've fallen, I'm killed . . ." Rostov asked and answered himself all in one instant. He was alone in the middle of the field. Instead of the moving horses and the hussars' backs, he saw around him the motionless earth and stubblefield. There was warm blood under him.

"No, I'm wounded, and my horse is killed." Rook tried to get up on his forelegs, but he sank again, crushing his rider's leg under his leg. Blood was flowing from the horse's head. The horse struggled, but could not get up. Rostov tried to get up, and fell down too. His sabretache had caught in the saddle. Where our men were, where were the French, he did not know. All around him there was no one.

Getting his leg free, he stood up. "Which side, where now was that line that had so sharply divided the two armies?" he asked himself, and could not answer. "Hasn't something gone wrong with me? Do such things happen, and what ought one to do in such cases?" he wondered as he was getting up. But at that instant he felt as though something superfluous was hanging on his benumbed left arm. The wrist seemed not to belong to it. He looked at his hand, carefully searching for blood on it. "Come, here are some men," he thought joyfully, seeing some men running towards him. "They will help me!" In front of these men ran a single figure in a strange shako and a blue coat, with a swarthy sunburnt face and a hooked nose. Then came two men, and many more were running up behind. One of them said some strange words, not Russian. Between some similar figures in similar shakoes behind stood a Russian hussar. He was being held by the arms; behind him they were holding his horse too.

"It must be one of ours taken prisoner. . . . Yes. Surely they couldn't take me too? What sort of men are they?" Rostov was still wondering, unable to believe his own eyes. "Can they be the French?" He gazed at the approaching French, and although only a few seconds before he had been longing to get at these Frenchmen and to cut them down, their being so near seemed to him now so awful that he could not believe his eyes. "Who are they? What are they running for? Can it be to me? Can they be running to me? And what for? To kill me? *Me*, whom every one's so fond of?" He recalled his mother's love, the love of his family and his friends, and the enemy's intention of killing him seemed impossible. "But they may even kill me." For more than ten seconds he stood, not moving from the spot, nor grasping his position. The foremost Frenchman with the hook nose was getting so near that he could see the expression of his face. And the excited, alien countenance of the man, who was running so lightly and breathlessly towards him, with his bayonet lowered, terrified Rostov. He snatched up his pistol, and instead of firing with it, flung it at the Frenchman and ran to the bushes with all his might. Not with the feeling of doubt and conflict with which he had moved at the Enns bridge, did he now run, but with the feeling of a hare fleeing from the dogs. One unmixed feeling of fear for his young, happy life took possession of his whole being. Leaping rapidly over the hedges with the same impetuosity with which he used to run when he played games, he flew over the field, now and then turning his pale, good-natured, youthful face, and a chill of horror ran down his spine. "No, better not to look," he thought, but as he got near to the bushes he looked round once more. The French had given it up, and just at the moment when he looked round the foremost man was just dropping from a run into a walk, and turning round to shout something loudly to a comrade behind. Rostov stopped. "There's some mistake," he thought; "it can't be that they meant to kill me." And meanwhile his left arm was as heavy as if a hundred pound weight were hanging on it. He could run no further. The Frenchman stopped too and took aim. Rostov frowned and ducked. One bullet and then another flew hissing by him; he took his left hand in his right, and with a last effort ran as far as the bushes. In the bushes there were Russian sharpshooters.

The infantry, who had been caught unawares in the copse, had run away, and the different companies all confused together had retreated in disorderly crowds. One soldier in a panic had uttered those words—terrible in war and meaningless: "Cut off!" and those words had infected the whole mass with panic.

"Out flanked! Cut off! Lost!" they shouted as they ran.

When their general heard the firing and the shouts in the rear he had grasped at the instant that something awful was happening to his regiment; and the thought that he, an exemplary officer, who had served so many years without ever having been guilty of the slightest shortcoming, might be held responsible by his superiors for negligence or lack of discipline, so affected him that, instantly oblivious of the insubordinate cavalry colonel and his dignity 'as a general, utterly oblivious even of danger and of the instinct of self-preservation, he clutched at the crupper of his saddle, and spurring his horse, galloped off to the regiment under a perfect hail of bullets that luckily missed him. He was possessed by the one desire to find out what was wrong, and to help and correct the mistake whatever it might be, if it were a mistake on his part, so that after twenty-two years of exemplary service, without incurring a reprimand for anything, he might avoid being responsible for this blunder.

Galloping successfully between the French forces, he reached the field behind the copse across which our men were running downhill, not heeding the word of command. That moment had come of moral vacillation which decides the fate of battles. Would these disorderly crowds of soldiers hear the voice of their commander, or, looking back at him, run on further? In spite of the despairing yell of the commander, who had once been so awe-inspiring to his soldiers, in spite of his infuriated, purple face, distorted out of all likeness to itself, in spite of his brandished sword, the soldiers still ran and talked together, shooting into the air and not listening to the word of command. The moral balance which decides the fate of battle was unmistakably falling on the side of panic.

The general was choked with screaming and gunpowder-smoke, and he stood still in despair. All seemed lost; but at that moment the French, who had been advancing against our men, suddenly, for no apparent reason, ran back, vanished from the edge of the copse, and Russian sharp-shooters appeared in the copse. This was Timohin's division, the only one that had retained its good order in the copse, and hiding in ambush in the ditch behind the copse, had suddenly attacked the French. Timohin had rushed with such a desperate yell upon the French, and with such desper-ate and drunken energy had he dashed at the enemy with only a sword in his hand, that the French flung down their weapons and fled without pausing to recover themselves. Dolohov, running beside Timohin, killed one French soldier at close quarters, and was the first to seize by the collar an officer who surrendered. The fleeing Russians came back; the battalions were brought together; and the French, who had been on the point of splitting the forces of the left flank into two parts, were for the moment held in check. The reserves had time to join the main forces, and the runaways were stopped. The general stood with Major Ekonomov at the bridge, watching the retreating companies go by, when a soldier ran up to him, caught hold of his stirrup and almost clung on to it. The soldier was wearing a coat of blue fine cloth, he had no knapsack nor shako, his head was bound up, and across his shoulders was slung a French cartridge case. In his hand he held an officer's sword. The soldier was pale, his blue eyes looked impudently into the general's face, but his mouth was smiling. Although the general was engaged in giving instructions to Major Ekonomov, he could not help noticing this soldier.

"Your excellency, here are two trophies," said Dolohov, pointing to the French sword and cartridge case. "An officer was taken prisoner by me. I stopped the company." Dolohov breathed hard from weariness; he spoke in jerks. "The whole company can bear me witness. I beg you to remember me, your excellency!"

"Very good, very good," said the general, and he turned to Major Ekonomov. But Dolohov did not leave him; he undid the bandage, and showed the blood congealed on his head.

"A bayonet wound; I kept my place in the front. Remember me, your excellency."

Tushin's battery had been forgotten, and it was only at the very end of the action that Prince Bagration, still hearing the cannonade in the centre, sent the staff-officer on duty and then Prince Andrey to command the battery to retire as quickly as possible. The force which had been stationed near Tushin's cannons to protect them had by somebody's orders retreated in the middle of the battle. But the battery still kept up its fire, and was not taken by the French simply because the enemy could not conceive of the reckless daring of firing from four cannons that were quite unprotected. The French supposed, on the contrary, judging from the energetic action of the battery, that the chief forces of the Russians were concentrated here in the centre, and twice attempted to attack that point, and both times were driven back by the grapeshot fired on them from the four cannons which stood in solitude on the heights. Shortly after Prince Bagration's departure, Tushin had succeeded in setting fire to Schöngraben.

"Look, what a fuss they're in! It's flaming! What a smoke! Smartly done! First-rate! The smoke! the smoke!" cried the gunners, their spirits reviving.

All the guns were aimed without instructions in the direction of the conflagration. The soldiers, as though they were urging each other on, shouted at every volley: "Bravo! That's something like now! Go it! . . . First-rate!" The fire, fanned by the wind, soon spread. The French columns, who had marched out beyond the village, went back, but as though in revenge for this mischance, the enemy stationed ten cannons a little to the right of the village, and began firing from them on Tushin.

In their childlike glee at the conflagration of the village, and the excitement of their successful firing on the French, our artillerymen only noticed this battery when two cannon-balls and after them four more fell among their cannons, and one knocked over two horses and another tore off the foot of a gunner. Their spirits, however, once raised, did not flag; their excitement simply found another direction. The horses were replaced by others from the ammunition carriage; the wounded were removed, and the four cannons were turned facing the ten of the enemy's battery. The other officer, Tushin's comrade, was killed at the beginning of the action, and after an hour's time, of the forty gunners of the battery, seventeen were disabled, but they were still as merry and as eager as ever. Twice they noticed the French appearing below close to them, and they sent volleys of grapeshot at them.

The little man with his weak, clumsy movements, was continually asking his orderly *for just one more pipe for that stroke,* as he said, and scattering sparks from it, he kept running out in front and looking from under his little hand at the French.

"Smash away, lads!" he was continually saying, and he clutched at the cannon wheels himself and unscrewed the screws. In the smoke, deafened by the incessant booming of the cannons that made him shudder every time one was fired, Tushin ran from one cannon to the other, his short pipe never out of his mouth. At one moment he was taking aim, then reckoning the charges, then arranging for the changing and unharnessing of the killed and wounded horses, and all the time shouting in his weak, shrill, hesitating voice. His face grew more and more eager. Only when men where killed and wounded he knitted his brows, and turning away from the dead man, shouted angrily to the men, slow, as they always are, to pick up a wounded man or a dead body. The soldiers, for the most part fine, handsome fellows (a couple of heads taller than their officer and twice as broad in the chest, as they mostly are in the artillery), all looked to their commanding officer like children in a difficult position, and the expression they found on his face was invariably reflected at once on their own.

Owing to the fearful uproar and noise and the necessity of attention and activity, Tushin experienced not the slightest unpleasant sensation of fear;

and the idea that he might be killed or badly wounded never entered his head. On the contrary, he felt more and more lively. It seemed to him that the moment in which he had first seen the enemy and had fired the first shot was long, long ago, yesterday perhaps, and that the spot of earth on which he stood was a place long familiar to him, in which he was quite at home. Although he thought of everything, considered everything, did everything the very best officer could have done in his position, he was in a state of mind akin to the delirium of fever or the intoxication of a drunken man.

The deafening sound of his own guns on all sides, the hiss and thud of the enemy's shells, the sight of the perspiring, flushed gunners hurrying about the cannons, the sight of the blood of men and horses, and of the puffs of smoke from the enemy on the opposite side (always followed by a cannon-ball that flew across and hit the earth, a man, a horse, or a cannon)—all these images made up for him a fantastic world of his own, in which he found enjoyment at the moment. The enemy's cannons in his fancy were not cannons, but pipes from which an invisible smoker blew puffs of smoke at intervals.

"There he's puffing away again," Tushin murmured to himself as a cloud of smoke rolled downhill, and was borne off by the wind in a wreath to the left. "Now, your ball—throw it back."

"What is it, your honour?" asked a gunner who stood near him, and heard him muttering something.

"Nothing, a grenade . . ." he answered. "Now for it, our Matvyevna," he said to himself. Matvyevna was the name his fancy gave to the big cannon, cast in an old-fashioned mould, that stood at the end. The French seemed to be ants swarming about their cannons. The handsome, drunken soldier, number one gunner of the second cannon, was in his dream-world "uncle"; Tushin looked at him more often than at any of the rest, and took delight in every gesture of the man. The sound—dying away, then quickening again—of the musketry fire below the hill seemed to him like the heaving of some creature's breathing. He listened to the ebb and flow of these sounds.

"Ah, she's taking another breath again," he was saying to himself. He himself figured in his imagination as a mighty man of immense stature, who was flinging cannon balls at the French with both hands.

"Come, Matvyevna, old lady, stick by us!" he was saying, moving back from the cannon, when a strange, unfamiliar voice called over his head. "Captain Tushin! Captain!"

Tushin looked round in dismay. It was the same staff-officer who had turned him out of the booth at Grunte. He was shouting to him in a breathless voice:

"I say, are you mad? You've been commanded twice to retreat, and you . . ."

"Now, what are they pitching into me for?" . . . Tushin wondered, looking in alarm at the superior officer.

"I . . . don't . . ." he began, putting two fingers to the peak of his cap. "I . . ."

But the staff-officer did not say all he had meant to. A cannon ball flying near him made him duck down on his horse. He paused, and was just going to say something more, when another ball stopped him. He turned his horse's head and galloped away.

"Retreat! All to retreat!" he shouted from a distance.

The soldiers laughed. A minute later an adjutant arrived with the same message. This was Prince Andrey. The first thing he saw, on reaching the place where Tushin's cannons were stationed, was an unharnessed horse with a broken leg, which was neighing beside the harnessed horses. The blood was flowing in a perfect stream from its leg. Among the platforms lay several dead men. One cannon ball after another flew over him as he rode up, and he felt a nervous shudder running down his spine. But the very idea that he was afraid was enough to rouse him again. "I can't be frightened," he thought, and he deliberately dismounted from his horse between the cannons. He gave his message, but he did not leave the battery. He decided to stay and assist in removing the cannons from the position and getting them away. Stepping over the corpses, under the fearful fire from the French, he helped Tushin in getting the cannons ready.

"The officer that came just now ran off quicker than he came," said a gunner to Prince Andrey, "not like your honour."

Prince Andrey had no conversation with Tushin. They were both so busy that they hardly seemed to see each other. When they had got the two out of the four cannons that were uninjured on to the platforms and were moving downhill (one cannon that had been smashed and a howitzer were left behind), Prince Andrey went up to Tushin.

"Well, good-bye till we meet again," said Prince Andrey, holding out his hand to Tushin.

"Good-bye, my dear fellow," said Tushin, "dear soul! good-bye, my dear fellow," he said with tears, which for some unknown reason started suddenly into his eyes.

The wind had sunk, black storm-clouds hung low over the battlefield, melting on the horizon into the clouds of smoke from the powder. Darkness had come, and the glow of conflagrations showed all the more distinctly in two places. The cannonade had grown feebler, but the snapping of musketry-fire in the rear and on the right was heard nearer and more often. As soon as Tushin with his cannons, continually driving round the wounded and coming upon them, had got out of fire and were descending the ravine, he was met by the staff, among whom was the staff-officer and Zherkov, who had twice been sent to Tushin's battery, but had not once reached it. They all vied with one another in giving him orders, telling him how and where to go, finding fault and making criticisms. Tushin gave no orders, and in silence, afraid to speak because at every word he felt, he could not have said why, ready to burst into tears, he rode behind on his artillery nag. Though orders were given to abandon the wounded, many of them dragged themselves after the troops and begged for a seat on the cannons. The jaunty infantry-officer—the one who had run out of Tushin's shanty just before the battle—was laid on Matvyevna's carriage with a bullet in his stomach. At the bottom of the hill a pale ensign of hussars, holding one arm in the other hand, came up to Tushin and begged for a seat.

"Captain, for God's sake. I've hurt my arm," he said timidly. "For God's sake. I can't walk. For God's sake!" It was evident that this was not the first time the ensign had asked for a lift, and that he had been everywhere refused. He asked in a hesitating and piteous voice. "Tell them to let me get on, for God's sake!"

"Let him get on, let him get on," said Tushin. "Put a coat under him, you, Uncle." He turned to his favourite soldier. "But where's the wounded officer?"

"We took him off; he was dead," answered some one.

"Help him on. Sit down, my dear fellow, sit down. Lay the coat there, Antonov."

The ensign was Rostov. He was holding one hand in the other. He was pale, and his lower jaw was trembling as though in a fever. They put him on Matvyevna, the cannon from which they had just removed the dead officer. There was blood on the coat that was laid under him, and Rostov's riding-breeches and arm were smeared with it.

"What, are you wounded, my dear?" said Tushin, going up to the cannon on which Rostov was sitting.

"No; it's a sprain."

"How is it there's blood on the frame?" asked Tushin.

"That was the officer, your honour, stained it," answered an artilleryman, wiping the blood off with the sleeve of his coat, and as it were apologising for the dirty state of the cannon.

With difficulty, aided by the infantry, they dragged the cannon uphill, and halted on reaching the village of Guntersdorf. It was by now so dark that one could not distinguish the soldiers' uniforms ten paces away, and the firing had begun to subside. All of a sudden there came the sound of firing and shouts again close by on the right side. The flash of the shots could be seen in the darkness. This was the last attack of the French. It was met by the soldiers in ambush in the houses of the village. All rushed out of the village again, but Tushin's cannons could not move, and the artillerymen, Tushin, and the ensign looked at one another in anticipation of their fate. The firing on both sides began to subside, and some soldiers in lively conversation streamed out of a side street.

"Not hurt, Petrov?" inquired one.

"We gave it them hot, lads. They won't meddle with us now," another was saying.

"One couldn't see a thing. Didn't they give it to their own men! No seeing for the darkness, mates. Isn't there something to drink?"

The French had been repulsed for the last time. And again, in the complete darkness, Tushin's cannons moved forward, surrounded by the infantry, who kept up a hum of talk.

In the darkness they flowed on like an unseen, gloomy river always in the same direction, with a buzz of whisper and talk and the thud of hoofs and rumble of wheels. Above all other sounds, in the confused uproar, rose the moans and cries of the wounded, more distinct than anything in the darkness of the night. Their moans seemed to fill all the darkness surrounding the troops. Their moans and the darkness seemed to melt into one. A little later a thrill of emotion passed over the moving crowd. Some one followed by a suite had ridden by on a white horse, and had said something as he passed.

"What did he say? Where we are going now? To halt, eh? Thanked us, what?" eager questions were heard on all sides, and the whole moving mass began to press back on itself (the foremost, it seemed, had halted), and a rumour passed through that the order had been given to halt. All halted in the muddy road, just where they were.

Fires were lighted and the talk became more audible. Captain Tushin, after giving instructions to his battery, sent some of his soldiers to look for an ambulance or a doctor for the ensign, and sat down by the fire his soldiers had lighted by the roadside. Rostov too dragged himself to the fire. His whole body was trembling with fever from the pain, the cold, and the damp. He was dreadfully sleepy, but he could not go to sleep for the agonising pain in his arm, which ached and would not be easy in any position. He closed his eyes, then opened them to stare at the fire, which seemed to him dazzling red, and then at the stooping, feeble figure of Tushin, squatting in Turkish fashion near him. The big, kindly, and shrewd eyes of Tushin were fixed upon him with sympathy and commiseration. He saw that Tushin wished with all his soul to help him, but could do nothing for him.

On all sides they heard the footsteps and the chatter of the infantry going and coming and settling themselves round them. The sound of voices, of steps, and of horses' hoofs tramping in the mud, the crackling firewood far and near, all melted into one fluctuating roar of sound.

It was not now as before an unseen river flowing in the darkness, but a gloomy sea subsiding and still agitated after a storm. Rostov gazed vacantly and listened to what was passing before him and around him. An infantry soldier came up to the fire, squatted on his heels, held his hands to the fire, and turned his face.

"You don't mind, your honour?" he said, looking inquiringly at Tushin. "Here I've got lost from my company, your honour; I don't know myself where I am. It's dreadful!"

With the soldier an infantry officer approached the fire with a bandaged face. He asked Tushin to have the cannon moved a very little, so as to let a store wagon pass by. After the officer two soldiers ran up to the fire. They were swearing desperately and fighting, trying to pull a boot from one another.

"No fear! you picked it up! that's smart!" one shouted in a husky voice.

Then a thin, pale soldier approached, his neck bandaged with a blood-stained rag. With a voice of exasperation he asked the artillerymen for water.

"Why, is one to die like a dog?" he said.

Tushin told them to give him water. Next a good-humoured soldier ran up, to beg for some red-hot embers for the infantry.

"Some of your fire for the infantry! Glad to halt, lads. Thanks for the loan of the firing; we'll pay it back with interest," he said, carrying some glowing firebrands away into the darkness.

Next four soldiers passed by, carrying something heavy in an overcoat. One of them stumbled.

"Ay, the devils, they've left firewood in the road," grumbled one.

"He's dead; why carry him?" said one of them.

"Come on, you!" And they vanished into the darkness with their burden.

"Does it ache, eh?" Tushin asked Rostov in a whisper.

"Yes, it does ache."

"Your honour's sent for to the general. Here in a cottage he is," said a gunner, coming up to Tushin.

"In a minute, my dear." Tushin got up and walked away from the fire, buttoning up his coat and setting himself straight.

In a cottage that had been prepared for him not far from the artillery-men's fire, Prince Bagration was sitting at dinner, talking with several commanding officers, who had gathered about him. The little old colonel with the half-shut eyes was there, greedily gnawing at a mutton-bone, and the general of twenty-two years' irreproachable service, flushed with a glass of vodka and his dinner, and the staff-officer with the signet ring, and Zherkov, stealing uneasy glances at every one, and Prince Andrey, pale with set lips and feverishly glittering eyes.

In the corner of the cottage room stood a French flag, that had been captured, and the auditor with the naïve countenance was feeling the stuff of which the flag was made, and shaking his head with a puzzled air, possibly because looking at the flag really interested him, or possibly because he did not enjoy the sight of the dinner, as he was hungry and no place had been laid for him. In the next cottage there was the French colonel, who had been taken prisoner by the dragoons. Our officers were flocking in to look at him. Prince Bagration thanked the several commanding officers, and inquired into details of the battle and of the losses. The general, whose regiment had been inspected at Braunau, submitted to the prince that as soon as the engagement began, he had fallen back from the copse, mustered the men who were cutting wood, and letting them pass by him, had made a bayonet charge with two battalions and repulsed the French.

"As soon as I saw, your excellency, that the first battalion was thrown into confusion, I stood in the road and thought, 'I'll let them get through and then open fire on them'; and that's what I did."

The general had so longed to do this, he had so regretted not having succeeded in doing it, that it seemed to him now that this was just what had happened. Indeed might it not actually have been so? Who could make out in such confusion what did and what did not happen?

"And by the way I ought to note, your excellency," he continued, recalling Dolohov's conversation with Kutuzov and his own late interview with the degraded officer, "that the private Dolohov, degraded to the ranks, took a French officer prisoner before my eyes and particularly distinguished himself."

"I saw here, your excellency, the attack of the Pavlograd hussars," Zherkov put in, looking uneasily about him. He had not seen the hussars at all that day, but had only heard about them from an infantry officer. "They broke up two squares, your excellency."

When Zherkov began to speak, several officers smiled, as they always did, expecting a joke from him. But as they perceived that what he was saying all redounded to the glory of our arms and of the day, they assumed a serious expression, although many were very well aware that what Zherkov was saying was a lie utterly without foundation. Prince Bagration turned to the old colonel.

"I thank you all, gentlemen; all branches of the service behaved heroically—infantry, cavalry, and artillery. How did two cannons come to be abandoned in the centre?" he inquired, looking about for some one. (Prince Bagration did not ask about the cannons of the left flank; he knew that all of them had been abandoned at the very beginning of the action.) "I think it was you I sent," he added, addressing the staff-officer.

"One had been disabled," answered the staff-officer, "but the other, I can't explain; I was there all the while myself, giving instructions, and I had scarcely left there. . . . It was pretty hot, it's true," he added modestly.

Some one said that Captain Tushin was close by here in the village, and that he had already been sent for.

"Oh, but you went there," said Prince Bagration, addressing Prince Andrey.

"To be sure, we rode there almost together," said the staff-officer, smiling affably to Bolkonsky.

"I had not the pleasure of seeing you," said Prince Andrey, coldly and abruptly. Every one was silent.

Tushin appeared in the doorway, timidly edging in behind the generals' backs. Making his way round the generals in the crowded hut, embarrassed as he always was before his superior officers, Tushin did not see the flag-staff and tumbled over it. Several of the officers laughed.

"How was it a cannon was abandoned?" asked Bagration, frowning, not so much at the captain as at the laughing officers, among whom Zherkov's laugh was the loudest. Only now in the presence of the angry-looking commander, Tushin conceived in all its awfulness the crime and disgrace of his being still alive when he had lost two cannons. He had been so excited that till that instant he had not had time to think of that. The officers' laughter had bewildered him still more. He stood before Bagration, his lower jaw quivering, and could scarcely articulate:

"I don't know . . . your excellency . . . I hadn't the men, your excellency."

"You could have got them from the battalions that were covering your position!" That there were no battalions there was what Tushin did not say, though it was the fact. He was afraid of getting another officer into trouble by saying that, and without uttering a word he gazed straight into Bagration's face, as a confused schoolboy gazes at the face of an examiner.

The silence was rather a lengthy one. Prince Bagration, though he had no wish to be severe, apparently found nothing to say; the others did not venture to intervene. Prince Andrey was looking from under his brows at Tushin and his fingers moved nervously.

"Your excellency," Prince Andrey broke the silence with his abrupt voice, "you sent me to Captain Tushin's battery. I went there and found two-thirds of the men and horses killed, two cannons disabled and no forces near to defend them."

Prince Bagration and Tushin looked now with equal intensity at Bolkonsky, as he went on speaking with suppressed emotion.

"And if your excellency will permit me to express my opinion," he went on, "we owe the success of the day more to the action of that battery and the heroic steadiness of Captain Tushin and his men than to anything else," said Prince Andrey, and he got up at once and walked away from the table, without waiting for a reply.

Prince Bagration looked at Tushin and, apparently loath to express his disbelief in Bolkonsky's off-handed judgment, yet unable to put complete faith in it, he bent his head and said to Tushin that he could go. Prince Andrey walked out after him.

"Thanks, my dear fellow, you got me out of a scrape," Tushin said to him.

Prince Andrey looked at Tushin, and walked away without uttering a word. Prince Andrey felt bitter and melancholy. It was all so strange, so unlike what he had been hoping for.

After the Final Victory

AGNES SMEDLEY

SHEN KUO-HWA, the little guerrilla boy, stood by my table, relating an exciting story about the battle of Machiachung three weeks before, when the Japanese had attacked the guerrilla base. During the retreat of the guerrillas, a bullet had passed through his upper arm and he had been in the hospital for two weeks.

He was ten years old. Standing entirely naked by my table, he seemed much frailer and smaller than any Chinese boy of ten. His thin, wistful face was turned up to mine. Behind him stood the small wooden tub in which he had just bathed, and near by was a brazier of gleaming charcoal. He was waiting for me to delouse his uniform, which was his only suit of clothing. He had no underclothing at all, but I had bought a shirt for him. While he talked, I would thrust the charcoal tongs in among the gleaming charcoal and, while they heated, I would wet the inside seams of the uniform. Then, as I drew the hot tongs down the seams, the steam would arise and the lice would crack.

"It won't take much longer," I told him, "for you are small." And I looked at him to see how he would take this remark.

"I'm small because I never had enough to eat, and because I was sick so much when I was a beggar boy."

"You're not so very big just now, but later on you will be a big, strapping fellow. Then what will you do?"

"I want to ride a horse and fight the Japanese devils." He spoke solemnly

While the tongs were heating again, I bent over and examined the deep red scar on his arm.

"That happened when we were crossing the highway," he explained again. "We had many killed and wounded men in that battle. But we captured three of the devils. One was in the hospital with me. He was afraid at first, but we treated him well and then he was not afraid.

"Look," the child said, lifting one leg and showing another scar. "That's where a dog bit me. When I was a beggar boy people used to set their dogs on me. I am always afraid of dogs. I think they are going to eat me." He was a small, fearful child when he spoke of dogs.

"Ai-yoh—but your uniform is filled with lice!" I exclaimed.

From: *Asia Magazine* by permission of the Author.

"Every one has lice in winter. Some orderlies have more than I."

"Lice are very dangerous. They give you dangerous diseases."

"Yes. Men often die here from louse sickness. One died yesterday, and then all the lice crawled off his body—he had many, *very* many."

"Was he in the hospital?"

"The hospital is too far away."

"Where was he when he died?"

"He lay on some straw."

"Did a doctor take care of him?"

"We have no doctor here. But the soldiers gave him water and food when he wanted anything."

I deloused the uniform and thought—of delousing stations to prevent typhus and relapsing fever. But the guerrilla detachment moved often, for Japanese garrisons were all about it and there was almost continual fighting. I looked down at the child and asked:

"Do you think you can keep free of lice? The reason men are dying is because of lice."

"In the army there is no way. We all sleep together to keep warm. When I am with you, it is all right. When you go, I will get lice again. Even when I was very small, before I joined the army, I had lice in the winter time. I used to watch them. There are two kinds of lice—red lice and white lice. When they are babies they have two legs only."

"When they crawl on me I think they have a million legs."

"That's because you have only a few. Then you itch. If you get many lice you don't itch; you just get a headache and we call it louse sickness. Many other orderlies like me have a headache all the time."

"Come now, get into your clothing. If you feel any tomorrow I will do it again. Tonight I will boil your shirt and then you can put it on."

The child put on his uniform, then solemnly and gratefully said, "You are both my father and my mother."

I drew him to me, held him between my knees and combed his hair. "Where did you get this big scar on your cheek?" I asked.

"When I was very small, bandits burned down our house and killed my father and injured my mother. I was burned then."

While we talked a Chinese woman reporter who was with me in the guerrilla detachment came in, with another little boy, who was her orderly. We were soon busy delousing the boy. The two children kept up an excited patter about this unusual event, about their daily lives, about the classes they attended each day where they learned to read and write. Often it was difficult to get them to act like children with us because the army had given them orderly work and they acted like little men. They cleaned our rooms in the morning, brought tea or water for washing, and kept our fires burning. Because we were guests, we had a charcoal fire. But the guerrillas were too poor to buy charcoal for others. It was winter time and the snow lay on the ground. The wind swished past our paper-covered windows. Our rooms were the only ones warm enough for a bath.

"What a miserable existence! This storm is miserable!" the woman reporter exclaimed, listening to the wind.

Shen Kuo-hwa was peering through a hole in the paper window. "The storm will not last long," he told her. "When the wind sounds like that and the snow lies like that on the ground, the snow will soon stop."

"How do you know?" she asked.

"When I tended cows for the big landlord I watched the snow and listened to the wind each winter. Before that I watched, too, for I was a beggar boy."

"When and where was all that?"

"In Honan, before I joined this army, I worked for a landlord for three years. My mother asked a small landlord to guarantee me to a big landlord, so I got a job tending cows. The landlord paid me eighty cents a year. Yes, he gave me food. If his sons threw away any clothing he gave some to me. My mother used my eighty cents to make me shoes for winter."

"How old were you?" The woman's voice was as sad as the wind outside.

"I was six when I got the job."

"How long were you a beggar boy?"

"I think it was two years. It was before I tended cows. It was after the bandits burned our home and killed my father and injured my mother. My two brothers had joined the army to make a living. So we had nothing. Then my mother told me to beg. She said I must find a rich man's house and beg before it. I was very little and I did not know how to beg. But I found a big house and many people went in and came out all day. I stood there all day but no one saw me. When it was dark a man who had gone in and come out many times saw me and told me to go home; he said all children ought to be in bed. I told him the bandits had burned our house and we had no bed and no food. Then he gave me a little money and I went to find my mother. After that I was a beggar boy for two years. It was very bad. People treat you very badly; they used to set their dogs on me and drive me away. I was sick very much."

"What did you do when you were sick?"

"I would find a place and lie down."

The delousing had finished and as he talked the child was leaning against me. Now he lowered his head and was silent. The bill of his small military cap hid his face. He made no motion and no sound, but tears were rolling down his cheeks and falling on my jacket. I lifted his chin in my hand and wiped the tears away. The other little orderly watched us, then said cheerfully: "Kuo-hwa is a very good orderly and makes no trouble with the other orderlies. He studies hard and has learned to read and write a lot."

This simple tribute caused Kuo-hwa to look gratefully at the other boy. He ceased crying. But he was a child so humble that he could not take credit for even learning to read and write.

"The army taught me," he replied. "Before I joined the army I tried to learn, but no one would teach me. I used to watch rich boys go to school with their book satchels. I learned to write the characters for one, two and three, but four and five were very hard and I could not get any one to help me. I asked a man once, but he pushed me and asked me what a beggar boy wanted to learn to read and write for. He said, "Get out!" But I learned to write "quality" because it is on boxes of goods before shops and it has three squares. I learned how to write "matches" and the name of the firm that makes matches. I would write with a stick or my finger, in the dust. But no one ever taught me to write my name. I learned that in the army. But I don't know much yet."

The other little orderly defended him stoutly: "I think he knows over two hundred characters," he told us. "Of course I know more because I am older and have been in the army longer. Kuo-hwa learns quickly. He is the best orderly in the army."

"You are a good orderly, too, and very willing," Kuo-hwa replied.

The woman reporter looked from one child to the other, her face eloquent with tenderness.

"How did you get into this army?" she asked Kuo-hwa.

"Wang Lao-han brought me. He is a good man. One day my brother's army came to Choshan on the Pinghan railway. My brother saw my mother begging on the streets, but he would not give her any money. My good brother was killed in the battle of Lukouchiao (Marco Polo Bridge). This bad brother said I was a fool for working for a landlord for eighty cents a year. He said I ought to get a good job that paid good money.

"While my brother's army was in Choshan I heard some soldiers talking. They said the Eighth Route Army was a poor man's army, every one learned how to read and write, and officers could not beat the soldiers. But they said the soldiers were paid only one dollar and a half a month. I thought I would join the Eighth Route Army, and I asked the soldiers where I could find it. They laughed and said it was far away. I asked a policeman where I could find it, but he said it was made up of bandits and he shook me by the arm and asked me why I wanted to find it. I said it was a poor man's army and I was a poor man."

"Never ask a policeman anything!" the other little orderly cautioned.

"After that, what did you do?" the woman reporter asked Kuo-hwa.

"Once in Choshan I saw an old man with a beard and a kind face, and though he was old he had on a military uniform. I asked him the same question, and he smiled and patted me on the head and said the Eighth Route Army was very far away and I was too small to join an army. I followed him and told him how I could walk and work, and how the landlord's servants sometimes beat me and made me do their work too. I followed him all day. His name was Wang Lao-han, and he was from this New Fourth Army Storm Guerrilla Detachment. He said it was a poor man's army, too, but it did not have enough food and clothing and could not pay much money.

"Wang Lao-han did not want me to follow him but when he went to a village outside Choshan he got tired of saying I must go back. Then I came with him here."

The storm ceased, but the snow lay in great drifts on the mountain paths. At such a time there would be no fighting. So the woman reporter sat by the fire in my room, a small boy on either side of her, and they talked. The boys brought their small pocket manuals, and she helped them study. While I wrote at the table, their low, soft voices filled the room like gentle music. Listening, sometimes I heard them drilling: "I am a human being. You are a human being. He is a human being." Then they would look at the bottom of the page for the discussion theme and read. "Why is there a distinction between the rich and the poor among human beings?" They would read further, "The peasants grow rice." And the discussion theme: "Why can workers and peasants not consume the things they produce?" Or they would discuss: "Why is reliance on another man unreliable?" "Why are the rich and the poor both anti-Japanese today?" "Why is Japanese imperialism the most ruthless in the world?"

The snow along the mountain paths became packed hard by the marching feet of soldiers. And one day the woman reporter and I returned to our rooms. "We are going with a regiment into the lake region," we told the boys. "When we return you can be our orderlies again."

Kuo-hwa stood with lowered head. He was a little soldier and seemed to be taking an order obediently, silently. Humble, he expected little, and was grateful that the guerrillas had allowed him to share their barren, dour life.

"Kuo-hwa," I said. "Can you keep free of lice while I am gone?"

"No," he replied. "There is no way. We must all sleep close together to keep warm."

"How far have you walked in the army?"

"Sometimes we march all night, in the dark, and I carry things like the others. I could go with you—" then he lowered his head and said dully —"if you want me."

The woman reporter and I looked at each other. Did we dare take these children into a region of great danger? The Children's Dramatic Corps was already in that region, she insisted. I thought of Kuo-hwa remaining here, where relapsing fever killed men each day.

"Kuo-hwa—we will ask permission for you both to come with us. We leave late this afternoon. Can you get ready?"

The child lifted his face to ours and both boys began talking eagerly. "We can always be ready in five minutes," they assured us.

Then the woman reporter and I, and our two small orderlies, went into the lake region near Hankow. And in going there, the armed escort with which we marched came suddenly face to face with the Japanese, and fought. The midnight darkness was split with the singing of bullets and the bursting of hand-grenades, and those of us who were not fighters were told to run quickly behind the shelter of hills. Kuo-hwa, the woman reporter, my secretary and two new volunteers without guns found themselves in one group, and none knew where I was. Kuo-hwa then began running about in the darkness, asking desperately if the devils had caught me. He told the others that he could go out into the night and shout, and that I would answer his voice, but that I would fear to answer any one else lest it be a Japanese devil.

The woman reporter took him by the hand and told him to remain silent because he was a child and could not find me.

Angrily he turned on her and said: "When she came to our army, they told me to serve her and they said I was responsible for her. It is my duty to the army to find and protect her!"

But when they all refused to allow him to venture into the darkness to find me, the little soldier became a sobbing child. They pitied him and said he could never find his way back. Once more he became the soldier. He ceased crying, looked at the encircling hills, at a few trees, and then for a long time at the stars above.

"I can find her and bring her back to this place," he stated.

Yet they refused. Later, when we all had assembled once more, the child came quickly to my side and placed his hands on my arm.

Knowing what he had tried to do, I said to him: "Yes—you were right; I would have answered you, but no one else." And then he was quiet and at peace. Often my impulse was to put my arms about him and comfort him. Always I hesitated, not knowing the effect. A bitter life had fashioned him into a small creature that lived within himself, alone. In the army there was comradeship in ideas and in general struggle, but each person— man or child—had to care for himself or fall behind in the march of life. Even the reading textbooks contained the discussion topic: "Why is reliance on another person unreliable?" Already my contact with this small life had disturbed a pattern that had been laid and I could not say if it was for the better.

In the weeks that followed, the woman reporter and I always found time to write in our notebooks. Kuo-hwa would often come up and stand watching us in silence. Once he asked us what we wrote, and then the woman reporter read to him and explained that we wrote not just what we saw, but what men said, and sometimes what we ourselves felt and thought.

Then we saw that the child was trying to do as we did. He would take any bit of paper or open a cast-off cigarette case and write on the inside of it. He would sit thinking, wet the lead of his pencil on his tongue and write; then think again. Once I picked up such a case and asked the woman reporter to read to me what he had written. She read these words:

"Got up before sun and walked on hill. Fog everywhere in trees. Sun came up big and red and fog went away. Went down hill and saw Wang Lao-han coming. I felt glad. But he forgot me and forgot he brought me to army. I feel sad. I went away."

Soon the time came when I had to leave the guerrilla army. For weeks I had thought of the problem of Kuo-hwa. If he remained in the army, he would receive some education, but it would be limited. From the rank of orderly he would later become a guard, from a guard a soldier, and from the rank of soldier he would become a commander. If he lived! But his body was too frail to withstand a dangerous disease. And, it seemed to me, in him were rare qualities. With the woman reporter I discussed a special school in western China, where life was simple and even austere, yet where the children were well-fed and well-clothed, where they did their own work, but where serious emphasis was laid on the teaching of science. Then I went to the commander and asked if I could adopt Kuo-hwa.

"Oh, of course," the commander replied, "if the boy is willing. But why choose him?"

"Because he has watched the growth of lice, the way the wind blows, the way the snow drifts, the position of the stars at night. He has given the stars names of his own. And he can describe well what he sees and thinks in writing."

A number of men, listening, smiled, and one said, "I can do all those things also." The commander's eyes narrowed and he remarked dryly: "So can I. What about adopting us also?" And a burly fellow leaning against the door added: "I know more about lice than your little devil Kuo-hwa. I don't know if I can write as well, but I have many other strong points."

That night the woman reporter and I talked with Kuo-hwa and told him about the school. He feared going among "rich little boys," but we told him it was not that kind of school. "You can come back to the army later and teach what you have learned," we urged. He said he would talk with the other little orderly and tell me the next day. And the next morning the two of them came, and Kuo-hwa gave his decision, from which we could not move him.

"We think all men must remain at the front," he said. "You can adopt me after the final victory."

Her Privates We

BY

PRIVATE 19022

By my troth, I care not; a man can die but once; we owe God a death . . . and let it go which way it will, he that dies this year is quit for the next.

SHAKESPEARE

THE darkness was increasing rapidly, as the whole sky had clouded, and threatened thunder. There was still some desultory shelling. When the relief had taken over from them, they set off to return to their original line as best they could. Bourne, who was beaten to the wide, gradually dropped behind, and in trying to keep the others in sight missed his footing and fell into a shell-hole. By the time he had picked himself up again the rest of the party had vanished; and, uncertain of his direction, he stumbled on alone. He neither hurried nor slackened his pace; he was light-headed, almost exalted, and driven only by the desire to find an end. Somewhere, eventually, he would sleep. He almost fell into the wrecked trench and after a moment's hesitation turned left, caring little where it led him. The world seemed extraordinarily empty of men, though he knew the ground was alive with them. He was breathing with difficulty, his mouth and throat seemed to be cracking with dryness, and his water-bottle was empty. Coming to a dug-out, he groped his way down, feeling for the steps with his feet; a piece of Wilson canvas, hung across the passage but twisted aside, rasped his cheek; and a few steps lower his face was enveloped suddenly in the musty folds of a blanket. The dug-out was empty. For the moment he collapsed there, indifferent to everything. Then with shaking hands he felt for his cigarettes, and putting one between his lips struck a match. The light revealed a candle-end stuck by its own grease to the oval lid of a tobacco-tin, and he lit it; it was scarcely thicker than a shilling, but it would last his time. He would finish his cigarette, and then move on to find his company.

There was a kind of bank or seat excavated in the wall of the dug-out, and he noticed first the tattered remains of a blanket lying on it, and then, gleaming faintly in its folds a small metal disk reflecting the light. It was the cap on the cork of a water-bottle. Sprawling sideways he reached it, the feel of the bottle told him it was full, and uncorking it he

From: *Her Privates We.* Courtesy of G. P. Putnam's Sons.

put it to his lips and took a great gulp before discovering that he was swallowing neat whiskey. The fiery spirit almost choked him for the moment, in his surprise he even spat some of it out; then recovering, he drank again, discreetly but sufficiently, and was meditating a more prolonged appreciation when he heard men groping their way down the steps. He recorked the bottle, hid it quickly under the blanket, and removed himself to what might seem an innocent distance from temptation.

Three Scotsmen came in; they were almost as spent and broken as he was, that he knew by their uneven voices; but they put up a show of indifference, and were able to tell him that some of his mob were on the left, in a dug-out about fifty yards away. They, too, had lost their way, and asked him questions in their turn; but he could not help them, and they developed among themselves an incoherent debate, on the question of what was the best thing for them to do in the circumstances. Their dialect only allowed him to follow their arguments imperfectly, but under the talk it was easy enough to see the irresolution of weary men seeking in their difficulties some reasonable pretext for doing nothing. It touched his own conscience, and throwing away the butt of his cigarette he decided to go. The candle was flickering feebly on the verge of extinction, and presently the dug-out would be in darkness again. Prudence stifled in him an impulse to tell them of the whiskey; perhaps they would find it for themselves; it was a matter which might be left for providence or chance to decide. He was moving towards the stairs, when a voice, muffled by the blanket, came from outside.

"Who are down there?"

There was no mistaking the note of authority and Bourne answered promptly. There was a pause, and then the blanket was waved aside, and an officer entered. He was Mr. Clinton, with whom Bourne had fired his course at Tregelly.

"Hullo, Bourne," he began, and then seeing the other men he turned and questioned them in his soft kindly voice. His face had the greenish pallor of crude beeswax, his eyes were red and tired, his hands were as nervous as theirs, and his voice had the same note of over-excitement, but he listened to them without a sign of impatience.

"Well, I don't want to hurry you men off," he said at last, "but your battalion will be moving out before we do. The best thing you can do is to cut along to it. They're about a hundred yards further down the trench. You don't want to straggle back to camp by yourselves; it doesn't look well either. So you had better get moving right away. What you really want is twelve hours solid sleep, and I am only telling you the shortest road to it."

They accepted his view of the matter quietly, they were willing enough; but, like all tired men in similar conditions, they were glad to have their action determined for them; so they thanked him and wished him goodnight, if not cheerfully, at least with the air of being reasonable men, who appreciated his kindliness. Bourne made as though to follow them out, but Mr. Clinton stopped him.

"Wait a minute, Bourne, and we shall go together," he said as the last Scotsman groped his way up the steeply-pitched stairs. "It is indecent to follow a kilted Highlander too closely out of a dug-out. Besides I left something here."

He looked about him, went straight to the blanket, and took up the water-bottle. It must have seemed lighter than he expected, for he shook it a little suspiciously before uncorking it. He took a long steady drink and paused.

"I left this bottle full of whiskey," he said, "but those bloody Jocks must have smelt it. You know, Bourne, I don't go over with a skinful, as some of them do; but, by God, when I come back I want it. Here, take a pull yourself; you look as though you could do with one."

Bourne took the bottle without any hesitation; his case was much the same. One had lived instantaneously during that timeless interval, for in the shock and violence of the attack, the perilous instant, on which he stood perched so precariously, was all that the half-stunned consciousness of man could grasp; and, if he lost his grip on it, he fell back among the grotesque terrors and nightmare creatures of his own mind. Afterwards, when the strain had been finally released, in the physical exhaustion which followed, there was a collapse, in which one's emotional nature was no longer under control.

"We're in the next dug-out, those who are left of us," Mr. Clinton continued. "I am glad you came through all right, Bourne. You were in the last show, weren't you? It seems to me the old Hun has brought up a lot more stuff, and doesn't mean to shift, if he can help it. Anyway we should get a spell out of the line now. I don't believe there are more than a hundred of us left."

A quickening in his speech showed that the whiskey was beginning to play on frayed nerves: it had steadied Bourne for the time being. The flame of the candle gave one leap and went out. Mr. Clinton switched on his torch, and shoved the water-bottle into the pocket of his raincoat.

"Come on," he said, making for the steps, "you and I are two of the lucky ones, Bourne; we've come through without a scratch; and if our luck holds we'll keep moving out of one bloody misery into another, until we break, see, until we break."

Bourne felt a kind of suffocation in his throat: there was nothing weak or complaining in Mr. Clinton's voice, it was full of angry soreness. He switched off the light as he came to the Wilson canvas.

"Don't talk so bloody wet," Bourne said to him through the darkness. "You'll never break."

The officer gave no sign of having heard the sympathetic but indecorous rebuke. They moved along the battered trench silently. The sky flickered with the flash of guns, and an occasional star-shell flooded their path with light. As one fell slowly, Bourne saw a dead man in field grey popped up in a corner of a traverse; probably he had surrendered, wounded, and reached the trench only to die there. He looked indifferently at this piece of wreckage. The grey face was senseless and empty. As they turned the corner they were challenged by a sentry over the dug-out.

"Good-night, Bourne," said Mr. Clinton quietly.

"Good-night, sir," said Bourne, saluting; and he exchanged a few words with the sentry.

"Wish to Christ they'd get a move on," said the sentry, as Bourne turned to go down.

The dug-out was full of men, and all the drawn, pitiless faces turned to see who it was as he entered, and after that flicker of interest relapsed into apathy and stupor again. The air was thick with smoke and the reek of guttering candles. He saw Shem lift a hand to attract his attention, and he managed to squeeze in beside him. They didn't speak after each had asked the other if he were all right; some kind of oppression weighed on them all, they sat like men condemned to death.

"Wonder if they'll keep us up in support?" whispered Shem.

Probably that was the question they were all asking, as they sat there in their bitter resignation, with brooding enigmatic faces, hopeless, but undefeated; even the faces of boys seeming curiously old; and then it changed suddenly: there were quick hurried movements, belts were buckled, rifles taken up, and stooping, they crawled up into the air. Shem and Bourne were among the first out. They moved off at once. Shells travelled overhead; they heard one or two bump fairly close, but they saw nothing except the sides of the trench, whitish with chalk in places, and the steel helmet and lifting swaying shoulders of the man in front, or the frantic uplifted arms of shattered trees, and the sky with the clouds broken in places, through which opened the inaccessible peace of the stars. They seemed to hurry, as though the sense of escape filled them. The walls of the communication trench became gradually lower, the track sloping upward to the surface of the ground, and at last they emerged, the officer standing aside, to watch what was left of his men file out, and form up in two ranks before him. There was little light, but under the brims of the helmets one could see living eyes moving restlessly in blank faces. His face, too, was a blank from weariness, but he stood erect, an ash-stick under his arm, as the dun-coloured shadows shuffled into some sort of order. The words of command that came from him were no more than whispers, his voice was cracked and not quite under control, though there was still some harshness in it. Then they moved off in fours, away from the crest of the ridge, towards the place they called Happy Valley.

They had not far to go. As they were approaching the tents a crump dropped by the mule-lines, and that set them swaying a little, but not much. Captain Malet called them to attention a little later; and from the tents, camp-details, cooks, snobs, and a few unfit men, gathered in groups to watch them, with a sympathy genuine enough, but tactfully aloof; for there is a gulf between men just returned from action, and those who have not been in the show as unbridgeable as that between the sober and the drunk. Captain Malet halted his men by the orderly-room tent. There was even a pretence to dress ranks. Then he looked at them, and they at him for a few seconds which seemed long. They were only shadows in the darkness.

"Dismiss!"

His voice was still pitched low, but they turned almost with the precision of troops on the square, each rifle was struck smartly, the officer saluting; and then the will which bound them together dissolved, the enervated muscles relaxed, and they lurched off to their tents as silent and as dispirited as beaten men. One of the tailors took his pipe out of his mouth and spat on the ground.

"They can say what they like," he said appreciatively, "but we're a bloody fine mob."

Once during the night Bourne started up in an access of inexplicable horror, and after a moment of bewildered recollection, turned over and tried to sleep again. He remembered nothing of the nightmare which had roused him, if it were a nightmare, but gradually his awakened sense felt a vague restlessness troubling equally the other men. He noticed it first in Shem, whose body, almost touching his own, gave a quick, convulsive jump, and continued twitching for a moment, while he muttered unintelligibly, and worked his lips as though he were trying to moisten them. The obscure disquiet passed fitfully from one to another, lips parted with the sound of a bubble bursting, teeth met grinding as the jaws worked, there were little whimperings which quickened into sobs, passed into long shuddering moans, or culminated in angry, half-articulate obscenities, and then relapsed, with fretful, uneasy movements and heavy breathing, into a more profound sleep. Even though Bourne tried to persuade himself that these convulsive agonies were merely reflex actions, part of an unconscious physical process, through which the disordered nerves sought to readjust themselves, or to perform belatedly some instinctive movement which an over-riding will had thwarted at its original inception, his own conscious mind now filled itself with the passions, of which the mutterings and twitchings heard in the darkness were only the unconscious mimicry. The senses certainly have, in some measure, an independent activity of their own, and remain vigilant even in the mind's eclipse. The darkness seemed to him to be filled with the shuddering of tormented flesh, as though something diabolically evil probed curiously to find a quick sensitive nerve and wring from it a reluctant cry of pain. At last, unable to ignore the sense of misery which filled him, he sat up and lit the inevitable cigarette. The formless terrors haunting their sleep took shape for him. His mind reached back into the past day, groping among obscure and broken memories, for it seemed to him now that for the greater part of the time he had been stunned and blinded, and that what he had seen, he had seen in sudden, vivid flashes, instantaneously: he felt again the tension of waiting, that became impatience, and then the immense effort to move, and the momentary relief which came with movement, the sense of unreality and dread which descended on one, and some restoration of balance as one saw other men moving forward in a way that seemed commonplace, mechanical, as though at some moment of ordinary routine; the restraint, and the haste that fought against it with every voice in one's being crying out to hurry. Hurry? One cannot hurry, alone, into nowhere, into nothing. Every impulse created immediately its own violent contradiction. The confusion and tumult in his own mind was inseparable from the senseless fury about him, each reinforcing the other. He saw great chunks of the German line blown up, as the artillery blasted a way for them; clouds of dust and smoke screened their advance, but the Hun searched for them scrupulously; the air was alive with the rush and flutter of wings; it was ripped by screaming shells, hissing like tons of molten metal plunging suddenly into water, there was the blast and concussion of their explosion, men smashed, obliterated in sudden eruptions of earth, rent and strewn in bloody fragments, shells that were like hell-cats humped and spitting, little sounds, unpleasantly close, like the plucking of tense strings, and something tangling his feet, tearing at his trousers and puttees as he stumbled over it, and then a face suddenly, an inconceivably distorted face, which raved and sobbed at him as he fell with it into a shell-hole. He saw with astonishment the bare stern of a Scotsman who had gone into action wearing only a kilt-apron; and then they righted themselves and looked at each other, bewildered and humiliated. There followed a moment of perfect lucidity, while they took a breather; and he found himself, though unwounded, wondering with an insane prudence where the nearest dressing-station was. Other men came up; two more Gordons joined them, and then Mr. Halliday, who flung himself on top of them and, keeping his head well down, called them a lot of bloody skullers. He had a slight wound in the fore-arm. They made a rush forward again, the dust and smoke clearing a little, and they heard the elastic twang of Mills bombs as they reached an empty trench, very narrow where shelling had not wrecked or levelled it. Mr. Halliday was hit again, in the knee, before they reached the trench, and Bourne felt something pluck the front of his tunic at the same time. They pulled Mr. Halliday into the trench and left him with one of the Gordons who had also been hit. Men were converging there, and he went forward with some of his own company again. From the moment he had thrown himself into the shell-hole with the Scotsman something had changed in him; the conflict and tumult of his mind had gone, his mind itself seemed to have gone, to have contracted and hardened within him; fear remained, an implacable and restless fear, but that, too, seemed to have been beaten and forged into a point of exquisite sensibility and to have become indistinguishable from hate. Only the instincts of the beast survived in him, every sense was alert and in that tension was some poignancy. He neither knew where he was nor whither he was going, he could have no plan because he could foresee nothing, everything happening was inevitable and unexpected, he was an act in a whole chain of acts; and, though his movements had to conform to those of others, spontaneously, as part of some infinitely flexible plan, which he could not comprehend very clearly even in regard to its immediate object, he could rely on no one but himself. They worked round a point still held by machine-guns, through a rather intricate system of trenches linking up shell-craters. The trenches were little more than bolt-holes, through which the machine-gunners, after they had held up the advancing infantry as long as possible, might hope to escape to some other appointed position further back, and resume their work, thus gaining time for the troops behind to ˙recover from the effect of the bombardment, and emerge from their hiding-places. They were singularly brave men, these Prussian machine-gunners, but the extreme of heroism, alike in foe or friend, is indistinguishable from despair. Bourne found himself playing again a game of his childhood, though not now among rocks from which reverberated heat quivered in wavy films, but in made fissures too chalky and unweathered for adequate concealment. One has not, perhaps, at thirty years the same zest in the game as one had at thirteen, but the sense of danger brought into play a latent experience which had become a kind of instinct with him, and he moved in those tortuous ways with the furtive cunning of a stoat or weasel. Stooping low at an angle in the trench he saw the next comparatively straight length empty, and when the man behind was close to him, ran forward still stooping. The advancing line, hung up at one point, inevitably tended to surround it, and it was suddenly abandoned by the few men holding it. Bourne, running, checked as a running Hun rounded the further angle precipitately, saw him prop, shrink back into a defensive posture, and fired without lifting the butt of his rifle quite level with his right breast. The man fell shot in the face, and someone screamed at Bourne to go on; the body choked the narrow angle, and when he put his foot on it, squirmed or moved, making him check again, fortunately, as a bomb exploded a couple yards round the corner. He turned, dismayed, on the man behind him, but behind the bomber he saw the grim bulk of Captain Malet, and his strangely exultant face; and Bourne, incapable of articulate speech, could only wave a hand to indicate the way he divined the Huns to have gone. Captain Malet swung himself above the ground, and the men, following, overflowed the narrow channel of the trench; but the two waves, which had swept round the machine-gun post, were now on the point of meeting; men bunched together, and there were some casualties among them before they went to ground again. Captain Malet gave him a word in passing, and Bourne, looking at him with dull uncomprehending eyes, lagged a little to let others intervene between them. He had found himself immediately afterwards next to Company-Sergeant-Major Glasspool, who nodded to him swiftly and appreciatively; and then Bourne understood. He was doing the right thing. In that last rush he had gone on and got into the lead, somehow, for a brief moment; but he realised himself that he had only gone on because he had been unable to stand still. The sense of being one in a crowd did not give him the same confidence as at the start, the present stage seemed to call for a little more personal freedom. Presently, just because they were together they would rush something in a hurry instead of stalking it. Two men of another regiment, who had presumably got lost, broke back momentarily demoralised, and Sergeant-Major Glasspool confronted them.

"Where the bloody hell do you reckon you're going?"

He rapped out the question with the staccato of a machine-gun; facing their hysterical disorder, he was the living embodiment of a threat.

"We were ordered back," one said, shamefaced and fearful.

"Yes. You take your bloody orders from Fritz," Glasspool, whitelipped and with heaving chest, shot sneering at them. They came to heel quietly enough, but all the rage and hatred in their hearts found an object in him, now. He forgot them as soon as he found them in hand.

"You're all right, chum," whispered Bourne, to the one who had spoken. "Get among your own mob again as soon as there's a chance."

The man only looked at him stonily. In the next rush forward something struck Bourne's helmet, knocking it back over the nape of his neck so that the chin-strap tore his ears. For the moment he thought he had been knocked out, he had bitten his tongue, too, and his mouth was salt with blood. The blow had left a deep dent in the helmet, just fracturing the steel. He was still dazed and shaken when they reached some building-ruins, which he seemed to remember. They were near the railway-station.

He wished he could sleep, he was heavy with it; but his restless memory made sleep seem something to be resisted as too like death. He closed his eyes and had a vision of men advancing under a rain of shells. They had seemed so toylike, so trivial and ineffective when opposed to that overwhelming wrath, and yet they had moved forward mechanically as though they were hypnotised or fascinated by some superior will. That had been one of Bourne's most vivid impressions in action, a man close to him moving forward with the jerky motion a clockwork toy has when it is running down; and it had been vivid to him because of the relief with which he had turned to it and away from the confusion and tumult of his own mind. It had seemed impossible to relate that petty, commonplace, unheroic figure, in ill-fitting khaki and a helmet like the barber's basin with which Don Quixote made shift on his adventures, to the moral and spiritual conflict, almost superhuman in its agony, within him. Power is measured by the amount of resistance which it overcomes, and, in the last resort, the moral power of men was greater than any purely material force, which could be brought to bear on it. It took the chance of death, as one of the chances it was bound to take; though, paradoxically enough, the function of our moral nature consists solely in the assertion of one's own individual will against anything which may be opposed to it, and death, therefore, would imply its extinction in the particular and individual case. The true inwardness of tragedy lies in the fact that its failure is only apparent, and as in the case of the martyr also, the moral conscience of man has made its own deliberate choice, and asserted the freedom of its being. The sense of wasted effort is only true for meaner and more material natures. It took the more horrible chance of mutilation. But as far as Bourne himself, and probably also, since the moral impulse is not necessarily an intellectual act, as far as the majority of his comrades were concerned, its strength and its weakness were inseparably entangled in each other. Whether a man be killed by a rifle-bullet through the brain, or blown into fragments by a high-explosive shell, may seem a matter of indifference to the conscientious objector, or to any other equally well-placed observer, who in point of fact is probably right; but to the poor fool who is a candidate for posthumous honours, and necessarily takes a more directly interested view, it is a question of importance. He is, perhaps, the victim of an illusion, like all who, in the words of Paul, are fools for Christ's sake; but he has seen one man shot cleanly in his tracks and left face downwards, dead, and he has seen another torn into bloody tatters as by some invisible beast, and these experiences had nothing illusory about them: they were actual facts. Death, of course, like chastity, admits of no degree; a man is dead or not dead, and a man is just as dead by one means as by another; but it is infinitely more horrible and revolting to see a man shattered and eviscerated, than to see him shot. And one sees such things; and one suffers vicariously, with the inalienable sympathy of man for man. One forgets quickly. The mind is averted as well as the eyes. It reassures itself after that first despairing cry: "It is I!"

"No, it is not I. I shall not be like that."

And one moves on, leaving the mauled and bloody thing behind: gambling, in fact, on that implicit assurance each one of us has of his own immortality. One forgets, but he will remember again later, if only in his sleep.

After all, the dead are quiet. Nothing in the world is more still than a dead man. One sees living men living, living, as it were, desperately, and then suddenly emptied of life. A man dies and stiffens into something like a wooden dummy, at which one glances for a second with a furtive curiosity. Suddenly he remembered the dead in Trones Wood, the unburied dead with whom one lived, he might say, cheek by jowl, Briton and Hun impartially confounded, festering, fly-blown corruption, the pasture of rats, blackening in the heat, swollen with distended bellies, or shrivelling away within their mouldering rags; and even when night covered them, one vented in the wind the stench of death. Out of one bloody misery into another, until we break. One must not break. He took in his breath suddenly in a shaken sob, and the mind relinquished its hopeless business. The warm smelly darkness of the tent seemed almost luxurious ease. He drowsed heavily; dreaming of womanly softness, sweetness; but their faces slipped away from him like the reflections in water when the wind shakes it, and his soul sank deeply and more deeply into the healing of oblivion.

Borodino

BY

COUNT LEO TOLSTOY

THE chief action of the battle of Borodino was fought on the space seven thousand feet in width between Borodino and Bagration's flèches. Outside that region, on one side there was the action on the part of Uvarov's cavalry in the middle of the day; on the other side, behind Utitsa, there was the skirmish between Poniatovsky and Tutchkov; but those two actions were detached and of little importance in comparison with what took place in the centre of the battlefield. The chief action of the day was fought in the simplest and the most artless fashion on the open space, visible from both sides, between Borodino and the flèches by the copse.

The battle began with a cannonade from several hundred of guns on both sides. Then, when the whole plain was covered with smoke, on the French side the two divisions of Desaix and Compans advanced on the right upon the flèches, and on the left the viceroy's regiments advanced upon Borodino. The flèches were a verst from the Shevardino redoubt, where Napoleon was standing; but Borodino was more than two versts further, in a straight line, and therefore Napoleon could not see what was passing there, especially as the smoke, mingling with the fog, completely hid the whole of that part of the plain. The soldiers of Desaix's division, advancing upon the flèches, were in sight till they disappeared from view in the hollow that lay between them and the flèches. As soon as they dropped down into the hollow, the smoke of the cannon and muskets on the flèches became so thick that it concealed the whole slope of that side of the hollow. Through the smoke could be caught glimpses of something black, probably men, and sometimes the gleam of bayonets. But whether they were stationary or moving, whether they were French or Russian, could not be seen from Shevardino.

The sun had risen brightly, and its slanting rays shone straight in Napoleon's face as he looked from under his hand towards the flèches. The smoke hung over the flèches, and at one moment it seemed as though it were the smoke that was moving, at the next, the troops moving in the smoke. Sometimes cries could be heard through the firing; but it was impossible to tell what was being done there.

Napoleon, standing on the redoubt, was looking through a fieldglass, and in the tiny circle of the glass saw smoke and men, sometimes his own, sometimes Russians. But where what he had seen was, he could not tell when he looked again with the naked eye.

From: *War and Peace.*

He came down from the redoubt, and began walking up and down before it.

At intervals he stood still, listening to the firing and looking intently at the battlefield.

It was not simply impossible from below, where he was standing, and from the redoubt above, where several of his generals were standing, to make out what was passing at the flèches; but on the flèches themselves, occupied now together, now alternately by French and Russians, living, dead, and wounded, the frightened and frantic soldiers had no idea what they were doing. For several hours together, in the midst of incessant cannon and musket fire, Russians and French, infantry and cavalry, had captured the place in turn; they rushed upon it, fell, fired, came into collision, did not know what to do with each other, screamed, and ran back again.

From the battlefield adjutants were continually galloping up to Napoleon with reports from his marshals of the progress of action. But all those reports were deceptive; both because in the heat of battle it is impossible to say what is happening at any given moment, and because many of the adjutants never reached the actual battlefield, but simply repeated what they heard from others, and also because, while the adjutant was galloping the two or three versts to Napoleon, circumstances had changed, and the news he brought already become untrue. Thus an adjutant came galloping from the viceroy with the news that Borodino had been taken and the bridge on the Kolotcha was in the hands of the French. The adjutant asked Napoleon should the troops cross the bridge. Napoleon's command was to form on the further side and wait; but long before he gave that command, when the adjutant indeed had only just started from Borodino, the bridge had been broken down and burnt by the Russians in the very skirmish Pierre had taken part in at the beginning of the day.

An adjutant, galloping up from the flèches with a pale and frightened face, brought Napoleon word that the attack had been repulsed, and Compans wounded and Davoust killed; while meantime the flèches had been captured by another division of the troops, and Davoust was alive and well, except for a slight bruise. Upon such inevitably misleading reports Napoleon based his instructions, which had mostly been carried out before he made them, or else were never, and could never, be carried out at all.

The marshals and generals who were closer to the scene of action, but, like Napoleon, not actually taking part in it, and only at intervals riding within bullet range, made their plans without asking Napoleon, and gave their orders from where and in what direction to fire, and where the cavalry were to gallop and the infantry to run. But even their orders, like Napoleon's, were but rarely, and to a slight extent, carried out.

For the most part what happened was the opposite of what they commanded to be done. The soldiers ordered to advance found themselves under grapeshot fire, and ran back. The soldiers commanded to stand still in one place seeing the Russians appear suddenly before them, either ran away or rushed upon them; and the cavalry unbidden galloped in after the flying Russians. In this way two cavalry regiments galloped across the Semyonovskoye hollow, and as soon as they reached the top of the hill, turned and galloped headlong back again. The infantry, in the same way, moved sometimes in the direction opposite to that in which they were commanded to move.

All decisions as to when and where to move the cannons, when to send infantry to fire, when to send cavalry to trample down the Russian infantry—all such decisions were made by the nearest officers in the ranks, without any reference to Ney, Davoust, and Murat, far less to Napoleon himself. They did not dread getting into trouble for nonfulfilment of orders, nor for assuming responsibility, because in battle what is at stake is what is most precious to every man—his own life; and at one time it seems as though safety is to be found in flying back, sometimes in flying forward; and these men placed in the very thick of the fray acted in accordance with the temper of the moment.

In reality all these movements forward and back again hardly improved or affected the position of the troops. All their onslaughts on one another did little harm; the harm, the death and disablement was the work of the cannon balls and bullets, that were flying all about the open space, where those men ran to and fro. As soon as they got out of that exposed space, over which the balls and bullets were flying, their superior officer promptly formed them in good order, and restored discipline, and under the influence of that discipline led them back under fire again; and there again, under the influence of the terror of death, they lost all discipline, and dashed to and fro at the chance promptings of the crowd.

Napoleon's generals, Davoust, Ney, and Murat, who were close to that region of fire, and sometimes even rode into it, several times led immense masses of orderly troops into that region. But instead of what had invariably happened in all their previous battles, instead of hearing that the enemy were in flight, the disciplined masses of troops came back in undisciplined, panic-stricken crowds. They formed them in good order again, but their number was steadily dwindling. In the middle of the day Murat sent his adjutant to Napoleon with a request for reinforcements.

Napoleon was sitting under the redoubt, drinking punch, when Murat's adjutant galloped to him with the message that the Russians would be routed if his majesty would let them have another division.

"Reinforcements?" said Napoleon, with stern astonishment, staring, as though failing to comprehend his words, at the handsome, boyish adjutant, who wore his black hair in floating curls, like Murat's own. "Reinforcements!" thought Napoleon. "How can they want reinforcements when they have half the army already, concentrated against one weak, unsupported flank of the Russians!"

"Tell the King of Naples," said Napoleon sternly, "that it is not mid-day, and I don't yet see clearly over my chess-board. You can go."

The handsome, boyish adjutant with the long curls heaved a deep sigh, and still holding his hand to his hat, galloped back to the slaughter.

Napoleon got up, and summoning Caulaincourt and Berthier, began conversing with them of matters not connected with the battle.

In the middle of the conversation, which began to interest Napoleon, Berthier's eye was caught by a general, who was galloping on a steaming horse to the redoubt, followed by his suite. It was Beliard. Dismounting from his horse, he walked rapidly up to the Emperor, and, in a loud voice, began boldly explaining the absolute necessity of reinforcements. He swore on his honour that the Russians would be annihilated if the Emperor would let them have another division.

Napoleon shrugged his shoulders, and continued walking up and down, without answering. Beliard began loudly and eagerly talking with the generals of the suite standing round him.

"You are very hasty, Beliard," said Napoleon, going back again to him. "It is easy to make a mistake in the heat of the fray. Go and look again and then come to me." Before Beliard was out of sight another messenger came galloping up from another part of the battlefield.

"Well, what is it now?" said Napoleon, in the tone of a man irritated by repeated interruptions.

"Sire, the prince . . ." began the adjutant.

"Asks for reinforcements?" said Napoleon, with a wrathful gesture. The adjutant bent his head affirmatively and was proceeding to give his message, but the Emperor turned and walked a couple of steps away, stopped, turned back, and beckoned to Berthier. "We must send the reserves," he said with a slight gesticulation. "Whom shall we send there? what do you think?" he asked Berthier, that "gosling I have made an eagle," as he afterwards called him.

"Claparède's division, sire," said Berthier, who knew all the divisions, regiments, and battalions by heart.

Napoleon nodded his head in assent.

The adjutant galloped off to Claparède's division. And a few moments later the Young Guards, stationed behind the redoubt, were moving out. Napoleon gazed in that direction in silence.

"No," he said suddenly to Berthier, "I can't send Claparède. Send Friant's division."

Though there was no advantage of any kind in sending Friant's division rather than Claparède's, and there was obvious inconvenience and delay now in turning back Claparède and despatching Friant, the order was carried out. Napoleon did not see that in relation to his troops he played the part of the doctor, whose action in hindering the course of nature with his nostrums he so truly gauged and condemned.

Friant's division vanished like the rest into the smoke of the battlefield. Adjutants still kept galloping up from every side, and all, as though in collusion, said the same thing. All asked for reinforcements; all told of the Russians standing firm and keeping up a hellish fire, under which the French troops were melting away.

Napoleon sat on a camp-stool, plunged in thought. M. de Beausset, the reputed lover of travel, had been fasting since early morning, and approaching the Emperor, he ventured respectfully to suggest breakfast to his majesty.

"I hope that I can already congratulate your majesty on a victory," he said.

Napoleon shook his head. Supposing the negative to refer to the victory only and not to the breakfast, M. de Beausset permitted himself with respectful playfulness to observe that there was no reason in the world that could be allowed to interfere with breakfast when breakfast was possible.

"Go to the . . ." Napoleon jerked out gloomily, and he turned his back on him. A saintly smile of sympathy, regret, and ecstasy beamed on M. de Beausset's face as he moved with his swinging step back to the other generals.

Napoleon was experiencing the bitter feeling of a lucky gambler, who, after recklessly staking his money and always winning, suddenly finds, precisely when he has carefully reckoned up all contingencies, that the more he considers his course, the more certain he is of losing.

The soldiers were the same, the generals the same, there had been the same preparations, the same disposition, the same proclamation, *"court et énergique."* He was himself the same,—he knew that; he knew that he was more experienced and skilful indeed now than he had been of old. The enemy even was the same as at Austerlitz and Friedland. But the irresistible wave of his hand seemed robbed of its might by magic.

All the old manœuvres that had invariably been crowned with success: the concentration of the battery on one point, and the advance of the reserves to break the line, and the cavalry attack of "men of iron," all these resources had been employed; and far from victory being secure, from all sides the same tidings kept pouring in of killed or wounded generals, of reinforcements needed, of the troops being in disorder, and the Russians impossible to move.

Hitherto, after two or three orders being given, two or three phrases delivered, marshals and adjutants had galloped up with radiant faces and congratulations, announcing the capture as trophies of whole corps of prisoners, of bundles of flags and eagles, of cannons and stores, and Murat had asked leave to let the cavalry go to capture the baggage. So it had been at Lodi, Marengo, Arcole, Jena, Austerlitz, Wagram, and so on, and so on. But now something strange was coming over his men.

In spite of the news of the capture of the flèches, Napoleon saw that things were not the same, not at all the same as at previous battles. He saw that what he was feeling, all the men round him, experienced in military matters, were feeling too. All their faces were gloomy; all avoided each others' eyes. It was only a Beausset who could fail to grasp the import of what was happening. Napoleon after his long experience of war knew very well all that was meant by an unsuccessful attack after eight hours' straining every possible effort. He knew that this was almost equivalent to a defeat, and that the merest chance might now, in the critical point the battle was in, be the overthrow of himself and his troops.

When he went over in his own mind all this strange Russian campaign, in which not a single victory had been gained, in which not a flag, nor a cannon, nor a corps had been taken in two months, when he looked at the concealed gloom in the faces round him, and heard reports that the Russians still held their ground—a terrible feeling, such as is experienced in a nightmare, came over him, and all the unlucky contingencies occurred to him that might be his ruin. The Russians might fall upon his left wing, might break through his centre; a stray ball might even kill himself. All that was possible. In his former battles he had only considered the possibilities of success, now an immense number of unlucky chances presented themselves, and he expected them all. Yes, it was like a nightmare, when a man dreams that an assailant is attacking him, and in his dream he lifts up his arm and deals a blow with a force at his assailant that he knows must crush him, and feels that his arm falls limp and powerless as a rag, and the horror of inevitable death comes upon him in his helplessness.

The news that the Russians were attacking the left flank of the French army aroused that horror in Napoleon. He sat in silence on a camp-stool under the redoubt, his elbows on his knees, and his head sunk in his hands. Berthier came up to him and suggested that they should inspect the lines to ascertain the position of affairs.

"What? What do you say?" said Napoleon. "Yes, tell them to bring my horse." He mounted a horse and rode to Semyonovskoye.

In the slowly parting smoke, over the whole plain through which Napoleon rode, men and horses, singly and in heaps, were lying in pools of blood. Such a fearful spectacle, so great a mass of killed in so small a space, had never been seen by Napoleon nor any of his generals. The roar of the cannon that had not ceased for ten hours, exhausted the ear and gave a peculiar character to the spectacle (like music accompanying living pictures). Napoleon rode up to the height of Semyonovskoye, and through the smoke he saw ranks of soldiers in uniforms of unfamiliar hues. They were the Russians.

The Russians stood in serried ranks behind Semyonovskoye and the redoubt, and their guns kept up an incessant roar and smoke all along their lines. It was not a battle. It was a prolonged massacre, which could be of no avail either to French or Russians. Napoleon pulled up his horse, and sank again into the brooding reverie from which Berthier had roused him. He could not stay that thing that was being done before him and about him, and that was regarded as being led by him and as depending on him, that thing for the first time, after ill success, struck him as superfluous and horrible. One of the generals, riding up to Napoleon, ventured to suggest to him that the Old Guard should advance into action. Ney and Berthier, standing close by, exchanged glances and smiled contemptuously at the wild suggestion of this general.

Napoleon sat mute with downcast head.

"Eight hundred leagues from France, I am not going to let my Guard be destroyed," he said, and turning his horse, he rode back to Shevardino.

Kutuzov, with his grey head hanging, and his heavy, corpulent frame sunk into a heap, was sitting on a bench covered with a rug, in the same place in which Pierre had seen him in the morning. He issued no orders, and simply gave or withheld his assent to what was proposed to him.

"Yes, yes, do so," he would say in reply to various suggestions. "Yes, yes, go across, my dear boy, and see," he would cry first to one and then to another of the adjutants near him; or, "No, better not; we'd better wait a bit," he would say. He listened to the reports brought him, and gave orders, when they were asked for. But as he heard the reports, he seemed to take little interest in the import of the words spoken; something else in the expression of the face, in the tone of the voice of the speaker, seemed to interest him more. From long years of military experience he had learned, and with the wisdom of old age he had recognised, that one man cannot guide hundreds of thousands of men struggling with death; that the fate of battles is not decided by the orders given by the commander-in-chief, nor the place in which the troops are stationed, nor the number of cannons, nor of killed, but by that intangible force called the spirit of the army, and he followed that force and led it as far as it lay in his power.

The general expression of Kutuzov's face was concentrated, quiet attention and intensity, with difficulty overcoming his weak and aged body.

At eleven o'clock they brought him the news that the French had been driven back again from the flèches they had captured, but that Bagration was wounded. Kutuzov groaned, and shook his head.

"Ride over to Prince Pyotr Ivanovitch and find out exactly about it," he said to one of the adjutants, and then he turned to the Prince of Würtemberg, who was standing behind him:

"Will your highness be pleased to take command of the first army?"

Soon after the prince's departure—so soon that he could not yet have reached Semyonovskoye—his adjutant came back with a message from him asking Kutuzov for more troops.

Kutuzov frowned, and sent Dohturov orders to take the command of the first army, and begged the prince to come back, saying that he found he could not get on without him at such an important moment. When news was brought that Murat had been taken prisoner, and the members of the staff congratulated Kutuzov, he smiled.

"Wait a little, gentlemen," he said. "The battle is won, and Murat's being taken prisoner is nothing very extraordinary. But we had better defer our rejoicings." Still he sent an adjutant to take the news to the troops.

When Shtcherbinin galloped up from the left flank with the report of the capture of the flèche, and Semyonovskoye by the French, Kutuzov, guessing from the sounds of the battlefield and Shtcherbinin's face, that the news was bad, got up as though to stretch his legs, and taking Shtcherbinin by the arm drew him aside.

"You go, my dear boy," he said to Yermolov, "and see whether something can't be done."

Kutuzov was in Gorky, the centre of the Russian position. The attack on our left flank had been several times repulsed. In the centre the French did not advance beyond Borodino. Uvarov's cavalry had sent the French flying from the left flank.

At three o'clock the attacks of the French ceased. On the faces of all who came from the battlefield, as well as of those standing round him, Kutuzov read an expression of effort, strained to the utmost tension. He was himself satisfied with the success of the day beyond his expectations. But the old man's physical force was failing him. Several times his head sank, as though he were falling, and he dropped asleep. Dinner was brought him.

The adjutant-general, Woltzogen, the man whom Prince Andrey had overheard saying that the war ought to be *"im Raum verlegen,"* and whom Bagration so particularly detested, rode up to Kutuzov while he was at dinner. Woltzogen had come from Barclay to report on the progress of the fight on the left flank. The sagacious Barclay de Tolly, seeing crowds of wounded men running back, and the ranks in disorder, and weighing all the circumstances of the case, made up his mind that the battle was lost, and sent his favourite adjutant to the commander-in-chief to tell him so.

Kutuzov was with difficulty chewing roast chicken, and his eyes were screwed up with a more cheerful expression as he glanced at Woltzogen.

With a half-contemptuous smile Woltzogen walked carelessly up to Kutuzov, scarcely touching the peak of his cap.

He behaved to his highness with a certain affected negligence, which aimed at showing that he, as a highly trained military man, left it to the Russians to make a prodigy of this useless old person, and was himself well aware what kind of a man he had to deal with. "The 'old gentleman' "— this was how Kutuzov was always spoken of in Woltzogen's German circle —"is making himself quite comfortable," he thought; and glancing severely at the dishes before Kutuzov, he began reporting to the old gentleman Barclay's message and his own impressions and views. "Every point of our position is in the enemy's hands, and they cannot be driven back, because there are not the troops to do it; the men run away and there's no possibility of stopping them," he submitted.

Kutuzov, stopping short in his munching, stared at Woltzogen in amazement, as though not understanding what was said to him. Woltzogen, noticing the old gentleman's excitement, said with a smile:

"I did not consider I had a right to conceal from your highness what I saw. . . . The troops are completely routed. . . ."

"You saw? You saw? . . ." cried Kutuzov, getting up quickly, and stepping up to Woltzogen. "How . . . how dare you! . . ." making a menacing gesture with his trembling hands, he cried, with a catch in his breath: "How dare you, sir, tell *me* that? You know nothing about it. Tell General Barclay from me that his information is incorrect, and that I, the commander-in-chief, know more of the course of the battle than he does."

Woltzogen would have made some protest, but Kutuzov interrupted him.

"The enemy has been repulsed on the left and defeated on the right flank. If you have seen amiss, sir, do not permit yourself to speak of what you do not understand. Kindly return to General Barclay and inform him of my unhesitating intention to attack the French tomorrow," said Kutuzov sternly.

All were silent, and nothing was to be heard but the heavy breathing of the gasping, old general. "Repulsed at all points, for which I thank God and our brave men. The enemy is defeated, and to-morrow we will drive him out of the holy land of Russia!" said Kutuzov, crossing himself; and all at once he gave a sob from the rising tears.

Woltzogen, shrugging his shoulders, and puckering his lips, walked away in silence, marvelling *"über diese Eingenommenheit des alten Herrn."*

"Ah, here he is, my hero!" said Kutuzov, as a stoutish, handsome, black-haired general came up the hillside. It was Raevsky, who had spent the whole day at the most important part of the battlefield.

Raevsky reported that the men were standing their ground firmly, and that the French were not venturing a further attack.

When he had heard him out, Kutuzov said in French: "You do not think, like some others, that we are obliged to retreat?"

"On the contrary, your highness, in indecisive actions it is always the most obstinate who remains victorious," answer Raevsky; "and my opinion . . ."

"Kaisarov," Kutuzov called to his adjutant, "sit down and write the order for to-morrow. And you," he turned to another, "ride along the line and announce that to-morrow we attack."

While he was talking to Raevsky and dictating the order, Woltzogen came back from Barclay and announced that General Barclay de Tolly would be glad to have a written confirmation of the order given by the field-marshal.

Kutuzov, without looking at Woltzogen, ordered an adjutant to make out this written order, which the former commander-in-chief very prudently wished to have to screen himself from all responsibility. And through the undefinable, mysterious link that maintains through a whole army the same temper, called the spirit of the army, and constituting the chief sinew of war, Kutuzov's words, his order for the battle next day, were transmitted instantaneously from one end of the army to the other.

The words and the phrases of the order were by no means the same when they reached the furthest links in the chain. There was, indeed, not a word in the stories men were repeating to one another from one end of the army to the other, that resembled what Kutuzov had actually said; but the drift of his words spread everywhere, because what Kutuzov had said was not the result of shrewd considerations, but the outflow of a feeling that lay deep in the heart of the commander-in-chief, and deep in the heart of every Russian.

And learning that to-morrow we were to attack the enemy, hearing from the higher spheres of the army the confirmation of what they wanted to believe, the worn-out, wavering men took comfort and courage again.

The fearful spectacle of the battlefield, heaped with dead and wounded, in conjunction with the heaviness of his head, the news that some twenty generals he knew well were among the killed or wounded, and the sense of the impotence of his once mighty army, made an unexpected impression on Napoleon, who was usually fond of looking over the dead and wounded, proving thereby, as he imagined, his dauntless spirit. On that day, the awful spectacle of the battlefield overcame this dauntless spirit, which he looked upon as a merit and a proof of greatness. He hastened away from the field of battle and returned to Shevardino. With a yellow, puffy, heavy face, dim eyes, a red nose, and a husky voice, he sat on a camp-stool, looking down and involuntarily listening to the sounds of the firing. With sickly uneasiness he awaited the end of this action, in which he considered himself the prime mover, though he could not have stopped it. The personal, human sentiment for one brief moment gained the ascendant over the artificial phantasm of life, that he had served so long. He imagined in his own case the agonies and death he had seen on the battlefield. The heaviness of his head and chest reminded him of the possibility for him too of agony and death. At that minute he felt no longing for Moscow, for victory or for glory. (What need had he for more glory?) The one thing he desired now was repose, tranquillity, and freedom. But when he was on the height above Semyonovskoye, the officer in command of the artillery proposed to him to bring several batteries up on to that height to increase the fire on the Russian troops before Knyazkovo. Napoleon assented, and gave orders that word should be brought him of the effect produced by this battery.

An adjutant came to say that by the Emperor's orders two hundred guns had been directed upon the Russians, but that they were still holding their ground.

"Our fire is mowing them down in whole rows, but they stand firm," said the adjutant.

"They want more of it!" said Napoleon in his husky voice.

"Sire?" repeated the adjutant, who had not caught the words.

"They want even more!" Napoleon croaked hoarsely, frowning. "Well, let them have it then."

Already, without orders from him, what he did not really want was being done, and he gave the order to do it simply because he thought the order was expected of him. And he passed back again into his old artificial world, peopled by the phantoms of some unreal greatness, and again (as a horse running in a rolling wheel may imagine it is acting on its own account) he fell back into submissively performing the cruel, gloomy, irksome, and inhuman part destined for him.

Some tens of thousands of men lay sacrificed in various postures and uniforms on the fields and meadows belonging to the Davidov family and the Crown serfs, on those fields and meadows where for hundreds of years the peasants of Borodino, Gorky, Shevardino, and Semyonovskoye had harvested their crops and grazed their cattle. At the ambulance stations the grass and earth were soaked with blood for two acres round. Crowds of men, wounded and unwounded, of various arms, with panic-stricken faces, dragged themselves, on one side back to Mozhaisk, on the other to Valuev. Other crowds, exhausted and hungry, were led forward by their officers. Others still held their ground and went on firing.

Over all the plain, at first so bright and gay with its glittering bayonets and puffs of smoke in the morning sunshine, there hung now a dark cloud of damp mist and smoke, and a strange, sour smell of saltpetre and blood. Storm clouds had gathered, and a drizzling rain began to fall on the dead, on the wounded, on the panic-stricken, and exhausted, and hesitating soldiers. It seemed to say: "Enough, enough; cease. . . . Consider. What are you doing?"

To the men on both sides, alike exhausted from want of food and rest, the doubt began to come whether they should still persist in slaughtering one another; and in every face could be seen hesitation, and in every heart alike there rose the question: "For what, for whom am I to slay and be slain? Slay whom you will, do what you will, but I have had enough!" This thought took shape towards evening in every heart alike. Any minute all those men might be horror-stricken at what they were doing, might throw up everything and run anywhere.

But though towards the end of the battle the men felt all the horror of their actions, though they would have been glad to cease, some unfathomable, mysterious force still led them on, and the artillerymen—the third of them left—soaked with sweat, grimed with powder and blood, and panting with weariness, still brought the charges, loaded, aimed, and lighted the match; and the cannon balls flew as swiftly and cruelly from each side and crushed human flesh, and kept up the fearful work, which was done not at the will of men, but at the will of Him who sways men and worlds.

Any one looking at the disorder in the rear of the Russian army would have said that the French had but to make one slight effort more and the Russian army would have been annihilated; and any one seeing the rear of the French army would have said that the Russians need but make a slight effort more and the French would be overthrown. But neither French nor Russians made that effort, and the flame of the battle burnt slowly out.

Trafalgar

BY

ROBERT SOUTHEY

THE station which Nelson had chosen was some fifty or sixty miles to the west of Cadiz, near Cape St. Mary. At this distance he hoped to decoy the enemy out, while he guarded against the danger of being caught with a westerly wind near Cadiz, and driven within the Straits. The blockade of the port was rigorously enforced, in hopes that the combined fleets might be forced to sea by want. The Danish vessels therefore, which were carrying provisions from the French ports in the bay, under the name of Danish property, to all the little ports from Ayamonte to Algeziras, from whence they were conveyed in coasting boats to Cadiz, were seized. Without this proper exertion of power the blockade would have been rendered nugatory by the advantage thus taken of the neutral flag. The supplies from France were thus effectually cut off. There was now every indication that the enemy would speedily venture out; officers and men were in the highest spirits at the prospect of giving them a decisive blow—such, indeed, as would put an end to all further contests upon the seas.

On the 9th Nelson sent Collingwood what he called in his diary the "Nelson touch." "I send you," said he, "my plan of attack, as far as a man dare venture to guess at the very uncertain position the enemy may be found in; but it is to place you perfectly at ease respecting my intentions, and to give full scope to your judgment for carrying them into effect. We can, my dear Coll, have no little jealousies. We have only one great object in view, that of annihilating our enemies, and getting a glorious peace for our country. No man has more confidence in another than I have in you, and no man will render your services more justice than your very old friend, Nelson and Bronte."

The order of sailing was to be the order of battle—the fleet in two lines, with an advanced squadron of eight of the fastest sailing two-deckers. The second in command, having the entire direction of his line, was to break through the enemy, about the twelfth ship from their rear; he would lead through the centre, and the advanced squadron was to cut off three or four ahead of the centre. This plan was to be adapted to the strength of the enemy, so that they should always be one-fourth superior to those whom they cut off. Nelson said that "his admirals and captains, knowing his precise object to be that of a close and decisive action, would supply any deficiency of signals and act accordingly. In case signals cannot be seen

From: *The Life of Nelson.*

or clearly understood, no captain can do wrong if he places his ship along-side that of an enemy."

About half-past nine in the morning of the 19th the *Mars*, being the nearest to the fleet of the ships which formed the line of communication with the frigates inshore, repeated the signal that the enemy were coming out of port. The wind was at this time very light, with partial breezes, mostly from the S. S. W. Nelson ordered the signal to be made for a chase in the south-east quarter. About two the repeating ships announced that the enemy were at sea. All night the British fleet continued under all sail, steering to the south-east. At daybreak they were in the entrance of the Straits, but the enemy were not in sight. About seven, one of the frigates made signal that the enemy was bearing north. Upon this the *Victory* hove to, and shortly afterwards Nelson made sail again to the northward. In the afternoon the wind blew fresh from the south-west, and the English began to fear that the foe might be forced to return to port.

A little before sunset, however, Blackwood, in the *Euryalus*, telegraphed that they appeared determined to go to the westward. "And that," said the Admiral in his diary, "they shall not do, if it is in the power of Nelson and Bronte to prevent them." Nelson had signified to Blackwood that he depended upon him to keep sight of the enemy. They were observed so well that all their motions were made known to him, and as they wore twice, he inferred that they were aiming to keep the port of Cadiz open, and would retreat there as soon as they saw the British fleet; for this reason he was very careful not to approach near enough to be seen by them during the night. At daybreak the combined fleets were distinctly seen from the *Victory's* deck, formed in a close line of battle ahead, on the starboard tack, about twelve miles to leeward, and standing to the south. Our fleet consisted of twenty-seven sail of the line and four frigates; theirs of thirty-three and seven large frigates. Their superiority was greater in size and weight of metal than in numbers. They had four thousand troops on board, and the best riflemen that could be procured, many of them Tyrolese, were dispersed through the ships.

Soon after daylight Nelson came upon deck. The 21st of October was a festival in his family, because on that day his uncle, Captain Suckling, in the *Dreadnought*, with two other line-of-battle ships, had beaten off a French squadron of four sail of the line and three frigates. Nelson, with that sort of superstition from which few persons are entirely exempt, had more than once expressed his persuasion that this was to be the day of his battle also, and he was well pleased at seeing his prediction about to be verified. The wind was now from the west—light breezes, with a long heavy swell. Signal was made to bear down upon the enemy in two lines, and the fleet set all sail. Collingwood, in the *Royal Sovereign*, led the lee line of thirteen ships; the *Victory* led the weather line of fourteen. Having seen that all was as it should be, Nelson retired to his cabin, and wrote the following prayer—

"May the great God whom I worship, grant to my country, and for the benefit of Europe in general, a great and glorious victory, and may no misconduct in any one tarnish it, and may humanity after victory be the predominant feature in the British fleet! For myself individually, I commit my life to Him that made me, and may His blessing alight on my endeavours for serving my country faithfully! To Him I resign myself, and the just cause which is entrusted to me to defend. Amen, Amen, Amen."

Blackwood went on board the *Victory* about six. He found him in good spirits, but very calm; not in that exhilaration which he felt upon entering into battle at Aboukir and Copenhagen; he knew that his own life would be particularly aimed at, and seems to have looked for death with almost as sure an expectation as for victory. His whole attention was fixed upon the enemy. They tacked to the northward, and formed their line on the larboard tack; thus bringing the shoals of Trafalgar and St. Pedro under the lee of the British, and keeping the port of Cadiz open for themselves. This was judiciously done; and Nelson, aware of all the advantages which he gave them, made signal to prepare to anchor.

Villeneuve was a skilful seaman, worthy of serving a better master and a better cause. His plan of defence was as well conceived and as original as the plan of attack. He formed the fleet in a double line, every alternate ship being about a cable's length to windward of her second ahead and astern. Nelson, certain of a triumphant issue to the day, asked Blackwood what he should consider as a victory. That officer answered that, considering the handsome way in which battle was offered by the enemy, their apparent determination for a fair trial of strength, and the situation of the land, he thought it would be a glorious result if fourteen were captured. He replied: "I shall not be satisfied with less than twenty." Soon afterwards he asked him if he did not think there was a signal wanting. Captain Blackwood made answer that he thought the whole fleet seemed very clearly to understand what they were about. These words were scarcely spoken before that signal was made which will be remembered as long as the language or even the memory of England shall endure—"ENGLAND EXPECTS EVERY MAN WILL DO HIS DUTY!" It was received throughout the fleet with a shout of answering acclamation, made sublime by the spirit which it breathed and the feeling which it expressed. "Now," said Lord Nelson, "I can do no more. We must trust to the great disposer of all events and the justice of our cause. I thank God for this great opportunity of doing my duty."

He wore that day, as usual, his admiral's frock-coat, bearing on the left breast four stars of the different orders with which he was invested. Ornaments which rendered him so conspicuous a mark for the enemy were beheld with ominous apprehension by his officers. It was known that there were riflemen on board the French ships, and it could not be doubted but that his life would be particularly aimed at. They communicated their fears to each other, and the surgeon, Mr. Beatty, spoke to the chaplain, Dr. Scott, and to Mr. Scott, the public secretary, desiring that some person would entreat him to change his dress or cover the stars; but they knew that such a request would highly displease him. "In honour I gained them," he had said when such a thing had been hinted to him formerly, "and in honour I will die with them." Mr. Beatty, however, would not have been deterred by any fear of exciting his displeasure from speaking to him himself upon a subject in which the weal of England, as well as the life of Nelson, was concerned; but he was ordered from the deck before he could find an opportunity. This was a point upon which Nelson's officers knew that it was hopeless to remonstrate or reason with him; but both Blackwood and his own captain, Hardy, represented to him how advantageous to the fleet it would be for him to keep out of action as long as possible, and he consented at last to let the *Leviathan* and the *Temeraire,* which were sailing abreast of the *Victory* be ordered to pass ahead.

Yet even here the last infirmity of this noble mind was indulged, for these ships could not pass ahead if the *Victory* continued to carry all her sail; and so far was Nelson from shortening sail, that it was evident he took pleasure in pressing on, and rendering it impossible for them to obey his own orders. A long swell was setting into the Bay of Cadiz. Our ships, crowding all sail, moved majestically before it, with light winds from the south-west. The sun shone on the sails of the enemy, but their well-formed line, with their numerous three-deckers, made an appearance which any other assailants would have thought formidable, but the British sailors only admired the beauty and the splendour of the spectacle, and in full confidence of winning what they saw, remarked to each other what a fine sight yonder ships would make at Spithead!

The French admiral, from the *Bucentaure,* beheld the new manner in which his enemy was advancing—Nelson and Collingwood, each leading his line; and pointing them out to his officers, he is said to have exclaimed that such conduct could not fail to be successful. Yet Villeneuve had made his own dispositions with the utmost skill, and the fleets under his command waited for the attack with perfect coolness. Ten minutes before twelve they opened their fire. Eight or nine of the ships immediately ahead of the *Victory,* and across her bows, fired single guns at her to ascertain whether she was yet within their range. As soon as Nelson perceived that their shot passed over him, he desired Blackwood and Captain Prowse, of the *Sirius,* to repair to their respective frigates, and on their way to tell all the captains of the line-of-battle ships that he depended on their exertions, and that, if by the prescribed mode of attack they found it impracticable to get into action immediately, they might adopt whatever they thought best, provided it led them quickly and closely alongside an enemy. As they were standing on the poop, Blackwood took him by the hand, saying he hoped soon to return and find him in possession of twenty prizes. He replied, "God bless you, Blackwood; I shall never see you again."

Nelson's column was steered about two points more to the north than Collingwood's, in order to cut off the enemy's escape into Cadiz. The lee line, therefore, was first engaged. "See," cried Nelson, pointing to the *Royal Sovereign,* as she steered right for the centre of the enemy's line, cut

through it astern of the *Santa Anna,* three-decker, and engaged her at the
muzzle of her guns on the starboard side; "see how that noble fellow
Collingwood carries his ship into action!" Collingwood, delighted at being
first in the heat of the fire, and knowing the feelings of his commander and
old friend, turned to his captain and exclaimed: "Rotherham, what would
Nelson give to be here!" Both these brave officers, perhaps, at this moment
thought of Nelson with gratitude for a circumstance which had occurred
on the preceding day. Admiral Collingwood, with some of the captains,
having gone on board the *Victory* to receive instructions, Nelson inquired
of him where his captain was, and was told in reply that they were not
upon good terms with each other. "Terms!" said Nelson; "good terms with
each other!" Immediately he sent a boat for Captain Rotherham, led him,
so soon as he arrived, to Collingwood, and saying, "Look, yonder are the
enemy!" bade them shake hands like Englishmen.

The enemy continued to fire a gun at a time at the *Victory* till they saw
that a shot had passed through her main-topgallant sail; then they opened
their broadsides, aiming chiefly at her rigging, in the hope of disabling her
before she could close with them. Nelson as usual had hoisted several flags,
lest one should be shot away. The enemy showed no colours till late in the
action, when they began to feel the necessity of having them to strike. For
this reason the *Santissima Trinidad,* Nelson's old acquaintance, as he used
to call her, was distinguishable only by her four decks, and to the bow of
this opponent he ordered the *Victory* to be steered. Meantime an incessant
raking fire was kept up upon the *Victory.* The Admiral's secretary was one
of the first who fell; he was killed by a cannon shot while conversing with
Hardy. Captain Adair, of the marines, with the help of a sailor, endeavoured to remove the body from Nelson's sight, who had a great regard
for Mr. Scott, but he anxiously asked, "Is that poor Scott that's gone?"
and being informed that it was indeed so, exclaimed, "Poor fellow!"

Presently a double-headed shot struck a party of marines who were drawn
up on the poop, and killed eight of them, upon which Nelson immediately
desired Captain Adair to disperse his men round the ship, that they might
not suffer so much from being together. A few minutes afterwards a shot
struck the fore-brace bits on the quarter-deck, and passed between Nelson
and Hardy, a splinter from the bit tearing off Hardy's buckle and bruising
his foot. Both stopped, and looked anxiously at each other: each supposed
the other to be wounded. Nelson then smiled, and said: "This is too warm
work, Hardy, to last long."

The *Victory* had not yet returned a single gun; fifty of her men had by
this time been killed or wounded, and her maintopmast, with all her
studding sails and their booms, shot away. Nelson declared that in all his
battles he had seen nothing which surpassed the cool courage of his crew
on this occasion. At four minutes after twelve she opened her fire from both
sides of her deck. It was not possible to break the enemy's lines without
running on board one of their ships; Hardy informed him of this, and
asked him which he would prefer. Nelson replied: "Take your choice,

Hardy; it does not signify much." The master was ordered to put the helm to port, and the *Victory* ran on board the *Redoubtable* just as her tiller-ropes were shot away. The French ship received her with a broadside, then instantly let down her lower-deck ports for fear of being boarded through them, and never afterwards fired a great gun during the action. Her tops, like those of all the enemy's ships, were filled with riflemen. Nelson never placed musketry in his tops; he had a strong dislike to the practice, not merely because it endangers setting fire to the sails, but also because it is a murderous sort of warfare, by which individuals may suffer and a commander now and then be picked off, but which never can decide the fate of a general engagement.

Captain Harvey, in the *Temeraire,* fell on board the *Redoubtable* on the side; another enemy was in like manner on board the *Temeraire;* so that these four ships formed as compact a tier as if they had been moored together, their heads all lying the same way. The lieutenants of the *Victory* seeing this, depressed their guns of the middle and lower decks, and fired with a diminished charge, lest the shot should pass through and injure the *Temeraire;* and because there was danger that the *Redoubtable* might take fire from the lower deck guns, the muzzles of which touched her side when they were run out, the fireman of each gun stood ready with a bucket of water, which, as soon as the gun was discharged, he dashed into the hole made by the shot. An incessant fire was kept up from the *Victory* from both sides, her larboard guns playing upon the *Bucentaure* and the huge *Santissima Trinidad.*

It had been part of Nelson's prayer that the British fleet should be distinguished by humanity in the victory he expected. Setting an example himself, he twice gave orders to cease firing upon the *Redoubtable,* supposing that she had struck, because her great guns were silent; for, as she carried no flag, there was no means of instantly ascertaining the fact. From this ship, which he had thus twice spared, he received his death. A ball fired from her mizzen-top, which in the then situation of the two vessels was not more than fifteen yards from that part of the deck where he was standing, struck the epaulette on his left shoulder, about a quarter after one, just in the heat of action. He fell upon his face, on the spot which was covered with his poor secretary's blood. Hardy, who was a few steps from him, turning round, saw three men raising him up. "They have done for me at last, Hardy!" said he. "I hope not!" cried Hardy. "Yes," he replied, "my backbone is shot through!"

Yet even now, not for a moment losing his presence of mind, he observed as they were carrying him down the ladder, that the tiller-ropes, which had been shot away, were not yet replaced, and ordered that new ones should be rove immediately. Then, that he might not be seen by the crew, he took out his handkerchief and covered his face and his stars. Had he but concealed these badges of honour from the enemy, England perhaps would not have had cause to receive with sorrow the news of the battle of Trafalgar. The cockpit was crowded with wounded and dying men, over whose bodies he was with some difficulty conveyed, and laid upon a pallet in the midshipmen's berth. It was soon perceived, upon examination, that the wound was mortal. This, however, was concealed from all except Captain Hardy, the chaplain, and the medical attendants. He himself being certain, from the sensation in his back and the gush of blood he felt momently within his breast, that no human care could avail him, insisted that the surgeon should leave him, and attend to those to whom he might be useful, "for," said he, "you can do nothing for me."

All that could be done was to fan him with paper, and frequently give him lemonade to alleviate his intense thirst. He was in great pain, and expressed much anxiety for the event of the action, which now began to declare itself. As often as a ship struck, the crew of the *Victory* hurrahed, and at every hurrah a visible expression of joy gleamed in the eyes and marked the countenance of the dying hero. But he became impatient to see Captain Hardy, and as that officer, though often sent for, could not leave the deck, Nelson feared that some fatal cause prevented him, and repeatedly cried, "Will no one bring Hardy to me? He must be killed! He is surely dead!"

An hour and ten minutes elapsed from the time when Nelson received his wound before Hardy could come to him. They shook hands in silence; Hardy in vain struggling to express the feelings of that most painful and yet sublimest moment. "Well, Hardy," said Nelson, "how goes the day with us?"—"Very well," replied Hardy; "ten ships have struck, but five of the van have tacked, and show an intention to bear down upon the *Victory*. I have called two or three of our fresh ships round, and have no doubt of giving them a drubbing."—"I hope," said Nelson, "none of our ships have struck." Hardy answered, "There was no fear of that." Then, and not till then, Nelson spoke of himself. "I am a dead man, Hardy," said he; "I am going fast; it will be all over with me soon. Come nearer to me." Hardy observed that he hoped Mr Beatty could yet hold out some prospect of life. "Oh no!" he replied, "it is impossible; my back is shot through. Beatty will tell you so." Captain Hardy then once more shook hands with him, and with a heart almost bursting hastened upon deck.

By this time, all feeling below the breast was gone; and Nelson, having made the surgeon ascertain this, said to him: "You know I am gone. I know it. I feel something rising in my breast"—putting his hand on his left side—"which tells me so." And upon Beatty's inquiring whether his pain was very great, he replied, "So great that he wished he was dead." "Yet," said he in a lower voice, "one would like to live a little longer too!" Captain Hardy, some fifty minutes after he had left the cockpit, returned, and again taking the hand of his dying friend and commander, congratulated him on having gained a complete victory. How many of the enemy were taken he did not know, as it was impossible to perceive them distinctly; but fourteen or fifteen at least. "That's well!" cried Nelson; "but I bargained for twenty." And then in a stronger voice he said, "Anchor, Hardy, anchor." Hardy upon this hinted that Admiral Collingwood would take upon himself the direction of affairs. "Not while I live, Hardy," said the dying Nelson, ineffectually endeavouring to raise himself from the bed; "Do you anchor."

His previous order for preparing to anchor had shown how clearly he foresaw the necessity of this. Presently calling Hardy back, he said to him in a low voice: "Don't throw me overboard"; and he desired that he might be buried by his parents, unless it should please the king to order otherwise. Then turning to Hardy: "Kiss me, Hardy," said he. Hardy knelt down and kissed his cheek, and Nelson said: "Now I am satisfied. Thank God, I have done my duty!" Hardy stood over him in silence for a moment or two, then knelt again and kissed his forehead. "Who is that?" said Nelson; and being informed, he replied: "God bless you, Hardy." And Hardy then left him for ever.

Nelson now desired to be turned upon his right side, and said: "I wish I had not left the deck, for I shall soon be gone." Death was indeed rapidly approaching. He said to the chaplain: "Doctor, I have *not* been a *great* sinner." His articulation now became difficult, but he was distinctly heard to say: "Thank God, I have done my duty!" These words he repeatedly pronounced. And they were the last words that he uttered. He expired at thirty minutes after four, three hours and a quarter after he had received his wound!

The Battle of Atlanta

LLOYD LEWIS

KNOWING that the new Confederate leader, Hood, would be aching for a chance to redeem his reputation as an attacker—the bold attacker who would show Joe Johnston the error of defensive warfare—in late July Sherman proposed to tempt his adversary. "Act with confidence . . . act offensively to show him that you dare him to the encounter," he wrote Logan as on the twenty-seventh the Army of the Tennessee swung to the right, and with its wagon wheels muffled in hay marched around the city aiming at a new position southwest of Atlanta. With Schofield stretching his Army of the Ohio on the north and northeast, Thomas on the west, this would give Hood but one avenue for bringing in supplies—the railroad to the south. On the twenty-eighth, as the Fifteenth Corps swept past the new trenches that Hood had erected in the neighborhood of Ezra Church and the Lickskillet Road, the Confederates accepted the dare. Out they came, yelling and shooting. Two miles away, Sherman heard the thunder. "Logan is feeling them, and I guess he has found them," he said. Presently one of Howard's staff officers galloped up to say that Logan was fighting off a heavy attack. "Good—that's fine—just what I wanted, just what I wanted," said Sherman, while Major Connolly stood close by, staring at him in admiration. "Tell Howard to invite them to attack, it will save us trouble, save us trouble, they'll only beat their own brains out, beat their own brains out." Connolly heard him "talk on gayly; he understood his own strategy was working."

"Hold 'em! Hold 'em!" Logan was howling, and his Fifteenth Corps, crouching behind a rail fence, beat off five attacks, and were holding their ground at nightfall. They had repulsed the Johnnies twelve times in a week. When Sherman arrived to compliment them, they showed him the field carpeted with dead and wounded enemies and lied proudly about it all, saying, "It was easy." The Fifty-fifth Illinois counted graycoats "in windrows, sometimes two or three deep." Howard, who had tactfully remained in the rear so that Logan might have all possible honor, said, "I never saw fighting like this before."

A prisoner confessed to men of the Fifty-fifth Illinois, "Our generals told us that the Fifteenth Corps had bragged long enough that they had never been whipped, and today we'd drive you to the river or hell before supper." From a Union rifle pit at the day's end a voice called, "Well, Johnny,

From: *Sherman: Fighting Prophet:* Copyright 1932 by Harcourt, Brace & Co.

how many of you are left?" "Oh, about enough for another killing," came the answer.

Desertions were increasing in the Confederate Army. Jefferson Davis advised Hood to avoid frontal attacks. Here and there privates shouted, "Give us Johnston!" That master of his art had been justified. He had known better than to expose his men so openly to the sharpshooters of the Northwest.

Sherman's men said that Uncle Billy had atoned for his Kenesaw mistake. In three pitched battles before Atlanta he had let the enemy make the attacks. Sherman wrote Halleck:

We have good corporals and sergeants and some good lieutenants and captains, and those are far more important than good generals. They all seem to have implicit confidence in me. They think I know where every road and by-path is in Georgia, and one soldier swore that I was born on Kenesaw Mountain.

It was not purely chance that gave Sherman the nickname of Uncle Billy. The fatherly Thomas was well called Pap, and Brigadier General Alpheus S. Williams of the Twentieth Corps was paternal enough at fifty-four to be universally known as Pop. Marse Robert and Marse Joe were fitting nicknames for Lee and Johnston among Southern privates, who were, on the whole, more respectful of their generals. Sherman's attitude of distant friendliness and unsentimentality made him seem like an uncle who watches over nephews zealously yet without paternalism. Had he been more dramatic he might have won such names as Hooker and Logan did—Fighting Joe and Black Jack. But Sherman was too practical and too scornful of heroics to become an idol.

The one Western general to become an idol was Logan. The men cheered and leaned forward to touch his stallion when he galloped past. He loved it; his hat seemed always to be off, his walrus mustachios streaming in the wind.

It was the correspondent of the *Washington National Tribune* who after the war gave the nation the romantic tale of Logan and the "Rebel" baby. As he advanced after the Battle of Ezra Church, surgeons told Logan of a neighboring accouchement. They wanted Logan to christen the baby. Excited at the thought of life entering so confidently into a world of death, Logan agreed to act as godfather. He found a cabin with its roof half shot away, and an interior looted by both armies. On the bed lay a white-faced girl whose husband, she said, had died in Lee's army. Beside her sat her mother, a crone who was smoking tobacco given her by the surgeons. Among the covers was a microscopic scarlet face—a girl baby.

"This looks damn rough," said Logan, and sent officers to bring poles and fix the roof, set them to sweeping out the place and building a fire. He asked his staff to empty their haversacks in a clean spot in a corner. When the last colonel was down off the roof, the old crone brought a gourdful of spring water, Logan took the infant in his arms, and the chaplain prepared to officiate. Shells crashed in the woods not far away. "What are you goin' to give her for a name?" quavered Grandma. "I want it to be right pert, now." The chaplain began to speak holy words. He came to the naming of the baby. "Shell-Anna," said Logan, and as he departed, he gave the grandmother a gold coin for the child, adding, "Put it in a safe place or some damned bummer will steal it in spite of everything."

War correspondents had no such hero tales of Sherman. They still disliked him, although he was now too successful to be hounded. One of them described him:

. . . no symptoms of heavy cares—his nose high, thin and planted with a curve as vehement as the curl of a Malay cutlass—tall, slender, his quick movements denoted good muscle added to absolute leanness, not thinness.

General Rusling thought Sherman

too busy to eat much. He ate hardtack, sweet potatoes, bacon, black coffee off a rough table, sitting on a cracker box, wearing a gray flannel shirt, a faded old blue blouse and trousers that he had worn since long before Chattanooga. He talked and smoked cigars incessantly, giving orders, dictating telegrams, bright and chipper.

He had seen to it that men fought off scurvy by eating turnip tops, dandelion greens, sassafras root, and pine-leaf tea. A country boy himself, he had learned the pioneer trick of subsisting in the wilderness. He noted that men sickened of the patent compounds with which the War Department sought to vary rations—desiccated vegetables, concentrated milk, meat biscuit, and curious extracts. It amused him to hear the soldiers jeer at "desecrated vegetables and consecrated milk." Often a strip of raw pork sprinkled with brown sugar and eaten on hardtack was the fare in isolated rifle pits. Around campfires men toasted hardtack, or pounded it into flour and mixed it with boiled rice to make griddle cakes to be eaten with molasses filched from plantations. Cracker crumbs fried in pork fat and seasoned were called hell-fire stew.

But the favorite food to be found in the commissariat was baked beans— beans prepared as by a ritual, thrown into an iron pot, covered with fat pork, sunk in a pit of coals, and kept baking all night. Sentries threw chunks on the fire, bayonets lifted out the kettle at dawn, and in the sunrise the beans and pork were found melted together—a rhapsodic memory for the years. Around the fiery pit soldiers lay, shadows flickering on their blankets, their minds gloating upon the millions of beans that had been eaten and the millions more waiting in warehouse caverns back in Nashville.

One hundred days after the start of the campaign, Cump wrote Ellen that his greatest triumph was not that of battle or strategy, but in so handling his supplies that not one of his men had missed a meal.

Vigilantly Sherman protected his slender railroad from the passengers who would have kept it from its primary task—the bringing of food. "A single messenger's bulk and weight in bread and meat would feed 100 men a day or one man 100 days," he said in denying the Governor of Minnesota the right to send extra commissioners to care for the wounded. There were already too many commissioners on the ground, one from each State, county, and congressional district in addition to the agents of the Sanitary and Christian commissions. Sherman denied powerful editors transportation for huge bundles of newspapers. He was, however, becoming more philosophic, temporarily at least, about the press. He wrote Thomas forbidding them to suppress "mischievous and treasonable newspapers" in Nashville:

I have no objection whatever, but in human nature there is so much of the mule left that prohibition of a newspaper increases its circulation . . . it would be like damming a few of the tributaries of the Kanawha to stop the flood of the Mississippi.
. . . the proper remedy is in punishing the men who publish malicious and false articles. . . . Thus, put in public stocks any venders of obscene or libelous sheets and give a good horse-whipping to any editor who would dare advise our soldiers to avoid their honorable contracts of enlistment.

Demanding cold logic and unsentimental reasoning from all others, in the campaign Sherman allowed himself to stray from his ideal when he thought of Federal prisoners starving in Southern prison pens. Before commencing his shift of forces to the southwest of Atlanta, he had sent two large groups of cavalry against the sole Confederate railroad entering the city. General Stoneman, commanding one of these forces, had begged Sherman to allow him to ride on to Macon and Andersonville, where some 30,000 prisoners were suffering. Evidently without stopping to question how so many weakened men, if rescued, could be brought back across a hundred and thirty miles of hostile territory, Sherman bade Stoneman Godspeed. When both groups of horsemen were defeated—Stoneman and many of his men captured—Sherman made explanation to Halleck, writing on August 7:

Nothing but natural and intense desire to accomplish an end so inviting to one's feelings would have drawn me to commit a military mistake at such a crisis, as that of dividing and risking my cavalry so necessary to the success of my campaign.

To the Sanitary Commission he wrote later, "I don't think I ever set my heart so strongly on any one thing as I did in attempting to rescue those prisoners."
With the return of the vanquished horsemen, Sherman thought of sending infantry against the railroad, but he decided that this would stretch his lines too thin; he gave it up, sent to Chattanooga for large siege guns, and began to bombard the city. In late June he had said that he had no thought of attacking Atlanta; his objective was the Confederate Army, and now in August, when it became necessary to focus his attention upon a citadel, he wrote Halleck, "I am too impatient for a siege," but "whether

we get inside Atlanta or not, it will be a used-up community by the time we are done with it."

Scouts and his own reason told him that the city was depopulated. "Most of the people are gone," he wrote Ellen on August 2; "it is now simply a big fort."

By August 10 he was writing Howard, "Let us destroy Atlanta and make it a desolation." He informed his generals that since Atlanta was a fortified town "whose inhabitants have, of course, got out," they must shell not only the Confederate lines, which were close to the suburbs, but the railroad depots, arsenals, and ammunition and provision warehouses in the city proper. Soon his infantrymen in their trenches lay under a canopy of hurtling iron. The ground shook night and day from the roar of 223 cannon.

The Twelfth Wisconsin was troubled by a gun in their rear that was deficient enough to drop its shells into Federal rather than Confederate trenches. "She slobbers at the mouth—take 'er away!" they shouted through cupped hands to the gunners. They rejoiced when the huge siege guns arrived from Chattanooga. Soon the largest of the new cannon began a monotonous dispatch of a shell at five-minute intervals. "There goes the Atlanta Express," said the men as it boomed.

Federal trenches were topped by sandbags, and at danger points signs read, "Keep down here! Don't stand on the works." At night both armies burned cotton balls, soaked in turpentine, between the lines to aid their sharpshooters in picking off soldiers who wormed through the open spaces stringing telegraph wire, ankle-high, between stumps. Other workers dug little pits, two feet deep, and covered them with twigs. Attacking was made difficult. Often in the evening brass bands played while Northerners and Southerners sang the same song. The campaign became everything that Sherman detested, immobile, tedious. He fidgeted because health and morale declined in trench and camp. He and his men craved the open country, the swinging march. "The enemy hold us by an inferior force," he told Schofield; "we are more besieged than they." His orders became irritable—"I don't hear those guns." . . . "Move up the pickets." . . . "Move up the guns."

A duel of nerves was being fought between himself and Hood—two impatient men. Hood weakened first. He sent Wheeler with almost all the cavalry to threaten Sherman's long railroad. Sherman's nerve held. The threat, he announced, was only a wild-goose chase. He had enough guards in blockhouses and repair gangs in cities along the way to keep the road mended no matter how often Wheeler dashed in to break it. His prediction came true. Wheeler, unable to do serious harm, galloped on into East Tennessee, where he could affect Sherman not at all. General Cox observed that Wheeler had yielded "to the common temptation of cavalry to make too much of the distance they may go behind the hostile lines."

Sherman recognized that Hood had made a capital blunder. Minus his horse scouts, the Confederate was now like a blind man. Quickly Sherman sent his own cavalry to break Hood's one remaining railway. He knew from past records that his horsemen would do railroad tracks as little damage as Wheeler's were doing, but Sherman pinned his faith on the general whom he selected to lead the cavalry raid—Brigadier General Hugh Judson Kilpatrick.

Kilpatrick was a headlong youth of twenty-nine whom Grant had sent Sherman from the Army of the Potomac in April—a bristling little man with a long red nose and longer and redder side-burns. At West Point, Little Kil had gone outside the curriculum to practice amateur acting, political oratory, and fisticuffs with Southern cadets who advocated secession. He had married on the day of his graduation in June, 1861, had ridden away to become the first regular-army officer to be wounded, also the first of the younger West-Pointers to command either a brigade or a division. A precipitate Celt he was, fearing no present and no future and believing that, if spared, he would some day become governor of his native New Jersey, and later on President of the United States. Much given to fictitious descriptions of his feats, his accounts of battles were as boastful and unreliable as were those of his ex-classmate and present rival, Joe Wheeler. Legends about him ran through the army. Men said he neither drank whisky nor gambled—but women! Don Juan of the cavalry! Not all of the romance attributed to him could have been true, however, for he carried with him much of the time Billy, a nephew of fourteen, whose lessons Little Kil heard in his tent. A few months after the Atlanta campaign, Union soldiers were laughing about the two Negro wenches who cooked for Kil, and the *Macon Telegraph* charged that he seated them at his dinner table—most likely an invention.

Sherman favored Kilpatrick over Garrard because the latter would, in Sherman's language, retreat "if he can see a horseman in the distance with a spyglass." Sherman admitted that Kilpatrick's treatment of his own horses entitled him to the name Kil-Cavalry, but when selecting him in November, 1864, to head a raid involving fighting, Sherman said, "I know that Kilpatrick is a hell of a damned fool, but I want just that sort of a man to command my cavalry on this expedition."

In August, 1864, however, Sherman imagined that Kilpatrick would work and toil as well as fight. In sending him to destroy the Confederate railroad, Sherman wrote Kil's superior, Schofield:

Tell Kilpatrick he cannot tear up too much track nor twist too much iron. It may save this army the necessity of making a long, hazardous flank march.

His orders to Kil were "not to fight but to work."

In a few days Kilpatrick was back from his raid, boasting that he had disabled the road for ten days at least; but next morning Sherman saw supply trains calmly puffing into Atlanta over the "demolished" tracks. Inquiry revealed that Kil had spent most of his time fighting and charging. Sadly Sherman dismounted his cavalry and put it into the trenches to free infantry for the dangerous march that must now be made. As Sherman slipped all but Slocum's corps from the west to the southeast, he was courting danger. Joe Johnston, hearing of it some days later in his retirement, said, "It is Sherman's one mistake of the whole summer." But Sherman, beginning the movement on the night of August 25, relied upon Hood's lack of cavalry scouts to keep the secret. Thomas thought the whole affair "extra-hazardous," since it obliged the army to cut loose from its base of supplies—the depot near the Chattahoochee—and to march with only ten days' rations. But as they rode with the men, Cump showed Tom privates gathering and husking roasting ears—he had timed his march to the ripening of the corn.

To Hood came spies saying that Sherman was marching with scant supplies. Not stopping to think of the roasting ears, Hood leaped to the conclusion that Sherman had abandoned the siege . . . Wheeler had cut the Federal line . . . Sherman was starving . . . retreating! Hood telegraphed Richmond of the "great victory" and planned a civic celebration in Atlanta. Trainloads of ladies, fluttering with joy, arrived from Macon, singing songs of triumph and dreaming of a victory ball.

On to the railroad over which the happy ladies had traveled came the Federals, with Sherman saying to Thomas, "I have Atlanta as certainly as if it were in my hand."

It was the thirtieth before Hood awakened to the fact that Sherman was attacking, not retreating. Quickly he sent Hardee with two corps to Jonesboro, some twenty miles south of the city, to protect the railroad. Then, while these troops clashed with the Fifteenth Corps outside the town, Hood learned that Schofield was on the tracks at Rough and Ready, halfway between Jonesboro and Atlanta. Quickly Hood brought half of Hardee's men back to Atlanta; he was attempting Pemberton's method at Vicksburg—to defend a city and fight an open battle at the same time. Paying no attention to Atlanta, other than to assure himself that Slocum was still watching it from the trenches on its north, Sherman brought Schofield and Thomas down the railroad—twisting iron—toward Jonesboro, and sent Howard to cut the tracks south of the town. On September 1, Hardee was in Sherman's net. The Fourteenth Corps, in Thomas's army, which the profane Jefferson C. Davis, supplanting Palmer, had turned into a most aggressive unit, assailed Hardee so fiercely that Sherman cried, "They're rolling 'em up like a sheet of paper!"

Sherman kept watching the left of the line, where Stanley's Fourth Corps —one of Thomas's—was expected. If it kept its appointment no earthly power could prevent the capture of Hardee's force. Sherman sent courier after courier to cry Stanley on. Finally he sent Thomas himself, and said later that it was "the only time during the campaign I can recall seeing General Thomas urge his horse into a gallop."

Meanwhile Davis's men almost annihilated a much smaller organization known as Govan's Arkansans, and, breaking through, fell upon the flank of an equally famous Confederate brigade, Granbury's Texans. Next day the surviving Arkansans—a pitiful handful—sent a bandaged delegation to ask if the Texans had "lost confidence" in them. Granbury's remnants said, "No."

In the race between Stanley and night, Stanley lost, finding himself tangled in dense forests, and in the darkness, Hardee slipped out of the bottle neck and circled south to intrench again at Lovejoy's Station, seven miles lower on the railroad. Stanley had cost Sherman a chance to establish himself as a notable leader in battle and in private Sherman was inclined to blame his lack of "dash and energy" for the enemy's escape. But in public Sherman blamed the impassable forests and said nothing against Stanley.

With such long stretches of the railroad in Union hands, it was certain that Hood must sooner or later evacuate the city. Sherman consoled himself for Hardee's escape by thinking of how his strategy had fooled Hood. The *Macon Telegraph* of November 23 reported how Sherman, talking with a Southern lady, had said:

I played Hood a real Yankee trick that time, didn't I? You can beat us fighting, madam, but we can out-maneuver you; your generals do not work half enough; we work day and nights and spare no labor nor pains to carry out our plans.

During the night of this Thursday, September 1, that ended the fighting at Jonesboro, citizens in the North sat by their lamps reading the platform that the Democrats had adopted at their Chicago convention earlier in the week and which declared that the war must be ended "in the name of humanity, liberty, and public welfare." McClellan was the candidate, with bright prospects of victory.

That same Thursday night Lincoln sat in the White House, outside whose windows the darkness was black indeed. The draft would go into effect on Monday! In the President's desk was a memorandum, penned a week before:

This morning, as for some days past, it seems exceedingly probable that this administration will not be reëlected.

Then it will be my duty to so coöperate with the President-elect as to save the Union between the election and the inauguration; as he will have secured his election on such ground that he cannot save it afterward.

In that same darkness Sherman paced beside a campfire upon which, now and then, he absent-mindedly tossed a Georgia pine knot. He strained his ears for sounds from Atlanta twenty-six miles away. Eleven o'clock; all quiet. Sherman sent couriers to order Slocum on the north of the city to feel Hood's defenses. Midnight; muttering thunder on the north wind—cannon? —and faint shudders that might be rifle volleys? Sherman pointed his nose into the wind like a hound. He walked to a farmhouse in which lights had burned earlier in the evening. Knocks brought a sleepy farmer into the yard. Had he lived there long? Yes. Had he ever heard those noises before? Yes, that was the way it sounded when there was fighting up at Atlanta.

The low rumblings died, but Sherman, returning to his campfire, stood listening, listening—alone in the nighttime, when he was freest, most alive. He was painting imaginary pictures on the vast black canvas above—pictures of Hood attacking Slocum . . . pictures of Hood blowing up his magazines and leaving the city . . . pictures of Hood falling upon the flank of Sherman's own army. If he could be sure what the thunder meant, he would know what to do. If Hood was evacuating, Sherman should rouse his army and strike forward to cut off the retreat.

Four in the morning—another muttering on the horizon. Sherman sent an aide to warn Schofield to be on the alert against attack. The sounds died. Sherman paced. The sky grew gray against the pine forests to the east. Officers stirred in their blankets. Sherman heard bugles blow. The great army awakened. Fires winked in the twilight of dawn. Coffee scented the air. With daylight, Sherman pressed forward, ordering a mass attack upon Hardee. "We want to destroy our enemy," he said.

Too late. Hardee had gone. At 8. A.M. Schofield sent word that *he* had heard those noises last night and thought Hood was destroying his stores. At 10 A.M. Schofield reported that a Negro, just in from Atlanta, said Hood was evacuating the city in great confusion. But at 8 P.M. Sherman was still wondering if the rumor was true. He had sent couriers to find out, but they had not yet returned. He knew how ready soldiers were to believe what they were anxious to hear. Perhaps the bulk of Hood's army was south of him. Nothing was certain. He now moved cautiously, indeed, he ordered his generals to avoid battle: "I do not wish to waste lives by an assault." At 9:30 that night came a courier from Schofield, stating that while everything was still indefinite, all reports indicated Hood's retirement during the night. At 11:20 Sherman wrote Schofield: "Nothing positive from Atlanta, and that bothers me."

Between midnight and 6 A.M. a courier arrived with Slocum's word of victory. Slocum, hearing the noises Thursday at midnight, had crowded forward at daybreak to find the Confederate trenches empty. Federals had broken into town to see the last of Hood's men departing at the other end of the city. Slocum had telegraphed Stanton: "General Sherman has taken Atlanta." The wire was in Lincoln's hands soon after 10 P.M. Friday, September 2. On Saturday the North was rocking with joy. The President set Sunday aside as a day of thanks to the Supreme Being for the victories of Farragut in Mobile Bay and Sherman at Atlanta.

At 5:30 P.M. on Sunday Halleck was handed the first word from Sherman:

So Atlanta is ours and fairly won. I shall not push farther on this raid, but in a day or two will move to Atlanta and give my men some rest. Since May 5th we have been in one constant battle or skirmish. . . .

Sherman had filed the message with the nearest telegraph operator at 6 A.M. on Saturday. From his bivouac he had sent the news to Thomas, who hurried over to see Slocum's note. Tom could scarcely believe his eyes. He studied it in delight, snapped his fingers, whistled, and tried, in his elephantine way, to caper. Sherman said, "He almost danced."

In the woods couriers ran with Sherman's announcement of victory. Sherman listened to the "wild hallooing and glorious laughter" of his men. They were thinking of how they had cut from the Confederacy Kentucky, Tennessee, Arkansas, Texas, Louisiana, Mississippi, Alabama—now Georgia and Florida were theirs for the marching. The Confederacy had been reduced to Virginia and the Carolinas.

Up North, boys rode horses down dirt roads between tall walls of plumed and whispering corn. They waved newspapers and shouted to gray-bearded farmers who were cutting weeds in rail-fence corners:

"Sherman's taken Atlanta! Atlanta's fallen!"

The men in fence corners threw down their scythes and waved their hats. On porches women listened to the shouting neighbor boys, then threw their aprons over their heads and ran into the house sobbing in joy.

Sherman's old enemies, the *Cincinnati Commercial* and the *New York Herald,* led the chorus of acclaim that rose. The *Herald* said his blows were "cyclopean." Soon Northern newspapers were reprinting the *Richmond Examiner's* condemnation of President Davis for his removal of Johnston from the command:

The result is disaster at Atlanta in the very nick of time when a victory alone could save the party of Lincoln from irretrievable ruin. . . . It will obscure the prospect of peace, late so bright. It will also diffuse gloom over the South.

Secretary of State Seward was saying, "Sherman and Farragut have knocked the bottom out of the Chicago platform."

In the Army of the Potomac sat a twenty-nine-year-old officer, Charles Francis Adams, Jr., listening to the artillery salutes that Grant was firing in honor of Sherman. Scion of a patrician and intellectual family of New England, son of the American ambassador to Great Britain, grandson of one President of the United States and great-grandson of another, young Charles Francis, Jr., felt the cold blood of the Adamses grow hot in his veins. He wrote his mother:

How superbly Sherman—Sherman "the unlucky"—has handled that army. It almost brings tears to my eyes to read of the boldness, the caution, the skill, the judgment, the profound military experience and knowledge of that movement, all resulting in its brilliant success and condensed in that one immortal line, "So Atlanta is ours and fairly won."

Why should not Sherman rank only second to Gustavus, Frederick and Napoleon? . . . Unquestionably it is THE campaign of this war, not more brilliant or so complete as Vicksburg but reviewed as a whole, with its unheard-of lines of supply and unceasing opposition, it rolls along like a sonorous epic. The enemy swarms on his flank and rear like mosquitoes, they do not turn him back a day. They stand across his path, he rolls around them and forces them back. At last he brings them to bay and all observers shout, "A deadlock!"

Lo, his cannon thunder in their rear and astonished and demoralized, outgeneralled and outfought, they save themselves in confessed defeat. It is superb. . . .

I only look at the campaign in an artist's point of view as a poem.

The Cavalry Charge at Omdurman

BY

WINSTON CHURCHILL

LONG before the dawn we were astir, and by five o'clock the 21st Lancers were drawn up mounted outside the zeriba. My squadron-leader Major Finn, an Australian by birth, had promised me some days before that he would give me "a show" when the time came. I was afraid that he would count my mission to Lord Kitchener the day before as quittance; but I was now called out from my troop to advance with a patrol and reconnoitre the ridge between the rocky peak of Jebel Surgham and the river. Other patrols from our squadron and from the Egyptian cavalry were also sent hurrying forward in the darkness. I took six men and a corporal. We trotted fast over the plain and soon began to breast the unknown slopes of the ridge. There is nothing like the dawn. The quarter of an hour before the curtain is lifted upon an unknowable situation is an intense experience of war. Was the ridge held by the enemy or not? Were we riding through the gloom into thousands of ferocious savages? Every step might be deadly; yet there was no time for overmuch precaution. The regiment was coming on behind us, and dawn was breaking. It was already half light as we climbed the slope. What should we find at the summit? For cool, tense excitement I commend such moments.

Now we are near the top of the ridge. I make one man follow a hundred yards behind, so that whatever happens, he may tell the tale. There is no sound but our own clatter. We have reached the crest line. We rein in our horses. Every minute the horizon extends; we can already see 200 yards. Now we can see perhaps a quarter of a mile. All is quiet; no life but our own breathes among the rocks and sand hummocks of the ridge. No ambuscade, no occupation in force! The farther plain is bare below us: we can now see more than half a mile.

So they have all decamped! Just what we said! All bolted off to Kordofan; no battle! But wait! The dawn is growing fast. Veil after veil is lifted from the landscape. What is this shimmering in the distant plain? Nay—it is lighter now—what are these dark markings beneath the shimmer? *They are there!* These enormous black smears are thousands of men; the shimmering is the glinting of their weapons. It is now daylight. I slip off my horse; I write in my field service notebook "The Dervish army is still in position a mile and a half south-west of Jebel Surgham."

From: *A Roving Commission.* Copyright 1930, 1939 by Scribners.

I send this message by the corporal direct as ordered to the Commander-in-Chief. I mark it XXX. In the words of the drill book "with all despatch" or as one would say "Hell for leather."

A glorious sunrise is taking place behind us; but we are admiring something else. It is already light enough to use field-glasses. The dark masses are changing their values. They are already becoming lighter than the plain; they are fawn-coloured. Now they are a kind of white, while the plain is dun. In front of us is a vast array four or five miles long. It fills the horizon till it is blocked out on our right by the serrated silhouette of Surgham Peak. This is an hour to live. We mount again, and suddenly new impressions strike the eye and mind. These masses are not stationary. They are advancing, and they are advancing fast. A tide is coming in. But what is this sound which we hear: a deadened roar coming up to us in waves? They are cheering for God, his Prophet and his holy Khalifa. They think they are going to win. We shall see about that presently. Still I must admit that we check our horses and hang upon the crest of the ridge for a few moments before advancing down its slopes.

But now it is broad morning and the slanting sun adds brilliant colour to the scene. The masses have defined themselves into swarms of men, in ordered ranks bright with glittering weapons, and above them dance a multitude of gorgeous flags. We see for ourselves what the Crusaders saw. We must see more of it. I trot briskly forward to somewhere near the sandhills where the 21st Lancers had halted the day before. Here we are scarcely 400 yards away from the great masses. We halt again and I make four troopers fire upon them, while the other two hold their horses. The enemy come on like the sea. A crackle of musketry breaks out on our front and to our left. Dust spurts rise among the sandhills. This is no place for Christians. We scamper off; and luckily no man nor horse is hurt. We climb back on to the ridge, and almost at this moment there returns the corporal on a panting horse. He comes direct from Kitchener with an order signed by the Chief of Staff. "Remain as long as possible, and report how the masses of attack are moving." Talk of Fun! Where will you beat this! On horseback, at daybreak, within shot of an advancing army, seeing everything, and corresponding direct with Headquarters.

So we remained on the ridge for nearly half an hour and I watched close up a scene which few have witnessed. All the masses except one passed for a time out of our view beyond the peak of Surgham on our right. But one, a division of certainly 6,000 men moved directly over the shoulder of the ridge. Already they were climbing its forward slopes. From where we sat on our horses we could see both sides. There was our army ranked and massed by the river. There were the gunboats lying expectant in the stream. There were all the batteries ready to open. And meanwhile on the other side, this large oblong gay-coloured crowd in fairly good order climbed swiftly up to the crest of exposure. We were about 2,500 yards from our own batteries, but little more than 200 from the approaching target. I called these Dervishes "The White Flags." They reminded me of the armies in the Bayeux tapestries, because of their rows of white and yellow standards held upright. Meanwhile the Dervish centre far out in the plain had come within range, and one after another the British and Egyptian batteries opened upon it. My eyes were rivetted by a nearer scene. At the top of the hill "The White Flags" paused to rearrange their ranks and drew out a broad and solid parade along the crest. Then the cannonade turned upon them. Two or three batteries and all the gunboats, at least thirty guns, opened an intense fire. Their shells shrieked towards us and burst in scores over the heads and among the masses of the White Flag-men. We were so close, as we sat spellbound on our horses, that we almost shared their perils. I saw the full blast of Death strike this human wall. Down went their standards by dozens and their men by hundreds. Wide gaps and shapeless heaps appeared in their array. One saw them jumping and tumbling under the shrapnel bursts; but none turned back. Line after line they all streamed over the shoulder and advanced towards our zeriba, opening a heavy rifle fire which wreathed them in smoke.

Hitherto no one had taken any notice of us; but I now saw Baggara horsemen in twos and threes riding across the plain on our left towards the ridge. One of these patrols of three men came within pistol range. They were dark, cowled figures, like monks on horseback—ugly, sinister brutes with long spears. I fired a few shots at them from the saddle, and they sheered off. I did not see why we should not stop out on this ridge during the assault. I thought we could edge back towards the Nile and so watch both sides while keeping out of harm's way. But now arrived a positive order from Major Finn, whom I had perforce left out of my correspondence with the Commander-in-Chief, saying "Come back at once into the zeriba as the infantry are about to open fire." We should in fact have been safer on the ridge, for we only just got into the infantry lines before the rifle-storm began.

It is not my purpose in this record of personal impressions to give a general account of the Battle of Omdurman. The story has been told so often and in such exact military detail that everyone who is interested in the subject is no doubt well acquainted with what took place. I shall only summarise the course of the battle so far as may be necessary to explain my own experiences.

The whole of the Khalifa's army, nearly 60,000 strong, advanced in battle order from their encampment of the night before, topped the swell of ground which hid the two armies from one another, and then rolled down the gently-sloping amphitheatre in the arena of which, backed upon the Nile, Kitchener's 20,000 troops were drawn up shoulder to shoulder to receive them. Ancient and modern confronted one another. The weapons, the methods and the fanaticism of the Middle Ages were brought by an extraordinary anachronism into dire collision with the organisation and inventions of the nineteenth century. The result was not surprising. As the successors of the Saracens descended the long smooth slopes which led to the river and their enemy, they encountered the rifle fire of two and a half divisions of trained infantry, drawn up two deep and in close order and supported by at least 70 guns on the river bank and in the gunboats, all firing with undisturbed efficiency. Under this fire the whole attack withered and came to a standstill, with a loss of perhaps six or seven thousand men, at least 700 yards away from the British-Egyptian line. The Dervish army, however, possessed nearly 20,000 rifles of various kinds, from the most antiquated to the most modern, and when the spearmen could get no farther, these riflemen lay down on the plain and began a ragged, unaimed but considerable fusillade at the dark line of the thorn-fence zeriba. Now for the first time they began to inflict losses on their antagonists, and in the short space that this lasted perhaps two hundred casualties occurred among the British and Egyptian troops.

Seeing that the attack had been repulsed with great slaughter and that he was nearer to the city of Omdurman than the Dervish army, Kitchener, immediately wheeled his five brigades into his usual echelon formation, and with his left flank on the river proceeded to march south towards the city, intending thereby to cut off what he considered to be the remnants of the Dervish army from their capital, their base, their food, their water, their home, and to drive them out into the vast deserts which stared on every side. But the Dervishes were by no means defeated. The whole of their left, having overshot the mark, had not even been under fire. The Khalifa's reserve of perhaps 15,000 men was still intact. All these swarms now advanced with undaunted courage to attack the British and Egyptian forces, which were no longer drawn up in a prepared position, but marching freely over the desert. This second shock was far more critical than the first. The charging Dervishes succeeded everywhere in coming to within a hundred or two hundred yards of the troops, and the rear brigade of Soudanese, attacked from two directions, was only saved from destruction by the skill and firmness of its commander, General Hector Macdonald. However, discipline and machinery triumphed over the most desperate valour, and after an enormous carnage, certainly exceeding 20,000 men, who strewed the ground in heaps and swathes "like snowdrifts," the whole mass of the Dervishes dissolved into fragments and into particles and streamed away into the fantastic mirages of the desert.

The Egyptian cavalry and the camel corps had been protecting the right flank of the zeriba when it was attacked, and the 21st Lancers were the only horsemen on the left flank nearest to Omdurman. Immediately after the first attack had been repulsed we were ordered to leave the zeriba, ascertain what enemy forces, if any, stood between Kitchener and the city, and if possible drive these forces back and clear the way for the advancing army. Of course as a regimental officer one knows very little of what is taking place over the whole field of battle. We waited by our horses during the first attack close down by the river's edge, sheltered by the steep Nile bank from the bullets which whistled overhead. As soon as the fire began to slacken and it was said on all sides that the attack had been repulsed, a General arrived with his staff at a gallop with instant orders to mount and advance. In two minutes the four squadrons were mounted and trotting out of the zeriba in a southerly direction. We ascended again the slopes of Jebel Surgham which had played its part in the first stages of the action, and from its ridges soon saw before us the whole plain of Omdurman with the vast mud city, its minarets and domes, spread before us six or seven miles away. After various halts and reconnoitrings we found ourselves walking forward in what is called "column of troops." There are four troops in a squadron and four squadrons in a regiment. Each of these troops now followed the other. I commanded the second troop from the rear, comprising between twenty and twenty-five Lancers.

Everyone expected that we were going to make a charge. That was the one idea that had been in all minds since we had started from Cairo. Of course there would be a charge. In those days, before the Boer War, British cavalry had been taught little else. Here was clearly the occasion for a charge. But against what body of enemy, over what ground, in which direction or with what purpose, were matters hidden from the rank and file. We continued to pace forward over the hard sand, peering into the mirage-twisted plain in a high state of suppressed excitement. Presently I noticed, 300 yards away on our flank and parallel to the line on which we were advancing, a long row of blue-black objects, two or three yards apart. I thought there were about a hundred and fifty. Then I became sure that these were men—enemy men—squatting on the ground. Almost at the same moment the trumpet sounded "Trot," and the whole long column of cavalry began to jingle and clatter across the front of these crouching figures. We were in the lull of the battle and there was perfect silence. Forthwith from every blue-black blob came a white puff of smoke, and a loud volley of musketry broke the odd stillness. Such a target at such a distance could scarcely be missed, and all along the column here and there horses bounded and a few men fell.

The intentions of our Colonel had no doubt been to move round the flank of the body of Dervishes he had now located, and who, concealed in a fold of the ground behind their riflemen, were invisible to us, and then to attack them from a more advantageous quarter; but once the fire was opened and losses began to grow, he must have judged it inexpedient to prolong his procession across the open plain. The trumpet sounded "Right wheel into line," and all the sixteen troops swung round towards the blue-black riflemen. Almost immediately the regiment broke into a gallop, and the 21st Lancers were committed to their first charge in war!

I propose to describe exactly what happened to me: what I saw and what I felt. I recalled it to my mind so frequently after the event that the impression is as clear and vivid as it was a quarter of a century ago. The troop I commanded was, when we wheeled into line, the second from the right of the regiment. I was riding a handy, sure-footed, grey Arab polo pony. Before we wheeled and began to gallop, the officers had been marching with drawn swords. On account of my shoulder I had always decided that if I were involved in hand-to-hand fighting, I must use a pistol and not a sword. I had purchased in London a Mauser automatic pistol, then the newest and the latest design. I had practised carefully with this during our march and journey up the river. This then was the weapon with which I determined to fight. I had first of all to return my sword into its scabbard, which is not the easiest thing to do at a gallop. I had then to draw my pistol from its wooden holster and bring it to full cock. This dual operation took an appreciable time, and until it was finished, apart from a few glances to my left to see what effect the fire was producing, I did not look up at the general scene.

Then I saw immediately before me, and now only half the length of a polo ground away, the row of crouching blue figures firing frantically, wreathed in white smoke. On my right and left my neighbouring troop leaders made a good line. Immediately behind was a long dancing row of lances couched for the charge. We were going at a fast but steady gallop. There was too much trampling and rifle fire to hear any bullets. After this glance to the right and left and at my troop, I looked again towards the enemy. The scene appeared to be suddenly transformed. The blue-black men were still firing, but behind them there now came into view a depression like a shallow sunken road. This was crowded and crammed with men rising up from the ground where they had hidden. Bright flags appeared as if by magic, and I saw arriving from nowhere Emirs on horseback among and around the mass of the enemy. The Dervishes appeared to be ten or twelve deep at the thickest, a great grey mass gleaming with steel, filling the dry watercourse. In the same twinkling of an eye I saw also that our right overlapped their left, that my troop would just strike the edge of their array, and that the troop on my right would charge into air. My subaltern comrade on the right, Wormald of the 7th Hussars, could see the situation too; and we both increased our speed to the very fastest gallop and curved inwards like the horns of the moon. One really had not time to be frightened or to think of anything else but these particular necessary actions which I have described. They completely occupied mind and senses.

The collision was now very near. I saw immediately before me, not ten yards away, the two blue men who lay in my path. They were perhaps a couple of yards apart. I rode at the interval between them. They both fired. I passed through the smoke conscious that I was unhurt. The trooper immediately behind me was killed at this place and at this moment, whether by these shots or not I do not know. I checked my pony as the ground began to fall away beneath his feet. The clever animal dropped like a cat four or five feet down on to the sandy bed of the watercourse, and in this sandy bed I found myself surrounded by what seemed to be dozens of men. They were not thickly packed enough at this point for me to experience any actual collision with them. Whereas Grenfell's troop, next but one on my left, was brought to a complete standstill and suffered very heavy losses, we seemed to push our way through as one has sometimes seen mounted police-men break up a crowd. In less time than it takes to relate, my pony had scrambled up the other side of the ditch. I looked round.

Once again I was on the hard, crisp desert, my horse at a trot. I had the impression of scattered Dervishes running to and fro in all directions. Straight before me a man threw himself on the ground. The reader must remember that I had been trained as a cavalry soldier to believe that if ever cavalry broke into a mass of infantry, the latter would be at their mercy. My first idea therefore was that the man was terrified. But simul-taneously I saw the gleam of his curved sword as he drew it back for a ham-stringing cut. I had room and time enough to turn my pony out of his reach, and leaning over on the off side I fired two shots into him at about three yards. As I straightened myself in the saddle, I saw before me another figure with uplifted sword. I raised my pistol and fired. So close were we that the pistol itself actually struck him. Man and sword disappeared below and behind me. On my left, ten yards away, was an Arab horseman in a bright-coloured tunic and steel helmet, with chain-mail hangings. I fired at him. He turned aside. I pulled my horse into a walk and looked around again.

In one respect a cavalry charge is very like ordinary life. So long as you are all right, firmly in your saddle, your horse in hand, and well armed, lots of enemies will give you a wide berth. But as soon as you have lost a stirrup, have a rein cut, have dropped your weapon, are wounded, or your horse is wounded, then is the moment when from all quarters enemies rush upon you. Such was the fate of not a few of my comrades in the troops immediately on my left. Brought to an actual standstill in the enemy's mass, clutched at from every side, stabbed at and hacked at by spear and sword, they were dragged from their horses and cut to pieces by the infuriated foe. But this I did not at the time see or understand. My impressions continued to be sanguine. I thought we were masters of the situ-ation, riding the enemy down, scattering them and killing them. I pulled my horse up and looked about me. There was a mass of Dervishes about forty or fifty yards away on my left. They were huddling and clumping them-selves together, rallying for mutual protection. They seemed wild with excitement, dancing about on their feet, shaking their spears up and down. The whole scene seemed to flicker. I have an impression, but it is too fleet-ing to define, of brown-clad Lancers mixed up here and there with this surging mob. The scattered individuals in my immediate neighbourhood made no attempt to molest me. Where was my troop? Where were the other troops of the squadron? Within a hundred yards of me I could not see a single officer or man. I looked back at the Dervish mass. I saw two or three riflemen crouching and aiming their rifles at me from the fringe of it. Then for the first time that morning I experienced a sudden sensation of fear. I felt myself absolutely alone. I thought these riflemen would hit me and the rest devour me like wolves. What a fool I was to loiter like this in the midst of the enemy! I crouched over the saddle, spurred my horse into a gallop and drew clear of the *mêlée*. Two or three hundred yards away I found my troop already faced about and partly formed up.

The other three troops of the squadron were reforming close by. Suddenly in the midst of the troop up sprang a Dervish. How he got there I do not know. He must have leaped out of some scrub or hole. All the troopers turned upon him thrusting with their lances: but he darted to and fro causing for the moment a frantic commotion. Wounded several times, he staggered towards me raising his spear. I shot him at less than a yard. He fell on the sand, and lay there dead. How easy to kill a man! But I did not worry about it. I found I had fired the whole magazine of my Mauser pistol, so I put in a new clip of ten cartridges before thinking of anything else.

I was still prepossessed with the idea that we had inflicted great slaughter on the enemy and had scarcely suffered at all ourselves. Three or four men were missing from my troop. Six men and nine or ten horses were bleeding from spear thrusts or sword cuts. We all expected to be ordered immediately to charge back again. The men were ready, though they all looked serious. Several asked to be allowed to throw away their lances and draw their swords. I asked my second sergeant if he had enjoyed himself. His answer was "Well, I don't exactly say I enjoyed it, Sir; but I think I'll get more used to it next time." At this the whole troop laughed.

But now from the direction of the enemy there came a succession of grisly apparitions; horses spouting blood, struggling on three legs, men staggering on foot, men bleeding from terrible wounds, fish-hook spears stuck right through them, arms and faces cut to pieces, bowels protruding, men gasping, crying, collapsing, expiring. Our first task was to succour these; and meanwhile the blood of our leaders cooled. They remembered for the first time that we had carbines. Everything was still in great confusion. But trumpets were sounded and orders shouted, and we all moved off at a trot towards the flank of the enemy. Arrived at a position from which we could enfilade and rake the watercourse, two squadrons were dismounted and in a few minutes with their fire at three hundred yards compelled the Dervishes to retreat. We therefore remained in possession of the field. Within twenty minutes of the time when we had first wheeled into line and began our charge, we were halted and breakfasting in the very watercourse that had so nearly proved our undoing. There one could see the futility of the much vaunted *Arme Blanche*. The Dervishes had carried off their wounded, and the corpses of thirty or forty enemy were all that could be counted on the ground. Among these lay the bodies of over twenty Lancers, so hacked and mutilated as to be mostly unrecognisable. In all out of 310 officers and men the regiment had lost in the space of about two or three minutes five officers and sixty-five men killed and wounded, and 120 horses—nearly a quarter of its strength.

Such were my fortunes in this celebrated episode. It is very rarely that cavalry and infantry, while still both unshaken, are intermingled as the result of an actual collision. Either the infantry keep their heads and shoot the cavalry down, or they break into confusion and are cut down or speared as they run. But the two or three thousand Dervishes who faced the 21st Lancers in the watercourse at Omdurman were not in the least shaken by the stress of battle or afraid of cavalry. Their fire was not good enough to stop the charge, but they had no doubt faced horsemen many a time in the wars with Abyssinia. They were familiar with the ordeal of the charge. It was the kind of fighting they thoroughly understood. Moreover, the fight was with equal weapons, for the British too fought with sword and lance as in the days of old.

A white gunboat seeing our first advance had hurried up the river in the hopes of being of assistance. From the crow's nest, its commander, Beatty, watched the whole event with breathless interest. Many years passed before I met this officer or knew that he had witnessed our gallop. When we met, I was First Lord of the Admiralty and he the youngest Admiral in the Royal Navy. "What did it look like?" I asked him. "What was your prevailing impression?" "It looked," said Admiral Beatty, "like plum duff: brown currants scattered about in a great deal of suet." With this striking, if somewhat homely, description my account of this adventure may fittingly close.

The Sun of Austerlitz

BY

GENERAL MARBOT

MOST military authors are apt to confuse the reader's mind by over-crowding their story with details. So much is this the case that, in the greater part of the works published on the wars of the Empire, I have been utterly unable to understand the history of many battles at which I was present, and of which all the phases were well known to me. In order to preserve due clearness in relating a military action, I think one ought to be content with indicating the respective conditions of the two armies before the engagement, and reporting only such facts as affected the decision. That is what I shall try to do in order to give you an idea of the battle of Austerlitz, as it is called, though it took place short of the village of that name. On the eve of the battle, however, the Emperors of Austria and Russia had slept at the château of Austerlitz, and when Napoleon drove them from this, he wished to heighten his triumph by giving that name to the battle.

You will see on a map that the Goldbach brook, which rises on the other side of the Olmütz road, falls into the small lake of Mönitz. This stream, flowing at the bottom of a little valley with pretty steep sides, separated the two armies. The Austro-Russian right rested on a hanging wood in rear of the Posoritz post-house beyond the Olmütz road; their centre occupied Pratzen and the wide plateau of that name; their left was near the pools of Satschan and the swampy ground in their neighborhood. The Emperor Napoleon rested his left on a hillock difficult of access, to which the Egyptian soldiers gave the name of the "Santon," because it had on the top a little chapel with a spire like a minaret. The French centre was near the marsh of Kobelnitz, the right was at Telnitz. But at this point the Emperor had placed very few people, in order to draw the Russians on to the marshy ground, where he had arranged to defeat them by concealing Davout's corps at Gross Raigern, on the Vienna road.

On the 1st of December, the day before the battle, Napoleon left Brunn early in the morning, spent the whole day in inspecting the positions, and in the evening fixed his headquarters in rear of the French centre, at a point whence the view took in the bivouacs of both sides, as well as the ground which was to be their field of battle next day. There was no other building in the place than a poor barn. The Emperor's tables and maps were placed there, and he established himself in person by an immense fire, surrounded

From: *The Adventures of General Marbot.* Scribners.

822

by his numerous staff and his guard. Fortunately there was no snow, and though it was very cold, I lay on the ground and went soundly to sleep. But we were soon obliged to remount and go the rounds with the Emperor. There was no moon, and the darkness of the night was increased by a thick fog which made progress very difficult. The chasseurs of the escort had the idea of lighting torches made of pine branches and straw, which proved very useful. The troops, seeing a group of horsemen thus lighted come towards them, had no difficulty in recognizing the imperial staff, and in an instant, as if by enchantment, we could see along the whole line all our bivouac fires lighted up by thousands of torches in the hands of the soldiers. The cheers with which, in their enthusiasm, they saluted Napoleon, were all the more animated for the fact that the morrow was the anniversary of his coronation, and the coincidence seemed of good omen. The enemies must have been a good deal surprised when, from the top of a neighboring hill, they saw in the middle of the night 60,000 torches lighted, and heard a thousand times repeated the cry of "Long live the Emperor!" accompanied by the sound of the many bands of the French regiments. In our camp all was joy, light, and movement, while on the side of the Austrians and Russians all was gloom and silence.

Next day, December 2, the sound of cannon was heard at daybreak. As we have seen, the Emperor had shown but few troops on his right; this was a trap for the enemy, with the view of allowing them to capture Telnitz easily, to cross the Goldbach there, then to go on to Gross Raigern and take possession of the road from Brunn to Vienna, and so to cut off our retreat. The Russians and Austrians fell into the snare perfectly, for, weakening the rest of their line, they clumsily crowded considerable forces into the bottom of Telnitz, and into the swampy valleys bordering on the pools of Satschan and Mönitz. But as they imagined, for some not very apparent reason, that Napoleon had the intention of retreating without delivering battle, they resolved, by way of completing their success, to attack us on our left towards the "Santon," and also on our centre before Puntowitz. By this means our defeat would be complete when we had been forced back on these two points, and found the road to Vienna occupied in our rear by the Russians. As it befell, however, on our left Marshal Lannes not only repulsed all the attacks of the enemy upon the "Santon," but drove him back on the other side of the Olmütz road as far as Blasiowitz. There the ground became more level, and allowed Murat's cavalry to execute some brilliant charges, the results of which were of great importance, for the Russians were driven out of hand as far as the village of Austerlitz.

While this splendid success was being won by our left wing, the centre, consisting of the troops under Soult and Bernadotte, which the Emperor had posted at the bottom of Goldbach ravine, where it was concealed by a thick fog, dashed forward towards the hill on which stands the village of Pratzen. This was the moment when that brilliant sun of Austerlitz, the recollection of which Napoleon so delighted to recall, burst forth in all its splendor. Marshal Soult carried not only the village of Pratzen, but also the

vast tableland of that name, which was the culminating point of the whole
country, and consequently the key of the battlefield. There, under the Emperor's eyes, the sharpest of the fighting took place, and the Russians were
beaten back. But one battalion, the 4th of the line, of which Prince Joseph,
Napoleon's brother, was colonel, allowing itself to be carried too far in
pursuit of the enemy, was charged and broken up by the Noble Guard and
the Grand Duke Constantine's cuirassiers, losing its eagle. Several lines of
Russian cavalry quickly advanced to support this momentary success of the
guards, but Napoleon hurled against them the Mamelukes, the mounted
chasseurs, and the mounted grenadiers of his guard, under Marshal Bes-
sières and General Rapp. The mêlée was of the most sanguinary kind; the
Russian squadrons were crushed and driven back beyond the village of
Austerlitz with immense loss. Our troopers captured many colors and prisoners, among the latter Prince Repnin, commander of the Noble Guard.
This regiment, composed of the most brilliant of the young Russian nobility, lost heavily, because the swagger in which they had indulged against
the French having come to the ears of our soldiers, these, and above all the
mounted grenadiers, attacked them with fury, shouting as they passed their
great sabres through their bodies: "We will give the ladies of St. Petersburg something to cry for!"

The painter Gérard, in his picture of the battle of Austerlitz, has taken
for his subject the moment when General Rapp, coming wounded out of
the fight, and covered with his enemies' blood and his own, is presenting to
the Emperor the flags just captured and his prisoner, Prince Repnin. I was
present at this imposing spectacle, which the artist has reproduced with
wonderful accuracy. All the heads are portraits, even that of the brave
chasseur who, making no complaint, though he had been shot through the
body, had the courage to come up to the Emperor and fall stone dead as he
presented the standard which he had just taken. Napoleon, wishing to honor
his memory, ordered the painter to find a place for him in his composition.
In the picture may be seen also a Mameluke, who is carrying in one hand
an enemy's flag and holds in the other the bridle of his dying horse. This
man, named Mustapha, was well known in the guard for his courage and
ferocity. During the charge he had pursued the Grand Duke Constantine,
who only got rid of him by a pistol-shot, which severely wounded the
Mameluke's horse. Mustapha, grieved at having only a standard to offer
to the Emperor, said in his broken French as he presented it: "Ah, if me
catch Prince Constantine, me cut him head off and bring it to Emperor!"
Napoleon, disgusted, replied: "Will you hold your tongue, you savage?"
But to finish the account of the battle. While Marshals Lannes, Soult, and
Murat, with the imperial guard, were beating the right and centre of the
allied army, and driving them back beyond the village of Austerlitz, the
enemy's left, falling into the trap laid by Napoleon when he made a show
of keeping close to the pools, threw itself on the village of Telnitz, captured
it, and, crossing the Goldbach, prepared to occupy the road to Vienna. But
the enemy had taken a false prognostic of Napoleon's genius when they

supposed him capable of committing such a blunder as to leave undefended a road by which, in the event of disaster, his retreat was secured; for our right was guarded by the divisions under Davout, concealed in the rear in the little town of Gross Raigern. From this point Davout fell upon the allies at the moment when he saw their masses entangled in the defiles between the lakes of Telnitz and Mönitz, and the stream.

The Emperor, whom we left on the plateau of Pratzen, having freed himself from the enemy's right and centre, which were in flight on the other side of Austerlitz, descended from the heights of Pratzen with a small force of all arms, including Soult's corps and his guard, and went with all speed towards Telnitz, and took the enemy's columns in rear at the moment when Davout was attacking in front. At once the heavy masses of Austrians and Russians, packed on the narrow roadways which lead beside the Goldbach brook, finding themselves between two fires, fell into an indescribable confusion. All ranks were mixed up together, and each sought to save himself by flight. Some hurled themselves headlong into the marshes which border the pools, but our infantry followed them there. Others hoped to escape by the road that lies between the two pools; our cavalry charged them, and the butchery was frightful. Lastly, the greater part of the enemy, chiefly Russians, sought to pass over the ice. It was very thick, and five or six thousand men, keeping some kind of order, had reached the middle of the Satschan lake, when Napoleon, calling up the artillery of his guard, gave the order to fire on the ice. It broke at countless points, and a mighty cracking was heard. The water, oozing through the fissures, soon covered the floes, and we saw thousands of Russians, with their horses, guns, and wagons, slowly settle down into the depths. It was a horribly majestic spectacle which I shall never forget. In an instant the surface of the lake was covered with everything that could swim. Men and horses struggled in the water amongst the floes. Some—a very small number—succeeded in saving themselves by the help of poles and ropes, which our soldiers reached to them from the shore, but the greater part were drowned.

The number of combatants at the Emperor's disposal in this battle was 68,000 men; that of the allied army amounted to 82,000 men. Our loss in killed and wounded was about 8,000; our enemies admitted that theirs, in killed, wounded, and drowned, reached 14,000. We had made 18,000 prisoners, captured 150 guns, and a great quantity of standards and colors.

After giving the order to pursue the enemy in every direction, the Emperor betook himself to his new headquarters at the post-house of Posoritz on the Olmütz road. As may be imagined, he was radiant, but frequently expressed regret that the very eagle we had lost should have belonged to the 4th regiment of the line, of which his brother Joseph was colonel, and should have been captured by the regiment of the Grand Duke Constantine, brother of the Emperor of Russia. The coincidence was, in truth, rather quaint, and made the loss more noticeable. But Napoleon soon received great consolation. Prince John of Lichtenstein came from the Emperor of Austria to request an interview, and Napoleon, understanding that this would result in a peace and would deliver him from the fear of seeing the Prussians march on his rear before he was clear of his present enemy, granted it.

Of all the divisions of the French imperial guard, it was the mounted chasseurs who suffered the heaviest loss in their great charge against the Russian guard on the Pratzen plateau. My poor friend, Captain Fournier, had been killed, and General Morland too. The Emperor, always on the lookout for anything that might kindle the spirit of emulation among the troops, decided that General Morland's body should be placed in the memorial building which he proposed to erect on the Esplanade des Invalides at Paris. The surgeons, having neither the time nor the materials necessary to embalm the general's body on the battlefield, put it into a barrel of rum, which was transported to Paris. But subsequent events having delayed the construction of the monument destined for General Morland, the barrel in which he had been placed was still standing in one of the rooms of the School of Medicine when Napoleon lost the Empire in 1814. Not long afterwards the barrel broke through decay, and people were much surprised to find that the rum had made the general's moustaches grow to such an extraordinary extent that they fell below his waist. The corpse was in perfect preservation, but, in order to get possession of it, the family was obliged to bring an action against some scientific man who had made a curiosity of it. Cultivate the love of glory and go and get killed, to let some oaf of a naturalist set you up in his library between a rhinoceros horn and a stuffed crocodile!

I did not receive any wound at the battle of Austerlitz, though I was often in a very exposed position; notably at the time of the cavalry mêlée on the Pratzen plateau. The Emperor had sent me with orders to General Rapp, whom I succeeded with great difficulty in reaching in the middle of that terrible hurly-burly of slaughterers and slaughtered. My horse came in contact with that of one of the Noble Guard, and our sabres were on the point of crossing, when we were forced apart by the combatants, and I got off with a severe contusion. But the next day I incurred a much greater danger of a very different kind from those which one ordinarily meets on the field of battle. It happened in this way. On the morning of the 3rd, the Emperor mounted and rode round the different positions where the fights of the day before had taken place. Having reached the shores of the Satschan lake, Napoleon dismounted, and was chatting with several marshals round a camp fire, when he saw floating a hundred yards from the embankment a large isolated ice floe, on which was stretched a poor Russian non-commissioned officer with a decoration. The poor fellow could not help himself, having got a bullet through his thigh, and his blood had stained the ice floe which supported him. It was a horrible sight. Seeing a numerous staff surrounded by guards, the man judged that Napoleon must be there; he raised himself as well as he could, and cried out that as soldiers of all countries became brothers when the fight was over, he begged his life of the powerful Emperor of the French. Napoleon's interpreter having translated this entreaty, he was touched by it, and ordered General Bertrand, his aide-de-camp, to do what he could to save the poor man. Straightway several men of the escort, and even two staff officers, seeing two great treestems on the bank, pushed them into the water, and then, getting astride of them, they thought that by moving their legs simultaneously they would drive these pieces of wood forward. But scarcely were they a fathom from the edge than they rolled over, throwing into the water the men who bestrode them. Their clothes were saturated in a moment, and as it was freezing very hard, the cloth of their sleeves and their trousers became stiff as they swam, and their limbs, shut up, as it were, in cases, could not move, so that several came near to being drowned, and they only got back to land with great difficulty, by the help of ropes which were thrown to them.

I bethought me then of saying that the swimmers ought to have stripped; in the first place, to preserve their freedom of movement, and secondly, to avoid having to pass the night in wet clothes. General Bertrand having heard this repeated it to the Emperor, who declared that I was right and that the others had shown more zeal than discretion. I do not wish to make myself out better than I am, so I will admit that just having taken part in a battle where I had seen thousands of dead and dying, the edge had been taken off my sensibility, and I did not feel philanthropic enough to run the risk of a bad cold by contesting with the ice floes the life of an enemy. I felt quite content with deploring his sad fate. But the Emperor's answer piqued me, and it seemed to me that I should be open to ridicule if I gave advice and did not dare to carry it into execution. So I leapt from my horse, and stripped myself naked and dashed into the water. I had gone fast in the course of the day and got hot, so that the chill struck me keenly, but I was young and vigorous and a good swimmer; the Emperor's presence encouraged me, and I struck out towards the Russian sergeant. At the same time my example, and probably the praise given me by the Emperor, determined a lieutenant of artillery, by name Roumestain, to imitate me.

While he was undressing I was advancing, but with a good deal more difficulty than I had foreseen. The older and stronger ice, which had been smashed to pieces the day before, had almost entirely disappeared, but a new skin had formed some lines in thickness, the sharp edges of which scratched the skin of my arms, breast, and neck in a very unpleasant fashion. The artillery officer, who had caught me up half-way, had not perceived it at all, having profited by the path which I had opened in the new ice. He called my attention to this fact, and generously demanded to be allowed to take his turn at leading, to which I agreed, for I was cruelly cut up. At last we reached the huge floe of old ice on which the poor Russian was lying, and thought that the most laborious part of our enterprise was achieved. There we were quite wrong, for as soon as we began to push the floe forward the layer of new ice which covered the surface of the water, being broken by contact with it, piled itself up in front, so as in a short time to form a mass which not only resisted our efforts, but began to break the edges of the big floe. The bulk of this got smaller every moment, and we began to fear that the poor man whom we were trying to save would be drowned before our eyes. The edges, moreover, of the floe were remarkably sharp, so that we had to choose spots on which to rest our hands and our chests as we pushed. We were at our last gasp. Finally, by way of a crowning stroke, as we got near the bank the ice split in several places, and the portion on which the Russian lay was reduced to a slab only a few feet in breadth, quite insufficient to bear his weight. He was on the point of sinking when my comrade and I, feeling bottom at length, slipped our shoulders under the ice slab, and bore it to the shore. They threw us ropes, which we fastened round the Russian, and he was at last hoisted on to the beach. We had to use the same means to get out of the water, for we were wearied, torn, bruised, and bleeding, and could hardly stand. My kind comrade Massy, who had watched me with the greatest anxiety throughout my swim, had been so thoughtful as to have his horse-cloth warmed before the camp fire, and as soon as I was out of the water he wrapped me in it. After a good rub down I put on my clothes and wanted to stretch out by the fire, but this Dr. Larrey forbade, and ordered me to walk about, to do which I required the help of two chasseurs. The Emperor came and congratulated the artillery lieutenant and me on our courage in undertaking and achieving the rescue of the wounded Russian, and calling his Mameluke Roustan, who always carried refreshments with him on his horse, he poured us out a glass of excellent rum, and asked us, laughing, how we had liked our bath. As for the Russian sergeant, the Emperor directed Dr. Larrey to attend to him, and gave him several pieces of gold. He was fed and put into dry clothes, and after being wrapped in warm rugs, he was taken to a house in Telnitz which was used as an ambulance, and transferred the next day to the hospital at Brunn. The poor lad blessed the Emperor as well as M. Roumestain and me, and would kiss our hands. He was a Lithuanian, a native, that is, of a province of the old Poland now joined to Russia. As soon as he was well he declared that he would never serve any other than the Emperor Napoleon, so he returned to France with our wounded and was enrolled in the Polish legion. Ultimately he became a sergeant in the lancers of the guard, and whenever I came across him he testified his gratitude in broken, but expressive, language.

My icy bath, and the really superhuman efforts which I had had to make to save the poor man, might have cost me dear if I had been less young and vigorous. M. Roumestain, who did not possess the latter advantage to the same extent as I, was seized that same evening with violent congestion of the lungs, and had to be taken to the hospital, where he passed several months between life and death. He never, indeed, recovered completely, and had to leave the service invalided some years later. As for myself, though I was very weak, I got myself hoisted on to my horse when the Emperor left the lake to go to the château of Austerlitz, where his headquarters now were. Napoleon always went at a gallop, and in my shaken state this pace did not suit me; still, I kept up, because the night was coming on and I was afraid of straying; besides which, if I had gone at a walk the cold would have got hold of me. When I reached the château it took several men to help me to dismount, a shivering fit seized me, my teeth were chattering, and I was quite ill. Colonel Dahlmann, lieutenant-colonel of the mounted chasseurs, who had just been promoted to general in place of Morland, grateful doubtless for the service I had rendered his late chief, took me into one of the outbuildings of the château, where he and his officers were established. After having given me some very hot tea, his surgeon rubbed me all over with warm oil; they swaddled me in many rugs and stuck me into a great heap of hay, leaving only my face outside. Gradually a pleasant warmth penetrated my numbed limbs. I slept soundly, and thanks to all this kind care, as well as to my twenty-three years, I found myself next morning fresh and in good condition, and was able to mount my horse and witness an extremely interesting spectacle.

The defeat which the Russians had undergone had thrown their army into such disorder that all who escaped the disaster of Austerlitz made haste to reach Galicia and get out of the victor's power. The rout was complete; we took many prisoners and found the roads covered with deserted cannon and baggage. The Emperor of Russia, who had made sure of victory, went away in hopeless grief, authorizing his ally Francis II to make terms with Napoleon. On the very evening of the battle, the Emperor of Austria, to save his country from utter ruin, begged an interview of the French Emperor, and Napoleon agreeing, had halted at the village of Nasiedlowitz. The interview took place on the 4th, near the mill of Poleny, between the French and Austrian lines. I was present at this memorable meeting. Napoleon, starting very early from the château with his staff, was the first at the place of meeting. He dismounted and was strolling about when, seeing the Emperor of Austria approaching, he went towards him and embraced him cordially. A strange sight for the philosopher to reflect on! An Emperor of Germany come to humble himself by suing for peace to the son of a small Corsican family, not long ago a sub-lieutenant of artillery, whom his talents, his good fortune, and the courage of the French soldier had raised to the summit of power, and made the arbiter of the destinies of Europe!

Oriskany: 1777

BY

WALTER D. EDMONDS

In the morning, Herkimer sent out a call for all commanding officers to come to his tent. While the men were cooking breakfast they arrived. They made a knot of uniforms, bright, lighthearted, against the dark hemlock boughs. Cox with his bellicose flushed face and staring eyes; Bellinger, raw-boned, simple, honest, looking worried; Klock, stodgy, chewing snuff and still smelling faintly of manure and already sweating; Campbell's gray face freshly shaved; Fisscher, dapper and dandy in his tailor-made coat and new cocked hat; and the blackcoated, clerkly, calculating Mr. Paris. Behind them assorted captains and majors waited, watching.

Cox had the first word, as he always did.

"Well, Herkimer. Going to give us marching orders?"

"Pretty soon."

"Why not now? The sooner we get going, the sooner we'll have Sillinger making tracks for home."

"Listen, the Oneidas told me last night that Brant and Butler have got the Indians somewhere up the road. They moved down after dark. Johnson's troops ought to be there by now."

"Fine," Cox said boisterously. "We can lick the Tories and then we can tend to the regulars. Like eggs and bacon for breakfast."

Herkimer looked thoughtfully from face to face, looking for support, perhaps, or perhaps just looking for what was there. Only Bellinger was attentive—and maybe Klock.

"We won't break camp for a while," Herkimer said. "I've sent Demooth and two men up to the fort. They'll send a party out and shoot off three cannon when they do. We'll move when we hear the guns."

For a moment no one said a word. But they all looked at Herkimer in the sunshine, while the morning birds cheeped in the surrounding trees.

"You mean we've got to sit here on our arses?" demanded Cox.

"If you like to wait like that," said Herkimer. "I do not mind."

"Personally," said Fisscher, "I'm getting sick of waiting."

Herkimer said nothing.

"It's a good idea," Bellinger said loyally.

"You getting scared too?" said Paris.

From: *Drums Along the Mohawk*, by permission of Little, Brown & Co. and the Atlantic Monthly Press.

Herkimer held up his hand with the pipe in it.

"There's no sense fighting among ourselves."

"What's the matter? We'll outnumber them. The whites. We can handle the Indians on the side."

"You've never seen an Indian ambush," said Herkimer.

"Oh, my God," cried Cox, "this isn't 1757! Can't you get that through your thick German head?"

Rumor had gone down the road that the gentry were having words. The men abandoned their fires to hear the fun. Many of them left their guns behind. They pushed off the road, surrounding the clearing, till the little German seated before his tent was the focal point of over a hundred pairs of eyes.

Gil Martin, coming with the rest, listened among strangers. For over an hour the silly fatuous remarks went on. Some said you could not hear a cannon that far; some said that the three men would surely get captured; some said that probably they'd never gone to the fort at all. That was Paris's voice.

Herkimer sat in their midst with the voices flinging back and forth above his head; his shirt was still unbottoned, showing his stained woolen undershirt. Now and then he took his pipe from his lips to answer some remark that had a rudiment of sense behind it; but the rest of the time he kept his head turned to the west, listening. Apparently he was unheeding; but the men close to him could see his cheeks flexing from time to time and the slow even reddening of his skin.

It was Cox who finally touched the match.

"By Jesus Christ," he shouted in his roaring voice, "It's plain enough. Either he's scared, or else he's got interest with the British. I didn't bring my regiment this far to set and knit like girls." He looked round with his staring eyes. "Who's coming along?"

Fisscher cried, "I am."

Suddenly all the officers were shouting; and the men, following their voices, filled the woods with shouts.

It seemed to Gil that nobody was looking at Herkimer but himself. He saw the old man sitting there, his face pained, his eyes worried. He saw him knock the pipe out on his hand, blow out his breath, and lift his head.

"Listen to me, you damned fools." He used German. He was getting on his feet and yanking his coat over his arms. But his voice was enough to stop them. "Listen," he went on in English. "You don't know what you're doing, you Fisscher, Cox, the bunch of you. But if you want to fight so bad, by God Almighty, I'll take you to it."

He climbed aboard the old white horse and sat there, looking down on them for a change.

"God knows what's going to happen. But I'll tell you one thing," he said bitterly. "The ones that have been yelling so much here will be the first to pull foot if we get jumped."

For a moment they gaped at him.

"Vorwaerts!" he shouted, and put the horse toward the creek. Some of them were still standing there when he splashed through and waited on the other side. Then the officers were running to their companies, yelling, "Fall in. Fall in."

The men went scrambling through the brush to find their guns and blankets.

"March! March!" The word was in all the woods where the abandoned breakfast fires still sent up their stems of smoke among the tree trunks. Up ahead at the ford, a drummer gave the double tap of the flam. It was like the first nervous beating of a drummer partridge. It was too early for such a sound, but there it was.

Then the whips began their rapid fire along the wagon train. The cart-wheels screeched in starting. The still heat in the woods was overflowed with shouts, stamping hoofs, the rattle and slam of carts along the corduroy, the treading feet. The dust rose over the column. All at once it was jerking, getting started, moving.

At the head of the army, Cox moved his big horse beside Herkimer's. His face was triumphant, almost good-humored once more, because he had planted his will on the column. He felt half sorry for the little German farmer. But he would help the little bugger out.

The rough road went nearly straight along the level ground of the Mohawk Valley's edge, following the course of the low hill. Now and then it dipped down sharply to get over a brook. But the bottom was solidly corduroyed. The wagons didn't get stuck. They had even moved up a little on the marching men.

Blue jays squawked and fluttered off, cool spots of angry blue against the leaves. Squirrels, chattering, raced from limb to limb. A porcupine took hold of a tree and climbed it halfway, and turned his head to see the thronging, jumbled mass that heaved and started, checked, and went again along the narrow road.

The men marched in two lines, one for either rut, their rifles on their shoulders, their hats in their hands. When they came to a brook, the thirsty fell out and drank. Nobody stopped them. When they were through they wiped their mouths and looked up, startled, to see their company replaced by another. They got out of the way of other thirsty men and floundered in the bushes to catch up. There was no room left on the road to pass.

Even George Herkimer's company of rangers, who were supposed to act as scouts, would stop at a spring. And when they went ahead they crashed in the undergrowth like wild cattle. There was nobody to stop them. There were no tracks. The woods were dusty. Branches, whipping on hot faces, stung like salt. The heat grew. Not a breath of air in the branches anywhere, not a cloud in the bits of sky high overhead, nothing but leaves, nothing in all the woods but their own uproarious, bursting, unstemmable progress on the narrow road.

Gil, pushed on from behind, pushing on George Weaver just ahead of him, heard the birds singing in the dark swamp ahead. The ground fell steeply to a quiet flowing brook with a cool moss bottom. He felt his own step quicken with the instinct to drink and cool himself. Looking over George Weaver's thick round shoulders, he had a glimpse of the road turning into a causeway of logs across the stream; of George Herkimer's rangers crowding down on the crossing to make it dryshod; of the Canajoharie regiment floundering in the swamp and drinking face down by the brook; of Cox turning his red sweaty face to Herkimer and bawling, "Where did you say Butler was?"; of the two banks, precipitous and thickly clothed with a young stand of hemlocks, so soft and cool and damp and dark that it made one wish to lie down there and rest. Now he felt the ground falling under his feet, and the resistless push at his back thrusting him out on the causeway. They had passed half of Cox's regiment and were plugging up the other side. The stamp of Klock's regiment came down the bank at their backs. Behind in the woods the jangle and rattle of the carts, the steady cracking of whips, and the little futile *rattle-tats* of Fisscher's drummers. All in the moment: "I meant to get a drink of water," Reall's voice was saying at his shoulder. "So did I," said Gil. "My God," said Weaver, "what was that?"

At the top of the hemlocks a little stab of orange was mushroomed out by a black coil of smoke. They heard the crack. Cox's voice, caught short in another remark, lifted beyond reason. His big body swayed suddenly against his horse's neck. The horse reared, screamed, and, as Cox slid sack-like off his back, crashed completely over.

A shrill silver whistle sounded. Three short blasts. The young hemlocks disgorged a solid mass of fire that made a single impact on the ear. Gil felt George Weaver slam against his chest, knocking him sidewise on top of Reall. A horse screamed again and went leaping into the scrub. As he got up, Gil saw the beast fall over on his head. It was Herkimer's old white horse, galvanized into senseless vigor. He felt his arm caught and Bellinger was shouting, "Give me a hand with the old man." The old man was sitting on the causeway, holding onto his knee with both hands. His face was gray and shining and his lips moved in it.

But the voice was lost.

Gil stood before him with his back to the slope and stared down into the ravine. The militia were milling along the brook, flung down along the bank, like sticks thrown up by a freshet, kneeling, lying on their bellies, resting their rifles on the bellies of dead men. They were oddly silent. But the air around them was swept by the dull endless crash of muskets and a weird high swell of yelling from the woods.

Then beyond them he saw the Indians in the trees, adder-like, streaked with vermilion, and black, and white. From the head of the rise the first orderly discharge went over his head with a compelling, even shearing of the air, as if a hand had swung an enormous scythe. He saw the green coats on men firing at him; but he bent down and grasped the general by the knees and heaved him on up the bank while Bellinger lugged him by the armpits.

The colonel was swearing in a strange way. He wiped his mouth on his sleeve and said, "By God, Fisscher has pulled foot!"

East of the causeway, where the rear guard had been, a dwindling tide of yells and firing fled backward into the woods. They dumped the general down behind a log and fell beside him. Gil put his rifle over the log and pulled the trigger on the first green coat that filled the sights. The butt bucked against his cheek. He yanked the rifle back and tilted his powder flask to the muzzle. He saw the man he had fired at lean forward slowly in the bushes, buckle at the hips, and thump face down. He felt his insides retract, and suddenly had a queer realization that they had just returned to their proper places; and he thought with wonder at himself, "That's the first shot I've fired."

"Peter."

"Yes, Honnikol."

"It looks as if the Indians were mostly chasing after Fisscher. You'd better try and fetch the boys up here."

The little German's voice was calm.

There was no sense at first in any of it. The opening volley had been fired at ten o'clock. For the next half hour the militia lay where they had dropped, shooting up against the bank whenever they saw a flash. Their line extended roughly along the road, beginning with the disrupted welter of the wagon train, and ending at the west, just over the rise of ground, where a mixed group of Canajoharie men, and Demooth's company of the German Flats regiment, and what was left of Herkimer's rangers, made a spearhead by hugging the dirt with their bellies and doing nothing to draw attention to themselves. If the Indians had stayed put or if Fisscher had not run away, the entire army would have been destroyed.

But the Indians could not resist the temptation of chasing the terrified Fisscher. More than half of them had followed his men as far as Oriskany Creek before they gave over the attempt. And a large proportion of the rest, seeing easy scalps ready for the taking, started sneaking down out of the timber. When, at last, Bellinger began to rally the men and get them up the slope, the Indians made no attempt to follow them, for they had discovered that killing horses was an intoxicating business.

The ascent of the slope was the first orderly movement of the battle. It also revealed the initial mistake of the British side. Their flanks made no connection with the Indians, and they had to retire from the edge of the ravine to the bigger timber. It gave the Americans a foothold. They pushed to right and left along the ravine and forward with their centre, until their line made a semicircle backed on the ravine.

No single company remained intact. It was impossible to give intelligent orders, or, if that had been possible, to get them carried out. The men took to trees and fired at the flashes in front of them. And this new disposition of the battle, which remained in force till nearly eleven, was the salvation of the militia. They began to see that they could hold their own. Also it was borne in on them that to go backward across the valley would be sheer destruction.

The general, by his own orders, had been carried still farther up the slope until he could sit on the level ground under a beech tree, and see out through the tall timber. His saddle had been brought up for him to sit on, and Dr. Petry sent for. While the doctor was binding up his shattered knee, Herkimer worked with his tinder box to get a light for his pipe. Then, finally established, he looked the battle over and gave his second order of the day.

"Have the boys get two behind each tree. One hold his fire and get the Indian when he comes in."

It was an axiomatic precaution that none of the militia would have thought of for themselves. Gil, moved up behind a fallen tree, heard a crash of feet behind him, turned his head to see a black-bearded, heavy-shouldered man plunge up to him carrying an Indian spear in one hand and a musket in the other.

"You got a good place here," said the man.

He drove the butt of the spear into the ground.

"It may come handy."

"Where'd you get it?"

"Off an Indian." He turned his head. "Back there. They're scalping the dead ones. There's one of the bastards now."

He pushed his gun across the log and fired.

"Christ! I missed him. You'd better do the long shots, Bub. You've got a rifle there. I ain't a hand at this stuff."

Gil had found a loophole in the roots. He poked his gun through and waited for a sign. While he waited he said, "My name's Martin."

"Gardinier," said the bearded man. "Captain in Fisscher's regiment. Don't ask me why. We didn't have the sense to run when he did. There's fifty of us left, but I don't know where they are. Old Herkimer told me to get up in front. He said he wanted to see us run away next time."

Gardinier cursed. Gil saw a shoulder, naked, and glistening with sweat, stick out on the side of a tree. He pressed the trigger, easily. The Indian yelped. They didn't see him, but they saw the underbrush thresh madly.

"Pretty, pretty," said Gardinier. "We ought to make a partnership. You take my musket and I'll load for you. Jesus, you ain't a Mason, are you?"

"No," said Gil.

"You ought to be." He touched Gil's shoulder with the rifle barrel. "Here's your rifle, Bub."

Gil caught a spot of red over a low-lying bough. A headdress. It was a pot shot, but he let it go. The Indian whooped and the next moment he was coming in long buck jumps straight for the log. He was a thin fellow, dark-skinned like a Seneca, and stark naked except for the paint on face and chest.

Gil felt his inside tighten and rolled over to see what had become of

Gardinier. But the heavy Frenchman was grinning, showing white teeth through his beard.

He had set down his musket and taken the spear. The Indian bounded high to clear the log and Gardinier braced the spear under him as he came down. The hatchet spun out of the Indian's hand. A human surprise re-formed his painted face. The spear went in through his lower abdomen and just broke the skin between his shoulders. He screamed once. But the Frenchman lifted him, spear and all, and shoved him back over the log.

"Hell," he said. "No sense in wasting powder."

Gil turned back to face the woods. The Indian, with the spear still sticking out of him, was trying to crawl under some cover. The odd thing was that he wasn't bleeding. But he kept falling down against the spear, as if his wrists had lost their strength.

"For God's sake shoot him."

The Frenchman stuck his head over the log.

"Jesus!" he remarked. He made no motion.

The Indian heaved himself up. He half turned toward the log. Then his mouth opened, and, as if a well had been tapped by the spear, and all this time had been necessary for the blood to find its level, it poured through the open mouth, down the painted chest, turning the front of his body wet and red.

Gil yelled, jumped up, and fired straight down into the pouring face. The Indian jerked back and flopped, raising the needles with his hands.

Gardinier said, "You hadn't ought to have done that. Wasting ball that way."

"For God's sake kill the next one, then."

"All right, all right. You don't need to get mad." But after a moment, he muttered, "I wish to God I'd pulled that spear out first, though. It was a handy tool."

All a man could see was the section of woods in front of him. The woods were dark with a green gloom, made by the high tops of the hemlocks, through which the sun came feebly. The heat was stifling. There was no movement of air. Only the bullets ripped passionate sounds out of the heat.

The ravine behind the militia had long since quieted with the death of the last horse. But now and then a solitary war whoop lifted in the trees to right or left; and the answering shot was like a period marking off the time.

In the American line, out of the disruption, figures began to grow into command that had no bearing on their rank. A man who shot better than his neighbors began to give orders. Jacob Sammons on the left began the first outward movement by taking twenty men in a quick charge against the Indian flank and halting them on a low knoll of beech trees. They started a cross fire against the white troops in front, and the militia in the centre, finding the woods cleared for a space, moved forward. Gil went with them. Gardinier stood up and scouted.

"There's a first-class maple up in front," he said.

They took it in a rush. Then they had a breathing space in which they could look back. They were surprised to find that this new view disclosed men lying on the intervening ground.

Back at the edge of the ravine, old Herkimer was still smoking his pipe. He had taken his hat off and his grizzled head showed plainly from where Gil and Gardinier had taken stand.

Gardinier laughed out loud.

"Look at the old pup," he said. "I wish Fisscher was here."

Both of them realized that they had one man they could depend on, though there was nothing one man could do for them. But it was a feeling all the same.

The lull did not endure.

In the woods ahead they heard a whistle shrilling. The firing had stopped, except for sporadic outbursts way to right and left, where a few Indians still persisted.

Then Herkimer's voice came to them surprisingly loud.

"Get out your hatchets, boys. They're going to try bayonets."

To Gil it seemed as though the fight had begun all over again. Lying behind a tree was one thing. Standing up in the open was something he had not thought of.

But Gardinier suddenly found something he could understand. He heaved his great bulk up and asked, "What you got, Bub?" When Gil merely stared, "Hatchet or bagnet, son?"

Gil reached for the hatchet at his belt with stiff fingers.

"All right. You give them one shot with your rifle. I've got a bagnet." He was fixing it to the muzzle of his army musket. He wheeled back and roared, "Come on."

He seemed surprised when some of his own company came round the trees behind.

Gil saw them coming. They all saw them, in the green gloom under the trees which covered their faces with a pale shine. They were like water coming toward the militia, flowing round the tree trunks, bending down the brush, an uneven line that formed in places and broke with the shape of the ground and formed.

There was a moment of silence on both sides as the militia rose up confronting them. It was almost as if the militia were surprised. Herkimer's warning had suggested to them that regular troops were going to attack. Instead they saw only the green coats that they knew belonged to Johnson's company of Tories, and men in hunting shirts and homespun like themselves.

As the line came nearer, they saw that some of these men were the Scotch from Johnstown who had fled with Sir John. They weren't Sillinger's army at all. They were the men who had passed threats of gutting the valley wide open. For a moment the militia could hardly believe what they were seeing.

Then it seemed as if the senseless glut of war would overflow. Men fired and flung their muskets down and went for each other with their hands. The American flanks turned in, leaving the Indians where they were. The woods filled suddenly with men swaying together, clubbing rifle barrels, swinging hatchets, yelling like the Indians themselves. There were no shots. Even the yelling stopped after the first joining of the lines, and men began to go down.

The immediate silence of the woods was broken afresh. Gil, jostled and flung forward, saw a face in front of him met by a musket stock. The face seemed to burst. He swung his hatchet feebly against the arm that clubbed the musket and felt the axe ripped from his fingers. The man he had struck cried out, a small clear sound as if enunciated in a great stillness. Then Gil's ears cleared and he heard a man crying and he stepped on a body and felt it wince under his boot. The wince threw him, and he hit the dirt with his knees, and at the same time a gun exploded in front of him and he thought his whole arm had been torn away.

The boughs of the hemlocks heeled away from him, and the back of his head struck the ground and a man walked over him, three steps, down the length of his body, and he felt sick and then he forgot entirely everything but the fact that he was dying.

He did not feel any more. He was lying on the ground. It seemed to him that every needle leaf and twig on the ground stood up with painful clearness beyond any plausible dimension. A little way off someone kept yelling, "For God's sake, oh, for God's sake." He thought that if he could look he could see what the sound was, but he could not look.

Then the forest darkened. There was a blinding flash. He felt a man's hands taking hold of his shoulders. He felt himself moving backward while his legs trailed behind him. He was jerked up and put on his feet, and he knew that it was raining. He thought, "The drought's broken."

Peal after peal of thunder shook the hemlocks. The rain fell directly down, hissing on the dry ground, and raising mist in the trees. There was no sound left but the pouring rain and the continuous devastating thunder. You couldn't see when you opened your eyes. Only the tree trunks rising close to you, shining black with wet and the falling rain and the distortion of the lightning glares that lit up crooked alleys in the woods and shut them off again.

He felt himself being shaken, and a voice was saying, "Can you walk, Bub?"

He tried to walk, but his feet were overcome with a preposterous weariness.

"Put them down, Bub, put them down. Flat on your feet and stand up. Have a drink; you're all right."

He opened his eyes again and saw the beard of Gardinier matted with rain, and the wild white teeth and staring eyes of the Frenchman.

"Brandy makes the world go round," said the Frenchman. "It makes the girl handy, it makes for boys and girls, Bub. It'll fix you. Hell, you ain't only creased in one arm, and me, I've lost an ear."

The side of his face was streaming blood into his collar.

"They've quit, Bub. They're all to hell and gone. We've licked the pus clean out of them. Come on. Doc will fix you."

He sat Gil down on a mound, and then Dr. Petry's big fleshy face, muttering, looking enraged and tired, bent down. The Doc was splashing alcohol of some sort on his arm. He was being bandaged. The stinging revived him, and he looked up and saw just above him old Herkimer, white in the face now, but still puffing at his pipe, which he held in his mouth inverted against the rain.

"They'll come back," Herkimer was saying. "They're bound to. But we'll rest while it rains."

A little way off a man was eating on a log. The rest were standing, lying on the ground, steaming in the rain. Everyone looked tired, a little sick, and ugly, as if there had been a trémendous drunk a while before.

Nobody was keeping watch. They merely stood there in the rain.

The rain passed as suddenly as it had broken. The men got up and kicked other men to get up, and picked up their rifles. They drew the priming and reprimed, or loaded entirely fresh.

Gil got to his feet shakily, surprised to find his rifle still in his hand. It seemed a long time since the rain. The woods had changed so that he did not know where west lay, or east, or any direction.

Then he saw that Herkimer had moved the position so that the militia were in the centre of the level ground between the first ravine and a smaller, shallower watercourse. Any new attack would have to take them on a narrow flank, or directly up the new slope on top of which their line was formed.

The first shots came scatteringly. The Indians were firing from long range. They seemed to have lost their taste for war. They were being very careful now. Everybody was being careful. The militia stood their ground, but kept to cover.

In a line running north and south through the new position, a broken mass of men lay on the ground, like an uneven windrow of some preposterous corn. They seemed almost equally made up of militia and the green-coated troops that had come through the hemlocks. They lay in queer positions, on their arms, grasping knife or hatchet or musket, the purpose still on the blank face like an overlying plaster; or else they lay on their backs, their empty hands flung out as if to catch the rain.

The militia stepped over this line impersonally. There was an Indian transfixed to a tree by a bayonet, waist high, with his legs dangling life-lessly against the ground. But he kept his eyes open and the eyes seemed to Gil to turn as he went by.

A little way along a face struck him as familiar. He looked at it again. The possessor of the face had fallen with his chin over a log so that the face was tilted up. Gil looked at it curiously before he recognized it for Christian Reall's face. He had been scalped. The top of his head looked flat and red; and the circumcision of the crown had allowed the muscles to give way so that his cheeks hung down in jowls, tugging his eyes open and showing enormous bloody underlids.

The two armies merely sniped at each other for an hour. Then the second attack by the enemy developed from the southwest along the level ground. At first the militia mistook them for reënforcements from the fort. The direction they came from and the fact that they had pinned up their hat brims to look like the tricorn hats of Continental soldiers were deceptive.

The militia broke cover, cheering, and rushed forward to shake hands, and the enemy let them come. There was no firing. It was only at the last moment that the sun came through the wet trees, dazzling all the ground and showing the bright green of the approaching company.

Gil was not in the direct contact of the two companies. From where he stood he seemed divorced from the whole proceeding.

But another company of green coats was coming round the first in his direction, with the same quiet march, and the same bright glitter on their advanced bayonets.

He became aware of the instinct to run away. It suddenly occurred to him that he was hungry. Not merely hungry as one is at supper or break-fast; but a persisting, all-consuming gnawing in his intestines that moved and hurt. He felt that it was not worth staying for. He was too tired. And the oncoming men looked tired. And it seemed to take forever for them to make a contact. But they came like people who couldn't stop themselves, while he himself could not make his feet move to carry him away.

They made less noise. The rainstorm which had broken the drought had not had power to take the dryness from their throats. They seemed to strike each other with preposterous slow weary blows, which they were too slow to dodge, and they fell down under them preposterously.

It couldn't last.

Gil found himself standing alone in the militia. There were a few men near him, but there was no one whose face he recognized. They kept look-ing at each other as if they would have liked to speak.

On the flank, the firing continued where the Indians still skirmished. But that, too, broke off except for stray shots, the last survivors of all the holocaust of firing.

The Indians were calling in the woods. A high barbaric word, over and over. "*Oonah, Oonah, Oonah.*" Suddenly a man shouted, "They've pulled foot!"

At first they thought another thunderstorm had started. Then they realized that what they had heard, with such surprising force, had been three successive cannon shots.

The messengers had reached the fort, and the garrison was making a diversion.

A deliberate understanding gradually dawned on all their faces. They leaned on their rifles and looked round. The woods were empty, but for themselves, for their dead, and for the enemy dead. The living enemy had run away.

Those that could walk began a retrograde movement to the knoll on which Herkimer was sitting under his tree. The old man was looking at them; his black eyes, yet ardent, passing feverishly from face to face, and then turning slowly to the lines of dead.

One of the officers spoke fatuously, "Do we go on to the fort now, Honnikol?" He paused, swallowed, and said, as if to excuse himself, "We know they know we're here."

The little German swung his eyes to the speaker. The eyes filled and he put his hand over them.

Peter Bellinger and Peter Tygert came up to him and touched his shoulder. They said to the officer, "We can't move forward."

They picked Herkimer up by the arms.

"I can't walk, boys." He swallowed his tears noisily. "There's still Sillinger up there. With the British regulars there ain't enough of us. I think we'd better go home."

He asked first that the live men be assembled and counted. It was a slow business, getting them to their feet and lining them up under the trees. The earth was still steaming from the rain. There was a sick smell of blood from the ravine.

The naming of men took too long. The officers went along the wavering lines, cutting notches in sticks for every ten men. They figured that after Fisscher pulled foot with the Mohawk company there had been about six hundred and fifty concerned in the ambush and battle. Out of them about two hundred were judged able to walk. There were forty more who were not dead. How many had been killed and how many taken prisoner no one could say.

Stretchers were made of coats and poles, and the worst wounded were piled onto them. Those who were not acting as bearers dully reprimed or loaded their guns. They started east.

It seemed a long way to the ravine where the battle had started. It seemed a long time, longer than they could remember, since they had seen it last. It was sunset by the time they reached Oriskany Creek.

From there men were sent ahead to order boats rowed up the Mohawk, to meet the wounded at the ford. The whole army lay down when they reached the ford. They lay in the darkness, along the edge of the sluggish river, until the boats came up. They were apathetic.

Only when the boats arrived did they get onto their feet and help put the wounded men in. Several of them afterwards remembered Herkimer's face in the light of the fire. He had stopped smoking, though the pipe was still fast in his teeth. He wasn't saying anything. He sat still, holding onto his knee.

At the time they had just stood around watching him being loaded aboard the boat and laid out in the bottom. Then they had been told to march through the ford, and along the road. They went wearily, too exhausted to talk, even to think. And tired as they were, they were forced to do the same march they had taken three days to make on the way up.

They did not look at the terrified white faces of the people when they came to the settlement. They were too exhausted to see. The word had already gone down the river. People were expecting the appearance of the enemy.

It was a calamity. The army had looked so big going west that nobody had thought they would not get through to the fort. Now they were back; they looked licked, and they acted licked, and they had not even met the regulars. It was pointless to think that the enemy had left the scene of battle before they had.

An officer, some said afterwards that it was Major Clyde, yelled from the foot of the fort stockade that they were dismissed. They were to go home and try to rest while they could. They should expect another summons very soon.

But the men did not stop to listen to him. Ever since they had come out of the woods at Schuyler they had been dropping from the ranks. The instinct to get home was irresistible. They weren't an army any more, and they knew it better than anyone could have told them.

The Marines at Soissons

BY

COLONEL JOHN W. THOMASON, JR.

I

In the town of Villers-Nancy, where the battalion billeted, they published this order to the troops:

No. 862'3

Ordre Général No. 318

Xe Armée
État-Major
3e Bureau   AuQGA 30 July 18

Officers, Non-Commissioned Officers and Soldiers of the Third United States Army Corps:

Shoulder to shoulder with your French comrades you were thrown into the counter-offensive battle which commenced on the 18th of July. You rushed to the attack as to a festival. Your magnificent courage completely routed a surprised enemy and your indomitable tenacity checked the counter-attacks of his fresh divisions. You have shown yourselves worthy sons of your great country, and you were admired by your comrades-in-arms.

Ninety-one guns, 7,200 prisoners, immense booty, 10 kilomètres of country liberated; this is your portion of the spoil of this victory. Furthermore, you have demonstrated your superiority over the barbarian enemy of all mankind. To attack him is to vanquish him.

American comrades! I am grateful to you for the blood so generously spilled on the soil of my country. I am proud to have commanded you during such days, and to have fought with you for the deliverance of the world.

(Signed)   MANGIN.

THE 1st Battalion lay in Croutte-sur-Marne. It drank deep of the golden July weather, and swam noisily in the Marne, which swung a blue and shining loop below the town. The battalion took but little interest in the war, which could be heard growling and muttering intermittently to the north and east. Indeed, the unpleasant Bois-de-Belleau-Bouresches area

From: *Fix Bayonets.* Copyright 1925, by Scribners.

was only a few hours' march distant, and Château-Thierry was just up the river. The guns were loud and continuous in that direction.

But the 2d American Division—Marines and troops of the Regular Army—had just finished a hitch of some thirty-eight days attacking and holding and attacking again, from Hill 142, on the left, through that ghastly wood which the French now called the "Bois de la Brigade de Marine," to Vaux, on the right; and in this battalion, as in the other units of the division, such men as had survived were quite willing to think about something else.

Division Headquarters were over Montreuil way, and thither certain distinguished individuals were ordered, to return with crosses on their faded blouses. This furnished pleasant food for gossip and speculation. Then, vin rouge and vin blanc were to be had, as well as fresh milk for the less carnally minded, and such supplements to the ration were always matters of interest. Also, there were certain buxom mademoiselles among the few civilian families who lingered here in the teeth of the war, and although every girl was watched by lynx-eyed elders early and late, their very presence was stimulating and they were all inclined to be friendly.

The most delightful diversion of all was discussion of the rumor that rose up and ran through the companies: "Got it hot from a bird that was talkin' to a dog-robber at Brigade H. Q.—the division is gonna be sent back to St. Denis for a month's rest, an' leaves, an' everything!" "Yeh! we gonna parade in Paris, too." It was ascertained that St. Denis was right near Paris. Platoon commanders were respectfully approached: "Beggin' the lootenant's pardon, but does the lootenant think that we—" The lieutenants looked wise and answered vaguely and asked the captains. All ranks hung upon the idea.

July 14 came. "Sort o' Frog Fourth o' July," explained a learned corporal, standing in line for morning chow.

"In Paris, they's parades, an' music, an' fireworks, an' all that kinder thing. Speakin' an' barbecues, like back home. Celebratin' the time the Frogs rose agin 'em an' tore down some noted brig or other they had. Now, if I wuz in Paree now, sittin' in front of the Caffey de Pay—!"

"Don't try to go there, Corp. J'seen the cellar they's got fer a brig here?—If you—"

"Don't see no flag-wavin' or such celebrations here. Seen one little Frog kid with his gas-mask an' a Frog flag down the street—no more. Why back home, even in tank towns like this, on the Fourth—"

As a matter of fact, Croutte took on this day no especial joy in the far-off fall of the Bastille. Croutte was in range of the Boche heavy artillery; one could perceive, at the end of this street where, in effect, the house of M'sieu' le Maire had been! An obus of two hundred and twenty centimètres. And others, regard you, near the bridge. Some descended into the river, the naughty ones, and killed many fish. Also, the avions—

Did it not appear to Messieurs les Officiers that the cannon were louder this day, especially toward Rheims? And as the day went on, it did appear so. In the afternoon a Boche came out of a cloud and shot down in flames the fat observation balloon that lived just up the river from Croutte. The rumor of St. Denis and fourteen-day leaves waned somewhat. Certainly there grew to be a feeling in the air. . . .

About one o'clock the morning of the 15th the Boche dropped nine-inch shells into the town. The battalion was turned out, and stood under arms in the dark while the battalion gas officer sniffed around busily to see if the shells were the gas variety. They were not, but the battalion, after the shelling stopped and the casualties were attended to, observed that in the east a light not of the dawn was putting out the stars. The eastern sky was all aflame with gun-flashes, and a growing thunder shook the still air.

The files remarked that they were glad not to be where all that stuff was lightin', and after breakfast projected the usual swimming parties. Aquatic sports were then vetoed by regretful platoon commanders, since it appeared that Battalion H. Q. had directed the companies to hold themselves in readiness for instant movement to an unspecified place. Thereupon the guns eastward took on a more than professional interest. The civilians looked and listened also. Their faces were anxious. They had heard that noise before. The hot July hours passed; the battalion continued to be held in readiness, and got practically no sleep in consequence. There was further shelling, and the guns were undoubtedly louder—and nearer.

Breakfast on the 16th was scant, and the cooks held out little encouragement for lunch. Lunch was an hour early, and consisted of beans. "Boys, we're goin' somewhere. We always gets beans to make a hike on." "Yeh! an' you always gets more than two-men rates—standin' in line for fourths, now!"—"What's that sergeant yellin' about—fill yo' canteens? Gonna get ving blonk in mine!"

At noon, the rolling kitchens packed up and moved off, nobody knew where. The battalion regarded their departure soberly. "Wish I hadn't et my reserve rations. . . ." The shadows were lengthening when the bugles blew "assembly" and the companies fell in, taking the broad white road that led down the river. At the next town—towns were thick along the Marne from Château-Thierry to Meaux—they passed through the other battalions of the 5th Marines, jeeringly at ease beside the road. Greetings were tossed about, and the files gibed at each other. "Where you bums goin'?" "Dunno—don' care—But you see the ole 1st Battalion is leadin', as usual!" "Aw . . . Close up! close up!"

Beyond them was the 6th Regiment of Marines, arms stacked in the fields by the river. Each battalion took the road in turn, and presently the whole Marine Brigade was swinging down the Marne in the slanting sunlight. Very solid and businesslike the brigade was, keen-faced and gaunt and hard from the great fight behind them, and fit and competent for greater battles yet to come. The companies were under strength, but they had the quality of veterans. They had met the Boche and broken him, and they knew they could do it again. The rumble of the guns was behind them, and the rumor of the leave area still ran strong enough to maintain a slow volubility among the squads. They talked and laughed, but they did not sing. Veterans do not sing a great deal.

It was getting dusk when the 1st Battalion of the 5th, leading, rounded a turn in the road and came upon an endless column of camions, drawn up along the river road as far as one could see. The companies became silent.

"Camions! They rode us to Chatto-Terry in them busses—" "Yeh! an' it was a one-way trip for a hell of a lot of us, too!" "Close up! Close up an' keep to the right of the road."

"Camions! That's a sign they want us bad, somewhere on the line," commented the lean first lieutenant who hiked at the head of the 49th Company. "Walter"—to the officer beside him—"I wonder what happened yesterday an' to-day, with all that shooting." "Don't know—but this Château-Thierry salient is mighty deep an' narrow, unless the Boche spread himself yesterday. . . . If we were to break into it, up near one of the corners . . ." "Yes! Well, we're right on the tip of it here—can jump either way—Lord! there's a lot of these conveyances."

Later the battalion knew what had happened on July 15, when the Boche made his final cast across the Champagne country toward Rheims and Épernay; and his storm divisions surged to the Marne, and stayed, and lapped around the foot of the gray Mountain of Rheims, and stayed. Just now the battalion cared for none of these things. It had no supper; it faced a crowded trip of uncertain duration, and was assured of various discomforts after that.

Well accustomed to the ways of war, the men growled horribly as they crammed into their appointed chariots, while the officers inexorably loaded the best part of a platoon into each camion, the dusk hiding their grins of sympathy. "Get aboard! get aboard! Where'll you put yo' pack? Now what the hell do I know about yo' pack—want a special stateroom an' a coon vallay, do yuh, yuh—!" The sergeants didn't grin. They swore, and the men swore, and they raged altogether. But, in much less time than it took to tell about it afterward, the men were loaded on. The officers were skilled and prompt in such matters.

Wizened Annamites from the colonies of France drove the camions. Presently, with clangor and much dust, they started their engines, and the camion train jolted off down the river road. A red moon shone wanly through the haze. The Marne was a silver thread through the valley of a dream, infinitely aloof from the gasoline-smelling tumult. . . . "Valley of the Marne! . . . the Marne . . . some of us will not see you again. . . ."

A camion, as understood by the French, is a motor-vehicle with small wheels and no springs to speak of. It finds every hole in the road, and makes an unholy racket; but it covers ground, the roadbed being of no consequence, as the suffering files bore witness. To the lieutenant of the 49th, nursing his cane on the driver's seat of a lurching camion, beside two Annamitish heathen who smelt like camels and chattered like monkeys, came scraps of conversation from the compressed platoon behind him. "Sardines is comfortable to what we is! . . ." "Chevawz forty—hommes eight! Lord forgive us, I uster kick about them noble box cars. . . ." ". . . They say it was taxicabs an' motor-trucks that won the first battle of the Marne—yeh! If they rushed them Frogs up packed like this, you know they felt like fightin' when they got out!" . . . "I feel like fightin' now!—take yo' laigs outer my shortribs, you big embuskay."

"Night before last they shelled us, an' we stood by last night—when do we sleep?—that's what I wanna know—" But sleeping isn't done in camions. The dust on the road rose thick and white around the train, and rode with it through the night. The face of the moon, very old and wise, peered down through the dust. They left the river, and by the testimony of the stars it seemed to the lieutenant that they were hurrying north. Always, on the right, the far horizon glowed with the fires of war—flares, signal-lights, gun-flashes from hidden batteries; the route paralleled the line. The lieutenant visualized his map: "Followin' the salient around—to the north—the north—Soissons way, or Montdidier. . . . The Boche took Soissons. . . ."

Quiet French villages along the road, stone houses like gray ghosts under the pale moon, and all lights hooded against Boche planes. Lone, empty stretches of road. Shadowy columns of French infantry, overtaken and passed. Horse-drawn batteries of 75s on the move. Swift staff cars that dashed by, hooting. Then, long files of horsemen, cloaked and helmeted, with a ghostly glint of lanceheads over them—French cavalry. Presently, dawn, with low clouds piling up in the rosy sky. And along the road, wherever there were groves, more cavalry was seen, at ease under the trees. Horses were picketed, lances and sabres stuck into the ground, and cooking-fires alight.

The Marines had not met the French horse before. They now looked approvingly upon them. Men and horses were alike big and well-conditioned. All morning the camions passed through a country packed with troops and guns, wherever there was cover from the sky. Something big was in the air.

It was mid-forenoon when the train stopped, and the battalion climbed out on cramped legs. "Fall in on the right of the road. . . . Platoon commanders, report. . . . Keep fifty yards' distance between platoons. . . . Squads right. . . . March!" and the companies moved off stiffly, on empty stomachs. The little dark Annamites watched the files pass with incurious eyes. They had taken many men up to battle.

II

Company by company, the 1st Battalion passed on, and behind them the other battalions of the 5th Marines took the road and, after them, the 6th. "None of the wagons, or the galleys—don't see the machine-gun outfits, either," observed the lieutenant of the 49th Company, looking back from the crest of the first low hill. Here the battalion was halted, having marched for half an hour, to tighten slings and settle equipment for the real business of hiking. "They may get up to-night, chow an' all—wonder how far we came, an' where we're goin'. No, sergeant—can't send for water here—my canteen's empty, too. All I know about it is that we seem to be in a hurry."

The dust of the ride had settled thick, like fine gray masks, on the men's faces, and one knew that it was just as thick in their throats! Of course the canteens, filled at Croutte, were finished. The files swore through cracked lips.

The battalion moved off again, and the major up forward set a pace all disproportionate to his short legs. When the first halt came, the usual ten-minute rest out of the hour was cut to five. "Aw hell! forced march!" "An' the lootenant has forgot everything but 'close up! close up!'—Listen to him—"

The camions had set them down in a gently rolling country, unwooded, and fat with ripening wheat. Far across it, to the north, blue with distance, stood a great forest, and toward this forest the battalion marched, talkative, as men are in the first hour of the hike, before the slings of the pack begin to cut into your shoulders. . . . "Look at them poppies in the wheat."— "They ain't as red as the poppies were the mornin' of the 6th of June, when we went up to Hill 142—" "Yep! Beginnin' to fade some. It's gettin' late in the season." "Hi—I'm beginnin' to fade some myself—this guerre is wearin' on a man . . . remember how they looked in the wheat that mornin', just before we hit the Maxim guns?—red as blood—" "Pore old Jerry Finnegan picked one and stuck it in the buckle of his helmet—I seen it in his tin hat after he was killed, there behin' the Hill. . . . I'll always think about poppies an' blood together, as long as I live—" This last from little Tritt, the lieutenant's orderly.

"Long as you live—that's good!" gibed Corporal Snair, of the Company Headquarters group. "Don't you know by now how expendable you bucks are?"—The lieutenant heard, and remembered it, oddly enough, in a crowded moment the next day, when he lost the two of them to a hard-fought Maxim gun.

No wind moved across the lonely wheatland; the bearded stalks waved not at all, and the sun-drenched air was hot and dead. Sweat made muddy runnels through the thick white dust that masked the faces of the men. Conversation languished; what was said was in profane monosyllables. Clouds came up, and there were showers of rain, with hot sunshine between. Uniforms steamed after each shower, and thirst became a torture. The man who had the vin blanc in his canteen fell out and was quite ill. "Hikin'—in—a dam'—Turkish bath—"

After interminable hours, the column came to the forest and passed from streaming sunshine into sultry shades. It was a noble wood of great high-branching trees, clean of underbrush as a park. Something was doing in the forest. Small-arms ammunition was stacked beside the road, and there were dumps of shells and bombs under the trees. And French soldiers everywhere. This road presently led into a great paved highway, and along it were more of the properties of war—row upon row of every caliber of shell, orderly stacks of winged aerial bombs, pile after pile of rifle and machine-gun ammunition, and cases of hand-grenades and pyrotechnics. There were picket-lines of cavalry, and park after park of artillery, light and heavy. There were infantrymen with stacked rifles.

Gunner and horseman and poilu, they looked amicably upon the sweating Marines, and waved their hands with naïve Gallic friendliness. The battalion came out of its weariness and responded in kind. "Say, where do they get that stuff about little Frenchmen? Look at that long-sparred horse soldier yonder—seven feet if he's an inch!"—"Them gunners is fine men, too. All the runts in the Frog army is in the infantry!"—"Well, if these Frawgs fights accordin' to their size, Gawd pity the old Boche when that cavalry gets after him—lances an' all!" "You said it! Them little five-foot-nothin' infantry, with enough on they backs, in the way o' tents an' pots an' pans, to set up light housekeepin' wit', and that long squirrel gun they carry, an' that knittin'-needle bayonet—! Remember how they charged at Torcy, there on the left—?"

The French were cooking dinner beside the road. For your Frenchmen never fights without his kitchens and a full meal under his cartridge-pouches. They go into the front line with him, the kitchens and the chow, and there is always the coffee avec rhum, and the good hot soup that smells so divinely to the hungry Americans, passing empty. "When we goes up to hit the old Boche, we always says adoo to the galleys till we comes out again—guess the idea is to starve us so we'll be mad, like the lions in them glad-i-a-tor-ial mills the corp'ril was tellin' about."—"Hell! we don't eat, it seems—them Frawgs might at least have the decency to keep their home cookin' where we can't smell it!"

The highway led straight through the forest. Many roads emptied into it, and from every road debouched a stream of horses, men, and guns. The battalion went into column of twos, then into column of files, to make room. On the left of the road, abreast of the Marines, plodded another column of foot—strange black men, in the blue greatcoats of the French infantry and mustard-yellow uniforms under them. Their helmets were khaki-colored, and bore a crescent instead of the bursting bomb of the French line. But they marched like veterans, and the Marines eyed them approvingly. Between the foot, the road was level-full of guns and transport, moving axle to axle, and all moving in the same direction. In this column were tanks, large and small, all ring-streaked and striped with camouflage, mounting one-pounders and machine-guns; and the big ones, short-barrelled 75s.

The tanks were new to the Marines. They moved with a horrific clanging and jangling, and stunk of petrol. "Boy, what would you do if you seen one of them little things comin' at you? The big ones is males, and the little ones is females, the lootenant says. . . ." "Chillun, we're goin' into somethin' big—Dunno what, but it's big!"

The sultry afternoon passed wearily, and at six o'clock the battalion turned off the road, shambling and footsore, and rested for two hours. They found water and filled canteens. A few of the hardier made shift to wash. "Gonna smear soapsuds an' lather all over me—the Hospital Corps men say it keeps off mustard-gas!" But most of the men dropped where the platoon broke ranks and slept. Battalion H. Q. sent for all company commanders.

Presently the lieutenant of the 49th returned, with papers and a map. He called the company officers around him, and spread the map on the ground. He spoke briefly.

"We're in the Villers-Cotterets woods—the Forêt de Retz. At H hour on D day, which I think is to-morrow morning, although the major didn't say, we attack the Boche here"—pointing—"and go on to here—past the town of Vierzy. Eight or nine kilomètres. Three objectives—marked—so—and so. The 2d Division with one of the infantry regiments leading, and the 5th Marines, attacks with the 1st Moroccan Division on our left. The Frog Foreign Legion is somewhere around too, and the 1st American Division. It's Mangin's Colonial Army—the bird they call the butcher.

"The 49th Company has the division's left, and we're to keep in touch with the French over there. They're Senegalese—the niggers you saw on the road, and said to be bon fighters. The tanks will come behind us through the woods, and take the lead as soon as we hit the open.

"No special instructions, except, if we are held up any place, signal a tank by wavin' a rag or something on a bayonet, in the direction of the obstacle, and the tank will do the rest.

"No rations, an' we move soon. See that canteens are filled. Now go and explain it all to your platoons, and—better take a sketch from this map—it's the only one I have. Impress it on everybody that the job is to maintain connection between the Senegalese on the left and our people. Tritt, I'm goin' to catch a nap—wake me when we move—"

It was dark when the battalion fell in and took the road again. They went into single file on the right, at the very edge of it, for the highway was jammed with three columns of traffic, moving forward. It began to rain, and the night, there under the thick branches, was inconceivably black. The files couldn't see the man ahead, and each man caught hold of the pack in front and went feeling for the road with his feet, clawing along with the wheels and the artillery horses and machine-gun mules. On the right was a six-foot ditch, too deep in mud to march in. The rain increased to a sheeted downpour and continued all night, with long rolls of thunder, and white stabs of lightning that intensified the dark. The picked might of France and America toiled on that road through the Villers-Cotterets forest that night, like a great flowing river of martial force. . . .

And after the 5th Marines have forgotten the machine-guns that sowed death in the wheat behind Hill 142, and the shrapnel that showered down at Blanc Mont, before St. Étienne, they will remember the march to the Soissons battle, through the dark and the rain. . . .

As guns and caissons slewed sideways across the files, or irate machine-gun mules plunged across the tangle, the column slowed and jammed and halted on heavy feet; then went on again to plunge blindly against the next obstacle. Men fell into the deep ditch and broke arms and legs. Just to keep moving was a harder test than battle ever imposed. The battalion was too tired to swear. "I'm to where—I have to think about movin' my feet—! Plant—the left foot—an'—advance the right—an'—bring up the—left foot—an'—"

No battle ever tried them half as hard as the night road to Soissons. . . .

The rain ceased, and the sky grew gray with dawn. The traffic thinned, and the battalion turned off on a smaller road, closed up, and hurried on. Five minutes by the side of the road to form combat packs and strip to rifle and bayonet. "Fall in quickly! Forward!"

Overhead the clouds were gone; a handful of stars paled and went out; day was coming. The battalion, lightened, hastened. They perceived, dimly, through a mist of fatigue, that a cloudless day was promised and that the world was wonderfully new washed and clean—and quiet! Not a gun any-where, and the mud on the road muffled the sound of hobnailed boots. "Double time! Close up! Close up, there!"

There had been fighting here; there were shell-holes, scarred and splintered trees. The battalion panted to a crossroads, where stone buildings lay all blasted by some gale of shell-fire. And by the road what looked like a well! The files swayed toward it, clutching at dry canteens—"Back in ranks! Back in ranks, you—!"

Then, barbed wire across the roadway, and battered shallow trenches to right and left, and a little knot of French and American officers, Major Turrill standing forward. The leading company turned off to the left, along the trenches. The 49th followed in column. "Turn here," ordered the major. "Keep on to the left until you meet the Moroccans, and go for-ward. . . ." The 49th went beyond the trench, still in column of route, picking its way through the woods. The lieutenant looked back at his men as he went; their faces were gray and drawn and old; they were staggering with weariness—"Fix bayonets—" and the dry click of the steel on the locking-ring ran along the ragged column, loud in the hush of dawn.

III

It was 4.35, the morning of July 18.

Miles of close-laid batteries opened with one stupendous thunder. The air above the tree-tops spoke with unearthly noises, the shriek and rumble of light and heavy shells. Forward through the woods, very near, rose up a continued crashing roar of explosions, and a murk of smoke, and a hell of bright fires continually renewed. It lasted only five minutes, that barrage, with every French and American gun that could be brought to bear firing at top speed. But they were terrible minutes for the unsuspecting Boche. Dazed, beaten down, and swept away, he tumbled out of his holes when it lifted, only to find the long bayonets of the Americans licking like flame across his forward positions, and those black devils, the Senegalese, raging with knives in his rifle-pits. His counter-barrage was slow and weak, and when it came the shells burst well behind the assaulting waves, which were already deep in his defenses.

The 49th Company, running heavily, sodden with weariness, was plunging through a line of wire entanglements when the guns opened. A French rifleman squatted in a hole under the wire, and a sergeant bent over him and shouted: "Combien—how far—damn it, how you say?—combien—kilomètre—à la Boche?" The Frenchman's eyes bulged. He did violent things with his arms. "Kilomèt'? *kilomètres?* Mon Dieu, cent mètres! Cent mètres!" Half the company, still in column, was struggling in the wire when, from the tangle right in front, a machine-gun dinned fiercely and rifle-fire ran to left and right through the woods.

It was well that the woods were a little open in that spot, so that the lieutenant's frantic signals could be seen, for no voice could have been heard. And it was more than well that every man there had been shot over enough not to be gun-shy. They divined his order, they deployed to the left, and they went forward yelling. That always remained, to the lieutenant, the marvel of the Soissons fight—how those men, two days without food, three nights without sleep, after a day and a night of forced marching, flung off their weariness like a discarded piece of equipment, and at the shouting of the shells sprang fresh and eager against the German line.

Liaison—to keep the touch—was his company's mission—the major's last order. To the left were only the smoky woods—no Senegalese in sight—and to the left the lieutenant anxiously extended his line, throwing out the last two platoons, while the leading one shot and stabbed among the first Boche machine-guns. He himself ran in that direction, cursing and stumbling in wire and fallen branches, having no time for certain Boches who fired at him over a bush. . . . Finally, Corbett, the platoon commander, leading to the left, turned and waved his arms. And through the trees he saw the Senegalese—lean, rangy men in mustard-colored uniforms, running with their bayonets all aslant. He turned back toward his company with the sweetest feeling of relief that he had ever known; he had his contact established; his clever and war-wise company would attend to keeping it, no matter what happened to him.

The battle roared into the wood. Three lines of machine-guns, echeloned, held it. Here the Forêt de Retz was like Dante's wood, so shattered and tortured and horrible it was, and the very trees seemed to writhe in agony. Here the fury of the barrage was spent, and the great trunks, thick as a man's body, were sheared off like weed-stalks; others were uprooted and lay gigantic along the torn earth; big limbs still crashed down or swayed half-severed; splinters and débris choked the ways beneath. A few German shells fell among the men—mustard-gas; and there in the wet woods one could see the devilish stuff spreading slowly, like a snaky mist, around the shell-hole after the smoke had lifted.

Machine-guns raved everywhere; there was a crackling din of rifles, and the coughing roar of hand-grenades. Company and platoon commanders lost control—their men were committed to the fight—and so thick was the going that anything like formation was impossible. It was every man for himself, an irregular, broken line, clawing through the tangles, climbing over fallen trees, plunging heavily into Boche rifle-pits. Here and there a well-fought Maxim gun held its front until somebody—officer, non-com, or private—got a few men together and, crawling to left or right, gained a flank and silenced it. And some guns were silenced by blind, furious rushes that left a trail of writhing khaki figures, but always carried two or three frenzied Marines with bayonets into the emplacement; from whence would come shooting and screaming and other clotted unpleasant sounds, and then silence.

From such a place, with four men, the lieutenant climbed, and stood leaning on his rifle, while he wiped the sweat from his eyes with a shaking hand. Panting, white or red after their nature—for fighting takes men differently, as whiskey does—the four grouped around him. One of them squatted and was very sick. And one of them, quite young and freckled, explored a near-by hole and prodded half a dozen Boches out of it, who were most anxious to make friends. The other three took interest in this, and the Boches saw death in their eyes. They howled like animals, these big hairy men of Saxony, and capered in a very ecstasy of terror. The freckled Marine set his feet deliberately, judging his distance, and poised his bayonet. The lieutenant grasped his arm— "No! No! take 'em back— they've quit. Take 'em to the rear, I tell you!" The freckled one obeyed, very surly, and went off through the tangle to the rear. The lieutenant turned and went on.

To left and right he caught glimpses of his men, running, crawling, firing as they went. In a clearing, Lieutenant Appelgate, of the 17th Company, on the right, came into view. He waved his pistol and shouted something. He was grinning. . . . All the men were grinning . . . it was a bon fight, after all. . . .

Then little Tritt, his orderly, running at his side, went down, clawing at a bright jet of scarlet over his collar. The war became personal again—a keening sibilance of flesh-hunting bullets, ringing under his helmet. He found himself prone behind a great fallen tree, with a handful of his men; bark and splinters were leaping from the round trunk that sheltered them.

"You"—to a panting half-dozen down the log—"crawl back to the stump and shoot into that clump of green bushes over there, where you see the new dirt—it's in there! Everything you've got, and watch for me up ahead. Slover"—to Sergeant Robert Slover, a small, fiery man from Tennessee—"come on."

They crawled along the tree. Back toward the stump the Springfields crackled furiously. Somewhere beyond the machine-gun raved like a mad thing, and the Boches around it threw hand-grenades that made much smoke and noise. The two of them left the protection of the trunk, and felt remarkably naked behind a screen of leaves. They crawled slowly, stopping to peer across at the bushes. The lieutenant caught the dull gleam of a round gray helmet, moved a little, and saw the head and the hands of the Boche who worked the gun. He pushed the sergeant with his foot and, moving very carefully, got his rifle up and laid his cheek against the stock. Over his sights, the German's face, twenty metres away, was intent and serious. The lieutenant fired, and saw his man half-rise and topple forward on the gun.

Then things happened fast. Another German came into view straining to tear the fallen gunner off the firing mechanism. Slover shot him. There was another, and another. Then the bush boiled like an ant-heap, and a feld-webel sprang out with a grenade, which he did not get to throw. It went off, just the same, and the Marines from the other end of the tree came with bayonets. . . . Presently they went on. . . . "There's a squad of them bastards to do orderly duty for the corp'ral an' little Tritt," said the sergeant. "Spread out more, you birds."

Afterward, sweating and panting, the freckled one who had started back with prisoners caught up with the lieutenant. "Lootenant, sir!" he gasped, wiping certain stains from his bayonet with his sleeve. "Them damn Heinies tried to run on me, an' I jest natcherly had to shoot 'em up a few—" and he looked guilelessly into the officer's eyes. "Why you—Hell! . . . fall in behind me, then, an' come along. Need another orderly."

He pondered absently on the matter of frightfulness as he picked his way along. There were, in effect, very few prisoners taken in the woods that morning. It was close-up, savage work. "But speakin' of frightfulness, one of these nineteen-year-olds, with never a hair to his face—" A spitting gust of machine-gun bullets put an end to extraneous musings.

Later, working to the left of his company, he was caught up in a fighting swirl of Senegalese and went with them into an evil place of barbed wire and machine-guns. These wild black Mohammedans from West Africa were enjoying themselves. Killing, which is at best an acquired taste with the civilized races, was only too palpably their mission in life. Their eyes rolled, and their splendid white teeth flashed in their heads, but here all resemblance to a happy Southern darky stopped. They were deadly. Each platoon swept its front like a hunting-pack, moving swiftly and surely together. The lieutenant felt a thrill of professional admiration as he went with them.

The hidden guns that fired on them were located with uncanny skill; they worked their automatic rifles forward on each flank until the doomed emplacement was under a scissors fire; then they took up the matter with the bayonet, and slew with lion-like leaps and lunges and a shrill barbaric yapping. They took no prisoners. It was plain that they did not rely on rifle-fire or understand the powers of that arm—to them a rifle was merely something to stick a bayonet on—but with the bayonet they were terrible, and the skill of their rifle grenadiers and automatic-rifle men always carried them to close quarters without too great loss.

They carried also a broad-bladed knife, razor-sharp, which disembowelled a man at a stroke. The slim bayonet of the French breaks off short when the weight of a body pulls down and sidewise on it; and then the knives come out. With reason the Boche feared them worse than anything living, and the lieutenant saw in those woods unwounded fighting Germans who flung down their rifles when the Senegalese rushed, and covered their faces, and stood screaming against the death they could not look upon. And—in a lull, a long, grinning sergeant, with a cruel acquiline face, approached him and offered a brace of human ears, nicely fresh, strung upon a thong. "B'jour, Americain! Voilà! Beaucoup souvenir ici—bon! Désirez-vous? Bon—!"

Later, on the last objective, there was a dignified Boche major of infantry, who came at discretion out of a deep dugout, and spoke in careful English: "Und I peg of you, Herr Leutnant, to put me under trusty guard of your Americans true-and-tried! Ja! These black savages, of the art of war most ignorant, they would kill us prave Germans in cold plood! . . . The Herr General Mangin, that"—here a poignant string of gutturals—"I tell you, Herr Leutnant, der very name of Mangin, it is equal to fünf divisions on unser front!"

Back with his own men again, the company whittled thin! Was there no limit to the gloomy woods? . . . Light through the trees yonder!—

The wood ended, and the attack burst out into the rolling wheat-land, where the sun shone in a cloudless sky and poppies grew in the wheat. To the right, a great paved road marched, between tall poplars, much battered. On the road two motor-trucks burned fiercely, and dead men lay around them. Across the road a group of stone farm-buildings had been shelled into a smoking dust-heap, but from the ruins a nest of never-die machine-guns opened flanking fire. The khaki lines checked and swirled around them, and there was a mounting crackle of rifle-fire . . . and the bayonets got in. The lines went forward to the low crest beyond, where, astride the road, was the first objective; and the assault companies halted here to reform. A few Boche shells howled over them, but the Boche were still pounding the wood, where the support battalions followed. The tanks debouched from the forest and went forward through the infantry.

In a hollow just ahead of the reformed line something was being dealt with by artillery, directed by the planes that dipped and swerved above the fight. The shells crashed down and made a great roaring murk of smoke and dust and flickering flames of red and green. The lieutenant, his report to the major despatched, and his company straightened out, along with men from other units and a handful of Senegalese who had attached themselves to him, ran an expert eye along his waiting squads, and allowed his mind to settle profoundly on breakfast. "Let's see—it's July, an' in Texas they'll be havin' cantaloupes, and coffee, an' eggs, an' bacon, an'—" Second Lieutenant Corbett, beside him, groaned like a man shot through the body, and he realized that he had been thinking aloud. Then Corbett seized his arm, and gasped: "Lordy! Look at—"

The shelling forward had abated, but the smoke and murk of it still hung low. Into this murk every man in the line was now peering eagerly. Advancing toward them, dimly seen, was a great body of Germans, hundreds upon hundreds, in mass formation—

Pure joy ran among the men. They took out cartridges, and arranged them in convenient piles. They tested the wind with wetted fingers, and set their sights, and licked their lips. "Range three-fifty—Oh, boy, ain't war wonderful! We been hearin' about this mass-formation stuff, an' now we gets a chance at it—!"

Then: "Aw, hell! Prisoners!" "The low-life bums, they all got their hands up!" "Lookit! One o' them tanks is ridin' herd over them—" It was the garrison of a strong point.

The artillery had battered them, and when it lifted, and they had come out of their holes, they found a brace of agile tanks squatting over their defenses with one-pounders and machine-guns. They had very sensibly surrendered, en masse, and were now ambling through the attacking lines to the rear.

The officers' whistles shrilled, and the attack went on. The woods fell away behind, and for miles to the left and right across the rolling country the waves of assault could be seen. It was a great stirring pageant wherein moved all the forces of modern war. The tanks, large and small, lumbered in advance. Over them the battle-planes flew low, searching the ground, rowelling the Boche with bursts of machine-gun fire. The infantry followed close, assault waves deployed, support platoons in column, American Marines and Regulars, Senegalese and the Foreign Legion of France, their rifles slanting forward, and the sun on all their bayonets. And behind the infantry, straining horses galloped with lean-muzzled 75s, battery on battery—artillery, over the top at last with the rifles. On the skirts of the attack hovered squadrons of cavalry the Marines had seen the day before, dragoons and lancers, marked from afar by the sparkle and glitter of lance-heads and sabres.

And forward through the wheat, the Boche lines broke and his strong points crumbled; standing stubbornly in one place; running in panic at another; and here and there attempting sharp counter-attacks; but everywhere engulfed; and the battle roared over him. The Boche was in mixed quality that day. Some of his people fought and died fighting; a great many others threw down their arms and bleated "Kamaraden" at the distant approach of the attackers.

The rest was no connected story. Only the hot exaltation of the fight kept the men on their feet. Wheat waist-high is almost as hard to get through as running water, and the sun was pitiless. To the left of the battalion, and forward, machine-guns fired from the Chaudun farm; the 17th Company went in and stamped the Maxims flat. In a little hollow there was a battery of 105s that fired pointblank upon the Marines, the gunners working desperately behind their gun-shields. The Marines worked to right and left and beat them down with rifle-fire, and later a gunnery sergeant and a wandering detachment of Senegalese turned one of these guns around and shelled the Vierzy ravine with it—range 900 yards—to the great annoyance of the Boche in that place.

Further, a hidden strong point in the wheat held them, and a tank came and sat upon that strong point and shot it into nothing with a one-pounder gun. Another place, hidden Saxons, laired behind low trip-wires in high wheat, raked the line savagely. There was crawling and shooting low among the poppies, and presently hand-to-hand fighting, in which the freckled boy saw his brother killed and went himself quite mad among the wounded and the corpses with his bayonet. . . .

Then, without being very clear as to how they got there, the lieutenant and his company and a great many others were at the Vierzy ravine, in the cross-fire of the machine-guns that held it.

The ravine was very deep and very precipitous and wooded. A sunken road led into it and, while the riflemen stalked the place cannily, a tank came up and disappeared down the sunken road. A terrific row of rifles and grenades arose, and a wild yelling. Running forward, the Marines observed that the tank was stalled, its guns not working; and a gray frantic mass of German infantry was swarming over it, prying at its plates with bayonets and firing into such openings as could be found. One beauty of the tank is that, when it is in such a difficulty, you can fire without fearing for your friends inside. The automatic-rifle men especially enjoyed the brief crowded seconds that followed. Then all at once the farther slope of the ravine swarmed with running Boches, and the Americans knelt or lay down at ease, and fired steadily and without haste. As they passed the tank a greasy, smiling Frenchman emerged head and shoulders and inquired after a cigarette. There were very many dead Germans in the ravine and on its slope when they went forward.

Wearily now, the exaltation dying down, they left the stone towers of Vierzy to the right, in the path of the Regulars of the 9th and 23d. On line northeast of it they halted and prepared to hold. It was a lonesome place. Very thin indeed were the assault companies; very far away the support columns. . . . "Accordin' to the map, we're here. Turn those Boche machine-guns around—guess we'll stay. Thank God, we must have grabbed off all their artillery, 'cept the heavies. . . ."

"Lootenant, come up here, for God's sake! Lord, what a slew o' Boches!" Beyond rifle-shot a strong gray column was advancing. There were machine-guns with it. It was not deployed, but its intention was very evident. . . . Here were thirty-odd Marines and a few strays from one of the infantry regiments—nobody in sight, flanks or rear——

But to the rear a clanging and a clattering, and the thudding of horse-hoofs!—"Graves, beat it back an' flag those guns." Graves ran frantically, waving his helmet. The guns halted in a cloud of dust, and a gunner lieutenant trotted up, jaunty, immaculate. He dismounted, in his beautiful pale-blue uniform and his gleaming boots and tiny jingling spurs, and saluted the sweating, unshaven Marine officer. He looked with his glasses, and he consulted his map, and then he smiled like a man who has gained his heart's desire. He dashed back toward his guns, waving a signal.

The guns wheeled around; the horses galloped back; there was a whirl and bustle behind each caisson, and two gunners with a field-telephone came running. It all happened in seconds.

The first 75 barked, clear and incisive, and the shell whined away . . . the next gun, and the next. . . . The little puff-balls, ranging shots, burst very near the Boche column. Then the battery fired as one gun—a long rafale of fire, wherein no single gun could be heard, but a drumming thunder.

Smoke and fire flowered hideously over the Boche column. A cloud hit it for a space. When the cloud lifted the column had disintegrated; there was only a far-off swarm of fleeing figures, flailed by shrapnel as they ran. And the glass showed squirming heaps of gray flattened on the ground. . . .

The gunner officer looked and saw that his work was good. "Bon, eh? Soixante-quinze—!" With an all-embracing gesture and a white-toothed smile, he went. Already his battery was limbered up and galloping, and when the first retaliatory shell came from an indignant Boche 155, the 75s were a quarter of a mile away. The Boche shelled the locality with earnestness and method for the next hour, but he did not try to throw forward another column. . . . "Man, I jest love them little 75s! Swa-sont-cans bon? Say, that Frog said a mouthful!"

The lieutenant wrote and sent back his final report: ". . . and final objective reached, position organized at . . ." and stopped and swore in amazement when he looked at his watch—barely noon! Sergeant Cannon's watch corroborated the time—"But, by God! The way my laigs feel, it's day after to-morrow, anyway!—" "Wake those fellows up—got to finish diggin' in—No tellin' what we'll get here—" Some of his people were asleep on their rifles. Some were searching for iron crosses among the dead. A sergeant came with hands and mouth full. "Sir, they's a bunch of this here black German bread and some stuff that looks like coffee, only ain't— in that dugout—" And the company found that Kriegsbrot and Kaffee Ersatz will sustain life, and even taste good if you've been long enough without food. . . .

The shadows turned eastward; in the rear bloated observation balloons appeared on the sky-line. "Them fellers gets a good view from there. Lonesome, though . . ." "Wonder where all our planes went—don't see none—" "Hell! Went home to lunch! Them birds, they don't allow no guerre to interfere with they meals. Now, that's what I got against this fighting stuff —it breaks into your three hots a day." "Boy, I'm so empty I could button my blouse on the knobs of my spine! Hey—yonder's a covey o' them a-vions now—low—strung out—Boche! Hit the deck!"

They were Boche—sinister red-nosed machines that came out of the eye of the sun and harrowed the flattened infantry, swooping one after another with bursts of machine-gun fire. Also they dropped bombs. Some of them went after the observation balloons, and shot more than one down, flaming, before they could be grounded. And not an Ally plane in sight, anywhere! To be just, there was one, in the course of the afternoon; he came from somewhere, and went away very swiftly, with five Germans on his tail. The lieutenant gathered from the conversation of his men that they thought the Frenchman used good judgment.

That afternoon the Boche had the air. He dropped bombs and otherwise did the best he could to make up, with planes, for the artillery that he had lost that morning. On the whole, he was infinitely annoying. There's something about being machine-gunned from the air that gets a man's goat, as the files remarked with profane emphasis. Much futile rifle-fire greeted his machines as they came and went, and away over on the right toward Vierzy the lieutenant saw one low-flying fellow crumple and come down like a stricken duck. This plane, alleged to have been brought down by a chaut-chaut automatic rifle, was afterward officially claimed by four infantry regiments and a machine-gun battalion. Late in the afternoon the French brought up anti-aircraft guns on motor-trucks and the terror of the air abated somewhat; but, while it lasted, the lieutenant heard——

"There comes—" (great rending explosion near by) "God-damighty! 'nother air-bomb?"

"Naw, thank God! That was only a shell!"

As dusk fell, the French cavalry rode forward through the lines. The lieutenant thoughtfully watched a blue squadron pass—"If spirits walk, Murat and Marshal Ney an' all the Emperor's cavalry are ridin' with those fellows. . . ."

In the early dawn of the next day the cavalry rode back. One squadron went through the company's position. It was a very small squadron, indeed, this morning. Half the troopers led horses with empty saddles. A tall young captain was in command. They were drawn and haggard from the night's work, but the men carried their heads high, and even the horses looked triumphant. They had, it developed, been having a perfectly wonderful time, riding around behind the German lines. They had shot up transport, and set fire to ammunition-dumps, and added greatly to the discomfort of the Boche. They thought they might go back again to-night. . . . They did.

The night of the 19th the galleys got up, and the men had hot food. Early the morning of the 20th the division was relieved and began to withdraw to reserve position, while fresh troops carried the battle on. The 1st Battalion of the 5th Marines marched back, in a misty dawn, across the ground they had fought over two days before. In the trampled fields, where the dead lay unburied, old French territorials were mowing the ripe wheat and shocking it up. The battle was far away. . . .

The battalion entered the woods and turned off the road toward the blue smoke of the galleys, from which came an altogether glorious smell of food. One of the company officers ran ahead of the 49th to find a place to stack arms and pile equipment. Presently he beckoned, and the lieutenant led his people to the place—a sort of clearing, along one side of which lay a great fallen tree. Under an outthrust leafy branch something long and stiff lay covered with a blanket.

"Stack arms . . . fall out!"

Graves, the officer who had gone ahead, was standing by the blanket. "Do you know who's under this?" he said. The lieutenant stooped and looked. It was little Tritt. . . .

After breakfast, some of the men enlarged the pit where the machine-gun had been and tidied it up. . . . They wrapped the body in a blanket and two German water-proof sheets that were handy, and buried the boy there.

". . . But before he got it, he knew that we were winning." The men put on their helmets and went away, to look for others who had stopped in the woods . . . to gather souvenirs.

"Well, he's where he ain't hungry, an' his feet don't hurt from hikin', an' his heavy marchin' order won't never cut into his shoulders any more. . . ." "No, nor no damn Boche buzzards drop air-bombs on him——"

"Wonder where we'll hit the old Boche next——"

The Battle of Ypres

BY

FRANK RICHARDS

THE first week in October we left the Aisne to march north, and were issued with topcoats but no packs. We folded our topcoats and tied them on our shoulder-straps with string. We marched by night and rested by day. My gambling money came in very handy: we could buy food in the villages where we rested. There were three of us mucking in and we lived like fighting cocks. Our clothes were beginning to show signs of wear, though, and some of the men were wearing civilian trousers which they had scrounged. A lot of us had no caps: I was wearing a handkerchief knotted at the four corners—the only headgear I was to wear for some time. We looked a ragtime lot, but in good spirits and ready for anything that turned up. About eighty per cent of us were Birmingham men: I never saw better soldiers or wished for better pals. Our Colonel was very strict but a good soldier: the Adjutant likewise. We all admired the Adjutant very much: he could give us all chalks on at swearing and beat the lot of us easily.

Our Company Commander had left us on the Retirement, and during the last day's march from the Aisne a new one took over the company: he was a First Battalion officer and the majority of us had never seen him before. We were loading a train when he first appeared on the scene and he commenced to rave and storm, saying that everything was being loaded up wrong and that we were a lot of ruddy idiots. Company-Sergeant-Major Stanway and Sergeant Fox, who was my platoon sergeant, were directing the loading of the train, and what they didn't know about loading trains was not worth knowing. Stanway had about fifteen years service and Fox about twelve, the greater part of which they had spent abroad. They were the two best non-commissioned officers I ever soldiered under. In any battalion of men there were always a number of bullies, and it's natural to expect one or two among the officers: our new Company Commander was agreed to be a first-class bully. Bullies as a rule are bad soldiers, but he was an exception to the rule.

We entrained that evening and arrived at St. Omer. We were on the move next morning, and a couple of days later we had a brush-up with some German Uhlans who were fine cavalrymen and excellent raiders; there were bands of them operating around the Bailleul area. One lot had done a good deal of damage to Steenwerk railway station, between Armentières and

From: *Old Soldiers Never Die.*

861

Bailleul, blowing up the points. We were advancing by platoons in extended order over open country when rifle-fire opened out from somewhere in front. We judged it to come from a fair sized wood about six hundred yards away, and laying down opened out with rapid fire at it. A few more shots were fired at us and then the firing ceased. We advanced again and through the wood but saw no one. No doubt the Uhlans had seen us advancing and opened fire with their carbines from inside the wood, then mounting their horses and using the wood as a screen had galloped safely out of sight. My platoon had no casualties, but Number 2 and Number 3 platoons had about half a dozen during the day. The men of Number 3 told us later in the day that they had killed four Uhlans and their horses as they had galloped out of a small wood on their right front about five hundred yards away.

One of our badly wounded men was taken to a lone farmhouse; McGregor, a stretcher-bearer, volunteered to stay the night with him. The next morning he told us that he had been through a bit of torture: the wounded man had been carried upstairs and during the night six Uhlans had rode up to the farm, tied their horses up outside and entered. They had made the old lady of the farm put them out food and drink. McGregor was wondering whether they would have a scrounge through the house after they had finished their meal. The wounded man was delirious too and might easily have given the show away. The Uhlans left as soon as they had finished their meal but McGregor reckoned that he had lost a stone in weight during that short time they were in the house.

We entered Bailleul in the afternoon and the people there were very glad to see us. The place had been in possession of the enemy for a few days and the Uhlans had intended to billet there that night. At this place Stevens rejoined the Battalion. His wanderings on the retirement had been similar to my own: he had also been to Le Mans and had been in hospital a week with fever and ague, after which he had been sent up country and had been serving with another unit for a fortnight. The next morning as we left Bailleul on our way to Vlamertinghe we saw about a dozen Uhlans galloping for all they were worth back from the outskirts. We fired a few shots but they were too far away for us to do any damage. The sight of one Uhlan would frighten the French people more than if half a dozen large shells were exploding in their villages. They told us that the Uhlans were brigands of the first water and would pinch anything they could carry with them. Although the French were our allies we used to do much the same. But we had to be careful: at this early date in the War the penalty for looting was death. We were at Vlamertinghe a few days and then marched for thirteen hours, arriving at a place named Laventie the following morning; we must have come a roundabout way to have taken that time. We moved off again at daybreak and relieved some French troops the further side of Fromelles on the Belgian frontier: two days later we retired back through Fromelles and dug our trenches about four hundred yards this side of that village.

Little did we think when we were digging those trenches that we were digging our future homes; but they were the beginnings of the long stretch that soon went all the way from the North Sea to Switzerland and they were our homes for the next four years. Each platoon dug in on its own, with gaps of about forty yards bet veen each platoon. B Company were in support, but one platoon of B were ᵥn the extreme right of the Battalion's front line. On our left were the 1st Middlesex, and on our right was a battalion of Indian native infantry. Our Company Commander used to visit the other three platoons at night; he, the Second-in-Command of the Company and the platoon officer stayed on the extreme right of our trench. We dug those trenches simply for fighting; they were breast-high with the front parapet on ground level and in each bay we stood shoulder to shoulder. We were so squeezed for room that whenever an officer passed along the trench one man would get behind the traverse if the officer wanted to stay awhile in that bay. No man was allowed to fire from behind the traverse: because the least deflection of his rifle would put a bullet through someone in the bay in front of him. Traverses were made to counteract enfilade rifle-fire. Sandbags were unknown at this time.

A part of our trench crossed a willow ditch and about forty yards in front of us we blocked this ditch with a little bank which was to be our listening post at night. The ditch was dry at present. Every order was passed up the trench by word of mouth, and we found in many instances that by the time an order reached the last man it was entirely different from what the first man had passed along. When our Company Commander passed along the trench we had to squeeze our bodies into the front parapet to allow him to pass. If a man did not move smart enough, out would come his revolver and he would threaten to blow the man's ruddy brains out. During this time he had a perfect mania for pulling his gun and threatening us one and all for the least trifling thing we done. Our platoon officer followed his example, but he used to pull his gun in a half ashamed manner. The platoon nicknamed them Buffalo Bill and Deadwood Dick. I got on very well with Deadwood Dick and he was a decent platoon officer. We always numbered off at night: one, two, one, two—odd numbers up, even numbers down, and change every hour. It made no difference whether we were down or up: we could only lay over the parapet by our rifles and with our heads resting on the wet ground try and snatch an hour's sleep.

About the third day we were there Buffalo Bill came up to our part of the trench: I got behind the traverse to allow him to get in the bay. He ordered us to keep a sharp look-out, as the enemy were attacking on our extreme right, and said that it was quite possible the attack would develop all along the front. About four hundred yards in front of us was a road leading into Fromelles. Just behind the road were some trees. I spotted a few of the enemy advancing among the trees and, forgetting for a moment that I was behind a traverse, I rose my rifle to fire, but recollected in time and put it down again. At the same time a man in the next bay below me opened fire. Buffalo Bill turned around. He was red in the face, the veins in his neck had swelled, and he looked for all the world like a cobra ready to strike. "You dog!" he shouted. "You fired!" I replied that I hadn't. He did not go for his gun but picked up a big clod of earth and threw it at me, hitting me on the chest. All my discipline vanished at that moment. "You dirty swine!" I said. By a bit of luck he didn't hear me, for at that moment the enemy's artillery happened to open out and shells began bursting all along our front; but I could hear *him* all right. "Get in that next bay," he roared. I squeezed myself in the next bay.

Some of the enemy had now come out of the trees and no doubt intended to advance a little way under cover of their barrage. But the shelling was not severe enough to prevent us opening out rapid fire at them. I don't think any one of them ran twenty yards before he was dropped. To good, trained, pre-War soldiers who kept their nerve, ten men holding a trench could easily stop fifty who were trying to take it, advancing from a distance of four hundred yards. The enemy now put up a tremendous barrage on our trench, but fortunately for us the shells were dropping short. Some more of the enemy had advanced at the run under cover of this barrage and had dropped down behind some little tumps of ground about two hundred and fifty yards away. I was watching the ground in front but it was very difficult to make anything out through the smoke and showers of dirt being blown up by the exploding shells. Buffalo Bill came into the bay I was in: he had his glasses out and was peering through them but seemed unable to see more than we had done. Most of us now had our heads well below the parapet, waiting for the barrage to lift. The enemy opened out with rifle-fire, and although they could not see us their bullets were kicking up the dirt all around. Buffalo Bill was as cool as a cucumber: he had plenty of guts, I'll say that for him. He passed down the trench warning us as soon as the barrage lifted to be prepared to stop an attack.

At last the barrage lifted: the shells were now exploding about a hundred yards behind us. We were all on the alert and stood to. The enemy rose up and started to advance. They were stopped at once: with the parapet as a rest for our rifles it was impossible to miss. The attack was over before it had hardly commenced. From somewhere under cover by the trees the enemy then opened out with rifle-fire on our trench and a couple of men in the next bay to me were shot through the head. We directed our fire in that direction. Stevens shouted to me to look at one of the men in our bay: he had his head well below the parapet and was firing in the air. We made him put his head well up and fire properly. The whole of the men in the bay threatened to shoot him dead if he done it again. If Buffalo Bill had seen him he wouldn't have given him that chance, but soon put daylight through him.

The left platoon of Indian native infantry on the extreme right of the Battalion had lost their white officer and the enemy's shelling had put the wind up them properly. While the enemy was advancing toward them our men on their left noticed that none of the Germans were falling; so they got a cross fire on them which soon held the attack up. The Indians were firing all the time as if they were mad, but they must have had their heads well below the parapet, like the man in our bay, and been firing up in the air. Every evening after, until the native infantry were relieved by a British battalion, twelve of our men were sent over to their trench with orders to stay the night there; they went over at dusk and returned at dawn. Every man of the twelve had served in India. One of the men told me later that the first night they went over they found the natives wailing and weeping; no one was on sentry and they hadn't attempted to remove their dead out of the trench. Our fellows cursed the natives in Hindustani and finding that of no avail commenced to kick and hit them about and also threatened to shoot or bayonet the lot of them if they did not put their heads over the parapet: in fact they put the wind up them more thoroughly than what the German shells had. It was quite possible that the natives might have hopped it in the dark, but if they had attempted to in the day they would have been mowed down by our own men as well as by the enemy. Native infantry were no good in France. Some writers in the papers wrote at the time that they couldn't stand the cold weather; but the truth was that they suffered from cold feet, and a few enemy shells exploding round their trenches were enough to demoralize the majority of them. But there was one thing about them: over three years later the Battalion passed through a village they had been billeted in, and I saw several half-caste mites playing in the street. One old Expeditionary Force man remarked to me that if the bloody niggers were no good at fighting they were good at something else that sounded much the same.

That night we heard the enemy working on our front, but we didn't know whether they were entrenching themselves or not. The next morning a heavy mist hung over everywhere and it was impossible to see ten yards ahead. Buffalo Bill decided to send a patrol out, consisting of a corporal and two men; in my battalion throughout the whole of the War no privates were ever warned to go out on patrol—volunteers were always called for. Corporal Pardoe, Private Miles and I went out on that patrol; our orders were simply to proceed as far as we could up the willow ditch and to discover what we could. We had gone a considerable way past our listening-post when we halted. Pardoe said: "How far do you think we have come?" "Over two hundred yards," said Miles, and I agreed with him. The mist was still heavy and we were listening intently. Presently we heard voices not far off and the sounds of men working. We were wondering whether to work up closer or to go back and report, when all of a sudden the mist blew away, and there, a little over a hundred yards in front of us, were new enemy trenches. The enemy were taking advantage of the mist and working on the parapet: some were a good thirty yards from their trench—they had been levelling some corn-stacks so as to have a clear line of fire. Pardoe got on one side of the ditch, and Miles and I on the other, and opened out with rapid fire. We had our rifles resting on the bank. The three of us had been marksmen all through our soldiering: each of us could get off twenty-five aimed rounds a minute and it was impossible to miss at that distance. We had downed half a dozen men before they realized what was happening; then they commenced to jump back in the trench. Those that were out in front started to run, but we bowled them over like rabbits. It put me in mind of firing at the "running man" on a peace-time course of musketry. Against we had expended our magazines which held ten rounds there wasn't a live enemy to be seen, and the whole affair had not lasted half a minute. We quickly reloaded our magazines, which took us a couple of seconds, turned around, and ran towards our trench, each of us in turn halting to fire five rounds covering fire at the enemy's trench.

The mist had now lifted everywhere: we could see our own trench quite plainly and bullets were zipping around us. Our men on the extreme left of the platoon had opened fire on the enemy's trench, but the men in line with the ditch were not allowed to fire for fear of hitting us (we learned this when we got back). We arrived at our listening-post, jumped the little bank and laid down, properly winded. We were not out of the soup yet: we still had forty yards to travel before we got back in our trench. We were safe from rifle-fire as long as we crawled on our bellies to the parapet but when we got to the end of the ditch we would have to jump out in the open before getting into the trench, and we knew full well that the enemy would be waiting for that move. We arrived at the end of the ditch and there we heard Buffalo Bill shouting over for us to remain where we were for a couple of minutes, and then to get back in the trench one by one. He passed word up the trench for the whole platoon to open out with rapid fire which would make the enemy keep their heads down and give us a decent chance to get home without being hit. We got back safely; I never knew how well I could jump until that morning. I was out of the ditch and into the trench in the twinkling of an eye: Duffy said that I cleared the parapet like a Grand National winner. The corporal made his report to Buffalo Bill who was delighted at our brush-up. Miles and I did not know what narrow squeaks we had had until someone noticed a bullet-hole through Miles's trousers and two more through the right sleeve of my tunic.

About an hour later Miles was busy sniping. In those early days of trench-warfare both sides were pretty reckless, and it was no uncommon sight on our front, and especially on our right front, to see a German pop up out of his trench and make a dart for the village. He did not always get there, and as time went on both sides respected the marksmanship of each other so much that no one dared to show a finger. Miles had just claimed to have popped a German over when he got a bullet through the head himself. That same evening Corporal Pardoe also got killed in the same way, after getting away with that stunt in the morning it was tough luck on the both of them.

Our dead we used to put on the back of the parapet and we carried them at night to a place just behind the line and buried them there. All companies carried their dead to the same place. If a dead man's clothes or boots were in good condition we never hesitated to take them off him, especially when they would fit a man. My own puttees were in ribbons, so I took the

Corporal's, which were in good condition. In a belt that Corporal Pardoe wore next to his skin they found about sixty English sovereigns, besides French money. None of it went back to his next-of-kin. I could have had some but I didn't want to touch it: I was satisfied with his puttees. We began to sap out to our left and right platoons and dug a trench from the officers' bay back to a dip in the ground about twenty yards from a farm-house. We used to fill our water-bottles at the farm at night, and each man's water-bottle had to last him twenty-four hours.

There was no such thing as cooked food or hot tea at this stage of the War, and rations were very scarce: we were lucky if we got our four biscuits a man daily, a pound tin of bully between two, a tin of jam between six, and the rum ration which was about a tablespoonful and a half. Even at this early period the jam was rotten and one firm that supplied it must have made hundreds of thousands of pounds profit out of it—the stuff they put in instead of fruit and sugar! One man swore that if ever he got back to England he would make it his first duty to shoot up the managing director and all the other heads of that particular firm. Tobacco, cigarettes and matches were also very scarce. We had plenty of small-arm ammunition but no rifle-oil or rifle-rag to clean our rifles with. We used to cut pieces off our shirts for use as rifle-rags, and some of us who had bought small tins of vaseline (in villages we passed through during our Aisne advance) for use on sore heels or chafed legs, used to grease our rifles with that. A rifle soon got done up without oil in these conditions. Our sanitary arrangements were very bad: we used empty bully-beef tins for urinating in, throwing it over the back of the parapet. If a man was taken short during the day he had to use the trench he was in and then throw it over the back of the trench and throw earth after it.

One night there was an enemy attack which we beat off and the next morning some corpses were to be seen lying just out in front of us: they were wearing spiked helmets. We crawled out the next night and went through their packs, taking anything they had of value from them. The spiked helmets we intended to keep as souvenirs, but we soon came to the conclusion that it was no good keeping souvenirs of that sort when any moment we may be dancing a two-step in another world. So we used them as latrine buckets, throwing them over the parapet at the back when we had used them. A few days later we had completed a trench back to a dip in the ground where we dug a square pit which we used as a latrine: we could go back in the day to it and be quite safe from rifle-fire.

The only artillery covering our front were two eighteen-pounders who had a limited number of shells to fire each day. They were so hard up for shells that they couldn't spare a shell to fire at a large straw rick on our right from which some enemy snipers were causing us casualties. The young artillery officer with the guns often used to come up to our trench during the night, and sometimes bring us tobacco and cigarettes: he was a very cheery soul. Two companies of Argyle and Sutherland Highlanders were in reserve to the whole of the Brigade front.

The 29th October, 1914, was a miserable rainy day. One young soldier remarked that he did not believe anyone was in support or reserve to us. But Duffy said, "What the hell does it matter about supports or reserves? We have plenty of small-arm ammunition, and as long as our rifles hold out we can stop any attack, especially if they make it during the day." The night before a party of Engineers had come up to our trench and had driven some posts in the ground about fifteen yards in front with one strand of barbed wire stretching across them. It looked like a clothes line during the day. We had put a covering party about thirty yards in front of them while they were doing the work. The Old Soldier of the platoon remarked that the British Government must be terribly hard up, what with short rations, no rifle-oil, no shells, and now sending Engineers up to the front line to stretch one single bloody strand of barbed wire out, which he had no doubt was the only single bloody strand in the whole of France, and which a bloody giraffe could rise up and walk under. It was enough to make good soldiers weep tears of blood, he said, the way things were going on. This was the first and last time Engineers put out wire in front of the Battalion: after this we always put out our own, no matter where we were.

Well, it was still raining on the night of the 29th when heavy rifle-fire broke out on the extreme right of our front. At the same time our listening-post sent back to say that the enemy were getting out of their trenches, so the post was called in at once, and presently we could see dim forms in front of us. Then our right platoon opened out with rapid fire. We opened out with rapid fire too. We were firing as fast as we could pull the trigger: no man can take a sight in the dark so we were firing direct in front of us. One of our eighteen-pounders had fired a star shell which enabled us to see the enemy dropping down on their stomachs. Five or six ordinary shells were fired too, and one of them set fire to the straw-rick on our right front which was soon burning merrily. The enemy in front of us were held up for the time being, so we opened fire on our right front where we could see some more of them quite clearly by the light of the burning rick. On the left of our left platoon the enemy had captured one platoon-frontage of trench from the Middlesex, but a company of the Argyles had been rushed up and soon recaptured it. The platoon of Middlesex holding that trench had lost a lot of men a few days before, and the trench was thinly manned.

One of our chaps in turning to get another bandolier of ammunition out of the box, noticed three men coming towards our trench from the back. "Halt! Hands up! Who are you?" he challenged. We turned around. We knew it was quite possible for some of the enemy to have got through the gap between us and our left platoon and come around the back of us. Instead of answering the challenge two of the men dropped on their stomachs and the other mumbled something which we did not understand. Two men opened fire at him and he dropped; then one of the men on the ground shouted: "You bloody fools! We're artillery signallers and you've shot our officer." We asked them why they did not answer when challenged. They said that they had left it to the officer to answer, and that they were running a telephone line out to our trench. He was the young officer who used to visit us: one bullet had gone through his jaw and the other through his right side. The two men carried him back and we all hoped that he would recover from his wounds; but we never heard any more news of him.

The attack was still going on: we kept up a continuous fire on our front, but one by one our rifles began to jam. Word was passed up the trench for Richards and Smith to go down to the officers' bay. When we two arrived there we were warned to stay in that bay for the night. In a short time mine and Smith's rifles were about the only two that were firing in the whole of the platoon. Then ours were done up too: the fact was that continual rain had made the parapet very muddy and the mud had got into the rifle mechanism, which needed oiling in any case, and continual firing had heated the metal so that between the one thing and the other it was impossible to open and close the bolts. The same thing had happened all along the Battalion front.

About a couple of hours before dawn, word was passed along the trench for every man to get out and lay down five paces in front of the parapet and be prepared to meet the enemy with the bayonet. When everyone was out Buffalo Bill walked up and down the platoon and told us all that we would have to fight to the last man. He had his sword in one hand and his revolver in the other; officers carried their swords in action at this time. We were all dead-beat, and if any man had slept two hours during the last seven days without being disturbed he had been a very lucky man. Smith said to me: "I expect this is our last time around, Dick, but I hope we take a few of them on the long journey with us." I replied that I was going to do my level best in that way. The straw-rick had practically burned itself out, but it had now stopped raining and we could see more clearly in front of us. The enemy were about thirty yards away. They had halted and begun talking together. One of them fired a rocket; it was a very poor one, it spluttered into sparks and fell only a few paces in front of them.

There was no firing all along our front. The enemy were not firing either; perhaps their rifles were done up the same as our own. In spite of the danger I had great difficulty in keeping my eyes open, and the man on the left of Smith had commenced to snore. Smith drove his elbow into his ribs. The Second-in-Command of the company had dozed off too. Buffalo Bill spoke to him sharply a few times before he answered; even the knowledge that it might be their last minute on earth did not prevent some of the men from dozing off. Sleep will beat any man and under any conditions. It was passed along for us to get up on our feet to receive the charge. But no charge came. It was getting a little lighter, and just before dawn broke the enemy turned around and hurried back to their trench; and we didn't have a single good rifle to fire a round at them. We had two machine-guns in the Battalion at this time, one in the centre and the other on the extreme right, and both had done good work during the night; but they were done up too, the same as our rifles.

We got back in our trench wet through to the skin (but we were getting used to that) and commenced to clean our rifles. This proved a difficult job; but the metal had cooled now and some of us who still had some vaseline left handed it around and we got them all in working order again. A sentry was posted in each bay and we snatched a few hours sleep, the best way we could. Our rations that day, October 30th, were three biscuits, a tin of bully between four, a spoonful of jam and our rum ration. To hungry, half-starved men it was a flea-bite. The Old Soldier remarked that the Government was trying to make us as fierce as Bengal tigers so that all the Germans we killed in future we would also devour as well. We could now see the effects of our night's work: a lot of the enemy dead lay out in front. One of the men in our left platoon threw his equipment off, jumped on the parapet with his hands above his head and then pointed to a wounded German who was trying to crawl to our lines. He then went forward, got hold of the wounded man and carried him in, the enemy clapping their hands and cheering until he had disappeared into our trench.

We were constantly sapping out to our left and right platoons whenever we had the chance and now had plenty of room in the trench. There was a decent orchard in the farm at the back of our trench, and Stevens and I used to slip over in the night and fill his pack full of apples—Stevens was the only man in the whole platoon with a pack. We had to fill our bellies with *something*. There was one cow and one pig left in the farm. Buffalo Bill had the pig killed and sent back to the company cooks with instructions to melt a lot of the fat down and cook the remainder; the pork came up the following night and we enjoyed it greatly although we had no bread to eat with it. The fat that was melted down we used for greasing our rifles with. With the exception of one dicksee of tea, which was stone-cold against it reached us, this was the only occasion that the cooks had to do anything for us the whole of the time we were there.

One morning the officers were about to have breakfast at the end of the trench leading to their bay, from where it was possible by stooping low in a ditch to get into the farm by daylight. One of the officers' servants, whose duty it was to milk the cow so that the officers could have milk in their tea, reported that the cow had broken loose and that they would have to do without milk that morning. Buffalo Bill jumped to his feet, revolver out, and roared at the man: "My God, you'll catch that cow and milk her or I'll blow your ruddy brains out!" The cow was grazing about twenty yards away where there was a dip in the ground. The man ran after her, the cow ran up the slope in the rear, the man following; if they kept on they would soon be in full view of the enemy. Buffalo Bill saw the danger the man would soon be in. He shouted: "Come back, you ruddy fool, and never mind the cow!" The man evidently did not hear him, but kept on. One or two bullets hit up the dirt around him. The enemy had been sending over a few light shells that morning, and now they sent over one or two more. One burst quite close to the cow. The cow got killed and the man received a nice wound in the leg which took him back to Blighty. I expect when he got home he blessed Buffalo Bill, also the cow and the German who shot him: even at this time we used to reckon that anyone who got a clean wound through the leg or arm was an extremely fortunate man.

One night some of the men in the company on our right were pinching chickens out of the farm when Buffalo Bill appeared on the scene. He roared like a lion and threatened to blow their ruddy brains out if he caught them again and told them that everything on the farm belonged to *him*. Not many hours later there wasn't a feathered fowl left on that farm: the men had pinched the lot. His favourite punishment from now on was forty-eight hours continual digging in a support trench. Yet he never troubled himself to see whether the punishment was being done or not, and in some instances that punishment was a blessing in disguise because we took things far easier behind than in the front trench. I never remembered him having any favourites: he treated all men in the same way—like dirt.

The enemy made a half-hearted attack on us a few nights after the 29th, but we stopped them before they had come far. After this we settled down to ordinary trench-warfare, and were finally relieved on the night of the 15th November. By this time we were as lousy as rooks. No man had washed or shaved for nearly a month, and with our beards and mud we looked a proper ragtime band of brigands.

Twenty-fours hours later, after a wash, shave and sleep we were different men, and in another twenty-four hours we had marched through Armentières and relieved some troops in trenches on the right of Houplines. We were relieved eight days later and billeted in a cotton factory in that place. We thought we were going to have a rest, but we were wrong: every night we had to go up the line digging communication trenches leading back from the front line. During this time we were issued with caps and packs. It was the first cap I had worn since August.

About one hundred of us were sent to a village outside Armentières, where the King inspected some of his Army. I hadn't seen the King since he was Prince of Wales, when early in 1905 he held a garden party in the grounds of Sikundra Taj, about six miles from Agra in India. I was present as a signaller at that party, and although over nine years had elapsed he did not look a day older. No king in the history of England ever reviewed more loyal or lousier troops than what His Majesty did that day. To look at us we were as clean as new pins, but in our shirts, pants and trousers were whole platoons of crawlers. His Majesty decorated one of our sergeants with the Distinguished Conduct Medal, who had won it at Fromelles.

There were fifty-eight Number One Field Punishment prisoners in the Battalion at this time. When out of action they were locked up and had to do all the dirty jobs that wanted doing, and were tied up two hours a day (by the ankles and wrists, generally) to the carts and wagons in the transport lines. Outside the factory on the one side of the street was a wall with some iron railings sunk in. One afternoon the fifty-eight prisoners were tied up to the railings and I should think three parts of the female population of Houplines and Armentières paraded that street in the afternoon. Some were sympathetic and some were laughing. The prisoners resented this very much, and one remarked that he didn't mind being tied up but he didn't want a bloody lot of frog-eating bastards gaping at him. There were some hard cases among the Number One's and the majority were continually in trouble, but these on the whole were the finest soldiers, in action, that I ever saw. During the first four months of the War, if a man was sentenced to imprisonment he left the Battalion to serve his sentence, but afterwards it was only an isolated case that was sent away. I have known men who were sentenced to five or ten years imprisonment stay with the Battalion, and in less than a month's time have their sentences washed out for gallant conduct in the field.

One man in my company whom we called Broncho was the hardest case of the lot. Whenever we were out of action he was always up in front of the Colonel for some crime or other. He was a grand front-line soldier, and most of his crimes were caused by overbearing non-commissioned officers. There was an old saying that in the Army they tamed lions; but Broncho was never tamed. I was one of the escort to him one morning when he was in front of the Colonel. His crime was too serious for the Company Commander to deal with. It was insubordination to an N.C.O.—he had told a corporal that he was no bloody good. The Colonel gave Broncho the usual twenty-eight days Number One and warned him that he would be put up against the wall and shot if he did not alter. Broncho then reminded the Colonel that it was the third time he had given him that warning and that he didn't care a damn whether he was shot or not. "March him out!" shouted the Colonel. He was brought up again next morning and sentenced to another twenty-eight days Number One for insubordination to his Commanding Officer.

But he got the whole lot washed out a fortnight later in the following manner. The enemy had been shelling so badly in the rear of us that all communication had broken down, and Buffalo Bill called for a volunteer to take a message back to Battalion Headquarters. Anyone who took the message back would have to make his way through the barrage and the communication trench had not yet been dug. Broncho shouted out: "I'll take the bloody message," and it was handed to him. It was a hundred to one he would be blown to bits before he had gone sixty yards—he not only arrived at Battalion Headquarters with the message but also came back with an answer. He was recommended for a decoration for this. A week previous when returning from a night-patrol one of the patrol had got badly wounded by unaimed fire; and it was Broncho who carried him back safely to the trench. For these two acts he had a term of imprisonment washed out and about six months accumulated Number Ones; but he got no decoration.

The third Battle of Ypres commenced on July 31st and our Division were sent to the Belgian coast. We travelled by train and barge and arrived at Dunkirk. A little higher up the coast was a place named Bray Dunes, where we stayed about a week, and the architect and I went for many a long swim in the sea. We moved closer to the line along the coast and arrived at a place which the majority of inhabitants had only just evacuated. In July a British division had relieved the Belgian troops around this part. Ever since November 1914 the people had been living in peace and security in the towns and villages in this area, but as soon as the British troops took over the enemy began shelling these places and the people cleared out. In one place we were in the people were in the act of leaving and complaining very bitterly because the arrival of British troops had caused a lot of shelling and forced them to leave their homes. In one pretty village by the sea there hadn't been enough of shells exploded in it to have frightened a poll parrot away, yet there wasn't a soul left there now. They were evidently not such good stickers as the French people who worried less about their lives than about their property and hung on to the last possible minute.

At Bray Dunes I got in conversation with a Canadian officer who was in charge of some men building a light railway. He said it was a good job that the States came in the War as the French were ready to throw the sponge up. A few days later two of our signallers overheard a full colonel of the Staff telling our Colonel that he did not know what would have happened if the United States had not come in when they did. It was common knowledge among the Staff that the whole of the French Army were more or less demoralized, and the States coming in had to a great extent been the means of restoring their morale. We got wind that our Division and another had been sent up the coast to try and break through the German Front and capture Ostend. This was freely discussed by the officers, but no break through was attempted owing to so little progress being made on the Ypres front.

One of the largest concentration prison camps I ever saw was erected in this area. It was estimated to hold between ten and fifteen thousand prisoners, but all I saw in it were two solitary prisoners who must have been very lonely in so large a place.

On the night the Battalion went in the line I went on leave. It was eighteen months since I had the last one and as usual I made the most of it. I didn't spend the whole of it in pubs: I spent two days going for long tramps in the mountains, which I thoroughly enjoyed after being so long in a flat country. I was presented with a gold watch, in recognition of winning the D.C.M., which I still have, but it has been touch-and-go with it several times since the War. Probably if there hadn't been an inscription on it I should have parted with it. This time every man of military age that I met wanted to shake hands with me and also ask my advice on how to evade military service, or, if they were forced to go, which would be the best corps to join that would keep them away from the firing line. They were wonderfully patriotic at smoking concerts given in honour of soldiers returning from the Front, but their patriotism never extended beyond that.

When I landed back at Boulogne I came across the man who had been shot through his cheeks at Bois Grenier in April 1915. If anything, that bullet had improved his appearance. He now had a nice little dimple on each side of his face. We had a chat. I asked what he was doing now and he said that he had a Staff job, as a military policeman around the Docks. He told me very seriously that if it was possible, and he had the name and address of the German that shot him, he would send him the largest parcel he could pack and a hundred-franc note as well. He was having the time of his life on his present job and had one of the smartest fillies in Boulogne, who was the goods in every way. As I left him I could not help thinking how lucky some men were and how unlucky were others.

When I arrived back I found that the Division had left the coastal area on short notice. All returning leave men of the Division were in a little camp outside Dunkirk. One night some German planes came over bombing and one of our searchlights kept a plane in its rays for some time. Anti-aircraft guns, machine-guns and Lewis guns, and we with our rifles were all banging at him, but he got away with it. Whilst everyone was busy firing at that one, his friends were busy dropping their bombs on Dunkirk. It was very rare that a plane flying at any height was brought down by anti-aircraft guns or rifle-fire but we lost a lot of planes on the Somme by rifle-fire when they came down very low, machine-gunning the enemy before our troops attacked. German planes used to do the same thing and seldom got away with it either.

I rejoined the Battalion in a village near Ypres and guessed that we would soon be in the blood tub. Ricco and Paddy had been made full corporals but Paddy had taken a lot of persuading before he consented to be made an N.C.O. He was sent back to Division Headquarters for a special course of signalling and was lucky enough to miss the next show we were in. Our Colonel went on leave and missed the show too. The name of our Acting-Colonel was Major Poore. He was not an old regimental officer but had been posted to us some six months before from the Yeomanry, I believe. He was a very big man, about fifty years of age, slightly deaf, and his favourite expression was "What, what!" He was a very decent officer. A tall, slender young lieutenant who had just returned from leave was made Assistant-Adjutant for the show. I believe he was given that job because he was an excellent map-reader. As we were marching along the road, Sealyham asked him if he had come across Mr. Sassoon during his leave. He replied that he hadn't and that he had spent a good part of his leave trying to find out where he was but had failed to get any news at all. This young officer had joined the Battalion about the same time as Mr. Sassoon and we old hands thought he was a man and a half to spend his leave looking for a pal. His name was Casson. I wrote it down first here as Carson, but an old soldiering pal tells me that I had it wrong. Mr. Casson was said to be a first-class pianist, but trench warfare did not give him much opportunity to show his skill at that. If he was as good a pianist as he was a cool soldier he must have been a treat to hear.

During the night we passed through a wood where a Very-light dump had been exploded by a German shell. It was like witnessing a fireworks display at home. We stayed in the wood for the night. Our Brigade were in reserve and ready to be called upon at any moment. Orders were given that no fires were to be lit. September 26th, 1917, was a glorious day from the weather point of view and when dawn was breaking Ricco and I who were crack hands at making smokeless fires had found a dump of pick-handles which when cut up in thin strips answered very well. We soon cooked our bacon and made tea for ourselves and the bank clerk and architect, and made no more smoke than a man would have done smoking a cigarette. We had at least made sure of our breakfast which might be the last we would ever have.

At 8 a.m. orders arrived that the Battalion would move off to the assistance of the Australians who had made an attack early in the morning on Polygon Wood. Although the attack was successful they had received heavy casualties and were now hard pressed themselves. Young Mr. Casson led the way, as cool as a cucumber. One part of the ground we travelled over was nothing but lakes and boggy ground and the whole of the Battalion were strung out in Indian file walking along a track about eighteen inches wide. We had just got out of this bad ground but were still travelling in file when the enemy opened out with a fierce bombardment. Just in front of me half a dozen men fell on the side of the track: it was like as if a Giant Hand had suddenly swept them one side. The Battalion had close on a hundred casualties before they were out of that valley. If a man's best pal was wounded he could not stop to dress his wounds for him.

We arrived on some rising ground and joined forces with the Australians. I expected to find a wood but it was undulating land with a tree dotted here and there and little banks running in different directions. About half a mile in front of us was a ridge of trees, and a few concrete pillboxes of different sizes. The ground that we were now on and some of the pillboxes had only been taken some hours previously. I entered one pillbox during the day and found eighteen dead Germans inside. There was not a mark on one of them; one of our heavy shells had made a direct hit on the top of it and they were killed by concussion, but very little damage had been done to the pillbox. They were all constructed with reinforced concrete and shells could explode all round them but the flying pieces would never penetrate the concrete. There were small windows in the sides and by jumping in and out of shell holes attacking troops could get in bombing range: if a bomb was thrown through one of the windows the pillbox was as good as captured.

There was a strong point called Black Watch Corner which was a trench facing north, south, east and west. A few yards outside the trench was a pillbox which was Battalion Headquarters. The bank clerk, architect and I got in the trench facing our front, and I was soon on friendly terms with an Australian officer, whom his men called Mr. Diamond. He was wearing the ribbon of the D.C.M., which he told me he had won in Gallipoli while serving in the ranks and had been granted a commission some time later. About a hundred yards in front of us was a bank which extended for hundreds of yards across the ground behind which the Australians were. Our chaps charged through them to take a position in front and Captain Mann, our Adjutant, who was following close behind, fell with a bullet through his head. The enemy now began to heavily bombard our position and Major Poore and Mr. Casson left the pillbox and got in a large shell hole which had a deep narrow trench dug in the bottom of it. They were safer there than in the pillbox, yet in less than fifteen minutes an howitzer shell had pitched clean in it, killing the both of them.

During the day shells fell all around the pillbox but not one made a direct hit on it. The ground rocked and heaved with the bursting shells. The enemy were doing their best to obliterate the strong point that they had lost. Mr. Diamond and I were mucking-in with a tin of Maconochies when a dud shell landed clean in the trench, killing the man behind me, and burying itself in the side of the trench by me. Our Maconochie was spoilt but I opened another one and we had the luck to eat that one without a clod of earth being thrown over it. If that shell had not been a dud we should have needed no more Maconochies in this world. I had found eight of them in a sandbag before I left the wood and brought them along with me. I passed the other six along our trench, but no one seemed to want them with the exception of the bank clerk and architect who had got into my way of thinking that it was better to enter the next world with a full belly than an empty one.

The bombardment lasted until the afternoon and then ceased. Not one of us had hardly moved a yard for some hours but we had been lucky in our part of the trench, having only two casualties. In two other parts of the strong point every man had been killed or wounded. The shells had been bursting right on the parapets and in the trenches, blowing them to pieces. One part of the trench was completely obliterated. The fourth part of the strong point had also been lucky, having only three casualties. Mr. Diamond said that we could expect a counter attack at any minute. He lined us up on the parapet in extended order outside the trench and told us to lie down. Suddenly a German plane swooped very low, machine-gunning us. We brought him down but not before he had done some damage, several being killed including our Aid Post Sergeant.

A few minutes later Dr. Dunn temporarily resigned from the Royal Army Medical Corps. He told me to get him a rifle and bayonet and a bandolier of ammunition. I told him that he had better have a revolver but he insisted on having what he had asked me to get. I found them for him and slinging the rifle over his shoulder he commenced to make his way over to the troops behind the bank. I accompanied him. Just before we reached there our chaps who were hanging on to a position in front of it started to retire back. The doctor barked at them to line up with the others. Only Captain Radford and four platoon officers were left in the Battalion and the Doctor unofficially took command.

We and the Australians were all mixed up in extended order. Everyone had now left the strong point and were lined up behind the bank, which was about three feet high. We had lent a Lewis-gun team to the 5th Scottish Rifles on our right, and when it began to get dark the Doctor sent me with a verbal message to bring them back with me, if they were still in the land of the living. When I arrived at the extreme right of our line I asked the right-hand man if he was in touch with the 5th Scottish. He replied that he had no more idea than a crow where they were, but guessed that they were somewhere in front and to the right of him. I now made my way very carefully over the ground. After I had walked some way I began to crawl. I was liable any moment to come in contact with a German post or trench. I thought I saw someone moving in front of me, so I slid into a shell hole and landed on a dead German. I waited in that shell hole for a while trying to pierce the darkness in front. I resumed my journey and, skirting one shell hole, a wounded German was shrieking aloud in agony; he must have been hit low down but I could not stop for no wounded man. I saw the forms of two men in a shallow trench and did not know whether they were the 5th Scottish or the Germans until I was sharply challenged in good Glasgow English. When I got in their trench they told me that they had only just spotted me when they challenged. The Lewis-gun team were still kicking and my journey back with them was a lot easier than the outgoing one.

I reported to the Doctor that there was a gap of about one hundred yards between the 5th Scottish Rifles and we; and he went himself to remedy it. The whole of the British Front that night seemed to be in a semi-circle. We had sent up some S O S rockets and no matter where we looked we could see our S O S rockets going up in the air: they were only used when the situation was deemed critical and everybody seemed to be in the same plight as ourselves. The bank clerk and I got into a shell hole to snatch a couple of hours rest, and although there were two dead Germans in it we were soon fast asleep. I was woke up to guide a ration party to us who were on their way. Dawn was now breaking and I made my way back about six hundred yards, where I met them. We landed safely with the rations.

Major Kearsley had just arrived from B Echelon to take command of the Battalion. The Brigadier-General of the Australians had also arrived and was sorting his men out. It was the only time during the whole of the War that I saw a brigadier with the first line of attacking troops. Some brigadiers that I knew never moved from Brigade Headquarters. It was also the first time I had been in action with the Australians and I found them very brave men. There was also an excellent spirit of comradeship between officers and men.

We were moving about quite freely in the open but we did not know that a large pillbox a little over an hundred yards in front of us was still held by the enemy. They must have all been having a snooze, otherwise some of us would have been riddled. Major Kearsley, the Doctor and I went out reconnoitring. We were jumping in and out of shell holes when a machine-gun opened out from somewhere in front, the bullets knocking up the dust around the shell holes we had just jumped into. They both agreed that the machine-gun had been fired from the pillbox about a hundred yards in front of us. We did some wonderful jumping and hopping, making our way back to the bank. The enemy's artillery had also opened out and an hour later shells were bursting all over our front and in the rear of us.

A sapping platoon of one sergeant and twenty men under the command of The Athlete were on the extreme left of the bank, and the Major and I made our way towards them. We found the men but not the officer and sergeant, and when the Major inquired where they were they replied that they were both down the dug-out. There was a concrete dug-out at this spot which had been taken the day before. I shouted down for them to come up, and the Major gave the young officer a severe reprimand for being in the dug-out, especially as he knew our men had just started another attack. Our chaps and the 5th Scottish Rifles had attacked on our right about fifteen minutes previously. The Major gave The Athlete orders that if the pillbox in front was not taken in fifteen minutes he was to take his platoon and capture it and then dig a trench around it. If the pillbox was captured during that time he was still to take his platoon and sap around it. I felt very sorry for The Athlete. This was the first real action he had been in and he had the most windy sergeant in the Battalion with him. Although The Athlete did not know it, this sergeant had been extremely lucky after one of his Arras stunts that he had not been court-martialled and tried on the charge of cowardice in face of the enemy.

We arrived back at our position behind the bank. We and the Australians were in telephone communication with no one; all messages went by runners. Ricco, the bank clerk and the architect were running messages, the majority of our Battalion runners being casualties. Sealyham was still kicking and Lane was back in B Echelon; it was the first time for over two years he had been left out of the line. The Sapping-Sergeant came running along the track by the bank and informed the Major that The Athlete had sent him for further instructions as he was not quite certain what he had to do. The Major very nearly lost his temper and told me to go back with the Sergeant and tell him what he had to do. Just as we arrived at the sapping-platoon we saw some of our chaps rushing towards the pillbox, which surrendered, one officer and twenty men being inside it.

C and D Companies were now merged into one company. They advanced and took up a position behind a little bank about a hundred yards in front of the pillbox. I informed The Athlete that he had to take his platoon and sap around the pillbox, and that this was a verbal message which Major Kearsley had given me for him. I left him and the Sergeant conferring together and made my way back by a different route.

The enemy were now shelling very heavily and occasionally the track was being sprayed by machine-gun bullets. I met a man of one of our companies with six German prisoners whom he told me he had to take back to a place called Clapham Junction, where he would hand them over. He then had to return and rejoin his company. The shelling was worse behind us than where we were and it happened more than once that escort and prisoners had been killed making their way back. I had known this man about eighteen months and he said, "Look here, Dick. About an hour ago I lost the best pal I ever had, and he was worth all these six Jerries put together. I'm not going to take them far before I put them out of mess." Just after they passed me I saw the six dive in one large shell hole and he had a job to drive them out. I expect being under their own shelling would make them more nervous than under ours. Some little time later I saw him coming back and I knew it was impossible for him to have reached Clapham Junction and returned in the time, especially by the way his prisoners had been ducking and jumping into shell holes. As he passed me again he said: "I done them in as I said, about two hundred yards back. Two bombs did the trick." He had not walked twenty yards beyond me when he fell himself: a shell-splinter had gone clean through him. I had often heard some of our chaps say that they had done their prisoners in whilst taking them back but this was the only case I could vouch for, and no doubt the loss of his pal had upset him very much.

During the afternoon the Major handed me a message to take to A Company, which consisted of the survivors of two companies now merged into one under the command of a young platoon officer. They had to advance and take up a position about two hundred yards in front of them. The ground over which I had to travel had been occupied by the enemy a little while before and the Company were behind a little bank which was being heavily shelled. I slung my rifle, and after I had proceeded some way I pulled my revolver out for safety. Shells were falling here and there and I was jumping in and out of shell holes. When I was about fifty yards from the Company, in getting out of a large shell hole I saw a German pop up from another shell hole in front of me and rest his rifle on the lip of the shell hole. He was about to fire at our chaps in front who had passed him by without noticing him. He could never have heard me amidst all the din around: I expect it was some instinct made him turn around with the rifle at his shoulder. I fired first and as the rifle fell out of his hands I fired again. I made sure he was dead before I left him. If he hadn't popped his head up when he did no doubt I would have passed the shell hole he was in. I expect he had been shamming death and every now and then popping up and sniping at our chaps in front. If I hadn't spotted him he would have soon put my lights out after I had passed him and if any of his bullets had found their mark it would not have been noticed among the Company, who were getting men knocked out now and then by the shells that were bursting around them. This little affair was nothing out of the ordinary in a runner's work when in attacks.

The shelling was very severe around here and when I arrived I shouted for the officer. A man pointed along the bank. When I found him and delivered the message he shouted above the noise that he had not been given much time; I had delivered the message only three minutes before they were timed to advance. During the short time they had been behind the bank one-third of the Company had become casualties. When I arrived back I could only see the Major. All the signallers had gone somewhere on messages and the Doctor was some distance away attending wounded men whom he came across. He seemed to be temporarily back in the R.A.M.C.

The Major asked me how my leg was. I replied that it was all right when I was moving about, but it became very stiff after I had been resting. During the two days many pieces and flying splinters of shells and bullets must have missed me by inches. But when a small piece of spent shrapnel had hit me on the calf of the leg I knew all about it. I thought at the time that someone had hit me with a coal hammer. I had the bottom of my trousers doubled inside the sock on the calf and also my puttee doubled in the same place which, no doubt, had helped to minimize the blow. If it had not been a spent piece it would have gone clean through the calf and given me a beautiful blighty wound, which I don't mind admitting I was still hoping for.

Ricco in returning from running a message to Brigade had come across the ration party of another battalion who had all been killed, and he had brought back with him a lovely sandbag full of officers' rations. There were several kinds of tinned stuffs and three loaves of bread. The bank clerk, architect and Sealyham had also arrived back and we all had a muck in. The way the bank clerk and architect got a tin of cooked sausages across their chests made me wonder whether their forefathers had not been pure-bred Germans. The officers who the bag of rations were intended for could never have enjoyed them better than we did.

Just as we finished our feed Major Kearsley called me and told me to follow him. I could see we were making our way towards where we had visited the sapping-platoon, but I could not see any men sapping around the pillbox and was wondering if they had been knocked out. When we arrived at the concrete dug-out some of the sapping-platoon were still outside it and some had become casualties, but The Athlete and the Sergeant were still down in the dug-out. I shouted down and told them to come up and the Major asked The Athlete the reason why he had not carried out his orders. He replied that the shelling had been so intense around the pillbox after it was taken that he decided to stop where he was until it slackened. Then he had seen our troops advance again and he was under the impression that the trench would not be needed. The Major again gave him a severe reprimand and told him to take what men he had left and sap around the pillbox as he had been ordered at first.

Shortly after, the Major said he was going to visit the positions our companies had lately taken. We set off on our journey and when we passed through the Australians they started shouting, "Come back, you bloody fools! They've got everything in line with machine-gun fire." We took no notice and by jumping in shell holes now and again we reached halfway there. We had only advanced a few yards further when in jumping into a large shell hole an enemy machine-gun opened out and the ground around us was sprayed with bullets. The Major was shot clean through the leg just above the ankle. As I dressed his wound we discussed the possibility of returning to the bank. I said that it would be dusk in two hours' time and that we had better wait until then. He replied that he could not do that as he would have to hand over the command of the Battalion, and also wanted to discuss matters with the Commanding Officer of the 5th Scottish Rifles, and that we would make our way back at once. He clambered out of the shell hole and I followed. He hopped back to the bank, taking a zig-zag course and I the same. How we were not riddled was a mystery: the machine-gun had been playing a pretty tune behind us.

We met the Doctor and Captain Radford, who had been sent for some time before, advancing along the bank. They had decided to shift Battalion Headquarters more on the left of the bank and they had just shifted in time. The spot where Battalion Headquarters had been was now being blown to pieces. Shells were bursting right along the bank and for a considerable way back and men were being blowed yards in the air. The Major said that the Battalion would be relieved at dusk and he would try to stick it until then; but the Doctor warned him, if he did, that it might be the cause of him losing his leg.

He then handed over the command to Captain Radford, who said that he would much prefer the Doctor taking command, as he seemed to have a better grip of the situation than what he had. But the Major said he could not do that as the Doctor was a non-combatant, but that they could make any arrangements they liked when he had left. We made our way to the 5th Scottish Rifles and met their colonel outside a little dug-out. He mentioned that only three young platoon-officers were left in his battalion. They went in the dug-out to discuss matters and when we left the Major had a difficult job to walk. The Casualty Clearing Station was at Clapham Junction and all along the track leading down to it lay stretcher-bearers and bandaged men who had been killed making their way back. Many men who had received what they thought were nice blighty wounds had been killed along this track. The previous day the track, in addition to being heavily shelled had also been under machine-gun fire. As we were moving along I counted over twenty of our tanks which had been put out of action. Mr. Diamond, whom I had not seen since the previous day, passed us with his arm in a sling and said, "Hello. I'm glad to see you alive." He had been hit through the muscle of his arm. Shells were bursting here and there and we could sniff gas. We put our gas helmets on for a little while and it was twilight when we reached Clapham Junction.

The Major told me that the Battalion was going back to Dickiebusch after it was relieved and that I had no need to return. He wrote me out a note to take back to the transport. He then said that he would have liked to have remained with the Battalion until they were relieved but he thought it best to follow the Doctor's advice, especially when he said that he might lose his leg. I told him not to take too much notice of the Doctor, who would have made a better general than a doctor, and that I had seen worse bullet-wounds than what he had which had healed up in a fortnight's time.

I hoped he would be back with the Battalion inside a couple of months. We shook hands and wished one another the best of luck and I made my way back to the transport.

The enemy bombed Dickiebusch that night but it was such a common occurrence around this area and I was so dead-beat that I took no notice of it. The following morning I rejoined the remnants of the Battalion and found that Ricco, the bank clerk, the architect and Sealyham were still kicking. They thought I had gone West and were as delighted to see me as I was them. We had lost heavily in signallers, but Tich was still hale and hearty

We were back in a village many miles from the Front, and one dark evening when I was standing outside my billet The Athlete came up to me and asked me if I would mind going for a walk with him. I thought it was a strange request for an officer to make to a private, especially when out of action, but I accompanied him. If he had been seen by a senior officer he might easily have been brought up for a breach of discipline. The Peer who had been back with Minimum Reserve had rejoined us, and also the Colonel from leave. When we were out of the village he said: "Richards, I'm in a fix, and what I am going to tell you is in confidence." He then told me that the previous day he had been sent for to appear in front of the Colonel, who informed him that he had received a very bad report on the way he had conducted himself in action on September 26th and 27th, and then read out the charges that had been made against him. He was then asked what explanation he could give in answer to the charges. He had explained to the best of his ability, and the Colonel had then dismissed him. He did not know whether he would be court-martialled or not. In case he was, he thought about calling upon me as a witness. I told him I was very sorry, but if he called upon me as a witness I was afraid I would do him more harm than good. I said that the sergeant he had with him was the most windy man in France and didn't care a damn who else got in the soup as long as he didn't, and that he should never have listened to his advice. The Athlete said that a young officer who had been left out in Minimum Reserve had since told him the same, and he wished he had realized it before. We then parted. When I arrived back at my billet the boys wanted to know where I had been, and when I told them I had picked up with a fair young maid they called me a scrounging old hound.

Two days later I called at the transport lines and an old soldier asked me if I thought The Athlete would be stuck against the wall and shot. I inquired what for. He then gave me full details of the case and said it was now stale news on the transport and was surprised I knew nothing about it. Our transport men were marvels; they knew everything that was happening on the Western Front. The Old Soldier when he was with the Battalion often used to say that they had a private telephone line to the Commander-in-Chief's bedroom.

The Athlete was not court-martialled, however, and later proved himself a very brave and capable officer, winning the Military Cross. In July 1918 he was wounded in a night raid on Beaumont-Hamel. I don't remember what became of the windy sergeant in the end; if he had had his just deserts he should have been given a couple of severe reprimands and then put against the wall and shot. All I know is that he later was with one of our new service battalions as a company-sergeant-major. It was only natural that a young inexperienced lieutenant would look for guidance from an experienced sergeant, but in this case it very nearly proved the undoing of what turned out to be a brave and capable officer.

WAR IS FOUGHT BY HUMAN BEINGS

An Occurrence at Owl Creek Bridge

BY

AMBROSE BIERCE

I

A MAN stood upon a railroad bridge in northern Alabama, looking down into the swift water twenty feet below. The man's hands were behind his back, the wrists bound with a cord. A rope closely encircled his neck. It was attached to a stout cross-timber above his head and the slack fell to the level of his knees. Some loose boards laid upon the sleepers supporting the metals of the railway supplied a footing for him and his executioners— two private soldiers of the Federal army, directed by a sergeant who in civil life may have been a deputy sheriff. At a short remove upon the same temporary platform was an officer in the uniform of his rank, armed. He was a captain. A sentinel at each end of the bridge stood with his rifle in the position known as "support," that is to say, vertical in front of the left shoulder, the hammer resting on the forearm thrown straight across the chest—a formal and unnatural position, enforcing an erect carriage of the body. It did not appear to be the duty of these two men to know what was occurring at the centre of the bridge; they merely blockaded the two ends of the foot planking that traversed it.

Beyond one of the sentinels nobody was in sight; the railroad ran straight away into a forest for a hundred yards, then, curving, was lost to view. Doubtless there was an outpost farther along. The other bank of the stream was open ground—a gentle acclivity topped with a stockade of vertical tree trunks, loopholed for rifles, with a single embrasure through which pro-truded the muzzle of a brass cannon commanding the bridge. Midway of the slope between bridge and fort were the spectators—a single company of infantry in line, at "parade rest," the butts of the rifles on the ground, the barrels inclining slightly backward against the right shoulder, the hands crossed upon the stock. A lieutenant stood at the right of the line, the point of his sword upon the ground, his left hand resting upon his right. Excepting the group of four at the centre of the bridge, not a man moved. The company faced the bridge, staring stonily, motionless. The sentinels, facing the banks of the stream, might have been statues to adorn the bridge. The captain stood with folded arms, silent, observing the work of his subor-dinates, but making no sign. Death is a dignitary who when he comes

From: *In the Midst of Life.* Albert and Charles Boni.

announced is to be received with formal manifestations of respect, even by those most familiar with him. In the code of military etiquette silence and fixity are forms of deference.

The man who was engaged in being hanged was apparently about thirty-five years of age. He was a civilian, if one might judge from his habit, which was that of a planter. His features were good—a straight nose, firm mouth, broad forehead, from which his long, dark hair was combed straight back, falling behind his ears to the collar of his well-fitting frock-coat. He wore a mustache and pointed beard, but no whiskers; his eyes were large and dark gray, and had a kindly expression which one would hardly have expected in one whose neck was in the hemp. Evidently this was no vulgar assassin. The liberal military code makes provision for hanging many kinds of persons, and gentlemen are not excluded.

The preparations being complete, the two private soldiers stepped aside and each drew away the plank upon which he had been standing. The sergeant turned to the captain, saluted and placed himself immediately behind that officer, who in turn moved apart one pace. These movements left the condemned man and the sergeant standing on the two ends of the same plank, which spanned three of the cross-ties of the bridge. The end upon which the civilian stood almost, but not quite, reached a fourth. This plank had been held in place by the weight of the captain; it was now held by that of the sergeant. At a signal from the former the latter would step aside, the plank would tilt and the condemned man go down between two ties. The arrangement commended itself to his judgment as simple and effective. His face had not been covered nor his eyes bandaged. He looked a moment at his "unsteadfast footing," then let his gaze wander to the swirling water of the stream racing madly beneath his feet. A piece of dancing driftwood caught his attention and his eyes followed it down the current. How slowly it appeared to move! What a sluggish stream!

He closed his eyes in order to fix his last thoughts upon his wife and children. The water, touched to gold by the early sun, the brooding mists under the banks at some distance down the stream, the fort, the soldiers, the piece of drift—all had distracted him. And now he became conscious of a new disturbance. Striking through the thought of his dear ones was a sound which he could neither ignore nor understand, a sharp, distinct, metallic percussion like the stroke of a blacksmith's hammer upon the anvil; it had the same ringing quality. He wondered what it was, and whether immeasurably distant or near by—it seemed both. Its recurrence was regular, but as slow as the tolling of a death knell. He awaited each stroke with impatience and—he knew not why—apprehension. The intervals of silence grew progressively longer; the delays became maddening. With their greater infrequency the sounds increased in strength and sharpness. They hurt his ear like the thrust of a knife; he feared he would shriek. What he heard was the ticking of his watch.

He unclosed his eyes and saw again the water below him. "If I could free my hands," he thought, "I might throw off the noose and spring into the stream. By diving I could evade the bullets and, swimming vigorously, reach the bank, take to the woods and get away home. My home, thank God, is as yet outside their lines; my wife and little ones are still beyond the invader's farthest advance."

As these thoughts, which have here to be set down in words, were flashed into the doomed man's brain rather than evolved from it the captain nodded to the sergeant. The sergeant stepped aside.

II

Peyton Farquhar was a well-to-do planter, of an old and highly respected Alabama family. Being a slave owner and like other slave owners a politician he was naturally an original secessionist and ardently devoted to the Southern cause. Circumstances of an imperious nature, which it is unnecessary to relate here, had prevented him from taking service with the gallant army that had fought the disastrous campaigns ending with the fall of Corinth, and he chafed under the inglorious restraint, longing for the release of his energies, the larger life of the soldier, the opportunity for distinction. That opportunity, he felt, would come, as it comes to all in war time. Meanwhile he did what he could. No service was too humble for him to perform in aid of the South, no adventure too perilous for him to undertake if consistent with the character of a civilian who was at heart a soldier, and who in good faith and without too much qualification assented to at least a part of the frankly villainous dictum that all is fair in love and war.

One evening while Farquhar and his wife were sitting on a rustic bench near the entrance to his grounds, a gray-clad soldier rode up to the gate and asked for a drink of water. Mrs. Farquhar was only too happy to serve him with her own white hands. While she was fetching the water her husband approached the dusty horseman and inquired eagerly for news from the front.

"The Yanks are repairing the railroads," said the man, "and are getting ready for another advance. They have reached the Owl Creek bridge, put it in order and built a stockade on the north bank. The commandant has issued an order, which is posted everywhere, declaring that any civilian caught interfering with the railroad, its bridges, tunnels or trains will be summarily hanged. I saw the order."

"How far is it to the Owl Creek bridge?" Farquhar asked.

"About thirty miles."

"Is there no force on this side the creek?"

"Only a picket post half a mile out, on the railroad, and a single sentinel at this end of the bridge."

"Suppose a man—a civilian and student of hanging—should elude the picket post and perhaps get the better of the sentinel," said Farquhar, smiling, "what could he accomplish?"

The soldier reflected. "I was there a month ago," he replied. "I observed that the flood of last winter had lodged a great quantity of driftwood against the wooden pier at this end of the bridge. It is now dry and would burn like tow."

The lady had now brought the water, which the soldier drank. He thanked her ceremoniously, bowed to her husband and rode away. An hour later, after nightfall, he repassed the plantation, going northward in the direction from which he had come. He was a Federal scout.

III

As Peyton Farquhar fell straight downward through the bridge he lost consciousness and was as one already dead. From this state he was awakened—ages later, it seemed to him—by the pain of a sharp pressure upon his throat, followed by a sense of suffocation. Keen, poignant agonies seemed to shoot from his neck downward through every fibre of his body and limbs. These pains appeared to flash along well-defined lines of ramification and to beat with an inconceivably rapid periodicity. They seemed like streams of pulsating fire heating him to an intolerable temperature. As to his head, he was conscious of nothing but a feeling of fulness—of congestion. These sensations were unaccompanied by thought. The intellectual part of his nature was already effaced; he had power only to feel, and feeling was torment. He was conscious of motion. Encompassed in a luminous cloud, of which he was now merely the fiery heart, without material substance, he swung through unthinkable arcs of oscillation, like a vast pendulum. Then all at once, with terrible suddenness, the light about him shot upward with the noise of a loud plash; a frightful roaring was in his ears, and all was cold and dark. The power of thought was restored; he knew that the rope had broken and he had fallen into the stream. There was no additional strangulation; the noose about his neck was already suffocating him and kept the water from his lungs. To die of hanging at the bottom of a river!—the idea seemed to him ludicrous. He opened his eyes in the darkness and saw above him a gleam of light, but how distant, how inaccessible! He was still sinking, for the light became fainter and fainter until it was a mere glimmer. Then it began to grow and brighten, and he knew that he was rising toward the surface—knew it with reluctance, for he was now very comfortable. "To be hanged and drowned," he thought, "that is not so bad; but I do not wish to be shot. No; I will not be shot; that is not fair."

He was not conscious of an effort, but a sharp pain in his wrist apprised him that he was trying to free his hands. He gave the struggle his attention, as an idler might observe the feat of a juggler, without interest in the outcome. What splendid effort!—what magnificent, what superhuman strength! Ah, that was a fine endeavor! Bravo! The cord fell away; his arms parted and floated upward, the hands dimly seen on each side in the growing light. He watched them with a new interest as first one and then the other pounced upon the noose at his neck. They tore it away and thrust it fiercely aside, its undulations resembling those of a water-snake. "Put it back, put it back!" He thought he shouted these words to his hands, for the undoing of the noose had been succeeded by the direst pang that he had yet experienced. His neck ached horribly; his brain was on fire; his heart, which had been fluttering faintly, gave a great leap, trying to force itself out at his mouth. His whole body was racked and wrenched with an insupportable anguish! But his disobedient hands gave no heed to the command. They beat the water vigorously with quick, downward strokes, forcing him to the surface. He felt his head emerge; his eyes were blinded by the sunlight; his chest expanded convulsively, and with a supreme and crowning agony his lungs engulfed a great draught of air, which instantly he expelled in a shriek!

He was now in full possession of his physical senses. They were, indeed, preternaturally keen and alert. Something in the awful disturbance of his organic system had so exalted and refined them that they made record of things never before perceived. He felt the ripples upon his face and heard their separate sounds as they struck. He looked at the forest on the bank of the stream, saw the individual trees, the leaves and the veining of each leaf—saw the very insects upon them: the locusts, the brilliant-bodied flies, the gray spiders stretching their webs from twig to twig. He noted the prismatic colors in all the dewdrops upon a million blades of grass. The humming of the gnats that danced above the eddies of the stream, the beating of the dragon-flies' wings, the strokes of the waterspiders' legs, like oars which had lifted their boat—all these made audible music. A fish slid along beneath his eyes and he heard the rush of its body parting the water.

He had come to the surface facing down the stream; in a moment the visible world seemed to wheel slowly round, himself the pivotal point, and he saw the bridge, the fort, the soldiers upon the bridge, the captain, the sergeant, the two privates, his executioners. They were in silhouette against the blue sky. They shouted and gesticulated, pointing at him. The captain had drawn his pistol, but did not fire; the others were unarmed. Their movements were grotesque and horrible, their forms gigantic.

Suddenly he heard a sharp report and something struck the water smartly within a few inches of his head, spattering his face with spray. He heard a second report, and saw one of the sentinels with his rifle at his shoulder, a light cloud of blue smoke rising from the muzzle. The man in the water saw the eye of the man on the bridge gazing into his own through the sights of the rifle. He observed that it was a gray eye and remembered having read that gray eyes were keenest, and that all famous marksmen had them. Nevertheless, this one had missed.

A counter-swirl had caught Farquhar and turned him half round; he was again looking into the forest on the bank opposite the fort. The sound of a clear, high voice in a monotonous singsong now rang out behind him and came across the water with a distinctness that pierced and subdued all other sounds, even the beating of the ripples in his ears. Although no soldier, he had frequented camps enough to know the dread significance of that deliberate, drawling, aspirated chant; the lieutenant on shore was taking a part in the morning's work. How coldly and pitilessly—with what an even, calm intonation, presaging, and enforcing tranquillity in the men—with what accurately measured intervals fell those cruel words:

"Attention, company! . . . Shoulder arms! . . . Ready! . . . Aim! . . . Fire!"

Farquhar dived—dived as deeply as he could. The water roared in his ears like the voice of Niagara, yet he heard the dulled thunder of the volley and, rising again toward the surface, met shining bits of metal, singularly flattened, oscillating slowly downward. Some of them touched him on the face and hands, then fell away, continuing their descent. One lodged between his collar and neck; it was uncomfortably warm and he snatched it out.

As he rose to the surface, gasping for breath, he saw that he had been a long time under water; he was perceptibly farther down stream—nearer to safety. The soldiers had almost finished reloading; the metal ramrods flashed all at once in the sunshine as they were drawn from the barrels, turned in the air, and thrust into their sockets. The two sentinels fired again, independently and ineffectually.

The hunted man saw all this over his shoulder; he was now swimming vigorously with the current. His brain was as energetic as his arms and legs; he thought with the rapidity of lightning.

"The officer," he reasoned, "will not make that martinet's error a second time. It is as easy to dodge a volley as a single shot. He has probably already given the command to fire at will. God help me, I cannot dodge them all!"

An appalling plash within two yards of him was followed by a loud, rushing sound, *diminuendo,* which seemed to travel back through the air to the fort and died in an explosion which stirred the very river to its deeps! A rising sheet of water curved over him, fell down upon him, blinded him, strangled him! The cannon had taken a hand in the game. As he shook his head free from the commotion of the smitten water he heard the deflected shot humming through the air ahead, and in an instant it was cracking and smashing the branches in the forest beyond.

"They will not do that again," he thought; "the next time they will use a charge of grape. I must keep my eye upon the gun; the smoke will apprise me—the report arrives too late; it lags behind the missile. That is a good gun."

Suddenly he felt himself whirled round and round—spinning like a top. The water, the banks, the forests, the now distant bridge, fort and men—all were commingled and blurred. Objects were represented by their colors only; circular horizontal streaks of color—that was all he saw. He had been caught in a vortex and was being whirled on with a velocity of advance and gyration that made him giddy and sick. In a few moments he was flung upon the gravel at the foot of the left bank of the stream—the southern bank—and behind a projecting point which concealed him from his enemies. The sudden arrest of his motion, the abrasion of one of his hands on the gravel, restored him, and he wept with delight. He dug his fingers into the sand, threw it over himself in handfuls and audibly blessed it. It looked like diamonds, rubies, emeralds; he could think of nothing beautiful which it did not resemble. The trees upon the bank were giant garden plants; he noted a definite order in their arrangement, inhaled the fragrance of their blooms. A strange, roseate light shone through the spaces among their trunks and the wind made in their branches the music of æolian harps. He had no wish to perfect his escape—was content to remain in that enchanting spot until retaken.

A whiz and rattle of grapeshot among the branches high above his head roused him from his dream. The baffled cannoneer had fired a random farewell. He sprang to his feet, rushed up the sloping bank, and plunged into the forest.

All that day he traveled, laying his course by the rounding sun. The forest seemed interminable; nowhere did he discover a break in it, not even a woodman's road. He had not known that he lived in so wild a region. There was something uncanny in the revelation.

By nightfall he was fatigued, footsore, famishing. The thought of his wife and children urged him on. At last he found a road which led him in what he knew to be the right direction. It was as wide and straight as a city street, yet it seemed untraveled. No fields bordered it, no dwelling anywhere. Not so much as the barking of a dog suggested human habitation. The black bodies of the trees formed a straight wall on both sides, terminating on the horizon in a point, like a diagram in a lesson in perspective. Overhead, as he looked up through this rift in the wood, shone great golden stars looking unfamiliar and grouped in strange constellations. He was sure they were arranged in some order which had a secret and malign significance. The wood on either side was full of singular noises, among which— once, twice, and again—he distinctly heard whispers in an unknown tongue.

His neck was in pain and lifting his hand to it he found it horribly swollen. He knew that it had a circle of black where the rope had bruised it. His eyes felt congested; he could no longer close them. His tongue was swollen with thirst; he relieved its fever by thrusting it forward from between his teeth into the cold air. How softly the turf had carpeted the untraveled avenue—he could no longer feel the roadway beneath his feet!

Doubtless, despite his suffering, he had fallen asleep while walking, for now he sees another scene—perhaps he has merely recovered from a delirium. He stands at the gate of his own home. All is as he left it, and all bright and beautiful in the morning sunshine. He must have traveled the entire night. As he pushes open the gate and passes up the wide white walk, he sees a flutter of female garments; his wife, looking fresh and cool and sweet, steps down from the veranda to meet him. At the bottom of the steps she stands waiting, with a smile of ineffable joy, an attitude of matchless grace and dignity. Ah, how beautiful she is! He springs forward with extended arms. As he is about to clasp her he feels a stunning blow upon the back of the neck; a blinding white light blazes all about him with a sound like the shock of a cannon—then all is darkness and silence!

Peyton Farquhar was dead; his body, with a broken neck, swung gently from side to side beneath the timbers of the Owl Creek bridge.

Joshua's Conquest of Jericho

THE BIBLE

Now after the death of Moses the servant of the Lord it came to pass, that the Lord spake unto Joshua the son of Nun, Moses' minister, saying,

Moses my servant is dead; now therefore arise, go over this Jordan, thou, and all this people, unto the land which I do give to them, even to the children of Israel. Every place that the sole of your foot shall tread upon, that have I given unto you, as I said unto Moses. From the wilderness and this Lebanon even unto the great river, the river Euphrates, all the land of the Hittites, and unto the great sea toward the going down of the sun, shall be your coast. There shall not any man be able to stand before thee all the days of thy life: as I was with Moses, so I will be with thee: I will not fail thee, nor forsake thee. Be strong and of a good courage: for unto this people shalt thou divide for an inheritance the land, which I sware unto their fathers to give them. Only be thou strong and very courageous, that thou mayest observe to do according to all the law, which Moses my servant commanded thee: turn not from it to the right hand or to the left, that thou mayest prosper whithersoever thou goest. Have not I commanded thee? Be strong and of a good courage; be not afraid, neither be thou dismayed: for the Lord thy God is with thee whithersoever thou goest.

Then Joshua commanded the officers of the people, saying, Pass through the host, and command the people, saying, Prepare you victuals; for within three days ye shall pass over this Jordan, to go in to possess the land, which the Lord your God giveth you to possess it.

And they answered Joshua, saying, All that thou commandest us we will do, and whithersoever thou sendest us, we will go.

And Joshua the son of Nun sent out of Shittim two men to spy secretly, saying, Go view the land, even Jericho. And they went, and came into an harlot's house, named Rahab, and lodged there.

And it was told the King of Jericho, saying, Behold, there came men in hither to night of the children of Israel to search out the country. And the King of Jericho sent unto Rahab, saying, Bring forth the men that are come to thee, which are entered into thine house: for they be come to search out all the country.

And the woman took the two men, and hid them, and said thus, There came men unto me, but I wist not whence they were: And it came to pass

From: *The Bible.*

about the time of shutting of the gate, when it was dark, that the men went out: whither the men went I wot not: pursue after them quickly; for ye shall overtake them. But she had brought them up to the roof of the house, and hid them with the stalks of flax, which she had laid in order upon the roof. And the men pursued after them the way to Jordan unto the fords; and as soon as they which pursued after them were gone out, they shut the gate.

And before they were laid down, she came up unto them upon the roof; And she said unto the men, I know that the Lord hath given you the land, and that your terror is fallen upon us, and that all the inhabitants of the land faint because of you. For we have heard how the Lord dried up the water of the Red Sea for you, when ye came out of Egypt; and what ye did unto the two kings of the Amorites, that were on the other side Jordan, Sihon and Og, whom ye utterly destroyed. And as soon as we had heard these things, our hearts did melt, neither did there remain any more courage in any man, because of you: for the Lord your God, He is God in heaven above, and in earth beneath. Now therefore, I pray you, swear unto me by the Lord, since I have shewed you kindness, that ye will also shew kindness unto my father's house, and give me a true token: And that ye will save alive my father, and my mother, and my brethren, and my sisters, and all that they have, and deliver our lives from death.

And the men answered her, Our life for yours, if ye utter not this our business. And it shall be, when the Lord hath given us the land, that we will deal kindly and truly with thee.

Then she let them down by a cord through the window: for her house was upon the town wall, and she dwelt upon the wall. And she said unto them, Get you to the mountain, lest the pursuers meet you; and hide yourselves there three days, until the pursuers be returned: and afterward may ye go your way.

And the men said unto her, We will be blameless of this thine oath which thou hast made us swear. Behold, when we come into the land, thou shalt bind this line of scarlet thread in the window which thou didst let us down by: and thou shalt bring thy father, and thy mother, and thy brethren, and all thy father's household, home unto thee. And it shall be, that whosoever shall go out of the doors of thy house into the street, his blood shall be upon his head, and we will be guiltless: and whosoever shall be with thee in the house, his blood shall be on our head, if any hand be upon him. And if thou utter this our business, then we will be quit of thine oath which thou hast made us to swear.

And she said, According unto your words, so be it. And she sent them away, and they departed: and she bound the scarlet line in the window.

And they went, and came unto the mountain, and abode there three days, until the pursuers were returned: and the pursuers sought them throughout all the way, but found them not. So the two men returned, and descended from the mountain, and passed over, and came to Joshua the son of Nun, and told him all things that befell them: And they said unto

Joshua, Truly the Lord hath delivered into our hands all the land; for even all the inhabitants of the country do faint because of us.

And Joshua rose early in the morning; and they removed from Shittim, and came to Jordan, he and all the children of Israel, and lodged there before they passed over.

And Joshua spake unto the priests, saying, Take up the ark of the covenant, and pass over before the people. And they took up the ark of the covenant, and went before the people.

And the Lord said unto Joshua, This day will I begin to magnify thee in the sight of all Israel, that they may know that, as I was with Moses, so I will be with thee. And thou shalt command the priests that bear the ark of the covenant, saying, When ye are come to the brink of the water of Jordan, ye shall stand still in Jordan.

And Joshua said unto the children of Israel, Come hither, and hear the words of the Lord your God. And Joshua said, Hereby ye shall know that the living God is among you, and that He will without fail drive out from before you the Canaanites, and the Hittites, and the Hivites, and the Perizzites, and the Girgashites, and the Amorites, and the Jebusites. Behold, the ark of the covenant of the Lord of all the earth passeth over before you into Jordan. Now therefore take you twelve men out of the tribes of Israel, out of every tribe a man. And it shall come to pass, as soon as the soles of the feet of the priests that bear the ark of the Lord, the Lord of all the earth, shall rest in the waters of Jordan, that the waters of Jordan shall be cut off from the waters that come down from above; and they shall stand upon an heap.

And it came to pass, when the people removed from their tents, to pass over Jordan, and the priests bearing the ark of the covenant before the people; And as they that bare the ark were come unto Jordan, and the feet of the priests that bare the ark were dipped in the brim of the water, (for Jordan overfloweth all his banks all the time of harvest), That the waters which came down from above stood and rose up upon an heap very far from the city Adam, that is beside Zaretan: and those that came down toward the sea of the plain, even the salt sea, failed, and were cut off: and the people passed over right against Jericho. And the priests that bare the ark of the covenant of the Lord stood firm on dry ground in the midst of Jordan, and all the Israelites passed over on dry ground, until all the people were passed clean over Jordan.

About forty thousand prepared for war passed over before the Lord unto battle, to the plains of Jericho.

On that day the Lord magnified Joshua in the sight of all Israel; and they feared him, as they feared Moses, all the days of his life.

And it came to pass, when Joshua was by Jericho, that he lifted up his eyes and looked, and, behold, there stood a man over against him with his sword drawn in his hand: and Joshua went unto him, and said unto him, Art thou for us, or for our adversaries?

And he said, Nay; but as captain of the host of the Lord am I now come.

And Joshua fell on his face to the earth, and did worship, and said unto him, What saith my lord unto his servant? And the captain of the Lord's host said unto Joshua, Loose thy shoe from off thy foot; for the place whereon thou standest is holy. And Joshua did so.

Now Jericho was straitly shut up because of the children of Israel: none went out, and none came in.

And the Lord said unto Joshua, See, I have given into thine hand Jericho, and the king thereof, and the mighty men of valour. And ye shall compass the city, all ye men of war, and go round about the city once. Thus shalt thou do six days. And seven priests shall bear before the ark seven trumpets of rams' horns: and the seventh day ye shall compass the city seven times, and the priests shall blow with the trumpets. And it shall come to pass, that when they make a long blast with the ram's horn, and when ye hear the sound of the trumpet, all the people shall shout with a great shout; and the wall of the city shall fall down flat, and the people shall ascend up every man straight before him.

And Joshua the son of Nun called the priests, and said unto them, Take up the ark of the covenant, and let seven priests bear seven trumpets of rams' horns before the ark of the Lord. And he said unto the people, Pass on, and compass the city, and let him that is armed pass on before the ark of the Lord.

And it came to pass, when Joshua had spoken unto the people, that the seven priests bearing the seven trumpets of rams' horns passed on before the Lord, and blew with the trumpets: and the ark of the covenant of the Lord followed them. And the armed men went before the priests that blew with the trumpets, and the rearward came after the ark, the priests going on, and blowing with the trumpets. And Joshua had commanded the people, saying, Ye shall not shout, nor make any noise with your voice, neither shall any word proceed out of your mouth, until the day I bid you shout; then shall ye shout. So the ark of the Lord compassed the city, going about it once: and they came into the camp, and lodged in the camp.

And Joshua rose early in the morning, and the priests took up the ark of the Lord. And seven priests bearing seven trumpets of rams' horns before the ark of the Lord went on continually, and blew with the trumpets: and the armed men went before them; but the rearward came after the ark of the Lord, the priests going on, and blowing the trumpets.

And the second day they compassed the city once, and returned into the camp: so they did six days.

And it came to pass on the seventh day, that they rose early about the dawning of the day, and compassed the city after the same manner seven times: only on that day they compassed the city seven times. And it came to pass at the seventh time, when the priests blew with the trumpets, Joshua said unto the people, Shout; for the Lord hath given you the city. And the city shall be accursed, even it, and all that are therein, to the Lord: only Rahab the harlot shall live, she and all that are with her in the house, because she hid the messengers that we sent. And ye, in any wise keep yourselves from the accursed thing, lest ye make yourselves accursed, when ye take of the accursed thing, and make the camp of Israel a curse, and trouble it. But all the silver, and gold, and vessels of brass and iron, are consecrated unto the Lord: they shall come into the treasury of the Lord.

So the people shouted when the priests blew with the trumpets: and it came to pass, when the people heard the sound of the trumpet, and the people shouted with a great shout, that the wall fell down flat, so that the people went up into the city, every man straight before him, and they took the city. And they utterly destroyed all that was in the city, both man and woman, young and old, and ox, and sheep, and ass, with the edge of the sword.

But Joshua had said unto the two men that had spied out the country, Go into the harlot's house, and bring out thence the woman, and all that she hath, as ye sware unto her.

And the young men that were spies went in, and brought out Rahab, and her father, and her mother, and her brethren, and all that she had; and they brought out all her kindred, and left them without the camp of Israel.

And they burnt the city with fire, and all that was therein: only the silver, and the gold, and the vessels of brass and of iron, they put into the treasury of the house of the Lord.

And Joshua saved Rahab the harlot alive, and her father's household, and all that she had; and she dwelleth in Israel even unto this day; because she hid the messengers, which Joshua sent to spy out Jericho.

And Joshua adjured them at that time, saying, Cursed be the man before the Lord, that riseth up and buildeth this city Jericho: he shall lay the foundation thereof in his firstborn, and in his youngest son shall he set up the gates of it.

So the Lord was with Joshua; and his fame was noised throughout all the country.

The Taking of Lungtungpen

BY

RUDYARD KIPLING

So we loosed a bloomin' volley,
　An' we made the beggars cut,
An' when our pouch was emptied out,
　We used the bloomin' butt,
　　Ho! My!
　Don't yer come anigh,
When Tommy is a playin' with the
　bayonit an' the butt.

Barrack Room Ballad.

MY FRIEND Private Mulvaney told me this, sitting on the parapet of the road to Dagshai, when we were hunting butterflies together. He had theories about the Army, and colored clay pipes perfectly. He said that the young soldier is the best to work with, "on account av the surpassing innocinse av the child."

"Now, listen!" said Mulvaney, throwing himself full length on the wall in the sun. "I'm a born scutt av the barrick room! The Army's mate an' dhrink to me, bekaze I'm wan av the few that can't quit ut. I've put in sivinteen years, an' the pipeclay's in the marrow av me. Av I cud have kept out av wan big dhrink a month, I wud have been a Hon'ry Lift'nint by this time—a nuisance to my betthers, a laughin' shtock to my equils, an' a curse to meself. Bein' fwhat I am, I'm Privit Mulvaney, wid no good-conduc' pay an' a devourin' thirst. Always barrin' me little frind Bobs Bahadur, I know as much about the Army as most men."

I said something here.

"Wolseley be shot! Betune you an' me an' that butterfly net, he's a ramblin', incoherent sort av a divil, wid wan oi on the Quane an' the Coort, an' the other on his blessed silf—everlastin'ly playing Saysar an' Alexandrier rowled into a lump. Now Bobs is a sinsible little man. Wid Bobs an' a few three-year-olds, I'd swape any army av the earth into a towel, an' throw it away afterward. Faith, I'm not jokin'! 'Tis the bhoys—the raw bhoys—that don't know fwhat a bullet manes, an' wudn't care av they did—that dhu the work. They're crammed wid bull-mate till they fairly *ramps* wid good livin'; and thin, av they don't fight, they blow each other's

From: *Soldiers Three.*

899

hids off. 'Tis the trut' I'm tellin' you. They shud be kept on water an' rice in the hot weather; but ther'd be a mut'ny av 'twas done.

"Did ye iver hear how Privit Mulvaney tuk the town av Lungtungpen? I thought not! 'Twas the Lift'nint got the credit; but 'twas me planned the schame. A little before I was inviladed from Burma, me an' four-an'-twenty young wans undher a Lift'nint Brazenose, was ruinin' our dijeshins thryin' to catch dacoits. An' such double-ended divils I niver knew! 'Tis only a *dah* an' a Snider that makes a dacoit. Widout thim, he's a paceful cultivator, an' felony for to shoot. We hunted, an' we hunted, an' tuk fever an' elephints now an' again; but no dacoits. Evenshually, we *puckarowed* wan man. 'Trate him tinderly,' sez the Lift'nint. So I tuk him away into the jungle, wid the Burmese Interprut'r an' my clanin'-rod. Sez I to the man, 'My paceful squireen,' sez I, 'you shquot on your hunkers an' dimonstrate to *my* frind here, where *your* frinds are whin they're at home?' Wid that I introjuced him to the clanin'-rod, an' he comminst to jabber; the Interprut'r interprutin' in betweens, an' me helpin' the Intilligence Departmint wid my clanin'-rod whin the man misremembered.

"Prisintly, I learn that, acrost the river, about nine miles away, was a town just dhrippin' wid *dahs*, an' bohs an' arrows, an' dacoits, an' elephints, an' *jingles*. 'Good!' sez I; 'this office will now close!'

"That night, I went to the Lift'nint an' communicates my information. I never thought much of Lift'nint Brazenose till that night. He was shtiff wid books an' the-ouries, an' all manner av thrimmin's no manner av use. 'Town did ye say?' sez he. 'Accordin' to the the-ouries av War, we shud wait for reinforcemints.'—'Faith!' thinks I, 'we'd betther dig our graves thin;' for the nearest throops was up to their shtocks in the marshes out Mimbu way. 'But,' says the Lift'nint, 'since 'tis a speshil case, I'll make an excepshin. We'll visit this Lungtungpen tonight.'

"The bhoys was fairly woild wid deloight whin I tould 'em; an', by this an' that, they wint through the jungle like buck-rabbits. About midnight we come to the shtrame which I had clane forgot to minshin to my orficer. I was on, ahead, wid four bhoys, an' I thought that the Lift'nint might want to the-ourise. 'Shtrip bhoys!' sez I. 'Shtrip to the buff, an' shwim in where glory waits!'—'But I *can't* shwim!' sez two of thim. 'To think I should live to hear that from a bhoy wid a board-school edukashin!' sez I. 'Take a lump av timber, an' me an' Conolly here will ferry ye over, ye young ladies!'

"We got an ould tree-trunk, an' pushed off wid the kits an' the rifles on it. The night was chokin' dhark, an' just as we was fairly embarked, I heard the Lift'nint behind av me callin' out. 'There's a bit av a *nullah* here, sorr,' sez I, 'but I can feel the bottom already.' So I cud, for I was not a yard from the bank.

" 'Bit av a *nullah*! Bit av an eshtuary!' sez the Lift'nint. 'Go on, ye mad Irishman! Shtrip bhoys!' I heard him laugh; an' the bhoys begun shtrippin' an' rollin' a log into the wather to put their kits on. So me an' Conolly shtruck out through the warm wather wid our log, an' the rest come on behind.

"That shtrame was miles woide! Orth'ris, on the rear-rank log, whispers we had got into the Thames below Sheerness by mistake. 'Kape on shwim-min', ye little blayguard,' sez I, 'an' Irriwaddy.'—'Silence, men!' sings out the Lift'nint. So we shwum on into the black dhark, wid our chests on the logs, trustin' in the Saints an' the luck av the British Army.

"Evenshually, we hit ground—a bit av sand—an' a man. I put my heel on the back av him. He skreeched an' ran.

"'*Now* we've done it!' sez Lift'nint Brazenose. 'Where the Divil *is* Lungtungpen?' There was about a minute and a half to wait. The bhoys laid a hould av their rifles an' some thried to put their belts on; we was marchin' wid fixed baynits av coorse. Thin we knew where Lungtungpen was; for we had hit the river-wall av it in the dhark, an' the whole town blazed wid thim messin' *jingles* an' Sniders like a cat's back on a frosty night. They was firin' all ways at wanst; but over our heads into the shtrame.

"'Have you got your rifles?' sez Brazenose. 'Got 'em!' sez Orth'ris. 'I've got that thief Mulvaney's for all my back-pay, an' she'll kick my heart sick wid that blunderin' long shtock av hers.'—'Go on!' yells Brazenose, whippin' his sword out. 'Go on an' take the town! An' the Lord have mercy on our sowls!'

"Thin the bhoys gave wan divastatin' howl, an' pranced into the dhark, feelin' for the town, an' blindin' an' stiffin' like Cavalry Ridin' Masters whin the grass pricked their bare legs. I hammered wid the butt at some bamboo-thing that felt wake, an' the rest come an' hammered contagious, while the *jingles* was jingling, an' feroshus yells from inside was shplittin' our ears. We was too close under the wall for thim to hurt us.

"Evenshually, the thing, whatever ut was, bruk; an' the six-an'-twenty av us tumbled, wan after the other, naked as we was borrun, into the town of Lungtungpen. There was a *melly* av a sumpshus kind for a whoile; but whether they tuk us, all white an' wet, for a new breed av divil, or a new kind av dacoit, I don't know. They ran as though we was both, an' we wint into thim, baynit an' butt, shriekin' wid laughin'. There was torches in the shtreets, an' I saw little Orth'ris rubbin' his showlther ivry time he loosed my long-shtock Martini; an' Brazenose walkin' into the gang wid his sword, like Diarmid av the Gowlden Collar—barring he hadn't a stitch av clothin' on him. We diskivered elephints wid dacoits under their bellies, an', what wid wan thing an' other, we was busy till mornin' takin' possession av the town of Lungtungpen.

"Then we halted an' formed up, the wimmen howlin' in the houses an' the Lift'nint blushin' pink in the light av the mornin' sun. 'Twas the most ondasint p'rade I iver tuk a hand in. Foive-an'-twinty privits an' a orficer av the Line in review ordher, an' not as much as wud dust a fife betune 'em all in the way of clothin'! Eight av us had their belts an' pouches on; but the rest had gone in wid a handful av cartridges an' the skin God gave them. *They* was as nakid as Vanus.

" 'Number off from the right!' sez the Lift'nint. 'Odd numbers fall out to dress; even numbers pathrol the town till relieved by the dressing party.' Let me tell you, pathrollin' a town wid nothin' on is an ex*pay*rience. I pathrolled for tin minutes, an' begad, before 'twas over, I blushed. The women laughed so. I niver blushed before or since; but I blushed all over my carkiss thin. Orth'ris didn't pathrol. He sez only, 'Portsmouth Barricks an' the 'Ard av a Sunday!' Thin he lay down an' rolled any ways wid laughin'.

"Whin we was all dhressed, we counted the dead—sivinty-foive dacoits besides the wounded. We tuk five elephints, a hunder' an' sivinty Sniders, two hunder' dahs, and a lot of other burglarious thruck. Not a man av us was hurt—excep' maybe the Lift'nint, an' he from the shock of his dasincy.

"The Headman av Lungtungpen, who surrinder'd himself asked the Interprut'r—'Av the English fight like that wid their clo'es off, what in the wurruld do they do wid their clo'es on?' Orth'ris began rowlin' his eyes an' crackin' his fingers an' dancin' a step-dance for to impress the Headman. He ran to his house; an' we spint the rest av the day carryin' the Lift'nint on our showlthers round the town, an' playin' wid the Burmese babies—fat, little, brown little divils, as pretty as picturs.

"Whin I was inviladed for the dysent'ry to India, I sez to the Lift'nint, 'Sorr,' sez I, 'you've the makin' in you av a great man; but, av you'll let an ould sodger spake, you're too fond of the-ourisin'.' He shuk hands wid me and sez, 'Hit high, hit low, there's no plazin' you, Mulvaney. You've seen me waltzin' through Lungtungpen like a Red Injin widout the war-paint, an' you say I'm too fond av the-ourisin'?'—'Sorr,' sez I, for I loved the bhoy; 'I wud waltz wid you in that condishin through *Hell*, an' so wud the rest av the men!' Thin I went downshtrame in the flat an' left him my blessin'. May the Saints carry ut where ut shud go, for he was a fine upstandin' young orficer.

"To reshume. Fwhat I've said jist shows the use av three-year-olds. Wud fifty seasoned sodgers have taken Lungtungpen in the dhark that way? No! They'd know the risk av fever an' chill. Let alone the shootin'. Two hunder' might have done ut. But the three-year-olds know little an' care less; an' where there's no fear, there's no danger. Catch thim young, feed thim high, an' by the honor av that great, little man Bobs, behind a good orficer, 'tisn't only dacoits they'd smash wid their clo'es off—'tis Con-ti-nental Ar-r-r-mies! They tuk Lungtungpen nakid; an' they'd take St. Pethersburg in their dhrawers! Begad, they would that!"

So saying, Mulvaney took up his butterfly-net, and returned to the barracks.

Ball-of-Fat

BY

GUY DE MAUPASSANT

FOR many days now the fag-end of the army had been straggling through the town. They were not troops, but a disbanded horde. The beards of the men were long and filthy, their uniforms in tatters, and they advanced at an easy pace without flag or regiment. All seemed worn-out and back-broken, incapable of a thought or a resolution, marching by habit solely, and falling from fatigue as soon as they stopped. In short, they were a mobilized, pacific people, bending under the weight of the gun; some little squads on the alert, easy to take alarm and prompt in enthusiasm, ready to attack or to flee; and in the midst of them, some red breeches, the remains of a division broken up in a great battle; some sombre artillery men in line with these varied kinds of foot soldiers; and, sometimes the brilliant helmet of a dragoon on foot who followed with difficulty the shortest march of the lines.

Some legions of free-shooters, under the heroic names of "Avengers of the Defeat," "Citizens of the Tomb," "Partakers of Death," passed in their turn with the air of bandits.

Their leaders were former cloth or grain merchants, ex-merchants in tallow or soap, warriors of circumstance, elected officers on account of their escutcheons and the length of their mustaches, covered with arms and with braids, speaking in constrained voices, discussing plans of campaign, and pretending to carry agonized France alone on their swaggering shoulders, but sometimes fearing their own soldiers, prison-birds, who were often brave at first and later proved to be plunderers and debauchees.

It was said that the Prussians were going to enter Rouen.

The National Guard who for two months had been carefully reconnoitering in the neighboring woods, shooting sometimes their own sentinels, and ready for a combat whenever a little wolf stirred in the thicket, had now returned to their firesides. Their arms, their uniforms, all the murderous accoutrements with which they had lately struck fear into the national heart for three leagues in every direction, had suddenly disappeared.

The last French soldiers finally came across the Seine to reach the Audemer bridge through Saint-Sever and Bourg-Achard; and, marching behind, on foot, between two officers of ordnance, the General, in despair, unable to do anything with these incongruous tatters, himself lost in the breaking-up of a people accustomed to conquer, and disastrously beaten, in spite of his legendary bravery.

A profound calm, a frightful, silent expectancy had spread over the city. Many of the heavy citizens, emasculated by commerce, anxiously awaited the conquerors, trembling lest their roasting spits or kitchen knives be considered arms.

All life seemed stopped; shops were closed, the streets dumb. Sometimes an inhabitant, intimidated by this silence, moved rapidly along next the walls. The agony of waiting made them wish the enemy would come.

In the afternoon of the day which followed the departure of the French troops, some uhlans, coming from one knows not where, crossed the town with celerity. Then, a little later, a black mass descended the side of St. Catharine, while two other invading bands approached by the way of Darnetal and Boisguillaume. The advance guard of the three bodies joined one another at the same moment in the Hotel de Ville square and, by all the neighboring streets, the German army continued to arrive, spreading out its battalions, making the pavement resound under their hard, rhythmic step.

Some orders of the commander, in a foreign, guttural voice, reached the houses which seemed dead and deserted, while behind closed shutters, eyes were watching these victorious men, masters of the city, of fortunes, of lives, through the "rights of war." The inhabitants, shut up in their rooms, were visited with the kind of excitement that a cataclysm, or some fatal upheaval of the earth, brings to us, against which all force is useless. For the same sensation is produced each time that the established order of things is over-turned, when security no longer exists, and all that protect the laws of man and of nature find themselves at the mercy of unreasoning, ferocious brutality. The trembling of the earth crushing the houses and burying an entire people; a river overflowing its banks and carrying in its course the drowned peasants, carcasses of beeves, and girders snatched from roofs, or a glorious army massacring those trying to defend themselves, leading others prisoners, pillaging in the name of the sword and thanking God to the sound of the cannon, all are alike frightful scourges which disconnect all belief in eternal justice, all the confidence that we have in the protection of Heaven and the reason of man.

Some detachments rapped at each door, then disappeared into the houses. It was occupation after invasion. Then the duty commences for the conquered to show themselves gracious toward the conquerors.

After some time, as soon as the first terror disappears, a new calm is established. In many families, the Prussian officer eats at the table. He is sometimes well bred and, through politeness, pities France, and speaks of his repugnance in taking part in this affair. One is grateful to him for this sentiment; then, one may be, some day or other, in need of his protection. By treating him well, one has, perhaps, a less number of men to feed. And why should we wound anyone on whom we are entirely dependent? To act thus would be less bravery than temerity. And temerity is no longer a fault of the commoner of Rouen, as it was at the time of the heroic defense, when their city became famous. Finally, each told himself that the highest judgment of French urbanity required that they be allowed to be polite to the strange soldier in the house, provided they did not show themselves familiar with him in public. Outside they would not make themselves known to each other, but at home they could chat freely, and the German might remain longer each evening warming his feet at their hearthstones.

The town even took on, little by little, its ordinary aspect. The French scarcely went out, but the Prussian soldiers grumbled in the streets. In short, the officers of the Blue Hussars, who dragged with arrogance their great weapons of death up and down the pavement, seemed to have no more grievous scorn for the simple citizens than the officers or the sportsmen who, the year before, drank in the same *cafés*.

There was nevertheless, something in the air, something subtle and unknown, a strange, intolerable atmosphere like a penetrating odor, the odor of invasion. It filled the dwellings and the public places, changed the taste of the food, gave the impression of being on a journey, far away, among barbarous and dangerous tribes.

The conquerors exacted money, much money. The inhabitants always paid and they were rich enough to do it. But the richer a trading Norman becomes the more he suffers at every outlay, at each part of his fortune that he sees pass from his hands into those of another.

Therefore, two or three leagues below the town, following the course of the river toward Croisset, Dieppedalle, or Biessart, mariners and fishermen often picked up the swollen corpse of a German in uniform from the bottom of the river, killed by the blow of a knife, the head crushed with a stone, or perhaps thrown into the water by a push from the high bridge. The slime of the river bed buried these obscure vengeances, savage, but legitimate, unknown heroisms, mute attacks more perilous than the battles of broad day, and without the echoing sound of glory.

For hatred of the foreigner always arouses some intrepid ones, who are ready to die for an idea.

Finally, as soon as the invaders had brought the town quite under subjection with their inflexible discipline, without having been guilty of any of the horrors for which they were famous along their triumphal line of march, people began to take courage, and the need of trade put new heart into the commerce of the country. Some had large interests at Havre, which the French army occupied, and they wished to try and reach this port by going to Dieppe by land and there embarking.

They used their influence with the German soldiers with whom they had an acquaintance, and finally, an authorization of departure was obtained from the General-in-chief.

Then, a large diligence, with four horses, having been engaged for this journey, and ten persons having engaged seats in it, it was resolved to set out on Tuesday morning before daylight, in order to escape observation.

For some time before, the frost had been hardening the earth and on

Monday, toward three o'clock, great black clouds coming from the north brought the snow which fell without interruption during the evening and all night.

At half past four in the morning, the travelers met in the courtyard of the Hotel Normandie, where they were to take the carriage.

They were still full of sleep, and shivering with cold under their wraps. They could only see each other dimly in the obscure light, and the accumulation of heavy winter garments made them all resemble fat curates in long cassocks. Only two of the men were acquainted; a third accosted them and they chatted: "I'm going to take my wife," said one. "I too," said another. "And I," said the third. The first added, "We shall not return to Rouen, and if the Prussians approach Havre, we shall go over to England." All had the same projects, being of the same mind.

As yet the horses were not harnessed. A little lantern, carried by a stable boy, went out one door from time to time, to immediately appear at another. The feet of the horses striking the floor could be heard, although deadened by the straw and litter, and the voice of a man talking to the beasts, sometimes swearing, came from the end of the building. A light tinkling of bells announced that they were taking down the harness; this murmur soon became a clear and continuous rhythm by the movement of the animal, stopping sometimes, then breaking into a brusque shake which was accompanied by the dull stamp of a sabot upon the hard earth.

The door suddenly closed. All noise ceased. The frozen citizens were silent; they remained immovable and stiff.

A curtain of uninterrupted white flakes constantly sparkled in its descent to the ground. It effaced forms, and powdered everything with a downy moss. And nothing could be heard in the great silence. The town was calm, and buried under the wintry frost, as this fall of snow, unnamable and floating, a sensation rather than a sound (trembling atoms which only seem to fill all space), came to cover the earth.

The man reappeared with his lantern, pulling at the end of a rope a sad horse which would not come willingly. He placed him against the pole, fastened the traces, walked about a long time adjusting the harness, for he had the use of but one hand, the other carrying the lantern. As he went for the second horse, he noticed the travelers, motionless, already white with snow, and said to them: "Why not get into the carriage? You will be under cover, at least."

They had evidently not thought of it, and they hastened to do so. The three men installed their wives at the back and then followed them. Then the other forms, undecided and veiled, took in their turn the last places without exchanging a word.

The floor was covered with straw, in which the feet ensconced themselves. The ladies at the back having brought little copper foot stoves, with a carbon fire, lighted them and, for some time, in low voices, enumerated the advantages of the appliances, repeating things that they had known for a long time.

Finally, the carriage was harnessed with six horses instead of four, because the traveling was very bad, and a voice called out:

"Is everybody aboard?"

And a voice within answered: "Yes."

They were off. The carriage moved slowly, slowly for a little way. The wheels were imbedded in the snow; the whole body groaned with heavy cracking sounds; the horses glistened, puffed, and smoked; and the great whip of the driver snapped without ceasing, hovering about on all sides, knotting and unrolling itself like a thin serpent, lashing brusquely some horse on the rebound, which then put forth its most violent effort.

Now the day was imperceptibly dawning. The light flakes, which one of the travelers, a Rouenese by birth, said looked like a shower of cotton, no longer fell. A faint light filtered through the great dull clouds, which rendered more brilliant the white of the fields, where appeared a line of great trees clothed in whiteness, or a chimney with a cap of snow.

In the carriage, each looked at the others curiously, in the sad light of this dawn.

At the back, in the best places, Monsieur Loiseau, wholesale wine merchant, of the Rue Grand-Pont, and Madame Loiseau were sleeping opposite each other. Loiseau had bought out his former patron who failed in business, and made his fortune. He sold bad wine at a good price to small retailers in the country, and passed among his friends and acquaintances as a knavish wag, a true Norman full of deceit and joviality.

His reputation as a sharper was so well established that one evening at the residence of the prefect, Monsieur Tournel, author of some fables and songs, of keen, satirical mind, a local celebrity, having proposed to some ladies, who seemed to be getting a little sleepy, that they make up a game of "Loiseau tricks," the joke traversed the rooms of the prefect, reached those of the town, and then, in the months to come, made many a face in the province expand with laughter.

Loiseau was especially known for his love of farce of every kind, for his jokes, good and bad; and no one could ever talk with him without thinking: "He is invaluable, this Loiseau." Of tall figure, his balloon-shaped front was surmounted by a ruddy face surrounded by gray whiskers.

His wife, large, strong, and resolute, with a quick, decisive manner, was the order and arithmetic of this house of commerce, while he was the life of it through his joyous activity.

Beside them, Monsieur Carré-Lamadon held himself with great dignity, as if belonging to a superior caste; a considerable man, in cottons, proprietor of three mills, officer of the Legion of Honor, and member of the General Council. He had remained, during the Empire, chief of the friendly opposition, famous for making the Emperor pay more dear for rallying to the cause than if he had combated it with blunted arms, according to his own story. Madame Carré-Lamadon, much younger than her husband, was the consolation of officers of good family sent to Rouen in garrison. She sat opposite her husband, very dainty, petite, and pretty, wrapped closely in furs and looking with sad eyes at the interior of the carriage.

Her neighbors, the Count and Countess Hubert de Breville, bore the name of one of the most ancient and noble families of Normandy. The Count, an old gentleman of good figure, accentuated, by the artifices of his toilette, his resemblance to King Henry IV, who, following a glorious legend of the family, had impregnated one of the De Breville ladies, whose husband, for this reason, was made a count and governor of the province.

A colleague of Monsieur Carré-Lamadon in the General Council, Count Hubert represented the Orléans party in the Department.

The story of his marriage with the daughter of a little captain of a privateer had always remained a mystery. But as the Countess had a grand air, received better than anyone, and passed for having been loved by the son of Louis-Philippe, all the nobility did her honor, and her salon remained the first in the country, the only one which preserved the old gallantry, and to which the *entrée* was difficult. The fortune of the Brevilles amounted, it was said, to five hundred thousand francs in income, all in good securities.

These six persons formed the foundation of the carriage company, the society side, serene and strong, honest, established people, who had both religion and principles.

By a strange chance, all the women were upon the same seat; and the Countess had for neighbors two sisters who picked at long strings of beads and muttered some *Paters* and *Aves*. One was old and as pitted with smallpox as if she had received a broadside of grapeshot full in the face. The other, very sad, had a pretty face and a disease of the lungs, which, added to their devoted faith, illumined them and made them appear like martyrs.

Opposite these two devotees were a man and a woman who attracted the notice of all. The man, well known, was Cornudet the democrat, the terror of respectable people. For twenty years he had soaked his great red beard in the *bocks* of all the democratic *cafés*. He had consumed with his friends and *confrères* a rather pretty fortune left him by his father, an old confectioner, and he awaited the establishing of the Republic with impatience, that he might have the position he merited by his great expenditures. On the fourth of September, by some joke perhaps, he believed himself elected prefect, but when he went to assume the duties, the clerks of the office were masters of the place and refused to recognize him, obliging him to retreat. Rather a good bachelor, on the whole, inoffensive and serviceable, he had busied himself, with incomparable ardor, in organizing the defense against the Prussians. He had dug holes in all the plains, cut down young trees from the neighboring forests, sown snares over all routes and, at the approach of the enemy, took himself quickly back to the town. He now thought he could be of more use in Havre where more entrenchments would be necessary.

The woman, one of those called a coquette, was celebrated for her *embonpoint,* which had given her the nickname of "Ball-of-Fat." Small, round, and fat as lard, with puffy fingers choked at the phalanges, like chaplets of short sausages; with a stretched and shining skin, an enormous bosom which shook under her dress, she was, nevertheless, pleasing and sought after, on account of a certain freshness and breeziness of disposition. Her face was a round apple, a peony bud ready to pop into bloom, and inside that opened two great black eyes, shaded with thick brows that cast a shadow within; and below, a charming mouth, humid for kissing, furnished with shining, microscopic baby teeth. She was, it was said, full of admirable qualities.

As soon as she was recognized, a whisper went around among the honest women, and the words "prostitute" and "public shame" were whispered so loudly that she raised her head. Then she threw at her neighbors such a provoking, courageous look that a great silence reigned, and everybody looked down except Loiseau who watched her with an exhilarated air.

And immediately conversation began among the three ladies, whom the presence of this girl had suddenly rendered friendly, almost intimate. It seemed to them they should bring their married dignity into union in opposition to that sold without shame; for legal love always takes on a tone of contempt for its free *confrère.*

The three men, also drawn together by an instinct of preservation at the sight of Cornudet, talked money with a certain high tone of disdain for the poor. Count Hubert talked of the havoc which the Prussians had caused, the losses which resulted from being robbed of cattle and from destroyed crops, with the assurance of a great lord, ten times millionaire whom these ravages would scarcely cramp for a year. Monsieur Carré-Lamadon, largely experienced in the cotton industry, had had need of sending six hundred thousand francs to England, as a trifle in reserve if it should be needed. As for Loiseau, he had arranged with the French administration to sell them all the wines that remained in his cellars, on account of which the State owed him a formidable sum, which he counted on collecting at Havre.

And all three threw toward each other swift and amicable glances.

Although in different conditions, they felt themselves to be brothers through money, that grand free-masonry of those who possess it, and make the gold rattle by putting their hands in their trousers' pockets.

The carriage went so slowly that at ten o'clock in the morning they had not gone four leagues. The men had got down three times to climb hills on foot. They began to be disturbed because they should be now taking breakfast at Tôtes and they despaired now of reaching there before night. Each one had begun to watch for an inn along the route, when the carriage foundered in a snowdrift, and it took two hours to extricate it.

Growing appetites troubled their minds; and no eating-house, no wine shop showed itself, the approach of the Prussians and the passage of the troops having frightened away all these industries.

The gentlemen ran to the farms along the way for provisions, but they did not even find bread, for the defiant peasant had concealed his stores for fear of being pillaged by the soldiers who, having nothing to put between their teeth, took by force whatever they discovered.

Toward one o'clock in the afternoon, Loiseau announced that there was a decided hollow in his stomach. Everybody suffered with him, and the violent need of eating, ever increasing, had killed conversation.

From time to time some one yawned; another immediately imitated him; and each, in his turn, in accordance with his character, his knowledge of life, and his social position, opened his mouth with carelessness or modesty, placing his hand quickly before the yawning hole from whence issued a vapor.

Ball-of-Fat, after many attempts, bent down as if seeking something under her skirts. She hesitated a second, looked at her neighbors, then sat up again tranquilly. The faces were pale and drawn. Loiseau affirmed that he would give a thousand francs for a small ham. His wife made a gesture, as if in protest; but she kept quiet. She was always troubled when anyone spoke of squandering money, and could not comprehend any pleasantry on the subject. "The fact is," said the Count, "I cannot understand why I did not think to bring some provisions with me." Each reproached himself in the same way.

However, Cornudet had a flask full of rum. He offered it; it was refused coldly. Loiseau alone accepted two swallows, and then passed back the flask saying, by way of thanks: "It is good all the same; it is warming and checks the appetite." The alcohol put him in good-humor and he proposed that they do as they did on the little ship in the song, eat the fattest of the passengers. This indirect allusion to Ball-of-Fat choked the well-bred people. They said nothing. Cornudet alone laughed. The two good sisters had ceased to mumble their rosaries and, with their hands enfolded in their great sleeves, held themselves immovable, obstinately lowering their eyes, without doubt offering to Heaven the suffering it had brought upon them.

Finally at three o'clock, when they found themselves in the midst of an interminable plain, without a single village in sight, Ball-of-Fat bending down quickly drew from under the seat a large basket covered with a white napkin.

At first she brought out a little china plate and a silver cup; then a large dish in which there were two whole chickens, cut up and imbedded in their own jelly. And one could still see in the basket other good things, some *pâtés,* fruits, and sweetmeats, provisions for three days if they should not see the kitchen of an inn. Four necks of bottles were seen among the packages of food. She took a wing of a chicken and began to eat it delicately, with one of those little biscuits called "Regence" in Normandy.

All looks were turned in her direction. Then the odor spread, enlarging the nostrils and making the mouth water, besides causing a painful contraction of the jaw behind the ears. The scorn of the women for this girl became ferocious, as if they had a desire to kill her and throw her out of the carriage into the snow, her, her silver cup, her basket, provisions and all.

But Loiseau with his eyes devoured the dish of chicken. He said: "Fortunately Madame had more precaution than we. There are some people who know how to think ahead always."

She turned toward him, saying: "If you would like some of it, sir? It is hard to go without breakfast so long."

He saluted her and replied: "Faith, I frankly cannot refuse; I can stand it no longer. Everything goes in time of war, does it not, Madame?" And then casting a comprehensive glance around, he added: "In moments like this, one can but be pleased to find people who are obliging."

He had a newspaper which he spread out on his knees, that no spot might come to his pantaloons, and upon the point of a knife that he always carried in his pocket, he took up a leg all glistening with jelly, put it between his teeth and masticated it with a satisfaction so evident that there ran through the carriage a great sigh of distress.

Then Ball-of-Fat, in a sweet and humble voice, proposed that the two sisters partake of her collation. They both accepted instantly and, without raising their eyes, began to eat very quickly, after stammering their thanks. Cornudet no longer refused the offers of his neighbor, and they formed with the sisters a sort of table, by spreading out some newspapers upon their knees.

The mouths opened and shut without ceasing, they masticated, swallowed, gulping ferociously. Loiseau in his corner was working hard and, in a low voice, was trying to induce his wife to follow his example. She resisted for a long time; then, when a drawn sensation ran through her body, she yielded. Her husband, rounding his phrase, asked their "charming companion" if he might be allowed to offer a little piece to Madame Loiseau.

She replied: "Why, yes, certainly, sir," with an amiable smile, as she passed the dish.

An embarrassing thing confronted them when they opened the first bottle of Bordeaux: they had but one cup. Each passed it after having tasted. Cornudet alone, for politeness without doubt, placed his lips at the spot left humid by his fair neighbor.

Then, surrounded by people eating, suffocated by the odors of the food, the Count and Countess de Breville, as well as Madame and Monsieur Carré-Lamadon, were suffering that odious torment which has preserved the name of Tantalus. Suddenly the young wife of the manufacturer gave forth such a sigh that all heads were turned in her direction; she was as white as the snow without; her eyes closed, her head drooped; she had lost consciousness. Her husband, much excited, implored the help of everybody. Each lost his head completely, until the elder of the two sisters, holding the head of the sufferer, slipped Ball-of-Fat's cup between her lips and forced her to swallow a few drops of wine. The pretty little lady revived, opened her eyes, smiled, and declared in a dying voice that she felt very well now. But, in order that the attack might not return, the sister urged her to drink a full glass of Bordeaux, and added: "It is just hunger, nothing more."

Then Ball-of-Fat, blushing and embarrassed, looked at the four travelers who had fasted and stammered: "Goodness knows! if I dared to offer anything to these gentlemen and ladies, I would——" Then she was silent, as if fearing an insult. Loiseau took up the word: "Ah! certainly, in times like these all the world are brothers and ought to aid each other. Come, ladies, without ceremony; why the devil not accept? We do not know whether we shall even find a house where we can pass the night. At the pace we are going now, we shall not reach Tôtes before noon tomorrow——"

They still hesitated, no one daring to assume the responsibility of a "Yes." The Count decided the question. He turned toward the fat, intimidated girl and, taking on a grand air of condescension, he said to her:

"We accept with gratitude, Madame."

It is the first step that counts. The Rubicon passed, one lends himself to the occasion squarely. The basket was stripped. It still contained a *pâté de foie gras, a pâté* of larks, a piece of smoked tongue, some preserved pears, a loaf of hard bread, some wafers, and a full cup of pickled gherkins and onions, of which crudities Ball-of-Fat, like all women, was extremely fond.

They could not eat this girl's provisions without speaking to her. And so they chatted, with reserve at first; then, as she carried herself well, with more abandon. The ladies De Breville and Carré-Lamadon, who were acquainted with all the ins and outs of good-breeding, were gracious with a certain delicacy. The Countess, especially, showed that amiable condescension of very noble ladies who do not fear being spoiled by contact with anyone, and was charming. But the great Madame Loiseau, who had the soul of a plebeian, remained crabbed, saying little and eating much.

The conversation was about the war, naturally. They related the horrible deeds of the Prussians, the brave acts of the French; and all of them, although running away, did homage to those who stayed behind. Then personal stories began to be told, and Ball-of-Fat related, with sincere emotion, and in the heated words that such girls sometimes use in expressing their natural feelings, how she had left Rouen:

"I believed at first that I could remain," she said. "I had my house full of provisions, and I preferred to feed a few soldiers rather than expatriate myself, to go I knew not where. But as soon as I saw them, those Prussians, that was too much for me! They made my blood boil with anger, and I wept for very shame all day long. Oh! if I were only a man! I watched them from my windows, the great porkers with their pointed helmets, and my maid held my hands to keep me from throwing the furniture down upon them. Then one of them came to lodge at my house; I sprang at his throat the first thing; they are no more difficult to strangle than other people. And I should have put an end to that one then and there had they not pulled me away by the hair. After that, it was necessary to keep out of sight. And finally, when I found an opportunity, I left town and—here I am!"

They congratulated her. She grew in the estimation of her companions, who had not shown themselves so hot-brained, and Cornudet, while listening to her, took on the approving, benevolent smile of an apostle, as a priest would if he heard a devotee praise God, for the long-bearded democrats have a monopoly of patriotism, as the men in cassocks have of religion. In his turn he spoke, in a doctrinal tone, with the emphasis of a proclamation such as we see pasted on the walls about town, and finished by a bit of eloquence whereby he gave that "scamp of a Badinguet" a good lashing.

Then Ball-of-Fat was angry, for she was a Bonapartist. She grew redder than a cherry and, stammering with indignation, said:

"I would like to have seen you in his place, you other people. Then everything would have been quite right; oh, yes! It is you who have betrayed this man! One would never have had to leave France if it had been governed by blackguards like you!"

Cornudet, undisturbed, preserved a disdainful, superior smile, but all felt that the high note had been struck, until the Count, not without some difficulty, calmed the exasperated girl and proclaimed with a manner of authority that all sincere opinions should be respected. But the Countess and the manufacturer's wife, who had in their souls an unreasonable hatred for the people that favor a Republic, and the same instinctive tenderness that all women have for a decorative, despotic government, felt themselves drawn, in spite of themselves, toward this prostitute so full of dignity, whose sentiments so strongly resembled their own.

The basket was empty. By ten o'clock they had easily exhausted the contents and regretted that there was not more. Conversation continued for some time, but a little more coldly since they had finished eating.

The night fell, the darkness little by little became profound, and the cold, felt more during digestion, made Ball-of-Fat shiver in spite of her plumpness. Then Madame de Breville offered her the little foot-stove, in which the fuel had been renewed many times since morning; she accepted it immediately, for her feet were becoming numb with cold. The ladies Carré-Lamadon and Loiseau gave theirs to the two religious sisters.

The driver had lighted his lanterns. They shone out with a lively glimmer showing a cloud of foam beyond, the sweat of the horses; and, on both sides of the way, the snow seemed to roll itself along under the moving reflection of the lights.

Inside the carriage one could distinguish nothing. But a sudden movement seemed to be made between Ball-of-Fat and Cornudet; and Loiseau, whose eye penetrated the shadow, believed that he saw the big-bearded man start back quickly as if he had received a swift, noiseless blow.

Then some twinkling points of fire appeared in the distance along the road. It was Tôtes. They had traveled eleven hours, which, with the two hours given to resting and feeding the horses, made thirteen. They entered the town and stopped before the Hotel of Commerce.

The carriage door opened! A well-known sound gave the travelers a start; it was the scabbard of a sword hitting the ground. Immediately a German voice was heard in the darkness.

Although the diligence was not moving, no one offered to alight, fearing some one might be waiting to murder them as they stepped out. Then the conductor appeared, holding in his hand one of the lanterns which lighted the carriage to its depth, and showed the two rows of frightened faces, whose mouths were open and whose eyes were wide with surprise and fear.

Outside beside the driver, in plain sight, stood a German officer, an excessively tall young man, thin and blond, squeezed into his uniform like a girl in a corset, and wearing on his head a flat, oilcloth cap which made him resemble the porter of an English hotel. His enormous mustache, of long straight hairs, growing gradually thin at each side and terminating in a single blond thread so fine that one could not perceive where it ended, seemed to weigh heavily on the corners of his mouth and, drawing down the cheeks, left a decided wrinkle about the lips.

In Alsatian French, he invited the travelers to come in, saying in a suave tone: "Will you descend, gentlemen and ladies?"

The two good sisters were the first to obey, with the docility of saints accustomed ever to submission. The Count and Countess then appeared, followed by the manufacturer and his wife; then Loiseau, pushing ahead of him his larger half. The last-named, as he set foot on the earth, said to the officer: "Good evening, sir," more as a measure of prudence than politeness. The officer, insolent as all powerful people usually are, looked at him without a word.

Ball-of-Fat and Cornudet, although nearest the door, were the last to descend, grave and haughty before the enemy. The fat girl tried to control herself and be calm. The democrat waved a tragic hand and his long beard seemed to tremble a little and grow redder. They wished to preserve their dignity, comprehending that in such meetings as these they represented in some degree their great country, and somewhat disgusted with the docility of her companions, the fat girl tried to show more pride than her neighbors, the honest women, and, as she felt that some one should set an example, she continued her attitude of resistance assumed at the beginning of the journey.

They entered the vast kitchen of the inn, and the German, having demanded their traveling papers signed by the General-in-chief (in which the name, the description, and profession of each traveler was mentioned), and having examined them all critically, comparing the people and their signatures, said: "It is quite right," and went out.

Then they breathed. They were still hungry and supper was ordered. A half hour was necessary to prepare it, and while two servants were attending to this they went to their rooms. They found them along a corridor which terminated in a large glazed door.

Finally, they sat down at table, when the proprietor of the inn himself appeared. He was a former horse merchant, a large, asthmatic man, with a constant wheezing and rattling in his throat. His father had left him the name of Follenvie. He asked:

"Is Miss Elizabeth Rousset here?"

Ball-of-Fat started as she answered: "It is I."

"The Prussian officer wishes to speak with you immediately."

"With me?"

"Yes, that is, if you are Miss Elizabeth Rousset."

She was disturbed, and reflecting for an instant, declared flatly:

"That is my name, but I shall not go."

A stir was felt around her; each discussed and tried to think of the cause of this order. The Count approached her, saying:

"You are wrong, Madame, for your refusal may lead to considerable difficulty, not only to yourself, but for all your companions. It is never worth while to resist those in power. This request cannot assuredly bring any danger; it is, without doubt, about some forgotten formality."

Everybody agreed with him, asking, begging, beseeching her to go, and at last they convinced her that it was best; they all feared the complications that might result from disobedience. She finally said:

"It is for you that I do this, you understand."

The Countess took her by the hand, saying: "And we are grateful to you for it."

She went out. They waited before sitting down at table.

Each one regretted not having been sent for in the place of this violent, irascible girl, and mentally prepared some platitudes, in case they should be called in their turn.

But at the end of ten minutes she reappeared, out of breath, red to suffocation, and exasperated. She stammered: "Oh! the rascal; the rascal!"

All gathered around to learn something, but she said nothing; and when the Count insisted, she responded with great dignity: "No, it does not concern you; I can say nothing."

Then they all seated themselves around a high soup tureen, whence came the odor of cabbage. In spite of alarm, the supper was gay. The cider was good, the beverage Loiseau and the good sisters took as a means of economy. The others called for wine; Cornudet demanded beer. He had a special fashion of uncorking the bottle, making froth on the liquid, carefully filling the glass and then holding it before the light to better appreciate the color. When he drank, his great beard, which still kept some of the foam of his beloved beverage, seemed to tremble with tenderness; his eyes were squinted, in order not to lose sight of his tipple, and he had the unique air of fulfilling the function for which he was born. One would say that there was in his mind a meeting, like that of affinities, between the two great passions that occupied his life—Pale Ale and Revolutions; and assuredly he could not taste the one without thinking of the other.

Monsieur and Madame Follenvie dined at the end of the table. The man, rattling like a cracked locomotive, had too much trouble in breathing to talk while eating, but his wife was never silent. She told all her impressions at the arrival of the Prussians, what they did, what they said, reviling them because they cost her some money, and because she had two sons in the army. She addressed herself especially to the Countess, flattered by being able to talk with a lady of quality.

When she lowered her voice to say some delicate thing, her husband would interrupt, from time to time, with: "You had better keep silent, Madame Follenvie." But she paid no attention, continuing in this fashion:

"Yes, Madame, those people there not only eat our potatoes and pork, but our pork and potatoes. And it must not be believed that they are at all proper—oh, no! such filthy things they do, saving the respect I owe to you! And if you could see them exercise for hours in the day! they are all there in the field, marching ahead, then marching back, turning here and turning there. They might be cultivating the land, or at least working on the roads of their own country! But no, Madame, these military men are profitable to no one. Poor people have to feed them, or perhaps be murdered! I am only an old woman without education, it is true, but when I see some endangering their constitutions by raging from morning to night, I say: "When there are so many people found to be useless, how unnecessary it is for others to take so much trouble to be nuisances! Truly, is it not an abomination to kill people, whether they be Prussian, or English, or Polish, or French? If one man revenges himself upon another who has done him some injury, it is wicked and he is punished; but when they exterminate our boys, as if they were game, with guns, they give decorations, indeed, to the one who destroys the most! Now, you see, I can never understand that, never!"

Cornudet raised his voice: "War is a barbarity when one attacks a peaceable neighbor, but a sacred duty when one defends his country."

The old woman lowered her head:

"Yes, when one defends himself, it is another thing; but why not make it a duty to kill all the kings who make these wars for their pleasure?"

Cornudet's eyes flashed. "Bravo my country-woman!" said he.

M. Carré-Lamadon reflected profoundly. Although he was prejudiced as a Captain of Industry, the good sense of this peasant woman made him think of the opulence that would be brought into the country were the idle and consequently mischievous hands, and the troops which were now maintained in unproductiveness, employed in some great industrial work that it would require centuries to achieve.

Loiseau, leaving his place, went to speak with the innkeeper in a low tone of voice. The great man laughed, shook, and squeaked, his corpulence quivered with joy at the jokes of his neighbor, and he bought of him six cases of wine for spring, after the Prussians had gone.

As soon as supper was finished, as they were worn out with fatigue, they retired.

However, Loiseau, who had observed things, after getting his wife to bed, glued his eye and then his ear to a hole in the wall, to try and discover what are known as "the mysteries of the corridor."

At the end of about an hour, he heard a groping, and, looking quickly, he perceived Ball-of-Fat, who appeared still more plump in a blue cashmere negligee trimmed with white lace. She had a candle in her hand and was directing her steps toward the great door at the end of the corridor. But a door at the side opened, and when she returned at the end of some minutes Cornudet, in his suspenders, followed her. They spoke low, then they stopped. Ball-of-Fat seemed to be defending the entrance to her room with energy. Loiseau, unfortunately, could not hear all their words, but finally, as they raised their voices, he was able to catch a few. Cornudet insisted with vivacity. He said:

"Come, now, you are a silly woman; what harm can be done?"

She had an indignant air in responding: "No, my dear, there are moments when such things are out of place. Here it would be a shame."

He doubtless did not comprehend and asked why. Then she cried out, raising her voice still more:

"Why? you do not see why? When there are Prussians in the house, in the very next room, perhaps?"

He was silent. This patriotic shame of the harlot, who would not suffer his caress so near the enemy, must have awakened the latent dignity in his heart, for after simply kissing her, he went back to his own door with a bound.

Loiseau, much excited, left the aperture, cut a caper in his room, put on his pajamas, turned back the clothes that covered the bony carcass of his companion, whom he awakened with a kiss, murmuring: "Do you love me, dearie?"

Then all the house was still. And immediately there arose somewhere, from an uncertain quarter, which might be the cellar but was quite as likely to be the garret, a powerful snoring, monotonous and regular, a heavy, prolonged sound, like a great kettle under pressure. M. Follenvie was asleep.

As they had decided that they would set out at eight o'clock the next morning, they all collected in the kitchen. But the carriage, the roof of which was covered with snow, stood undisturbed in the courtyard, without horses and without a conductor. They sought him in vain in the stables, in the hay, and in the coach-house. Then they resolved to scour the town, and started out. They found themselves in a square, with a church at one end and some low houses on either side, where they perceived some Prussian soldiers. The first one they saw was paring potatoes. The second, further off, was cleaning the hairdresser's shop. Another, bearded to the eyes, was tending a troublesome brat, cradling it and trying to appease it; and the great peasant women, whose husbands were "away in the army," indicated by signs to their obedient conquerors the work they wished to have done: cutting wood, cooking the soup, grinding the coffee, or what not. One of them even washed the linen of his hostess, an important old grandmother.

The Count, astonished, asked questions of the beadle who came out of the rectory. The old man responded:

"Oh! those men are not wicked; they are not the Prussians we hear

about. They are from far off, I know not where; and they have left wives
and children in their country; it is not amusing to them, this war, I can tell
you! I am sure they also weep for their homes, and that it makes as much
sorrow among them as it does among us. Here, now, there is not so much
unhappiness for the moment, because the soldiers do no harm and they
work as if they were in their own homes. You see, sir, among poor people
it is necessary that they aid one another. These are the great traits which
war develops."

Cornudet, indignant at the cordial relations between the conquerors and
the conquered, preferred to shut himself up in the inn. Loiseau had a joke
for the occasion: "They will re-people the land."

Monsieur Carré-Lamadon had a serious word: "They try to make
amends."

But they did not find the driver. Finally, they discovered him in a *café*
of the village, sitting at table fraternally with the officer of ordnance. The
Count called out to him:

"Were you not ordered to be ready at eight o'clock?"

"Well, yes; but another order has been given me since."

"By whom?"

"Faith! the Prussian commander."

"What was it?"

"Not to harness at all."

"Why?"

"I know nothing about it. Go and ask him. They tell me not to harness,
and I don't harness. That's all."

"Did he give you the order himself?"

"No, sir, the innkeeper gave the order for him."

"When was that?"

"Last evening, as I was going to bed."

The three men returned, much disturbed. They asked for M. Follenvie,
but the servant answered that that gentleman, because of his asthma, never
rose before ten o'clock. And he had given strict orders not to be wakened
before that, except in case of fire.

They wished to see the officer, but that was absolutely impossible, since,
while he lodged at the inn, M. Follenvie alone was authorized to speak to
him upon civil affairs. So they waited. The women went up to their rooms
again and occupied themselves with futile tasks.

Cornudet installed himself near the great chimney in the kitchen, where
there was a good fire burning. He ordered one of the little tables to be
brought from the *café*, then a can of beer, he then drew out his pipe, which
plays among democrats a part almost equal to his own, because in serving
Cornudet it was serving its country. It was a superb pipe, an admirably
colored meerschaum, as black as the teeth of its master, but perfumed,
curved, glistening, easy to the hand, completing his physiognomy. And he
remained motionless, his eyes as much fixed upon the flame of the fire as
upon his favorite tipple and its frothy crown; and each time that he drank,

he passed his long, thin fingers through his scanty, gray hair, with an air of satisfaction, after which he sucked in his mustache fringed with foam.

Loiseau, under the pretext of stretching his legs, went to place some wine among the retailers of the country. The Count and the manufacturer began to talk politics. They could foresee the future of France. One of them believed in an Orléans, the other in some unknown savior for the country, a hero who would reveal himself when all were in despair: a Guesclin, or a Joan of Arc, perhaps, or would it be another Napoleon First? Ah! if the Prince Imperial were not so young!

Cornudet listened to them and smiled like one who holds the word of destiny. His pipe perfumed the kitchen.

As ten o'clock struck, M. Follenvie appeared. They asked him hurried questions; but he could only repeat two or three times without variation, these words:

"The officer said to me: 'M. Follenvie, you see to it that the carriage is not harnessed for those travelers to-morrow. I do not wish them to leave without my order. That is sufficient.' "

Then they wished to see the officer. The Count sent him his card, on which M. Carré-Lamadon wrote his name and all his titles. The Prussian sent back word that he would meet the two gentlemen after he had breakfasted, that is to say, about one o'clock.

The ladies reappeared and ate a little something, despite their disquiet. Ball-of-Fat seemed ill and prodigiously troubled.

They were finishing their coffee when the word came that the officer was ready to meet the gentlemen. Loiseau joined them; but when they tried to enlist Cornudet, to give more solemnity to their proceedings, he declared proudly that he would have nothing to do with the Germans; and he betook himself to his chimney corner and ordered another liter of beer.

The three men mounted the staircase and were introduced to the best room of the inn, where the officer received them, stretched out in an arm-chair, his feet on the mantel-piece, smoking a long, porcelain pipe, and enveloped in a flamboyant dressing-gown, appropriated, without doubt, from some dwelling belonging to a common citizen of bad taste. He did not rise, nor greet them in any way, not even looking at them. It was a magnificent display of natural blackguardism transformed into the military victor.

At the expiration of some moments, he asked: "What is it you wish?"

The count became spokesman: "We desire to go on our way, sir."

"No."

"May I ask the cause of this refusal?"

"Because I do not wish it."

"But, I would respectfully observe to you, sir, that your General-in-chief gave us permission to go to Dieppe; and I know of nothing we have done to merit your severity."

"I do not wish it—that is all; you can go."

All three having bowed, retired.

The afternoon was lamentable. They could not understand this caprice of the German; and the most singular ideas would come into their heads to trouble them. Everybody stayed in the kitchen and discussed the situation endlessly, imagining all sorts of unlikely things. Perhaps they would be retained as hostages—but to what end?—or taken prisoners—or rather a considerable ransom might be demanded. At this thought a panic prevailed. The richest were the most frightened, already seeing themselves constrained to pay for their lives with sacks of gold poured into the hands of this insolent soldier. They racked their brains to think of some acceptable falsehoods to conceal their riches and make them pass themselves off for poor people, very poor people. Loiseau took off the chain to his watch and hid it away in his pocket. The falling night increased their apprehensions. The lamp was lighted, and as there was still two hours before dinner, Madame Loiseau proposed a game of Thirty-one. It would be a diversion. They accepted. Cornudet himself, having smoked his pipe, took part for politeness.

The Count shuffled the cards, dealt, and Ball-of-Fat had thirty-one at the outset; and immediately the interest was great enough to appease the fear that haunted their minds. Then Cornudet perceived that the house of Loiseau was given to tricks.

As they were going to the dinner table, Monsieur Follenvie again appeared, and, in wheezing, rattling voice, announced:

"The Prussian officer orders me to ask Mademoiselle Elizabeth Rousset if she has yet changed her mind."

Ball-of-Fat remained standing and was pale; then suddenly becoming crimson, such a stifling anger took possession of her that she could not speak. But finally she flashed out: "You may say to the dirty beast, that idiot, that carrion of a Prussian, that I shall never change it; you understand, never, never, never!"

The great innkeeper went out. Then Ball-of-Fat was immediately surrounded, questioned, and solicited by all to disclose the mystery of his visit. She resisted, at first, but soon becoming exasperated, she said: "What does he want? You really want to know what he wants? He wants to sleep with me."

Everybody was choked for words, and indignation was rife. Cornudet broke his glass, so violently did he bring his fist down upon the table. There was a clamor of censure against this ignoble soldier, a blast of anger, a union of all for resistance, as if a demand had been made on each one of the party for the sacrifice exacted of her. The Count declared with disgust that those people conducted themselves after the fashion of the ancient barbarians. The women, especially, showed to Ball-of-Fat a most energetic and tender commiseration. The good sisters who only showed themselves at mealtime, lowered their heads and said nothing.

They all dined, nevertheless, when the first *furore* had abated. But there was little conversation; they were thinking.

The ladies retired early, and the men, all smoking, organized a game at cards to which Monsieur Follenvie was invited, as they intended to put a few casual questions to him on the subject of conquering the resistance of this officer. But he thought of nothing but the cards and, without listening or answering, would keep repeating: "To the game, sirs, to the game." His attention was so taken that he even forgot to expectorate, which must have put him some points to the good with the organ in his breast. His whistling lungs ran the whole asthmatic scale, from deep, profound tones to the sharp rustiness of a young cock essaying to crow.

He even refused to retire when his wife, who had fallen asleep previously, came to look for him. She went away alone, for she was an "early bird," always up with the sun, while her husband was a "night owl," always ready to pass the night with his friends. He cried out to her: "Leave my creamed chicken before the fire!" and then went on with his game. When they saw that they could get nothing from him, they declared that it was time to stop, and each sought his bed.

They all rose rather early the next day, with an undefined hope of geting away, which desire the terror of passing another day in that horrible inn greatly increased.

Alas! the horses remained in the stable and the driver was invisible. For want of better employment, they went out and walked around the carriage.

The breakfast was very doleful; and it became apparent that a coldness had arisen toward Ball-of-Fat, and that the night, which brings counsel, had slightly modified their judgments. They almost wished now that the Prussian had secretly found this girl, in order to give her companions a pleasant surprise in the morning. What could be more simple? Besides, who would know anything about it? She could save appearances by telling the officer that she took pity on their distress. To her, it would make so little difference!

No one had avowed these thoughts yet.

In the afternoon, as they were almost perishing from *ennui,* the Count proposed that they take a walk around the village. Each wrapped up warmly and the little party set out, with the exception of Cornudet, who preferred to remain near the fire, and the good sisters, who passed their time in the church or at the curate's.

The cold, growing more intense every day, cruelly pinched their noses and ears; their feet became so numb that each step was torture; and when they came to a field it seemed to them frightfully sad under this limitless white, so that everybody returned immediately, with hearts hard pressed and souls congealed.

The four women walked ahead, the three gentlemen followed just behind. Loiseau, who understood the situation, asked suddenly if they thought that girl there was going to keep them long in such a place as this. The Count, always courteous, said that they could not exact from a woman a sacrifice so hard, unless it should come of her own will. Monsieur Carré-Lamadon remarked that if the French made their return through Dieppe, as they were likely to, a battle would surely take place at Tôtes. This reflection made the two others anxious.

"If we could only get away on foot," said Loiseau.

The Count shrugged his shoulders: "How can we think of it in this snow? and with our wives?" he said. "And then, we should be pursued and caught in ten minutes and led back prisoners at the mercy of these soldiers."

It was true, and they were silent.

The ladies talked of their clothes, but a certain constraint seemed to disunite them. Suddenly at the end of the street, the officer appeared. His tall, wasp-like figure in uniform was outlined upon the horizon formed by the snow, and he was marching with knees apart, a gait particularly military, which is affected that they may not spot their carefully blackened boots.

He bowed in passing near the ladies and looked disdainfully at the men, who preserved their dignity by not seeing him, except Loiseau, who made a motion toward raising his hat.

Ball-of-Fat reddened to the ears, and the three married women resented the great humiliation of being thus met by this soldier in the company of this girl whom he had treated so cavalierly.

But they spoke of him, of his figure and his face. Madame Carré-Lamadon who had known many officers and considered herself a connoisseur of them, found this one not at all bad; she regretted even that he was not French, because he would make such a pretty hussar, one all the women would rave over.

Again in the house, no one knew what to do. Some sharp words, even, were said about things very insignificant. The dinner was silent, and almost immediately after it, each one went to his room to kill time in sleep.

They descended the next morning with weary faces and exasperated hearts. The women scarcely spoke to Ball-of-Fat.

A bell began to ring. It was for a baptism. The fat girl had a child being brought up among the peasants of Yvetot. She had not seen it for a year, or thought of it; but the idea of a child being baptized threw into her heart a sudden and violent tenderness for her own, and she strongly wished to be present at the ceremony.

As soon as she was gone, everybody looked at each other, then pulled their chairs together, for they thought that finally something should be decided upon. Loiseau had an inspiration: it was to hold Ball-of-Fat alone and let the others go.

M. Follenvie was charged with the commission, but he returned almost immediately, for the German, who understood human nature, had put him out. He pretended that he would retain everybody so long as his desire was not satisfied.

Then the commonplace nature of Madame Loiseau burst out with:

"Well, we are not going to stay here to die of old age. Since it is the trade of this creature to accommodate herself to all kinds, I fail to see how she has the right to refuse one more than another. I can tell you she has received all she could find in Rouen, even the coachmen! Yes, Madame, the prefect's coachman! I know him very well, for he bought his wine at our house. And to think that to-day we should be drawn into this embarrassment by this affected woman, this minx! For my part, I find that this officer conducts himself very well. He has perhaps suffered privations for a long time; and doubtless he would have preferred us three; but no, he is contented with common property. He respects married women. And we must remember too that he is master. He has only to say 'I wish,' and he could take us by force with his soldiers."

The two women had a cold shiver. Pretty Madame Carré-Lamadon's eyes grew brilliant and she became a little pale, as if she saw herself already taken by force by the officer.

The men met and discussed the situation. Loiseau, furious, was for delivering "the wretch" bound hand and foot to the enemy. But the Count, descended through three generations of ambassadors, and endowed with the temperament of a diplomatist, was the advocate of ingenuity.

"It is best to decide upon something," said he. Then they conspired.

The women kept together, the tone of their voices was lowered, each gave advice and the discussion was general. Everything was very harmonious. The ladies especially found delicate shades and charming subleties of expression for saying the most unusual things. A stranger would have understood nothing, so great was the precaution of language observed. But the light edge of modesty, with which every woman of the world is barbed, only covers the surface; they blossom out in a scandalous adventure of this kind, being deeply amused and feeling themselves in their element, mixing love and sensuality as a greedy cook prepares supper for his master.

Even gaiety returned, so funny did the whole story seem to them at last. The Count found some of the jokes a little off color, but they were so well told that he was forced to smile. In his turn, Loiseau came out with some still bolder tales, and yet nobody was wounded. The brutal thought, expressed by his wife, dominated all minds: "Since it is her trade, why should she refuse this one more than another?" The genteel Madame Carré-Lamadon seemed to think that in her place, she would refuse this one less than some others.

They prepared the blockade at length, as if they were about to surround a fortress. Each took some rôle to play, some arguments he would bring to bear, some maneuvers that he would endeavor to put into execution. They decided on the plan of attack, the ruse to employ, the surprise of assault, that should force this living citadel to receive the enemy in her room.

Cornudet remained apart from the rest, and was a stranger to the whole affair.

So entirely were their minds distracted that they did not hear Ball-of-Fat enter. The Count uttered a light "Ssh!" which turned all eyes in her direction. There she was. The abrupt silence and a certain embarrassment hindered them from speaking to her at first. The Countess, more accustomed to the duplicity of society than the others, finally inquired:

"Was it very amusing, that baptism?"

The fat girl, filled with emotion, told them all about it, the faces, the attitudes, and even the appearance of the church. She added: "It is good to pray sometimes."

And up to the time for luncheon these ladies continued to be amiable toward her, in order to increase her docility and her confidence in their counsel. At the table they commenced the approach. This was in the shape of a vague conversation upon devotion. They cited ancient examples: Judith and Holophernes, then, without reason, Lucrece and Sextus, and Cleopatra obliging all the generals of the enemy to pass by her couch and reducing them in servility to slaves. Then they brought out a fantastic story, hatched in the imagination of these ignorant millionaires, where the women of Rome went to Capua for the purpose of lulling Hannibal to sleep in their arms, and his lieutenants and phalanxes of mercenaries as well. They cited all the women who have been taken by conquering armies, making a battlefield of their bodies, making them also a weapon, and a means of success; and all those hideous and detestable beings who have conquered by their heroic caresses, and sacrificed their chastity to vengeance or a beloved cause. They even spoke in veiled terms of that great English family which allowed one of its women to be inoculated with a horrible and contagious disease in order to transmit it to Bonaparte, who was miraculously saved by a sudden illness at the hour of the fatal rendezvous.

And all this was related in an agreeable, temperate fashion, except as it was enlivened by the enthusiasm deemed proper to excite emulation.

One might finally have believed that the sole duty of woman here below was a sacrifice of her person, and a continual abandonment to soldierly caprices.

The two good sisters seemed not to hear, lost as they were in profound thought. Ball-of-Fat said nothing.

During the whole afternoon they let her reflect. But, in the place of calling her "Madame" as they had up to this time, they simply called her "Mademoiselle" without knowing exactly why, as if they had a desire to put her down a degree in their esteem, which she had taken by storm, and make her feel her shameful situation.

The moment supper was served, Monsieur Follenvie appeared with his old phrase: "The Prussian officer orders me to ask if Mademoiselle Elizabeth Rousset has yet changed her mind."

Ball-of-Fat responded dryly: "No, sir."

But at dinner the coalition weakened. Loiseau made three unhappy remarks. Each one beat his wits for new examples but found nothing; when the Countess, without premeditation, perhaps feeling some vague need of rendering homage to religion, asked the elder of the good sisters to tell them some great deeds in the lives of the saints. It appeared that many of their acts would have been considered crimes in our eyes; but the Church gave absolution of them readily, since they were done for the glory of God, or for the good of all. It was a powerful argument; the Countess made the most of it.

Thus it may be by one of those tacit understandings, or the veiled complacency in which anyone who wears the ecclesiastical garb excels, it may be simply from the effect of a happy unintelligence, a helpful stupidity, but in fact the religious sister lent a formidable support to the conspiracy. They had thought her timid, but she showed herself courageous, verbose, even violent. She was not troubled by the chatter of the casuist; her doctrine seemed a bar of iron; her faith never hesitated; her conscience had no scruples. She found the sacrifice of Abraham perfectly simple, for she would immediately kill father or mother on an order from on high. And nothing, in her opinion, could displease the Lord, if the intention was laudable. The Countess put to use the authority of her unwitting accomplice, and added to it the edifying paraphrase and axiom of Jesuit morals: "The need justifies the means."

Then she asked her: "Then, my sister, do you think that God accepts intentions, and pardons the deed when the motive is pure?"

"Who could doubt it, Madame? An action blamable in itself often becomes meritorious by the thought it springs from."

And they continued thus, unraveling the will of God, foreseeing His decisions, making themselves interested in things that, in truth, they would never think of noticing. All this was guarded, skillful, discreet. But each word of the saintly sister in a cap helped to break down the resistance of the unworthy courtesan. Then the conversation changed a little, the woman of the chaplet speaking of the houses of her order, of her Superior, of herself, of her dainty neighbor, the dear sister Saint-Nicephore. They had been called to the hospitals of Havre to care for the hundreds of soldiers stricken with smallpox. They depicted these miserable creatures, giving details of the malady. And while they were stopped, *en route,* by the caprice of this Prussian officer, a great number of Frenchmen might die, whom perhaps they could have saved! It was a specialty with her, caring for soldiers. She had been in Crimea, in Italy, in Austria, and, in telling of her campaigns, she revealed herself as one of those religious aids to drums and trumpets, who seem made to follow camps, pick up the wounded in the thick of battle, and, better than an officer, subdue with a word great bands of undisciplined recruits. A true, good sister of the rataplan, whose ravaged face, marked with innumerable scars, appeared the image of the devastation of war.

No one could speak after her, so excellent seemed the effect of her words.

As soon as the repast was ended they quickly went up to their rooms, with the purpose of not coming down the next day until late in the morning.

The luncheon was quiet. They had given the grain of seed time to germinate and bear fruit. The Countess proposed that they take a walk in the afternoon. The Count, being agreeably inclined, gave an arm to Ball-of-Fat and walked behind the others with her. He talked to her in a familiar, paternal tone, a little disdainful, after the manner of men having girls in their employ, calling her "my dear child," from the height of his social position, of his undisputed honor. He reached the vital part of the question at once:

"Then you prefer to leave us here, exposed to the violences which follow a defeat, rather than consent to a favor which you have so often given in your life?"

Ball-of-Fat answered nothing.

Then he tried to reach her through gentleness, reason, and then the sentiments. He knew how to remain "The Count," even while showing himself gallant or complimentary, or very amiable if it became necessary. He exalted the service that she would render them, and spoke of their appreciation; then suddenly became gaily familiar, and said:

"And you know, my dear, it would be something for him to boast of that he had known a pretty girl; something it is difficult to find in his country."

Ball-of-Fat did not answer but joined the rest of the party. As soon as they entered the house she went to her room and did not appear again. The disquiet was extreme. What were they to do? If she continued to resist, what an embarrassment!

The dinner hour struck. They waited in vain. Monsieur Follenvie finally entered and said that Mademoiselle Rousset was indisposed, and would not be at the table. Everybody pricked up his ears. The Count went to the innkeeper and said in a low voice:

"Is he in there?"

"Yes."

For convenience, he said nothing to his companions, but made a slight sign with his head. Immediately a great sigh of relief went up from every breast and a light appeared in their faces. Loiseau cried out:

"Holy Christopher! I pay for the champagne, if there is any to be found in the establishment." And Madame Loiseau was pained to see the proprietor return with four quart bottles in his hands.

Each one had suddenly become communicative and buoyant. A wanton joy filled their hearts. The Count suddenly perceived that Madame Carré-Lamadon was charming, the manufacturer paid compliments to the Countess. The conversation was lively, gay, full of touches.

Suddenly Loiseau, with anxious face and hand upraised, called out: "Silence!" Everybody was silent, surprised, already frightened. Then he listened intently and said: "S-s-sh!" his two eyes and his hands raised toward the ceiling, listening, and then continuing, in his natural voice: "All right! All goes well!"

They failed to comprehend at first, but soon all laughed. At the end of a quarter of an hour he began the same farce again, renewing it occasionally during the whole afternoon. And he pretended to call to some one in the story above, giving him advice in a double meaning, drawn from the fountain-head—the mind of a commercial traveler. For some moments he would assume a sad air, breathing in a whisper: "Poor girl!" Then he would murmur between his teeth, with an appearance of rage: "Ugh! That scamp of a Prussian." Sometimes, at a moment when no more was thought about it, he would say, in an affected voice, many times over: "Enough! enough!" and add, as if speaking to himself. "If we could only see her again, it isn't necessary that he should kill her, the wretch!"

Although these jokes were in deplorable taste, they amused all and wounded no one, for indignation, like other things, depends upon its surroundings, and the atmosphere which had been gradually created around them was charged with sensual thoughts.

At the dessert the women themselves made some delicate and discreet allusions. Their eyes glistened; they had drunk much. The Count, who preserved, even in his flights, his grand appearance of gravity, made a comparison, much relished, upon the subject of those wintering at the pole, and the joy of ship-wrecked sailors who saw an opening toward the south.

Loiseau suddenly arose, a glass of champagne in his hand, and said: "I drink to our deliverance." Everybody was on his feet; they shouted in agreement. Even the two good sisters consented to touch their lips to the froth of the wine which they had never before tasted. They declared that it tasted like charged lemonade, only much nicer.

Loiseau resumed: "It is unfortunate that we have no piano, for we might make up a quadrille."

Cornudet had not said a word, nor made a gesture; he appeared plunged in very grave thoughts, and made sometimes a furious motion, so that his great beard seemed to wish to free itself. Finally, toward midnight, as they were separating, Loiseau, who was staggering, touched him suddenly on the stomach and said to him in a stammer: "You are not very funny, this evening; you have said nothing, citizen!" Then Cornudet raised his head brusquely and, casting a brilliant, terrible glance around the company, said: "I tell you all that you have been guilty of infamy!" He rose, went to the door, and again repeated: "Infamy, I say!" and disappeared.

This made a coldness at first. Loiseau, interlocutor, was stupefied; but he recovered immediately and laughed heartily as he said: "He is very green, my friends. He is very green." And then, as they did not comprehend, he told them about the "mysteries of the corridor." Then there was a return of gaiety. The women behaved like lunatics. The Count and Monsieur Carré-Lamadon wept from the force of their laughter. They could not believe it.

"How is that? Are you sure?"

"I tell you I saw it."

"And she refused——"

"Yes, because the Prussian officer was in the next room."

"Impossible!"

"I swear it!"

The Count was stifled with laughter. The industrial gentleman held his sides with both hands. Loiseau continued:

"And now you understand why he saw nothing funny this evening! No, nothing at all!" And the three started out half ill, suffocated.

They separated. But Madame Loiseau, who was of a spiteful nature, remarked to her husband as they were getting into bed, that "that *grisette*" of a little Carré-Lamadon was yellow with envy all the evening. "You know," she continued, "how some women will take a uniform, whether it be French or Prussian! It is all the same to them! Oh! what a pity!"

And all night, in the darkness of the corridor, there were to be heard light noises, like whisperings and walking in bare feet, and imperceptible creakings. They did not go to sleep until late, that is sure, for there were threads of light shining under the doors for a long time. The champagne had its effect; they say it troubles sleep.

The next day a clear winter's sun made the snow very brilliant. The diligence, already harnessed, waited before the door, while an army of white pigeons, in their thick plumage, with rose-colored eyes, with a black spot in the center, walked up and down gravely among the legs of the six horses, seeking their livelihood in the manure there scattered.

The driver, enveloped in his sheep-skin, had a lighted pipe under the seat, and all the travelers, radiant, were rapidly packing some provisions for the rest of the journey. They were only waiting for Ball-of-Fat. Finally she appeared.

She seemed a little troubled, ashamed. And she advanced timidly toward her companions, who all, with one motion, turned as if they had not seen her. The Count, with dignity, took the arm of his wife and removed her from this impure contact.

The fat girl stopped, half stupefied; then, plucking up courage, she approached the manufacturer's wife with "Good morning, Madame," humbly murmured. The lady made a slight bow of the head which she accompanied with a look of outraged virtue. Everybody seemed busy, and kept themselves as far from her as if she had had some infectious disease in her skirts. Then they hurried into the carriage, where she came last, alone, and where she took the place she had occupied during the first part of the journey.

They seemed not to see her or know her; although Madame Loiseau, looking at her from afar, said to her husband in a half-tone: "Happily, I don't have to sit beside her."

The heavy carriage began to move and the remainder of the journey commenced. No one spoke at first. Ball-of-Fat dared not raise her eyes. She felt indignant toward all her neighbors, and at the same time humiliated at having yielded to the foul kisses of this Prussian, into whose arms they had hypocritically thrown her.

Then the Countess, turning toward Madame Carré-Lamadon, broke the difficult silence:

"I believe you know Madame d'Etrelles?"

"Yes, she is one of my friends."

"What a charming woman!"

"Delightful! A very gentle nature, and well educated, besides; then she is an artist to the tips of her fingers, sings beautifully, and draws to perfection."

The manufacturer chatted with the Count, and in the midst of the rattling of the glass, an occasional word escaped such as "coupon—premium —limit—expiration."

Loiseau, who had pilfered the old pack of cards from the inn, greasy through five years of contact with tables badly cleaned, began a game of bezique with his wife.

The good sisters took from their belt the long rosary which hung there, made together the sign of the cross, and suddenly began to move their lips in a lively murmur, as if they were going through the whole of the "Oremus." And from time to time they kissed a medal, made the sign anew, then recommenced their muttering, which was rapid and continued.

Cornudet sat motionless, thinking.

At the end of three hours on the way, Loiseau put up the cards and said: "I am hungry."

His wife drew out a package from whence she brought a piece of cold veal. She cut it evenly in thin pieces and they both began to eat.

"Suppose we do the same," said the Countess.

They consented to it and she undid the provisions prepared for the two couples. It was in one of those dishes whose lid is decorated with a china hare, to signify that a *pâté* of hare is inside, a succulent dish of pork, where white rivers of lard cross the brown flesh of the game, mixed with some other viands hashed fine. A beautiful square of Gruyère cheese, wrapped in a piece of newspaper, preserved the imprint "divers things" upon the unctuous plate.

The two good sisters unrolled a big sausage which smelled of garlic; and Cornudet plunged his two hands into the vast pockets of his overcoat, at the same time, and drew out four hard eggs and a piece of bread. He removed the shells and threw them in the straw under his feet; then he began to eat the eggs, letting fall on his vast beard some bits of clear yellow, which looked like stars caught there.

Ball-of-Fat, in the haste and distraction of her rising, had not thought of anything; and she looked at them exasperated, suffocating with rage, at all of them eating so placidly. A tumultuous anger swept over her at first, and she opened her mouth to cry out at them, to hurl at them a flood of injury which mounted to her lips; but she could not speak, her exasperation strangled her.

No one looked at her or thought of her. She felt herself drowned in the scorn of these honest scoundrels, who had first sacrificed her and then rejected her, like some improper or useless article. She thought of her great basket full of good things which they had greedily devoured, of her two chickens shining with jelly, of her *pâtés*, her pears, and the four bottles of Bordeaux; and her fury suddenly falling, as a cord drawn too tightly breaks, she felt ready to weep. She made terrible efforts to prevent it, making ugly faces, swallowing her sobs as children do, but the tears came and glistened in the corners of her eyes, and then two great drops, detaching themselves from the rest, rolled slowly down like little streams of water that filter through rock, and, falling regularly, rebounded upon her breast. She sits erect, her eyes fixed, her face rigid and pale, hoping that no one will notice her.

But the Countess perceives her and tells her husband by a sign. He shrugs his shoulders, as much as to say:

"What would you have me do, it is not my fault."

Mme. Loiseau indulged in a mute laugh of triumph and murmured: "She weeps for shame."

The two good sisters began to pray again, after having wrapped in a paper the remainder of their sausage.

Then Cornudet, who was digesting his eggs, extended his legs to the seat opposite, crossed them, folded his arms, smiled like a man who is watching a good farce, and began to whistle the "Marseillaise."

All faces grew dark. The popular song assuredly did not please his neighbors. They became nervous and agitated, having an appearance of wishing to howl, like dogs, when they hear a barbarous organ. He perceived this but did not stop. Sometimes he would hum the words:

> *Sacred love of country*
> *Help, sustain th' avenging arm;*
> *Liberty, sweet Liberty*
> *Ever fight, with no alarm.*

They traveled fast, the snow being harder. But as far as Dieppe, during the long, sad hours of the journey, across the jolts in the road, through the falling night, in the profound darkness of the carriage, he continued his vengeful, monotonous whistling with a ferocious obstinacy, constraining his neighbors to follow the song from one end to the other, and to recall the words that belonged to each measure.

And Ball-of-Fat wept continually; and sometimes a sob, which she was not able to restrain, echoed between the two rows of people in the shadows.

Hands Across the Sea

BY

ALEXANDER WOOLLCOTT

THE night of the strange, swift inspection, held under a fitful light at all of the camps which American troops had pitched in the mud of Brittany.

IN THE World War, when chance made me a spellbound witness of some great occasions, some part of me—the incorrigible journalist, I suppose—kept saying: "This will be something to remember. This will be something to remember." Well, it seems I was wrong about that. I find I do not often think of the war at all, and when I do, it is the small, unimportant days that come drifting back, the ones that have no part in history at all. For example, of late my thoughts have taken unaccountably to joggling back along the road to Savenay, an ancient Breton village of steep, cobbled streets, and windmills that still, I suppose, turn sleepily against the sunset sky. And here I am, bent to the task of telling you about the evening of the strange inspection there.

It was at Savenay, in August of '17, that the base hospital recruited at the Post-Graduate in New York was established, with an enlisted personnel consisting, to an impressive extent, of bouncing undergraduates from Princeton and Rutgers who had enlisted early in May in order to escape the June exams. This frustrated group was part of a shipment of two thousand soldiers who sailed stealthily from Hoboken on a hot morning in July aboard the *Saratoga,* which aged transport got as far as Staten Island before being rammed and sunk. A week later, the same outfit tried again with another boat and got as far as Savenay. Then followed an interminable and corrupting wait through that bleak autumn of '17 when the war seemed to stretch ahead of us as a sterile condition of life of which we, at least, would never see the end. A time when only the real stalwarts were strong enough to keep from becoming silly or servile or both. A time of inaction and suspense and only the most sporadic and belated news from home. A time when no rumor could be too monstrous to be believed.

I emphasize this matter of rumors riding on every wind which came up the valley of the Loire only so that you may remember what tinder we all were for wild surmise, and what an outbreak of fantastic speculation there must have been one frosty December afternoon when, just after sundown, the bugles began blowing a summons which none of us, as we came tumbling out of quarters, could account for. "Line up, everybody! Line up! Line up!" This from the sergeants, all conscientiously gruff and authoritative, exhorting us and pushing us in any order into hastily formed queues which at once began shuffling docilely along in the quick-gathering darkness. Within sight, there were several such lines, each apparently working its way up to an appointed table, where there seemed to be muster-rolls spread out. We caught the gleam from officers' caps, bent in candle-lit conference. At the table, the line would pause for a moment, then move on and be swallowed up in the darkness. During this pause a light would flash on and off, on and off, like a winking beacon. What was up? It seemed to be some new kind of inspection. A curious hour for any kind. It was like a nightmare pay-day. But we had just *been* paid the week before. Perhaps the fool quartermaster wanted his francs back. Too late. Too late. There was smothered laughter, and a few foul but constructive suggestions as to what the quartermaster could do if he felt so inclined. A distant line had started up a song, and in a moment you could hear nothing else in the courtyard. It was that fine old pessimistic refrain to the tune of "Glory Hallelujah":

> *Every day we sign the pay-roll*
> *Every day we sign the pay-roll*
> *Every day we sign the pay-roll*
> *But we never get a*
> *God-damned cent.*

By this time my place in line was so far advanced that I could see something of what was going on. As each soldier reached the table, his name would be checked on the roll. Then he would be told to spread his hands on the table, palms down. An electric flash would spotlight them. The officers all bent low to examine them. Then palms up. Again the light. Again the close inspection. And that was all. No more than that. Well, for Christ's sake, was it leprosy they thought we had *this* time? The soldier would move on, bewildered. The next man would take his place. A moment later my own hands were spread out. By now the entire outfit was humming with surmise. It was a kind of off-stage hubbub with only the recurrent word "hands" distinguishable. Hands. Hands. Hands. Why did they want to see our hands? From the gossipy orderly in the adjutant's office we learned there had been a telephone call from the base and within half an hour, every hand in that outfit was being checked. Patients', orderlies', doctors', cooks', mechanics', everybody's. Except the nurses'.

We drifted out through the gate onto the road to Nantes. It lay hard as flint in the frost, white as snow in the light of the new-risen moon. Across the fields was a camp of the Seventeenth Engineers. There, too, the same puzzled line was forming, writhing. The same candle-lit table, the same winking flashlight. They were looking at all the American hands in Savenay.

We later learned that, at that same moment, in Nantes, some thirty kilo-meters away, and in all the camps pitched in the frozen mud outside St. Nazaire, the same swift inspection was going on. Also, still later, we learned why. In a barn near the port that afternoon, a fourteen-year-old girl in a torn black smock had been found unconscious. She had been raped. They could learn from her only that she had been dragged there by a soldier in a brown uniform, and that, while she was struggling with him, she had caught his hand and bitten it. Bitten it until she tasted blood.

Well, that is the story. Not, as you see, an important one. It was un-related to the major forces launched to make the world safe for democracy. But, every now and again, some sight of a line shuffling in the torch-lit darkness—a not altogether unfamiliar sight in *this* rescued democracy— some Proustian invocation of a bygone moment brings it all back to me.

And the end of the story? You want to know, perhaps, whether they found a man with a bitten hand. Yes, they did.

I Bombed the Barges

BY

THE CAPTAIN OF A BLENHEIM BOMBER

THE narrator is a twenty-eight-year-old Scot who has raided nearly all the invasion ports, from Flushing to Brest, on some night or another since the first British onslaught began in early September.

If anything, Air Ministry bulletins have minimized the scale and intensity of these R.A.F. attacks, which went on from twilight to dawn without intermission until the last week of October. The imminence of the invasion threat probably inspired the sustained ferocity of the raids. They have laid waste every port and harbor from Holland to the Atlantic seaboard of France and smashed all German hopes of a landing in Britain and an early conclusion to the war. Air power—the battering ram of the Luftwaffe—brought the German Army to the Channel ports; air power—the might of the R.A.F.—stopped it there.

Since the British expected to find considerable fighter opposition at these ports, Blenheim bombers were used in preference to heavy night bombers like the Wellingtons, Whitleys, and Hampdens. The R.A.F. has plenty of Blenheims, which are fighter-bombers and which could more than make up in speed and maneuverability what they might sacrifice in sheer load capacity.

As it happened, the R.A.F. found little fighter opposition. But according to the pilots, the ground defenses were hotter than anything encountered in their raids over German territory. It is believed that large numbers of mobile A.A. batteries were taken away from home defense in Germany and packed around the Channel ports. At any rate, pilots on "sorties" into Germany reported a much easier time while the bombing of the barges was proceeding. In addition, most of the A.A. guns and ammunition captured from the French, Belgians, and Dutch were packed into the restricted areas round these ports. And the Blenheim's special qualities of speed and "handling" came in useful in facing and breaking through such a hell-fire of ground defense.

The nickname given by bomber crews to the coastline of the invasion ports is "Blackpool Front." Blackpool, in Lancashire, is Britain's Coney Island, famous in pre-war days for grandiose illuminations and firework spectacles.

The pilot who tells this story is a rather rangy young man with a droll

From: *Their Finest Hour,* Ed. by Graebner & Michie. Copyright 1941. By permission of Harcourt, Brace & Co.

sense of humor and speech full of telling metaphors. Before the war he was a constructional engineer employed in his father's firm, which has built, among other things, most of the cinemas for a big group in Britain.

He is a completely professional type and grimly deplores the exigencies of this war, which has brought him to "knocking things down when I would rather be building them up." But apparently he can do both equally well.

This is the Captain's story: It was three o'clock in the morning. An hour before, I was sleeping peacefully in my warm bed at the airdrome; now I was encased in noisy, vibrating metal walls, rumbling southeast under the stars over the dark, hidden fields and sleeping villages of England. At 9,000 feet I turned on my oxygen supply and instructed my rear gunner and the bomb-aimer to do likewise. It was freezing-cold and we've learned from experience that oxygen helps warm the blood.

We were heading for Ostend. As I watched the vague, greenish glimmer from the radium-painted instrument dials, I ran over in my mind all that we had been told at the "briefing" that evening. Again I visualized the photograph which our Intelligence Officer had shown us: the rows of 100-foot barges, ten in a line, ten rows deep, lying in each of the four harbor basins. From the height at which the picture was taken, they looked like matchsticks loosely bundled together.

I again pictured the three arms of the jetties separating the basins, three black lines jutting out toward the harbor entrance and probably packed with military stores and men. But it was the barges I was after, and I began to review our method of attack. I decided I would not bomb up the basins. If I was even a tiny bit out, my bombs might miss the water space and hit the jetties. No, I would bomb diagonally across all four basins. Then *some* of the stick of bombs would be certain to hit barges.

I thought of my chances of getting in for a low attack without being spotted. They were good, because I was the leading aircraft of my squadron. The others were following me at three-minute intervals and behind them were squadrons from two other stations. It was to be a proper "do." We were to put Ostend out of the invasion business for some time to come.

But since I would be the first visitor that night, I hoped that the usual "reception committee" would not be at work and that I would be able to throttle back well out to sea and glide in unobserved. I knew some of our boys had been busy already at Dunkirk and Calais, but I still hoped that the panic there would not have affected the German gunners at Ostend.

Reflecting about these matters, I began to get a little worried. It was pitch black outside, but I wondered whether even the faint glow from the instrument panels would affect our vision. I'm a stickler on this subject of darkness. I won't have any light at all inside my aircraft on a night raid. It's not that we might be spotted by enemy watchers but that I need about twenty minutes to get my full night vision and the slightest glint of light puts me off for another twenty minutes. And if we were to make a surprise attack, both the bomb-aimer and I would have to be at our best to pick up the target and the outline of the jetties on such a moonless night. And it would have to be done almost instantly after we crossed the enemy coastline. If we didn't pick it up and bomb at once, I would have to open up the motors again for another run on to the barges. Then the band would begin to play and low bombing would be out of the question.

Just then my navigator switched on his shrouded hand torch to scan the map on his table. He sits in front of me and the table is hidden from my view by my instrument panel, but a tiny reflected glow touched the side windows of the cabin. I told him urgently to hurry with his position check and douse the torch, and then kicked myself for being so brusque. He was a good bomb-aimer, quick, calm and accurate, and this was his last trip with me, as he was leaving the squadron to go on a pilot's course. A good bomb-aimer makes all the difference in getting your job done quickly and successfully and getting the hell out of it. I was fed up at losing him, so I chatted to him mildly for a while about various details.

We were over the sea now, heading for Ostend. I could tell that by the different sound of the motors, which always change their note over the sea. I did the last-minute jobs, setting the bomb fuses and pressing down the bomb-selection switches so the packets would all leave in a stick. It won't be long now, I thought, settling down in the seat.

I put her up in a long, slow climb to 15,000, at which height I would begin my glide in from about ten miles out. I warned my navigator to make a close check on our speed and course so that he could tell me the right moment to throttle back and start down.

Halfway across the Channel, I saw the glow of fires, the flash of bombs, bursting shells, and a great cascade of tracers, "flaming onions," and other muck coming up on my right along the French coast, where other British bombers were hitting hard. But to my left and straight ahead there was complete darkness. "Still good," I thought, and concentrated on my flying and the instruments. The navigator left his bench and squatted forward over the bomb sight. He began to check various readings with me over the phones. Just then my rear gunner, perched in his lonely cubbyhole amidships, called out "Fighter!" I listened anxiously through the crackle of the phones. Then the direction. "Red [port beam] below." Instantly I kicked the rudder over and climbed, so as to give the gunner a fair go at it. I leveled and waited. Then the gunner again: "He's out of range. But he's seen us. He's stalking us, sir."

There was nothing to do but go down again and turn widely off course, hoping to lose him. For it was no use attemping to argue with him. I had a job to do. Meanwhile I made rapid calculations. If I did not shake him off quickly, all my plans for a silent approach to the barges would be upset and the following aircraft from my squadron would be on top of me. I thumped the handle of my stick with impatience. We dived, swerved, swung around again, and hoped for the best. As luck would have it, my gunner soon announced that the fighter had gone. I got back on my course, giving full throttle to make up for lost time.

The whole of "Blackpool Front" was now in near view. It was an amazing spectacle. The Calais docks were on fire. So was the waterfront of Boulogne, and glares extended for miles. The whole French coast seemed to be a barrier of flame broken only by intense white flashes of exploding bombs and varicolored incendiary tracers soaring and circling skyward.

The rear gunner, who had hardly uttered a word throughout the entire trip, was shouting excitedly through the "intercom." "Gawd! Look at that —and that!" I grinned to myself as he went burbling on. He never talks as a rule, never complains or tries to open up a line of gossip, as many rear gunners do, afflicted by the loneliness and cold of their job. Throughout many a raid he has spoken to me only when he has had to answer routine questions. As he once put it to me with a grin, "Sometimes I sits and thinks, and sometimes I just sits."

We were getting near now. But not a peep, not a glimmer from the darkness ahead. I made some last-minute adjustments and called to the navigator, who called out "Now!"

I throttled back and put the nose down. Pressing my head against the windows, I strained and peered out to pick up the first glimpse of the Ostend harbor works. The navigator had gone forward to squat over his bomb sight in the nose. The semi-silence after the steady roar of the motors was almost startling. The air stream rushing past us rose in a high, steady, whistling scream as we plunged down. I thought of the waiting gun crews hidden there far ahead in the darkness, the massed soldiers on the quays and in the barges, unaware of our coming. I felt exultant, tremendous. I felt like singing above the vast avenging crescendo of my bomber driving through the sky.

And then I thought, "They'll hear us! They'll hear us!" The drone of the motors was cut, but the scream of the air stream was now deafening. The Blenheim was trembling as we touched the top speed of the dive. In that instant the navigator called, "Left, left!" As I obeyed instantly with rudder pressure, I saw the harbor too—a black outline on the darkness. It rushed nearer and upward. "Steady! Ri-i-ght! Steady!" chanted the bomb-aimer. We were over the harbor front. I fought the stick, flickering my gaze to ground and back to the quivering altimeter needle. Down to 500. There were the four jetty arms. We were dead on line. A searchlight shot up to the right of us, miles out and too late. I had an instant's thought of my bomb-aimer crouched forward with his hand on the lever of the "Mickey Mouse" [R.A.F. slang for bomb-release device], his eyes glued on those barge-filled basins sliding down between the drift wires on the bomb sight. Then came the great, surging kick on the stick as the bombs left the plane. A second later he was through to me on the phones and calmly announced, "Bombs gone."

My waiting hand threw open the throttle levers in a flash. The motors thundered out. Hauling back on the stick, kicking at the rudder, we went up in a great, banking climb. As we went, I stared down and out through the windows. There they were! One, two, three, four vast flashes as my bombs struck. In the light of the last one, just as lightning will suddenly paint a whole landscape, I saw the outline of the jetties in vivid relief. Between them the water boiled with thin black shapes. They were barges flung end up and fragments turning slowly over and over in the air.

Then came a most gigantic crash. We were nearly 2,000 feet up now and well away from the jetties, but the whole aircraft pitched over, as if a giant blow had struck us underneath. A vivid flash enveloped us and lingered, as sound burst round our ears. It was a blinding white flash like a great sheet of daylight stuck in between the dark. While all hell broke loose around us, I fought like mad to get control of the bomber. But all the time my mind was blankly wondering—half stunned as I was—what the devil had we hit. Afterward I learned that the last bomb had struck a group of mines stacked on a jetty waiting to be loaded aboard the mine-layers. Photographs taken the next morning showed two stone jetties blown away to the water's edge, all barges vanished from the inner basins, and devastation over a mile radius!

Then the searchlights got me. I plunged inland to dodge them, but they held, and the sky all round us was packed with every kind of muck arching over us and all around. It was a bad few minutes, and once or twice I thought we would never get out. In their mass of colored bursts the flak [German anti-aircraft fire] was crazily beautiful but horrible. The whole interior of my aircraft was lit up. I saw my navigator sitting up at my feet rubbing his head. He had been flung out of his compartment when we turned over in that great explosion.

There was a new kind of fiery flak which followed us and stuck close on either side. It resembled the three colored balls of a pawnbroker's sign. They frightened me. I watched them diving and climbing wildly, and dodged as best I could. They were probably clues to my position for their fighters, but they looked damnably dangerous. Somehow—I don't know how—we were out. I turned again and headed out to sea. Taking stock of ourselves, I called up the rear gunner. "I'm O.K.," he said, "but I didn't expect a ride in a rocket." My navigator said that he had been laid out when he was flung at my feet, but all he had now was a bad headache. Turning again along the coast, I saw more and more great flashes as others of my squadron went into Ostend. The whole sky was packed with A.A. bursts and I counted twenty great fires at different places round the harbor. Against the flames, the whole town stood out clearly. Most of the squadron, I reflected, would have had a free run in from the sea while the batteries were concentrating on me inland. In the din of that first great explosion their approaching engines would not have been heard. They couldn't have wished for a brighter target.

Then we swung around and headed for home. Behind us, yet another of the German Army's invasion ports was a bonfire on the skyline. The dawn was coming up across my right shoulder. England lay in her guarded sleep just ahead of us. The engines droned on. We were tired but somehow peaceful and happy as we quietly munched our rations.

The Italian Debacle at Guadalajara

BY

F. G. TINKER, JR.

On March eighth we received two more replacement pilots—Lecha and Blanche. They were each given about an hour in which to practise take-offs and landings so that they could get used to the rather rough landing field. Also to give LaCalle a chance to see what kind of pilots they were. Blanche turned out to be an exceptionally good pilot. Lecha was only fair, having had very little previous flying time.

That night Chang told us a very interesting story about Blanche. He had been over in Spanish Morocco when the rebellion broke out, had pretended to be a Fascist sympathizer, and was assigned to the job of co-piloting a large seaplane bomber, the chief pilot being a Spanish Rebel captain. One of the plane's two mechanics was also a Loyalist sympathizer, so the two of them got together and did a little secret plotting. At the first favorable opportunity, Blanche gave the signal by shooting the chief pilot dead and taking over the controls himself. While he was doing this, his consort was busy shooting up the other mechanic and the rear machine gunner. Whereupon Blanche set a course for Loyalist territory and landed the plane in the habor at Valencia, where he was received with wild acclaim. The grateful Government immediately made him a first lieutenant in the Loyalist Air Force, and he flew seaplanes for a while until he decided to try his hand in fighting planes. The Government immediately granted his request and sent him to Los Alcázares for training. When he completed the course there he was sent to the *Escuadrilla de LaCalle,* and we were certainly glad to have him.

At that particular time LaCalle was having a bit of trouble finding someone to lead the third patrol, which Berthial had been leading. He wanted to give me the job, but I fell back on my ignorance of the Spanish language as an excuse for staying with Whitey and Chang. When he saw the way in which Blanche handled his plane, he immediately made him the third patrol leader. All hands concurred in the opinion that he had made a very wise choice.

On this day we received word that the enemy had started a drive on the front to the north of us—the Guadalajara front. The attack was started from the Fascist-held town of Sigüenza, which is forty-odd miles northeast of Guadalajara. It consisted of three columns, highly mechanized, advancing down the main highway connecting Madrid and Zaragoza. It was, as we found out later, the beginning of the famous Italian offensive on the Guadalajara front. At any rate, they managed to advance several miles before nightfall that day. The Government troops put up a strong resistance with machine guns and light field pieces, but they were gradually forced back by Mussolini's tanks.

March ninth was a rather eventful day. Early in the morning our alarm flares started us off, and hardly had the last plane cleared the ground when we saw three bimotored Junkers coming out of a low-lying layer of clouds which began just north of the field and extended northward as far as the eye could see. They also saw us climbing up, and the sight so rattled them that they dropped their bombs in the river and fled. We managed to get in a few long-distance shots at them, but they were too fast for us to overtake.

The Italian troops made considerable headway that day. Early in the morning they captured three small towns near the main highway—Almadrones, Argecilla, and Ledanca—and continued their advance. All this time it was raining heavily, which was to our advantage. Their central column was pushing down the main highway sweeping all opposition before it. Our soldiers lacked the equipment for combatting tanks and armored cars; but after about a third of this column had crossed a bridge near an important crossroad, the bridge was washed out by the flood due to the unusually heavy rains. This kept the majority of this most important column out of action for several hours during the most critical part of the advance while the bridge was being repaired. The vanguard of the central column continued its advance for three or four miles, but it was not strong enough to consolidate its newly-captured positions and was forced to retreat. The washing-out of this bridge was a great blow to the Italians, since it frustrated the entire advantage of their mechanized army—speed and surprise.

In the meantime the Italians to the east of the main highway had also been making considerable progress. They surrounded the town of Brihuega and captured it shortly after nightfall. They had advanced so rapidly that they were within the city limits before the Government commander was even aware that they were in the vicinity. As Brihuega is only about fifteen miles from Guadalajara, there were some awfully long faces around our dining table that night. And our spirits weren't at all uplifted by the two- or three-hour bombardment we were treated to that night. That was the only occasion I can remember when there was no singing or laughing in a bomb shelter during a bombardment. Even the usually cheerful Cristina and Maria were looking a little sad and thoughtful that night.

The following morning was dismal and rainy, with clouds almost down on the valley floor. However, the ceiling lifted for a while, so LaCalle sent Whitey out on a reconnaissance flight over the Italian territory. When he returned he reported that many troops were moving on enemy roads back of the lines. We immediately loaded up with bombs and got all set to take off. Just about that time, though, the ceiling dropped back to zero again and stayed there the rest of the day. All we could do was sit there grinding our teeth and listening to the heavy artillery booming away in the distance. LaCalle would come around every now and then and give us the latest news from the front.

The news on this day wasn't as disheartening as that of the day before. Our high command had taken advantage of the enemy's delay, caused by the bridge washout, to send up reinforcements as fast as they could get them there. Among these reinforcements were the eleventh and twelfth brigades of the international column, which were sent up during the night. They immediately entrenched themselves in the valleys and arroyos which extended westward from Brihuega. Our espionage system also discovered that Italian headquarters had been moved up to the little town of Trijueque, located on the main highway due west of Brihuega. It rained so heavily and continuously on this day that neither side was able to do very much fighting.

Whitey, Chang, and I went into Madrid that night and almost got bombed on our way back at the little town of Torrejón de Ardoz. The Junkers were trying to bomb the railroad station there, but instead they hit the area about halfway between the station and the highway, which were about two hundred yards apart. We just barely had time to jump into the ditch before the bombs started falling. We stayed there for about half an hour before continuing on our way to Azuqueca, where we were bawled out by LaCalle for being twenty minutes late; but we had the shrapnel-slashed top of our car to back up our story, so we were exonerated.

The eleventh of March was another wet day, with occasional heavy clouds coming along scraping the ground. About the middle of the morning we loaded up with bombs, nevertheless, and took off between rain squalls for our first look at the Guadalajara front. We cruised along over the very low clouds, with only an occasional glimpse of the ground below, and fortunately found an opening just over the place we were supposed to bomb, so down we went. We dropped our bombs at an altitude of about 600 feet and then went the rest of the way down with all four machine guns hammering away. The Italian troops were certainly in a bad way down there. The continual rains had made a regular quagmire out of that entire section of the country, and they were practically without protection from our aerial attack. What trenches they had been able to dig filled up with water almost as soon as they were dug. They didn't seem to have any anti-aircraft guns at all at that time, although a few of their field guns opened up an ineffective fire on us. We could see the poor devils scurrying through the mud in all directions as we came down spraying them with bullets. We made only one pass at them, as we had instructions to hurry back to the field before the ceiling fell to zero again.

That afternoon we learned that there was very little fighting going on at the front. The adverse weather conditions kept the Italians from using their machinery, so they were practically stalled. Their trucks, armored cars, and even their tanks were forced to stay on the main highways. Our side was taking advantage of the situation to rush in reinforcements and armament. The Government had managed to get in some modern, rapid-fire, large-caliber guns, enabling our men to play havoc with the enemy's stalled motor units. These guns would have done much more damage but for the fact that the men were unaccustomed to their operation.

About two hours before sundown we loaded up with bombs and took off again. This proved to be a tactical error; hardly had we left the ground when the clouds converged and we found ourselves right in the middle of a terrific thunder, lightning, and hail storm. LaCalle gave the landing signal and went over to the river and dropped his bombs—we had orders never to land with bombs, as several pilots had been killed that way—the rest of us doing likewise. By that time there were planes all over the sky—flying through the rain, hail, and lightning flashes. Our patrol stayed in formation until Chang pulled his head down in his cockpit so that he could reach his bomb release. He then slid over and almost rammed my plane, missing it by about six feet. This rattled him so much that he sheered off into the rain and never did find Whitey and me again.

LaCalle landed safely, but the rest of them were having difficulties; two or three were trying to land at the same time and nearly had collisions. Whitey and I watched this performance for a while, the storm getting worse all the time, and then decided to head for Albacete while we still had a chance. Neither one of us had a map, but somehow or other we managed to get there. We landed about an hour later, wondering how many of our squadron mates had got down safely.

As soon as we identified ourselves we were taken to the pilots' house, which was about two miles from the field. There we met the Russian Commander-in-chief, General Douglas, and several of our Russian friends whom we had met at Alcalá. They located a Russo-English interpreter, and when they heard our story called up Alcalá immediately to tell them that the two Americans were safe. They also told them to pass the word along to LaCalle at Azuqueca. After that we were led down to the very sumptuous dining room. The place had formerly been a duke's hunting lodge and was furnished and decorated like a palace. After an excellent meal we sat around talking to the American wife—Mrs. Rose-Marie—of an American pilot who was flying transport planes for the Government. She could also speak Russian, so our Russian friends were able to join in the conversation. After a couple of hours of this we were shown to our quarters and turned in for the night.

Early the next morning we went out to the field and discovered that we were to fly back to Alcalá with no less a personage than General Douglas himself. We naturally assumed that we would be assigned to the job of flying protection over some slow-moving transport plane. Our eyes almost popped out of our heads when we saw the general come out and climb into a fighting plane just like the ones we were flying ourselves. We had heard of generals in the United States flying—but they merely flew long enough to qualify for the 50 per cent extra pay to be derived thereby. But here was a general actually flying himself up to the front in a single-seater fighting plane!

Anyway, we took off with the general, in V formation, and were over Alcalá about an hour later. When he gave the break-up signal we sheered off, as previously instructed, and headed for Guadalajara. When we landed there, it was just as though two prodigal sons had returned. Our two mechanics, Chamorro and Juanas, were overjoyed to see us. They had given us up for lost when we failed to return the day before, and had only halfway believed LaCalle when he told them that we were safe in Albacete. They even had brand-new packages of American cigarettes ready for us; and American cigarettes were rather scarce at that time.

When we went in to make our report to LaCalle we received a half-hearted calling-down for leaving the vicinity of the field so soon. However, we could see that he was pleased to see us back safely. In fact, Chang later informed us that he had heard LaCalle bragging to the Russians about how two of his pilots had been able to find the field at Albacete in such adverse weather conditions without a map. We also found out that the rest of the boys had climbed up above the clouds and flown around until the squall passed. Then they had all come down and landed safely, with the exception of Chang, who had got himself lost and finally tried to land in some farmer's newly-plowed field. Naturally, his plane had nosed over. He was not hurt in the crash, however, and had been retrieved shortly before midnight.

The squadron had already made one flight across the lines that morning, and we had arrived just in time for the second one. On this flight we had a double mission to fulfil. We were to protect a squadron of our heavy bombers while they bombed, and then, when they finished, go down and do our dive-bombing and machine-gunning; or, in other words, mop up after them. We climbed to 8000 feet directly over our field and waited until the heavy bombers came along. They were flying at about 3200 feet, so we came down to 6500 feet and accompanied them across the lines. Even from that height we could see that a great battle was in progress down below. The flashes of field artillery from both sides were almost continuous. The appearance of our aerial fleet turned out to be the beginning of the end as far as the already-retreating Italians were concerned.

Three of our heavy bombers made a direct hit on and around the crossroad northwest of Brihuega and completely ruined it. They also wrecked fifteen or twenty trucks and cars which were trying to retreat and had become involved in a traffic jam there. A huge truck, whirling end over end through the air, made a most impressive sight. As soon as our bombers were safely back in our territory we dove down on the poor devils ourselves and cut loose with both bombs and machine guns. After that we went up to about 1000 feet and started cruising around.

This crossroad was the only avenue of retreat for the motorized units of the central and part of the eastern Italian columns. The fields were so muddy that they were forced to stay on the two roads leading from this crossroad to Brihuega and Trijueque. Even the foot soldiers had trouble retreating through the mud, which, being very sticky, accumulated in large lumps on their feet.

As no enemy planes appeared, we had nothing at all to do except watch the progress of the battle below and help to demoralize the Italians. Immediately after the aerial bombardment, our tanks (Russian) started to advance slowly through the mire, followed by cavalry, which proved to be worth its weight in gold in this engagement. By that time the Italians were so demoralized that it was almost terrible to behold. Rifles and ammunition belts were abandoned to facilitate running and away they went. That misery loves company was illustrated by the way the fleeing wretches tended to group together as they ran. That was very bad judgment indeed, because at the first sign of a group of men, down would come one of our fighting planes with all four guns chattering away. That was part of the instructions we had received before leaving the field. A description of one of these murderous dives will give you an idea of what the foot soldiers may expect in the war to come.

I spotted one especially large group of Italians in wild retreat before a couple of tanks. My first move was to maneuver my plane to a down-wind position from them—the wind was blowing in the same direction they were running—and then push its nose over into about a sixty-degree dive. At that altitude—1000 feet—the men looked like a mass of ants on the ground, even through my telescopic sight. At about 700 feet I opened fire with one upper and one lower machine gun. This was so that I could see, by the tracer bullets, whether or not I was on the target. The stream of bullets was just ahead of the fleeing group, so I opened up with the other two guns and pulled the plane's nose up a little.

By this time I could see the individuals plainly; they had also become aware of my presence. Then they did the worst thing they could have done—started running in the opposite direction. I could see dead-white faces swivel around and, at sight of the plane, comprehension would turn them even whiter. I could see their lips drawing back from their teeth in stark terror. Some of them tried to run at right angles, but it was too late; already they were falling like grain before a reaper. I pushed the rudder back and forth gently, so that the bullets would cover a wider area, then pulled back on the stick—just as gently—thus lengthening the swath. I pulled out of the dive about twenty feet off the ground, zoomed up to rejoin the squadron, and started looking for more victims. We kept this up until our gasoline and bullets were so low that we were forced to return to the field.

Late in the afternoon the weather cleared up enough for us to make another trip across the lines. Once more we loaded up with bombs and climbed above the lower layer of clouds. Just as we got into position for bombing, we spotted a squadron of Italian fighting planes—Fiats—headed in our direction. LaCalle failed to see them and went right on about his bombing. We thought he was merely ignoring them, so we followed him down and did our bombing and machine-gunning. When we got back to the field we found that both our patrol and the third patrol had been fired on—one plane in each patrol coming back full of holes.

Chang's plane was the one shot up in our patrol—it had thirty-five or forty bullet holes in it. He had been, as usual, lagging back out of position in the formation. The funny thing about it was that he thought someone in the third patrol had been shooting at him; he had not seen the Fiats at all. In fact, he didn't even know that he had been under fire until he landed and his mechanic pointed out that his plane was full of holes. Then he immediately wanted to go over and fight everyone in the third patrol. It took all of Whitey's eloquence and mine to convince him that he had actually been under fire from enemy planes.

That night we received very good news from the front lines. Our troops had advanced as far as the crossroad and were busy consolidating their positions. They had captured a large number of enemy cars and trucks which had been unable to get past the bombed crossroad. The territory the Italians still held on the west of the main highway was so mountainous that the use of anything on wheels was out of the question. We had inflicted an enormous amount of damage on the enemy that morning. Our heavy bombers had destroyed several columns of trucks on the highways and our own bombardment and machine gunnery had entirely broken the morale of the Italian first-line troops.

The same bad weather was in evidence the next day. In the morning LaCalle sent Whitey and me across the lines on a reconnaissance flight to check up on the movements of the enemy. We spotted several convoys of trucks and two or three long freight trains between Jadraque and Sigüenza. We also discovered that they now had anti-aircraft guns, as we were fired at several times. All of this we marked down on our maps so there would be no chance of forgetting anything. On our way back to the field we saw three bombers off in the distance headed toward enemy territory. Whether they were ours or their's we never did find out. We had had strict instructions from LaCalle to do nothing except reconnoiter and protect ourselves.

That afternoon we loaded up with bombs, and just as we were getting ready to take off, our two red flares went floating up. Fortunately, we were all sitting in our planes with our motors idling, so we all went off at once— except two or three who habitually lagged behind. Just as Whitey and I came around in our first turn we saw three bimotored Junkers come out from behind the clouds overhead. They saw us at once, and their gunners immediately opened fire, although they were a good 4800 feet above us. The pilot of the Junkers on the right was evidently a bit nervous, because he deserted the formation and started for his own territory full blast. (I have often wondered what happened to him when he reached his camp.) The other two held course and speed, and tried to carry out their mission. They were trying to hit the railroad station, but they overshot, and their bombs landed right in the middle of the old Hispano-Suiza buildings at the end of the field—just as the above-mentioned laggards were taking off over that area.

Although we were weighed down with bombs, Whitey and I started climbing at once, and were soon up to the level of the two remaining planes; but as soon as we got up to their level they dived into the thick clouds and started for home. We finally saw one of them streaking through the clouds below and went after it—opening fire as soon as we lined up our sights on it. Its rear machine gunner also opened fire on us: we could see his tracer bullets coming our way. However, we hit either him or his gun, because after about ten seconds of firing his stream of tracer bullets ended abruptly. We fired at that plane until it scrambled to safety in the next cloud. Then we went back to rejoin the formation.

The rest of the squadron had all tried to close in with the single plane which had left the formation, but it had too great a start. Blanche, the new leader of the third patrol, managed to fire at it a few seconds before one of its gunners shot the tail off his plane. He immediately bailed out and pulled his parachute rip cord. Then we were horrified to see the parachute string out above him and fail to open. The entire squadron saw him strike the ground, about 6500 feet below, with terrific force. LaCalle re-formed the squadron and we went on across the lines and carried out our bombing mission—using up the rest of our bullets on the enemy troops as we were returning.

Chang had gone down to the spot where Blanche struck and had memorized the location thoroughly before returning to the field. By the time we returned he had already started out after the body in our patrol car. They returned about half an hour later. For the rest of the time during which we used that particular car we had a rather grim reminder of our ex-squadron mate in the form of a large bloodstain on the rear cushion. His parachute had failed to open because it had been wet, so they immediately started checking up on all our parachutes.

The front-line reports we received that night were more cheering than ever. It seemed that our infantry had made two very effective counter-attacks. The first had been made against the town of Trijueque and had been supported by tanks and planes. The support from the air had consisted of two squadrons of bombers protected by a squadron of mono-planes. They had made five trips across the lines that day and had done outstanding work. The tanks, as usual, had advanced after each bombard-ment. The second attack, above Brihuega, had cut the enemy lines between Brihuega and Torija. This placed the Italians occupying Brihuega in the most dangerous position.

That night Whitey, Chang, and I took a run in to Madrid after the evening meal. We met all our American newspaper friends and indulged in another hot bath. When we got back home we discovered that we had missed an unusually good bombardment. Three houses on the edge of the little town had been destroyed. In fact, the more timid of the town's citizens were still in bed when we got there an hour after it happened. Before we turned in, LaCalle came around and told me that I was going to lead the third patrol whether I wanted to or not. Blanche's death that day had again left it without a leader.

Buchmendel

BY

STEFAN ZWEIG

HAVING just got back to Vienna, after a visit to an out-of-the-way part of the country, I was walking home from the station when a heavy shower came on, such a deluge that the passers-by hastened to take shelter in doorways, and I myself felt it expedient to get out of the downpour. Luckily there is a café at almost every street-corner in the metropolis, and I made for the nearest, though not before my hat was dripping wet and my shoulders were drenched to the skin. An old-fashioned suburban place, lacking the attractions (copied from Germany) of music and a dancing-floor to be found in the centre of the town; full of small shop-keepers and working folk who consumed more newspapers than coffee and rolls. Since it was already late in the evening, the air, which would have been stuffy anyhow, was thick with tobacco-smoke. Still, the place was clean and brightly decorated, had new satin-covered couches, and a shining cash-register, so that it looked thoroughly attractive. In my haste to get out of the rain, I had not troubled to read its name—but what matter? There I rested, warm and comfortable, though looking rather impatiently through the blue-tinted window panes to see when the shower would be over, and I should be able to get on my way.

Thus I sat unoccupied, and began to succumb to that inertia which results from the narcotic atmosphere of the typical Viennese café. Out of this void, I scanned various individuals whose eyes, in the murky room, had a greyish look in the artificial light; I mechanically contemplated the young woman at the counter as, like an automaton, she dealt out sugar and a teaspoon to the waiter for each cup of coffee; with half an eye and a wandering attention I read the uninteresting advertisements on the walls—and there was something agreeable about these dull occupations. But suddenly, and in a peculiar fashion, I was aroused from what had become almost a doze. A vague internal movement had begun; much as a toothache sometimes begins, without one's being able to say whether it is on the right side or the left, in the upper jaw or the lower. All I became aware of was a numb tension, an obscure sentiment of spiritual unrest. Then, without knowing why, I grew fully conscious. I must have been in this café once before, years ago, and random associations had awakened memories of the walls, the tables, the chairs, the seemingly unfamiliar smoke-laden room.

The more I endeavoured to grasp this lost memory, the more obstinately did it elude me; a sort of jellyfish glistening in the abysses of consciousness, slippery and unseizable. Vainly did I scrutinize every object within the range of vision. Certainly when I had been here before the counter had had neither marble top nor cash-register; the walls had not been panelled with imitation rosewood; these must be recent acquisitions. Yet I had indubitably been here, more than twenty years back. Within these four walls, as firmly fixed as a nail driven up to the head in a tree, there clung a part of my ego, long since overgrown. Vainly I explored, not only the room, but my own inner man, to grapple the lost links. Curse it all, I could not plumb the depths!

It will be seen that I was becoming vexed, as one is always out of humour when one's grip slips in this way, and reveals the inadequacy, the imperfections, of one's spiritual powers. Yet I still hoped to recover the clue. A slender thread would suffice, for my memory is of a peculiar type, both good and bad; on the one hand stubbornly untrustworthy, and on the other incredibly dependable. It swallows the most important details, whether in concrete happenings or in faces, and no voluntary exertion will induce it to regurgitate them from the gulf. Yet the most trifling indication—a picture postcard, the address on an envelope, a newspaper cutting—will suffice to hook up what is wanted as an angler who has made a strike and successfully imbedded his hook reels in a lively, struggling, and reluctant fish. Then I can recall the features of a man seen once only, the shape of his mouth and the gap to the left where he had an upper eye-tooth knocked out, the falsetto tone of his laugh, and the twitching of the moustache when he chooses to be merry, the entire change of expression which hilarity effects in him. Not only do these physical traits rise before my mind's eye, But I remember, years afterwards, every word the man said to me, and the tenor of my replies. But if I am to see and feel the past thus vividly, there must be some material link to start the current of associations. My memory will not work satisfactorily on the abstract plane.

I closed my eyes to think more strenuously, in the attempt to forge the hook which would catch my fish. In vain! In vain! There was no hook, or the fish would not bite. So fierce waxed my irritation with the inefficient and mulish thinking apparatus between my temples that I could have struck myself a violent blow on the forehead, much as an irascible man will shake and kick a penny-in-the-slot machine which, when he has inserted his coin, refuses to render him his due.

So exasperated did I become at my failure, that I could no longer sit quiet, but rose to prowl about the room. The instant I moved, the glow of awakening memory began. To the right of the cash-register, I recalled, there must be a doorway leading into a windowless room, where the only light was artificial. Yes, the place actually existed. The decorative scheme was different, but the proportions were unchanged. A square box of a place, behind the bar—the card-room. My nerves thrilled as I contemplated the furniture, for I was on the track, I had found the clue, and soon I should know all. There were two small billiard-tables, looking like silent ponds covered with green scum. In the corners, card-tables, at one of which two bearded men of professorial type were playing chess. Beside the iron stove, close to a door labelled "Telephone," was another small table. In a flash, I had it! That was Mendel's place, Jacob Mendel's. That was where Mendel used to hang out, Buchmendel. I was in the Café Gluck! How could I have forgotten Jacob Mendel? Was it possible that I had not thought about him for ages, a man so peculiar as wellnigh to belong to the Land of Fable, the eighth wonder of the world, famous at the university and among a narrow circle of admirers, magician of book-fanciers, who had been wont to sit there from morning till night, an emblem of bookish lore, the glory of the Café Gluck? Why had I had so much difficulty in hooking my fish? How could I have forgotten Buchmendel?

I allowed my imagination to work. The man's face and form pictured themselves vividly before me. I saw him as he had been in the flesh, seated at the table with its grey marble top, on which books and manuscripts were piled. Motionless he sat, his spectacled eyes fixed upon the printed page. Yet not altogether motionless, for he had a habit (acquired at school in the Jewish quarter of the Galician town from which he came) of rocking his shiny bald pate backwards and forwards and humming to himself as he read. There he studied catalogues and tomes, crooning and rocking, as Jewish boys are taught to do when reading the Talmud. The rabbis believe that, just as a child is rocked to sleep in its cradle, so are the pious ideas of the holy text better instilled by this rhythmical and hypnotizing movement of head and body. In fact, as if he had been in a trance, Jacob Mendel saw and heard nothing while thus occupied. He was oblivious to the click of billiard-balls, the coming and going of waiters, the ringing of the telephone bell; he paid no heed when the floor was scrubbed and when the stove was refilled. Once a red-hot coal fell out of the latter, and the flooring began to blaze a few inches from Mendel's feet; the room was full of smoke, and one of the guests ran for a pail of water to extinguish the fire. But neither the smoke, the bustle, nor the stench diverted his attention from the volume before him. He read as others pray, as gamblers follow the spinning of the roulette board, as drunkards stare into vacancy; he read with such profound absorption that ever since I first watched him the reading of ordinary mortals has seemed a pastime. This Galician second-hand book dealer, Jacob Mendel, was the first to reveal to me in my youth the mystery of absolute concentration which characterizes the artist and the scholar, the sage and the imbecile; the first to make me acquainted with the tragical happiness and unhappiness of complete absorption.

A senior student introduced me to him. I was studying the life and doings of a man who is even today too little known, Mesmer the magnetizer. My researches were bearing scant fruit, for the books I could lay my hands on conveyed sparse information, and when I applied to the university librarian for help he told me, uncivilly, that it was not his business to hunt up references for a freshman. Then my college friend suggested taking me to Mendel.

"He knows everything about books, and will tell you where to find the information you want. The ablest man in Vienna, and an original to boot. The man is a saurian of the book-world, an antediluvian survivor of an extinct species."

We went, therefore, to the Café Gluck, and found Buchmendel in his usual place, bespectacled, bearded, wearing a rusty black suit, and rocking as I have described. He did not notice our intrusion, but went on reading, looking like a nodding mandarin. On a hook behind him hung his ragged black overcoat, the pockets of which bulged with manuscripts, catalogues, and books. My friend coughed loudly, to attract his attention, but Mendel ignored the sign. At length Schmidt rapped on the table-top, as if knocking at a door, and at this Mendel glanced up, mechanically pushed his spectacles on to his forehead, and from beneath his thick and untidy ashen-grey brows there glared at us two dark, alert little eyes. My friend introduced me, and I explained my quandary, being careful (as Schmidt had advised) to express great annoyance at the librarian's unwillingness to assist me. Mendel leaned back, laughed scornfully, and answered with a strong Galician accent:

"Unwillingness, you think? Incompetence, that's what's the matter with him. He's a jackass. I've known him (for my sins) twenty years at least, and he's learned nothing in the whole of that time. Pocket their wages— that's all such fellows can do. They should be mending the road, instead of sitting over books."

This outburst served to break the ice, and with a friendly wave of the hand the bookworm invited me to sit down at his table. I reiterated my object in consulting him; to get a list of all the early works on animal magnetism, and of contemporary and subsequent books and pamphlets for and against Mesmer. When I had said my say, Mendel closed his left eye for an instant, as if excluding a grain of dust. This was, with him, a sign of concentrated attention. Then, as though reading from an invisible catalogue, he reeled out the names of two or three dozen titles, giving in each case place and date of publication and approximate price. I was amazed, though Schmidt had warned me what to expect. His vanity was tickled by my surprise, for he went on to strum the keyboard of his marvellous memory, and to produce the most astounding bibliographical notes. Did I want to know about sleepwalkers, Perkins's metallic tractors, early experiments in hynotism, Braid, Gassner, attempts to conjure up the devil, Christian Science, theosophy, Madame Blavatsky? In connexion with each item there was a hailstorm of book-names, dates, and appropriate details. I was beginning to understand that Jacob Mendel was a living lexicon, something like the general catalogue of the British Museum Reading Room, but able to walk about on two legs. I stared dumbfounded at this bibliographical phenomenon, which masqueraded in the sordid and rather unclean domino of a Galician second-hand book dealer, who, after rattling off some eighty titles (with assumed indifference, but really with the satisfaction of one who plays an unexpected trump), proceeded to wipe his spectacles with a handkerchief which might long before have been white.

Hoping to conceal my astonishment, I inquired:

"Which among these works do you think you could get for me without too much trouble?"

"Oh, I'll have a look round," he answered. "Come here tomorrow and I shall certainly have some of them. As for the others, it's only a question of time, and of knowing where to look."

"I'm greatly obliged to you," I said; and, then, wishing to be civil, I put my foot in it, proposing to give him a list of the books I wanted. Schmidt nudged me warningly, but too late. Mendel had already flashed a look at me—such a look, at once triumphant and affronted, scornful and overwhelmingly superior—the royal look with which Macbeth answers Macduff when summoned to yield without a blow. He laughed curtly. His Adam's apple moved excitedly. Obviously he had gulped down a choleric, an insulting epithet.

Indeed he had good reason to be angry. Only a stranger, an ignoramus, could have proposed to give him, Jacob Mendel, a memorandum, as if he had been a bookseller's assistant or an underling in a public library. Not until I knew him better did I fully understand how much my would-be politeness must have galled this aberrant genius—for the man had, and knew himself to have, a titanic memory, wherein, behind a dirty and un-distinguished-looking forehead, was indelibly recorded a picture of the title-page of every book that had been printed. No matter whether it had issued from the press yesterday or hundreds of years ago, he knew its place of publication, its author's name, and its price. From his mind, as if from the printed page, he could read off the contents, could reproduce the illustrations; could visualize, not only what he had actually held in his hands, but also what he had glanced at in a bookseller's window; could see it with the same vividness as an artist sees the creations of fancy which he has not yet reproduced upon canvas. When a book was offered for six marks by a Regensburg dealer, he could remember that, two years before, a copy of the same work had changed hands for four crowns at a Viennese auction, and he recalled the name of the purchaser. In a word, Jacob Mendel never forgot a title or a figure; he knew every plant, every in-fusorian, every star, in the continually revolving and incessantly changing cosmos of the book-universe. In each literary specialty, he knew more than the specialists; he knew the contents of the libraries better than the li-brarians; he knew the book-lists of most publishers better than the heads of the firms concerned—though he had nothing to guide him except the magical powers of his inexplicable but invariably accurate memory.

True, this memory owed its infallibility to the man's limitations, to his extraordinary power of concentration. Apart from books, he knew nothing of the world. The phenomena of existence did not begin to become real for him until they had been set in type, arranged upon a composing stick, collected and, so to say, sterilized in a book. Nor did he read books for their meaning, to extract their spiritual or narrative substance. What aroused his passionate interest, what fixed his attention, was the name, the price, the format, the title-page. Though in the last analysis unproductive and uncreative, this specifically antiquarian memory of Jacob Mendel, since it was not a printed book-catalogue but was stamped upon the grey matter of a mammalian brain, was, in its unique perfection, no less remarkable a phenomenon than Napoleon's gift for physiognomy, Mezzofanti's talent for languages, Lasker's skill at chess-openings, Busoni's musical genius. Given a public position as a teacher, this man with so marvellous a brain might have taught thousands and hundreds of thousands of students, have trained others to become men of great learning and of incalculable value to those communal treasure-houses we call libraries. But to him, a man of no account, a Galician Jew, a book-pedlar whose only training had been received in a Talmudic school, this upper world of culture was a fenced precinct he could never enter; and his amazing faculties could only find application at the marble-topped table in the inner room of the Café Gluck. When, some day, there arises a great psychologist who shall classify the types of that magical power we term memory as effectively as Buffon classified the genera and species of animals, a man competent to give a detailed description of all varieties, he will have to find a pigeonhole for Jacob Mendel, forgotten master of the lore of book-prices and book-titles, the ambulatory catalogue alike of incunabula and the modern commonplace.

In the book-trade and among ordinary persons, Jacob Mendel was regarded as nothing more than a second-hand book dealer in a small way of business. Sunday after Sunday, his stereotyped advertisement appeared in the "Neue Freie Presse" and the "Neues Wiener Tagblatt." It ran as follows: "Best prices paid for old books, Mendel, Obere Alserstrasse." A telephone number followed, really that of the Café Gluck. He rummaged every available corner for his wares, and once a week, with the aid of a bearded porter, conveyed fresh booty to his headquarters and got rid of old stock—for he had no proper bookshop. Thus he remained a petty trader, and his business was not lucrative. Students sold him their textbooks, which year by year passed through his hands from one "generation" to another; and for a small percentage on the price he would procure any additional book that was wanted. He charged little or nothing for advice. Money seemed to have no standing in his world. No one had ever seen him better dressed than in the threadbare black coat. For breakfast and supper he had a glass of milk and a couple of rolls, while at midday a modest meal was brought him from a neighbouring restaurant. He did not smoke; he did not play cards; one might almost say he did not live, were it not that his eyes were alive behind his spectacles, and unceasingly fed his enigmatic brain with words, titles, names. The brain, like a fertile pasture, greedily sucked in this abundant irrigation. Human beings did not interest him, and of all human passions perhaps one only moved him, the most universal—vanity.

When someone, wearied by a futile hunt in countless other places, applied to him for information, and was instantly put on the track, his self-gratification was overwhelming; and it was unquestionably a delight to him that in Vienna and elsewhere there existed a few dozen persons who respected him for his knowledge and valued him for the services he could render. In every one of these monstrous aggregates we call towns, there are here and there facets which reflect one and the same universe in miniature—unseen by most, but highly prized by connoisseurs, by brethren of the same craft, by devotees of the same passion. The fans of the book-market knew Jacob Mendel. Just as anyone encountering a difficulty in deciphering a score would apply to Eusebius Mandyczewski of the Musical Society, who would be found wearing a grey skull-cap and seated among multifarious musical MSS., ready, with a friendly smile, to solve the most obstinate crux; and just as, today, anyone in search of information about the Viennese theatrical and cultural life of earlier times will unhesitatingly look up the polyhistor Father Glossy; so, with equal confidence did the bibliophiles of Vienna, when they had a particularly hard nut to crack, make a pilgrimage to the Café Gluck and lay their difficulty before Jacob Mendel.

To me, young and eager for new experiences, it became enthralling to watch such a consultation. Whereas ordinarily, when a would-be seller brought him some ordinary book, he would contemptuously clap the cover to and mutter, "Two crowns"; if shown a rare or unique volume, he would sit up and take notice, lay the treasure upon a clean sheet of paper; and, on one such occasion, he was obviously ashamed of his dirty, ink-stained fingers and mourning finger-nails. Tenderly, cautiously, respectfully, he would turn the pages of the treasure. One would have been as loath to disturb him at such a moment as to break in upon the devotions of a man at prayer; and in very truth there was a flavour of solemn ritual and religious observance about the way in which contemplation, palpation, smelling, and weighing in the hand followed one another in orderly succession. His rounded back waggled while he was thus engaged, he muttered to himself, exclaimed "Ah" now and again to express wonder or admiration, or "Oh, dear" when a page was missing or another had been mutilated by the larva of a book-beetle. His weighing of the tome in his hand was as circumspect as if books were sold by the ounce, and his snuffling at it as sentimental as a girl's smelling of a rose. Of course it would have been the height of bad form for the owner to show impatience during this ritual of examination.

When it was over, he willingly, nay enthusiastically, tendered all the information at his disposal, not forgetting relevant anecdotes, and dramatized accounts of the prices which other specimens of the same work had fetched at auctions or in sales by private treaty. He looked brighter, younger, more lively at such times, and only one thing could put him seriously out of humour. This was when a novice offered him money for his expert opinion. Then he would draw back with an affronted air, looking for all the world like the skilled custodian of a museum gallery to whom an American traveller has offered a tip—for to Jacob Mendel contact with a rare book was something sacred, as is contact with a woman to a young man who has not had the bloom rubbed off. Such moments were his platonic love-nights. Books exerted a spell on him, never money. Vainly, therefore, did great collectors (among them one of the notables of Princeton University) try to recruit Mendel as librarian or book-buyer. The offer was declined with thanks. He could not forsake his familiar headquarters at the Café Gluck. Thirty-three years before, an awkward youngster with black down sprouting on his chin and black ringlets hanging over his temples, he had come from Galicia to Vienna, intending to adopt the calling of rabbi; but ere long he forsook the worship of the harsh and jealous Jehovah to devote himself to the more lively and polytheistic cult of books. Then he happened upon the Café Gluck, by degrees making it his workshop, headquarters, post-office—his world. Just as an astronomer, alone in an observatory, watches night after night through a telescope the myriads of stars, their mysterious movements, their changeful medley, their extinction and their flaming-up anew, so did Jacob Mendel, seated at his table in the Café Gluck, look through his spectacles into the universe of books, a universe that lies above the world of our everyday life, and, like the stellar universe, is full of changing cycles.

It need hardly be said that he was highly esteemed in the Café Gluck, whose fame seemed to us to depend far more upon his unofficial pro-fessorship than upon the godfathership of the famous musician, Christoph Willibald Gluck, composer of *Alcestis* and *Iphigenia*. He belonged to the outfit quite as much as did the old cherrywood counter, the two billiard-tables with their cloth stitched in many places, and the copper coffee-urn. His table was guarded as a sanctuary. His numerous clients and customers were expected to take a drink "for the good of the house," so that most of the profit of his far-flung knowledge flowed into the big leathern pouch slung round the waist of Deubler, the waiter. In return for being a centre of attraction, Mendel enjoyed many privileges. The telephone was at his service for nothing. He could have his letters directed to the café, and his parcels were taken in there. The excellent old woman who looked after the toilet brushed his coat, sewed on buttons, and carried a small bundle of underlinen every week to the wash. He was the only guest who could have a meal sent in from the restaurant; and every morning Herr Standhartner, the proprietor of the café, made a point of coming to his table and saying "Good morning!"—though Jacob Mendel, immersed in his books, seldom noticed the greeting. Punctually at half-past seven he arrived, and did not leave till the lights were extinguished. He never spoke to the other guests, never read a newspaper, noticed no changes; and once, when Herr Stand-hartner civilly asked him whether he did not find the electric light more agreeable to read by than the malodorous and uncertain kerosene lamps they had replaced, he stared in astonishment at the new incandescents. Although the installation had necessitated several days' hammering and bustle, the introduction of the glow-lamps had escaped his notice. Only through the two round apertures of the spectacles, only through these two shining and sucking lenses, did the milliards of black infusorians which were the letters filter into his brain. Whatever else happened in his vicinity was disregarded as unmeaning noise. He had spent more than thirty years of his waking life at this table, reading, comparing, calculating, in a continuous waking dream, interrupted only by intervals of sleep.

A sense of horror overcame me when, looking into the inner room behind the bar of the Café Gluck, I saw that the marble top of the table where Jacob Mendel used to deliver his oracles was now as bare as a tombstone. Grown older since those days, I understood how much disappears when such a man drops out of his place in the world, were it only because, amid the daily increase in hopeless monotony, the unique 'grows continually more precious. Besides, in my callow youth a profound intuition had made me exceedingly fond of Buchmendel. It was through the observation of him that I had first become aware of the enigmatic fact that supreme achievement and outstanding capacity are only rendered possible by mental concentration, by a sublime monomania that verges on lunacy. Through the living example of this obscure genius of a second-hand book dealer, far more than through the flashes of insight in the works of our poets and other imaginative writers, had been made plain to me the persistent possibility of a pure life of the spirit, of complete absorption in an idea, an ecstasy as absolute as that of an Indian yogi or a medieval monk; and I had learned that this was possible in an electric-lighted café and adjoining a telephone box. Yet I had forgotten him, during the war years, and through a kindred immersion in my own work. The sight of the empty table made me ashamed of myself, and at the same time curious about the man who used to sit there.

What had become of him? I called the waiter and inquired.

"No, Sir," he answered, "I'm sorry, but I never heard of Herr Mendel. There is no one of that name among the frequenters of the Café Gluck. Perhaps the head-waiter will know."

"Herr Mendel?" said the head-waiter dubiously, after a moment's reflection. "No, Sir, never heard of him. Unless you mean Herr Mandl, who has a hardware store in the Florianigasse?"

I had a bitter taste in the mouth, the taste of an irrecoverable past. What is the use of living, when the wind obliterates our footsteps in the sand directly we have gone by? Thirty years, perhaps forty, a man had breathed, read, thought, and spoken within this narrow room; three or four years had elapsed, and there had arisen a new king over Egypt, which knew not Joseph. No one in the Café Gluck had ever heard of Jacob Mendel, of Buchmendel. Somewhat pettishly I asked the head-waiter whether I could have a word with Herr Standhartner, or with one of the old staff.

"Herr Standhartner, who used to own the place? He sold it years ago, and has died since. . . . The former head-waiter? He saved up enough to retire, and lives upon a little property at Krems. No, Sir, all of the old lot are scattered. All except one, indeed, Frau Sporschil, who looks after the toilet. She's been here for ages, worked under the late owner, I know. But she's not likely to remember your Herr Mendel. Such as she hardly know one guest from another."

I dissented in thought.

"One does not forget a Jacob Mendel so easily!"

What I said was:

"Still, I should like to have a word with Frau Sporschil, if she has a moment to spare."

The "Toilettenfrau" (known in the Viennese vernacular as the "Schocoladefrau") soon emerged from the basement, white-haired, run to seed, heavy-footed, wiping her chapped hands upon a towel as she came. She had been called away from her task of cleaning up, and was obviously uneasy at being summoned into the strong light of the guest-rooms—for common folk in Vienna, where an authoritative tradition has lingered on after the revolution, always think it must be a police matter when their "superiors" want to question them. She eyed me suspiciously, though humbly. But as soon as I asked her about Jacob Mendel, she braced up, and at the same time her eyes filled with tears.

"Poor Herr Mendel . . . so there's still someone who bears him in mind?"

Old people are commonly much moved by anything which recalls the days of their youth and revives the memory of past companionships. I asked if he was still alive.

"Good Lord, no. Poor Herr Mendel must have died five or six years ago. Indeed, I think it's fully seven since he passed away. Dear, good man that he was; and how long I knew him, more than twenty-five years; he was already sitting every day at his table when I began to work here. It was a shame, it was, the way they let him die."

Growing more and more excited, she asked if I was a relative. No one had ever inquired about him before. Didn't I know what had happened to him?

"No," I replied, "and I want you to be good enough to tell me all about it."

She looked at me timidly, and continued to wipe her damp hands. It was plain to me that she found it embarrassing, with her dirty apron and her tousled white hair, to be standing in the full glare of the café. She kept looking round anxiously, to see if one of the waiters might be listening.

"Let's go into the card-room," I said, "Mendel's old room. You shall tell me your story there."

She nodded appreciatively, thankful that I understood, and led the way to the inner room, a little shambling in her gait. As I followed, I noticed that the waiters and the guests were staring at us as a strangely assorted pair. We sat down opposite one another at the marble-topped table, and there she told me the story of Jacob Mendel's ruin and death. I will give the tale as nearly as may be in her own words, supplemented here and there by what I learned afterwards from other sources.

"Down to the outbreak of war, and after the war had begun, he continued to come here every morning at half-past seven, to sit at this table and study all day just as before. We had the feeling that the fact of a war going on had never entered his mind. Certainly he didn't read the newspapers, and didn't talk to anyone except about books. He paid no attention when (in the early days of the war, before the authorities put a stop to such things) the newspaper-venders ran through the streets shouting, 'Great Battle on the Eastern Front' (or wherever it might be), 'Horrible Slaughter,' and so on; when people gathered in knots to talk things over, he kept himself to himself; he did not know that Fritz, the billiard-marker, who fell in one of the first battles, had vanished from this place; he did not know that Herr Standhartner's son had been taken prisoner by the Russians at Przemysl; never said a word when the bread grew more and more uneatable and when he was given bean-coffee to drink at breakfast and supper instead of hot milk. Once only did he express surprise at the changes, wondering why so few students came to the café. There was nothing in the world that mattered to him except his books.

"Then disaster befell him. At eleven one morning, two policemen came, one in uniform, and the other a plainclothes man. The latter showed the red rosette under the lapel of his coat and asked whether there was a man named Jacob Mendel in the house. They went straight to Herr Mendel's table. The poor man, in his innocence, supposed they had books to sell, or wanted some information; but they told him he was under arrest, and took him away at once. It was a scandal for the café. All the guests flocked round Herr Mendel, as he stood between the two police officers, his spectacles pushed up under his hair, staring from each to the other bewildered. Some ventured a protest, saying there must be a mistake—that Herr Mendel was a man who wouldn't hurt a fly; but the detective was furious, and told them to mind their own business. They took him away, and none of us at the Café Gluck saw him again for two years. I never found out what they had against him, but I would take my dying oath that they must have made a mistake. Herr Mendel could never have done anything wrong. It was a crime to treat an innocent man so harshly."

The excellent Frau Sporschil was right. Our friend Jacob Mendel had done nothing wrong. He had merely (as I subsequently learned) done something incredibly stupid, only explicable to those who knew the man's peculiarities. The military censorship board, whose function it was to supervise correspondence passing into and out of neutral hands, one day got its clutches upon a postcard written and signed by a certain Jacob Mendel, properly stamped for transmission abroad. This postcard was addressed to Monsieur Jean Labourdaire, Libraire, Quai de Grenelle, Paris—to an enemy country, therefore. The writer complained that the last eight issues of the monthly "Bulletin bibliographique de la France" had failed to reach him, although his annual subscription had been duly paid in advance. The jack-in-office who read this missive (a high-school teacher with a bent for the study of the Romance languages, called up for "war-service" and sent to employ his talents at the censorship board instead of wasting them in the trenches) was astonished by its tenor. "Must be a joke," he thought. He had to examine some two thousand letters and postcards every week, always on the alert to detect anything that might savour of espionage, but never yet had he chanced upon anything so absurd as that an Austrian subject should unconcernedly drop into one of the imperial and royal letter-boxes a postcard addressed to someone in an enemy land, regardless of the trifling detail that since August 1914 the Central Powers had been cut off from Russia on one side and from France on the other by barbed-wire entanglements and a network of ditches in which men armed with rifles and bayonets, machine-guns and artillery, were doing their utmost to exterminate one another like rats. Our school-master enrolled in the Landsturm did not treat this first postcard seriously, but pigeon-holed it as a curiosity not worth talking about to his chief. But a few weeks later there turned up another card, again from Jacob Mendel, this time to John Albridge, Bookseller, Golden Square, London, asking whether the addressee could send the last few numbers of the "Antiquarian" to an address in Vienna which was clearly stated on the card.

The censor in the blue uniform began to feel uneasy. Was his "class" trying to trick the schoolmaster? Were the cards written in cipher? Possible, anyhow; so the subordinate went over to the major's desk, clicked his heels together, saluted, and laid the suspicious documents before "properly constituted authority." A strange business, certainly. The police were instructed by telephone to see if there actually was a Jacob Mendel at the specified address, and, if so, to bring the fellow along. Within the hour, Mendel had been arrested, and (still stupefied by the shock) brought before the major, who showed him the post-cards, and asked him with drill-sergeant roughness whether he acknowledged their authorship. Angered at being spoken to so sharply, and still more annoyed because his perusal of an important catalogue had been interrupted, Mendel answered tartly:

"Of course I wrote the cards. That's my handwriting and signature. Surely one has a right to claim the delivery of a periodical to which one has subscribed?"

The major swung half-round in his swivel-chair and exchanged a mean-ing glance with the lieutenant seated at the adjoining desk.

"The man must be a double-distilled idiot" was what they mutely conveyed to one another.

Then the chief took counsel within himself whether he should discharge the offender with a caution, or whether he should treat the case more seriously. In all offices, when such doubts arise, the usual practice is, not to spin a coin, but to send in a report. Thus Pilate washes his hands of responsibility. Even if the report does no good, it can do no harm, and is merely one useless manuscript or typescript added to a million others.

In this instance, however, the decision to send in a report did much harm, alas, to an inoffensive man of genius, for it involved asking a series of questions, and the third of them brought suspicious circumstances to light.

"Your full name?"

"Jacob Mendel."

"Occupation?"

"Book-pedlar" (for, as already explained, Mendel had no shop, but only a pedlar's license).

"Place of birth?"

Now came the disaster. Mendel's birthplace was not far from Petrikau. The major raised his eyebrows. Petrikau, or Piotrkov, was across the frontier, in Russian Poland.

"You were born a Russian subject. When did you acquire Austrian nationality? Show me your papers."

Mendel gazed at the officer uncomprehendingly through his spectacles.

"Papers? Identification papers? I have nothing but my hawker's license."

"What's your nationality, then? Was your father Austrian or Russian?"

Undismayed, Mendel answered:

"A Russian, of course."

"What about yourself?"

"Wishing to evade Russian military service, I slipped across the frontier thirty-three years ago, and ever since I have lived in Vienna."

The matter seemed to the major to be growing worse and worse.

"But didn't you take steps to become an Austrian subject?"

"Why should I?" countered Mendel. "I never troubled my head about such things."

"Then you are still a Russian subject?"

Mendel, who was bored by this endless questioning, answered simply:

"Yes, I suppose I am."

The startled and indignant major threw himself back in his chair with such violence that the wood cracked protestingly. So this was what it had come to! In Vienna, the Austrian capital, at the end of 1915, after Tarnow, when the war was in full blast, after the great offensive, a Russian could walk about unmolested, could write letters to France and England, while the police ignored his machinations. And then the fools who wrote in the newspapers wondered why Conrad von Hotzendorf had not advanced in seven-leagued boots to Warsaw, and the general staff was puzzled because every movement of the troops was immediately blabbed to the Russians.

The lieutenant had sprung to his feet and crossed the room to his chief's table. What had been an almost friendly conversation took a new turn, and degenerated into a trial.

"Why didn't you report as an enemy alien directly the war began?"

Mendel, still failing to realize the gravity of his position, answered in his singing Jewish jargon:

"Why should I report? I don't understand."

The major regarded this inquiry as a challenge, and asked threateningly: "Didn't you read the notices that were posted up everywhere?"

"No."

"Didn't you read the newspapers?"

"No."

The two officers stared at Jacob Mendel (now sweating with uneasiness) as if the moon had fallen from the sky into their office. Then the telephone buzzed, the typewriters clacked, orderlies ran hither and thither, and Mendel was sent under guard to the nearest barracks, where he was to await transfer to a concentration camp. When he was ordered to follow the two soldiers, he was frankly puzzled, but not seriously perturbed. What could the man with the gold-lace collar and the rough voice have against him? In the upper world of books, where Mendel lived and breathed and had his being, there was no warfare, there were no misunderstandings, only an ever-increasing knowledge of words and figures, of book-titles and authors' names. He walked good-humouredly enough downstairs between the soldiers, whose first charge was to take him to the police station. Not until, there, the books were taken out of his overcoat pockets, and the police impounded the portfolio containing a hundred important memoranda and customers' addresses, did he lose his temper, and begin to resist and strike blows. They had to tie his hands. In the struggle, his spectacles fell off, and these magical telescopes, without which he could not see into the wonderworld of books, were smashed into a thousand pieces. Two days later, insufficiently clad (for his only wrap was a light summer cloak), he was sent to the internment camp for Russian civilians at Komorn.

I have no information as to what Jacob Mendel suffered during these two years of internment, cut off from his beloved books, penniless, among roughly nurtured men, few of whom could read or write, in a huge human dunghill. This must be left to the imagination of those who can grasp the torments of a caged eagle. By degrees, however, our world, grown sober after its fit of drunkenness, has become aware that, of all the cruelties and wanton abuses of power during the war, the most needless and therefore the most inexcusable was this herding together behind barbed-wire fences of thousands upon thousands of persons who had outgrown the age of military service, who made homes for themselves in a foreign land, and who (believing in the good faith of their hosts) had refrained from exercising the sacred right of hospitality granted even by the Tunguses and Araucanians—the right to flee while time permits. This crime against civilization was committed with the same unthinking hardihood in France, Germany, and Britain, in every belligerent country of our crazy Europe.

Probably Jacob Mendel would, like thousands as innocent as he, have perished in this cattle-pen, have gone stark mad, have succumbed to dysentery, asthenia, softening of the brain, had it not been that, before the worst happened, a chance (typically Austrian) recalled him to the world in which a spiritual life became again possible. Several times after his disappearance, letters from distinguished customers were delivered for him at the Café Gluck. Count Schönberg, sometime lord-lieutenant of Styria, an enthusiastic collector of works on heraldry; Siegenfeld, the former dean of the theological faculty, who was writing a commentary on the works of St. Augustine; Edler von Pisek, an octogenarian admiral on the retired list, engaged in writing his memoirs—these and other persons of note, wanting information from Buchmendel, had repeatedly addressed communications to him at his familiar haunt, and some of these were duly forwarded to the concentration camp at Komorn. There they fell into the hands of the commanding officer, who happened to be a man of humane disposition, and was astonished to find what notables were among the correspondents of this dirty little Russian Jew, who, half-blind now that his spectacles were broken and he had no money to buy new ones, crouched in a corner like a mole, grey, eyeless, and dumb. A man who had such patrons must be a person of importance, whatever he looked like. The C.O. therefore read the letters to the short-sighted Mendel, and penned answers for him to sign—answers which were mainly requests that influence should be exercised on his behalf. The spell worked, for these correspondents had the solidarity of collectors. Joining forces and pulling strings they were able (giving guarantees for the "enemy alien's" good behaviour) to secure leave for Buchmendel's return to Vienna in 1917, after more than two years at Komorn—on the condition that he should report daily to the police. The proviso mattered little. He was a free man once more, free to take up his quarters in his old attic, free to handle books again, free (above all) to return to his table in the Café Gluck. I can describe the return from the underworld of the camp in the good Frau Sporschil's own words:

"One day—Jesus, Mary, Joseph; I could hardly believe my eyes—the door opened (you remember the way he had) little wider than a crack, and through this opening he sidled, poor Herr Mendel. He was wearing a tattered and much-darned military cloak, and his head was covered by what had perhaps once been a hat thrown away by the owner as past use. No collar. His face looked like a death's head, so haggard it was, and his hair was pitifully thin. But he came in as if nothing had happened, went straight to his table, and took off his cloak, not briskly as of old, for he panted with the exertion. Nor had he any books with him. He just sat there without a word, staring straight in front of him with hollow, expressionless eyes. Only by degrees, after we had brought him the big bundle of printed matter which had arrived for him from Germany, did he begin to read again. But he was never the same man."

No, he was never the same man, not now the miraculum mundi, the magical walking book-catalogue. All who saw him in those days told me the same pitiful story. Something had gone irrecoverably wrong; he was broken; the blood-red comet of the war had burst into the remote, calm atmosphere of his bookish world. His eyes, accustomed for decades to look at nothing but print, must have seen terrible sights in the wire-fenced human stockyard, for the eyes that had formerly been so alert and full of ironical gleams were now almost completely veiled by the inert lids, and looked sleepy and red-bordered behind the carefully repaired spectacle-frames. Worse still, a cog must have broken somewhere in the marvellous machinery of his memory, so that the working of the whole was impaired; for so delicate is the structure of the brain (a sort of switchboard made of the most fragile substances, and as easily jarred as are all instruments of precision) that a blocked arteriole, a congested bundle of nerve-fibres, a fatigued group of cells, even a displaced molecule, may put the apparatus out of gear and make harmonious working impossible. In Mendel's memory, the keyboard of knowledge, the keys were stiff, or—to use psychological terminology—the associations were impaired. When, now and again, some-one came to ask for information, Jacob stared blankly at the inquirer, failing to understand the question, and even forgetting it before he had found the answer. Mendel was no longer Buchmendel, just as the world was no longer the world. He could not now become wholly absorbed in his reading, did not rock as of old when he read, but sat bolt upright, his glasses turned mechanically towards the printed page, but perhaps not reading at all, and only sunk in a reverie. Often, said Frau Sporschil, his head would drop on to his book and he would fall asleep in the daytime, or he would gaze hour after hour at the stinking acetylene lamp which (in the days of the coal famine) had replaced the electric lighting. No, Mendel was no longer Buchmendel, no longer the eighth wonder of the world, but a weary, worn-out, though still breathing, useless bundle of beard and ragged garments, which sat, as futile as a potato-bogle, where of old the Pythian oracle had sat; no longer the glory of the Café Gluck, but a shameful scarecrow, evil-smelling, a parasite.

That was the impression he produced upon the new proprietor, Florian Gurtner from Retz, who (a successful profiteer in flour and butter) had cajoled Standhartner into selling him the Café Gluck for eighty thousand rapidly depreciating paper crowns. He took everything into his hard peasant grip, hastily arranged to have the old place redecorated, bought fine-looking satin-covered seats, installed a marble porch, and was in nego-tiation with his next-door neighbour to buy a place where he could extend the café into a dancing-hall. Naturally while he was making these embel-lishments, he was not best pleased by the parasitic encumbrance of Jacob Mendel, a filthy old Galician Jew, who had been in trouble with the au-thorities during the war, was still to be regarded as an "enemy alien," and, while occupying a table from morning till night, consumed no more than two cups of coffee and four or five rolls. Standhartner, indeed, had put in a word for this guest of long standing, had explained that Mendel was a person of note, and, in the stock-taking, had handed him over as having a perma-nent lien upon the establishment, but as an asset rather than a liability. Florian Gurtner, however, had brought into the café, not only new furni-ture, and an up-to-date cash-register, but also the profit-making and hard temper of the post-war era, and awaited the first pretext for ejecting from his smart coffee-house the last troublesome vestige of suburban shabbiness.

A good excuse was not slow to present itself. Jacob Mendel was impoverished to the last degree. Such banknotes as had been left to him had crumbled away to nothing during the inflation period; his regular clientele had been killed, ruined, or dispersed. When he tried to resume his early trade of book-pedlar, calling from door to door to buy and to sell, he found that he lacked strength to carry books up and down stairs. A hundred little signs showed him to be a pauper. Seldom, now, did he have a midday meal sent in from the restaurant, and he began to run up a score at the Café Gluck for his modest breakfast and supper. Once his payments were as much as three weeks overdue. Were it only for this reason, the head-waiter wanted Gurtner to "give Mendel the sack." But Frau Sporschil intervened, and stood surety for the debtor. What was due could be stopped out of her wages!

This staved off disaster for a while, but worse was to come. For some time the head-waiter had noticed that rolls were disappearing faster than the tally would account for. Naturally suspicion fell upon Mendel, who was known to be six months in debt to the tottering old porter whose services he still needed. The head-waiter, hidden behind the stove, was able, two days later, to catch Mendel red-handed. The unwelcome guest had stolen from his seat in the card-room, crept behind the counter in the front room, taken two rolls from the bread-basket, returned to the card-room, and hungrily devoured them. When settling-up at the end of the day, he said he had only had coffee; no rolls. The source of wastage had been traced, and the waiter reported his discovery to the proprietor. Herr Gurtner, delighted to have so good an excuse for getting rid of Mendel, made a scene, openly accused him of theft, and declared that nothing but the goodness of his own heart prevented his sending for the police.

"But after this," said Florian, "you'll kindly take yourself off for good and all. We don't want to see your face again at the Café Gluck."

Jacob Mendel trembled, but made no reply. Abandoning his poor belongings, he departed without a word.

"It was ghastly," said Frau Sporschil. "Never shall I forget the sight. He stood up, his spectacles pushed on to his forehead, and his face white as a sheet. He did not even stop to put on his cloak, although it was January, and very cold. You'll remember that severe winter, just after the war. In his fright, he left the book he was reading open upon the table. I did not notice it at first, and then, when I wanted to pick it up and take it after him, he had already stumbled out through the doorway. I was afraid to follow him into the street, for Herr Gurtner was standing at the door and shouting at him, so that a crowd had gathered. Yet I felt ashamed to the depths of my soul. Such a thing would never have happened under the old master. Herr Standhartner would not have driven Herr Mendel away for pinching one or two rolls when he was hungry, but would have let him have as many as he wanted for nothing, to the end of his days.

Since the war, people seem to have grown heartless. Drive away a man who had been a guest daily for so many, many years. Shameful! I should not like to have to answer before God for such cruelty!"

The good woman had grown excited, and, with the passionate garrulousness of old age, she kept on repeating how shameful it was, and that nothing of the sort would have happened if Herr Standhartner had not sold the business. In the end I tried to stop the flow by asking her what had happened to Mendel, and whether she had ever seen him again. These questions excited her yet more.

"Day after day, when I passed his table, it gave me the creeps, as you will easily understand. Each time I thought to myself: 'Where can he have got to, poor Herr Mendel?' Had I known where he lived, I would have called and taken him something nice and hot to eat—for where could he get the money to cook food and warm his room? As far as I knew, he had no kinsfolk in the wide world. When, after a long time, I had heard nothing about him, I began to believe that it must be all up with him, and that I should never see him again. I had made up my mind to have a mass said for the peace of his soul, knowing him to be a good man, after twenty-five years' acquaintance.

"At length one day in February, at half-past seven in the morning, when I was cleaning the windows, the door opened, and in came Herr Mendel. Generally, as you know, he sidled in, looking confused, and not 'quite all there'; this time, somehow, it was different. I noticed at once the strange look in his eyes; they were sparkling, and he rolled them this way and that, as if to see everything at once; as for his appearance, he seemed nothing but beard and skin and bone. Instantly it crossed my mind: 'He's forgotten all that happened last time he was here; it's his way to go about like a sleepwalker noticing nothing; he doesn't remember about the rolls, and how shamefully Herr Gurtner ordered him out of the place, half in mind to set the police on him.' Thank goodness, Herr Gurtner hadn't come yet, and the head-waiter was drinking coffee. I ran up to Herr Mendel, meaning to tell him he'd better make himself scarce, for otherwise that ruffian" [she looked round timidly to see if we were overheard, and hastily amended her phrase], "Herr Gurtner, I mean, would only have him thrown into the street once more. 'Herr Mendel,' I began. He started, and looked at me. In that very moment (it was dreadful), he must have remembered the whole thing, for he almost collapsed, and began to tremble, not his fingers only, but to shiver and shake from head to foot. Hastily he stepped back into the street, and fell in a heap on the pavement as soon as he was outside the door. We telephoned for the ambulance, and they carried him off to a hospital, the nurse who came saying he had high fever directly she touched him. He died that evening. 'Double pneumonia,' the doctor said, and that he never recovered consciousness—could not have been fully conscious when he came to the Café Gluck. As I said, he had entered like a man walking in his sleep. The table where he had sat day after day for thirty-six years drew him back to it like a home."

Frau Sporschil and I went on talking about him for a long time, the two last persons to remember this strange creature, Buchmendel: I to whom in youth the book-pedlar from Galicia had given the first revelation of a life wholly devoted to the things of the spirit; she, the poor old woman who was caretaker of a café-toilet, who had never read a book in her life, and whose only tie with this strangely matched comrade in her subordinate, poverty-stricken world had been that for twenty-five years she had brushed his overcoat and had sewn on buttons for him. We, too, might have been considered strangely assorted, but Frau Sporschil and I got on very well together, linked, as we sat at the forsaken marble-topped table, by our common memories of the shade our talk had conjured up— for joint memories, and above all loving memories, always establish a tie. Suddenly, while in the full stream of talk, she exclaimed:

"Lord Jesus, how forgetful I am. I still have the book he left on the table the evening Herr Gurtner gave him the key of the street. I didn't know where to take it. Afterwards, when no one appeared to claim it, I ventured to keep it as a souvenir. You don't think it wrong of me, Sir?"

She went to a locker where she stored some of the requisites for her job, and produced the volume for my inspection. I found it hard to repress a smile, for I was face to face with one of life's little ironies. It was the second volume of Hayn's *Bibliotheca Germanorum erotica et curiosa*, a compendium of gallant literature known to every book-collector. "Habent sua fata libelli!" This scabrous publication, as legacy of the vanished magician, had fallen into toilworn hands which had perhaps never held any other printed work than a prayer-book. Maybe I was not wholly successful in controlling my mirth, for the expression of my face seemed to perplex the worthy soul, and once more she said:

"You don't think it wrong of me to keep it, Sir?"

I shook her cordially by the hand.

"Keep it, and welcome," I said. "I am absolutely sure that our old friend Mendel would be only too delighted to know that someone among the many thousand he has provided with books, cherishes his memory."

Then I took my departure, feeling a trifle ashamed when I compared myself with this excellent old woman, who, so simply and so humanely, had fostered the memory of the dead scholar. For she, uncultured though she was, had at least preserved a book as a memento; whereas I, a man of education and a writer, had completely forgotten Buchmendel for years— I, who at least should have known that one only makes books in order to keep in touch with one's fellows after one has ceased to breathe, and thus to defend oneself against the inexorable fate of all that lives—transitoriness and oblivion.

I Capture Vladivostok

BY

FRAZIER HUNT

IT ISN'T every war correspondent who can capture a city. I don't mean to say that I got one all by myself, but at least I was the first man in. And different from the immortal Kipling's tale of how "Privit Mulvaney tuk the town of Lungtungpen," I had my pants on when I took mine.

I've never written the story before and I doubt if I would do it now if Frank Martinek, one-time U. S. Naval Intelligence Officer in Vladivostok, had not told what youthful critics, not quite dry behind the ears, like to call "the dénouement" of the yarn in introducing me to a Chicago audience.

I had landed in the colorful and war-weary Siberian port from a miserable little Japanese tub, that had bobbled across the sea of Japan like a champagne cork. It was the last day of 1919, and Vladivostok was being held by a bob-tail White Guard army, supported by Japanese troops. Ten thousand homesick, disgusted American soldiers were scattered for a thousand miles up and down the single line of steel that pointed toward Moscow. Admiral Kolchak, dictator and White savior, once head of the British- and Japanese-supported anti-Bolshevik hopes, had just had a rather frightful accident: his own troops had mutinied, held a drum-head court-martial, and quietly led him out to a convenient wall and filled him full of lead (although I believe it is actually steel bullets they use in such emergencies).

The whole White Guard movement in Siberia was crumbling rapidly, and old Czarist officials, Japanese generals, Cossack *atamans,* and thick-skinned British advisers did not know what to do about it. The American commander, the incorruptible, wise Major General Graves, however, did know exactly what to do; simply keep his troops out of mixing in the internal affairs of Russia, and see to it that the 50,000 Japanese soldiers there did not move the hills and the rivers. It was a cinch they were going to try to move everything else.

I was primed for this situation like an Indiana pump in frosty weather. In the previous winter I had spent two months with the North Russian Expedition in the desolate country around Archangel. I had ridden almost a thousand miles by sled up frozen rivers and through forests of glistening Christmas trees, visiting American outposts and snow-bound fronts.

When I left the unsavory mess, I was bitter and resentful. I could not

From: *We Cover the World,* Ed. by Eugene Lyons. By permission of Harcourt, Brace & Co.

stand the sight of American doughboys being commanded to do British officers' dirty work. A five-thousand-word exposé cable that I had sneaked out and filed at the cable-head in Narvik, Norway, had been read in the United States Senate, and, I think, had had some little to do with the promise of the White House to remove the American troops as soon as the ice went out.

Following this pleasant adventure in the shadow of the Arctic Circle, I had worked my way through the Allied blockade into the heart of the Soviets. For two months I had enjoyed the exclusive privilege of working the greatest news gold mine in history. . . . And now I was at the other end of the world in a second intervention mess, and ready for trouble.

It took less than a day for me to see that this American Expeditionary Force was run in quite a different manner than the North Russia fiasco. A Lieutenant General of the Japanese Army had unanimously elected himself Commander-in-Chief of the Allied Forces, and, before General Graves had arrived, had sent the two American regiments, hustled up from Manila, westward to pick up a fight with the anti-White peasant outfits called Partizans. But the very day General Graves disembarked, he called in his troops, and figuratively set the high-ranking little gentleman from Nippon squarely on his west end. So my anticipated story of how American soldiers were a second time doing filthy jobs for someone else evaporated into the cold, dry air. And I needed a few good pieces to keep the Chicago *Tribune* contented.

Now I have always operated on the general theory that the best place to get a story is directly from the people who are mixed up in it. So it was that after I had been a few days in Vladivostok I decided to get out with the fighting Red Siberian moujiks, and see for myself how they were feeling about their revolution, their war with the Whites, and their near-war with the Japanese. For my interpreter I found a gentle, old-fashioned Social-Democrat, named Kolko, who years before had escaped from a Siberian prison, then denned up in New York until the first revolution had broken, and was now a sort of anti-White spy around Vladivostok.

We had a great time for ten days living with the Partizans. As I look back over a long series of "great times," I'm inclined to say this is tops on my purple list. We rode, slept, drank vodka, and sang with these young peasant soldiers—and I made speeches to bearded old grandpappies on how friendly America really was, and how I wished them luck with their Japanese problem.

I'd do this volunteer lecturing in school houses, or crowded peasant homes, or anywhere they'd ask me. At first most of them would be suspicious of me, but when they understood that I'd been in Moscow, and that I was really on their side, they were like eager children. They'd ask all sorts of questions about America, and how people lived and ran their affairs in a free country. Most of the time they'd keep the soldiers from coming in, and there would be only Kolko, the interpreter, and myself and the grizzled old fellows in their sheepskin coats and felt boots.

I was surprised, too, at the depth of the feeling of the youthful Partizan soldiers. They knew what they were fighting for; they were against the return of the ways of the Czar, and against the interference of the Japanese. They still felt that they wanted some form of assembly and democratic constitution, but the futile efforts of Kerensky, and the coming of Kolchak and the intervention, had shaken their faith in half-way measures.

They were thrilled by the magic of the word "soviet." They thought that possibly that was what they needed, too. And somehow or other they knew that Lenin was their true leader. . . . When they heard that I had met Lenin and had talked with him for a few minutes, they barraged me with a hundred questions. The revolution was vague and shadowy in their minds, but at least it meant land and freedom for them.

Probably it is a bit far-fetched, but time and again I could not help but think how similar this must have been to the mood and dreams of Putnam's men and the Green Mountain boys—when the name of George Washington thrilled the hearts of hungry, beaten soldiers with the same imagery and the same fervor that Lenin's name was doing now, 140 years later, and ten thousand miles to the westward. I'd like to have been a correspondent in those days, too.

Then one day, far back in the snow-covered hills, I joined up with a small Partizan detachment that had five Japanese soldier prisoners, who were eating them out of house and home. They had captured the lads from a "Makaka" garrison some twenty miles away. Incidentally, to call a Japanese soldier a "Makaka" was like calling him a so-and-so and not smiling when you did it. The Japs had been doing a little village-burning, and bayonet practice among the peasant villages, and all the emotional tinder for a nice little war was laid out ready to be lit.

The young Red commander couldn't figure out anything to do with his five prisoners except humanely to shoot them. I explained through my interpreter that it would be a fine lesson in hospitality if he'd turn these boys over to me and let me put them in Lieutenant General Oi's lap, with the word that his troops didn't have to shoot every Partizan soldier they got their hands on. Finally, we traded the lot for my watch.

It was all good, clean fun, and in due time I got back to Vladivostok with my Japanese quintuplets. The able little Japanese commander rubbed his bald pate while I gave him a lengthy discourse on the beauty of letting his soldiers have their target practice on something else besides captured Siberians

Then I heard that down Nikolsk-way real fighting was about to start between the Japanese-supported Whites and the Red Partizans. Kolko and I took the twice-a-week train the hundred *versts* or so toward this latest front.

We missed the show by four hours—but it wasn't much of a war to brag about at that. The Whites had quickly surrendered, and while there was some question as to what to do with the old Czarist officers, the White troopers themselves had gladly melted into the Partizan forces.

And now they were moving to attack and capture the key city of Vladivostok, still in the hands of the Whites. Two troop trains were being made up directly in front of the station. They would be pulling out very soon.

We hurried back to the Red commander. "Tell him I must go in on that first train," I instructed Kolko.

But the commander shook his head. "There'll be some heavy fighting before we get there," he answered. "The Whites have plenty of artillery and they'll try to stop us."

But I insisted that I'd like to go along; that I had to go. Then it was that the commander got his brilliant idea. "You might ride in the armored car we've just captured," he suggested. "It'll be ahead of the engine on the first train, but it ought to be safe enough in there."

I pumped his hand. I patted his shoulder. It was too good to be true: a war in an armored car. Send me there right now!

He called a smiling kid soldier and rolled out a few yards of orders; then we followed the boy down the track to a home-made armored car, with steel plates bolted to the sides. In the armor were cut a half-dozen oblong slits. I noticed the muzzles of machine guns sticking out from two or three of these loopholes.

Behind the armored car an ancient, wood-burning engine was champing at the bit—or whatever it is engines do. Ahead of the armored car there was nothing but snow, and two steel rails gleaming in the late afternoon sunlight—and way off down the track other boys were getting ready to blow this pleasant little armored car to kingdom come. It seemed a very silly idea, but it was a bit romantic at that.

Our guide ducked under the car and disappeared through a trap-door in the floor. We followed, and pulled ourselves into the car. Two tin lanterns, with candles stuck in them, hung from the ceiling. In the flickering light I could make out six or seven men. A young lad, certainly not over nineteen years old, stepped up and our guide reeled off his instructions. The car commander turned to me, welcomed me with a handshake and a broad smile. Then one by one I shook hands with the two machine-gun crews. Someone pushed up an ammunition box and I took off my old fur-lined trench coat, folded it on top of the box, and sat down. Next I broke out a package of cigarettes and passed them around, leaving the remainder of the package on a second ammunition box. I could have had the car after that.

We settled back in the stifling heat. A pot-bellied stove in the center of the car was roaring. It was 20 degrees below zero outside, but we were baking here inside our steel oven.

The young commander said something, then slipped down through the trap-door. Silence settled over the car. A giant tow-headed boy, astride the seat of a Maxim-Vickers, started humming a Slav song in the inevitable minor chords. Soon we were all dreaming of our worlds outside this hot armored car. . . . Time drifted by. Then the young chief pushed his head up through the door, popped in, and closed the steel trap behind him. His voice was pitched high with excitement.

"We're starting, comrades!" he announced dramatically. "Let every man do his duty! If anyone falters, he knows what to expect!"

Almost immediately we heard the muffled tones of an engine bell and the echoes of men's voices. Then came a violent bump that all but sent us sprawling from our cartridge-box seats. At last we were actually rolling. One of the wheels was a bit flat and it soured the song the other wheels were singing. I'm sure each of us was making up his own words. Mine were: "This is life! . . . This is life! . . . This is life!!"

The young commander pulled up an ammunition case close by mine. It was evident that he was of a little different breed than these square-faced Slav peasants, with their wide cheek bones and their heavy bodies. Finally Kolko and I got him to talking about himself: he was from Petrograd and his father had in the Czar's days been Captain of a Russian battleship. He was now a Red Admiral. This boy, Ivan Vasilievitch Trestiakoff, had been a naval cadet for a year, then when the revolution broke he had joined up with the Bolshies, and had been swept by one of the strange tides of war to this distant land of Far Eastern Siberia.

I asked him what he wanted to do. He answered straight off. "When we've finished the Whites and driven out the Japs, I would like to take my armored car to Petrograd and say: 'Here I am, Papa, with my brave machine gunners.' "

He took a turn around the little car. Then he came back and went on with his talk: "These Whites thought we were all stupid fools. Well, we were foolish like a fox. You know how they always had trouble getting their engines to run. Our people in the railroad shops saw to that. They're running all right now."

As a matter of fact this particular engine of ours that was pushing us into the night and its black uncertainty, wasn't running any too well. Or maybe it was something else that kept us starting and stopping every few miles. We'd get a series of good healthy bumps from both operations. Sometimes we'd pull up and for what seemed like hours we'd stand dead still. Then there would be that clanking engine bell, and the shouting, and we'd get a couple of bumps, then off we go again. We were not troubled with any fancy air-brakes on this make-shift troop train.

In one of these long stops our young chief slipped down through the manhole in the bottom of the car. He wore a short, curved sword that he'd taken from some dead Cossack, and it would catch on the sides of the narrow trap-door when he'd climb in or out. It was the only side arm he had, and I thought seriously of giving him my own 45-caliber Colt automatic army pistol which I carried deep in the right hand pocket of my breeches. But General Graves had presented it to me, and I couldn't get myself around to parting with it.

Our commander was gone for some minutes, and when he finally stuck his head up through the hole he had a broad grin on his face. In his right hand he held a stubby automatic. He announced that we had stopped opposite a station platform, and that he'd just lifted the pistol from an unsuspecting civilian. He dug up a heavy cord, looped it around his neck, tied the ends to the pistol butt, and stuck the gun in his belt. He was a real officer now; he had both a sword and a pistol.

Before long we got our regular bumping, and slowly pushed our way on toward our unknown fate. Kolko and I moved over next to the tow-headed machine gunner. He'd been fighting with the Partizan troops for almost a year now. He'd had a bad break, and he was disconsolate. "I'm thinking about my wife all the time," he explained. "We'd only been married a month when I had to join up with the Partizans. I just can't hardly think of anything else but how I'd like to have her right now."

We offered him our condolences. Maybe he could go home before so very long. If he didn't get there pretty soon some other man might be keeping her warm on these cold nights. . . . He only shook his head sadly when we suggested that possibility.

Leaning against the wall was a red-bearded boy who wore his sheepskin jacket despite the incredible heat of this steel baking oven. He was a new recruit; he'd join up with the Partizans only that morning. "I was afraid to desert from the Whites," he explained to us. "You see I live in the country near Nikolsk and they might have punished my family."

A third peasant soldier cut in: "Kolchak and the 'Makakas' made us all Partizans. While we were fighting for Kolchak, the Japs were burning our villages and killing our people. When we finish off the Whites, we'll give them something. America understands us. They are men like we are. If America would only help us we could whip the Japs. We never had anything against the Americans. They did a little something against us at the start when they first got here, but that didn't amount to much. They're our friends now."

The blond giant, with the wide mouth and the shining teeth, and the big yen for his wife, muscled into the conversation. "Did you hear about that American who brought back five Jap prisoners we had and turned them over to the Jap General? He told him that was the way we treated our prisoners, and for him to quit killing ours."

I didn't say anything. It was too hot and stuffy in that car to be even your own hero. I drifted back to my old seat on the ammunition case.

The boy commander started talking about some mystical thing he called *svoboda*—freedom. He would have made quite a rabble-rouser if he'd put his mind to it.

We jogged along through the interminable hours. The two lanterns swaying from their hooks, cast weird shadows. The little stove threw off enough heat to barbecue a mule.

We'd talk a few sentences and then we'd turn to our own dreams. Once in a while the tow-headed homesick lover on the Maxim-Vickers saddle seat would hum a song. Maybe the others would join, and again maybe they wouldn't.

The young commander would make his rounds, and examine the two heavy guns. Their barrels were blanketed, and their water coolers warm and ready for action. He was a true machine gunner. He'd pet the guns and call them "baby." You could get action from the seat of a Maxim-Vickers—especially if you put your heart in your work.

He was a bit of a romantic, too. "Wish you could take a picture so you'd remember us," he suggested. Then he began looking around the car again. "I'd like to give you a souvenir of some kind or other, but I can't find any," he went on.

Then he got his inspiration. He hurried to the far end of the car and pulled the lid off a box.

"Here's something to take home," he said in eager earnestness. Then he rolled a pineapple hand grenade on the floor straight toward my feet.

I didn't know much about hand grenades, but I'd seen plenty of men who'd been mangled by them. At least I knew they weren't to play hand-ball with. . . . I watched this little package of bad news as it bounced and rolled toward me. I started to count ten: most grenades were supposed to burst on the fatal ten. Then a sort of sickly grin spread over my face. I was conscious that my comrades were watching me—me, the over-sized American who was supposed to know all the answers.

I casually reached down and picked up the grenade. If it was going to explode it might as well do the job right and not just mess around. I knew a few Russian words, and, with the steel pineapple cupped in my two hands, I nodded to the young commander and said, "Thanks, comrade!"

I looked it over with feigned professional interest. I saw that the pin was in its proper place and securely bent over. I knew, now, that we were safe; it couldn't go off as long as that pin was in its place. Then, with just a trace of bravado, I shoved the gift in my trousers pocket, opposite the one that held my Colt.

I imagine it was an hour later, when we'd got up near Razdolne, that we bumped to another stop. Again there was a long wait. Through the gun slits we could make out, far down the tracks, what looked to be a bonfire. After a while our commander lifted the trap-door and slipped down through it.

Within three or four minutes he came back. He was excited and his dark eyes were snapping. "The White cadets are entrenched 300 yards down the track with three-inch guns," he shouted. "We'll have a fight now."

He pushed the tow-headed gunner off the saddle seat of the gun in the front of the car, pulled the blankets off the barrel, and squared himself for action. There was tense silence in the car. Any second now we might be pushing forward toward that dull red glow and into those three-inch guns.

I reached back of me and felt the steel sides of the car. I remembered that the armor plate was not more than three-eighths of an inch thick. That would be pie for a three-inch high explosive. I'd seen the twisted, pathetic wrecks of dozens of armor-plated tanks that tried to stop German 77's up in the Soissons area in France. One direct hit on this car of ours and they wouldn't be able to tell which had been me and which the blond gunner with the yen for his bride.

My throat was parched and I smacked my dry lips. The heat, the cigarette smoke, and the foul air, smelling of unwashed bodies and sheepskin jackets, was even smarting my eyes. I wanted to get out of here. I didn't want to be blown to bits by some nervous White cadet, pulling a lanyard that would send an unlucky shell, with my number on it, to its unnecessary mission.

The voice of the commander broke the long hot silence. Kolko whispered that he had said he would slip out and find what was happening. The blond giant took his old seat on the machine-gun and the boy hurried to the trap-door and disappeared.

He was gone for what seemed a very long time. Then his Cossack cap popped up from the man-hole and his white teeth showed in the candle-light. He shouted something in Russian.

"What's that? What'd he say?" I demanded of Kolko.

My interpreter did not answer me. He had jumped to his feet and was shouting to the commander. The gunners were talking loudly and excitedly.

"What's doing?" I questioned. But no one paid the slightest attention to me.

"What in hell did he say?" I demanded again, grabbing Kolko's sleeve. But he had no time to answer me.

"God damn it! What'd he say?" I yelled, striking at him.

Kolko came out of his trance. "He said the cadets had surrendered!" he gulped and answered. "The road to Vladivostok is open!"

I joined in the cheering. Two or three of the men were hugging each other. The tow-headed gunner gleefully shouted that maybe he'd get to see his bride again before very long.

Slowly we settled back to our waiting game. Then we got the go-ahead bump and crept on toward what the doughboys called "Bloodyvostok."

I awoke from sleep with a jerk. We were coming to a stop. The boy commander peered out through a loophole. Kolko translated what he said: "It's getting light. . . . Looks like we're almost in Vladivostok."

I stretched my cramped legs. I drew a deep breath of the foul, dead air and immediately regretted it. I couldn't stand this car any longer. I'd rather freeze than toast, and I'd rather be shot in the open than smothered to death in a heated vacuum.

Again the commander disappeared through the manhole. I slipped on my fur-lined coat and cap, pulled on my great gloves, and told Kolko I was going to get out of here. He presented arguments and recited pledges. I answered that I didn't give a damn about anything except to leave this steel pigsty. . . . He pick up his coat and started to follow me. But I wouldn't let him come. I explained that I'd only get some fresh air, look around and report back.

I crawled out between the wheels. We were in a gap in the snow-blanketed hills that surrounded the magnificent "Golden Horn." We couldn't be more than three or four miles from the railroad station.

Dawn was just breaking, but here in the Far North it would be a late dawn. It was almost eight o'clock. Several groups of men were evidently conferring by the side of the train, a car or two below the engine. I snooped around to see what I could see. A narrow steel ladder on the rear of our armored car, that led to the roof, caught my eye. I climbed up and made a quick survey. The car had a flat wooden roof. I scrambled down, ducked between the wheels, and stuck my head up through the trap-door. The hot blast and the stench was almost like a smash in the face. I told Kolko not to worry about me, that I was going to stay outside in the clear air. He said he'd join me, but I begged him not to: his outfit was not as warm as mine. Then I slipped out, returned to the ladder, and mounted it to the top of the car. Carefully I tucked the skirts of my long coat under me, and with my legs dangling over the front end sat squarely on the roof. Vladivostok was straight ahead of me.

The engine bell rang, men shouted and scurried to their coaches, and off we started. Suddenly I realized that I was doing a very silly thing. If there was fighting at the station I'd be the first man to be picked off. But the air was champagne to me, and I was intoxicated with this blessed oxygen, and the lovely morning, and the whole thrilling business of living gaily and dangerously.

We were getting into town now. A little group of workmen along the track cheered and waved as we went by. Then there was more shouting, and waving.

I was taking the salute. I was the man on the white horse at the head of the procession. I chuckled to myself. From my high seat at the front of the No. 1 car, I sang out *"Tovarish!"*—"Comrade!" to everyone we passed.

Now we were pushing into the station. There was a wild crowd of cheering men here. They had no uniforms but they were waving rifles, and yelling.

I looked down from my box seat. Two or three officers in American uniforms were in the crowd next to the track. I recognized my friend Frank Martinek, of the Naval Intelligence. The train ground to a stop. Then they saw me and yelled a welcome.

Frank shouted up to me: "We surrender! Will you accept our unconditional surrender?"

"I will!" I shouted back. "And may God have pity on your miserable souls!"

I hurried to the back of the car and scrambled down the little ladder. Martinek, and my tried true friends, Lieutenant Colonel Bob Eichelberger and Major Sidney Graves, pounded me on the back.

"Young man," Frank hilariously insisted, "this is the first time in history that a war correspondent ever captured a town!" The others roared and pommeled me.

But a little later when I sent off my story I had to admit that the anti-

Whites had pulled their *coup d'état* and taken over the town just before dawn, and that even the Japanese had been forced to accept the turnover.

I might have captured only a captured town, but at least I had my pants on, and, as I have already said, that's something Kipling's private Mulvaney lacked.

P.S.: I never was able to find out whether or not that tow-headed machine gunner got home to his wife before it thawed that spring. I've always hoped that he did.

"Up Periscope!"

BY

AN OFFICER OF H. M. SUBMARINE STURGEON

ON THE evening of September 2, the small British submarine *Sturgeon*, 740 tons, commanded by Lieutenant George David Archibald Gregory, was on patrol on the *inside* of a German mine field off the north coast of Denmark. There it intercepted and sunk a 10,000-ton German transport which was traveling toward Norway with four thousand German troops, guns, and ammunition. It is believed that most of these soldiers perished, for many hundreds of bodies were later washed up on the coast of Norway.

The troopship had an escort of destroyers and aircraft. There was half a gale blowing at the time, it was nearly dark, and the submarine was in a bad position to attack when the convoy was first sighted. But Lieutenant Gregory stalked the ship for some time, and by extraordinarily good marksmanship (which he describes as "luck") he managed to strike home with his torpedoes from a distance of over two miles. Gregory had previously received the D.S.O. for submarine work on "hazardous duties."

Gregory is thirty, married, with one child. He is a Scot, son of a gunner colonel, and has been in the Submarine Service for nine years. He thinks it is "the best game there is."

This is the story of the *Sturgeon:* When we slid out into the North Sea from our home base on that late August afternoon, I had no idea of the amazing piece of luck which awaited us. For, contrary to general belief, we in "The Trade" [Navy's name for the Submarine Service] get precious little real excitement as a rule and hardly a target to shoot at from one month's end to another. Whereas a U-boat captain has only to poke his nose out of his home waters to find the sea stiff with targets, we usually find "enemy waters" empty from the beginning of our patrol to the end of it. No fat convoys, no crowded troopships, no enemy warships stripped for action and looking for trouble.

For most of us our patrols have meant long weeks of boredom and routine. We hunt in a void which seldom offers a chance of action to alleviate the monotony. By day we comb the endless sea miles of our assigned "beat," traveling just under periscope death and popping up every few minutes to have a look round. It's "Up periscope. . . . Down periscope" all the hours of daylight.

At night we rest on the surface to recharge the batteries. The off-duty men come along then to stand in little groups smoking and gossiping under the open hatch of the conning tower. This is the time, too, for "hot cooking," because the fresh night air drives away the stale air and the all-pervading stink of Diesel oil from the engines.

As usual, the first few days of this trip were quiet. When we reached the outer fringe of our patrol area—a spot well within enemy waters—the weather was steadily getting worse, but we saw nothing. Then we began to inch our way through what the Germans had declared to be a mine field. Eventually we reached waters which we judged would be a very good place to intercept anything coming from the German eastern ports. Patrolling up and down, we saw nothing the first few days except one or two aircraft, which didn't worry us very much because the sea was too rough for them to spot the faint feathering of our periscope. It is in calm weather that we have to be careful of aircraft, for then they can see not only the periscope feather but our shadow below the surface of the water.

On the fifth day of our patrol, just as it was getting dark, I noticed one aircraft in the distance which seemed to be taking a lot of interest in the sea beneath. It kept buzzing around within a three-mile radius. I was feeling pretty annoyed that we had seen nothing so far, and this aircraft was a bit of a nuisance, because we wanted to keep at periscope depth for the last of the daylight. Handing over to his No. 1 [first lieutenant], the captain went along to our little wardroom to check over some reports.

He had hardly sat down when the No. 1 reported that the two men at the hydrophones had picked up the faint, far-off beat of ship's engines. He jumped up and raced into the control room. The hydrophone men had got a bearing on those distant engines. They reported the sound of several ships. "To hell with that aircraft," I thought. "We're coming up to have a jolly good look round." Sure enough came the order "Up periscope."

Through the eyepiece I first saw only the green translucent wash of the sea, but then, as the glass cleared the surface waves, I spotted a German destroyer silhouetted against the after glare of the dying sun. Seven-eighths of the horizon was dark, but there in the one clear patch was the enemy ship. The order "Diving stations" was given.

The captain watched the destroyer for a minute or two and then passed another order to the coxswain, perched unemotionally at the hydroplane wheel, to bring her up a few feet. I had another quick glance as the captain passed the eyepiece to me. Droplets of sea water flew down across the crystal-bright surface of the lens as I swung the periscope round a bit. And there, just behind the first destroyer, another ship loomed up! This was a large, handsome transport. Behind was another small destroyer. They were about three miles off to the northwest of me, clearly heading toward Oslo.

This was a tremendous moment for us. Here was the thing we had been waiting for during all these wearisome patrols. And it was big game, too.

But the captain had to think fast. The light was going, and we were in about the worst possible position to attack. The enemy ships were just ahead of us on our beam and steaming a parallel course, but in the opposite direction. We had to alter course quickly and travel unseen to a position from which, on a converging track, our torpedoes would have the maximum chance of striking home. I remembered the captain taking his eye away from the lens for a moment and seeing the No. 1 and the men in the control room watching him eagerly. "A big one," he said to them briefly, "with a destroyer escort."

Another look at the swiftly oncoming ships, a glance at the bearing figures on the periscope, a last summing up of our position, and he issued the order, "Blow all torpedo tubes." [Drive water out of tubes and insert torpedoes ready for firing.] He stayed at the lens for another moment, getting a last "fix" and giving the information and orders which would bring us to our next position: "Bearing red seven 0; I am 20 degrees starboard; port wheel five knots. . . . Steer 350 degrees. . . . DOWN PERISCOPE."

The next few minutes, as the boat slowly turned under water to get on to the new course, we worried ourselves sick. Had we estimated the enemy course and speed aright? How long were we going to be getting round? Where would they be when we put the periscope up again?

Impatiently, the captain watched the torpedo tubes' signal lights. I heard him snap out to our No. 1, "When the hell are Nos. 2 and 4 going to be ready?" But before he had even finished the sentence the "readiness" signals flashed up. I watched the silent men at the depth-control valves. The electric driving motors whined louder, flooding into the silence in the control room. Then again he called, "UP PERISCOPE!"

There they were—much nearer, but at a new angle. The Germans had altered course slightly. "We might miss them yet," I thought. So the captain yelled another series of hurried orders, which, with the answers, went something like this:

CAPTAIN (at periscope): Bearing, green 25 degrees.

THIRD HAND (at instrument showing bearing of submarine to target): You are now 25 degrees starboard, sir.

CAPTAIN: Oh, Lord, no! He's more than that. Give him 45 degrees.

THIRD HAND: Enemy's new course then on 40 degrees.

CAPTAIN: DOWN PERISCOPE. Starboard wheel. Nine knots. Steer 310 degrees. Down 50 feet.

COXSWAIN: Fifty feet, sir.

CAPTAIN: Slow both. [Slowing engines so periscope will not feather too much on breaking water.] Periscope depth. UP PERISCOPE!"

The rest was a matter of seconds. We were closing rapidly, and even at our distance of about two and a half miles and in the last of the light the white water could be seen breaking away from the speeding transport's bow. She was dead on our line of sight. "Stand by!" ordered the captain without taking his eye away from the lens. He pressed the button of his stopwatch and counted as the angle was closing. "One . . . two . . . three." Then: "FIRE!" The rating who had been standing by the firing panel, head cocked expectantly toward him, pushed home the switches.

I felt the boat shudder as the torpedoes left her and sped on their way. I had a last look. The transport, curiously it seemed to me, was steaming serenely on against that patch of light to the northwest. Then the captain bellowed, "DOWN PERISCOPE." . . . "Down 60 feet." We waited in dead silence, our eyes fixed on the minute hand of the control-room clock. It seemed to creep round the dial. One minute went by, then two, and my doubts and uncertainties began to grow agonizing. I strained my ears for a distant sound, but heard only the hum and ticktock of the giro near the helmsman, the faint noises of the sea outside the hull, and the glug-glug of the ballast tanks as we kept our depth. "We've missed," I thought gloomily. "We've missed her." We would not have another chance. We could not attack again at the altered angle.

In that instant, when I had given up all hope, I heard a distant muffled bang. Then another and another. All the light bulbs flickered for a moment or two. A gentle tremor shook the deck plates beneath me. The captain from his swivel seat near the instrument panels sprang up and ordered the submarine to periscope depth. He had a quick look and then silently handed the glass to me. I thought first that the coating of sea spume would never clear from the glass, but then in a flash the whole terrific picture leaped into view. An enormous column of black smoke reared high above the transport. To the left and right of it, giant fireballs, which must have been exploding ammunition, arched outward against the background of darkening sky. The captain turned to the men in the control room, who were staring at him questioningly. "She's gone," he said. Their faces broke into broad grins. One of the ratings slid out of the control room to take the "buzz" [news] along to the men forward. He watched that distant scene for a moment more and then, just as I had replaced him at the eye-piece, I suddenly spotted the escort aircraft making a beeline back along our torpedo tracks toward us. These tracks must still have been faintly visible, for less than three minutes had passed since that first distant bang. Down we shot once more.

For the next few minutes we waited anxiously, wondering if the aircraft had seen us and had called up the destroyers. Any moment we expected the thud and shake of the depth charges. At the captain's hand signal the men in the control room froze into stillness. Those at hydrophones bent over their gear listening hard. The first few minutes were awful. But nothing happened, so he decided to come up and have another look.

It was now completely dark, and I saw the transport was on fire from stem to stern. The reflection from the flames seemed to make a patch across the waters toward me. And against the vast red glow I could pick out the silhouettes of the destroyers passing and repassing. I watched the flaming ship for a long time as we cruised gently along at periscope depth. After an hour, when we saw that she was obviously a goner, the captain gave the order to dive down deep and reload torpedo tubes.

We stayed down about an hour, still hearing nothing except the very distant sound of ship's engines. As it was getting rather late and the air was thickening, we decided to surface cautiously. Unfortunately we came up "beam on" to the target position. I was first onto the bridge through the conning-tower hatch, and as I got there we were suddenly lit up from end to end in the blinding glare of a searchlight. That moment was perhaps the worst of the whole episode. I stood absolutely glued to the bridge rail for a second or two. Then the searchlight moved on. They hadn't seen us! The searchlights were obviously combing the sea for survivors, and after a while they began to dim. The destroyers were moving away from us.

I stayed on the bridge while the watch was posted and filled my lungs with the good fresh air. Suddenly I felt more tired than I have ever been in my life. On the distant dark horizon there was an occasional flicker of signal and recognition lights from enemy vessels, which had no doubt come out to meet the escort destroyers. But there was no sound except the noise of the rising gale and the breaking seas. We cruised slowly on, recharging our batteries. The normal routine of the boat started again. Up through the conning-tower hatch I could catch the smell of bacon and eggs frying for breakfast. It was quiet again and all the tension was over. There was one minor tragedy, however, before that night was over. The rating ordered up to polish the great object glass of the periscope reported that there was no petrol left in the small bottle, which is all we are allowed to carry in submarines. It is essential that this glass should take the highest possible polish so that water droplets will not adhere to the surface and spoil peri-scope vision. There was nothing to do but hand over the last two inches that remained in my only bottle of fine old brandy. That was a terrible blow. But I watched that rating like a lynx to see that all the brandy went on the polishing cloth and not down his throat.

Father Duffy

BY

ALEXANDER WOOLLCOTT

THE funeral of a great priest as reported by one who had come to know him during his genial missions "in partibus infidelium."

AFTER her last tour in *The Rivals,* that celebrated Mrs. Malaprop who was the grandmother of these latter-day Barrymores used to sit rocking on her veranda at Larchmont. Joseph Jefferson, himself getting on towards seventy, would rock beside her. "What mystifies me, Joe," she said one day, "is why you should traipse all the way across New England just to visit an old woman like me." He told her why. You see, she was the only person left in the world who called him Joe. You who are young now cannot hope to postpone until so ripe an age the first sense of your own world coming to an end. By the time you have reached the middle years, it may well be that people dearer to you than anyone can ever be again will already be ashes scattered to the winds. Thereafter, one by one, the friends slip away. Death seems to come oftener into your street than he used to do, now knocking at the house next door, now touching on the shoulder the neighbor you were talking to only yesterday at sundown. You grow quite accustomed to the sound of his step under your window.

It is a life thus successively and irremediably impoverished which you yourself give up at last—the less reluctantly, I daresay. At least that is the feeling I have when I try looking squarely at the fact that I shall never again read a new page by Lytton Strachey, never again hear the wonder of Mrs. Fiske's voice in the theater, never again experience on Christmas Eve, as in so many jolly years gone by, the heart-warming benediction of Father Duffy's smile. I seem to remember it more often than not as a mutinous smile, the eyes dancing, the lips puckering as if his conscientious sobriety as a priest were once more engaged in its long, losing fight with his inner amusement at the world—his deeply contented amusement at the world. I thought that smile one of the pleasantest sights in America, and I find unbearable the thought that I shall not see it again.

They buried Father Duffy from St. Patrick's at the end of June in 1932. The huge cathedral might as well have been a tiny chapel for all it could hope to hold those of us who wanted to say good-bye to him. As I waited in the cool, candle-lit dusk of the church for the procession to make its way up the sunny avenue, all around me lips were moving in prayer and gnarled fingers were telling their rosaries. But even the heathen could at least count over their hours with him. There were many of us there, outsiders who, without belonging to his outfit, had nevertheless been attached to him for rations—of the spirit. One had only to stop for a moment and speak to him on the street to go on one's way immensely set up, reassured by what he was that there might be a good deal, after all, to this institution called the human race.

While we waited, my own wry thoughts jumped back to that desperate October in 1918 when his regiment, the old 69th of New York, was cut to ribbons in the Argonne. Especially I recalled the black day when Colonel Donovan was carried out of the battle on a blanket—Wild Bill, who was the very apple of the Padre's eye. Father Duffy had always scolded him for his gaudy recklessness, and there he was at last with his underpinnings shot from under him. As they carried him into the dressing-station he had just strength enough left to shake a defiant fist. "Ah, there, Father," he said, "you thought you'd have the pleasure of burying me!" Father Duffy shook a fist in reply. "And I will yet," he said. But it was not to be that way. For here, fourteen years later, was Wild Bill and a thousand others of the old regiment coming up the avenue to bury Father Duffy.

One by one there came back to me all the times our paths had crossed in France and on the Rhine. He would always have tall tales to tell of his Irish fighters, who, with death all around them, heard only the grace of God purring in their hearts. It delighted him that they spoke of the Ourcq as the O'Rourke, and he enjoyed their wonderment at the French presumption in dignifying so measly a creek by calling it a river. He loved the story of one wounded soldier who waved aside a proffered canteen. "Give it to the Ourcq. It needs it more than I do." And he loved all stories wherein the uppity were discomfited. On the Rhine he relished the spectacle of Pershing vainly trying to unbend a bit and play the little father to his troops. The Commander-in-Chief paused before one Irish doughboy who had three wound stripes on his arm. "Well, my lad," asked the great man in benevolent tones, "and where did you get those?" "From the supply sergeant, Sir," the hero answered, and Father Duffy grinned from ear to ear.

Most often he would talk not of France and the war at all, but of New York. He liked nothing better than to sit in the shell-hole with Clancey and Callahan and Kerrigan and talk about New York. I have stood beside him ankle-deep in the Argonne mud and, above the noise of the rain pattering on our helmets, heard him speculate about the gleam of Fifth Avenue in the October sunshine and say how he would like to see once more that grand actress who called herself Laurette Taylor, but who, mind you, was born a Cooney. And for him the most electric moment in all the war came on a night of June moonlight in Lorraine when the troops of the old 69th discovered that the shiny new outfit which was relieving them was also from New York. The war had picked them both up by the scruff of the neck, carried them across the world, and dropped them in the French mud, and here they were passing each other on the road. At that time the Rainbow had been in the line only a few weeks, and the Baccarat Sector was a tranquil one. The real slaughter of July and October lay ahead of them but at least they could feel battle-scarred and scornful when compared with these green boys of the 77th, fresh from the transports. Being themselves volunteers, they jeered at the newcomers as conscripts, who retorted, to their surprise, by calling them draft dodgers. There was some excitement as old neighbors would identify each other in the moonlight, and one unforgettable moment when Father Duffy saw two brothers meet. In their emotion they could only take pokes at each other and swear enormously. Then, lest all these ructions draw the attention of the enemy artillery to this relief, order was somehow restored and the march went on, mingling prohibited, speech of any kind forbidden. So these passing regiments just hummed to each other very softly in the darkness. "Give my regards to Broadway." The rhythm staccato, the words unnecessary. "Remember me to Herald Square." The tune said the words for all of them. "Tell all the boys in Forty-second Street that I will soon be there." In the distance the sound grew fainter and fainter. Father Duffy had a lump in his throat.

For he was the great New Yorker. Born in Canada, Irish as Irish, schooled in Maynooth, he was surely the first citizen of our town. This city is too large for most of us. But not for Father Duffy. Not too large, I mean, for him to invest it with the homeliness of a neighborhood. When he walked down the street—any street—he was like a *curé* striding through his own village. Everyone knew him. I have walked beside him and thought I had never before seen so many *pleased* faces. The beaming cop would stop all traffic to make a path from curb to curb for Father Duffy. Both the proud-stomached banker who stopped to speak with him on the corner and the checkroom boy who took his hat at the restaurant would grin transcendently at the sight of him. He would call them both by their first names, and you could see how proud they were on the account. Father Duffy was of such dimensions that he made New York into a small town.

No wonder all the sidewalk space as far as one could see was needed for the overflow at his funeral. To my notion, the mute multitude in the June sunlight made the more impressive congregation. To alien ears the Latin passages of the Mass seem as automatic and as passionless as the multiplication table, and at least those who could not get in missed the harangue delivered from the pulpit with the vocal technique of a train announcer. One woman I know saw an unused bit of pavement and asked a huge policeman if she might not stand there. He told her the space was reserved. "But," she explained, as if offering credentials, "I was a personal friend of Father Duffy's." The policeman's answer was an epitaph. "That is true, Ma'am," he said, "of everyone here today."

The War Years

BY

JAMES HILTON

I

THE War years.

The first shock, and then the first optimism. The Battle of the Marne, the Russian steam-roller, Kitchener.

"Do you think it will last long, sir?"

Chips, questioned as he watched the first trial game of the season, gave quite a cheery answer. He was, like thousands of others, hopelessly wrong; but, unlike thousands of others, he did not afterward conceal the fact. "We ought to have—um—finished it—um—by Christmas. The Germans are already beaten. But why? Are you thinking of—um—joining up, Forrester?"

Joke—because Forrester was the smallest new boy Brookfield had ever had—about four feet high above his muddy football boots. (But not so much a joke, when you came to think of it afterward; for he was killed in 1918—shot down in flames over Cambrai.) But one didn't guess what lay ahead. It seemed tragically sensational when the first Old Brookfieldian was killed in action—in September. Chips thought, when that news came: A hundred years ago boys from this school were fighting *against* the French. Strange, in a way, that the sacrifices of one generation should so cancel out those of another. He tried to express this to Blades, the Head of School House; but Blades, eighteen years old and already in training for a cadet-ship, only laughed. What had all that history stuff to do with it, anyhow? Just old Chips with one of his queer ideas, that's all.

1915. Armies clenched in deadlock from the sea to Switzerland. The Dardanelles. Gallipoli. Military camps springing up quite near Brookfield; soldiers using the playing fields for sports and training; swift developments of Brookfield O.T.C. Most of the younger masters gone or in uniform. Every Sunday night, in the Chapel after evening service, Chatteris read out the names of old boys killed, together with short biographies. Very moving; but Chips, in the black pew under the gallery, thought: They are only names to him; he doesn't see their faces as I do. . . .

1916. . . . The Somme Battle. Twenty-three names read out one Sunday evening.

From: *Goodbye, Mr. Chips.* By permission of Little, Brown and Co. and the Atlantic Monthly Press.

Toward the close of that catastrophic July, Chatteris talked to Chips one afternoon at Mrs. Wickett's. He was overworked and overworried and looked very ill. "To tell you the truth, Chipping, I'm not having too easy a time here. I'm thirty-nine, you know, and unmarried, and lots of people seem to think they know what I ought to do. Also, I happen to be diabetic, and couldn't pass the blindest M.O., but I don't see why I should pin a medical certificate on my front door."

Chips hadn't known anything about this; it was a shock to him, for he liked Chatteris.

The latter continued: "You see how it is. Ralston filled the place up with young men—all very good, of course—but now most of them have joined up and the substitutes are pretty dreadful, on the whole. They poured ink down a man's neck in prep one night last week—silly fool—got hysterical. I have to take classes myself, take prep for fools like that, work till midnight every night, and get cold-shouldered as a slacker on top of everything. I can't stand it much longer. If things don't improve next term I shall have a breakdown."

"I do sympathize with you," Chips said.

"I hoped you would. And that brings me to what I came here to ask you. Briefly, my suggestion is that—if you felt equal to it and would care to—how about coming back here for a while? You look pretty fit, and, of course, you know all the ropes. I don't mean a lot of hard work for you —you needn't take anything strenuously—just a few odd jobs here and there, as you choose. What I'd like you for more than anything else is not for the actual work you'd do—though that, naturally, would be very valuable—but for your help in other ways—in just *belonging* here. There's nobody ever been more popular than you were, and are still—you'd help to hold things together if there were any danger of them flying to bits. And perhaps there *is* that danger. . . ."

Chips answered, breathlessly and with a holy joy in his heart: "I'll come. . . ."

II

He still kept on his rooms with Mrs. Wickett; indeed, he still lived there; but every morning, about half-past ten, he put on his coat and muffler and crossed the road to the School. He felt very fit, and the actual work was not taxing. Just a few forms in Latin and Roman History—the old lessons— even the old pronunciation. The same joke about the Lex Canuleia—there was a new generation that had not heard it, and he was absurdly gratified by the success it achieved. He felt a little like a music-hall favorite returning to the boards after a positively last appearance.

They all said how marvelous it was that he knew every boy's name and face so quickly. They did not guess how closely he had kept in touch from across the road.

He was a grand success altogether. In some strange way he did, and they all knew and felt it, help things. For the first time in his life he felt *necessary*—and necessary to something that was nearest his heart. There is no sublimer feeling in the world, and it was his at last.

He made new jokes, too—about O.T.C. and the food-rationing system and the anti-air-raid blinds that had to be fitted on all the windows. There was a mysterious kind of rissole that began to appear on the School menu on Mondays, and Chips called it *abhorrendum*—"meat to be abhorred." The story went round—heard Chip's latest?

Chatteris fell ill during the winter of '17, and again, for the second time in his life, Chips became Acting Head of Brookfield. Then in April Chatteris died, and the Governors asked Chips if he would carry on "for the duration." He said he would, if they would refrain from appointing him officially. From that last honor, within his reach at last, he shrank instinctively, feeling himself in so many ways unequal to it. He said to Rivers: "You see, I'm not a young man and I don't want people to—um—expect a lot from me. I'm like all these new colonels and majors you see everywhere— just a war-time fluke. A ranker—that's all I am really."

1917. 1918. Chips lived through it all. He sat in the headmaster's study every morning, handling problems, dealing with plaints and requests. Out of vast experience had emerged a kindly, gentle confidence in himself. To keep a sense of proportion, that was the main thing. So much of the world was losing it; as well keep it where it had, or ought to have, a congenial home.

On Sundays in Chapel it was he who now read out the tragic list, and sometimes it was seen and heard that he was in tears over it. Well, why not, the School said; he was an old man; they might have despised anyone else for the weakness.

One day he got a letter from Switzerland, from friends there; it was heavily censored, but conveyed some news. On the following Sunday, after the names and biographies of old boys, he paused a moment and then added:—

"Those few of you who were here before the War will remember Max Staefel, the German master. He was in Germany, visiting his home, when war broke out. He was popular while he was here, and made many friends. Those who knew him will be sorry to hear that he was killed last week, on the Western Front."

He was a little pale when he sat down afterward, aware that he had done something unusual. He had consulted nobody about it, anyhow; no one else could be blamed. Later, outside the Chapel, he heard an argument:—

"On the Western Front, Chips said. Does that mean he was fighting for the Germans?"

"I suppose it does."

"Seems funny, then, to read his name out with all the others. After all, he was an *enemy*."

"Oh, just one of Chip's ideas, I expect. The old boy still has 'em."

Chips, in his room again, was not displeased by the comment. Yes, he still had 'em—those ideas of dignity and generosity that were becoming increasingly rare in a frantic world. And he thought: Brookfield will take them, too, from me; but it wouldn't from anyone else.

Once, asked for his opinion of bayonet practice being carried on near the cricket pavilion, he answered, with that lazy, slightly asthmatic intonation that had been so often and so extravagantly imitated: "It seems—to me—umph—a very vulgar way of killing people."

The yarn was passed on and joyously appreciated—how Chips had told some big brass hat from the War Office that bayonet fighting was vulgar. Just like Chips. And they found an adjective for him—an adjective just beginning to be used: he was pre-War.

III

And once, on a night of full moonlight, the air raid warning was given while Chips was taking his lower fourth in Latin. The guns began almost instantly, and, as there was plenty of shrapnel falling about outside, it seemed to Chips that they might just as well stay where they were, on the ground floor of School House. It was pretty solidly built and made as good a dugout as Brookfield could offer; and as for a direct hit, well, they could not expect to survive that, wherever they were.

So he went on with his Latin, speaking a little louder amid the reverberating crashes of the guns and the shrill whine of anti-aircraft shells. Some of the boys were nervous; few were able to be attentive. He said, gently: "It may possibly seem to you, Robertson—at this particular moment in the world's history—umph—that the affairs of Cæsar in Gaul some two thousand years ago—are—umph—of somewhat secondary importance—and that—umph—the irregular conjugation of the verb *tollo* is—umph—even less important still. But believe me—umph—my dear Robertson—that is not really the case." Just then there came a particularly loud explosion—quite near. "You cannot—umph—judge the importance of things—umph —by the noise they make. Oh dear me, no." A little chuckle. "And these things—umph—that have mattered—for thousands of years—are not going to be—snuffed out—because some stink merchant—in his laboratory—invents a new kind of mischief." Titters of nervous laughter; for Buffles, the pale, lean, and medically unfit science master, was nicknamed the Stink Merchant. Another explosion—nearer still. "Let us—um—resume our work. If it is fate that we are soon to be—umph—interrupted, let us be found employing ourselves in something—umph—really appropriate. Is there anyone who will volunteer to construe?"

Maynard, chubby, dauntless, clever, and impudent said: "I will, sir."

"Very good. Turn to page forty and begin at the bottom line."

The explosions still continued deafeningly; the whole building shook as if it were being lifted off its foundations. Maynard found the page, which was some way ahead, and began, shrilly:—

"*Genus hoc erat pugnae*—this was the kind of fight—*quo se Germani exercuerant*—in which the Germans busied themselves. Oh, sir, that's good —that's really very funny indeed, sir—one of your very best—"

Laughing began, and Chips added: "Well—umph—you can see—now —that these dead languages—umph—can come to life again—sometimes— eh? Eh?"

Afterward they learned that five bombs had fallen in and around Brookfield, the nearest of them just outside the School grounds. Nine persons had been killed.

The story was told, retold, embellished. "The dear old boy never turned a hair. Even found some old tag to illustrate what was going on. Something in Cæsar about the way the Germans fought. You wouldn't think there were things like that in Cæsar, would you? And the way Chips laughed . . . you know the way he *does* laugh . . . the tears all running down his face . . . never seen him laugh so much. . . ."

He was a legend.

With his old and tattered gown, his walk that was just beginning to break into a stumble, his mild eyes peering over the steel-rimmed spectacles, and his quaintly humorous sayings, Brookfield would not have had an atom of him different.

November 11, 1918.

News came through in the morning; a whole holiday was decreed for the School, and the kitchen staff were implored to provide as cheerful a spread as war-time rationing permitted. There was much cheering and singing, and a bread fight across the Dining Hall. When Chips entered in the midst of the uproar there was an instant hush, and then wave upon wave of cheering; everyone gazed on him with eager, shining eyes, as on a symbol of victory. He walked to the dais, seeming as if he wished to speak; they made silence for him, but he shook his head after a moment, smiled, and walked away again.

It had been a damp, foggy day, and the walk across the quadrangle to the Dining Hall had given him a chill. The next day he was in bed with bronchitis, and stayed there till after Christmas. But already, on that night of November 11, after his visit to the Dining Hall, he had sent in his resignation to the Board of Governors.

When school reassembled after the holidays he was back at Mrs. Wickett's. At his own request there were no more farewells or presentations, nothing but a handshake with his successor and the word "acting" crossed out on official stationery. The "duration" was over.

Soldiers of the Republic

BY

DOROTHY PARKER

THAT Sunday afternoon we sat with the Swedish girl in the big café in
Valencia. We had vermouth in thick goblets, each with a cube of honeycombed gray ice in it. The waiter was so proud of that ice he could hardly
bear to leave the glasses on the table, and thus part from it forever. He
went to his duty—all over the room they were clapping their hands and
hissing to draw his attention—but he looked back over his shoulder.

It was dark outside, the quick, new dark that leaps down without dusk
on the day; but, because there were no lights in the streets, it seemed as set
and as old as midnight. So you wondered that all the babies were still up.
There were babies everywhere in the café, babies serious without solemnity
and interested in a tolerant way in their surroundings.

At the table next ours, there was a notably small one; maybe six months
old. Its father, a little man in a big uniform that dragged his shoulders
down, held it carefully on his knee. It was doing nothing whatever, yet he
and his thin young wife, whose belly was already big again under her sleazy
dress, sat watching it in a sort of ecstasy of admiration, while their coffee
cooled in front of them. The baby was in Sunday white; its dress was
patched so delicately that you would have thought the fabric whole had not
the patches varied in their shades of whiteness. In its hair was a bow of new
blue ribbon, tied with absolute balance of loops and ends. The ribbon was
of no use; there was not enough hair to require restraint. The bow was
sheerly an adornment, a calculated bit of dash.

"Oh, for God's sake, stop that!" I said to myself. "All right, so it's got
a piece of blue ribbon on its hair. All right, so its mother went without
eating so it could look pretty when its father came home on leave. All right,
so it's her business, and none of yours. All right, so what have you got to
cry about?"

The big, dim room was crowded and lively. That morning there had been
a bombing from the air, the more horrible for broad daylight. But nobody
in the café sat tense and strained, nobody desperately forced forgetfulness.
They drank coffee or bottled lemonade, in the pleasant, earned ease of Sunday afternoon, chatting of small, gay matters, all talking at once, all hearing and answering.

From: *The New Yorker.* By permission of the Author.

There were many soldiers in the room, in what appeared to be the uniforms of twenty different armies until you saw that the variety lay in the differing ways the cloth had worn or faded. Only a few of them had been wounded; here and there you saw one stepping gingerly, leaning on a crutch or two canes, but so far on toward recovery that his face had color. There were many men, too, in civilian clothes—some of them soldiers home on leave, some of them governmental workers, some of them anybody's guess. There were plump, comfortable wives, active with paper fans, and old women as quiet as their grandchildren. There were many pretty girls and some beauties, of whom you did not remark, "There's a charming Spanish type," but said, "What a beautiful girl!" The women's clothes were not new, and their material was too humble ever to have warranted skillful cutting.

"It's funny," I said to the Swedish girl, "how when nobody in a place is best-dressed, you don't notice that everybody isn't."

"Please?" the Swedish girl said.

No one, save an occasional soldier, wore a hat. When we had first come to Valencia, I lived in a state of puzzled pain as to why everybody on the streets laughed at me. It was not because "West End Avenue" was writ across my face as if left there by a customs officer's chalked scrawl. They like Americans in Valencia, where they have seen good ones—the doctors who left their practices and came to help, the calm young nurses, the men of the International Brigade. But when I walked forth, men and women courteously laid their hands across their splitting faces and little children, too innocent for dissembling, doubled with glee and pointed and cried, "*Olé!*" Then, pretty late, I made my discovery, and left my hat off; and there was laughter no longer. It was not one of those comic hats, either; it was just a hat.

The café filled to overflow, and I left our table to speak to a friend across the room. When I came back to the table, six soldiers were sitting there. They were crowded in, and I scraped past them to my chair. They looked tired and dusty and little, the way that the newly dead look little, and the first things you saw about them were the tendons in their necks. I felt like a prize sow.

They were all in conversation with the Swedish girl. She has Spanish, French, German, anything in Scandinavian, Italian, and English. When she has a moment for regret, she sighs that her Dutch is so rusty she can no longer speak it, only read it, and the same is true of her Rumanian.

They had told her, she told us, that they were at the end of forty-eight hours' leave from the trenches, and, for their holiday, they had all pooled their money for cigarettes, and something had gone wrong, and the cigarettes had never come through to them. I had a pack of American cigarettes —in Spain rubies are as nothing to them—and I brought it out, and by nods and smiles and a sort of breast stroke, made it understood that I was offering it to those six men yearning for tobacco. When they saw what I meant, each one of them rose and shook my hand. Darling of me to share my cigarettes with them on their way back to the trenches. Little Lady Bountiful. The prize sow.

Each one lit his cigarette with a contrivance of yellow rope that stank when afire and was also used, the Swedish girl translated, for igniting grenades. Each one received what he had ordered, a glass of coffee, and each one murmured appreciatively over the tiny cornucopia of coarse sugar that accompanied it. Then they talked.

They talked through the Swedish girl, but they did to us that thing we all do when we speak our own language to one who has no knowledge of it. They looked us square in the face, and spoke slowly, and pronounced their words with elaborate movements of their lips. Then, as their stories came, they poured them at us so vehemently, so emphatically that they were sure we must understand. They were so convinced we would understand that we were ashamed for not understanding.

But the Swedish girl told us. They were all farmers and farmers' sons, from a district so poor that you try not to remember there is that kind of poverty. Their village was next that one where the old men and the sick men and the women and children had gone, on a holiday, to the bullring; and the planes had come over and dropped bombs on the bullring, and the old men and the sick men and the women and the children were more than two hundred.

They had all, the six of them, been in the war for over a year, and most of that time they had been in the trenches. Four of them were married. One had one child, two had three children, one had five. They had not had word from their families since they had left for the front. There had been no communication; two of them had learned to write from men fighting next them in the trench, but they had not dared to write home. They belonged to a union, and union men, of course, are put to death if taken. The village where their families lived had been captured, and if your wife gets a letter from a union man, who knows but they'll shoot her for the connection?

They told about how they had not heard from their families for more than a year. They did not tell it gallantly or whimsically or stoically. They told it as if— Well, look. You have been in the trenches, fighting, for a year. You have heard nothing of your wife and your children. They do not know if you are dead or alive or blinded. You do not know where they are, or if they are. You must talk to somebody. That is the way they told about it.

One of them, some six months before, had heard of his wife and his three children—they had such beautiful eyes, he said—from a brother-in-law in France. They were all alive then, he was told, and had a bowl of beans a day. But his wife had not complained of the food, he heard. What had troubled her was that she had no thread to mend the children's ragged clothes. So that troubled him, too.

"She has no thread," he kept telling us. "My wife has no thread to mend with. No thread."

We sat there, and listened to what the Swedish girl told us they were saying. Suddenly one of them looked at the clock, and then there was excitement. They jumped up, as a man, and there were calls for the waiter and rapid talk with him, and each of them shook the hand of each of us. We went through more swimming motions to explain to them that they were to take the rest of the cigarettes—fourteen cigarettes for six soldiers to take to war—and then they shook our hands again. Then all of us said *"Salud!"* as many times as could be for six of them and three of us, and then they filed out of the café, the six of them, tired and dusty and little, as men of a mighty horde are little.

Only the Swedish girl talked, after they had gone. The Swedish girl has been in Spain since the start of the war. She has nursed splintered men, and she has carried stretchers into the trenches and, heavier laden, back to the hospital. She has seen and heard too much to be knocked into silence.

Presently it was time to go, and the Swedish girl raised her hands above her head and clapped them twice together to summon the waiter. He came, but he only shook his head and his hand, and moved away.

The soldiers had paid for our drinks.

The Chauffeurs of Madrid

BY

ERNEST HEMINGWAY

WE HAD a lot of different chauffeurs in Madrid. The first one was named Tomas, was four feet eleven inches high and looked like a particularly unattractive, very mature dwarf out of Velasquez put into a suit of blue dungarees. He had several front teeth missing and seethed with patriotic sentiments. He also loved Scotch whisky.

We drove up from Valencia with Tomas and, as we sighted Madrid rising like a great white fortress across the plain from Alcala de Henares, Tomas said, through missing teeth, "Long live Madrid, the Capital of my Soul!"

"And of my heart," I said, having had a couple myself. It had been a long cold ride.

"Hurray!" shouted Tomas and abandoned the wheel temporarily in order to clap me on the back. We just missed a lorry full of troops and a staff car.

"I am a man of sentiment," said Tomas.

"Me, too," I said, "but hang on to that wheel."

"Of the noblest sentiment," said Tomas.

"No doubt of it, comrade," I said, "but just try to watch where you're driving."

"You can place all confidence in me," said Tomas.

But the next day we were stalled in a muddy road up near Brihuega by a tank, which had lurched around a little too far on a hairpin bend, and held up six other tanks behind it. Three rebel planes sighted the tanks and decided to bomb them. The bombs hit the wet hillside above us lifting mud geysers in sudden, clustered, bumping shocks. Nothing hit us and the planes went on over their own lines. In the field glasses, standing by the car, I could see the little Fiats that protected the bombers, very shining looking, hanging up in the sun. We thought some more bombers were coming and everybody got away from there as fast as possible. But no more came.

Next morning Tomas couldn't get the car to start. And every day when anything of that sort happened, from then on, no matter how well the car had run coming home at night, Tomas never could start her in the morning. The way he felt about the front became sort of pitiful, finally, along with

By permission of the Author.

his size, his patriotism, and his general inefficiency, and we sent him back to Valencia, with a note to the press department thanking them for Tomas, a man of the noblest sentiments and the finest intentions; but they could send us something just a little braver.

So they sent one with a note certifying him as the bravest chauffeur in the whole department. I don't know what his name was because I never saw him. Sid Franklin, who bought us all our food, cooked breakfasts, typed articles, wangled petrol, wangled cars, wangled chauffeurs, and covered Madrid and all its gossip like a human dictaphone, evidently instructed this chauffeur very strongly. Sid put forty litres of petrol in the car, and petrol was the correspondent's main problem, being harder to obtain than Chanel's and Molyneux's perfumes or Bols gin, took the chauffeur's name and address, and told him to hold himself ready to roll whenever he was called. We were expecting an attack.

Until we called him he was free to do whatever he wanted. But he must leave word at all times where we could reach him. We did not want to use up the precious petrol riding around in Madrid in the car. We all felt good now, because we had transport.

The chauffeur was to check in at the hotel the next night at seven-thirty to see if there were any new orders. He didn't come and we called up his rooming house. He had left that same morning for Valencia with the car and the forty litres of petrol. He is in jail in Valencia now. I hope he likes it.

Then we got David. David was an Anarchist boy from a little town near Toledo. He used language that was so utterly and unconceivably foul that half the time you could not believe what your ears were hearing. Being with David has changed my whole conception of profanity. He was absolutely brave and he had only one real defect as a chauffeur. He couldn't drive a car. He was like a horse which has only two gaits: walking and running away. David could sneak along, in second speed, and hit practically no one in the streets, due to his clearing a swathe ahead of him with his vocabulary. He would also drive with the car wide open, hanging to the wheel, in a sort of fatalism that was, however, never tinged with despair. We solved the problem by driving for David ourselves. He liked this and it gave him a chance to work his vocabulary. His vocabulary was terrific.

He liked the war and he thought shelling was beautiful. "Look at that! Olé! That's the stuff to give the unmentionable unspeakable absolutely unutterables," he would say in delight. "Come on, let's get closer!" He was watching his first battle in the Casa del Campo and it was like a super-fireworks show to him. The spouting clouds of stone and plaster dust that pulsed up as the Government shells landed on a house the Moors held with machine guns, and the great, tremendous, slither automatic rifles, machine guns and rapid fire combine into at the moment of the assault moved David very deeply. "Ayee! Ayee!" he said. "That's war. That's really war!"

He liked the tearing rush of the incomers just as much as the crack and the chu-chu-chu-ing air-parting rustle of sound that came from the battery which was firing over our heads on to the rebel positions.

"Olé," said David, as a 75 burst a little way down the street.

"Listen," I said. "Those are the bad ones. Those are the ones that kill us."

"That's of no importance," David said. "Listen to that unspeakable unmentionable noise."

Well, I went back to the hotel, finally, to write a dispatch and we sent David around to a place near the Plaza Mayor to get some petrol. I had almost finished the dispatch when in came David.

"Come and look at the car," he said. "It's full of blood. It's a terrible thing." He was pretty shaky. He had a dark face and his lips trembled.

"What was it?"

"A shell hit a line of women waiting to buy food. It killed seven. I took three to the hospital."

"Good boy."

"But you can't imagine it," he said. "It's terrible. I did not know there were such things."

"Listen, David," I said. "You're a brave boy. You must remember that. But all day you have been brave about noises. What you see now is what those noises do. Now you must be brave about the noises knowing what they can do."

"Yes, man," he said. "But it is a terrible thing just the same to see."

David was brave though. I don't think he ever thought it was quite as beautiful again as he did that first day; but he never shirked any of it. On the other hand he never learned to drive a car. But he was a good, if fairly useless, kid and I loved to hear his awful language. The only thing that developed in David was his vocabulary. He went off to the village where the motion picture outfit were making a film and, after having one more particularly useless chauffeur that there is no point in going into, we got Hipolito. Hipolito is the point of this story.

Hipolito was not much taller than Tomas but he looked carved out of a granite block. He walked with a roll, putting his feet down flat at each stride; and he had an automatic pistol so big it came half way down his leg. He always said, "Salud" with a rising inflection as though it were something you said to hounds. Good hounds that knew their business. He knew motors, he could drive and if you told him to show up at six a.m., he was there ten minutes before the hour. He had fought at the taking of Montana barracks in the first days of the war and he had never been a member of any political party. He was a trade union man for the last twenty years in the Socialist Union, the U.G.T. He said, when I asked him what he believed in, that he believed in the Republic. He was our chauffeur in Madrid and at the front during a nineteen-day bombardment of the capital that was almost too bad to write anything about. All the time he was as solid as the rock he looked to be cut from, as sound as a good bell and as regular and accurate as a railway man's watch. He made you realize why

Franco never took Madrid when he had the chance. Hipolito and the others like him would have fought from street to street, and house to house, as long as anyone of them was left alive; and the last ones left would have burned the town. They are tough and they are efficient. They are the Spaniards that once conquered the Western World. They are not romantic like the Anarchists and they are not afraid to die. Only they never mention it. The Anarchists talk a little too much about it, the way Italians do.

On the day we had over 300 shells come into Madrid so the main streets were a glass-strewn, brick-dust powdered, smoking shambles, Hipolito had the car parked in the lee of a building in a narrow street beside the hotel. It looked like a good safe place and after he had sat around the room while I was working until he was thoroughly bored, he said he'd go down and sit in the car. He hadn't been gone ten minutes when a six inch shell hit the hotel just at the junction of the main floor and the sidewalk. It went deep in out of sight and didn't explode. If it had burst there would not have been enough of Hipolito and the car to take a picture of. They were about fifteen feet away from where the shell hit. I looked out of the window, saw he was all right, and then went downstairs.

"How are you?" I was fairly average breathless.

"Fine," he said.

"Put the car further down the street."

"Don't be foolish," he said. "Another one wouldn't drop there in a thousand years. Besides it didn't explode."

"Put it farther along the street."

"What's the matter with you?" he asked. "You getting windy?"

"You've got to be sensible."

"Go ahead and do your work," he said. "Don't worry about me."

The details of that day are a little confused because after nineteen days of heavy shelling some of the days get merged into others; but at one o'clock the shelling stopped and we decided to go to the Hotel Gran Via, about six blocks down, to get some lunch. I was going to walk by a very tortuous and extremely safe way I had worked out utilizing the angles of least danger, when Hipolito said, "Where are you going?"

"To eat."

"Get in the car."

"You're crazy."

"Come on, we'll drive you down the Gran Via. It's stopped. They are eating their lunch too."

Four of us got into the car and drove down the Gran Via. It was solid with broken glass. There were great holes all down the sidewalks. Buildings were smashed and we had to walk around a heap of rubble and a smashed stone cornice to get into the hotel. There was not a living person on either side of this street which had been always Madrid's Fifth Avenue and Broadway combined. There were many dead. We were the only motor car.

Hipolito put the car up a side street and we all ate together. We were still eating when Hipolito finished and went up to the car. There was some more shelling sounding, in the hotel basement, like muffled blasting, and when we finished the lunch of bean soup, paper thin sliced sausage and an orange, we went upstairs, the streets were full of smoke and clouds of dust. There was new smashed cement work all over the sidewalk. I looked around the corner for the car. There was rubble scattered all down that street from a new shell that had just hit overhead. I saw the car. It was covered with dust and rubble.

"My God," I said, "they've got Hipolito."

He was lying with his head back in the driver's seat. I went up to him feeling very badly. I had got very fond of Hipolito.

Hipolito was asleep.

"I thought you were dead," I said. He woke up and wiped a yawn on the back of his hand.

"Que va, hombre," he said. "I am always accustomed to sleep after lunch if I have time."

"We are going to Chicote's bar," I said.

"Have they got good coffee there?"

"Excellent."

"Come on," he said. "Let's go."

I tried to give him some money when I left Madrid.

"I don't want anything from you," he said.

"No," I said. "Take it. Go on. Buy something for the family."

"No," he said. "Listen, we had a good time, didn't we?"

You can bet on Franco, or Mussolini, or Hitler, if you want. But my money goes on Hipolito.

A Man's Bound to Fight

BY

COLONEL JOHN W. THOMASON, JR.

THAT evening, deep in the gloomy Wilderness, a sulphurous yellow sunset filtering unearthly light through the raddled trees, Captain Praxiteles Swan returned heavily from an inspection of the Brigade lines—lines but half as long as they were that morning—and prepared to set his pickets out. He was Brigade outpost officer now. He had speech with a captured New Yorker, a medical officer, who, from his garments and his forearms, appeared to have been working in a slaughter-house.

"Why," said the surgeon, much discontented, borrowing a chew of tobacco, "don't you fellows get this over with? Win the war, or let us win it, and then we'll all go home. I've a practice, back home, that's going completely to hell—Oh, I have no patience with you. You hit our center this morning—kill Wadsworth—kill Alexander—kill any amount of small fry—drive us back on our wagons. Then you chop down on our left and roll us up like a blanket—give you my word, this is our Corps hospital, and old Hancock himself was right here speaking to me, a little while ago. It's my belief he left here to arrange return passage over the Rapidan! Then you let up on us. I tell you, my Southern friend, this sort of thing can't go on. It's silly. What made you stop?"

Praxiteles looked at him somberly. "Longstreet," he said, "Longstreet's shot. Last year it was Jackson. At Gettysburg it was Hood. It can't go on, you're right."

"Sho!" said the medical officer, and made clucking sounds with his tongue which might have been sympathy. "Too many good men getting killed, on both sides. Why don't you quit? We've all had a great sufficiency of this fighting. It don't seem to get us anywhere. Why, I was right in this very same neighborhood last year. And we've got a better man than Joe Hooker, now. What you fighting for, anyway?"

Praxiteles leaned on his saber—he was very tired. "Young man," he answered, slowly, "when I came up here, in '61, I had State's Rights on my mind. I never gave much thought to the politics of it. I'm a minister of the Gospel when I'm home. Now, I don't know. I hear the boys talk. Reckon, if we're fighting for anything, we're fighting for General Lee—"

From: *Lone Star Preacher*: Copyright 1941. Scribners.

He straightened up and put both hands on the hilt of his saber. His voice grew big in the shadow of the Wilderness.

"A man's bound to fight," he declared, "for what he believes in. He's bound to keep on fighting—that part of it's with him. But whether he wins or not—that's with God.

"I reckon we'll keep on fighting, while there's any of us left——"

Squadron Scramble!

BY

BYRON KENNERLY

AS TOLD TO GRAHAM BERRY

AFTER a week of being confined to the ground by bad weather, we were awakened one night by the blasts of high-explosive bombs and the "whap! whap!" percussion of antiaircraft fire. Our brick officers' quarters rocked and shook with the crescendo. This meant that the storms which had grounded the Nazis were breaking, that Jerry probably would be back during the daylight hours to make up for lost time, and that we would see action after a week of restless waiting.

The thunderous pounding stopped shortly after midnight and we snatched a bit of sleep.

An hour before dawn the batman brought in the cup of tea, now our "official" getting up drink. Luke climbed out of bed and we began the cumbersome ritual of getting into our flying togs.

I stuck my head out the window and discovered it wasn't cold enough for the fur-lined Irving suit. We dressed in thick silk teddy bears and fireproof sidkas. Pulling on our boots, into which we stuffed maps, and carrying helmets, Mae Wests and gloves and mittens, we headed downstairs for breakfast. We found most of the boys unusually voluble, keyed up at the prospect of action.

Breakfast done we hurried out into the approaching dawn to check the aircraft and to see if the bombing had harmed the airdrome. It hadn't, although my sergeant pilot informed me that a near-by dummy airfield, on which were four dummy planes made of old wooden boxes, had been blasted to bits.

As I crawled into the Hurricane's cockpit, my mechanic sang out his customary, "She's hot and ready, sir." Since Jerry was afraid to send over bomber formations during the day, I set the gunsights for thirty-two and one-half feet, the wing span of an Me. 109. We were more apt to run into them than any other type of Nazi aircraft.

Laying the parachute on the wing where it could be grabbed quickly, I hurried—you do everything in a hurry over here excepting the waiting—to the airdrome office and signed the "700 sheet," first making sure that every member of my ground crew had his name down. Luke and Flight Lieutenant B., the other two pilots of Red Section, signed up. B., as section leader, telephoned operations, "Red Section now in readiness."

We went into the dispersal hut; nothing to do but wait expectantly. For awhile the favorite between-flight diversion was teaching the British pilots how to shoot dice. They were too lucky so we dropped this game for dominoes or cards.

About two hours passed. Suddenly the long-expected metallic voice—the one we'd waited a week to hear—snapped over the Tannoy loud-speaker:

"Squadron ————, Red Section. Scramble!"

That was us! I caught Luke's triumphant grin as he jumped up. He and I ran out to our aircraft, pulling on helmets and gloves. I grabbed my 'chute and climbed into its harness. My big Merlin Rolls Royce motor already was ticking beautifully.

I got aboard and adjusted the Sutton harness, fastening it loosely so I could lean forward to fight off blackouts. I revved up the motor, holding the brakes on. Attaching the oxygen tube to the tank and plugging the radio cord to the R.T. set, I eased off the brakes.

Like a long-caged bird anxious for the sky's freedom, the big Hurricane rolled down the runway, gathering speed with each revolution of the propeller. Flipping the magneto switches to test them, I adjusted the propeller at full fine and set the carburetor boost. The motor was only about two-thirds open on the take-off. B. was ahead and Luke beside me. In a vic we hopped off, boosting the planes into a steep climb. Luke and I were concentrating so intensely on B.'s wing tips that he could have flown us into a mountain and we'd never have seen it.

B. called operations by its code name of the day, Battle Control, and reported we were air-borne.

Later operations asked, "Hello, Red Leader. Battle Control calling. Are you receiving me?"

"Hello, Battle Control, Red Leader answering. Receiving you loud and clear. Over."

"Hello, Red Leader. Vector 110. Is that understood?"

"Hello, Battle Control, Red Leader answering. Understand vector 110. Listening out."

Now we knew where we were going. We'd been circling for altitude until we got the vector. I set the compass at 110, which would bring us over the North Sea. We knew we'd been assigned to one of two jobs, either to patrol or to get a bomber that was preying on a convoy. These are the usual North Sea assignments.

At 9,000 feet a cloud bank swallowed us. It took us two minutes to reach it. Luke and I were flying very tight, our wing tips three feet back of and inside B.'s ailerons. You've got to fly this way in the soup or you'll lose one another. And a lone Hurricane is just a piece of cake for Jerry. In the last war, air battles consisted of spectacular two-plane dogfights. Today these are the exception. Most modern fighting is done in teams, and the R.A.F. has developed formation flying and combat teamwork to the highest degree of efficiency the world has ever known.

I felt a bumping and scraping. It was my wing tip touching B.'s wing. The thought of a crumpled wing was most unpleasant. Three times I'd found paint from his wing on mine. I moved back into position and turned the oxygen on.

At 14,000 feet we burst through the clouds into the bright world of the upper air, a world with fantastic cloud landscapes of cottony valleys and billowy mountains. The scene dazzled me. This was the battleground of the second World War. At 20,000 feet we leveled off. I was a little light-headed from the quick climb, although I had kept the oxygen intake at 5,000 feet ahead of the actual altitude. A dial shows the amount of oxygen you are taking in. The higher the altitude, the more oxygen you turn on.

No enemy aircraft were visible, But B. ordered the section into line astern. You never could tell when Jerry would come swarming out of the clouds. Luke and I swung our Hurricanes in a line behind B., Luke being in the "rear man Charley" spot, protecting our tails. Then the radio crackled:

"Hello, Red Leader. Battle Control calling. Are you receiving me?"

B. reported he was.

"Hello, Red Leader. Angels one zero. Bandit."

An enemy aircraft at 10,000 feet! It must be a prowler over the North Sea. Down we shot into the clouds again. I boosted the throttle and the Hurricane jumped ahead, keeping close behind B. I turned the safety catch on the firing button, snapped on the gunsight and looked over the instruments quickly, my subconscious mind doing most of the work. The motor was heating a bit, but there was no time to do anything about it. Since I had my gunsight adjusted for the wing span of an Me. 109, I knew I would have to reset it before making an attack. Apparently there was only one bandit, and it must be a bomber whose wing span might be double that of a Messerschmitt fighter.

We came under the clouds at 11,000 feet and leveled off. Better stay near the stratus until we sized up the situation. Below was a great slab of sea, with a ragged, dark coastline to the west. England. About twelve miles offshore were black streaks which resembled a stream of ants. They were ships in a convoy.

There! About five miles ahead and 3,000 feet below scooted a black bug. I squinted to make out what it was. It looked like a Dornier 17 heavy bomber, one of the nastiest aircraft to tackle. Manned by four or five men, it was heavily gunned and armored. I glanced up. There might be an escort of Messerschmitts just inside that sullen cloud curtain. No time for reconnoitering. We slanted toward the bomber—yes, it was a Dornier. We didn't want him to see us until we got closer. If only he took his time getting the range of the convoy, we could swoop down and nail him before he did any damage. I hoped none of the Spitfire boys were around to try and spoil our chase.

Suddenly the bomber dropped his nose in a steep dive toward the convoy. He must have spotted us and he wanted to get a vessel or two before going home. I saw the black cross on top of his starboard wing as he went into the plunge. His two big propellers glinted menacingly for a moment, like a wolf baring his teeth.

B. yelled, "Tallyho!" and dove after him. I followed pulling the teat, the auxiliary throttle that cut loose all 1,250 horsepower. We vaulted downstairs, our Merlins screaming. Just then the unhurried voice of operations reported over the radio: "Hello, Red Leader. Battle Control calling. You should be in vicinity of Tunbridge Wells and bandit." Tunbridge Wells, a small English town, was the code name for this convoy.

B. called, "Hello, Battle Control. Red Leader answering. We're chasing bandit!" Operations dropped his formal answer, merely saying, "Good luck."

It was a race now to see who got to the convoy first. The Dornier was away below us and was hard to see, being painted blue-gray, the color of the sea. The Germans had a tricky habit of camouflaging their planes for every special job. We were gaining fast. Suddenly my Hurricane rocked violently. It steaded and started rocking again. I spotted a puff of smoke from a vessel in the convoy. He was shooting at the bomber, but his anti-aircraft shells were bursting somewhere near us.

The firing stopped as the Dornier and we approached the long line of ships. The Dornier cut loose a whole stick of four bombs. He wasn't wasting his time aiming and I knew the bombs would fall wide. We were about three-quarters of a mile from him now. B. veered off from the direct chase, diving for the first freighters in the convoy, trying to cut the Dornier off from his prey. Seeing that we were too close, the Jerry banked away toward home, dropping his other bomb stick and an aerial torpedo to lighten his load. The bombs sent up harmless geysers of water a mile from the nearest freighter. The torpedo, I knew, broke when it hit the water after being dropped from 2,000 feet. We had won the first round. Now to get the Dornier. We banked after him.

He had dropped so close to the sea that it looked as if he would ram into it. He leveled off a scant twenty feet above the choppy waves, his starboard wing tip almost cutting the water as he turned directly toward his base. These Dorniers could move fast. Quickly I set the gunsight for a fifty-nine-foot wing span.

Close to the water the Dornier was a tough target. We couldn't dive on him or we would ram into the sea. The only attack to make was directly astern, trying to pick off the top turret gunner before he blasted us. Then we could get at the pilot.

We were closing in fast. He was less than a mile away. B. began leveling off and I hauled back a little on the stick, to stay astern of him. It was hard to pull against the 400-plus-mile-an-hour wind velocity. I could see the Dornier's gunner now in his plastic glass blister, his hands on his twin cannon triggers.

As we came gradually out of the dive, centrifugal force dragged on my body. My hands grew heavy and my jaw sagged. Mustn't black out! I took a deep breath and yelled—anything to build up blood pressure so the blood wouldn't leave my brain. Another danger presented itself. We were much too close to the water. If we ever hit the propeller backwash of the bomber, it would bounce us into the sea.

The German opened fire, smoke from his tracers looping up at B., who threw his Hurricane into a criss-cross to throw off the Jerry's aim. B. started firing; his tracer bullets showed he was firing into the blister. Then B. was past the gunner and it was my turn.

I moved the stick right, then left, and alternated foot pressure on the rudder to keep the gunner in the sights. I could even see his tense face. His lips were parted, his teeth clenched as he sawed his fire-spouting cannons back and forth. I pressed the firing button with my thumb, hurling explosives, ball, incendiary, armor-piercing, and tracer bullets at him. The noise was like muffled high-pitched drums and the plane vibrated and slowed from the recoil. The tracers' chemical smoke trails showed the fire sweeping under the Dornier.

Abandoning caution to get a more accurate aim, I stopped the criss-cross and nosed the Hurricane right at him. He was only about 100 yards away now. There was a loud pow! And a splintering sound, like hailstones on a drum. He must have hit me. But I couldn't see where. My bullets were streaming into his blister, tearing great rents in the plastic glass.

Just as I swept over him, he fell back, arms upraised. I slipped up and to the side. A black curtain dropped over my eyes as I came around, almost in a vertical bank. I eased the stick forward to come to, knowing that Luke was giving the pilot the works.

I glanced back to see Luke almost cutting off the Dornier's tail with his prop, he was flying so close to him. The bomber was still flying. We didn't get him on the first attack.

As I followed B. down for another attack I heard Luke yell over the radio, "Red Leader. Red Three calling. Bandits over the French Coast!" I looked to the east. Nine planes in three vics were coming toward us, one vic far in advance of the others. The Dornier must have radioed for help. The planes still were several miles away but it wouldn't take a minute for them to get here. We had to work fast.

B.'s Hurricane thundered down on the Dornier's tail. I saw two Germans dragging the gunner's body from his seat. They were going to replace him. If they succeeded in doing this before we got the pilot, the Dornier was as good as safe on its home airdrome. The pilot would be protected by the new rear gunner until the Jerry fighter planes arrived. B. dove low over the Dornier's tail and gave the pilot's cockpit a long burst, sliding up and to the side again. Before I could start firing, the Dornier's wings wiggled slightly, the nose dropped slowly. He smacked the water, sheets of spray exploding up from his fuselage. He bounced twice and settled on the choppy sea. B. got him that time. Soon he would sink.

Heading upstairs in a hurry after B., I spotted the first Jerry section of three aircraft slanting down to attack us. These aircraft were smaller than an Me. 109 and they were painted white. I had never seen them before. They must be the new, faster Heinkel 113 fighters we'd heard about.

I closed in behind B. and Luke was right on my tail. We were low on petrol and bullets and we had finished our job, so the better part of valor was to head for home quickly. Besides our planes had been damaged and might not be able to stand the terrific strain of combat. Below us the remainder of the Dornier crew launched a rubber life boat.

B. leveled off to gain speed and pointed for home. I followed, nearly deafened by the scream of air through the cowling where the cannon shell had penetrated, and by the shriek from the machine-gun mouths where the patches had been shot away.

The Jerries kept coming, so B. banked quickly and started circling. Now Jerry couldn't get on our tail because each one of us was protecting the other's tail. The three Heinkels veered away. They didn't like our circle.

"Red Two and Three, Red One calling. Maintain tight formation, line astern!"

As one Heinkel got a little below us, B. suddenly straightened out and dove for it. Luke and I were right behind him. B. got in a long burst. The two other Heinkels immediately dove for B. I picked one Jerry and Luke the other. I got in one quick burst of fire on my Heinkel's tail. Then it power-dived out of range. In fact all three Heinkels veered off and hurried away. We quickly reformed behind B. Apparently they weren't too anxious to tangle.

B. called Battle Control, got the response and announced, "Hello, Battle Control. Red Leader calling. Dornier 17 down. See pilots in rubber boat. Bandits in vicinity." Operations might send a launch or flying boat after them.

Luke and I both reported that our petrol was running low. Luke added that his port wing had been badly ripped. I hoped everything would hold together until we landed.

We left the sea and the Jerries, vowing to be back for them later, and started flying over England. Operations was vectoring us home. Although the countryside was honeycombed with airdromes, we couldn't spot one from up here. Clever artists had blended buildings, airdromes, and gun emplacements with paint and secret camouflaging materials to look like a checkerboard of innocent farm plots, separated by hedges. Operations informed us we were above our airdrome and we circled down over what looked like a pasture, with hedges and haystacks. At 800 feet we made out the runway. Circling the field, we lowered our landing gear and flaps and came in at 100 miles an hour for a power landing. We slid across the field and my wheels rumbled pleasantly on the runway as the plane settled down. We were back! The clock showed we'd been gone only forty minutes!

We taxied to our camouflaged, sandbagged hangars, where the ground crews greeted us with cheers. They had heard the shriek of wind through the gun ports. I felt let down and tired from nervous exhaustion. My hands were clammy and the helmet seemed very heavy and tight. There was much conversation as we climbed out and inspected the damage. The crews swarmed over the aircraft and found that all three planes bore marks of the fight. The shell that had burst in my ship struck just ahead of the hatch and not six inches from where my forehead had been pressed against the gunsight rest. A close call. The floor was filled with glass fragments. Luke and I were assigned new planes until ours were repaired.

After checking the new aircraft, we made out combat reports and notified operations that we were in readiness again. Then we returned to the dispersal hut to wait for something else to happen.

ONE afternoon as the gray light over the airdrome was thickening into dusk, Luke and I had just settled down to a typical friendly argument with a British pilot over the merits of various fighter planes when our talk was cut short by the loud speaker:

"Squadron ———, Red and Blue sections. Squadron ———, Green and White sections. Scramble!"

The Britisher smiled hopefully as he jumped up with, "Twelve of us going up. It's a big flap this time!" It had to be or they wouldn't risk sending us aloft so late in the day.

A dozen of us, six Americans and six Britishers, ran out to our aircraft. The Britishers were the Spitfire boys. I climbed into a new Hurricane. The motor on mine was being overhauled. I was a little dubious about the new plane, not knowing its little habits. Each aircraft has its own.

Both sections of the Spitfire squadron roared down the runway and the six planes took off as one. Those boys were beautiful formation flyers.

M., the leader of our flight, taxied out, the two aircraft in his section coming into a vic behind him. They took off and we followed immediately. In two tight vics, one right behind the other, we thundered upward into a cloud canopy which was made almost as black as night by coal smoke from factories. M.'s tail was directly under my propeller. It was so dark I couldn't see his wings.

On the radio I heard him get vectored to 270, operations adding, "Buster!" This meant step on it. M.'s tail drew away. I pulled the teat a little and came up close. Our planes were just inches apart. I felt a vibration. Must be Luke's wing tip up against mine. Visibility was too poor now for him to see me motion him back. A quick glance showed Luke's wing edging back a little. He had felt the impact too.

Operations called again, reporting, "Angels two five. Many, many bandits!"

Many enemy aircraft at 25,000 feet! The altimeter read 12,000 feet. I turned on the oxygen, spinning the dial to 17,000 feet.

I fervently hoped operations was vectoring us right. There were two balloon barrages in this vicinity and it would be just too bad if we got snagged in one. I wondered if my guns were hot enough to fire, if the rest of the boys in the formation were getting the right information, and understood it, and if the motor, this new motor I'd never tried out before, would respond to the big job required of it in combat. You don't actually worry about these things, but you can't help their flashing through your mind.

Suddenly we burst through the black cloud bank into the brilliance of the evening sky. The sun was almost resting on a crimson mattress. Admiration of the beauty about us was cut off by operations:

"Hello, Red Leader. Locust Control calling. Are you receiving me?"

"Hello, Locust Control. Red Leader answering. Receiving you loud and clear. Over," M. answered.

"Hello, Red Leader. Locust Control calling. Bandits five miles to port at angels two zero. Buster!"

We were flying at 22,000 feet. We didn't see them. They must be under that big ragged hole in the clouds. M. called for echelon starboard. Our Hurricanes moved into single file, each plane to the right of the plane in front. M. banked to the left and one after the other we followed.

There were the Jerries! Three swarms of black specks several thousand feet above. They were the Messerschmitt fighter convoys. They were always above us. I could just make them out. There must be fifty of them. But we were not looking for them. I glanced below as we roared over the big cloud rift. There was our quarry. Fifteen big murky green bombers. Junker 88's, flying in three stepped-up, line-astern formations. It was the toughest formation to attack because the bombers were flying in three groups, one above the other. In our dive we had to run the gantlet of cannon and machine-gun blasts from each level.

Far off in the golden mist I saw other clusters of planes. They must be over the English Channel. I couldn't tell whether they were German or British. Behind us were more planes. They were closer and camouflaged green and tan. They were Spitfires from some other airdrome, a welcome addition to the sky picture!

M. was angling for a beam attack. I set and turned on the gunsight, caught a glimpse of the reassuring glow and set the button in firing position. Striking down at the side of the bombers would give us the biggest target. Besides, the Ju.88's weren't armored there. There was a cool feeling in my stomach and my mouth got very dry. The dryness may have been caused by the oxygen. I was taking in deep breaths of it. There was a swarm of Messerschmitt 109's directly overhead, and following us like hawks stalking their prey. They wouldn't dive until we did. Then they would be on our tail in a flash. I could see in the gathering dusk the black crosses on the underside of their square-cut wings.

Suddenly M. waggled his wings and peeled off, zooming down in a sixty-degree power dive with a "Tallyho!" Number two and number three followed screaming after him. I pulled the teat wide open and shoved the stick from me. The Hurricane jumped ahead and shrieked downstairs.

The three Hurricanes on front broke formation and leveled off, each picking a separate target. I came out of my dive and got a bomber in the sights, the front Jerry in the middle formation. We must pick off the front bombers, for in one of them was the flight leader. If we got him, the rest of the formation would turn for home. But so long as he was still in action, they would keep right on to their objective.

Over the whining crescendo of airplane motors I heard in the earphones a "Yipee! Hi—Yoooo-oo!" It was one of our boys giving his cowboy battle yell. He had forgotten and left his radio on send, so we heard him.

As we roared in on them, the bombers didn't try to get out of the way. I was watching for some evasive action to throw our aim off. My target loomed larger and larger in the sights as I started rolling over. His murky camouflaging almost blended with the darkness. My thumb was itching to press the firing button. But he was still too far away. Smoke trails poured from the bomber as the gunner opened fire at me.

The stick vibrated in my hand. Bullets from somewhere were cutting into an aileron. I could tell this because the vibration was a sideways motion. It couldn't be from a bomber below. I wasn't in range yet. The rear-view mirror showed a Messerschmitt fighter on my tail. But he was too far off to hit me. The jerking stopped. The bullets must have come from the top formation of bombers. They were almost overhead.

No time to investigate. My target was only 350 yards away. My thumb squeezed down on the firing button. Tracer smoke showed the bullets falling short and too far ahead of the pilot's cabin. I tried to pull her nose in on the target. The Hurricane responded sluggishly. From the way her starboard wing dragged I knew it was the aileron on that wing that was damaged. Probably the fabric had been shot off. I tried to keep the gunsight just ahead of his nose so the pilot would run into the hail of death. I gave him another burst. There! The tracer smoke poured into the pilot's plastic cabin. I bore down on the trigger as if trying to force more bullets into him. As I pulled down and rocketed upside down across the bomber's belly, it started to roll over. That meant I had probably got him!

As the Hurricane started into the break-away, I caught sight of two Messerschmitts on my tail. I gazed a split second too long into the rear-vision mirror. The Hurricane was roaring directly at another bomber. I hadn't spotted it in the gloom. I gave it one quick, wicked burst at almost point-blank range as the Hurricane dropped away in a sickening dive.

Just as I felt the blood draining from my head I heard a "pow"! A cannon shell from the bomber ripped through the hatch just above my head, showering the cockpit with glass and miniature shrapnel fragments. Wind whistled in the cockpit and I had to drop my head far forward so that my helmet wouldn't get ripped off by the blast.

My head and shoulders were getting unbearably heavy. Centrifugal force pulled my jaw down. Even the chin strap couldn't keep it up. I groaned trying to take a deep breath. My eyelids became too heavy to keep open and consciousness faded away.

When I came to a few seconds later there were several screaming, diving planes around. There went a Spitfire in flames. The letters on the fuselage identified it as Hank, one of the English boys at our airdrome. Poor devil! No time for mourning now, though. It may be my turn next.

As I pulled gradually out of the dive, two streamers of fire whipped past the starboard wing. Tracers from a Messerschmitt! I had almost forgotten them. In fact, I thought my 7,000-foot dive would have carried me far away from their guns. Yes, one of them was right behind, his guns blinking like lights. There was just enough daylight left for him to see me if he was close. And he was much too close. I banked over in a tight turn. He was right after me. I twisted and writhed, but Jerry wouldn't shake loose. His bullets thrummed a tattoo somewhere on the fuselage. If an incendiary bullet started to work, it was all over. The Hurricane responded to the controls slowly because of the ruined aileron. That was why Jerry could follow me.

Only one thing was left to do—go into a spin. With the aileron damaged, the Hurricane might not come out of it, but it would be a lot better to take that chance than to sit still and get shot in the back. I gunned the throttle and jerked the stick toward me. Instantly the lift on the wings was gone. The Hurricane stalled at nearly 300 miles an hour and whipped over and down in a shrieking spin. Consciousness again left me, but I knew Jerry had zoomed past overhead.

As I began to come to it seemed as if a dozen huge propellers were spinning in my head. I shook my head to throw off the nauseating sensation and took a deep breath of oxygen. As my vision cleared, I realized that the ship was still spinning. The altimeter read 3,000 feet. I'd have to bring her out of it fast. Wondering if the bad aileron would let her come out, I shoved the stick forward and reversed the controls. Nothing happened. The altimeter showed 2,500 feet. The Hurricane was dropping at a little more than 200 miles an hour, the speedometer indicated, the spin having slowed her down.

Still holding the stick over, I grabbed for the hatch with my left hand and tried to jerk it back. It was time to jump. In an awful instant, I realized the cannon shell had jammed the hatch. Clenching my teeth and trying to swallow a panicky emotion that kept welling up in my throat, I shoved the throttle, opening it wide, and pulled the teat. It was kill or cure this time. The plane gathered speed.

Slowly—and I could hardly believe it—the controls grew firm and the spin slowed. Then it stopped as the speedometer needle climbed to 250 M.P.H.,—275—300. Quickly I eased the throttle and brought the stick back slowly on the left side. I must keep the starboard wing up. If she dove again it would be my last ride. I didn't even know if I were coming out of this dive before ramming into the ground.

The altimeter read a scant 800 feet. I was flying entirely by instruments now as it was dark everywhere except for the glowing instrument panel.

At 300 feet the Hurricane leveled off and I gasped a deep breath, lifting my head a little to let the air blast cool it. Snapping the radio switch to send, I called operations, asking for an emergency homing. I flipped the key to receive and listened, wondering whether the radio still worked. It did! The steady, unruffled voice of operations ordered:

"Talk for ten seconds."

This was to enable operations to get a bearing on me. I mumbled something into the mike, hardly aware of what it was. Then there was silence except for the roar of the motor and the wind screaming through the hatch and gun mouths.

It seemed hours, but in reality it was about fifty seconds when operations notified that I was over an airdrome. There was nothing but blackness below as I banked the Hurricane carefully in a descending turn. As the altimeter dropped below the 1,500-foot mark, a red-and-white Very rocket shot up from somewhere beneath. A welcome sight, these colors of the day! On a telegraph key I tapped out in Morse code "A" and "T," the letters of the day. The dots and dashes blinked from the amber light under my plane—that is, if they hadn't been shot off.

Apparently they hadn't for almost immediately a row of dim lights flashed on, marking the runway of the airdrome. By their yellow color I knew the lights were oil pots. This meant there was a ground haze, oil lights penetrating it better than electric lamps. Inexperienced pilots sometimes try to land on this haze—which hugs the ground to a depth of about four feet—because the top of it looks like the ground surface.

I lowered the landing wheels and flaps and nosed the Hurricane down, keeping the starboard wing up slightly. The plane slanted to the border of the runway and I edged her through the thick haze at 100 miles an hour. She hit the ground with the port wheel, bounced up, slid through the air a moment, then settled down on the runway. I shoved gently on the brakes and she eased to a stop. Suddenly I felt very much all in.

The duty pilot and a crew of mechanics and armorers raced up to take the ship over. They pried open the badly damaged hatch and informed me that I was fifteen miles from the home airdrome. Her starboard aileron was more than half gone, part of the rudder had been shot away, three control wires were badly frayed, the cowling was smashed in near the hatch, and there were innumerable bullet holes through the fuselage and wings. Still she brought me in safely. That's a Hurricane for you!

After telephoning home, I climbed into a truck and spent a bumpy half-hour before reaching our officers' lounge. I arrived in time for a victory celebration. Pilots from our airdrome had brought down two bombers sure and one probable, as well as two fighters. The only one not there to help with the festivities was Hank. We drank a toast to his memory.

Later that night in our room Luke took Hank's photograph off the wall.

"Guess we'd better put him away until after the war," Luke said, placing the picture in his suitcase. Then he added, "This is one more casualty that is going to cost Jerry plenty!"

We solemnly shook hands on it.

A Name and a Flag

BY

COLONEL JOHN W. THOMASON, JR.

It is one of the last stories they tell of Praxiteles Swan, and of the Texas Brigade in the Army of Northern Virginia—how he went with Major Howdy Martin to beard Mr. Jefferson Davis in his private cabinet over a matter that was important to them, in the last dark winter of the Confederate War. If you are diligent in business, Praxiteles used to remark, you stand before Kings—you do not stand before mean men. And Jefferson Davis was as near a King as the Confederacy could afford.

Praxiteles used to comment, when the old folks talked of the war and why we lost it, that he felt Jeff Davis did the best he could—as well as anybody, and better than most. Certainly, on the one occasion he, Praxiteles, had reason to confer with the President, Mr. Davis was remarkably sensible in his judgments.

For it fell out, about Christmastime of '64, that a rumor not of Yankee issue came to vex the shrunken gray regiments that stood between Grant and Richmond. Longstreet's Corps held the north side of the James; A. P. Hill covered Petersburg, and the II Corps was distributed, some with Gordon in the lines, others towards the Valley under Jubal Early. There were many indications that the war was running down—but the men in the miserable, sodden trenches, and in the bleak hutments behind them, took very little interest in such matters. They were preoccupied with professional military details, and with the problem of keeping alive. They maintained a desultory bickering with equally uncomfortable blue formations over against them, and foraged desperately to supplement the slender rations, and remained tough-minded and generally cheerful throughout. Let the politicians worry about the rest of it, was their word. An astonishingly large number of private letters from the front, that last bleak winter, shine with a persistent hopefulness; indicate, also, oyster roasts and occasional turkeys. They did not starve and they did not despair. The Yankee excursions in the West, deep thinkers among them asserted, had over-extended the Federal resources. Come spring, they'd better look to themselves! It is always that way in war; the people at the point of contact take the most cheerful view. The people beind the lines are the first to cry havoc and the first to cry for peace. Of course there were desertions—an appalling number of desertions. Some pretty good men were quitting; and

From: *Lone Star Preacher*. Copyright 1941. Scribners.

the folks back home—even the preachers and the women—appeared to have the blues. But on the line, the word the Texas troops were really grieved to hear dealt with a projected reorganization of the army.

The basis of the Provisional Army of the Confederate States was the old militia structure. From this came most of the volunteer regiments and brigades which fought the opening actions. The orders of battle about the time of 1st Manassas listed brigades and divisions by number, and regiments after their state designations. But the Confederate soldier was an individual, distrustful of anything that smacked of regimentation; jealous and ardent for his sectional ties; and peculiarly susceptible to leadership. Thus, by the end of 1861, brigades were generally known by the names of their brigadiers, and their states; and divisions, then and afterwards, were named for their generals; and this applied even to Corps. The names of their armies were officially regional. The Confederate service was a personal service. The 1st Virginia Brigade, for instance, glorious at First Manassas, and on other fields, was never anything but the Stonewall brigade. There were Benning's Georgians and Law's Alabamians, and Pickett's Division was so designated; and I Corps was Longstreet's Corps—and your old men always said "Lee's Army." After the formation of the permanent Confederate government, and the adoption of a consistent military policy, in 1862, with conscription as its leading feature, the Provisional Army created very few new regiments or brigades. Late volunteers and conscripts alike went into existing formations; and this was the foundation for Confederate excellence in battle. Each regiment of soldiers had a solid core of veterans, with traditions and *esprit* to match. The pride they had in themselves was something fierce and alive, unflagging to the end.

But, as the old stock was ground away between the millstones of war, and as the replacement material in the depots dwindled and failed, the numbers and strengths in the units under arms faded also. Regiments, that bleak winter of '64, fell to 100 men or so—300 or 400 rifles made an unusually strong brigade. A division order of battle might, and usually did, list five brigades, yet muster no more in actual fighting strength than two Northern regiments. Operations officers and clerks alike made moan; and the War Department, dreamily pondering academic details, busied itself with the drafting of an order that would abolish at once the annoying sectional and personal designations, do away with these high-stomached corporals' guards masquerading as combat units, and regroup officers and men into actual, rather than skeleton, organizations.

It was the rumor of this impending anonymity which struck fire in the camps of the 400 odd veterans of Hood's old Texas Brigade. They had every proper sentiment of respect and affection for their companions in arms out of Virginia, the Carolinas, Tennessee, and the Gulf States. But Texas, by God, was something else again. Officers and men took council together, over a score of smoky campfires; and determined on measures. They would make a protest. It was felt that their spokesmen should be persons of loud voice and imposing presence, worthy of the Brigade in bearing as well as in combat background. It was felt that they should have enough rank to brush aside slick young aides-de-camp and door-keepers, yet not enough seniority to make them timid before higher authority. It was decided, in brief, that Major Howdy Martin and Captain Praxiteles Swan, veterans of every battle from Elthan's Landing to the Darbytown Road, both of them humble before God, and brash in every other relation, were ideal representatives. The two officers said they'd take the job. They made ready to go to Richmond, and present the matter to the Secretary of War, and, if necessary, to the President.

The old men who told this tale a lifetime afterwards still chuckled when they desribed the grooming and titivating which the Major and the Elder underwent for the occasion. Uniforms had become mighty shabby on the Northside lines, and the Richmond merchants had no stocks to replenish a man's outfit. Howdy Martin went unabashed in a skin-tight pair of Yankee-blue trousers, taken from a miraculous Yankee quartermaster who had been in life almost as big as the Major. Some large officer loaned a uniform coat which, after a little stretching at the shoulder seams, would serve. It was simple to sew a major's star on the collar; and Howdy's winter beard made a shirt quite unnecessary. His boots were a difficulty; they were cracked and broken so that his toes showed—but nothing could be done about boots, and his feet were too big for any Yankee's they captured, a fact regretfully conceded and accepted; although the pickets went out after dark two nights, and brought in specimens. His hat, a slant-brimmed Kilpatrick, was on the small side, but his brass-mounted dragoon revolvers, one on each hip, and his long cavalry saber, were sufficiently imposing; and once a man saw his adventurous nose jutting from his great beard, and his bright hard eyes, deep-set under bushy brows, and the whole confident frontier strut of the man, the details didn't matter.

Praxiteles, who wore a good coat all his life, and good boots, was in better case, but not much better. The crude darning showed painfully over his right hip and inside his right sleeve, where his pistol holster had worn away the cloth, and low on his left hip where saber slings had chafed. His breeches were frankly patched at knee and seat; good, weather-tight patches, but unsightly. However, his leather and his weapons were fine and bright, and you had to look close to see that his beaver was broken about the crown. Somebody loaned him a clean paper collar, and, as regimental officers went in that army, he considered himself well turned out. Secretly, he conceded that this was important to him. Old Howdy didn't care—but Praxiteles Swan cared, and made himself as smart as he could in any company.

The Brigade Commander, who was the senior Colonel—John Gregg, dead on the Darbytown Road, not having been replaced, and never would be— said, dubiously, he reckoned they could go, and sent them on to Division Headquarters. Major General Field, a meticulous administrator, disapproved, but forwarded the request to Longstreet, at I Corps. Longstreet, the old regular, said, "No, not by a damn sight—" No officer or man from his corps was going to a higher echelon with a complaint against orders, actual or impending. Orders were orders, he told them severely. The Articles of War were explicit on the circulation of petitions. Such procedure smacked of mutiny. Longstreet could be mighty severe on subjects like that.

But Longstreet knew his Texans; and he had not forgotten how meanly his couriers were treated by the Richmond war lords; the chosen valiant men in whose hands he sent the captured battleflags of Chickamauga to the President, after that hard battle. The story was, not even an adjutant met them at the depot; Winder's military police harassed them; the Yankee standards were carried through the streets of the capital in a dray, behind a Negro and a mule, and slung into the corner of an office. The War Department found no time for Longstreet's orphans, at all. This the general considered briefly; then held up a hand to check the outburst he saw gathering in Praxiteles Swan's angry eye, and behind Major Howdy Martin's purpled face.

"Of course," he added, "if you two gentlemen wish a brief season of refreshment in Richmond after labor—why, the front's right quiet now. Your services are very well known to me. Why don't you take a little furlough in town? And if you should chance to meet Mr. Secretary of War—whoever he is at the moment—in the Ballard House bar; or encounter Mr. President Davis in a social way—why any Southern officer has the right to state his private views, in any company. And if you choose to discuss professional matters—your blood be on your own shirt fronts! Major Goree, see about their passes—and before they go out into this weather, remember, Major, it's confoundedly cold."—There was a warm humanity about old Longstreet, Praxiteles always said. They mounted their horses and rode some miles to Richmond, in time for a latish dinner, for which Howdy Martin paid with a 100-dollar Confederate bill, and gave the waiter the change. Money was mighty low: the more you had, the less it seemed to be worth. Their coattail pockets were full of it.

Encouraged by what Howdy Martin described as ample vittles, they discussed ways and means. They could go to the office of the adviser to the President, General Bragg; but they didn't like what they knew of Bragg: no nourishment there, Praxiteles thought. They could go to the Adjutant General, Cooper; but he was a terrible fellow for orders, everybody said. And the Secretary of War, of course. But the President was over them all; and when you came right down to it, he ran the army. Everybody knew that. "Why bother with the spoon-vittles?" asked Howdy Martin. "Elder, let's go right for the meat. Minnows air safe—we air out after whales!" Praxiteles agreed that this was horse sense. They walked the few blocks to the gloomy house where the President had his offices. The streets were empty, and the December sky was low and dark. Nobody was outside who didn't have to be. It was coming on to sleet, and the short winter day was drawing in. At the Confederate White House the sentry, tramping the sidewalk briskly to avoid freezing on his beat, kept his hands in his armpits and his piece under his arm; a length of old shawl was tied around his ears and his wrists were blue with cold. He started to unjoint himself for ceremony, but Praxiteles stopped him— "Ne' mind Son. We'll just go in"— A mournful Negro doorman, in white gloves and a swallowtail, admitted them. A smart young staff officer, passing through the hall, raised his brows at them and would have let it go at that, but they loomed enormous in the dim light, and their eyes held him.

"Well, gentlemen? Major Martin? Captain Swan? Texas Brigade? Oh yes, those cotton states fellows. See the President? See Mr. Jefferson Davis? You have—haven't an appointment?" The staff officer said he'd never heard of such a thing. He leaned against the wall, shaken. He managed to convey that Mr. Jefferson Davis was mighty busy—a mighty busy man these days. Only saw folks by appointment.

"He'll see us," said Howdy Martin. "We've come in from the Northside, in all this weather——"

"We're grieved to discommode him," began Praxiteles Swan. "But there's a little matter"—his voice began to rise.

"Whar's his room?" demanded Howdy Martin, in his battle-pitch. The officer was visibly distressed. "Not so loud—please, gentlemen! I'll speak to Colonel——"

"You'll speak to nobody! Whar's his room?"

"If you'll just be patient, gentlemen! I'll arrange—here; this way." He led them upstairs, to the second floor. There was a hall, and chairs and sofas along it; men in fine civilian broadcloth, with papers in green-baize bags, and sleek men in uniform, half a dozen or so, occupied the seats. They eyed the two rough soldiers with distaste. The young aide slipped away. The Texans looked at each other. Which door? Howdy insisted. But there were four doors, and all of them closed.

Praxiteles Swan took thought, and his temper abated. He had waited in the anterooms of the great, in that other existence of his, more than Major Howdy Martin had waited.

"No sense," he said, mildly, "in bulling into this. I reckon Mr. Davis has a lot on his mind. We can wait a spell——"

"Don't want to wait," said Howdy. "I'm riled up now—I caint express myself now the way the boys would like me to. Did I sit here in this crib, an' all these nice folks around with little shoes on their feet, an' clean paper collars—why, Elder, the strength will go right out of me. I tell you, I'm——"

A door opened, the door facing them. A medium-sized general, with a bluish, bilious face, bushy eyebrows, and irascible dark eyes, came out, stuffing papers into his pockets. He looked at them without seeing them, or the other people who got to their feet for him. "General Bragg," said Praxiteles—"saw him after Chickamauga."— Howdy Martin, his saber clanking loudly, was across the hall in three long strides, and through the door. Praxiteles followed him, as duty bound, but he didn't like it. He didn't like it. There was this matter of the fitness of things— He closed the door gently behind him.

There were three men around a desk. Lamps bathed the room in yellow light. Already the day was gone, outside the windows. Behind the desk, erect, slender, and with a dignity that made you forget his medium stature —he could have stood up straight under Praxiteles' arm—Mr. Jefferson Davis, President of the Confederate States, looked coldly upon these intruders. A dapper civilian, that would be Burton Harrison, straightened up from some papers, and gave them quizzical regard, his head tilted to one side. A tall officer with the yellow collar and cuffs of the cavalry, a handsome, bearded man with a bearing hauntingly familiar, took a step towards them.

Praxiteles Swan, watching the President's austere, high-nosed face, tried to recall a thing remembered from long ago——

Spring of 1861. The sandy road through the pines and the sweetgums, from Huntsville to Montgomery. Riding down that road to join the war— riding with old General Sam Houston. And the general said, in that blunt voice of his, "I'll tell you about Jeff Davis. Cold-blooded as a lizard, proud as Lucifer—what he touches will not prosper—" Sam Houston knew his man. The war wasn't prospering—the maps on the desk were maps of Wilmington, last open port of the Confederacy—of Cape Fear River and Fort Fisher. But, Praxiteles conceded, this man was not defeated. There were plenty of officials in high places who were beaten now. But not Mr. Jefferson Davis. The man was tempered steel—whether you admired his judgment or not. You could kill such people; you couldn't defeat them. Months afterwards, when Praxiteles heard that Davis had been captured in flight, he needed nobody to tell him that Davis was going west in the hope that he would find enough men of his own hard fiber, to keep on fighting.

All this went through Praxiteles' head, while Mr. Davis spoke. His voice was thin and keen, and cold as the wind outside.

"Officers having business here are usually announced," he informed them. "To what urgency do I owe this honor?" The timbre of the voice raised the hackles on Praxiteles' neck. Howdy Martin planted his feet, squared his great shoulders, and inflated his chest.

"Mr. President, I'll make myself known. I'm Major Martin, of Hood's Texas Brigade. This here is Elder—Captain Swan, of that same command. Mr. President, I'll make a long story short, as the fellow says. The boys out on the Northside, in the lines, hev been told a tale that they don't understand. They hev heard tell of something that bothers them. Mr. President, they hev kind of deputized me, an' the Elder—Captain, there— me not bein' a man of smooth speech, as the Good Book puts it—to come in here and find out about it."

A faint shadow of expression, gone as quickly as it showed, flicked across the President's face. Behind his icy front, he had a certain feeling for combat soldiers—wanted, he said always, to serve in the field himself. "What is it, Major," he inquired, "that has thus upset my Texans? If it is properly a matter for my attention——"

"Mr. President, I'll tell you—if it ain't for your attention, I don't know whose attention it's for. They tell us, Seh, in ouah camp, that the War Department is getting ready to issue an order, to take away our state names—to break us up, and mix us around, and to number us, by regiments an' brigades an' divisions, like any bunch of conscripts brought in by a posse!

"Mr. President, the Texas Brigade come up here in the summer of 1861. Right after Manassas. We popped our first caps at Elthan's Landing. We was the boys that broke the line at Gaines's Mill. Second Manassas, Mr. President!" (The windows rattled and the lamps flickered.) "Sharpsburg— you slick civilian, there, did you ever hear tell of the cornfield at Sharpsburg? Fredericksburg! Gettysburg! Chickamauga! The Wilderness! An' Spottsylvania. Cold Harbor! An' the Darbytown Road! I tell you, Mr. President, we have left our dead on every field this army has fought—from the James River up into Pennsylvania—an' as far west as north Georgia! And outside of a few boys who straggled too far forward at Gettysburg, we have buried our dead ourselves!" (This was important to soldiers—it meant, you held your ground.) "We have our battle flags that our women gave us—Mr. President"—he was terribly passionate—"they air Texas Flags. Texas ladies made them. Texas boys have fought under them. Those names I named you, they air on those flags. Will you take 'em away from us, an' give us a number in place of them? And a number in place of our Texas name?

"Mr. President, we Texicans have obeyed orders. We aim to keep on fighting while the war lasts. But Mr. President, we air the Texas Brigade, an' so we will remain——"

He stopped talking and the silence fairly thundered. Then Praxiteles added quietly—"That's what the boys wanted you to know, Mr. President. Our minds air made up." It was like the still small voice after the hurricane.

Jefferson Davis was moved—only his aides knew how much. He was not a man who showed emotion. Now he said: "Major Martin. Captain Swan. The details of Army Administration would not interest you. It is your good fortune, sirs, that you need take the soldier's view, only. But you may return to your men, out there, and tell them for me: So long as there are any of them alive to carry their state colors, they will be known as Texans, of the Texas regiments, of Hood's Texas Brigade.

"Now, Major Martin—Captain Swan—it has been a pleasure to receive you here. But I am not master of my own time—" He took their hands, first the Major's, then the Captain's. He bowed formally; his hand was thin and cold, with a nervous strength. And the tall Cavalry General, who said his name was Custis Lee, showed them to the door.

The two, in the sleety night, found nothing to say to each other. They thought they might as well go on back to the command. They got their horses from the livery stable. The sleet had changed to a wet snow, driven on a bitter wind. The widely spaced street lights were blanketed, and made luminous yellow spheres of radiance, that gave no light at all. The horses' hooves were muffled on the road. They seemed, to themselves, riding with their heads bent against the wind, the last lonely souls in a world of cold and sleep.

They came to a crossroads where all directions looked the same. "Which road, Elder, which road?" asked Major Martin impatiently. "I'm kind of turned around."

Praxiteles lifted his beard from his chest and answered, out of a dark dream. "Either road will take us where we're going. It don't matter now— Same distance and no choice——"

Off to the west and south the rain was falling through the naked boughs of tall trees that stood gaunt around a place called Appomattox.

A Personal View of Waterloo

BY

STENDHAL

That day the army, which had just won the battle of Ligny, was marching straight on Brussels. It was the eve of the battle of Waterloo. Towards midday, the rain still continuing to fall in torrents, Fabrizio heard the sound of the guns; this joy made him completely oblivious of the fearful moments of despair in which so unjust an imprisonment had plunged him. He rode on until late at night, and, as he was beginning to have a little common sense, went to seek shelter in a peasant's house a long way from the road. This peasant wept and pretended that everything had been taken from him; Fabrizio gave him a crown, and he found some barley. "My horse is no beauty," Fabrizio said to himself, "but that makes no difference, he may easily take the fancy of some *adjudant*," and he went to lie down in the stable by its side. An hour before dawn Fabrizio was on the road, and, by copious endearments, succeeded in making his horse trot. About five o'clock, he heard the cannonade: it was the preliminaries of Waterloo.

Fabrizio soon came upon some *vivandières,* and the extreme gratitude that he felt for the gaoler's wife of B—— impelled him to address them; he asked one of them where he would find the 4th Hussar Regiment, to which he belonged.

"You would do just as well not to be in such a hurry, young soldier," said the *cantinière,* touched by Fabrizio's pallor and glowing eyes. "Your wrist is not strong enough yet for the sabre-thrusts they'll be giving to-day. If you had a musket, I don't say, maybe you could let off your round as well as any of them."

This advice displeased Fabrizio; but however much he urged on his horse, he could go no faster than the *cantinière* in her cart. Every now and then the sound of the guns seemed to come nearer and prevented them from hearing each other speak, for Fabrizio was so beside himself with enthusiasm and delight that he had renewed the conversation. Every word uttered by the *cantinière* intensified his happiness by making him understand it. With the exception of his real name and his escape from prison, he ended by confiding everything to this woman who seemed such a good soul. She was greatly surprised and understood nothing at all of what this handsome young soldier was telling her.

"I see what it is," she exclaimed at length with an air of triumph. "You're

From: *Le Chartreuse de Parme.*

a young gentleman who has fallen in love with the wife of some captain in the 4th Hussars. Your mistress will have made you a present of the uniform you're wearing, and you're going after her. As sure as God's in heaven, you've never been a soldier; but, like the brave boy you are, seeing your regiment's under fire, you want to be there too, and not let them think you a chicken."

Fabrizio agreed with everything; it was his only way of procuring good advice. "I know nothing of the ways of these French people," he said to himself, "and if I am not guided by someone I shall find myself being put in prison again, and they'll steal my horse."

"First of all, my boy," said the *cantinière,* who was becoming more and more of a friend to him, "confess that you're not one-and-twenty: at the very most you might be seventeen."

This was the truth, and Fabrizio admitted as much with good grace.

"Then, you aren't even a conscript; it's simply because of Madame's pretty face that you're going to get your bones broken. Plague it, she can't be particular. If you've still got some of the *yellow-boys* she sent you, you must first of all buy yourself another horse; look how your screw pricks up his ears when the guns sound at all near; that's a peasant's horse, and will be the death of you as soon as you reach the line. That white smoke you see over there above the hedge, that's the infantry firing, my boy. So prepare for a fine fright when you hear the bullets whistling over you. You'll do as well to eat a bit while there's still time."

Fabrizio followed this advice and, presenting a napoleon to the *vivandière,* asked her to accept payment.

"It makes one weep to see him!" cried the woman; "the poor child doesn't even know how to spend his money! It would be no more than you deserve if I pocketed your napoleon and put Cocotte into a trot; damned if your screw could catch me up. What would you do, stupid, if you saw me go off? Bear in mind, when the *brute* growls, never to show your gold. Here," she went on, "here's 18 francs, 50 centimes, and your breakfast costs you 30 sous. Now, we shall soon have some horses for sale. If the beast is a small one, you'll give ten francs, and, in any case, never more than twenty, not if it was the horse of the Four Sons of Aymon."

The meal finished, the *vivandière,* who was still haranguing, was interrupted by a woman who had come across the fields and passed them on the road.

"Hallo there, hi!" this woman shouted. "Hallo, Margot! Your 6th Light are over there on the right."

"I must leave you, my boy," said the *vivandière* to our hero; "but really and truly I pity you; I've taken quite a fancy to you, upon my word I have. You don't know a thing about anything, you're going to get a wipe in the eye, as sure as God's in heaven! Come along to the 6th Light with me."

"I quite understand that I know nothing," Fabrizio told her, "but I want to fight, and I'm determined to go over there towards that white smoke."

"Look how your horse is twitching his ears! As soon as he gets over there, even if he's no strength left, he'll take the bit in his teeth and start galloping, and heaven only knows where he'll land you. Will you listen to me now? As soon as you get to the troops, pick up a musket and a cartridge pouch, get down among the men and copy what you see them do, exactly the same: But, good heavens, I'll bet you don't even know how to open a cartridge."

Fabrizio, stung to the quick, admitted nevertheless to his new friend that she had guessed aright.

"Poor boy!" He'll be killed straight away; sure as God! It won't take long. You've got to come with me, absolutely," went on the *cantinière* in a tone of authority.

"But I want to fight."

"You shall fight too; why, the 6th Light are famous fighters, and there's fighting enough to-day for everyone."

"But shall we come soon to the regiment?"

"In a quarter of an hour at the most."

"With this honest woman's recommendations," Fabrizio told himself, "my ignorance of everything won't make them take me for a spy, and I shall have a chance of fighting." At this moment the noise of the guns redoubled, each explosion coming straight on top of the last. "It's like a Rosary," said Fabrizio.

"We're beginning to hear the infantry fire now," said the *vivandière*, whipping up her little horse, which seemed quite excited by the firing.

The *cantinière* turned to the right and took a side road that ran through the fields; there was a foot of mud in it; the little cart seemed about to be stuck fast: Fabrizio pushed the wheel. His horse fell twice; presently the road, though with less water on it, was nothing more than a bridle path through the grass. Fabrizio had not gone five hundred yards when his nag stopped short: it was a corpse, lying across the path, which terrified horse and rider alike.

Fabrizio's face, pale enough by nature, assumed a markedly green tinge; the *cantinière,* after looking at the dead man, said, as though speaking to herself: "That's not one of our Division." Then, raising her eyes to our hero, she burst out laughing.

"Aha, my boy! There's a titbit for you!" Fabrizio sat frozen. What struck him most of all was the dirtiness of the feet of this corpse which had already been stripped of its shoes and left with nothing but an old pair of trousers all clotted with blood.

"Come nearer," the *cantinière* ordered him, "get off your horse, you'll have to get accustomed to them; look," she cried, "he's stopped one in the head."

A bullet, entering on one side of the nose, had gone out at the opposite temple, and disfigured the corpse in a hideous fashion. It lay with one eye still open.

"Get off your horse then, lad," said the *cantinière,* "and give him a shake of the hand to see if he'll return it."

Without hesitation, although ready to yield up his soul with disgust, Fabrizio flung himself from his horse and took the hand of the corpse which he shook vigorously; then he stood still as though paralyzed. He felt that he had not the strength to mount again. What horrified him more than anything was that open eye.

"The *vivandière* will think me a coward," he said to himself bitterly. But he felt the impossibility of making any movement; he would have fallen. It was a frightful moment; Fabrizio was on the point of being physically sick. The *vivandière* noticed this, jumped lightly down from her little carriage, and held out to him, without saying a word, a glass of brandy which he swallowed at a gulp; he was able to mount his screw, and continued on his way without speaking. The *vivandière* looked at him now and again from the corner of her eye.

"You shall fight to-morrow, my boy," she said at length; "to-day you're going to stop with me. You can see now that you've got to learn the business before you can become a soldier."

"On the contrary, I want to start fighting at once," exclaimed our hero with a sombre air which seemed to the *vivandière* to augur well. The noise of the guns grew twice as loud and seemed to be coming nearer. The explosions began to form a continuous bass; there was no interval between one and the next, and above this running bass, which suggested the roar of a torrent in the distance, they could make out quite plainly the rattle of musketry.

At this point the road dived down into a clump of trees. The *vivandière* saw three or four soldiers of our army who were coming towards her as fast as their legs would carry them; she jumped nimbly down from her cart and ran into cover fifteen or twenty paces from the road. She hid herself in a hole which had been left where a big tree had recently been uprooted. "Now," thought Fabrizio, "we shall see whether I am a coward!" He stopped by the side of the little cart which the woman had abandoned, and drew his sabre. The soldiers paid no attention to him and passed at a run along the wood, to the left of the road.

"They're ours," said the *vivandière* calmly, as she came back, quite breathless, to her little cart. . . . "If your horse was capable of galloping, I should say: push ahead as far as the end of the wood, and see if there's anyone on the plain." Fabrizio did not wait to be told twice, he tore off a branch from a poplar, stripped it and started to lash his horse with all his might; the animal broke into a gallop for a moment, then fell back into its regular slow trot. The *vivandière* had put her horse into a gallop. "Stop, will you, stop!" she called after Fabrizio. Presently both were clear of the wood. Coming to the edge of the plain, they heard a terrifying din, guns and muskets thundered on every side, right, left, behind them. And as the clump of trees from which they emerged grew on a mound rising nine or ten feet above the plain, they could see fairly well a corner of the battle; but still there was no one to be seen in the meadow beyond the wood. This meadow was bordered, half a mile away, by a long row of willows, very bushy; above the willows appeared a white smoke which now and again rose eddying into the sky.

"If I only knew where the regiment was," said the *cantinière,* in some embarrassment. "It won't do to go straight ahead over this big field. By the way," she said to Fabrizio, "if you see one of the enemy, stick him with the point of your sabre, don't play about with the blade."

At this moment, the *cantinière* caught sight of the four soldiers whom we mentioned a little way back; they were coming out of the wood on to the plain to the left of the road. One of them was on horseback.

"There you are," she said to Fabrizio. "Hallo there!" she called to the mounted man, "come over here and have a glass of brandy." The soldiers approached.

"Where are the 6th Light?" she shouted.

"Over there, five minutes away, across that canal that runs along by the willows; why, Colonel Macon has just been killed."

"Will you take five francs for your horse, you?"

"Five francs! That's not a bad one, *ma!* An officer's horse I can sell in ten minutes for five napoleons."

"Give me one of your napoleons," said the *vivandière* to Fabrizio. Then going up to the mounted soldier: "Get off, quickly," she said to him, "here's your napoleon."

The soldier dismounted, Fabrizio sprang gaily on to the saddle, the *vivandière* unstrapped the little portmanteau which was on his old horse.

"Come and help me, all of you!" she said to the soldiers, "is that the way you leave a lady to do the work?"

But no sooner had the captured horse felt the weight of the portmanteau than he began to rear, and Fabrizio, who was an excellent horseman, had to use all his strength to hold him.

"A good sign!" said the *vivandière,* "the gentleman is not accustomed to being tickled by portmanteaus."

"A general's horse," cried the man who had sold it, "a horse that's worth ten napoleons if it's worth a liard."

"Here are twenty francs," said Fabrizio, who could not contain himself for joy at feeling between his legs a horse that could really move.

At that moment a shot struck the line of willows, through which it passed obliquely, and Fabrizio had the curious spectacle of all those little branches flying this way and that as though mown down by a stroke of the scythe.

"Look, there's the *brute* advancing," the soldier said to him as he took the twenty francs. It was now about two o'clock.

Fabrizio was still under the spell of this strange spectacle when a party of generals, followed by a score of hussars, passed at a gallop across one corner of the huge field on the edge of which he had halted: his horse neighed, reared several times in succession, then began violently tugging the bridle that was holding him. "All right, then," Fabrizio said to himself.

The horse, left to his own devices, dashed off hell for leather to join the escort that was following the generals. Fabrizio counted four gold-laced hats. A quarter of an hour later, from a few words said by one hussar to the next, Fabrizio gathered that one of these generals was the famous Marshal Ney. His happiness knew no bounds; only he had no way of telling which of the four generals was Marshal Ney; he would have given everything in the world to know, but he remembered that he had been told not to speak. The escort halted, having to cross a wide ditch left full of water by the rain overnight; it was fringed with tall trees and formed the left-hand boundary of the field at the entrance to which Fabrizio had bought the horse. Almost all the hussars had dismounted; the bank of the ditch was steep and very slippery and the water lay quite three or four feet below the level of the field. Fabrizio, distracted with joy, was thinking more of Marshal Ney and of glory than of his horse, which, being highly excited, jumped into the canal; thus splashing the water up to a considerable height. One of the generals was soaked to the skin by the sheet of water, and cried with an oath: "Damn the f—— brute!" Fabrizio felt deeply hurt by this insult. "Can I ask him to apologise?" he wondered. Meanwhile, to prove that he was not so clumsy after all, he set his horse to climb the opposite bank of the ditch; but it rose straight up and was five or six feet high. He had to abandon the attempt; then he rode up stream, his horse being up to its head in water, and at last found a sort of drinking-place. By this gentle slope he was easily able to reach the field on the other side of the canal. He was the first man of the escort to appear there; he started to trot proudly down the bank; below him, in the canal, the hussars were splashing about, somewhat embarrassed by their position, for in many places the water was five feet deep. Two or three horses took fright and began to swim, making an appalling mess. A serjeant noticed the manœuvre that this youngster, who looked so very unlike a soldier, had just carried out.

"Up here! There is a watering-place on the left!" he shouted, and in time they all crossed.

On reaching the farther bank, Fabrizio had found the generals there by themselves; the noise of the guns seemed to him to have doubled; and it was all he could do to hear the general whom he had given such a good soaking and who now shouted in his ear:

"Where did you get that horse?"

Fabrizio was so much upset that he answered in Italian:

"*L'ho comprato poco fa.* (I bought it just now.)"

"What's that you say?" cried the general.

But the din at that moment became so terrific that Fabrizio could not answer him. We must admit that our hero was very little of a hero at that moment. However, fear came to him only as a secondary consideration; he was principally shocked by the noise, which hurt his ears. The escort broke into a gallop; they crossed a large batch of tilled land which lay beyond the canal. And this field was strewn with dead.

"Red-coats! red-coats!" the hussars of the escort exclaimed joyfully, and at first Fabrizio did not understand; then he noticed that as a matter of fact almost all these bodies wore red uniforms. One detail made him shudder with horror; he observed that many of these unfortunate red-coats were still alive; they were calling out, evidently asking for help, and no one stopped to give it them. Our hero, being most humane, took every possible care that his horse should not tread upon any of the red-coats. The escort halted; Fabrizio, who was not paying sufficient attention to his military duty, galloped on, his eyes fixed on a wounded wretch in front of him.

"Will you halt, you young fool!" the serjeant shouted after him. Fabrizio discovered that he was twenty paces on the generals' right front, and precisely in the direction in which they were gazing through their glasses. As he came back to take his place behind the other hussars, who had halted a few paces in rear of them, he noticed the biggest of these generals who was speaking to his neighbour, a general also, in a tone of authority and almost of reprimand; he was swearing. Fabrizio could not contain his curiosity; and, in spite of the warning not to speak, given him by his friend the gaoler's wife, he composed a short sentence in good French, quite correct, and said to his neighbour:

"Who is that general who is *chewing up* the one next to him?"

"Gad, it's the Marshal!"

"What Marshal?"

"Marshal Ney, you fool! I say, where have you been serving?"

Fabrizio, although highly susceptible, had no thought of resenting this insult; he was studying, lost in childish admiration, the famous Prince de la Moskowa, the "Bravest of the Brave."

Suddenly they all moved off at full gallop. A few minutes later Fabrizio saw, twenty paces ahead of him, a ploughed field the surface of which was moving in a singular fashion. The furrows were full of water and the soil, very damp, which formed the ridges between these furrows kept flying off in little black lumps three or four feet into the air. Fabrizio noticed as he passed this curious effect; then his thoughts turned to dreaming of the Marshal and his glory. He heard a sharp cry close to him; two hussars fell struck by shot; and, when he looked back at them, they were already twenty paces behind the escort. What seemed to him horrible was a horse streaming with blood that was struggling on the ploughed land, its hooves caught in its own entrails; it was trying to follow the others: its blood ran down into the mire.

"Ah! So I am under fire at last!" he said to himself. "I have seen shots fired!" he repeated with a sense of satisfaction. "Now I am a real soldier." At that moment, the escort began to go hell for leather, and our hero realised that it was shot from the guns that was making the earth fly up all round him. He looked vainly in the direction from which the balls were coming, he saw the white smoke of the battery at an enormous distance, and, in the thick of the steady and continuous rumble produced by the artillery fire, he seemed to hear shots discharged much closer at hand: he could not understand in the least what was happening.

At that moment, the generals and their escort dropped into a little road filled with water which ran five feet below the level of the fields.

The Marshal halted and looked again through his glasses. Fabrizio, this time, could examine him at his leisure. He found him to be very fair, with a big red face. "We don't have any faces like that in Italy," he said to himself. "With my pale cheeks and chestnut hair, I shall never look like that," he added despondently. To him these words implied: "I shall never be a hero." He looked at the hussars; with a solitary exception, all of them had yellow moustaches. If Fabrizio was studying the hussar's of the escort, they were all studying him as well. Their stare made him blush, and, to get rid of his embarrassment, he turned his head towards the enemy. They consisted of widely extended lines of men in red, but, what greatly surprised him, these men seemed to be quite minute. Their long files, which were regiments or divisions, appeared no taller than hedges. A line of red cavalry were trotting in the direction of the sunken road along which the Marshal and his escort had begun to move at a walk, splashing through the mud. The smoke made it impossible to distinguish anything in the direction in which they were advancing; now and then one saw men moving at a gallop against this background of white smoke.

Suddenly, from the direction of the enemy, Fabrizio saw four men approaching hell for leather. "Ah! We are attacked," he said to himself; then he saw two of these men speak to the Marshal. One of the generals on the latter's staff set off at a gallop towards the enemy, followed by two hussars of the escort and by the four men who had just come up. After a little canal which they all crossed, Fabrizio found himself riding beside a serjeant who seemed a good-natured fellow. "I must speak to this one," he said to himself, "then perhaps they'll stop staring at me." He thought for a long time.

"Sir, this is the first time that I have been present at a battle," he said at length to the serjeant. "But is this a real battle?"

"Something like. But who are you?"

"I am the brother of a captain's wife."

"And what is he called, your captain?"

Our hero was terribly embarrassed; he had never anticipated this question. Fortunately, the Marshal and his escort broke into a gallop. "What French name shall I say?" he wondered. At last he remembered the name of the inn-keeper with whom he had lodged in Paris; he brought his horse up to the serjeant's, and shouted to him at the top of his voice:

"Captain Meunier!" The other, not hearing properly in the roar of the guns, replied: "Oh, Captain Teulier? Well, he's been killed." "Splendid," thought Fabrizio. "Captain Teulier; I must look sad."

"Good God!" he cried; and assumed a piteous mien. They had left the sunken road and were crossing a small meadow, they were going hell for leather, shots were coming over again, the Marshal headed for a division of cavalry. The escort found themselves surrounded by dead and wounded men; but this sight had already ceased to make any impression on our hero; he had other things to think of.

While the escort was halted, he caught sight of the little cart of a *cantinière,* and his affection for this honourable corps sweeping aside every other consideration, set off at a gallop to join her.

"Stay where you are, curse you," the serjeant shouted after him.

"What can he do to me here?" thought Fabrizio, and he continued to gallop towards the *cantinière.* When he put spurs to his horse, he had had some hope that it might be his good *cantinière* of the morning; the horse and the little cart bore a strong resemblance, but their owner was quite different, and our hero thought her appearance most forbidding. As he came up to her, Fabrizio heard her say: "And he was such a fine looking man, too!" A very ugly sight awaited the new recruit; they were sawing off a cuirassier's leg at the thigh, a handsome young fellow of five feet ten. Fabrizio shut his eyes and drank four glasses of brandy straight off.

"How you do go for it, you boozer!" cried the *cantinière.* The brandy gave him an idea: "I must buy the goodwill of my comrades, the hussars of the escort."

"Give me the rest of the bottle," he said to the *vivandière.*

"What do you mean," was her answer, "what's left there costs ten francs, on a day like this."

As he rejoined the escort at a gallop:

"Ah! You're bringing us a drop of drink," cried the serjeant. "That was why you deserted, was it? Hand it over."

The bottle went round, the last man to take it flung it in the air after drinking. "Thank you, chum!" he cried to Fabrizio. All eyes were fastened on him kindly. This friendly gaze lifted a hundredweight from Fabrizio's heart; it was one of those hearts of too delicate tissue which require the friendship of those around it. So at last he had ceased to be looked at askance by his comrades, there was a bond between them! Fabrizio breathed a deep sigh of relief, then in a bold voice said to the serjeant:

"And if Captain Teulier has been killed, where shall I find my sister?" He fancied himself a little Machiavelli to be saying Teulier so naturally instead of Meunier.

"That's what you'll find out to-night," was the serjeant's reply.

The escort moved on again and made for some divisions of infantry. Fabrizio felt quite drunk; he had taken too much brandy, he was rolling slightly in his saddle: he remembered most opportunely a favourite saying of his mother's coachman: "When you've been lifting your elbow, look straight between your horse's ears, and do what the man next you does." The Marshal stopped for some time beside a number of cavalry units which he ordered to charge; but for an hour or two our hero was barely conscious of what was going on round about him. He was feeling extremely tired, and when his horse galloped he fell back on the saddle like a lump of lead.

Suddenly the serjeant called out to his men: "Don't you see the Emperor, curse you!" Whereupon the escort shouted: *"Vive l'Empereur!"* at the top of their voices. It may be imagined that our hero stared till his eyes started out of his head, but all he saw was some generals galloping, also followed by an escort. The long floating plumes of horsehair which the dragoons of the bodyguard wore on their helmets prevented him from distinguishing their faces. "So I have missed seeing the Emperor on a field of battle, all because of those cursed glasses of brandy!" This reflexion brought him back to his senses.

They went down into a road filled with water, the horses wished drink. "So that was the Emperor who went past then?" he asked the man next to him.

"Why, surely, the one with no braid on his coat. How is it you didn't see him?" his comrade answered kindly. Fabrizio felt a strong desire to gallop after the Emperor's escort and embody himself in it. What a joy to go really to war in the train of that hero! It was for that that he had come to France. "I am quite at liberty to do it," he said to himself, "for after all I have no other reason for being where I am but the will of my horse, which started galloping after these generals."

What made Fabrizio decide to stay where he was was that the hussars, his new comrades, seemed so friendly towards him; he began to imagine himself the intimate friend of all the troopers with whom he had been galloping for the last few hours. He saw arise between them and himself that noble friendship of the heroes of Tasso and Ariosto. If he were to attach himself to the Emperor's escort, there would be fresh acquaintances to be made, perhaps they would look at him askance, for these other horsemen were dragoons, and he was wearing the hussar uniform like all the rest that were following the Marshal. The way in which they now looked at him set our hero on a pinnacle of happiness; he would have done anything in the world for his comrades; his mind and soul were in the clouds. Everything seemed to have assumed a new aspect now that he was among friends, he was dying to ask them various questions. "But I am still a little drunk," he said to himself, "I must bear in mind what the gaoler's wife told me." He noticed on leaving the sunken road that the escort was no longer with Marshal Ney; the general whom they were following was tall and thin, with a dry face and an awe-inspiring eye.

This general was none other than Comte d'A——, the Lieutenant Robert of the 15th of May, 1796. How delighted he would have been to meet Fabrizio del Dongo!

It was already some time since Fabrizio had noticed the earth flying off in black crumbs on being struck by shot; they came in rear of a regiment of cuirassiers, he could hear distinctly the rattle of the grapeshot against their breastplates, and saw several men fall.

The sun was now very low and had begun to set when the escort, emerging from a sunken road, mounted a little bank three or four feet high to enter a ploughed field. Fabrizio heard an odd little sound quite close to him: he turned his head, four men had fallen with their horses; the general himself had been unseated, but picked himself up, covered in blood. Fabrizio looked at the hussars who were lying on the ground: three of them were still making convulsive movements, the fourth cried: "Pull me out!" The serjeant and two or three men had dismounted to assist the general who, leaning upon his aide-de-camp, was attempting to walk a few steps; he was trying to get away from his horse, which lay on the ground struggling and kicking out madly.

The serjeant came up to Fabrizio. At that moment our hero heard a voice say behind him and quite close to his ear: "This is the only one that can still gallop." He felt himself seized by the feet; they were taken out of the stirrups at the same time as someone caught him underneath the arms; he was lifted over his horse's tail and then allowed to slip to the ground, where he landed sitting.

The aide-de-camp took Fabrizio's horse by the bridle; the general, with the help of the serjeant, mounted and rode off at a gallop; he was quickly followed by the six men who were left of the escort. Fabrizio rose up in a fury, and began to run after them shouting: "*Ladri! Ladri!* (Thieves! Thieves!)" It was an amusing experience to run after horse-stealers across a battlefield.

The escort and the general, Comte d'A——, disappeared presently behind a row of willows. Fabrizio, blind with rage, also arrived at this line of willows; he found himself brought to a halt by a canal of considerable depth which he crossed. Then, on reaching the other side, he began swearing again as he saw once more, but far away in the distance, the general and his escort vanishing among the trees. "Thieves! Thieves!" he cried, in French this time. In desperation, not so much at the loss of his horse as at the treachery to himself, he let himself sink down on the side of the ditch, tired out and dying of hunger. If his fine horse had been taken from him by the enemy, he would have thought no more about it; but to see himself betrayed and robbed by that serjeant whom he liked so much and by those hussars whom he regarded as brothers! That was what broke his heart. He could find no consolation for so great an infamy, and, leaning his back against a willow, began to shed hot tears. He abandoned one by one all those beautiful dreams of a chivalrous and sublime friendship, like that of the heroes of the *Gerusalemme Liberata*. To see death come to one was nothing, surrounded by heroic and tender hearts, by noble friends who clasp one by the hand as one yields one's dying breath! But to retain one's enthusiasm surrounded by a pack of vile scoundrels! Like all angry men Frabrizio exaggerated. After a quarter of an hour of this melting mood, he noticed that the guns were beginning to range on the row of trees in the shade of which he sat meditating. He rose and tried to find his bearings. He scanned those fields bounded by a wide canal and the row of pollard willows: he thought he knew where he was. He saw a body of infantry crossing the ditch and marching over the fields, a quarter of a league in front of him. "I was just falling asleep," he said to himself; "I must see that I'm not taken prisoner." And he put his best foot foremost. As he advanced, his mind was set at rest; he recognized the uniforms, the regiments by which he had been afraid of being cut off were French. He made a right incline so as to join them.

After the moral anguish of having been so shamefully betrayed and robbed, there came another which, at every moment, made itself felt more keenly; he was dying of hunger. It was therefore with infinite joy that after having walked, or rather run for ten minutes, he saw that the column of infantry, which also had been moving very rapidly, was halting to take up a position. A few minutes later, he was among the nearest of the soldiers.

"Friends, could you sell me a mouthful of bread?"

"I say, here's a fellow who thinks we're bakers!"

This harsh utterance and the general guffaw that followed it had a crushing effect on Fabrizio. So war was no longer that noble and universal uplifting of souls athirst for glory which he had imagined it to be from Napoleon's proclamations! He sat down, or rather let himself fall on the grass; he turned very pale. The soldier who had spoken to him, and who had stopped ten paces off to clean the lock of his musket with his handkerchief, came nearer and flung him a lump of bread; then, seeing that he did not pick it up, broke off a piece which he put in our hero's mouth. Fabrizio opened his eyes, and ate the bread without having the strength to speak. When at length he looked round for the soldier to pay him, he found himself alone; the men nearest to him were a hundred yards off and were marching. Mechanically he rose and followed them. He entered a wood; he was dropping with exhaustion, and already had begun to look round for a comfortable resting-place; but what was his delight on recognising first of all the horse, then the cart, and finally the *cantinière* of that morning! She ran to him and was frightened by his appearance.

"Still going, my boy," she said to him; "you're wounded then? And where's your fine horse?" So saying she led him towards the cart, upon which she made him climb, supporting him under the arms. No sooner was he in the cart than our hero, utterly worn out, fell fast asleep.

Nothing could awaken him, neither the muskets fired close to the cart nor the trot of the horse which the *cantinière* was flogging with all her might. The regiment, attacked unexpectedly by swarms of Prussian cavalry, after imagining all day that they were winning the battle, was beating a retreat or rather fleeing in the direction of France.

The colonel, a handsome young man, well turned out, who had succeeded Macon, was sabred; the battalion commander who took his place, an old man with white hair, ordered the regiment to halt. "Damn you," he cried to his men, "in the days of the Republic we waited till we were forced by the enemy before running away. Defend every inch of ground, and get yourselves killed!" he shouted, and swore at them. "It is the soil of the Fatherland that these Prussians want to invade now!"

The little cart halted; Fabrizio awoke with a start. The sun had set some time back; he was quite astonished to see that it was almost night. The troops were running in all directions in a confusion which greatly surprised our hero; they looked shame-faced, he thought.

"What is happening?" he asked the *cantinière*.

"Nothing at all. Only that we're in the soup, my boy; it's the Prussian cavalry mowing us down, that's all. The idiot of a general thought at first they were our men. Come, quick, help me to mend Cocotte's trace; it's broken."

Several shots where fired ten yards off. Our hero, cool and composed, said to himself: "But really, I haven't fought at all, the whole day; I have only escorted a general.—I must go and fight," he said to the *cantinière*.

"Keep calm, you shall fight, and more than you want! We're done for.

"Aubry, my lad," she called out to a passing corporal, "keep an eye on the little cart now and then."

"Are you going to fight?" Fabrizio asked Aubry.

"Oh, no, I'm putting my pumps on to go to a dance!"

"I shall follow you."

"I tell you, he's all right, the little hussar," cried the *cantinière*. "The young gentleman has a stout heart." Corporal Aubry marched on without saying a word. Eight or nine soldiers ran up and joined him; he led them behind a big oak surrounded by brambles. On reaching it he posted them along the edge of the wood, still without uttering a word, on a widely extended front, each man being at least ten paces from the next.

"Now then, you men," said the corporal, opening his mouth for the first time, "don't fire till I give the order: remember you've only got three rounds each."

"Why, what is happening?" Fabrizio wondered. At length, when he found himself alone with the corporal, he said to him: "I have no musket."

"Will you hold your tongue? Go forward there: fifty paces in front of the wood you'll find one of the poor fellows of the Regiment who've been sabred; you will take his cartridge-pouch and his musket. Don't strip a wounded man, though; take the pouch and musket from one who's properly dead, and hurry up or you'll be shot in the back by our fellows." Fabrizio set off at a run and returned the next minute with a musket and a pouch.

"Load your musket and stick yourself behind this tree, and whatever you do don't fire till you get the order from me. . . . Great God in heaven!" the corporal broke off, "he doesn't even know how to load!" He helped Fabrizio to do this while going on with his instructions. "If one of the enemy's cavalry gallops at you to cut you down, dodge round your tree and don't fire till he's within three paces: wait till your bayonet's practically touching his uniform.

"Throw that great sabre away," cried the corporal. "Good God, do you want it to trip you up? Fine sort of soldiers they're sending us these days!" As he spoke he himself took hold of the sabre which he flung angrily away.

"You there, wipe the flint of your musket with your handkerchief. Have you never fired a musket?"

"I am a hunter."

"Thank God for that!" went on the corporal with a loud sigh. "Whatever you do, don't fire till I give the order." And he moved away.

Fabrizio was supremely happy. "Now I'm going to do some real fighting," he said to himself, "and kill one of the enemy. This morning they were sending cannon-balls over, and I did nothing but expose myself and risk getting killed; that's a fool's game." He gazed all round him with extreme curiosity. Presently he heard seven or eight shots fired quite close at hand. But receiving no order to fire he stood quietly behind his tree. It was almost night; he felt he was in a *look-out,* bear-shooting, on the mountain of Tramezzina, above Grianta. A hunter's idea came to him: he took a cartridge from his pouch and removed the ball. "If I see him," he said, "it won't do to miss him," and he slipped this second ball into the barrel of his musket. He heard shots fired close to his tree; at the same moment he saw a horseman in blue pass in front of him at a gallop, going from right to left. "It is more than three paces," he said to himself, "but at that range I am certain of my mark." He kept the trooper carefully sighted with his musket and finally pressed the trigger: the trooper fell with his horse. Our hero imagined he was stalking game: he ran joyfully out to collect his bag. He was actually touching the man, who appeared to him to be dying, when, with incredible speed, two Prussian troopers charged down on him to sabre him. Fabrizio dashed back as fast as he could go to the wood; to gain speed he flung his musket away. The Prussian troopers were not more than three paces from him when he reached another plantation of young oaks, as thick as his arm and quite upright, which fringed the wood. These little oaks delayed the horsemen for a moment, but they passed them and continued their pursuit of Fabrizio along a clearing. Once again they were just overtaking him when he slipped in among seven or eight big trees. At that moment his face was almost scorched by the flame of five or six musket shots fired from in front of him. He ducked his head; when he raised it again he found himself face to face with the corporal.

"Did you kill your man?" Corporal Aubry asked him.

"Yes; but I've lost my musket."

"It's not muskets we're short of. You're not a bad b——; though you do look as green as a cabbage you've won the day all right, and these men here have just missed the two who were chasing you and coming straight at them. I didn't see them myself. What we've got to do now is to get away at the double; the Regiment must be half a mile off, and there's a bit of a field to cross, too, where we may find ourselves surrounded."

As he spoke, the corporal marched off at a brisk pace at the head of his ten men. Two hundred yards farther on, as they entered the little field he had mentioned, they came upon a wounded general who was being carried by his aide-de-camp and an orderly.

"Give me four of your men," he said to the corporal in a faint voice, "I've got to be carried to the ambulance; my leg is shattered."

"Go and f—— yourself!" replied the corporal, "you and all your generals. You've all of you betrayed the Emperor to-day."

"What," said the general, furious, "you dispute my orders. Do you know that I am General Comte B——, commanding your Division," and so on. He waxed rhetorical. The aide-de-camp flung himself on the men. The corporal gave him a thrust in the arm with his bayonet, then made off with his party at the double. "I wish they were all in your boat," he repeated with an oath; "I'd shatter their arms and legs for them. A pack of puppies! All of them bought by the Bourbons, to betray the Emperor!" Fabrizio listened with a thrill of horror to this frightful accusation.

About ten o'clock that night the little party overtook their regiment on the outskirts of a large village which divided the road into several very narrow streets; but Fabrizio noticed that Corporal Aubry avoided speaking to any of the officers. "We can't get on," he called to his men. All these streets were blocked with infantry, cavalry, and, worst of all, by the limbers and wagons of the artillery. The corporal tried three of these streets in turn; after advancing twenty yards he was obliged to halt. Everyone was swearing and losing his temper.

"Some traitor in command here, too!" cried the corporal: "if the enemy has the sense to surround the village, we shall all be caught like rats in a trap. Follow me, you." Fabrizio looked round; there were only six men left with the corporal. Through a big gate which stood open they came into a huge courtyard; from this courtyard they passed into a stable, the back door of which let them into a garden. They lost their way for a moment and wandered blindly about. But finally, going through a hedge, they found themselves in a huge field of buckwheat. In less than half an hour, guided by the shouts and confused noises, they had regained the high road on the other side of the village. The ditches on either side of this road were filled with muskets that had been thrown away; Fabrizio selected one: but the road, although very broad, was so blocked with stragglers and transports that in the next half-hour the corporal and Fabrizio had not advanced more than five hundred yards at the most; they were told that this road led to Charleroi. As the village clock struck eleven:

"Let us cut across the field again," said the corporal. The little party was reduced now to three men, the corporal and Fabrizio. When they had gone a quarter of a league from the high road: "I'm done," said one of the soldiers.

"Me, too!" said another.

"That's good news! We're all in the same boat," said the corporal; "but do what I tell you and you'll get through all right." His eye fell on five or six trees marking the line of a little ditch in the middle of an immense corn-field. "Make for the trees!" he told his men; "lie down," he added when they had reached the trees, "and not a sound, remember. But before you go to sleep, who's got any bread?"

"I have," said one of the men.

"Give it here," said the corporal in a tone of authority. He divided the bread into five pieces and took the smallest himself.

"A quarter of an hour before dawn," he said as he ate it, "you'll have the enemy's cavalry on your backs. You've got to see you're not sabred. A man by himself is done for with cavalry after him on these big plains, but five can get away; keep in close touch with me, don't fire till they're at close range, and to-morrow evening I'll undertake to get you to Charleroi." The corporal roused his men an hour before daybreak and made them recharge their muskets. The noise on the high road still continued; it had gone on all night: it was like the sound of a torrent heard from a long way off.

"They're like a flock of sheep running away," said Fabrizio with a guileless air to the corporal.

"Will you shut your mouth, you young fool!" said the corporal, greatly indignant. And the three soldiers who with Fabrizio composed his whole force scowled angrily at our hero as though he had uttered blasphemy. He had insulted the nation.

"That is where their strength lies!" thought our hero. "I noticed it before with the Viceroy at Milan; they are not running away, oh, no! With these Frenchmen you must never speak the truth if it shocks their vanity. But as for their savage scowls, they don't trouble me, and I must let them understand as much." They kept on their way, always at an interval of five hundred yards from the torrent of fugitives that covered the high road. A league farther on, the corporal and his party crossed a road running into the high road in which a number of soldiers were lying. Fabrizio purchased a fairly good horse which cost him forty francs, and among all the sabres that had been thrown down everywhere made a careful choice of one that was long and straight. "Since I'm told I've got to stick them," he thought, "this is the best." Thus equipped, he put his horse into a gallop and soon overtook the corporal who had gone on ahead. He sat up in his stirrups, took hold with his left hand of the scabbard of his straight sabre, and said to the four Frenchmen:

"Those people going along the high road look like a flock of sheep . . . they are running like frightened sheep. . . ."

In spite of his dwelling upon the word *sheep,* his companions had completely forgotten that it had annoyed them an hour earlier. Here we see one of the contrasts between the Italian character and the French; the Frenchman is no doubt the happier of the two; he glides lightly over the events of life and bears no malice afterwards.

We shall not attempt to conceal the fact that Fabrizio was highly pleased with himself after using the word *sheep.* They marched on, talking about nothing in particular. After covering two leagues more, the corporal, still greatly astonished to see no sign of the enemy's cavalry, said to Fabrizio:

"You are our cavalry; gallop over to that farm on the little hill; ask the farmer if he will *sell* us breakfast: mind you tell him there are only five of us. If he hesitates, put down five francs of your money in advance; but don't be frightened, we'll take the dollar back from him after we've eaten."

Fabrizio looked at the corporal; he saw in his face an imperturbable gravity and really an air of moral superiority; he obeyed. Everything fell out as the commander in chief had anticipated; only, Fabrizio insisted on their not taking back by force the five francs he had given to the farmer.

"The money is mine," he said to his friends; "I'm not paying for you, I'm paying for the oats he's given my horse."

Fabrizio's French accent was so bad that his companions thought they detected in his words a note of superiority; they were keenly annoyed, and from that moment a duel began to take shape in their minds for the end of the day. They found him very different from themselves, which shocked them; Fabrizio, on the contrary, was beginning to feel a warm friendship towards them.

They had marched without saying a word for a couple of hours when the corporal, looking across at the high road, exclaimed in a transport of joy: "There's the Regiment!" They were soon on the road; but, alas, round the eagle were mustered not more than two hundred men. Fabrizio's eye soon caught sight of the *vivandière:* she was going on foot, her eyes were red and every now and again she burst into tears. Fabrizio looked in vain for the little cart and Cocotte.

"Stripped, ruined, robbed!" cried the *vivandière,* in answer to our hero's inquiring glance. He, without a word, got down from his horse, took hold of the bridle and said to the *vivandière:* "Mount!" She did not have to be told twice.

"Shorten the stirrups for me," was her only remark.

As soon as she was comfortably in the saddle she began to tell Fabrizio all the disasters of the night. After a narrative of endless length but eagerly drunk in by our hero who, to tell the truth, understood nothing at all of what she said but had a tender feeling for the *vivandière,* she went on:

"And to think that they were Frenchmen who robbed me, beat me, destroyed me. . . ."

"What! It wasn't the enemy?" said Fabrizio with an air of innocence which made his grave, pale face look charming.

"What a fool you are, you poor boy!" said the *vivandière,* smiling through her tears; "but you're very nice, for all that."

"And such as he is, he brought down his Prussian properly," said Corporal Aubry, who, in the general confusion round them, happened to be on the other side of the horse on which the *cantinière* was sitting. "But he's proud," the corporal went on. . . . Fabrizio made an impulsive movement. "And what's your name?" asked the corporal; "for if there's a report going in I should like to mention you."

"I'm called Vasi," replied Fabrizio, with a curious expression on his face. "Boulot, I mean," he added, quickly correcting himself.

Boulot was the name of the late possessor of the marching orders which the gaoler's wife at B—— had given him; on his way from B—— he had studied them carefully, for he was beginning to think a little and was no longer so easily surprised. In addition to the marching orders of Trooper Boulot, he had stowed away in a safe place the precious Italian passport according to which he was entitled to the noble appellation of Vasi, dealer in barometers. When the corporal had charged him with being proud, it had been on the tip of his tongue to retort: "I proud! I, Fabrizio Volterra, Marchesino del Dongo, who consent to go by the name of a Vasi, dealer in barometers!"

While he was making these reflexions and saying to himself: "I must not forget that I am called Boulot, or look out for the prison fate theatens me with," the corporal and the *cantinière* had been exchanging a few words with regard to him.

"Don't say I'm inquisitive," said the *cantinière*, ceasing to address him in the second person singular, "it's for your good I ask you these questions. Who are you, now, really?"

Fabrizio did not reply at first. He was considering that never again would he find more devoted friends to ask for advice, and he was in urgent need of advice from someone. "We are coming into a fortified place, the governor will want to know who I am, and ware prison if I let him see by my answers that I know nobody in the 4th Hussar Regiment whose uniform I am wearing!" In his capacity as an Austrian subject, Fabrizio knew all about the importance to be attached to a passport. Various members of his family, although noble and devout, although supporters of the winning side, had been in trouble a score of times over their passports; he was therefore not in the least put out by the question which the *cantinière* had addressed to him. But as, before answering, he had to think of the French words which would express his meaning most clearly, the *cantinière*, pricked by a keen curiosity, added, to induce him to speak: "Corporal Aubry and I are going to give you some good advice."

"I have no doubt you are," replied Fabrizio. "My name is Vasi and I come from Genoa; my sister, who is famous for her beauty, is married to a captain. As I am only seventeen, she made me come to her to let me see something of France, and form my character a little; not finding her in Paris, and knowing that she was with this army, I came on here. I've searched for her everywhere and haven't found her. The soldiers, who were puzzled by my accent, had me arrested. I had money then, I gave some to the *gendarme,* who let me have some marching orders and a uniform, and said to me: 'Get away with you, and swear you'll never mention my name.'"

"What was he called?" asked the *cantinière*.

"I've given my word," said Fabrizio.

"He's right," put in the corporal, "the *gendarme* is a sweep, but our friend ought not to give his name. And what is the other one called, this captain, your sister's husband? If we knew his name, we would try to find him."

"Teulier, Captain in the 4th Hussars," replied our hero.

"And so," said the corporal, with a certain subtlety, "from your foreign accent the soldiers took you for a spy?"

"That's the abominable word!" cried Fabrizio, his eyes blazing. "I who love the Emperor so and the French people! And it was that insult that annoyed me more than anything."

"There's no insult about it; that's where you're wrong; the soldiers' mistake was quite natural," replied Corporal Aubry gravely.

And he went on to explain in the most pedantic manner that in the army one must belong to some corps and wear a uniform, failing which it was quite simple that people should take one for a spy. "The enemy sends us any number of them; everybody's a traitor in this war." The scales fell from Fabrizio's eyes; he realised for the first time that he had been in the wrong in everything that had happened to him during the last two months.

"But make the boy tell us the whole story," said the *cantinière,* her curiosity more and more excited. Fabrizio obeyed. When he had finished:

"It comes to this," said the *cantinière,* speaking in a serious tone to the corporal, "this child is not a soldier at all; we're going to have a bloody war now that we've been beaten and betrayed. Why should he go and get his bones broken free, gratis and for nothing?"

"Especially," put in the corporal, "as he doesn't even know how to load his musket, neither by numbers, nor in his own time. It was I put in the shot that brought down the Prussian."

"Besides, he lets everyone see the colour of his money," added the *cantinière;* "he will be robbed of all he has as soon as he hasn't got us to look after him."

"The first cavalry non-com. he comes across," said the corporal, "will take it from him to pay for his drink, and perhaps they'll enlist him for the enemy; they're all traitors. The first man he meets will order him to follow, and he'll follow him; he would do better to join our Regiment."

"No, please, if you don't mind, corporal!" Fabrizio exclaimed with animation; "I am more comfortable on a horse. And, besides, I don't know how to load a musket, and you have seen that I can manage a horse."

Fabrizio was extremely proud of this little speech. We need not report the long discussion that followed between the corporal and the *cantinière* as to his future destiny. Fabrizio noticed that in discussing him these people repeated three or four times all the circumstances of his story: the soldiers' suspicions, the *gendarme* selling him marching orders and a uniform, the accident by which, the day before, he had found himself forming part of the marshal's escort, the glimpse of the Emperor as he galloped past, the horse that had been *scoffed* from him, and so on indefinitely.

With feminine curiosity the *cantinière* kept harking back incessantly to the way in which he had been dispossessed of the good horse which she had made him buy.

"You felt yourself seized by the feet, they lifted you gently over your horse's tail, and sat you down on the ground!" "Why repeat so often," Fabrizio said to himself, "what all three of us know perfectly well?" He had not yet discovered that this is how, in France, the lower orders proceed in quest of ideas.

"How much money have you?" the *cantinière* asked him suddenly. Fabrizio had no hesitation in answering. He was sure of the nobility of the woman's nature; that is the fine side of France.

"Altogether, I may have got left thirty napoleons in gold, and eight or nine five-franc pieces."

"In that case, you have a clear field!" exclaimed the *cantinière.* "Get right away from this rout of an army; clear out, take the first road with ruts on it that you come to on the right; keep your horse moving and your back to the army. At the first opportunity, buy some civilian clothes. When you've gone nine or ten leagues and there are no more soldiers in sight, take the mail-coach, and go and rest for a week and eat beefsteaks in some nice town. Never let anyone know that you've been in the army, or the police will take you up as a deserter; and, nice as you are, my boy, you're not quite clever enough yet to stand up to the police. As soon as you've got civilian clothes on your back, tear up your marching orders into a thousand pieces and go back to your real name: say that you're Vasi. And where ought he to say he comes from?" she asked the corporal.

"From Cambrai on the Scheldt: it's a good town and quite small, if you know what I mean. There's a cathedral there, and Fénelon."

"That's right," said the *cantinière*. "Never let on to anyone that you've been in battle, don't breathe a word about B———, or the *gendarme* who sold you the marching orders. When you're ready to go back to Paris, make first for Versailles, and pass the Paris barrier from that side in a leisurely way, on foot, as if you were taking a stroll. Sew up your napoleons inside your breeches, and remember, when you have to pay for anything, shew only the exact sum that you want to spend. What makes me sad is that they'll take you and rob you and strip you of everything you have. And whatever will you do without money, you that don't know how to look after yourself . . ." and so on.

The good woman went on talking for some time still; the corporal indicated his support by nodding his head, not being able to get a word in himself. Suddenly the crowd that was packing the road first of all doubled its pace, then, in the twinkling of an eye, crossed the little ditch that bounded the road on the left and fled helter-skelter across country. Cries of "The Cossacks! The Cossacks!" rose from every side.

"Take back your horse!" the *cantinière* shouted.

"God forbid!" said Fabrizio. "Gallop! Away with you! I give him to you. Do you want something to buy another cart with? Half of what I have is yours."

"Take back your horse, I tell you!" cried the *cantinière* angrily; and she prepared to dismount. Fabrizio drew his sabre. "Hold on tight!" he shouted to her; and gave two or three strokes with the flat of his sabre to the horse, which broke into a gallop and followed the fugitives.

Our hero stood looking at the road; a moment ago, two or three thousand people had been jostling along it, packed together like peasants at the tail of a procession. After the shout of: "Cossacks!" he saw not a soul on it; the fugitives had cast away shakoes, muskets, sabres, everything. Fabrizio, quite bewildered, climbed up into a field on the right of the road and twenty or thirty feet above it; he scanned the line of the road in both directions, and the plain, but saw no trace of the Cossacks. "Funny people, these French!" he said to himself. "Since I have got to go to the right," he thought, "I may as well start off at once; it is possible that these people have a reason for running away that I don't know." He picked up a musket, saw that it was charged, shook up the powder in the priming, cleaned the flint, then chose a cartridge-pouch that was well filled and looked round him again in all directions; he was absolutely alone in the middle of this plain which just now had been so crowded with people. In the far distance he could see the fugitives who were beginning to disappear behind the trees, and were still running. "That's a very odd thing," he said to himself, and remembering the tactics employed by the corporal the night before, he went and sat down in the middle of a field of corn. He did not go farther because he was anxious to see again his good friends the *cantinière* and Corporal Aubry.

In this cornfield, he made the discovery that he had no more than eighteen napoleons, instead of thirty as he had supposed; but he still had some small diamonds which he had stowed away in the lining of the hussar's boots, before dawn, in the gaoler's wife's room at B——. He concealed his napoleons as best he could, pondering deeply the while on the sudden disappearance of the others. "Is that a bad omen for me?" he asked himself. What distressed him most was that he had not asked Corporal Aubry the question: "Have I really taken part in a battle?" It seemed to him that he had, and his happiness would have known no bounds could he have been certain of this.

"But even if I have," he said to himself, "I took part in it bearing the name of a prisoner, I had a prisoner's marching orders in my pocket, and, worse still, his coat on my back! That is the fatal threat to my future: what would the Priore Blanès say to it? And that wretched Boulot died in prison. It is all of the most sinister augury; fate will lead me to prison." Fabrizio would have given anything in the world to know whether Trooper Boulot had really been guilty; when he searched his memory, he seemed to recollect that the gaoler's wife had told him that the hussar had been taken up not only for the theft of silver plate but also for stealing a cow from a peasant and nearly beating the peasant to death: Fabrizio had no doubt that he himself would be sent to prison some day for a crime which would bear some relation to that of Trooper Boulot. He thought of his friend the *parroco* Blanès: what would he not have given for an opportunity of consulting him! Then he remembered that he had not written to his aunt since leaving Paris. "Poor Gina!" he said to himself. And tears stood in his eyes, when suddenly he heard a slight sound quite close to him: a soldier was feeding three horses on the standing corn; he had taken the bits out of their mouths and they seemed half dead with hunger; he was holding them by the snaffle. Fabrizio got up like a partridge; the soldier seemed frightened. Our hero noticed this, and yielded to the pleasure of playing the hussar for a moment.

"One of those horses belongs to me, f—— you, but I don't mind giving you five francs for the trouble you've taken in bringing it here."

"What are you playing at?" said the soldier. Fabrizio took aim at him from a distance of six paces.

"Let go the horse, or I'll blow your head off."

The soldier had his musket slung on his back; he reached over his shoulder to seize it.

"If you move an inch, you're a dead man!" cried Fabrizio, rushing upon him.

"All right, give me the five francs and take one of the horses," said the embarrassed soldier, after casting a rueful glance at the high road, on which there was absolutely no one to be seen. Fabrizio, keeping his musket raised in his left hand, with the right flung him three five franc pieces.

"Dismount, or you're a dead man. Bridle the black, and go farther off with the other two. . . . If you move, I fire."

The soldier looked savage but obeyed. Fabrizio went up to the horse and passed the rein over his left arm, without losing sight of the soldier, who was moving slowly away; when our hero saw that he had gone fifty paces, he jumped nimbly on to the horse. He had barely mounted and was feeling with his foot for the off stirrup when he heard a bullet whistle past close to his head: it was the soldier who had fired at him. Fabrizio, beside himself with rage, started galloping after the soldier who ran off as fast as his legs could carry him, and presently Fabrizio saw him mount one of his two horses and gallop away. "Good, he's out of range now," he said to himself. The horse he had just bought was a magnificent animal, but seemed half starved. Fabrizio returned to the high road, where there was still not a living soul; he crossed it and put his horse into a trot to reach a little fold in the ground on the left, where he hoped to find the *cantinière*; but when he was at the top of the little rise he could see nothing save, more than a league away, a few scattered troops. "It is written that I shall not see her again," he said to himself with a sigh, "the good, brave woman!" He came to a farm which he had seen in the distance on the right of the road. Without dismounting, and after paying for it in advance, he made the farmer produce some oats for his poor horse, which was so famished that it began to gnaw the manger. An hour later, Fabrizio was trotting along the high road, still in the hope of meeting the *cantinière,* or at any rate Corporal Aubry. Moving all the time and keeping a look-out all round him, he came to a marshy river crossed by a fairly narrow wooden bridge. Between him and the bridge, on the right of the road, was a solitary house bearing the sign of the White Horse. "There I shall get some dinner," thought Fabrizio. A cavalry officer with his arm in a sling was guarding the approach to the bridge; he was on horseback and looked very melancholy; ten paces away from him, three dismounted troopers were filling their pipes.

"There are some people," Fabrizio said to himself, "who look to me very much as though they would like to buy my horse for even less than he cost me." The wounded officer and the three men on foot watched him approach and seemed to be waiting for him. "It would be better not to cross by this bridge, but to follow the river bank to the right; that was the way the *cantinière* advised me to take to get clear of difficulties. . . . Yes," thought our hero, "but if I take to my heels now, to-morrow I shall be thoroughly ashamed of myself; besides, my horse has good legs, the officer's is probably tied; if he tries to make me dismount I shall gallop." Reasoning thus with himself, Fabrizio pulled up his horse and moved forward at the slowest possible pace.

"Advance, you, hussar!" the officer called to him with an air of authority. Fabrizio went on a few paces and then halted.

"Do you want to take my horse?" he shouted.

"Not in the least; advance."

Fabrizio examined the officer; he had a white moustache, and looked the best fellow in the world; the handkerchief that held up his left arm was drenched with blood, and his right hand also was bound up in a piece of bloodstained linen. "It is the men on foot who are going to snatch my bridle," thought Fabrizio; but, on looking at them from nearer, he saw that they too were wounded.

"On your honour as a soldier," said the officer, who wore the epaulettes of a colonel, "stay here on picket, and tell all the dragoons, chasseurs and hussars that you see that Colonel Le Baron is in the inn over there, and that I order them to come and report to me." The old colonel had the air of a man broken by suffering; with his first words he had made a conquest of our hero, who replied with great good sense:

"I am very young, sir, to make them listen to me; I ought to have a written order from you."

"He is right," said the colonel, studying him closely; "make out the order, La Rose, you've got the use of your right hand."

Without saying a word, La Rose took from his pocket a little parchment book, wrote a few lines, and, tearing out a leaf, handed it to Fabrizio; the colonel repeated the order to him, adding that after two hours on duty he would be relieved, as was right and proper, by one of the three wounded troopers he had with him. So saying he went into the inn with his men. Fabrizio watched them go and sat without moving at the end of his wooden bridge, so deeply impressed had he been by the sombre, silent grief of these three persons. "One would think they were under a spell," he said to himself. At length he unfolded the paper and read the order, which ran as follows:

"Colonel Le Baron, 6th Dragoons, Commanding the 2nd Brigade of the 1st Cavalry Division of the XIV Corps, orders all cavalrymen, dragoons, chasseurs and hussars, on no account to cross the bridge, and to report to him at the White Horse Inn, by the bridge, which is his headquarters.

"Headquarters, by the bridge of La Sainte, June 19, 1815.

"For Colonel Le Baron, wounded in the right arm,
and by his orders,
"LA ROSE, *Serjeant*."

Fabrizio had been on guard at the bridge for barely half an hour when he saw six chasseurs approaching him mounted, and three on foot; he communicated the colonel's order to them. "We're coming back," said four of the mounted men, and crossed the bridge at a fast trot. Fabrizio then spoke to the other two. During the discussion, which grew heated, the three men on foot crossed the bridge. Finally, one of the two mounted troopers who had stayed behind asked to see the order again, and carried it off, with:

"I am taking it to the others, who will come back without fail; wait for them here." And off he went at a gallop; his companion followed him. All this had happened in the twinkling of an eye.

Fabrizio was furious, and called to one of the wounded soldiers, who appeared at a window of the White Horse. This soldier, on whose arm Fabrizio saw the stripes of a cavalry sergeant, came down and shouted to him: "Draw your sabre, man, you're on picket." Fabrizio obeyed, then said: "They've carried off the order."

"They're out of hand after yesterday's affair," replied the other in a melancholy tone. "I'll let you have one of my pistols; if they force past you again, fire it in the air; I shall come, or the colonel himself will appear."

Fabrizio had not failed to observe the serjeant's start of surprise on hearing of the theft of the order. He realised that it was a personal insult to himself, and promised himself that he would not allow such a trick to be played on him again.

Armed with the serjeant's horse-pistol, Fabrizio had proudly resumed his guard when he saw coming towards him seven hussars, mounted. He had taken up a position that barred the bridge; he read them the colonel's order, which seemed greatly to annoy them; the most venturesome of them tried to pass. Fabrizio, following the wise counsel of his friend the *vivandière*, who, the morning before, had told him that he must thrust and not slash, lowered the point of his long, straight sabre and made as though to stab with it the man who was trying to pass him.

"Oh, so he wants to kill us, the baby!" cried the hussars, "as if we hadn't been killed quite enough yesterday!" They all drew their sabres at once and fell on Fabrizio: he gave himself up for dead; but he thought of the serjeant's surprise, and was not anxious to earn his contempt again. Drawing back on to his bridge, he tried to reach them with his sabre-point. He looked so absurd when he tried to wield this huge, straight heavy-dragoon sabre, a great deal too heavy for him, that the hussars soon saw with what sort of soldier they had to deal; they then endeavoured not to wound him but to slash his clothing. In this way Fabrizio received three or four slight sabre-cuts on his arms. For his own part, still faithful to the *cantinière's* precept, he kept thrusting the point of his sabre at them with all his might. As ill luck would have it, one of these thrusts wounded a hussar in the hand: highly indignant at being touched by so raw a recruit, he replied with a downward thrust which caught Fabrizio in the upper part of the thigh. What made this blow effective was that our hero's horse, so far from avoiding the fray, seemed to take pleasure in it and to be flinging himself on the assailants. These, seeing Fabrizio's blood streaming along his right arm, were afraid that they might have carried the game too far, and, pushing him against the left-hand parapet of the bridge, crossed at a gallop. As soon as Fabrizio had a moment to himself he fired his pistol in the air to warn the colonel.

Four mounted hussars and two on foot, of the same regiment as the others, were coming towards the bridge and were still two hundred yards away from it when the pistol went off. They had been paying close attention to what was happening on the bridge, and, imagining that Fabrizio had fired at their comrades, the four mounted men galloped upon him with raised sabres: it was a regular cavalry charge. Colonel Le Baron, summoned by the pistol-shot, opened the door of the inn and rushed on to the bridge just as the galloping hussars reached it, and himself gave them the order to halt.

"There's no colonel here now!" cried one of them, and pressed on his horse. The colonel in exasperation broke off the reprimand he was giving them, and with his wounded right hand seized the rein of this horse on the off side.

"Halt! You bad soldier," he said to the hussar; "I know you, you're in Captain Henriot's squadron."

"Very well, then! The captain can give me the order himself! Captain Henriot was killed yesterday," he added with a snigger, "and you can go and f—— yourself!"

So saying, he tried to force a passage, and pushed the old colonel who fell in a sitting position on the roadway of the bridge. Fabrizio, who was a couple of yards farther along upon the bridge, but facing the inn, pressed his horse, and, while the breast-piece of the assailant's harness threw down the old colonel who never let go the off rein, Fabrizio, indignant, bore down upon the hussar with a driving thrust. Fortunately the hussar's horse, feeling itself pulled towards the ground by the rein which the colonel still held, made a movement sideways, with the result that the long blade of Fabrizio's heavy-cavalry sabre slid along the hussar's jacket, and the whole length of it passed beneath his eyes. Furious, the hussar turned round and, using all his strength, dealt Fabrizio a blow which cut his sleeve and went deep into his arm: our hero fell.

One of the dismounted hussars, seeing the two defenders of the bridge on the ground, seized the opportunity, jumped on to Fabrizio's horse and tried to make off with it by starting at a gallop across the bridge.

The serjeant, as he hurried from the inn, had seen his colonel fall, and supposed him to be seriously wounded. He ran after Fabrizio's horse and plunged the point of his sabre into the thief's entrails; he fell. The hussars, seeing no one now on the bridge but the serjeant, who was on foot, crossed at a gallop and rapidly disappeared. The one on foot bolted into the fields.

The serjeant came up to the wounded men. Fabrizio was already on his feet; he was not in great pain, but was bleeding profusely. The colonel got up more slowly; he was quite stunned by his fall, but had received no injury. "I feel nothing," he said to the serjeant, "except the old wound in my hand."

The hussar whom the serjeant had wounded was dying.

"The devil take him!" exclaimed the colonel. "But," he said to the serjeant and the two troopers who came running out, "look after this young man whose life I have risked, most improperly. I shall stay on the bridge myself and try to stop these madmen. Take the young man to the inn and tie up his arm. Use one of my shirts."

The whole of this adventure had not lasted a minute. Fabrizio's wounds were nothing; they tied up his arm with bandages torn from the colonel's shirt. They wanted to make up a bed for him upstairs in the inn.

"But while I am tucked up here on the first floor," said Fabrizio to the serjeant, "my horse, who is down in the stable, will get bored with being left alone and will go off with another master."

"Not bad for a conscript!" said the serjeant. And they deposited Fabrizio on a litter of clean straw in the same stall as his horse.

Then, as he was feeling very weak, the serjeant brought him a bowl of mulled wine and talked to him for a little. Several compliments included in this conversation carried our hero to the seventh heaven.

Fabrizio did not wake until dawn on the following day; the horses were neighing continuously and making a frightful din; the stable was filled with smoke. At first Fabrizio could make nothing of all this noise, and did not even know where he was: finally, half-stifled by the smoke, it occurred to him that the house was on fire; in the twinkling of an eye he was out of the stable and in the saddle. He raised his head; smoke was belching violently from the two windows over the stable; and the roof was covered by a black smoke which rose curling into the air. A hundred fugitives had arrived during the night at the White Horse; they were all shouting and swearing. The five or six whom Fabrizio could see close at hand seemed to him to be completely drunk; one of them tried to stop him and called out to him: "Where are you taking my horse?"

When Fabrizio had gone a quarter of a league, he turned his head. There was no one following him; the building was in flames. Fabrizio caught sight of the bridge; he remembered his wound, and felt his arm compressed by bandages and very hot. "And the old colonel, what has become of him? He gave his shirt to tie up my arm." Our hero was this morning the coolest man in the world; the amount of blood he had shed had liberated him from all the romantic element in his character.

"To the right!" he said to himself, "and no time to lose." He began quietly following the course of the river which, after passing under the bridge, ran to the right of the road. He remembered the good *cantinière's* advice. "What friendship!" he said to himself, "what an open nature!"

After riding for an hour he felt very weak. "Oho! Am I going to faint?" he wondered. "If I faint, someone will steal my horse, and my clothes, perhaps, and my money and jewels with them." He had no longer the strength to hold the reins, and was trying to keep his balance in the saddle when a peasant who was digging in a field by the side of the high road noticed his pallor and came up to offer him a glass of beer and some bread.

"When I saw you look so pale, I thought you must be one of the wounded from the great battle," the peasant told him. Never did help come more opportunely. As Fabrizio was munching the piece of bread his eyes began to hurt him when he looked straight ahead. When he felt a little better he thanked the man. "And where am I?" he asked. The peasant told him that three quarters of a league farther on he would come to the township of Zonders, where he would be very well looked after. Fabrizio reached the town, not knowing quite what he was doing and thinking only at every step of not falling off his horse. He saw a big door standing open; he entered. It was the Woolcomb Inn. At once there ran out to him the good lady of the house, an enormous woman; she called for help in a voice that throbbed with pity. Two girls came and helped Fabrizio to dismount; no sooner had his feet touched the ground than he fainted completely. A surgeon was fetched, who bled him. For the rest of that day and the days that followed Fabrizio scarcely knew what was being done to him, he slept almost without interruption.

The sabre wound in his thigh threatened to form a serious abscess. When his mind was clear again, he asked them to look after his horse, and kept on repeating that he would pay them well, which shocked the good hostess and her daughters. For a fortnight he was admirably looked after and he was beginning to be himself again when he noticed one evening that his hostess seemed greatly upset. Presently a German officer came into his room: in answering his questions they used a language which Fabrizio did not understand, but he could see that they were speaking about him; he pretended to be asleep. A little later, when he thought that the officer must have gone, he called his hostesses.

"That officer came to put my name on a list, and make me a prisoner, didn't he?" The landlady assented with tears in her eyes.

"Very well, there is money in my dolman!" he cried, sitting up in bed; buy me some civilian clothes and to-night I shall go away on my horse. You have already saved my life once by taking me in just as I was going to drop down dead in the street; save it again by giving me the means of going back to my mother."

At this point the landlady's daughters began to dissolve in tears; they trembled for Fabrizio; and, as they barely understood French, they came to his bedside to question him. They talked with their mother in Flemish; but at every moment pitying eyes were turned on our hero; he thought he could make out that his escape might compromise them seriously, but that they would gladly incur the risk. A Jew in the town supplied a complete outfit, but when he brought it to the inn about ten o'clock that night, the girls saw, on comparing it with Fabrizio's dolman, that it would require an endless amount of alteration. At once they set to work; there was no time to lose. Fabrizio showed them where several napoleons were hidden in his uniform, and begged his hostesses to stitch them into the new garments.

With these had come a fine pair of new boots. Fabrizio had no hesitation in asking these kind girls to slit open the hussar's boots at the place which he shewed them, and they hid the little diamonds in the lining of the new pair.

One curious result of his loss of blood and the weakness that followed from it was that Fabrizio had almost completely forgotten his French; he used Italian to address his hostesses, who themselves spoke a Flemish dialect, so that their conversation had to be conducted almost entirely in signs. When the girls, who for that matter were entirely disinterested, saw the diamonds, their enthusiasm for Fabrizio knew no bounds; they imagined him to be a prince in disguise. Aniken, the younger and less sophisticated, kissed him without ceremony. Fabrizio, for his part, found them charming, and towards midnight, when the surgeon had allowed him a little wine in view of the journey he had to take, he felt almost inclined not to go. "Where could I be better off than here?" he asked himself. However, about two o'clock in the morning, he rose and dressed. As he was leaving the room, his good hostess informed him that his horse had been taken by the officer who had come to search the house that afternoon.

"Ah! The swine!" cried Fabrizio with an oath, "robbing a wounded man!" He was not enough of a philosopher, this young Italian, to bear in mind the price at which he himself had acquired the horse.

Aniken told him with tears that they had hired a horse for him. She would have liked him not to go. Their farewells were tender. Two big lads, cousins of the good landlady, helped Fabrizio into the saddle: during the journey they supported him on his horse, while a third, who walked a few hundred yards in advance of the little convoy, searched the roads for any suspicious patrol. After going for a couple of hours, they stopped at the house of a cousin of the landlady of the Woolcomb. In spite of anything that Fabrizio might say, the young men who accompanied him refused absolutely to leave him; they claimed that they knew better than anyone the hidden paths through the woods.

"But to-morrow morning, when my flight becomes known, and they don't see you anywhere in the town, your absence will make things awkward for you," said Fabrizio.

They proceeded on their way. Fortunately, when day broke at last, the plain was covered by a thick fog. About eight o'clock in the morning they came in sight of a little town. One of the young men went on ahead to see if the post-horses there had been stolen. The postmaster had had time to make them vanish and to raise a team of wretched screws with which he had filled his stables. Grooms were sent to find a pair of horses in the marshes where they were hidden, and three hours later Fabrizio climbed into a little cabriolet which was quite dilapidated but had harnessed to it a pair of good post-horses. He had regained his strength. The moment of parting with the young men, his hostess's cousins, was pathetic in the extreme; on no account, whatever friendly pretext Fabrizio might find, would they consent to take any money.

"In your condition, sir, you need it more than we do," was the invariable reply of these worthy young fellows. Finally they set off with letters in which Fabrizio, somewhat emboldened by the agitation of the journey, had tried to convey to his hostesses all that he felt for them. Fabrizio wrote with tears in his eyes, and there was certainly love in the letter addressed to little Aniken.

In the rest of the journey there was nothing out of the common. He reached Amiens in great pain from the cut he had received in his thigh; it had not occurred to the country doctor to lance the wound, and in spite of the bleedings an abscess had formed. During the fortnight that Fabrizio spent in the inn at Amiens, kept by an obsequious and avaricious family, the Allies were invading France, and Fabrizio became another man, so many and profound were his reflections on the things that had happened to him. He had remained a child upon one point only: what he had seen, was it a battle; and, if so, was that battle Waterloo? For the first time in his life he found pleasure in reading; he was always hoping to find in the newspapers, or in the published accounts of the battle, some description which would enable him to identify the ground he had covered with Marshal Ney's escort, and afterwards with the other general. During his stay at Amiens he wrote almost every day to his good friends at the Woolcomb. As soon as his wound was healed, he came to Paris.

Falling Through Space

BY

RICHARD HILLARY

SEPTEMBER 3rd dawned dark and overcast, with a slight breeze ruffling the waters of the Estuary. Hornchurch airdrome, twelve miles east of London, wore its usual morning pallor of yellow fog, lending an air of added grimness to the dim shapes of the Spitfires around the boundary. From time to time a balloon would poke its head grotesquely through the mist, as though looking for possible victims, before falling back like some tired monster.

We came out onto the tarmac at about eight o'clock. During the night our machines had been moved from the Dispersal Point over to the hangars. All the machine tools, oil, and general equipment had been left on the far side of the airdrome. I was worried. We had been bombed a short time before, and my plane had been fitted out with a brand-new cockpit hood. This hood unfortunately would not slide open along its groove; and with a depleted ground staff and no tools, I began to fear it never would. Unless it did open, I shouldn't be able to bail out in a hurry if I had to. Miraculously, "Uncle George" Denholm, our Squadron Leader, produced three men with a heavy file and lubricating oil, and the corporal-fitter and I set upon the hood in a fury of haste. We took it turn by turn, filing and oiling, oiling and filing, until at last the hood began to move. But agonizingly slowly: by ten o'clock, when the mist had cleared and the sun was blazing out of a clear sky, the hood was still sticking firmly half-way along the groove; at ten-fifteen, what I had feared for the last hour happened. Down the loud-speaker came the emotionless voice of the controller: "603 Squadron take off and patrol base; you will receive further orders in the air: 603 Squadron take off as quickly as you can, please." As I pressed the starter and the engine roared into life, the corporal stepped back and crossed his fingers significantly. I felt the usual sick feeling in the pit of the stomach, as though I were about to row a race, and then I was too busy getting into position to feel anything.

Uncle George and the leading section took off in a cloud of dust; Brian Carberry looked across and put up his thumbs. I nodded and opened up, to take off for the last time from Hornchurch. I was flying No. 3 in Brian's section, with Stapme Stapleton on the right: the third section consisted of only two machines, so that our Squadron strength was eight. We headed southeast, climbing all out on a steady course. At about 12,000 feet we came up through the clouds: I looked down and saw them spread out below me like layers of whipped cream. The sun was brilliant and made it difficult to see even the next plane when turning. I was peering anxiously ahead, for the controller had given us warning of at least fifty enemy fighters approaching very high. When we did first sight them, nobody shouted, as if we had all seen them at the same moment. They must have been 500 to 1,000 feet above us and coming straight on like a swarm of locusts. I remember cursing and going automatically into line astern: the next moment we were in among them and it was each man for himself. As soon as they saw us they spread out and dived, and the next ten minutes was a blur of twisting machines and tracer bullets. One Messerschmitt went down in a sheet of flame on my right, and a Spitfire hurtled past in a half-roll; I was weaving and turning in a desperate attempt to gain height, with the machine practically hanging on the airscrew. Then, just below me and to my left, I saw what I had been praying for—a Messerschmitt climbing and away from the sun. I closed in to 200 yards, and from slightly to one side gave him a two-second burst: fabric ripped off the wing and black smoke poured from the engine, but he did not go down. Like a fool, I did not break away, but put in another three-second burst. Red flames shot upwards and he spiralled out of sight. At that moment, I felt a terrific explosion which knocked the control stick from my hand, and the whole machine quivered like a stricken animal. In a second, the cockpit was a mass of flames: instinctively, I reached up to open the hood. It would not move. I tore off my straps and managed to force it back; but this took time, and when I dropped back into the seat and reached for the stick in an effort to turn the plane on its back, the heat was so intense that I could feel myself going. I remember a second of sharp agony, remember thinking, "So this is it!" and putting both my hands up to my eyes. Then I passed out.

When I regained consciousness I was free of the machine and falling rapidly. I pulled the rip-cord of my parachute and checked my descent with a jerk. Looking down, I saw that my left trouser leg was burnt off, that I was going to fall into the sea, and that the English coast was far away. About twenty feet above the water, I attempted to undo my parachute, failed, and flopped into the sea with it billowing round me. I was told later that the machine went into a spin at about 25,000 feet and that at 10,000 feet I fell out—unconscious. This may well have been so, for I discovered later a large cut on the top of my head, presumably collected while bumping round inside.

The water was not unwarm and I was pleasantly surprised to find that my life-jacket, my "Mae West" kept me afloat. I locked at my watch: it was not there. Then, for the first time, I noticed how burnt my hands were: down to the wrist, the skin was dead white and hung in shreds: I felt faintly sick from the smell of burnt flesh. By closing one eye, I could see my lips, jutting out like motor tires. The side of my parachute harness was cutting into me particularly painfully, so that I guess my right hip was burnt. I made a further attempt to undo the harness, but owing to the pain of my hands, soon desisted. Instead, I lay back and reviewed my position. I was a long way from land; my hands were burnt, and so, judging from the pain of the sun, was my face; it was unlikely that anyone on shore had seen me come down and even more unlikely that a ship would come by; I could float for possibly four hours in my Mae West. I began to feel that I had perhaps been premature in considering myself lucky to have escaped from the machine. After about half an hour my teeth started chattering, and to quiet them I kept up a regular tuneless chant, varying it from time to time with calls for help. There can be few more futile pastimes than yelling for help alone in the North Sea, with a solitary seagull for company, yet it gave me a certain melancholy satisfaction, for I had once written a short story in which the hero, falling from a liner, had done just this. (It was rejected.)

The water now seemed much colder and I noticed with surprise that the sun had gone in though my face was still burning. I looked down at my hands, and not seeing them, realized that I had gone blind. So I was going to die. It came to me like that—I was going to die, and I was not afraid. This realization came as a surprise. The manner of my approaching death appalled and horrified me, but the actual vision of death left me unafraid: I felt only a profound curiosity and a sense of satisfaction that within a few minutes or a few hours I was to learn the great answer. I decided that it should be in a few minutes. I had no qualms about hastening my end and reaching up, I managed to unscrew the valve of my Mae West. The air escaped in a rush and my head went under water. It is said by people who have all but died in the sea that drowning is a pleasant death. I did not find it so. I swallowed a large quantity of water before my head came up again, but derived little satisfaction from it. I tried again, to find that I could not get my face under. I was so enmeshed in my parachute that I could not move. For the next ten minutes, I tore my hands to ribbons on the spring-release catch. It was stuck fast. I lay back exhausted, and then I started to laugh. By this time I was probably not entirely normal and I doubt if my laughter was wholly sane, but there was something irresistibly comical in my grand gesture of suicide being so simply thwarted.

Goethe once wrote that no one, unless he had led the full life and realized himself, completely, had the right to take his own life. Providence seemed determined that I should not incur the great man's displeasure.

Another thing often said is that a dying man relives his whole life in one rapid kaleidoscope. I merely thought gloomily of the Squadron returning, of my mother at home, and of the few people who would miss me. Outside my family, I could count them on the fingers of one hand. What did gratify me enormously was to find that I indulged in no frantic abasements or prayers to the Almighty. It is an old jibe of God-fearing people that the irreligious always change their tune when about to die: I was pleased to think that I was proving them wrong. Because I seemed to be in for an indeterminate period of waiting, I began to feel a terrible loneliness and sought for some means to take my mind off my plight. I took it for granted that I must soon become delirious, and I attempted to hasten the process: I encouraged my mind to wander vaguely and aimlessly, with the result that I did experience a certain peace. But when I forced myself to think of something concrete, I found that I was still only too lucid. I went on shuttling between the two with varying success until I was picked up. I remember as in a dream hearing somebody shout: it seemed so far away and quite unconnected with me. . . .

Then willing arms were dragging me over the side; my parachute was taken off (and with such ease!); a brandy flask was pushed between my lips; a voice said, "O.K., Joe, it's one of ours and still kicking"; and I was safe. I was neither relieved nor angry: I was past caring.

It was to the Margate lifeboat that I owed my rescue. Watchers on the coast had seen me come down, and for three hours they had been searching for me. Owing to wrong directions, they were just giving up and turning back for land when ironically enough one of them saw my parachute. They were then fifteen miles east of Margate.

While in the water I had been numb and had felt very little pain. Now that I began to thaw out, the agony was such that I could have cried out. The good fellows made me as comfortable as possible, put up some sort of awning to keep the sun from my face, and phoned through for a doctor. It seemed to me to take an eternity to reach shore. I was put into an ambulance and driven rapidly to a hospital. Through all this I was quite conscious, though unable to see. At the hospital they cut off my uniform, I gave the requisite information to a nurse about my next of kin, and then, to my infinite relief, felt a hypodermic syringe pushed into my arm.

I can't help feeling that a good epitaph for me at that moment would have been four lines of Verlaine:

> *Quoique sans patrie et sans roi,*
> *Et très brave ne l'étant guère,*
> *J'ai voulu mourir à la guerre.*
> *La mort n'a pas voulu de moi.*

A man who has been rejected by death is easily tempted to take up the pen.

Pearl Harbor

BY

BLAKE CLARK

AT HICKAM FIELD, the air field so near Pearl Harbor that it is virtually the same target, a long row of hangars and bombers invited the Japanese. The attack combined bombing and strafing. The enemy planes bombed the hangars and strafed the quarter-mile-long row of planes drawn up in front of the hangars in orderly parade formation.

A bomb-hit on a hangar announced the news to the thousands on the post. Men came pouring out from all nine wings of the barracks—men in slacks, men in shorts, some in their underwear only, some without anything on at all. What was going on? Another mock war? No, bombs! Everyone ran for his battle station.

Colonel Ferguson was in a building up the street from the hangar line. He ran out into the open, saw the damaged planes, and jumped into the gutter. While strafers bounced bullets off the road by his side, the Colonel crawled down the gutter to the line. There he directed the tactical squadrons who were arriving a hundred to a hundred and fifty at a time on the double quick.

"Disperse those planes!" was the order.

Up and back, up and back, the Japanese squadron was flying, strafing the airplanes on the wings. The men ran on heedless of the rain of bullets. Some of the men faltered and fell.

A general's aide was already on the line. He was trying to taxi one of the big bombers. Strafers had put one motor out of commission. It was no easy job to taxi such a heavy plane with only one motor going. He did it by racing the one engine until it pulled its side of the plane forward. Then he slammed on the opposite brake, which forced the other wing up. Wading and crawfishing along under enemy fire, he brought the plane across the landing mat to comparative safety.

While the fire department fought flames at the tail end of some of the planes, daring crew men jumped upon the wings, disconnected the engines, and pulled their eight or nine hundred pounds' weight to the edge of the apron. Fine engines were saved by their quick thinking.

Inside one hangar twenty-one Hawaiians were fighting fire. Planes roared hoarsely, machine guns stuttered overhead. In the middle of the smoke-filled hangar, Solomon Naauao, 245-pound athlete, trained the water from his fire-hose on the fuselage of a four-motor flying fortress, pushing back the gasoline fire that leaped out from the fuselage onto the wings. Solomon is a giant Hawaiian, a true son of a warrior. Short, thick, black hair fits his massive head like a fur cap. He was hoping the Chief would come soon with the foamite. Water was not much good against gasoline.

One end of the burning hangar fell through to the floor, revealing a sky dotted with three approaching Japanese bombers. They were flying just a few feet above the hangar. The first one passed directly above Solomon and his fellow-fighters. Solomon heard an explosion and felt hot pain.

"Lord help me!" he prayed, falling to the concrete floor. The whole inner side of his right leg was blown away.

With his arms and sound leg he crawled through the smoke, away from the flames. When two soldiers picked him up, he learned that five others with him had been wounded, three more blown to pieces. They left him in the doorway to wait for the ambulance just coming in. As he lay there, Japanese planes flew slowly above, just clearing the hangar, and strafed the men running to carry him to the ambulance. Others quickly picked him up and sped him to the hospital.

Sergeant Dwyer got a machine gun out of ordnance, put a corporal in charge of it, and dashed back for another. A bomb fell, and its deadly fragments flew. He got his second gun and set it up on the parade ground. He felt wet and looked at his shirt. It was soaked with blood. The sergeant remembered that something he had thought was a stone had hit him when the bomb exploded. He was taken to the hospital with a shattered shoulder.

A lieutenant ran toward a plane. A Japanese flew over, strafing. The lieutenant fell to the ground, mortally wounded. A young corporal by his side lifted him to an ambulance, sped back across the apron, leaped in the plane, and taxied it out.

The raid lasted fifteen or twenty minutes. As soon as it ceased, activity burst upon the streets and flooded them. Ambulances and all the cars that could be pressed into service as ambulances were whizzing up and back from the bombed area. School buses, army station wagons, American Factors delivery trucks, and private cars helped to deliver the wounded and to rush surgical supplies from Honolulu to the hospitals.

Before half their work was completed, they were caught in the second and most destructive raid. Two rows of high-flying bombers dropped over twenty heavy and light demolition bombs from a height of ten to twelve thousand feet. They landed in the most populous section of Hickam Field. For what seemed a full minute after the bombs had landed, there was a dead silence in which nothing happened. Then the new mess hall, large enough for six complete basketball courts inside, the photograph laboratory, the guard house, the fire station, the barracks built to house thousands, an immense hangar—everything in the entire area—seemed to rise intact from the earth, poise in mid-air, and fall apart, dropping back to the earth in millions of fragments and clouds of dust.

The third wave came strafing. Ground defenses were going full blast and accounted for several of the raiders. Guns were set up on the parade ground, on the hangar line, and even around the flagpole at post headquarters. One man—no one knows how—had lugged a machine gun up on top of one of the unbombed hangars and was perched up there, popping away at the strafing planes.

Green men under fire acted like veterans. All moved swiftly to their places without any confusion or disorder. The cooks ran back into the kitchen to remove all the stored food to a safer place. The kitchen was hit. The Staff Sergeant in charge was struck on the head by a piece of shrapnel. He ripped off his shirt, tied up his head to stop the blood, and went on directing the work.

Outside, a corporal was speeding across the parade ground to help man a machine gun. It was entirely in the open, without any protection whatever. Halfway there he was strafed by a low-flying Japanese pilot. Mortally wounded, he kept on, trying to get to the machine gun. He fell dead on the way.

His place was quickly taken. Eager privates ran out and took over the gun. They did this time and again, dashing out under fire and taking over free machine guns, even though the men who were operating them had just been strafed and killed.

On the apron opposite the hangars a lone man was firing a 30-caliber machine gun which he had carried out and set up on the mount of a B-18 bomber. It was unstable, because the mount was made for an aerial gun. He braced it against his shoulder and kept up a steady stream of fire. An enemy plane flew low, strafed the plane he was in with incendiary bullets, and set it on fire. There was no way for the lone machine gunner to get out of his position in the nose of the bomber. All behind him was a flaming death trap. Spectators not far away said that he did not even try to get out, but kept on firing. Long after the leaping flames had enveloped the nose of the plane, they saw the red tracer bullets from his machine gun mounting skyward.

There was humor with the tragedy. When the Japanese came over Hickam the third time, they placed a bomb squarely on the "Snake Ranch," the boys' name for their recently opened beer garden. A first sergeant of a truck company had endured the first two waves bravely enough, but this was too much. He dashed out of his barricade, shook his fist at the sky, and shouted, "You dirty S. O. B.'s! You've bombed the most important building on the Post!"

A group of U.S. bombers, all unarmed, were just flying in from the mainland when the bewildered pilots suddenly found themselves pounced upon by a fleet of armed and shooting bombers. Many of the Americans did not see the Rising Sun on the planes and simply could not imagine what had broken loose above their heads. What kind of Hawaiian welcome was this?

The planes were to be delivered to one particular field, but they dispersed in every direction and landed wherever they could.

All that happened at the air fields was only a prelude to the drama of Pearl Harbor. For years the Japanese have wanted to smash this Gibraltar of the Pacific. It stands in the way of any successful attack on the mainland United States. "If we could only 'get' Pearl Harbor," the Japanese militarists tell themselves, "we could raid the West Coast of the United States at will." And they could. Every detail of strategy in the attack showed that Pearl Harbor was the real objective. Planes were used in attacking it that never bothered to approach the landing fields. The attack lasted from 7:55 A.M. to 9:15 A.M. and there were probably 150 Japanese planes—torpedo planes, strafers, dive bombers, and high-altitude horizontal bombers.

I cannot tell you how many ships were lying in Pearl Harbor on that peaceful Sunday morning. That is a naval secret. I can tell you the names of the *Oklahoma*, the *Utah*, and the *Arizona*, because they have been mentioned in dispatches and in the newspapers. I cannot tell anything more specific. But you know that Pearl Harbor is the United States' largest naval base, and that its spacious waters can float every ship of any navy in the world. Battleships were there, those great warships named for the states in our union, anchored in the harbor. Destroyers lay near them, minelayers, cruisers, and all the types of ships that the great navy of America boasts. On each were boys and men of the United States Navy from virtually every city and county of the forty-eight states, from towns with such outlandish names as Wahoo, Nebraska, and Hominy, Oklahoma.

A great surprise was in store for them, the greatest in their lives, and the most astounding in the life of the U.S. Navy. From somewhere, exactly where they did not know, a wave of torpedo planes flying in from the direction of Honolulu, swift, low over the calm waters of the Harbor, eased down toward the ships, and released their torpedoes, glittering like fish in the sun, plunging with a loud splash into the sea.

You can tell a torpedo plane by the way it approaches its target. It comes down at an angle, levels off, and drops its torpedo as near the target as possible. The Japanese squadron of torpedo planes came in two waves. Each plane had its object carefully selected in advance, or so it seemed, for the approaching planes separated and each went to a definite attack.

From the crow's nest of one of the battleships, a sailor saw one of the ugly mustard-colored planes heading toward the side of his ship. He saw its deadly "fish," like a great shark, propeller for a tail, splash into the water below. The plane roared upward, barely clearing the deck of the ship. The sailor, paralyzed by the horrible fascination of awaiting the inevitable, watched the wake of the torpedo, coming straight for his ship. Massive battleship, of thousands of tons, it rocked as if hit by a mighty fist. Almost simultaneously with the horrendous roar which accompanied the blow, quantities of oil flew all over the ship. The oil caught on fire. In two minutes the deck of the ship was covered with flames, as if it were an oil tanker that had been hit. Flames leaped as high as the crow's nest on which the lone sailor stood. Billows of heavy, oily smoke enveloped him. It was like sticking his head in a burning chimney flue to look over. Terrific heat, smoke, the gas from the bomb blinded and choked him. He fell to the floor of the crow's nest and hid his face in his arms. Cries of the burned and wounded below came up to him. He raised himself and tried to look down. Cinders and flakes of burning paint flew into his eyes and blinded him. Gropingly, he climbed upon the edge of the crow's nest and leaped into the oil-covered, flaming water below, just missing the deck. He swam under water as long as he could, then came up for breath. In a moment the burning oil forced him under again. It was only a short way to Ford Island, but when he clambered up on the beach, every hair had been singed from his head. Yet he went on fighting.

The captain of another ship was below in his cabin when the first explosion came. He leaped to the porthole. The water, ordinarily eight or nine feet below, was only six inches from his face, and covered with oil. At that moment the ship was hit again. Water gushed into the cabin. He snapped the catch underneath the porthole just in time. As he did, the ship listed farther, and through the glass he saw the water come above the porthole. He turned to the door and heard the rush of water down the passageway. When he opened it, the torrent of water surged over the floor of his room. By the time he had fought his way to the top of the ladder, the whole compartment below him was filled with oil and water. He was like a rat caught in a sewer.

As the captain stepped out on deck, ready to run for his battle station, a bomber flying almost directly above him dropped an incendiary bomb. Instantly hundreds of fragments of red-hot steel were flying at him, and all over the ship. He leaped behind the combing of the hatch and was not hit.

In the next second a bomb hit, knocking one of the ship's airplanes from its catapult. As it crashed to the deck, one of its pontoons broke off and came hurtling toward him. It hit the hatch-combing behind which he crouched, and flew off into the water. It would have been death to move. To walk out now was to enter a wall of shrapnel and machine-gun fire.

This hell lasted until the first wave of airplanes withdrew—perhaps twenty minutes. Suddenly the noise ceased, and the captain could hear voices on the nearby shore of Ford Island. The ship was listing. The order came to abandon ship. Behind the hatch, on the side of the ship away from Ford Island, a young ensign and two enlisted men were struggling to release a life raft. It had been caught in the deck rigging, and they could not approach it from their side. The captain stepped up to it and, with that super-strength that comes in such moments, shoved it out. From the raft, the captain, the ensign, and the two men rescued others who had abandoned the ship and were swimming around in the oily water. Many of them were so completely covered with the heavy fuel oil that they could not open their eyes. Several were vomiting, sick from swallowing oil and salt water. While they were struggling at their rescue work, a Japanese plane, one of the second wave, swooped down and strafed them, but missed. The rescuers collected twenty-eight men and took them ashore to the Navy Yard, opposite Ford Island.

The *Oklahoma* had turned over. The *Arizona* was lost. Flames were leaping up from the *Downes,* the *Cassin,* and others. Men were killed and unded, dying on every air field, in Pearl Harbor, and in the streets of Honolulu. Airplanes, ships, and homes were afire, but the Japanese imperialists lit a new fire that day which, praise be to the allied armies, will sweep over the world, carrying democracy and liberation even to Japan's own people.

Even that day, the attackers got a taste of what is to come. Once the first shock had passed, America swerved and hit back. From every part of the island, defense forces rose to action.

Before the attack, a seaman first-class was writing a letter near one of the machine-gun nests. When the first Japanese plane came over, he manned the machine gun and fired away, scoring several hits. He got his first plane before "General Quarters," the call to battle stations, was sounded.

In the wardroom of a 1500-ton destroyer, an Academy ensign and three reserve ensigns heard the announcement from the bridge telephone: "The *Utah* has been torpedoed by Japanese aircraft!"

Immediately they sounded General Quarters and manned their battle stations. As senior officer, the Academy ensign gave orders to get under way at once. One of the reserve officers took the bridge with the senior officer, another took the guns, and the third became damage-control officer.

Five minutes later they opened against the enemy with their machine guns. Japanese plans were diving at ships in the harbor. Two minutes later Ensign —— brought his large caliber anti-aircraft battery into action.

Below decks, the chief machinist mate, acting as engineering officer, lit off another boiler. Fortunately, they already had steam under one. The chief boatswain's mate led his repair party into the job of clearing ship for action.

Within a short time they were heading for the channel. A gun jammed. The chief gunner's mate ordered all his men away from the gun shield and out of the handling room. At the risk of being blown to bits, he cleared the jammed shell, called the men back, and continued firing.

As they moved downstream, they kept up a hot fire with their main battery and machine guns. Four planes went down in smoke. Two planes dived over the destroyer, trying to reach the battleships beyond. Machine guns got them.

Abeam Fort Weaver, the Academy ensign called for more knots. The chief gave them.

They sped out of the harbor, heading for their area.

The chief radioman got a good contact on his listening apparatus. "Submarine!"

They maneuvered the destroyer for the attack and dropped two depth charges. Then they regained contact and dropped two more.

A large oil-slick appeared on the sea and bubbles covered the surface for two hundred feet. At first they thought the submarine was surfacing, so Ensign —— trained the battery to starboard to be ready for it.

Suddenly a third contact was reported. Apparently the submarine was heading for a cruiser near by.

The destroyer made an emergency turn and attacked. From the racks the ensigns loosed another pair of depth charges. When they swung around again they saw another oil-slick. They had sunk a second submarine.

From then on they screened the cruiser. Though she had expended hundreds of rounds of high-explosive shells and thousands of rounds of machine-gun bullets, the destroyer's young officers returned her to Pearl Harbor without a single casualty.

Officers and men worked together and set each other inspiring examples. A first lieutenant of one ship exposed himself continuously to the enemy strafing while directing operations on the quarterdeck and boatdeck. He ordered men not engaged to keep back in sheltered areas, but he himself remained constantly exposed in order to direct the work of damage control and putting out fires.

His example was followed by the boatswain's mate, who was sent to the booth of the officer of the deck to phone the central engine room to put more pressure on the fire mains. While he was phoning, a bomb struck near the booth and enveloped him in flames. He stayed at the phone to get the message through.

An ensign on the same ship manned a three-inch battery until the ammunition supply was blocked by fire and water. Any place on a burning ship is dangerous, but the ammunition supply room is the most dangerous of all. Nevertheless the ensign organized a party of volunteers to go below. There they worked swiftly and silently, in constant danger of being blown to bits. They carried ammunition through the fire, supplying other batteries to fight off the Japanese. A bomb exploded, and the shrapnel flying from it mortally wounded the brave ensign. His men wanted to carry him above, but he ordered them to abandon him.

"It's too late to save me," he said. "Save yourselves!" He died by his post.

On every ship men leaped to their battle stations and poured out reprisal fire from anti-aircraft and machine guns. One of the ships hit began turning over; its fighting crew followed it around as it capsized, firing their guns until they went under water. They swam to the dock, cheering a more fortunate ship than their own as it cleared the harbor.

All guns were put into use. A country lad from the West, a lowly "boot-seaman," had a standard rifle shoved in his hand.

"Get out and shoot!" was the command.

A small dive bomber came in, poised to drop a bomb. The boy had not been trained to handle a heavy rifle, but he had "done lots of huntin' " in his day. He took a bead and fired. One of the freak accidents of the war occurred. Apparently the boy's bullet hit the detonator of the bomb the Japanese was about to drop, for the plane simply burst in mid-air and dis-integrated before their eyes. The boy fainted.

On one of the ships, a chaplain robed in his ecclesiastical gowns was setting up his reader's stand in preparation for the morning service when a bomb explosion announced the attack. He dashed to the door where they were dealing out arms, and grabbed a machine gun. Using his reader's stand for a prop, he set up the gun and fired away, refusing to let go until the attack was over.

A chief gunner was lying in his bunk recovering from yellow fever shots. The first torpedo hit just forward below him. He was thrown to the ceiling, and landed with a wrenched back. Fuel oil was coming in. Forgetting his back, he ran to the magazine to help get anti-aircraft ammunition going up to his battle station. Men there were being overcome by fumes from the fuel oil, and were falling on the deck. A man sent to the phone to call for help was enveloped in the fumes and fell to the deck before he could reach the phone. The gunner took the phone and called the Sky Control.

"Men for the five-inch anti-aircraft!" he shouted.

He turned to the guns, but there was no more ammunition. He dashed back to the ammunition room. The floor was strewn with asphyxiated men. He started getting out ammunition himself, and fell to the floor in a faint.

A wounded gunner woke that afternoon on a mess table in the marine grounds, his back hurting. He was naked. Rescuers had removed his oil-soaked clothes. He leaped from the table; ran to the supply room; got a shirt, shoes, and trousers; and ran back to his ship.

Two marines were manning a machine gun. A Japanese plane flew low and dropped a bomb which exploded on deck. A burning fragment from it sank into the back of the marine firing. While his mate tugged at the jagged steel and pulled it from his flesh, the marine kept firing his gun at the attackers.

This was the real spirit of Pearl Harbor.

Three Men On a Raft

BY

HAROLD F. DIXON
Aviation Chief Machinist's Mate, U. S. N.

I GUESS you would call me superstitious. Most sailors are, and I've been a sailor and an aviator for 22 years. The funny thing is that for a few days before Jan. 16, as our ship sailed southward in the Pacific, I had had a peculiar feeling that something was going to happen. It was hard to pin down the feeling but numerous little things went wrong. For instance, after I had left the mess table at noon on that last day, something told me to go back and eat two or three more stalks of celery. I figured I might need them. Then as I walked out by the sick bay, a pharmacist's mate stopped me and asked me to look inside. There on the surgeon's table lay one of my best friends. He was out of his head, his legs and arms waving in the air. Strangely enough, I had the feeling that it was really I who was lying there on that table and that I was in great agony and entirely naked. All of this eventually came to pass.

The patrol that day was uneventful. Late in the afternoon, however, rain clouds and scattered squalls occasionally hid the ocean, and somehow or other I lost our ship. For hours I flew the plane over the area where I thought the ship ought to be but at last the gas was almost gone. There was nothing to do but land our plane in the water. This I did, bringing her in on a power stall.

We had figured we would have plenty of time to get out our raft and put rations and water aboard before the plane sank but there was to be no such good luck. Much sooner than we expected the plane was down and the three of us were swimming in the water, held up by our life jackets. Fortunately, I had been able to get the rubber life raft inflated by opening the carbon-dioxide chamber, which automatically sucked air into the air chamber. When we finally got it upright and crawled onto it, even though it was only 8 ft. by 4 ft., the raft made a pretty seaworthy craft.

It's interesting how you remember certain things about the crises in your life. My concern was solely to get that plane down in a good power stall and to get out on the wing and inflate the life raft. Tony Pastula, I knew, was saying a little prayer. Then, too, my most vivid recollection of that terrible half hour was watching the flashlight which Gene Aldrich had rescued from the plane sinking down through the water after Gene dropped it. Down,

down and down it went—a bright spot in the crystal-clear tropical waters. At least, I thought, if there are sharks around here, they'll probably follow that light down instead of attacking us.

On the raft that first night we were a tired and bedraggled crew. Tony Pastula had been firmly convinced he was going to be killed in the crash. Gene Aldrich, whom we called Henry from the radio serial *Henry Aldrich,* was convinced that our boat, made of thin rubberized fabric, would burst and sink at almost any time. As a matter of fact, this remained one of our greatest worries, especially later when Gene was stabbing fish over the side with his pocketknife and sharks were cruising just a foot or two under our floating raft.

We were all up early the next morning to keep a sharp lookout for any rescue ships or planes. Sure enough, at about 8:30 a. m. a tiny speck appeared in the distance, heading our way. It was a searching plane from our ship. Gradually it approached, then passed a half mile to the south. Both Gene and Tony were excited. Gene, in particular, jumped up, waved his arms and took off his blue shirt to wave that too. But it did no good. The plane continued on its way, leaving us unspotted behind.

When that plane passed my heart sank and a moment of deep, black fear entered. I am an oldtimer in the Navy. The nation is at war and our force was in the immediate vicinity of enemy positions. The admiral, I knew, would never risk his whole force for the rescue of one plane. For us it was a hard pill to swallow, but it was simple military logic.

Inwardly I was calculating how we were going to get out of the pickle we were in. To the west and north of our position were Japanese islands. I wanted to avoid them at all costs because the Japs, I knew, were in no mood to take prisoners. To the east were uninhabited islands which would not do us much good to reach. Our only hope seemed to be in maneuvering our boat some 500 miles to the south and west where there were inhabited friendly islands. Also along such a route I thought we might be able to pick up an American convoy or perhaps even a naval task force.

That first day I spent observing how our boat acted in the wind and the water. Being flat and smooth-bottomed, it sailed smartly down wind and, with virtually no tendency to yaw, stayed steadily lengthwise to the trough of the sea. Its length thus acted as a sail. I even figured out how to judge our speed. To 8 ft. of heavy cord from the tool pocket I tied a metal identification disk from Tony's key ring and, by tossing this out to drift and carefully observing it, I could gauge the speed. By this method and the more simple one of throwing rags overboard and counting the seconds as they went by, I arrived at the conclusion that 12 knots of wind gave us a drift of approximately 2.5 knots, while 6 knots of wind gave us a drift of one knot.

We were, of course, at the complete mercy of the wind. Whenever it blew from the northeast, our spirits rose because we knew that eventually it would blow us to safety, but when it shifted and came in from the southwest, we were depressed because then we were heading for disaster and probably death. To stop drifting in the wrong direction, I invented a sea anchor. Around the entire outside edge of the raft was a half-inch Manila rope. I removed this rope and tied one end to the raft's gas-inductor manifold and the other to my pneumatic life jacket. With this sea anchor we could cut the speed of our drift in the wrong direction to less than one knot for every 16 knots of wind.

There was only one other technical problem to solve. We had to have a map of our progress. I knew the approximate position where our plane crashed, and from our log which indicated speed and from the sun by day and the moon and stars by night which all indicated direction, I could tell pretty accurately where we were going. I eventually made a map on the front of one of the pneumatic life jackets. Fortunately, I had a small celluloid aerial navigator's scale, which had an excellent mileage scale. With such a map I was able to keep a chart of our progress.

So we three settled down to the business of living at sea on a tiny raft. One of the first things we found out was that it was going to be almost impossible to sleep. If you want to know what it was like on that raft, do the following things:

1) Lie on your back with your knees well drawn up. (There was not enough room to stretch out our legs.) Make sure, of course, that you are lying on a hard mattress with no springs underneath.

2) Have a good strong man rap you with a full swing of a baseball bat across the back of the head and shoulders. Two such raps every three seconds will duplicate the action of the waves pounding against the bottom of the boat.

3) Have a boy with a 3-gal. galvanized pail dash cold water on your face at irregular intervals.

4) Have four empty dump trucks run circles around you continually for sound effects.

5) Try all of this for 34 days continually. It will get very monotonous.

When our plane sank it went down so fast we had been able to salvage virtually nothing. Our life jackets, a 45-cal. pistol, a pocketknife, a pair of pliers and our wallets—that was all. No food. No water. Along about the fifth day the lack of water began to bother us seriously. The wind had been blowing us along at a fast clip in the general direction of south, but we had had no rain. Occasionally in those first few days we had seen rain clouds on the horizon. At times real squalls passed within a few hundred yards of us. But still we remained dry. Our salivary glands dried up and we had a parched feeling in our mouths that made it difficult to swallow. All that morning we had watched showers approaching, then fading away again. Hour after hour we sat in the broiling sun. The day before we had all gone into the water for a five-minute soak, but now there were sharks playing around the boat and we didn't dare venture over the side. So instead of a swim we kept our clothes soaked in salt water, rewetting them every few minutes to keep our bodies cool.

All that morning we sat and waited for rain. We knew that if we didn't get rain we wouldn't last long, that death by thirst is one of the most terrible forms of torture. It was then that Gene suggested we should pray for help. I had been thinking about that, too, but had been almost ashamed to make the suggestion. I now know that such a hesitation was wrong. We had all been brought up in good Christian families, but Gene and I, as so many military men, had drifted away from God. Tony was a Roman Catholic and more religious than either of the rest of us. Now, in the midst of our great trial and tribulation, we all felt the need for God.

So in the blazing sun, pushed by the trade winds, surrounded by sharks and the rolling waves, we held the first of what soon became a daily prayer service. Each of us stuttered and mumbled his way through an old prayer, then asked God to bless our loved ones back home and to take care of them, if we should die, and also to look after our shipmates at sea and to protect them in His mercy. I was particularly worried because I had $100 in my wallet which I had originally intended to send to my wife in San Diego, but I had forgotten and now, I thought, the money will never do her any good. From God also, we asked for rain to drink.

In His almighty goodness, God was gracious to us. Hardly had we stopped praying when overhead there appeared a tremendous black cloud, and down from the heavens poured the rain. The deluge lasted five minutes and we had our first drink in days.

Late that afternoon, God seemed still to be with us. As I was bringing my chart up to date and marking off another day on the port oarlock, where we made a mark for every day at sea, the wind shifted abruptly to the northeast. This was just what we wanted, especially as it held that way through the bright starry night. Neither Gene nor Tony could tell directions from the stars and they would ask me every few minutes how the wind was holding. I tried to give them instructions in the constellations, but they seemed to lack the natural aptitude of the born navigator. They are the kind of men who will always get lost in the woods. I advised them both to keep out of the tall timber.

Tony was more unhappy than the rest of us during these first few days. Most of the time he lay in the bottom of the boat apparently sleeping, keeping his own counsel and never speaking unless spoken to. Later it developed that he was firmly convinced we were doomed and that there was no use in trying to put up a struggle. Later on, as he realized that I could control the drift of the boat and that we actually had a pretty good chance of reaching an inhabited island, he snapped completely out of it.

On the evening of the sixth day we decided to hold another prayer meeting, to see whether this one would work as well as the one the day before had worked. We badly needed more rain and also something to eat. The meeting started with the singing of *When The Roll Is Called Up Yonder* and the *Little Brown Church In The Vale*—that is, we sang such words as we could remember and filled in the rest with humming. Then, once more we asked for rain and food, and for blessings on our families and our shipmates.

The next day, as if again in response to our prayers, we caught a fish. All morning great swarms of fish had been playing and feeding around us, many of them coming up to inspect us, apparently being attracted by the orange coloring of the raft.

Aldrich got a fish by simply leaning over the side and stabbing it with the pocketknife as it swam past. Tony was in the bottom of the boat dozing, as usual. With one continuous movement, Gene swung the blade through the fish and then brought the fish into the boat and dropped it on Tony. That woke him up. He rolled over on top of the fish and held it down until it quit struggling.

None of us had ever eaten raw fish, but we knew that before this trip was over we were going to have to, so we decided to make the try right then and there. The fish, which looked like a large perch, was cut into three pieces and we ate as much as we could. It didn't taste very good but it was food. That afternoon we had another heavy shower and more water to drink.

As I said in the beginning, I am a sailor and I am superstitious. The prayer meetings and the resultant water and food had made me both more religious and more superstitious. I also remembered as a kid having read the *Rime Of The Ancient Mariner*—especially the part that goes:

> *"At length did cross an Albatross,*
> *Through the fog it came;*
> *As if it had been a Christian soul,*
> *We hailed it in God's name.*

> *"And a good south wind sprung up behind;*
> *The Albatross did follow,*
> *And every day, for food or play,*
> *Came to the mariners' hollo!*

> *"God save thee, ancient Mariners,*
> *From the fiends that plague thee thus!—*
> *Why look'st thou so?"—"With my cross-bow*
> *I shot the Albatross!"*

We, too, shot an albatross. It was on the afternoon of the same day that we got our first fish. I was lying in the bottom of the boat, when suddenly right next to my face there was a terrific explosion. An albatross had landed on the stern of the boat and Gene, who was sitting on the forward thwart, slowly and steadily reached down and picked up the 45-cal. pistol and fired it right by my ear. The albatross, hit amidships, had fallen off the stern. Quickly I jumped up and leaped over the side, retrieving the bird and getting back in the boat before the raft had drifted 20 ft. We skinned the bird and, after eating the liver and the heart, put it away with what was left of the morning's fish. We wrapped both the bird and the fish in a few rags.

That night we remembered the old tradition that to kill an albatross brings bad luck. At midnight, when time came for my watch, I noticed a strange silvery blue light coming from the bow of the boat. On closer examination, I saw it came from the rags around the food. So I carefully unwrapped the rags, and lo and behold the albatross glowed like a flashlight, lighting up the whole boat and surrounding water. The tail in particular glowed like an electric-light bulb. We were astonished but figured that the glow must have come from the phosphorous in the food which the albatross had been eating. In any case, we were sure that we were not going to eat the bird. We certainly didn't want to glow like that. So we tossed both the albatross and the fish overboard.

The boys didn't think much more about this incident, but I did. I was worried about killing the albatross, and I looked around for another one which would fly close and keep us company day after day. For a long time I didn't see such a bird. We saw plenty of albatrosses but none which seemed to take a special interest in us. They were, however, undisputed monarchs of the sea we traveled over. To an aviator such as I, their movements were a source of never-ending delight. Wheeling and circling in the wind, taking advantage of the upcurrents from the big swells, they never went into spins, but were always able merely to slip off on one wing, go into a short slip, then quickly pick up speed again.

Some days later what I had been fearing happened. We ran into a calm. It rained. The sun came out. It rained again. But always it was calm. All of us were worried that we would never get any nearer to that inhabited island which was at the end of our personal rainbows.

Then we saw a huge old gray albatross. He came in in great circles, flying about the boat in majestic swoops. Finally he flew straight in toward us, landing on the water nearby. He had no fear of us, looked us over carefully and began dunking his head in the water. When he finally went away he swung off to the north, looking back as if wishing us good luck. He somehow made me feel that he would return and that eventually he would bring us good weather and good winds.

The good weather did not come immediately. In the continuing calm I had to figure out some way of rowing our boat. I still had my shoes with their thick rubber soles and low heels, so with the knife I cut away the uppers, thus making ideal paddles. With them, the three of us took turns paddling for 18 consecutive hours.

The next day the albatross returned, and virtually every day thereafter. Sometimes he came alone and sometimes he brought his mate—a smaller and darker bird. Usually he would sit on the water nearby, looking solemnly at us before taking off northward again. I often thought how good he would taste.

At length he brought us luck. That night, from a rainy sky and a smooth sea, the wind came to us right out of the east, strong and sweet and pure. We were glad to feel it in our faces and to know that once more we were sweeping on to deliverance and safety.

Sometimes as I look back now on those 34 days of sailing the ocean, time and events, and rains and suns, and heavy seas and flat calms merge together and nothing comes out clearly but a feeling of hunger, and thirst, and sadness. Yet there are some things I remember well. Like the day Aldrich caught the shark and then later how his hand was almost bitten off.

The shark was caught the day after we had shot the albatross. During the morning, which was hot and sunny, several small yellowish brown sand-sharks were playing around the boat. As time went on they got pretty bold and one of them finally ventured right up next to us. With his pocketknife, Gene stabbed at it, catching it in the gills. Tony, as usual, was in the bottom of the boat and the floundering shark, which was perhaps 4 ft. long, landed right on top of him as Gene yanked it out of the water. Tony was frightened but luckily had presence of mind enough to roll on the shark. After about ten minutes enough of the fight had gone out of the fish for me to try to cut it open.

For awhile I sawed and hacked at it by myself but its skin was much too tough for one man to handle. At length Tony was forced to hold the tail and Gene the head, while I slit open the stomach. First we cut out the liver, divided it into three large pieces, and ate that. But still we were hungry. Next we further explored the stomach, finding to our surprise two 6-in. sardines, one of which had been bitten entirely in two when the shark had swallowed it. Because Aldrich had caught the shark, we gave him one whole sardine, while Tony and I shared the rest. Never in my life have I tasted better meat than that shark liver, which even when raw resembled chicken liver, or the sardines, which tasted to our ravenous appetites like the tastiest kind of herring. Finally we devoured the rest of the shark's innards. By now, we had thoroughly lost what prejudices we may have had against eating raw fish.

Then I had an idea. The most nourishing part of the shark was certainly its blood. So we held up the shark's tail and head, forming a pocket in the middle of the body into which the blood poured. It was thin and watery and had a strong flavor, but we drank it. Finally we ate as much of the shark's flesh as we could stand, and put the rest of it away in the bow until the next day.

All that day the sun shone hot and all that day the shark meat rested in the bow of that little raft. I thought it would be completely spoiled, but on the morrow I found that the sun, instead of spoiling the meat, had merely cooked and dehydrated it. The salt water, with which it had been soaked during the night, had also helped flavor it and taken out much of the ammonia taste. In any case it tasted much better than before. We ate all the meat we could pull loose from the skin and bones, but we could not do much with the tough lower tail section.

Incidentally, one thing the shark did for us was to act as a physic. After eating it, all three of us had the only bowel movement we were to have in our 34 days at sea.

It was that night that Aldrich was bitten by a shark. Toward midnight he was on watch, and being anxious to feel any drift of the boat in the very light wind, he stuck his hand in the water. No sooner had he done so, than . . . *whoosh* . . . up came a shark and grabbed him by the fingers. In his fright he yanked his hand so hard that he pulled the shark right out of water, across the boat and tossed it over the other side. In the darkness we could not see how badly Gene was hurt, but we were naturally frightened, especially since he might bleed to death if the wound was bad. Fortunately I had a handkerchief with which I bound his finger and the bleeding subsided.

In the morning, however, we saw that the wound could have been a lot worse. The shark's teeth had raked down the index finger cutting the nail completely through in two places. The root of the nail was badly mangled and it was apparent that he would soon lose the nail. The rest of his fingers were cut in some places almost to the bone. Later when infection set in in the nail of the index finger, I was forced to cut right through it to relieve the pressure. The swelling immediately went down, and with the help of the salt water, the wounds were well on the way to healing by the time we reached land.

With each passing day we thought our chances of rescue were growing better. We thought this, perhaps foolhardily, in view of the obvious fact that we were growing weaker and that we were getting very little food indeed. Besides the sun was hotter as we worked southward. During this time we unfortunately worked farther to the eastward than we had hoped and farther than I had indicated on my map. When we finally made land, I was off some 100 miles in my dead reckoning, but it must be remembered I had absolutely no navigation instruments of any kind except for the small aerial navigation calculator. All of our watches—and also our gun—were soon lost by the corrosion of salt water.

The problem of food remained serious. We were getting enough water but scarcely enough vitamins to keep up our strength. We were all losing weight fast, and for the first time I began to worry whether we would have the physical strength to sail the boat all the way south to the inhabited islands. Occasionally, of course, we did get more food. Aldrich sat continually on the edge of the raft, his patience never giving out, trying to stab another fish. Finally one day, about a week after the first perchlike fish, he got another exactly like it. Our hunger, which had been intense for four or five days after eating the shark, had begun to subside. But we ate the fish with relish and without delay. That was the last fish we were to catch on the whole trip.

During one night I caught a bird. After a heavy shower, we had just finished bailing out and I was lying in the bottom of the boat trying to get a little rest. Suddenly I heard a scratching noise on the stern of the raft just above my head. It was a bird. Noiselessly and slowly I slid my hand up inside and as close to the edge of the boat as possible, grabbing the bird by the leg. In the morning we discovered that it was a young tern and that its flesh was tender and delicious, tasting considerably like chicken.

I might as well add here that the only other food, in addition to the fish, shark and bird already mentioned, which we had on the trip, was two coconuts. We picked up the coconuts as they drifted past the boat. Unfortunately we let one coconut drift past when we thought it was the nose of a seal.

By now I began to figure we were in the neighborhood of islands or reefs. All around us were hundreds of varieties of birds and fish, indicating that some sort of breeding grounds such as shallow water or reefs must be near. Nearby, too, feeding on the fish were plenty of leopard sharks, vicious creatures that often threatened to upset our boat. Once we had to fight one of them away by punching him in the nose. Another one we managed to shoot and kill with our pistol before the weapon had become too rusty for use.

It was now the 29th day at sea. We were all weak. No longer was there much conversation. Mostly we lay back in our cramped and uncomfortable positions, not caring much longer what happened. Deep in our hearts we were all beginning to resign ourselves to our fate. It looked as if we would die of hunger and weakness long before we spotted land.

That day we got a bad wind and the boat tipped over. It seemed like the end, but somehow or other we had strength enough left to turn the boat over on its right side and climb back in. We thought maybe we had reached the bottom of our luck. On the morning of the 33rd day we struck the beginning of a hurricane, which drove us swiftly on toward the southwest. It was a terrible day. The huge combers poured gallons and gallons of water into our little raft. In our weakness and unhappiness we hardly had strength or spirit enough to bail. But somehow, bail we did. The rain whistled around us. The skies were dark. The waves roared louder and louder and louder.

To bail more effectively, we took off all our clothes, leaving us stark naked in the howling storm. There we were, I thought, completely returned to the primeval, naked and alone, fighting the unbridled forces of nature. Suddenly the boat tipped over and all our clothes were lost. All we saved was the sole of one shoe and two billfolds.

After the storm the sun came out, fierce and burning. Our bodies, unprotected by any clothes, burned and peeled and burned again. We were discouraged and wanted to give up. But we shook hands and went on.

Bv now our minds were growing weak with hunger. Sometimes they strayed away and imagined queer things. Tony imagined he heard choral voices singing. The voices were low and sweet and beautiful. They sang sentimental songs of home. Once he asked, "Don't you hear those voices singing?" I heard nothing but the winds and the waves.

All over our red, inflamed bodies, our bones stuck out. I couldn't hold my eyes open for more than a few seconds, and could hardly focus them at all.

We had had to give up a night watch out of sheer physical weakness. During darkness, we huddled close together in the bottom of the raft for warmth. There we thought slowly and solemnly of death. We could hardly feel that anything else awaited us at the end of our voyage.

On the morning of the 34th day Aldrich was up on the bow. The weather was clear. Suddenly he said, "Chief, I see a field of corn." Gene is from Missouri, a farm boy, and I thought, "Now he has gone completely crazy." Fifteen minutes later, however, he said it again, "Chief, I see a beautiful field of corn." So I stood up as best I could, while the other two helped me, and waited until we rode the crest of a wave. What I saw made my heart jump and sing with the purest, greatest joy it has ever known. There, lying ahead, was a green island. The field of corn was a shoreline of waving palm trees. "Boys," I said, "you can thank God. It's an island."

All that day we rowed toward the beautiful green patch of land. As Tony paddled, a shark struck at him. He said, "Chief, a shark's got me." I said, "Did he bite you?" He said, "No." I said, "Keep rowing."

Toward afternoon the sky began to cloud over. A certain strange silence and an increasing wind, with rain, told me that we were at the edge of a hurricane. I knew that if we didn't get ashore now, we probably never would. In our little raft, we could not survive a hurricane.

In the late afternoon we made it. We came right in over the reef, in a burst of crashing surf. Our raft shot out from under us, and we were tossed head over heels into the shallow water near shore. The raft was already waiting there for us.

We still didn't know, of course, whether the island was friendly or Japanese. So, although we could barely stagger and none of us could stand up straight, we marched ashore in military fashion, stark naked. If there were Japs there, we did not want to be crawling. We wanted them to have to shoot us, like men-o'-warsmen.

As it turned out, there were no Japs. It was a friendly island, controlled by a Resident Commissioner. The next morning, after we had spent the night in a little native shack, covering our bodies with coconut mats, a native found us and notified the Commissioner, who gave us food and water, and helped me contact the commanding officer of my ship.

That night all three of us slept in a real bed, our bodies stretched as nearly full length as we could get them after the weeks of living on the cramped raft. Outside our windows we could hear the full force of the hurricane, snapping trees and pounding up a terrible surf outside the reef. I knew we had reached shore just in the nick of time. One more day and the hurricane would have done what starvation, thirst, wind, sun and sharks had failed to do.

Midway

BY

WALTER B. CLAUSEN

THE first eyewitness account of the Battle of Midway Island, detailing its most violent stages, was related by a wounded United States naval aviator who told of floating in the sea and watching a line of burning Japanese ships pass by.

He told of a thunderous—and highly successful—attack by United States dive-bombers and torpedo planes on Japanese aircraft carriers. He saw the certain destruction of a flaming carrier of the 26,900-ton *Kaga* Class and the probable sinking of two other blazing Japanese carriers, one of them also of the *Kaga* Class. And he watched the desperate circlings of Japanese naval planes, unable to settle on their blazing and battered mother ships.

Admiral Chester W. Nimitz, Commander in Chief of the Pacific Fleet, revealed the story of the aviator, Ensign George H. Gay, Jr., 25-year-old torpedo-plane pilot of Houston, Texas. Ensign Gay's wounds were not serious.

For twenty-four hours Ensign Gay, careful to conceal himself from vengeful Japanese fliers by hiding his head under a cushion from his wrecked plane, drifted in the sea and obtained one of the most amazing eyewitness stories of a major naval engagement in the history of sea warfare.

Ensign Gay occupied what naval men called a "fish eye view" of the attack on three Japanese carriers. His squadron met fierce enemy fighter-plane opposition while driving home a torpedo assault on one of the larger carriers in the Japanese fleet early on June 4, opening day of the Battle of Midway.

He was the only one of the crew of three to survive the crash of his ship. In the water, he clung to his boat bag and covered his head with the cushion.

What happened thereafter is a naval epic.

Taking off from his fleet carrier with his squadron, Ensign Gay approached the objective in mid-morning. Visibility was unlimited. Below lay three Japanese carriers, less than ten miles extending between the first and last of the enemy ships, which were screened by a considerable force of cruisers and destroyers.

The flier took stock of the astounding drama below him. Two *Kaga* Class carriers had been taking on their aircraft. Another smaller carrier lay be-

By permission of The Associated Press.

tween them, also receiving planes that were fighting the far-flung battle of Midway.

One of the larger carriers already burned fiercely, while Japanese cruisers and destroyers wheeled around it waiting to rescue personnel.

Twenty minutes later the American dive-bombers rocketed into view.

In the face of terrific anti-aircraft fire and enemy fighter attack, the United States planes leveled for the assault. Ensign Gay heard his machine-gunner say he had been hit. But the approach continued. Near the great Japanese carrier, the pilot launched his projectile, then swung sharply over the target and sped astern as fast as his plane could go.

Suddenly an explosive shell from a Zero fighter ripped through his torpedo plane's rudder controls. The detonation seared Ensign Gay's left leg. Almost simultaneously, a small-caliber bullet struck his upper left arm.

Coolly, Ensign Gay brought his heavy plane into a stall and pancaked into the sea several miles astern of the enemy carrier. His gunner was dead, and in the emergency landing his radio man was unable to pull free.

At 11 A.M., the pilot, alone, watched the tail surfaces of his plane disappear. Now a bit of luck held with him. Out of the sinking wreckage floated the bag containing the deflated rubber life raft—and a black cushion on which the bombardier kneels while working.

Ensign Gay figured his chances quickly and accurately. There had been reports that the Japanese were strafing helpless pilots bailing out by parachute, and that they were machine-gunning men in such life rafts as had floated clear of his own plane.

The flier declined to offer himself as such a victim. He ducked under the cushion as enemy fighters swarmed overhead. Not knowing the extent of his wounds, he felt cautiously at his arm. The bullet, which apparently had struck him at the spent end of its trajectory, dropped out in his hand.

"For some reason," he recalled, "I put it in my mouth. Maybe I wanted a souvenir. Anyhow, I lost it before long."

He bandaged his injured leg under water. Then, from his "fish-eye view" at sea level, he saw two other Japanese carriers hit squarely by United States bombs.

Tremendous fires burst from these vessels. Great billows of smoke churned upward with the flames flaring from the apex in dark columns.

Internal explosions sent new gushes of smoke and fire belching from the carriers at momentary intervals, he said.

As the ferocious Pacific Fleet attack ended, the second *Kaga* Class carrier was on fire from bow to stern.

Surface craft gave Ensign Gay some narrow brushes. One enemy destroyer appeared to be driving straight at him as she sped to aid a stricken carrier. He thought it would run him down, but at the last instant it swirled past him harmlessly.

A heavy cruiser steamed by less than 500 yards from him. Ensign Gay saw her crew lining the rail, their white uniforms gleaming against the battle-paint, grimly watching the destruction of their force.

As the afternoon waned, the Japanese made frantic efforts to stem the damage. An enemy cruiser sought to stand alongside a crippled carrier, but seemed unable to approach close enough. Ensign Gay observed this vessel's big guns commence to rake the wounded carrier, presumably to scuttle her.

Some time later a destroyer managed to come alongside the still floating carrier to remove survivors. Overhead, Ensign Gay said, Japanese planes appeared to be circling in a vain attempt to land on the smashed carrier. They would pass above her, then soar out of sight, and return.

Darkness fell, and he never learned what became of them.

In the twilight, "maybe a little earlier than was wise," Ensign Gay inflated his life raft from his carbon dioxide bottle. He said he had his fill of salt water.

Working calmly, the young pilot had to make emergency patches on several bullet holes in the rubber boat before it would sustain him safely. He clambered in. The long night began.

Far to the north, great glowing patches appeared in the sky. Ensign Gay thought these might have been the searchlights of Japanese rescue vessels seeking to pick up carrier personnel.

There did not seem to be much else to do, so he "tried to catch a few winks of sleep."

Toward morning he was awakened from fitful slumber by three explosions that he believed might have been demolition charges.

Several hours after sun-up a Navy patrol plane, winging out on a search, spotted his rubber boat. Later, the plane returned and picked up the flier.

A Navy doctor asked what treatment he had for his burns and he replied: "Well, I soaked 'em in salt water for ten hours."

They headed back to the base. The surface of the battle area was littered with black Japanese life rafts, presumably used by the enemy when they abandoned ship. Great patches of oil floated on the debris-strewn sea, Ensign Gay said.

He reported that the one carrier of the *Kaga* class could be listed as a "certain loss," while the two other carriers were "probable." These were later pursued by United States forces engaged in finishing off the crippled units of the Japanese fleet.